A PRACTICAL APPROACH TO

EMPLOYMENT LAW

A PRACTICAL APPROACH TO
EMPLOYMENT LAW

NINTH EDITION

John Bowers QC

BARRISTER

Principal of Brasenose College, Oxford
Former co-head of Littleton Chambers

OXFORD

UNIVERSITY PRESS

OXFORD

UNIVERSITY PRESS

Great Clarendon Street, Oxford, OX2 6DP,
United Kingdom

Oxford University Press is a department of the University of Oxford.
It furthers the University's objective of excellence in research, scholarship,
and education by publishing worldwide. Oxford is a registered trade mark of
Oxford University Press in the UK and in certain other countries

© John Bowers 2017

The moral rights of the author have been asserted

Eighth Edition published in 2009
Ninth Edition published in 2017
Impression: 1

Crown copyright material is reproduced under Class Licence
Number C01P0000148 with the permission of OPSI
and the Queen's Printer for Scotland

Published in the United States of America by Oxford University Press
198 Madison Avenue, New York, NY 10016, United States of America

British Library Cataloguing in Publication Data
Data available

Library of Congress Control Number: 2016960272

ISBN 978-0-19-876654-4

Printed and bound by
CPI Group (UK) Ltd, Croydon, CR0 4YY

Links to third party websites are provided by Oxford in good faith and
for information only. Oxford disclaims any responsibility for the materials
contained in any third party website referenced in this work.

FOREWORD

John Bowers QC had, when in full-time practice, the inimitable reputation as the counsel who could be relied upon to know, and to cover, every relevant authority on any particular topic in the wide field of Employment and Discrimination law, and he exercised the same authority in his learned academic works, always ensuring that the conclusions to be drawn from any cited case were fully understood. Somehow, in updating this book for the new edition, from his Lodgings as a distinguished Principal of Brasenose, he has achieved the impossible task of filleting all his learning, and rendering it comprehensible for the reader, be he or she a layman, lawyer, or judge, while still ensuring that the benefit of his encyclopaedic knowledge is fully imparted. There is no employment law topic which is not given new and insightful consideration in this edition, and I note in particular the coverage given to Human Rights, which will be of great value in the years to come, as statute law comes to terms with the impact of Brexit. This book is now an even more necessary companion and guide for those seeking answers in the ever burgeoning area of Employment law.

Sir Michael Burton, President of the Investigatory Powers Tribunal and
Chairman of the Central Arbitration Committee: High Court Judge 1998–2016,
President of the Employment Appeal Tribunal 2002–2005

PREFACE

As I write this Introduction, the main unknown is the impact on employment law of the UK leaving the European Union. Brexit may have a major impact in our area although the Prime Minister has indicated that existing workers' rights will be upheld. The scope of this promise is unclear. The tribunal system is still reeling from the massive drop in claims since fees for employment claims were introduced by the Coalition Government. The labour market is changing rapidly with more precarious employment patterns typified by the "gig economy" and zero hours' contracts.

This is the ninth edition of this book and includes for the first time the Equality Act 2010. This emphasises the link between human dignity and business interests. I think no one has summed up so pithily the role of employment law than Lord Hoffmann in *Johnson v Unisys Ltd* [2001] ICR 480, at 495h: "Employment law requires a balancing of the interests of employers and employees, with proper regard not only to the individual dignity and worth of employees but also to the general economic interest."

This is the first edition I have written from Oxford where I love my role as Principal of Brasenose College. The College has a very long and distinguished line of employment lawyers as Fellows and alumni: I think of Prof Otto Kahn Freund, the late and much missed Judge Jeremy Mc Mullen, Judge Jeffrey Burke, Prof Mark Freedland (albeit only for a year) Prof Hugh Collins and Prof Anne Davies. We also have as an alumnus Lord Justice Beatson who both in the EAT and Court of Appeal has contributed to the development of employment law. I have learnt a lot from all of them, as well as the present students and Fellows of the College and students here as I did from my pupils at the Bar and fellow advocates.

I thank Sir Michael Burton for his generous introduction and my wife Prof Suzanne Franks and children Emma, Hannah and Ben. I dedicate the book to the memory of my mother Irene Bowers who sadly died two years ago and who (along with my Dad) made everything possible for me. My father Alf (a hero of the Russian convoys in World War II) is happily still going strong in Cleethorpes at 96.

John Bowers
November 2016, Oxford
John Bowers QC
November 2016

CONTENTS SUMMARY

	Table of Cases	xix
	Table of Statutes	lxxi
	Table of Statutory Instruments	lxxxi
	List of Abbreviations	lxxxv
1	History	1
2	The Status of Employee	8
3	The Individual Contract of Employment and Its Sources	27
4	Rights and Obligations of Employer and Employee	47
5	Statutory Regulation of Wages and Hours	68
6	The Duty of Fidelity and Restraint of Trade Clauses	89
7	Equal Pay	106
8	Discrimination	129
9	Part-time and Fixed-term Workers	178
10	Maternity, Parental, and Domestic Care Rights, and Flexible Working	182
11	Continuity of Employment	200
12	The Scope of Statutory Protection: Unfair Dismissal and Redundancy	213
13	Termination of Contract and Wrongful Dismissal	228
14	Unfair Dismissal	246
15	Public Interest Disclosures: Dismissal and Detriment Claims	344
16	Redundancy Payments	351
17	Consultation about Redundancy	373
18	Transfers of Undertakings	385
19	Trade Unions and Collective Bargaining	418
20	Protection of Trade Union and Cognate Activities	450
21	Strikes and Other Industrial Action	468
22	Picketing and Public Order	512
23	Employment Law and Human Rights	524
	Index	539

CONTENTS

Table of Cases   xix
Table of Statutes   lxxi
Table of Statutory Instruments   lxxxi
List of Abbreviations   lxxxv

---

1   HISTORY

    A   THE BACKGROUND TO THE MODERN ERA   1.01

    B   THE 1960s AND THE DONOVAN REPORT   1.03

    C   THE INDUSTRIAL RELATIONS ACT 1971 AND INDUSTRIAL STRIFE   1.06

    D   THE 'SOCIAL CONTRACT': TRADE UNION AND LABOUR RELATIONS
       ACT 1974 AND THE EMPLOYMENT PROTECTION ACT 1975   1.08

    E   CONSERVATIVE LEGISLATION 1980-95   1.11

    F   A THIRD WAY? LABOUR LEGISLATION 1997-2009   1.24

    G   THE CAMERON GOVERNMENTS   1.29

---

2   THE STATUS OF EMPLOYEE

    A   THE PURPOSE OF DEFINING THE EMPLOYEE   2.01

    B   THE TESTS OF EMPLOYEE STATUS   2.06

    C   OTHER WORK RELATIONSHIPS   2.35

    D   DEFINITION OF WORKERS   2.66

    E   QUESTION OF LAW OR FACT?   2.77

---

3   THE INDIVIDUAL CONTRACT OF EMPLOYMENT AND ITS SOURCES

    A   THE COLLECTIVE BARGAIN   3.04

    B   IMPLIED TERMS   3.21

    C   RULES OF EMPLOYMENT   3.36

    D   CUSTOM AND PRACTICE   3.40

    E   STATUTE   3.43

    F   AWARDS   3.44

    G   CAPACITY   3.45

    H   FORMATION AND VARIATION OF CONTRACT   3.46

    I   THE EFFECT ON CONTRACT OF A TRANSFER OF UNDERTAKING   3.61

    J   WRITTEN STATEMENT OF TERMS   3.62

4 RIGHTS AND OBLIGATIONS OF EMPLOYER AND EMPLOYEE

A   PAY   4.02

B   COOPERATION   4.23

C   CARE AND SAFETY   4.29

D   TIME OFF AND HOLIDAYS   4.35

E   FOLLOWING INSTRUCTIONS   4.42

F   BREACH OF CONTRACT   4.46

G   DISCIPLINE   4.48

H   LAY-OFF AND SHORT-TIME WORKING   4.53

I   MOBILITY AND FLEXIBILITY CLAUSES   4.73

J   REFERENCES AND PRE-EMPLOYMENT MEDICALS   4.76

K   MEDICAL REPORTS   4.79

L   RIGHT TO BE ACCOMPANIED AT DISCIPLINARY AND GRIEVANCE
        PROCEDURES   4.81

5 STATUTORY REGULATION OF WAGES AND HOURS

A   DEDUCTIONS FROM WAGES   5.01

B   ITEMISED PAY STATEMENT   5.15

C   THE NATIONAL MINIMUM WAGE   5.19

D   WORKING TIME REGULATIONS   5.47

E   SUNDAY TRADING   5.76

6 THE DUTY OF FIDELITY AND RESTRAINT OF TRADE CLAUSES

A   DUTY TO ACCOUNT AND DISCLOSE   6.03

B   COMPETITION WITH THE EMPLOYER WHILE EMPLOYED BY HIM   6.08

C   GARDEN LEAVE INJUNCTIONS   6.13

D   RESTRAINING THE EX-EMPLOYEE   6.21

E   CONFIDENTIAL INFORMATION   6.23

F   PATENTS   6.41

G   RESTRAINT OF TRADE CLAUSES   6.48

7 EQUAL PAY

A   INTRODUCTION   7.01

B   THE EQUALITY CLAUSE AND LIKE WORK   7.11

C   JOB EVALUATION   7.67

D   EQUAL VALUE CLAIMS   7.78

E   CLAIMING EQUAL PAY   7.82

F   MATERNITY   7.93

G   COLLECTIVE ENFORCEMENT   7.94

H   EUROPEAN LAW   7.96

I   THE NATURE OF THE RIGHT   7.101

J   EQUAL TREATMENT IN RESPECT OF PENSIONS IN UK LAW—SECTION 67   7.105

8 **DISCRIMINATION**

A   INTRODUCTION   8.01

B   MEANING OF PROTECTED CHARACTERISTICS   8.13

C   FORMS OF DISCRIMINATION   8.69

D   THE SCOPE OF PROHIBITED DISCRIMINATION   8.138

E   CLAIMANTS AND RESPONDENTS   8.162

F   'REVERSE DISCRIMINATION'   8.172

G   ENFORCEMENT MECHANISMS   8.174

9 **PART-TIME AND FIXED-TERM WORKERS**

A   PART-TIME WORKERS REGULATIONS   9.01

B   FIXED-TERM WORKERS   9.17

C   AGENCY WORKERS   9.21

10 **MATERNITY, PARENTAL, AND DOMESTIC CARE RIGHTS,
   AND FLEXIBLE WORKING**

A   ORDINARY MATERNITY LEAVE   10.07

B   ADDITIONAL MATERNITY LEAVE   10.21

C   STATUTORY MATERNITY AND PATERNITY PAY   10.29

D   PATERNITY LEAVE   10.35

E   ADOPTION LEAVE AND PAY   10.38

F   ANTENATAL CARE   10.39

G   SUSPENSION ON MATERNITY GROUNDS   10.40

H   SHARED PARENTAL LEAVE   10.46

I   CONTRACTUAL RIGHTS   10.54

J   DEPENDANT CARE LEAVE   10.55

K   DISMISSAL   10.66

L   DETRIMENT   10.77

M   FLEXIBLE WORKING   10.78

11   CONTINUITY OF EMPLOYMENT

   A   BACKGROUND   11.01

   B   MONTHS AND YEARS OF SERVICE   11.06

   C   WEEKS IN WHICH THERE IS NO CONTRACT OF EMPLOYMENT   11.07

   D   CHANGE OF EMPLOYER   11.30

   E   ESTOPPEL   11.51

**12   THE SCOPE OF STATUTORY PROTECTION: UNFAIR DISMISSAL
       AND REDUNDANCY**

   A   QUALIFYING PERIOD   12.04

   B   LIMITS IN TIME   12.07

   C   ILLEGALITY   12.25

   D   GEOGRAPHICAL LIMITATIONS   12.34

   E   THE NATURE OF THE EMPLOYER   12.42

   F   THE NATURE OF THE EMPLOYMENT   12.43

   G   EXCLUSION BY AGREEMENT   12.44

   H   MISCELLANEOUS   12.58

13   TERMINATION OF CONTRACT AND WRONGFUL DISMISSAL

   A   AUTOMATIC TERMINATION BY SUPERVENING EVENT   13.02

   B   TERMINATION BY NOTICE   13.03

   C   TERMINATION BY BREACH   13.10

   D   TERMINATION BY DISMISSAL   13.20

   E   REMEDIES FOR WRONGFUL DISMISSAL   13.40

14   UNFAIR DISMISSAL

   A   THE BACKGROUND   14.01

   B   OUTLINE   14.06

   C   DISMISSAL   14.10

   D   EFFECTIVE DATE OF TERMINATION   14.92

   E   THE REASON FOR DISMISSAL   14.94

   F   FAIRNESS OF DISMISSAL: GENERAL   14.106

   G   INCAPABILITY   14.112

   H   MISCONDUCT   14.136

   I   PROCEDURE   14.172

   J   REDUNDANCY   14.191

   K   SOME OTHER SUBSTANTIAL REASON   14.213

L	ILLEGALITY	14.242
M	SPENT OFFENCES	14.245
N	DISMISSAL DURING STRIKE OR LOCK-OUT	14.247
O	DISMISSAL BY REASON OF RECOGNITION ACTION	14.276
P	DISMISSAL FOR ASSERTION OF A STATUTORY RIGHT	14.278
Q	JURY SERVICE	14.284
R	DISMISSAL: PRESSURE ON EMPLOYER TO DISMISS	14.286
S	REMEDIES	14.287
T	UNFAIR DISMISSAL: OVERVIEW	14.362

15 PUBLIC INTEREST DISCLOSURES: DISMISSAL AND DETRIMENT CLAIMS

A	DISCLOSURE	15.03
B	WIDER DISCLOSURE	15.13
C	DETRIMENT	15.17
D	THE REASON TEST	15.18
E	BURDEN OF PROOF	15.19
F	SCOPE	15.20
G	JOINT LIABILITY	15.21
H	TIME LIMIT	15.24

16 REDUNDANCY PAYMENTS

A	INTRODUCTION	16.01
B	DEFINITION OF REDUNDANCY	16.08
C	OFFER OF NEW EMPLOYMENT	16.33
D	DISQUALIFICATION FROM REDUNDANCY PAYMENT	16.50
E	CALCULATION OF REDUNDANCY PAYMENT	16.56
F	CLAIMING A REDUNDANCY PAYMENT	16.68
G	INSOLVENCY	16.69

17 CONSULTATION ABOUT REDUNDANCY

A	DEFINITION OF REDUNDANCY	17.07
B	TRADE UNION RECOGNITION	17.09
C	ELECTED EMPLOYEE REPRESENTATIVES	17.16
D	CONSULTATION IN GOOD TIME BEFORE DISMISSALS TAKE PLACE	17.23
E	MEANING OF ESTABLISHMENT	17.33
F	INFORMED CONSULTATION	17.38
G	THE DEFENCE OF 'SPECIAL CIRCUMSTANCES'	17.41

H   SANCTION: THE PROTECTIVE AWARD   17.44

I   WHO ARE THE UNION'S AUTHORISED REPRESENTATIVES?   17.55

18   **TRANSFERS OF UNDERTAKINGS**

A   A RELEVANT TRANSFER   18.04

B   WHOSE CONTRACTS ARE TRANSFERRED?   18.43

C   EFFECT OF TRANSFER ON THE CONTRACT OF EMPLOYMENT   18.59

D   THE POSITION OF THE EMPLOYEE   18.85

E   DISMISSAL ON TRANSFER OF UNDERTAKING   18.99

F   CONSULTATION WITH THE RECOGNISED UNIONS
    OR ELECTED REPRESENTATIVES   18.116

G   TRADE UNION RIGHTS   18.126

19   **TRADE UNIONS AND COLLECTIVE BARGAINING**

A   THE BRITISH SYSTEM OF COLLECTIVE BARGAINING   19.01

B   THE LEGAL STATUS OF TRADE UNIONS AND EMPLOYERS' ASSOCIATIONS 19.03

C   LISTING   19.07

D   INDEPENDENCE OF TRADE UNIONS   19.11

E   THE RIGHT TO JOIN A TRADE UNION   19.18

F   UNION LIABILITY IN TORT   19.43

G   ENFORCEMENT OF COLLECTIVE BARGAINS   19.49

H   THE AUXILIARY ROLE OF THE LAW   19.55

I   RECOGNITION   19.57

J   RIGHT OF TRADE UNIONS TO INFORMATION IN SUPPORT
    OF COLLECTIVE BARGAINING   19.103

K   INFORMATION AND CONSULTATION ON TRAINING   19.116

L   THE ADVISORY, CONCILIATION AND ARBITRATION SERVICE (ACAS)   19.121

M   CENTRAL ARBITRATION COMMITTEE (CAC)   19.131

N   CODES OF PRACTICE   19.134

O   HEALTH AND SAFETY AND COLLECTIVE BARGAINING   19.138

P   EUROPEAN WORKS COUNCILS   19.141

20   **PROTECTION OF TRADE UNION AND COGNATE ACTIVITIES**

A   THE RIGHTS   20.01

B   ACTIVITIES   20.08

C   WHAT TIME IS APPROPRIATE FOR TRADE UNION ACTIVITIES?   20.26

D   DETRIMENT   20.28

E   PROOF   20.32

F   TIME OFF FOR TRADE UNION DUTIES   20.35

G   TIME OFF FOR TRADE UNION ACTIVITIES   20.52

H   TIME OFF FOR INDUSTRIAL RELATIONS TRAINING   20.54

I   TIME OFF FOR HEALTH AND SAFETY REPRESENTATIVES   20.55

J   PROTECTION OF HEALTH AND SAFETY ACTIVITIES   20.57

K   RIGHTS OF PENSION FUND TRUSTEES   20.67

L   REMEDIES   20.69

21 STRIKES AND OTHER INDUSTRIAL ACTION

A   A RIGHT TO STRIKE?   21.01

B   INDUSTRIAL ACTION AND THE INDIVIDUAL CONTRACT   21.06

C   THE LEGALITY OF INDUSTRIAL ACTION: THE QUESTIONS FOR THE COURT   21.16

D   INDUCING BREACH OF CONTRACT   21.18

E   INTERFERENCE WITH CONTRACT   21.44

F   INTIMIDATION   21.57

G   CONSPIRACY   21.62

H   TRADE DISPUTE IMMUNITY   21.71

I   STATUTORY CONTROL OF SECONDARY ACTION   21.103

J   STRIKE BALLOTS   21.106

K   UNION RECRUITMENT STRIKES   21.154

L   STATUTORY RESTRICTIONS ON INDUSTRIAL ACTION   21.155

M   CONSUMER ACTIONS   21.157

N   EU LAW ON FREEDOM OF ESTABLISHMENT   21.158

O   INJUNCTIONS   21.159

22 PICKETING AND PUBLIC ORDER

A   INDUSTRIAL BACKGROUND   22.01

B   OFFENCES AND PICKETING   22.05

C   CIVIL LIABILITY   22.29

D   IMMUNITY   22.36

E   THE CODE OF PRACTICE   22.47

23 EMPLOYMENT LAW AND HUMAN RIGHTS

A   THE IMPACT IN EMPLOYMENT LAW   23.01

Index   539

TABLE OF CASES

1 Pump Court Tax Chambers v Horton, *The Times*, 30 August 2004 . . . . .8.170
102 Social Club and Institute Ltd v Bickerton [1977] ICR 91. . . . . .2.39

A. Dakri & Co Ltd v Tiffen [1981] IRLR 57 . . . . 4.57, 4.69
A. Links & Co v Rose [1991] IRLR 353. . . . . .14.125
AB v A Chief Constable [2014] IRLR 700 . . . . .4.76
ADI (UK) Ltd v Willer [2001] IRLR 542 . . . . .18.28
AEI Cables Ltd v McLay [1980] IRLR 84. . . . . .14.151
AG v Blake [2001] IRLR 36 . . . . .6.04
AMICUS v City Building (Glasgow) LLP [2009] IRLR 253. .18.116
AMICUS v GBS Tooling Ltd [2005] IRLR 683 . . . . .17.51
AON Training Ltd v Dore [2005] IRLR 89. . . . . .14.325
ASLEF v UK [2007] IRLR 361 . . . . .19.23
A.T. Poeton (Gloucester Plating) Ltd v Horton [2000] ICR 1208. . . . . .6.31
AUEW v Sefton Engineering Co Ltd [1976] IRLR 318. . . . . .17.13
A v B [2003] IRLR 405 . . . . .14.167, 14.169
AB v A Chief Constable [2014] IRLR 700 . . . . .4.76
Abadeh v BT [2001] IRLR 23 . . . . .8.58
Abbey National Plc v Chagger [2010] ICR 397. . . . . 8.198, 8.205
Abbey National plc v Fairbrother [2007] IRLR 320. . . . . .3.25
Abbots & Standley v Wesson-Glynwed Steels Ltd [1982] IRLR 51 . . . . 14.108, 14.208
Abdoulaye v Regie Nationale des Usines Renault [2001] ICR 527 . . . . .7.98
Abdulaziz Cabales & Balkandali v UK (1985) 7 EHRR 471 . . . . .23.71
Abernethy v Mott Hay and Anderson [1974] ICR 323 . . . . .14.94
Abertawe Bro Morgannwg University Health Board v Ferguson [2013] ICR 1108 . . . . .5.17
Abler v Sodexho MM Catering Gesellschaft mbH [2004] IRLR 168. . . . . .18.32
Abrahams v Performing Rights Society Ltd [1995] ICR 1028. .13.73
Acrow (Automation) Ltd v Rex Chain Belts Inc [1971] WLR 1676 . . . . .21.52
Adams &Others v Lancashire CC and BET Catering Services Ltd [1996] ICR 935. . . . . . .18.70
Adams v British Airways plc [1996] IRLR 574. . . . . 3.53, 19.50
Adams v Charles Zub Associates Ltd [1978] IRLR 551 . . . . .14.39
Adams v Derby City Council [1986] IRLR 163 . . . . .14.94
Adams v GKN Sankey Ltd [1980] IRLR 416 . . . . .14.93
Adams v Union Cinemas Ltd [1939] 3 All ER 136 . . . . .13.03
Adamson v B & L Cleaning Services Ltd [1995] IRLR 193 . . . . .6.11
Adda International Ltd v Curcio [1976] ICR 407. . . . . .14.322
Addis v Gramophone Co Ltd [1909] AC 488 . . . . .13.59
Addison v Ashby [2003] IRLR 783. . . . . .5.51
Addison v London Philharmonic Orchestra [1981] ICR 261 . . . . 2.25, 2.55
Adekeye v Post Office [1993] IRLR 324 . . . . .8.177
Aderemi v London & South Eastern Railway Ltd [2013] ICR 591. . . . . .8.34
Adeshina v St Georges University Hospitals NHS Foundation Trust [2015] IRLR 704 . . . 14.188
Adin v Sedco Forex International Resources Ltd [1997] IRLR 280 . . . . .3.26
Adlam v Salisbury and Wells Theological College [1985] ICR 786 . . . . 8.175, 20.70
Aegon UK Corporate Services Ltd v Roberts [2010] ICR 596. .7.102
Affleck v Newcastle Mind [1999] IRLR 405. . . . . 2.54, 11.50
Ahmed v UK (1982) 4 EHRR 126. . . . . .23.40
Ahmed v UK [1999] IRLR 188 . . . . .23.49
Ainsworth v Glass Tubes and Components Ltd [1977] IRLR 74 . . . . .7.17
Air Canada v Lee [1978] ICR 1202; [1978] IRLR 392 . . . . 14.61, 16.39
Airbus UK Ltd v Webb [2008] IRLR 309 . . . . .14.178

Airey v Ireland (1979–89) 2 EHRR 305 . . . . .23.14
Airfix Footwear Ltd v Cope [1978] ICR 1210. . . . . .2.25
Airlie v City of Edinburgh District Council [1996] IRLR 516 .3.17
Akavan Erityisalojen Keskusliitto v Fujitsu Siemens Computers Oy [2010] ICR 444. . . . .18.123
Al Jumard v Clywd Leisure Ltd [2008] IRLR 345 . . . . .8.204
Albert J. Parsons & Sons Ltd v Parsons [1979] ICR 271. . . . . .2.56
Albion Shipping v Arnold [1981] IRLR 525 . . . . .7.38
Alboni v Ind Coope Retail Ltd [1998] IRLR 131 . . . . .14.99
Alcan Extrusions Ltd v Yates [1996] IRLR 327 . . . . .14.11
Alemo-Herron v Parkwood Leisure Ltd [2010] ICR 793; [2013] ICR 1116 . . . . .18.127
Alexander v Home Office [1988] ICR 685 . . . . .8.206
Alexander v STC plc [1990] ICR 29 . . . . .13.46
Alexander v STC Ltd No 2 [1991] IRLR 287 . . . . 3.10, 3.16
Ali v Christian Salvesen Food Services Limited [1997] IRLR 17 . . . . .3.08
Ali v McDonagh [2002] ICR 1026 . . . . .8.170
Ali v Southwark LBC [1988] ICR 567. . . . . .13.46
Allaway v Reilly [2007] IRLR 864 . . . . .8.165
Allders International Ltd v Parkins [1981] IRLR 68 . . . . 14.31, 14.151
Allen & Son v Coventry [1979] IRLR 399 . . . . .11.49
Allen v Amalgamated Construction Co Ltd [2000] IRLR 119, ECJ. 18.09
Allen v Flood [1898] AC 1. . . . . 21.03, 21.06, 21.19, 21.31, 21.46
Allen v GMB [2008] IRLR 690. . . . . .8.105
Allen v Hammett [1982] IRLR 89. . . . . .14.341
Allen v Morrisons Facilities Services Ltd [2014] ICR 792. . . . . .18.123
Alliance Paper Group plc v Prestwich [1996] IRLR 25. . . . . 6.50, 6.69
Allied Dunbar (Frank Weisinger) Ltd v Frank Weisinger [1988] IRLR 60 . . . . .6.48
Allinson v Drew Simmons Engineering Ltd [1985] ICR 488. . . . . .4.72
Amalgamated Society of Boilermakers v George Wimpey Ltd [1977] IRLR 95 . . . . .17.41, 17.50
American Cyanamid Ltd v Ethicon [1975] AC 396. . . . . 6.71, 21.161, 21.164
Amey Services Ltd v Cardigan [2008] IRLR 279 . . . . .7.17
Amey v Peter Symonds College [2014] IRLR 206 . . . . .4.21
Amos v MaxArc Ltd [1973] IRLR 285 . . . . 16.21, 16.31
Anderson & McAlonie v Dalkeith Engineering Ltd [1984] IRLR 429 . . . . 16.10, 18.106, 18.111
Andrews v King [1991] ICR 846. . . . . .2.77
Anged v Fasga [2012] ICR 1211 . . . . .5.65
Angestelltenbetriebsrat der Wiener v Wiener Gebietskrankenkasse [2000] ICR 1134 . . . . . .7.29
Angus Jowett & Co Ltd v NUTGW [1985] IRLR 326. 18.121, 18.122
Aniagwu v London Borough of Hackney [1999] IRLR 303 . . . . .12.18
Anya v University of Oxford [2001] IRLR 377. . . . . 8.185, 8.186
Anyanwu v South Bank Student Union [2001] ICR 391 . . . . .8.165
Aparau v Iceland Frozen Foods [1996] IRLR 119. . . . . 3.26, 3.36, 3.74, 4.75
Apelgun-Gabriels v London Borough of Lambeth [2002] IRLR 116 . . . . .12.18
Apex Leisure Hire Ltd v Barratt [1984] ICR 452 . . . . .18.55
Appiah v Governing Body of Bishop Douglass RC High School [2007] IRLR 264 . . . . . . .8.184
Appleyard v Smith (Hull) Ltd [1972] IRLR 19 . . . . .14.243
Arch Initiatives v Greater Manchester West Mental Health NHS Foundation
    Trust [2016] IRLR 406. . . . . .18.35
Archbold Freightage v Wilson [1974] IRLR 10. . . . . .14.351
Archer v Cheshire & Northwich Building Society [1976] IRLR 424 . . . . .14.171
Archibald v Fife Council [2004] IRLR 651. . . . . 8.129 8.141
Archibald v Rossleigh Commercials Ltd [1975] IRLR 231 . . . . .16.21
Argent v Minister of Social Security [1968] 3 All ER 208 . . . . .2.25
Arjona Camacho v Securitas Seguridad España SA [2016] ICR 389. . . . . .8.207
Armstrong v Newcastle upon Tyne NHS Hospital Trust [2006] IRLR 124 . . . . .7.22, 7.35, 7.54
Arnold v Beecham Group Ltd [1982] IRLR 307. . . . . 7.76, 7.77

Arrowsmith v Jenkins [1963] 2 QB 561 .... .22.06
Arrowsmith v UK (1980) 3 EHRR 218 .... .23.38
Arthur v Attorney-General [1999] ICR 631 .... .8.170
Arthur v London Eastern Railway Ltd [2008] IRLR 58 .... .15.24
Ashcroft v Haberdashers' Aske's Boys' School [2008] IRLR 375 .... .12.23
Asociaţia ACCEPT v Consiliul Naţional pentru Combaterea Discriminării
  [2013] ICR 938 .... .8.188
Aspden v Webbs Poultry & Meat Group (Holdings) Ltd [1996] IRLR 521 ...... .3.34
Associated British Ports v TGWU [1989] IRLR 399 .... .21.54, 21.83, 21.93, 21.99,
                                                      21.161, 21.163–21.165
Associated Newspapers Group Ltd v Flynn (1970) 10 KIR 17 .... .21.93
Associated Newspapers v Wade [1979] ICR 664 .... .21.52, 21.53, 21.101
Associated Tyre Specialists (Eastern) Ltd v Waterhouse [1976] IRLR 386 .... .4.26
Association de médiation sociale v Union des sydicats [2014] ICR 411 .... .17.06
Association of HSD (Hatfield) Employees v Certification Officer [1978] ICR 2 .... 19.11
Association of Patternmakers and Allied Craftsmen v Kirvin Ltd
  [1978] IRLR 318 .... .17.23, 17.43
Association of Scientific, Technical and Managerial Staffs v Hawker Siddeley
  Aviation Ltd [1977] IRLR 418 .... .17.50
Association of University Teachers v University of Newcastle upon Tyne
  [1988] IRLR 10 .... .16.20
Athinaïki Chartopoïïa AE v Panagiotidis [2007] IRLR 284 .... .17.36
Atkinson v George Lindsay & Co [1980] IRLR 19 .... .14.196
Atos Origin IT Services Ltd v Haddock [2005] ICR 277 .... .8.198
Attorney-General for New South Wales v Perpetual Trustee Co Ltd
  [1955] AC 457 .... .2.36
Attorney-General v The Observer [1988] 2 WLR 805 .... .6.40
Attwood v Lamont [1920] 3 KB 571 .... .6.59
Auguste Noël Ltd v Curtis [1990] ICR 604 .... .14.178
Austin v Metropolitan Police Commissioner [2007] EWCA Civ 989 .... .22.08
Australian Mutual Provident Society v Allan (1978) 52 ALJR 407 .... .2.30
Autoclenz Ltd v Belcher [2011] IRLR 820 .... .2.03, 2.12, 2.14, 3.52
Avon and Somerset Police v Emery [1981] ICR 229 .... .7.47
Avon County Council v Howlett [1983] IRLR 171 .... 4.17, 5.12
Avonmouth Construction Co Ltd v Shipway [1979] IRLR 14 .... .14.211
Ayub v Vauxhall Motors Ltd [1978] IRLR 428 .... .14.179
Aziz v Trinity Taxis Ltd [1988] ICR 534 .... .8.112

BA plc v Unite the Union [2010] IRLR 809 .... .21.151, 21.152
BA v Grundy [2008] IRLR 815 .... .7.66
BA v Mak [2011] ICR 735 .... .12.37
BA v Williams [2012] IRLR 1014 .... .5.67
BAC Ltd v Austin [1978] IRLR 322 .... .4.26
BAC v Austin [1978] IRLR 332 .... .14.27
BAE Systems (Operations) Ltd v Konczak [2014] IRLR 676 .... .8.198
BALPA v Jet 2 [2015] IRLR 543 .... 3.16, 19.60
BBC v Beckett [1983] IRLR 43 .... .14.41
BBC v Farnworth [1998] ICR 1116 .... .16.25
BBC v Hearn [1978] 1 All ER 111 .... .21.52, 21.86, 21.88, 21.100
BBC v Roden [2015] IRLR 627 .... .23.16
BBC Scotland v Souster [2001] IRLR 150 .... .8.20
BCCI SA v Ali [1999] IRLR 226; [2002] IRLR 460; [2003] IRLR 292 .... 6.06, 12.53
BCCI v Ali (No 3) [1999] IRLR 508 .... .3.30
BHS Ltd v Burchell [1978] IRLR 379 .... .14.157
BL Cars v Lewis [1983] IRLR 58 .... .14.201

BMA v Chaudhary [2007] IRLR 800 . . . . .8.184
BMK v Logue [1993] ICR 601. . . . . .14.93
BP Chemicals Ltd v Gillick [1995] IRLR 128 . . . . .8.10
BP plc v Elstone [2010] ICR 879 . . . . .15.07
BP Tanker Co v Jeffries [1974] IRLR 260. . . . . .14.126
BSC Sports & Social Club v Morgan [1987] IRLR 391 . . . . .14.110
BSG Property Services and Mid Beds DC v Tuck [1996] IRLR 134 . . . . .18.112
BT Managed Services Ltd v Edwards [2016] ICR 733 . . . . .18.50
BT plc v CWU [2003] EWHC 937 . . . . .21.137
BTC v Gourley [1956] AC 185 . . . . .13.74
BUSM Co Ltd v Clarke [1978] ICR 70 . . . . .14.312
B v UK (1985) 45 D&R 41 . . . . .23.50
Babar Indian Restaurant v Rawat [1985] IRLR 57. . . . . .16.22
Babcock FATA Ltd v Addison [1987] IRLR 173. . . . . 14.316, 14.322
Babula v Waltham Forest College [2007] IRLR 346. . . . . 15.10, 15.11
Bacica v Muir [2006] IRLR 35 . . . . .2.69
Bailey v BP Oil (Kent Refinery) Ltd [1980] IRLR 287. . . . . .14.110
Bailey v BP Oil Ltd [1980] IRLR 287 . . . . .14.183
Bailey v Home Office [2005] IRLR 369 . . . . .7.53
Bainbridge v Westinghouse Brake & Signal Co Ltd (1966) 1 ITR 5 . . . . .16.48
Baker v Gill (1971) 6 ITR 61. . . . . .16.35
Baker v Kaye [1997] IRLR 219 . . . . .4.77
Balamoody v UKCC [2002] ICR 646 . . . . .8.80
Baldwin v Brighton & Hove City Council [2007] IRLR 232, EAT 3.30, 14.28, 14.34
Baldwin v British Coal Corporation [1995] IRLR 139 . . . . 3.42, 13.05
Balfour Beatty Engineering Services Ltd. v UNITE [2010] ICR 822 . . . . .21.119
Balfour Beatty Power Networks Ltd v Wilcox [2006] IRLR 258 . . . . 18.16, 18.33
Balfour Kilpatrick Ltd v Acheson [2003] IRLR 683 . . . . .20.58
Balfour v Foreign and Commonwealth Office [1994] ICR 277. . . . . .23.21
Balgobin v London Borough of Tower Hamlets [1987] IRLR 401 . . . . .8.169
Balkaya v Kiesel Abbruch– und Recycling Technik GmbH [2015] ICR 1110. . . . . .2.75
Balston Ltd v Headline Filters Ltd [1987] FSR 330. . . . . 6.11, 6.35
Bamsey v Albion Engineering Ltd [2004] IRLR 457. . . . . 5.63, 16.57
Banaszczyk v Booker Ltd [2016] IRLR 273 . . . . .8.60
Banerjee v City and East London AHA [1979] IRLR 147. . . . . 14.219, 14.225
Bank voor Handel en Scheepvaart NV v Slatford [1953] 1 QB 248 . . . . .2.19
Barber & ors v RJB Mining (UK) Limited [1999] IRLR 308 . . . . .5.54
Barber v NCR (Manufacturing) Ltd [1993] ICR 95 . . . . .7.64
Barber v Somerset CC [2004] IRLR 475. . . . . .4.32
Barber v Staffordshire CC [1996] IRLR 209. . . . . .7.03
Bărbulescu v Romania [2016] IRLR 235. . . . . .23.33
Barclay v City of Glasgow DC [1983] IRLR 313. . . . . .14.71
Barclays Bank plc v Kapur (No 2) [1995] IRLR 8. . . . . .8.85
Barley v Amey Roadstone Corporation Ltd [1977] IRLR 299 . . . . 14.312, 17.34
Barley v Amey Roadstone Ltd [1977] ICR 546. . . . . .20.77
Barnes v Leavesley [2001] ICR 38. . . . . .14.63
Barratt Construction Ltd v Dalrymple [1984] IRLR 385 . . . . .14.211
Barratt Developments Ltd v UCATT [1978] ICR 319. .17.34, 17.48
Barratt v Thomas Glover & Co Ltd (1970) 5 ITR 95 . . . . .16.48
Barrel Plating Co Ltd v Danks [1976] 3 All ER 652 . . . . .14.322
Barrett v National Coal Board [1978] ICR 1102. . . . . .3.20
Barretts & Baird (Wholesale) Ltd v IPCS [1987] IRLR 3 . . . . 21.44, 21.54, 21.55, 21.159
Barros D'Sa v University Hospital Coventry and Warwickshire NHS Trust
    [2001] IRLR 691. . . . . .13.28
Barry v Midland Bank plc [1999] ICR 859 . . . . 7.62, 8.104

Barton v Investec Ltd [2003] IRLR 332 . . . . .8.180
Basildon & Thurrock NHS Foundation Trust v Weerasinghe [2016] ICR 30. . . . . .8.86
Basnett v J. & A. Jackson Ltd [1976] ICR 63 . . . . .13.75
Bass Leisure Ltd v Thomas [1994] IRLR 104 . . . . 4.75, 16.16
Bass Taverns Ltd v Burgess [1995] IRLR 596 . . . . .20.09
Batchelor v British Railways Board [1987] IRLR 136. 13.19, 14.93
Bates VAN Winkelhof v Clyde & Co LLP [2014] ICR 730. . . . . .2.69
Bauman v Hulton Press Ltd [1952] 2 All ER 1121 . . . . .13.03
Bauman v Hulton Press Ltd [1952] WN 556. . . . . .4.56
Bayoomi v British Railways Board [1981] IRLR 431 . . . . .8.195
Beal v Beecham Group Ltd [1982] ICR 460 . . . . .20.46
Bear Scotland Ltd v Fulton [2015] IRLR 15 . . . . 5.67, 5.74
Beard v St Joseph's School [1978] ICR 1234. . . . . .14.236
Beart v HM Prison Service [2003] IRLR 238 . . . . .8.134
Beaverbrook Newspapers Ltd v Keys [1978] IRLR 34 . . . . .21.52, 21.93, 21.101, 21.165
Beckett Investment Management Group Ltd v Hall [2007] IRLR 793. . . . . .6.59
Beckmann v Dynamco Whicheloe Macfarlane Ltd [2002] IRLR 578. . . . . .18.71
Bective Electrical Co Ltd v Warren (1968) 3 ITR 119. . . . . .16.18
Beecham Ltd v Beal (No 2) [1983] IRLR 317 . . . . .20.47
Beetham v Trinidad Cement Ltd [1960] AC 132. . . . . .21.83
Belgian Linguistics case (1968) 1 EHRR 252 . . . . .23.72
Bell v Devon & Cornwall Police Authority [1978] IRLR 283. . . . . .14.182
Bell v Lever Brothers [1932] AC 161 . . . . .6.05
Belling & Lee v Burford [1982] ICR 454. . . . . .12.19
Beloff v Pressdram Ltd [1973] 1 All ER 241 . . . . 2.19, 6.39
Benson v Secretary of State for Trade and Industry [2003] ICR 1082 . . . . .16.74
Bent's Brewery Co Ltd v Hogan [1945] 2 All ER 570. . . . . .21.100
Bentley Engineering Co Ltd v Crown [1976] IRLR 146 . . . . 11.18, 11.43
Bentley Engineering Co Ltd v Mistry [1978] IRLR 436; [1979] ICR 47. . . . . 14.164, 14.182
Benton v Sanderson Kayser Ltd [1989] ICR 136; [1989] IRLR 19 . . . . 14.59, 16.37
Bentwood Bros (Manchester) Ltd v Shepherd [2003] ICR 1000. . . . . .8.198
Benveniste v University of Southampton [1989] IRLR 122. . . . . .7.49
Berg and Busschers v Besselsen [1989] IRLR 447 . . . . .18.12
Berriman v Delabole Slate Ltd [1984] ICR 636. . . . . .18.107
Berry v Aynsley Trust Ltd (1976) 127 NLJ 1052. . . . . .13.75
Berwick Salmon Fisheries Co Ltd v Rutherford [1991] IRLR 203 . . . . .11.21
Bessenden Properties Ltd v Corness [1977] ICR 821 . . . . 14.203, 14.351
Betriu Montull v Instituto Nacional de la Seguridad Social [2013] ICR 1323 . . . . .10.18
Betts v Brintel Helicopters Ltd [1997] IRLR 361 . . . . 18.23, 18.98
Bevan Harris Ltd v Gair [1981] IRLR 520 . . . . .14.121
Bick v Royal West of England School for the Deaf [1976] IRLR 326 . . . . .8.24
Biggs v Somerset CC [1995] ICR 811; [1996] ICR 364. 7.03, 12.16
Bigham v GKN Kwikform Ltd [1992] ICR 113. . . . . .14.269
Bilka-Kaufhaus GmbH v Weber von Hartz (Case 170/84) [1984]
    IRLR 317 . . . . .7.40, 7.60, 8.104
Billington v Michael Hunter & Sons Ltd EAT, 16 October 2003 . . . . .3.31
Bingham v Hobourn Engineering Ltd [1992] IRLR 29. . . . . .14.326
Birch v University of Liverpool [1985] ICR 470 . . . . .14.73
Bird v British Celanese Ltd [1945] KB 336 . . . . .4.57
Bird v Sylvester [2008] IRLR 232 . . . . .8.155
Birmingham Mosque Trust Ltd v Alavi [1992] ICR 435. . . . . .2.37
Birmingham Optical plc v Johnson [1996] ICR 459 . . . . 12.22
Blackbay Ventures Ltd v Gahir [2014] ICR 747 . . . . .15.23
Blackburn v Chief Constable of West Midlands Police [2009] IRLR 135. . . . . .7.63
Blakely v Chemetron Ltd (1972) 7 ITR 224 . . . . .16.30

Bleuse v MBT Transport Ltd [2008] ICR 488 . . . . .12.41
Bliss v South East Thames Regional Health Authority [1985] IRLR 308 . . . . .3.26, 14.31,
14.41, 14.51
Blue Chip Trading Ltd v Helbawi [2009] IRLR 128 . . . . .12.33
Blue Circle Staff Association v Certification Officer [1977] ICR 224 . . . . .19.15
Blue Star Ship Management Ltd v Williams [1979] IRLR 16 . . . . .14.135
Blundell v Christie Hospital NHS Trust [1996] ICR 347 . . . . .14.189
Blundell v Governing Body of St Andrews RC Primary School [2007] IRLR 652 . . . . .10.18
Blyth v The Scottish Liberal Club [1983] IRLR 24 . . . . .13.30, 13.33
Board of Governors, National Heart and Chest Hospital v Nambiar
[1981] IRLR 196 . . . . 14.93, 14.98
Boardman v Nugent Care Society [2013] ICR 927 . . . . 13.31, 14.110
Bodha v Hampshire AHA [1982] ICR 200 . . . . .12.17
Bohon-Mitchell v Common Professional Examination Board and the Council
of Legal Education [1978] IRLR 525 . . . . .8.101
Bolton School v Evans [2007] IRLR 140 . . . . 15.03, 15.18
Bolton v Mahadeva [1972] 2 All ER 1322 . . . . .4.04
Bolwell v Redcliffe Homes Ltd [1999] IRLR 485 . . . . .18.01
Bombardier Aerospace v McConnell [2008] IRLR 51 . . . . .20.77
Bonner v Gibert Ltd [1989] IRLR 475 . . . . .16.52
Boorman v Allmakes Ltd [1995] IRLR 553 . . . . .14.309
Booth v USA [1999] IRLR 16 . . . . .11.23
Boots Co plc v Lees-Collier [1986] IRLR 485 . . . . .14.290
Borders Regional Council v Maule [1993] IRLR 199 . . . . .4.39
Boston Deep Sea Fishing and Ice Co v Ansell
(1888) 39 ChD 339 . . . . 4.04, 6.03, 13.33, 13.38, 14.95
Bosworth v Angus Jowett and Co Ltd [1977] IRLR 374 . . . . .4.56
Botzen v Rotterdamsche Droogdok Maatschappij BV [1986] 2 CMLR 50 . . . . .18.45
Bouchaala v Trusthouse Forte Hotels Ltd [1980] ICR 721 . . . . .14.244
Boulting v ACTT [1963] 2 QB 606 . . . . .19.20
Boulton & Paul Ltd v Arnold [1994] IRLR 532 . . . . .14.322
Bournemouth University HEC v Buckland [2011] QB 323 . . . . 14.11, 14.26
Bouzourou v Ottoman Bank [1930] AC 271 . . . . .4.43
Bovey v Hospital for Sick Children [1978] IRLR 241 . . . . .10.54
Bowater Containers Ltd v McCormack [1980] IRLR 50 . . . . .14.226
Bowater v Northwest London Hospitals Trust [2011] IRLR 331 . . . . .14.110
Bowden v Tuffnells Parcels Express Ltd [2001] IRLR 838 . . . . .5.55
Bowes & Partners v Press [1894] 1 QB 202 . . . . .21.10
Boxfoldia Ltd v NGA (1982) [1988] IRLR 383; [1988] ICR 752 . . . . 4.35, 21.06, 21.08, 21.112
Boxfoldia v National Graphical Association (1982) [1988] ICR 752 . . . . .19.43
Boychuk v H.J. Symons Holdings Ltd [1977] IRLR 395 . . . . .14.143
Boys' and Girls' Welfare Society v McDonald [1996] IRLR 129 . . . . .14.158
Brace v Calder [1895] 2 QB 253 . . . . .13.02
Bracebridge Engineering Ltd v Darby [1990] IRLR 3 . . . . .14.39
Bradford Hospitals NHS Trust v Al-Shabib [2003] IRLR 4 . . . . 8.80, 8.95
Bradley v NALGO [1991] ICR 359 . . . . .19.38
Bradshaw v Rugby Portland Cement Co Ltd [1972] IRLR 46 . . . . 14.155, 14.323
Brandon and Goold v Murphy Bros [1983] IRLR 54 . . . . .14.171
Brassington v Cauldon Wholesale Ltd [1978] IRLR 479 . . . . .20.70
Breach v Epsylon Industries Ltd [1976] IRLR 180 . . . . .4.56
Brekkes Ltd v Cattel [1972] Ch 105 . . . . .21.44
Brennan v J.H. Dewhurst Ltd [1983] IRLR 357 . . . . .8.141
Brennan v W. Ellward (Lancs) Ltd [1976] IRLR 378 . . . . .20.19
Brent LBC v Fuller [2011] ICR 806 . . . . .14.110
Brigden v American Express Bank [2000] IRLR 94 . . . . .4.47

Briggs v ICI (1968) 3 ITR 276 . . . . .4.73
Briggs v Oates [1990] ICR 473 . . . . .13.02
Briggs v Oates [1990] IRLR 472, [1990] ICR 473 . . . . .6.64
Brimelow v Casson [1924] 1 Ch 302 . . . . .21.38
British Aerospace Ltd v Green [1995] IRLR 433 . . . . .14.200
British Airports Authority v Ashton [1983] 1 WLR 1079 . . . . 22.31, 22.41
British Airways Engine Overhaul Ltd v Francis [1981] IRLR 9 .20.09
British Airways plc v Grundy (No 2) [2008] IRLR 815 . . . . .8.104
British Airways plc v Noble [2006] IRLR 533 . . . . .5.63
British Airways plc v UNITE [2010] ICR 1316 . . . . .21.120
British Airways plc v Valencia [2014] IRLR 683 . . . . .14.298
British Coal Corporation v Cheesbrough [1990] ICR 317 . . . . .16.60
British Coal Corporation v McGinty [1988] IRLR 7 . . . . .20.79
British Coal Corporation v Smith [1996] IRLR 404 . . . . .7.16
British Fuels Ltd v Meade & Baxendale [1998] IRLR 706 . . . . 18.79, 18.80
British Gas plc v McCarrick [1991] IRLR 30 . . . . .14.153
British Gas plc v Sharma [1991] ICR 19 . . . . .8.195
British Gas Services Ltd v McCaull [2001] IRLR 60 . . . . .8.177
British Home Stores Ltd v Burchell [1978] IRLR 379 . . . . .14.110
British Industrial Plastics Ltd v Ferguson [1938] 4 All ER 504 .21.26
British Labour Pump Co Ltd v Byrne [1979] ICR 347 . . . . .14.110
British Leyland (UK) Ltd v Swift [1981] IRLR 91 . . . . .14.110, 14.153
British Leyland Ltd v Ashraf [1978] ICR 979 . . . . .14.77
British Leyland Ltd v Powell [1978] IRLR 57 . . . . .7.27
British Leyland UK Ltd v McQuilken [1978] IRLR 245 . . . . 3.16, 14.39
British Motor Trades Association v Salvadori [1949] Ch 556 . . . . .21.39
British Nursing Association v Inland Revenue [2002] IRLR 472 .5.30
British Railways Board v National Union of Railwaymen [1989] IRLR 349 . . . . .21.117
British Reinforced Concrete Co Ltd v Lind (1917) 116 LT 243 .6.41
British Road Services Ltd v Loughran [1997] IRLR 92 . . . . .7.53
British Telecommunications plc v Roberts [1996] IRLR 601 . . . . .8.29
British Telecommunications plc v Sheridan [1990] IRLR 27 . . . . .14.110
British Telecommunications plc v Ticehurst [1992] ICR 383 . . . . 4.25, 21.14
British United Shoe Machinery Co Ltd v Clarke [1977] IRLR 29 . . . . .14.211
Britool Ltd v Roberts [1993] IRLR 481 . . . . .20.19
Brittains Arborfield Ltd v Van Uden [1977] ICR 211 . . . . 14.322, 14.330
Broadbent v Crisp [1974] ICR 248 . . . . .2.71
Broaders v Kalkare Property Maintenance Ltd [1990] IRLR 421 . . . . .12.30
Bromby and Hoare Ltd v Evans [1972] ITR 76 . . . . .16.31
Bromley v H. & J. Quick Ltd [1988] ICR 623 . . . . .7.73
Brompton v AOC International Ltd [1997] IRLR 638 . . . . .3.26
Brookes v Borough Care Services [1998] IRLR 636 . . . . .18.07
Brooks v Olyslager OMS (UK) Limited [1998] IRLR 590 . . . . .6.29
Broome v DPP [1974] AC 587 . . . . 22.06, 22.41, 22.45
Brown v JBD Engineering Ltd [1994] IRLR 568 . . . . .14.41
Brown v LB of Croydon [2007] IRLR 259 . . . . .8.184
Brown v Rentokil [1998] IRLR 445 . . . . .8.30
Brown v Southall and Knight [1980] IRLR 130 . . . . 11.25, 14.93
Brown v Stockton on Tees BC [1988] IRLR 263 . . . . .14.191
Brown v Stuart Scott & Co [1981] ICR 166 . . . . .14.102
Brown v TNT Express Ltd [2001] ICR 182 . . . . .8.77
Browning v Crumlin Valley Collieries Ltd [1926] 1 KB 522 . . . . .4.54
Bruce v Wiggins Teape (Stationery) Ltd [1994] IRLR 536 . . . . .5.03
Brumfitt v MOD [2005] IRLR 4 . . . . .23.27
Brunnhofer v Bank der Österreichischen Postsparkasse [2001] IRLR 571 . . . . .7.65

Brunnhofer v Bank der Österreichischen Postsparkasse AG [2001] IRLR 571 . . . . . . .7.29, 7.103
Buchanan v Tilcon Ltd [1983] IRLR 417 . . . . .14.198
Buchanan-Smith v Schleicher & Co International Ltd [1996] ICR 613 . . . . .18.47
Budgen & Co v Thomas [1976] IRLR 174 . . . . .14.182
Bull v Pitney-Bowes Ltd [1967] 1 WLR 273 . . . . .6.63
Bunce v Postworth Ltd t/a Skyblue [2005] IRLR 557 . . . . .2.13
Burdett-Coutts v Hertfordshire CC [1984] IRLR 91 . . . . 3.54, 3.59
Burlo v Langley [2007] IRLR 145 . . . . 14.316, 14.320
Burrow Down Support Services Ltd v Rossiter [2008] ICR 1172 .5.30
Burton Group Ltd v Smith [1977] IRLR 351 . . . . .3.11
Busch v Klinikum Neustadt GmbH & Co [2003] IRLR 626 . . . . .8.29
Business Seating (Renovations) Ltd v Broad [1989] ICR 729 . . . . .6.60
Byrne Bros (Formwork) Ltd v Baird [2002] IRLR 96 . . . . .2.13
Byrne v BOC Ltd [1994] IRLR 505 . . . . .14.187
Byrne v City of Birmingham DC [1988] ICR 480 . . . . .11.15
Byrne v Financial Times Ltd [1991] IRLR 417 . . . . .7.35

C.A. Parsons & Co Ltd v McLoughlin [1978] IRLR 65 . . . . .14.148
CCSU v UK (1988) 50 DR 228 . . . . .23.64
CJD v Royal Bank of Scotland [2014] IRLR 25 . . . . .14.136
CLECE SA v Martin Valor [2011] ICR 1319 . . . . .18.19
CPL Distribution Ltd v Todd [2003] IRLR 28 . . . . .18.47
CPS Recruitment v Bowen and Secretary of State for Employment [1982] IRLR 54 . . . . . .14.56
Cable & Wireless plc v Muscat [2006] IRLR 354 . . . . .2.06
Cadman v JHSE [2006] ECR I-9583 . . . . .7.41
Cadoux v Central Regional Council [1986] IRLR 131 . . . . .3.17
Cain v Leeds Western HA [1990] ICR 585 . . . . .14.151
Calder v Rowntree Mackintosh Confectionery Ltd [1993] ICR 81 .7.43
Caledonian Mining Co Ltd v Bassett and Steel [1987] IRLR 165 .14.70
Callaghan v Glasgow City Council [2001] IRLR 724 . . . . .8.129
CalMac Ferries Ltd v Wallace [2014] ICR 453 . . . . .7.36
Calveley v Merseyside Police [1989] 1 All ER 1025 . . . . .13.27
Cambridge & Peterborough NHS Foundation Trust v Crouchman [2009] ICR 1306 . . . . 12.22
Cambridge and District Cooperative Society Ltd v Ruse [1993] IRLR 156 . . . . 16.46, 16.48
Camden & Islington Community Services NHS Trust v Kennedy [1996] IRLR 381 . . . . . .12.08
Camden Nominees Ltd v Forcey [1940] Ch 352 . . . . .21.39
Camellia Tanker SA v ITF [1976] ICR 274 . . . . .21.29
Camelo v Sheerlyn Productions Ltd [1976] ICR 531 . . . . .16.33
Camelot v Centaur Communications Limited [1998] IRLR 80 . . . . .6.26
Campbell v Dunoon & Cowal Housing Association Ltd [1993] IRLR 496 . . . . . 14.192, 14.312
Campbell v Frisbee [2003] ICR 141 . . . . .6.39
Canniffe v East Riding of Yorkshire Council [2000] IRLR 555 . . . . .8.169
Canning v Niaz [1983] IRLR 431 . . . . .18.106
Cantor Fitzgerald (UK) Ltd v Wallace [1992] IRLR 215 . . . . .6.49, 6.51, 6.69
Cantor Fitzgerald International v Bird [2003] IRLR 867 . . . . .14.47
Cantor Fitzgerald International v Callaghan [1999] IRLR 234 . . . . .14.34
Capita Hartshead Ltd v Byard [2012] ICR 1256 . . . . .14.110
Capita Health Solutions Ltd v McLean [2008] IRLR 595 . . . . .18.94
Capital Energy Solutions v Arnold [2015] ICR 611 . . . . .17.07
Capital Foods Retail Ltd v Corrigan [1993] IRLR 430 . . . . .12.14
Capper Pass Ltd v Lawton [1976] IRLR 366 . . . . 7.25, 7.41
Cardiff City Council v Condé [1978] IRLR 218 . . . . .14.184
Cardinal Vaughan Memorial School Governors v Alie [1987] ICR 406 . . . . .14.57
Carl v University of Sheffield [2009] IRLR 617 . . . . .9.08
Carlin v St Cuthberts Co-op Association Ltd [1974] IRLR 188 . . . . .14.94

Carmichael v National Power plc [2000] IRLR 43 . . . . .2.09
Carr v Alexander Russell Ltd [1976] IRLR 220 . . . . .14.170
Carrington v Harwich Dock Co Ltd [1998] ICR 1112 . . . . .11.07
Carrington v Helix Lighting Ltd [1990] IRLR 6. . . . . .8.191
Carron Company v Robertson (1967) 2 ITR 484 . . . . .16.45
Carter v Law Society [1973] ICR 113 . . . . .2.69
Cartiers Superfoods Ltd v Laws [1978] IRLR 315 . . . . .14.322
Cartwright v G. Clancey Ltd [1983] ICR 552 . . . . .4.65
Cassell v Broome [1972] AC 1027 . . . . .8.206
Cassidy v Ministry of Health [1951] 2 KB 343 . . . . .2.17
Cast v Croydon College [1998] ICR 500 . . . . .10.27
Catamaran Cruisers Ltd v Williams [1994] IRLR 386 . . . . 2.06, 14.229
Catherall v Michelin Tyres plc [2003] ICR 28 . . . . .14.69
Catherine Haigh Harlequin Hair Design v Seed [1990] IRLR 175 . . . . .14.102
Cavanagh v William Evans Ltd [2012] ICR 1231 . . . . .13.18
Cavendish Munro Professional Risks Management Ltd v Gould [2010] ICR 325 . . . . .15.04
Cawley v South Wales Electricity Board [1985] IRLR 89 . . . . 14.31, 14.53
Cayne v Global Natural Resources plc [1984] 1 All ER 225 .21.161
Celtec Ltd v Astley [2005] IRLR 647, ECJ 18.58, 18.95, 18.96
Celtec v Anstey [2001] IRLR 788 . . . . .11.40
Centrum voor Gelijkheid van Kansen en voor Racismebestrijding v Firma
    Feryn NV [2008] IRLR 732; [2008] ECR-I 5187l 8.71, 8.141
Cerberus Software Ltd v Rowley [2001] IRLR 160 . . . . .13.73
Chakki v United Yeast Co Ltd [1982] ICR 140 . . . . .14.85
Chamberlain Solicitors v Emokpae [2004] IRLR 592 . . . . .8.181
Chant v Aquaboats Ltd [1978] 3 All ER 102 . . . . .20.13
Chantrill v W. F. Shortland Ltd [1974] IRLR 333 . . . . .14.171
Chaplin v Rawlinson [1991] ICR 553 . . . . .14.312
Chapman and another v CPS Computer Group plc [1987] IRLR 462, CA 18.76
Chapman v Goonvean and Rostowrack China Clay Ltd [1973] ICR 310 . . . . .16.29
Chapman v Letherby & Christopher Ltd [1981] IRLR 440 . . . . .14.93
Chapman, Lowry & Puttick Ltd v Cox, EAT 270/85 . . . . .14.31
Chappell v Times Newspapers Ltd [1975] ICR 145 . . . . 13.44, 21.12
Chare née Julien v France (App No 14461/88) DR 141 . . . . .23.35
Charles Lang & Sons Ltd v Aubrey [1977] IRLR 354 . . . . .14.102
Charles Robertson Ltd v White [1995] ICR 349 . . . . .14.347
Charles v SRC (1977) 12 ITR 208 . . . . .14.178
Charlton v Charlton Thermosystems (Romsey) Ltd [1995] ICR 56 . . . . .18.33
Charnock v Barrie Muirhead Ltd [1984] ICR 641 . . . . .11.43
Charnock v Court [1899] 2 Ch 35 . . . . .22.41
Chattopadhay v Holloway School [1981] IRLR 487 . . . . .8.192
Cheall v UK (1986) 8 EHRR 74 . . . . .23.63
Cheall v Vauxhall Motors [1979] IRLR 253 . . . . .20.70
Cheeseman v Bowater Paper Ltd [1971] 3 All ER 513 . . . . .13.75
Cheesman v R. Brewer Contracts Ltd [2001] IRLR 144 . . . . .18.33
Chelsea Football Club & Athletic Co Ltd v Heath [1981] IRLR 73 . . . . 14.307, 14.334
Cheng Yuen v Royal Hong Kong Golf Club [1998] ICR 131 . . . . .2.25
Chief Constable of Dumfries & Galloway Constabulary v Adams [2009] IRLR 612 . . . . . .8.60
Chief Constable of Lincolnshire Police v Stubbs [1999] IRLR 81 . . . . .8.168
Chief Constable of Lothian & Borders Police v Cumming [2010] IRLR 109 . . . . .8.60
Chief Constable of North Wales v Evans [1983] 1 WLR 141 . . . . .13.21
Chief Constable of South Yorkshire v Jelic [2010] IRLR 744 .8.130
Chief Constable of W Yorkshire Police v Homer [2012] ICR 704 . . . . .8.98
Chief Constable of West Midlands Police v Harrod 8.105
Chief Constable of West Yorkshire Police v Khan [2001] IRLR 830 . . . . .8.113

Chief Constable of West Yorkshire Police v Vento [2001] IRLR 124 . . . . .8.80
Chief Constable of West Yorkshire Police v Vento (No 2) [2002] IRLR 177 . . . . .8.195
Chiltern House Ltd v Chambers [1990] IRLR 8 . . . . .5.12
Chisholm v Kirklees Borough Council [1993] ICR 826 . . . . .7.60
Christie v John E Haith Ltd [2003] IRLR 670 . . . . .7.37
Chrystie v Rolls Royce Ltd [1976] IRLR 336 . . . . .14.189
Chubb Fire Security Ltd v Harper [1983] IRLR 311 . . . . .14.228
Church v West Lancashire NHS Trust [1998] IRLR 5 . . . . .16.25
Churchill v A. Yeates & Sons Ltd [1983] IRLR 187 . . . . .12.19
City and Hackney Health Authority v Crisp [1990] ICR 95 . . . . .14.301
City and Hackney Health Authority v NUPE [1985] IRLR 252 .21.14
City of Birmingham v Beyer [1977] IRLR 211 . . . . .20.15
City of Bradford MBC v Arora [1991] IRLR 165 . . . . .8.206
City of Edinburgh Council v Wilkinson [2010] IRLR 756 . . . . .7.20
City of Edinburgh DC v Stephen [1977] IRLR 135 . . . . .14.171
Clancy v Cannock Chase Technical College [2001] IRLR 331 . . . . 14.296, 14.328
Claridge v Daler Rowney Ltd [2008] ICR 1267 . . . . .3.25
Clark & Tokeley Ltd v Oakes [1998] IRLR 577 . . . . .11.40
Clark v BET plc [1997] IRLR 348 . . . . .13.58
Clark v Civil Aviation Authority [1991] IRLR 412 . . . . .14.181, 14.187
Clark v Clark Construction Initiatives Ltd [2008] IRLR 364 . . . . .2.59
Clark v NATSOPA [1985] IRLR 494 . . . . .19.23
Clark v Nomura International plc [2000] IRLR 766 . . . . .3.26
Clark v Oxfordshire Health Authority [1998] IRLR 125 . . . . .2.09
Clarke v Eley (IMI) Kynoch Ltd [1982] IRLR 482 . . . . 8.101, 14.203
Clarke v Hampshire Electro-Plating Co Ltd [1992] ICR 312 . . . . .8.177
Clarke v Redcar & Cleveland BC [2006] IRLR 324 . . . . .12.50
Clarke v Trimoco Motor Group Ltd [1993] ICR 238 . . . . 14.94, 14.182
Clarks of Hove Ltd v Bakers Union [1978] ICR 1076 . . . . 17.42
Clay Cross (Quarry Services) Ltd v Fletcher [1979] ICR 1 . . . . 7.31, 7.38, 7.39
Cleeve Link Ltd v Bryla [2014] ICR 264 . . . . .4.51
Cleveland Ambulance NHS Trust v Blane [1997] ICR 851 . . . . .20.70
Cleveland CC v Springett [1985] IRLR 131 . . . . .17.12
Clifford v Union of Democratic Mineworkers [1991] IRLR 518 . . . . .2.77
Clouston & Co Ltd v Corry [1906] AC 122 . . . . .13.33
Clymo v London Borough of Wandsworth [1989] IRLR 241 . . . . 8.101, 8.155
Coales v John Wood & Co [1986] IRLR 129 . . . . .5.17
Coalter v Walter Craven [1980] IRLR 262 . . . . .14.341
Coates v Modern Methods and Materials Ltd [1982] ICR 763 . . . . .14.249, 14.262, 14.264
Cobley v Forward Technology [2003] ICR 1051 . . . . .14.238
Cockram v Air Products plc [2014] ICR 1065 . . . . .14.47
Cofone v Spaghetti House Ltd [1980] ICR 155 . . . . 5.16, 16.60
Cohen v London Borough of Barking [1976] IRLR 416 . . . . .14.236
Coleman v Attridge Law [2008] IRLR 722 . . . . .8.116
Coleman v Magnet Joinery Ltd [1974] IRLR 343 . . . . .14.292
Coleman v S & W Baldwin [1977] IRLR 342 . . . . .14.34
Coleman v Toleman's Delivery Service Ltd [1973] IRLR 6 . . . . .14.293
Colen v Cebrian (UK) Ltd [2004] ICR 568 . . . . 12.26, 12.29
Coles v Ministry of Defence [2016] ICR 55 . . . . .9.21
College of Ripon & York v Hobbs [2002] IRLR 185 . . . . .8.33
Collier v Smith's Dock Ltd (1969) 4 ITR 338 . . . . .16.45
Collino v Telecom Italia SPA [2002] ICR 38 . . . . .18.21
Collison v British Broadcasting Corporation [1998] ICR 669, EAT 11.53, 12.50
Colwyn Borough Council v Dutton [1980] IRLR 420 . . . . .14.286
Commerzbank AG v Keen [2007] IRLR 13 . . . . .3.26, 4.47, 13.58

Commission for Racial Equality v Dutton [1989] IRLR 8 ....8.18
Commission for Racial Equality v Imperial Society of Teachers of Dancing
 [1983] IRLR 315...8.167
Commission of European Communities v UK [1994] IRLR 412; [1994] ICR 664 ...... 1.23, 18.118
Commission of the European Communities v Belgium [1993] IRLR 404, ECJ 7.60
Commission of the European Communities v UK [1994] ICR 664...................17.04
Commission of European Communities v UK [2006] IRLR 888 ....5.49
Commission of the European Communities v United Kingdom [1984] IRLR 29 ....7.06
Commissioners of Inland Revenue v Morgan [2002] IRLR 776................. 8.75, 8.113
Commissioners of Inland Revenue v Post Office Ltd [2003] IRLR 199 ....2.25, 2.71
Commotion Ltd v Rutty [2006] ICR 290 ....10.83
Community Dental Centres Ltd v Sultan-Darmon [2010] IRLR 1024 ....2.68
Company's Application, Re [1989] 3 WLR 265 ....6.39
Compass Group plc v Ayodele [2011] IRLR 802................................8.105
Connely v Liverpool Corporation (1974) 9 ITR 51.............................14.175
Connex South Eastern Ltd v National Union of Rail Maritime and Transport
 Workers [1999] IRLR 249...21.128
Connolly v Sellers Arenascene Ltd [2001] ICR 760.............................2.58
Connor v Comet Radiovision Services Ltd, EAT 650/81 ....14.341
Conoco (UK) Ltd v Neal [1989] IRLR 51....................................14.301
Consistent Group Ltd v Kalwak [2008] IRLR 505 ....2.14
Constantine v McGregor Cory Ltd [2000] ICR 938............................14.322
Construction Industry Training Board v Leighton [1978] IRLR 60 ....3.75
Conteh v Parking Partners Ltd [2011] ICR 341...............................8.109
Contract Bottling Ltd v Cave [2015] ICR 146................................14.322
Converfoam (Darwen) Ltd v Bell [1981] IRLR 195............................14.134
Converfoam (Darwen) v Bell [1981] IRLR 195................................14.87
Conway v Matthew Wright & Nephew Ltd [1977] IRLR 89 ....14.170, 14.184
Conway v Wade [1909] AC 506 ....21.83, 21.90, 21.100
Cook v MSHK Ltd [2009] IRLR 838 ....14.46
Cook v Square D Ltd [1992] ICR 263.......................................4.29
Cook v Thomas Linnell & Sons Ltd [1977] IRLR 132...........................14.115
Cooner v P. S. Doal & Sons [1988] IRLR 338................................16.60
Cooper v Firth Brown Ltd [1963] 1 WLR 418 ....13.75
Cooper v Isle of Wight College [2008] IRLR 125..............................4.05
Cooperative Wholesale Society v Squirrell (1974) 9 ITR 191.....................14.325
Coors Brewers v Adcock [2007] IRLR 440...................................5.06
Copsey v WWB Devon Clays Ltd [2005] IRLR 810............................23.40
Copson v Eversure Accessories Ltd [1974] ICR 636 ....14.327
Cordant Security Ltd v Singh [2016] IRLR 4 ....8.151
Cordell v FCO [2012] ICR 280...8.133
Corner v Buckinghamshire CC [1978] IRLR 320..............................4.39
Cornwall CC v Prater [2006] ICR 73 ....11.05
Corps of Commissionaires Management Ltd v Hughes [2009] IRLR 122 ....5.49
Corton House Ltd v Skipper [1981] IRLR 78 ....11.26
Cory Lighterage Ltd v TGWU [1973] ICR 339................................21.84
Cotswold Developments Construction Ltd v Williams [2006] IRLR 181..............2.69
Council of Civil Service Unions v Minister for the Civil Service [1985] IRLR 28........14.103
Council of Engineering Institutions v Maddison [1977] ICR 30...................12.44
Council of the Isles of Scilly v Brintel Helicopters Ltd [1995] IRLR 6 ....18.10
County Council of Hereford and Worcester v Neale [1986] IRLR 168..............14.110
Courage Take Home Trade Ltd v Keys [1986] IRLR 427........................12.50
Courtaulds Northern Spinning Ltd v Moosa [1984] IRLR 43 ....14.313, 14.322, 14.340, 14.342
Courtaulds Northern Spinning Ltd v Sibson and TGWU
 [1988] IRLR 305...........................3.23, 3.36, 3.74, 4.75, 14.34

Courtaulds Northern Textiles Ltd v Andrew [1979] IRLR 84 . . . . .14.28
Courtney v Babcock & Wilcox (Operations) Ltd [1977] IRLR 30 . . . . .14.345
Coutts & Co v Cure [2005] ICR 1098 . . . . .9.17
Cowan v Pullman Spring Filled Co Ltd (1967) 2 ITR 650 . . . . .16.62
Coward v John Menzies (Holdings) Ltd [1977] IRLR 428 . . . . .14.141
Cowell v Quilter Goodison Ltd [1989] IRLR 392. . . . . .2.64
Cowley v Manson Timber Ltd [1994] ICR 252. . . . . .14.287
Cox v Sun Alliance Life Ltd [2001] IRLR 449 . . . . .4.78
Cox v Wildt Mellor Bromley Ltd [1978] IRLR 15 . . . . .14.201
Coxon v Rank Xerox (UK) Ltd [2003] ICR 628 . . . . .14.182
Cranleigh Precision Engineering Ltd v Bryant [1965] 1 WLR 129 . . . . .6.26
Crawford v Swinton Insurance Brokers Ltd [1990] ICR 85 . . . . .18.109
Crédit Suisse Asset Management Ltd v Armstrong [1996] IRLR 450. . . . . .6.20
Credit Suisse First Boston (Europe) Ltd v Lister [1998] IRLR 700 . . . . .18.82
Creffield v BBC [1975] IRLR 23 . . . . .14.155
Cresswell v Board of Inland Revenue [1984] ICR 508 . . . . 3.56, 4.20, 4.43
Croft v Royal Mail Group Ltd [2003] IRLR 592 . . . . .8.169
Crofter Handwoven Harris Tweed Co Ltd v Veitch [1942] AC 435 . . . . 21.46, 21.66
Crofts v Cathay Pacific Airways [2005] IRLR 624 . . . . .12.36
Croke v Hydro Aluminum Worcester Ltd [2007] ICR 1303 . . . . .15.20
Crompton v Truly Fair (International) Ltd [1975] ICR 359 . . . . .11.36
Cross v British Airways [2005] IRLR 423 . . . . .8.105
Cross v Highlands and Islands Enterprise [2001] IRLR 336. . . . . .4.30
Crossley v Faithful & Gould Holdings Ltd [2004] IRLR 377. .3.26
Crosville Motor Services Ltd v Ashfield [1986] IRLR 475 . . . . .20.22
Crosville Wales Ltd v Tracey [1993] IRLR 60. . . . . .14.269
Crown Agents v Lawal [1978] IRLR 542 . . . . .14.93
Crowson Fabrics Ltd v Rider [2008] IRLR 28 . . . . .6.09
Crowson Fabrics Ltd v Rider [2008] IRLR 288 . . . . 6.05, 6.22
Croydon Health Authority v Jaufurally [1986] ICR 4. . . . . 12.17, 12.22
Cruickshank v VAW Motorcast Ltd [2002] IRLR 23 . . . . 8.32, 8.60
Cruikshank v Hobbs [1977] ICR 725 . . . . .14.203
Cuckson v Stones (1858) 1 E & E 248. . . . . .4.19
Cumbria CC v Dow (No 1) [2008] IRLR 91. . . . . .7.35
Cumbria County Council v Carlisle-Morgan [2007] IRLR 314 . . . . .15.21
Cunard SS Co Ltd v Stacey [1955] 2 Lloyd's Rep 247. . . . . .21.26
Curr v Marks & Spencer plc [2003] IRLR 74. . . . . .11.23
Cutter v Powell (1795) 101 ER 573 . . . . .4.04

DC Builders v Rees [1966] 2 QB 617. . . . . .21.60
DCA v Jones [2008] IRLR 128 . . . . .8.174
DEFRA v Robertson [2005] ICR 750 . . . . .7.22
DPP v Jones [1999] 2 All ER 257 . . . . .22.18
D v M [1996] IRLR 291 . . . . .6.66
Dabell v Vale Industrial Services (Nottingham) Ltd [1988] IRLR 439 . . . . 11.37, 18.33
Dacas v Brook Street Bureau (UK) Ltd [2003] IRLR 358 . . . . 2.30, 2.51
Daily Mirror Newspapers v Gardner [1968] 2 QB 762. . . . . 21.37, 21.52
Dairy Crest Ltd v Pigott [1989] ICR 92. . . . . .6.51
Dairy Produce Packers Ltd v Beverstock [1981] IRLR 265 .14.149
Dal v A. S. Orr [1980] IRLR 413 . . . . .3.54
Dale v IRC [1954] AC 11. . . . . .2.39
Daley v A. E. Dorsett [1981] IRLR 385 . . . . 14.329, 14.353
Daley v Allied Suppliers [1983] IRLR 14. . . . . .2.45
Dalgleish v Kew House Farm Ltd [1982] IRLR 251 . . . . .13.09
Dalton v Burton's Gold Medal Biscuits Ltd [1974] IRLR 45. . . . . .14.150

Dance v Dorothy Perkins [1978] ICR 760 . . . . .7.17

Daniels Elliott & Hare v Thomas Glover Ltd (1966) 1 ITR 283 . . . . .16.48

Danosa v LKB Līzings [2011] 2 CMLR 2 . . . . .2.74

Dansk Jurist v Indenrigs – og Sundhedsministeriet [2014] ICR 1 .7.10

Darnell v UK (1994) 18 EHRR 205 . . . . .23.13

Darnton v University of Surrey [2003] ICR 615 . . . . .15.09

Darr v LRC Products Ltd [1993] IRLR 257 . . . . .14.309

Davidson and Maillou v Comparisons [1980] IRLR 360, EAT 6.09

Davidson and Maillou v Comparisons Ltd [1980] IRLR 360 . . . . .14.238

Davidson v Pillay [1979] IRLR 275 . . . . .12.28

Davies v Davies (1887) 36 ChD 359 . . . . 4.51, 6.65

Davies v Hotpoint Ltd [1994] IRLR 538 . . . . .5.03

Davies v M.J. Wyatt (Decorators) Ltd [2000] IRLR 759 . . . . .5.62

Davies v McCartneys [1989] IRLR 439 . . . . .7.40

Davies v Neath Port Talbot County BC [1999] IRLR 769 . . . . 7.03, 20.36

Davies v Presbyterian Church of Wales [1986] IRLR 194 . . . . .2.32, 2.77

Davies v Sandwell MBC [2013] IRLR 374 . . . . .14.122

Davis Contractors Ltd v Fareham UDC [1956] AC 696 . . . . .14.80

Davis v New England College of Arundel [1977] ICR 6 . . . . 2.25, 2.26, 2.28

Dawkins v Department of the Environment [1993] IRLR 284 . . . . .8.18

Dawney, Day & Co Limited v De Braconier d'Alphen [1997] IRLR 443 . . . . .6.51

Day v SOGAT (1982) [1986] ICR 640 . . . . .19.29

Daynecourt Insurance Brokers Ltd v Iles [1978] IRLR 335 . . . . .14.102

De Brito v Standard Chartered Bank Ltd [1978] ICR 650 . . . . .7.28

De Francesco v Barnum (1890) 43 ChD 165 . . . . 3.45, 13.41

De Grasse v Stockwell Tools Ltd [1992] IRLR 269 . . . . 14.109, 14.208

De Keyser Ltd v Wilson [2001] IRLR 324 . . . . 8.121, 23.17, 23.35

De Souza v Automobile Association [1986] IRLR 103 . . . . .8.152

Dean v Eastbourne Fishermen's and Boatmen's Protection Society Ltd [1977] ICR 556 . . .16.58

Deane v Craik, *The Times*, 16 March 1962 . . . . .3.11

Deane v Ealing LBC [1993] ICR 32 . . . . .8.206

Dedman v British Building & Engineering Appliances Ltd [1974] ICR 53,
    [1974] IRLR 379 . . . . 12.08, 12.12, 12.13, 12.17

Deeley v British Rail Engineering Ltd [1979] IRLR 5; [1980] IRLR 147 . . . . 3.48, 14.139

Defrenne v Sabena [1976] ECR 455 . . . . .7.19, 7.97

Degnan v Redcar & Cleveland BC [2005] IRLR 615 . . . . .7.103

Delanair Ltd v Mead [1976] ICR 522 . . . . .16.26

Delaney v Staples [1992] ICR 483; [1992] ICR 331 .5.05, 5.06, 13.04

Dellas v Premier Ministre [2006] IRLR 225 . . . . .5.31

Demir v Turkey [2009] IRLR 766 . . . . .21.02

Dench v Flynn & Partners [1998] IRLR 653 . . . . .14.322

Denco Ltd v Joinson [1991] IRLR 63 . . . . .14.171

Denmark Productions Ltd v Boscobel Productions Ltd [1969] 1 QB 699 . . . . .14.90

Denton v Neepsend Ltd [1976] IRLR 164 . . . . .16.48

Department for Work & Pensions v Thompson [2004] IRLR 348 .8.83

Department of the Environment v Fox [1979] ICR 736 . . . . 2.38, 8.170

Derby CC v Marshall [1979] ICR 731 . . . . .14.34

Derby Specialist Fabrication Ltd v Burton [2001] IRLR 69; [2001] ICR 833 . . . . . . 8.175, 8.148

Devonald v Rosser and Sons [1906] 2 KB 708 . . . . .4.56

Devonshire v Trico-Folberth Ltd [1989] IRLR 396 . . . . .14.322

Dhaliwal v British Airways Board [1985] ICR 513 . . . . .14.167

Dhunna v Creditsights Ltd [2013] ICR 909 [2015] ICR 105 . . . . .12.40

Dibro v Hore [1990] IRLR 129, [1990] ICR 370 . . . . .7.77

Dickins v 02 plc [2009] IRLR 59 . . . . .4.32

Diennet v France (1995) 21 EHRR 554 . . . . .23.19

Dietman v London Borough of Brent [1987] IRLR 259 . . . . .13.67
Digital Equipment Co Ltd v Clements (No 2) [1997] IRLR 141;
    [1998] ICR 258 . . . . 14.322, 14.334, 14.346
Dignity Funerals Ltd v Bruce [2005] IRLR 189 . . . . .14.334
Dimbleby & Sons Ltd v NUJ [1984] 1 WLR 427 . . . . 21.16, 21.50, 21.80, 21.87, 21.164
Dimskal Shipping Co SA v International Transport Workers Federation
    [1992] ICR 37; [1992] IRLR 78 . . . . .21.76
Dines v Initial Services Ltd [1994] IRLR 336 . . . . .18.33
Diocese of Southwark v Coker [1998] ICR 140, CA 2.34
Diosynth Ltd v Thomson [2006] IRLR 284 . . . . .14.178
Discount Tobacco & Confectionery Ltd v Williamson [1993] ICR 371 . . . . .5.07
Discount Tobacco Ltd v Armitage [1990] IRLR 14. . . . . .20.10
Distillers Co (Bottling Services) Ltd v Gardner [1982] IRLR 47. . . . . 14.149, 14.158, 14.182
Dixon and Shaw v West Ella Developments Ltd [1978] IRLR 151 . . . . .20.08
Dixon v Wilson Walton Engineering Ltd [1979] ICR 438. . . . . .14.262
Dobie v Burns International Security Services (UK) Ltd [1984] IRLR 329. . . . . .14.241
Doble v Firestone Tyre Co Ltd [1981] IRLR 300 . . . . .14.15
Doherty v British Midland Airways Ltd [2006] IRLR 90. . . . . .14.36
Donelan v Kerrby Constructions Ltd [1983] ICR 237. . . . . .16.60
Donkor v Royal Bank of Scotland Ltd [2016] IRLR 268 . . . . .8.75
Doyle v Northumbria Probation Committee [1992] ICR 121 . . . . .13.52
Drage v Governing Body of Greenford High School [2000] ICR 899. . . . . .14.93
Dresdner Kleinwort Wasserstein Ltd v Adebayo [2005] IRLR 514. . . . . .8.180
Drew v St Edmundsbury BC [1980] ICR 513 . . . . 20.14, 20.19
Driver v Cleveland Structural Engineering Co Ltd [1994] ICR 372 . . . . .20.30
Dryden v Greater Glasgow Health Board [1992] IRLR 469, EAT .3.39
Drym Fabricators Ltd v Johnson [1981] ICR 274 . . . . .2.55
Dudley Bower Building Services Ltd v Lowe [2003] IRLR 260 . . . . .18.27
Duff v Evan Thomas Radcliffe & Co Ltd [1979] ICR 720 . . . . .11.25
Duffin v Secretary of State for Employment [1983] ICR 766 . . . . .16.68
Duffy v Eastern Health and Social Services Board [1992] IRLR 25 . . . . .8.200
Dugdale v Kraft Foods Ltd [1977] 1 All ER 454. . . . . 7.28, 7.41
Duke v GEC Reliance Ltd [1988] ICR 339 . . . . .7.03
Duke v Reliance Systems [1982] ICR 44 . . . . .3.41
Dumfries & Galloway Council v North [2013] ICR 993 . . . . .7.24
Duncombe v Secretary of State for Children, Schools and Families (No 2)
    [2011] ICR 1312 . . . . .12.38
Dundon v GPT Ltd [1995] IRLR 403 . . . . .20.30
Dunk v George Waller & Sons Ltd [1970] 2 QB 163 . . . . .13.65
Dunlop Pneumatic Tyre Co Ltd v New Garage & Motor Co Ltd [1915] AC 79. . . . . .4.51
Dunlop Tyres Ltd v Blowers [2001] IRLR 629 . . . . .3.49
Dunn v AAH Ltd [2010] IRLR 709 . . . . .13.32
Dunnachie v Kingston upon Hull CC [2004] IRLR 727. . . . . 14.318, 14.331
Dunning and Sons (Shopfitters) Ltd v Jacomb [1973] ICR 448. .14.116
Duport Steels Ltd v Sirs [1980] 1 All ER 529 . . . . .21.101, 21.165
Durrant v North Yorkshire AHA [1979] IRLR 401 . . . . .7.25
D'Urso v Ercole Marelli Elettromeccanica General SpA [1992] IRLR 13. . . . . .18.109
Dutton & Clark Ltd v Daly [1985] IRLR 363. . . . . .14.39
Dutton v Hawker Siddeley Aviation Ltd [1978] ICR 1057; [1978] IRLR 390. . . . . . . 4.38, 16.47
Dynamex Friction Ltd v AMICUS [2008] IRLR 515 . . . . .18.106

EAD Solicitors LLP v Garry Abrams Ltd [2016] ICR 380 . . . . .8.116
EBAC Ltd v Wymer [1995] ICR 466. . . . . .16.34
EBR Attridge LLP v Coleman [2010] ICR 24 . . . . .8.09
ECM (Vehicle Delivery Service) Ltd v Cox [1999] IRLR 559 . . . . 18.28, 18.33

E Ivor Hughes Educational Foundation v Morris [2015] IRLR 696 . . . . .17.41
EOC v Birmingham CC [1989] AC 1155 . . . . .8.85
Eagland v British Telecommunications plc [1993] ICR 644 . . . . .3.76
Eagle Place Services Ltd v Rudd [2010] IRLR 486 . . . . .8.53
Ealing LBC v Race Relations Board [1972] AC 34 . . . . .8.21
Earl v Slater & Wheeler Ltd (Airlyne) [1972] ICR 508;
    [1972] IRLR 115 . . . . 14.159, 14.172, 14.182
East Berkshire Health Authority v Matadeen [1992] IRLR 336 . . . . .14.110, 14.171
East England Schools CIC v Palmer [2014] IRLR 191 . . . . .6.55
East Hertfordshire DC v Boyten [1977] IRLR 347 . . . . .14.173
East Lindsey DC v Daubney [1977] ICR 566 . . . . .14.125
East Suffolk Local Health Services NHS Trust v Palmer [1997] ICR 425 . . . . .16.39
East Sussex CC v Walker (1972) 6 ITR 280 . . . . .14.68
Eastwood v Magnox Electric plc [2004] ICR 1064 . . . . .3.33
Eaton Ltd v King [1995] IRLR 75 . . . . .14.198
Eaton Ltd v Nuttall [1977] IRLR 71 . . . . 7.27, 7.70, 7.72
Eaton v Robert Eaton Ltd and Secretary of State for Employment [1988] IRLR 83 . . . . .2.56
Ebbw Vale Steel, Iron and Coal Co v Tew (1935) 79 SJ 593 .21.13
Edie v HCL Insurance BPO Services Ltd [2015] ICR 713 . . . . .8.105
Edinburgh Council v Brown [1999] IRLR 208 . . . . .19.50
Edwards v Chesterfield Royal Hospital NHS Foundation Trust
    [2012] ICR 201 . . . . 13.55, 13.61
Edwards v Clinch [1981] 3 WLR 707 . . . . .2.38
Edwards v Governors of Hanson School [2001] IRLR 723 . . . . .14.127
Edwards v Mid Suffolk District Council [2001] IRLR 190 . . . . .8.121
Edwards v Skyways Ltd [1964] 1 WLR 349 . . . . 3.51, 19.50
Edwards v SOGAT [1971] Ch 354 . . . . .13.71
Edwards v Surrey Police [1999] IRLR 456 . . . . .14.50
Egg Stores (Stamford Hill) Ltd v Leibovici [1977] ICR 260 . . . . .14.84
Eke v Commissioners of Customs and Excise [1981] IRLR 334 . . . . .8.154
Ekpe v Metropolitan Police Commissioner [2001] IRLR 605 .8.60
Electrical and Engineering Association v Ashwell-Scott [1976] IRLR 319 . . . . .17.39
Electrolux Ltd v Hutchinson [1976] IRLR 410 . . . . .7.27
Electronic Data Processing Ltd v Wright [1986] IRLR 8 . . . . .14.299
Elkouil v Coney Island Ltd [2002] IRLR 174 . . . . .14.322
Elliot Brothers (London) Ltd v Colverd [1979] IRLR 92 . . . . .14.151
Ellis v Brighton Co-operative Society [1976] IRLR 419 . . . . .14.226
Ellis v Lucas [1967] Ch 858 . . . . .2.36
Elsey v Smith [1983] IRLR 292 . . . . 22.23, 22.41
Ely v YKK Fasteners (UK) Ltd [1994] ICR 164 . . . . .14.94
Emerald Construction Co Ltd v Lowthian [1966] 1 WLR 691 . . . . 21.26, 21.37, 21.47
Enderby v Frenchay HA (No 2) [2000] ICR 612 . . . . .7.103
Enderby v Frenchay Health Authority [1993] IRLR 591 . . . . .7.53
Enessy Co SA v Minoprio [1978] IRLR 489 . . . . .14.295
England v Bromley LBC [1978] ICR 1 . . . . .7.76
English v Thomas Sanderson [2009] IRLR 206 . . . . .8.107
Environmental Agency v Rowan [2008] IRLR 20 . . . . .8.129
Esparon v Slavikovska [2014] ICR 1037 . . . . .5.30
Essa v Laing Ltd [2004] ICR 746 . . . . .8.198
Esso Petroleum Co Ltd v Harper's Garage (Stourport) Ltd [1968] AC 269 . . . . .6.48
Essop v Home Office [2015] ICR 1063 . . . . .8.102
European Operations at Gatwick) Ltd v Moore & Botterill [2000] IRLR 296 . . . . 10.41, 10.45
Evans v Elemeta Holdings Ltd [1982] IRLR 143 . . . . .14.228
Evans v George Galloway & Co Ltd [1974] IRLR 167 . . . . .14.322
Evans v Malley Organisation Ltd [2003] ICR 443 . . . . 11.23, 16.63

Evans v RSA Consulting Ltd [2011] ICR 37 . . . . .2.30
Evenden v Guildford City Association Football Club [1975] ICR 36 . . . . 3.73, 11.52
Evening Standard Co v Henderson [1978] IRLR 64 . . . . 6.14, 13.42
Eversheds Legal Services v De Belin [2011] ICR 1137. . . . . .10.73
Everwear Candlewick Ltd v Isaac (1974) 8 ITR 334. . . . . .14.316
Evesham v W Herts HA [2000] IRLR 257 . . . . .7.103
Evesham v West Herts Health Authority [2000] IRLR 257 . . . . .7.11
Eweida v BA [2013] IRLR 231 . . . . 8.68, 23.43
Examite Ltd v Whittaker [1977] IRLR 312 . . . . .21.80
Express & Star Ltd v Bunday [1988] ICR 379 . . . . .14.258
Express & Star Ltd v NGA [1986] IRLR 222. . . . . .19.45
Express and Echo Publications Limited v Tanton [1999] IRLR 367. . . . . .2.13
Express Newspapers Ltd v McShane [1980] ICR 42. . . . . 21.71, 21.101, 21.165

F. C. Shepherd & Co Ltd v Jerrom [1986] IRLR 358 . . . . 13.19, 14.53, 14.89, 14.348
F. Kennedy v Werneth Ring Mills Ltd [1977] ICR 206. . . . . .16.47
F. Lafferty Construction Ltd v Duthie [1985] IRLR 487 . . . . .14.208
F. Little v Charterhouse Magna Assurance Co Ltd [1980] IRLR 1. . . . . 16.17
FOCSA Services (UK) Ltd v Birkett [1996] IRLR 32 . . . . .13.66
FSS Travel & Leisure Systems Limited v Johnson [1998] IRLR 383, CA 6.24
Faccenda Chicken Ltd v Fowler [1986] IRLR 69 . . . . 6.27, 6.35
Fairfield Ltd v Skinner [1992] ICR 836. . . . . .5.07
Faramus v Film Artistes' Association [1964] AC 925 . . . . .19.20
Fareham College Corporation v Walters [2009] IRLR 991. . . . . .8.129
Farmeary v Veterinary Drug Co Ltd [1976] IRLR 322. . . . . .20.77
Farnan v Sunderland AFC [2016] IRLR 185. . . . . .13.35
Farnsworth v McCoid [1999] IRLR 626. . . . . .20.18
Farquharson v Ross (1966) 1 ITR 335 . . . . .16.33
Farr v Hoveringham Gravels Ltd [1972] IRLR 104 . . . . .14.233
Farrant v The Woodroffe School [1998] ICR 184. . . . . .14.142
Farrell Matthews & Weir v Hansen [2005] ICR 509 . . . . .5.04
Farrow v Wilson (1869) LR 4 CP 744. . . . . .13.02
Faust v Power Packing Casemakers Ltd [1983] IRLR 117. . . . . .14.253
Fecitt v NHS Manchester [2012] ICR 372 . . . . 15.18, 15.23
Federatie Nederlasnmdse Vakbeweging [2006] ICR 962 . . . . .5.48
Federation of Offshore Workers' Trade Unions v Norway (App No 38190/97) 23.68
Fenoll v Centre d'aide par le travail La Jouvene [2016] IRLR 67 . . . . .2.75
Ferguson v John Dawson & Partners (Contractors) Ltd [1976] 1 WLR 1213;
    [1976] 3 All ER 817 . . . . 2.27, 2.29, 2.77, 3.01
Ferodo Ltd v Barnes [1976] IRLR 302 . . . . .14.159
Field v Receiver of Metropolitan Police [1907] 2 KB 853 . . . . .22.17
Financial Techniques (Planning Services) Ltd v Hughes [1981] IRLR 32 . . . . .3.51
Financial Techniques v Hughes [1981] IRLR 32. . . . . .14.41
Finnie v Top Hat Frozen Foods Ltd [1985] ICR 433. . . . . 14.317, 14.322
First West Yorkshire Ltd v Haigh [2008] IRLR 182 . . . . 14.125, 14.127
Fisher v California Cake & Cookie Ltd [1997] IRLR 212 . . . . .14.322
Fisher v Oldham Corporation [1930] 2 KB 364 . . . . .2.36
Fisher v York Trailer Co Ltd [1979] ICR 834 . . . . 14.258, 14.268
Fisscher v Voorhuis Hengelo BV [1994] IRLR 662 . . . . .7.88
Fitzgerald v Hall, Russell & Co Ltd [1970] AC 984 . . . . .11.14
Fitzgerald v University of Kent at Canterbury [2004] ICR 737 CA. 12.50, 14.93
Fitzpatrick v British Railways Board 1992] ICR 221 . . . . .20.16
Flack v Kodak Ltd [1986] IRLR 255. . . . . .11.20
Fleming v Secretary of State for Trade and Industry [1997] IRLR 682, Ct of Sess. 2.57
Fletcher v Blackpool Fylde & Wyre Hospitals NHS Trust [2005] IRLR 689 . . . . .10.30

Fletcher v NHS Pensions Agency [2005] ICR 1458. . . . . .8.29
Ford Motor Co Ltd v Hudson [1978] ICR 482 . . . . .14.286
Ford Motor Co v AEU [1969] 2 QB 302. . . . . .19.50
Ford v Warwickshire County Council [1983] IRLR 126 . . . . 11.10, 11.16, 11.18
Foreningen af Arbejdsledere I Danmark v Daddy's Dance Hall A/S
    [1988] IRLR 315. . . . . 18.09, 18.12, 18.41, 18.78, 18.80
Forex Neptune (Overseas) Ltd v Miller [1987] ICR 170. . . . . .7.47
Forman Construction Ltd v Kelly [1977] IRLR 469. . . . . .14.203
Forshaw v Archcraft Ltd [2005] IRLR 600. . . . . .14.234
Foster Bryant Surveying Ltd v Bryant [2007] IRLR 425. . . . . .6.11
Fougère v Phoenix Motor Ltd [1976] ICR 495 . . . . .14.322
Four Seasons Healthcare Ltd v Maughan [2005] IRLR 324. . . . . .14.89
Fox Bros (Clothes) Ltd v Bryant [1978] IRLR 485 . . . . .13.02
Fox v British Airways plc [2013] ICR 1257. . . . . .14.334
Fox v C. Wright (Farmers) Ltd [1978] ICR 98. . . . . .16.57
Frames Snooker Centre v Boyce [1992] IRLR 472 . . . . .14.163
Framlington Group plc v Anderson and Others [1995] 1 CCLC 475 . . . . .6.11
Francisco Hernández Vidal SA v Gómez Pérez [1999] IRLR 132 . . . . .18.17
Francome v Mirror Group Newspapers [1984] 2 All ER 408. . . . . .6.39
Frank Wright & Co (Holdings) v Punch [1980] IRLR 217. . . . . .14.41
Frankling v BPS Public Sector Ltd [1999] IRLR 34. . . . . .18.70
Franks v Reuters Ltd [2003] ICR 1188 . . . . .2.51
Fraser v Thames TV Ltd [1983] 2 WLR 917. . . . . .6.24
Freeman v Sovereign Chicken Ltd [1991] ICR 853 . . . . .12.50
Freemans plc v Flynn [1984] IRLR 486. . . . . .14.300
Freeth v Burr (1874) 9 CP 208. . . . . .13.30
French v Barclays Bank plc [1998] IRLR 646 . . . . 3.29, 13.64
Freud v Bentalls Ltd [1982] IRLR 443 . . . . .14.208
Friend v Civil Aviation Authority [2002] IRLR 819 . . . . .14.345
Friend v PMA Holdings Ltd [1976] ICR 330 . . . . .16.58
Frith Accountants Ltd v Law [2014] ICR 805. . . . . .14.312
Futty v D & D Brekkes Ltd [1974] IRLR 130. . . . . .14.13
Fyfe v Scientific Furnishings Ltd [1989] IRLR 331 . . . . 14.349, 14.351

GAB Robbins (UK) Ltd v Triggs [2008] IRLR 317. . . . . 14.40, 14.334
G.D. Searle & Co Ltd v Celltech Ltd [1982] FSR 92. . . . . .6.24
GEC Machines Ltd v Gilford [1982] ICR 72. . . . . .14.202
GFI Group Inc v Eaglestone [1994] IRLR 119 . . . . .6.18
GKN (Cwmbran) Ltd v Lloyd [1972] ICR 214 . . . . .13.44
GKN Sankey Ltd v National Society of Motor Mechanics [1980] IRLR 8. . . . . .17.48
GLC v Canning [1980] IRLR 378. . . . . .14.39
GMB & AMICUS v Beloit Walmsley Ltd [2004] IRLR 18. . . . . .17.43
GMB v Man Truck and Bus UK Ltd [2000] IRLR 636. . . . . .17.08
GMB v Rankin and Harrison [1992] IRLR 514 . . . . .17.43
GUS Home Shopping Ltd v Green [2001] IRLR 75. . . . . .10.28
G. W. Stephens & Son v Fish [1989] ICR 324. 11.10, 11.17, 14.47
GWK v Dunlop (1926) 42 TLR 376 . . . . .21.23
Gallagher v Alpha Catering Services Ltd [2005] IRLR 102 . . . . .5.56
Gallagher v Post Office [1970] 3 All ER 714. . . . . 3.16, 3.27
Gallear v Watson [1979] IRLR 306. . . . . .14.353
Gallop v Newport CC (No 2) [2016] IRLR 395 . . . . .8.118
Galt v Philp [1984] IRLR 156 . . . . .22.24
Garamukana v Solent NHS Trust [2016] IRLR 476 . . . . .23.29
Gardiner v London Borough of Merton [1980] IRLR 472 . . . . 11.42, 11.44
Gardiner v Newport County Borough Council [1974] IRLR 262. . . . . .14.155

Gardiner-Hill v Roland Berger Technics Ltd [1982] IRLR 498 .... 14.325, 14.354
Gardner (F.C.) Ltd v Beresford [1978] IRLR 63 ....14.31
Gardner v Peaks Retail Ltd [1975] IRLR 244....................................20.13
Garner v Grange Furnishing Ltd [1977] IRLR 206 .... 4.26, 13.12, 14.340
Garratt v MGN Ltd [2011] ICR 880...3.52
Garricks Caterers Ltd v Nolan [1980] IRLR 259 ....14.133
Garry v London Borough of Ealing [2001] IRLR 681 ....8.154
Gascol Conversions Ltd v Mercer [1974] ICR 420 ....3.69
Gate Gourmet London Ltd v TGWU [2005] IRLR 881 ....19.44
Gateway Hotels Ltd v Stewart [1988] IRLR 287......................... 18.102, 18.111
Gbaja-Biamila v DHL International (UK) Ltd [2000] ICR 730 ....8.213
General and Municipal Workers' Union v Wailes Dove Bitumastic Ltd
　　[1977] IRLR 45..17.55
General Aviation Services UK Ltd v TGWU [1974] ICR 35 ....21.93
General Billposting Co Ltd v Atkinson [1909] AC 118........................ 6.64, 6.67
General Dynamics Information Technology Ltd v Carranza [2015] ICR 169..........14.180
General Engineering Services Ltd v Kingston and St Andrew Corporation
　　[1988] 3 All ER 867 ....21.14
General of the Salvation Army v Dewsbury [1984] ICR 498.......................11.06
Genower v Ealing, Hammersmith & Hounslow AHA [1980] IRLR 297........ 14.43, 14.226
Geo Moore & Co Ltd v Menzies (1989) 386 IRLIB 21..............................6.64
George Wimpey Ltd v Cooper [1977] IRLR 205 ....14.24
Geys v Société Générale, London Branch [2013] ICR 117....................13.17, 14.19
Gibb v Maidstone & Tunbridge Wells NHS Trust [2010] IRLR 786 ....12.57
Gibbons v Associated British Ports [1985] IRLR 376.............................3.14
Gibson v British Transport Docks Board [1982] IRLR 278 .... 14.160, 14.167, 14.338
Gibson v Lawson [1891] 2 QB 545 .... 22.23
Gibson v Motortune Ltd [1990] ICR 740 .... 11.07, 11.32
Gibson v Sheffield CC [2010] ICR 708 ....7.56
Gilbank v Miles [2006] IRLR 538 ....8.212
Gilbert v Kembridge Fibres Ltd [1984] IRLR 52.................................12.50
Gilgrove Ltd v Hay [2012] ICR 1171; [2013] ICR 1139 ....3.53
Gill and Coote v El Vinos Co Ltd [1983] IRLR 206..............................8.154
Gill v Cape Contracts [1985] IRLR 499 ....3.47
Gillespie v Northern Health and Social Services Board [1996] ICR 498 ....10.30
Ging v Ellward Lancashire Ltd (1978) 13 ITR 265..............................14.322
Giraud UK Ltd v Smith [2000] IRLR 763.................................. 4.51, 5.09
Gisda Cyf v Barratt [2010] IRLR 1073...12.09
Glasenapp v Germany (1986) 9 EHRR 25 ....23.48
Glasgow City Council v UNISON [2014] IRLR 532 ....7.23
Gledhow Autoparts Ltd v Delaney [1965] 1 WLR 1366...........................6.52
Glenboig Union Fireclay Co Ltd v Stewart (1971) 6 ITR 14......................13.02
Glendale Managed Services v Graham [2003] IRLR 46...................... 3.14, 3.26
Glitz v Watford Electric Co Ltd [1979] IRLR 89 ....14.141
Global Plant Ltd v Secretary of State for Social Services [1972] QB 139 ....2.25
Gloucester Working Men's Club & Institute v James [1986] ICR 603 ....8.175
Gloystarne & Co Ltd v Martin [2001] IRLR 15.................................12.50
Gogay v Herts CC [2000] IRLR 703..3.31
Golden Cross Hire Co Ltd v Lovell [1979] IRLR 267......................14.150, 14.171
Golding and Howard v Fire Auto & Marine Insurance Co Ltd (1968) 3 ITR 372........13.02
Goodeve v Gilsons [1985] ICR 401...12.43
Goodfellow v NATSOPA [1985] IRLR 3 ....19.22
Goodwin Ltd v Fitzmaurice [1977] IRLR 393 .... 14.192, 20.33
Goodwin v Patent Office [1999] IRLR 4.. 8.53, 8.60
Goodwin v UK (2002) 35 EHRR 18..8.16

Goold Ltd v McConnell [1995] IRLR 516 . . . . .3.26
Gorictree Ltd v Jenkinson [1984] IRLR 391. . . . . 16.10, 18.106
Gorman v London Computer Training Centre [1978] IRLR 22 . . . . .14.224
Gorse v Durham CC [1971] 2 All ER 666. . . . . .21.14
Gotch & Partners v Guest (1966) 1 ITR 65 . . . . .16.47
Gould v Stuart [1896] AC 575. . . . . .2.40
Gouriet v UPW [1978] AC 435 . . . . 21.93, 21.155, 21.168, 22.20
Gover v Propertycare Ltd [2006] ICR 1073 . . . . .14.322
Governing Body of Addey & Stanhope School v Vakkante [2003] ICR 290 . . . . .8.214
Governing Body of the Northern Ireland Hotel and Catering College v NATFHE
    [1995] IRLR 83. . . . . .17.31
Government Communications Staff Federation v Certification Officer
    [1993] IRLR 260. . . . . .19.16
Govia Thameslink Railway Ltd v ASLEF [2016] IRLR 686. . . . . .21.149
Graham Oxley Tool Steels Ltd v Firth [1980] IRLR 135 . . . . .14.31
Graham v ABF Ltd [1986] IRLR 90 . . . . 14.201, 14.208
Grainger plc v Nicholson [2010] ICR 360. . . . . .8.65
Grant v HM Land Registry [2011] IRLR 748. . . . . .8.107
Grant v South-West Trains Limited [1998] IRLR 188, QBD 3.39
Gray Dunn and Co Ltd v Edwards [1980] IRLR 23 . . . . .3.13
Gray v Grimsby Town FC [1979] ICR 364 . . . . .14.116
Gray v Shetland Norse Preserving Co Ltd [1985] IRLR 53. . . . . 14.199, 14.203
Great Western Railway v Bater [1920] 3 KB 266 . . . . .2.36
Greater Manchester Police Authority v Lea [1990] IRLR 372 .8.104
Green & Son (Castings) Ltd v ASTMS & AUEW [1984] IRLR 135. . . . . .17.27, 17.35
Green v A & I Fraser (Wholesale Fish Merchants) Ltd [1985] IRLR 55 . . . . .14.203
Greenall Whitley plc v Carr [1985] IRLR 289 . . . . .14.98
Greenaway Harrison Ltd v Wiles [1994] IRLR 380 . . . . .14.37
Greencroft Social Club and Institute v Mullen [1985] ICR 796 . . . . .8.104
Greenslade v Hoveringham Gravels Ltd [1975] IRLR 114 . . . . .14.151
Greenwood v NWF Retail Ltd [2011] ICR 896. . . . . .14.322
Greg May (CF&C) Ltd v Dring [1990] IRLR 19. . . . . .5.03
Gregory v Ford [1951] 1 All ER 121 . . . . .4.44
Gregory v Tudsbury Ltd [1982] IRLR 267 . . . . .10.39
Gregory v Wallace [1998] IRLR 387. . . . . .13.72
Greig v Insole [1978] 3 All ER 449 . . . . 6.62, 21.26, 21.39, 21.47
Greig v Sir Alfred McAlpine & Son (Northern) Ltd [1979] IRLR 372 . . . . .14.201
Gridquest Ltd v Blackburn [2002] IRLR 168 . . . . .5.62
Griffin and Others v South West Water Services Ltd [1994] IRLR 1 . . . . .17.05
Griffin v Plymouth Hospital NHS Trust [2014] IRLR 963. . . . . .14.326
Griggs v Duke Power Co (1971) 401 US 424. . . . . .8.96
Grootcon (UK) Ltd v Keld [1984] IRLR 302. . . . . .14.241
Group 4 Nightspeed Ltd v Gilbert [1997] IRLR 398 . . . . .5.09
Grundy (Teddington) Ltd v Plummer and Salt [1983] IRLR 98; [1983] ICR 367 . . . .14.110, 14.199
Grundy v British Airways plc [2008] IRLR 74 . . . . .7.35
Grundy v Sun Printing and Publishing Association (1916) 33 TLR 77. . . . . .13.03
Gryf Lowczowski v Hinchingbrooke Healthcare NHS Trust [2006] IRLR 100. . . . . .13.46, 14.90
Gubala v Crompton Parkinson Ltd [1977] IRLR 10. . . . . .8.210
Gunton v Richmond-upon-Thames LBC [1980] ICR 755 . . . . .13.50
Gurney-Gorres v Securicor Aviation [2006] IRLR 305 . . . . .8.33
Gutridge v Sodexo Ltd [2009] IRLR 721 . . . . 7.92, 18.75
Gwynedd CC v Jones [1986] ICR 833. . . . . .8.19

H. Campey & Son Ltd v Bellwood [1987] ICR 311 . . . . .14.268
HK Danmark v Dansk almennyttigt Boligselskab [2013] ICR 851. . . . . .8.35

HK Danmark v Experian A/S [2014] ICR 27 . . . . .7.10
HM Land Registry v Benson [2012] ICR 628 . . . . .8.105
HM Prison Service v Ibimidin [2008] IRLR 940 . . . . .8.155
HM Prison Service v Johnson [2007] IRLR 951 . . . . .8.183
HM Prison Service v Salmon [2001] IRLR 425 . . . . .8.202
HM Revenue & Customs v Lorne Stewart [2015] ICR 708 . . . . .5.42
HM Revenue & Customs v Stringer [2009] IRLR 677 . . . . .5.74
H v Belgium (1988) 10 EHRR 339 . . . . .23.19
H v France (1990) 12 EHRR 74 . . . . .23.12
Hackney LBC v Sivanandan [2011] ICR 1374 [2013] ICR 672 .14.336
Haddow v ILEA [1979] ICR 202 . . . . .4.35
Haden v Cowen [1982] IRLR 314 . . . . .16.24
Hadjioannou v Coral Casinos Ltd [1981] IRLR 352 . . . . .14.151
Hadmor Productions Ltd v Hamilton [1983] 1 AC 191 . . . . . . 21.31, 21.48, 21.74, 21.84, 21.93
Hagen v ICI Chemicals and Polymers Ltd [2002] IRLR 31 . . . . .4.27
Haine v Day [2008] IRLR 642 . . . . .17.54
Hairsine v Kingston upon Hull CC [1992] ICR 212 . . . . .20.36
Halford v UK [1997] IRLR 471 . . . . .23.30
Halfpenny v IGC Medical Systems Ltd [1999] ICR 834 . . . . .10.06
Hall v Lorimer [1994] IRLR 171 . . . . .2.24
Hall v Woolston Hall Leisure Ltd [2000] IRLR 578 . . . . .8.214, 12.29
Hamilton v Argyll and Clyde Health Board [1993] IRLR 99 . . . . .13.37
Hamilton v Futura Floors [1990] IRLR 478 . . . . .3.12
Hammersmith and Queen Charlotte's Special Health Authority v Cato [1987] IRLR 483 . . . .7.98
Hammond v Haigh Castle & Co Ltd [1973] ICR 148 . . . . .12.08
Hampson v Department of Education and Science [1989] IRLR 69 . . . . .8.104
Hancill v Marcon Engineering Ltd [1990] ICR 103 . . . . .11.48
Handley v H. Mono Ltd [1979] ICR 147 . . . . .7.42
Hanley v Pease & Partners [1915] 1 KB 698 . . . . .4.54
Hannan v TNT-IPEC (UK) Ltd [1986] IRLR 165 . . . . .14.94
Hanson v Fashion Industries (Hartlepool) Ltd [1980] IRLR 393 . . . . .11.13, 11.27, 12.45
Harber v North London Polytechnic [1990] IRLR 198 . . . . .12.14
Hardwick v Leeds AHA [1975] IRLR 319 . . . . .14.353
Hardy v Polk (Leeds) Ltd [2004] IRLR 420 . . . . .14.322
Hardy v Tourism South East [2005] IRLR 242 . . . . .17.08
Hardys & Hansons plc v Lax [2005] IRLR 726 . . . . .8.104, 8.105
Hare v Murphy Brothers [1974] ICR 603 . . . . .14.89
Harford v Swiftrim Ltd [1987] ICR 439 . . . . .11.47
Harlow v Artemis Int Corp Ltd [2008] IRLR 629 . . . . .3.16, 3.52, 3.74
Harman v Flexible Lamps Ltd [1980] IRLR 418 . . . . .14.66, 14.83
Harmer v Cornelius (1858) 5 CBNS 236 . . . . .4.33
Harold Fielding Ltd v Mansi [1974] 1 All ER 1035 . . . . .11.49
Harper v National Coal Board [1980] IRLR 260 . . . . .14.215, 14.238
Harrington v Kent CC [1980] IRLR 353 . . . . .14.9
Harris & Russell Ltd v Slingsby [1973] ICR 454 . . . . .14.21
Harris (Ipswich) Ltd v Harrison [1978] IRLR 382 . . . . .14.159
Harrison Bowden Ltd v Bowden [1994] ICR 186 . . . . .18.101
Harrison v Kent County Council [1995] ICR 434 . . . . .20.23
Harrods Ltd v Remick [1998] ICR 156 . . . . .8.146
Hart v Marshall [1977] ICR 539 . . . . .14.86
Hartlebury Printers Ltd, Re [1992] ICR 560 . . . . .17.24
Hartley v King Edward VI College [2015] ICR 1143 . . . . .4.21
Harvard Securities plc v Younghusband [1990] IRLR 17 . . . . .14.101
Harvest Press Ltd v McCaffrey [1999] IRLR 778 . . . . .20.59
Hashwani v Jivraj [2011] ICR 1004 . . . . .2.69, 2.72, 2.76

Hasley v Fair Employment Agency [1989] IRLR 106 . . . . .11.42
Havenhand v Thomas Black Ltd (1968) 3 ITR 271. . . . . .16.43
Hawes & Curtis Ltd v Arfan [2012] ICR 1244. . . . . .12.08
Hawker Siddeley Power Engineering Ltd v Rump [1979] IRLR 42. . . . . .14.34
Hawkins v Bell [1996] IRLR 258 . . . . .12.14
Hawley v Fieldcastle & Co Ltd [1982] IRLR 223. . . . . .2.45
Hay v George Hanson (Building Contractors) Ltd [1996] IRLR 427 . . . . .18.86
Hayward v Cammell Laird Shipbuilders Ltd [1986] IRLR 287 . . . . .7.81, 7.101
Healey v Société Anonyme Française Rubastic [1917] 1 KB 946 . . . . .6.05
Health Computing Ltd v Meek [1980] IRLR 437. . . . . .21.100
Heath v J. F. Longman (Meat Salesmen) Ltd [1973] ICR 407. . . . . .14.266
Heath v Metropolitan Police Commissioner [2005] ICR 32 . . . . .8.171
Heath v Metropolitan Police Commissioner [2005] ICR 329 . . . . .23.23
Heathmill Multimedia ASP Ltd v Jones [2003] IRLR 856 . . . . .4.84
Heaton's Transport Ltd v TGWU [1972] ICR 308 . . . . .3.10
Hebden v Forsey and Son [1973] ICR 607 . . . . .14.87
Hellyer Bros Ltd v Atkinson [1992] IRLR 540 . . . . .14.66
Helmet Integrated Systems v Tunnard and Others [2007] IRLR 126. . . . . .6.11
Hempell v W.H. Smith & Sons Ltd [1986] IRLR 95. . . . . .16.34
Hencke v Gemeinde Schierke [1996] IRLR 701 . . . . .18.21
Henderson v Connect (South Tyneside) Ltd [2010] IRLR 466 .14.238
Henderson v Granville Tours Ltd [1982] IRLR 494 . . . . .14.109, 14.167
Hendricks v Commissioner of Police for the Metropolis [2003] IRLR 96 . . . . .8.177
Hendry v Scottish Liberal Club [1977] IRLR 5 . . . . .14.246
Hendy v Ministry of Justice [2014] IRLR 856 . . . . .4.86
Hennessey v Craigmyle & Co Ltd and ACAS [1986] ICR 461 . . . . .12.50
Henry v London General Transport Services Ltd [2001] IRLR 132;
    [2002] IRLR 472. . . . . .3.12, 3.41
Henthorn and Taylor v CEGB [1980] IRLR 361. . . . . .21.12
Herbert Clayton & Jack Waller Ltd v Oliver [1930] AC 209 . . . . .4.56
Herbert Morris v Saxelby [1916] 1 AC 688. . . . . .6.48
Hetherington v Dependable Products Ltd (1971) 6 ITR 1. . . . . .16.68
Hewage v Grampian Health Board [2012] ICR 1054 . . . . .8.77
Hewcastle Catering Ltd v Ahmed and Elkanah [1992] ICR 626. . . . . .12.33
Hewlett Packard Ltd v O'Murphy [2002] IRLR 4 . . . . .2.51
Hickman v Maisey [1900] 1 QB 752. . . . . .22.32
Hicks v Humphrey (1967) 2 ITR 214 . . . . .14.15
High Table Ltd v Horst [1997] IRLR 513. . . . . .16.16
Highlands Fabricators Ltd v McLaughlin [1985] ICR 183 . . . . .14.269
Hill v CA Parsons and Co Ltd [1972] 1 Ch 305 . . . . .13.43
Hill v Governing Body of Great Tey Primary School [2013] ICR 691. . . . . 14.322, 23.52
Hill v Levey (1858) 157 ER 366 . . . . .3.11
Hilton International Hotels (UK) Ltd v Faraji [1994] IRLR 267 . . . . 14.320, 14.334
Hilton International Hotels (UK) Ltd v Protopapa [1990] IRLR 316 . . . . .14.37
Hilton v Shiner Ltd [2001] IRLR 728 . . . . .3.30, 14.34
Hindle Gears Ltd v McGinty [1984] IRLR 477 . . . . 14.249, 14.262, 14.264, 14.265
Hindle v Percival Boats Ltd (1969) 4 ITR 86. . . . . .16.32
Hinton v University of East London [2005] ICR 1260 . . . . .12.54
Hitchcock v Post Office [1980] ICR 100. . . . . .2.25
Hitchcock v St Ann's Hosiery (1971) 6 ITR 98. . . . . .16.48
Hivac Ltd v Park Royal Scientific Instruments Ltd [1946] Ch 169 .6.08
Hodges v Webb [1920] Ch 70 . . . . .21.59
Hoenig v Isaacs [1952] 2 All ER 176, CA 4.04
Hogg v Dover College [1990] ICR 39 . . . . 3.55, 14.11
Holden v Bradville Ltd [1985] IRLR 483 . . . . .14.208

Holland v London Society of Compositors (1924) 40 TLR 440 . . . . .3.11
Hollier v Plysu Ltd [1983] IRLR 260 . . . . .14.348
Hollis Metal Industries Ltd v GMB [2008] IRLR 187 . . . . .18.03
Hollister v NFU [1979] ICR 542. . . . . 14.226, 14.227
Holman v Johnson (1775) 1 Cowp 341. . . . . 12.25
Holroyd v Gravure Cylinders Ltd [1984] IRLR 259 . . . . .14.340
Holterman Ferho Explotatie BV v Spies Von Büllesheim [2016] IRLR 140 . . . . .2.75
Homan v A1 Bacon Co Ltd [1996] ICR 721. . . . . .14.334
Home Counties Dairies Ltd v Shilton [1970] 1 WLR 526. . . . . .6.57
Home Office v Ayres [1992] ICR 175 . . . . 4.20, 5.12
Home Office v Bailey and Others [2005] IRLR 757. . . . . .7.69
Home Office v Holmes [1984] IRLR 299 . . . . .8.101
Home Office v Robinson [1982] ICR 31 . . . . 2.36, 12.58
Hone v Six Continents Retail Ltd [2006] IRLR 49. . . . . .4.32
Hong Kong Fir Shipping v Kawasaki Kisen Kaisha [1962] 2 QB 26. . . . . .13.11
Hooper v British Railways Board [1988] IRLR 517 . . . . 14.124, 14.133
Hoover Ltd v Forde [1980] ICR 239. . . . . 14.149, 14.189, 14.342
Hopkins v Norcross plc [1994] IRLR 18. . . . . .13.75
Hopley-Dodd v Highfield Motors (Derby) Ltd (1969) 4 ITR 289. . . . . .13.02
Horcal Ltd v Gatland [1983] IRLR 459 . . . . 6.06, 6.22
Horizon Holidays Ltd v Grassi [1987] ICR 851 . . . . 14.317, 14.322
Horizon Recruitment v Vincent [2010] ICR 491. . . . . .12.56
Horkulak v Cantor Fitzgerald International [2003] IRLR 756. . . . . .3.31
Hornby v Close (1867) 2 LRQB 153 . . . . .19.03
Horrigan v Lewisham LBC [1978] ICR 15, EAT. 3.27, 3.55
Horsey v Dyfed CC [1982] IRLR 395 . . . . .8.94
Horsley Smith and Sherry Ltd v Dutton [1977] IRLR 172 . . . . .14.102
Horwood v Millar's Timber & Trading Co Ltd [1917] 1 KB 305. . . . . .4.51
Hospital Medical Group Ltd v Westwood [2013] ICR 415. . . . . .2.70
Hotson v Wisbech Conservative Club [1984] IRLR 422. . . . . .14.94
Hough v Leyland DAF Ltd [1991] ICR 696. . . . . 17.23, 17.24
Hounga v Allen [2014] ICR 847 . . . . .12.31
Hounslow LBC v Klusova [2008] ICR 39 . . . . .12.32
Housing Maintenance Solutions Ltd v McAteer [2015] ICR 87 .18.58
Hovell v Ashford & St Peter's Hospital NHS Trust [2009] IRLR 734 . . . . .7.75, 7.78
Howard v Muillrise Ltd [2005] ICR 435. . . . . .17.21
Howard v NGA [1985] ICR 101 . . . . .19.29
Howarth Timber (Leeds) Ltd v Biscomb [1986] IRLR 52. . . . . .14.108
Howgate v Fane Acoustics Ltd [1981] IRLR 16 . . . . .14.93
Howlett Marine Services Ltd v Bowlan [2001] IRLR 201 . . . . .17.46
Howman & Son v Blyth [1983] IRLR 139 . . . . 3.25, 4.06
Hoyland v ASDA Stores Ltd [2005] IRLR 438 . . . . .10.30
Hoyland v Asda Stores Ltd [2006] IRLR 468. . . . . .7.09
Hubbard v Pitt [1975] ICR 308. . . . . 22.18, 22.32, 22.37
Huber v France (1998) 26 EHRR 457. . . . . .23.21
Huddersfield Parcels Ltd v Sykes [1981] IRLR 115 . . . . .14.209
Huet v Université de Bretagne occidentale [2012] ICR 694. . . . . .9.19
Hughes v Gwynedd AHA [1978] ICR 161 . . . . 14.18, 14.71
Hugh-Jones v St John's College, Cambridge [1979] ICR 848 . . . . .2.44
Hunter v Canary Wharf Ltd [1997] AC 655. . . . . 22.30
Hunter v McCarrick [2013] ICR 235 . . . . .18.35
Hunter v Smith's Dock Co Ltd [1968] 2 All ER 81 . . . . .11.13
Huntley v Thornton [1957] 1 All ER 234. . . . . 21.63, 21.67, 21.91
Hurley v Mustoe [1981] IRLR 208 . . . . 8.101, 8.104
Hurst v Kelly [2013] ICR 1225 . . . . .8.165

Hussain v King's College Hospital NHS Trust [2002] ICR 1433 . . . . .8.11
Hussein v Saints Complete House Furnishers Ltd [1979] IRLR 337. . . . . .8.101
Hutchinson v Enfield Rolling Mills Ltd [1981] IRLR 318. . . . . 14.130, 14.339
Hutchison v Westward TV Ltd [1977] ICR 279 . . . . .8.174
Hyde Housing Association Ltd v Layton [2016] ICR 26. . . . . .18.20
Hyland v J.H. Barker (North-West) Ltd [1985] IRLR 403 . . . . 11.03, 12.26
Hynd v Armstrong [2007] IRLR 338 . . . . .14.94

ICTS (UK) Ltd v Tchoula [2000] IRLR 643 . . . . .8.198, 8.209, 8.213
ICTS UK Ltd v Mahdi [2016] ICR 274 . . . . .18.36
ILEA v Gravett [1988] IRLR 497 . . . . 14.157, 14.164, 14.293
ILEA v Lloyd [1981] IRLR 394. . . . . .14.114, 14.119
IRC v Ainsworth [2005] ICR 1149; [2005] EWCA Civ 441 . . . . .5.04, 5.64, 5.74
IRC v Brander & Cruikshank [1971] 1 All ER 36. . . . . .2.36
ITT Components (Europe) Ltd v Kolah [1977] ICR 740. . . . . .16.58
Ibekwe v London General Transport Services Ltd [2003] IRLR 697 . . . . .3.26
Ibex Trading Ltd v Walton [1994] ICR 907 . . . . .18.101
Iceland Frozen Foods Ltd v Jones [1982] IRLR 439 . . . . 14.110
Igbo v Johnson Matthey Chemicals Ltd [1986] IRLR 215 . . . . 12.46, 14.79
Igen Ltd v Wong [2005] ICR 931 . . . . .8.183
Igen v Wong [2005] IRLR 258 . . . . .8.74
Iman Sadeque v Bluebay Asset Management (Services) Ltd [2013] IRLR 344 . . . . .6.10
Imperial Metal Industries (Kynoch) Ltd v AUEW [1978] IRLR 407. . . . . .19.131
Independent Insurance Co Ltd v Aspinall [2011] ICR 1234 . . . . 17.18
Industrial Rubber Products Ltd v Gillon [1977] IRLR 389. . . . . .14.233
Industrial Rubber Products v Gillon [1977] IRLR 389. . . . . .14.34
Inex Home Improvements Ltd v Hodgkins [2016] ICR 71 . . . . .18.62
Ingram v Foxon [1984] ICR 685 . . . . 11.23, 11.28
Initial Electronic Security Systems Ltd v Avdic [2005] IRLR 671. . . . . .12.08
Initial Services Ltd v Putterill [1968] 1 QB 396. . . . . .6.39
Institution of Professional Civil Servants v Secretary of State for Defence
    [1987] IRLR 373. . . . . 18.117
Intel Corp UK Ltd [2007] IRLR 35. . . . . .4.32
International Computers v Kennedy [1981] IRLR 28 . . . . .14.17
International Consulting Services (UK) Ltd v Hart [2000] IRLR 227 . . . . .6.53
International Sports Co Ltd v Thomson [1980] IRLR 340. . . . . .14.128
International Transport Workers' Federation v Viking Line ABP
    [2008] IRLR 143. . . . . 21.158, 23.69
Irani v Southampton and South West Hampshire Health Authority
    [1985] IRLR 203. . . . . 13.44, 13.46
Ironmonger v Movefield Ltd t/a Deering Appointments [1988] IRLR 461 . . . . .2.49
Irvine v Prestcold Ltd [1981] IRLR 281 . . . . .8.195
Isle of Wight Tourist Board v Coombes [1976] IRLR 413 . . . . .14.31
Isleworth Studios Ltd v Rickard [1988] IRLR 137 . . . . .14.322
Item Software (UK) Ltd v Fassihi [2003] IRLR 769 . . . . 6.07, 14.95
Ixora Trading Inc v Jones [1990] FSR 251 . . . . .6.33

J. H. Walker Ltd v Hussain [1996] IRLR 10. . . . . .8.101
J.A. Mont (UK) Ltd v Mills [1993] IRLR 172. . . . . 6.12, 6.57
J. & J. Stern v Simpson [1983] IRLR 52 . . . . .14.13
J. Lyons & Sons v Wilkins [1899] 1 Ch 255 . . . . 22.18, 22.22, 22.37
JP Morgan Europe Ltd v Chweidan [2012] ICR 268. . . . . .8.53
J.S. Buckley Ltd v Maslin [1977] ICR 425 . . . . .16.60
J Sainsbury plc v Hitt [2003] ICR 111. . . . . .14.110
J. Sainsbury Ltd v Savage [1980] IRLR 109 . . . . .14.93

J.T. Stratford and Son Ltd v Lindley [1965] AC 269 . . . . 21.07, 21.23, 21.28, 21.46, 21.47,
21.51, 21.73, 21.91, 21.100, 21.161
J v DLA Piper UK LLP [2010] ICR 1052. . . . . .8.46
Jäamställdhetsombudsmannen v Örebo läns landsting [2001] ICR 249. . . . . .7.98
Jack Allen (Sales and Service) Ltd v Smith [1999] IRLR 19 . . . . .6.70
Jackson v Computershare Investor Services plc [2008] IRLR 70 .18.68
Jackson v General Accident, Fire and Life Assurance Co Ltd [1977] IRLR 338. . . . . .14.196
Jackson v Ghosh [2003] IRLR 824 . . . . .12.36
Jagdeo v Smiths Industries Ltd [1982] ICR 47. . . . . .4.29
Jakowlew v Nestor Primecare Services Ltd [2015] IRLR 813. . . . . .18.50
Jalota v IMI [1979] IRLR 313. . . . . 8.190, 8.191
James and Jones v National Coal Board (1969) 4 ITR 70. . . . . .16.49
James v Eastleigh BC [1989] 3 WLR 123 . . . . 8.80, 8.91
James v LB of Greenwich [2008] IRLR 302 . . . . .2.52
James v Redcats (Brands) Ltd [2007] IRLR 296. . . . . .5.22
James v Redcats (Brands) Ltd [2007] IRLR 296. . . . . .2.72
James v Waltham Holy Cross UDC [1973] IRLR 202 . . . . 14.117, 14.121, 14.184
James W. Cook & Co (Wivenhoe) Ltd v Tipper [1991] IRLR 386 . . . . 12.23, 14.322
Janata Bank Ltd v Ahmed [1981] IRLR 457. . . . . 3.54, 4.33, 4.46
Janciuk v Winerite Ltd [1998] IRLR 63 . . . . .13.54
Jeetle v Elster [1985] IRLR 227. . . . . 11.37, 11.49
Jeffrey v Laurence Scott [1977] IRLR 466 . . . . .14.46
Jenkins v Kingsgate (Clothing Productions) Ltd (No 2) [1981] IRLR 388 . . . . . . 7.05, 7.35, 7.42
Jenkins v P&O European Ferries (Dover) Ltd [1991] ICR 652 .14.263
Jennings v Salford Community Service Agency [1981] IRLR 76. . . . . .11.04
Jenvey v Australian Broadcasting Corp [2003] ICR 79. . . . . .3.26
Jewell v Neptune Concrete Ltd [1975] IRLR 147 . . . . .4.69
Jiad v Byford [2003] IRLR 232 . . . . .8.155
Jiménez Melgar v Ayuntamiento de Los Barrios [2001] IRLR 848. . . . . .8.29
John Brown Engineering Ltd v Brown [1997] IRLR 90 . . . . .14.202
John Lewis v Coyne [2001] IRLR 139 . . . . .14.171
John Michael Design plc v Cooke [1987] ICR 445 . . . . .6.72
John Mill and Sons v Quinn [1974] IRLR 107 . . . . .14.330
John Snaith, Re [1982] IRLR 157 . . . . .13.26
Johnson & Bloy (Holdings) Ltd v Wolstenholme Rink plc and Fallon
[1987] IRLR 499. . . . . 6.29, 6.36
Johnson & Johnson Medical Ltd v Filmer [2002] ICR 292 . . . . .8.129
Johnson Matthey Metals Ltd v Harding [1978] IRLR 248. . . . . .14.151
Johnson v Nottinghamshire Combined Police Authority [1974] ICR 170. . . . . .16.30
Johnson v Ryan [2000] ICR 236 . . . . .2.38
Johnson v Unisys Ltd [2001] ICR 480. . . . . 3.23, 3.32, 13.59, 14.330
Johnstone v Bloomsbury Health Authority [1991] IRLR 118, [1991] ICR 269. . . . . .3.34
Jones v 3M Healthcare Ltd [2002] ICR 341 . . . . .23.71
Jones v Associated Tunnelling Co Ltd [1981] IRLR 477. . . . . 3.36, 3.74, 4.75, 16.17
Jones v Aston Cabinet Co Ltd [1973] ICR 292 . . . . .16.48
Jones v F. Sirl & Son (Furnishers) Ltd [1997] IRLR 493. . . . . .14.68
Jones v Friends Provident Life Office [2004] IRLR 783 . . . . .8.146
Jones v Gwent CC [1992] IRLR 521. . . . . .13.27
Jones v H. Sherman Ltd (1969) 4 ITR 63 . . . . .4.56
Jones v Lee [1980] ICR 310. . . . . .13.44
Jones v Mid-Glamorgan County Council [1997] IRLR 685, CA 14.68
Jones v Tower Boot Co Ltd [1997] ICR 254 . . . . .8.168
Joshi v Sandercock EAT 1140/02 . . . . .5.36
Joshua Wilson & Bros Ltd v USDAW [1978] IRLR 120. . . . . .17.11
Jouini v Princess Personal Service GmbH [2007] IRLR 1005. .18.18

Jowett v Earl of Bradford (No 2) [1978] ICR 431 . . . . .14.110
Judge v Crown Leisure Ltd [2005] IRLR 823 . . . . .3.51
Jupiter General Insurance Co v Shroff [1937] 3 All ER 67 . . . . 4.33, 13.33

Kalac v Turkey (1999) 27 EHRR 152 . . . . .23.42
Kamara v DPP [1974] AC 104 . . . . .21.63
Kane v Raine & Co [1974] ICR 300 . . . . .16.44
Kapadia v London Borough of Lambeth [2000] IRLR 14 . . . . 8.50, 8.59
Kapfunde v Abbey National plc [1998] IRLR 584 . . . . .4.77
Kaplan v International Alliance of Theatrical Operatives, 525 F(2d) 1354 . . . . .8.189
Kapur v Barclays Bank [1991] ICR 208 . . . . 8.152, 8.177
Kapur v Shields [1976] ICR 26 . . . . .12.03
Katsikas v Konstantinidis [1993] IRLR 179 . . . . .18.86
Kaur v MG Rover Group Ltd [2005] IRLR 40 . . . . .3.16
Kavanagh v Crystal Palace FC Ltd [2014] ICR 25 . . . . .18.104
Kavanagh v Hiscock [1974] QB 600 . . . . 22.07, 22.08
Keegan v Newcastle United FC Ltd [2010] IRLR 94 . . . . .14.31
Kelly v University of Southampton [2008] ICR 357 . . . . .12.32
Kelman v Care Contract Services Ltd [1995] ICR 260 . . . . 18.10, 18.33
Kelman v G. J. Oram [1983] IRLR 432 . . . . .14.238
Kenneth McRae & Co Ltd v Dawson [1984] IRLR 5 . . . . .14.39
Kenny v Hampshire Constabulary [1999] IRLR 76 . . . . .8.136
Kenny v South Manchester College [1994] IRLR 336 . . . . .18.33
Kenny v Vauxhall Motors Ltd [1985] ICR 535 . . . . .3.11
Kent CC v Gilham [1985] IRLR 16 . . . . 14.102, 14.214
Kent CC v Gilham (No 2) [1985] ICR 233 . . . . .14.110
Kent Management Services v Butterfield [1992] ICR 272 . . . . .5.04
Keppel Seghers UK Ltd v Hinds [2014] ICR 1105 . . . . .15.20
Kerry Foods Ltd v Creber [2000] IRLR 10 . . . . 18.24, 18.28
Kerry Foods Ltd v Lynch [2008] IRLR 680 . . . . .3.33
Kestongate Ltd v Miller [1986] ICR 672 . . . . .18.5
Keys v Shoefayre Ltd [1978] IRLR 476 . . . . .14.34
Khan v Royal Mail Group Ltd [2014] IRLR 947 . . . . .8.74
Khanum v Mid-Glamorgan AHA [1978] IRLR 215 . . . . .14.182
Kidd v Axa Equity & Law Life Assurance Society plc [2000] IRLR 30 . . . . .4.78
Kidd v DRG (UK) Ltd [1985] IRLR 90 . . . . .14.203
Kigass Aero Components Ltd v Brown [2002] IRLR 312 . . . . .5.64
Kimberley Group Housing Ltd v Hambley [2008] IRLR 682 . . . . .18.37
King v Eaton Ltd [1996] IRLR 199 . . . . .14.209
King v Eaton Ltd (No 2) [1998] IRLR 686 . . . . .14.322
Kingston upon Hull CC v Dunnachie No 3 [2003] IRLR 843 . . . . .14.322
Kingston v British Railways Board [1984] IRLR 146 . . . . 14.156, 14.238
Kinzley v Minories Finance Ltd [1988] ICR 113 . . . . .14.319
Kirby v Manpower Services Commission [1980] IRLR 229 . . . . .8.154
Kirkham v NATSOPA [1981] IRLR 244 . . . . .19.22
Klarenberg v Ferrotron Technologies GmbH [2009] ICR 1263 . . . . .18.19
Knapton v ECC Card Clothing Ltd [2006] IRLR 756 . . . . .14.328
Knight v Attorney-General [1979] ICR 194 . . . . 2.38, 8.170
Knudsen v Norway (1985) 142 DR 247 . . . . .23.40
Kolfor Plant Ltd v Wright [1982] IRLR 311 . . . . .10.54
König v Germany (1979–80) 2 EHRR 170 . . . . .23.19
Kores Manufacturing Ltd v Kolok Manufacturing Ltd [1959] 1 Ch 108 . . . . .6.69
Kosiek v Germany (1987) 9 EHRR 328 . . . . .23.48
Kowalska v Freie und Hansestadt Hamburg [1992] ICR 29 . . . . 7.98, 7.100
Kraft Foods Ltd v Fox [1978] ICR 311 . . . . .14.340

Krasner v McMath [2005] IRLR 995 . . . . .17.54
Kucuk v Land Nordrhein-Westfalen [2012] ICR 682 . . . . .9.19
Kücükdeveci v Swedex GmbH & Co [2010] ECR I-36 . . . . .8.105
Kulkarni v Milton Keynes Hospital NHS Foundation Trust [2010] ICR 101 . . . . .3.52
Kutz-Bauer v Freie und Hansestadt Hamburg [2003] IRLR 368 . . . . .7.60
Kuzel v Roche Products Ltd [2007] IRLR 309 [2008] EWCA Civ 380;
    [2008] ICR 279. . . . . .14.94, 15.19, 20.33
Kwik Fit (GB) Ltd v Lineham [1992] IRLR 156 . . . . .14.72
Kykot v Smith Hartley [1975] IRLR 372. . . . . .16.30

Ladbroke Courage Holidays Ltd v Asten [1981] IRLR 59 . . . . .14.193, 14.230, 16.31
Ladbroke Racing Ltd v Arnott [1983] IRLR 154 . . . . .14.151
Ladbroke Racing Ltd v Mason [1978] ICR 49 . . . . .14.338
Ladup Ltd v Barnes [1982] IRLR 7. . . . . .14.340
Laffin and Callaghan v Fashion Industries (Hartlepool) Ltd [1978] IRLR 448 . . . . .14.270
Laing (John) & Son Ltd v Best (1968) 3 ITR 3 . . . . .16.49
Laird v A K Stoddart Ltd [2001] IRLR 591 . . . . .5.43, 5.63
Lake v BTP [2007] ICR 301 . . . . .8.171, 15.20
Lakshmi v Mid Cheshire Hospital NHS Trust [2008] IRLR 956 . . . . .3.16, 3.31
Lamont v Fry's Metals Ltd [1985] ICR 566 . . . . .16.20
Lancashire Fires Limited v SA Lyons & Co Limited [1997] IRLR 113. . . . . .6.30
Land and Wilson v West Yorkshire MCC [1981] IRLR 87 . . . . .14.17, 14.20
Land Registry v Grant [2011] ICR 1390 . . . . .8.155
Landeshauptstadt Kiel v Jaeger [2003] IRLR 804. . . . . .5.53
Landsorganisationen i Danmark v Ny Mølle Kro [1989] IRLR 37. . . . . .18.00, 18.12
Langston v AUEW [1974] 1 All ER 980 . . . . .4.58
Langston v AUEW (No 2) [1974] ICR 510 . . . . .14.293
Langston v Cranfield University [1998] IRLR 172 . . . . .14.199
Lansing Linde v Kerr [1991] 1 All ER 25 . . . . .6.30, 6.36, 6.71
Lanton Leisure Ltd v White and Gibson [1987] IRLR 119. . . . . .14.93
Larkin v Belfast Harbour Commissioners [1908] 2 IR 214. . . . . .22.41
Larkin v Long [1915] AC 814 . . . . .21.81
Lassman v De Vere University Arms Hotel [2003] ICR 44 . . . . .14.69
Laughton and Hawley v Bapp Industrial Supplies Ltd [1986] IRLR 245 . . . . .6.09, 1.171
Laval un Partneri Ltd v Svenska Byggnadsarbetareförbundet [2008] IRLR 160. . . . . .21.158
Lavarack v Woods of Colchester Ltd [1967] 1 QB 278 . . . . .13.64, 13.72
Law Hospital NHS Trust v Rush [2001] IRLR 611. . . . . .8.59
Law Society v Bahl [2003] IRLR 640 . . . . .8.187
Lawrence David Ltd v Ashton [1989] IRLR 22. . . . . .6.71
Lawrence v Cooklin Kitchen Fitments Ltd (1966) 1 ITR 398 .16.60
Lawrence v Regent Office Care Ltd [1999] IRLR 148. . . . . .7.21
Lawrie-Blum v Land Baden-Württemberg [1986], ECLI:EU:C:1986:284. . . . . .2.74
Laws v London Chronicle (Indicator Newspapers) Ltd [1959] 1 WLR 69 . . . . .13.30, 13.33
Lawson v Britfish Ltd [1987] ICR 726 . . . . .7.15
Lawson v Serco Ltd [2006] IRLR 289. . . . . .12.34, 12.36
Lawton v BOC Transhield Ltd [1987] ICR 7 . . . . .4.76
Le Compte v Belgium (1982) 5 EHRR 183 . . . . .23.19
Leach v Office of Communication [2012] ICR 1270, CA 14.169, 23.11
Leander v Sweden (1987) 9 EHRR 433. . . . . .23.31
Leary v NUVB [1971] Ch 34. . . . . .19.41
Lee Ting Sang v Chung ChiKeung [1990] ICR 409. . . . . .2.22, 2.23, 2.77
Lee v GEC Plessey Telecommunications [1993] IRLR 383 .3.09 3.71
Lee v IPC Business Press Ltd [1984] ICR 306 . . . . .14.329, 14.354
Leech v Preston BC [1985] ICR 192 . . . . .14.93
Leeds Dental Team Ltd v Rose [2014] ICR 9 . . . . .14.33

Leeds Private Hospital v Parkin [1992] ICR 571....................................8.77
Lees v The Orchard [1978] IRLR 20..14.159
Leicestershire CC v UNISON [2006] IRLR 810.................................17.08
Leonard v Southern Derbyshire Chamber of Commerce [2001] IRLR 19 ....8.60
Leonard v Strathclyde Buses Ltd [1998] IRLR 693.............................14.312
Les Ambassadeurs Club v Bainda [1982] IRLR 5 ....14.347
Lesney Products & Co Ltd v Nolan [1977] ICR 235 ....16.29
Letheby & Christopher Ltd v Bond [1988] ICR 480............................11.17
Leverton v Clwyd CC [1989] IRLR 28 ....7.15
Levett v Biotrace International plc [1999] ICR 818...........................13.57
Levez v T.H. Jennings (Harlow Pools) Ltd [1999] IRLR 764, [1999] ICR 521 .....7.03, 7.83, 7.90
Lewis and Britton v E. Mason & Sons [1994] IRLR 4 ....14.251, 14.253
Lewis Shops Group Ltd v Wiggins [1973] ICR 335............................14.113
Lewis v Motorworld Garages Ltd [1985] IRLR 465..................... 14.32, 14.49
Lewis v Surrey County Council [1987] IRLR 509 ....11.19
Leyland Vehicles Ltd v Reston [1980] IRLR 376.............................16.62
Liddell's Coaches v Cook [2013] ICR 547...................................18.35
Lifeguard Assurance Ltd v Zadrozny [1977] IRLR 56 ....14.314
Lightfoot v D.J. Sporting [1996] IRLR 64 ....12.30
Lightways (Contractors) Ltd v Associated Holdings Ltd [2000] IRLR 24 ....18.33
Lincoln v Hayman [1982] 1 WLR 488 ....13.75
Lincs CC v Hopper [2002] ICR 1301 ....2.36
Linfood Cash & Carry Ltd v Thomson [1989] IRLR 235............. 14.110, 14.167, 14.170
Liskojärvi v Oy Liikenne Ab [2002] ICR 155 ....18.18
List Design Group Ltd v Douglas [2003] IRLR 14 ....5.04
Lister v Romford Ice and Cold Storage Co Ltd [1957] AC 55................3.23, 3.27
Litster v Forth Dry Dock Engineering Co Ltd [1989] ICR 341; [1989] IRLR 161 ....11.40, 18.57
Little v Charterhouse Magna Assurance Co [1980] IRLR 19.....................14.34
Littlewoods Organisation Ltd v Egenti [1976] ICR 516 ....14.177
Living Design (Home Improvements) Ltd v Davidson [1994] IRLR 69............. 6.61, 6.66
Livingstone v Hepworth Refractories Ltd [1992] ICR 287......................12.50
Lloyd v Brassey (1969) 4 ITR 100...16.00
Lloyd v Taylor Woodrow Construction Ltd [1999] IRLR 782 ....14.208
Lloyds Bank Ltd v Secretary of State for Employment [1979] ICR 258 ....11.26
Lock International plc v Beswick [1989] IRLR 481 ....6.38
Lock v British Gas Trading Ltd [2014] ICR 813 .... 5.67, 5.74
Lockwood v DWP [2014] ICR 1257 ....8.75
Logan Salton v Durham CC [1989] IRLR 99 .... 12.50, 14.67
Logan v Commissioners of Customs and Excise [2004] IRLR 63...................14.47
Loman and Henderson v Merseyside Transport Services Ltd (1967) 3 KIR 726 .... 3.20, 16.59
London & Birmingham Railway Ltd v ASLEF [2011] ICR 848 ....21.140
London Ambulance Service v Charlton [1992] ICR 773........................20.48
London and Solent Ltd v Brooks, Daily Telegraph, 27 October 1988...................6.54
London Borough of Hackney v Adams [2003] IRLR 402.........................20.71
London Borough of Harrow v Cunningham [1996] IRLR 256............... 14.151, 14.154
London Borough of Harrow v Knight [2003] IRLR 140.........................15.18
London Borough of Newham v Ward [1985] IRLR 509..........................14.93
London Borough of Southwark v O'Brien [1996] IRLR 420 ....5.12
London Borough of Wandsworth v National Association of Schoolmasters/
    Union of Women Teachers [1993] IRLR 344 ....21.87
London Clubs Management Ltd v Hood [2001] IRLR 723 ....8.135
London Export Corp v Jubilee Coffee Roasting Co [1958] 2 All ER 411 ....3.41
London Fire & Civil Defence Authority v Betty [1994] IRLR 384..................14.127
London International College Ltd v Sen [1993] IRLR 333 ....12.14
London Transport Executive v Clarke [1981] IRLR 166........................21.11

London Underground Ltd v Edwards [1999] ICR 494 ....8.98
London Underground Ltd v Ferenc-Batchelor [2003] ICR 656.......................4.84
London Underground Ltd v Noel [1999] IRLR 621 ....12.21
London Underground Ltd v RMT [1996] ICR 170.............................21.116
Long v Smithson (1918) 88 LJ KB 223 ....21.26
Longden v Ferrari Ltd and Another [1994] IRLR 157 ....18.40
Lonrho plc v Fayed [1992] AC 448 ....21.63
Lonrho v Shell Petroleum Co Ltd (No 2) [1982] AC 173..............21.53, 21.63
Lord Advocate v De Rosa [1974] 2 All ER 849..............................11.31
Lotus Cars Ltd v Sutcliffe and Stratton [1982] IRLR 381.....................16.57
Loughran and Kelly v Northern Ireland Housing Executive [1998] IRLR 593...........8.10
Louies v Coventry Hood and Seating Co [1990] IRLR 324 ....14.182
Lovie Ltd v Anderson [1999] IRLR 164 ....14.159
Lowdens v Keaveney [1903] 2 IR 82..22.06
Lowndes v Specialist Heavy Engineering [1976] IRLR 246 ....14.184
Loxley v BAE Systems [2008] ICR 1348.....................................8.105
Lucas v Henry Johnson (Packers & Shippers) Ltd [1986] ICR 384..............16.33
Lucas v Lawrence Scott and Electromotors Ltd [1983] IRLR 61 ....14.334
Luce v London Borough of Bexley [1990] ICR 159...........................20.53
Luckings v May and Baker [1975] IRLR 151 ....14.133
Luke v Stoke on Trent CC [2007] IRLR 305................................3.26
Lumley v Gye (1853) 2 E & B 216...21.19
Lumley v Wagner (1852) 1 De GM & G 604 ....13.16, 13.42
Lunt v Merseyside TEC [1999] IRLR 458....................................12.52
Lupetti v Wrens Old House Ltd [1984] ICR 348.............................8.175
Lyddon v Engefield Brickwork Ltd [2008] IRLR 198 ....5.63
Lyford v Turquand (1966) 1 ITR 554 ....16.60
Lynock v Cereal Packaging Ltd [1988] ICR 670.............................14.129
Lyon v St James Press Ltd [1976] ICR 413 ....20.08, 20.09
Lyons v DWP Job Centre Plus [2014] ICR 668 ....10.20, 10.71, 14.335

MBS Ltd v Calo [1983] IRLR 189...14.334
MDH Ltd v Sussex [1986] IRLR 123 ....14.210
MPB Structures Ltd v Munro [2003] IRLR 350...............................5.63
MSF v GEC Ferranti (Defence Systems) Ltd (No 2) [1994] IRLR 113 ....17.40
MSF v Refuge Assurance plc [2002] IRLR 324.......................17.28, 17.36
Mabrizi v National Hospital for Nervous Diseases [1990] IRLR 133...........14.290, 14.299
Macari v Celtic FC [1999] IRLR 787 ....4.42
MacCulloch v ICI [2008] ICR 1334 ....8.104
Macer v Aberfast Ltd [1990] ICR 234......................................18.57
MacFarlane v Glasgow City Council [2001] IRLR 7 ....2.13
Macfisheries v Findlay [1985] ICR 160.........................16.20, 16.27, 16.30
Machine Tool Industry Research Association v Simpson [1988] IRLR 212 ....12.20, 12.23
MacLea v Essex Lines Ltd (1933) 45 Ll LR 254 ....3.41
Maclean v Workers Union [1929] 1 Ch 602 ....19.42
MacLelland v NUJ [1975] ICR 116..19.41
Macmillan Inc v Bishopsgate Investment Trust plc [1993] IRLR 793...............6.75
MacPherson v London Borough of Lambeth [1988] IRLR 470 ....4.20
Madarassay v Nomura International plc [2007] IRLR 246 ....8.74, 8.184
Madden v Preferred Technical Group CHA Ltd [2005] IRLR 46....................8.71
Maher v Fram Gerrard Ltd [1974] ICR 31 ....14.19
Mahlburg v Land Mecklenburg-Vorpommern [2001] ICR 1032 ....8.29
Maintenance Co Ltd v Dormer [1982] IRLR 491............................14.171
Makin v Greens Motor (Bridport) Ltd, *The Times*, 18 April 1986...........14.13, 14.72
Malcolm v Lewisham LBC [2008] 1 AC 1399 ....8.118

Malik v Bank of Credit and Commerce International SA (in compulsory liquidation)
  [1997] ICR 606; [1997] IRLR 462 . . . . 3.28, 3.29, 13.59
Malins v Post Office [1975] ICR 60 . . . . .2.40
Malloch v Aberdeen Corporation [1971] 1 WLR 1578. 13.21, 13.51
Mallone v BPB Industries Ltd [2002] ICR 1045 . . . . .3.26
Malone v BA [2011] ICR 125 . . . . .3.18
Managers (Holborn) Ltd v Hohne [1977] IRLR 230 . . . . .14.34
Manchester College v Hazel [2014] ICR 989 . . . . .18.107
Mandla v Dowell Lee [1983] 2 AC 548. . . . . 8.17, 8.104
Manifold Industries Ltd v Sims [1991] IRLR 242 . . . . .14.263
Manpower Ltd v Hearne [1983] IRLR 281. . . . . .14.313
Mansard Precision Engineering Co Ltd v Taylor [1978] ICR 44. . . . . .6.08
Mansfield Hosiery Mills Ltd v Bromley [1977] IRLR 301 . . . . .14.312
Marabu Porr, The [1979] 2 Lloyd's Rep 331 . . . . .21.80
Marbe v George Edwardes (Daly's Theatres) Ltd [1928] 1 KB 269. . . . . .13.65
Marcus v George Wimpey Co Ltd [1974] IRLR 356. . . . . .14.322
Marion White Ltd v Francis [1972] 3 All ER 22. . . . . .6.56
Maris v Rotherham Corporation [1974] 2 All ER 776 . . . . 14.338, 14.345
Market Investigations Ltd v Minister of Social Security [1969] 2 WLR 1 . . . . .2.22, 2.25
Marks and Spencer v Williams Ryan [2005] IRLR 562 . . . . 12.22
Marley (UK) Ltd v Anderson [1996] IRLR 163 . . . . 12.23, 12.24
Marley Homecare Ltd v Dutton [1981] IRLR 380 . . . . .14.151
Marley Tile Co Ltd v Shaw [1980] ICR 72 . . . . .20.12, 20.17, 20.27
Marley v Forward Trust Group Ltd [1986] IRLR 369 . . . . .3.07
Márquez Samohano v Universitat Pompeu Fabra [2014] ICR 609 . . . . .9.19
Marriott v Oxford and District Cooperative Society (No 2)
  [1970] 1 QB 186 . . . . 3.55, 14.10, 14.19
Marriott v Oxford and District Co-operative Society (No 2) [1970] 1 QB 186 . . . . 13.10, 16.39
Marsden v Fairey Stainless Ltd [1979] IRLR 103 . . . . .14.60
Marsh v National Autistic Society [1993] ICR 453. . . . . 13.19, 13.44
Marshall (Cambridge) Ltd v Hamblin [1994] ICR 363. . . . . .13.04
Marshall Specialist Vehicles Ltd v Osborne [2003] IRLR 67 .3.26
Marshall v Alexander Sloan and Co Ltd [1981] IRLR 264. . . . . .4.45
Marshall v Harland & Wolff [1972] ICR 10. . . . . .14.81
Marshall v Industrial Systems & Control Ltd [1992] IRLR 294. . . . . 6.17, 6.21, 14.171
Marshall v NM Financial Management Ltd [1997] IRLR 449. . . . . 6.48, 6.60
Marshall v Southampton and South West Hampshire HA [1986] ICR 335 . . . . .2.40
Marshalls Clay Products v Caulfield [2003] IRLR 552. . . . . .5.63
Marsland v Francis Dunn Ltd (1967) 2 ITR 353. . . . . .16.14
Martin v Automobile Proprietary Ltd [1979] IRLR 64. . . . . .14.233
Martin v Devonshire's Solicitors [2011] ICR 352 . . . . .8.90
Martin v Lancashire CC [2001] ICR 197 . . . . .18.67
Martin v MBS Fastenings (Glynwed) Distribution Ltd [1983] ICR 511 . . . . .14.12
Martin v Solus Schall [1979] IRLR 7 . . . . .14.184
Martin v South Bank University [2004] IRLR 75, ECJ. 18.72
Martin v Southern Health and Social Care Trust [2010] IRLR 1048. . . . . .5.50
Martin v Yeomen Aggregates Ltd [1983] IRLR 49 . . . . .14.13
Massey v Crown Life Insurance Company [1978] IRLR 31 . . . . 2.28, 2.30, 2.31
Massey v UNIFI [2007] IRLR 902. . . . . .19.38
Mathewson v R. B. Wilson Dental Laboratory Ltd [1988] IRLR 512 . . . . .14.155
Matthews v Kent & Medway Towns Fire Authority [2004] IRLR 697,
  [2006] IRLR 367 . . . . 9.06, 9.12
Mattu v University Hospitals Coventry & Warwicks NHS Trust [2013] ICR 27. . . . . . . .23.11
Maund v Penwith DC [1984] IRLR 24 . . . . 14.94, 20.33
Mayeur v Association Promotion de L'Information Messine [2000] IRLR 788 . . . . .18.21

Mba v Merton lbc [2014] ICR 357 ....8.68
McAlwane v Boughton Estates Ltd [1973] 2 All ER 299 ....14.66
McAndrew v Prestwick Circuits Ltd [1988] IRLR 514......................14.34, 14.352
McAulay v Cementation Chemicals Ltd [1972] IRLR 71 ....14.293
McAuley v Eastern Health & Social Services Board [1991] IRLR 467.................7.72
McCall v Castleton Crafts Ltd [1979] IRLR 218 ....14.176
McCarthy v British Insulated Callenders Cables plc [1985] IRLR 9.................14.334
McCarthys Ltd v Smith [1980] IRLR 210.....................................7.18, 7.97
McCartney v Oversley House Management [2006] IRLR 514........................5.31
McClaren v Home Office [1990] IRLR 338 ....3.51, 13.23
McClelland v Northern Ireland General Health Services Board [1957] 2 All ER 129 .....13.27
McClintock v DCA [2008] IRLR 29...8.66
McClory v Post Office [1993] IRLR 159...3.26
McConnell v Bolik [1979] IRLR 422 ....12.28
McConnell v Police Authority for Northern Ireland [1997] IRLR 625.................8.208
McCormick v Horsepower Ltd [1981] IRLR 217 ....14.267
McCrea v Cullen & Davison Ltd [1988] IRLR 30 ....16.19
McCreadie v Thomson & MacIntyre (Patternmakers) Ltd [1971] 2 All ER 113..........16.43
McCree v Tower Hamlets London Borough Council [1992] ICR 99 .... 5.06, 5.12
McDougall v Richmond Adult Community College [2007] IRLR 771.................8.39
McFall & Co v Curran [1981] IRLR 45 14346
McGhee v TGWU [1985] IRLR 198...19.22
McGowan v Scottish Water [2005] IRLR 167 ....23.35
McGrath v Rank Leisure Ltd [1985] ICR 527..................................18.110
McIntosh v British Rail (1967) 2 ITR 26 ....16.47
McKenzie v Crosville Motor Services Ltd [1989] IRLR 516................. 14.263, 14.264
McKindley v William Hill (Scotland) Ltd [1985] IRLR 492.........................16.39
McLean v Rainbow Homeloans Ltd [2007] IRLR 14............................14.283
McLeod v Hellyer Brothers Ltd [1987] IRLR 232 ....2.10, 2.78, 11.16
McLory v Post Office [1992] ICR 758..13.20
McMaster v Manchester Airport plc [1998] IRLR 112............................14.93
McMeechan v Secretary of State for Employment [1997] ICR 549 .... 2.49, 2.78
McMenamin (Inspector of Taxes) v Diggles [1991] ICR 641 ....2.38
McMenemy v Capita Business Services Ltd [2006] IRLR 761 ....9.10
McMillan v Airedale NHS Foundation Trust [2015] ICR 747 .... 4.50, 13.45
McNeill v Charles Crimin (Electrical Contractors) Ltd [1984] IRLR 17 .... 14.34, 14.42
McNicol v Balfour Beatty Rail Maintenance Ltd [2002] ICR 1498 ....8.55
McPherson v Rathgael Centre for Children and Young People and Northern Ireland Office
    (Training Schools Branch) [1991] IRLR 206................................7.17
McPhie & McDermott v Wimpey Waste Management Ltd [1981] IRLR 31 ....14.158
McQuade v Scotbeef Ltd [1975] IRLR 332......................................20.17
Meade v Haringey LBC [1979] 2 All ER 1016 ....21.53
Mears v Safecar Security Ltd [1982] IRLR 183...........................3.75, 4.06
Medhurst v Dental Estimates Board Branch of NALGO and NALGO
    [1990] IRLR 459..19.33
Meek v Allen Rubber Co Ltd and Secretary of State for Employment [1980] IRLR 21 ....16.38
Meek v Port of London Authority [1918] 1 Ch 415..............................3.41
Meikle v McPhail [1983] IRLR 35 .... 18.102, 18.106
Meikle v Notts CC [2005] ICR 1 ....14.40
Melhuish v Redbridge CAB [2005] IRLR 419 ....2.15
Melon v Hector Powe Ltd [1981] ICR 43 .... 11.33, 11.35
Mennell v Newell & Wright (Transport Contractors) Ltd [1997] ICR 1039 ....14.283
Menzies v Smith & McLaurin Ltd [1980] IRLR 180 ....20.54
Mercia Rubber Mouldings v Lingwood [1974] IRLR 82 ....14.218
Merckx v Ford Motor Co Belgium SA [1996] IRLR 467 ....18.88

Mercury Communications Ltd v ScottGarner [1984] Ch 37......................21.97
Meridian Ltd v Gomersall [1977] ICR 597; [1977] IRLR 425 .... 14.151, 14.292
Merino Gomez v Continental Industrias del Caucho SA [2004] IRLR 407 ....10.14
Merkur Island Shipping Corporation v Laughton [1983] IRLR 218;
    [1983] 2 AC 570 .... 21.16, 21.24, 21.45, 21.49
Mersey Dock and Harbour Co v Verrinder [1982] IRLR 152............. 22.18, 22.31, 22.39
Merseyside & North Wales Electricity Board v Taylor [1975] IRLR 60...............14.133
Messenger Newspaper Group Ltd v NGA [1984] IRLR 397........................22.31
Metall und Rohstoff AG v Donaldson Lufkin & Jenrette Inc [1989] 3 All ER 14 ....21.63
Meter U Ltd v Ackroyd [2012] ICR 834 ....18.108
Metrobus [2010] IRLR 173......................................21.135
Metroline Travel Ltd v Unite the Union [2012] IRLR 749 ....21.122
Metropolitan Police Commissioner v Keohane [2014] ICR 1073 ....10.71
Metropolitan Resources Ltd v Churchill Dulwich Ltd [2009] IRLR 700......... 18.38, 18.39
Meyer Dunmore International Ltd v Rogers [1978] IRLR 167......................14.148
Mezey v SW London & St Georges Mental Health NHS Trust
    [2010] IRLR 512...13.29, 13.34, 13.48
Micklefield v SAC Technology Ltd [1990] IRLR 218 ....13.57
Mid Staffs General Hospitals NHS Trust v Cambridge [2003] IRLR 566 ....8.129
Middlebrook Mushrooms Ltd v TGWU [1993] ICR 612 ....21.51
Middlesbrough BC v Surtees No 2 [2008] ICR 349 ....7.81
Midland Cold Storage v Steer [1972] Ch 630 ....21.31
Midland Electric Manufacturing Co Ltd v Kanji [1980] IRLR 185 ....14.78
Midland Plastics v Till [1983] IRLR 9 ....14.267
Mihalis Angelos, The [1971] 1 QB 164......................................13.11
Miles v Linkage Community Trust Ltd [2008] IRLR 60 ....5.71
Miles v Wakefield Metropolitan District Council [1987] ICR 368......... 4.18, 14.252, 21.14
Millam v Print Factory (London) 1991 Ltd [2007] IRLR 526 ....18.08
Millar v IRC [2006] IRLR 112..8.33
Millbank Financial Services Ltd v Crawford [2014] IRLR 18....................15.05
Millbrook Furnishing Ltd v McIntosh [1981] IRLR 309 ....4.59, 14.25, 14.34
Miller v Executors of John Graham [1978] IRLR 309 ....14.113
Miller v Hamworthy Engineering Ltd [1986] ICR 846................3.59, 4.46, 4.55
Miller v Interserve Industrial Services Ltd [2013] ICR 445......................20.30
Milsom v Leicestershire County Council [1978] IRLR 433 ....5.16
Mingeley v Pennock & Ivory [2004] IRLR 373 ....8.10
Ministry of Defence v Bristow [1996] ICR 544...............................8.198
Ministry of Defence v Cannock [1994] IRLR 509 ....8.197
Ministry of Defence v Crook and Irving [1982] IRLR 488.......................20.54
Ministry of Defence v DeBique [2010] IRLR 471.............................8.102
Ministry of Defence v Hay [2008] ICR 1247 ....8.33
Ministry of Defence v Hunt [1996] ICR 554................................8.198
Ministry of Defence v Jeremiah [1980] ICR 13................. 8.76, 8.149, 8.195
Ministry of Defence v Kemeh [2014] ICR 625 ....8.199
Ministry of Defence v Mutton [1996] ICR 590...............................8.206
Ministry of Defence v Sullivan [1994] ICR 193 .... 8.197, 8.200
Ministry of Defence v Wallis [2010] IRLR 1035; [2011] ICR 617...................12.36
Ministry of Justice v Burton [2016] IRLR 100 ....9.13
Ministry of Justice v O'Brien [2013] ICR 499...............................9.14
Ministry of Justice v Parry [2013] ICR 311.................................23.11
Ministry of Justice v POA [2008] IRLR 380........................ 21.12, 21.167
Minnevitch v Café de Paris [1936] 1 All ER 884 ....4.59
Miriki v Bar Council [2002] ICR 505......................................8.186
Mirror Group Newspaper Ltd v Gunning [1986] IRLR 27.......................8.11
Mirror Group Newspapers Ltd v Gunning [1986] IRLR 27........................2.66

Mitchell v Arkwood Plastics (Engineering) Ltd [1993] ICR 471 . . . . .14.126
Modern Injection Moulds Ltd v Price [1976] ICR 370 . . . . .14.211
Mogul Steamship Co v McGregor, Gow and Co [1892] AC 25 . . . . 21.64, 21.66
Mohar v Granitstone Galloway Ltd [1974] ICR 273 . . . . .14.323
Moncur v International Paint Co Ltd [1978] IRLR 223 . . . . .14.340
Monie v Coral Racing Ltd [1981] ICR 109 . . . . 14.94, 14.160
Mono Pumps Ltd v Froggatt and Radford [1987] IRLR 368 . . . . .14.329
Monsanto plc v TGWU [1987] ICR 269 . . . . .21.112
Monterosso Shipping Ltd v International Transport Workers' Federation
    [1982] ICR 675 . . . . .19.50
Moody v Telefusion Ltd [1978] IRLR 311 . . . . .14.241
Moon v Homeworthy Furniture (Northern) Ltd [1977] ICR 117 . . . . .14.192
Moorcock, The (1889) 14 PD 64 . . . . .3.23
Moore v C & A Modes [1981] IRLR 71 . . . . .14.155
Moore v Duport Furniture Products Ltd [1982] ICR 84 . . . . .12.50
Moores v Bude-Stratton Town Council [2000] IRLR 676 . . . . .14.37
Moorthy v HM Revenue & Customs [2016] IRLR 259 . . . . .13.74
Morgan v Electrolux [1991] IRLR 8 . . . . .14.170
Morgan v Fry [1968] 2 QB 710 . . . . 4.35, 21.08–21.10, 21.60
Morgan v Manser [1948] 1 KB 184 . . . . .14.88
Morgan v Staffordshire University [2002] IRLR 190 . . . . .8.56
Morgan v Welsh Rugby Union [2011] IRLR 376 . . . . .14.199
Morgan v West Glamorgan CC [1995] IRLR 68 . . . . .5.12
Morganite Crucible v Street [1972] ICR 110 . . . . .16.49
Morganite Electrical Carbon Ltd v Donne [1987] IRLR 363 . . . . 14.299, 14.351
Morgans v Alpha Plus Security Ltd [2005] IRLR 234 . . . . .14.334
Morissens v Belgium (1988) D&R 127 . . . . 23.21, 23.50
Morley v C. T. Morley Ltd [1985] ICR 499 . . . . .14.73
Morley v Heritage plc [1993] IRLR 400 . . . . .4.41
Morley's of Brixton Ltd v Minott [1982] IRLR 270 . . . . .14.167
Morran v Glasgow Council of Tenants Association [1998] IRLR 67 . . . . .13.66
Morris Angel Ltd v Hollande [1993] ICR 71 . . . . .18.74
Morris v Acco Co Ltd [1985] ICR 30 . . . . .14.312
Morris v John Grose Group Ltd [1998] IRLR 499 . . . . .18.101
Morris v Secretary of State for Employment [1985] IRLR 297 . . . . .16.77
Morris v Walsh Western UK Ltd [1997] IRLR 563 . . . . .11.23
Morrish v Henlys (Folkestone) Ltd [1973] ICR 482 . . . . 4.44, 14.144
Morrison & Poole v Ceramic Engineering Co Ltd (1966) 1 ITR 404 . . . . .16.47
Morrison v ATGWU [1989] IRLR 361 . . . . .14.340
Morrow v Safeway Stores plc [2002] IRLR 10 . . . . .14.32
Morse v Wiltshire County Council [1998] IRLR 352 . . . . .8.134
Morton Sundour Fabrics Ltd v Shaw (1967) 2 ITR 84 .14.15, 14.18
Morton v Chief Adjudication Officer [1988] IRLR 444 . . . . .14.359
Motherwell Railway Club v McQueen [1989] ICR 418 . . . . .14.292
Motorola Ltd v Davidson [2001] IRLR 4 . . . . .2.50
Mowlem Northern Ltd v Watson [1990] IRLR 500 . . . . .14.75
Moyer-Lee v Cofely Workplace Ltd [2015] IRLR 879 . . . . .17.37
Moyes v Hylton Castle Working Men's Social Club & Institute Ltd [1986] IRLR 482 . . .14.182
Mugford v Midland Bank plc [1997] IRLR 209 . . . . .14.207
Mulcahy v R (1868) LR 3 HL 306 . . . . .21.62
Munif v Cole & Kirby Ltd [1973] ICR 486 . . . . .14.341
Munir v Jang Publications Ltd [1989] IRLR 224 . . . . .14.250
Munro v UK (1987) 52 DR 158 . . . . .23.15
Murco Petroleum Ltd v Forge [1987] IRLR 50 . . . . .14.31
Murphy v A. Birrell & Sons Ltd [1978] IRLR 458 . . . . .11.22

Murphy v Epsom College [1983] IRLR 395; [1984] IRLR 271 . . . . .14.94, 14.221, 16.21
Murray MacKinnon v Forno [1983] IRLR 7. . . . . .14.108
Murray v British Rail [1976] IRLR 382 . . . . .14.182
Murray v Foyle Meats Ltd [1999] IRLR 562. . . . . 16.23, 16.26
Murray v Leisureplay plc [2005] IRLR 946 . . . . .13.73
Murray v Newham CAB [2001] ICR 708 . . . . .8.140
Murray v Powertech (Scotland) Ltd [1992] IRLR 257 . . . . .8.200
Mustafa v Trekl Highways Services Ltd [2016] IRLR 326 . . . . .18.62

NACODS v Gluchowski [1996] IRLR 252 . . . . .19.22
NALGO v Courteney-Dunn [1992] IRLR 114 . . . . .19.38
NALGO v Killorn and Simm [1990] IRLR 464 . . . . .19.33
NALGO v National Travel (Midlands) Ltd [1978] ICR 598. .17.28
N.C. Watling & Co Ltd v Richardson [1978] ICR 1049. . . . . .14.110
NRG Victory Reinsurance Ltd v Alexander [1992] ICR 675 .12.50
NUMAST v P&O Scottish Ferries [2005] ICR 1270 . . . . .18.33
NWL Ltd v Woods [1979] 3 All ER 614. . . . . .21.00, 21.86, 21.102, 21.162, 21.164
Nabi v British Leyland (UK) Ltd [1980] 1 All ER 667 . . . . .13.75
Naeem v Secretary of State for Justice [2016] ICR 289. . . . . .8.99
Nagarajan v London Regional Transport [1999] IRLR 572. .8.112
Nagle v Feilden [1966] 2 QB 633 . . . . .19.20
Nagy v Weston [1965] 1 WLR 280. . . . . .22.06
Nairne v Highlands and Islands Fire Brigade [1989] IRLR 366 . . . . .14.292
Nambalat v Taher [2013] ICR 1025 . . . . .5.25
Napier v National Business Agency Ltd [1951] 2 All ER 264 .12.26
Narich Pty Ltd v Commissioner of Pay-roll Tax [1984] ICR 286 . . . . 2.25, 2.31
National Coal Board v Galley [1958] 1 WLR 16. . . . . .3.06, 3.48, 21.13
National Coal Board v National Union of Mineworkers [1986] IRLR 439 . . . . 3.11, 3.16, 19.51
National Coal Board v Sherwin & Spruce [1978] IRLR 122 . . . . 7.28, 7.101
National Sailors and Firemen's Union of GB and Ireland v Reed [1926] 1 Ch 536. . . . . . .21.92
National Union of Gold, Silver and Allied Trades v Albury Brothers Ltd
  [1978] IRLR 504. . . . . 17.10, 17.13, 19.57
National Union of Public Employees v General Cleaning Contractors
  [1976] IRLR 362. . . . . .17.23
National Union of Rail, Maritime and Transport Workers v London Underground Ltd
  [2001] IRLR 229. . . . . 21.134, 21.136
National Union of Rail, Maritime and Transport Workers v Midland Mainline Ltd
  [2001] IRLR 813. . . . . .21.115
National Union of Rail, Maritime and Transport Workers v Serco Ltd
  [2011] IRLR 399. . . . . .21.121
National Union of Tailors and Garment Workers v Charles Ingram & Co Ltd
  [1977] IRLR 14. . . . . .17.11
National Union of Teachers v Avon County Council [1978] IRLR 55 . . . . .17.27
National Vulcan Engineering Insurance Group Ltd v Wade [1978] IRLR 25. . . . . 7.35, 7.51
Navy, Army and Air Force Institutes v Varley [1976] IRLR 408 . . . . .7.41
Naylor v Orton & Smith Ltd [1983] IRLR 233. . . . . .14.262
Nazir v Asim [2010] ICR 1225 . . . . .8.74
Neary v Service Children's Education [2010] IRLR 1030. . . . . .12.35
Neepsend Steel Ltd v Vaughan [1972] 3 All ER 725. . . . . .4.72
Neigel v France (1997) 21 EHRR 424. . . . . .23.20
Nelson v BBC (No 2) [1979] IRLR 346. . . . . 14.338, 14.341
Nelson v BBC [1977] ICR 649 . . . . 14.94, 16.24
Nelson v Carillion Service Ltd [2003] IRLR 428 . . . . .7.35
Nerva v R. L. & G. Ltd [1997] ICR 11. . . . . .14.323
Nesbitt v Secretary of State for Trade & Industry [2007] IRLR 847 . . . . .2.59

Nethermere (St Neots) Ltd v Taverna and Gardiner [1984] IRLR 240 . . . . 2.07, 2.77
Network Rail Infrastructure Ltd v Griffiths-Henry [2006] IRLR 865 . . . . 8.180
New Century Cleaning Co Ltd v Church [2000] IRLR 27 . . . . 5.04
New ISG Ltd v Vernon [2008] IRLR 115 . . . . 18.97
New Testament Church of God v Stewart [2007] IRLR 178, [2008] IRLR 134 . . . . 2.32
Newcastle upon Tyne CC v Allan [2005] ICR 1170 . . . . 7.104
Newcastle upon Tyne Hospitals NHS Foundation Trust v Armstrong [2010] ICR 674 . . . . . 7.58
Newham London Borough Council v NALGO [1993] ICR 189 . . . . 21.110, 21.132
Newman v Polytechnic of South Wales Students Union [1995] IRLR 72 . . . . 14.93
Newns v British Airways plc [1992] IRLR 575 . . . . 4.26, 18.98
News Group Newspapers v SOGAT 82 [1986] ICR 716 . . . . 19.45, 22.18, 22.29, 22.30,
                                                                           22.31, 22.40, 22.42, 22.44
Newsham v Dunlop Textiles Ltd (No 2) (1969) 4 ITR 268 . . . . 11.13
Newstead v Dept of Transport and HM Treasury [1988] ICR 332 . . . . 7.99
NHS Direct NHS Trust v Gunn [2015] IRLR 799 . . . . 18.67
Nicholl v Nocorrode Ltd [1981] IRLR 163 . . . . 11.05
Nicoll v Cutts [1985] BCLC 322 . . . . 13.02, 16.70
Nicoll v Falcon Airways Ltd [1962] 1 Lloyd's Rep 24 . . . . 13.03
Niemitz v Germany (1993) 16 EHRR 97 . . . . 23.30
Nimz v Freie und Hansestadt Hamburg [1991] IRLR 222 . . . . 7.100
Noble v David Gold and Son (Holdings) Ltd [1980] IRLR 252 . . . . 8.84
Nokes v Doncaster Amalgamated Collieries Ltd [1940] AC 1014 . . . . 3.61, 11.30, 18.01
Noone v North West Thames Regional Health Authority
    [1988] IRLR 530 . . . . 8.195, 8.199, 8.213
Norbrook Laboratories (GB) Ltd v Shaw [2014] ICR 540 . . . . 15.03
Norbrook Laboratories Ltd v King [1984] IRLR 200 . . . . 21.102
Nordenfelt v Maxim Nordenfelt Guns and Ammunition Ltd [1894] AC 535 . . . . 6.52
Norfolk CC v Bernard [1979] IRLR 220 . . . . 14.155
Norgett v Luton Industrial Co-operative Society Ltd [1976] IRLR 30 . . . . 12.22
Norris v Southampton City Council [1982] IRLR 141 . . . . 14.90
North Cumbria Acute Hospitals NHS Trust v Potter [2009] IRLR 176 . . . . 7.22
North Cumbria University Hospitals NHS Trust v Fox [2010] IRLR 804 . . . . 7.91
North East Coast Ship Repairers Ltd v Secretary of State for Employment
    [1978] IRLR 149 . . . . 16.32
North Essex Health Authority v David-John [2004] ICR 112 . . . . 8.11
North Riding Garages Ltd v Butterwick (1967) 2 ITR 229 . . . . 16.26, 16.30
North v Pavleigh Ltd [1978] IRLR 461 . . . . 4.62
North Western Health Board v McKenna [2005] IRLR 895 . . . . 10.30
North Yorkshire CC v Fay [1985] IRLR 247 . . . . 14.236
Northern General Hospital NHS Trust v Gale [1994] IRLR 292 . . . . 18.47
Northern Joint Police Board v Power [1997] IRLR 610 . . . . 8.20
Northgate HR Ltd v Mercy [2008] IRLR 222 . . . . 14.199, 17.45
Norton Tool Co Ltd v Tewson [1972] ICR 501 . . . . 14.314, 14.316, 14.322, 14.329
Norwest Holst Group Administration Ltd v Harrison [1984] IRLR 419 . . . . 3.58, 14.37
Notcutt v Universal Equipment (London) Ltd [1986] 1 WLR 641 . . . . 14.83
Nothman v Barnet LBC [1979] IRLR 35 . . . . 14.362
Nothman v London Borough of Barnet (No 2) [1980] IRLR 65 . . . . 14.293
Nottingham University v Fishel [2000] IRLR 471 . . . . 6.03
Nottinghamshire CC v Bowly [1978] IRLR 252 . . . . 14.155
Nottinghamshire CC v Lee [1979] IRLR 294 . . . . 16.32
Nova Plastics Ltd v Froggatt [1982] IRLR 146 . . . . 6.09
Nunn v Royal Mail Group Ltd [2011] ICR 162 . . . . 14.94

O'Brien v Associated Fire Alarms Ltd (1968) 3 ITR 18 . . . . 16.17
O'Brien v Ministry of Justice [2010] IRLR 883; [2013] ICR 499 . . . . 9.03

O'Brien v Prudential Assurance Co Ltd [1979] IRLR 140 . . . . 14.134, 14.238
O'Dea v ISC Chemicals Ltd [1995] IRLR 599 . . . . 1.322, 20.31
O'Donoghue v Redcar and Cleveland Borough Council [2001] IRLR 615. . . . . .14.322
O'Hanlon v HM Revenue and Customs [2007] IRLR 404. . . . . .8.132
O'Hare and Rutherford v Rotaprint Ltd [1980] IRLR 47. . . . . .16.32
O'Kelly v Trusthouse Forte plc [1983] 3 WLR 605. . . . . .2.47, 2.77, 2.78
O'Laiore v Jackel International Ltd [1990] ICR 197; [1991] ICR 718 . . . . 13.64, 13.75, 14.299,
14.301, 14.334
O'Neill v Merseyside Plumbing Ltd [1973] ICR 96. . . . . .16.21
O'Reilly v Hotpoint Ltd (1970) 5 ITR 68 . . . . .4.57
O'Reilly v Welwyn and Hatfield District Council [1975] IRLR 334. . . . . .14.353
OBG Ltd v Allan [2007] IRLR 21. . . . . 21.27, 21.35
Oakland v Wellswood (Yorkshire) Ltd [2009] IRLR 250 . . . . .18.84
Oakley v The Labour Party [1988] IRLR 34. . . . . .14.231
Obermeier v Germany (1991) 13 EHRR 290 . . . . .23.12
Octavius Atkinson & Sons Ltd v Morris [1989] IRLR 158. . . . . 13.19, 14.212
Ole Rygaard v Dansk Arbejdsgiverforening, acting on behalf of Strø Mølle Akustik A/S
[1996] IRLR 51. . . . . .18.14
Oliver v J.P. Malnick & Co [1983] IRLR 456. . . . . .8.10
Olsen v Gear Bulk Services Ltd [2015] IRLR 185. . . . . .12.40
Omilaju v Waltham Forest LBC [2005] IRLR 35 . . . . .14.40
Onu v Akwiwu [2016] IRLR 719 . . . . 8.20, 8.22
Onyango v Berkeley [2013] IRLR 338. . . . . .15.07
Optare Group Ltd v TGWU [2007] IRLR 932. . . . . .17.32
Optical Express Ltd v Williams [2007] IRLR 936 . . . . .16.36
Optikinetics Ltd v Whooley [1999] ICR 984 . . . . .14.344
Optimum Group Services plc v Muir [2013] IRLR 339 . . . . .4.308
Orr v Milton Keynes Council [2011] ICR 704 . . . . .14.168
Orr v Vaughan [1981] IRLR 63. . . . . 14.193, 14.230
Orthet Ltd v Vince Cain [2004] IRLR 85 . . . . .13.74
Österreichischer Gewerkschaftsbund v Wirtschaftskammer Österreich
[2014] ICR 1152 . . . . .18.127
Ottimo Property Services Ltd v Duncan [2015] ICR 859 . . . . .18.35
Ottoman Bank Ltd v Chakarian [1930] AC 277. . . . . .4.43
Oudahar v Esporta Group Ltd [2011] ICR 140. . . . . .20.73
Outlook Supplies Ltd v Penny [1978] IRLR 12. . . . . .7.47
Owen & Briggs v James [1981] IRLR 133. . . . . .8.85
Oyarce v Cheshire CC [2008] IRLR 653. . . . . .8.184

P Bork International v Foreningen af Arbejdsledere i Danmark [1989] IRLR 41 . . . . 18.09,
18.12, 18.100
PBDS National Carriers v Filkins [1979] IRLR 356 . . . . 21.94, 21.101
P&O European Ferries (Dover) Ltd v Byrne [1989] IRLR 254 .14.267
PSM International plc v Whitehouse [1992] IRLR 279. . . . . 6.38, 6.72
P v Commissioner of Police for the Metropolis [2016] IRLR 301. . . . . .8.171
P v NASUWT [2001] IRLR 532 . . . . .21.114, 21.117
P v Nottinghamshire CC [1992] IRLR 362. . . . . .14.166
P v The National Association of School Masters/Union of Women Teachers
[2001] ICR 1241 . . . . .21.88
Pacitti Jones v O'Brien [2005] IRLR 888 . . . . .12.08
Page One Records Ltd v Britton [1967] 3 All ER 822. . . . . .13.42
Paggetti v Cobb [2003] IRLR 861. . . . . .14.322
Paine and Moore v Grundy (Teddington) Ltd [1981] IRLR 267. . . . . .14.203
Palmanor Ltd v Cedron [1978] ICR 1008. . . . . 4.26, 14.323
Palmer v Southend-on-Sea BC [1984] IRLR 119. . . . . .12.11

Palomo Sanchez v Spain [2011] ECHR 1319 . . . . .23.59
Palumbo v Stylianou (1966) 1 ITR 407 . . . . .2.64
Parker & Farr Ltd v Shelvey [1979] IRLR 435 . . . . .14.346
Parker Bakeries Ltd v Palmer [1977] IRLR 215 . . . . .14.166
Parker Foundry Ltd v Slack [1992] ICR 302 . . . . .14.338
Parkins v Sodexho Ltd [2002] IRLR 109 . . . . .15.06
Parkinson v March Consulting Ltd [1998] ICR 276 . . . . .14.99
Parliamentary Commissioner for Administration v Fernandez [2004] IRLR 22 . . . . .7.54
Parr v Whitbread & Co plc [1990] ICR 427; [1990] IRLR 39 . . . . 14.151 14.162
Parry v Holst & Co Ltd (1968) 3 ITR 317 . . . . 3.54, 16.18
Parry v National Westminster Bank plc [2005] IRLR 19 . . . . .14.301
Parsons (C.A.) & Co v McLoughlin [1978] IRLR 65 . . . . .14.171
Parsons v BNM Laboratories Ltd [1964] 1 QB 9 . . . . .13.75
Patefield v Belfast City Council [2000] IRLR 664 . . . . .8.29
Patel v Nagesan [1995] IRLR 370 . . . . .14.14
Patel v Oldham MBC [2010] ICR 603 . . . . .8.37
Paterson v Commissioner of Police of the Metropolis [2007] IRLR 763 . . . . 8.40, 8.60
Paton Calvert & Co Ltd v Westerside [1979] IRLR 108 . . . . .16.49
Patterson v Castlereagh BC [2015] IRLR 721 . . . . .5.67
Patterson v Legal Services Commission [2004] IRLR 153 . . . . .8.11
Patterson v Messrs Bracketts [1977] IRLR 137 . . . . .14.130
Paul v East Surrey District Health Authority [1995] IRLR 30 .14.151
Pay v UK [2009] IRLR 139 . . . . .23.24
Payne v Secretary of State for Employment [1989] IRLR 352 . . . . .11.47
Peake v Automotive Products Ltd [1978] QB 23 . . . . 8.76, 8.149
Pearson v Kent County Council [1992] ICR 20 . . . . .11.12
Pedersen v Camden London Borough [1981] IRLR 173 . . . . .3.48, 14.34, 14.42
Pendlebury v Christian Schools North West Ltd [1985] ICR 174 . . . . .13.19
Peninsula Business Services Ltd v Sweeney [2004] IRLR 49 . . . . .3.26
PennWell Publishing (UK) Ltd v Ornstein [2007] IRLR 700 . . . . .6.32
Penprase v Mander Bros Ltd [1973] IRLR 167 . . . . .14.322
Pepper & Hope v Daish [1980] IRLR 13 . . . . .14.34
Pepper v Webb [1969] 2 All ER 216 . . . . 13.12, 13.37
Percy v Church of Scotland Board of National Mission [2006] IRLR 195 . . . . .2.32
Performing Right Society v Mitchell and Booker (Palais de Danse) Ltd
    [1924] 1 KB 762 . . . . .2.16
Perkin v St George's Healthcare NHS Trust [2005] IRLR 934 . . . . 14.145, 14.322
Perth & Kinross Council v Donaldson [2004] IRLR 121 . . . . 18.27, 18.33
Peters (Michael) Ltd v Farnfield and Peters (Michael) Group plc
    [1995] IRLR 190 . . . . 18.53, 18.54
Petrie v MacFisheries [1940] 1 KB 258 . . . . .3.39
Pfaffinger v City of Liverpool Community College [1996] IRLR 508 . . . . .16.11
Phillips v Alhambra Palace Co [1901] 1 KB 59 . . . . .13.02
Phillips v Xtera Communications Ltd [2012] ICR 171 . . . . .17.20
Photo Production Ltd v Securicor Transport Ltd [1980] AC 827 . . . . 13.14, 13.16
Photostatic Copiers (Southern) Ltd v Okuda and Japan Office Equipment Ltd
    [1995] IRLR 11 . . . . .18.89
Pickstone v Freemans plc [1986] IRLR 335 . . . . .7.80
Piddington v Bates [1960] 3 All ER 660 . . . . .22.08
Piggott Brothers & Co Ltd v Jackson [1991] IRLR 309 . . . . .14.110
Pillinger v Manchester AHA [1979] IRLR 430 EAT 16.21
Pinewood Repro Ltd v Page [2011] ICR 508 . . . . .14.204
Pink v White and White & Co (Earls Barton) Ltd [1985] IRLR 489 . . . . .16.24
Pinkney v Sandpiper Drilling Ltd [1989] ICR 389 . . . . .11.42
Pirelli General Cable Works Ltd v Murray [1979] IRLR 190 . . . . 14.182, 14.287

Plasticisers Ltd v Amos, EAT 13/76 ....14.175
Plumb v Duncan Print Group Ltd [2016] ICR 125 ....5.66
Polentarutti v Autokraft Ltd [1991] ICR 757 ....14.340
Polkey v Dayton Services Ltd [1988] ICR 142.............14.107, 14.172, 14.195,
14.209, 14.322, 14.334, 14.346
Pollard v Teako (Swiss) Ltd (1967) 2 ITR 357 ....16.75
Poparm Ltd v Weekes [1984] IRLR 388 ....11.47
Port of London Authority v Payne and Others [1994] IRLR 9 ....14.291, 14.294
Port of Tilbury (London) Ltd v Birch and Others [2005] IRLR 92...............14.326
Porter and Nanayakkara v Queen's Medical Centre (Nottingham University Hospital)
[1993] IRLR 486...18.105
Porter v Bandridge [1978] IRLR 271...12.17
Portsea Island Mutual Cooperative Society v Rees [1980] ICR 26 ....14.170
Post Office Counters v Heavey [1990] ICR 1 ....14.108
Post Office v Crouch [1974] 1 WLR 89..20.09
Post Office v Fennell [1981] IRLR 221 ....4.151
Post Office v Jones [2001] IRLR 34 ....8.137
Post Office v Moore [1981] ICR 623..12.08
Post Office v Mughal [1977] IRLR 178 ....14.119
Post Office v Roberts [1980] IRLR 347...14.32
Post Office v Sanhotra [2000] ICR 866...12.20
Post Office v Strange [1981] IRLR 515 ....14.34
Post Office v Union of Communications Workers [1990] IRLR 143...........21.113, 21.116
Post Office v UPW [1974] ICR 378..20.26
Pothecary Witham Weld v Bullimore [2010] IRLR 57 ....8.115
Potter v Hunt Contractors Ltd [1992] ICR 337..................................5.07
Potter v R KJ Temple plc, *The Times*, 11 February 2004 ....14.93
Powdrill v Watson and Talbot v Cadge [1995] IRLR 267...................16.71, 16.73
Powell v London Borough of Brent [1987] IRLR 466..............................13.46
Powell v OMV Exploration & Production Ltd [2014] ICR 63 ....12.40
Power v Panasonic UK Ltd [2003] IRLR 15 ....8.43
Powerhouse Retail Ltd v Burroughs [2006] IRLR 381 ....18.75
Powrmatic v Bull [1977] IRLR 144..14.327
Prais v EC Commission [1976] ECR 1589 ....23.41
Premier Motors (Medway) Ltd v Total Oil (GB) Ltd [1984] ICR 58.................18.06
President of the Methodist Conference v Parfitt [1984] ICR 176 ....2.32
Preston v President of the Methodist Conference [2013] ICR 833 ....2.33
Preston v Wolverhampton Healthcare NHS Trust [1988] ICR 227...........3.55, 7.85–7.87
Prestwick Circuits Ltd v McAndrew [1990] IRLR 191.................3.35, 14.34, 14.350
Priddle v Dibble [1978] ICR 149 ....14.238
Pringle v Lucas Industrial Equipment Ltd [1975] IRLR 266......................14.147
Printers & Finishers Ltd v Holloway [1965] 1 WLR 1 ....6.24
Pritchard-Rhodes Ltd v Boon [1979] IRLR 19 ....16.68
Pritchett & Dyjasek v J. McIntyre Ltd [1987] IRLR 18 ....14.182
Procter v British Gypsum Ltd [1992] IRLR 7 ....14.151
Project Management Institute v Latif [2007] IRLR 579..........................8.129
Property Guards Ltd v Taylor and Kershaw [1982] IRLR 17 ....14.246, 14.342
Provident Financial Group plc and Whitegates Estate Agency Ltd v Hayward
[1989] IRLR 84...4.56, 6.14
Pruden v Cunard Ellerman Ltd [1993] IRLR 317.................................12.08
Prudential Assurance Co v Lorenz (1971) 11 KIR 78 ....21.32
Puglia v C. James & Sons [1996] IRLR 70.............................14.320, 14.334
Pujante Rivera v Gestora Clubs Dir SL [2016] IRLR 51 ....17.07
Pulham v Barking & Dagenham LBC [2010] ICR 335 ....7.57
Pulham v LB of Barking & Dagenham [2010] ICR 333 ....8.105

Purdy v Willowbank International Ltd [1977] IRLR 388...........................4.63
Putsman v Taylor [1920] 3 KB 637 ....6.59
Puttick v John Wright & Sons (Blackwall) Ltd [1972] ICR 45 ....11.25
Puttick v John Wright & Sons (Blackwall) Ltd [1972] ICR 457 ....4.69

Qua v John Ford Morrison [2003] ICR 482 ....10.64
Qualcast (Wolverhampton) Ltd v Ross [1979] IRLR 98.............................14.186
Quashie v Stringfellow Restaurants Ltd [2013] IRLR 99 ....2.25
Quinlan v B&Q plc EAT 138/97..8.59
Quinn v Calder Industrial Materials [1996] IRLR 126..............................3.42
Quinn v Leathem [1901] AC 495...21.46, 21.64, 21.77
Quinnen v Hovell [1984] IRLR 227 ....8.10
Quirk v Burton Hospitals NHS Trust [2002] ICR 602................................7.88
Qureshi v Victoria University of Manchester [2001] ICR 863 ....8.73, 8.81

RBS v Ashton [2011] ICR 632..8.129
RCO Support Services & Aintree Hospital Trust v UNISON [2000] IRLR 624.... 18.28, 18.30
RDF Media Group plc v Clements [2008] IRLR 207 ....14.29, 14.34
R.F. Hill Ltd v Mooney [1981] IRLR 258...14.34
RHP Bearings Ltd v Brookes [1979] IRLR 452.............................20.43, 20.45
RNLI v Bushaway [2005] IRLR 674...2.06
RR Donnelley Global Document Solutions Group plc v Besagni [2014] ICR 1008 ......18.107
RS Components Ltd v Irwin [1973] ICR 535 ....14.217, 14.232
RSPCA v Cruden [1986] ICR 205...14.151, 14.347
R (Age UK) v Secretary of State for Business Innovation and Skills [2010] ICR 260 ....8.03
R (on application of BBC) v CAC [2003] IRLR 460 ....2.69
R (on application of Cable & Wireless Services UK Ltd) v CAC [2008] IRLR 425 ....19.68
R (on application of Laporte) v Chief Constable of Gloucestershire Constabulary
    [2007] 2 AC 105 ....22.07
R (on application of the NUJ) v CAC [2006] IRLR 53...............................19.63
R (on the application of Age UK) v Secretary of State for BIS [2009] IRLR 1017.........8.105
R (on the application of Boots Management Services Ltd) v CAC
    [2014] IRLR 887...19.63, 19.92
R (on the application of European Roma Rights Centre) v Immigration officers at Prague
    airport [2005] IRLR 115...8.92
R (on the application of Hottak) v Secretary of State for Foreign and Commonwealth
    Affairs [2015] IRLR 827...12.41
R (on the application of Kirk) v Middlesbrough BC [2010] IRLR 699 ....23.11
R (on the application of McNally) v Secretary of State for Education [2002] ICR 15......13.26
R (on the application of NUJ) v CAC [2006] IRLR 53.............................23.62
R (on the application of Ultraframe (UK) Ltd) v CAC [2005] IRLR 641 ....19.74
R (Shoesmith) v Ofsted [2011] ICR 1195 ....23.18
R v Attorney-General for Northern Ireland, ex p Burns [1999] IRLR 315..............5.69
R v BBC, ex p Lavelle [1982] IRLR 404 ....13.25
R v British Coal Corporation and Secretary of State for Trade and Industry,
    ex p Price and Others [1994] IRLR 72 ....17.26
R v CAC, ex p Kwik Fit (GB) Ltd [2002] IRLR 395 ....19.68, 19.132
R v CAC, ex p TI Tube Divisional Services Ltd [1978] IRLR 183....................19.132
R v Chief Constable of Thames Valley Police, ex p Cotton [1990] IRLR 344 ....13.21
R v Civil Service Appeal Board, ex p Bruce [1988] ICR 649.........................2.41
R v Civil Service Appeal Board, ex p Cunningham [1990] IRLR 503 ....12.58
R v Derbyshire CC, ex p Noble [1990] ICR 808....................................13.52
R v East Berkshire Health Authority, ex p Walsh [1984] ICR 743 ....13.22,13.51
R v Hampshire CC, ex p Ellerton [1985] ICR 317 ....13.26
R v Jones [1974] ICR 310 ....22.23

R v Lord Chancellor's Department, ex p Nangle [1991] ICR 743......................2.41
R v Secretary of State for Employment, ex p EOC [1994] ICR 317...................9.01
R v Secretary of State for Employment, ex p Seymour Smith [1997] IRLR 315;
    [1999] IRLR 253...12.05
R v Secretary of State for Employment, ex p Seymour Smith (No 2) [2000] ICR 244 .....12.05
R v Secretary of State for the Home Department, ex p Benwell [1985] IRLR 6 ....13.23
R v Secretary of State for the Home Department, ex p Broom [1986] QB 198...........13.23
R v Secretary of State for Trade and Industry, ex p BECTU [2001] IRLR 559..........5.47
R(G) v X School [2012] 1 AC 167.......................................23.11
Radford v De Froberville [1977] 1 WLR 1262................................13.53
Radford v NATSOPA [1972] ICR 484 ....19.42
Rai v Somerfield Stores [2004] IRLR 124...................................14.16
Rainey v Greater Glasgow Health Board Eastern District [1985] IRLR 414 ....7.39
Ralton v Havering College of Further & Higher Education [2001] IRLR 738..... 18.64, 18.81
Ramdoolar v Bycity Ltd [2005] ICR 368 ....10.66
Rank Xerox (UK) Ltd v Goodchild [1979] IRLR 185................. 14.97, 14.189, 14.190
Rank Xerox (UK) Ltd v Skyczek [1995] IRLR 568.............................14.301
Rank Xerox v Churchill [1988] IRLR 280 ....4.75
Rao v Civil Aviation Authority [1992] IRLR 203.........................EAT 14.189
Rao v Civil Aviation Authority [1994] IRLR 240..........................CA 14.312
Rashid v ILEA [1977] ICR 157..11.16
Rasool v Hepworth Pipe Co Ltd (No 1) [1980] ICR 494 ....14.254
Raspin v United News Shops Ltd [1999] IRLR 9 ....13.66
Ratcliffe v Dorset CC [1978] IRLR 191 ....4.39
Rath v Cruden Construction Ltd [1982] IRLR 9 ....20.20
Rathakrishnan v Pizza Express (Restaurants) Ltd [2016] ICR 283..................8.174
Ravat v Halliburton Manufacturing and Services Ltd [2012] ICR 389 ....12.39
Rayware Ltd v TGWU [1989] IRLR 134 ....22.40
Read v Phoenix Preservation Ltd [1985] IRLR 93 ....14.167, 14.182
Ready Case Ltd v Jackson [1981] IRLR 312................... 14.41, 14.56, 14.239
Ready Mixed Concrete (South East) Ltd v Minister of Pensions and National Insurance
    [1968] 2 QB 497 ....2.20
Reda v Flag Ltd [2002] IRLR 747.................................3.26, 13.03
Redbridge LBC v Fishman [1978] ICR 569............................ 14.01, 14.140
Redcar & Cleveland BC v Bainbridge [2007] IRLR 984....... 7.17, 7.48, 7.55, 7.59, 7.69, 7.77
Redfearn v Serco Ltd [2006] IRLR 623 ....8.116
Redfearn v UK [2012] ECHR 1878.......................................14.105
Redrow Homes (Yorkshire) Ltd v Buckborough [2009] IRLR 34....................2.14
Rees v Apollo Watches [1996] ICR 466 ....8.29
Regent Security Services Ltd v Power [2008] IRLR 66..........................18.42
Regents of the University of California v Bakke 438 US 265 (1978).................8.172
Reid v Camphill Engravers Ltd [1990] IRLR 268.........................14.47, 14.49
Reid v Rush & Tompkins Group plc [1989] IRLR 265..........................4.29
Reigate v Union Manufacturing Co Ltd [1918] 1 KB 592........................3.23
Reiss Engineering Co Ltd v Harrison [1985] IRLR 232 ....6.43
Rekvényi v Hungary (2000) 30 EHRR 519 ....23.51
Rentokil v Mackin [1989] IRLR 286......................................14.152
Retarded Children's Aid Society v Day [1978] ICR 437 .... 14.110, 14.171, 14.174
Revenue and Customs Commissioners v Annabel's (Berkley Square) Ltd
    [2008] ICR 1076...5.42
Revenue and Customs Commissioners v Leisure Employment Services Ltd
    [2007] ICR 1056...5.38
Rex Stewart Jefferies Parker Ginsberg Ltd v Parker [1988] IRLR 483 ....6.59, 6.64, 13.05
Reynolds v CLFIS (UK) Ltd [2015] ICR 1010................................8.88
Reynolds v Shipping Federation [1924] 1 Ch 28.............................21.66

Rice v Fon-a-Car [1980] ICR 133 . . . . .8.146
Richards v Bulpitt & Sons Ltd [1975] IRLR 134 . . . . .14.151
Richmond Precision Engineering Ltd v Pearce [1985] IRLR 179 . . . . 14.228, 18.110
Rickard v P.B. Glass Supplies [1990] ICR 150 . . . . .5.12
Ridge v Baldwin [1964] AC 40 . . . . 13.21, 13.51
Ridgway v Hungerford Market (1835) 3 Ad & El 173 . . . . .14.95
Riežniece v Zemkopības Ministrija [2013] ICR 1096 . . . . .10.18
Rigby v Ferodo Ltd [1987] IRLR 51 . . . . .3.54, 3.59, 13.19
Rihal v LB of Ealing [2004] IRLR 642 . . . . .8.192
Riley v Tesco Stores Ltd [1980] IRLR 103 . . . . .12.13
Rinner Kühn v FWW Spezial-Gebäudereinigung [1989] IRLR 493 . . . . .7.60
Roach v CSB (Moulds) Ltd [1991] ICR 349 . . . . .11.07
Roadburg v Lothian Regional Council [1976] IRLR 283 . . . . .8.210
Roadchef Ltd v Hastings [1988] IRLR 142 . . . . .14.317
Robb v London Borough of Hammersmith and Fulham [1991] ICR 514 . . . . .13.47
Robert Cort & Son Ltd v Charman [1981] IRLR 437 . . . . 13.66, 14.93
Robert Whiting Designs Ltd v Lamb [1978] ICR 89 . . . . .14.339
Roberts v Essoldo Circuit (Control) Ltd (1967) 2 ITR 351 . . . . .6.43
Robertson v Bexley Community Centre [2003] IRLR 434 . . . . .8.174
Robertson v Blackstone Franks Investment Management Ltd [1998] IRLR 376 . . . . .5.04
Robertson v British Gas Corporation [1983] ICR 351 . . . . 3.14, 3.71
Robinson Steele v R D Retail Services Ltd [2006] IRLR 386 . . . . .5.63
Robinson v British Island Airways Ltd [1978] ICR 304 . . . . .14.226
Robinson v Carrickfergus BC [1983] IRLR 122 . . . . .14.198
Robinson v Crompton Parkinson Ltd [1978] ICR 401 . . . . 4.26, 14.31
Robinson v Flitwick Frames Ltd [1975] IRLR 261 . . . . .14.233
Robinson v Post Office [2000] IRLR 804 . . . . .8.174
Robinson v Tescom Corporation [2008] IRLR 408 . . . . .14.141
Robinson v Ulster Carpet Mills Ltd [1991] IRLR 348 . . . . .14.205
Rock Refrigeration Ltd v Jones [1996] IRLR 675 . . . . .6.67
Rockfon A/S v Specialarbejderforbundet i Danmark [1996] IRLR 168 . . . . .17.36
Roger Bullivant Ltd v Ellis [1987] IRLR 49 . . . . 6.26, 6.37
Rogers v Booth [1935] 2 All ER 751 . . . . .2.36
Rogers v Chloride Systems Ltd [1992] IRLR 198 . . . . .14.265
Rollo v Minister of Town and Country Planning [1947] 2 All ER 488 . . . . .17.40
Rolls Royce Motors Ltd v Dewhurst [1985] IRLR 184 . . . . .14.199
Rolls Royce plc v Unite the Union [2011] ICR 1 . . . . .8.105
Rolls Royce v Walpole [1980] IRLR 343 . . . . .14.129
Rookes v Barnard [1963] 1 QB 623; [1964] AC 1129 . . . . 1.04, 8.206, 21.07, 21.62
Rose v Dodd [2005] IRLR 977 . . . . .13.02
Rose v Henry Trickett & Sons Ltd (No 2) (1971) 6 ITR 211 . . . . .16.35
Rosseyer Motors Ltd v Bradshaw (1972) 7 ITR 3 . . . . .16.43
Rossiter v Pendragon plc [2001] IRLR 256 . . . . .18.92
Rovenska v General Medical Council [1997] IRLR 367 . . . . .8.177
Rowbotham v Arthur Lee & Sons Ltd [1974] IRLR 377 . . . . .16.18
Rowe v Radio Rentals Ltd [1982] IRLR 177 . . . . .14.189
Rowley, Holmes and Co v Barber [1977] ICR 387 . . . . .11.30
Rowstock Ltd v Jessemey [2014] ICR 550 . . . . .8.114
Royal Mail Group Ltd v CWU [2010] ICR 83 . . . . .18.123
Royal National Orthopaedic Hospital Trust v Howard [2003] IRLR 849 . . . . .12.55
Royal Society for the Protection of Birds v Croucher [1984] IRLR 425 . . . . .14.166
Royle v Trafford Borough Council [1984] IRLR 184 . . . . .4.20
Rubel Bronze & Metal Co Ltd, Re [1918] 1 KB 315 . . . . .13.30
Rubel Bronze & Metal Co, Re [1918] 1 KB 315 . . . . .13.12
Rubenstein v McGloughlin [1996] IRLR 557 . . . . 14.320, 14.334

Rugamer v Sony Music Entertainment UK Ltd [2001] IRLR 644. .8.54
Rummler v Dato-Druck GmbH [1987] IRLR 32 . . . . .7.74
Rushton v Harcros Timber and Building Supplies Ltd [1993] ICR 230 . . . . .14.322
Russell v Duke of Norfolk [1949] 1 All ER 109 . . . . .13.26
Russell v Transocean International Resources Ltd [2012] ICR 185 . . . . .5.63
Rutherford v Seymour Pierce Ltd [2010] IRLR 606 . . . . .3.23
Ryan v Shipboard Maintenance Ltd [1980] IRLR 16 . . . . .11.04
Rybak v Jean Sorelle Ltd [1991] ICR 127 . . . . .12.23
Ryford Ltd v Drinkwater [1996] IRLR 16. . . . . 20.35, 20.72
Rynda (UK) Ltd v Rhijnsburger [2015] ICR 1300 . . . . .18.36

SBJ Stephenson v Mandy [2000] IRLR 233 . . . . 6.16, 6.34
SCA Packaging Ltd v Boyle [2009] IRLR 53. . . . . 8.30, 8.38
SE Sheffield CAB v Grayson [2004] IRLR 343 . . . . .2.15
SG&R Valuation Services Co LLC v Boudrais [2008] IRLR 770. . . . . .6.16
SI (Systems and Instrumentation) Ltd v Grist and Riley [1983] IRLR 39 . . . . 11.37, 18.33
SIMAP v Conselleria Sanidide Consumo de Generalidad Valenciana [2000] IRLR 845 . . . .5.53
SITA (GB) Ltd v Burton [1997] IRLR 501 . . . . .18.90
SNR Denton UK LLP v Kirwan [2013] ICR 101. . . . . 18.34, 18.36
S & U Stores Ltd v Lee (1969) 4 ITR 227 . . . . .16.60
Saatchi and Saatchi v Saatchi and Saatchi and Others, unreported (ChD),
    13 February 1995 . . . . .6.11
Saavedra v Aceground Limited t/a Terrazza Est [1995] IRLR 199, EAT. 5.04
Sadek v MPS [2005] IRLR 57. . . . . .2.69
Sadler v Imperial Life of Canada Ltd [1988] IRLR 388 . . . . .6.60
Safeway Stores plc v Burrell [1997] IRLR 200 . . . . 16.25, 16.26
Sagar v Ridehalgh & Son Ltd [1931] 1 Ch 310 . . . . .3.41
Sahota v Home Office [2010] ICR 772 . . . . .10.68
Sahota v Home Office [2010] ICR 772 . . . . .8.89
Salford Royal NHS Foundation Trust v Roldan [2010] IRLR 721 . . . . .14.157
Salmon v Castlebeck Care (Teesdale) Ltd [2015] ICR 735 . . . . .18.61
Saltman Engineering Co v Campbell Engineering Co [1963] 2 All ER 413 . . . . .6.26
Salveson v Simons [1994] ICR 409 . . . . .12.30
Sánchez Hidalgo v Asociación de Servicios Aser and Sociedad Cooperativa Minerva
    [1999] IRLR 136. . . . . .18.17
Sanders v Ernest A. Neale Ltd [1974] ICR 565 . . . . 13.16, 13.44, 16.14, 16.52
Sanders v Parry [1967] 2 All ER 803. . . . . .6.09
Sandhu v Department of Education and Science [1978] IRLR 208. . . . . .14.242
Sandhu v Jan de Rijk Transport Ltd [2007] ICR 1137 . . . . 14.13, 14.65
Santamera v Express Cargo Forwarding [2003] IRLR 273. .14.182
Santokh Singh v Guru Nanak Gurdwara [1990] ICR 309 . . . . 2.37, 2.78
Sarkar v West London Health NHS Trust [2010] EWCA Civ 28 . . . . .14.110
Sarkatzis Herrero v Insttituto Madrileno de la Salud [2006] IRLR 296. . . . . .10.77
Sarker v South Tees Acute Hospitals NHS Trust [1997] IRLR 328 . . . . .13.20
Sarti Ltd v Polito [2008] ICR 1279 . . . . .5.13
Sartor v P&O European Ferries Ltd [1992] IRLR 273 . . . . .14.187
Saunders v APCOA Parking UK Ltd EAT, 18 March 2003. .20.71
Saunders v Bakers, Food and Allied Workers' Union [1986] IRLR 16 . . . . .19.29
Saunders v Richmond LBC [1977] IRLR 362. . . . . .8.140
Savage v Saxena [1998] IRLR 182. . . . . .14.354
Savoia v Chiltern Herb Farms Ltd [1982] IRLR 166. . . . . 14.52, 14.350
Saxton v National Coal Board (1970) 6 ITR 196 . . . . .3.20
Scala Ballroom (Wolverhampton) Ltd v Ratcliffe [1958] 3 All ER 220. . . . . .21.67
Scally v Southern Health and Social Services Board [1991] ICR 771 . . . . .3.26
Scarlett v Godfrey Abbot Group Ltd [1978] IRLR 456. . . . . .11.09

Scattolon v Ministero dell'Istruzione [2012] ICR 740. . . . . .18.63
Schmidt and Dahlström v Sweden (1979–80) 1 EHRR 632 . . . . .23.66
Schmidt v Spar [1995] ICR 23. . . . . 18.24, 18.33
Schüth v Germany, 23 September 2010. . . . . .23.29
Scope v Thornett [2007] IRLR 155. . . . . .14.322
Scott Packing and Warehousing Co Ltd v Paterson [1978] IRLR 16. . . . . .14.240
Scott v Coalite Fuels and Chemicals [1988] IRLR 131 . . . . 14.42, 14.73
Scott v Creager [1979] IRLR 162 . . . . .5.18
Scott v Formica Ltd [1975] IRLR 104. . . . . .14.68
Scottbridge Construction Ltd v Wright [2003] IRLR 7. . . . . .5.30
Scottish and Newcastle Breweries Ltd v Halliday [1986] IRLR 291. . . . . .14.351
Scottish Cooperative Wholesale Society Ltd v Lloyd [1973] ICR 137. . . . . .14.324
Scottish Daily Record Ltd v Laird [1996] IRLR 665. . . . . .14.158
Scottish Midland Cooperative Society Ltd v Cullion [1991] IRLR 261 . . . . .14.158
Scottish Special Housing Association v Cooke [1979] IRLR 264 . . . . .14.157, 14.160
Scottish Special Housing Association v Linnen [1979] IRLR 265. . . . . .14.166
Scotts Co (UK) Ltd v Budd [2004] ICR 299 . . . . 13.04, 13.06
Secretary of State for Employment v ASLEF (No 2) [1972] 2 QB 455 . . . . 3.38, 4.19, 4.23,
                                                          13.33, 14.252, 21.14
Secretary of State for Employment v Banks [1983] ICR 48. . . . . .16.68
Secretary of State for Employment v Cohen [1987] IRLR 169 . . . . .11.05
Secretary of State for Employment v Cooper [1987] ICR 766. . . . . .16.76
Secretary of State for Employment v Cox [1984] IRLR 437 . . . . .16.82
Secretary of State for Employment v Deary and Cambridgeshire CC [1984] IRLR 180. . . .12.46
Secretary of State for Employment v Globe Elastic Thread Co Ltd
  [1979] 2 All ER 1077; [1979] ICR 706 . . . . 3.73, 11.53
Secretary of State for Employment v Haynes [1980] ICR 371; [1980] IRLR 270 . . . . 13.08,
                                           16.60, 16.76
Secretary of State for Employment v Jobling [1980] ICR 380. . . . . .16.76
Secretary of State for Employment v John Woodrow & Sons (Builders) Ltd
  [1983] IRLR 11. . . . . .16.60
Secretary of State for Employment v Mann [1996] IRLR 4 . . . . .17.54
Secretary of State for Employment v Newbold and David Armstrong (Catering Services) Ltd
  [1981] IRLR 305. . . . . .11.46
Secretary of State for Employment v Spence [1986] IRLR 248. . . . . 18.56, 18.57
Secretary of State for Employment v Staffordshire CC [1989] IRLR 117 . . . . .14.93
Secretary of State for Employment v Wilson and BCCI [1996] IRLR 330 . . . . .16.76
Secretary of State for Employment and Productivity v Vic Hallam Ltd
  (1970) 5 ITR 108 . . . . .17.34
Secretary of State for Justice v Lown [2016] IRLR 22 . . . . .14.110
Secretary of State for Schools v Fletcher [2011] ICR 495 . . . . .9.18
Secretary of State for Scotland v Scottish Prison Officers' Association
  [1991] IRLR 371. . . . . .21.109
Secretary of State for Trade and Industry v Bottrill [1999] ICR 592, CA. 2.57
Secretary of State for Trade and Industry v Cook [1997] IRLR 288. . . . . .18.89
Secretary of State for Trade and Industry v Slater [2007] IRLR 928 . . . . .18.83
Secretary of State for Work & Pensions v Higgins [2014] ICR 341 . . . . .8.102
Secretary of State for Work and Pensions v Alam [2010] ICR 665 . . . . .8.129
Securicor Ltd v Smith [1989] IRLR 356 . . . . .14.110, 14.151
Securicor Omega Express Ltd v GMB [2004] IRLR 9 . . . . .17.28
Sefton BC v Wainwright [2015] ICR 65 . . . . .10.70
Sehmi v Gate Gourmet London Ltd [2009] IRLR 807 . . . . 14.256, 14.257
Seide v Gillette Industries Ltd [1980] IRLR 427. . . . . 8.17, 8.85
Seldon No 2 [2014] IRLR 748. . . . . .8.105
Seldon v Clarkson Wright & Jakes [2012] ICR 716 . . . . .8.105

Selfridges Ltd v Malik [1998] ICR 268 . . . . .14.301
Seligman & Latz v McHugh [1979] IRLR 130 . . . . .14.34
Sengupta v Republic of India [1983] ICR 221 . . . . .12.42
Senior Heat Treatment Ltd v Bell [1997] IRLR 614 . . . . 18.86, 18.93
Shamoon v Chief Constable of the RUC [2003] ICR 337 . . . . .8.71, 8.80, 8.153
Sharifi v Strathclyde Regional Council [1992] IRLR 259 . . . . .8.200
Sharma v Manchester CC [2008] IRLR 336 . . . . .9.11
Sharp v Caledonia Group Services Ltd [2006] IRLR 4 . . . . .7.65
Sharpe v Worcester Diocesan Board of Finance Ltd [2015] ICR 1241 . . . . .2.34, 2.68
Shawkat v Nottingham City Hospital NHS Trust [1999] IRLR 340
    [2001] IRLR 555 . . . . .16.26
Shawkat v Nottingham City Hospital NHS Trust (No 2) [2001] ICR 7 . . . . .16.21
Shedden v Youth Hostel Association (Scotland) (1966) 1 ITR 32 . . . . .14.15
Sheffield v Oxford Controls Co [1979] IRLR 133 . . . . .14.69
Sheikh v Chief Constable of Greater Manchester Police [1989] 2 All ER 684 . . . . . . 2.44, 8.170
Shepherds Investments Ltd v Walters [2007] IRLR 110 . . . . .6.03
Sherard v AUEW [1973] IRLR 188 . . . . .21.92
Sheriff v Klyne Tugs (Lowestoft) Ltd [1999] IRLR 481 . . . . .8.211
Shields Furniture Ltd v Goff [1973] ICR 187 . . . . 3.58, 16.39
Shields v E. Coomes (Holdings) Ltd [1978] IRLR 263 . . . . .7.26
Shindler v Northern Raincoat Co Ltd [1960] 1 WLR 1038 . . . . .4.28
Shipping Company Uniform Inc. v ITWF [1985] ICR 245 . . . . .21.114
Shirlaw v Southern Foundries (1926) Ltd [1939] 2 KB 206 . . . . .3.22
Shook v London Borough of Ealing [1986] IRLR 46 . . . . 13.19, 14.51, 14.133
Short v J. & W. Henderson Ltd (1946) 62 TLR 427 . . . . .2.18
Short v Poole Corporation [1926] Ch 66 . . . . .13.27
Shove v Downs Surgical plc [1984] IRLR 17 . . . . 13.53, 13.56, 13.74
Showboat Entertainment Centre Ltd v Owens [1984] IRLR 7 . . . . .8.116
Sidabras v Lithuania [2004] ECHR 395 . . . . .23.36
Sidhu v Aerospace Composite Technology Ltd [2001] ICR 167 . . . . 8.77, 8.168
Siggs & Chapman (Contractors) Ltd v Knight [1984] IRLR 83 . . . . .14.182
Sillars v Charrington Fuels Ltd [1989] IRLR 152 . . . . .11.21
Silver v Jel Group of Companies (1966) 1 ITR 238 . . . . .16.48
Silvey v Pendragon plc [2001] IRLR 686 . . . . .13.56
Sim v Rotherham Metropolitan Borough Council [1986] ICR 897 . . . . .3.26, 4.20, 21.14
Simbian Ltd v Christensen [2001] IRLR 77 . . . . .6.19
Simmonds v Dowty Seals Ltd [1978] IRLR 211 . . . . .14.141
Simmons v Hoover Ltd [1977] QB 284; 1977] ICR 61 . . . . 3.27, 4.35, 13.33, 16.53, 21.10
Simon v Brimham Associates [1987] IRLR 307 . . . . 8.17, 8.85
Simpson v Endsleigh Insurance Services Ltd [2011] ICR 75 . . . . .10.18
Simpson v Reid & Findlater [1983] IRLR 40 . . . . .14.198
Simrad Ltd v Scott [1997] IRLR 147 . . . . .14.322
Sinclair v Neighbour [1967] 2 QB 279 . . . . 6.03, 13.33
Singh v British Steel Corporation [1974] IRLR 131 . . . . .3.10
Singh v London Country Bus Services Ltd [1976] IRLR 176 .14.135
Skillen v Eastwoods Froy Ltd (1967) 2 ITR 112 . . . . .16.60
Skyrail Oceanic Ltd v Coleman [1980] ICR 596; [1981] IRLR 398 . . . . 8.199, 14.238
Slack v Greenham (Plant Hire) Ltd [1983] IRLR 271 . . . . .12.50
Slater and Secretary for Employment v John Swain Ltd [1981] IRLR 303 . . . . .14.93
Slaughter v C. Brewer & Sons Ltd [1990] ICR 730;
    [1990] IRLR 426 . . . . 14.322, 14.340, 14.342
Smith v Blandford Gee Cementation Ltd [1970] 3 All ER 154 . . . . .11.54
Smith v Cherry Lewis Ltd [2005] IRLR 86 . . . . .17.51
Smith v Churchills Stairlifts plc [2006] IRLR 41 . . . . .8.135
Smith v City of Glasgow District Council [1987] IRLR 326 . . . . .14.94

Smith v Hayle Town Council [1978] IRLR 413.............................20.33, 20.34
Smith v Morrisroes & Sons Ltd [2005] ICR 59......................................5.63
Smith v Oxfordshire Learning Disability NHS Trust [2009] ICR 1395.................5.39
Smith v Safeway plc [1996] IRLR 4 ....8.82
Smith, Kline & French Laboratories v Coates [1977] IRLR 220 ....14.327, 14.353
Smithies v National Association of Operative Plasterers [1909] 1 KB 310 ....21.26
Smiths Industries Aerospace and Defence Systems v Brookes [1986] IRLR 434.........14.133
Smiths Industries Aerospace and Defence Systems v Rawlings [1996] IRLR 656.....20.31, 20.64
Smyth v Croft Inns Ltd [1996] IRLR 84..8.116
Snoxell v Vauxhall Motors Ltd [1977] IRLR 123......................................7.46
Software 2000 Ltd v Andrews [2007] IRLR 568 ....14.322
Solectron Scotland Ltd v Roper [2004] IRLR 4 ....18.81
Solihull Metropolitan Borough v National Union of Teachers [1985] IRLR 211 ....21.08,
                                                    21.27, 21.31, 21.144, 21.166
Somerset CC v Pike [2009] IRLR 870..8.102
Sood Enterprises Ltd v Healy [2013] ICR 1361.......................................5.66
Sood v GEC Elliott Process Automation Ltd [1979] IRLR 416.........................20.40
Soros v Davison [1994] IRLR 264...14.312
Soteriou v Ultrachem Ltd [2004] IRLR 870 ....23.23
Sothern v Franks Charlesly & Co [1981] IRLR 278 ....14.18
Souter v Balfour Ltd (1966) 1 ITR 383..16.47
South Ayrshire Council v Morton [2001] IRLR 28.....................................7.22
South Manchester Abbeyfield Society Ltd v Hopkins [2011] ICR 254 ....5.32
South Tyne MBC v Anderson [2007] IRLR 715 ....7.23
South Wales Miners' Federation v Glamorgan Coal Co Ltd [1905] AC 239.............21.39
South West Launderettes Ltd v Laidler [1986] ICR 455 ....11.47
Southampton City College v Randall [2006] IRLR 18 ....8.130
Southern Cross Healthcare Co Ltd v Perkins [2011] ICR 285.........................3.72
Southwark LBC v Afolabi [2003] ICR 800 ....8.175
Southwark LBC v Whillier [2001] ICR 1016, CA....................................20.34
Sovereign Distribution v TGWU [1989] IRLR 334...................................17.50
Sovereign House Security Services Ltd v Savage [1989] IRLR 115 ....14.18
Spackman v London Metropolitan University [2007] IRLR 744 ....4.20
Spafax Ltd v Harrison [1980] IRLR 442..6.50
Specht v Land Berlin [2014] ICR 966 ....8.105
Specialarbejderforbundet i Danmark v Dansk Industri [1996] IRLR 648 ....7.100
Speciality Care plc v Pachella [1996] IRLR 248 ....20.10
Speed Seal Products Ltd v Paddington [1985] 1 WLR 1327 ....6.39
Spence v BRB [2001] ICR 232...12.58
Spencer v Gloucestershire CC [1985] IRLR 393.............................16.45, 16.49
Spencer v Marchington [1988] IRLR 392..6.52
Spencer v Paragon Wallpapers Ltd [1977] ICR 301 ....14.123, 14.133
Spijkers v Gebroeders Benedik Abattoir CV [1986] 2 CMLR 296.........18.11, 18.24, 18.33
Spillers-French Holdings Ltd v USDAW [1980] ICR 31 ....17.00, 17.48
Spink v Express Food Group Ltd [1990] IRLR 320 ....14.182
Spinpress Ltd v Turner [1986] ICR 433..4.72
Spring v Guardian Assurance plc [1994] ICR 596.....................................4.76
Springbank Sand & Gravel Ltd v Craig [1973] IRLR 278 ....14.121
Springboard Sunderland Trust v Robson [1992] ICR 554...............................7.69
Squibb UK Staff Association v Certification Officer [1979] ICR 235.................19.14
St Helens MBC v Derbyshire [2007] ICR 841.......................................8.150
St John of God (Care Services) Ltd v Brooks [1992] IRLR 546 ....14.229
Stacey v Babcock Power Ltd [1986] IRLR 3 ....14.99
Stadt Lengerich v Helmig [1995] IRLR 216, ECJ 7.00, 7.61
Staffordshire CC v Donovan [1981] IRLR 108 ....14.68

Staffordshire Sentinel Newspapers Ltd v Potter [2004] IRLR 752 . . . . .2.13
Stanley Cole (Wainfleet) Ltd v Sheridan [2003] ICR 297 . . . . .14.34
Stapp v The Shaftesbury Society [1982] IRLR 326. . . . . .14.93
Star Sea Transport Corp of Monrovia v Slater [1978] IRLR 507 CA 21.101
Stedman v UK (1997) 23 EHRR 168 . . . . .23.41
Steel v Union of Post Office Workers [1977] IRLR 288 . . . . .8.100
Steen v ASP Packaging Ltd [2014] ICR 56. . . . . .14.345
Stein v Associated Dairies Ltd [1982] IRLR 447. . . . . .14.180
Steinicke v Bundesanstalt für Arbeit [2003] IRLR 892. . . . . .7.60
Stenhouse Australia Ltd v Phillips [1974] AC 391. . . . . .6.49
Stephenson & Co (Oxford) Ltd v Austin [1990] ICR 609. .14.52
Stephenson v Delphi Diesel Systems Ltd [2003] ICR 471 . . . . .2.51
Stevedoring and Haulage Services Ltd v Fuller [2001] IRLR 627 . . . . .2.11
Stevens v UK [1986] D&R 245 . . . . .23.47
Stevenson v Golden Wonder Ltd [1977] IRLR 474. . . . . .14.171
Stevenson v URTU [1977] ICR 893; [1977] 2 All ER 941 . . . . .2.36, 13.24, 13.26, 13.49
Stevenson, Jordan and Harrison Ltd v Macdonald and Evans [1952] 1 TLR 101. . . . . 2.00, 2.19
Stewart v AUEW [1973] ICR 128 . . . . .21.84
Stocks v Magna Merchants Ltd [1973] ICR 530. . . . . .13.75
Stockton on Tees BC v Aylott [2010] ICR 127 . . . . .8.79
Stoker v Lancashire County Council [1992] IRLR 75. . . . . .14.189
Stokes and Roberts v Wheeler-Green Ltd [1979] IRLR 211 . . . . 20.09, 20.14
Stone v Charrington & Co [1977] ICR 24 . . . . .20.77
Strange Ltd v Mann [1965] 1 All ER 1069 . . . . .14.65
Strathclyde Regional Council v Neil [1984] IRLR 11 . . . . .6.73
Strathclyde Regional Council v Wallace [1998] ICR 205 . . . . 7.05, 7.54, 7.64
Street v Derbyshire Unemployed Workers Centre [2004] IRLR 687. . . . . .15.12
Stringer v HMRC [2009] IRLR 214 . . . . 5.04, 5.64
Strouthos v London Underground Ltd [2004] IRLR 636 . . . . .14.182
Strudwick v IBL [1988] ICR 796. . . . . .11.47
Sturdy Finance Ltd v Bardsley [1979] IRLR 65. . . . . .14.349
Sulemany v Habib Bank Ltd [1983] ICR 60 . . . . .20.77
Sumison v BBC [2007] IRLR 678. . . . . .5.61
Sunderland CC v Brennan [2012] ICR 1216 . . . . .7.44
Sunderland Polytechnic v Evans [1993] IRLR 196 . . . . .5.12
Sunley Turriff Holdings Ltd v Thomson [1995] IRLR 184. .18.52
Surrey Police v Marshall [2003] IRLR 843 . . . . .8.121
Susie Radin Ltd v GMB [2004] IRLR 400 . . . . 17.51, 18.122
Sutcliffe & Eaton Ltd v Pinney [1977] IRLR 349. . . . . .14.243
Sutcliffe v Hawker Siddeley Aviation Ltd (1974) 9 ITR 58 DC. 16.18
Sutherland v Hatton [2002] IRLR 263 . . . . .4.30
Sutton & Gates (Luton) Ltd v Boxall [1978] IRLR 486 . . . . .14.340
Sutton v Revlon Overseas CorporationLtd [1973] IRLR 173 . . . . .16.27
Süzen v Zehnacker Gebäudereinigung GmbH Krankenhausservice
    [1997] IRLR 255. . . . . 18.15, 18.23, 18.24, 18.33
Swedish Engine Drivers' Union v Sweden (1979–80) 1 EHRR 617. . . . . 23.60, 23.61
Sweeney v J. & S. Henderson (Concessions) Ltd [1999] IRLR 306. . . . . .11.07
Sweetin v Coral Racing [2006] IRLR 252. . . . . 3.26, 18.122
Sweetlove v Redbridge & Waltham Forest AHA [1979] IRLR 195. . . . . .14.353
Swift v Chief Constable of Wiltshire Constabulary [2004] IRLR 541 . . . . .8.41
Swithland Motors plc v Clarke [1994] ICR 231 . . . . .8.177
Sybron Corporation v Rochem Ltd [1983] IRLR 253 . . . . 6.05, 6.06
Sylvester v Standard Upholstery Co Ltd (1967) 2 ITR 507. .1.63
System Floors (UK) Ltd v Daniel [1982] ICR 54. . . . . .3.71
Systems Reliability Holdings plc v Smith [1990] IRLR 377 . . . . 6.48, 6.65

TBA Industrial Products Ltd v Locke [1984] IRLR 48 . . . . .14.327
TBA Industrial Products v Morland [1982] ICR 686 . . . . .14.93
TGWU v Courtenham Products Ltd [1977] IRLR 9. . . . . 17.13
TGWU v Howard [1992] ICR 106; [1992] IRLR 170. . . . . 14.312, 20.75
T. Lucas & Co v Mitchell [1972] 3 All ER 689. . . . . .6.52
TNT Express Ltd v Downes [1994] ICR 1 . . . . .14.342
TSB Bank plc v Harris [2000] IRLR 157 . . . . .4.76
TSC Europe (UK) Limited v Massey [1999] IRLR 22. . . . . .6.69
Tadd v Eastwood [1983] IRLR 320. . . . . 3.17, 3.26
Taff Vale Railway Company v Amalgamated Society of Railway Servants
    [1901] AC 426. . . . . .19.04
Talke Fashions Ltd v Amalgamated Society of Textile Workers and Kindred Trades
    [1977] ICR 833. . . . . .17.47
Tan v Berry Brothers and Rudd Ltd [1974] ICR 586. . . . . .14.123
Tanks & Drums Ltd v TGWU [1992] ICR 1. . . . . .21.150
Tanna v Post Office [1981] ICR 374 . . . . .8.11
Tanner v D.T. Kean Ltd [1978] IRLR 110. . . . . .14.13
Tapere v S London & Maudsley NHS Trust [2009] IRLR 972. . . . . .18.87
Taplin v C. Shippam Ltd [1978] IRLR 450. . . . . .20.78
Tarleton v McGawley (1793) 1 Peake 270. . . . . .21.57
Tarmac Roadstone Holdings Ltd v Peacock (1973) 8 ITR 300. . . . . .16.57
Tarnesby v Kensington, Chelsea and Westminster AHA [1981] IRLR 369. . . . . .14.88
Taylor v Alidair Ltd [1978] IRLR 82. . . . . .14.114
Taylor v Butler Machine Tool Ltd [1976] IRLR 133. . . . . 14.191, 20.09
Taylor v Caldwell (1863) B & S 826 . . . . .14.88
Taylor v East Midlands Offender Employment [2000] IRLR 760. . . . . .5.63
Taylor v John Webster Buildings Civil Engineering [1999] ICR 561. . . . . .14.322
Taylor v Kent CC (1969) 4 ITR 294 . . . . .16.47
Taylor v Lowe [2000] IRLR 760. . . . . .4.05
Taylor v Parsons Peebles NEI Bruce Peebles [1981] IRLR 119 . . . . .14.151
Taylor v XLN Telecom Ltd [2010] IRLR 499. . . . . .8.201
Taylorplan Services Ltd v Jackson [1996] IRLR 184. . . . . .12.08
Tayside Regional Council v McIntosh [1982] IRLR 272. . . . . .14.135
Teesside Times Ltd v Drury [1980] IRLR 72 . . . . .11.38
Tejani v Superintendent Registrar for the District of Peterborough [1986] IRLR 50 . . . . . . .8.87
Tele Danmark A/S v Handels- og Kontorfunktionærernes Forbund i Danmark
    [2001] IRLR 853. . . . . .8.29
Tele-Trading Ltd v Jenkins [1990] IRLR 430 . . . . .14.339
Temco Service Industries v Imzilyen [2002] IRLR 214. . . . . .18.18
Terry v East Sussex CC [1976] ICR 536 . . . . .14.236
Tesco Group of Companies (Holdings) Ltd v Hill [1977] IRLR 63 . . . . 14.182, 14.189
Tesco Stores Ltd v Pook [2004] IRLR 61 . . . . .6.07
Thaine v LSE [2010] ICR 1422 . . . . .14.336
Thames Water Utilities v Reynolds [1996] IRLR 186. . . . . 4.05, 5.08
Therm-A-Stor Ltd v Atkins [1983] IRLR 78. . . . . .20.18
Thomas & Betts Manufacturing Co Ltd v Harding [1980] IRLR 255 . . . . 14.203, 14.211
Thomas Marshall (Exports) Ltd v Guinlé [1978] Ch 227. . . . . .6.25, 6.33, 13.16
Thomas Scott & Sons (Bakers) Ltd v Allen [1983] IRLR 329. . . . . .20.50
Thomas v Jones [1978] ICR 274 . . . . .16.13
Thomas v National Coal Board [1987] ICR 75. . . . . .7.25
Thomas v National Union of Mineworkers (South Wales Area)
    [1985] IRLR 136. . . . . .1.45, 19.136, 21.50, 21.64,
                                                            22.04, 22.11, 22.19, 22.22,
                                                            22.30, 22.32, 22.33, 22.44
Thomas Wragg & Sons Ltd v Wood [1976] ICR 313 . . . . .16.49
Thompson v Bristol Channel Ship Repairers (1969) 4 ITR 262 . . . . .11.18

Thompson v Eaton Ltd [1976] ICR 336 .... 14.255, 14.260
Thompson v London Central Bus Co Ltd [2016] IRLR 9 .... 8.116
Thompson v SCS Consulting Ltd [2001] IRLR 801, EAT 18.57, 18.115
Thompson v Woodland Designs Ltd [1980] IRLR 423 .... 14.263
Thomson v Alloa Motor Co Ltd [1983] IRLR 403 .... 14.136
Thomson v Deakin [1952] Ch 646 .... 21.23, 21.24, 21.26, 21.28, 21.33, 21.67
Thorndyke v Bell Fruit (North Central) Ltd [1979] IRLR 1 .... 8.101, 8.210
Timeplan Education Group Ltd v National Union of Teachers [1997] IRLR 457 .... 21.27
Times Newspapers Ltd v Bartlett (1976) 11 ITR 106 .... 14.34
Times Newspapers Ltd v Fitt [1981] ICR 637 .... 12.44
Times Newspapers Ltd v O'Regan [1977] IRLR 101 .... 12.22
Timex Corporation v Thomson [1981] IRLR 522 .... 14.292
Timothy James Consulting Ltd v Wilton [2015] IRLR 368 .... 13.74
Tipper v Roofdec Ltd [1989] IRLR 419 .... 11.04, 11.11
Tiptools Ltd v Curtis [1973] IRLR 276 .... 14.189
Titchener v Secretary of State for Trade and Industry [2002] ICR 225 .... 16.77
Tocher v General Motors (Scotland) Ltd [1981] IRLR 55 EAT 12.45, 16.47
Tomlinson v Dick Evans 'U' Drive Ltd [1978] IRLR 77 .... 12.26
Tomlinson v LM & S Railway [1944] 1 All ER 537 .... 13.20
Torquay Hotel Co Ltd v Cousins [1969] 2 Ch 106 .... 21.22, 21.37, 21.47, 21.52,
                                                                    21.72, 21.91
Torr v British Railways Board [1977] IRLR 185 .... 14.156
Tower Hamlets Health Authority v Anthony [1989] IRLR 394 .... 14.180
Tower Hamlets LBC v Wooster [2009] IRLR 980 .... 8.198
Townson v Northgate Group Ltd [1981] IRLR 382 .... 14.312
Tracey v Crosville Wales Ltd [1997] ICR 862 .... 14.343
Tradewinds Airways Ltd v Fletcher [1981] IRLR 272 .... 14.316, 14.321, 14.322, 14.324
Tradition Securities and Futures SA v X [2008] IRLR 934 .... 12.41
Trafford v Sharpe & Fisher (Building Supplies) Ltd [1994] IRLR 325 .... 18.103, 1.109
Tramp Shipping Corporation v Greenwich Marine Inc [1975] ICR 261 .... 14.251
Transco v O'Brien [2002] IRLR 441 .... 14.35, 14.41
Transport and General Workers' Union v Ledbury Preserves (1928) Ltd
    [1986] IRLR 492 .... 17.27, 17.49
Treganowan v Robert Knee [1975] ICR 405 .... 14.238
Trend v Chiltern Hunt Ltd [1977] ICR 612 .... 14.345
Trevelyans (Birmingham) Ltd v Norton [1991] ICR 488 .... 12.14, 12.22
Trico Folbeith Ltd v Devonshire [1989] IRLR 396 .... 14.322
Trotter v Forth Ports Authority [1991] IRLR 419 .... 13.05
Trusler v Lummus Co Ltd [1972] IRLR 35 .... 14.293
Trusthouse Forte Hotels Ltd v Murphy [1977] IRLR 186 .... 14.158
Trusthouse Forte Leisure Ltd v Aquilar [1976] IRLR 251 .... 14.153, 14.158, 14.219
Tsoukka v Potomac Restaurants Ltd (1968) 3 ITR 259 .... 16.60
Tucker v British Leyland Motor Corporation [1978] IRLR 493 .... 4.41
Tullett Prebon plc v BGC Brokers LP [2010] IRLR 648 .... 14.30
Tullett Prebon v El-Hajjali [2008] IRLR 760 .... 5.09, 14.51
Tunnel Holdings Ltd v Woolf [1976] ICR 387 .... 14.15
Turley v Allders Department Stores Ltd [1980] IRLR 4 .... 8.26
Turner v East Midlands Trains Ltd [2013] ICR 525 .... 23.28
Turner v Goldsmith [1891] 1 QB 544 .... 4.56
Turner v Mason (1845) 14 M&W 112 .... 4.42
Turner v Pleasurama Casinos Ltd [1976] IRLR 151 .... 14.121
Turner v Sawdon [1901] 2 KB 653 .... 4.54
Turner v Vestric Ltd [1980] ICR 528 .... 14.238
Turner v Wadham Stringer Commercials (Portsmouth) Ltd [1974] ICR 277 .... 14.94
Turriff Construction Ltd v Bryant (1967) 2 ITR 292 .... 3.69
Turvey v C.W. Cheyney & Sons Ltd [1979] IRLR 105 .... 14.61, 16.39

Tyagi v BBC World Service [2001] IRLR 465 . . . . .8.177
Tynan v Balmer [1967] 1 QB 91 . . . . 22.19, 22.32, 22.41
Tyne and Clyde Warehouses Ltd v Hamerton [1978] ICR 661 . . . . .2.28
Tyne and Wear PTE (t/a Nexus) v Best [2007] ICR 523 . . . . .7.54
Tyrolean Airways v Betriebsrat Bord der Tyrolean Airways [2013] ICR 71 . . . . .8.101

UBAF Bank Ltd v Davis [1978] IRLR 442 . . . . 14.177, 14.346
UBS Wealth Management (UK) Ltd v Vestra Wealth LLP [2008] IRLR 96 . . . . .6.37
UCLH v UNISON [1999] ICR 204. . . . . .23.67
UK Atomic Energy Authority v Claydon [1974] IRLR 6. . . . . 16.16
UK Coal Mining Ltd v National Union of Mineworkers (Northumberland Area)
       [2008] IRLR 4. . . . . .17.25
UNIFI v Union Bank of Nigeria plc [2001] IRLR 713 . . . . .19.60
UNISON v Allen [2007] IRLR 975. . . . . .18.75
UNISON v Somerset CC [2010] ICR 498 . . . . .18.118
UNISON v UK [2002] IRLR 497 . . . . 21.99, 23.67
USA v Silk (1946) 331 US 704. . . . . .2.20
Ulsterbus Ltd v Henderson [1989] IRLR 251 . . . . 14.182
Union Cartage Co Ltd v Blunden [1977] ICR 420 . . . . 12.22
Union of Construction Allied Trades and Technicians v Brain [1980] IRLR 35;
       [1981] IRLR 225. . . . . .14.137, 14.142
Union of Construction Allied Trades and Technicians v H. Rooke and Son (Cambridge) Ltd
       [1978] IRLR 204. . . . . 17.41
Union of Shop, Distributive and Allied Workers v Leancut Bacon Ltd
       [1981] IRLR 295. . . . . 17.43
Union of Shop, Distributive and Allied Workers v Sketchley [1981] IRLR 291 . . . . 17.15
Union Traffic Ltd v TGWU [1989] ICR 98 . . . . 21.51, 21.166, 22.33, 22.40
United Bank Ltd v Akhtar [1989] IRLR 507. . . . . 3.35, 4.75, 14.34, 16.17
United Distillers v Conlin [1992] IRLR 503 . . . . 14.110, 14.151, 14.153
Universe Tankships Inc of Monrovia v ITWF [1983] AC 366. . . . . 21.75, 21.87
University College at Buckingham v Phillips [1982] ICR 318 . . . . .14.167
University College Hospital NHS Trust v UNISON [1999] IRLR 31 . . . . . . .21.82, 21.93, 21.99
University Council of the Vidyodaya University v Silva [1965] 1 WLR 77 . . . . .13.51
University of Aston in Birmingham v Malik [1984] ICR 492 . . . . 11.16
University of Cambridge v Murray [1993] IRLR 460 . . . . .12.08
University of Central England v NALGO [1993] IRLR 81 . . . . .21.125
University of Huddersfield v Wolff [2004] IRLR 534 . . . . .8.182
University of Nottingham v Eyett [1999] IRLR 87 . . . . .3.26
University of Oxford v Humphreys [2000] IRLR 183. . . . . .18.91
University of Stirling v UCU [2015] ICR 567 . . . . .17.07
Unkles v Milanda Bread Co [1973] IRLR 76 . . . . .14.151, 14.171
Ur-Rehman v Ahmad [2013] ICR 2. . . . . .8.205

Vakante v Governing Body of Addey and Stanhope School (No 2) [2005] ICR 231. . . . . . .12.32
Valor Newhome Ltd v Hampson [1982] ICR 407. . . . . .14.196
van der Mussele v Belgium [1984] 6 EHRR 163 . . . . .23.05
van Droogenbroeck v Belgium [1982] 4 EHRR 433 . . . . .23.06
Vaughan v Weighpack [1974] ICR 261 . . . . .14.322
Vaux and Associated Breweries Ltd v Ward (1968) 3 ITR 385 . . . . .16.21
Vauxhall Motors Ltd v Ghafoor [1993] ICR 376 . . . . .14.182
Vauxhall Motors Ltd v TGWU [2006] IRLR 674. . . . . .17.29
Veakins v Kier Islington Ltd [2010] IRLR 132 . . . . .8.108
Vehicle Delivery Service) Ltd v Cox [1999] IRLR 559 . . . . .18.24
Vento v Chief Constable of West Yorkshire Police (No 2) [2003] ICR 318 . . . . .8.203
Vestergaard Frandsen A/S v Bestnet Europe Ltd [2013] ICR 981 . . . . .6.28

Vicary v BT [1999] IRLR 680 . . . . .8.59
Vickers Ltd v Smith [1977] IRLR 11 . . . . .14.110, 14.196
Villalba v Merrill Lynch & Co Inc [2006] IRLR 437 . . . . 7.65, 8.112
Villella v MFI Furniture Centres Ltd [1999] IRLR 468 . . . . .14.87
Vine v National Dock Labour Board [1956] 1 QB 658 . . . . .13.49
Virdi v Commissioner of Police of the Metropolis [2007] IRLR 24 . . . . .8.177
Visa International Service Association v Paul [2004] IRLR 42 .3.31
Vogt v Germany (1996) 21 EHRR 205 . . . . 23.21, 23.48
Voith Turbo Ltd v Stowe [2005] IRLR 228 . . . . .14.318
Vokes Ltd v Bear [1974] ICR 1 . . . . .14.210
Volkov v Ukraine [2013] IRLR 480 . . . . .23.18

W. Devis & Sons Ltd v Atkins [1977] AC 931 . . . . 13.38, 14.00, 14.09,
                14.94, 14.95, 14.164, 14.306, 14.311,
                  14.322, 14.337, 14.345
W. & J. Wass Ltd v Binns [1982] ICR 486 . . . . .14.110
W. Weddel & Co Ltd v Tepper [1980] ICR 286 . . . . .14.110, 14.158
WAC Ltd v Whillock [1990] IRLR 22 . . . . .6.58
W.E. Cox Toner International Ltd v Crook [1981] IRLR 443 .14.47
WHPT Housing Association Ltd v Secretary of State for Social Services [1981] ICR 737 . . .2.23
Wadcock v London Borough of Brent [1990] IRLR 223 . . . . .13.47
Waddington v Leicester Council for Voluntary Service [1977] 2 All ER 633;
 [1977] IRLR 3 . . . . 7.28, 7.50
Wadham Stringer Commercials (London) Ltd v Brown [1983] IRLR 46 . . . . 14.25, 14.31
Wadi v Cornwall & Isles of Scily Family Practitioner Committee [1985] ICR 492 . . . . .8.11
Wadley v Eager Electrical Ltd [1986] IRLR 93 . . . . .14.239
Waine v R. Oliver (Plant Hire) Ltd [1977] IRLR 434 . . . . .4.57
Wakeman v Quick Corporation [1999] IRLR 424 . . . . .8.87
Walker v Josiah Wedgwood & Sons Ltd [1978] IRLR 105 . . . . .14.39
Walker v Northumberland County Council [1995] IRLR 35 . . . . .4.30
Wallace Bogan & Co v Cove [1997] IRLR 453, CA 6.22
Walley v Morgan (1969) 4 ITR 122 . . . . .16.11
Walls Meat Co Ltd v Khan [1979] ICR 52 . . . . 12.15, 12.17
Wallwork v Fielding [1922] KB 66 . . . . .4.57
Walmsley v C. & R. Ferguson Ltd [1989] IRLR 112 . . . . .14.62
Walmsley v UDEC Refrigeration Ltd [1972] IRLR 80 . . . . .4.43
Walter Braund (London) Ltd v Murray [1991] IRLR 100 .14.334
Walton v Independent Living Organisation Ltd [2003] ICR 688 . . . . .5.30
Waltons and Morse v Dorrington [1997] IRLR 48 . . . . .3.26
Wandsworth London Borough Council v D'Silva [1998] IRLR 193, CA 3.39, 4.07
Wang v University of Keele [2011] ICR 1251 . . . . .12.10
Warburton v Taff Vale Railway Co (1902) 18 TLR 420 . . . . .4.54
Ward Lock & Co v Operative Printers' Assistants Society (1906) 22 TLR 327 . . . . 22.22
Wardle v Credit Agricole Corporate & Investment Bank [2011] ICR 1290 . . . . .14.322
Warner Bros Pictures Inc v Nelson [1937] 1 KB 209 . . . . .13.42
Warner Holidays Ltd v Secretary of State for Social Services [1983] ICR 440 . . . . . . .2.26, 2.77
Warner v Armfield Retail & Leisure Ltd [2014] ICR 239 . . . . .8.131
Warnes v Cheriton Oddfellows Social Club [1993] IRLR 58 . . . . .14.37
Warren v Mendy [1989] ICR 525 . . . . 6.72, 13.42
Warrilow v Robert Walker Ltd [1984] IRLR 304 . . . . 14.345, 14.348
Washington Arts Association Ltd v Forster [1983] ICR 346 .11.47
Waters v Commissioner of Police of the Metropolis [1997] ICR 1073 . . . . .8.168
Waters v Metropolitan Police Commissioner [2000] IRLR 720 . . . . .4.29
Watson v Bowaters UK Pulp & Paper Mills Ltd (1967) 2 ITR 278 . . . . .16.47
Watson v Prager [1991] ICR 603 . . . . .6.62

Watts v Rubery Owen Conveyancer Ltd [1977] 2 All ER 1 . . . . .16.68
Weathersfield Ltd v Sargent [1999] IRLR 94. . . . . 8.116, 14.48
Webb (Duncan) Offset (Maidstone) Ltd v Cooper [1995] IRLR 633 . . . . .18.51
Webb v Emo Air Cargo (UK) Ltd [1993] IRLR 2 . . . . 7.03, 8.26, 8.27, 10.71
Webley v Department for Work and Pensions [2005] ICR 577. .9.17
Weinberger v Inglis [1919] AC 606 . . . . .19.42
Welton v Deluxe Retail Ltd [2013] ICR 428 . . . . .11.07
Welton v Deluxe Retail Ltd [2013] ICR 428 . . . . .11.13
Wendelboe v LJ Music ApS [1985] ECR 457. . . . . .18.102
Werhof v Freeway Traffic Systems GmbH & Co KG [2006] IRLR 400 . . . . .18.126
Wershof v Metropolitan Police Commissioner [1978] 3 All ER 540. . . . . .22.10
Wessex Dairies Ltd v Smith [1935] 2 KB 80 . . . . .6.21
West Kent College v Richardson [1999] ICR 511 . . . . .14.99
West London Mental Health NHS Trust v Chhabra [2014] IRLR 227. . . . . .13.29
West Midland Co-operative Society Ltd v Tipton [1986] IRLR 112. . . . . 14.93, 14.97
West Midlands Passenger Transport Executive v Singh [1988] ICR 614. . . . . .8.191
West Thames RHA and London Ambulance Service [1990] IRLR 62 . . . . .4.20
West v Kneels Ltd [1987] ICR 146 . . . . .14.93
Western Excavating (ECC) Ltd v Sharp [1978] QB 761;
    [1978] 1 All ER 713 . . . . .13.11, 14.11, 14.24, 14.27, 14.45, 18.85
Westminster City Council v Cabaj [1996] IRLR 399 . . . . .14.189
Westminster City Council v UNISON [2001] ICR 1046; [2001] IRLR 524. . . . . . 21.82, 21.135
Westward Circuits Ltd v Read [1973] ICR 301 NIRC 12.07
Westwood v Secretary of State for Employment [1984] IRLR 20. . . . . 13.70, 16.76
Wheeler v Patel and J. Golding Group of Companies [1987] IRLR 211 . . . . 18.58, 18.102
Whent v T. Cartledge Ltd [1997] IRLR 153 . . . . .19.50
Whitbread & Co plc v Mills [1988] IRLR 501 . . . . 14.98, 14.186
Whitbread & Co plc v Thomas [1988] ICR 135 . . . . .14.162
Whitbread plc v Hall [2001] ICR 699; [2001] IRLR 275 . . . . .14.110, 14.182
White v London Transport Executive [1981] IRLR 261 . . . . .14.31
White v Pressed Steel Fisher Ltd [1980] IRLR 176 . . . . .20.55
White v Reflecting Roadstuds Ltd [1991] ICR 733 . . . . .14.34
White v South London Transport Ltd [1998] ICR 293 . . . . .14.98
Whitehouse v Blatchford & Sons Ltd [1999] IRLR 492 . . . . .18.114
Whitley District Men's Club v Mackay [2001] IRLR 595. . . . . .5.63
Whittlestone v BJP Home Support Ltd [2014] ICR 275 . . . . .5.31
Wibberley v Staveley Iron & Chemical Co Ltd (1966) 1 ITR 55. . . . . .16.60
Wickens v Champion Employment [1984] ICR 365 . . . . .2.49
Wickramasinghe v UK (1998) 22 EHRR 318 . . . . .23.19
Widdicombe v Longcombe [1998] ICR 710 . . . . 14.18, 14.93
Wignall v British Gas Corporation [1984] IRLR 493 . . . . .20.49
Wijesundera v Heathrow 3PL Logistics Ltd [2014] ICR 523 .8.215
Wilcox v Humphreys & Glasgow [1975] ICR 333 . . . . .14.179
Wilding v BT [2002] IRLR 524. . . . . .14.350
Wileman v Minilec Engineering Ltd [1988] IRLR 144 .8.200, 8.213
Wilkins v Cantrell & Cochrane (GB) Ltd [1978] IRLR 483 .14.261
Wilkinson v Lugg [1990] ICR 599 . . . . .12.30
William Hill Organisation Limited v Tucker [1998] IRLR 313 . . . . .6.15
William Robinson & Co Ltd v Heuer [1898] 2 Ch 451. . . . . .13.16
Williams v Compair Maxam Ltd [1982] IRLR 83 . . . . .14.110, 14.197, 14.199,
                                                                                                   14.201, 14.206
Williams v J Walter Thompson Group Ltd [2005] IRLR 376. . . . . .8.137
Williams v National Theatre Board Ltd [1982] ICR 715 . . . . .14.269
Williams v Watsons Luxury Coaches Ltd [1990] IRLR 164. . . . . .14.81 14.83
Williams v Western Mail and Echo Ltd [1980] ICR 366. . . . . .14.264

Willment Brothers Ltd v Oliver [1979] IRLR 393..............................14.327
Willoughby v CF Capital plc [2012] ICR 1038 ....14.13
Willow Oak Developments Ltd v Silverwood [2006] IRLR 28....................14.234
Wilson & Clyde Coal Co v English [1938] AC 57............................4.29
Wilson & Others v UK [2002] IRLR 568 ....23.62
Wilson & Palmer v UK [2002] IRLR 568 .... 20.02, 20.13
Wilson v Health and Safety Executive [2010] ICR 302........................7.41
Wilson v National Coal Board (1980) 130 NLJ 114...........................13.75
Wilson v Post Office [2000] IRLR 834 .... 14.94, 14.165
Wilson v Racher [1974] ICR 428...13.36
Wilson v St Helens Borough Council [1996] IRLR 320 ....18.77, 18.79, 18.100, 18.109
Wilson v UK (2002) 35 EHRR 20...19.00
Wilson-Undy v Instrument Co Ltd [1976] ICR 508 ....16.48
Wiltshire Police Authority v Wynn [1980] ICR 649 ....2.44
Wiluszynski v London Borough of Tower Hamlets [1989] IRLR 259............. 4.04, 4.20
Windle v Secretary of State for Justice [2015] ICR 156...........................2.72
Winnett v Seamarks Bros [1978] ICR 1240; [1978] IRLR 387 .... 11.27, 14.267, 20.19
Winterhalter Gastronom Ltd v Webb [1973] IRLR 120 ....14.120, 14.312, 14.322
Wishart v NACAB [1990] ICR 794.....................................13.46
Wishart v National Coal Board [1974] ICR 460..............................11.24
Withers v Flackwell Heath Football Supporters Club [1981] IRLR 307..............2.23
Wood Group Heavy Industrial Turbines v Crossan [1998] IRLR 680 ....14.295
Wood v Coverage Care Ltd [1996] IRLR 264...............................14.246
Wood v Leeds AHA [1974] ICR 535..2.40
Wood v York City Council [1978] IRLR 228 ....11.03
Woodcock v Cumbria Primary Care Trust [2012] ICR 1126 ....8.105
Woodhouse v Peter Brotherhood Ltd [1972] 2 QB 520..........................11.34
Woods v WM Car Services (Peterborough) Ltd [1982] IRLR 413......... 14.25, 14.31, 14.42
Worringham v Lloyds Bank Ltd [1979] IRLR 440, [1981] IRLR 178 ECJ...............7.97
Worsley v Cooper [1939] 1 All ER 290.....................................6.26
Wray v JW Lees & Co (Brewers) Ltd [2012] ICR 43............................5.30
Wren v Eastbourne DC [1993] IRLR 425 .... 18.22, 18.33
Wren v Wiltshire CC (1969) 4 ITR 251....................................16.31
Wright v Dunlop Rubber Co Ltd (1971) 11 KIR 311 ....4.29
Wright v Governing Body of Bilton High School [2002] ICR 1463 ....8.129
Wright v North Ayrshire Council [2014] ICR 77 ....14.48
Writers' Guild of Great Britain v BBC [1974] ICR 234...........................2.71
Wyatt v Kreglinger and Ferneau [1933] 1 KB 793......................... 6.63, 6.74
Wynnwith Engineering Co Ltd v Bennett and Others [2002] IRLR 170 .... 18.25, 18.26

X v Mid Sussex CAB [2013] ICR 249......................................2.15
X v Sweden (1959) 2 YB 354..23.09
X v UK (1984) 6 EHRR 583 ....23.38
X v Y [2004] IRLR 625..23.26

YKK Europe Ltd v Heneghan [2010] ICR 611 ....12.36
Yate Foundry Ltd v Walters [1984] ICR 44..................................14.348
Yeboah v Crofton [2002] IRLR 634 .... 8.166, 14.110
Yemm v British Steel plc [1994] IRLR 117 ....5.12
Yetton v Eastwoods Froy [1967] 1 WLR 104 ....13.71
York City & District Travel Ltd v Smith [1990] IRLR 213.........................5.07
Yorkshire Engineering & Welding Ltd v Burnham [1974] ICR 77 ....13.75
Young and Woods Ltd v West [1980] IRLR 20..............................2.31
Young v Canadian Northern Railway Co [1931] AC 83..........................3.16
Young v Carr Fasteners Ltd [1979] IRLR 420.................................20.44

Young v National Power plc [2001] ICR 328 ....7.88
Young, James, and Webster v UK [1981] IRLR 408 ....23.54, 23.58
Youngs of Gosport v Kendall [1977] ICR 907 ....14.322
Yusuf v Aberplace Ltd [1984] ICR 850 ....14.238

Zafar v Glasgow City Council [1998] IRLR 3 ....8.81
Zarb and Samuels v British & Brazilian Produce Co (Sales) Ltd
    [1978] IRLR 78.. 11.46, 11.47
Zarczynska v Levy [1979] 1 All ER 814 ....8.116
Zucker v Astrid Jewels Ltd [1978] IRLR 385 ....20.08

TABLE OF STATUTES

(European Convention on Human Rights is tabled under Sch 1 of Human Rights Act 1998)

Access to Medical Reports Act 1988
  s 1. . . . . 4.79
Airforce Act 1955 . . . . .21.155
Aliens Restriction (Amendment) Act 1919
  s 3(2) 21.155
Apportionment Act 1870
  s 2. .4.05, 5.08
Army Act 1955 . . . . .21.155

Baking Industry (Hours of Work)
  Act 1954 . . . . 20.48

Children Act 1989. . . . . 10.48
Children (Scotland) Act 1995 1048
Children and Families Act 2014 . . . . 1.29,
                        10.05, 10.50
Children and Young Persons Act 1933. . . .5.51
  s 18(1). 3.45
Children and Young Persons Act 1963
  s 37. . . . . 3.45
Civil Contingencies Act 2004
  s 23(3)(b) 21.156
Civil Liability (Contribution)
  Act 1978 . . . . 4.34
Civil Rights Act 1964 . . . . .8.96, 8.189
Companies Act 1985
  s 492(3) 16.70
Companies Act 2006. . . . . 11.48
  Pt 10. . . . . 2.60
  s 188. .2.61, 2.62
  s 188(4) 2.63
  s 189. .2.61, 2.62
  s 227. . . . . 2.60
Conspiracy and Protection of Property
  Act 1875 . . . . 21.77, 22.21, 22.37
  s 3. .21.62, 21.69
Contracts of Employment
  Act 1963 . . . . .103, 3.62, 13.04
Copyright, Designs and Patents Act 1988
  s 11. . . . . 6.47
  s 215. . . . . 6.47
Criminal Justice Act 1991. . . . .
  s 17(2). 21.155
Criminal Justice and Immigration Act 2008
  s 138. . . . . 21.30, 21.155
  s 139. . . . . 21.30, 21.155

Criminal Justice and Public Order
  Act 1994 .21.155
  s 127. . . . . 21.30
Criminal Law Act 1977
  s 1(3) 21.69

Data Protection Act 1998 . . . . 1.24
Deregulation Act 2015
  s 2. . . . . 8.194
Disability Discrimination Act 1995
  (DDA 1995). 8.130
Dockyard Services Act 1986
  s 1. . . . . .18.117

Employment Act 1980. . . . . 1.12, 1.13,
                        14.06, 21.74
  s 4. . . . . 19.22
  s 14. . . . . 20.01
  s 17(2). 21.04
Employment Act 1982. . . . . 14.06
  s 10. . . . . 20.01
  s 18(2) 21.79
  s 19(1) 21.56
Employment Act 1988. . . . . . .1.18, 4.52, 4.80,
                        14.06, 21.85
Employment Act 1989. . . . . 1.19
Employment Act 1990. . . . . .1.20, 20.23
  s 4. . . . . .21.105
Employment Act 2002. . . . . 10.04
  s 31(2) 14.356
  s 34 . . . . 14.107
  s 38. . . . . 3.76
  Sch 2 . . . . .14.181, 14.185, 14.356
Employment Act 2008. . . . . 14.356
Employment Protection Act 1975
  (EPA 1975) 10.01, 14.06, 19.138
  Pt IV. 17.01
  s 99. . . . . .17.24
  ss 99–107. .17.01
  Sch II 1.12
Employment Protection (Consolidation)
  Act 1978 (EPCA) 19.55
  s 11. . . . . 3.75
  s 84 . . . . 16.33
  s 140. . . . . .14.74
  Sch 13 . . . . .11.38, 14.251

Employment Relations Act 1999 . . . . 1.24,
19.02, 20.06, 21.117
s 10. . . . . 4.81, 14.183
s 10(2B)(a) 4.82
s 10(2B)(b) 4.82
s 10(3) 4.81, 4.82
s 10(6) 4.82
s 13(4) 4.83
s 13(5) 4.83
s 12. . . . . 4.82
s 23 . . . . 2.73
s 32. . . . . 12.34
s 34 . . . . 14.304, 16.65, 20.25, 20.74
s 34(4) 14.310
s 37(1). 14.310
s 94(1) 12.36
Employment Relations Act 2004
s 36. . . . . 4.82
Employment Rights Act 1996 (ERA 1996)
Pt 1 (ss 1–12) 3.62
s 1(3) 3.63
s 1(4) 3.63
ss 1–12. . . . . 3.62
s 2(1) 3.66
s 2(2) 3.66
s 2(3) 3.63
s 2(4) 3.66
s 2(5) 3.64
s 2(6) 3.64
s 3. . . . . 3.63, 4.52
s 4(3)–(5) 3.67
s 4(7) 3.67
s 6. . . . . 3.65
s 7. . . . . 3.66
s 8. . . . . 5.15
s 9(2) 5.16
s 12. . . . . 5.18
Pt II (ss 13–27). 2.69, 5.01, 5.13
s 13. . . . . 4.22, 5.01, 5.12
s 13(5) 4.22
s 14(5) 21.12
s 14(6) 5.12
s 18(1). 5.11
s 18(2)–(4) 10.20
s 18(6) 10.20
s 23 . . . . 5.11, 5.74
s 24(2) 5.14
s 27. . . . . 5.04
s 27A 2.81
s 28. . . . . 5.19
s 28(1) 4.62
s 28(3) 4.62
ss 28–35. . . . . 4.61
s 29(2) 4.63
s 29(3) 4.63

s 29(5) 4.63
s 30(1)–(3) 4.65
s 31. . . . . 4.64
s 34 . . . . 4.66
Pt IV (ss 36–43ZB) 5.76
s 36(2) 5.77
s 36(3) 5.77
s 36(5) 5.78
s 41. . . . . 5.78
s 42(4) 5.80
s 43. . . . . .5.80, 15.06
Pt IVA (ss 43A–43L) 15.01
s 43B(1) 15.11
s 43C 15.08
s 43D 15.08
s 43F. 15.08
s 43H 15.14
s 43J 15.06
s 43K 15.06
s 43K(1)(a) 15.20
s 43M 14.284
s 44 . . . . 20.57
s 44(2) 20.59
s 44(3) 20.59
s 45(1). 5.79
s 45(5) 5.79
s 46(1) 20.67
s 47(1). 18.124
s 47(1A) 18.124
s 47B 12.06, 15.17, 15.22
s 47C 10.77
s 47D 10.84
s 48(2) 20.61
s 48(3) 15.24
s 48(3)(a) 20.61
s 48(4)(b) 20.61
s 49(2)–(5) 20.62
s 50. . . . . 4.39
s 52. . . . . 4.38
s 55. . . . . 10.39
s 57A 10.55
s 57A(1) 10.56
s 57A(3) 10.59
s 57A(4) 10.60
s 57B 10.55
s 57ZA. 10.39
ss 58–60
s 61. . . . . 18.125
s 61(1). 18.124
s 64(1) 4.14
s 64(5) 4.14
ss 64–68. . . . . 4.13
s 65(1) 12.06
s 65(3) 4.15
s 65(4)(a) 4.15

s 65(4)(b) 4.15
s 66. . . . . 10.42
s 66(1) 10.40
s 66(2) 10.67
ss 66–68. . . . . .10.40, 10.42
s 67. . . . . 10.43
s 67(1) 10.41, 10.42
s 68. . . . . 10.42, 10.44, 10.45
s 68A 10.45
s 68B 10.45
s 70. . . . . 4.16
s 70(2) 10.44
s 70(3) 10.44
s 70(4)–(7) 10.42
s 71(4) 10.16
s 71(4)(c). 10.18
s 71(5) 10.16
s 71(7) 10.19
s 76. . . . . 10.72
s 77(3) 10.41
s 80A 10.35
s 80F 10.78
s 80F(4) 10.79
s 80G 10.79
s 80H(1). 10.83
s 80I 10.83
s 86. . . . . 13.04, 14.281, 16.61, 16.76
s 86(2) 13.04
s 86(3) 13.04, 13.05
s 87. . . . . 13.04
s 88(1) 13.06
ss 88–91. . . . . 13.06
s 89(2) 13.07
s 91(1). 13.07
s 91(2) 13.07
s 91(4) 13.07
s 92(4) 10.75
s 92(6) 14.93
s 93(1) 10.76
Pt X (ss 94–134A) 14.06
s 94 . . . . 14.07, 14.79
s 95. 14.67, 14.79
s 95(1). 14.11, 18.92
s 95(1)(a). 14.13–14.21
s 95(1)(b) 14.22
s 95(1)(c). 14.23
s 95(2) 14.56
s 97(2) 14.93
s 98. . . . . 14.103, 14.145
s 98(1)(b) 14.223, 14.224
s 98(2)(c) 14.224
s 98(3)(a) 14.112
s 98(3)(b) 14.112
s 98(4) 14.106, 14.110, 14.191,
                        14.194, 14.196, 15.19

s 98A 14.107
s 98A(1) 14.107
s 98B 14.285
s 100. . . . . 20.63
s 100(3) 20.63
s 101. . . . . 5.79, 5.80
s 102. . . . . 20.67
s 102(2) 16.64
s 103(2) 18.124
s 103A 15.16, 15.19
s 104. . . . . 5.80, 14.278, 14.282
s 104(1) 14.278
s 104(2) 14.282
s 104(3) 14.279
s 104(4)(b) 14.281
s 104C 10.84
s 105. . . . . 14.191, 20.63
s 105(4) 5.79
s 106. . . . . 14.220
s 107. . . . . 14.286
s 108. . . . . .12.06, 20.64
s 110(3) 12.48
s 111. . . . . 14.282
s 111(2). 12.11
s 111(3). 12.08
s 114(2). 14.288
s 115(1). 14.298
s 116(5). 14.297
s 117(4). 14.300
s 118. . . . . 14.302
s 119. . . . . 14.302
s 119(2) 14.303
s 119(3) 14.304
s 120 . . . . 14.305
s 121. . . . . 14.305
s 122(1) 14.306
s 122(2) 14.306, 14.337
s 122(4) 14.309
s 123(1) 14.310
s 123(5) 14.286
s 123(6) 14.337
s 123(7) 14.334
s 124(1ZA). 14.310
s 126 . . . . 14.334
s 128 .19.98, 20.76
s 128(1) 20.65
s 129 . . . . 19.98
Pt XIV, ch I (s 135) 11.02
s 135. . . . . .14.223, 18.106
s 136(1) 14.11
s 136(3) 14.55
s 136(5) 14.63
s 138. . . . . .16.33, 16.34
s 138(1) 16.33
s 138(3) 14.59

s 138(4) 16.37
s 138(4)–(6) 16.35
s 138(6) 14.59
s 139....... 14.191, 14.223, 14.224, 16.52
s 139(1)..................... 16.09, 16.32
s 139(2) 16.32
s 140(1) 16.51, 16.54
s 140(2) 16.54
s 141(2)......................... 16.41
s 141(3)(b) 16.41
s 142............................ 16.55
s 143(2) 16.54
s 143(2)(c)...................... 16.54
s 147............................ 4.71
s 147(1)......................... 14.62
s 147(2)......................... 14.62
ss 147–152 .... 14.62
s 148............................ 4.72
s 152(1) 4.72
s 152(1)(a) 14.62
s 153(4) 11.42
s 159............................ 12.42
s 160(1) 12.42
s 161(1)......................... 12.43
s 163(5) 16.56
s 164............................ 16.68
s 164(2) 16.68
s 165............................ 16.67
s 165(3)......................... 16.67
s 165(4)......................... 16.67
s 166(5) 16.81
s 167............................ 16.81
s 170............................ 16.81
s 182............................ 16.76
s 184(1)(a)...................... 16.76
s 184(1)(b) 16.76
s 184(1)(d) 16.76
s 184(1)(e)...................... 16.76
s 186(1)..................... 16.76, 16.77
s 189............................ 16.82
s 191............................ 12.42
s 192............................ 20.07
s 199(1) 12.43
s 199(2) 12.43
s 200 .... 20.07
s 203............... 12.44–12.47, 12.50,
            12.52, 14.67, 14.74, 14.78
s 203(1)(b) 12.50
s 203(2) 12.56
s 203(3) 12.51
s 205A 2.80
s 209(1) 12.58
s 210(5) 11.05
ss 210–219...................... 14.251
s 211(1)(a)...................... 11.06

s 212(3) 11.09
s 214(2) 16.66
s 215(1)......................... 11.03
s 215(2) 11.03, 11.29, 16.66
s 217(1)......................... 11.29
s 218(2) 11.30, 11.32
s 218(3)......................... 11.30
s 218(4)......................... 11.30
s 218(6) 11.30
s 218(7) 11.45
s 218(8) 11.44
s 219............................ 21.16
s 221(1)......................... 16.63
s 221(2) 16.63
s 221(3) 16.60, 16.63
ss 221–227...................... 4.16
ss 221–229...................... 16.56
s 224(2) 16.63
s 226 .... 16.61
s 228 .... 21.17
s 230(1) 2.02
s 230(2) 2.43
s 230(3) 2.69
s 231............................ 11.41
s 234 .... 16.57
s 235(1) 16.60
s 235(4) 14.258
s 235(5) 14.251
Sch 13, para 9 .... 11.10
Enterprise and Regulatory Reform
     Act 2013 .... 1.29, 12.44
Equal Pay Act 1970 .... 1.10, 7.01, 7.05,
                              8.02, 18.75
s 1.............................. 7.80
s 1(3) 7.39, 7.40, 7.43, 7.50, 7.51
s 1(5) 7.73
s 1(6) 7.16, 7.24
s 2(4) 7.90
s 2(5) 7.85, 7.90
Equality Act 2006
s 11............................. 8.216
s 13............................. 8.216
s 16............................. 8.216
s 20 .... 8.216
s 21............................. 8.216
s 21(5) 8.216
s 22 .... 8.217
s 23 .... 8.216, 8.217
s 30(1) 8.219
Equality Act 2010 .... 2.66, 7.01
s 5.............................. 8.14
s 6(1) 8.31
s 7.............................. 8.15
s 9.............................. 8.17
s 9(4) 8.17

s 10(1) 8.62
s 10(2) 8.62
s 13(1) 8.70
s 13(2) 8.70
s 13(3) 8.70
s 13(5) 8.70
s 13(6) 8.70
s 14. . . . . 8.06
s 15(1). 8.118
s 15(1)(a). 8.86
s 15(2) 8.118
s 16. . . . . 8.16
s 19(1) 8.96
s 19(2) 8.96
s 19(2)(b) 8.99
s 20(2) 8.123
s 20(7) 8.124
s 20(9) 8.125
s 26 . . . . 8.106
s 26(2) 8.106
s 26(4) 8.106
s 27(1). 8.111
s 27(2) 8.111
s 27(2)(a)–(d) 8.112
s 27(3) 8.111
s 39. . . . . 7.07, 8.139
s 39(1) 8.139
s 39(2) 8.139
s 41. . . . . 2.49
s 41(1). 8.145
s 47. . . . . 8.170
s 55. . . . . 8.170
s 60. . . . . 8.119
s 60(3) 8.119
s 65. . . . . 7.08
s 65(1) 7.11
s 65(2) 7.12
s 65(3) 7.12
s 65(4) 7.67
s 65(6) 7.79, 7.80
s 65(8) 7.78
s 66. . . . . 7.07
s 66(2) 7.11
s 66(4) 8.196
s 67. . . . . 7.07
s 69. . . . . 7.07
s 69(1). 7.32
s 69(1)(b) 7.33
s 69(2) 7.32
s 69(3) 7.33
s 69(6) 7.34
s 70. . . . . 7.07
s 70(1) 7.12
s 71. . . . . 7.07
s 72 . . . . 7.09

s 73. . . . . 7.93
s 74(2)–(4) 7.93
s 79(3) 7.13
s 79(9) 7.21
s 80(2) 7.08
s 80(2)(a) 7.09
s 83. . . . . 8.10
s 96(1) 8.170
s 96(2) 8.170
s 108. . . . . 8.162
s 108(4) 8.125
s 109(2) 8.163
s 111(1). 8.164
s 111(8). 8.164
s 112. . . . . 8.164
s 118. . . . . .8.174
s 123 . . . . .8.174
s 124(2)(a) 8.193
s 124(3) 8.194
s 124(6) 8.196
s 128(1) 7.83
s 129(1) 7.83
s 130(3) 7.84
s 130(4) 7.84
s 136. . . . . 8.179
s 140. . . . . .8.174
s 140(3) 8.176
s 142(1). 8.220
s 144(1) 8.220
s 158. . . . . 8.173
s 158(6) 8.173
s 159. . . . . 8.173
s 205. . . . . 8.170
Sch 1 . . . . 8.57
Sch 1, para 2 . . . . 8.36
Sch 1, para 3 . . . . 8.48
Sch 1, para 5 . . . . 8.49, 8.51
Sch 1, para 6 . . . . 8.44
Sch 1, para 8 . . . . 8.52
Sch 8, para 20 . . . . 8.126
Sch 9, para 1(1) 8.156
Sch 9, para 11. 5.25
European Communities Act 1972
   s 2(2) 2.73

Gender Recognition Act 2004. . . . . 8.16
Growth and Infrastructure
   Act 2013 . . . . .1.29, 2.80

Health and Safety at Work, etc
   Act 1974 (HSAWA). 8.137, 19.138
   s 2(7) 19.138
   s 16. . . . . .4.14, 10.40
Highways Act 1980
   s 137. . . . . .22.06

Human Rights Act 1998 . . . . .1.24, 1.25
  s 3. . . . . 23.27
  s 13. . . . . 23.45
  Sch 1 European Convention on Human
    Rights (ECHR)
  Art 3 . . . . 23.01
  Art 4 . . . . .23.01, 23.02
  Art 6 . . . 23.01, 23.03, 23.10, 23.11, 23.23
  Art 6(1) 23.08, 23.20, 23.21
  Art 8 . . . . 23.01, 23.24, 23.27–23.29,
                    23.33–23.36, 23.71
  Art 8(2) 23.31
  Art 9 . . . . .23.01, 23.37, 23.40,
                    23.41, 23.43
  Art 9(1) 23.38
  Art 10. . . . . .21.53, 23.01, 23.34,
                 23.46, 23.48, 23.49
  Art 11. . . . . 19.23, 19.63,
                21.121, 22.01, 23.01,
                23.53, 23.56, 23.61
  Art 11(1). 23.60–23.65
  Art 11(2) 23.57, 23.65, 23.67
  Art 14. . . . . 23.01, 23.70, 23.72

Incitement to Disaffection Act 1934
  s 1. . . . . .21.155
Income and Corporation Taxes Act 1988
  s 467 . . . . .19.10
  Sch D 2.03
  Sch E 2.03
Income Tax (Earnings and Pensions) Act 2003
  s 403 . . . . 13.74
Industrial Relations Act 1971 . . . . 1.12, 4.23,
               12.02, 14.01, 14.10,
               16.07, 19.05, 21.18,
               21.78, 22.37
  ss 6–18 . . . . 1.06
  ss 27–32 . . . . 1.06
  ss 34–36 . . . . 1.06
  s 65. . . . . 1.06
  ss 138–45 . . . . 1.06
Industrial Training Act 1964. . . . . 1.03
Insolvency Act 1986
  s 19. . . . . 16.71
  s 40 . . . . 16.70
  s 44 . . . . 16.72
  s 175. . . . . 16.69
  s 328. . . . . 16.69
  s 421. . . . . 16.75
  Sch 6 . . . . 16.69

Jobseekers Act 1995 . . . . 4.67
  ss 1–25 . . . . 4.67
  s 2(1)(c). 4.67
  s 4(1)(b) 4.67
  ss 9–11 . . . . 4.67

  s 35. . . . . 4.09
  Sch 1, paras 3, 4. . . . . 4.68

Merchant Shipping Act 1894. . . . . 2.65
Merchant Shipping Act 1970. . . . . 2.65
Merchant Shipping Act 1988. . . . . 2.65
Merchant Shipping Act 1995
  s 58. . . . . .21.155

National Minimum Wage Act 1998
  (NMWA). 1.24, 5.19
  s 1(2)(c). 5.23
  s 2. . . . . 5.25
  ss 5–8. . . . . 5.46
  ss 17–26 . . . . 5.44
  s 19A(1) 5.45
  s 19A(6) 5.45
  s 34(2) 5.21
  s 35(1). 5.22
  s 35(2) 5.22
  s 36. . . . . 5.24
  s 37. . . . . 5.24
  s 38. . . . . 5.24
  s 39. . . . . 5.24
  ss 43–45 . . . . 5.20
  s 54(3) 5.22, 5.22
Naval Discipline Act 1953. . . . . .21.155

Official Secrets Act 1989. . . . . 6.23

Patents Act 1977 . . . . 6.41
  s 39. . . . . 6.42
  s 40 .6.44, 6.46
  s 41(1). 6.44
Pension Schemes Act 1993. . . . . 18.134
Pensions Act 1995 . . . . 7.06
  s 62(2) 7.105
  s 63(4) 7.105
Pensions Act 2004. . . . . 18.73
Police Act 1964
  s 51(3). 22.07
Police Act 1996
  s 64 . . . . 20.07
  s 91. . . . . .21.155
Political Parties, Elections and
  Referendums Act 2000
  s 54(2)(d) .19.10
  s 54(2)(h) .19.10
Post Office Act 1953 . . . . .21.168
  s 58. . . . . .21.155
  s 68. . . . . .21.155
Protection from Harassment
  Act 1997 . . . . 22.30
  s 1. . . . . 22.27, 22.28, 22.35
  s 1(3) 22.28
  s 3. . . . . 22.35

s 4. . . . . .22.27, 22.28

s 4(3) 22.28

s 7. . . . . 22.27

Public Health Act 1936

   s 205. . . . . 10.13

Public Interest Disclosure Act 1998. . . . .1.24,

                         12.06, 15.01

Public Order Act 1986

   s 1(1). 22.17

   s 2. . . . . 22.15

   s 3. . . . . 22.16

   s 4. . . . . 22.12

   s 4A 8.110, 22.14

   s 5. . . . . 22.13

   ss 11–16 . . . . 22.06

   s 14. . . . . 22.26

   s 16. . . . . 22.26

   Sch 2 . . . . 22.25

Race Relations Act 1965 . . . . 8.02

Race Relations Act 1968 . . . . 8.21

Race Relations Act 1976 . . . . 1.10, 2.45, 8.02

Redundancy Payments Act 1965. . . 14.10, 16.52

Registered Designs Act 1949

   s 2(1B) 6.47

Regulation of Investigatory Powers Act 2000 .

   s 1(3) 23.30

Rehabilitation of Offenders Act 1974 . . .3.46,

                  14.103, 14.245

Reserve Forces (Safeguard of Employment)

   Act 1985 . . . . 11.29

Restrictive Practices Act 1956 . . . . 21.52

Sex Discrimination Act 1975 (SDA) 1.10,

                 1.19, 7.05, 12.29

   s 3(1) 8.24

   s 77 . . . . 7.94

   s 82(1) 2.32

Sex Discrimination Act 1986. . . . . 7.94

Sex Disqualification (Removal)

   Act 1919 . . . . 8.01

Small Business, Enterprise and Employment

   Act 2015 . . . . .2.81, 5.45

Social Security Act 1985

   Sch 2 . . . . .19.114

Social Security Contributions and Benefits

   Act 1992

   s 164(6) 10.34

   Sch 11, para 2(g) 4.09

Social Security Pensions Act 1975 . . . . .19.114

State Immunity Act 1978

   s 4(1) 12.42

Sunday Trading Act 1994 . . . . 5.76

Telecommunications Act 1984

   s 44 . . . . .21.155

s 45. . . . . .21.155

Telegraph Act 1863

   s 45. . . . . .21.155

Trade Disputes Act 1906 . . . . . . 21.41, 21.56,

                  21.77, 22.37

Trade Disputes and Trade Union

   Act 1927 . . . . 1.02

Trade Disputes and Trade Union

   Act 1946 . . . . 1.02

Trade Union Act 1871 . . . . 19.04, 19.07

Trade Union Act 1876 . . . . 19.04

Trade Union Act 1984 . . . . 1.14, 21.78

   Pt II 21.106

Trade Union Act 2016 . . . . 20.66, 21.111,

            21.122–21.127, 21.141,

                 22.01, 22.46

   s 4. . . . . 21.122

   s 14. . . . . 20.66

Trade Union and Labour Relations Act 1974

   (TULRA 1974) 14.06, 19.55,

            22.19, 22.37, 23.54

   s 1. . . . . 1.08

   s 13(1)(a). 21.41

   s 13(1)(b) 21.61

   s 13(2) 21.56

   s 13(3) 21.74

   s 13(3)(b) 21.73

   s 17(1). 21.164

   s 29(1) 21.85, 21.86

Trade Union and Labour Relations

   (Amendment) Act 1976. . . . . 21.41,

                21.78, 23.54

Trade Union and Labour Relations

   (Consolidation) Act 1992

   (TULR(C)A) 1.21, 12.58,

            14.06, 17.01, 21.75

   Pt I 21.130

   s 2. . . . . 19.07

   s 2(4) 19.10

   s 3(4) 19.08

   s 4. . . . . 19.09

   s 5. . . . . .19.14

   ss 5–9. . . . . 19.13

   s 8(1) 19.17

   s 8(4) 19.17

   s 9. . . . . 19.09

   s 10(1) 19.04, 19.06

   s 11. . . . . 19.06

   s 15. . . . . 21.04

   s 16. . . . . 21.04

   s 19. . . . . 21.72

   s 20 . . . . 19.44

   s 21(3). 19.45

   s 21(5) 19.46

   s 22 . . . . 19.43

   s 23 . . . . 19.48

s 32(ZA)...................... 21.153
s 62....................... 21.145, 21.146
ss 64–67.................. 19.30, 21.05
s 65(2) 19.32
s 65(6) 19.34
s 66........................... 19.36
s 66(2) 19.36
s 67(3) 19.37
s 67(5) 19.37
s 67(6) 19.38
s 67(7) 19.38
s 67(8) 19.39
s 70B 19.116
s 70B(1) 19.117
s 70B(6) 19.119
s 70B(7) 19.117
s 70C 19.120
s 70C(3)–(5).................. 19.120
s 119......................... 20.35
s 137......................... 20.23
s 139......................... 20.25
s 140(1)(b) 20.25
s 140(2) 20.25
s 140(4) 20.25
s 142(1)....................... 20.25
s 145..........................19.101
s 145A 20.02
s 145B 20.03
s 145E(3) 20.03
s 146.............. 20.01, 20.08, 20.29
s 146(2) 20.26
s 147......................... 20.29
s 148......................... 20.29
s 148(1)....................... 20.34
s 149(2) 20.70
s 150(1) 20.70
s 152........ 20.01, 20.08, 20.22, 20.75
s 152(2) 20.26
s 153.....................20.01, 20.31
s 155(2) 20.75
s 161......................... 20.01
s 162(1)....................... 20.78
s 164......................... 20.78
s 165......................... 20.79
s 168.....................20.42, 20.44
s 168(1)....................... 20.35
s 168A 20.51
s 170......................... 20.52
s 170(1)....................... 20.53
s 170(2) 20.26
s 172......................... 20.72
s 172A 20.66
s 174......................... 19.23
s 174(2)....................... 19.24
s 174(4)....................... 19.24

s 174(4A) 19.24
s 174(4H) 19.41
s 176(2)....................... 19.27
s 176(5)....................... 19.26
s 176(6) 19.26, 19.28
s 178.........................19.105
s 178(2) 19.57
s 178(3 ....17.09
s 179.................... 18.126, 19.51
s 180(1) 3.19
s 181.................. 19.13, 19.118
s 181(1)....................... 19.109
s 182.........................19.110
s 182(1)(f).....................19.110
s 182(2)(b) 19.110
s 183.........................19.111
s 183(3) 19.133
ss 183–185 ....19.131
s 184.........................19.111
s 184(2) 19.133
s 186.........................19.102
s 187.........................19.102
s 188.............17.08, 17.22, 17.23
s 188(1A) 17.30
s 188(3) 17.49
s 188(4) 17.38
s 188(6) 17.38
s 188(7) 17.41
s 188(7B) 17.18
s 188A 17.16, 17.22
s 189(1)....................... 17.22
s 189(3) 17.44
s 189(4) 17.44, 17.49
s 189(6) 17.41
s 190(1) 17.44
s 192(2)(a) 17.46
s 195.........................17.07
s 196.........................17.55
s 197(1) 17.31
s 199......................... 19.134
s 203.........................19.135
s 203(1)(a) 19.135
s 203(1)(b) 19.137
s 207(1) 19.136
s 207A 14.107, 14.356
s 209 .... 19.55
s 210(1)....................... 19.124
s 210A 19.71
s 212(1)(a)..................... 19.129
s 212(2) 19.130
s 213......................... 19.128
s 214......................... 19.129
s 215(3) 19.129
s 219........14.273, 21.41, 22.24, 22.34
s 219(1)(b 21.61

s 219(2) 21.68
s 220 . . . . 21.42, 21.43, 22.34, 22.36
s 220(1)(a) 22.40
s 220(1)(b) 22.39
s 220(2) 22.39
s 220(3) 22.39
s 220(4) 22.39
s 220A(2) 22.46
s 221. . . . . 21.164
s 223 . . . . 14.272
s 224 . . . . 21.78, 22.34, 22.38
s 225(1) 21.154
s 226 . . . . 21.109
s 226(2) 21.122
s 226A 21.133, 21.134
s 226A(2)(c) 21.139
ss 226–232. . . . . .21.145
ss 226–234. . . . . 21.106
s 227. . . . . 21.152
s 227(1) 21.114
s 228 . . . . 21.125
s 228A 21.127
s 229(2) 21.128
s 229(2A) 21.128
s 229(3) 21.149
s 229(4) 21.128
s 230(1) 21.130
s 230(2) 21.117
s 230(4) 21.131
s 231. . . . . 21.120
s 231A 21.138
s 232A 21.114
s 232B 21.117, 21.152
s 233(3) 21.132, 21.150
s 234 . . . . .21.111
s 234(1) 21.111
s 234A 21.134, 21.142
s 234A(4)(b) 21.142
s 234A(5A) 21.143
s 235A 21.157
s 235A(1) 21.126
s 235A(3) 21.157
s 236 . . . . 13.41, 21.159
s 237. . . . . 14.271
ss 237–239 . . . . 12.08, 14.247,
14.251, 14.251, 14.252,
14.340, 21.11

s 238 . . . . 14.247
s 238(5) 14.93
s 238A 14.273
s 238A(3) 14.273
s 238A(4) 14.273
s 238A(5) 14.273
s 238A(7D). 14.274
s 238A(8) 14.275
s 238B 14.274
s 240(1) 21.155
s 241. . . . . 22.21, 22.22
s 244 . . . . 20.35, 21.85,
21.95, 21.102
s 244(1) 21.77
s 244(2) 21.94
s 244(3) 21.95
s 244(5) 21.80
s 245. . . . . 2.42
s 247(3) 19.121
s 259(1) 19.131
s 263(6) 19.131
s 288 . . . . 21.125
s 295. . . . . 2.02
s 296(1) 2.69
Sch A1 . . . . 3.06, 14.276, 19.13,
19.58–19.99, 19.117,
19.131, 19.135
Sch A1, para 159 . . . . 14.277
Sch A1, para 161 . . . . 14.277
Sch A1, para 161(1)(2) 14.276
Sch A2 . . . . 14.356
Sch 3, para 7 . . . . .9.132
Trade Union Reform and Employment
Rights Act 1993
(TURERA 1993). 1.22, 7.94,
10.01, 10.07,
14.06, 17.05
s 34(2) 17.41
Truck Act 1896 . . . . 5.01

Unfair Contract Terms Act 1977
s 2(2) 4.29
s 3. . . . . 4.47

Wages Act 1986. . . . . 2.69, 5.12, 14.283

TABLE OF STATUTORY INSTRUMENTS

Agency Workers Regulations. 2.53

Civil Procedure Rules 1998 (SI 1998/3132)
  Pt 25. . . . . 21.160
Collective Redundancies and Transfer
  of Undertakings (Amendment)
  Regulations 2014 (SI 2014/16) 18.99
Collective Redundancies and Transfer of
  Undertakings (Protection of Employment)
  (Amendment) Regulations
  1995 (SI 1995/2587) 17.04,
                                18.02, 18.119
  reg 10(2). 18.119
  reg 14 . . . . 18.120
  reg 15(1). 18.120
  reg 15(2). 18.121
Collective Redundancies and Transfer
  of Undertakings (Protection of
  Employment) (Amendment)
  Regulations 1999 (SI 1999/1925) . . .17.06
Conduct of Employment Agencies
  Regulations 2003 . . . . 2.53

Employment Protection (Continuity
  of Employment) Regulations 1996
  (SI 1996/3147). 11.28
Employment Protection (Recoupment
  of Jobseeker's Allowance and Income
  Support) Regulations 1996
  (SI 1996/2349) 4.66, 14.358
Employment Relations Act 1999 (Blacklists)
  Regulations 2010 (SI 2010/493)
  reg 3. . . . . 20.06
  reg 8(1)(b). 20.06
Employment Tribunals (Extension
  of Jurisdiction) Order 1994
  (SI 1994/1623). 5.05, 13.08
Employment Tribunals (Interest) Order
  1990 (SI 1990/479) 14.361
Employment Tribunals (Constitution and
  Rules of Procedure) Regulations 2013
  (SI 2013/1237)
  Sch 3 . . . . 7.06
Equal Pay (Amendment) Regulations 1983
  (SI 1983/1794). 1.15
Equal Pay Act (Amendment) Regulations
  2003 (SI 2003/1656) 7.86
Equality Act 2010 (Disability) Regulations
  2010 (SI 2010/2128)
  reg 3. . . . . 8.42

reg 4. . . . . 8.42
European Public Limited Liability
  Company Regulations 2004
  (SI 2004/2326) 19.150
Exclusivity Terms in Zero Hours
  Contracts (Redress) Regulations 2015
  (SI 2015/2021). 14.104

Fixed-term Employees (Prevention of Less
  Favourable Treatment) Regulations
  2002 (SI 2002/2034)
  reg 2(1)(a). .9.17
  reg 3(1). 9.17
  reg 3(3). 9.17
  reg 8 . . . . 9.20
Flexible Working Regulations 2014
  (SI 2014/1389)
  reg 4. . . . . 10.79
Flexible Working (Procedural Requirements)
  Regulations 2002 (SI 2002/3207)
  reg 3. . . . . 10.82
  reg 4. . . . . 10.82
  reg 6. . . . . .10.82, 10.83
  reg 7. . . . . 10.83
  reg 12. . . . . 10.82

Health and Safety (Consultation with
  Employees) Regulations 1996
  (SI 1996/1513). 19.140, 20.65

Information and Consultation of
  Employees Regulations 2004
  (SI 2004/3426) 19.148
  reg 20(7) 19.149
  reg 23(2). 19.149

Jobseeker's Allowance Regulations 1996
  (SI 1996/207) 4.67
  regs 31–45 . . . . 4.67
  regs 46–48. 4.68
  reg 56. . . . . 4.67
  reg 79. . . . . 4.67
  reg 80. . . . . 4.67
  reg 81. . . . . 4.67

Legal Executives (Compromise Agreements
  (Description of Person) Order 2004
  (SI 2004/754) 12.51
Local Government (Political Restrictions)
  Regulations 1990 (SI 1990/851) . . . 23.49

Maternity and Parental Leave Regulations
   1999 (SI 1999/3312)
   reg 2(1). 10.10
   reg 4(1)(a). 10.08
   reg 4(1)(b). 10.09
   reg 4(2). 10.09, 10.10
   reg 4(3). 10.11
   reg 4(4). 10.10
   reg 6(3). 10.21
   reg 7(1). 10.12
   reg 7(2). 10.13
   reg 8. . . . . 10.13
   reg 9. . . . . .10.17
   reg 11(1)–(4). 10.15, 10.22
   reg 13. . . . . 10.48
   reg 17. . . . . 10.23, 10.24, 10.49
   reg 20(1). 10.74
   reg 20(2). 10.69
   reg 20(7) 10.74
   reg 21. . . . . 10.54
Maternity and Parental Leave Regulations
   2006 (SI 2006/2014). 10.04

National Health Service Regulations
   1992 . . . . 8.11
National Minimum Wage Regulations 1999
   (SI 1999/584) (NMWR) 5.19
   reg 2. . . . . 5.28
   reg 4A. 5.23
   reg 6. . . . . 5.36
   reg 7. . . . . 5.36
   reg 8. . . . . 5.26
   reg 9. .5.26, 5.37
   reg 10. .5.40–5.42
   reg 10(1). 5.42
   reg 11. . . . . 5.25
   reg 12. . . . . 5.42
   reg 14. . . . . 5.38
   reg 15. . . . . 5.38
   reg 15(2)(b). 5.33
   reg 16. . . . . 5.38
   reg 30. .5.26, 5.27
   regs 31–35 . . . . 5.29
   reg 32(2). 5.29
   reg 34. . . . . 5.33
   reg 34(1). 5.33
   reg 34(2). 5.33
   reg 35. . . . . 5.30
   reg 36. .5.26, 5.28
   reg 37. . . . . 5.34
   regs 39–43 . . . . 5.34
   reg 42. . . . . 5.28
   reg 44. .5.26, 5.28
   reg 45. . . . . 5.35
   reg 57. . . . . 5.25

   reg 59. . . . . 5.44
National Minimum Wage Regulations 2015
   (SI 2015/621 . . . . .5.19, 5.28
   reg 9(1)(b). 5.36
National Minimum Wage (Offshore
   Employment) Order 1999
   (SI 1999/1128). 5.24

Occupational Pension Schemes
   (Disclosure of Information) Regulations
   1996 (SI 1996/1655) 19.115
Occupational Pension Schemes
   (Equal Treatment) Regulations 1995
   (SI 1995/3183). 7.107
   regs 13–15 . . . . .7.107
Occupational and Personal Pension
   Schemes (Disclosure of Information)
   Regulations 2013
   (SI 2013/2734). 19.151

Part-time Workers (Prevention of Less
   Favourable Treatment) Regulations
   2000 (SI 2000/1551). 7.43
   reg 1(2). 9.09
   reg 2(1). 9.04
   reg 2(3). 9.05
   reg 2(3)(a)–(f). 9.06
   reg 2(3)(f). 9.05
   reg 5(1). 9.07
   reg 5(2)(b). 9.14
   reg 5(3). 9.09
   reg 6. . . . . 9.15
   reg 7. . . . . .14.103
   reg 8(2). 9.16
Paternity and Adoption Leave Regulations
   2002 (2002/2788). 10.35
Prices and Charges (Notification of
   Increases and Information)
   Order 1977 (SI 1977/1281). 16.60
Public Interest (Prescribed Persons) Order
   2014 (SI 2014/2418) 15.08

Redundancy Payments (Continuity of
   Employment in Local Government, etc.)
   (Modification) Order 1999
   (SI 1999/2277) 11.44
Redundancy Payments (Local Government)
   (Modification) Order 1983
   (SI 1983/1160). 11.44
Redundancy Payments Office Holders
   Regulations 1965
   (SI 1965/2007) 12.58
Rehabilitation of Offenders Act 1974
   (Exceptions) Order 1975
   (SI 1975/1023). 14.246

Rehabilitation of Offenders Act 1974
(Exceptions) (Amendment) Order
1986 (SI 1986/1249) 14.246

Safety Representatives and
Committees Regulations 1977
(SI 1977/1500). 19.138
reg 4(2). 20.55
Safety Representatives and Committees
(Amendment) Regulations 1992
(SI 1992/2051). 19.138
Sex Discrimination and Equal Pay
(Remedies) Regulations 1993
(SI 1993/2798). 14.361
Sex Discrimination and Equal Pay
(Miscellaneous Amendments)
Regulations 1996 (SI 1996/438 . . . . . . .7.78
Shared Parental Leave General Regulations
2014 (SI 2014/3050) 10.47, 10.50
Social Security (General Benefit)
Amendment Regulations 1984
(SI 1984/1259). 16.76
Statutory Maternity Pay (General)
Regulations 1986 (SI 1986/1960) . . . 10.31
reg 7. . . . . 16.82
reg 11. . . . . 10.33
reg 30. . . . . 16.82
Statutory Maternity Pay (General)
Amendment Regulations 1996
(SI 1996/1335). 10.30
Statutory Sick Pay (General) Regulations 1982
(SI 1982/894)
reg 7(1)(a). 4.12

Trade Union Recognition (Method of
Collective Bargaining) Order 2000
(SI 2000/1300) 19.80
Transfer of Employment (Pension Protection)
Regulations 2005 (SI 2005/649) . . . 18.73
Transfer of Undertakings (Protection of
Employment) Regulations 1981
(SI 1981/1794). 1.15, 3.15, 3.61,
18.01, 18.08
reg 5(3). 18.57
reg 5(4A) 18.86
reg 8(2). 18.78
reg 10. . . . . .18.117
reg 10(2). .18.117
Transfer of Undertakings (Protection
of Employment) Regulations 2006
(SI 2006/246)
(TUPE Regulations 2006) 11.32,
14.38, 17.03, 18.01,
18.02, 19.100

reg 3(1)(b). 18.34, 18.35
reg 3(2). 18.04
reg 3(3)(a)(ii). 18.35
reg 3(6)(a). 18.40
reg 4. . . . . 18.65, 18.83, 18.84
reg 4(1). 18.44, 18.55, 18.59
reg 4(2). 18.60
reg 4(2)(b) 18.63
reg 4(3). 18.57
reg 4(4). 18.82
reg 4(4)(a). 18.21
reg 4(7). 18.85, 18.86, 18.96
reg 4(9). 18.91, 18.94
reg 5. . . . . 18.126, 19.54
reg 5(1). 18.89
reg 5(5). 18.92
reg 6. . . . . 17.14, 18.128, 19.100
reg 7. . . . . 18.130, 18.134
reg 7(2). 14.220, 18.78
reg 8. . . . . 18.60
reg 8(5). 18.83
reg 8(6). 18.84
reg 9. . . . . 18.81
reg 10(6A) 18.125
reg 11. . . . . 18.130, 18.133
reg 11(1). 18.129
reg 13(2). 18.116, 18.117, 18.123
reg 15(9). 18.60, 18.66
Transnational Information and Consultation
of Employees Regulations 1999
(SI 1999/3323). 14.103, 19.141

Working Time Regulations 1998. . . . . . .1.24,
4.41, 5.47, 10.25,
19.13, 23.07
reg 2. . . . . 5.51, 5.70
reg 2(1). 5.68
reg 4. . . . . 5.49, 5.54
reg 4(1). 5.54
reg 4(2). 5.54
reg 4(6). 5.49
reg 7. . . . . 5.68
reg 8. . . . . 5.49
reg 10. . . . . 5.49
reg 11. . . . . 5.49
reg 12. . . . . 5.49
reg 13. . . . . 5.49
reg 13(3). 5.61
reg 15. . . . . 5.61
reg 16(1). 5.63
reg 18(2)(a). 5.55
reg 18(2)(c). 5.55
reg 19. . . . . 5.55
reg 20. . . . . 5.57

reg 20(1).......................... 5.55
reg 20(2)....................5.58, 5.59
reg 21............................ 5.56
reg 24A 5.56
reg 25A........................... 5.55
reg 29............................ 5.72
reg 30......................5.71, 5.74

Working Time (Amendment) Regulations
    1999 (SI 1999/3372) 5.70, 5.73
Working Time (Amendment)
    Regulations 2001
    (SI 2001/3256) 5.47
Working Time (Amendment) Regulations
    2003 .... 5.55

LIST OF ABBREVIATIONS

ACAS   Advisory Conciliation and Arbitration Service
All ER   All England Law Reports

BIS   (Department for) Business, Innovation and Skills

CA   Court of Appeal
CAC   Central Arbitration Committee
CO   Certification Officer
COET   Central Office of Employment Tribunals
CRE   Commission for Racial Equality

DC   Divisional Court of Queen's Bench Division
DDA   Disability Discrimination Act 1995
DRC   Disability Rights Commission
DRCA   Disability Rights Commission Act 1999

EA   Employment Acts 1980–1989
EA 2010   Equality Act 2010
EAT   Employment Appeal Tribunal
ECJ   European Court of Justice
EOC   Equal Opportunities Commission
EPA   Employment Protection Act 1975
EPCA   Employment Protection (Consolidation) Act 1978
ERA   Employment Rights Act 1996
EU   European Union

HC   High Court
HMSO   Her Majesty's Stationery Office

ICR   Industrial Cases Reports
ILJ   Industrial Law Journal
ILO   International Labour Organization
IRLR   Industrial Relations Law Reports
ITR   Industrial Tribunal Reports

LQR   Law Quarterly Review
LSG   Law Society Gazette

MLR   Modern Law Review

NIRC   National Industrial Relations Court
NLJ   New Law Journal

ROET   Regional Office of Employment Tribunals
RRA   Race Relations Act 1976

SDA   Sex Discrimination Act 1975
SJ   Solicitors Journal

TUA   Trade Union Act 1913
TUC   Trades Union Congress
TULRA Trade Union and Labour Relations Act 1974

TULR(A)A	Trade Union and Labour Relations (Amendment) Act 1976
TULR(C)A	Trade Union and Labour Relations (Consolidation) Act 1992
TURERA	Trade Union Reform and Employment Rights Act 1993
WTR	Work Time Regulations 1998

1

HISTORY

A THE BACKGROUND TO
THE MODERN ERA 1.01

B THE 1960s AND
THE DONOVAN REPORT 1.03

C THE INDUSTRIAL RELATIONS ACT 1971 AND
INDUSTRIAL STRIFE 1.06

D THE 'SOCIAL CONTRACT': TRADE UNION
AND LABOUR RELATIONS ACT 1974

AND THE EMPLOYMENT PROTECTION
ACT 1975 . . . . 1.08

E CONSERVATIVE LEGISLATION
1980-95 . . . . 1.11

F A THIRD WAY? LABOUR LEGISLATION
1997-2009 . . . . 1.24

G THE CAMERON GOVERNMENTS 1.29

I do not think that you will find any other country in which, in important sections of the economy, the trade unions had attained a considerable bargaining strength long before their members had obtained the franchise—no country, in other words, in which, through their own early history, the unions got so much used to the reliance on industrial rather than on political pressure, on collective bargaining outside the law rather than on legislation. (Professor O Kahn-Freund, 7 BJIR 3.)

Labour is not a commodity. (ILO Declaration of Philadelphia 1944.)

Employment law and trade union law must be viewed against a long historical perspective in order to understand its modern context.

A THE BACKGROUND TO THE MODERN ERA

The substantive history of employment law stretches back to the Middle Ages and this **1.01** has been considered further in previous editions. Here we only consider the main modern issues without which modern employment law cannot be properly understood.

The modern story began with the failure of the General Strike in 1926 which demor- **1.02** alised the unions, and the Government reacted with the Trade Disputes and Trade Union Act 1927. This Act made illegal strikes which had any object other than the furtherance of a purely trade dispute, especially if it was a sympathy strike by workers in a different industry, or designed to coerce the Government by inflicting harm on the wider community. The closed shop was outlawed in local and public employment, and public employees were restricted in the unions they could join. These measures had little effect, owing to the relative quiescence of the unions in the subsequent twenty years. More important was the accompanying requirement that union members had to actively 'contract in' to pay the union political levy, and this considerably reduced union funds available to the Labour Party. Not surprisingly the newly elected 1945 Labour Government proceeded to reverse this provision in the Trade Disputes and Trade Union Act 1946.

B THE 1960s AND THE DONOVAN REPORT

1.03 It was in the 1960s that for the first time employment protection legislation was passed
on a large scale to improve the lot of individual workers. The Contracts of Employment
Act 1963 decreed the provision by the employer to each employee of a written statement
of contractual terms; the Industrial Training Act 1964 sought better training provisions
and set up industrial tribunals to adjudicate on its levy provisions; and the Redundancy
Payments Act 1965 for the first time provided statutory compensation on dismissal.

1.04 The main focus of union fears was on the collective side with the unexpected decision in
Rookes v Barnard [1964] AC 1129. Here, the House of Lords applied the tort of intimidation well away from its traditional ground of threats of assault to include threats of
breach of contract. The furore surrounding this *cause célèbre* was one of the reasons
for the appointment in 1965 of the Royal Commission on Trade Unions and Employers'
Associations under the chairmanship of Lord Donovan, a law lord. It was established 'to
consider relations between management and employees and the role of trade unions and
employers' associations in promoting the interests of their members and in accelerating
the social and economic advance of the nation ...'.

1.05 The report was published in 1968, and detected a major industrial problem in the 'irrevers-
ible shift' from formal industry-wide collective bargaining to informal and often chaotic
arrangements led by increasingly powerful shop stewards. It favoured machinery based
on consensus and provided the background to the subsequent feverish legislative activity.
But the immediate response of the Labour Government, which received the report, did
not reach the statute book. Its controversial White Paper, *In Place of Strife*, published
in January 1969, split the Labour and trade union movements, especially because of its
'penal clauses' which, in aiming to stamp out unofficial strikes by criminal sanctions,
went beyond the Donovan recommendations.

C THE INDUSTRIAL RELATIONS ACT 1971 AND INDUSTRIAL STRIFE

1.06 The new Conservative Government elected in 1970 had no qualms about reform. Their
Industrial Relations Act 1971 was more radical than the position the Donovan Report
had suggested, and, based in large measure on a Conservative Party pamphlet, *Fair Deal
at Work*, it sought to translate several concepts from Continental and American labour
law. The Act put the law at the centre stage in collective bargaining. The Act thus:

(a) *controlled the closed shop* by outlawing any obligation of trade union membership
as a condition for job applicants (the so-called pre-entry closed shop) and allowed
other forms of 100 per cent unionism only with the approval of the Commission on
Industrial Relations and a ballot of affected workers (ss 6–18);

(b) accorded rights to employees not to be excluded or expelled from a union by *arbitrary or unreasonable discrimination* and not to be subjected to unreasonable disciplinary action. These were supplemented by a provision that members should not be
penalised for refusing to take part in unlawful industrial action and ensuring natural
justice for union members by 'guiding principles' (s 65);

(c) provided that the NIRC could order a *cooling-off period and ballot* for those strikes
which would be gravely injurious to the national economy, create a risk of disorder,
or endanger lives (ss 138–45);

(d) made collective bargains for the first time prima facie *legally enforceable* (ss 34–6)
although there was an exception by the will of both parties, and most bargains

negotiated in the period of the Act contained the phrase 'This is not a legally enforceable agreement' (the TINALEA clause); and

(e) introduced the right not to be *unfairly dismissed* (ss 27–32), which still exists in similar form today, and also accorded the cognate right to trade union members not to be discriminated against.

It also became illegal for any person to call a strike without proper notice unless he was **1.07** an official of a registered trade union. This sought to prevent unofficial disputes, and of most concern to trade union leaders was the provision in s 96 that *unregistered* unions would be liable to have their funds sequestered if sued for such 'unfair industrial practices', which was the new name for torts committed by trade unions.

D THE 'SOCIAL CONTRACT': TRADE UNION AND LABOUR RELATIONS ACT 1974 AND THE EMPLOYMENT PROTECTION ACT 1975

The Labour Government was returned to power in 1974, following a damaging national **1.08** miners' strike; it proceeded to dismantle the edifice of the Industrial Relations Act which had proved unable to control mounting unrest. Thus, s 1 of the quickly enacted Trade Union and Labour Relations Act 1974 wholly repealed the 1971 Act, although the rest of the statute proceeded to re-enact many of its features, albeit with modifications. The unfair dismissal provisions were strengthened, and listing of unions continued, although no longer providing the gateway to any significant union rights. The immunity of trade unions and individuals in trade dispute cases broadly returned to the position in 1906, although there was a new restriction on the use by employers of injunctions, and the efficacy of no-strike agreements was limited.

This legislation was part of the Labour Government's 'social contract' with the unions, its **1.09** *quid pro quo* for union wage restraint. Industrial tribunals were given several new jurisdictions, and a new appeal body was created—the Employment Appeal Tribunal (EAT), which differed from the NIRC in that it had neither a primary jurisdiction nor dealt with collective disputes.

The Equal Pay Act, actually passed in 1970, was brought into force in 1975 along with the **1.10** Sex Discrimination Act (Chapters 7 and 8), which sought to supplement it by prohibiting discrimination against job applicants and employees on the grounds of sex and/or marital status. A new Race Relations Act 1976 widened the scope of the similar enactments of 1965 and 1968, in particular giving the individual employee the right to complain to industrial tribunals. The late 1960s and the 1970s also experienced a major growth in trade unionism, especially in local government and the health service among white-collar and professional employees.

E CONSERVATIVE LEGISLATION 1980–95

The next three years saw mounting criticism by employers and various pressure groups of **1.11** the 1974–76 legislation. It was claimed that they greatly increased wage costs at a time of recession, and discouraged employers from taking on more employees, thus defeating their own ostensible objects. Many also reacted sharply against the actions of the unions in the so-called 'winter of discontent' of 1978–79, when a whole series of strikes (especially in the public sector) paralysed the nation, and were accompanied by widespread secondary picketing—that is, directed against employers not directly involved in the relevant dispute.

1.12 After the election of a new Conservative Government, the Employment Act 1980 thus sought to restrict the powers of the unions and the ambit of individual rights but without mounting the headlong assault on the unions seen in the 1971 legislation. The 1980 Act:

(a) enabled the Secretary of State for Employment to give public funds to unions for the holding of *secret ballots*, and to issue employment codes of practice (19.134);

(b) limited the effectiveness of the *closed shop* by enlarging those situations in which dismissal for failure to join a specified union is unfair, granting the employer the right in this situation to reclaim whatever compensation he may have to pay out from the union signatory of the agreement, and issuing a restrictive code of practice;

(c) gave individuals the right to complain of *unreasonable exclusion or expulsion* from a union in a closed shop (19.31);

(d) limited the effectiveness of *unfair dismissal* (the qualifying period already having been increased by statutory order);

(e) made illegal *secondary industrial action* and secondary picketing directed at an employer not in dispute with the union (22.38); and

(f) abolished statutory recognition procedures and Sch II of the Employment Protection Act 1975 with its provision for extension of collectively bargained and general level terms.

1.13 Many, however, considered that the Employment Act 1980 did not go far enough to restrain the unions and redress the industrial balance which they thought had been tilted in the unions' favour between 1974 and 1979. The main features of the Employment Act 1982 introduced by Norman Tebbit as Secretary of State for Employment concerned:

(a) removing immunity from trade union funds;

(b) subjecting closed shops to periodic review, and prohibiting union membership only clauses in contracts and tender documents; and

(c) increasing compensation for employees unfairly dismissed in consequence of a closed shop.

1.14 The Trade Union Act 1984 was intended by the Government to 'give unions back to their members'. The statute provided for ballots to be held for the election of the principal executive committee, before industrial action, and to maintain the union's political fund. The effect was to take the courts further into the internal affairs of trade unions.

1.15 Increasingly the effect of European law was being felt in the employment law arena. The Thatcher Government was, however, impelled by European directives to implement two important pieces of legislation which were not to its liking. Both were introduced by statutory instrument: the Transfer of Undertakings (Protection of Employment) Regulations 1981 (SI 1981/1794) which gives employees various rights on takeovers, and the Equal Pay (Amendment) Regulations 1983 (SI 1983/1794) which gives women the right to claim equal pay when their work is of equal value to a man's instead of merely when he and she perform like work.

1.16 After ten years of Conservative government, the trade unions were weaker than at any point since the war. They had lost some 2 million members, been buffeted by the courts, and were uncertain of their strategy to fight back. The wounds opened by the year-long miners' strike in 1984–85, which ended with defeat for Arthur Scargill's National Union of Mineworkers, took long to heal.

1.17 The Government's continuing ideological approach to employment law may be seen in the statement in their Green Paper *Lifting the Burden* (Cm 9571, 1985, at 29): 'priority should be given to action to reduce the administrative and legislative burdens on business, particularly on small and medium-sized enterprises'.

The next employment legislation following this pronouncement, however, dealt with **1.18** other government preoccupations. The Employment Act 1988 gave further rights to trade union members over union funds and, to prevent strikes not supported by a valid ballot, altered the rules on election and political fund ballots, tightened the provisions on the closed shop, and introduced the Commissioner for the Rights of Trade Union Members. This statute provided the backdrop to increased litigation on the wording and scope of strike ballots, including major litigation in 1989 concerning the dock and railways strikes, both of which resulted in court victories for the unions.

The Employment Act 1989 followed hard on the heels of the 1988 statute, but notwith- **1.19** standing its title, dealt mainly with amendments to the Sex Discrimination Act 1975.

The Employment Act 1990 was a further move from the consensus view of industrial **1.20** relations and included the abolition of the pre-entry closed shop, further restriction on secondary action, and widening the powers of the Commissioner for the Rights of Trade Union Members. The liability of trade unions was also extended to cover the acts of their committees and officials, including shop stewards, unless disowned by the union, and employees lost the right to claim unfair dismissal if at the time they are engaged in unofficial industrial action.

The Trade Union and Labour Relations (Consolidation) Act 1992 consolidated statutory **1.21** collective labour law.

The next piece of industrial legislation was again controversial and constituted a return by **1.22** the Major Government to the attack on trade unionism which characterised the Thatcher years. The Trade Union Reform and Employment Rights Act 1993 placed further restrictions on the rights of employees to strike and strictly regulated the financial affairs of trade unions. Although it contained some provisions to extend workers' rights, these derived almost entirely from the impulse of European directives. Indeed this was the first general piece of primary industrial legislation which derived a majority of its provisions from European Community law, in particular on maternity rights, transfer of undertakings, and proof of employment relationship.

Michael Portillo in early 1995 issued a Green Paper which proposed radical reform of **1.23** employment tribunal procedure (*Resolving Employment Rights Disputes: Options for Reform*, December 1994) and announced that all minimum hours thresholds were to be abolished. The Government had to introduce legislation to ensure that consultation took place over redundancies and transfer of undertakings whether or not a union is recognised by the employer. This was in order to implement the ECJ decision in *Commission of European Communities v UK* [1994] IRLR 412, and regulations were introduced in 1995.

F A THIRD WAY? LABOUR LEGISLATION 1997–2009

The first two years of the Government led by Tony Blair (himself a former employment **1.24** lawyer) saw the passage of the Working Time Regulations 1998, the Public Interest Disclosure Act 1998, the Data Protection Act 1998, and the National Minimum Wage Act 1998. The Human Rights Act 1998 also had a major effect in the employment context. The Employment Relations Act 1999 implemented many of the proposals first published in the White Paper, *Fairness at Work* (Cm 3968, May 1998). The underlying aim, as explained in the White Paper, was to create 'a framework in which the development of strong partnerships at work can flourish as the best way of improving fairness at work'. Its contents fell into six main areas:

(a) new statutory procedures for the recognition and derecognition of trade unions for collective bargaining;
(b) provisions relating to protection for trade union membership and non-membership;
(c) changes to the law on industrial action;
(d) new rights and changes in family-related employment rights;
(e) a new right for workers to be accompanied in disciplinary and grievance hearings; and
(f) other changes in individual employment rights.

It did not, however, challenge the main thrust of the Thatcherite settlement on strikes and picketing.

1.25 The Human Rights Act 1998 has had a major impact on employment law in such areas as religious rights and the right to freedom of association and privacy.

1.26 The second Blair Government introduced another Employment Act in 2002, bringing important changes to the law on family rights, including a new right to paid paternity leave, reform to aspects of employment tribunals, including the possibility for the first time of widespread costs orders, and enabling provisions relating to fixed-term contracts and flexible working.

1.27 In 2000 the EU proclaimed the EU Charter of Fundamental Rights. The general legacy from the EU is somewhat mixed: insofar as there is a uniting theme in the legislation emanating from Brussels it is the policy of 'flexicurity', a confection or mixture of flexibility of the workforce and security (as seen, eg, in the Posted Workers Directive).

1.28 The last substantive piece of employment legislation in the second Blair term was the Employment Relations Act 2004, which followed the review of the Employment Relations Act 1999. The changes made were, however, minimal and reflect the general satisfaction of both sides of industry with the 1999 settlement on recognition. The Employment Act 2008 was the first statute of the Gordon Brown premiership and primarily repeals the statutory disciplinary and grievance provisions introduced in 2004.

G THE CAMERON GOVERNMENTS

1.29 The first Cameron-led Government was a Coalition which proceeded gingerly in the substantive employment law area, although its introduction of fees for employment tribunal claims in July 2013 greatly reduced their numbers; since then the number of cases lodged has reduced by 30 per cent. The second Government had no such inhibitions and the Trade Union Bill was very radical and controversial. The Government, however, backtracked on reforms it envisaged to check-off and political fund contributions. The Act as enacted largely deals with turnouts in strike ballots and the required majorities. Some of the employment measures in recent years have been buried away in more general statutes such as the Enterprise and Regulatory Reform Act 2013, the Growth and Infrastructure Act 2013, and the Children and Families Act 2014.

1.30 It is too early to say how the May Government will deal with employment law although the exit from the European Union gives them the opportunity to liberalise the employment sphere even more.

One of the most significant features, even since the first edition of this book was pub- **1.31** lished, has been the steep decline in trade union membership, particularly in the private sector, which has arisen because of the legislative background and also the decline in large manufacturing industries where there would have been thousands of workers operating from one site. Another key development has been the transfer of risk from employers to workers, described as 'demutualization' by Profs Freedland and Kountourtis in *The Legal Construction of Personal Work Relations*, OUP, 2011. Another major cause of concern is the introduction of fees for employees' and their unions' employment tribunal cases.

2

THE STATUS OF EMPLOYEE

A THE PURPOSE OF DEFINING THE
  EMPLOYEE 2.01

B THE TESTS OF EMPLOYEE STATUS 2.06
  Mutuality of obligation 2.06
  The control test 2.16
  The integration test 2.19
  The economic reality test 2.20

C OTHER WORK RELATIONSHIPS 2.35
  Office holders 2.36
  Crown servants 2.40
  Apprentices .2.43
  Students, cadets, and youth schemes . . . 2.44

Labour only sub-contractors and
  casual workers .2.46
  Agency workers 2.48
  Unincorporated associations and
  workers' cooperatives 2.54
  Directors 2.56
  Partners 2.64
  Merchant seamen 2.65

D DEFINITION OF WORKERS 2.66
  The client exception 2.70

E QUESTION OF LAW OR FACT? 2.77
  Employee shareholders 2.80
  Zero hours contracts 2.81

It is often easy to recognise a contract of service when you see it but difficult to say wherein the difference [between it and a contract for services] lies. (Denning LJ in *Stevenson, Jordan and Harrison Ltd v Macdonald and Evans* [1952] 1 TLR 101.)

A THE PURPOSE OF DEFINING THE EMPLOYEE

2.01 Most working people have a contract of employment and are employees or, in the archaic word, servants. A builder building an extension to a house, a watchmaker repairing a watch or a plumber mending a tap is, however, more likely to be engaged on a contract for services, an independent contractor. He labours for a short time and the hirer is interested not in controlling what he does while he does it but only in the finished product or service. The self-employed person may bargain with the hirer in a way that the employee normally cannot, unless he is highly skilled or his services are in short supply.

2.02 It is fundamental to statutory and common law employment law to identify who is an employee and who is an independent contractor, yet statute provides only an outline distinction between these two modes in which a man may sell his labour and the rest is filled in by the common law (the Trade Union and Labour Relations (Consolidation) Act (TULR(C)A) 1992, s 295). The Employment Rights Act 1996, s 230(1), defines an 'employee' as 'an individual who has entered into or works under (or, where the employment has ceased, worked under) a contract of employment'. The answer to the question largely depends on conflicting tests established at common law over several decades and with varying emphases at different times particularly because of the different purposes which they serve. They were first formulated to decide on vicarious liability, that is, when an employer is liable to a third party for the torts of his employees. The distinction is now vital more generally, since only employees qualify for:

(a) benefits such as jobseeker's allowance, for industrial injuries, and for sickness;
(b) employment protection rights such as guaranteed pay, unfair dismissal, redundancy payments, rights to notice, and time off;
(c) health and safety provisions, including the Factories Acts;
(d) protection of wages on insolvency of the employer; and
(e) the benefit of the employer's common law duty of care.

The distinction is most importantly used on a day-to-day basis for taxation, since while employees are taxed under Sch E of the Income and Corporation Taxes Act 1988, the self-employed enjoy generally more favourable treatment by Sch D. The courts here are naturally astute to crack down on avoidance techniques. Until recently the courts have only departed from the contractual approach by preventing the use of labelling to achieve a result. Now the Supreme Court decision in *Autoclenz Ltd v Belcher* [2011] IRLR 820 permits a more interventionist approach, so that the courts can really identify the parties' true agreement. **2.03**

The common law tests of employee status are theoretically the same for this multiplicity of purposes. Yet the policy considerations behind a decision under each heading are rather different. Thus, in determining vicarious liability, the court will be most concerned with the adequate protection of third parties and the nature of control retained by the putative employer; while in respect of national insurance contributions and tax, the policy uppermost in the court's mind may be the prevention of avoidance of duties owed. **2.04**

One of the primary aims of the law is to distinguish between commercial and business relations on the one hand and dependent employment contracts on the other. Collins, Ewing, & McColgan in *Labour Law*, CUP, 2012, at 186 put it thus: 'The law of unfair dismissal is concerned with the abuse of managerial disciplinary power and so it should apply only to those types of contract where the terms of the contract create an authority relation and the associated risk of an abuse of power.' The other important new element is that EU law takes a wide view of the employment relationship. **2.05**

B THE TESTS OF EMPLOYEE STATUS

Mutuality of obligation

The bare essentials of a contract of employment are the obligations to provide work for remuneration and the obligation to perform it coupled with control. It does not matter that the arrangements for payment are made directly or indirectly through an agency (*Cable & Wireless plc v Muscat* [2006] IRLR 354; see also *RNLI v Bushaway* [2005] IRLR 674). Indeed a person may qualify as an employee even though he provides services through the medium of a limited company (*Catamaran Cruisers Ltd v Williams* [1994] IRLR 386). While the formation of such a company may be strong evidence of a change of status away from employment, that fact has to be evaluated in the context of all the other facts which have been found to apply. **2.06**

There must in all cases be an obligation on each side, that is on the employer to provide work and on the employee to carry out that work (*Nethermere (St Neots) Ltd v Taverna and Gardiner* [1984] IRLR 240). Dr Mark Freedland sees the contract of employment as consisting of the wage–work bargain and the global or umbrella contract: *The Contract of Employment*, Clarendon Press, 1976. **2.07**

2.08 It is necessary that mutuality of obligation exists in order for a contract of employment to arise at all. There is, however, ongoing controversy over the true place of mutuality of obligation; whether it is necessary in order to show that there is a contract at all or whether it merely demonstrates that it is one of employment.

2.09 This fundamental point was stressed by the Court of Appeal in *Clark v Oxfordshire Health Authority* [1998] IRLR 125 where the real issue was whether the actual periods of work carried out by the claimant could be spanned. This was especially important when the claimant was a 'bank nurse' with the respondent health authority. She was taken on under a general or global contract of employment but was actually offered work only as and when it was available, and there was no obligation on either side to provide work or to work. Notwithstanding that she worked for three years for the health authority with gaps totalling some four and a half months, the Court of Appeal held that she was not an employee because there was no mutuality of obligation since she could refuse work as she wished between the periods when she agreed to a contract. In *Carmichael v National Power plc* [2000] IRLR 43, an agreement between two tour guides and the respondent that the former would work on a 'casual as required' basis was not sufficient to give rise to mutually binding obligations. Lord Irvine LC said it was necessary to consider not only the documents recording the relationship but also the way in which the relationship had worked in practice in deciding that, outside the period of the actual work being done, there was not the irreducible minimum of obligation on the part of the two parties so that no relationship of employment was created.

2.10 In *McLeod v Hellyer Brothers Ltd* [1987] IRLR 232, the Court of Appeal gave very detailed attention to the concept of an 'umbrella' or 'global' contract of employment. The five appellants in the two consolidated appeals were Hull trawlermen. Prior to January 1984, they had each worked over a long period exclusively for the respective respondents. They had served on the terms of a series of 'crew agreements' which were signed on each engagement on board a fishing vessel. In between sailings, they had registered as unemployed and received social security benefits. In January 1984 the vessels were taken out of commission and the employees each claimed a redundancy payment. The Court of Appeal rejected the claimants' contention that they were throughout employed under a global contract of employment which spanned the intervening periods between crew agreements. This was because it was not possible to infer from the parties' conduct the existence in between crew agreements of a trawlerman's obligation 'to serve'. The heads of a series of individual contracts could not simply be counted together. Here the men had not placed themselves under any legally binding obligation either to make themselves available for the respective respondents in between crew agreements or not to accept employment from another trawler owner during such periods. Indeed the evidence was that they actually did sign on for other trawler owners in these periods so there could not be any such obligation.

2.11 The issue for the tribunal will thus often be whether such workers are governed by a general contract covering the whole period. In *Stevedoring and Haulage Services Ltd v Fuller* [2001] IRLR 627, for example, the Court of Appeal found that an employment tribunal had erred in holding that the claimant casual workers were working under an umbrella contract of employment rather than under a series of individual engagements, notwithstanding that the document setting out the terms under which they were offered and accepted work expressly provided that they were being engaged on an *ad hoc* and casual basis with no obligation on the company to offer work and no obligation on the applicants to accept it. It was not correct to say that those terms which provided for an irreducible minimum of obligation on each side had been implied from the way in which parties had conducted themselves since the inception of the agreement. Tuckey LJ said that 'at best the parties assumed moral obligations of loyalty where both recognised that their mutual economic interest lay in being accommodating to one another'.

Ability to delegate

A key test militating against a person being an employee is the ability to delegate. It is **2.12** also important that the putative employee agrees to carry out the obligations demanded of him *personally* and not through others. A power to substitute is usually anathema to a contract of employment but tribunals must be astute to recognise substitution cases or clauses denying any obligation to accept or provide work in employment contracts which are really sham contracts and where they do not reflect the reality of the employment relationship (*Autoclenz Ltd v Belcher* [2011] IRLR 820).

Thus, in *Express and Echo Publications Limited v Tanton* [1999] IRLR 367, the Court of **2.13** Appeal held that no contract of employment existed because a clause in the 'agreement for services' provided that if the worker was unable to carry out his work as a driver personally, he was to arrange a substitute at his own expense. In *Byrne Bros (Formwork) Ltd v Baird* [2002] IRLR 96, however, the power to appoint substitutes was qualified and exceptional and thus fell short of a blanket licence to supply the contractual service through a substitute (*Staffordshire Sentinel Newspapers Ltd v Potter* [2004] IRLR 752) (see also 2.48–2.49). It thus did not prevent the person being a worker. A provision allowing for some limited ability to delegate does not, however, inescapably lead to a conclusion that the contract is one for services and not a contract of service. In *MacFarlane v Glasgow City Council* [2001] IRLR 7, where qualified gymnastics instructors working at recreational and sports centres could truly arrange for replacements from a register of coaches maintained by the council, there was still a contract of employment and *Tanton* could be distinguished. That was an extreme case. The substitution was only permissible if they were not able to attend. Further, the council could veto a replacement, and in some cases organised the replacement itself (see also *Bunce v Postworth Ltd t/a Skyblue* [2005] IRLR 557).

Sham contracts

In *Consistent Group Ltd v Kalwak* [2008] IRLR 505, the Court of Appeal stressed that **2.14** it was not for the employment tribunal to recast the parties' bargain which they had made so that if they provide for substitutes this should be respected. To diverge from that agreement can only be done by a clear finding that the real agreement was to that different effect and that the relevant term in the contract was included so as to present a misleadingly different impression (see also *Redrow Homes (Yorkshire) Ltd v Buckborough* [2009] IRLR 34). This was put into perspective in the important case of *Autoclenz Ltd v Belcher* [2011] ICR 1157. The Supreme Court decided that there should be a special approach to sham arrangements in putative employment contracts. The claimants were car cleaners or valeters. Their contracts said in terms that they were independent subcontractors, responsible for their own taxes, and were doing casual work as required and that suitably qualified substitutes were permitted to operate. The contract also said that they would supply their own cleaning equipment. The evidence was that the employer did not expect in practice that any substitutes would be offered work. The Supreme Court said that 'the relative bargaining power of the parties must be taken into account in deciding whether the terms of any written agreement in truth represent what was agreed and the true agreement will often have to be gleaned from all the circumstances of the case of which the written agreement is only a part'. The decision was that here the power of substitution was a sham and they were in truth employees. The importance of the case is that it gives rise to the possibility of identifying the true agreement between the parties which may differ from the written terms.

The volunteer

2.15 A question frequently arises whether a volunteer is an employee both in domestic and European law. It is necessary to identify an arrangement under which in exchange for valuable consideration, the volunteer is contractually obliged to render services for the employer and the employer has to provide work for the volunteer personally to do (*SE Sheffield CAB v Grayson* [2004] IRLR 343; *Melhuish v Redbridge CAB* [2005] IRLR 419). An unpaid volunteer at an advice bureau pursuant to a volunteer agreement was not a worker within Directive 2000/78 as occupation did not envisage voluntary activity. Further, there was a deliberate choice made by the European Council not to cover voluntary work in the Directive (*X v Mid Sussex CAB* [2013] ICR 249).

The control test

2.16 Since it was in the context of vicarious liability that the courts first considered who was an employee, it was natural that they saw its touchstone as whether the master (as he was then called) controlled or had the right to control not only what the worker did but also the *manner* in which he did it (*Performing Right Society v Mitchell and Booker (Palais de Danse) Ltd* [1924] 1 KB 762). An independent contractor, on the other hand, was seen as being hired to achieve a certain result but had a complete discretion as to how to effect it. This control test also served to differentiate the servant from an agent, who similarly can choose exactly how he goes about tasks given to him by his principal. Thus, while a domestic servant was an employee, a blacksmith was an independent contractor.

2.17 As the pace of technological change hastened, however, it became increasingly unrealistic to conceive of the employer as having the knowledge to control many of his increasingly highly skilled employees. A surgeon, a research chemist, or an airline pilot will have know-how far beyond that possessed by the management that employs them. It is, however, an aspect of public policy that someone should normally assume vicarious liability for the worker's negligence to others to ensure a claimworthy defendant. The breakthrough towards a more realistic approach came in a series of cases in the late 1940s in which hospitals were held vicariously liable for the acts of surgeons, radiographers, and other specialists (eg *Cassidy v Ministry of Health* [1951] 2 KB 343).

2.18 The single control test was thus variegated to a series of indications of control. Lord Thankerton, in *Short v J. & W. Henderson Ltd* (1946) 62 TLR 427, looked at whether the putative master had:

(a) power of selection of his servant;
(b) right to control the method of doing the work; and
(c) right of *suspension* and dismissal.

Only if these questions were answered in the affirmative, and the worker received wages or other remuneration, would a contract of employment exist. As this notion has developed the two general criteria now in general use for distinguishing employees from independent contractors are: (a) the integration test and (b) the economic reality test, although these are usually presented in the form of factors to be taken into account rather than formal requirements which must be ticked off.

The integration test

2.19 Denning LJ in *Stevenson, Jordan and Harrison Ltd v Macdonald and Evans* [1952] 1 TLR 101 (a copyright case) considered that the decisive question was whether the person under consideration was *fully integrated* into the employer's organisation. A ship's master, a chauffeur, and a reporter on the staff of a newspaper are thus all employed under a contract *of* service; but a ship's pilot, a taxi driver, and a newspaper contributor are hired under a contract *for* services. Denning LJ detected that: 'one feature which seems to run through the instances is that, under a contract of service a man is employed as part of the business and his work is done as an integral part of the business but under a contract for services his work, although done for the business is not integrated into it but only accessory to it'. In a later case (*Bank voor Handel en Scheepvaart NV v Slatford* [1953] 1 QB 248), Lord Denning reformulated the question as whether the worker was 'part and parcel' of the employer's organisation (see also *Beloff v Pressdram Ltd* [1973] 1 All ER 241). The great drawback of this approach, however, lies in its failure to define exactly what is meant by 'integration' and 'organisation', so that it has to be addressed on a case-by-case basis.

The economic reality test

The courts have now recognised that no single test or series of criteria can be decisive. **2.20** Instead they have adopted something like the American notion of an 'economic reality' composite test (see *USA v Silk* (1946) 331 US 704) and the clearest illustration is the very full judgment in *Ready Mixed Concrete (South East) Ltd v Minister of Pensions and National Insurance* [1968] 2 QB 497. The case concerned the appellant company's liability for social security contributions of its workers for which it was responsible only if the workers had contracts of service. The workers drove ready mixed concrete lorries which they were buying on hire purchase agreement from the appellant company, which required, in a detailed contract of thirty pages, that they must, *inter alia:*

(a) use the lorry only on company business;
(b) maintain it in accordance with the company's instructions; and
(c) obey all reasonable orders.

Although this suggested a measure of close control by the company, there were no require- **2.21** ments about hours of work and the times at which the drivers took holidays. Moreover, they could generally hire out the driving of their vehicle to another, and were paid, subject to a yearly minimum, according to the amount of concrete which they transported. McKenna J identified three conditions for a contract *of* service which have often been repeated:

(a) the servant agrees that in consideration of a wage or other remuneration he will provide his own work and skill in performing some service for his master;
(b) he agrees expressly or impliedly that in performance of that service he will be subject to the other's control in a sufficient degree to make that other the master; and
(c) the other provisions of the contract are consistent with it being a contract of service.

On the facts of the case, the judge decided that the workers were independent contractors, most particularly because the third test (c) was not satisfied since most of the terms pointed to it as a contract *for* services.

It is the meaning of (c) in this list which has, indeed, caused most difficulty in the subse- **2.22** quent case law. In *Market Investigations Ltd v Minister of Social Security* [1969] 2 WLR 1, for example, which was approved by the Privy Council in *Lee Ting Sang v Chung Chi-Keung* [1990] ICR 409, Cooke J paraphrased the fundamental test as whether the person performing services is in business on his own account. If the answer was yes, the contract was *for* services; but it was not so in the instant case, where the respondents engaged interviewers for a short time during which they were free to work when they wished, and were permitted to perform tasks for other companies. The learned judge said that:

> No exhaustive list has been compiled and perhaps no exhaustive list can be compiled of considerations which are relevant in determining [the] question, nor can strict rules be laid down as to the relative weight which the various considerations may carry in particular cases.

2.23 Indeed, in some cases it has been recognised that the only sure test is to ask whether an ordinary person would think there was a contract of service (see also *Withers v Flackwell Heath Football Supporters Club* [1981] IRLR 307). In *WHPT Housing Association Ltd v Secretary of State for Social Services* [1981] ICR 737, Webster J saw the essence of the distinction as the fact that the employee provided himself to serve, while the independent contractor only provides his services (see also *Lee Ting Sang v Chung Chi-Keung* [1990] ICR 409).

2.24 It has indeed been emphasised that there is no single path to determining whether or not contracts are of service or for services. In *Hall v Lorimer* [1994] IRLR 171, the Court of Appeal agreed with Mummery J that:

> It is not a mechanical exercise of running through items on a check list to see whether they are present in, or absent from, a given situation. The object of the exercise is to paint a picture from the accumulation of detail. The overall effect can only be appreciated by standing back from the detailed picture which has been painted, by viewing it from a distance and making an informed, considered, qualitative appreciation of the whole.

The factors indicating status

2.25 In most modern cases the courts will consider a whole range of factors which may point in different directions but which must be considered in the round and a conclusion reached on them as a matter of fact and degree. This list provides some indication of the factors considered by the courts as attributes of employees and independent contractors (see eg *Market Investigations Ltd v Minister of Social Security* [1969] 2 QB 173 at 185):

(a) *Ownership of tools* and instruments by the worker points in the direction of self-employment.

(b) Payment of *wages and sick pay* indicates that the person under consideration is an employee, since the independent contractor usually receives a lump sum for the job and bears any risk of ill health himself. As Lord Widgery put it in *Global Plant Ltd v Secretary of State for Social Services* [1972] QB 139:

> If a man agrees to perform an operation for a fixed sum and thus stands to lose if the work is delayed and to profit if it is done quickly, that is the man who on the face of it appears to be an independent contractor working under a contract for services.

This factor was of some importance in the case of *Hitchcock v Post Office* [1980] ICR 100, where a sub-postmaster, who provided the shop for his sub-post office, was held to be self-employed even though he had to carry out Post Office instructions and had to advise the head postmaster if absent for three days. The decision was supported by the facts that he could delegate his duties to others, and bore the risk of profit or loss.

(c) The presence or absence of *residual control* (considered already) 'is still an important factor but it is not the only one' (Slynn J in *Hitchcock*, above). In *Addison v London Philharmonic Orchestra* [1981] ICR 261, orchestral musicians were held to be independent contractors since 'the obligations imposed on them were the very minimum to ensure that the work is done. Personal attendance at rehearsals and self-discipline were "simply prerequisites of a concert artist's work and did not decisively point to a contract of service"'. While hospital administrators cannot tell the surgeon how he should perform his operations, they can ensure that serious consequences follow if he were to decide to perform them in the middle of a field and they thus maintain some degree of control. As Cooke J said in *Market Investigations Ltd v Minister of Social Security* [1969] 2 WLR 1: 'The most that can be said is that control will no doubt always have to be considered, although it can no longer be regarded as the sole decisive factor.' The more *discretion* accorded to *when* his work will be performed, the more likely it is that the worker is under a contract for services (eg *Narich Pty Ltd v Commissioner of Pay-roll Tax* [1984] ICR 286 and *Commissioners of Inland Revenue v Post Office Ltd* [2003] IRLR 199), where the provision of their own premises and equipment, the right to provide their own staff, and the right to run their own businesses subject to keeping separate accounts mitigated against a finding of either worker or employer status.

(d) Deduction of *PAYE and national insurance contributions* points to employment, but this is not decisive (*Davis v New England College of Arundel* [1977] ICR 6, *Airfix Footwear Ltd v Cope* [1978] ICR 1210). If, however, the person is registered for VAT purposes, this points the other way.

(e) A casual and short-term engagement suggests the status of independent contractor, especially when the worker retains the right to, or actually does, work elsewhere (*Argent v Minister of Social Security* [1968] 3 All ER 208). In *Hall v Lorimer* [1994] IRLR 171, the respondent, a vision-mixer, customarily worked for twenty or more different companies at any one time and the vast majority of his assignments lasted for only a single day. Moreover, he ran the risk himself of bad debts being created and he incurred very substantial expenditure in carrying out his engagements. It was thus held that he was self-employed and not an employee.

(f) The fact that an individual works at his own premises may be an indicator of self-employment, although that is less forceful as a consideration nowadays given the increase in home working. The facts in *Quashie v Stringfellow Restaurants Ltd* [2013] IRLR 99 were that Ms Quashie was a lap dancer in a nightclub. Customers bought vouchers to pay her for dances. At the end of each evening she gave these vouchers to the club cashier who gave her money after deducting fees. She would be out of pocket if she did not earn enough. The Court of Appeal decided that there was true economic risk here so that she was not an employee of the club.

(g) Whether payments are made by the putative employer, and it will count against a determination of employment if they are made by, for example, a third party (see the Privy Council in *Cheng Yuen v Royal Hong Kong Golf Club* [1998] ICR 131).

Self-description

Often the parties to a contract describe themselves as hirer and independent contractor **2.26** to avoid employee status. This is, however, in no way decisive in determining the true characterisation in law, since the courts consider the substance of the relationship and not its form (*Davis v New England College of Arundel* [1977] ICR 6). This is especially true where there are public obligations involved, such as social security contributions (*Warner Holidays Ltd v Secretary of State for Social Services* [1983] ICR 440). The description may, however, have some limited persuasive value. The issue which most commonly comes before the court is where the parties have (a) chosen a self-employed relationship for reasons of tax or national insurance, but (b) the worker later seeks the benefits of employee status in order to gain statutory employment protection rights, usually when the relationship has ended. The cases on this point are by no means easy to reconcile.

In *Ferguson v John Dawson and Partners (Contractors) Ltd* [1976] 3 All ER 817, for **2.27** example, the worker was told on his very informal hiring as a 'general labourer' that he would become part of a 'lump' labour force. There were no 'cards' and no deductions were to be made for tax and national insurance. He nevertheless had to obey the company's instructions concerning what to do and when to do it. When he was seriously injured in the course of his work, the success of his claim for industrial injuries benefit, and damages for breach of statutory duty, depended solely on whether he was an employee, all other criteria being fulfilled. Megaw and Browne LJJ decided that he *was* so entitled, notwithstanding the arrangements voluntarily entered into. The self-description of the parties was only one factor to be taken into account. Lawton LJ dissented and took a rather more stringent view. It was, he thought, open to anyone to decide how he was to sell his labour and 'contrary to public policy to allow a man to say that he was self-employed for the purposes of avoiding the incidence of tax, then a servant for the purpose of claiming compensation'. He thought that the parties were estopped from reneging on the agreement which they had made.

2.28 Two later cases followed the majority approach rather than that adopted by Lawton LJ: *Davis v New England College of Arundel* (above) and *Tyne and Clyde Warehouses Ltd v Hamerton* [1978] ICR 661. The Court of Appeal has, however, since drawn a distinction between the *Ferguson* case and situations where there is an actual and considered, albeit agreed, change in status. Thus, in *Massey v Crown Life Insurance Company* [1978] IRLR 31, the claimant had been employed for two years by the respondents as a branch manager. He then entered into a new arrangement with them whereby he registered himself as John L Massey and Associates with the Registry of Business Names (although he did not in fact form a company), and his one-man business was appointed manager. The main effect was that the respondents no longer made tax or other deductions from fees paid to Mr Massey. The Inland Revenue agreed to treat him as self-employed, notwithstanding that his duties largely remained the same. When he was removed with one month's notice, he was held not entitled to bring a claim for unfair dismissal, since he was self-employed.

2.29 Lord Denning MR distinguished *Ferguson*'s case on its facts because:

> there is a perfectly genuine agreement entered into at the instance of Mr Massey on the footing that he is 'self-employed'. He gets the benefit of it by avoiding tax deductions and getting his pension contributions returned. I do not see that he can come along afterwards and say it is something else in order to claim that he has been unfairly dismissed. Having made his bed as being 'self-employed' he must lie on it.

The written contract here 'becomes the best material from which to gather the true relationship between the parties'. On the other hand, 'the parties cannot alter the truth of [the] relationship by putting a different label on it and use it as a dishonest device to deceive the Revenue'.

2.30 Lawton LJ thought that the existence of the written contract distinguished the case from the majority decision in *Ferguson*, and he agreed with Lord Denning's public policy reasoning. Although *Massey* has been followed by the Privy Council in *Australian Mutual Provident Society v Allan* (1978) 52 ALJR 407, and see to the same effect *Dacas v Brook Street Bureau (UK) Ltd* [2003] IRLR, little has been done to clarify the exact distinction between the facts in *Ferguson* and *Massey* (see also on implied contract: *Evans v RSA Consulting Ltd* [2011] ICR 37).

2.31 However, the Court of Appeal decision in *Young and Woods Ltd v West* [1980] IRLR 201 suggests that *Massey* should be confined to its facts. The respondent, a skilled sheet metal worker chose self-employment, again for tax reasons, but since he was paid on an hourly rate, had normal working hours and use of the appellants' equipment, he was classified as an employee by the Court of Appeal so that he was eligible to claim unfair dismissal. The important feature for Stephenson LJ was that the claimant was not 'in business on his own account'. He distinguished *Massey* on two grounds: firstly that the claimant in that case had two contracts, one of service as manager of the branch office and the other for services under a general agency agreement; and secondly that the self-employment resulted from a deliberate change of relationship. He concurred with the other members of the Court of Appeal in disapproving of the general operation of the doctrine of estoppel in this area, saying, 'I am satisfied that the parties can resile from the position which they have deliberately and openly chosen to take up and ... to reach any other conclusion would be in effect to permit the parties to contract out of the Act.' In *Narich Pty Ltd v Commissioner of Pay-roll Tax* [1984] ICR 286, the Privy Council looked behind the terms of an agreement between a weight-watching franchise company and their lecturers. It claimed to create independent contractors, but the court decided that the relationship was in truth one of employment. In reality the company was entitled to control and direct not only the nature and scope of the task allotted to the lecturer but also the precise manner in which it was performed.

Ministers of religion

An associate minister's relationship with the Church of Scotland could qualify as employ- **2.32** ment under s 82(1) SDA since it was a contract 'personally to execute work'. Here there was an offer and acceptance of a church post for a specific period with specific provision for the appointee's duties and remuneration, travel expenses, holidays, and accommodation. Holding an office and being an employee were not inconsistent (*Percy v Church of Scotland Board of National Mission* [2006] IRLR 195; *New Testament Church of God v Stewart* [2007] IRLR 178, [2008] IRLR 134). The fact that the worker has very considerable freedom and independence as to how she performs the duty of her office does not take her outside the definition. In *President of the Methodist Conference v Parfitt* [1984] ICR 176, the Court of Appeal emphasised the spiritual nature of the relationship between the applicant Methodist minister and the Methodist Conference. There was no contract of any sort between them. In *Davies v Presbyterian Church of Wales* [1986] IRLR 194, the appellant was a pastor of the Presbyterian Church of Wales until his dismissal in May 1981. A tribunal held that he was entitled to bring a claim of unfair dismissal but the House of Lords ultimately allowed the Church's appeal. Here there was no contract between the appellant and the Church. The Book of Rules of the Methodist Church which governed the pastor did not contain terms of employment, and his duties were not contractual or enforceable, being dictated by conscience and not law.

In a further consideration of the issue by the Supreme Court, the key issues in deciding **2.33** whether a minister of religion served under a contract of employment were held to be the manner in which the minister was engaged and the character of rules or terms governing the minister's service. The question whether an arrangement was a legally binding contract depended on the intentions of the parties and the mere fact that the arrangement included payment of a stipend, the provision of accommodation, and the performance of recognised duties did not resolve that issue. The Constitution and Standing Orders of the Methodist Church showed that the manner in which a minister was engaged was incapable of being analysed in terms of contractual formation. The appointment depended on a unilateral decision by the Conference. The stipend and manse were due to the minister by virtue only of his admission into Full Connexion (*Preston v President of the Methodist Conference* [2013] ICR 833). The rights and duties of ministers arose entirely from their status in the constitution of the church and not from any contract. It arose from the life-long relationship into which they had entered when they were ordained.

2.34 A similar position has been reached after much litigation in respect of the Church of England. *Diocese of Southwark v Coker* [1998] ICR 140, CA, concerned a curate of the Church of England who complained to a tribunal that he had been unfairly dismissed. *Coker* followed *Davis* in holding that the applicant was not employed. Mummery LJ stressed that there must be an objectively ascertained intention to create a contractual relationship, giving rise to legally enforceable obligations. In *Sharpe v Worcester Diocesan Board of Finance Ltd* [2015] ICR 1241 the Supreme Court decided that there was in general no different test for religious officers than for others, but concluded that the claimant, a Church of England priest, assumed the office not simply because he was selected but because he was installed, and as part of that installation he made an oath of canonical obedience in exchange for which the Church provided him with facilities to discharge his calling. The Church had little power to control the way in which he discharged his functions or to remove him from his post. He did not enter into any agreement to work for the Church since the office of rector was part of ecclesiastical law and not the result of a contractual arrangement.

C OTHER WORK RELATIONSHIPS

2.35 There are several special work situations to consider.

Office holders

2.36 The most widely cited general definition of an office is that formulated by Rowlatt J in *Great Western Railway v Bater* [1920] 3 KB 266 (a taxation case), that it is 'a subsisting, permanent, substantive position which had its existence independently from the person who filled it, which went on and was filled in succession by successive holders'. The clearest examples are trustees (eg *Attorney-General for New South Wales v Perpetual Trustee Co Ltd* [1955] AC 457); bailiffs; trade union officers (*Stevenson v URTU* [1977] ICR 893); officers of the Salvation Army (*Rogers v Booth* [1935] 2 All ER 751); company directors (*Ellis v Lucas* [1967] Ch 858); police officers (*Fisher v Oldham Corporation* [1930] 2 KB 364); prison officers (*Home Office v Robinson* [1982] ICR 31); company registrars (*IRC v Brander & Cruikshank* [1971] 1 All ER 36); and a registrar of births, marriages, and deaths (*Lincs CC v Hopper* [2002] ICR 1301).

2.37 Clergymen, of whatever religion, are usually classified as holding an office (*Santokh Singh v Guru Nanak Gurdwara* [1990] ICR 309; *Birmingham Mosque Trust Ltd v Alavi* [1992] ICR 435).

2.38 The courts have also decided that JPs and rent officers fall within the definition of office holder (*Knight v Attorney-General* [1979] ICR 194; *Department of the Environment v Fox* [1979] ICR 736; *Johnson v Ryan* [2000] ICR 236), but not a civil engineer who conducted public inquiries on behalf of the Department of Environment because of the lack of continuity and permanence of his position (*Edwards v Clinch* [1981] 3 WLR 707), nor a senior barristers' clerk (*McMenamin (Inspector of Taxes) v Diggles* [1991] ICR 641).

2.39 In the case of policemen, in *Attorney General of New South Wales v Perpetual Trustee Co* [1955] AC 457, Lord Simonds said: 'His authority is original not delegated and is exercised at his own discretion by virtue of the office; he is a ministerial officer exercising statutory rights independent of contract' (see also *102 Social Club and Institute Ltd v Bickerton* [1977] ICR 911).

Crown servants

Crown servants are engaged under or for the purposes of a government department and **2.40**
this makes it a wider category than civil servants alone (*Wood v Leeds AHA* [1974] ICR
535, applied in *Marshall v Southampton and South West Hampshire HA* [1986] ICR 335
by the European Court of Justice). The main reason for distinguishing a separate category
of such workers is that it is still undecided whether they have a contract at all (see *Malins
v Post Office* [1975] ICR 60), because, at common law, the Crown is able to dismiss
at pleasure unless it is expressly otherwise provided by statute (*Gould v Stuart* [1896]
AC 575). The significance of this has declined with the growth of statutory employment
rights (see especially ERA 1996, s 191). In defining them for this purpose the statute talks
of their terms of employment, thus studiously avoiding any assumption of contract.

This important issue arose again in *R v Lord Chancellor's Department, ex p Nangle* **2.41**
[1991] ICR 743, when an executive grade civil servant sought judicial review of decisions
that complaints of sexual harassment against him were well founded. The application was
dismissed on the bases that:

(a) the proper question on whether the parties had entered into legal relations was not
    what the parties themselves believed but an objective construction of the documents
    by which the applicant was appointed, and the Civil Service Pay and Conditions of
    Service Code showed that the parties had entered into obligations, rights, and entitle-
    ments consistent with a contract of employment;
(b) therefore the documents were to be construed as creating a contract of employment; and
(c) even if there were no legal relationship the mere absence of a private law remedy did
    not give rise to public law relief.

The Divisional Court thus declined to follow its previous decision in *R v Civil Service
Appeal Board, ex p Bruce* [1988] ICR 649, and decided that civil servants do work under
contracts of employment.

The position of Crown servants has received specific treatment since 1988 in relation to **2.42**
strike action. The root of most legal proceedings to restrain industrial action is a breach
of the contract of employment. Since it is not clear whether Crown servants had contracts
of employment of which a breach might be induced, s 245 of the TULR(C)A 1992 deems
Crown servants to have such contracts but only for the purpose of the economic torts.

Apprentices

Apprenticeship is a relationship which consists of more than employment, since the **2.43**
apprentice agrees to be engaged for the purpose also of learning and the master agrees to
teach the apprentice. Many old rules surrounding apprenticeships, such as the master's
duty to provide medical care and right to chastise, apply to the institution which is much
less widely adopted now than in former years. It is now included in most statutory definitions of employment (ERA 1996, s 230(2)) and has the same consequences for vicarious
liability.

Students, cadets, and youth schemes

Some others provide services only to a limited degree, which are *ancillary* to their main **2.44**
role of learning. Thus, a student's essays for his tutor are not services in this sense, however hard he labours on them, and even though he has some sort of contract with the
university it is not one of service. The same applies to a research student who is engaged

on a specific project (*Hugh-Jones v St John's College, Cambridge* [1979] ICR 848) and a police cadet (*Wiltshire Police Authority v Wynn* [1980] ICR 649. On special constables, see *Sheikh v Chief Constable of Greater Manchester Police* [1989] 2 All ER 684).

2.45 A similar result was reached in *Daley v Allied Suppliers* [1983] IRLR 14, in which it was held that a person taking part in a work experience scheme as part of the then Youth Opportunities Programme was not a person employed within the meaning of the then Race Relations Act 1976. There was no contract binding the applicants and respondents together notwithstanding that they owed *some* obligations towards each other. If there were a contract it was one of training, enabling the applicant to acquire certain skills and experience (see to the same effect *Hawley v Fieldcastle & Co Ltd* [1982] IRLR 223).

Labour only sub-contractors and casual workers

2.46 Especially common in the building industry is the practice of the 'lump', whereby an individual contractor supplies his labour to complete a job and is paid in a lump sum on completion of that job. Such workers often move on and off the 'cards' (ie from employment to this form of self-employment and back again) with regularity, performing the same work in both capacities. This is done with the acquiescence of the 'hirers', the main contractors, who thereby have less administrative paperwork and do not pay secondary national insurance contributions or industrial training levies.

2.47 The treatment of casual workers generally has been the subject of several important cases at high levels of authority. The most detailed discussion of the position of casual workers is found in the Court of Appeal's judgment in *O'Kelly v Trusthouse Forte plc* [1983] 3 WLR 605. The appellants worked as wine butlers at the Grosvenor House Hotel. They were known as 'regular casuals' and were given preference in the work rotas over other casual staff. They had no other employment. The employment tribunal found that many factors were consistent with a contract of service but one thing was missing, mutuality of obligation. The respondent had no obligation to provide work, and if the workers could obtain alternative work, they were free to take it. The preferential rota position was not a contractual promise. Their Lordships were not attracted by the proposition that there was in fact a series of short contracts of service. Even if there was an umbrella contract that created a permanent relationship despite the intermittent nature of the performance of work, that umbrella contract was not one of employment.

Agency workers

2.48 A growing sector of the economy is manned by agency workers. There are some 1.5 million people who gain work through agencies.

2.49 They are unlikely to be made expressly employees of the employment agency, especially when they work on a temporary basis. In *Wickens v Champion Employment* [1984] ICR 365, the main considerations militating against employee status for agency workers were that the agency had no obligation to find work for its workers and the contracts did not create a relationship with the necessary elements of continuity and care (see also *Ironmonger v Movefield Ltd t/a Deering Appointments* [1988] IRLR 461). This may not, however, apply to a specific engagement which has been entered into under a temporary worker's general terms of employment with an employment agency. For the purposes of the specific engagement, a temporary worker may thus be an employee of the agency even though he is not an employee with respect to his general terms of employment by the agency (*McMeechan v Secretary of State for Employment* [1997]

ICR 549). Agency labour may be used to cover sudden increases in demand. There are special provisions to accommodate this in that s 41 of the Equality Act 2010 renders the end user ('the principal') subject to the duty not to discriminate. Article 4(1) of the EU Temporary Agency Work Directive provides that 'prohibitions or restrictions on the use of temporary agency work shall be justified only on grounds of general interest relating in particular to the protection of temporary agency workers, the requirements of health and safety at work or the need to ensure that the labour market functions properly and abuses are prevented'.

These relationships may be highly complex and difficult to unravel. In *Motorola Ltd v*   **2.50**
Davidson [2001] IRLR 4, Mr Davidson responded to an advertisement for jobs as analysers to repair mobile telephones with Motorola at their plant in Bathgate. The recruitment process was carried out by Melville Craig Group Ltd, which had an operating agreement with Motorola for the supply of temporary workers. Mr Davidson was taken on by Melville Craig and assigned to work at Motorola's site. Under the terms of his contract he was bound to comply with all reasonable instructions and requests by Motorola. The Employment Appeal Tribunal held that the tribunal was correct in deciding that Motorola had a sufficient degree of control over Mr Davidson that he could probably be regarded as their employee in circumstances in which, although the appellant had no direct legal right of control under a contract which they had made with him, he was bound by the terms of his contract with the employment agency who then assigned his service to Motorola to comply with all reasonable instructions and requests made. It was appropriate to consider practical aspects of control that fell short of legal rights.

In certain circumstances, an offer of work by an employment agency, even at another's   **2.51**
workplace, which is accepted by the individual but the remuneration is to be paid by the agency, could satisfy the requirement of mutual obligation. Whether in any given situation significant control exists to constitute the one party as the employer is a matter for the tribunal to decide on the facts. There must, however, be a contractual nexus of some kind between employee and putative employer for the relationship of employment to be found to exist (*Hewlett Packard Ltd v O'Murphy* [2002] IRLR 4). According to *Franks v Reuters Ltd* [2003] ICR 1188, the tribunal has to consider not only the relevant documents but also the complete picture including the surrounding circumstances, the subsequent conduct of the parties, and the way in which the parties operated and understood the situation (*Stephenson v Delphi Diesel Systems Ltd* [2003] ICR 471; *Dacas v Brook Street Bureau (UK) Ltd* [2004] IRLR 358).

The question to be asked in a tripartite setting is usually whether it is necessary to imply   **2.52**
mutual contractual obligations between the end user to provide the worker with work and the worker to perform the work for the end user and, on the facts in *James v LB of Greenwich* [2008] IRLR 302, it was held that there was not. Ms James worked for the council as a housing support worker but she obtained the post through an employment agency. It was unnecessary to imply a contract in order to explain why the worker was supplying services to the client and why the agency paid the worker.

The Conduct of Employment Agencies Regulations 2003 requires employment agencies to   **2.53**
specify in a contract the employment status (or otherwise) of any individual who obtains work through the agency. The Agency Workers Regulations are considered elsewhere.

Unincorporated associations and workers' cooperatives

The identity of the employer may be problematic where there is not a corporate employer.   **2.54**
In general, such workers are employed by the relevant management committee and

its members are as constituted from time to time (*Affleck v Newcastle Mind* [1999] IRLR 405).

2.55 The Employment Appeal Tribunal in *Drym Fabricators Ltd v Johnson* [1981] ICR 274 considered that workers involved in a cooperative which is registered as a limited company are likely to be employees. A different result was, however, reached in the case of orchestras which functioned as musical cooperatives, since the musicians were entitled to do other work and effectively provided services in business on their own account. They were subjecting themselves to self-discipline in the orchestra rather than control in the recognised sense of employer direction (*Addison v London Philharmonic Orchestra* [1981] ICR 261).

Directors

2.56 A director is an officer of his company but may also (and usually does) have a contract of service, whether an express service agreement or one implied at law. In *Albert J. Parsons & Sons Ltd v Parsons* [1979] ICR 271, the Court of Appeal held that there was no contract of employment in the case of a full-time working director who was paid by director's fees only and had not been treated as employed for purposes of national insurance. In *Eaton v Robert Eaton Ltd and Secretary of State for Employment* [1988] IRLR 83, in which the EAT held that the applicant director was not an employee of the respondent, Kilner Brown J said that the main factors in determining the question were:

(a) the use of any descriptive term such as managing director;
(b) whether there was an express contract of employment or a board minute constituting an agreement to employ;
(c) whether remuneration was by way of salary as opposed to director's fee;
(d) whether that remuneration was fixed in advance rather than paid on an *ad hoc* basis;
(e) whether remuneration was by way of entitlement rather than gratuitous; and
(f) the function actually performed by the director.

2.57 An important issue is whether the director is a majority shareholder (see *Fleming v Secretary of State for Trade and Industry* [1997] IRLR 682, Ct of Sess, and *Secretary of State for Trade and Industry v Bottrill* [1999] ICR 592 CA), but this is not decisive of the result. The employment tribunal should not attach a significance to that fact which excludes proper consideration of all other relevant factors.

2.58 The facts that a person had skills as an entrepreneur and stood to gain if a company prospered were not inimical to his being an employee according to the Court of Appeal in *Connolly v Sellers Arenascene Ltd* [2001] ICR 760. The employment tribunal was also wrong to find that the fact that the company's banker required the claimant to remain with the group as controlling shareholder had any bearing on the issue.

2.59 The tribunal may disregard a purported contract of employment between a company and controlling shareholder where the company is a sham and where the contract was entered into for an ulterior purpose, such as to secure statutory payment from the Secretary of State, or where the parties do not in fact conduct their relationship in accordance with the contract (*Clark v Clark Construction Initiatives Ltd* [2008] IRLR 364). That may be because they never really intended that it should be so conducted or because the relationship has ceased to reflect the contractual terms (see also *Nesbitt v Secretary of State for Trade & Industry* [2007] IRLR 847).

2.60 The Companies Act 2006 made major changes to the requirements in relation to the contracts of directors. Section 227 introduces a definition of 'directors' service contract' which is common to the whole of Pt 10 of the Act which deals with fair dealing by directors. The definition includes letters of appointment to the office of director. There are exemptions for contracts requiring a director to work outside the United Kingdom and for contracts with less than twelve months to run.

A term of notice two years or longer cannot be agreed by a company unless it has been **2.61** approved by resolution of the members of the company and, where the director is director of a holding company, by resolution of members of that company (ss 188–9 CA 2006). The significant change from the previous legislation is the length of the guaranteed term which needs approval by resolution—this used to be five years but has been reduced to two. This change is designed to bring the statutory rules into line with modern corporate governance recommendations that directors' contracts be renewed annually, or at least bi- or tri-annually.

A provision agreed by a company in breach of s 188 will be void to the extent of the con- **2.62** travention, and the contract will be deemed to contain a term entitling the company to terminate it at any time by the giving of reasonable notice (s 189).

If more than six months before the end of the guaranteed term of a director's employ- **2.63** ment the company enters into a further service contract (other than a right arising out of the original contract), the section applies as if there were added to the guaranteed term of the new contract the unexpired period of the guaranteed term of the original contract (s 188(4)).

Partners

A partner is not an employee of his firm (*Palumbo v Stylianou* (1966) 1 ITR 407 and **2.64** *Cowell v Quilter Goodison Ltd* [1989] IRLR 392).

Merchant seamen

Merchant seamen used to be governed by a totally different regime from other workers. **2.65** The antique procedures of the Merchant Shipping Act 1894 have been partially reformed by the Merchant Shipping Acts 1970 and 1988.

D DEFINITION OF WORKERS

Since the mid-1970s some statutory provisions have extended to the employed and self- **2.66** employed alike, and this is becoming more common, especially in rights derived from EU law. Moreover, the Equality Act 2010 prohibits discrimination against those employed 'under a contract of service or of apprenticeship or personally to execute any work or labour' (see *Mirror Group Newspapers Ltd v Gunning* [1986] IRLR 27).

A worker may claim: national minimum wage; WTR rights; not to be discriminated **2.67** against on grounds of trade union membership or for working part-time; agency worker rights; the right to be accompanied at a disciplinary or grievance hearing; and rights of the whistleblower and in respect of health and safety.

To be a worker there must be a contract with another party and there was not between **2.68** a bishop and a priest of the Church of England (*Sharpe v Worcester Diocesan Board of Finance Ltd* [2015] ICR 1241, see above). Further, a person was held not to be a worker in *Community Dental Centres Ltd v Sultan-Darmon* [2010] IRLR 1024, when there was no mutuality of obligation; no obligation to perform services personally; and an unfettered right to appoint a substitute in the case of a dentist.

2.69 The former Wages Act 1986 (now ERA 1996, Pt II) applies to contracts of service, apprenticeships or 'any other contract ... whereby the individual undertakes to do or perform personally any work or services for another party to the contract whose status is not by virtue of the contract that of a client or customer of any profession or business undertaking carried on by the individual' (ERA 1996, s 230(3); see also the TULR(C)A 1992, s 296(1); *Carter v Law Society* [1973] ICR 113). To be a profession, it is not necessary that there be some form of regulation by a supervisory body (*R (on application of BBC) v CAC* [2003] IRLR 460) but this is an issue that can be taken into account. A worker may include a member of a profession (*Sadek v MPS* [2005] IRLR 57) but it would not cover a painter and decorator who was taxed under the Construction Industry Scheme, had business accounts prepared by an accountant, was free to work for others and had in fact done so, and who received an hourly rate which included an allowance for overheads (*Bacica v Muir* [2006] IRLR 35). The EAT said that the definition of worker would normally exclude those who are self-employed (also *Cotswold Developments Construction Ltd v Williams* [2006] IRLR 181). A limited liability partner was a worker as she undertook to perform personally certain work (*Bates Van Winkelhof v Clyde & Co LLP* [2014] ICR 730). The requirement of subordination was rejected. Lady Hale said that the subordination requirement in *Jivraj* was 'introduced in order to distinguish the intermediate category [of workers] from people who were dealing with clients or customers on their own account'.

The client exception

2.70 As to whether a person was within the exception for a client, see the case of a hair restoration surgeon in *Hospital Medical Group Ltd v Westwood* [2013] ICR 415. Although Dr Westwood, who provided advice and treatment to patients suffering from hair loss, ran his own business he was 'integrated' into the clinic's work in that he was presented by Hospital Medical Group as 'its' surgeon and because it was an abuse of language to describe the Group as a customer or client of Dr Westwood's business.

2.71 Since a worker must 'perform personally' his services, the definition has been held to exclude:

(a) anyone who agrees to perform a task but can then delegate it to another (*Broadbent v Crisp* [1974] ICR 248);

(b) persons such as writers who undertake no obligation to produce any work (*Writers' Guild of Great Britain v BBC* [1974] ICR 234); and

(c) sub-postmasters since they have the choice whether or not to do the work themselves; in any event they are carrying on a business undertaking (*Commissioners of Inland Revenue v Post Office Ltd* [2003] IRLR 199).

2.72 It is not correct to view all those who are non-employees as being in business on their own account: *James v Redcats (Brands) Ltd* [2007] IRLR 296. Mutuality of obligation is not relevant to the existence of a 'contract personally to do work' (*Windle v Secretary of State for Justice* [2015] ICR 156). However, a restriction was put on the extent of the concept in *Jivraj v Hashwani* [2011] ICR 1004. This concerned an arbitrator and whether insistence on his being part of a particular religious group was lawful. The Supreme Court decided that the relationship had to require subordination, whereas an arbitrator was an independent provider of services.

Section 23 of the Employment Relations Act 1999 gives wide power to the Secretary of **2.73**
State to confer any employment rights on individuals 'who are of a specified description'.
Thus, the definition of those who can claim unfair dismissal could be significantly widened to include independent contractors or anyone carrying out work requiring personal
service. This also applies to other rights conferred by the TULR(C)A 1992, the ERA
1996, the ERA 1999, and s 2(2) of the European Communities Act 1972. As yet no date
has been set for implementation.

The European approach

The CJEU has produced a European definition of worker as a 'person employed to provide **2.74**
services under the direction of another'. In the leading case of *Lawrie-Blum v Land Baden-
Württemberg* [1986], ECLI:EU:C:1986:284, the Court decided that 'the essential feature
of an employment relationship ... is that for a certain period of time a person performs
services for and under the direction of another person for which he receives remuneration'
(see also *Danosa v LKB Līzings* [2011] 2 CMLR 2).

Further, for European purposes it includes a company director (*Balkaya v Kiesel* **2.75**
Abbruch– und Recycling Technik GmbH [2015] ICR 1110; see also *Fenoll v Centre
d'aide par le travail La Jouvene* [2016] IRLR 67; *Holterman Ferho Explotatie BV v Spies
Von Büllesheim* [2016] IRLR 140).

For religion and belief the European jurisprudence drew a clear distinction between those **2.76**
who were in substance employed and those who were independent providers of services
who were not in a relationship of subordination with the person who received the services; an arbitrator's role was that of an independent provider of services (*Hashwani v
Jivraj* [2011] ICR 1004).

E QUESTION OF LAW OR FACT?

There is an important issue as to the extent to which the question of employment status is **2.77**
one of fact or law as this governs the degree to which the higher courts will intervene to
correct a decision. Browne LJ in *Ferguson v John Dawson & Partners (Contractors) Ltd*
[1976] 1 WLR 1213 was firmly of the view that it was an issue of fact and thus not open
to challenge on appeal. The Court of Appeal authority suggests that the question is one
of law but that it involves matters of degree and fact which are essentially for the employment tribunal to determine (*O'Kelly v Trusthouse Forte plc* [1983] 3 WLR 605; *Clifford
v Union of Democratic Mineworkers* [1991] IRLR 518). In *Nethermere (St Neots) Ltd v
Taverna and Gardiner* [1984] IRLR 240, the Court of Appeal applied the administrative
law test to the effect that the EAT could not interfere with a tribunal's decision unless it
had misdirected itself in law or its decision was one which no tribunal properly directing
itself on the relevant facts could have reached (also *Warner Holidays Ltd v Secretary of
State for Social Services* [1983] ICR 440). See also *Davies v Presbyterian Church of Wales*
[1986] IRLR 194; *Lee Ting Sang v Chung Chi-Keung* [1990] ICR 409; *Andrews v King*
[1991] ICR 846.

In *McLeod v Hellyer Brothers Ltd* [1987] IRLR 232 (for the facts see **2.10**, above), the **2.78**
question of whether the appellants were employees depended partly on the interpretation
of various written documents and partly on inferences to be drawn from the parties' conduct. The appellate court was thus entitled to interfere with the decision of the employment tribunal only if the tribunal had misdirected itself in law or the decision was one
which no tribunal properly instructed could have reached. The Court of Appeal did not

consider the reasoning of the majority in *O'Kelly*'s case to be overruled by the House of Lords in the *Davies* case, which applied where the case turned entirely on the construction of a document and as a matter of law there was only one correct answer (see also *Santokh Singh v Guru Nanak Gurdwara* [1990] ICR 309 and *McMeechan v Secretary of State for Employment* [1997] ICR 549).

2.79 There are two new classes of worker which are necessitated by recent legislation: employee shareholders and zero hours contracts.

Employee shareholders

2.80 Employee shareholders may give up major employment rights in exchange for shares in the employer company. The rights which may be signed away are the right not to be unfairly dismissed (with exceptions for discriminatory dismissals), the right to redundancy pay, and the right to request flexible working. Those rights derived from EU law cannot be waived. They may have to give longer notice in some circumstances such as returning after maternity. The quid pro quo is that the employee receives at least £2,000 worth of shares in the employing company. The employee must have received independent legal advice before taking up the status and should be given a seven-day period to reconsider (s 205A ERA, inserted by the Growth and Infrastructure Act 2013).

Zero hours contracts

2.81 A new s 27A ERA implemented by the Small Business, Enterprise and Employment Act 2015 defines for the first time zero hours contracts as a contract

under which

(a) the undertaking to do or perform work or services is an undertaking to do so conditionally on the employer making work available to the worker and

(b) there is no certainty that any such work or services will be made available to the worker.

2.82 The only special provision for this type of contract is that by s 27A(3) any provision is unenforceable which prohibits the worker working for another whether at all or without the employer's consent.

2.83 A zero hours contract means that the employee promises to be ready and available for work but the employer only promises to pay for the time actually worked as the employer requires.

3

THE INDIVIDUAL CONTRACT
OF EMPLOYMENT AND ITS SOURCES

A THE COLLECTIVE BARGAIN 3.04

The effect of the collective bargain
on the individual contract of
employment 3.06

The basis of incorporation 3.10

Termination of collective agreement 3.14

Terms which are inappropriate for
incorporation 3.16

Incorporation of no-strike clauses 3.19

Levels of bargaining 3.20

B IMPLIED TERMS 3.21

C RULES OF EMPLOYMENT 3.36

D CUSTOM AND PRACTICE 3.40

E STATUTE 3.43

F AWARDS 3.44

G CAPACITY 3.45

H FORMATION AND VARIATION
OF CONTRACT 3.46

Formation of contract of employment . . .3.46

Intention to create legal relations 3.51

Construction of the contract 3.52

Variation 3.54

I THE EFFECT ON CONTRACT OF A TRANSFER
OF UNDERTAKING 3.61

J WRITTEN STATEMENT OF TERMS 3.62

The details 3.62

Supplementary provisions 3.65

The status of the statement 3.69

Remedy for failure to supply written
statement of terms 3.75

> The modern model of the employment contract, as a voluntary consensual relationship sanctioned by the civil law, is suffused with an individualism that ignores the economic reality behind the bargain. (KW Wedderburn, *The Worker and the Law*, Penguin, 1986, 3rd edn at 142.)

3.01 The contract of employment, although one of the most important of all legal agreements, is also one of the most informal and formless. This is partly because it is virtually impossible to cover all issues which may arise at work in a document, and partly derives from the trade union movement's traditional suspicion of legally drawn express bargains (although this has reduced in recent years). There is also the continuation of informal hiring practices (eg *Ferguson v John Dawson & Partners (Contractors) Ltd* [1976] 1 WLR 1213). Although the general contractual principles apply, they have to be modified to some degree to take into account the formless nature of the agreement and the inequality of bargaining power between employer and employee and that they carry on for a long time. Often of more significance than the formal contract is what is known as the psychological contract, that is the understandings which underlie it. As has been said, the classical model of parties negotiating the terms of agreement 'is discordant with social practice' (Collins, Ewing, & McColgan, *Labour Law*, CUP, 2012, at 99). Only those with scarcity value or special talents are likely to be able to negotiate their own pay and benefits.

3.02 Most workers do not bargain individually with the employer at all; instead they have to take what terms are offered to them. The relationship is thus in truth one of subordination, partially or wholly—forced acceptance of the employer's terms if the employee wants the job, except where he has a strong bargaining position due to scarcity, high status, or qualifications. In those cases detailed service agreements are the norm. Otherwise the employee is unlikely to receive more than a short paper or letter setting out his terms and conditions. Most contracts are standard in form and in effect, but may derive from and incorporate several other documents and be drawn from many sources. Further, the courts have formulated many implied terms to supplement the express terms of the employment relationship, and there are many laws which are protective of employees and which operate by incorporating terms into the contract of employment (eg guarantee pay, minimum wages, equal pay). Within most employment relationships there will be an express, oral, or written contract which is then supplemented by important implied terms.

3.03 In this chapter, we examine the several sources of the terms of the contract of employment. We will then consider:

(a) the capacity to make the contract;
(b) the formation of the contract;
(c) the effect of a takeover; and
(d) the written statement of terms.

A THE COLLECTIVE BARGAIN

> A collective agreement is a treaty between social powers. It is ... a peace treaty and at the same time a normative treaty. (O Kahn-Freund, *Labour and the Law*, Sweet & Maxwell, 1983, 3rd edn at 123.)

3.04 The most important terms in the employee's contract derive for many workers not from an individual bargain with his employer but from a collective agreement entered into by a union recognised for this purpose at his place of work. The importance of this element has, however, declined in recent years as has union density, especially in the private sector.

3.05 Very often an individual's statement of terms will do no more than refer him to the relevant collective agreement which is likely to deal with, in particular, wages, hours, holidays, and the guaranteed week, as its most important substantive rules. This is its legislative or normative function, but it also has another important aspect concerning relations between the union and the employer, including negotiating rights, grievance procedures, and also a means for renegotiating the agreement, usually at fixed intervals. Notwithstanding the decline in trade union membership, 64 per cent of public sector workers and 17 per cent of private sector employees had pay set by collective bargaining in 2013 (BIS, *Trade Union Membership 2013*).

The effect of the collective bargain on the individual contract of employment

3.06 The unions and employers cannot sue each other on the collective bargain save in the rare cases in which the parties agree that the terms are enforceable at law or under Sch A1 to the Trade Union and Labour Relations (Consolidation) Act (TULR(C)A) 1992, which provides that collective agreements for recognition are legally enforceable but that the only remedy will be specific performance (see further 19.81). In any event, the terms may still be legally binding between employer and employee on an individual basis, although the law is somewhat pragmatic as to how and why such incorporation is achieved. There must be some 'bridge' between the collective bargain and individual contract for its incorporation into the latter, and this is often achieved by way of express reference in the actual contract or in the written statement of terms. Thus, in *National Coal Board v Galley* [1958] 1 WLR 16, the individual contract fairly typically provided 'wages shall be regulated by such national agreement and the county wages agreement for the time being in force and this agreement shall be subject to these agreements and to any other agreements relating to or in connection with or subsidiary to the wages agreement'. This also means that the contract need not be amended every time that such negotiations take place.

Incorporation will be readily implied from the universal observance of the collective **3.07** bargain in the employee's workplace, even though the individual employee may neither know of the pact, nor be a member of the union which negotiates it. There will frequently be no other basis for the employment, but regular observance by itself is not always decisive. Knowledge of the terms by the particular employee is usually not necessary so long as the terms can be ascertained (see *Marley v Forward Trust Group Ltd* [1986] IRLR 369).

Although most basic employment terms will usually be covered in the collective bargain, **3.08** the absence of an issue even in a broad collective bargain does not raise an inference that there has been an omission which is so obvious that it should be incorporated into individual contracts of employment. In these circumstances, the implication to be drawn may be, rather, that the issue which has been omitted was too controversial or complicated to justify its incorporation in the collective bargain (*Ali v Christian Salvesen Food Services Limited* [1997] IRLR 17).

Consideration will normally be spelt out quite readily. In *Lee v GEC Plessey* **3.09** *Telecommunications* [1993] IRLR 383, there was held to be sufficient consideration for the introduction of an enhanced severance package in that thereafter the employee continued in the employment of the employer, thereby abandoning any argument that the increase should have been greater and removing a potential area of dispute between employer and employee.

The basis of incorporation

While it is prima facie attractive from a conceptual standpoint to view the union as **3.10** bargaining as an agent for its members, the practical problem is that this would restrict the union to acting only on behalf of employees for the time being, thus implying that a later hired worker was not so bound. There would also be a serious difficulty if a union member as a principal purported to withdraw his authority from the union to act as his agent on a particular issue (see generally *Heaton's Transport Ltd v TGWU* [1972] ICR 308; *Singh v British Steel Corporation* [1974] IRLR 131; *Harris v Richard Lawson Autologistics Ltd* [2002] ICR 765). The courts have thus been reluctant to find the solution to the problem in an express relationship of agency. The underlying question is: Did the parties intend to incorporate relevant parts of the collective agreement into the individual's contract? (*Alexander v STC Ltd No 2* [1991] IRLR 287).

In *Holland v London Society of Compositors* (1924) 40 TLR 440, Lush J held that the **3.11** union acts as a principal and not its members' agent in bargaining. But Arnold J voiced the most widespread view when he said in *Burton Group Ltd v Smith* [1977] IRLR 351, at para 21:

> There is no reason at all why, in a particular case, union representatives should not be the agent of an employee to make a contract, or to receive a notice, or otherwise effect a binding transaction on his behalf. But that agency does not stem from the mere fact that they

are union representatives and that he is a member of the union; it must be supported in the particular case by the creation of some specific agency.

(See eg *Deane v Craik*, The Times, 16 March 1962.) It is also generally recognised that non-unionists as well as union members are covered by an effective collective bargain, unlike in the United States. The most pragmatic approach is that collective bargains are implied into individual contracts by way of conduct (*Hill v Levey* (1858) 157 ER 366, Watson B), or as Professor Kahn-Freund has put it, that they become 'crystallised custom'. In the case of informal hiring, there may be no other possible terms which could be applied (see *Kenny v Vauxhall Motors Ltd* [1985] ICR 535; *National Coal Board v National Union of Mineworkers* [1986] IRLR 439).

3.12 Collective bargains are not, however, automatically to be incorporated into the individual contract merely because the employer is a member of an employers' association which is party to the collective agreement in the absence of a custom in the trade that such terms would be observed (*Hamilton v Futura Floors* [1990] IRLR 478; *Henry v London General Transport Services Ltd* [2002] IRLR 472).

3.13 An indirect effect of the collective bargain is illustrated by *Gray Dunn and Co Ltd v Edwards* [1980] IRLR 23, where it was held that where employers negotiate a detailed agreement with a recognised union (here concerning a disciplinary code), they are entitled to assume that all unionised employees know of and are bound by its provisions. The Court of Appeal thought that 'there could be no stability in industrial relations if this were not so'. British collective bargains do not, however, operate as a code, as do most Continental systems, so that it is possible for individual employees to have terms less favourable to the employee than those provided for in the agreement between union and management.

Termination of collective agreement

3.14 Where a collectively bargained bonus scheme (or any other provision) has been incorporated into the individual contract of employment, the employer cannot unilaterally determine that scheme (*Robertson v British Gas Corporation* [1983] ICR 351; *Glendale Managed Services v Graham* [2003] IRLR 465). On the other hand, in *Gibbons v Associated British Ports* [1985] IRLR 376, the termination of a collective agreement had no effect at all on the terms of remuneration incorporated into an individual's contract of employment. The inescapable conclusion was that the collectively agreed six-day guarantee, designed to compensate dock workers for loss of profitable shift work, was an integral part of the term of remuneration.

3.15 On a transfer of an undertaking, whether by sale or some other disposition or by operation of law, the transferee company is obliged to observe the terms of any collective bargain which has been negotiated by the transferor (Transfer of Undertakings (Protection of Employment) Regulations 2006) (see Chapter 18).

Terms which are inappropriate for incorporation

3.16 Some terms of the collective bargain are not susceptible to 'translation' into the individual contract, because they relate to obligations which have been entered into by the union collectively, such as union recognition (*Gallagher v Post Office* [1970] 3 All ER 714), or redundancy procedure. Thus, in *British Leyland UK Ltd v McQuilken* [1978] IRLR 245, the appellant company agreed with the union representing the majority of its workers on a phased discontinuance of its experimental department in Glasgow. Skilled employees would have a choice of retraining or redundancy. Some workers who had chosen the latter later changed their minds, and the employees claimed that the employer was breaking their contracts by infringing the collective bargain. Lord McDonald held, however, that the collective implied agreement 'was a long-term plan dealing with policy rather than the rights of individual employees under their contract of employment'. The court looked for authority to a 1930s Privy Council decision that an agreement between a Canadian railway company and a trade union providing, in a redundancy situation, for staff with the shortest service to be dismissed first, was not part of the individual contract (*Young v Canadian Northern Railway Co* [1931] AC 83), since '[this agreement] does not appear to be a document adapted for conversion into or incorporation with a service agreement'. The courts draw a distinction between terms in a collective agreement which are designed and intended to govern the relationship between the employer and the union which are not incorporated, and those designed and intended to benefit individuals which may be incorporated (*NCB v NUM*, above; *Alexander v STC plc* [1990] ICR 291; *Kaur v MG Rover Group Ltd* [2005] IRLR 40; *BALPA v Jet 2* [2016] IRLR). There may, for example, be some parts of a disciplinary policy which are inapt for incorporation: *Lakshmi v Mid Cheshire Hospital NHS Trust* [2008] IRLR 956; *Harlow v Artemis Int Corp Ltd* [2008] IRLR 629.

These two cases illustrate the general principles applied to the interplay of collective agreements and individual contracts: **3.17**

(a) A collective agreement between the *Daily Telegraph* and the Institute of Journalists which established a disputes procedure and provided that it should be the only means of resolving a dispute between the parties was also held not to be incorporated into the individual contract of employment (*Tadd v Eastwood* [1983] IRLR 320).

(b) In *Cadoux v Central Regional Council* [1986] IRLR 131, the Court of Session decided that a provision for a non-contributory life assurance scheme was not a contractual right. The employee's letter of appointment recorded that 'the post is subject to the Conditions of Service laid down by the National Joint Council for Local Authorities, Administrative, Professional, Technical and Clerical Services (Scottish Council) and as supplemented by the Authorities' Rules and *as amended from time to time*'. When the council unilaterally withdrew the scheme, the plaintiff sought a declaration that he was contractually entitled to it. This was refused since the local authority's rules were made unilaterally and could be changed at will (see also *Airlie v City of Edinburgh District Council* [1996] IRLR 516).

In a specific elaboration of the principle in connection with air travel, a collective agreement headed 'Minimum planned crew complements' provided 'All services will be planned to the current industrially agreed complements for each aircraft type' and included a table setting out the crew numbers for each type of aircraft. The defendant unilaterally reduced crew complements. It was held that where these provisions were inherently vague or merely an expression of policy or aspiration or plainly dealt with such collective matters as conciliation arrangements they would not be apt for incorporation into individual contracts. While crew complements did impact to some extent on the working conditions of the employees, when set against the potentially disastrous effect on the business if an individual employee could with impunity refuse to fly without the agreed complement, it was not contractually binding as the parties could not have so intended it to be so (*Malone v BA* [2011] ICR 125). **3.18**

Incorporation of no-strike clauses

The only statutory modification of the rules of incorporation is s 180(1) of the TULR(C)A 1992, which severely restricts the binding inclusion in a collective agreement of clauses **3.19** which inhibit the taking of industrial action, or have the effect of doing so. These are very rarely found in practice in any event. Such a provision may be incorporated in the individual contract only if the following stringent conditions are satisfied:

(a) the collective agreement is in writing;
(b) it contains an express statement that such a clause is incorporated into the individual contract;
(c) it is reasonably accessible at the workplace and available during working hours;
(d) each trade union party to the agreement is independent (see 19.12 for definition); and
(e) the individual contract expressly or impliedly incorporates such a term.

Levels of bargaining

3.20 Where there are different levels of collective bargaining, the courts have tended to look at the national agreement for incorporation into the individual contract. The courts take this view probably because the national agreement is the more comprehensive and legal-appearing document. Thus, in *Loman and Henderson v Merseyside Transport Services Ltd* (1967) 3 KIR 726, the road haulage national agreement provided guaranteed weekly pay on the foundation of a 40-hour week, yet at the Barking depot of the respondent warehousing company a local agreement offered 68 hours. The Divisional Court, however, held that the latter was 'in the nature of a gentleman's agreement for ironing out local difficulties and providing an incentive for cooperation ...'. This was notwithstanding that the local agreement was much more directly effective, on the ground that employees who refused overtime would have been removed (but cf *Barrett v National Coal Board* [1978] ICR 1102 and *Saxton v National Coal Board* (1970) 6 ITR 196). In recent years major national agreements have declined in importance (see 19.02).

B IMPLIED TERMS

3.21 Professor M Freedland in *The Personal Employment Contract*, OUP, 2003, at 186, says that underlying the general principles governing the construction of contracts of employment it is useful to identify 'an overarching principle of fair management and performance'. Implied terms seek to cover the need to adapt to changing circumstances in what is envisaged to be a long-term relationship.

3.22 The classic exposition of the process of implication of contractual terms in contracts generally was given by MacKinnon LJ in *Shirlaw v Southern Foundries (1926) Ltd* [1939] 2 KB 206 at 227:

> Prima facie that which in any contract is left to be implied and need not be expressed is something so obvious that it goes without saying; so that, if, while the parties were making their bargain, an officious bystander were to suggest some express provision for it in their agreement, they would testily suppress him with a common 'Oh, of course!'.

3.23 This also accords with Bowen LJ's oft quoted *dictum* in *The Moorcock* (1889) 14 PD 64 (a commercial case), that an implied term must be 'founded on presumed intention and upon reason'. An alternative test provides for implication of terms which are 'necessary in the business sense to give efficacy to the contract' (*Reigate v Union Manufacturing Co Ltd* [1918] 1 KB 592 per Scrutton LJ; *Rutherford v Seymour Pierce Ltd* [2010] IRLR 606). In any case, the term must also be precise enough to be enforced by the courts (*Lister v Romford Ice and Cold Storage Co Ltd* [1957] AC 555; *Courtaulds Northern Spinning*

Ltd v Sibson and TGWU [1988] IRLR 305; see also *Johnson v Unisys Ltd* [2001] ICR 480 especially at paras 35, 77–9).

Certain standard implied terms have emerged in the employment area, because of the **3.24** essentially similar nature of all relationships between employer and employee. Whether the courts always concentrate on the intention of the parties as they profess to do is rather dubious, especially as the interests of employer and employee so widely and obviously diverge.

Professor O Kahn-Freund said 'It is however sheer utopia to postulate a common inter- **3.25** est in the substance of labour relations' (*Labour and the Law*, Sweet & Maxwell, 1983, 3rd edn at 28). Thus, the employee's implied duties of care, fidelity and coopera- tion may not, in fact, be expressly desired at all, but they are considered necessary to be implied by the courts (see *Howman & Son v Blyth* [1983] IRLR 139 on implication of reasonable terms, and *Liverpool CC v Irwin*, above). There was, moreover, until recently, little authority on some of the most important implied terms because litiga- tion in the civil courts on the contract of employment was relatively rare. The adoption of the breach of contract test for constructive unfair dismissal, however, stimulated the growth of important implied terms based on reasonable industrial practice in the employment tribunals, which will be considered later under that rubric (14.23). In recent years the rapid development of the implied term of trust and confidence has indeed done much to reform traditional notions of the contractual status of employees (see eg *Abbey National plc v Fairbrother* [2007] IRLR 320; *Claridge v Daler Rowney Ltd* [2008] ICR 1267).

The wide scope of implication may be gauged from the following decisions of high author- **3.26** ity in favour of implied terms that:

(a) Teachers have an implied duty to act professionally, which includes covering for ab- sent colleagues (*Sim v Rotherham Metropolitan Borough Council* [1986] ICR 897).
(b) The employer must notify employees of their rights under a complex pension scheme which had been negotiated between the relevant representative bodies when there was a valuable right contingent on action being taken by the employee to avail him- self of that benefit (*Scally v Southern Health and Social Services Board* [1991] ICR 771), but this does not mean that there is always a duty to take reasonable steps to bring to the attention of the employee the existence of a valuable right (*University of Nottingham v Eyett* [1999] IRLR 87) and this duty may be fulfilled by attaching let- ters to employees' payslips; the employer does not have to ensure that the information was actually communicated to the employee, merely to take reasonable steps to in- form him about his rights (*Ibekwe v London General Transport Services Ltd* [2003] IRLR 697). Further, there is no general duty on the employer to advise his employees (*Crossley v Faithful & Gould Holdings Ltd* [2004] IRLR 377).
(c) The employer will reasonably and promptly afford a reasonable opportunity to ob- tain redress of grievances (*Goold Ltd v McConnell* [1995] IRLR 516) but an em- ployer cannot be in breach of an implied duty to deal expeditiously with a grievance if that grievance has not been effectively communicated to him (*Sweetin v Coral Racing* [2006] IRLR 252).
(d) The employer must not deprive the employee of health insurance by the manner of the employee's dismissal or by the employer's actions subsequent to the employee leav- ing his position (*Adin v Sedco Forex International Resources Ltd* [1997] IRLR 280; *Brompton v AOC International Ltd* [1997] IRLR 638).
(e) The employer will provide and monitor for employees, so far as is reasonably practic- able, a working environment that is reasonably suitable for the performance by them

of their contractual duties (eg *Waltons and Morse v Dorrington* [1997] IRLR 488, which concerned a smoking ban).

(f) An employer must not, even in the case of a discretion that on the face of the contract is unfettered, act in such a way as no reasonable employer would act. In *Clark v Nomura International plc* [2000] IRLR 766, for example, the employer was in breach of contract by not awarding the claimant, a senior derivatives trader, a discretionary payment for the nine-month period prior to his dismissal during which he had earned profits for the company in excess of £6 million (see also *Commerzbank AG v Keen* [2007] IRLR 132).

(g) Once an employer had determined that an employee would be dismissed by reason of redundancy, such that dismissal for any other reason would defeat the employee's rights to contractual benefits which accrued when there was a redundancy dismissal, the employer could not dismiss for a reason other than redundancy, unless the dismissal was for good cause; otherwise it would deny the employee the benefits promised by the redundancy scheme (*Jenvey v Australian Broadcasting Corp* [2003] ICR 79; *Mallone v BPB Industries Ltd* [2002] ICR 1045).

(h) Where a contract provides that National Joint Council rates will normally be paid, the employer must inform the employee if and when there is to be a departure from the normal situation (*Glendale Managed Services v Graham* [2003] IRLR 465; cf *Reda v Flag Ltd* [2002] IRLR 747).

(i) To work at workplaces other than that to which the employee was assigned (*Luke v Stoke on Trent CC* [2007] IRLR 305).

(j) To take such action, as having regard to the availability of its human and financial resources may be reasonably practicable in the particular circumstances prevailing at the material time, to avoid either imposing a workload on the employee or acquiescing in the assumption by the employee of a workload that it was reasonably foreseeable may cause physical or mental injury (*Marshall Specialist Vehicles Ltd v Osborne* [2003] IRLR 672).

(k) The employer had a duty to take reasonable care for the claimant's economic well-being, which required it to alert the claimant to the effect that resigning would have on his entitlement to benefits under a long-term disability insurance scheme (*Crossley v Faithful & Gould Holdings Ltd* [2004] IRLR 377).

(l) An employee who used the disputes procedure negotiated between his union and employers would not sue any person who took part in those proceedings for defamation (*Tadd v Eastwood* [1983] IRLR 320).

(m) An employee must undergo a psychiatric examination (*Bliss v South East Thames Regional Health Authority* [1985] IRLR 308).

(n) Suspension could take place only after the employer provided the employee with full information as to the reason for the suspension and applied natural justice (*McClory v Post Office* [1993] IRLR 159). There was, however, an implied term that the employer's right to suspend would not be exercised on unreasonable grounds and that the suspension would continue only for so long as there were reasonable grounds for its so doing.

(o) A mobility clause was necessary in the contract of employment of a cashier for a frozen food chain, when there was no express mobility clause in her contract (*Aparau v Iceland Frozen Foods* [1996] IRLR 119).

(p) The employer should take reasonable steps to notify the employee of any unusual and onerous terms in the contract of employment (*Peninsula Business Services Ltd v Sweeney* [2004] IRLR 49).

The courts and tribunals have, however, refused to imply terms (either on the grounds of **3.27** unreasonableness or lack of common intention) that:

(a) the employer will indemnify the employee against liability in negligence (*Lister v Romford Ice and Cold Storage Co Ltd* [1957] AC 515);

(b) the employer will recognise a trade union for the purposes of collective bargaining (*Gallagher v Post Office* [1970] 2 All ER 712);

(c) the employee will work overtime because he has done so for the previous ten years (*Horrigan v Lewisham LBC* [1978] ICR 15);

(d) the employee has a right to strike (*Simmons v Hoover Ltd* [1977] ICR 61); and

(e) the employee has a generalised 'right to work' (see 4.53–4.57).

The duty of the employer to maintain trust and confidence with the employee must be **3.28** considered separately as it is one of the dynamic features of modern employment law. The House of Lords in *Malik v Bank of Credit and Commerce International SA (in compulsory liquidation)* [1997] IRLR 462 held in an application by the respondent to strike out the employees' statement of claim that it was a viable claim that the respondent had breached this term due to the corrupt and dishonest way in which it had operated, which had left the appellants with a stigma attached to their reputations. They contended that it was thus more difficult to find employment, notwithstanding the fact that they were themselves entirely innocent of wrongdoing. Lord Steyn said 'the implied obligation as formulated is apt to cover the great diversity of situations in which a balance has to be struck between an employer's interest in managing his business as he sees fit and the employee's interests in not being unfairly and improperly exploited'.

Accordingly, the appellants were held to be entitled to proceed to claim damages for the **3.29** financial loss which had been suffered by them, although after a full trial they failed to prove their case. *Malik* was subsequently applied in *French v Barclays Bank plc* [1998] IRLR 646, which concerned the respondent bank's withdrawal of a discretionary loan made to its employee.

If the employer acts in a way that is likely to destroy or seriously damage the relationship **3.30** of confidence and trust between employer and employee, the court should go on to ask whether there was a reasonable and proper cause for the behaviour (*Hilton v Shiner Ltd* [2001] IRLR 728; see also *BCCI v Ali (No 3)* [1999] IRLR 508). To establish a breach, the employee must show conduct by the employer 'which, objectively considered, is likely to seriously undermine the necessary trust and confidence in the employment relationship' (*Baldwin v Brighton & Hove City Council* [2007] IRLR 232, EAT).

There was under this head a breach of this term when: **3.31**

(a) the employer hastily suspended the employee in order to investigate allegations of sexual abuse (*Gogay v Herts CC* [2000] IRLR 703) and put forward allegations which were imprecise. The question to be asked is whether there is a reasonable and proper cause for the employer's action. Here, it was putting the matter too high to say there was even an allegation of sexual abuse; suspension was an immediate, knee-jerk reaction;

(b) an employer failed to notify the employee whilst she was on maternity leave of a vacancy for which she would have applied had she been aware of it (*Visa International Service Association v Paul* [2004] IRLR 42). It was irrelevant that she would not have been shortlisted for the post had she applied;

(c) an employee was told that she was likely to face dismissal but may instead resign on a generous resignation package (*Billington v Michael Hunter & Sons Ltd*

EAT, 16 October 2003; *Horkulak v Cantor Fitzgerald International* [2003] IRLR 756); and

(d) there was a disciplinary hearing and a request was made on apparently reasonable grounds for it to be adjourned, and the employer declined to adjourn it in the absence of good reason not to do so (*Lakshmi v Mid Cheshire Hospital NHS Trust* [2008] IRLR 956).

3.32 In many cases the breach of the implied duty of trust and confidence operates in advance of the dismissal, such as in the conduct of disciplinary or grievance hearings, but it is important that a dividing line be set down so as not to subvert the careful statutory scheme governing termination. In *Johnson v Unisys Ltd* [2001] ICR 480 the majority of the House of Lords held that the contractual duty of trust and confidence did not apply to the point of dismissal or the manner in which employment was terminated. Their Lordships reasoned that the implied term of trust and confidence is concerned with *preserving* the continuing relationship of employment and not linked to its termination. It is also inimical to the express term that a certain amount of notice may be given and it is against the intention of Parliament to provide such a remedy in addition to those for unfair dismissal.

3.33 This spawned much satellite litigation which was designed to draw the line between causes of action that constituted dismissal and those which operated during the course of employment where the implied term could be used. Thus, in *Eastwood v Magnox Electric plc* [2004] ICR 1064, the House of Lords decided that where an employee had acquired a common law cause of action in respect of the employer's failure to act fairly prior to his unfair dismissal, whether actual or constructive, such that it could be said to exist independently of his subsequent dismissal, and it led to financial loss, he could pursue that action for breach of an implied term. In the two cases before them, the House allowed these claims to proceed: (a) stress-related illness and inability to work alleged to have been caused by a campaign by the employers to demoralise the claimants; and (b) psychiatric injury caused by the employer following suspension and the failure during the next five months to inform the employee of allegations made against him or to carry out a proper investigation. There is, however, no breach of the duty of trust and confidence where the action consists in giving lawful notice of termination and an offer of immediate re-engagement (*Kerry Foods Ltd v Lynch* [2008] IRLR 680).

3.34 Express and implied terms must be capable of coexistence in the contract without coming into conflict (*Johnstone v Bloomsbury Health Authority* [1991] IRLR 118, [1991] ICR 269; *Aspden v Webbs Poultry & Meat Group (Holdings) Ltd* [1996] IRLR 521). Further, implied terms may always be excluded or modified by express agreement unless there is any relevant statutory restraint on this (see 3.36).

3.35 There is also a difference (although it may be a subtle distinction) between implying a term into a contract which negatives an express clause (which is not permitted) and implying one which controls the exercise of the employer's otherwise unfettered discretion which may occur. An example in the latter category would be the court controlling the express power of the employer to insist upon a move of the place of work by ensuring that the employer gives reasonable notice of any such change (*United Bank Ltd v Akhtar* [1989] IRLR 507; *Prestwick Circuits Ltd v McAndrew* [1990] IRLR 191).

C RULES OF EMPLOYMENT

3.36 Many companies produce detailed employment handbooks, which typically include disciplinary provisions but may also take in sickness, safety provisions, employee sports facilities, and holidays. They are usually given contractual effect by way of express or implied incorporation or custom and practice, and may be communicated by intranet, noticeboard, special handbook, sheet of paper, or even word of mouth. A typical format is where the employee signs a declaration that he accepts the conditions of employment as set out in the employment handbook, and such acceptance may be implied if the employee starts work and has reasonable notice of them. However, this depends on:

(a) the nature of the document, if any, in which the rules are communicated;
(b) the methods used to bring such document to the employees' attention; and
(c) whether notice was given before or at the time of the formation of the contract (*Jones v Associated Tunnelling Co Ltd* [1981] IRLR 477; see also *Courtaulds Northern Spinning Ltd v Sibson and TGWU* [1988] IRLR 305; *Aparau v Iceland Frozen Foods plc* [1996] IRLR 119).

The contents of employment handbooks are not, however, all to be treated as contractual **3.37** terms—some because, being uncertain and ambiguous like many collective bargains, they are not appropriate for incorporation, or otherwise because they are inherently variable, and solely within the prerogative of the employer.

In the leading case, *Secretary of State for Employment v ASLEF (No 2)* [1972] 2 QB **3.38** 455, the Court of Appeal had to determine whether the respondent union's 'work to rule' was in breach of contract. In disputing this, the union claimed that it was merely following the employer's rule book to the letter. The Court of Appeal held, however, that the rules of British Rail, which contained a mass of detailed instructions in 239 rules on 280 pages, were not all contractually binding. Some were clearly out of date, others trivial. Generally, Lord Denning MR said:

> Each man signs a form saying that he will abide by the rules, but these rules are in no way terms of the contract of employment. They are only instructions to a man as to how he is to do his work.

The employer might thus alter the rules at will and the boundaries of his prerogative are thereby increased. If the employee refuses to obey a changed rule he might still, however, be lawfully dismissed at common law and (depending on all the circumstances) probably fairly dismissed by statute. The employee must obey lawful and reasonable orders (see 4.42–4.45).

It may confidently be assumed, however, that those sections of work rule books which **3.39** deal with particulars which are required to be set out in the statutory statement of terms will be part of the contract. Otherwise the test to be applied is what the parties intend to be contractual terms. In *Petrie v MacFisheries* [1940] 1 KB 258, a notice about sick pay posted on the factory notice board was held to have contractual effect, even though the employees had never had their attention specifically drawn to it; while in *Dryden v Greater Glasgow Health Board* [1992] IRLR 469, EAT, a smoking ban was held to be a work rule, with the result that the employee could not claim that the ban constituted a material breach of her contract of employment (see also *Wandsworth London Borough Council v D'Silva* [1998] IRLR 193, CA; *Grant v South-West Trains Limited* [1998] IRLR 188, QBD; and 4.48–4.51).

D CUSTOM AND PRACTICE

Many day-to-day features of employment, and the way things are done in the workplace, **3.40** office, or factory, are governed as much by long-held custom and practice as by express contractual terms. Indeed, most terms were reached in this way in the nineteenth century before collective bargaining took over in many cases.

3.41 To be legally recognised by the courts, a custom must be 'reasonable, certain and notorious', and a term will be implied by custom only if there is nothing in the express or necessarily implied terms of the contract to prevent such inclusion (*London Export Corp v Jubilee Coffee Roasting Co* [1958] 2 All ER 411). The custom must be proved by the party asserting it on the balance of probabilities. In the leading case of *Sagar v Ridehalgh & Son Ltd* [1931] 1 Ch 310, the Court of Appeal decided that customary deductions from a weaver's wages which had been made in the same way for thirty years were contractual terms. Most mills in the area had the same custom of making deductions for work that had been performed according to the management without reasonable care and skill. The process of incorporation, according to Romer LJ, was that the employee 'entering the Appellant's service upon the same terms as the other weavers employed by them, ... must be deemed to have subjected himself to those terms whatever those terms might turn out to be' (see also *Duke v Reliance Systems* [1982] ICR 449). Knowledge of the practice by each worker was not necessary. However, in *Meek v Port of London Authority* [1918] 1 Ch 415, the long-established deduction of income tax was not incorporated into the employee's contract because employees did not know of it. The latter would appear to be the better approach as it seems unfair to impose on employees terms of which they are ignorant. Custom and practice may also be the basis for the incorporation of a collective agreement (*Henry v London General Transport Services Ltd* [2001] IRLR 132). Thus, in *MacLea v Essex Lines Ltd* (1933) 45 Ll LR 254, Acton J said:

> In the shipping industry, when people are engaged in this way simply by being told to join a ship without more ado, it is always assumed on both sides, that the engagement is on the terms and conditions of the National Maritime Board.

Indeed, many collective agreements, particularly at local level, are simply a distillation of established custom and practice.

3.42 The EAT emphasised in *Quinn v Calder Industrial Materials* [1996] IRLR 126 that the real question in determining whether there is an enforceable custom is not the number of occasions on which an employer has adopted a particular practice or calculation, but whether an intention to be bound contractually could be discerned from the policy as communicated by the employer (see to the same effect *Baldwin v British Coal Corporation* [1995] IRLR 139, especially para 30).

E STATUTE

3.43 Statute often protects the employee by means of implication of terms into the contract of employment, usually by generalising what is already best practice in collective agreements or individual bargains. Thus, the rights to guarantee pay, equal pay, notice, and maximum working hours are given effect in this way. This means that the employee may enforce the contract by proceedings for breach of contract in the civil courts, or, if the claim is outstanding on the termination of the contract, in the employment tribunal. Conversely some contractual terms are rendered void by statute, for example, a clause excluding rights to claim unfair dismissal or redundancy pay, terms which are discriminatory or, at common law, a term ousting the jurisdiction of the courts.

F AWARDS

3.44 Some employees' terms derive from an award of an arbitration panel or some other third party. Thus, the Central Arbitration Committee, for breach of the duty to disclose information to trade unions, may determine fair terms which are thereby automatically incorporated into the individual contracts of employment of affected workers (19.131). A similar process of implication arises where an *ad hoc* arbitrator or the CAC itself acts under a voluntary reference of a dispute made by ACAS.

G CAPACITY

Rules of capacity to make contracts of employment are much less significant today than in former times. There are, however, some residual matters of importance relating to infants under 18, which are found in the Infants Relief Act 1874, and are most important in relation to apprentices. An infant generally can be sued on an agreement only in respect of necessary goods or a contract for the benefit of the infant. The proper question in relation to a contract of employment is not whether any one stipulation is for his benefit. Instead, the court must look at the whole contract having regard to the circumstances of the case (*De Francesco v Barnum* (1890) 43 ChD 165). There are also particular statutory restrictions on the employment of some children. Thus, a child under 14 may not be employed at all (Children and Young Persons Act 1933, s 18(1)). Further restrictions are placed on the employment of the young in entertainment (Children and Young Persons Act 1963, s 37), while more broadly, local authorities have powers to gain information about the employment of children within their jurisdiction and prevent their taking unsuitable jobs and employment at unsuitable times. **3.45**

H FORMATION AND VARIATION OF CONTRACT

Formation of contract of employment

Like all other contracts, the contract of employment is constituted by offer and acceptance supported by consideration. The offer in the great majority of cases comes from the employer, and is then accepted in writing by the employee, or simply by the conduct of the employee in actually turning up for work. There are few analogous restrictions on the prerogative of management to hire workers, as exist in respect of dismissal. The exceptions relate to various protected characteristics (Chapter 8) and under the Rehabilitation of Offenders Act 1974. **3.46**

There are also some unusual situations in which persons may sue another even though no contract of employment as such has been entered into. Where employees were enticed to leave one job on the promise that they would be offered other highly paid positions, which did not materialise, they were entitled to damages for breach of warranty or a collateral contract (*Gill v Cape Contracts* [1985] IRLR 499). **3.47**

Although terms must be relatively certain for them to be enforced, the courts will go some way to construe any ambiguity there may be. The courts may thus look at an advertisement and letter of appointment to spell out terms or to construe ambiguities in the terms agreed (*Deeley v British Rail Engineering Ltd* [1979] IRLR 5; *Pedersen v Camden London Borough* [1981] IRLR 173). Thus, a judge upheld a promise to work 'such days or part days in each week as may reasonably be required by the management', defining it as demanding work for a reasonable number of days (*National Coal Board v Galley* [1958] 1 WLR 16). However, in a case in 1902 the court refused to enforce a contract for services in return for 'a West End salary to be actually agreed between us' (Wedderburn, *The Worker and the Law, op cit*, at 194). **3.48**

Where the terms of the contract of employment are truly ambiguous it is open to the court to look at the practice adopted by the parties and to attach considerable importance to **3.49** it as indicating a proper interpretation of contractual terms. Thus, it was quite appropriate to consider the practice of paying treble time which had existed for over thirty years (*Dunlop Tyres Ltd v Blowers* [2001] IRLR 629).

3.50 Contracts of employment need not themselves be in writing unless, very unusually, there is no consideration provided; then a deed is necessary. Form is important also in the cases of apprentices and merchant seamen. More importantly, statute requires a written statement of the most important terms of the contract of employment to be provided to the employee (3.62ff).

Intention to create legal relations

3.51 The parties must also intend the agreement and individual terms thereof to create legal relations. In *Financial Techniques (Planning Services) Ltd v Hughes* [1981] IRLR 32, the question arose as to whether that which was advertised as a 'sophisticated remuneration package' for a tax consultant was enforceable as part of the contract, or payable only at the discretion of the employers. The Court of Appeal tended to the former view because of the terms of the advertisement which attracted the applicant to take up the position, and because he was at no time informed that it was *not* to form part of the contract. In *Edwards v Skyways Ltd* [1964] 1 WLR 349 a pension clause was held to be enforceable even though it was stated to be *ex gratia* (see also *McClaren v Home Office* [1990] IRLR 338 in the case of prison officers; *Judge v Crown Leisure Ltd* [2005] IRLR 823).

Construction of the contract

3.52 One of the crucial issues is the extent to which different rules should be applied to the contract of employment from other contracts. For example, the general principle is that evidence should not be admitted to interpret a written agreement but this may be more difficult to apply in a context as informal as many contracts of employment. As we have seen in the last chapter, in *Autoclenz Ltd v Belcher* [2011] ICR 1157, the Supreme Court decided that there should be a special approach to shams in employment contracts. In *Harlow v Artemis Int Corp Ltd* [2008] IRLR 629, McCombe J commented that employment contracts today consist of all sorts of material put together by human resources officers rather than lawyers and designed to be read in an informal and common sense manner in the context of a relationship affecting ordinary people in their everyday lives. Thus, close arguments arising out of nuance of language, possibly of importance in more formal contracts, are singularly inappropriate in such a context unless it is made clear in a document that an important point of distinction is being made. Generally, however, in construing a contractual term the tribunal has to decide objectively what is meant and that is to ascertain what a reasonable onlooker apprised of the background would have thought it meant (*Kulkarni v Milton Keynes Hospital NHS Foundation Trust* [2010] ICR 101; see also *Garratt v MGN Ltd* [2011] ICR 880).

3.53 Construction of contract is a matter of law (*Adams v BA* [1996] IRLR 574; see also *Gilgrove Ltd v Hay* [2012] ICR 1171; [2013] ICR 1139).

Variation

3.54 The contract of employment is one of the most dynamic of legal agreements, changing frequently during its course as circumstances alter. Any variation in contractual terms, however, requires the assent, express or tacit, of both parties and should be supported by consideration. This tacit consent may be represented by the employee simply carrying on working under altered conditions. Many contracts contain wide flexibility clauses so that a change of the actual duties performed may lie within the four corners of the contractual job description, for example that the employee will perform such duties as are from time to time assigned to him by the board of directors or managing director. If not, it is important to keep in mind Donaldson LJ's remark in *Janata Bank Ltd v Ahmed* [1981] IRLR 457 at para 50, that 'the continuously changing contract is unknown to law' (see also *Parry v Holst & Co Ltd* (1968) 3 ITR 317; *Dal v A. S. Orr* [1980] IRLR 413). If, however, the employer unilaterally enforces a variation without active consent or acquiescence, he repudiates the contract of employment and the employee is put to his election whether to accept the fundamental breach, and resign, or to carry on working and seek damages (*Burdett-Coutts v Hertfordshire CC* [1984] IRLR 91; *Rigby v Ferodo Ltd* [1987] IRLR 516).

It is sometimes necessary to distinguish between a mere variation and a wholly new contract by reason of breach of the old one; thus a unilateral deduction by the management from the employee's pay and/or hours usually amounts to a fundamental breach of contract and its termination (cf *Hogg v Dover College* [1990] ICR 39), while on an agreed variation, the contract continues (see also *Preston v Wolverhampton Healthcare NHS Trust* [1988] ICR 227). Often the employee proceeds to work, perhaps oblivious of the breach or under some form of undue influence to ignore it. Judges have, however, been vigilant in appropriate cases not to spell out agreements to apparent new terms in these circumstances. For example, in *Horrigan v Lewisham London Borough Council* [1978] ICR 15 EAT, notwithstanding that the employee had worked overtime for ten years, Arnold J commented: **3.55**

> It is fairly difficult, in the ordinary way, to imply a variation of contract, and it is very necessary, if one is to do so, to have very solid facts which demonstrate that it was necessary to give business efficacy to the contract, that the contract should come to contain a new term implied by way of variation.

This is a particularly important issue in changes of job duties, the contractual scope of which is vital to decisions, for example, on constructive dismissal or redundancy payments. In *Marriott v Oxford and District Cooperative Society (No 2)* [1970] 1 QB 186, the appellant had been employed by the respondents as an electrical supervisor for two years when they found that there was insufficient work for him. They were prepared to offer him another post at £3 less per week and he took this under protest, worked for three or four weeks, but then terminated his contract by notice. In response to his claim for a redundancy payment, the respondent claimed that it had *not* terminated the agreement by insisting on his taking the new job (as was necessary for him to claim his statutory rights), but had merely varied it. Lord Denning MR found that (at 191C):

> He never agreed to the dictated terms. He protested against them. He submitted to them because he did not want to be out of employment. By insisting on new terms to which he never agreed, the employer did, I think, terminate the old contract of employment.

The issue is also important in relation to the introduction of new technology and the extent to which employees can be expected to adapt to new techniques within their contractual terms. In the old case of *Cresswell v Board of Inland Revenue* [1984] ICR 508, the defendants' introduction of computers did not, it was held, change the nature of the job done by PAYE staff. The Revenue were entitled to withhold payment for employees who refused to cooperate with the new system. Walton J thought that employees had no right to preserve their working conditions unchanged throughout **3.56** the course of their employment. They could reasonably be expected, after proper training, to adapt to new techniques especially where, as here, there was no evidence of real difficulty. He thought that the jobs would remain 'recognisably the same job but done in a different way'.

3.57 Employers frequently seek unilaterally to vary terms by giving to the employee the notice to which he is entitled under his contract. The case law suggests that the employer must make it clear that he is terminating one contract and offering another, otherwise there is a risk that the employee can claim in the courts or tribunals rights foregone under the old arrangements.

3.58 In *Shields Furniture Ltd v Goff* [1973] ICR 187, the National Industrial Relations Court reiterated that work under an alternative offer for a trial period does not constitute acceptance of those terms, and in *Sheet Metal Components Ltd v Plumridge* [1974] ICR 373, Sir John Donaldson said: 'the courts have rightly been slow to find that there has been a consensual variation where an employee has been faced with the alternative of dismissal and where the variation has been adverse to his interests' (see also *Norwest Holst Group Administration Ltd v Harrison* [1984] IRLR 419).

3.59 In *Burdett-Coutts v Hertfordshire County Council* (above), the employers sought to change the hours of six dinner ladies by means of a circular letter. The claimants, who were entitled to twelve weeks' notice of termination, sought a declaration that the purported variation was invalid, to which the defendants responded that the letter should be read as a termination of the employment coupled with an offer of new terms. Kenneth Jones J could not so read the letter which referred to 'detailed notice of variations in your contract of service'. The employees had elected not to accept the repudiation and could now claim the total wages to which they were entitled under the contract. The House of Lords confirmed in *Rigby v Ferodo Ltd* [1987] IRLR 516 that an employer's unilateral reduction of an employee's wages does not automatically bring the contract to an end. Where the employee had not accepted such a repudiation as terminating the contract, the damages recoverable were not limited to the amount of shortfall from the contractual wage over the employee's notice period, but the whole period to trial (see also *Miller v Hamworthy Engineering Ltd* [1986] ICR 846).

3.60 Employers who wish to change terms and conditions in anything more than a minor way should give proper notice to terminate one contract and offer another, although this carries with it the concomitant risk that the employee may claim unfair dismissal (see 14.11).

I THE EFFECT ON CONTRACT OF A TRANSFER OF UNDERTAKING

3.61 The common law doctrine that contracts of employment do not continue on a takeover, sought to recognise that 'employees are not serfs and cannot be transferred as though they were property' (*Nokes v Doncaster Amalgamated Collieries Ltd* [1940] AC 1014). Although this was designed to protect the employee, it could act as a boomerang in the context of modern employment protection rights, but until 1 May 1982 the only modification was in the context of continuity for various employment protection rights. Since then, pursuant to the EEC Directive on Acquired Rights 77/187, the Transfer of Undertakings (Protection of Employment) Regulations 1981, now replaced by the 2006 Regulations, has altered the position in the case of a transfer of undertaking, 'whether by sale or some other disposition or operation of law'. This is fully considered in Chapter 18.

J WRITTEN STATEMENT OF TERMS

The details

Most employees have the important right to receive a written statement of some of the **3.62** most important terms of their contracts of employment. This is the foundation on which employment protection rights may be built and was first introduced, in a limited form, in the Contracts of Employment Act 1963. The detail to be included was substantially increased by various Acts and is now found in the Employment Rights Act (ERA) 1996, ss 1–12.

The statement must be given within two months of starting work and must include the **3.63** following details (ERA 1996, s 1(3) and (4)):

(a) The *names of employer and employee.*

(b) The *date when employment began* and whether any previous service counts as continuous with the present contract. This has important implications for such rights as redundancy payment and unfair dismissal (see Chapters 14 and 15).

(c) A *brief description of the work* for which the employee is employed (ERA 1996, s 1(4)(f)), which may state simply 'administrative officer'. It is, however, in the interests of the employee not to allow undue width to the description since he might then be dismissed for refusing to perform duties within the title. Further, he will not be redundant if his duties are changed considerably but remain within the job title. The job title is also important when considering constructive dismissal and equal pay claims. In some senses it is the most important element in the written statement.

(d) The *scale or rate of remuneration* or the method of calculating it. This includes fringe benefits which are an increasingly important element of payment. The employee is also entitled to an itemised pay statement every time he is paid (5.15–5.18).

(e) Whether remuneration is to be *paid weekly*, monthly, or at some other interval.

(f) Normal *hours of work.*

(g) Entitlement to public and other *holidays* and holiday pay (see *Morley v Heritage plc* [1993] IRLR 400).

(h) Provision for *sickness* and injury, and, in particular, sick pay.

(i) *Pension rights*, especially whether a contracting out certificate has been given under the Social Security Pensions Act 1975.

(j) The *length of notice* which the employer and employee must give in order to terminate the contract of employment (ERA 1996, s 1(4)(e)); but the employee may be referred to 'the law [that is in the case of minimum periods of notice] or to the provisions of any collective agreement directly affecting the terms and conditions of the employment ...' (ERA 1996, s 2(3)).

(k) If the contract is for a *fixed period* the date of the end of the period must be stated (ERA 1996, s 1(4)(g)).

(l) In the case of *non-permanent employment*, 'the period for which it is expected to continue' (ERA 1996, s 1(4)(g)).

(m) Either *the place of work* or, where the employee is required or permitted to work at various places, an indication of that fact and the address of the employer (ERA 1996, s 1(4)(h)).

(n) '[A]ny *collective agreements* which directly affect the terms and conditions of the employment including, where the employer is not a party, the persons by whom they were made' (ERA 1996, s 1(4)(j)).

(o) In the case of an employee *required to work outside the UK for a period of more than a month*, the period of such work, the currency of remuneration, any additional remuneration or benefit by reason of the requirement to work outside the UK, and 'any terms and conditions relating to his return to the UK' (ERA 1996, s 1(4)(k)).

The statement must also contain a note specifying any disciplinary rules which are applicable to the employee, or refer him to a reasonably accessible document setting them out. The employee should also be notified of a person to whom he can apply if he is dissatisfied with any disciplinary decision, and how such application should be made (ERA 1996, s 3). Any further steps are to be specified, and the employer is well advised to include as much detail as possible as protection against unfair dismissal claims. By s 3(1)(aa), introduced by the Employment Act 2002, the statement must specify any procedure applicable to the taking of disciplinary decisions relating to the employee or to dismissal or refer the employee to a document specifying such a procedure, which is reasonably accessible to the employee.

3.64   Where before the end of two months after the start of employment, the employee 'is to begin work outside the UK for more than one month' the statement must be given to him before he leaves the UK to begin so to work (ERA 1996, s 2(5)) and such a statement must be given notwithstanding that the employment ends before the period in which the statement was to be given (ERA 1996, s 2(6)).

Supplementary provisions

3.65   There are several important aspects about the written statement. The employer may satisfy the provision by offering to the employee a *copy* of the whole contract or providing reasonable access to one while he is at work (s 6). A notice on the intranet or the well-viewed staff notice board referring to a collective agreement would be sufficient.

3.66   It must be clearly stated if there are *no relevant particulars* under any of the above headings (s 2(1)). This is to encourage employers to develop proper and clear terms and procedures. The Secretary of State has power to specify additional matters to be included, and all the terms must be correct not more than one week before the statement is given (s 7). Only matters relating to sickness and most pension schemes may now be contained in 'some other document which is reasonably accessible to the employee' (ERA 1996, s 2(2)). The following particulars conversely must be given in a single document (ERA 1996, s 2(4)):

(a) the names of employer and employee;
(b) the date when employment began;
(c) the date on which the employee's period of continuous employment began;
(d) the scale of remuneration or the method of calculating remuneration;
(e) the intervals at which remuneration is to be paid;
(f) any terms and conditions relating to hours of work;
(g) entitlement to holidays and details about accrued holiday pay;
(h) the title of the job which the employee is employed to do or a brief description of the work for which the employee is employed; and
(i) either the place of work or, where the employee is required or permitted to work at various places, an indication of that fact and the address of the employer.

3.67   Any *changes* in terms must be communicated in the same manner as was the original statement and at the earliest opportunity, and in any event within a month of the alteration or, where the change arises from the requirement to work outside the UK for more than a month, the time when the employee leaves the UK (ERA 1996, s 4(3)). This may be either by means of a new statement or in a collective bargain, provided that it is reasonably accessible in respect of sickness, pensions, disciplinary rules, and notice provisions (s 4(4) and (5)). In one case, the medium of the company journal (*King v Post Office* [1973] ICR 120) was found to be acceptable. A total failure to notify the terms does not, however, render any changes ineffective, and where the employer changes in name only, or where the identity changes but continuity is preserved by statute, this may be stated as a change in particulars, rather than necessitating the provision of a whole new statement (s 4(7)).

New particulars need not be given when an employee is re-employed within six months **3.68** of ending an earlier employment if he comes back on the same terms and conditions and he had already been given particulars.

The status of the statement

The general aim of the provision is to encourage the development of explicit and clear **3.69** terms about the most important elements of the employee's contract. It is intended to be a *mirror* of that agreement but it is *not* the contract itself. This is reflected in the right of either employer or employee to complain to an employment tribunal in case of dispute as to whether the correct particulars together with any changes have been communicated. Lord Parker CJ said in *Turriff Construction Ltd v Bryant* (1967) 2 ITR 292: 'It is of course quite clear that the statement ... is not the contract; it is not even conclusive evidence of the contract.' However, since very often there will be precious little other information available, especially in writing, about the agreement, it is quite natural that the statement should frequently be treated as the contract itself. This is particularly so where the employee has signed a receipt for the document: in *Gascol Conversions Ltd v Mercer* [1974] ICR 420, Lord Denning MR went so far as to state that by reason of the parole evidence rule (which applies to all contracts), ' "the statutory statement" being reduced to writing is the *sole evidence* that it is permissible of contract and its terms'.

It is not, however, clear from the report of the case whether the document in question was **3.70** just a written statement or purported to be the contract itself. If the former, it is submitted that the decision is not to be followed.

The most widely cited statement of the effect of the written statement is found in *System* **3.71** *Floors (UK) Ltd v Daniel* [1982] ICR 54 where Browne-Wilkinson J said that it:

> provides very strong prima facie evidence of what were the terms of the contract between the parties but does not constitute a written contract between the parties. Nor are the statements of the terms finally conclusive; at most they place a heavy burden on the employer to show that the actual terms of the contract are different from those which he has set out in the statutory statement.

(Approved in *Robertson v British Gas Corporation* [1983] ICR 351; *Lee v GEC Plessey Telecommunications* [1993] IRLR 383.) The particulars may not, however, be used as evidence about the meaning of a written term.

There is no jurisdiction in a tribunal to interpret terms when deciding on the contents **3.72** of the written statement (*Southern Cross Healthcare Co Ltd v Perkins* [2011] ICR 285). That goes beyond their remit.

It was thought at one time that the written statement had explicit legal effect by giving **3.73** rise to an estoppel (so that the employer could not contradict it) if an employee relied on it to his detriment. For example, in *Evenden v Guildford City Association Football Club* [1975] ICR 367, the employer stated that employment with a previous employer counted towards continuous service and he was not permitted to renege on that assurance. This case was, however, overruled by the House of Lords in *Secretary of State for Employment* *v Globe Elastic Thread Co Ltd* [1979] ICR 706, a case with similar facts, on the grounds that estoppel could not confer on a statutory tribunal a jurisdiction beyond that which is given by the empowering Act in respect of continuity of employment. The case concerned the giving of a *redundancy rebate* under statute by the Secretary of State who was of course not himself privy to the contract of employment, and it may still be argued that an estoppel may arise between employer and employee when there is no third party involved. For the decision was that, in the words of Lord Wilberforce, 'a personal estoppel between employer and employee which is the most that this could be, could not bind the Secretary of State' (see 16.75ff).

3.74   A failure to object to erroneous statements of terms is not to be taken as acceptance of such terms at least where the terms are of no immediate practical importance (*Jones v Associated Tunnelling Co Ltd* [1981] IRLR 477; see also *Courtaulds Northern Spinning Ltd v Sibson and TGWU* [1988] IRLR 305; *Aparau v Iceland Frozen Foods plc* [1996] IRLR 119; *Harlow v Artemis International Corp Ltd* [2008] IRLR 629).

Remedy for failure to supply written statement of terms

3.75   An employee who is dissatisfied because no written particulars have been supplied to him has always been able to refer the matter to an employment tribunal, which has power to determine what particulars the statement *should* have contained (ERA 1996, s 11(1)). There was some initial doubt about the existence of a power to rectify an error or to construe a misunderstanding between the parties (see *Construction Industry Training Board v Leighton* [1978] IRLR 60). The Court of Appeal in *Mears v Safecar Security Ltd* [1982] IRLR 183, however, held that what was then EPCA 1978, s 11 gave jurisdiction to the tribunal to confirm the details already given, or to amend or replace them by substituted particulars if they did not reflect the contract as agreed. The tribunal could add those particulars not given which *should* have been given. To decide what to so add, it must first decide whether the term in question has been expressly agreed by word of mouth or by necessary implication. If it has not been so agreed, the tribunal must imply and insert the missing term, and in doing so, should consider all the facts and circumstances of the relationship between employer and employee, including the way in which they had worked the contract since it commenced.

3.76   The employment tribunal, however, has no power to include terms as to holidays, holiday pay, sick pay, pensions, or disciplinary rules where none exist by agreement between the parties since the contract is not required to contain such terms (*Eagland v British Telecommunications plc* [1993] ICR 644). This is not to say, though, that the tribunal may not identify a term by reference to an agreement evidenced by the conduct of the parties. The Court of Appeal also rejected the suggestion that in some cases it was open to the tribunal to 'invent terms' where none had been agreed. The tribunal may award extra compensation of between two and four weeks' pay for failure to give proper written particulars (s 38 Employment Act 2002).

4

RIGHTS AND OBLIGATIONS
OF EMPLOYER AND EMPLOYEE

A PAY 4.02
   Quantum meruit 4.02
   Express and implied terms as
   to payment 4.03
B COOPERATION 4.23
C CARE AND SAFETY 4.29
D TIME OFF AND HOLIDAYS 4.35
   Time off 4.37
   Holidays 4.41
E FOLLOWING INSTRUCTIONS 4.42
F BREACH OF CONTRACT 4.46
G DISCIPLINE 4.48
   Common law .4.51
   Statute 4.52

H LAY-OFF AND SHORT-TIME
   WORKING 4.53
   Lay-off at common law 4.54
   Income maintenance at common law 4.59
   Guarantee pay by statute 4.60
   Jobseeker's allowance 4.67
   Redundancy payment 4.69
I MOBILITY AND FLEXIBILITY
   CLAUSES 4.73
J REFERENCES AND PRE-EMPLOYMENT
   MEDICALS 4.76
K MEDICAL REPORTS 4.79
L RIGHT TO BE ACCOMPANIED AT
   DISCIPLINARY AND GRIEVANCE
   PROCEDURES 4.81

There can be no employment relationship without a power to command and a duty to obey, that is, without this element of subordination in which lawyers rightly see the hallmark of the contract of employment. (Professor O Kahn-Freund, *Labour and the Law, op cit* para 3.1, at 17.)

We examine in this chapter the most important terms in the contract of employment, **4.01** looking in particular at what would be implied in the absence of detailed agreement. We also consider disciplinary provisions and lay-off. Statutory control of pay and hours is dealt with in Chapter 5.

A PAY

Quantum meruit

The essential element in the exchange for the employee is pay for hours worked. Generally, **4.02** remuneration is negotiated expressly by way of a collective or individual bargain on a yearly or biennial basis, but so essential is it to the contract, that in the absence of express agreement there is still a right to reasonable remuneration. The court will, if it needs to (which is an unusual event), assess what the employee's labours are reasonably worth by way of a quasi-contractual claim for *quantum meruit*. The implied term is, however, excluded if there is any contractual term on the subject, even if it is merely an article of association of the company giving entitlement to 'such amount as the directors may determine' (*Re Richmond Gate Property Co Ltd* [1965] 1 WLR 335).

Express and implied terms as to payment

4.03 There are more generally implied terms and statutory provisions governing:

(a) pay when only part of the contract is completed;
(b) payment during illness;
(c) medical suspension;
(d) payment during lay-off (4.53ff);
(e) maternity pay (10.29ff); and
(f) paid time off for trade union duties (20.35ff).

We will here consider the first four items, the others being treated under their appropriate subject headings. The itemised pay statement is considered at paras 5.15–5.18.

Payment when only part completed

4.04 Considerable conceptual problems surround the right to payment of an employee who completes only part of his contract. Confusion primarily derives from the eighteenth-century case of *Cutter v Powell* (1795) 101 ER 573. A second mate on a voyage from Jamaica to Liverpool was to be paid 30 guineas, provided he completed the voyage, but instead he died three weeks before the end of the two-month journey. The Court of King's Bench held that his widow was not entitled to any payment on a *quantum meruit* action or otherwise in respect of the part he had completed. Although the decision might have been different had there not been an express term for completion included on a promissory note, the statement of law was generalised in later cases. Thus, in *Boston Deep Sea Fishing and Ice Co v Ansell* (1888) 39 ChD 339, it was held that, at common law, an employee was not entitled to any pro rata payment in respect of any uncompleted period of service. This means that, if X is employed and paid Monday to Friday, and leaves on the Wednesday, he can recover no wages for days worked. An exception has, however, developed where the employer has received substantial performance even though not all the services bargained for are completed and then payment is due (*Hoenig v Isaacs* [1952] 2 All ER 176 CA; *Bolton v Mahadeva* [1972] 2 All ER 1322; cf *Wiluszynski v London Borough of Tower Hamlets* [1989] IRLR 259).

4.05 Further, the injustice of the general rule has been mitigated somewhat by the Apportionment Act 1870, s 2, which provides that 'all annuities (which includes salaries and pensions) ... and other periodical payments in the nature of income ... shall ... be considered as accruing from day-to-day, and should be apportioned in respect of time accordingly'. Thus, generally, a proportion of the contractual amount can now be gained. Judicial interpretation has not conclusively decided that 'salaries' as mentioned in the statute includes wages (see *Thames Water Utilities v Reynolds* [1996] IRLR 186; cf *Taylor v Lowe* [2000] IRLR 760; *Cooper v Isle of Wight College* [2008] IRLR 125).

Sick pay

4.06 The scope of the implied right to receive sick pay was reviewed by the EAT in *Mears v Safecar Security Ltd* [1982] ICR 626. Nothing was said about sick pay on the appellant's engagement as a security guard, and when he had been away ill in the past no money was paid to him. The employment tribunal thought that there was a presumption in favour of payment being made, but that this was subject to deduction of all statutory sickness benefit. The Court of Appeal rejected any such presumption. It was thus necessary to look at all the facts and circumstances. Whether payment was to be implied depended on:

(a) the *knowledge* of the parties on making the contract;
(b) whether the contract is one where payment is due if the employee is ready and *willing to work*;
(c) whether payment of wages is consideration for *faithful service* at other times;
(d) the *nature* of the contract;
(e) whether employment is on a *short-term* basis or for a fixed-term of years; and
(f) what the parties did during the *currency* of the contract.

Here, the appellant had been told by his workmates that he would not be paid during a period of sickness, and he had never before sent in sick notes so that a right to payment could not be implied (cf *Howman & Son v Blyth* [1983] IRLR 139).

The fact that the employer has a code of practice on staff sickness does not necessarily **4.07** mean that the code is contractually binding; it could merely be setting out good practice which managers should (but not necessarily must) follow. This means that the employer is entitled unilaterally to alter the code (*Wandsworth London Borough Council v D'Silva* [1998] IRLR 193).

The common law position is of somewhat less consequence since the introduction of **4.08** statutory sick pay. In outline, the scheme provides that the employer must pay sick pay for the first twenty-eight weeks of illness and only after that is the employee entitled to state sickness benefit.

The employee may not claim statutory sick pay for the first three days of any period of **4.09** sickness, and the following employees are excluded altogether from claiming it: pensioners; employees for less than three months; those who earn too little to pay national insurance contributions; and a person not employed by reason of a stoppage of work due to a trade dispute at his workplace unless the employee had not participated in the dispute and had no direct interest in its outcome. Paragraph 2(g) of Sch 11 to the Social Security Contributions and Benefits Act 1992 provides that employees will not be entitled to statutory sick pay if there is a stoppage of work due to a trade dispute at the employee's place of employment. Trade dispute for these purposes is defined by s 35 Jobseekers Act 1995.

To be able to claim, the employee must be suffering from some disease or physical or men- **4.10** tal disablement rendering him incapable of performing any work which he can reasonably be expected to do under his contract. Two periods of incapacity are treated as one if they are separated by not more than two weeks. Where an employee's contract is terminated in order to evade the employer's liability for sick pay, the entitlement continues as long as the sickness lasts. Although most workers labour from Monday to Friday, there are many variations to this theme, and the employer and employee may agree as to what are the qualifying days for sick pay purposes. In the absence of agreement, the regulations lay down the agreed normal working days as qualifying days.

The amount is paid at a daily rate but this depends on the amount of normal weekly earn- **4.11** ings. The general rule takes the last normal pay day before the entitlement to statutory sick pay arises and then averages the weekly earnings over the period of at least eight weeks before that date. The rates are reviewed annually. The payment is taxable and the claimant must pay national insurance contributions on it.

To claim statutory sick pay, the employee or his agent has to inform the employer that he **4.12** is unfit for work. The employer can fix a time limit for such notification, but must give reasonable publicity to it. If he says nothing, the notice must be in writing. It is treated as given if duly posted. In the absence of a published time limit, the employee has one month in which to give notice, with a discretionary extension for good cause up to ninety days (reg 7(1)(a) of the Statutory Sick Pay (General) Regulations 1982 (SI 1982/894), as amended). Although the employer cannot require that the sick employee notifies him in person of his illness, the employer may otherwise lay down the mode of notification. He cannot, however, require medical evidence or notification on a special form (reg 7 of the 1982 General Regulations). In due course, the employer may seek other relevant information, such as medical evidence, from the employee. The employee may conversely ask for a statement of his entitlement to statutory sick pay.

Medical suspension pay

4.13 As part of its policy of preserving income during difficult periods for employees, the ERA 1996, ss 64–8 give the right to payment to an employee who is suspended by his employer on medical grounds.

4.14 To qualify, the reason for suspension may be statutory requirements or any code of practice issued under s 16 of the Health and Safety at Work, etc Act 1974. These require suspension in the event of certain dangers arising from, for example, the handling of tin, enamel, chemicals, etc. The employee must then be paid while suspended for a period up to twenty-six weeks (ERA 1996, s 64(1)) 'only if and so long as he ... continues to be employed by his employer, but is ... not provided with work or does not perform the work he normally performed before the suspension' (s 64(5)).

4.15 The right is excluded where the employee:

(a) is incapable by reason of disease or bodily or mental impairment, since he can then gain state sickness benefit (s 65(3));

(b) unreasonably refuses a suitable offer of alternative work (s 65(4)(a)); or

(c) does not comply with reasonable requirements laid down by his employer to ensure that his services are available (s 65(4)(b)).

4.16 The appropriate week's pay is calculated in accordance with ss 221–7 of ERA 1996 like the other major employment protection rights (see 16.63) and if the employer does not pay what he owes, the employee can complain to an employment tribunal within three months (s 70). Moreover, the section is without prejudice to the case of the employee whose employer has suspended him without having any contractual right to do so. He has the usual contractual remedies, including a claim of constructive dismissal.

Overpayment by mistake

4.17 Difficulties arise where an employee has been overpaid by mistake and the employer seeks to reclaim these sums. In *Avon County Council v Howlett* [1983] IRLR 171, Mr Howlett, a teacher, was regularly overpaid whilst off work following an accident, in the sum of £1,007. When this was discovered, the county council sought recovery of the money in the High Court. The Court of Appeal synthesised legal and equitable considerations in formulating the general principle to the effect that the employer is estopped from claiming restitution of such sums where the payment was accompanied by an express or implicit representation which led the recipient to believe that he was entitled to treat the money as his own. Here the defendant was permitted to retain the overpayment since after such intimation and without notice of claim, he had so changed his position that it would be inequitable now to require him to make the repayment. The mistake made by the Authority was a mistake of *fact*, namely that the relevant pay clerks were unaware of the fact that (or had forgotten that) more than six months had elapsed, rather than by misinterpretations of the relevant regulations. The result would have been different if the defendant had still retained the sum paid by the employer, he had spent it on an obvious change in his style of living, or overpayment was owing substantially to the payee's own fault.

Deductions from pay for industrial action

When an employer is faced with disruption by his workforce which is short of a strike, he **4.18** may withhold a proportion (or all) of the pay for the period of disruption. This was determined in *Miles v Wakefield Metropolitan District Council* [1987] ICR 368 by the House of Lords. The case concerned a superintendent registrar of births, marriages, and deaths whose conditions were governed by statute. He normally worked thirty-seven hours per week, three of them on Saturday mornings. Between August 1981 and October 1982, on the instructions of his union as part of industrial action, he refused to carry out marriages on Saturday mornings and the council accordingly withheld 3/37ths of his pay. Whether office-holders were liable to have salary withheld for breach of statutory obligations was a question of the true construction of the relevant statute. Here the council had said nothing to undermine its statement that it would not accept partial performance; there was no obligation on the council to prevent him from working.

There is some Court of Appeal authority of the opposite tenor, since Lord Denning MR **4.19** said in *Secretary of State for Employment v ASLEF (No 2)* [1972] 2 QB 443:

> Is a man entitled to wages for his work when he, with others, is doing his best to make it useless? Surely not. Wages are to be paid for services rendered, not for producing deliberate chaos. The breach goes to the whole of the consideration as it was put by Lord Campbell CJ in *Cuckson v Stones* (1858) 1 E & E 248 at 255 ...

The House of Lords thus emphasised that an office-holder who had not performed cer- **4.20** tain of his duties during a period of industrial action was not entitled to remuneration in respect of that period in the absence of proof that he was ready to work in accordance with his contract. The principle is further illustrated in the following cases:

(a) in *Cresswell v Board of Inland Revenue* [1984] ICR 508, Walton J determined that a person who was refusing to accept the new computerised PAYE system had no right to be paid (see also *Royle v Trafford Borough Council* [1984] IRLR 184);

(b) in *Sim v Rotherham Metropolitan Borough Council* [1987] Ch 216, Scott J determined that teachers were under a contractual duty to comply with cover arrangements for absent colleagues, and the defendant local authorities could justify deductions of £2.00 to £3.37 made from the teachers' salaries during the teachers' industrial action as an equitable set-off arising from their breaches of contract;

(c) in *Wiluszynski v London Borough of Tower Hamlets* [1989] IRLR 259, however, the local authority was held not to be entitled to withhold pay from an estates officer in the Housing Directorate who was merely boycotting inquiries from council members. This was a small part of his job description. Michael Davies J held that the breach was minimal. Moreover, the council had allowed him to perform the substantial part of his services, so that it was not entitled later to withhold his salary for such period. The Court of Appeal overturned this decision of the High Court on the basis that the council could not physically prevent the plaintiff from attending work and performing his duties, and the doctrine of substantial performance was inapplicable (see also *MacPherson v London Borough of Lambeth* [1988] IRLR 470; *Home Office v Ayres* [1992] ICR 175);

(d) the court will not grant an interim order requiring employers to pay to employees engaged in strike action their wages and overtime payments which the employers were holding in respect of those periods in which the employers had refused to accept partial performance of the contractual duties of the employees (*Jakeman v South West Thames RHA and London Ambulance Service* [1990] IRLR 62, arising out of the 1989 ambulance workers' dispute); and

(e) an employee who took part in industrial action might have 30 per cent deducted from his pay, and the notion of *quantum meruit* could not realistically apply in the context of collective industrial action short of a strike (*Spackman v London Metropolitan University* [2007] IRLR 744).

If a refusal to work continues for only part of a day the Apportionment Act 1870 has no application; it serves to apportion wages for a week or more only.

4.21 It was also held to be appropriate under the Apportionment Act to decide that pay for a sixth form college teacher did not accrue over weekends (*Amey v Peter Symonds College* [2014] IRLR 206; see also *Hartley v King Edward VI College* [2015] ICR 1143).

4.22 Further protection given to employees by s 13 of the ERA 1996 (see 5.01–5.10) is rendered inapplicable in the case of deductions from a worker's wage for taking part in a strike or other industrial action (s 13(5)). The employer is thus entitled to refuse to pay for time spent or involved in industrial action.

B COOPERATION

4.23 The courts have frequently implied into the contract a duty of cooperation between employer and employee, notwithstanding the potential for direct conflict between their interests. Most of the older authorities deal with the obligation that this imposes on an employee, and a general statement is to be found in *Secretary of State for Employment v ASLEF (No 2)* [1972] 2 QB 455. The issue arose because under the Industrial Relations Act 1971 which was then in force, the Secretary of State for Employment could order a cooling-off period of a strike where, *inter alia*, employees were acting 'in breach of contract'. The union claimed that its work to rule was not a breach but instead entailed meticulous *observance* of British Rail's own rule book; it thus claimed that it was following their agreement to the letter. Lord Denning MR, however, identified a breach 'if the employee, with others, takes steps wilfully to disrupt the undertaking, to produce chaos so that it will not run as it should, then each one who is a party to those steps is guilty of a breach of contract'. He gave 'a homely instance' of what he had in mind as a breach (at 491F):

> Suppose I employ a man to drive me to the station. I know there is sufficient time, so that I do not tell him to hurry. He drives me at a slower speed than he need, with the deliberate object of making me lose the train, and I do lose it. He may say that he has performed the letter of the contract; he has driven me to the station; but he has wilfully made me lose the train, and that is a breach of contract beyond all doubt.

4.24 Lord Denning disapproved of the term suggested by Donaldson P at first instance that the employee should *actively* assist the employer to operate his organisation. It was thus going too far to suggest 'a duty to behave fairly to his employer and do a fair day's work'. Although far-reaching, the Master of the Rolls' proposition was not a positive doctrine: 'A man is not bound positively to do more for his employer than his contract requires. He can withdraw his goodwill if he pleases.' Buckley LJ implied a term that 'an employee must serve the employer faithfully with a view to promoting those commercial interests for which he is employed'.

4.25 The general principle is indeed that the employee must serve the employer and his interests faithfully. The Court of Appeal held in *British Telecommunications plc v Ticehurst*

[1992] ICR 383, that it was necessary to imply such a term 'in the case of a manager who is given charge of the work of other employees and who therefore must necessarily be entrusted to exercise her judgement and discretion in giving instructions to others and in supervising their work. Such a discretion, if the contract is to work properly must be exercised faithfully in the interests of the employers' (at 398e).

More recent authorities, primarily under the impulse of finding a breach of contract for **4.26** constructive dismissal, have emphasised the mirror-image obligation of the employer to cooperate with the employee, and not to make his task in any way to be more difficult. Thus, a breach has been identified when employers have criticised managers in front of subordinates; used foul language; made groundless accusations of theft; and failed to show proper respect for a senior employee (see *Associated Tyre Specialists (Eastern) Ltd v Waterhouse* [1976] IRLR 386; *Palmanor Ltd v Cedron* [1978] IRLR 303; *Robinson v Crompton Parkinson Ltd* [1978] ICR 401; and *Garner v Grange Furnishing Ltd* [1977] IRLR 206, respectively). As Phillips J stated *obiter* in *BAC Ltd v Austin* [1978] IRLR 322 at 334:

> It must ordinarily be an implied term of the contract of employment that employers do not behave in a way which is intolerable or in a way which employees cannot be expected to put up with any longer.

(See also 14.23ff; *Newns v British Airways plc* [1992] IRLR 575.)

In *Hagen v ICI Chemicals and Polymers Ltd* [2002] IRLR 31, Elias J decided that the **4.27** company was under a duty to take reasonable care to ensure that statements made to the employees regarding a transfer of an undertaking were true. There was an implied contractual duty to take reasonable care where the employer was proposing that the employees transfer their employment, the transferor will impact upon the future economic interests of the employees, the transfer will be unlikely to take place if a significant body of the employees object, the employer has access to certain information which is unavailable to the employees, and the employer knows that its information or advice will carry considerable weight with the employees. There is, however, no positive duty resting on an employer to make employees aware of their pension rights or other terms and conditions of their employment.

Another duty which may be placed under this broad rubric of the duty of coopera- **4.28** tion is that the employer must not put it out of his power to comply with a contract of employment he has entered into. Thus, in *Shindler v Northern Raincoat Co Ltd* [1960] 1 WLR 1038, the plaintiff was managing director of the respondents until their shares were acquired by another company which then removed him as a director. His employment as managing director was thus automatically terminated, and notwithstanding that the articles of association of the company clearly permitted this, Diplock J thought that it was in breach of an implied term that it would not deprive itself of the opportunity of using the employee's services. A similar duty rests on the employee.

C CARE AND SAFETY

Every employer must take reasonable care for the safety of his employees. This is a spe- **4.29** cialised application of the general law of negligence, but also takes effect as an implied term of the contract for employment. The consequence may be a different measure of damages (*Wright v Dunlop Rubber Co Ltd* (1971) 11 KIR 311). The House of Lords in *Wilson & Clyde Coal Co v English* [1938] AC 57 categorised three aspects of the generalised duty:

(a) to select proper staff;
(b) to provide adequate material; and
(c) to provide a safe system of working.

Moreover, s 2(2) of the Unfair Contract Terms Act 1977 prohibits the exclusion or restriction of liability for negligence in the case of loss or damage unless it is reasonable in favour of the employee. There is, however, no specific implied term that an employee should not be transferred to work involving a serious risk to her health in addition to the general contractual duties already discussed (*Jagdeo v Smiths Industries Ltd* [1982] ICR 47). An employer is also not obliged to insure the employee against the effects of unusual or dangerous work (*Reid v Rush & Tompkins Group plc* [1989] IRLR 265; cf *Cook v Square D Ltd* [1992] ICR 263). If an employer knows that acts being done by employees during their employment may cause physical or mental harm to a particular fellow employee, and he does nothing to supervise him or prevent such acts when it is in his power to do so, it is arguable that he may be in breach of his duty to that employee (*Waters v Metropolitan Police Commissioner* [2000] IRLR 720).

4.30 An employer also owes a duty to his employees not to cause them psychiatric damage by reason of the volume or character of the work that they are required to perform. In *Walker v Northumberland County Council* [1995] IRLR 35, a social worker who suffered two nervous breakdowns due to the intolerable stress and pressure placed on him by his employers, succeeded in claiming from his employers for his second breakdown. The High Court held that it was reasonably foreseeable that he would suffer a second breakdown as his employers had not improved his conditions of work following his first breakdown (see also *Cross v Highlands and Islands Enterprise* [2001] IRLR 336). This principle was, however, significantly limited by the Court of Appeal in a series of conjoined cases under the title *Sutherland v Hatton* [2002] IRLR 263 which held that the employer was entitled to assume that the employee can withstand the normal pressures of the job unless he knows of some particular problem or vulnerability of the employee. An employee who returns to work after a period of sickness without making further disclosure or explanation to his employer is usually implying that he believes himself to be fit enough to return to the work which he was doing before the absence. To trigger the duty on an employer to take steps to safeguard an employee from impending harm to his health arising from stress at work, the indications of stress on the part of the employee must be plain enough for any reasonable employer to realise that he should do something about it. The central test is whether a harmful reaction to the pressures of the workplace is reasonably foreseeable in the individual concerned.

4.31 The employer must take reasonable steps bearing in mind the probability of harm, its likely magnitude, and the costs and practicability of preventing it.

4.32 Such a stress reaction will have two components: (i) an injury to health which (ii) is attributable to stress at work. There are no occupations which should be regarded as intrinsically dangerous to mental health. It is not the job itself but rather the interaction between the individual and the job which causes harm. This was further considered when the cases went further under the name *Barber v Somerset CC* [2004] IRLR 475 and restricted to the extent that the House of Lords indicated that the overriding test was 'the conduct of the reasonable and prudent employer taking positive thought for the safety of his workers in the light of what he knows or ought to know' (see also *Intel Corp UK Ltd* [2007] IRLR 356; *Hone v Six Continents Retail Ltd* [2006] IRLR 49; *Dickins v 02 plc* [2009] IRLR 59).

Generally the employee must exercise reasonable care in carrying out his duties (see origi- **4.33** nally *Harmer v Cornelius* (1858) 5 CBNS 236), but the court seeks 'the standards of men and not those of angels' (*Jupiter General Insurance Co v Shroff* [1937] 3 All ER 67; *Janata Bank v Ahmed* [1981] IRLR 457). The employee also impliedly represents to the employer that he is reasonably competent to do his job (*Harmer v Cornelius* (1858) 5 CBNS 236). He can thus be lawfully dismissed instantly if he is in breach of this duty. This harsh common law position is, however, mitigated by the statutory unfair dismissal jurisdiction which affords various procedural safeguards to an incompetent employee as well as to others (see 14.113ff), and is now of much more consequence.

If the employee is sued in tort and the employer is vicariously liable they are treated as **4.34** joint tortfeasors under the Civil Liability (Contribution) Act 1978, and the court may thus award such contribution between them as it finds 'just and equitable having regard to the extent of their responsibility for the damage'.

D TIME OFF AND HOLIDAYS

The central obligation of the employee is to work. He cannot normally delegate this **4.35** duty to another, and he must not deliberately disable himself from performance of the work. The most important consequence is that a strike is prima facie a breach of contract (*Simmons v Hoover Ltd* [1977] QB 284; *Haddow v ILEA* [1979] ICR 202). It is only saved from such a conclusion if the employees give due notice of their intention to termi-nate their contracts, which rarely happens (*Morgan v Fry* [1968] 2 QB 710; cf *Boxfoldia Ltd v NGA (1982)* [1988] IRLR 383).

In examining the employee's service we will here consider: **4.36**

(a) statutory rights to time off work; and
(b) the right to holidays as a matter of contract.

Statutory control of working time is considered in Chapter 5.

Time off

Statute provides certain rights for employees to take time off. Three of these rights, of **4.37** trade union officials to carry out their duties with pay, of trade union members to partici-pate in trade union activities without the right to be paid, and of union learning repre-sentatives, are more appropriately considered as examples of the legal encouragement to collective bargaining (20.52ff). Another permits time off for antenatal care, and is dealt with under the wider question of maternity provision (10.39).

Two others are more widely available. Section 52 of the ERA 1996 accords to an employee **4.38** who has served over two years and who is dismissed for redundancy, the right to reason-able time off at the normal hourly rate to look for other work or make arrangements for training. What is 'reasonable' depends on the prospects of getting other work, but it is not essential for the employee to give details of his proposed interviews as a precondition of being released (*Dutton v Hawker Siddeley Aviation Ltd* [1978] ICR 1057).

Section 50 of the ERA 1996 permits reasonable time off to an employee who is a member **4.39** of a local authority, magistracy, statutory tribunal, police authority, a board of prison visitors or a prison visiting committee, a relevant health or education body, or a rel-evant environment agency, amongst others. This provision is designed to encourage a broader cross section of society to serve on such bodies. The criteria for determining the *reasonable* amount of time off include: how much time off is required for the performance of the relevant office; how much time the employee has already been permitted; the circumstances of the employer's business; and the effect of the employee's absence on the employer. There is no obligation on the employer to pay the employee for such time off since most of these public bodies provide loss of earnings allowances. It is not enough, on the other hand, for the employer merely to alter the times of the employee's work so that, for example, a lecturer's times of lectures do not clash with council meetings—the employee must actually have *time off* (*Ratcliffe v Dorset CC* [1978] IRLR 191; see also *Borders Regional Council v Maule* [1993] IRLR 199).

4.40 A complaint must be made to an employment tribunal within three months of the default of granting time off, so that it can award just and equitable compensation for such failure (s 51). It may not, however, impose conditions to be attached to the leave; a tribunal which declared that in future all of the days of absence over ten days should be by way of unpaid leave was rebuked by the EAT (*Corner v Buckinghamshire CC* [1978] IRLR 320).

Holidays

4.41 In *Tucker v British Leyland Motor Corporation* [1978] IRLR 493, a county court judge held that, in the absence of express provision or regular usage to the contrary, an hourly paid employee is entitled to a day's holiday on recognised public holidays without fear of dismissal as an absentee. In *Morley v Heritage plc* [1993] IRLR 400, the Court of Appeal determined that it was not an implied term of a contract of employment that if the employee's employment terminated without his having taken any part of his holiday entitlement the company would pay him in lieu thereof. The most important regulation of holidays is under the Working Time Regulations 1998 (see 5.63).

E FOLLOWING INSTRUCTIONS

4.42 At common law the employee is, in general, obliged to obey all of the lawful orders of the employer. That he might be summarily dismissed if he did not comply is the greatest bulwark of the managerial prerogative which is at the heart of the traditional employment relationship. An employee who fails to carry out a lawful and legitimate instruction is in material breach of contract irrespective of the propriety of the motive of the employer in giving the instruction (*Macari v Celtic FC* [1999] IRLR 787). In the modern law, the unfair dismissal jurisdiction has established significant procedural safeguards for the employee, and even at common law some of the harshest early decisions (eg in *Turner v Mason* (1845) 14 M&W 112) would not be reached today, since they reflect a very different view of the rights of employers.

4.43 Instructions, however, must now be tempered by reasonableness to be effective. *Ottoman Bank Ltd v Chakarian* [1930] AC 277 was a particularly strong case since the employers ordered the plaintiff, an Armenian, to stay in Constantinople where he had previously been sentenced to death and it was held that he was within his rights in refusing. On the other hand, in *Bouzourou v Ottoman Bank* [1930] AC 271, a Christian employee was obliged to obey an order to work at a branch in Asia Minor, notwithstanding the well-known hostility of the Turkish Government to his religion. It has also been held to be a breach of contract to refuse an order to visit Ireland because of general fear of IRA activity (*Walmsley v UDEC Refrigeration Ltd* [1972] IRLR 80). An employee is also obliged to adapt reasonably to new work methods required of him by the employer (*Cresswell v Board of Inland Revenue* [1984] ICR 508).

A dismissal for failure to obey an illegal order is always unlawful, so that in *Morrish* **4.44**
v Henlys (Folkestone) Ltd [1973] ICR 482, where an employee was ordered to falsify
the account books at the garage where he worked, his refusal was not in breach of contract. The same result was reached in *Gregory v Ford* [1951] 1 All ER 121, where the
employee said he would not take on the road a vehicle which was not covered by third
party insurance.

A sick employee is only excused from performing such orders as are rendered impos- **4.45**
sible by reason of the illness. His illness does not act as a general solvent or suspension
of duties, so that a commercial traveller was in breach in failing to remove merchandise
from her car during a period of illness (*Marshall v Alexander Sloan and Co Ltd* [1981]
IRLR 264).

F BREACH OF CONTRACT

Broadly, the consequences of a breach of contract by the employee are that: **4.46**

(a) He may be *disciplined* in accordance with contractual procedures (4.48–4.51).
(b) The employer may *sue for damages* for breach in the county or High Court (or if the
    breach is outstanding on the termination of employment in the employment tribunal),
    but this rarely happens because the amount of damages recoverable is usually min-
    imal (but see *Janata Bank Ltd v Ahmed* [1981] IRLR 457 and *Miller v Hamworthy
    Engineering Ltd* [1986] IRLR 461, which concerned an imposed salary cut for short-
    time working).
(c) The employer may apply for an *injunction* to prevent the employee's breach. This is
    most commonly found where the employee is infringing restrictive covenants or using
    trade secrets, but the courts will not make an order the effect of which is that the
    employee must continue to work for the employer against his will and will not do so
    where damages would be an adequate remedy.
(d) If the breach is very serious the employer may *summarily dismiss the employee*,
    although this may make him liable for a claim for damages if such dismissal is wrong-
    ful or unfair.

Terms may be challenged as invalid under the Unfair Contract Terms Act 1977. The **4.47**
individual must, in order to claim under the Act, show that he 'deals as a consumer'
with the other party. 'Consumer' is defined as a person who neither makes a contract
in the course of a business nor holds himself out as doing so, but in circumstances
where the other person does make the contract in the course of a business. Morland J
held that this could apply to a contract of employment agreed by the employer in the
course of business (*Brigden v American Express Bank* [2000] IRLR 94). Section 3 of
the Unfair Contract Terms Act, however, does not apply to a contract term for remuneration of an employee since he is not dealing with his employer as a consumer, nor
does he deal on its 'written standard terms of business': *Commerzbank AG v Keen*
[2007] IRLR 132.

G DISCIPLINE

'Fairness and transparency are promoted by developing and using rules and procedure **4.48**
for handling disciplinary and grievance situations. These should be set down in writing,
specific and clear' (ACAS Code No 1; Disciplinary and Grievance Procedures 2009).

4.49 The major sanction in order to maintain discipline amongst employees, of course, is dismissal (which will be considered in Chapter 10), but lesser penalties are adopted for less serious breaches of work rules. These include reprimands, suspension, demotion, transfer and the temporary withdrawal of privileges. Such disciplinary actions are only lawful so long as they are expressly or impliedly incorporated into the individual's contract of employment. Moreover, there are additional provisions striking down and modifying agreed terms at common law. The ACAS Code of Practice and Procedure 2009 also lays down detailed guidance primarily for the unfair dismissal jurisdiction. For deductions from wages, see 5.01–5.10.

4.50 In the absence of special provision in the contract of employment, there is no right to increase the disciplinary sanction on appeal (*McMillan v Airedale NHS Foundation Trust* [2015] ICR 747).

Common law

4.51 Terms are unlawful at common law which:

(a) contain servile incidents, rendering the employee no better than a slave (*Horwood v Millar's Timber & Trading Co Ltd* [1917] 1 KB 305; *Davies v Davies* (1887) 36 ChD 359); or

(b) provide for imposition of a penalty, that is a compulsory payment of money in the event of a breach of contract which does not represent a genuine pre-estimate of the damage likely to result from that breach (*Dunlop Pneumatic Tyre Co Ltd v New Garage & Motor Co Ltd* [1915] AC 79). This rule is common to all contracts. A clause in a contract which provided that 'failure to give the prior notice and work it out will result in a reduction from your final payment equivalent to the number of days short' was held to be an unlawful penalty clause. It was not a genuine pre-estimate of loss or damage. If the actual loss were nil, the employee would be liable for the calculable sum, but if the actual loss was greater than the calculable sum, he could face an unlimited claim for the balance. It was a case of 'heads I win, tails you lose' (*Giraud UK Ltd v Smith* [2000] IRLR 763; *Tullett Prebon Group Ltd v El Hajjali* [2008] IRLR 760). A deduction must be lawful and it will not be so if it is a penalty; one of the ways of testing whether it was a penalty is to contrast the difference between the sum stipulated and the most that would be likely to be awarded for damages for the breach. The position had to be addressed at the time when the contract was entered into (*Cleeve Link Ltd v Bryla* [2014] ICR 264).

Statute

4.52 The formulation of detailed disciplinary rules is encouraged by the Employment Rights Act 1996, s 3, which requires employers to specify them in the written particulars and to indicate a person to whom the employee can apply if dissatisfied with a particular disciplinary decision. Between 2004 and 5 April 2009 if the principles of prescriptive statutory disciplinary processes were not complied with, the resulting dismissal would be automatically unfair and the award could be increased by the ET. The Employment Act 2008 repealed all of the provisions about statutory disciplinary and grievance procedures but gave the tribunal a discretion to increase or decrease compensation to reflect the employee's and employer's conduct in relation to the guidance given in the ACAS Code of Practice about handling disciplinary and grievance issues.

H LAY-OFF AND SHORT-TIME WORKING

Everyone has the right to work, to free choice of employment, to just and favourable con- **4.53** ditions of work and to protection against unemployment (Art 23i, Universal Declaration of Human Rights, 1948).

Employees may be placed on short-time working with reduced or no pay, due to lack of orders, economic depression, or natural breaks in production. This practice was particularly widespread in the older industries such as shipbuilding and construction, where the legacy of casual working is still most apparent. It raises important legal problems in respect of the employer's contractual right to lay off workers, and maintenance by employees of income during such periods. We first examine the complications of the common law and then several statutory interventions, as follows:

(a) contractual rights to payment;
(b) guaranteed pay from the employer backed by statute;
(c) jobseeker's allowance; and
(d) redundancy payment.

Income support which may also be available is beyond the scope of this book.

Lay-off at common law

At common law, the employer is in breach of contract if he lays off an employee with- **4.54** out pay, unless there is an express or implied term permitting the lay-off (*Warburton v Taff Vale Railway Co* (1902) 18 TLR 420; *Hanley v Pease & Partners* [1915] 1 KB 698). A lay-off with pay is normally lawful since the employer is under no duty to provide work, but he must continue to pay employees even in the absence of their actually working. As A.L. Smith MR put it in *Turner v Sawdon* [1901] 2 KB 653: 'It is within the province of the (employer) to say that he will go on paying wages, but that he is under no obligation to provide work.' In *Browning v Crumlin Valley Collieries Ltd* [1926] 1 KB 522, a mine owner was held not to be in breach of contract in laying off his colliery workers when repair work had to be done to return the mine to a safe condition.

In *Miller v Hamworthy Engineering Ltd* [1986] IRLR 461, the employer relied on a pro- **4.55** vision in the staff terms and conditions for 'adjustments' to monthly salary for 'overtime, lost time or other alterations' to defend a claim for full wages when the employer did not provide work. The Court of Appeal held that this did not apply to an employee who was willing and able to work but not working merely because of the company's inability to provide him with work.

The courts have, however, gone some way towards implying a duty on the employer to **4.56** provide work in these three broad categories:

(a) Where the consideration for the employee's work is 'a salary plus the opportunity of becoming better known', as in the case of an actor (*Herbert Clayton & Jack Waller Ltd v Oliver* [1930] AC 209).
(b) Where the employee is engaged on skilled work, such as a chief engineer, and his skills may only be maintained with a reasonable amount of work (*Breach v Epsylon Industries Ltd* [1976] IRLR 180; also *Bosworth v Angus Jowett and Co Ltd* [1977] IRLR 374, sales director). In *Provident Financial Group plc and Whitegates Estate Agency Ltd v Hayward* [1989] IRLR 84, Dillon LJ said that the principle would apply to, for example, chartered accountants.

(c) Where remuneration is given partly by way of commission, so that the deprival of work reduces the amount which is earned, for example a commercial traveller (*Turner v Goldsmith* [1891] 1 QB 544), or journalist (*Bauman v Hulton Press Ltd* [1952] WN 556). In the Court of Appeal decision of *Devonald v Rosser and Sons* [1906] 2 KB 708 for instance, the employee's wages fluctuated with the number of items she completed, and when the employer refused to let her work during the period of notice to which she was entitled, she succeeded in an action for breach of contract. Although decided before *Browning*, this exception is more in tune with modern ideas on lay-offs than is the general principle. Thus, in *Jones v H. Sherman Ltd* (1969) 4 ITR 63, the court held that the employer had no right at common law to lay off a bookmaker manager when there was no racing.

4.57 An obligation not to put workers on short-time work has also been held to arise in other cases by way of: trade custom (*Bird v British Celanese Ltd* [1945] KB 336); collective agreements (*O'Reilly v Hotpoint Ltd* (1970) 5 ITR 68); or statute (*Wallwork v Fielding* [1922] KB 66, cf *Waine v R. Oliver (Plant Hire) Ltd* [1977] IRLR 434). An express contractual right to lay off is, however, likely to be restricted to lay-off for a reasonable period of time (*A. Dakri & Co Ltd v Tiffen* [1981] IRLR 57). If the employee is appointed expressly to a particular position, it may amount to constructive dismissal to remove the employee's duties of that engagement.

4.58 There have also been various generalised *dicta* about an implied 'right to work' in cases concerning entry to trade unions and professional bodies. It was in this context that Lord Denning MR in *Langston v AUEW* [1974] 1 All ER 980 tentatively suggested that in the case of skilled workers there is an obligation to provide a reasonable amount of work.

Income maintenance at common law

4.59 Even where lay-off is lawful, payment must normally continue throughout a period spent without work. In *Devonald*'s case (above) an attempt to establish 'custom and practice' to the contrary failed, significantly on the ground that it would be 'unreasonable' for the employer to close his factory down at any time without offering pay while the employees remained obliged to work if they were called upon to do so. Moreover, where there is an express term allowing the withholding of pay, the courts have generally construed it restrictively, for example *Minnevitch v Café de Paris* [1936] 1 All ER 884, and for a temporary period (*Millbrook Furnishing Ltd v McIntosh* [1981] IRLR 309). There are, however, two exceptions to this approach:

(a) where the lay-off is for reasons wholly *beyond the control* of the employer, such as lack of materials, a power breakdown, or mechanical mishap (see *Devonald*'s case), when the law impliedly *excludes* a right to payment; and

(b) where there is an *express term* permitting lay-off without pay.

Guarantee pay by statute

4.60 The uncertainty of these rights at common law, and the difficulty of enforcing them in the county court and High Court, stimulated the development in collective agreements of the concept of a guaranteed week securing payment during short-time working. The EPA 1975 thus stepped in to imply a restricted right to guarantee payments in every contract of employment, and in doing this the Government had the secondary aim of transferring some of the liability for loss due to intermittent work from the state to employers (which is the same policy as is apparent in statutory sick pay and statutory maternity pay).

Conditions of entitlement

Now contained in ss 28–35 of the Employment Rights Act 1996, the guarantee payment **4.61** is in a sense a temporary daily redundancy payment.

The claim must be made in respect of a 'workless day', that is a period of twenty-four **4.62** hours from midnight to midnight (s 28(1) and (3)), when the employee would have normally worked, so that like the jobseeker's allowance it does not apply to a normal idle day or holiday. To qualify, the reason for the lack of work must be:

(a) the diminution of the employer's need for the kind of work the employee does; or
(b) any other occurrence which affects the normal working of the business.

The latter, rather vague phrase has been little elucidated by litigation, but appears to comprise at least a fall in orders, lack of raw materials, power failure, bad weather and the bankruptcy of a major customer. It does not, according to the employment tribunal in *North v Pavleigh Ltd* [1978] IRLR 461, extend to the lay-off without pay because of the employer's desire to comply with Jewish holidays.

Exclusions

The right to payment is forfeited if: **4.63**

(a) The workless day is due to a *strike, lock-out or other industrial action* affecting any employee of the employer or an associated employer (s 29(3)) and this exception is now wider than the exclusions for jobseeker's allowance and income support.
(b) The employer has offered *suitable alternative employment* and the employee has unreasonably refused it (s 29(4)). It is irrelevant that the employee is not contractually obliged to perform the tasks, and a job may be considered to be suitable for a short time but not permanently (see *Purdy v Willowbank International Ltd* [1977] IRLR 388); otherwise the principles are similar to those applied in the defence to redundancy payment (16.32ff).
(c) The employee does not comply with *reasonable requirements* imposed by the employer such as that he telephone the employer each day at 10 a.m. to enquire whether work will be available (s 29(5)).
(d) The employee has been engaged for a period of *three months* or less (s 29(2)).

The following categories of workers are excluded from the right to claim: share fishermen (s 199(2)) and employees spending less than twelve weeks in employment on specific tasks (s 29(2)(b)).

Amount of payment

The employee is entitled, where none of the above exclusions applies, in any period of **4.64** three months, to as many days' guaranteed payments as he usually works in a week, subject to a maximum of five (s 31). Thus, if he normally has Friday, Saturday, and Sundays off work, he would be entitled to up to four days of payment in any quarter, but if he normally worked a six-day week, his entitlement would still be five.

The appropriate amount of payment is calculated by multiplying the employee's normal **4.65** working hours by the 'guaranteed hourly rate' (s 30(1)). For those who work regular hours each week, one divides the basic rate of pay, plus bonus, commission, and contractual overtime, by the hours worked (s 30(2)). If, on the other hand, he is on shift work, or works different hours each week, a 12-week average is taken (s 30(3)). The figures thus produced are subject to a daily maximum payment reviewed annually (ss 31, 208). Thus, if the employee normally works seven hours a day and earns £8 an hour, he is entitled at most to the maximum guarantee per day. Should (s)he labour seven hours a day at £2 per hour his entitlement would be £14 per day. From this there must always be deducted any contractual entitlement, whether by guarantee week agreement or otherwise, but only such a payment which derives from the employer and not, say, a trade union or sickness benefit (s 32) (see *Cartwright v G. Clancey Ltd* [1983] ICR 552). The statutory payment is also subject to income tax in the normal way.

4.66   If an employer does not comply with his obligations under these provisions, the employee may present a complaint to an employment tribunal within three months of his default, and the tribunal may then order the employer to pay the amount due (s 34). If, in the meantime, the employee has claimed jobseeker's allowance the sum which is paid out may be recouped. Since it may be a considerable time before the guarantee payment complaint is adjudicated upon, the worker can claim benefit and then pay back to the State from the money which he eventually receives as guarantee pay (Employment Protection (Recoupment of Jobseeker's Allowance and Income Support) Regulations 1996 (SI 1996/ 2349)).

Jobseeker's allowance

4.67   The Jobseekers Act 1995 and the Jobseeker's Allowance Regulations 1996 (SI 1996/207, as amended on several occasions) abolished the long-established unemployment benefit and replaced it with the less generous, 'contribution-based' jobseeker's allowance. Income support for unemployed persons has likewise been subsumed into the new scheme as 'income-based' jobseeker's allowance. A claimant's entitlement to jobseeker's allowance is subject to the conditions set out in the legislation (see ss 1–25 of the Act and the whole of the Regulations). The principal characteristics of the jobseeker's allowance are as follows:

(a)   Jobseeker's allowance is payable on a weekly rather than a daily basis (s 1(3)). However, where a claimant is entitled to the benefit only for part of a week, the amount which he or she receives will be calculated in accordance with the 'part-week' provisions contained in reg 150 of the 1996 Regulations.

(b)   The claimant must have entered into a jobseeker's agreement which remains in force (s 1(2)(b)). See ss 9–11 of the Act and regs 31–45 of the Regulations.

(c)   A claimant loses entitlement for any week in which his or her income exceeds the 'prescribed amount' calculated in accordance with reg 56 of the Regulations (s 2(1)(c) of the Act).

(d)   The amount of jobseeker's allowance which a claimant receives in any week depends on:
   (i)   his or her age, that is whether he or she is under 18, 18–24 years of age, or 25 and over (s 4(1)(a) and (2) of the Act and reg 79 of the Regulations);
   (ii)   any deductions in respect of earnings and pension payments received (s 4(1)(b) of the Act and regs 80 and 81 of the Regulations).

(e)   A claimant's entitlement ends after 182 days (ie six months). If necessary, he or she will then be assessed under the provisions relating to 'income-based' jobseeker's allowance, similar in most respects to those previously governing income support for the unemployed.

4.68   Entitlement to jobseeker's allowance begins only after three workless days ('waiting days') have passed (see Sch 1, para 4 to the Act and reg 46 of the Regulations). This rule is modified where an employee is subject to a pattern of intermittent working, such as lay-off or short-time; otherwise, such an employee might wait three days each time and never gain entitlement. The period may be aggregated by taking any two days in one week and adding them to any other day within the next twelve weeks. Such an employee can put the two days in the bank or 'deep freeze', taking them out when on the third necessary day work is unavailable. After this, jobseeker's allowance is claimable, and the worker does not then have to wait a further three days if he or she is laid off again, provided those are days on which the employee would normally work. Thus, if Iago is laid off every Monday and Friday, days when he is accustomed to work, he will be entitled to jobseeker's allowance from the Friday of the second week, because the first two days are treated as one jobseeking period and the next two are linked thereto, thus making up three waiting days. On the other hand, if an employee is laid off for only one day a week, and always on the same day, he will not be able to add them together (see Sch 1, paras 3 and 4 to the Act and regs 46–8 of the Regulations).

Redundancy payment

Normally a dismissal is a prerequisite for claiming a redundancy payment (Chapter 12). **4.69** An employee who is sacked with the expectation that he will be re-employed if and when work picks up is still dismissed and there is no problem about his claiming a redundancy payment. Further, where a lay-off is in breach of contract, the employee is entitled to react to the employer's breach by resigning and claiming constructive dismissal (eg *Puttick v John Wright & Sons (Blackwall) Ltd* [1972] ICR 457; *Jewell v Neptune Concrete Ltd* [1975] IRLR 147). Where the employer is in breach of contract in that he has laid off the employee for more than a reasonable period, the employee may claim a redundancy payment even though he has not complied with the elaborate statutory procedure (*A. Dakri & Co Ltd v Tiffen* [1981] IRLR 57).

The legislators went further since they considered that even without a normal statutory **4.70** dismissal a time must come when the employee can say 'enough is enough' and claim a redundancy payment. Otherwise the employer might effectively exclude his liability— by waiting for employees to resign owing to long periods of intermittent work rather than sacking them. The legislative extension provides the only circumstance where an employee can simply resign, not reacting to his employer's contractual breach, and still claim his statutory right to a redundancy payment.

By s 147 of the ERA 1996, an employee may mount the first hurdle towards securing **4.71** a redundancy payment (a dismissal) when there has been a stipulated period of short-time and/or lay-off. The statute provides that an employee is *laid off* in any week when he is entitled to no pay and on *short-time* when he earns less than half his normal week's pay. The provisions relate solely to an employee who is paid only for work he does and they depend on *pay* rather than hours worked; thus if an employee is entitled to three-quarters of his normal weekly remuneration even though he works on only one day in the week (perhaps by reason of a collective agreement), he is not treated as on short-time. This applies only to contractual remuneration and not what he might receive by way of guarantee payment, unemployment, or income support. *Continuity of employment* is also preserved during short-time and lay-off since they will be periods of 'temporary absences from work' although absence caused wholly or mainly by a *strike or lock-out* is disregarded (11.07–11.20).

The employee can commence this long route to a redundancy payment after: (i) four or **4.72** more consecutive weeks of short-time or lay-off; or (ii) six or more such weeks in any period of thirteen weeks. These weeks may consist partly of lay-off, partly of short-time, and he must then give notice to his employer within four weeks of the end of these respective periods that he *intends to claim* a redundancy payment (s 148). An employee's claim will be rejected if he has been laid off for less, even one day less, than four weeks at the time he presents his claim (*Allinson v Drew Simmons Engineering Ltd* [1985] ICR 488; see also *Spinpress Ltd v Turner* [1986] ICR 433). The notice acts as conditional resignation, but actually to gain the payment he must give one week's notice of actual termination of his contract of employment or such longer period as is expressly required of him in the contract of employment. The employee is able to see whether his claim to payment will be disputed before taking the drastic step of resigning, for the employer may serve, within seven days of the employee's communication, a counter-notice that he will contest liability to payment. Full-time work may soon resume again and as part of the statutory compromise the employer may resist payment if it is reasonably to be expected that the employee will, within four weeks, enter into thirteen consecutive weeks' employment without either short-time working or lay-off (s 152(1)) (see *Neepsend Steel Ltd v Vaughan* [1972] 3 All ER 725). He may expect new orders to come in, or that the business will be taken over. However, if the employee for the next four weeks is laid off or on short-time at all, he is conclusively presumed to be entitled to a redundancy payment.

I MOBILITY AND FLEXIBILITY CLAUSES

4.73 In some cases the description of job and place of work does not tell anything like the whole contractual story because of the presence of express or implied terms providing for flexibility on the part of the employer. It is not unusual to find a works rule book containing a provision for the working of forty hours per week or such time as may be communicated to employees by notice from time to time. The employee who works in Land's End may be surprised to find a clause in small print that he is expected to work anywhere in Great Britain, but he would still be expected to transfer to John O'Groats. Where there is any doubt in the contractual language used, however, the courts in construing such provisions adopt a test of reasonableness, so that in *Briggs v ICI* (1968) 3 ITR 276, a provision that 'you will accept the right of management to transfer you to another job with a higher or lower rate of pay whether day work, night work or shift work', was held by Lord Parker CJ to 'only entitle management to transfer the process worker to another job within the Billingham factory and only as a process worker'.

4.74 The issue most often arises in relation to redundancy payments which are made only if there is no longer a requirement for work of the particular kind which is carried on by the claimant; it is thus necessary to specify carefully what bundle of duties is comprised in the particular job (16.19ff), and where it is located.

4.75 In *Jones v Associated Tunnelling Co Ltd* [1981] IRLR 477, the EAT pointed out that a contract of employment could not be wholly silent on the place of work. The following considerations were relevant in implying such a term: the nature of the employer's business; whether or not the employee has, in fact, been moved during his employment; what he was told when engaged; and whether there is any provision to cover the employee's expenses when he was working out of daily reach of home. This principle was approved by the Court of Appeal in *Courtaulds Northern Spinning Ltd v Sibson and TGWU* [1988] IRLR 305, where it was held that in the case of an HGV driver it was implied that he would work at any depot within reasonable daily reach of his home. Conversely, in the case of *Aparau v Iceland Frozen Foods plc* [1996] IRLR 119, the EAT held that it was not necessary for there to be an implied mobility clause in the contract of employment of a cashier, when there was no express mobility clause (see also *Rank Xerox v Churchill* [1988] IRLR 280; *United Bank Ltd v Akhtar* [1989] IRLR 507; *Bass Leisure Ltd v Thomas* [1994] IRLR 104).

J REFERENCES AND PRE-EMPLOYMENT MEDICALS

An employer has a general right to give or to refuse a reference for an employee. Where **4.76** an employer gives a reference, however, he owes a duty of care to those persons (prospective employers) whom he can reasonably foresee may rely on any such reference. In *Spring v Guardian Assurance plc* [1994] ICR 596, the House of Lords decided that an employer who gave such a reference in respect of a former employee owed to that employee a duty to take reasonable care in its preparation and would be liable to him in negligence if he failed to do so and the employee thereby suffered damage. It was not (as had been argued by the employer) contrary to public policy to impose liability in this area on the ground that it might inhibit the giving of full and frank references. Lords Slynn and Woolf also found that this would be a breach of an implied term in the contract (see also *Lawton v BOC Transhield Ltd* [1987] ICR 7). In *TSB Bank plc v Harris* [2000] IRLR 157 the bank gave the employee a final warning in relation to her conduct, but she had also been the subject of complaints from customers which had not been shown to her (although she was aware of two of them). The bank reference required for a job elsewhere mentioned seventeen complaints. When she found out the reason for her job applications being rejected, the employee resigned on the basis of a breach of the implied term of trust and confidence. The employer was found to be in breach of contract because the reference was too full (see also *AB v A Chief Constable* [2014] IRLR 700).

A medical practitioner retained by a company to carry out pre-employment medical **4.77** assessments is not under any duty of care to a job applicant in assessing suitability for employment even though it is reasonably foreseeable that the applicant might suffer economic loss if a careless error in the doctor's assessment leads to the loss of opportunity of taking employment. The Court of Appeal thus held in *Kapfunde v Abbey National plc* [1998] IRLR 584, overruling the High Court decision in *Baker v Kaye* [1997] IRLR 219 on this point.

It is a breach of the duty of care to provide a reference in respect of the claimant to **4.78** subsequent employers which relied upon allegations of dishonest conduct if those allegations were not properly investigated (*Cox v Sun Alliance Life Ltd* [2001] IRLR 449). Although in order to discharge the duty of care an employer is not obliged to carry on with an enquiry into an employee's conduct after the employee has resigned, if an investigation is discontinued unfavourable comments should be confined to matters which have been investigated before the resignation. There is, however, no duty to provide for an employee a reference which is fair, full, and comprehensive; rather an employer must take reasonable care not to give misleading information about him, whether as a result of the unfairly selective provision of information or by the inclusion of facts and opinions, in such a manner as to give rise to a false or misleading inference in the mind of a reasonable recipient (*Kidd v Axa Equity & Law Life Assurance Society plc* [2000] IRLR 301).

K MEDICAL REPORTS

By s 1 of the Access to Medical Reports Act 1988, the employee has a right of access 'to **4.79** any medical report relating to the individual which is to be, or has been, supplied by a medical practitioner for employment purposes or insurance purposes'. There are various exemptions, the most important of which is when the disclosure of any part of the report 'would in the opinion of the practitioner be likely to cause serious harm to the physical

or mental health of the individual or others or would indicate the intentions of the practitioner in respect of the individual'.

4.80 This was revoked by the Employment Act 2008 but after 6 April 2009 the tribunal may consider whether the employee has presented a grievance in determining compensation under the various employment protection rights.

L RIGHT TO BE ACCOMPANIED AT DISCIPLINARY AND GRIEVANCE PROCEDURES

4.81 Section 10 of the Employment Relations Act 1999 accords a right for workers to be accompanied at disciplinary and grievance hearings where:

(a) a worker is required or invited by his employer to attend a disciplinary or grievance hearing; and

(b) the worker reasonably requests to be accompanied at the hearing.

The worker is entitled to choose the companion provided that he chooses someone who is either a fellow worker, or an employed official of a trade union (as defined in the TULR(C)A 1992), or a lay official whom 'the union has reasonably certified in writing as having experience of or as having received training in acting as a worker's companion at disciplinary or grievance hearings' (s 10(3)). If the chosen companion will not be available at the time specified by the employer, but the worker notifies an alternative time which is reasonable and within five working days of the day proposed by the employer, the hearing must be postponed to the time which is specified by the worker.

4.82 The companion has the following rights:

(a) to address the hearing in order to put the worker's case; sum up the case; and respond on the worker's behalf to any view expressed at the hearing (s 10(2B)(a) as amended by s 36 of the Employment Relations Act 2004);

(b) to confer with the worker during the hearing (s 10(2B)(b));

(c) to have paid time off to attend the hearing (s 10(6)); and

(d) not to be dismissed or suffer a detriment (s 12) for exercising these rights.

Importantly, however, the companion has no right to answer questions on behalf of the worker nor to address the hearing if the worker indicates at that hearing that he does not wish his companion to do so. Further, he must not use the powers conferred on him to prevent the employer from explaining his case or prevent any other person at the hearing from making a contribution. Once a worker has made a reasonable request to be accompanied to a disciplinary hearing, the employer has to accept the companion chosen by the worker subject to the safeguard which is contained in s 10(3) (*Roberts v GB Oils Ltd* [2014] ICR 462).

4.83 A disciplinary or grievance hearing is defined as a hearing which is held in the course of a disciplinary or grievance procedure established or adopted by an employer which:

(a) in the case of a disciplinary hearing, could result directly in the employer administering a formal warning to the worker or taking some other action in respect of him (s 13(4)); and

(b) in the case of a grievance hearing, 'concerns the performance of a duty by the employer in relation to a worker' (s 13(5)).

4.84 Whether there was a disciplinary hearing depends on findings of fact by the tribunal, which could look at the form and the substance of what took place, the process of decision-making and the possible consequences that might follow by way of action or sanction. A formal warning includes a disciplinary warning that became part of the employee's record. 'The taking of some other action in respect of the worker by his employer' in the subsection was to be read as meaning some sort of action similar to a warning, namely a disciplinary sanction, but did not include training, counselling, and advice. Where what was described as an informal oral warning became part of the employee's record, it was in reality a formal warning (*London Underground Ltd v Ferenc-Batchelor* [2003] ICR 656). A disciplinary hearing does not include a meeting which is held to reach a redundancy decision (*Heathmill Multimedia ASP Ltd v Jones* [2003] IRLR 856).

A 'worker' is widely defined for these purposes by s 13 so as to include: **4.85**

(a) an employee;
(b) a person working under any other contract where the individual undertakes to do or perform personally any work or services for another whose status is not that of a client or customer of any profession or business undertaking carried on by the individual;
(c) an agency worker;
(d) a home worker; and
(e) a person in Crown employment, except members of the naval, military, air, or reserve forces of the Crown.

A fair process does not necessarily have to involve a full trial process (*Hendy v Ministry of Justice* [2014] IRLR 856). **4.86**

A worker may complain to an employment tribunal if the employer either fails to comply or 'threatens to fail to comply' with the new right to be accompanied. The complaint must be brought within three months of the failure or threat or, if not reasonably practicable, within such period as is reasonable. Compensation will be limited to two weeks' pay (subject to the weekly maximum, now £479). **4.87**

5

STATUTORY REGULATION
OF WAGES AND HOURS

A DEDUCTIONS FROM WAGES 5.01

    The policy 5.01

    Deductions 5.03

    Retail employment 5.11

    Exceptions 5.12

B ITEMISED PAY STATEMENT 5.15

C THE NATIONAL MINIMUM WAGE 5.19

    Coverage 5.19

    Amount 5.25

    Hours to be taken into account 5.26

    Calculating the payment made 5.36

    Records and enforcement 5.44

D WORKING TIME REGULATIONS 5.47

    Coverage 5.51

    What is working time? 5.52

    General exclusions 5.55

    Annual leave 5.61

    Night workers .5.68

    Exclusion by agreement 5.70

    Enforcement 5.71

    Employment protection provisions 5.75

E SUNDAY TRADING 5.76

A DEDUCTIONS FROM WAGES

The policy

5.01 The Truck Act 1896 sought to protect vulnerable employees and prevent deductions from wages to take account of defective workmanship. These provisions were repealed by the Wages Act 1986 which is now consolidated as Pt II of the ERA 1996. By s 13 of the ERA 1996, an employer may not make any deduction from any wages of any worker unless the deduction is required or authorised by statute (eg PAYE and national insurance contributions) or by contract, or alternatively unless the worker has previously signified in writing his agreement or consent to making it.

5.02 The jurisdiction over deductions is now the second largest source of complaints to employment tribunals after unfair dismissal.

Deductions

5.03 It is necessary first to analyse what is a wage, and what qualifies as a deduction from that wage. The employment tribunal must determine what amount is *properly payable* and so whether the sum actually paid is a deduction therefrom (eg *Greg May (CF&C) Ltd v Dring* [1990] IRLR 19; see also *Bruce v Wiggins Teape (Stationery) Ltd* [1994] IRLR 536; *Davies v Hotpoint Ltd* [1994] IRLR 538).

5.04 Section 27 of the ERA 1996 defines 'wages' very widely as any sums payable by the employer to the worker in connection with the employment including 'any fee, bonus, commission, holiday pay or other emolument referable to his employment, whether payable under his contract or otherwise'. This includes commission which is expressed to be discretionary and non-contractual (*Kent Management Services v Butterfield* [1992] ICR 272; cf *New Century Cleaning Co Ltd v Church* [2000] IRLR 27) and a previously agreed proportion of a restaurant's service charge (*Saavedra v Aceground Limited t/a Terrazza Est* [1995] IRLR 199, EAT; cf 5.15–5.18 below). A non-contractual bonus fell within the definition of wages where there was a legal obligation resting on the employer to pay the bonus and a legal entitlement to receive it on the employee so that once an employer told the employee he was going to receive the bonus he was obliged to pay it (*Farrell Matthews & Weir v Hansen* [2005] ICR 509). Commissions which become payable after termination of the contract are also treated as 'wages' (*Robertson v Blackstone Franks Investment Management Ltd* [1998] IRLR 376). The failure to make payment for annual leave was held to give rise to a deduction claim (*List Design Group Ltd v Douglas* [2003] IRLR 14) but this was overruled by the Court of Appeal in *IRC v Ainsworth* [2005] ICR 1149 because it could not have been Parliament's intention that the deductions provisions should apply in the case of a subsequently created statutory right which came with its own enforcement regime. In *Stringer v HMRC* [2009] IRLR 214 (as *Ainsworth* was then named) the ECJ held that the entitlement of every worker to paid annual leave must be regarded as a particularly important principle of Community social law from which there can be no derogations and whose implementation by the competent national authorities must be confined within the limits in the Directive. Article 7(1) precludes national legislation which provides that the right to paid annual leave is extinguished at the end of the leave year and/or a carry-over period laid down by national law even where the worker could not exercise his right to paid annual leave because he was on sick leave during the whole or part of the leave year.

The House of Lords in *Delaney v Staples* [1992] ICR 483 decided that payment in lieu of notice is not included in the definition of 'wages'. The essential characteristic of the concept of wages is that wages are consideration for work done or to be done under a contract of employment, whereas 'if a payment is not referable to an obligation on the employee under a subsisting contract of employment to render his services' it does not qualify (at 488d–e). The primary consequence of this important ruling was that claims for payment in lieu of notice had to be brought in the county court or High Court, but this anomalous position was modified by the Employment Tribunals (Extension of Jurisdiction) Order 1994 (SI 1994/1623), which (subject to certain exceptions) extends the jurisdiction of employment tribunals to contractual claims existing at the time of termination of employment up to a maximum of £25,000 per claim (a limit which has not been increased since it was introduced). **5.05**

A deduction means that there is a failure or refusal to pay the amount agreed to be properly payable by way of remuneration (*Delaney v Staples* [1991] IRLR 112, CA). There are these subrules: **5.06**

(a) It must be a specified sum which is properly payable and not a claim for damages, for example, to replace a bonus system; to count it must be a reasonably quantifiable sum (*Coors Brewers v Adcock* [2007] IRLR 440).
(b) It does not matter that the *reason* for the refusal to pay is that the employer disputes that the sum is properly due.
(c) It is also a deduction unilaterally to abolish a wages supplement, so that in *McCree v Tower Hamlets London Borough Council* [1992] ICR 99, the employer was not able to avoid the effect of the Act by absorbing a sum into pay increases with a view to showing that there was no deduction at all.

Agreement to deduct

5.07 In order to be effective in permitting a deduction, agreement must have been reached *before* the conduct or events on account of which the deduction is made, rather than on or after the date when the deduction is taken from the wages, and must have been notified to the employee in writing before the date of deduction. In *Discount Tobacco & Confectionery Ltd v Williamson* [1993] ICR 371, the employee was manager of a store in which, in December 1988 and February 1989, there were large stock deficiencies. In March 1989 he signed a document giving to the employer the right to deduct £3,500 from his pay at the rate of £20 per week. In May 1989 there was a further deficiency. It was held that the employer could deduct only in relation to the last event (see *Potter v Hunt Contractors Ltd* [1992] ICR 337; *Fairfield Ltd v Skinner* [1992] ICR 836). Similar provisions apply to the employer's right to receive payments from his employee, but not to agreements that the employer is to pay over a certain amount to a third party such as a trade union under the check-off procedure for which there are special provisions. The variation itself may be agreed orally (*York City & District Travel Ltd v Smith* [1990] IRLR 213).

5.08 As part of its decision on deductions, the employment tribunal may indeed have to answer complex questions about the assessment of wages under particular contracts. In *Thames Water Utilities v Reynolds* [1996] IRLR 186, for example, when the employee was made redundant he was owed eight days' holiday pay. He had been engaged on an annual salary, and the employers paid him 8/365ths of that salary. The employee brought a deductions claim before the tribunal, arguing that the apportionment should have been made on the basis of the number of *working* days in a year (and not calendar days), which would have meant that he should have been paid 8/260ths of his salary. The tribunal, applying the Apportionment Act 1870, s 2, upheld his claim, but the EAT allowed the employer's appeal. The correct interpretation of the section (which states that, unless the contrary is intended, money due is to be 'considered as accruing from day to day') is that it applies to calendar days, not working days (see also *Taylor v Lowe* [2000] IRLR 780).

5.09 In *Giraud UK Ltd v Smith* [2000] IRLR 763, the employer had an unlimited right to make deductions if the worker failed to work out his notice after resigning and this was accordingly within the exemption. On the other hand, in *Tullett Prebon v El-Hajjali* [2008] IRLR 760, a provision requiring a newly hired worker with specialist skills to pay a substantial sum if he failed to start work was a valid attempt to pre-estimate the employer's loss.

5.10 Timing is crucial in making a claim. It is only at the stage when the employer fails to pay a sum due by way of remuneration at the appropriate time—that is, the contractual time for payment—that the claim for an unlawful deduction may arise. The fact that payment is normally made earlier than when it is due is irrelevant (*Group 4 Nightspeed Ltd v Gilbert* [1997] IRLR 398).

Retail employment

5.11 Special rules apply to the employer of a worker in *retail* employment, defined as involving the supply of goods and services directly to members of the public. Such an employer must not deduct in respect of cash shortages or stock deficiencies more than one-tenth of the gross amount which is payable to the worker on a particular pay day (save on the final pay day of the employment or payment in lieu of notice) (ERA 1996, s 18(1)), and must make a written demand for payment. Any complaint about unauthorised deductions must be made to an employment tribunal within three months of the incident in question (the

ERA 1996, s 23). No contracting out of the provisions is permitted save by an agreement reached after action has been taken by an ACAS Conciliation Officer.

Exceptions

These provisions on deductions do not, however, apply to: **5.12**

(a) overpayment of wages or expenses. In *Home Office v Ayres* [1992] ICR 175, the Home Office overpaid a prison officer £830 over two months. There was, however, no explanation given by the employer for the changing rate of pay, and the employee assumed that the money had been paid correctly and spent it on normal living expenses. The employers deducted the moneys in future wage payments and the employee successfully challenged this under the Wages Act 1986, relying on *Avon CC v Howlett* [1983] IRLR 171. This was reconsidered in *Sunderland Polytechnic v Evans* [1993] IRLR 196, and it was held that there was no requirement that the word 'lawful' be implied before 'deductions' in the ERA 1996, s 13. As to the definition of expenses, in *London Borough of Southwark v O'Brien* [1996] IRLR 420, the EAT held that payment of a mileage allowance to the employee would be construed as expenses rather than remuneration, notwithstanding that the allowance received was greater than the amount which was actually spent on petrol by the employee, if the allowance was specifically intended to pay for petrol;

(b) deductions in consequence of statutory disciplinary proceedings (not applying in the main to private employers but to services such as the police or fire service: *Chiltern House Ltd v Chambers* [1990] IRLR 88);

(c) a statutory requirement on the employer to pay over specified sums to a statutory authority (*McCree v Tower Hamlets London Borough Council* [1992] ICR 99);

(d) any arrangement agreed to by the employee whereby the employer is to pay over amounts notified to a third party;

(e) any payment on account of the worker taking part in a strike or other industrial action;

(f) any payment to satisfy a court judgment or tribunal decision (ERA 1996, s 14(6)); or

(g) errors in computation (but this does not include a conscious decision not to make a payment (cf *Yemm v British Steel plc* [1994] IRLR 117; *Morgan v West Glamorgan CC* [1995] IRLR 68).

There is no restriction on making claims in the civil court for unpaid wages even though **5.13** a claim could be brought under Pt II of the ERA 1996 on the same facts (*Rickard v P.B. Glass Supplies* [1990] ICR 150). The deduction jurisdiction cannot, however, be used where a decision needs to be taken about the entitlement to statutory sick pay where the determination of the sum lies exclusively with the Board of Inland Revenue (*Sarti Ltd v Polito* [2008] ICR 1279).

The Employment Act 2008 adds a new s 24(2) ERA so that the tribunal may award **5.14** 'such amount as the tribunal considers appropriate in all the circumstances to compensate the worker for any financial loss sustained by him which is attributable to the matter complained of'.

B ITEMISED PAY STATEMENT

Section 8 of the ERA 1996 gives to every employee the right to a written pay statement at **5.15** or before every payment of wages or salary. It must distinguish:

(a) the gross amount of wages or salary;

(b) the net amount payable;

(c) where different parts of the net amount are paid in different ways, the amount and method of each part payment; and

(d) any variable or fixed deductions therefrom.

5.16 In the case of fixed deductions (eg union contributions, or payments in respect of fines or maintenance), a new statement need not be given at each time payment is made. Instead, a single communication may cover a maximum of twelve months, but should always be specific, the label 'miscellaneous deductions' being inadequate (*Milsom v Leicestershire County Council* [1978] IRLR 433; see ERA 1996, s 9(2)). It should include the amount of the deduction, the intervals at which it is to be made and its purpose. This necessitates some definition of wages and it has been held that waiters' tips are not generally to be regarded as wages, so that the taking of sums by the employers in accordance with an internal company agreement is not a deduction which has to be notified (*Cofone v Spaghetti House Ltd* [1980] ICR 155).

5.17 The employee need not ask for such a statement (*Coales v John Wood & Co* [1986] IRLR 129); it must be given without request.

5.18 If the statement is not produced or there is a dispute over the terms it contains, an employment tribunal may: (a) declare the particulars which should have been included; and (b) order the employer to make up the unnotified deductions which have been made up to a period of thirteen weeks immediately preceding the application (ERA 1996, s 12). This is a penal provision and thus is to be construed restrictively. In *Scott v Creager* [1979] IRLR 162, the employment tribunal took into account that the respondent was a dentist with a busy professional practice, short of time to fulfil his statutory duty, that the requirement was then new and that he had to pay the solicitors for the costs of defending the claim, and thus made no award.

C THE NATIONAL MINIMUM WAGE

Coverage

5.19 The right to receive the national minimum wage came into effect on 1 April 1999 following the implementation of the National Minimum Wage Act (NMWA) 1998 and the National Minimum Wage Regulations (NMWR) 1999 (SI 1999/584). Both have been amended and the present Regulations are National Minimum Wage Regulations 2015 SI No 621 (although there were few changes of substance from the predecessor Regulations). The Act provides that a 'worker' shall be remunerated at no less than the national minimum wage, as long as he is above compulsory school age and works, or ordinarily works, in the United Kingdom. Section 17 of the NMWA implies this into the contract of every worker who is within scope. There is no qualifying period for the right. The term 'worker' is defined in exactly the same way as in the Working Time Regulations (see 5.51), so will include all workers save for those who are obviously self-employed. This applies to *former* workers by the National Minimum Wage (Enforcement Notices) Regulations 2003. The best estimate is that about 5 per cent of the British workforce earns at national minimum wage levels. Importantly by s 28 of the Act there is a presumption that the minimum wage is not being paid unless the contrary is proved.

5.20 The NMWA specifically excludes from protection share fishermen (s 43), voluntary workers (s 44), and prisoners working under the prison rules (s 45). In addition, those working in religious communities are excluded. This is defined as individuals who are residential members of religious and other similar communities where the community is a charity, its purpose is to practise or advance a religious or similar belief, and all or some of the members live together for that purpose.

The NMWA contains special provisions with regard to agency workers, which effectively **5.21** prevent such individuals from being excluded from the ambit of the Act by virtue of the absence of a worker's contract between the individual and the agent and the principal. In these circumstances, by s 34(2) of the NMWA, such a contract shall be deemed to exist between the individual and the agent or principal. The identity of the other party to this 'deemed contract' depends upon the arrangements which are in place for the payment of the individual concerned (s 34(2)).

Personal work

In keeping with the wide ambit of the coverage of the NMWA, the usual definition of **5.22** 'worker' contained in s 54(3) of the Act is also extended in the case of homeworkers. This extension is achieved by removing the requirement that the work is executed 'personally' (NMWA, s 35(1)). The term 'homeworker' is also broad and encompasses an individual who 'contracts with a person, for the purposes of that person's business, for the execution of work to be done in a place not under the control or management of that person' (NMWA, s 35(2)). A homeworker need not actually work physically at his home but merely in a place which is not under the control or management of the other party: *James v Redcats (Brands) Ltd* [2007] IRLR 296.

The requirement that the individual has ceased to be of compulsory school age contained **5.23** in NMWA s 1(2)(c) is developed further in the NMWR, so that there are different rates for apprentices, those aged under eighteen, those eighteen but not yet twenty-one, and those who are twenty-one or over but not yet twenty-five, and then for those over twenty-five (which is known as the living wage and is based on median earnings) (NMWR, reg 4A).

The protection of the NMWA is also substantially extended to Crown employment (s 36), **5.24** House of Lords and House of Commons staff (ss 38, 39), but not to the armed forces (s 37). The National Minimum Wage (Offshore Employment) Order 1999 (SI 1999/1128) extended the provisions of the Act to people working in the territorial waters of the United Kingdom.

Amount

The national minimum wage is currently (as from 1 October 2016) £7.20 per hour for **5.25** those aged over twenty-five (reg 11, known as the national living wage), £6.70 for those between twenty-one and twenty-four, and £5.30 per hour for eighteen to twenty-one-year-olds (reg 13, the development rate). There is an exception for these gradations from the age discrimination provisions (Equality Act 2010 Sch 9 para 11). Work does not include work in relation to an employer's family household (reg 57). There are also exemptions for certain training schemes such as those funded by the Government or the European Social Fund. Under s 2 of the 1998 Act, the Secretary of State is empowered to make regulations which may amend these provisions. The minimum wage need not be paid to a 'member of the family' and the test of treatment as a 'member of the family' requires an overall approach to family membership with the accommodation which is provided to the member as only one of several relevant factors. With regard to the provision of accommodation, the test is not whether a particular standard is provided but whether the worker is treated as a member of the employer's family household. As to sharing tasks, the work involved has to relate to the employer's family household but is not concerned solely with chores within the home which are undertaken by family members which fall outside the scope of the paid duties of the worker; a person receiving free accommodation and meals might be expected to perform more household duties than other family members. The performance of onerous duties may also be inconsistent with treatment as a member of the family (*Nambalat v Taher* [2013] ICR 1025).

Hours to be taken into account

5.26   The regulations governing how the hourly rate of pay is determined are necessarily complex and require that a distinction be drawn between what is and what is not *work*. The important concept underlying them is the pay reference period (regs 8, 9), which will normally be a month unless this is expressly stated to be otherwise. It is then necessary to calculate the number of hours worked in a specific pay period. This is calculated differently depending on what the type of work is which the worker carries out, and the various categories which are delineated by statute are salaried hours work, time work, output work, or unmeasured work (regs 30, 36, 44, respectively).

5.27   Time work is defined by NMWR, reg 30, as work that is paid for according to set or varying hours or periods of time and which is not salaried hours work. This will include circumstances in which the worker's pay is set according to a measure of output per hour or other period of time during the whole of which the worker is required to work. This would therefore cover the pieceworker in the factory who is required to clock in and out at specified times. Pay may go up and down depending on the amount of hours worked. Those on zero hours contracts fall under this heading.

5.28   The other types of work are:

(a) Salaried hours work, which is defined in NMWR, reg 2, as being work done under a contract to do salaried hours work under which the worker is entitled to no payment in addition to his annual salary other than a performance bonus. A contract to perform salaried hours work is a contract under which the worker is entitled to be paid for an ascertainable basic number of hours in a year, and in respect of these basic hours he is entitled to be paid an annual salary by equal weekly or monthly instalments regardless of how many hours the individual actually works in that period. The fact that overtime may be worked in return for additional payments does not prevent the contract from qualifying as a salaried hours work contract. Office work would normally fit in this rubric.

(b) Output work is defined in NMWR, reg 36, by exclusion as work which is paid for under a worker's contract that is not time work and which, apart from the national minimum wage, is paid for under the contract wholly by reference to the number of pieces which are made or processed by the worker, or number of tasks performed. Output work will therefore cover circumstances in which the worker is engaged on piecework or commission work without the obligation to work certain hours.

    Under the regime of 'rated output' work, the employer must determine the 'mean hourly output rate' on an actual or estimated basis. This will be used when working out the hourly pay rate of the worker. The employer must make an estimate of the mean speed at which the output work is done on 'a sample of the employer's workers which is so far as reasonably practicable, representative as respects the speed at which they work, of the speed at which the workers who produce the measure of output work; ... the average speed is reasonably adjusted to take into account the likely

difference in time involved in the worker doing the output work in the worker's physical conditions in comparison to the test which was carried out' (reg 42).

(c) Unmeasured work is defined in NMWR, reg 44, and is a sweeping-up provision. Such
work is defined as any work which is not time work, salaried hours work, or output
work, including, in particular, work in respect of which there are no specified hours
and where the worker is required to work when needed.

It is fundamental to determine what actually constitutes 'work' for the purposes of
the 2015 Regulations, and there are specific provisions as to what will count as hours
worked, in order to decide whether a worker has been paid the national minimum wage
for it. Again, whether an activity constitutes work will depend on the basis on which the
worker is paid, according to the four categories set out above.

Time work

The provisions determining which time counts for the purposes of time work are con-   **5.29**
tained in NMWR, regs 31 to 35. Time at which the worker is actually working is obviously included. To this must be added time when the worker is available at or near his
place of work for the purpose of doing time work and is required to be available for such
work, but the time of availability to be counted 'only includes hours when the worker is
awake for the purposes of working even if the worker by arrangement sleeps at or near a
place of work and the employer provides suitable facilities for sleeping' (reg 32(2)). This
is a controversial area.

On-call provisions are difficult to fit into the statutory structure. Employees operating the   **5.30**
employer's emergency booking service from home during night-time hours were 'working' notwithstanding that between telephone calls they could undertake other activities,
such as watching television or reading. They were held to be engaged on 'time work'
within the meaning of the NMWR and were entitled to be paid at the minimum rate for
all hours that they were on duty (*British Nursing Association v Inland Revenue* [2002]
IRLR 472). In determining when a worker is working, the essential task of a tribunal is
to look at the ingredients of a particular case, that is, the type of work that is involved
and the different elements thereof, to see if they can properly be described accurately as
'work'. Aspects which may be looked at in this respect include the nature of the work
in its substance and the extent to which the employee's activities are restricted by not
performing a particular task. Thirdly, although the way in which the parties approach
their mutual obligations and the manner in which remuneration is calculated are not
conclusive, calculation of pay by reference to a shift would provide some illustration of
the nature of the obligation for which remuneration is being made. Fourthly, bearing in
mind that ascertaining what is 'work' is part of a process which is required to be gone
through in order to calculate mathematically the number of hours to which the minimum
wage requirements apply, one of the guiding principles should be the extent to which the
period during which work is being performed is readily ascertainable. In *Scottbridge
Construction Ltd v Wright* [2003] IRLR 7, the Court of Session decided that a night
watchman was entitled to remuneration not only in respect of those hours when he was
required to be awake for the purpose of performing a particular task but for all of the
time when he was required to be on the employer's premises in his role of night watchman. The tribunal had confused its estimate of the time during which he was generally
active with an overall consideration of what was required of him as a night watchman at
any time (see also *Burrow Down Support Services Ltd v Rossiter* [2008] ICR 1172; *Wray
v JW Lees & Co (Brewers) Ltd* [2012] ICR 43). Work that was paid for by reference to
something other than time, even though payment might be expressed to be by the day,
was not, however, 'time work' (*Walton v Independent Living Organisation Ltd* [2003]

ICR 688). Here it was payment by the tasks required that was unmeasured work. If the reason why the employer requires the employee to be on the premises is to fulfil a statutory obligation to have a suitable person there (at a residential care home) 'just in case', the work would be time work (*Esparon v Slavikovska* [2014] ICR 1037).

Hours which are specifically picked out as not treated as work include absence from work, taking part in industrial action, and rest breaks (reg 35).

5.31 Sleepovers were considered as time working in a circumstance where the employee carried out shifts from 1pm to 7am to provide care if needed for three disabled young people. The answer to the question whether this was work did not depend on the actual level of activity involved by the worker. In *Whittlestone v BJP Home Support Ltd* [2014] ICR 275, specific hours were required of the worker on pain of discipline if they were not spent there. No distinction should be drawn between core hours and others in the contract as they were all working hours. The client was on a rota and the worker was obliged to visit each client in turn during the course of the day with inevitable travelling time between and that time was within the general control of the employer who was arranging the assignments that were to be counted as time work (see also *McCartney v Oversley House Management* [2006] IRLR 514; see also in ECJ *Dellas v Premier Ministre* [2006] IRLR 225).

5.32 There is a clear difference between cases where an employee is *working* merely by being present at the employer's premises and those where the employee is provided with sleeping accommodation and is merely *on call*. Here the claimants were merely on call at night outside contracted hours and could not be said to be working (*South Manchester Abbeyfield Society Ltd v Hopkins* [2011] ICR 254).

5.33 Special provisions are made in respect of travelling time for time work (NMWR, reg 34). Time spent travelling for the purpose of duties carried out by the worker will normally be treated as time work. There is an exception where the travelling which is carried on is incidental to the duties 'to the extent that the time is time when the worker would not otherwise be working' (NMWR, reg 34(1)). Where the travelling is from the home of the worker to his place of work (NMWR, reg 15(2)(b)) the time is excluded from the calculation. By reg 34(2) hours treated as such when the worker would 'otherwise be working' include '(a) hours when the worker is travelling for the purpose of carrying out assignments to be carried out at different places between which the worker is obliged to travel and which are not places occupied by the employer; (b) hours when the worker is travelling where it is uncertain whether the worker would otherwise be working because the worker's hours of work vary either as to their length or in respect of the time at which they are performed'.

Output work

5.34 The general rule with regard to output work in NMWR, reg 37, is that the 'output work worked by a worker in a pay reference period shall be the total number of hours spent by the worker during the pay reference period in doing output work ...'. There are special rules for training and travelling time and as to the meaning of average hourly output rate (regs 39 to 43).

Unmeasured work

5.35 In common with the position for output work, the parties may come to a 'daily average' agreement for unmeasured work for the purpose of calculating the hours worked. The general rule for unmeasured work in the absence of such an agreement is contained in NMWR, reg 45, which provides that the unmeasured work which is done by a worker in a pay reference period shall be the total of the number of hours which have been spent by him during the pay reference period in carrying out the contractual duties required of him under his contract to do such work. There are special rules as to training, travelling, industrial action, and the daily average agreement.

Calculating the payment made

Regulation 7 NMWR provides the general determination as to whether the national **5.36** minimum wage has been paid in this form: 'a worker is to be treated as remunerated by the employer in a pay reference period at the hourly rate determined by the calculation- R/H where R is the remuneration in the pay reference period. H is the hours of work in the pay reference period'. The pay reference period is a maximum of one month or if less than this the period by which pay is determined (reg 6). The calculation is made on the basis of gross pay (*Joshi v Sandercock* EAT 1140/02). Regulation 9(1)(b) of the 2015 Regulations provides that any payments that are earned during one pay reference period but are received in the following period are to be allocated to the period in which they are earned.

In order to calculate what counts as pay for the purposes of the national minimum wage, **5.37** it is thus first necessary to determine the 'total of remuneration' for the purposes of NMWR, reg 9. This figure is the sum of money payments determined in accordance with NMWR, reg 9, and is produced by adding together all money payments which have been paid by the employer to the worker in the pay reference period, as well as any money payments which have been paid by the employer to the worker in the following pay reference period in respect of the relevant pay reference period, whether in respect of work or not.

Accommodation

Benefits in kind (such as free gym membership or luncheon vouchers) are generally **5.38** excluded from this calculation, but the one exception to this rule is an amount in respect of accommodation. However, even then the circumstances in which such a benefit can be taken into account, and the amount which may be attributable to it, are strictly controlled. In order to qualify towards payment of the national minimum wage, the provision of accommodation must satisfy the requirements of NMWR, regs 14 and 15, that the employer must not be entitled to make any deduction from the wages of the worker or to receive any payment from him. If these requirements are satisfied the amounts to be taken into account are determined by NMWR, reg 16, which effectively limits the value to be ascribed to the benefit at £5.35 per day (see *Revenue and Customs Commissioners v Leisure Employment Services Ltd* [2007] ICR 1056).

The very concept of an allowance needs to be analysed: it is a payment attributable to an **5.39** element which is distinct from the worker's performance of his basic job. Other elements treated by the parties as deserving separate recognition remain payable as additional elements so that a sleep-in payment which is a payment for performing the sleep-in duty is inherently different from, for example, a separate payment if the employee has a disturbed night (*Smith v Oxfordshire Learning Disability NHS Trust* [2009] ICR 1395).

The NMWR also specifically exclude certain elements from being treated as 'payments' **5.40** by the employer. These include any payment by way of an advance of wages or a loan (reg 10(a)), any pension payments (reg 10(b)), any payment of an award made by a court or a tribunal or a similar settlement, other than a payment due under the worker's contract (reg 10(c)), any payment referable to the worker's redundancy (reg 10(d)), and any payment by way of an award under a suggestions scheme (reg 10(e)).

5.41 Overtime and shift premia payments need to be subtracted under NMWR, reg 10(i) to (k). This will cover any payment made to the worker on account of the fact that he has to perform the work at a particular time, on bank holidays etc. In such circumstances the higher premium rate of pay must be disregarded.

5.42 Other elements to be excluded are any money payment which is made by the employer to the worker representing an amount paid by customers by way of a service charge, tip, gratuity, or cover charge that is not paid through the payroll (see NMWR, reg 10(m)). Payments to an employee from a tronc of tips were not to be treated as payments by the employer because when the money went from the employer to the troncmaster (who holds tips) it was paid to the troncmaster's account (*Revenue and Customs Commissioners v Annabel's (Berkeley Square) Ltd* [2008] ICR 1076). The BEIS Code of Best Practice requires that businesses display prior to the point of purchase their policy on tips and service charge and that they inform workers fully about how such payments are distributed.

In addition, any payments or deductions which are calculated to cover payments made by the worker in the course of his work are excluded (NMWR, reg 10(l)). However, the general rule that deductions made by the employer are to be subtracted from the relevant total of remuneration is specifically excluded in certain cases. These exclusions are provided for in NMWR, reg 12, so that such deductions are permitted where the deduction is made on the basis of the conduct of the worker, or any other event, in respect of which he is contractually liable (see *HMRC v Lorne Stewart* [2015] ICR 708). In addition, deductions are permitted with respect to loan advances or advances of wages, recovery of a previous accidental overpayment of wages, and any reduction 'in respect of the purchase by the worker of any shares, other securities or share option, or of any share in a partnership'. Similar provisions also apply to the payments which are not to be subtracted from the total of remuneration (NMWR, reg 12).

5.43 In *Laird v A K Stoddart Ltd* [2001] IRLR 591 there was no breach of the NMWR when the employer varied the claimant's terms by consolidating 40p of a 70p an hour attendance allowance into the basic hourly rate of £3.27 to produce a new hourly rate of £3.67. An attendance allowance on its own would have had to be excluded. This could not be achieved without agreement, however, since the attendance allowance could be taken into account in determining what was properly payable for the purposes of deductions.

Records and enforcement

5.44 The 1999 Regulations impose a duty on the employer to keep records of all workers who qualify for the national minimum wage, 'sufficient to establish that he is remunerating the worker at a rate at least equal to the National Minimum Wage' (reg 59) and a worker has the right, subject to the provisions of s 10 of the Act, to inspect and examine the records relating to him. A worker is able by the 1998 Act to bring a claim before the employment tribunal if he believes that he is not receiving the national minimum wage. This can also be brought as a contractual claim. There is another claim if he is unfairly dismissed or victimised for asserting his rights thereto under the Act (ss 17–26).

5.45 A wages officer may serve a notice of underpayment requiring the employer to pay to the worker the sum due for any one or more pay reference periods before the relevant day but not more than six years earlier. Such a notice must also require the employer to pay a financial penalty to the Secretary of State within twenty-eight days (s 19A(1)) of

200 per cent of the total underpayments. There is a floor of £100 (s 19A(6)) and a maximum of £20,000 per worker as from 2014 by amendments made in the Small Business, Enterprise and Employment Act. There are provisions for suspension of this penalty if criminal proceedings have been instituted. There is a route for appeal to the employment tribunal within four weeks of service and the tribunal may amend or rescind. The reality is that enforcement of the minimum wage legislation has been thus far woefully inadequate.

The 1998 Act also established the Low Pay Commission and provides for what matters **5.46** may be referred to it (ss 5–8).

D WORKING TIME REGULATIONS

The Working Time Regulations 1998 (SI 1998/1833) are an unusual crossover between **5.47** employment law and health and safety law, and were introduced to implement in the UK the EU Working Time Directive passed on 23 November 1993 and the EU Young Workers Directive passed on 22 June 1994. Subsequent amendments have been made, most notably the removal of the 13-week minimum period of employment in order to claim annual leave after the judgment of the European Court of Justice in *R v Secretary of State for Trade and Industry, ex p BECTU* [2001] IRLR 559 (Working Time (Amendment) Regulations 2001 (SI 2001/3256)) and the removal of various exclusions including doctors in training as from 2004. The work/life balance is often thought of as being especially applicable to women but these provisions are more general. There are thirty-four ILO Conventions dealing with working time.

The aim of the Regulations is specifically to improve health and safety (*Federatie* **5.48** *Nederlasnmdse Vakbeweging* [2006] ICR 962) and according to the Government's public consultation document, 'a better balance between work and home', 'greater choice over hours of work', and 'improvements in health'.

The key provisions in the Regulations are as follows: **5.49**

(a) a maximum for weekly hours of forty-eight per week over a 'reference period', (normally) seventeen weeks, although this can be extended by agreement to twenty-six weeks (reg 4; the averaging of working time is laid down in reg 4(6));
(b) daily rest breaks of eleven hours in a twenty-four-hour period (reg 10) and a young worker may not work between 10pm and 6am;
(c) where the pattern of work puts the health and safety of a worker at risk, in particular because the work is monotonous or the work rate is predetermined, the employer must ensure that the employee is given adequate rest breaks (reg 8);
(d) weekly rest breaks of one day off per week, which need not be a Sunday (reg 11);
(e) a rest break of twenty minutes if the worker works more than six hours' work at one time (reg 12); and
(f) annual leave of four weeks (reg 13).

These are the minimum 'floor of rights' which may be built on by agreement (see *Corps of Commissionaires Management Ltd v Hughes* [2009] IRLR 122) and the employee must benefit from the rest as opposed to compensation (*Commission of European Communities v UK* [2006] IRLR 888).

It may not be possible to guarantee rest breaks for workers engaged in certain activities, **5.50** in particular those which concern services relating to the reception, treatment, or care provided by hospitals or similar establishments (see eg *Martin v Southern Health and Social Care Trust* [2010] IRLR 1048).

Coverage

5.51 There is a wide definition of 'worker' under the 1998 Regulations, since it includes personal work for another party to the contract but specifically excludes professional/client or supplier/customer relationships (see reg 2). All agency workers are included by reg 36 and there is a deeming of the paying party as the employer for these purposes. There is special provision for young workers between 15 and 18 years of age; a newspaper boy aged 15 was excluded because he was a child and governed by the Children and Young Persons Act 1933 (*Addison v Ashby* [2003] IRLR 783).

What is working time?

5.52 The definition of 'working time' is the key building block in the Regulations and it has caused some difficulties of interpretation. It is stated in the 1998 Regulations themselves to mean:

(a) time spent working at the employer's disposal; and
(b) time spent carrying out the worker's activity/duties; or
(c) as defined under a relevant agreement (by extension not by limitation); or
(d) a period during which the worker is receiving relevant training (reg 2(1)).

5.53 One of the difficult areas concerns employees who are on call, as it does in the minimum wage legislation. In *SIMAP v Conselleria Sanidide Consumo de Generalidad Valenciana* [2000] IRLR 845, the European Court of Justice held that time spent on call by doctors in family healthcare teams must be regarded as working time within the Directive where their presence at the health centre is actually required by the employers. On the other hand, where doctors are on call by being contacted without having to be at the health centre, only time spent on the actual provision of primary care services must be regarded as working time. In that situation, even if they are at the disposal of their employer in that it must be possible to contact them, they can manage their time with fewer constraints and pursue their own interests. This also applies to a doctor even though he was permitted to rest at the place of work (*Landeshauptstadt Kiel v Jaeger* [2003] IRLR 804).

5.54 The scope of reg 4 in respect of maximum weekly working time arose soon after the Regulations came into force in *Barber & ors v RJB Mining (UK) Limited* [1999] IRLR 308. Pit deputies employed by the respondent were required to work in excess of the statutory maximum period in the seventeen weeks following the coming into force of the Regulations. The pit deputies argued that reg 4(1) created a free-standing right that could be the subject of civil proceedings in the High Court, and that they should not be required to work again until such time as their average working hours fell within the limit specified in reg 4(1). The High Court accepted this argument, further stating that Parliament clearly intended that reg 4(1) should be incorporated into all contracts of employment (subject to the exceptions already mentioned). However, the High Court did not accept the pit deputies' other arguments, namely that the Court had jurisdiction to decide whether the respondent had taken reasonable steps to ensure compliance with the forty-eight-hour limit under reg 4(2), or that it could grant injunctions to prevent the respondent from subjecting the pit deputies to detriment and to restrain the respondent from requiring the pit deputies to work. This was the preserve of the employment tribunals and the procedures specifically detailed in the Regulations (see 5.71–5.73 below).

General exclusions

There are general exclusions from the scope of the Working Time Regulations 1998 for: **5.55**

(a) cases where the duration of working time is not measured or predetermined or can be determined by the worker himself, such as might be the case for 'managing executives or other persons with autonomous decision-taking powers' (reg 20(1));

(b) junior doctors in training (reg 18(2)(c)) in respect of whom there are special provisions in reg 25A;

(c) those working in the merchant shipping and fishing sectors to whom the European Agreement on the organisation of working time of seafarers 1998 applies (reg 18(a));

(d) some activities of the armed forces, police and civil protection services which 'inevitably conflict with the provisions of these Regulations' (reg 18(2)(a));

(e) domestic servants (reg 19);

(f) family workers (reg 20(1)(b)); and

(g) workers officiating at religious ceremonies in churches and religious communities (reg 20(1)),

in respect of maximum weekly work, length of night work, and daily and weekly rests. This also includes non-mobile workers in the road transport sector by the Working Time (Amendment) Regs 2003, thus reversing the decision in *Bowden v Tuffnells Parcels Express Ltd* [2001] IRLR 838.

The night work and rest provisions do not apply in several other particular circumstances **5.56** by reason of reg 21, where the worker's activities are such that his place of work and of residence are distant from one another; where the worker is engaged in security and surveillance activities requiring a permanent presence, or the worker's activities involve the need for continuity of service or production in particular fields of activity such as reception, treatment, or care provided by hospitals, dock or airport work, or in press and television, the carriage of passengers on regular urban transport services where the worker works in railway transport and his activities are intermittent (see eg *Gallagher v Alpha Catering Services Ltd* [2005] IRLR 102); he spends his working time on-board trains or his activities are linked to transport timetables and to ensuring the continuity and regularity of traffic. Peter Gibson LJ said that 'a rest break is an uninterrupted period of at least 20 minutes which is neither a rest period nor working time and which the worker can use as he pleases'. The provisions on night work, daily and weekly rest, and rest breaks do not apply (or apply in modified form) to mobile workers (reg 24A), that is, a person employed as a member of travelling or flying personnel by an undertaking that operates transport services for passengers or goods by road or air.

Regulation 20 refers to 'managing executives or others with autonomous decision-taking **5.57** powers'. This provision, the wording of which is lifted from the Directive, generated much debate, principally as to what level of seniority a worker had to have before it could be said that he was autonomous.

The amended reg 20(2) introduces a category of workers in respect of whom 'part of the **5.58** working time is measured or predetermined ... but the specific characteristics of the activity are such that, without being required to do so by the employer, the worker may also do work the duration of which is not measured or predetermined'. For such persons, the regulations governing the forty-eight-hour week and hours of night work 'apply only to so much of his work as is measured or predetermined'. A worker falling within reg 20(2) is *not*, however, excluded from the provisions governing night work.

5.59 Thus, a worker may have fixed core hours of forty per week. He habitually works for an additional fifteen per week, making an average of fifty-five per week. If it can be said that the additional fifteen hours were not hours which he was 'required to do by the employer' then that work falls within the new reg 20(2) and there would be no breach of the 1998 Regulations involved in his exceeding forty-eight per week. However, unless he agreed an opt-out, he could not be 'required' to work for more than forty-eight hours on average.

5.60 The agreement may be for a specified term or indefinite but the employee may terminate by written notice of a maximum of three months or in default of agreement of seven days.

Annual leave

5.61 There may be a relevant agreement between employer and employee as to the date on which the leave year starts, but in default of such an agreement, where the worker started before the 1998 Regulations came into force, the start date is the commencement date of the Regulations (reg 13(3)). If the worker started with the particular employer after the 1998 Regulations commenced, the relevant date is that of commencement of employment. The leave must be allowed to be taken by the employer and there is no provision for payment in lieu of such leave, save on termination of employment. If there is such a termination in the course of the leave year, an amount which is proportionate to the leave year worked must be given as pro rata payment (reg 15). If too much holiday has been given in a particular year, there may be some provision for pay-back by agreement. The taking of holiday operates by notice by the employee of when he wishes to take it and a counternotice by the employer as to dates on which holiday may be taken. The consistent designation of Saturday as a leave day was not unlawful (*Sumison v BBC* [2007] IRLR 678).

5.62 The EAT held that there may be a contractual element of holiday pay, even though it was part of a rolled-up rate (*Gridquest Ltd v Blackburn* [2002] IRLR 168) but this was overturned on appeal ([2002] IRLR 607) on the basis that the employer could not *unilaterally* decide that the week's pay is a payment not only for the hours worked during the week but includes an element of holiday pay; the week's pay is for the work done and it could only be held to include an amount for something else such as holiday pay if it is specifically agreed between employer and employee that it would be for that purpose. In *Davies v M.J. Wyatt (Decorators) Ltd* [2000] IRLR 759, the employers decided unilaterally to reduce the hourly rate of pay of all employees in order to assist in meeting the cost of providing paid annual leave, but it was held that this was an unauthorised deduction from wages, even though it was designed to discharge the employer's liability under the WTR to provide paid holidays.

5.63 The following further principles have been laid down in the case law:

  (a) Employers may vary the claimant's terms of employment by consolidating 40 pence of a 70 pence-an-hour attendance allowance into the basic hourly rate (*Laird v A.K. Stoddart Ltd* [2001] IRLR 591).
  (b) An agreement that provides for the most to be paid in respect of outstanding leave entitlement in the event of termination of employment, even for dishonesty, is void by reason of reg 35(1) (*Whitley District Men's Club v Mackay* [2001] IRLR 595).
  (c) It is wrong, when an employee was entitled to ten days' holiday, to gross up the entitlement to two working weeks to take into account the two weekends during the period (*Taylor v East Midlands Offender Employment* [2000] IRLR 760). The correct approach was to divide the gross annual salary by 365 to give a day's pay, then to multiply that by 14.

(d) In the Scottish EAT case of *MPB Structures Ltd v Munro* [2003] IRLR 350 it was held that payment must be made not only for annual leave but also *in association* with that leave; it was thus not lawful that it merely be rolled up and form part of the wage paid throughout the working year but this was disapproved by the EAT in England in *Marshalls Clay Products v Caulfield* [2003] IRLR 552. A contractual provision for rolled-up holiday pay which identifies an express amount or percentage by way of addition to basic pay is thus not unlawful under reg 16(1) WTR. A term providing for payment of holiday pay in respect of an express holiday entitlement but accruing throughout the year, suffices. The EAT formulated five categories of case that thus fell to be distinguished:

(i)   where the contract is silent as to holiday pay;

(ii) where the contract purports to exclude any liability for or entitlement to holiday pay;

(iii) where the contract has rates which are said to include holiday pay but there is no indication or specification of an amount;

(iv) where the contract provides for a basic wage or rate topped up by a specific amount or percentage for holiday pay;

(v)   'contracts where holiday pay is allocated to and during specific periods of holiday'.

The first three are in breach of the Regulations but the fourth and fifth are not. The EAT also gave general guidance for the future including these points: 'The rolled-up holiday pay must be clearly incorporated into the individual contract ... The allocation of the percentage or amount to holiday pay must be clearly identified in the contract and preferably also in the payslip ... Records of holidays taken must be kept'. During the first year of employment the amount of leave a worker may take is limited to that which has accrued on a month-by-month basis, so that by the end of month three he may take a quarter of the entitlement (reg 15A). The Court of Appeal decided in favour of the employer because there was nothing in the language of Article 7 of the European Directive that imposed an obligation to pay a worker in respect of his leave at the time such leave is taken (*Caulfield v Marshalls Clay Products Ltd* [2004] IRLR 564).

The Court of Appeal in *Bamsey v Albion Engineering Ltd* [2004] IRLR 457 decided that reg 16 of the WTR (which refers to the definition of the week's pay) incorporates the rules of interpretation by which the employees were entitled to holiday pay calculated only on the basis of their contractual 39-hour basic working week even though they regularly worked substantial amounts of overtime which they were contractually obliged to do but the employers were not obliged to provide.

(e) In order to be valid as 'rolled-up pay' there must be a genuine agreement between employer and employee for holiday pay as representing a true addition to the contractual rate of pay for time worked. The best way to evidence that is for the provision to be clearly incorporated into the contract of employment; the percentage or amount allocated to holiday pay or particulars sufficient to enable it to be calculated or identified in the contract and preferably also on the pay slip; records to be kept of holidays taken and for practicable steps to be taken to ensure that workers take their holidays before the end of the relevant holiday year (*Smith v Morrisroes & Sons Ltd* [2005] ICR 596). In *Lyddon v Engefield Brickwork Ltd* [2008] IRLR 198, the EAT, however, emphasised that the principles set out in *Smith* were to be treated as guidance only and the fundamental question to be answered was whether there was a consensual agreement identifying a specific sum as properly attributable to periods of holiday.

(f) An additional payment must in fact be received in respect of leave which is truly add-itional to the amount for work actually done (*Robinson Steele v R D Retail Services Ltd* [2006] IRLR 386).

(g) It is sufficient if the employers used an agreed method for calculating shift pay which ensured that employees were paid the same when they were on holiday as they were when they were at work (*British Airways plc v Noble* [2006] IRLR 533).

(h) Where there was a pattern of two weeks of work followed by two weeks of break from work, the appropriate annual leave entitlement was in respect of time when the employee was due to be working. This could be during the two weeks of breaks from work (*Russell v Transocean International Resources Ltd* [2012] ICR 185).

5.64 An important issue is the interrelationship between the period off sick and holidays. The EAT originally decided that a worker on long-term sick leave may claim holiday pay under the WTR, because the only requirement is that someone be a worker, not that any work needs to be done (*Kigass Aero Components Ltd v Brown* [2002] IRLR 312) but this was overruled by the Court of Appeal in *IRC v Ainsworth* [2005] ICR 1149 because leave in truth meant leave from the pressures of daily work, and in the case of an employee who was not required to work during the relevant period by reason of ill health, provision of such leave served no useful purpose. The ECJ decision was called *Stringer v HMRC* [2009] IRLR 214 and rejected the Court of Appeal's view that the right to holidays related only to the health of those who are working. Thus, national legislation must either provide for annual leave to be taken during the leave year in question or if it does not allow this, where the reason the worker has not taken annual leave in the year is because they are off work sick, the worker must be allowed to carry over their leave. An employee is entitled to payment for outstanding accrued holiday pay even where he has been dismissed for dishonesty and the contract excluded payment in such circumstances.

5.65 The issue was finally resolved by the CJEU. In *ANGED v FASGA* [2012] ICR 1211, the CJEU decided that it would be contrary to the purpose of annual leave not to allow a person who had become unfit for work during a period of annual leave subsequently to take leave for a period corresponding to the period of unfitness to work.

5.66 Further:

(a) it is not necessary that an employee demonstrate he is physically unable to take an-nual leave before he is treated as unable to exercise the right to annual leave;

(b) the provision allowing an employee to take leave in the leave year has to be read as permitting an employee on sick leave to take his annual leave within eighteen months of the end of the leave year (*Plumb v Duncan Print Group Ltd* [2016] ICR 125); and

(c) domestic law has to be interpreted in such a way as to ensure an outcome consistent with the objective pursued by EU law. It is inconsistent with EU law to require an employee to make a request to take annual leave during a period of sick leave (*Sood Enterprises Ltd v Healy* [2013] ICR 1361).

Payment terms

5.67 A key question is clearly what is the payment which is to be awarded for annual leave. Non-guaranteed overtime must be paid during four weeks' annual leave by reason of Art 7 of the Directive. This was considered by the CJEU in *BA v Williams* [2012] IRLR 1014. The CJEU drew a distinction between remuneration, including remuneration based on personal or professional status for all activities whether basic and 'inconvenient', under-taken during employment, on the one hand, and, on the other hand, payments intended exclusively to cover occasional or ancillary costs, that is, costs which would not be incurred during holiday periods. It was for the national court to assess into which of the two categories any payment falls. The CJEU decided that 'the assessment must be carried out on the basis of an average over a reference period which is judged to be representative'. This would be a period which was judged to be representative of 'normal' working and remuneration rather than a calculation based on what the employee might have earned during the holiday period had she been working.

In terms of applying this in the domestic arena, the subsequent case of *Bear Scotland Ltd v Fulton* [2015] IRLR 15 held that 'normal pay' is that which is normally received. There the pattern of work had been settled. The tribunal were entitled to decide that it had been so regularly required for payments made in respect of it to have been normal remuneration. It was possible to interpret the domestic Working Time Regulations to meet these require-ments of Article 7 of the EU Working Time Directive since this interpretation did not go against the grain of the domestic legislation. This interpretation was not required for the additional annual leave provided by reg 13A which was a purely domestic provision. There has been further exegesis of this in the following:

(a) It is appropriate to take commission into account in pay especially where it represents on average over 60 per cent of the employee's remuneration (*Lock v British Gas Trading Ltd* [2014] ICR 813).

(b) There is no reason in principle why voluntary overtime should not be included as part of a determination of entitlement to paid annual leave (*Patterson v Castlereagh BC* [2015] IRLR 721). It is a question of fact whether or not voluntary overtime is nor-mally carried out by the worker and with the appropriately permanent feature of the remuneration to trigger its inclusion in the calculation.

Night workers

Special provision is made for night working. Night work is defined as a period the duration of which is not less than seven hours, and includes a period between mid-night and 5am. This actual period in a particular case may be determined by a rel-evant agreement, or if not so defined then it is the period between 11pm and 6am. A night worker is someone who 'as a normal course, works at least three hours of his daily working time during night time', or 'who is likely, during night time, to work at least such proportion of his annual working time as may be specified' in a collec-tive or workforce agreement (reg 2(1)). A night worker's normal hours of work in any reference period must not exceed eight for each twenty-four hours and the employer must take all reasonable steps to ensure that this limit is complied with (reg 6(1)). Workers are also to have the opportunity to undergo free health assessments before being assigned to night work (reg 7). **5.68**

In *R v Attorney-General for Northern Ireland, ex p Burns* [1999] IRLR 315, an employee of a private company brought a *Francovich*-style action against the UK Government on the basis that the Working Time Directive had not been properly implemented. Ms Burns sought a declaration that the UK was in breach of the Directive and that she should be deemed to be a night worker. The Government argued that she was not qualified as a night worker under the Directive because the Directive required for such qualification that the worker should work night shifts either only or 'predominantly'. Kerr J decided that she was a night worker because the requirement that such a worker be one who works at least three hours during the night 'as a normal course' 'involved no more than that this should be a *regular feature* of her employment'. **5.69**

Exclusion by agreement

5.70 There are various kinds of agreements which may be used to exclude rights (as defined in reg 2):

(a) a 'relevant agreement' is an umbrella term for—
 (i) a workforce agreement,
 (ii) a collective agreement which becomes part of the contract,
 (iii) a legally enforceable agreement;

(b) a 'workforce agreement' is an agreement signed by workforce representatives or, in the case of employers of twenty employees or more or where there are fewer than twenty employees, where a majority of the employees sign. It must last no more than five years and the employer must provide a copy to all employees covered (Sch 1);

(c) an individual opt-out agreement is the only method to exclude the limit on maximum weekly working time (reg 5); and any such individual agreement can be determined unilaterally by the worker on seven days' notice, save that by the terms of that agreement the necessary notice of termination may be increased to three months. Following the Working Time (Amendment) Regulations 1999, the agreement need not be in writing: the employer need only show that it has 'first obtained the worker's agreement'; and

(d) a collective or workforce agreement may 'modify or exclude' these provisions:
 (i) the eight-hour limit on night work;
 (ii) the eleven-hour rest period in every twenty-four; and
 (iii) the twenty-four-hour rest period.

Enforcement

5.71 There are two separate enforcement mechanisms, reflecting the different nature of rights accorded by the Working Time Regulations 1998. Entitlements such as the right to paid leave are enforced by the individual employee in the employment tribunal (reg 30) and applications are to be made within three months of the act complained of, save in exceptional circumstances. On the level of award for breach, see *Miles v Linkage Community Trust Ltd* [2008] IRLR 602.

5.72 Limits imposed on the length of the working week, on the other hand, are subject to enforcement by the health and safety authorities, that is, the Health and Safety Executive, and in other cases by local authorities as offences (reg 29). There may also be a civil claim in tort by an employee for breach of statutory duty if the employee suffers damage to his health by reason of a failure to enforce the limits. The forty-eight-hour limit is enforced by criminal sanctions, and an employer may face fines of up to a maximum on summary conviction, or an unlimited fine on indictment for breach.

5.73 Records must be kept by employers which are adequate to show whether time limits for maximum weekly working time, night working, and assignment to night work have been complied with (reg 9), and they should be retained for two years from the time when they were made. Following the Working Time (Amendment) Regulations 1999 (SI 1999/3372), it is not necessary for an employer of workers who have opted out of the forty-eight-hour week to keep records of their working hours.

5.74 In *Commissioners of Inland Revenue v Ainsworth* [2005] EWCA Civ 441 the Court of Appeal held that reg 30 of the WTR 1998 gives the exclusive jurisdiction for a complaint under that legislation. As such, it is subject to a three-month time limit from the date of the last deduction (unless the tribunal uses its discretion to extend time). The claimant had tried to bring his claim under s 23 of the ERA 1996 as one of a series of deductions but there is no corresponding provision concerning a 'series of deductions' in WTR and accordingly any claims must be brought promptly. This is not affected by the ECJ decision (see 5.64). Failure to pay holiday pay under the WTR can amount to unauthorised deductions (*HM Revenue & Customs v Stringer* [2009] IRLR 677). The statutory purpose of the definition of wages is wide and inclusive. The principle of equivalence in EU law requires a wide interpretation. It is not the case that historic underpayments constitute a 'series of deductions' (*Bear Scotland Ltd v Fulton* [2015] IRLR 15). Parliament did not intend that jurisdiction could be regained because a later non-payment occurring more than three months later could be characterised as having similar features. If a period of annual leave took place which did not in fact see an underpayment that would break the series. The sense of the legislation is that any series punctuated from the next succeeding series by a gap of more than three months is one in respect of which the passage of time has extinguished the jurisdiction (see also *Lock v British Gas Trading Ltd No 2* [2016] IRLR 316).

Employment protection provisions

There are various employment protection rights accorded under the Working Time **5.75**
Regulations 1998, in particular that a worker can complain if he suffers detriment for pursuing his entitlements, although this right does not extend to job applicants; and unfair dismissal is also available on the same principle.

E SUNDAY TRADING

The Sunday Trading Act 1994 contained important protections for those not wishing to **5.76**
work on Sundays; it is now the ERA 1996, Pt IV, to which all statutory provisions here refer. There are two categories of such employees, 'protected shop workers' and 'opted out shop workers', around which the protections operate. 'Shop work' means work in a shop in England or Wales on a day on which the shop is open for the serving of customers (s 232(2)). Retail trade or business includes a barber or hairdresser, hiring goods otherwise than for use in the course of a trade or business, and retail sales by auction, but does not cover catering businesses, or the sale at theatres and places of amusement of programmes, catalogues, and similar items.

By s 36(2) and (3) of the ERA 1996, a 'protected shop worker' must have been in employ- **5.77**
ment as a shop worker on 25 August 1994, must not have been employed to work only on a Sunday, and must have been a shop worker throughout the period of continuous employment between the coming into force of the Act and the termination of the employment. Alternatively, the employee will fall within this rubric if he is not and cannot be required to work on Sundays pursuant to his contract of employment.

By s 41, an 'opted out shop worker' is one who under his contract of employment is or **5.78**
may be required to work on Sundays but is not employed to work only on Sundays and who has given to the employer a signed opted out notice stating that he objects to working on Sundays. By s 36(5), such a protected worker loses that status if he gives an opting *in* notice and makes an agreement with the employer to work on Sundays or a particular Sunday.

'Protected shop workers' and 'opted out shop workers' who are dismissed for refusing to **5.79**
work on Sundays have protection from dismissal (s 101) and selection for redundancy on

that ground (s 105(4)), and must not be put under a detriment (s 45(1)). This concept may include a failure by the employer to promote the shop worker, or a denial of overtime or training opportunities, but does not extend to the failure to give remuneration or other contractual benefits for Sunday shop work which other shop workers have done but this employee has not (s 45(5)).

5.80 There is no qualifying period to gain this right and the dismissal is automatically unfair (s 101). An employer must give employees taken on to work *inter alia* on Sundays a written statement in a prescribed form to tell them of their statutory rights (s 42(4)). Contracting out is prohibited subject to the normal exceptional cases (s 43). Rights under this Act are statutory rights for the purposes of unfair dismissal by reason of the assertion of statutory rights (ERA 1996, s 104).

6

THE DUTY OF FIDELITY AND RESTRAINT OF TRADE CLAUSES

A DUTY TO ACCOUNT AND DISCLOSE 6.03

B COMPETITION WITH THE EMPLOYER WHILE EMPLOYED BY HIM 6.08

C GARDEN LEAVE INJUNCTIONS 6.13

D RESTRAINING THE EX-EMPLOYEE 6.21

E CONFIDENTIAL INFORMATION 6.23

What is confidential information? 6.24

Express restraints on release of confidential information 6.35

Springboard injunctions 6.37

Exceptions to confidentiality 6.39

F PATENTS 6.41

G RESTRAINT OF TRADE CLAUSES 6.48

Area of restraint 6.52

The principles applied to the construction of covenants 6.56

Severance 6.59

Restraint in the public interest 6.62

Repudiatory breaches 6.64

Restraint on solicitation of employees . . .6.68

Injunctions as relief 6.70

Repayment clauses 6.73

Several duties owed by the employee may be comprised under the general rubric of 'fidel- **6.01** ity'. What they have in common is that, without them, the employee's service to the employer would be undermined; their precise character, however, differs according to the status and position of the employee, and is much influenced by principles developed by courts of equity. There have been significant developments in this field in recent years, fuelled by competition amongst employers to recruit highly skilled employees, especially in the financial services and high-tech sectors. Moreover, the basic implied obligations are often taken further by express agreement found in the particular contract. If there is a fundamental underlying rule, it may be summarised as honesty in the service of the employer.

The area is difficult to expound coherently because few cases proceed to a full trial but **6.02** rather they are disposed of on applications for interim injunctions when the employer need show only, in most cases, that he has an arguable case, and often the judge proceeds to consider only preserving the balance of convenience until the trial may be held.

A DUTY TO ACCOUNT AND DISCLOSE

The employee must strictly account to his employer for all money and property received **6.03** during the course of his employment, and can be disciplined in the event of any dishonesty. A blatant example of a breach is illicit 'borrowing' from the employer's till (*Sinclair v Neighbour* [1967] 2 QB 279). In *Boston Deep Sea Fishing & Ice Co v Ansell* (1888) 39 ChD 339, the principle was taken somewhat further. The defendant, who was managing director of company A, also owned shares in company B, which supplied ice to A, and received a bonus on these shares for all sales gained. Such secret profits were in breach of his duty to account to company A and he was held to have been lawfully dismissed. The case might, however, be narrowly distinguished since Ansell was a director and under strict fiduciary duties, as well as an employee (see also *Reading v AG* [1951] AC 507). The employment relationship is not in itself a fiduciary relationship in the strict sense, since its purpose is not to place the employee in a position where he is obliged to pursue his employer's interests at the expense of his own. The relationship is contractual and the powers imposed are conferred by the employer himself (*Shepherds Investments Ltd v Walters* [2007] IRLR 110). The case of *Nottingham University v Fishel* [2000] IRLR 471 set some limits to the duty of fidelity. Dr Fishel was an academic embryologist who carried out research and conducted a research clinic for his employer but also provided services in return for payment at other clinics. The university's contention that there was a breach of contract in this 'outside' work failed because it was not part of his role to attract contracts from overseas clinics. Thus, he was not in breach of the duty when he took those contracts for himself.

6.04 Taking an account of profits will be appropriate only in exceptional circumstances where the normal civil remedies of damages, specific performance, and injunction, coupled with a characterisation of sub-contractual obligations as fiduciary, do not provide an adequate response to a breach of contract. The claimant's interest in performance of a contract may make it just and equitable to grant such a remedy, but only where other relief would not provide full relief. In *AG v Blake* [2001] IRLR 36 it was held to be a just response to the breach of contract with the security services by the spy Blake, in publishing his autobiography in flagrant disregard of his undertaking not to divulge official information in book form. Each case depends on its own facts.

6.05 The cases concerning the employee's duty to disclose misdeeds are not, however, easy to reconcile. In *Healey v Société Anonyme Française Rubastic* [1917] 1 KB 946, Avory J said: 'I cannot accept the view that an omission to confess or to disclose his own misdoing was in itself a breach of the contract on the part of the plaintiff.' The duty to disclose misconduct was considered in *Sybron Corporation v Rochem Ltd* [1983] IRLR 253. At issue was the occupational pension of the chief manager who was discovered after his retirement to have been involved in a directly competing company while still employed. The plaintiff claimed that the pension had been given as a result of a mistake of fact and sought restitution. The Court of Appeal decided that the company was indeed entitled to recover the money. Stephenson LJ distinguished the House of Lords decision in *Bell v Lever Brothers* [1932] AC 161, which held that there was no duty on the employee to disclose *his own* misconduct, although he had a duty to report the misdeeds of *others* especially where he was senior enough to realise that what they were doing was wrong and he was responsible for reporting on their activities each month. An employee is not bound, as a matter of general principle, to inform his employer if and when he is doing outside work in breach of his contract. An employee is not normally considered without more to be a fiduciary if this is defined in strict equitable terms although he will owe some duties of fidelity to the employer (*Crowson Fabrics Ltd v Rider* [2008] IRLR 288).

6.06 The case of *Sybron* may be usefully contrasted with *Horcal Ltd v Gatland* [1983] IRLR 459. The defendant, the managing director of the plaintiff building contractors, was negotiating to purchase the shares of the company when a Mrs Kingsbury telephoned him asking that work be done on her home. He gave an estimate on the company's notepaper but kept the proceeds of the contract for himself. When the company found this out they sought recovery of £5,000 paid to him in respect of his past services. The Court of Appeal did not consider that the failure to disclose the incident was sufficient to avoid the termination payment made, but he was held not to be entitled to his last salary cheque because during that period he had not served the company honestly and faithfully (see also *BCCI SA v Ali* [1999] IRLR 226; [2002] IRLR 460).

In *Item Software (UK) Ltd v Fassihi* [2003] IRLR 769 it was held that *Bell* was 'not an   **6.07** absolute rule'. There may, however, be a 'super added' duty where there is a separate and independent aspect of the employee's duties that required the employee to disclose certain facts. In the instant case, the employee was involved in negotiations between the employer and its clients and his contractual obligations of fidelity and care required him to disclose important information known to him and which was relevant to those negotiations. If he had learned that a rival distributor was trying to sabotage the negotiations, it would have been his duty to tell the employers. The fact that it was he himself who was seeking to do so did not relieve him of that duty. There is a duty to disclose one's own misdeeds that amount to breach of fiduciary duties (*Tesco Stores Ltd v Pook* [2004] IRLR 618).

B COMPETITION WITH THE EMPLOYER WHILE EMPLOYED BY HIM

The courts are naturally vigilant to protect an employer whose employee acts directly   **6.08** in competition with him in work time, but on the other hand, they will not prohibit the individual's legitimate spare time activities (see *Mansard Precision Engineering Co Ltd v Taylor* [1978] ICR 44). Lord Greene MR indicated how far the courts would intervene to protect this delicate balance in *Hivac Ltd v Park Royal Scientific Instruments Ltd* [1946] Ch 169:

> It would be deplorable if it were laid down that an employee could consistently with his duty to his employer, knowingly deliberately and secretly set himself to do in his spare time something which would inflict great harm on his employer's business.

In the instant case, two weekday employees of the plaintiff company spent their Sundays working on highly specialised tasks for the defendant firm which also manufactured midget valves and was in direct competition with the plaintiff. An injunction was granted against continuing this arrangement, notwithstanding that there was no evidence of the actual misuse of confidential information, because their actions infringed the general duty of fidelity. Lord Greene MR and Morton LJ referred to the danger of a future transfer of information, and emphasised the secret nature of their work.

In *Sanders v Parry* [1967] 2 All ER 803, a solicitor employed as an assistant by another,   **6.09** made an agreement with an important client of his employer to work for him, and Havers J restrained this as a breach of the employee's duty of fidelity. There are, however, some contracts of a routine nature in which there is no question of exclusive services being required. Many employees 'moonlight', that is, work for one employer in the morning and for another by night, with the full acquiescence of the employers. In *Nova Plastics Ltd v Froggatt* [1982] IRLR 146 an odd-job man was held not to be in breach of contract when he worked for a competitor of his employer in his spare time (see also *Laughton and Hawley v Bapp Industrial Supplies Ltd* [1986] IRLR 245; *Davidson and Maillou v Comparisons* [1980] IRLR 360, EAT; *Crowson Fabrics Ltd v Rider* [2008] IRLR 288).

The duty of fidelity requires an employee not to engage in competitive activities. Where   **6.10** the boundary is to be drawn between legitimate preparatory activity and illegitimate competitive activity, however, is often a difficult question (eg *Iman Sadeque v Bluebay Asset Management (Services) Ltd* [2013] IRLR 344). It may require an employee to report to their employer a competitive threat of which they become aware, but whether it does so is fact sensitive and will depend upon such matters as the terms of the contract, the nature of the employee's role and responsibilities, the nature of the threat, and the circumstances in which the employee becomes aware of it. There is no reason in principle why the duty of loyalty should be attenuated during a period of garden leave.

6.11   There is no prohibition on an employee preparing to leave, or even setting up a company to compete with the employer after leaving, but there is a restriction on actual competition while the employee is still employed (*Balston Ltd v Headline Filters Ltd* [1987] FSR 330; *Framlington Group plc v Anderson and Others* [1995] 1 CCLC 475; *Saatchi and Saatchi v Saatchi and Saatchi and Others*, unreported (ChD), 13 February 1995). The Court of Appeal in *Foster Bryant Surveying Ltd v Bryant* [2007] IRLR 425 said that it was difficult accurately to encapsulate the circumstances in which a retiring director may or may not be found to have breached his fiduciary duty; the problem was fact sensitive. In *Adamson v B & L Cleaning Services Ltd* [1995] IRLR 193, however, competing for a tender against the employer while still employed was held to be in breach of contract but in the absence of a contractual provision to the contrary, *preparing* to compete by developing a competitive product in one's spare time may not be a breach of fiduciary or other duties (*Helmet Integrated Systems v Tunnard and Others* [2007] IRLR 126).

6.12   This doctrine cannot, however, be applied to situations arising after the contract has terminated (*J.A. Mont (UK) Ltd v Mills* [1993] IRLR 172). At that point there is no continuing duty of good faith, and the fact that the former employee is remunerated during the period of restraint makes no difference.

C GARDEN LEAVE INJUNCTIONS

6.13   The court frequently grants injunctions to prevent employees taking up employment with another company before their notice periods have expired. This is a fast growing area of litigation.

6.14   It began in *Evening Standard Co v Henderson* [1978] IRLR 64, where a senior production manager on the *Evening Standard* was restrained from working for the short-lived London evening newspaper rival, Mr Maxwell's *London Daily News*, after he had purported to resign on giving less than his contractual period of notice. The court received an undertaking from the employer that it would continue to provide the employee with his full remuneration and other contractual benefits without insisting that he should actually work. The injunction was granted because there was still trust and confidence existing between employer and employee. The case was distinguished in *Provident Financial Group plc and Whitegates Estate Agency Ltd v Hayward* [1989] IRLR 84: that employee, who gave short notice, was going to work for a company which did not directly compete with the previous employer although it was in an associated field. Whether an injunction should be granted in such a case was a matter for the court's discretion, and it was refused on these facts. This was notwithstanding the presence of a contractual term that the employer could suspend the employee from performing work on condition that he received full pay and benefit. Whether relief should be granted in a particular case depended on the *detriment* which the employer would suffer if the clause was not enforced by an injunction.

6.15   The important issue raised in *William Hill Organisation Limited v Tucker* [1998] IRLR 313 was the linked question of whether the employer was under a duty to provide the employee, a senior dealer with specialised experience, with work during his notice period. The Court of Appeal held that there was such a duty, as his post was specific and unique, and the skills necessary to the proper discharge of its duties required frequent use so as not to atrophy.

Whether there is a general 'right to work' and thus not to be left in the 'garden' will **6.16** depend on the particular contract and the surrounding circumstances of the profession (see also *SBJ Stephenson v Mandy* [2000] IRLR 233; *SG&R Valuation Services Co LLC v Boudrais* [2008] IRLR 770).

For an injunction to be an appropriate remedy there must also be a real risk that the **6.17** employee would foster the prospects of a rival (see *Marshall v Industrial Systems & Control Ltd* [1992] IRLR 294). The court must examine whether the new employment which is proposed to be taken by the employee would materially and adversely affect the old employer's business. Dillon LJ expressed the fear that 'the practice of long periods of garden leave is obviously capable of abuse'.

An example of the court exercising its discretionary jurisdiction to cut down a period of **6.18** garden leave set out in the contract is *GFI Group Inc v Eaglestone* [1994] IRLR 119. The contract of employment of an options broker restrained the employee from engaging in any business other than that of the employer during the twenty-week period of notice. The court recognised that his customer connection had been expensively created at the employer's expense and that there would be a substantial loss of goodwill if the employee left. Holland J was not, however, prepared to grant an injunction for the whole period which was sought by the employer since two other employees who were on shorter notice periods had already left to join the competitor to whom this employee was bound and substantial damage had already been done to the employer's connections. Therefore the order would be made to last for only thirteen weeks.

The interconnection between garden leave and restrictive covenants is complex. A restric- **6.19** tive covenant preventing an employee from engaging in any employment during the term of the contract was to be treated as continuing during a period of garden leave (*Simbian Ltd v Christensen* [2001] IRLR 77).

There is no general principle that time spent on garden leave should be credited against **6.20** the duration of express restrictive covenants, but the existence of such a clause may be a factor in determining the validity of a restraint clause, and there may be an exceptional case where a long garden leave period already served by the time that an attempt is made to enforce a restrictive covenant could provide a good reason for the court not to enforce a restraint clause at all (*Crédit Suisse Asset Management Ltd v Armstrong* [1996] IRLR 450).

D RESTRAINING THE EX-EMPLOYEE

An employee is normally in breach of his duty of fidelity where he leaves a job and then **6.21** uses his ex-employer's resources or confidential information to assist him to set up in competition with that employer. Thus, in *Wessex Dairies Ltd v Smith* [1935] 2 KB 80, a milk rounds-man who canvassed his employer's customers on his last day to give their business to him thereafter was held to have broken his contract (see *Marshall v Industrial Systems & Control*, above).

To copy out a list of customers whilst still employed will almost always be a breach. **6.22** Building up goodwill with customers which may incidentally be valuable if the employee were to set up a business himself on his own account is, on the other hand, quite lawful. In order to prevent even the possibility of such occurring, employers should insert into the contract express restrictive clauses (6.48–6.72). In the absence of such an express restrictive covenant there is no restriction on soliciting former customers to be implied (eg *Horcal Ltd v Gatland* [1983] IRLR 459). This applies in the same way to solicitors soliciting clients from their old firm, as to employees in any other trade or profession (*Wallace Bogan & Co v Cove* [1997] IRLR 453, CA). An ex-employee cannot, however, be restrained from using his own accumulated expertise, skills, and knowledge which have been acquired during the employment (*Crowson Fabrics Ltd v Rider* [2008] IRLR 288).

E CONFIDENTIAL INFORMATION

6.23 If an employee uses information which is confidential to his employer, both he and the recipients of the details may be liable in damages, and can be restrained by an injunction. Some employees are also at risk of criminal liability for breach of the Official Secrets Act 1989.

What is confidential information?

6.24 The main problem lies in identifying the proper parameters of confidential information and distinguishing it from the employee's 'individual skill and experience', acquired in the course of employment, which he may legitimately put to use in future for others. It is easier to know what it is when one sees it than to describe it in detail (like the proverbial elephant). It covers confidential information of a non-technical or non-scientific basis. In *Printers & Finishers Ltd v Holloway* [1965] 1 WLR 1, Cross J stated that an injunction would be appropriate 'if the information in question can fairly be regarded as a separate part of the employee's stock of knowledge which a man of ordinary honesty and intelligence would recognise to be the property of his old employer and not his own to do as he liked with' (see also *G.D. Searle & Co Ltd v Celltech Ltd* [1982] FSR 92; *Fraser v Thames TV Ltd* [1983] 2 WLR 917; *FSS Travel & Leisure Systems Limited v Johnson* [1998] IRLR 383, CA).

6.25 In *Thomas Marshall (Exports) Ltd v Guinlé* [1978] Ch 227, Megarry V-C developed criteria which have been much contested ever since, including whether the owner reasonably believes that the release of the information will be injurious to him or advantageous to his rivals and whether the owner reasonably believes that the information is not already in the public domain. The information was to be judged in the light of the usage and practices of the industry involved. The secret need not in any way be unique or complicated, and it is no defence for an employee to contend that a third party has already made it public. Megarry V-C held that the following matters were confidential: prices paid, details of manufacturers and suppliers, customer requirements, contract negotiations, and details of fast moving lines.

6.26 The employee was not injuncted when the information in question was the paper which was used by the employer (*Worsley v Cooper* [1939] 1 All ER 290), but the following have been considered trade secrets and their passing-on restrained:

  (a) the correct type of plastic clamp strip designed to hold together the inner and outer walls of a swimming pool (*Cranleigh Precision Engineering Ltd v Bryant* [1965] 1 WLR 1293);

  (b) drawings of a machine tool which, although readily available, required the use of specialist know-how (*Saltman Engineering Co v Campbell Engineering Co* [1963] 2 All ER 413);

  (c) customer lists (eg *Roger Bullivant Ltd v Ellis* [1987] IRLR 491); and

(d) company accounts. In *Camelot v Centaur Communications Limited* [1998] IRLR 80, the Court of Appeal held that Camelot was entitled to an order to recover year-end reports from the defendant publishers after they had been leaked by a Camelot employee, on the basis that Camelot had a legitimate and continuing interest in enforcing an obligation of loyalty and confidentiality against an employee who had made unauthorised disclosure and use of documents acquired by him in his employment. It was held that Camelot had a reason which was sufficiently strong to outweigh the public interest in the press being able to protect the anonymity of its sources.

The leading case is *Faccenda Chicken Ltd v Fowler* [1986] IRLR 69, although its scope **6.27** remains controversial. Mr Fowler had been employed by Faccenda Ltd as its sales manager until he resigned along with several other employees, and set up a business competing with the plaintiff company selling fresh chickens from refrigerated vehicles. The employees who left had no express restrictive clauses in their contracts, but the plaintiff claimed that they had broken the duty of confidentiality by using its sales information to its disadvantage. Goulding J thought that there were three classes of case to be distinguished:

(a) information which because of its trivial character and/or easy accessibility from public sources of information could not be regarded by reasonable people as confidential, such as a published patent specification;
(b) information which an employee was to treat as confidential because he was expressly told to do so or because, from its character, it was obviously confidential but which once learned necessarily remained in his head and became part of his own skill and knowledge. As long as his employment continued, he could not otherwise use or disclose such information without breach of contract, but when he left such employment he could use it in competition with his former employer. It could, however, be protected by an express restrictive clause; and
(c) information which is so secret that even though it might be learned by heart, it could not be used for the benefit of anyone but the employer.

The information in the instant case, the prices that customers were paying and the routes by which they could be visited, fell into the second category so that an injunction was inappropriate.

Whilst agreeing with the result, the Court of Appeal differed from Goulding J in that it **6.28** thought that in determining whether any information fell within the implied term of confidentiality, it was necessary to consider all the circumstances of the case and in particular:

(a) the nature of the employment;
(b) the nature of the information: it could only be protected if it could be classed as a trade secret or as material which was in all the circumstances of such a highly confidential nature as to require the same protection as a trade secret;
(c) whether the employer impressed upon the employee the confidentiality of the information; and
(d) whether the information could easily be isolated from other information which the employee was free to use or disclose.

Neill LJ gave as examples of truly confidential information the price to be charged for a new model of car or the prices negotiated for various grades of oil in a highly competitive market. The key modern formulation is that in *Vestergaard Frandsen A/S v Bestnet Europe Ltd* [2013] ICR 981 where Lord Neuberger said:

> Particularly in a modern economy, the law has to maintain a realistic and fair balance between (i) effectively protecting trade secrets (and other intellectual property rights) and (ii)

not unreasonably inhibiting competition in the market place. The importance to the economic prosperity of the country of research and development in the commercial world is self evident ... On the other hand, the law should not discourage former employees from benefitting society and advancing themselves by imposing unfair potential difficulties on their honest attempts to compete with their former employers.

6.29   Other truly confidential information was at issue in *Johnson & Bloy (Holdings) Ltd v Wolstenholme Rink plc and Fallon* [1987] IRLR 499. The plaintiff obtained an injunction to prevent a former director from using or disclosing details of the secret formula it used to manufacture gold ink in its printing process. Even though Mr Fallon could no doubt remember the process, it did not for that reason form part of his ordinary skill and knowledge. The Court of Appeal held, however, in *Brooks v Olyslager OMS (UK) Limited* [1998] IRLR 590, that information relating to a company's solvency, its ability to carry on business for a period of time, and its relationship with its holding company, was not a trade secret following the termination of the employee's employment (although such information could have been covered by an express duty of good faith while the employment was continuing).

6.30   In *Lancashire Fires Limited v SA Lyons & Co Limited* [1997] IRLR 113, the Court of Appeal held that the employer did not have to point out the precise limits of that which he sought to protect as confidential in order to satisfy category (c) above, as this will often be quite obvious. In setting out the criteria for holding information to be confidential, in *Lansing Linde v Kerr* [1991] 1 All ER 251, Staughton LJ required that the information be used in a trade or business and that the owner must limit the dissemination of it, or at least not encourage or permit widespread publication. It can thus include not only secret formulae for the manufacturers of products but also, in an appropriate case, the names of customers and the goods which they buy from the employer.

6.31   Another important illustration of these principles can be seen in *A.T. Poeton (Gloucester Plating) Ltd v Horton* [2000] ICR 1208. The plaintiff electroplaters employed a sales engineer for twenty-one months. A few months after he left employment he set up his own company as an electroplater, and the plaintiff claimed that he had wrongfully taken away confidential information in respect of the plating process. It had not, however, imposed a restrictive covenant or patented the process, and the Court of Appeal said that the court in these circumstances should not be astute to find that confidential information was tucked away in a wider clause. The information could not easily be isolated from other information acquired during the course of employment. The only inference which was justified on the evidence was that the defendant took away the salient features of the apparatus as part of his general knowledge without any deliberate memorisation.

6.32   *PennWell Publishing (UK) Ltd v Ornstein* [2007] IRLR 700 concerned an issue which frequently arises: a contact list drawn up over many years by a senior employee which was maintained on the company's computers. Before the employee left to work for a competing business, he downloaded his contact list. The employer successfully claimed that the list was company property, and not that of its former employee, even though the list contained contacts that pre-dated his employment with it. This was derived from ownership of the database upon which the information was collated. The position should, however, have been rendered clearer by express terms in the contract of employment dealing with the ownership of client contact information and a clear computer policy setting out company policy for the introduction of personal data on computer databases.

Other criteria to be taken into account in reaching the decision include: **6.33**

(a) whether the disclosure of the information to a competitor would be likely to cause real or significant damage to the employer; and
(b) the usage and practice of the particular trade and industry (*Thomas Marshall v Guinlé* [1979] Ch 227 at 248e–g).

For an injunction to issue there must be a high degree of specificity of the information which it is sought to restrain (*Ixora Trading Inc v Jones* [1990] FSR 251). This case also warns against use of confidential information cases as in effect a back-door restrictive covenant, or to harass employees who are leaving (at p261).

The distinction between information which is deliberately learned by the employee and **6.34** that which is innocently carried in the employee's head cannot, however, itself be decisive of what information can be legitimately protected after the termination of employment and what cannot (*SBJ Stephenson Ltd v Mandy* [2000] IRLR 233).

Express restraints on release of confidential information

In *Faccenda*, the Court of Appeal appeared to decide that information in the second **6.35** category that the employee carried in his head could not be protected by a restrictive covenant unless there was a trade secret to protect, but this was doubted in *Balston v Headline Filters Ltd* [1987] FSR 330.

In *Johnson & Bloy (Holdings) Ltd and Johnson & Bloy Ltd v Wolstenholme Rink plc* **6.36** *and Fallon* [1987] IRLR 499, Parker LJ said that, in so far as it might be thought that Scott J in *Balston* was laying down as a proposition of law that anything which is inevitably in somebody's head when they leave employment is something which they are free to use, that was wrong. There must indeed be a 'sufficiently high degree of confidentiality to amount to a trade secret' (*Lansing Linde Ltd v Kerr*, above).

Springboard injunctions

In many cases the effect of abuse of confidential information by the ex-employee is to give **6.37** the ex-employee, and his new employer to whom he gives it, a head start in his own venture or that which he sets up for his new employer so that he gets ahead of the game. The proper remedy for this may be an injunction which is limited to the period for which the head start has been gained, in so far as the court is able to calculate and predict this feature. In *Roger Bullivant Ltd v Ellis* [1987] IRLR 491, the Court of Appeal determined that such an injunction restraining former employees from entering into contracts with persons whose names and addresses formed part of information which was gained in breach of the duty of confidence should last only as long as the employees had gained an unfair advantage arising out of the breach of confidence. The appropriate order should be fashioned in such a way as to restrain defendants from obtaining an unjust head start in actions detrimental to the provider of the confidential information. Springboard relief is not confined to cases where former employees threaten to abuse confidential information but is available to prevent any future or further serious economic loss to a previous employer caused by former staff members taking an unfair advantage of any serious breaches of their contract of employment. That unfair advantage must, however, still exist at the time when the injunction is sought and it must be shown that it would continue until restrained (*UBS Wealth Management (UK) Ltd v Vestra Wealth LLP* [2008] IRLR 965).

One of the most effective remedies in confidentiality cases is the civil search order, which **6.38** allows the employer to search the home or business premises of the employee. However, the courts have indicated that such orders should be used sparingly in employment cases (*Lock International plc v Beswick* [1989] IRLR 481; see also *PSM International v Whitehouse* [1992] IRLR 279).

Exceptions to confidentiality

6.39 Information, whether confidential or not, may always be revealed by the employee if it discloses 'iniquity or misconduct on the part of his employer'. Thus, in *Initial Services Ltd v Putterill* [1968] 1 QB 396, a sales manager was held to be entitled to disclose an agreement to maintain prices which was contrary to the Restrictive Trade Practices Act 1965. Ungoed-Thomas J more broadly defined the circumstances when public interest demands disclosure as 'matters carried out or contemplated in breach of the country's security or in breach of law, including statutory duty, fraud or otherwise destructive of the country or its people, including matters medically dangerous to the public' (*Beloff v Pressdram Ltd* [1973] 1 All ER 241 at 260; see also *Speed Seal Products Ltd v Paddington* [1985] 1 WLR 1327). Further, it is not a breach of duty to disclose matters of wrongdoing to City regulatory bodies such as the Financial Services Authority, or the HM Revenue & Customs (*Re a Company's Application* [1989] 3 WLR 265) but information may be confidential even though it shows that a crime has been committed (*Francome v Mirror Group Newspapers* [1984] 2 All ER 408; see also *Campbell v Frisbee* [2003] ICR 141) (see Bowers, Fodder, Lewis, and Mitchell, *Whistleblowing: The New Law*, OUP, 2016, 3rd edn).

6.40 Information also ceases to be confidential when it becomes widely known to the public. This was the essence of the 'Spycatcher' decision (*Attorney-General v The Observer* [1988] 2 WLR 805).

F PATENTS

6.41 The common law duty of fidelity used to provide the legal basis of the ownership of inventions made by the employee in his employer's time. The courts emphasised that the employer had first call on the employee's time and any designs made during working hours thus belonged to the employer (*British Reinforced Concrete Co Ltd v Lind* (1917) 116 LT 243). Often collective agreements and individual bargaining modified its scope and now the Patents Act 1977 covers the field and greatly improves the position of the employee.

6.42 Section 39 provides that an invention made by an employee shall between him and his employer be taken to belong to the employer only if:

(a) the invention was made in the course of the normal duties of the employee and the circumstances were such that an invention might reasonably be expected to result from the carrying out of his duty; and

(b) the employee has a special obligation to further the interests of the employer's undertaking because of his duties and particular responsibility arising therefrom; or

(c) although the invention was not made in the normal course of duties it was made in the course of duty specifically assigned to the employee such that an invention would be expected to result.

In all other cases the patent vests in the employee.

6.43 The phrase 'the normal course of duties' is thus crucial. In *Reiss Engineering Co Ltd v Harrison* [1985] IRLR 232, Falconer J decided that an employee's normal duties under the Act are those which he is actually employed to carry out. The plaintiff, a manager of a valve department, was not employed to design or invent. He had no special obligation imposed by the statute to further the interests of the employer's undertaking. The extent of the latter depended on the status of the employee and his attendant responsibilities and duties. The plaintiff's invention accordingly belonged to him.

Even where it is lawfully patented by the employer, a worker may apply to a court or **6.44** to the Comptroller of Patents on the grounds that the patent is of 'outstanding benefit' to the employer and for that reason the employee deserves compensation for his effort (s 40). He is then entitled, by s 41(1), to a 'fair share having regard to all the circumstances of the benefit which the employer has derived, or may be reasonably expected to derive, from the patent'.

The criteria for 'fair share' are: **6.45**

(a) the nature of the employee's duties, his remuneration, and other advantages from his employer or the invention;
(b) the employee's effort and skill in making the invention;
(c) the effort and skill of any third party involved; and
(d) the significance of any contributions of the employer towards the invention (s 41(4)).

Since the coming into force of the 1977 Act, compensation may be awarded more gener- **6.46** ally where the employee has assigned to the employer for inadequate return any of the employee's rights in the invention belonging to himself (s 40). Again, the appropriate compensation is such as will secure for the employee a 'fair share' of the benefit the employer has derived or may reasonably be expected to derive from the patent. The one exception to the above rules is where there is a relevant collective agreement in force concerning the issue, and there is no requirement that this arrangement be more favourable to the employee than statute. On the other hand, an employee may not validly contract out of the rights conferred by the Act.

Where original works are the subject of copyright, s 11 of the Copyright, Designs and **6.47** Patents Act 1988 provides that the employer is first owner of it if the maker was employed by him under a contract of service, the work was made in the course of employment, and the employee was employed for the purpose of making such a work. When performed outside employment hours, copyright remains in the employee (Registered Designs Act 1949, s 2(1B); Copyright, Designs and Patents Act 1988, s 215).

G RESTRAINT OF TRADE CLAUSES

The restraint of trade doctrine in essence holds the ring between the freedom of the **6.48** employee and the desire of the employer to protect its business. Many employers, especially those in the professions and the financial sector, further protect themselves against damaging competition and misuse of confidential information by an express restrictive covenant. Typically an accountancy practice would include a clause that assistant accountants will not work for another practice within five miles during the first two years of leaving. This also facilitates proof of breach of the implied duties already considered, which otherwise is often difficult. The general common law rule against restraint of trade operates in this area just as in contracts between vendor and purchaser of a business (*Esso Petroleum Co Ltd v Harper's Garage (Stourport) Ltd* [1968] AC 269). Lord Atkinson said, in *Herbert Morris v Saxelby* [1916] 1 AC 688, at 699: 'It is in the public interest that a man should be free to exercise his skill and experience to the best advantage for the benefit of himself and of all others who desire to employ him.' A covenant in an agreement for the sale of a business is, however, more likely to be upheld than one in a contract of employment (*Allied Dunbar (Frank Weisinger) Ltd v Frank Weisinger* [1988] IRLR 60; *Systems Reliability Holdings plc v Smith* [1990] IRLR 377). The restraint of trade doctrine may also apply, for example, to a clause prohibiting a self-employed financial consultant from receiving commission after termination of his agency agreement if he competed with his employer within one year (*Marshall v NM Financial Management Ltd* [1997] IRLR 449). If the covenant is itself an unreasonable restraint of trade, the court will not permit commission to be withheld on that basis.

6.49 In employment cases, the court essentially attempts to hold the ring between the interest of the employee to be employed in the future as he wishes, and the employer's interest to preserve his business from disclosures and attacks on the existing customer connection by an ex-employee. Thus, the restrictive clauses must go no further than is reasonable for the protection of the employer's business interests and the general public interest must also be considered. Otherwise, as the House of Lords put it, 'the employee is entitled to use to the full any personal skill or experience even if this has been acquired in the service of his employer ...' (*Stenhouse Australia Ltd v Phillips* [1974] AC 391 at 400D; see also *Cantor Fitzgerald (UK) Ltd v Wallace* [1992] IRLR 215).

6.50 The court will generally review the covenants of a managing director of a company who had negotiated the sale of the business in a different light to those of a more junior employee (*Alliance Paper Group plc v Prestwich* [1996] IRLR 25). A restrictive covenant is more likely to be upheld where it prevents the employee from actually soliciting former customers, as opposed to stopping the employee from working at all. Most generally, Stephenson LJ concluded in *Spafax Ltd v Harrison* [1980] IRLR 442, para 25:

> An employer is entitled to take and enforce promises from an employee which the employer can prove are reasonably necessary to protect him, the employer, his trade connection, trade interests and goodwill, not from competition by the employee if he leaves his employment, or from his then using the skill and knowledge with which his employment had equipped him to compete, but from his then using his personal knowledge of his employer's customers or his personal influence over them, or his knowledge of his employer's trade secrets, or advantages acquired from his employment, to his employer's disadvantage.

6.51 Each case depends on its own facts and one case should not be treated as decisive of the result of another even though the terms of the covenant are similar (*Dairy Crest Ltd v Pigott* [1989] ICR 92). Where the true skills and art of a job lie in the make-up of the person performing it (the employee's personality, temperament, and ability to get on with people) there is some authority that the employer will not be able to establish a proprietary right by way of customer connections which had been built up during the course of employment where this is truly the result of the personal qualities of the employee (*Cantor Fitzgerald (UK) Ltd v Wallace* [1992] IRLR 215); but the better view is that restrictive covenants in such circumstances should be upheld (see *Dawney, Day & Co Limited v De Braconier d'Alphen* [1997] IRLR 443).

Area of restraint

Restricting employment in a particular area

6.52 The area of restraint placed on the employee must be reasonable in all the circumstances; thus a worldwide restraint may be valid only where the employer's business was of a similar extent, as in the leading case of *Nordenfelt v Maxim Nordenfelt Guns and Ammunition Ltd* [1894] AC 535. The question whether covenants restricting the taking of employment in a particular area are valid depends on the size of the area and its relationship to the employer's connections (*Gledhow Autoparts Ltd v Delaney* [1965] 1 WLR 1366; *T. Lucas & Co v Mitchell* [1972] 3 All ER 689). In *Spencer v Marchington* [1988] IRLR 392, for example, a covenant restraining a former employee from engaging in an employment agency business within a radius of twenty-five miles from her previous employer's premises was held to be too wide to be enforceable.

Non-solicitation or non-dealing covenants

A clause was held not to be too vague in so far as it restrained an employee from **6.53** dealing or contracting with any company or person who during the twelve months immediately prior to the termination of the employment was negotiating with the employer for the supply of services of the type with which the employee was concerned, and where the employee or one of his subordinates had dealt with that person (*International Consulting Services (UK) Ltd v Hart* [2000] IRLR 227). Because of the complexity of the subject matter of negotiations and the long period over which they were often conducted, the claimant legitimately regarded the connection with customers arising from negotiations as forming part of the goodwill of its business which required protection.

The courts will, in most cases, carefully consider the nature of the market in which **6.54** the employee was engaged. Thus, the narrower and more specialist the market, the more likely it is that a non-dealing covenant will be upheld, given that clients will in those circumstances naturally gravitate to the ex-employee who opens a new, competing company in such a case (*London and Solent Ltd v Brooks, Daily Telegraph*, 27 October 1988).

In *East England Schools CIC v Palmer* [2014] IRLR 191, the argument by the defend- **6.55** ant was that the market in matching teacher applicants with schools that had vacancies was inherently 'promiscuous' in that the employee would not have built up relationships either with schools or with teachers as neither had loyalty to a particular agency. The High Court decided, however, that there was here a legitimate proprietary interest requiring protection. As the building up of relationships with schools and teachers had been an integral part of the role envisaged for the employee, she would have acquired valuable information about schools and candidates in the course of her employment that was not publicly available, such as information about the personalities concerned, about their likes, dislikes, and foibles, and about their special requirements which would be useful to a competitor. The fact that the relationship between schools and teachers on the one hand and the claimant on the other was known to have been a fragile one had made it more rather than less necessary and legitimate for the employer to have sought to protect it because it made the prospect of a successful solicitation by the ex-employee more likely.

The principles applied to the construction of covenants

As the general approach to construction, Lord Denning MR said that the courts will not **6.56** strain to hold a restraint invalid; if it is reasonable in concept, the courts will construe it in a reasonable manner (see *Marion White Ltd v Francis* [1972] 3 All ER 22).

This has led in some cases to a narrow reading of restrictive clauses. Thus, in *Home* **6.57** *Counties Dairies Ltd v Shilton* [1970] 1 WLR 526, an agreement not 'to serve or sell milk or dairy produce' was limited to the defendant's former employment as a milkman. Courts should also not too diligently strive to find within restrictive covenants *ex facie* too wide implicit limitations such as would justify their imposition (*J.A. Mont (UK) Ltd v Mills* [1993] IRLR 172).

6.58   It clearly is not, however, the role of the courts to correct errors or supply omissions in the drafting of restrictive covenants (*WAC Ltd v Whillock* [1990] IRLR 22). Thus, where a person was restrained from personally carrying on business in competition with the ex-employing company but there was no restriction on his right to be a director or shareholder of another company which carried on such business, the court would not enforce the covenant as though it did include the latter restriction.

Severance

6.59   The courts may also sever a part of the restraint and uphold only the remaining lawful part, but it will do so only if 'the severed parts are independent of one another and can be severed without the severance affecting the meaning of the part remaining' (Lord Sterndale in *Attwood v Lamont* [1920] 3 KB 571; see also *Putsman v Taylor* [1920] 3 KB 637; *Rex Stewart Jefferies Parker Ginsberg Ltd v Parker* [1988] IRLR 483; *Beckett Investment Management Group Ltd v Hall* [2007] IRLR 793).

6.60   In *Sadler v Imperial Life of Canada Ltd* [1988] IRLR 388, the court held that severance was permissible only if three conditions were satisfied: (i) the unenforceable provision was capable of being removed without the necessity of adding to or modifying the wording of what remained; (ii) the remaining terms continued to be supported by adequate consideration; and (iii) the removal of the unenforceable provision did not so change the character of the contract that it became 'not the sort of contract that the parties entered into at all' (see also *Business Seating (Renovations) Ltd v Broad* [1989] ICR 729; *Marshall v NM Financial Management Ltd* [1997] IRLR 449).

6.61   In *Living Design (Home Improvements) Ltd v Davidson* [1994] IRLR 69, the Court of Session considered a clause which was commonly found in restrictive covenants that: 'In the event that any such restriction should be found to be void but would be valid if some part thereof could be deleted or the period or area of application reduced, such restriction shall apply with such modification as may be necessary to make it valid and effective.' Lord Coulsfield held that this did not permit the rewriting of a covenant which was otherwise too wide to be valid. Pursuant to that clause there could be severance only on orthodox principles, and even then only where what was struck out was of trivial importance or technical and not part of the main import or substance of the provision.

Restraint in the public interest

6.62   The restraint must also generally be in the public interest, which effectively depends on the exercise of the judge's discretion in each case. In practice, few covenants have been invalidated on this basis. Slade J in *Greig v Insole* [1978] 3 All ER 449 held, however, that a ban by the Test and County Cricket Board on cricketers who played in a rival series of cricket matches organised in Australia by Kerry Packer could not be enforced because its benefits at most were speculative and would deprive the public of watching first class cricket players. Another example from an area other than employment is *Watson v Prager* [1991] ICR 603 on restrictions imposed on licensed boxers.

6.63   It was also on this ground that in *Wyatt v Kreglinger and Fernau* [1933] 1 KB 793, the Court of Appeal decided that a pension agreement was void because of a condition that the defendant should not again take a job in the wool trade (see also *Bull v Pitney-Bowes Ltd* [1967] 1 WLR 273).

Repudiatory breaches

The position is quite different, however, if there has been a repudiation by the employer **6.64** of the contract of employment. These propositions emerge from the considerable body of case law which has considered the effect of repudiatory breaches on the enforceability of restrictive covenants:

(a) An employer who has breached the employee's contract, perhaps by failing to give proper notice of termination, or, it seems, in breach of a procedural provision in the contract (*Geo Moore & Co Ltd v Menzies* (1989) 386 IRLIB 21) is not able to enforce a restraint clause (*General Billposting Co Ltd v Atkinson* [1909] AC 118; see also *Briggs v Oates* [1990] IRLR 472, [1990] ICR 473, as a case of premature termination by reason of a change in partners in a solicitors' firm).

(b) The same applies when an employee is given pay in lieu of notice and there is no provision in his contract that he must accept the same as opposed to being given the opportunity to work out his notice (*Rex Stewart Jefferies Parker Ginsberg Ltd v Parker* [1988] IRLR 483).

A clause is often inserted within the restrictive covenant to the effect that the parties con- **6.65** sider the clause as drawn to be reasonable, but if the court does not so find it reasonable the parties agree that it be modified so as to render it enforceable. This clause has not been tested in a reported case as part of the *ratio* of a decision, but in *Systems Reliability Holdings plc v Smith* [1990] IRLR 377, Harman J doubted the willingness of the courts to enforce such a clause. This is consistent with the general principle that the court will not draft a clause for the parties (*Davies v Davies* (1887) 36 Ch D 357) but rather review its drafting for reasonableness.

Further, the court in *Living Design (Home Improvements) Ltd v Davidson* [1994] IRLR **6.66** 69 decided that a covenant which was designed to operate whether or not the contract was lawfully terminated was invalid even if in the particular case the contract was lawfully terminated. The law was thrown into some disarray, however, by the decision in *D v M* [1996] IRLR 291, to the effect that a clause was invalid in so far as it purported to apply after termination 'for whatever reason whatsoever'.

This was itself overruled by the Court of Appeal in *Rock Refrigeration Ltd v Jones* [1996] **6.67** IRLR 675, where Phillips LJ also suggested that *General Billposting* itself might be ripe for reconsideration.

Restraint on solicitation of employees

Covenants restricting the poaching of staff will only be lawful in general in highly skilled **6.68** knowledge-based industry where there is competition for key workers.

A restraint on solicitation of employees will be enforceable if it is reasonable **6.69** within the general doctrine of restraint of trade (*Kores Manufacturing Ltd v Kolok Manufacturing Ltd* [1959] 1 Ch 108; *Cantor Fitzgerald (UK) Ltd v Wallace* [1992] IRLR 215; *Alliance Paper Group plc v Prestwich* [1996] IRLR 25; *Dawney*, cited in 6.51 above). A restraint clause of this nature was too wide, however, where it restricted the solicitation of any employee and was extended to apply to employees engaged after the termination of the defendant's employment (*TSC Europe (UK) Limited v Massey* [1999] IRLR 22).

Injunctions as relief

6.70 The normal remedy for any breaches of a restrictive covenant is an injunction, but as usual a court will not grant an injunction where this is in effect tantamount to an order for specific performance of the contract of employment (*Whitwood Chemical Co v Hardman* [1891] 2 Ch 416, see 13.44–13.49). There is a question as to the proper approach to the exercise of discretion by the court in such cases. The claimant must, however, in each case demonstrate that there is 'a perceived actual or potential harm which is real and not fanciful which would justify interim restraint to avoid such harm being inflicted' (*Jack Allen (Sales and Service) Ltd v Smith* [1999] IRLR 19).

6.71 The Court of Appeal in *Lawrence David Ltd v Ashton* [1989] IRLR 22 decided that the general test in *American Cyanamid* applies to interim injunctions in restraint of trade cases, so that the question of whether to grant an injunction in such cases should normally be decided solely on the basis of whether the claimant has a serious issue to be tried, and then whether the balance of convenience or justice is in favour of the grant of an interim order. This may tilt the balance in favour of claimant employers. Only if the case may not be brought to trial before the expiry of the covenant should the exception to *American Cyanamid* be adopted and the court consider the likelihood of success (eg *Lansing Linde Ltd v Kerr* [1991] IRLR 80). Normally a speedy trial should be ordered in such cases (on the general application of *American Cyanamid* principles).

6.72 In *John Michael Design plc v Cooke* [1987] ICR 445, the Court of Appeal decided that once the court had concluded that a covenant was as a prima facie conclusion binding, it was not then proper to pick and choose the clients named in that covenant to which the injunction should or should not relate and it was proper to restrain an ex-employee from doing business with an ex-customer of his employer even though that customer had made it plain that he would not in fact deal again with the ex-employer (see, on the scope of injunctions, *PSM International plc v Whitehouse* [1992] IRLR 279; see *Warren v Mendy* [1989] ICR 525).

Repayment clauses

6.73 Novel points arose in *Strathclyde Regional Council v Neil* [1984] IRLR 11, where the employee raised a series of objections to a contractual provision that she had to return to the employer for at least two years after a paid training leave. If she did not do so she would have to 'refund ... an amount proportionate to the unexpired portion of the contracted minimum period of service'. The Scottish court rejected each objection in turn:

(a) this was not an unlawful restrictive clause since the employee was not restrained from using her skills after leaving the council;

(b) there was no restraint on her liberty beyond that normally involved in a contract of service;

(c) there was no evidence of such compulsion as would invalidate her contractual consent; and

(d) the terms of repayment were not a penalty.

The refusal to pay commission to an ex-employee or agent because of his new employer or **6.74** principal may be invalid by reason of the restraint of trade doctrine (*Wyatt v Kreglinger and Ferneau* [1933] 1 KB 793).

An employee who is on secondment to another employer owes the same duties of obedi- **6.75** ence and good faith to the employer to whom he is seconded during the period of secondment as to his contractual employer (*Macmillan Inc v Bishopsgate Investment Trust plc* [1993] IRLR 793).

7

EQUAL PAY

A INTRODUCTION 7.01
B THE EQUALITY CLAUSE AND LIKE WORK . . . 7.11
  The 'same establishment' in UK law 7.13
  The comparator in UK law 7.17
  The comparator and the establishment
  in EU law 7.19
  What is 'like work'? 7.25
  Genuine material factor 7.30
C JOB EVALUATION 7.67
  Meaning of job evaluation 7.72
  Challenges to job evaluation study 7.76
D EQUAL VALUE CLAIMS 7.78

  What is work of equal value? 7.80
E CLAIMING EQUAL PAY 7.82
F MATERNITY 7.93
G COLLECTIVE ENFORCEMENT 7.94
H EUROPEAN LAW 7.96
  Article 141 . . . . 7.96
  Meaning of pay 7.98
I THE NATURE OF THE RIGHT 7.101
J EQUAL TREATMENT IN RESPECT
  OF PENSIONS IN UK
  LAW—SECTION 67 . . . . 7.105

The principle of equal pay excludes not only the application of provisions leading to direct sex discrimination, but also the application of provisions which maintain different treatment between men and women at work as a result of criteria not based on sex where those differences of treatment are not attributable to objective factors which are unrelated to sex discrimination. (*Stadt Lengerich v Helmig* [1995] IRLR 216, ECJ, para 20.)

A INTRODUCTION

7.01 The aim of the Equal Pay Act 1970, as stated in its preamble, was to 'prevent discrimination as regards terms and conditions of employment between men and women'. It was intended to eliminate the clearly lower pay which has been given to women for centuries, and was the first legal embodiment of the equal pay principle which became TUC policy in 1888, was the subject of a Royal Commission in 1944–46, and has been ILO policy for decades. The number of cases has shot up in recent years with many series of mass claims which are especially prevalent in the local government and health service areas of the public sector and supermarkets in the private sector. The law is now found in the Equality Act 2010.

7.02 Notwithstanding the legal framework, the wage gap stubbornly remains 9.6 per cent for full-time employees and 19.7 per cent for full- and part-time employees combined.

7.03 The statute also represents Britain's enactment of the directly enforceable obligation contained in Art 141 (ex 119) of the EU Treaty, equal pay for equal work. The English courts have on several occasions referred cases to the European Court of Justice (now CJEU) for interpretation of the principle in the European legislation. These aspects will be dealt with later in this chapter (7.96–7.100), although the dominance of European law in the area of equal pay and sex discrimination is reflected by the fact that the early part of this chapter contains extensive reference to cases decided by the European Court of Justice, or by English courts and tribunals implementing principles laid down by the European Court. Indeed, in 1999 the EAT struck down two parts of the domestic legislation on the ground that they were inconsistent with Art 141 (*Davies v Neath Port Talbot CBC* [1999] IRLR 769; *Levez v T.H. Jennings (Harlow Pools) Ltd* [1999] IRLR 764). The direct effect of EU law operates to overrule inconsistencies or ambiguities to be found in domestic statutes rather than provide free-standing rights (*Biggs v Somerset CC* [1995] ICR 811; *Barber v Staffordshire CC* [1996] IRLR 209). It is desirable that domestic and Community law operate in harmony but this must not be at the expense of interpreting UK statutes in a distortion of their language (*Duke v GEC Reliance Ltd* [1988] ICR 339; *Webb v Emo Air Cargo (UK) Ltd* [1993] IRLR 27).

Closely allied with this principle are various maternity rights for pregnant employees which have been recently revised (Chapter 10). **7.04**

The Equal Pay Act was passed even before the UK acceded to membership of the EU, and **7.05** was brought into force on 29 December 1975 (giving to employers a five-year transitional period) having already been amended by the Sex Discrimination Act 1975. These two statutes are intended to form one harmonious code (see eg *Strathclyde Regional Council v Wallace* [1998] ICR 205; *Jenkins v Kingsgate (Clothing Productions) Ltd (No 2)* [1981] IRLR 388), the Equal Pay Act applying to contractual terms and the Sex Discrimination Act applicable to all other issues.

The Equal Pay Act was amended in 1983 to implement fully in English law the European **7.06** Communities Directive 75/117 on Equal Pay by enabling an employee to insist that a job evaluation study be carried out. The 1983 amending Regulations were introduced after the European Court of Justice ruled that the 1970 Act did not satisfy the requirement that 'the principle of equal pay for men and women ... means for the same work and for work to which equal value is attributed, the elimination of all discrimination on grounds of sex with regard to all aspects and conditions of remuneration' (*Commission of the European Communities v United Kingdom* [1984] IRLR 29). The important procedural consequences of the Regulations are now found in Sch 3 to the Employment Tribunals Rules of Procedure 2013. The Pensions Act 1995 further introduced the principle of equal treatment between men and women in occupational pension schemes. Sitting alongside the Act, the EOC published a Code of Practice on Equal Pay in 1997 which was updated in 2003.

The important dividing line with sex discrimination is drawn by s 70 of the Equality Act **7.07** 2010, which states that where an equal pay claim may be brought within s 66 or s 67 subject to any s 69 defence the claimant cannot choose instead to bring a sex discrimination claim under s 39. If no such claim is possible because there is no appropriate comparator, s 71 permits a claim under s 39 if the discrimination is direct.

Promotion, transfer, and non-contractual benefits come within the terms of other parts **7.08** of the Equality Act 2010, while equal pay under s 65 relates solely to what is regulated by way of the contract between employer and employee. Thus, by s 80(2) EA 2010:

The terms of a person's work are—

(a) if the person is employed, the terms of the person's employment that are in the person's contract of employment, contract of apprenticeship or contract to do work personally;

(b) if the person holds a personal or public office, the terms of the person's appointment to the office.

7.09 A bonus may be regulated by the contract and thus fall within these provisions even though it is discretionary if it is derived from terms in the contract (*Hoyland v Asda Stores Ltd* [2006] IRLR 468). By s 72 Equality Act 2010, the provisions apply to a person who '(a) is employed, or (b) holds a personal or public office'. By s 80(2)(a) this includes a contract of apprenticeship and a contract to do work personally.

7.10 The provisions are complex, now surrounded by much difficult case law, and operate on four levels, which will be considered in turn:

(a) the implication of an 'equality clause' into the contract of employment;
(b) the application of job evaluation studies;
(c) equal value claims; and
(d) the amendment of discriminatory collective agreements.

There is running through all this an issue about what constitutes pay which is to be equalised. This is largely worked out in the European cases. Availability pay is not a social security scheme but qualifies as pay for the purposes of the European Directives (*Dansk Jurist v Indenrigs – og Sundhedsministeriet* [2014] ICR 1; see also *HK Danmark v Experian A/S* [2014] ICR 27).

B THE EQUALITY CLAUSE AND LIKE WORK

7.11 The methods of comparison are set out in s 65(1) Equality Act 2010 so that:

A's work is equal to that of B if it is—

(a) like B's work,
(b) rated as equivalent to B's work, or
(c) of equal value to B's work.

This means that if any aspect of the woman's terms and conditions is or becomes less favourable to the woman than a term of a similar kind in the man's contract, the term is modified so as to be as favourable; if there is no corresponding term, the contract is deemed to include one (s 66(2)). Thus, if men have a right to four weeks' holiday and women to three, and the women are found to be engaged on like work, their entitlement must be increased to four. If women have no right to holidays at all, a term to that effect must be inserted at once. The defining principle is thus equality and not comparability: so that 'where a woman has established a claim for equal pay by reference to a particular male comparator, she is entitled to be paid the salary he received at the date of her claim, not to be placed on a higher rate of pay than the comparator to reflect her relative seniority in her own job' (*Evesham v West Herts Health Authority* [2000] IRLR 257). Failure to give equal pay is not a tort but a breach of an implied term in the contract, that term being implied by statute.

7.12 The defining concept of 'like work' is stated by s 65(2) so that A's work is like B's work if:

(a) A's work and B's work are the same or broadly similar, and
(b) such differences as there are between their work are not of practical importance in relation to the terms of their work.

By s 65(3):

on a comparison of one person's work with another's for the purposes of subsection (2), it is necessary to have regard to—

(a) the frequency with which differences between their work occur in practice, and
(b) the nature and extent of the differences.

By s 70(1):

> This section applies in relation to a term of a person's work—
>
> (a) that relates to pay, but
> (b) in relation to which a sex equality clause or rule has no effect.

The 'same establishment' in UK law

The comparators must be employed at the same establishment by the same employer or **7.13** an associate of that employer (s 79(3)), or at an establishment where common terms or conditions are observed either generally or for employees of the relevant class (s 79(4)). The word 'establishment' has caused problems of definition here as it has in respect of redundancy consultation procedures (17.33–17.37).

Example Crest Department Stores Ltd has two branches. All the checkout assistants at **7.14** Branch A are women but at Branch B some are male—the males receive a higher rate of pay: a woman at Branch A may compare herself to a man at Branch B if, but only if, the same general terms, possibly because of a collective agreement, apply to both places.

It is thus not a fatal objection to the bringing of an equal pay claim that none of the **7.15** comparators was employed at the same establishment as the claimant. Those employed at other establishments must, however, be engaged on the same 'terms and conditions of service' or broadly similar terms as the comparator in order to be able to claim, and this includes contractual obligations such as hours worked and length of holidays. In *Leverton v Clwyd CC* [1989] IRLR 28, the House of Lords determined that a nursery nurse was engaged on similar terms to eleven male clerical officers notwithstanding that their hours and holidays were different. It was a question of fact whether there were common terms and conditions at the two establishments. Terms covered by the same collective agreement are the paradigm but not the only case under the rubric (see also *Lawson v Britfish Ltd* [1987] ICR 726).

The definition of 'common terms and conditions' within what was then s 1(6) of the **7.16** Equal Pay Act engaged the attention of the House of Lords in *British Coal Corporation v Smith* [1996] IRLR 404, where canteen workers employed by British Coal who were predominantly women sought to compare their pay and conditions with surface mine-workers who were men. They were faced by the defence that they were not employed in the same employment for the purposes of the Act. The House of Lords upheld the commonsense approach taken by the tribunal: 'common terms and conditions' within s 1(6) means terms and conditions which are substantially comparable on a broad basis, rather than the same terms and conditions subject only to differences which are *de minimis*. The terms must, however, be sufficiently similar for a fair comparison to be made. There was sufficient material for the tribunal to determine that the facts satisfied the statutory test since the two groups of employees were both governed by the same national collective agreements even though there were local variations relating to an incentive bonus and concessionary coal.

The comparator in UK law

It is for the claimant to choose the comparator: *Amey Services Ltd v Cardigan* [2008] **7.17** IRLR 279. As Maurice Kay LJ put it in *Redcar & Cleveland BC v Bainbridge* [2007] IRLR 984, 'By its very nature, equal pay assumes a process of comparison.' The claimant for equal pay may normally freely choose with whom she is to be compared for the purposes of like work (*Ainsworth v Glass Tubes and Components Ltd* [1977] IRLR 74).

The Northern Ireland Court of Appeal in *McPherson v Rathgael Centre for Children and Young People and Northern Ireland Office (Training Schools Branch)* [1991] IRLR 206, however, left open the important question whether a claimant could select a comparator who was anomalous in some respect (see also *Dance v Dorothy Perkins* [1978] ICR 760). The search for a precise comparator in the past proved very difficult in those areas where women are generally underpaid, and for which the statute was most needed. In particular, employment in many textile, catering, and retail businesses is the preserve of women, so that no man is employed on like work.

7.18 This problem also led to women comparing their wages with a man who *had* been employed in the past but who was no longer employed at the time of a tribunal application, and this important issue of whether this was permissible was resolved eventually in favour of comparison with a former employee by the European Court of Justice in *McCarthys Ltd v Smith* [1980] IRLR 210. This is now provided for in the Act itself.

The comparator and the establishment in EU law

7.19 Article 141 is wider than the Equality Act 2010, in that it allows a comparison where the claimant and her comparator(s) are employed 'in the same establishment or service, whether private or public' as *Defrenne v Sabena* (see 7.97) held.

7.20 Establishment must be given a purposive construction to comply with EU law (*City of Edinburgh Council v Wilkinson* [2010] IRLR 756). A Council would prima facie be a single establishment only if the facts demonstrated that there were subsets of its operations which ought properly to be regarded as separate establishments would that presumption be set aside.

7.21 In *Lawrence v Regent Office Care Ltd* [1999] IRLR 148, the court rejected the claimants' submission that, as caterers employed by a private company, they were entitled to base their claim for equal pay on a comparison of their terms and conditions with those of male employees of North Yorkshire County Council, their former employer. Although accepting that it was not necessary, for the purposes of Art 141, that the claimant and her comparator be employed by the same or even an associated employer, the EAT explained that the two must at least be, 'in a loose and non-technical sense', employed in the same establishment and service. Article 141 was not so broad as to countenance comparison with someone employed by a different organisation, where the only connection was the nature of the work being done. This case was referred to the European Court of Justice [2002] IRLR 822, which held that in order for a comparison to be made the terms must be derived from a single source under Art 141 such that there was a body which is responsible for the inequality and could restore equal treatment. By s 79(9):

> For the purposes of this section, employers are associated if—
>
> (a) one is a company of which the other (directly or indirectly) has control, or
> (b) both are companies of which a third person (directly or indirectly) has control.

7.22 The nature of the single source has proved elusive. An NHS Hospital Trust could not be treated as a single source for the purposes of Art 141 (*Armstrong v Newcastle upon Tyne NHS Hospital Trust* [2006] IRLR 124). The bare fact that the claimant and comparator were in common employment was neither a necessary nor sufficient basis for a comparison under statute and it was necessary to consider in each case whether the terms and conditions of the claimant and comparator were established by a person or body which had responsibility for the claimed inequality, and the capacity to restore equal treatment. Here the evidence was that each department did its own negotiating (*DEFRA v*

Robertson [2005] ICR 750; see also *South Ayrshire Council v Morton* [2001] IRLR 28). The Equality Act does not itself require the incorporation of the doctrine of single source (*North Cumbria Acute Hospitals NHS Trust v Potter* [2009] IRLR 176). The Secretary of State for Health was not the single source of terms in the NHS as the claimants in *Potter* contended.

Gradually, the cases became more liberal in favour of employees (see also *Glasgow City Council v UNISON* [2014] IRLR 532). In *South Tyne MBC v Anderson* [2007] IRLR 715, it was held that employees within the general employment of a local authority could compare themselves with those engaged in community schools because they were all employed on the same collective agreement. The terms were held to be common in that they were sufficiently similar for a broad comparison to be made. **7.23**

It was also open to make comparisons between workers who did not and never would work in the same workplace; whilst the hypothesis under s 1(6) was that the comparators were transferred to do their present jobs in a different location, it was not a requirement that there should be a real possibility in fact of such a transfer taking place (*Dumfries & Galloway Council v North* [2013] ICR 993). **7.24**

What is 'like work'?

The question of whether there is 'like work' is generally a matter of degree for the tribunal (eg *Durrant v North Yorkshire AHA* [1979] IRLR 401), and it was suggested in early cases, such as *Capper Pass Ltd v Lawton* [1976] IRLR 366, that the words should be interpreted broadly in order to make the Act workable. Tribunals were thus advised not to undertake too minute an examination, or be constrained to find work to be dissimilar because of insubstantial differences. Thus, there was like work in *Lawton* between a female cook who made ten to twenty lunches for directors in their dining room, and two assistant male chefs who provided rather more meals in the works canteen. The crucial point was that the basic processes involved in the jobs were the same. In *Thomas v National Coal Board* [1987] ICR 757, the EAT held that women canteen assistants could not claim to be on 'like work' with a male canteen worker who worked permanently at night and alone. The tribunal had decided that the added responsibility of night work was a difference of practical importance, and the EAT would not interfere with that finding of fact. **7.25**

The Court of Appeal gave general guidance on this area in *Shields v E. Coomes (Holdings) Ltd* [1978] IRLR 263, where the claimant was employed as a counterhand in the respondent's betting shop. She was paid 62p per hour, while the men received £1.06, but the employer alleged that there was a difference in duties which justified the large variation in pay, since the men were expected by their contracts to help in case of trouble. This was not enough. The tribunal should first ask whether the work was the same or broadly similar, then, using its industrial experience, examine the nature and extent of any differences, and especial emphasis should be placed on the frequency or otherwise with which differences occurred in practice. In fact, there was no evidence here that a man had *ever* had to deal with a disturbance or incidents of violence, and every indication that the women had their own ways of dealing with difficult customers. Indeed, Lord Denning MR said (at 267): 'He may have been a small nervous man who would not say "boo to a goose". She may have been as fierce and formidable as a battle axe.' **7.26**

In *British Leyland Ltd v Powell* [1978] IRLR 57, the EAT formulated the proper test as 'whether the two employments would have been placed into the same category on an evaluation exercise', and Phillips J took a similar approach in the complex case of *Electrolux* **7.27**

Ltd v Hutchinson [1976] IRLR 410. There, men and women worked on the same track in the manufacture of refrigerators and freezers; but while all the men were paid on grade 10 rates, 599 out of the 600 women received rather lower wages in class 01. The company argued that the men had additional contractual obligations: they had to transfer to totally different tasks on demand, and work overtime as and when required. The EAT focused on how frequently the men in fact *did* other work; how often they were required to work on Sunday; and what kind of work they did in these unsocial hours. They came to the conclusion that in reality the work was like work. In *Eaton Ltd v Nuttall* [1977] IRLR 71, however, a male production scheduler handling 1,200 items worth between £5 and £1,000 each and a women scheduler handling 2,400 items below £2.50 were held not to be engaged on broadly similar work—for an error on the part of the man would be of much greater consequence. Handling substantial sums of money may prevent work being like, as may involvement on heavier work. Each case clearly depends on its own facts.

7.28 The following have been held insufficient as differences to make two jobs dissimilar for the purposes of analysing 'like work':

(a) that the work is performed at different times or in different places, although this may constitute a genuine material difference (7.30ff) (*Dugdale v Kraft Foods Ltd* [1977] 1 All ER 454);

(b) that two canteen ladies served breakfast to patrons at their tables, while the comparator male did not (*NCB v Sherwin & Spruce* [1978] IRLR 122); and

(c) that a male driver sometimes drove outside the precincts of the appellant's factory whereas the female applicant did not.

Difference in responsibility may be sufficient to differentiate jobs so that they are not like work (*De Brito v Standard Chartered Bank Ltd* [1978] ICR 650; *Waddington v Leicester Council for Voluntary Service* [1977] 2 All ER 633).

7.29 The limits of like work were exposed as a matter of EU law in the ECJ decision in *Angestelltenbetriebsrat der Wiener v Wiener Gebietskrankenkasse* [2000] ICR 1134. This concerned a claim for equal pay between graduate psychologists employed as physiotherapists and graduate doctors. Although the two groups performed seemingly identical activities, in treating their respective patients they drew on knowledge and skills which were acquired in very different disciplines; and even though doctors and psychologists both performed work of physiotherapy, the former were qualified to perform in addition to other tasks in a field which was not open to the latter. They could thus not be regarded as being in comparable situations. The fact that employees are classified in the same job category under a collective agreement is not itself sufficient for concluding that they perform the same work or work of equal value. This must be ascertained from many factors, including such matters as (i) the nature of the activities actually entrusted to each of the employees (*Brunnhofer v Bank der Österreichischen Postsparkasse AG* [2001] IRLR 571); (ii) the training requirements for carrying them out and working conditions.

Genuine material factor

7.30 Even if the comparative job is held to be like work, the employer has a defence if he can prove that a pay differential was due to a material factor.

7.31 This provision demonstrates that the Act is in effect aimed at differences in terms due to sex alone (or in combination with other features), for it would be a strange result if there was no possibility of paying different wages to recognise that a man (although employed on a similar job) in fact deserved more than the woman because of personal qualities or qualifications. Thus, while the like work or work of equal value concepts focus on the make-up of the job, the defence of genuine material difference essentially looks to the person filling it. The so-called 'personal equation', as Lawton LJ put it in *Clay Cross (Quarry Services) Ltd v Fletcher* [1979] ICR 1, at 9:

> ... embraces what appertains to her in her job, such as the qualifications she brought to it, the length of time she has been in it, the skill she has acquired, the responsibilities she has undertaken, and where and under what conditions she has to do it.

By s 69(1):   **7.32**

> The sex equality clause in A's terms has no effect in relation to a difference between A's terms and B's terms if the responsible person shows that the difference is because of a material factor reliance on which—
> (a) does not involve treating A less favourably because of A's sex than the responsible person treats B, and
> (b) if the factor is within subsection (2), is a proportionate means of achieving a legitimate aim.

This is further elaborated in s 69(2) such that 'A factor is within this subsection if A shows that, as a result of the factor, A and persons of the same sex doing work equal to A's are put at a particular disadvantage when compared with persons of the opposite sex doing work equal to A's.'

The reference in s 69(1)(b) to the factor having to be a 'proportionate means of achieving a   **7.33** legitimate aim' is an addition in the Equality Act but the case law under the Equal Pay Act had almost reached that far under the formula of genuine material difference other than sex. There may be bridging provisions to bring a disadvantaged group (usually women) up to the standards of the advantaged. By s 69(3) 'For the purposes of subsection (1), the long-term objective of reducing inequality between men's and women's terms of work is always to be regarded as a legitimate aim.'

Further, by s 69(6) 'For the purposes of this section, a factor is not material unless it is a   **7.34** material difference between A's case and B's.'

The courts here thus ask two basic questions with differing burdens of proof: **7.35**

(a) Has the employer shown that any variation was genuinely due to (ie caused by) a material factor existing between the two?
(b) Is that material difference genuinely owing to a reason other than sex taking into account the need that the factor must be a proportionate means of achieving a legitimate aim?

The burden of proof of demonstrating the criteria of the defence throughout rests on the employer (*Byrne v Financial Times Ltd* [1991] IRLR 417). However, in the case of an allegation of indirect discrimination the complainant has the burden of proving on the balance of probabilities that the matter complained of has a disproportionate adverse impact (*Nelson v Carillion Service Ltd* [2003] IRLR 428; *Armstrong v Newcastle upon Tyne NHS Hospital Trust* [2006] IRLR 124; *Cumbria CC v Dow (No 1)* [2008] IRLR 91; *Grundy v British Airways plc* [2008] IRLR 74). This is the normal burden as applied in civil cases (*National Vulcan Engineering Insurance Group Ltd v Wade* [1978] IRLR 225). It is not, however, enough to resist the defence that the employers did not *intend* to discriminate (*Jenkins v Kingsgate Ltd (No 2)* [1981] IRLR 388).

There must be an explanation for the difference that involved consideration of why each   **7.36** party was paid as he or she was (*CalMac Ferries Ltd v Wallace* [2014] ICR 453).

7.37 It is also quite possible for there to be a genuine material factor even if that same feature also was put forward as (but did not amount to) a difference making the jobs of the applicant and her comparator unequal, according to the EAT in *Christie v John E Haith Ltd* [2003] IRLR 670.

7.38 The Court of Appeal placed a vital restriction on the concept of genuine material difference in *Clay Cross (Quarry Services) v Fletcher* (above). The claimant, Mrs Fletcher, was a clerk earning £35 per week, but since the comparator male had received £43 per week in his existing job, Clay Cross Ltd paid him more in order to attract his services. It claimed that the previous pay constituted a genuine material difference, but the Lord Justices held that only 'the personal equation' might justify such discrimination, since the subsection went on to say that the distinction was 'between her case and his'. Here, extrinsic market forces were in effect determining the rate for the job, and Lord Denning MR remarked that, 'an employer cannot avoid his obligations under the Act by saying: "I paid him more because he asked for more", or "I paid her less because she was willing to come for less"'. To do so would render the statute virtually impotent. He went on: 'These are the very reasons why there was unequal pay before the statute.' This decision does not apply where comparisons are made between employees working at different times (*Albion Shipping v Arnold* [1981] IRLR 525). Then the economic circumstances of the business are relevant.

7.39 The *Fletcher* case was distinguished on narrow grounds (although understandably), however, in *Rainey v Greater Glasgow Health Board Eastern District* [1985] IRLR 414. When a prosthetic fitting service was set up within the Scottish NHS, it was agreed that the prosthetists would be paid on the Medical Physics and Technicians pay scale, but in order to attract a sufficient number of experienced prosthetists from the private sector, they were offered the same pay as they had been receiving. Further, a different structure of increase was adopted. A woman complained that a man who had joined from the private sector was paid £2,790 more than she was for the same work. The Court of Session, with one dissentient, thought that the circumstances of the higher pay were sufficiently 'personal' to fall within s 1(3), and were similar to the 'red circle' cases (7.45ff). The circumstances in which the man attained the higher pay were curious, exceptional and unique. The question whether it was 'material' was a matter for the employment tribunal. The House of Lords agreed in the result ([1986] 3 WLR 1017). Lord Keith of Kinkel considered that the decision of the Court of Appeal in *Fletcher* was 'unduly restrictive of the proper interpretation of s 1(3)'. The difference had to be 'material', which his Lordship would construe as meaning 'significant and relevant'. This required consideration of all the circumstances of the case.

7.40 In the light of the decision of the ECJ in *Bilka-Kaufhaus GmbH v Karin Weber von Hartz* [1986] IRLR 317, it was not necessary to construe the former s 1(3) as conferring greater rights on a worker than does Art 141 (ex 119) of the Treaty of Rome. Thus, 'the relevant difference for purposes of [the former] s 1(3) may relate to circumstances other than the personal qualifications or merits of the male and female workers who are the subject of comparison'. In *Rainey*, the difference between the case of the appellant and the comparator was that 'the former is a person who entered the National Health Service ... directly while the latter is a person who entered it from employment with a private contractor. The fact that one is a woman and the other a man is an accident' (see also *Davies v McCartneys* [1989] IRLR 439).

7.41 There are several distinct 'differences' which the courts have had frequent occasion to consider. Greater length of service is clearly a material factor (*Capper Pass v Lawton* [1977] ICR 83), just as working at different times of the day normally is not so (*Dugdale* *v Kraft Foods* [1977] ICR 48). In *Navy, Army and Air Force Institutes v Varley* [1976] IRLR 408, a distinction in hourly pay between workers based in London and the rather cheaper Nottingham area was held to be a genuine and material difference. An incorrect grading which arose because of an initial mistake as to the male comparator's qualifications could not amount to a material factor. Most controversy has surrounded treatment of part-time workers (7.42), sham bonuses, protection of earnings (7.45), and grading systems (7.50). In *Cadman v JHSE* [2006] ECR I-9583, the ECJ held that length of service is a legitimate criterion for an employer to use in setting pay and does not need to be justified. *Wilson v Health and Safety Executive* [2010] ICR 302 confirmed this. As a general rule EU law did not require an employer to provide objective justification for adopting service-related pay scales; justification would, however, be required where an equal pay claimant provided evidence capable of raising serious doubts that such a criterion was appropriate in order to attain the objective of rewarding experience.

Part-time workers

The treatment of part-timers was in the nature of a test case for the Act because of the predominance of women in the part-time labour market, and some of the early cases did much to retard their progress towards equal pay (eg *Handley v H. Mono Ltd* [1979] ICR 147). In *Jenkins v Kingsgate Ltd (No 2)* [1981] IRLR 388, however, the EAT took a more radical view. The employer had to show that the difference in pay between full-time male workers and part-time women was reasonably necessary in order to obtain some result which the employer desired for economic or other reasons. A bare statement to this effect by the employer was, however, not enough, and the case was remitted to the employment tribunal to determine whether the difference in pay was indeed necessary in order to enable the employers to reduce absenteeism and to obtain maximum utilisation of their plant as claimed. **7.42**

In the European Court of Justice ([1981] ICR 592) the prohibition of differences in rates of pay related to differences which were based exclusively on the sex of the employee. Thus, a difference in rates of remuneration between full-time and part-time employees did not offend Art 119 (now 141), provided that the difference was attributable to factors which were objectively justified and did not relate directly or indirectly to discrimination based on sex. On remission to the Employment Appeal Tribunal ([1981] 1 WLR 1485), Browne-Wilkinson P decided that even if the employer satisfied Art 119 (now 141), s 1(3) went further. It must show that the 'difference was reasonably necessary in order to obtain some result (other than cheap female labour) which the employer desires for economic or other reasons' (see also *Calder v Rowntree Mackintosh Confectionery Ltd* [1993] ICR 811). There are specific protections for part-timers in the Part-time Workers Regulations 2000 (SI 2000/1551) but the principles still apply in an equal pay claim (see 9.01–9.11). **7.43**

Sham bonus schemes

In many local authorities bonuses which started in the 1960s as a way of rewarding productivity had often become hardened by the 2000s into payments which were to be made come what may. They were overwhelmingly paid to men. Bonus schemes had been seen by both the management and workforce to be a fixed part of salary and were no longer productivity based (*Sunderland CC v Brennan* [2012] ICR 1216). **7.44**

Pay protection

In industrial relations jargon, earnings are said to be 'red-circled' when jobs are regraded, a new pay and grading structure is introduced, or a long-serving employee is moved, and his (and it is usually a man's) pay is protected at the previous rate or status in order to **7.45** avoid breach of his contract, or perhaps industrial unrest. New employees performing the same function will, however, receive the normal lower rate for the grade. Very often the long-serving or sick employee is a man, and the grade in which he is placed is solely or mainly female. This creates a major challenge for the implementation of equal pay.

7.46   A good example of the phenomenon is *Snoxell v Vauxhall Motors Ltd* [1977] IRLR 123. As part of a major company pay restructuring in 1970, designed partly to facilitate equal pay, the position of quality controller was downgraded but the males then in post had their wages protected in their inferior jobs. The claimant women who had been employed for many years as inspectors of machine parts sought equal pay with these men who were now doing a similar job. The EAT stated that the evocation of the red circle was not in itself decisive: the correct approach entailed eliciting and analysing all of the circumstances of the case, including the situation prior to the formation of the protected class of employees. An employer could never establish a genuine material difference if past discrimination blatantly contributed to the now protected differential, as indeed it had in *Snoxell*'s case. Phillips J, moreover, thought it desirable 'whenever possible for "red circles" to be phased out and eliminated'.

7.47   Other relevant factors included 'whether (the red circle) group ... is a closed group; whether the red circling has been the subject of negotiations with the representatives of the work people, and the views of the women taken into account; or whether the women are able equally with the men to transfer between the grades'. It is legitimate for a higher rate to continue to be paid where a man is transferred for reasons of illness or age (see also *Outlook Supplies Ltd v Penny* [1978] IRLR 12; *Avon and Somerset Police v Emery* [1981] ICR 229; *Forex Neptune (Overseas) Ltd v Miller* [1987] ICR 170).

7.48   In *Redcar & Cleveland BC v Bainbridge* [2008] IRLR 776, the Court of Appeal held that the protection of pay to male employees whose pay was higher on the day when a new pay and grading scheme (by reason of bonus payments being made to groups which were largely populated by men) came into effect was sexually discriminatory when the reason for the women not being paid as highly as the men was the failure of the employers to implement equal pay. This was capable of being a legitimate aim because the discrimination was indirect and it was a legitimate aim to cushion the blow for the employees on the changeover, but it was not justified in this case primarily because the employers knew that they were in breach of an equality clause and had not carried out any costing as to whether they could pay similar payments to the women.

7.49   Once the reason which led to a woman being paid less than a man has been removed, it is no longer possible for the employer to justify the difference in pay on that ground. For example, when the employee in *Benveniste v University of Southampton* [1989] IRLR 122 was appointed a lecturer, the University was subject to financial restraint and it was agreed that she would be offered a salary well below the level normally paid. When those financial constraints came to an end she was still not paid equally with men employed on like work. The Court of Appeal determined that it was 'not right that the appellant should continue to be paid on a lower scale once the reason for payment at the lower scale has been removed ... The material difference between the appellant's case and the case of the comparator's evaporated when the financial constraints were removed.'

Grading systems

7.50   The courts have also considered grading systems in a series of cases, starting with *Waddington v Leicester Council for Voluntary Service* [1977] IRLR 32. The claimant there was a female community worker who had responsibility for a male play leader.

She was, however, paid some £400 less than he was because she was on a different local authority pay scale. Phillips J stated: 'Where men and women are employed on like work, and the variation is in the rate of remuneration and the remuneration is fixed in accordance with a nationally or widely negotiated wage scale ... there will usually be a strong case for saying that the case falls within [the former] s 1(3).' While the scales are not conclusive, 'when one is dealing with nationally negotiated scales, in general use by local authorities, it seems unlikely that a problem caused by grading is very likely to give rise to a remedy under the Equal Pay Act'.

This case was approved by the Court of Appeal in *National Vulcan Ltd v Wade* [1978] **7.51** IRLR 225. The EAT had found fatal in the appellant's grading scheme the fact that 'the assignment of a particular individual, and therefore his remuneration, depended upon the personal assessment of the individual, which was of necessity a subjective judgment'. Lord Denning, however, overruling this decision took a much less interventionist stance; employers will have a defence under s 1(3) providing only that any scheme is 'genuinely operated'. It was a matter of policy, since 'a grading scheme according to skill, ability and experience is an integral part of good business management ... If it were to go forth that these grading systems are inoperative and operate against the Equal Pay Act, it would, I think, be disastrous for the ordinary running of efficient business'.

Not by reason of sex

To be a valid defence, the relevant difference must not, however, be by reason of sex, **7.52** whether direct or indirect.

The approach of the European Court of Justice may be seen in the important case of **7.53** *Enderby v Frenchay Health Authority* [1993] IRLR 591 which gave rise to a form of discrimination which was not obviously within the existing categories of direct or indirect but which usually goes under the sobriquet of Enderby-type discrimination. The ECJ decided that there is a prima facie case of sex discrimination where valid statistics disclose an appreciable difference in pay between two jobs of equal value, one of which is carried out almost exclusively by women and the other predominantly by men. It is for the national court to assess whether the statistics appear to be significant in that they cover enough individuals and do not illustrate purely fortuitous and short-term phenomena. Art 141 then requires the employer to show that the difference in pay is based on objectively justified factors unrelated to discrimination on grounds of sex. Further, the genuine material difference must justify the *whole* difference in pay and not merely a part of it. To demonstrate a prima facie case, the group does not have to be made up almost exclusively of women (see *British Road Services Ltd v Loughran* [1997] IRLR 92 and *Bailey v Home Office* [2005] IRLR 369).

Significantly, the House of Lords stated that the requirement of an 'objective justification' **7.54** will apply only where the material factor relied upon is tainted by sex discrimination, or is presumed to be so. For example, it was not necessary to justify a local education authority's policy of suspending pay increases for staff who took on the extra duties of a 'principal teacher'. Although the female claimants received lower pay than did their male comparators, this was owing to budgetary constraints rather than the difference in sex— a point further illustrated by the fact that a majority of the unpromoted teachers were actually male. No objective justification was required in such circumstances (*Strathclyde Regional Council v Wallace* [1998] ICR 205; see also *Parliamentary Commissioner for Administration v Fernandez* [2004] IRLR 22; *Armstrong v Newcastle upon Tyne NHS Trust* [2006] IRLR 124; and *Tyne and Wear PTE (t/a Nexus) v Best* [2007] ICR 523 on the proper use of statistics).

7.55 It was reiterated in *Redcar & Cleveland BC v Bainbridge* [2008] IRLR 776 that the fact that pay was negotiated by non-discriminatory different collective bargaining could be a genuine material difference defence (but it may be susceptible to the contention that their make-up is sex tainted as was often the case).

7.56 Indeed, where there are compelling statistics showing a disparately adverse impact on women of a particular practice, the inference of sex taint would be readily drawn (*Gibson v Sheffield CC* [2010] ICR 708).

7.57 Another example is *Pulham v Barking & Dagenham LBC* [2010] ICR 335, where the Council operated a scheme rewarding loyalty and experience under which employees were paid salary increments if they had twenty-five years' continuous service and had attained the age of fifty-five. The scheme was phased out when single status was intro- duced on 1 April 2007. The claimant claimed that her exclusion from the scheme was in breach of the regulations. The EAT held that although the elimination of past-recognised discrimination had to be immediate and full and its continuation in the form of transi- tional arrangements could not be justified, where an employer was faced with the coming into force of legislation affecting arrangements which had previously been perfectly law- ful it was open to him to justify the incorporation of an element of pay protection into the adjustments which were necessary to confirm the new law; it was here not enough that the arrangements represented the outcome of negotiations with the unions but it had itself to carry out the necessary proportionality exercise.

7.58 Discrimination could be shown by establishing that the market rate which the Trust's predecessor had sought to match in a competitive tendering exercise reflected the fact that the work in question was regarded as 'women's work' but it also had to be shown that the decision taker had appreciated that fact and had been willing to take advan- tage of it (*Newcastle upon Tyne Hospitals NHS Foundation Trust v Armstrong* [2010] ICR 674).

7.59 A tribunal is not entitled to conclude that even though the bonuses to refuse workers genuinely reflected increased productivity, it would have been possible for the employers to have adopted some other kind of bonus scheme which could have achieved equality and that the employer's failure to pay such a bonus could not be justified: *Redcar & Cleveland BC v Bainbridge* [2007] IRLR 91. The courts do not require the employers to manufac- ture some alternative means of paying the claimants.

Justification

7.60 In *Bilka-Kaufhaus GmbH v Karin Weber von Hartz* [1987] ICR 110, at 126, the ECJ held that it was not sufficient for the employer to show that there was no *intention* to discriminate for it to defend a claim. It was for the national court to decide whether it was objectively justified on economic grounds, and 'if [it] finds that the measures chosen by Bilka correspond to a real need on the part of the undertaking, are appropriate with a view to achieving the objectives pursued and are necessary to that end, the fact that the measures affect a far greater number of women than men is not sufficient to show that they constitute an infringement of Article 119 [now 141]' (see *Rinner Kühn v FWW Spezial-Gebäudereinigung* [1989] IRLR 493; *Chisholm v Kirklees Borough Council* [1993] ICR 826; *Commission of the EC v Belgium* [1993] IRLR 404, ECJ; *Kutz-Bauer v Freie und Hansestadt Hamburg* [2003] IRLR 368; *Steinicke v Bundesanstalt für Arbeit* [2003] IRLR 892).

7.61 There was, however, no liability in *Stadt Lengerich v Helmig* [1996] ICR 35, where all of the employees who worked more than the ordinary number of working hours for full-time workers received an overtime supplement but part-time workers did not: the ECJ held that there was no discrimination incompatible with Art 119 (now 141) or the Equal Treatment Directive when part-time employees received the same overall pay for the same number of hours worked (ECJ judgment, para 27).

If there is disparate impact the cause must *justify* the actual disparate impact to qualify **7.62** under this rubric. There is thus a twofold test: does the claimant(s) show that a group which is predominantly female is treated less favourably than a group doing like work or work of equal value of whom a majority are men? If so, the burden shifts to the employer to show that the difference is 'objectively justified' on a non-discriminatory basis. If market forces are relied upon the employer must show that these are gender neutral if he is to succeed in establishing the defence (see also for a less exacting test *Barry v Midland Bank plc* [1999] ICR 859).

The primary issue on determining proportionality is how the aim of the employer could **7.63** be achieved, not whether the employer should have *different* aims (*Blackburn v Chief Constable of West Midlands Police* [2009] IRLR 135).

In *Barber v NCR (Manufacturing) Ltd* [1993] ICR 95, for example, the evidence showed **7.64** the historical process by which the difference in hourly rates between two groups had been arrived at but did not show any objective factor which justified or even supported the result which had been produced, and thus did not suffice as a genuine material factor (but see *Strathclyde Regional Council v Wallace* at 7.54).

In *Sharp v Caledonia Group Services Ltd* [2006] IRLR 4, the EAT held that in every case **7.65** it was necessary for the employer to justify the difference but this was rejected by a later EAT panel in *Villalba v Merrill Lynch & Co Inc* [2006] IRLR 437 as not being required by the ECJ decision in *Brunnhofer v Bank der Österreichischen Postsparkasse* [2001] IRLR 571.

There is also no rule of law that justification must have formed part of the initial decision- **7.66** making process but while justification in retrospect is admissible, it will probably start from a lower evidential base (*BA v Grundy* [2008] IRLR 815).

C JOB EVALUATION

Another way of claiming equal pay is by the ascription of equal value to the jobs in issue **7.67** on a job evaluation scheme. Section 65(4) of the Equality Act 2010 regulates comparison between different jobs by way of a job evaluation scheme so that:

A's work is rated as equivalent to B's work if a job evaluation study—

(a) gives an equal value to A's job and B's job in terms of the demands made on a worker, or
(b) would give an equal value to A's job and B's job in those terms were the evaluation not made on a sex-specific system.

The definition of a sex-specific system is 'if, for the purposes of one or more of the demands made on a worker, it sets values for men different from those it sets for women'. This has not changed from the formula adopted in the forerunner Equal Pay Act 1970.

Example Alan and Betty work for Crest Stores as a travel agent and butcher respectively. **7.68** A job evaluation study awards both 30 points, but the employers still pay Alan £3 more per week. An employment tribunal must accept that the two are employed on like work, so that Alan may only be paid more if there is a genuine material difference in the personal equation, for example, as a result of his longer experience in the store.

7.69 A job evaluation scheme is thus an alternative route to equal pay for a claimant and attempts to be as scientific and objective as it is possible to be. Its criteria are commonly agreed between management and unions and are of particular application to clerical staff. Yet its limitations must be appreciated, since it classifies jobs, not the people who fill them. It may be followed in effect by a subjective merit assessment of the individual's qualities. A job evaluation study merely provides a building block which may indicate the underlying structure of wages on which individual variations may then be built. It may be then necessary to have regard to the full results of the scheme, including the final allocation of grades at the foot of score sheets such that there may be equality under this rubric in terms of an equal grade even though there is no precise equality of points in order to achieve that grade (*Springboard Sunderland Trust v Robson* [1992] ICR 554; cf *Home Office v Bailey and Others* [2005] IRLR 757). Claimants may thus make claims in respect of comparators who were placed in a lower band but received more pay since, although it was not expressly so stated in the Act, there was an obvious requirement to modify the precise language of the Equal Pay Act by writing words in (*Redcar & Cleveland BC v Bainbridge* [2007] IRLR 984).

7.70 The chief types of job evaluation schemes generally in use are:

(a) job ranking, where 'each job is considered as a whole and is then given a ranking in relation to all other jobs';

(b) paired comparisons, where points are awarded on a comparison between pairs of jobs and then a rank order is produced;

(c) job classification, whereby all other jobs are compared with benchmark grades;

(d) points assessment, 'the most common system' which 'breaks down each job into a number of factors—for example, skills, responsibility, physical and mental requirements and working conditions'; and

(e) factor comparison, which differs from points assessment only in that it uses a limited number of factors based on key jobs with fair wages (taken from the discussion in *Eaton Ltd v Nuttall* [1977] 3 All ER 1131).

7.71 The main legal questions which have emerged concern the meaning of, and the challenges to, job evaluation study, and the necessity of putting schemes into effect when completed.

Meaning of job evaluation

7.72 The study must be 'thorough in analysis and capable of impartial application' (according to *Eaton Ltd v Nuttall* (above)). Further, 'it should be possible by applying the study to arrive at the position of a particular employee at a particular point in a particular salary grade without taking other matters into account'. It must not require management to take a subjective view as to the grading of an employee (see also *McAuley v Eastern Health & Social Services Board* [1991] IRLR 467).

7.73 The Court of Appeal in *Bromley v H. & J. Quick Ltd* [1988] ICR 623 decided that an analytical method must be applied in carrying out the job evaluation scheme. This means that the jobs of the claimants must be valued with those of comparators in terms of various demands on the workers under the various headings set out in the former s 1(5) of the Equal Pay Act 1970. Thus, assessments which are made on a 'whole job' basis which do not involve individual comparisons under those headings do not amount to a valid job evaluation study for the purposes of s 1(5).

7.74 The Equal Pay Directive does not preclude using as criteria in job evaluation schemes muscular effort or exertion, or the degree to which work is physically heavy (primarily thought of as male traits), if the tasks involved do in fact objectively require a certain level of physical strength. The system used must as a whole, however, preclude all discrimination on the grounds of sex by taking into account other criteria. The European Court of Justice so held in *Rummler v Dato-Druck GmbH* [1987] IRLR 32, and went on to decide that it was for national courts to determine whether the job classification system in its entirety did meet those criteria. The case also decided that a pay system based on the degree of strength required may be justified under the Directive, but the scheme should, where the nature of the work permits, take into account criteria for which women workers may have a particular aptitude, such as manual dexterity. Otherwise, the scheme may be found to be discriminatory in its overall effect.

The mere fact that a claimant scores fewer points than her comparator in a job evaluation **7.75** study does not mean that a tribunal is obliged to conclude that her job is not of equal value unless there is the support of an appointed independent expert. A tribunal may be persuaded that a very small points difference, especially in the context of a wide-ranging job evaluation study which has focused on benchmark jobs and has not involved a direct comparison of the jobs in issue, does not reflect a material difference in the value of the two jobs. Although equal value does not mean nearly equal value, the analysis of job value is not a science and a slavish attachment to marks which have been scored suggests a degree of precision which the assessment of job value cannot bear (*Hovell v Ashford & St Peter's Hospital NHS Trust* [2009] IRLR 734).

Challenges to job evaluation study

Where there is a valid and proper study, it is impermissible for the employment tribunal or **7.76** an employer to override it, or implement only part of it. A broad attack on a scheme was attempted in *England v Bromley LBC* [1978] ICR 1, where the then widely used 'London Scheme' was adopted to grade the respondent council's employees, but it was adjusted for 'special factors'. The male claimant clerks received the same number of points in the main scheme as their female comparators, but were awarded less for 'special factors'. Phillips J closed the door to challenge thus: 'What the claimant cannot do is to base his claim on the footing that if the evaluation study had been carried out differently ... he would be entitled to the relief claimed. He must take the study as it is' (see also *Arnold v Beecham Group Ltd* [1982] IRLR 307). The single exception is where the factors used in making the evaluation are in themselves discriminatory.

A job evaluation study is not completed unless and until the parties who agreed to carry **7.77** out the study have accepted its validity (*Arnold v Beecham Group Ltd* [1982] IRLR 307). It is admissible before an employment tribunal even though it was carried out *after* the complaints to the tribunal had been presented, provided that the comparison is made between jobs which were carried out by the claimant and the comparator at the date of commencement of the proceedings (*Dibro v Hore* [1990] IRLR 129, [1990] ICR 370). Further, such a study does not have retrospective effect (*Redcar & Cleveland BC v Bainbridge* [2008] IRLR 776) so as to entitle the claimants to rely on it with respect to rated as equivalent claims for a period prior to an implementation of the job evaluation study.

D EQUAL VALUE CLAIMS

Before the coming into force of the amending Regulations in 1996, a claimant could **7.78** require an evaluation of the value of jobs to be carried out by an independent expert appointed from a panel nominated by ACAS, provided that the claim overcame some preliminary hurdles before an expert was appointed. This was amended by the Sex Discrimination and Equal Pay (Miscellaneous Amendments) Regulations 1996 (SI 1996/438), which in some circumstances gave the employment tribunal power to decide equal value cases itself, to place time limits on the expert, and to replace him if he did not perform to the standards laid down. This sought to address major concerns about the length of time taken by such cases. In reality, tribunals would only decide issues of equal value themselves in the most straightforward of cases. The tribunal must decide whether it will be assisted by an independent expert's report. The fact that it may in some cases properly find two jobs to be of equal value without obtaining a report does not mean it is obliged to follow that course if it feels prejudiced by the lack of expert assistance (*Hovell v Ashford & St Peter's Hospital NHS Trust* [2009] IRLR 734).

7.79 By s 65(6):

> A's work is of equal value to B's work if it is—
>
> (a) neither like B's work nor rated as equivalent to B's work, but
> (b) nevertheless equal to B's work in terms of the demands made on A by reference to factors such as effort, skill and decision-making.

Again this differs little from the formula which had been contained in the Equal Pay Act 1970.

What is work of equal value?

7.80 The EAT in *Pickstone v Freemans plc* [1986] IRLR 335 reached the somewhat surprising decision that if a woman is employed on like work with *one* man, she may not bring a claim of equal *value* with a person employed in a different position. This was a narrow reading of the amended s 1 of the Equal Pay Act, which applies the equal value procedures 'where a woman is employed on work which, not being work in relation to which paragraph (a) or (b) above applies, is ... of equal value to that of a man in the same employment' (which is very similar to the new s 65(6)). The House of Lords ([1988] ICR 697), however, applied a purposive construction of the English statute rather than relying on the European material. Thus, the fact that one or more men are engaged on 'like work' with the claimant woman does not prevent an equal value claim.

7.81 The expert is given no specific statutory criteria on which to assess equal value. In *Hayward v Cammell Laird Shipbuilders Ltd* [1986] IRLR 287, the expert found that the work of a cook was of equal value to that of a painter, joiner, and thermal insulation engineer, and the tribunal made the consequential orders. The employment tribunal said that it would interfere with the conclusion reached by an expert only if the expert had gone badly wrong in the assessment. It rejected the employer's attack on the expert's analysis of jobs in terms of demands under five factors which he ranked as low, moderate, or high. The employers claimed that this was crude and imprecise, and criticised the fact that he had spent only one day in the relevant shipyard and kitchens whilst preparing the report. The tribunal considered that the appropriate provision 'does not appear to look for the question of equal value to be dealt with by way of precise mathematical calculation'. They thought that one of the most effective ways to attack the independent expert's report was to commission and present an expert's report of one's own. The tribunal makes an assessment of equal value with the assistance of the independent expert; the final determination is for the tribunal and may be informed by partisan experts on evaluation methodology: *Middlesbrough BC v Surtees No 2* [2008] ICR 349.

E CLAIMING EQUAL PAY

Like most discrimination claims, while the proceedings are individual in nature, they are **7.82** usually brought in the nature of test cases, the pay of hundreds of other similarly placed employees commonly depending on the outcome. Moreover, the Commission for Equality and Human Rights may also provide general advice and assistance to claimants.

A claim for equal pay may be presented to an employment tribunal by the individual **7.83** employee affected at any time before the expiration of six months after leaving the relevant employment (s 129(1)), and then under the terms of the Act arrears of remuneration could be awarded for up to six years but five in Scotland (as required by the ECJ judgment *Levez v T.H. Jennings (Harlow Pools Ltd) (No 2)* [1999] IRLR 764) (see also 7.99). A claim may also come before a county court, which may refer the matter to the tribunal if this is a more convenient forum (s 128(1)).

There are exceptions where the period of six months begins at a later stage, that is, when **7.84** there has been a stable work case, which is defined as 'where the proceedings relate to a period during which there was a stable working relationship between the worker and the responsible person (including any time after the terms of work had expired)' (s 130(3)). In a concealment case, the relevant period is 'six months beginning with the day on which the worker discovered (or could with reasonable diligence have discovered) the qualifying fact'. This is defined as where 'the responsible person deliberately concealed a qualifying fact from the worker and the worker did not discover (or could not with reasonable diligence have discovered) the qualifying fact' (s 130(4)).

This derives from European case law. In *Preston v Wolverhampton Healthcare NHS* **7.85** *Trust* [2001] ICR 217, the ECJ ultimately decided that it was for the domestic legal system of each member state to determine the procedural conditions governing actions intended to protect Community law rights, provided that such conditions did not make enforcement of those rights impossible or excessively difficult in practice and were not less favourable than those applicable to a similar claim of a domestic nature. The rule, then contained in s 2(5) of the Equal Pay Act 1970, that the right to be admitted to a pension scheme might have an effect from a date no earlier than two years before the beginning of proceedings, made any action by individuals in reliance on Community law impossible in practice. The period of six months to bring proceedings, however, was not incompatible with Community law. Where contracts of employment were concluded at regular intervals in respect of the same employment within a stable employment relationship, the six-month period ran from the end of the last contract forming part of that relationship. The features of a stable employment relationship as laid down in EU law are:

(a) a succession of short-term contracts, meaning three or more contracts for an academic year or shorter;
(b) contracts concluded at regular intervals, in which they are clearly predictable and can be calculated precisely or where the employee is called upon frequently whenever a need arises;
(c) contracts relating to the same employment; and
(d) contracts to which the same pension scheme applies.

As a result of the *Preston* decision the Equal Pay Act 1970 was amended by the Equal **7.86** Pay Act (Amendment) Regulations 2003 (SI 2003/1656), so that there are separate categories of concealment and disability cases which differ from the norm. A concealment case is one where the employer deliberately concealed from the woman any fact that is relevant to the contravention to which the complaint relates and without knowledge of which the woman could not reasonably have been expected to present the complaint and the woman did not discover the qualifying fact (or could not with reasonable diligence have discovered it) until after the last day of the period of service during which the claim arose. In any such case the qualifying date is the date nine months after the woman discovered the qualifying fact or could with reasonable diligence have discovered it.

7.87   Such a relationship ceases for this purpose when a succession of short-term contracts is superseded by a permanent contract (*Preston v Wolverhampton Healthcare NHS Trust (No 3)* [2004] IRLR 96). Where it is clear from contractual documents that the parties have agreed to effect changes by a fresh contract that is decisive of the issue, the courts must give effect to the parties' chosen mechanism for change. The fact that an employer issues a document which purports to be a new contract will not suffice (*Cumbria CC v Dow (No 2)* [2008] IRLR 109).

7.88   Time starts running from the termination of employment even though the employee was not working in the job in respect of which equal pay is claimed at that time (*Young v National Power plc* [2001] ICR 328). The temporal limitation applied in relation to benefits which were paid under an occupational pension scheme, although not to the right to belong to a scheme itself, which fell within the protection afforded by Art 119 (now 141) (*Quirk v Burton Hospitals NHS Trust* [2002] ICR 602; see also *Fisscher v Voorhuis Hengelo BV* [1994] IRLR 662).

7.89   A disability case which may extend time under the Act is where the woman was under a disability during the nine months after the last day of the period of service during which the claim arose or the day on which she discovered (or could with reasonable diligence have discovered) the qualifying fact deliberately concealed from her by the employer. In the unusual situation of a case which is both a concealment and disability case the later date applies.

7.90   In *Levez v T.H. Jennings (Harlow Pools) Ltd* [1999] ICR 521, the ECJ held that although the two-year compensation limit for claims under what was then s 2(5) of the Equal Pay Act 1970 was not itself incompatible with this rule, the fact that a tribunal had no discretion to extend it where the employer misled the employee, therefore causing her to delay making her claim, was unacceptable. The EAT held that s 2(5) could not be relied on when the case was remitted to it ([1999] IRLR 764). This, in turn, brought into question the compatibility of the six-month time limit under s 2(4) of the Equal Pay Act 1970 with European law.

7.91   Stable employment may include an uninterrupted succession of contracts (*North Cumbria University Hospitals NHS Trust v Fox* [2010] IRLR 804). There, new terms imposed following the NHS national collective bargain called Agenda for Change did not interrupt the stability of the employment relationship.

7.92   The overlap between TUPE and equal pay limitation periods was considered in *Gutridge v Sodexo Ltd* [2009] IRLR 721. The claims in respect of the pre-transfer period were time barred under the six-month period. The employee cannot have any greater rights against the transferee than she had against the transferor. The employee had to make her claim within six months of termination of employment with the transferor. A right to equal pay survives transfer as a matter of TUPE law. Once the Act applies and the contract is modified to include an equality clause, the contract remains so modified even after a TUPE transfer.

F MATERNITY

The equal pay principles are extended to periods of maternity leave by s 73(1) such that 'If   **7.93**
the terms of the woman's work do not (by whatever means) include a maternity equality
clause, they are to be treated as including one.' This has the same impact as the normal
equality clause. The conditions are set out in s 74(2) to (4) so that:

(2) After the time referred to in subsection (1) but before the end of the protected period—
   (a) her pay increases, or
   (b) it would have increased had she not been on maternity leave.
(3) The maternity-related pay is not—
   (a) what her pay would have been had she not been on maternity leave, or
   (b) the difference between the amount of statutory maternity pay to which she is entitled
       and what her pay would have been had she not been on maternity leave.
(4) The terms of her work do not provide for the maternity-related pay to be subject to—
   (a) an increase as mentioned in subsection (2)(a) or
   (b) an increase that would have occurred as mentioned in subsection (2)(b)).

G COLLECTIVE ENFORCEMENT

The 1970 Act more broadly facilitated the amendment of whole collective agreements,   **7.94**
pay structures, wages regulation orders, and agricultural wages orders, where such
contained a provision applying specifically to men only or women only (s 3). Reference
could, under the 1970 Act, be made by union, management, or the Secretary of State
for Employment, to the Central Arbitration Committee which could give advice, and
ultimately declare what amendments must be made to remove the discriminatory features. The Sex Discrimination Act 1986 repealed this provision and introduced the different, more limited procedure under s 77 of the Sex Discrimination Act 1975, by which a
county court might make an order for removing or modifying a discriminatory term. This
was further amended by the TURERA 1993 in response to criticism by the European
Commission that the existing regime was in breach of the Equal Treatment Directive. By
the revised s 77, a term of a contract is void where:

(a) its inclusion renders the making of the contract unlawful by virtue of the Act;
(b) it is included in furtherance of an act rendered unlawful by the Act; or
(c) it provides for the doing of any act which would be rendered unlawful by the Act.

This applies if the term is directly or indirectly discriminatory against men, women, or
married persons by reason of sex or marital status. An application may also be made to
an employment tribunal.

In *UNISON v Brennan* [2008] IRLR 492, the only reported case on the section, the EAT   **7.95**
held that the principles of effectiveness were infringed because the claimants could not
pursue a claim for a declaration in the High Court.

H EUROPEAN LAW

Article 141

Article 141 (ex 119) of the Treaty of Rome provides that the European Council 'shall adopt   **7.96**
measures to ensure the application of the principle of equal opportunities and equal treatment

of men and women in matters of employment and occupation, including the principle of equal pay for equal work or work of equal value'. The preamble to the Article aims 'to ensure States with equal pay do not suffer a competitive disadvantage in inter-Community competition as compared with undertakings established in States which have not yet eliminated discrimination'. This is extended in concept by Directive 75/117 (the 'Equal Pay Directive') which states that 'the principle of equal pay' means for the same work or for work to which *equal value* is attributed, the elimination of all discrimination on the grounds of sex with regard to all aspects and conditions of remuneration. Directive 76/207 (the 'Equal Treatment Directive') seeks equal treatment and non-discrimination for men and women in regard to employment, promotion, working conditions, and vocational training.

7.97 The European legislation is important in Britain in two distinct ways—its direct enforceability in British courts, and because those courts might gain assistance from it in interpreting national legislation. The European Court has held Art 141 (ex 119) to be directly effective in national courts in *Defrenne v Sabena* [1976] ECR 455, *McCarthys v Smith* [1980] IRLR 210, and *Worringham v Lloyds Bank Ltd* [1979] IRLR 440, [1981] IRLR 178 ECJ. This is important because of its wider scope than the present English law, for example, in the ever-expanding notion of the single source spanning different establishments or employers. We have considered already the concepts of comparator and establishment (see 7.11–7.22 above).

Meaning of pay

7.98 The key to the understanding of the full impact of European law is an appreciation of the wide scope given to 'pay' which must be equalised between men and women. The definition of pay does not relate to a particular time of payment during the course of employment, as contended by the employers, but demands a direct connection between the payment and the employment (*Hammersmith and Queen Charlotte's Special Health Authority v Cato* [1987] IRLR 483). Pay, however, includes:

(a) a severance grant (*Kowalska v Freie und Hansestadt Hamburg* [1992] ICR 29);

(b) a lump sum payment to women on maternity leave in lieu of performance-related salary increases, taking part in training, and to reflect the fact that their period of service was reduced by the length of absence (*Abdoulaye v Regie Nationale des Usines Renault* [2001] ICR 527); and

(c) an inconvenient hours supplement which constituted compensation to the worker for the disruption and inconvenience caused by working unsocial hours (*Jäamställdhetsombudsmannen v Örebo läns landsting* [2001] ICR 249).

7.99 Article 141 covers 'consideration' which the worker receives directly or indirectly; there must be a benefit paid to a worker or a contribution paid by the employer to a pension scheme on behalf of the employee. In *Newstead v Dept of Transport and HM Treasury* [1988] ICR 332, the ECJ held that a civil servant who under a compulsory pension scheme had to pay 1.5 per cent of his gross salary to a widow's pension fund, whereas a female employee did not have to, did not fall within Art 141. This concerned a deduction of contributions from pay and was not a difference in pay itself within the scope of the Article. There was no breach of the Equal Treatment Directive, which did not apply to social security matters.

7.100 Article 141 has been held to preclude:

(a) the application of a provision of a collective agreement under which part-time workers are excluded from the benefit of a severance payment in the case of termination of the employment relationship when it is clear that in fact a considerably smaller percentage of men than of women worked part-time, unless the employer shows that the provision is justified by objective factors unrelated to any discrimination on the grounds of sex (*Kowalska v Freie und Hansestadt Hamburg* [1990] IRLR 447);

(b) a collective agreement under which the seniority of workers performing at least three-quarters of normal working time was to be fully taken into account for reclassification in a higher salary grade, whereas only half of such seniority was to be taken into account for workers whose working hours were between one-half and three-quarters of those normal working hours, where the latter group of employees comprised a considerably smaller percentage of men than women. The only justification would be factors which depend for their objectivity in particular on the relationship between the nature of the duties performed and the experience afforded by the performance of those duties, after a certain number of hours had been worked (*Nimz v Freie und Hansestadt Hamburg* [1991] IRLR 222); and

(c) piece-work schemes in which pay depended entirely or in large measure on the individual output of each worker. The mere fact that there was a difference of average pay of two groups, one consisting mainly of women and the other mainly of men, however, did not suffice to establish discrimination (*Specialarbejderforbundet i Danmark v Dansk Industri* [1996] IRLR 648).

I THE NATURE OF THE RIGHT

The right conferred by the Act to equal treatment does not require equality in *aggregate* **7.101** pay and conditions; it is to be considered on a term-by-term basis. As Phillips J said in *National Coal Board v Sherwin & Spruce* [1978] IRLR 122, the Act:

> ... does not mean that men, or women, cannot be paid extra for working at night or at weekends or at other inconvenient times; if the additional remuneration is justified by the inconvenience of the time at which it is done the claim will not succeed. For while every contract of employment is deemed to include an equality clause, it only has the effect so that the terms of the woman's contract shall be treated as so modified not to be less favourable than the man's ...

(See also *Hayward v Cammell Laird Shipbuilders* [1986] ICR 862.)

In *Aegon UK Corporate Services Ltd v Roberts* [2010] ICR 596, the EAT decided that **7.102** pension benefits were to be treated as part of the claimant's overall remuneration package. The benefit of a final salary pension scheme was to be translated into money terms and assessed as deferred remuneration; where a claimant had obtained permanent employment following dismissal the tribunal could not apply different principles of causation to different aspects of the remuneration package.

The female claimant must not be put in a better position than that enjoyed by the chosen **7.103** comparator (eg *Evesham v W Herts HA* [2000] IRLR 257). Each aspect of remuneration must be compared separately in order to achieve genuine transparency in assessing equality of pay (*Brunnhofer v Bank der Österreichischen Postsparkasse AG* [2001] IRLR 571). Terms have to be modified for equal pay purposes on a term-by-term basis; if the comparator's contract contained a term which was beneficial and which had no equivalent in the claimant's contract, the claimant's contract was altered so as to include the beneficial term (*Enderby v Frenchay HA (No 2)* [2000] ICR 612; see also *Degnan v Redcar & Cleveland BC* [2005] IRLR 615).

7.104 Non-economic loss (eg injury to feelings) is not recoverable on a claim for equal pay since this is a claim purely in contract and not for a statutory tort (*Newcastle upon Tyne CC v Allan* [2005] ICR 1170).

J EQUAL TREATMENT IN RESPECT OF PENSIONS IN UK LAW—SECTION 67

7.105 The Pensions Act 1995 requires equal treatment in pensions benefits and uses a similar structure to the Equal Pay Act 1970, so that the provisions apply where a member is employed on like or similar work to, or work of equal value to that of, a member of the other sex. It applies to the terms on which persons become members of a scheme and how members of the scheme are treated (Pensions Act 1995, s 62(2)). Unusually, there is a specific direction that the Act should be 'construed as one' with the Equal Pay Act (Pensions Act 1995, s 63(4)).

7.106 The rule will not apply if the difference is due to a factor which is not sex-related but is a difference between the man's and the woman's cases such as a difference in job status. Equal treatment is required for pensionable service only on or after 17 May 1990, the date of the *Barber* decision.

7.107 The Occupational Pension Schemes (Equal Treatment) Regulations 1995 (SI 1995/3183) allow a court or tribunal on a complaint of failure to comply with the equal treatment rule, to grant a declaration and make an order requiring the employer to provide additional resources for the pension scheme. There is no power, however, to make a financial award to an individual complainant unless he or she is a pensioner. The Regulations also provide for three exceptions to the equality rule, for bridging pensions, the effects of indexation, and the continued use of actuarial factors in relation to contributions and additional benefits (regs 13–15).

8

DISCRIMINATION

A INTRODUCTION 8.01

B MEANING OF PROTECTED CHARACTERISTICS . . . 8.13

   Age 8.14

   Gender reassignment 8.15

   Race 8.17

   Marital status 8.24

   Pregnancy 8.25

   Disability 8.31

   Severe disfigurement 8.48

   Mental impairment 8.54

   Treatment 8.57

   What are normal activities? 8.59

   Religion and belief 8.62

C FORMS OF DISCRIMINATION 8.69

   Direct discrimination 8.70

   Indirect discrimination 8.96

   Harassment 8.106

   Intentional harassment 8.110

   Victimisation 8.111

   'Transferred' or associative
discrimination 8.116

   Discrimination arising from
disability 8.118

D THE SCOPE OF PROHIBITED
   DISCRIMINATION 8.138

   Arrangements for deciding to whom to
offer employment 8.140

   Not offering employment 8.142

   Opportunities for promotion, transfer,
or training 8.143

   Contract workers 8.145

   Dismissal 8.147

   Any other detriment 8.149

   Exceptions 8.156

E CLAIMANTS AND RESPONDENTS 8.162

   Relationships which have ended 8.162

   Respondents 8.163

F 'REVERSE DISCRIMINATION' 8.172

G ENFORCEMENT MECHANISMS 8.174

   Individual complaint 8.174

   Problems of proof 8.178

   Burden of proof and inferences 8.179

   The scope of the inquiry 8.185

   Remedies 8.193

   Commission enforcement 8.216

States must take measures against any distinction, exclusion or preference made on the basis of race, sex, religion, political opinion, national extraction or social origin which has the effect of nullifying or impairing equality of opportunity or treatment in employment or occupation. (ILO Convention Concerning Discrimination in Respect of Employment or Occupation 1958 No 111.)

A INTRODUCTION

The common law did not in itself prohibit discrimination, and while the Sex Disqualification **8.01** (Removal) Act has been on the statute book since 1919, its coverage is minimal. Thus, as Britain became a multi-racial country and the women's movement gained momentum, Parliament belatedly determined to put into domestic law the nation's obligations under ILO Convention No 111, the UN International Convention on Social and Cultural

Rights, and the European Convention on the Protection of Human Rights, in respect of anti-discrimination laws.

8.02 The first major race relations legislation was the Race Relations Act 1965. This was modelled on the American Civil Rights Act 1964, and stimulated by a series of reports on the low status of blacks in Britain and the first racial violence. It was, however, mainly concerned with public order and incitement to racial hatred, and outlawed discrimination only in places of public resort. It was extended to employment three years later, and the new Act also introduced the definition of direct discrimination which still exists today. It was only in 1976 that an individual right of access to employment tribunals was introduced. The Race Relations Act 1976 followed closely the model of the Sex Discrimination Act, which had been passed the previous year to supplement the Equal Pay Act 1970 beyond the area of contractual entitlements. It had a counterpart enforcement agency independent of government, the Equal Opportunities Commission (EOC), with similar powers. The Government has now created the Commission for Equality and Human Rights (CEHR) to unite the previous bodies.

8.03 The scope of the legislation has been extended primarily under the influence of successive European directives, especially in the area of sex discrimination. EU discrimination law was revolutionised by the implementation of the Race Directive 2000/43, which brings race into the EU competence for the first time, and the Employment Directive 2000/78, which sets out the principle of equal treatment in sexual orientation, religion or belief, disability, and age. The Age Discrimination Regulations survived a crucial general challenge in *R (Age UK) v Secretary of State for Business Innovation and Skills* [2010] ICR 260. The Government convinced the Administrative Court that it had social policy concerns in protecting the integrity of the labour market. In 1999, the EU passed a Race Directive and a framework Employment Directive dealing with other protected grounds. With the Brexit Referendum vote, the UK may draw back from some of these provisions.

8.04 The Equality Act 2010 consolidated existing measures and made some changes too. Importantly, it brought into the same Act provisions about all of the protected characteristics, although age and disability have rather different requirements.

8.05 We are all used to differentiating between things or between people every day in many different circumstances. Indeed, to be discriminating in some senses is considered a virtue, and it remains perfectly lawful to reject an applicant for a job because, for example, he cannot spell, is a member of the Labour Party, supports Grimsby Town Football Club, or has green hair. The Equality Act 2010 now outlaws discrimination in employment, education, housing, or the provision of goods, facilities, and services on the grounds of these protected characteristics set out in:

Section 4—

- age;
- disability;
- gender reassignment;
- marriage and civil partnership;
- pregnancy and maternity;
- race;
- religion or belief;
- sex;
- sexual orientation.

8.06 Section 14 of the Equality Act 2010 recognises dual discrimination 'because of a combination of two relevant protected characteristics', but in March 2011 it was announced that this would not be implemented for reasons which are obscure (see *MOD v De Bique* [2010] IRLR 471).

The following different types of discrimination are found in the 2010 Act: **8.07**

(a) Direct;
(b) Indirect;
(c) Victimisation;
(d) Harassment;
(e) Failure to make a reasonable adjustment; and
(f) Discrimination arising from a disability which may be justified.

This account concentrates solely on discrimination in employment, and refers to cases **8.08** decided on the pre-2010 law where they are still relevant. Although most of the discrimination provisions are now common across the board of all protected characteristics, there are important differences in treatment of some of them, especially in relation to disabled status and age.

In this area European legislation is important if not pre-eminent. A court or tribunal **8.09** might go beyond the strict limits of statutory construction and read words into a statute to give effect to European Community legislation which the statute was intended to implement. This includes the proscription of associative discrimination, although this is now specifically provided for in domestic legislation (*EBR Attridge LLP v Coleman* [2010] ICR 242). This was held to prevent discrimination on the grounds of disability whether or not the claimant himself was the person suffering from the disability. There would be an addition to be made so that the same were compatible with European law to the effect that 'A person directly discriminates against a person if he treats him less favourably than he treats or would treat another person by reason of the disability of another person'.

Importantly, employment is widely defined for all purposes of discrimination law as **8.10** 'employment under a contract of service or of apprenticeship' or a contract 'personally to do work' (s 83). It does not, however, apply to volunteers. The Equality Act thus protects independent contractors. There must, however, still be a mutual obligation to offer or accept work between the parties for such protection (*Mingeley v Pennock & Ivory* [2004] IRLR 373). This includes within its scope a painter or a plumber; an articled clerk (*Oliver v J.P. Malnick & Co* [1983] IRLR 456); a self-employed salesman of fancy goods on a pitch in a department store remunerated on a commission basis (*Quinnen v Hovell* [1984] IRLR 227); and a lawyer applying to be included on a public authority's panel of solicitors (*Loughran and Kelly v Northern Ireland Housing Executive* [1998] IRLR 593; see also *BP Chemicals Ltd v Gillick* [1995] IRLR 128).

It excludes, however, a postmaster, since he is responsible merely for seeing that the work **8.11** of the Post Office is carried on and does not have to perform any of the duties himself (*Tanna v Post Office* [1981] ICR 374); an independent wholesale newspaper distributor who enjoyed an agency for the Mirror Group (*Mirror Group Newspaper Ltd v Gunning* [1986] IRLR 27); a legal aid contractor (*Patterson v Legal Services Commission* [2004] IRLR 153); a doctor who was not under a contractual arrangement but rather was linked by the statutory scheme with the Family Practitioner Committee or Medical Practitioners Committee (*Wadi v Cornwall & Isles of Scilly Family Practitioner Committee* [1985] ICR 492); and a general practitioner who provided medical services to a health authority under the National Health Service Regulations 1992 because the terms of service were statutory not contractual (*North Essex Health Authority v David-John* [2004] ICR 112).

The Act extends to arrangements for the purpose of determining who should be offered the employment and that is given a broad construction (*Hussain v King's College Hospital NHS Trust* [2002] ICR 1433).

8.12   It was always clear that the domestic legislation did not incorporate volunteers. It was, however, less certain in respect of the wider definition found in European law. The House of Lords held, however, that the EU Directive does not require the extension of the protection against disability discrimination to be extended to voluntary workers who do not work under any form of contract (*X v Mid Sussex CAB* [2010] IRLR 101). The definition in EU law of workers includes the existence of mutual rights and duties which are not applicable where there is no contract and remuneration in the case of true volunteers.

B   MEANING OF PROTECTED CHARACTERISTICS

8.13   There is some elaboration which is now necessary of what the protected characteristics mean because several of them are not straightforward. Specific elaborations of these protected characteristics are found in the statute or case law.

Age

8.14   In relation to age, by s 5 of the Equality Act:

  (a) a reference to a person who has a particular protected characteristic is a reference to a person of a particular age group;
  (b) a reference to persons who share a protected characteristic is a reference to persons of the same age group.

The concept of age itself in general is the issue for the law, not any *particular* age, so that the EU Directive and the Equality Act are not aimed at protecting older or younger workers as such but at prohibiting age as being part of an employer's reasoning process for the various types of prohibited conduct. This may be difficult in the age context where the workforce is made up of persons of a number of different ages and no specific age is discernible as preponderant. For example, if a claimant alleges that a redundancy policy has in fact been influenced by a desire to remove older workers, no specific age is likely to be specified as the basis for the policy.

Gender reassignment

8.15   A person has the protected characteristic of gender reassignment if the person is proposing to undergo, is undergoing, or has undergone a process (or part of a process) for the purpose of reassigning the person's sex by changing physiological or other attributes of sex (s 7).

8.16   The Gender Recognition Act 2004 was introduced as a result of the ECtHR's decision in *Goodwin v UK* (2002) 35 EHRR 18. Further, by s 16, a person discriminates 'if in relation to an absence of B's that is because of gender reassignment A treats B less favourably than A would treat B if B's absence was because of sickness or injury' or 'B's absence was for some other reason and it was not reasonable for B to be treated less favourably'. The absence is relevant 'if it is because the person is proposing to undergo, is undergoing or has undergone the process' of gender reassignment.

Race

By s 9, race is widely defined and   **8.17**

includes—

(a) colour;
(b) nationality;
(c) ethnic or national origins.

By s 9(4) 'The fact that a racial group comprises two or more distinct racial groups does not prevent it from constituting a particular racial group.'

Those who may claim on the grounds of ethnic origins include Jews (*Seide v Gillette Industries Ltd* [1980] IRLR 427; *Simon v Brimham Associates* [1987] IRLR 307) and Sikhs (finally determined by the House of Lords in *Mandla v Dowell Lee* [1983] 2 AC 548). The House of Lords in *Mandla* held that the adjective 'ethnic' did not (as the Court of Appeal had thought) require that the group be distinguished by some fixed or inherited racial characteristic. The concept was appreciably wider than the strictly racial or biological divide. The group, in order to qualify, need only regard itself and be regarded by others as a separate and distinct community by virtue of characteristics commonly associated with a common racial origin. Such a group could include converts to a religion. This was decided before the extension of protection to religion as such.

Gypsies constitute a racial group (*Commission for Racial Equality v Dutton* [1989]   **8.18** IRLR 8). Rastafarians are not an ethnic group, however (*Dawkins v Department of the Environment* [1993] IRLR 284). Although they are a separate group with identifiable characteristics, they have not established a separate identity by reference to their ethnic origins. They also do not have a long shared history since it goes back only some sixty years.

Race cannot be defined by the characteristic of language alone. Thus, there is no racial   **8.19** group of English-speaking Welsh, so that a condition requiring that applicants for jobs should be able to speak Welsh could not constitute unlawful indirect discrimination on the grounds of race (*Gwynedd CC v Jones* [1986] ICR 833).

The distinction between nationality and national origins causes some confusion.   **8.20** Nationality is not defined exclusively by reference to citizenship (*BBC Scotland v Souster* [2001] IRLR 150) and includes discrimination against Scots, Irish, or English (*Northern Joint Police Board v Power* [1997] IRLR 610), but they are not *ethnic* groups (*Souster*). Although one's nationality and national origins are likely to be the same in most cases, a person may have a different nationality to his *national origins* if, for example, he was born in the West Indies but has now gained British citizenship. It does not cover those discriminated against because of their immigration status (*Onu v Akwiwu* [2016] IRLR 719).

Nationality was added to the definition in 1976 because of the narrow interpretation of   **8.21** 'national origins' (which alone had been in the Race Relations Act 1968) in *Ealing LBC v Race Relations Board* [1972] AC 342. There the claimant was a British citizen but of Polish origin. The defendant council admitted discriminating against him on the grounds of his *origins* in establishing its house waiting list, but the House of Lords held that this was not illegal since it was not included in the definition of nationality.

Discrimination against migrant domestic workers does not, however, map precisely onto   **8.22** discrimination on grounds of nationality; whilst the claimants' immigration status might be intimately associated with their non-British nationality, that was simply because only people with non-British nationality would be migrant domestic workers (*Onu v Akwiwu* [2014] ICR 571).

8.23   The Equality Act 2010 provides that caste may be added to this list as a protected ground by statutory instrument but so far none has been enacted.

Marital status

8.24   The Equality Act extends to discrimination against married persons, although only in respect of employment (SDA 1975, s 3(1)). It remains lawful, however, to discriminate against *single* people in any way. In *Bick v Royal West of England School for the Deaf* [1976] IRLR 326, the claimant could not claim when she was sacked on 30 January because she intended to marry the next day, for at the appropriate time she was not married. Not only does this detract from the general symmetry of the discrimination statutes, but it may not wholly fulfil Britain's obligations under the 1975 EEC Directive that 'there shall be no discrimination whatsoever on ground of sex, either directly or indirectly by reference in particular to *marital or family status*' (emphasis added).

Pregnancy

8.25   Originally, claims for discrimination on grounds of pregnancy or maternity leave had to be brought as indirect discrimination claims on the grounds of sex, but now there are separate provisions which are considered in Chapter 10.

8.26   It was at one time thought that the *pregnant* woman was left unprotected if the ground for differentiation was her pregnancy (eg *Turley v Allders Department Stores Ltd* [1980] IRLR 4), but this was corrected in the landmark decision of the ECJ in *Webb v EMO Air Cargo (UK) Ltd* [1995] ICR 1021.

8.27   Essentially, the *Webb* case stands as authority for the following principles:

   (a) differentiation by reason of pregnancy constitutes sex discrimination;
   (b) there is a distinction between dismissal for pregnancy per se and illness; and
   (c) the comparison with a man's physical condition is inappropriate.

8.28   The CJEU in *Dekker* extended the protection for pregnancy to cover pregnancy-related illness, during the pregnancy itself and up to the end of maternity leave.

8.29   The following principles have also been laid down in this area primarily derived from European law:

   (a) The prohibition of dismissal on the grounds of pregnancy applies to both fixed-term contracts and contracts concluded for an indefinite period (*Jiménez Melgar v Ayuntamiento de Los Barrios* [2001] IRLR 848), and this extends where the employee has not told the employer that she is pregnant (*Tele Danmark A/S v Handels- og Kontorfunktionærernes Forbund i Danmark* [2001] IRLR 853) (see also *Rees v Apollo Watches* [1996] ICR 466; *British Telecommunications plc v Roberts* [1996] IRLR 601; *Mahlburg v Land Mecklenburg-Vorpommern* [2001] ICR 1032).
   (b) There was discrimination against a contract worker on grounds of sex when the employer replaced her with a permanent employee when she went on maternity leave,

even though it could have lawfully replaced her with a permanent employee at any time she was in post. If she had not taken leave at that time the Council would in fact have retained her in post indefinitely (*Patefield v Belfast City Council* [2000] IRLR 664).

(c) It is contrary to Art 2(1) of the Equal Treatment Directive to require an employee who wishes to return to work before the end of parental leave to answer whether she is pregnant even though she will be unable to carry out all of her duties because of legislative provisions (*Busch v Klinikum Neustadt GmbH & Co* [2003] IRLR 626).

(d) Treating pregnant women workers or women on maternity leave in the same way as other employees in circumstances in which they were disadvantaged because of their pregnancy or maternity was applying the same treatment to different situations and was therefore discriminatory as a matter of EU law (*Fletcher v NHS Pensions Agency* [2005] ICR 1458); it was not permissible to say, as the employer contended, that the treatment was on grounds of absence from a midwives' training course rather than pregnancy since the basic question was the effective and predominant cause of the act complained of.

The ECJ provided comprehensive guidance on dismissals for a pregnancy-related illness **8.30** in *Brown v Rentokil* [1998] IRLR 445. Unlike in *Webb*, the ECJ concluded that there was no difference between these and dismissals resulting from the pregnancy itself. Both are unlawful. Moreover, a comparison with the treatment of a sick male employee will be relevant only where the illness arises *after* the end of the maternity leave period.

Disability

The definition of disability is complex and often highly contested. Section 6(1) of the **8.31** Equality Act provides that:

A person (P) has a disability if—

(a) P has a physical or mental impairment, and
(b) the impairment has a substantial and long-term adverse effect on P's ability to carry out normal day-to-day activities.

The definition is not altogether easy to apply. The model adopted reflects a medical rather than social approach to disability (*SCA Packaging Ltd v Boyle* [2009] IRLR 53).

The axis around which the definition operates is a 'physical or mental impairment which **8.32** has a substantial and long-term adverse effect on [a person's] ability to carry out normal day-to-day activities'. The material time at which to consider the question of disability is the date of the alleged discriminatory act (*Cruickshank v VAW Motorcast Ltd* [2002] IRLR 24). The disability must be one from which the claimant in fact suffers.

'Impairment', which is a crucial governing word, is curiously left undefined. The EAT, in **8.33** *College of Ripon & York v Hobbs* [2002] IRLR 185, at para 32, said that 'The Act contemplates (certainly in relation to mental impairment) that an impairment can be something that results from an illness as opposed to being the illness ... It can thus be cause or effect'. A physical impairment may be established without reference to a particular illness (*Millar v IRC* [2006] IRLR 112); thus, an amputee could establish disability without there needing to be an actual illness. The impairment may be an illness or result from an illness so that the effects of or preliminaries to tuberculosis would be enough (*MOD v Hay* [2008] ICR 1247).

In examining day-to-day activities, the tribunal must focus not on what the employee **8.34** could do but what he maintained that he could *not* do as a result of his impairment (*Aderemi v London & South Eastern Railway Ltd* [2013] ICR 591).

8.35 This maps onto the European provisions but not precisely. Disability under the EU Directive is an evolving concept and includes a condition which was caused by an illness which was medically diagnosed as curable or incurable where that illness entailed a long-term limitation, resulting in particular from physical, mental, or psychological impairments which, in interaction with various barriers, might hinder the full and effective participation in professional life on an equal basis with other workers. Disability as a matter of EU law does not necessarily imply complete exclusion from work or professional life but rather is a hindrance to professional activity. It could encompass a person who is fit to work only part-time (*HK Danmark v Dansk almennyttigt Boligselskab* [2013] ICR 851).

8.36 In domestic law, the impairment must be long-lasting in order to qualify. Schedule 1 EA, para 2 states:

> (1) The effect of an impairment is long-term if—
>   (a) it has lasted for at least 12 months,
>   (b) it is likely to last for at least 12 months, or
>   (c) it is likely to last for the rest of the life of the person affected.

Further, by subsection (2) 'If an impairment ceases to have a substantial adverse effect on a person's ability to carry out normal day-to-day activities, it is to be treated as continuing to have that effect if that effect is likely to recur.'

8.37 While the cause is not relevant to the establishment of an impairment, there must be a causative link between an impairment and its effect when assessing whether the adverse effects were 'substantial' (*Patel v Oldham MBC* [2010] ICR 603). Careful analysis of any medical evidence is important since the medical expert must be asked to address this test and comment on the effect of the impairment on function.

8.38 The requirement of an 'adverse effect' does not mean that a person need be absolutely *incapable* of performing a particular activity. It is enough that he or she can carry out that activity but only with great difficulty; the ability will have been impaired. A substantial adverse *effect* is likely to recur if it is more probable than not that it will do so; that is the relevant question rather than whether the *illness* itself is likely to recur. 'Likely' in the subsection is used in the sense of 'could well happen' rather than 'probable' or 'more likely than not' (*SCA Packaging Ltd v Boyle* [2009] IRLR 746).

8.39 In *McDougall v Richmond Adult Community College* [2007] IRLR 771, the Court of Appeal held that the likelihood of recurrence must be judged at the date of the alleged act of discrimination, and that subsequent events cannot be taken into account.

8.40 The proper approach to establishing whether the disadvantage was substantial is to compare the effect of the disability on the individual and to consider how (s)he in fact carries out the activity compared with how (s)he would do it if (s)he was not suffering the impairment. If that difference is more than the kind that one might expect taking a cross-section of the population, then the effects are substantial (*Paterson v Commissioner of Police of the Metropolis* [2007] IRLR 763).

8.41 The Act contemplates that an illness may run its course to a conclusion but leave behind an impairment (*Swift v Chief Constable of Wiltshire Constabulary* [2004] IRLR 541). This provision protects those with disfigurements which may not affect the ability to work but which might lead employers to discriminate by, for example, refusing to appoint an applicant because the applicant had such a disfigurement. An example of severe disfigurement is a 'strawberry' birthmark, or scarring from burns.

The definition, however, specifically excludes tattoos; body piercing for decorative or **8.42** other non-medical purposes; nicotine, alcohol, and (non-medical) drug dependency; certain behavioural problems; and hay fever. Further, by virtue of the Regulations, a person also does not fall within the definition if he or she exhibits a tendency to set fires, a tendency to steal, a tendency to physical or sexual abuse of other persons, exhibitionism, or voyeurism (regs 3 & 4 Equality Act (Disability) Regulations 2010). This also excludes hay fever save where it aggravates the effect of another condition.

Save to this extent, it is not material to a decision as to whether a person has a disability **8.43** to consider the *cause* of the impairment. Thus, where it was alcoholism which led to depression, it was the depression that was the impairment, and the fact that addiction to alcohol is specifically excluded as a disability was irrelevant (*Power v Panasonic UK Ltd* [2003] IRLR 151). It may be evidentially difficult to separate what is a core impairment and what is the cause.

By Sch 1, para 6, cancer, HIV infection, and multiple sclerosis are each a disability. **8.44**

The 'Guidance on Matters to be Taken into Account in Determining Questions Relating **8.45** to the Definition of Disability' issued by the Office for Disability Issues says that whereas addictions such as alcoholism are not impairments, conditions they produce or which are associated with it, such as liver diseases or depression, may well be.

Depression is an impairment but a low mood as a reaction to adverse circumstances was **8.46** held not to be, although this is clearly a difficult distinction to apply (*J v DLA Piper UK LLP* [2010] ICR 1052). The ET must take into account evidence from the claimant's GP and/or any other treating physician. A GP is entitled to express an opinion on whether someone is suffering from depression.

There are certain extended definitions expressly provided for to which we now turn. **8.47**

Severe disfigurement

By Sch 1, para 3, EA 2010 '(1) An impairment which consists of a severe disfigurement is **8.48** to be treated as having a substantial adverse effect on the ability of the person concerned to carry out normal day-to-day activities.'

Effect of medical treatment

By Sch 1, para 5, EA 2010: **8.49**

   (1) An impairment is to be treated as having a substantial adverse effect on the ability of the person concerned to carry out normal day-to-day activities if—
     (a) measures are being taken to treat or correct it, and
     (b) but for that, it would be likely to have that effect.

For this purpose, ' "Measures" includes, in particular, medical treatment and the use of **8.50** a prosthesis or other aid.' It is necessary to distinguish between permanent improvement (taken into account in evaluating condition) and temporary amelioration (not taken into account); counselling and psychiatric assistance may count as treatment for these purposes (*Kapadia v London Borough of Lambeth* [2000] IRLR 14).

Special provision is made for sight in that by Sch 1, para 5(3): **8.51**

   Sub-paragraph (1) does not apply—
   (a) in relation to the impairment of a person's sight, to the extent that the impairment is, in the person's case, correctable by spectacles or contact lenses or in such other ways as may be prescribed.

Discrimination

8.52 By Sch 1, para 8:

> (1) This paragraph applies to a person (P) if—
>> (a) P has a progressive condition,
>> (b) as a result of that condition P has an impairment which has (or had) an effect on P's ability to carry out normal day-to-day activities, but
>> (c) the effect is not (or was not) a substantial adverse effect.
> (2) P is to be taken to have an impairment which has a substantial adverse effect if the condition is likely to result in P having such an impairment.

8.53 In general terms, in *Goodwin v Patent Office* [1999] IRLR 4, Morison J said that the tribunal should ask four questions:

> (1) Does the applicant have an impairment which is either mental or physical? ...
> (2) Does the impairment affect the applicant's ability to carry out normal day-to-day activities ... and does it have an adverse effect? ...
> (3) Is the adverse effect (upon the applicant's ability) substantial? ...
> (4) Is the adverse effect (upon the applicant's ability) long-term?

(As to the proper comparator in disability cases, see *Eagle Place Services Ltd v Rudd* [2010] IRLR 486; *JP Morgan Europe Ltd v Chweidan* [2012] ICR 268.)

Mental impairment

8.54 One important issue is the dividing line between physical and mental impairment. This depends on whether the nature of the impairment itself is physical or mental, not on whether the physical or mental function or activity is affected, since a physical impairment may affect mental activities as well as physical ones and vice versa (*Rugamer v Sony Music Entertainment UK Ltd* [2001] IRLR 644). Short of satisfactory medical evidence of a diagnosed or diagnosable clinical condition or other mental disorder of a recognised type, the evidence simply of a restriction on a person's level of function or activity, accompanied by a general suggestion that this is (or may be) a manifestation of some psychological state, will not meet the statutory threshold for establishing mental impairment.

8.55 In *McNicol v Balfour Beatty Rail Maintenance Ltd* [2002] ICR 1498, the employee stated that he suffered from a compression injury to the spine. There was no medical evidence that established any physical cause for his back pain. The employment tribunal said that the pain might have resulted from the functional or psychological overlay. The Court of Appeal decided that 'impairment' was to bear its ordinary and natural meaning, and it was for the employment tribunal to decide whether there was such a physical or mental impairment.

8.56 Mental impairment cases present special difficulties. In *Morgan v Staffordshire University* [2002] IRLR 190, the EAT laid down guidance for considering mental impairment cases, including these principles:

> (a) the parties should not expect members of employment tribunals to have anything more than a layman's rudimentary familiarity with psychiatric classification, so that matters need to be spelt out;
> (b) such terms as 'anxiety', 'stress', and 'depression' will not suffice to establish mental impairment unless there is credible and informed evidence that in the particular circumstances so loose a description identifies a clinically well-recognised illness; and
> (c) employment tribunals should not form a view on mental impairment simply from the way in which the claimant gives evidence before them.

Treatment

Impairments which can be medically treated or corrected may still be deemed as having **8.57** a substantial adverse effect and there is specific provision that: 'An impairment which would be likely to have a substantial adverse effect ... but for the fact that measures are being taken to treat or correct it, is to be treated as having that effect' (Equality Act Schedule 1).

In *Abadeh v BT* [2001] IRLR 23, the EAT said that: **8.58**

> Where the medical evidence satisfies the employment tribunal that the effect of the continuing medical treatment is to create a permanent improvement rather than a temporary improvement, such permanent improvement should be taken into account, as measures are no longer needed to treat or correct it once the permanent improvement has been established.

What are normal activities?

The emphasis is thus placed upon day-to-day activities rather than on specific work- **8.59** related activities, although, inevitably, the two may involve the same basic skills and abilities (see *Vicary v BT* [1999] IRLR 680). However, a person who can no longer carry out a work activity but can still continue to carry out day-to-day activities may not be covered by the Act. For example, an employee who could not lift heavy objects, but who was capable of lifting everyday objects, was found not to have a disability for the purpose of the Act (*Quinlan v B&Q plc* EAT 138/97; see also *Kapadia v London Borough of Lambeth* [2000] IRLR 14; *Law Hospital NHS Trust v Rush* [2001] IRLR 611).

These further principles have been expressed in the case law: **8.60**

(a) The tribunal should not ignore symptoms which have been caused when at work even though the work itself may be specialised and unusual, for example, a core maker in a foundry, so long as the disability and its consequences may be measured in terms of the ability of the claimant to undertake those activities (*Cruickshank v VAW Motorcast Ltd* [2002] IRLR 23).

(b) The activities should not be disregarded simply because they are predominantly the preserve of one sex, for example, putting rollers in hair or applying make-up (*Ekpe v Metropolitan Police Commissioner* [2001] IRLR 605).

(c) The fact that a person could carry on such activities did not mean that his or her ability had not been impaired; the tribunal has to determine whether the effect is more than trivial (*Goodwin v Patent Office* [1999] IRLR 4).

(d) The tribunal must concentrate on what the claimant cannot do or can do only with difficulty rather than on the things that he or she can do (*Leonard v Southern Derbyshire Chamber of Commerce* [2001] IRLR 19).

(e) What is 'normal' cannot sensibly depend on whether the majority of people carry out the activity. The antithesis for the purpose of the Act is thus between that which is normal and that which is abnormal or unusual as a regular activity judged by an objective standard (*Ekpe v Metropolitan Police Commissioner* [2001] IRLR 605).

(f) Although particular duties performed by an employee in the course of work cannot be equated with normal day-to-day activities, the work may include some normal day-to-day activities; the fact that the claimant continued to work in the hospital where she was employed did not permit the inference to be drawn that her evidence about difficulties at home was not credible or reliable (*Law Hospital NHS Trust v Rush* [2001] IRLR 611; *Banaszczyk v Booker Ltd* [2016] IRLR 273—lifting and moving cases of up to 25kg).

(g) Dyslexia may be a disability, and carrying out an assessment or examination (which becomes more difficult by reason of that condition) is normal day-to-day activity (*Paterson v Commissioner of Police of the Metropolis* [2007] IRLR 763).

(h) The phrase 'Normal day-to-day activities' does not refer to special skills such as a skilled silversmith or watchmaker. It also does not exclude any feature of the activities that exist because the person is at work: this may include working on a night shift since this is common in the UK (*Chief Constable of Dumfries & Galloway Constabulary v Adams* [2009] IRLR 612).

(i) A refusal to allow a claimant to progress in her professional life does not have in itself an adverse effect on normal day-to-day activities (*Chief Constable of Lothian & Borders Police v Cumming* [2010] IRLR 109).

8.61   What is 'normal' cannot sensibly depend on whether the majority of people carry on the activity. Further, the question of what is a normal day-to-day activity has to be addressed without regard to whether it was normal for the particular claimant. Thus, travelling by underground or aeroplane was a day-to-day activity. The claimant's mobility had to be considered not by reference to individual forms of transport but by looking at transport as a whole.

Religion and belief

8.62   By s 10(1), religion means 'any religion and a reference to religion includes a reference to a lack of religion'. Belief means 'any religious or philosophical belief and a reference to belief includes a reference to a lack of belief' (s 10(2)).

8.63   The Explanatory Notes to the draft Regulations state: 'This does not include any philosophical or political belief unless that belief is similar to a religious belief. The Courts and Tribunals may consider a number of factors when deciding what is a religion or belief (eg collective worship, clear belief system, profound belief reflecting way of life or view of the world).' Further, by para 51, it includes denominations or sects within a religion such as Protestants and Catholics within Christianity.

8.64   Lord Toulson in *R (Hodgkin) v Registrar General* [2013] UKSC 77 described religion 'in summary as a spiritual or non-secular belief system, held by a group of adherents, which claims to explain mankind's place in the universe and relationship with the infinite and to teach its adherents how they are to live their lives in conformity with the spiritual understanding associated with the belief system ... I mean a belief system which goes beyond that which can be perceived by the senses or ascertained by the application of science ... Such a belief system may or may not involve belief in a supreme being but it does involve a belief that there is more to be understood about mankind's nature and relationship to the universe than can be gained from the senses or from science'.

8.65   A philosophical belief is a belief genuinely held and not merely an opinion or viewpoint as to a weighty and substantial aspect of human life and behaviour that has a certain level of cogency, seriousness, cohesion, and importance, is worthy of respect in a democratic society, and is not incompatible with human dignity or in conflict with the human rights of others (*Grainger plc v Nicholson* [2010] ICR 360).

8.66   There must be a religious or philosophical belief in which one actually believes; it is not enough to have an opinion based on some real or perceived logic or based on information or lack of information available (*McClintock v DCA* [2008] IRLR 29).

8.67   In most cases political views will qualify as an opinion rather than a belief and thus not be covered. Fundamental political beliefs such as Marxism or Fascism may qualify.

A Christian employee refused to work two weekends in three at a residential home for **8.68** disabled children and claimed that she had been discriminated against on the grounds of religion. The ET dismissed the claim on weighing the discriminatory impact of the requirement on the claimant against the reasonable needs of the employer. The Court of Appeal decided that the ET had erred in taking into account the facts that the employer had made efforts to accommodate the claimant for two years and the employer had been prepared to enable her to attend church on Sundays and that the belief that Sunday should be a day of rest was 'not a core component of the Christian faith'. None of these were relevant but it was justified because the employer had no viable and practicable alternative way of running the care home effectively other than requiring the claimant to work on Sundays. The majority held that it was necessary to read the concept of justification compatibly with Art 9 so that group disadvantage did not arise. Thus, it did not matter whether the claimant was disadvantaged along with others or not (*Mba v Merton lbc* [2014] ICR 357). The landmark case of *Eweida v BA* [2013] IRLR 231 is considered in Chapter 23 on human rights.

C FORMS OF DISCRIMINATION

There exist four main forms of discrimination, but common to all is the key factor of **8.69** comparison between persons, and broadly the statute requires that like must be compared with like so that the 'relevant circumstances are the same or not materially different' between comparators.

Direct discrimination

Direct discrimination is the most blatant form of differentiation on protected grounds **8.70** and is what most laypeople mean by discrimination. It occurs by s 13(1) of the EA 2010 when 'a person (A) discriminates against another (B) if, because of a protected characteristic, A treats B less favourably than A treats or would treat others'.

There are then different criteria for different protected characteristics (some being asymmetric) so that:

(a) There is a justification defence in the case of age by s 13(2) so that A does not discriminate against B if A can show A's treatment of B to be a proportionate means of achieving a legitimate aim.
(b) By s 13(3) of the EA 2010: 'If the protected characteristic is disability, and B is not a disabled person, A does not discriminate against B only because A treats or would treat disabled persons more favourably than A treats B.'
(c) By s 13(5) of the EA 2010: 'If the protected characteristic is race, less favourable treatment includes segregating B from others.'
(d) By s 13(6) of the EA 2010:

> (6) If the protected characteristic is sex—
>> (a) less favourable treatment of a woman includes less favourable treatment of her because she is breast-feeding;
>> (b) in a case where B is a man, no account is to be taken of special treatment afforded to a woman in connection with pregnancy or childbirth.

The relevant comparison: The comparison must be such that 'the relevant circumstances **8.71** in the one case are the same, or not materially different in the other'. This has been frequently discussed in case law. In *Shamoon v Chief Constable of the RUC* [2003] ICR

337, Lord Hope said that 'A comparison of the cases of persons of a different sex ... must therefore be such that all the circumstances which are relevant to the way they were treated in the one case are the same or not materially different in the other', but it need not be a precise clone (*Madden v Preferred Technical Group CHA Ltd* [2005] IRLR 46). In *Bain v Bowles* [1991] IRLR 356, the Court of Appeal emphasised that this was merely an interpretive provision in order to ensure that like is compared with like, and is not intended to operate as an exception to the statute. Therefore, where a magazine did not accept an advertisement which had been placed by a man for a housekeeper which it would have accepted from a woman, these were not relevant circumstances which took the facts outside the SDA 1975 and the respondent had unlawfully discriminated against the claimant. In *Centrum voor Gelijkheid van Kansen en voor Racismebestrijding v Firma Feryn NV* [2008] ECR-I 51871, the ECJ decided that a public statement that 'immigrants' need not bother applying for work was contrary to the then Race Directive.

8.72 **Example** Alan and Betty both apply to Crest Supermarkets for the job of supermarket manager. Alan is chosen because he has been manager for ten years at another store, while Betty has only worked as the assistant manager for three years. This is not unlawful discrimination since the *reason* for failing to appoint Betty is not sex but Alan's experience. If the qualifications were the same, and Alan was appointed because he is a man, there is a prima facie case of sex discrimination.

8.73 The following order of questions was formulated by Mummery J for employment tribunals to ask in a typical discrimination case in *Qureshi v Victoria University of Manchester* [2001] ICR 863(n):

(a) Did the act complained of actually occur? In some cases there will be a head-on conflict of direct oral evidence. The tribunal will have to decide who to believe. If it does not believe the applicant and his witnesses, the applicant has failed to discharge the burden of proving the act complained of and the case will fail at that point. If the applicant is believed, has he brought his application in time and, if not, is it just and equitable to extend the time?

(b) If the act complained of occurred in time, was there a difference in race involving the applicant?

(c) If a difference in race was involved, was the applicant treated less favourably than the alleged discriminator treated or would treat other persons of a different racial group in the same, or not materially different, relevant circumstances?

(d) If there was difference in treatment involving persons of a different race, was that treatment 'on racial grounds'? Were racial grounds an effective cause of the difference in treatment? What explanation of the less favourable treatment is given by the respondent?

8.74 In order to provide an answer to each of these questions, the tribunal must make findings of primary fact, either on the basis of direct (or positive) evidence or by inference from circumstantial evidence. This must be considered, however, in the light of the subsequent judgments on burden of proof in *Igen v Wong* [2005] IRLR 258 and *Madarassay v Nomura International plc* [2007] IRLR 246 (see 8.184). (*Hewage v Grampian Health Board* [2012] ICR 1054 approved *Igen and Madarassy SC*; also *Khan v Royal Mail Group Ltd* [2014] IRLR 947; *Nazir v Asim* [2010] ICR 1225.)

8.75 Many institutions have been accused in the media of institutional racism. There is, however, no viable claim for institutional racism under the Act in and of itself, and it is essential to apply the statutory language to the facts if this be alleged (*Commissioners of Inland Revenue v Morgan* [2002] IRLR 776). As to the proper comparator for direct age discrimination, see *Lockwood v DWP* [2014] ICR 1257; *Donkor v Royal Bank of Scotland Ltd* [2016] IRLR 268.

Less favourable treatment

In most cases, the issue of what constitutes less favourable treatment will cause no prob- **8.76** lems. In the controversial sex discrimination case, *Peake v Automotive Products Ltd* [1978] QB 233, however, the Court of Appeal appeared to require a hostile motivation on the part of the employer for it to arise. This threatened to limit greatly the scope of the Act. Lord Denning, however, soon joined in the narrowing of the *ratio* of the decision in *Ministry of Defence v Jeremiah* [1980] ICR 13. The claimants were again men, this time employed at the appellant's ordnance factory. They had volunteered for overtime, which meant that they had to work in very dirty conditions in the 'colour bursting shell shop', making shells which exploded in red or orange for artillery practice. Women did not have to do this, partly because it was thought that such conditions would affect their hair. The Court of Appeal upheld the men's claim of discrimination; Lord Denning MR accepted that *Peake* could only be considered correctly decided on the basis that there the difference in treatment (five minutes less work per day) was *de minimis*.

The tribunal must consider not only how the employer does treat a member of another **8.77** group, but also how he *would* so treat such a person; and in the latter case it is not necessary to find actual evidence of what would happen but the tribunal should proceed on the basis of inference (*Leeds Private Hospital v Parkin* [1992] ICR 571). In certain cases, the comparison need not even be demonstrated by evidence as to how a comparator was or would have been treated because the very action complained of is in itself less favourable treatment on the grounds of sex. This did not, however, apply to a failure to investigate an allegation of a racially inspired attack. In *Sidhu v Aerospace Composite Technology Ltd* [2001] ICR 167, the employer's policy of dismissing an employee who was found guilty of using violent or abusive language without having regard to any provocation or any mitigating circumstances was not race specific. It had to be shown that someone from a different race was or would be treated differently (see also *Brown v TNT Express Ltd* [2001] ICR 182). The question whether or not particular individuals were appropriate comparators for the purposes of claims of discrimination is one of fact and degree for the employment tribunal (*Hewage v Grampian Health Board* [2012] ICR 1054).

Hypothetical comparator

The appropriate comparison may be with a hypothetical person, since it covers not only **8.78** actual treatment but also a comparison with how another person *would be* treated. It is, however, vital to prove that an effective cause of the treatment was the relevant protected characteristic of the complainant or an associate of the complainant.

It is not necessary to consider a hypothetical comparator in each case, especially if it **8.79** has not been pleaded (*Stockton on Tees BC v Aylott* [2010] ICR 1278). If a hypothetical comparator was to be taken it should be someone who behaved in the same way as the claimant but did not suffer from the claimant's disability rather than someone who had not acted in the way that had caused the employer to treat the claimant as he did.

The various questions run together. In *Shamoon v Chief Constable of the RUC* [2003] **8.80** ICR 337, Lord Nicholls indicated that it may not always be possible to decide whether there is less favourable treatment without deciding the question of 'the reason why' action was taken. This is especially so when a hypothetical comparator is used in the claim. It is thus not necessary for the tribunal in each case to go through a sequential process of reasoning, that is, first identifying whether there was less favourable treatment and then considering the reason(s) for it. The employment tribunal may thus construct an inference of the hypothetical comparator from how the employers treated actual non-identical but not wholly dissimilar cases (eg *Chief Constable of West Yorkshire Police v Vento* [2001] IRLR 124; *Balamoody v UKCC* [2002] ICR 646; *Bradford Hospitals NHS Trust v Al-Shabib* [2003] IRLR 4) (see *James v Eastleigh* below at 8.91).

8.81 The fact that the employer fell below the standards of a reasonable employer does not infer treatment on discriminatory grounds. The conduct of a hypothetical reasonable employer is, however, irrelevant to this determination (*Zafar v Glasgow City Council* [1998] IRLR 36). Similarly in *Qureshi v London Borough of Newham* [1991] IRLR 264, the Court of Appeal held that a mere failure by an employer to follow the terms of its equal opportunities policy did not in itself found a discrimination claim. The defect in the reasoning of the tribunal was an assumption that the policy would have been properly applied to persons of different racial origin from the claimant, which was not necessarily so.

Dress code

8.82 An important test of this concept of differential treatment is an appearance code which, for example, requires the hair of male employees not to be longer than collar-length whereas the same restriction does not apply to women. There may be good reason why this occurs. In *Smith v Safeway plc* [1996] IRLR 4, it was held that such a code was not sexually discriminatory since it merely laid down a requirement for conventional appearance and did not result in men being treated less favourably than women. Phillips and Peter Gibson LJJ said that 'there is an important distinction between discrimination between the sexes and discrimination against one or other of the sexes. It is the latter that is forbidden by [the SDA]'. The effect of any one item in an appearance code had to be considered in the context of the code as a whole. The Court of Appeal thus held that it was not discriminatory to ban unconventionally long hair or hair in a ponytail for men when such length of hair or ponytail was not unconventional for a woman. The company's rules for men and women, although differing in detail, had as a common feature requirements as to appearance that excluded the unconventional.

8.83 Similarly, a dress code to the effect that all those subject to it were required to dress 'in a professional and businesslike way' did not necessarily discriminate against a man who refused to wear a collar and tie, and received a warning for it. The appropriate question for the tribunal to consider was whether in the context of an overarching requirement of this sort the level of smartness that the employer required, applying contemporary standards of conventional dresswear, could only be achieved for men by requiring them to wear a collar and tie: if it could be achieved by men dressing otherwise, the lack of flexibility in the dress code would suggest less favourable treatment (*Department for Work & Pensions v Thompson* [2004] IRLR 348).

Because of the protected characteristic

8.84 The Equality Act 2010 uses as the crucial phrase in order to establish liability 'because of' the relevant protected characteristic, whereas the predecessor Acts it replaced referred to '*on the ground of*'. It is not anticipated that this would have a major impact on the interpretation of the Act and indeed the Explanatory Notes to the Act said that it was not intended to do so. It is not necessary to determine that any difference in treatment was for the protected reason, and not for another and *valid* reason. In *Noble v David Gold and Son (Holdings) Ltd* [1980] IRLR 252, for example, the allocation of women to lighter work was a result of the employer's practical experience rather than because of their sex.

Where there are two reasons which are put forward for treatment of the claimant, the **8.85** discriminatory ground must be *an effective cause* of the treatment but not necessarily the only one (*Owen & Briggs v James* [1981] IRLR 133; *Seide v Gillette Industries Ltd* [1980] IRLR 427; *Barclays Bank plc v Kapur (No 2)* [1995] IRLR 87; *Simon v Brimham Associates* [1987] IRLR 307). There is no need for the discriminator to have a malign motivation (*EOC v Birmingham CC* [1989] AC 1155).

Once a tribunal had identified the treatment complained of it had to focus on the words **8.86** 'because of something' in s 15(1)(a) and identify the 'something' and then separately to decide whether that something arose 'in consequence' of the claimant's disability before asking whether the treatment complained of was 'because of' that (*Basildon & Thurrock NHS Foundation Trust v Weerasinghe* [2016] ICR 305).

A good example of this scenario is found in the case of *Tejani v Superintendent Registrar* **8.87** *for the District of Peterborough* [1986] IRLR 502. There a request by a Superintendent Registrar of Births, Deaths, and Marriages to a person born or residing abroad to produce his passport was not race discrimination according to the Court of Appeal. The request was not made because of the claimant's racial or national origins within the statute. On the facts found, the Registrar treated alike everyone who came from abroad (see also *Wakeman v Quick Corporation* [1999] IRLR 424).

We now consider a series of principles which surround the primary question. There may **8.88** be difficult issues of corporate responsibility in this area. In a case where the employee was dismissed and the dismissing officer made reference to the age of the employee, the EAT held that in order to show that the dismissal was in no sense whatsoever decided upon on the grounds of age, the tribunal had to consider the mental processes of others in the company whose views had a significant influence on the decision to dismiss and that the tribunal was wrong not to have done so. The Court of Appeal, however, overturned this decision on the basis that the individual employee who did the act complained of had himself to have been motivated by the protected characteristic and there was no basis on which his act could be said to be discriminatory on the basis of someone else's motivation (*Reynolds v CLFIS (UK) Ltd* [2015] ICR 1010).

The question of what was said and with what effect is one for the tribunal to decide as the **8.89** judge of fact; it is necessary to have in mind in this respect the fact that an act complained of might have occurred in the context of or in connection with a protected characteristic, did not necessarily mean that it was done *on the grounds of* or because of that characteristic (*Sahota v Home Office* [2010] ICR 772).

There are particular issues which arise in respect of victimisation (generally to be consid- **8.90** ered below). There are cases where an employer has dismissed an employee or subjected him to some other detriment in response to the doing of a protected act but where it could be said as a matter of common sense and justice that the reason for dismissal was not the protected act as such but some particular feature of it which could properly be regarded as separable, such as the manner in which the employee made the complaint relied on as the protected act (*Martin v Devonshire's Solicitors* [2011] ICR 352). The proper test was whether the proscribed ground or protected act had had a significant influence on the outcome.

In the very important case of *James v Eastleigh BC* [1989] 3 WLR 123, the two central **8.91** concepts of less favourable treatment on the grounds of sex were considered in the context of a rather unusual claim for direct discrimination in relation to the provision of facilities which adopted a criterion which was itself discriminatory so that it was in reality serving as a proxy for a protected characteristic. The claimant was a man who had retired and he and his wife both regularly visited a leisure centre run by the defendant local authority. They were both aged sixty-one. The wife was admitted free of charge to the leisure centre as she was above the then retirement age for women but the claimant had to pay for the privilege. The precise basis of differentiation was that free admittance was only available to persons who had reached state pension age, which was then sixty-five in the case of the man and sixty for females, already thus a differentiation on grounds of sex. The Court of Appeal held that in a case of direct discrimination, it was necessary to consider *why* the defendant treated the claimant less favourably than (an)other(s). Here, the aim of the Council in giving free admittance was to provide benefits to those with limited resources. They reasoned that since neither the overt condition imposed nor any covert reason was related directly to the sex of the claimant it could not be said that the defendant was afforded less favourable treatment 'on the ground of' sex. The House of Lords, however, overturned the decision by a three to two majority. The appropriate test was simply to ask 'would the complainant have received the same treatment from the defendant but for his or her sex'. The subjective motive, intention, or reason was irrelevant. The use of the statutory pension age as a criterion in this case was thus directly discriminatory as a proxy for sex, and could not be justified as it would have been open to the defendant to do in the case of indirect discrimination.

8.92 An important application of many of these concepts may be seen in the judicial review application of *R (on the application of European Roma Rights Centre) v Immigration officers at Prague airport*. This case went to the House of Lords ([2005] IRLR 115), which unanimously held that the policy of more intrusive questioning of Roma for immigration purposes than non-Roma did directly discriminate on grounds of the Roma's race. The approach taken by the majority of the Court of Appeal impermissibly incorporated the essence of justification into the analysis of whether there was discrimination. The policy was in fact inherently and systematically discriminatory.

Generalised assumptions

8.93 The words of the statute also encompass cases where the reason for discrimination is a *generalised assumption* that people of a particular protected characteristic possess or lack certain characteristics. This is often described as stereotyping. In *Coleman v Skyrail Oceanic Ltd* [1981] IRLR 398, for example, a booking clerk in the respondent's travel agency was dismissed when she married a man who was employed by a rival tour operator, even though she promised not to divulge confidential information, and there was no evidence that she had done so during her engagement. The Court of Appeal (with Shaw LJ dissenting) held that the employer's very *assumption* that the man was the breadwinner, without further investigation of the personal situation, was, in itself, discriminatory. The husband in fact was earning only a modest wage, and there was no evidence that his employers were reluctant to dismiss *him*. The Court also noted that in 56.2 per cent of households married women contributed to their income.

8.94 It was also unlawful for the same reason for the respondents in *Horsey v Dyfed CC* [1982] IRLR 395 to refuse to second the claimant to a training course in the London area where her husband was employed because they assumed that she would remain in London when her course was completed and not return to work for the respondents in Wales. It was an inescapable inference to be drawn that the respondent would have treated a married *man* differently from the way in which it treated the applicant. The EAT did not, however, say that an employer could never act on the basis that a wife would give up her job to join her husband. What the employer could not do was to *assume* that this was so. The employer must look at the particular circumstances of each case.

What is in effect the converse of this approach may be seen in *Bradford Hospitals NHS* **8.95**
Trust v Al-Shabib [2003] IRLR 4. The EAT held that although it may sometimes be
legitimate for a tribunal to take into account differences in behaviour between people,
which reflect racial and cultural differences, it is wrong for a tribunal to make findings
based on the existence of such differences unless there is some evidential basis for them
such as expert evidence. For a tribunal simply to assume that a particular ethnic group
has a specific characteristic is wrong. A very broad distinction to the effect that there is a
difference between Anglo-Saxon and Iraqi behaviour is thus impermissible.

Indirect discrimination

The concept of indirect discrimination, which was first introduced in the SDA 1975 and **8.96**
then included in the RRA 1976, crucially recognises that inequality does not result from
intentional overt acts only, which is the model of *direct* discrimination. Some of the most
insidious institutional discrimination indeed operates at a more subtle level, by way of
tests or requirements, which, although applying to both sexes or all races, in effect discriminate against one. This is itself often the legacy of past discrimination. The United
States Supreme Court found the concept to be implicit in the very fabric of the prohibition
against discrimination in the Civil Rights Act 1964. The essence of its leading judgment
in *Griggs v Duke Power Co* (1971) 401 US 424 is that 'Practices, procedures, tests ... neutral on their face ... cannot be maintained if they operate to freeze the status quo of past
discrimination'. Thus, a height requirement in a company rule book may indirectly discriminate against women, although those who inserted the provision did not at all advert
to its effect on them, and short men would be treated similarly. The concept is modified in
the case of disability. Section 19(1) of the Equality Act 2010 renders a common definition
for most forms of protected characteristics as follows: 'A person (A) discriminates against
another (B) if A applies to B a provision, criterion or practice which is discriminatory in
relation to a relevant protected characteristic of B's.'

By s 19(2): **8.97**

> ... a provision, criterion or practice is discriminatory in relation to a relevant protected char-
> acteristic of B's if—
>
> (a) A applies, or would apply, it to persons with whom B does not share the characteristic,
> (b) it puts, or would put, persons with whom B shares the characteristic at a particular dis-
> advantage when compared with persons with whom B does not share it,
> (c) it puts, or would put, B at that disadvantage, and
> (d) A cannot show it to be a proportionate means of achieving a legitimate aim.

This provides a common formulation to replace the previously disparate provisions to be **8.98**
found in respect of different characteristics (see *London Underground Ltd v Edwards*
[1999] ICR 494). Lady Hale said in *Chief Constable of W Yorkshire Police v Homer*
[2012] ICR 704, para 14:

> The new formulation [of indirect discrimination] was ... intended to do away with the need
> for statistical comparisons where no statistics might exist ... now all that is needed is a par-
> ticular disadvantage when compared with other people who do not share the characteristic
> in question.

The Supreme Court decided that 'to be proportionate, a measure has to be both an appropriate means of achieving the legitimate aim and (reasonably) necessary in order to do so'.

In a controversial decision, *Naeem v Secretary of State for Justice* [2016] ICR 289, the **8.99**
Court of Appeal held that it was permissible for s 19(2)(b) to consider the reason for the
disparity in the sense of the factors which had caused it to occur in order to show that the

apparent disparate impact was the result of non-discriminatory factors. On the facts of the case, which concerned differences between Muslim and Christian chaplains because of their different lengths of service and the fact that there had been no need for employed Muslim chaplains in the prison service before 2002, it could not be said that it was the use of the length of service criterion that put Muslim chaplains at a disadvantage. Thus, the shorter average length of service of Muslim chaplains was attributable to a factor—the lack of need for employed Muslim chaplains before 2002—that was not the result of any discriminatory practice by the Prison Service. This rendered the practice not to be indirect discrimination.

8.100 The early case of *Steel v Union of Post Office Workers* [1977] IRLR 288 still demonstrates the importance of such an action in rooting out the effects of past discrimination and may provide in its result a contract to *Naeem*. Mrs Steel had been employed as a postwoman since 1961, but until 1975 women could hold only temporary and not permanent positions, and this deprived her of the seniority which would have given her priority in allocation of the best postal rounds. She complained when she was turned down for a particularly favourable 'walk' in favour of a man who had greater seniority as a 'permanent' postman, although he had only joined the service in 1973. The EAT found the Post Office's practice prima facie to amount to indirect discrimination, and remitted the case to the tribunal to 'weigh up in particular the needs of the enterprise against the discriminatory effect of the requirement or condition'.

Provision, criterion, practice

8.101 The following were held to be requirements or conditions under the pre-existing law (and are examples of what would clearly qualify under the new, looser rubric):

(a) a request that a person return to work full-time (*Home Office v Holmes* [1984] IRLR 299; cf *Clymo v London Borough of Wandsworth* [1989] IRLR 241);

(b) a practice that part-time workers should be dismissed first under a redundancy selection agreement (*Clarke v Eley (IMI) Kynoch Ltd* [1982] IRLR 482);

(c) a refusal to employ a person with young children, since this would affect considerably more married than unmarried persons (*Thorndyke v Bell Fruit (North Central) Ltd* [1979] IRLR 1; *Hurley v Mustoe* [1981] IRLR 208);

(d) a refusal to hire persons resident in Liverpool 8 postal district where 50 per cent of the population were black (*Hussein v Saints Complete House Furnishers Ltd* [1979] IRLR 337);

(e) the requirement of the Council of Legal Education that graduates from overseas universities should complete three years' study at its School of Law while those from British and Irish institutions need only serve two (*Bohon-Mitchell v Common Professional Examination Board and the Council of Legal Education* [1978] IRLR 525);

(f) language tests which exclude large numbers from ethnic minority groups;

(g) a rule that holidays were not to be taken during the employer's busiest season, since Muslims were unable to take time off for the important Eid religious festival (*J. H. Walker Ltd v Hussain* [1996] IRLR 10)—this would now be covered by discrimination on grounds of religion; and

(h) a provision in a collective agreement, which only took into account for the purposes of grading in the employment categories provided in that agreement the professional experience acquired as a cabin crew member of a specific airline while excluding substantively identical experience acquired in the service of another airline belonging to the same group of companies, entailed a difference in treatment according to the date of recruitment by the employer concerned that was not inextricably nor indirectly linked to the age of the employees even if a conceivable consequence of the application of the criterion at issue could in some individual cases be that advancement for those moving within the group of companies would occur at a later age than those who remained with one company. Thus, there was no indirect discrimination on age grounds (*Tyrolean Airways v Betriebsrat Bord der Tyrolean Airways* [2013] ICR 71).

The following further principles have been established: **8.102**

(a) It is necessary to consider in an indirect discrimination case why the employee failed to comply with the provision and in this particular case of *Essop v Home Office* [2015] ICR 1063 it was a core skills assessment. The claimant had to show why the particular provision, criterion, or practice disadvantaged the group sharing the protected characteristic and each claimant had to prove that he had suffered the same disadvantage: this could include statistical evidence as a method of showing this. This decision is, however, controversial and at the time of writing is due to be heard by the Supreme Court.

(b) It is clear that it is not always necessary to rely on statistics to demonstrate disparate impact after the EA 2010, whereas it was before its enactment (*MOD v DeBique* [2010] IRLR 471).

(c) It is necessary to identify the provision, criterion, or practice which is at issue, the persons who were not according to the protected characteristic disabled with whom comparison was being made, the nature and extent of the substantial disadvantage suffered by the employee, and the step or steps which it was reasonable for the employer to take to avoid that disadvantage (*Secretary of State for Work & Pensions v Higgins* [2014] ICR 341).

(d) The pool to be taken into account should not consist of people who had no interest in the advantage or disadvantage in question: the appropriate pool must instead be one that suitably tests the particular discrimination complained of (*Somerset CC v Pike* [2009] IRLR 870).

Justification

It is clear that some provisions are imposed on quite reasonable grounds, and it is unfair   **8.103**
and inefficient to prohibit them completely even though they may have an adverse effect on certain protected groups. The employer may thus impose conditions and requirements which have a disproportionate impact on a protected characteristic if he can show that they are 'proportionate means of achieving a legitimate aim', as justification is now defined in the EA 2010. This is derived from the European case law and it cannot be automatically assumed that all of the old case law will still be relevant (this case law is covered in detail in the Eighth Edition).

This is also the formulation for direct age discrimination which is the sole basis of *direct*   **8.104**
discrimination which may be justified. These principles remain relevant:

(a) In *Hampson v Department of Education and Science* [1989] IRLR 69, Balcombe LJ stated that it 'requires an objective balance between the discriminatory effect of the condition and the reasonable needs of the party who applies the condition', although this argument was not considered by the House of Lords [1990] IRLR 302; see also *Greater Manchester Police Authority v Lea* [1990] IRLR 372.

(b) The test of justification is generally objective, not resting solely on what the employer considers to be justifiable. The question is largely one of fact for the employment tribunal to consider (*Mandla*'s case (see 8.17); *Greencroft Social Club and Institute v Mullen* [1985] ICR 796; *Singh v British Rail Engineering Ltd* [1986] ICR 22).

(c) A blanket rule which incorporates discriminatory assumptions may prove very difficult to justify. Thus, in *Hurley v Mustoe* [1981] IRLR 208, where a restaurant manager sought to uphold a general refusal to employ waitresses with young children, it was not sufficient to claim that it was necessary for his small business that employees be reliable. A condition excluding *all* members of a class from employment cannot be justified on the ground that *some* members of that class are unreliable. The employer must investigate the reliability of each member of that class just like all others on their merits. This does not, however, inflexibly require that there be external or what might be called independent evidence of justification.

(d) In *British Airways plc v Grundy (No 2)* [2008] IRLR 815, the Court of Appeal held that a difference in terms and conditions between two sets of cabin crew (both of which were predominantly female) but to different extents could not be justified by the fact that the differences had resulted from a collective agreement designed to reward the 'greater contractual commitment' of the advantaged group where the disadvantaged group consisted largely of women who had chosen the particular pattern of working so as to manage their childcare responsibilities.

(e) In *MacCulloch v ICI* [2008] ICR 1334, Elias J laid down guidance as to the principles of justification in age cases (paras 10–12):

(1) The burden of proof is on the respondent to establish justification: see *Starmer v British Airways* [2005] IRLR 862 at [31].

(2) The classic test was set out in *Bilka-Kaufhaus GmbH v Weber von Hartz* (Case 170/84) [1984] IRLR 317 in the context of indirect sex discrimination. The ECJ said that the court or tribunal must be satisfied that the measures must 'correspond to a real need ... are appropriate with a view to achieving the objectives pursued and are necessary to that end' (para 36). This involves the application of the proportionality principle. It has subsequently been emphasised that the reference to 'necessary' means 'reasonably necessary': see *Barry v Midland Bank* ... per Lord Nicholls at para 5.

(3) The principle of proportionality requires an objective balance to be struck between the discriminatory effect of the measure and the needs of the undertaking. The more serious the disparate adverse impact, the more cogent must be the justification for it: *Hardys & Hansons plc v Lax* [2005] IRLR 726 per Pill LJ at paras 19–34, Thomas LJ at 54–55 and Gage LJ at 60.

(4) It is for the employment tribunal to weigh the reasonable needs of the undertaking against the discriminatory effect of the employer's measure and to make its own assessment of whether the former outweigh the latter. There is no 'range of reasonable response' test in this context: *Hardys & Hansons plc v Lax* [2005] IRLR 726, CA.

8.105 Age has special characteristics in terms of justification, in particular because of the societal expectations of retirement and the competing pressures on business, and these lead to these principles being formulated in respect of age:

(a) the question of proportionality involves a consideration of the impact on the affected claimant or class and whether a fair balance has been achieved between the competing considerations. In respect of a challenge to parts of the originally enacted Age Regulations, the court would give very considerable weight in this respect to the expertise of the Government in a field of economical and social policymaking where the court has no relevant experience or institutional competence (*R (on the application of Age UK) v Secretary of State for BIS* [2009] IRLR 1017).

(b) In *Kücükdeveci v Swedex GmbH & Co* [2010] ECR I-365, the employee received notice of termination calculated on three years' service for the employer. She had in fact worked for the company for ten years but service before the age of twenty-five was not taken into account. The Government contended that this rule protected the job security of older workers and reflected the greater flexibility of the younger staff. The Court did not accept this argument, stating that the rule did not apply equally to younger workers because it put at a disadvantage those who entered the labour market early.

(c) It is acceptable according to the CJEU for an employer to introduce a protection arrangement where a system of promotion was changed from one which was directly based on age to that of experience. The protection of the acquired rights of a category of persons such as this constituted an overriding reason which was in the public interest and legitimate (*Specht v Land Berlin* [2014] ICR 966).

(d) As to normal retirement age, there may be a policy against agreeing to extensions of time after normal retirement age but it must not be applied as an inflexible rule (*Compass Group plc v Ayodele* [2011] IRLR 802). An employer does not have to give reasons for refusing such a request.

(e) The Supreme Court, in the landmark decision of *Seldon v Clarkson Wright & Jakes* [2012] ICR 716, said that a distinction had to be drawn between, on the one hand, the social policy objectives of a public interest nature which could justify direct age discrimination and, on the other hand, purely individual reasons which were particular to the employer's situation which in general terms could not qualify. Thus, the objectives of inter-generational fairness and preserving the dignity of older workers by avoiding unseemly debates about capacity to continue were capable of being legitimate aims depending on the circumstances of the employment concerned and provided that the means chosen were appropriate and necessary. Where it was justified to have a general rule, the treatment resulting from it would usually be justified. The ET ultimately found that the employer's aims of retention and workforce planning had objectively justified the age of sixty-five for retirement in a solicitors' practice and this conclusion was upheld on appeal by the EAT (*Seldon No 2* [2014] IRLR 748; see also *Pulham v LB of Barking & Dagenham* [2010] ICR 333).

(f) The social policy aims may be broad, including the maintenance of economic competitiveness and, in times of high unemployment, the fair distribution of employment opportunities amongst the population as a whole, ensuring that workers have an adequate opportunity to provide for their retirement and the like. A wide margin is naturally afforded to Member States in formulating these social policy aims (*R (on the application of Age UK) v Secretary of State for BIS* [2009] IRLR 1017; see also Chief Constable of West Midlands Police v Harrod [2015] IRLR 790).

(g) In *Rolls Royce plc v Unite the Union* [2011] ICR 1, the Court of Appeal decided that while a redundancy points system based on length of service indirectly discriminated against younger employees as a group, the length of service criterion was just one of a number of criteria in the overall context of such selection which was not determinative and had been agreed between the employer and the union in order to pursue the objective of a selection process that was fair; viewed objectively it was a 'proportionate means of achieving a legitimate aim', that is, the reward of loyalty and the overall desirability of achieving a stable workforce in the context of a fair process of redundancy selection.

Further, Sch 22, para 1, provides wide exceptions in the case of age, disability, and religion where the person is required to act as it does by statute, but sex discrimination is only permitted when it is *necessary* to comply with specific provisions on the protection of pregnancy, maternity, and other risks specifically affecting women (para 2). Otherwise such statutory requirements will be overridden. Schedule 9, para 10, permits benefits to be related to length of service, without the need to consider justification. Where the person with the shorter service has worked in excess of five years the employer 'must reasonably believe' that the reward for long service 'fulfils a business need'.

(h) *Treatment of cost*: Economic reasons can be considered under this rubric but there is an inherent tension in this area of law. Thus, reduction of cost alone cannot in itself be regarded as a legitimate aim. For example, to employ young employees only on the basis that they are cheaper to engage would not be acceptable as justification. This issue was explored in *Cross v British Airways* [2005] IRLR 423, a case where retirement provisions were attacked as being of indirectly discriminatory effect. One of the factors in the employer's justification for the treatment was the likely cost of changing the policy. The EAT held that, following several ECJ decisions, cost alone could not be a justification. It could, however, form one of the reasons along with others albeit that it was a reason to which less weight would be attached. It was, however, legitimate for an employer to impose a budget on the amount to be spent on a redundancy scheme (*HM Land Registry v Benson* [2012] ICR 628). In terms of balancing resources, a business is entitled to seek to break even year on year (*Edie v HCL Insurance BPO Services Ltd* [2015] ICR 713). The saving or avoidance of costs would not, without more, amount to the achieving of a legitimate aim (*Woodcock v Cumbria Primary Care Trust* [2012] ICR 1126). It could, however, be so if it was combined with another reason to amount to justification.

(i)   *Agreement with the unions*: In *Loxley v BAE Systems* [2008] ICR 1348, the EAT said:

> the fact that an agreement is made with the trade unions is potentially a relevant consideration when determining whether treatment is proportionate.

This point, however, has to be approached with some care in that there is no sense that the parties can simply agree what the position is with respect to justification. It must be subject to the scrutiny of the tribunal.

(j)   As a general matter, a tribunal is required to make its own judgment as to whether, on a fair and detailed analysis of the working practices and business considerations involved, the relevant practice was reasonably necessary and should not apply a range of reasonable responses tests such as is adopted in unfair dismissal cases (*Hardy & Hansons plc v Lax* [2005] ICR 1565).

(k)   The proportionate means is not inherently narrow and a number of different actions may each be part and a necessary but not equal part of the means of achieving the chosen aim (*Allen v GMB* [2008] IRLR 690).

Harassment

8.106   The European Union Code of Practice on 'The Dignity of Men and Women at Work' defines sexual harassment as 'unwanted conduct of a sexual nature or other conduct based on sex affecting the dignity of men and women at work'. Sexual harassment was enacted in UK law as from October 2005 and is now incorporated as s 26 of the Equality Act 2010 so that:

  (1) A person (A) harasses another (B) if—
  (a) A engages in unwanted conduct related to a relevant protected characteristic, and
  (b) the conduct has the purpose or effect of—
    (i) violating B's dignity, or
    (ii) creating an intimidating, hostile, degrading, humiliating or offensive environment for B.

There is another form of harassment by s 26(2): if—

  (a) A engages in unwanted conduct of a sexual nature, and
  (b) the conduct has the purpose or effect referred to in subsection (1)(b).

A third variant is in subsection (3): if—

  (a) A or another person engages in unwanted conduct of a sexual nature or that is related to gender reassignment or sex,

(b) the conduct has the purpose or effect referred to in subsection (1)(b), and

(c) because of B's rejection of or submission to the conduct, A treats B less favourably than A would treat B if B had not rejected or submitted to the conduct.

As a general point, subsection (4) requires:

... each of the following must be taken into account—

(a) the perception of B;

(b) the other circumstances of the case;

(c) whether it is reasonable for the conduct to have that effect.

The whole notion behind this provision is that there should be no unlawfulness when **8.107** unreasonable offence is taken to action or words (*Grant v HM Land Registry* [2011] IRLR 748). In *English v Thomas Sanderson* [2009] IRLR 206, a man could be harassed on grounds of sexual orientation when his colleagues repeatedly referred to his being gay and engaged in banter even though all concerned knew he was not. The Court of Appeal by a majority decided that Parliament did not intend that a person had to declare their sexual orientation before bringing a claim.

To constitute harassment the action must be oppressive and unacceptable rather than **8.108** merely unattractive, unreasonable, or regrettable (*Veakins v Kier Islington Ltd* [2010] IRLR 132).

The creating of a hostile environment could take place over a period of time: third party **8.109** behaviour may have created it in part but the actions of the employer may make it worse, in which case it could be said to be 'created' by the actions of both and 'unwanted conduct' could include inaction, but it must in any event be an action which was taken on the relevant grounds (*Conteh v Parking Partners Ltd* [2011] ICR 341).

Intentional harassment

The offence of intentional harassment is found in s 4A of the Public Order Act 1986 which, **8.110** whilst wider in its terms, was intended to respond to concern over the increasing incidence of racial harassment. It renders a person guilty of an offence if he, with intent, causes another person harassment, alarm, or distress by using threatening, abusive, or insulting words or behaviour or disorderly conduct or by displaying any writing, sign, or other visible representation which is threatening, abusive, or insulting. It is a defence for an accused person to prove that his conduct was reasonable in all of the circumstances of the case. Incidents in the workplace are included within its scope and the offence carries a maximum penalty of six months' imprisonment or a fine not exceeding level 5. It is an arrestable offence.

Victimisation

By s 27(1): **8.111**

(1) A person (A) victimises another person (B) if A subjects B to a detriment because—

(a) B does a protected act, or

(b) A believes that B has done, or may do, a protected act.

Section 27(2) states that:

(2) Each of the following is a protected act—

(a) bringing proceedings under this Act;

(b) giving evidence or information in connection with proceedings under this Act;

(c) doing any other thing for the purposes of or in connection with this Act;

(d) making an allegation (whether or not express) that A or another person has contravened this Act.

By s 27(3), 'Giving false evidence or information, or making a false allegation, is not a protected act if the evidence or information is given, or the allegation is made, in bad faith.' A breach of an equality clause or rule is included in the definition (s 27(5)). It is also sufficient if the employer suspects one of these things.

8.112 In order to succeed in a claim of victimisation, the claimant must show that one of the acts in s 27(2)(a) to (d) above which is done by the claimant (such as bringing an earlier complaint of discrimination) has influenced the alleged victimiser in his unfavourable treatment of the claimant (*Aziz v Trinity Taxis Ltd* [1988] ICR 534). However, the House of Lords has made it clear that the alleged victimiser need not be 'consciously motivated' by the relevant issues (*Nagarajan v London Regional Transport* [1999] IRLR 572; also *Villalba v Merrill Lynch & Co Inc* [2006] IRLR 437).

8.113 Like other forms of discrimination, victimisation is not governed by the discriminator's motive or intention, so that there is no point in drawing a distinction between some-one's 'conscious' or 'unconscious' motivation. It is enough, the House of Lords observed, that one of the protected acts was an important cause of the less favourable treatment accorded to the person victimised. Thus, a refusal by a police force to give to an officer a reference when he applied to another force because he had a race discrimination com-plaint outstanding was not victimisation (*Chief Constable of West Yorkshire Police v Khan* [2001] IRLR 830; see also *Commissioners of Inland Revenue v Morgan* [2002] IRLR 776). The reference was not withheld 'by reason that' the claimant had brought discrimination proceedings, but rather because the employer temporarily needed to pre-serve his position in the outstanding proceedings. Lord Nicholls said that employers who acted 'honestly and reasonably in taking steps to preserve their position in pending dis-crimination proceedings' would 'not be doing so because of the fact that the complainant has brought discrimination proceedings but ... because currently and temporarily they need ... to take steps to preserve their position in the outstanding proceedings'. The spe-cific phrase now used in the EA 2010 is 'because of' but it is unlikely that this will make any difference to decisions. What is clear is that there is no need in a victimisation claim for a specific comparator.

8.114 The failure of the Equality Act 2010 to proscribe victimisation occurring after the termi-nation of employment was held to be an inadvertent drafting error by the Court of Appeal in *Rowstock Ltd v Jessemey* [2014] ICR 550. It was intended that it should have been covered so that words would be read in to accommodate it.

8.115 On the burden of proof and victimisation, see *Pothecary Witham Weld v Bullimore* [2010] IRLR 572.

'Transferred' or associative discrimination

8.116 The general definition of direct discrimination as less favourable treatment 'because of' the protected characteristic in the Equality Act 2010 is designed to make it clear that discrimination because of association with someone who has the protected characteristic or perception that he has the protected characteristic is covered. Under the pre-2010 law this was controversial but it was held that the prohibition included sacking an employee for serving a black customer (*Zarczynska v Levy* [1979] 1 All ER 814; see also *Showboat Entertainment Centre Ltd v Owens* [1984] IRLR 7; *Weathersfield Ltd v Sargent* [1999] IRLR 94; *Smyth v Croft Inns Ltd* [1996] IRLR 84; *Redfearn v Serco Ltd* [2006] IRLR 623; for fuller discussion see earlier editions of this work). This is also the case in EU law. In an important decision of the ECJ (which caused the consequential change in domestic law), *Coleman v Attridge Law* [2008] IRLR 722, it was held that discrimination against a person who cared for a disabled boy constituted discrimination on grounds of disability. The prohibition of direct discrimination on the grounds of disability is thus not limited only to those who are themselves disabled. The protected characteristic did not have to be enjoyed by the person who was the subject of the detrimental treatment, so that it might be of a person who was not the claimant but which was a company formed by the individual (*EAD Solicitors LLP v Garry Abrams Ltd* [2016] ICR 380; also *Thompson v London Central Bus Co Ltd* [2016] IRLR 9).

Having considered the forms of discrimination which are common to all the protected **8.117** characteristics, it is now necessary to discuss those which are limited to a single such characteristic.

Discrimination arising from disability

There are particular provisions applicable to the disabled designed to reverse the regres- **8.118** sive decision of the House of Lords in *Malcolm v Lewisham LBC* [2008] 1 AC 1399. Thus, the employee can claim not only where the discrimination arises by reason of the disability itself but something arising because of it, such as an employee becoming less productive or being off sick more often than other employees.

By s 15(1):

(1) A person (A) discriminates against a disabled person (B) if—
    (a) A treats B unfavourably because of something arising in consequence of B's disability, and
    (b) A cannot show that the treatment is a proportionate means of achieving a legitimate aim.

By s 15(2), 'Subsection (1) does not apply if A shows that A did not know, and could not reasonably have been expected to know, that B had the disability' (see *Gallop v Newport CC (No 2)* [2016] IRLR 395).

Enquiries about disability

There are also special provisions regarding enquiries which are made about disability and **8.119** health. By s 60:

(1) A person (A) to whom an application for work is made must not ask about the health of the applicant (B)—
    (a) before offering work to B, or
    (b) where A is not in a position to offer work to B, before including B in a pool of applicants from whom A intends (when in a position to do so) to select a person to whom to offer work.

Section 60(3) makes clear that 'A does not contravene a relevant disability provision merely by asking about B's health; but A's conduct in reliance on information given in response may be a contravention of a relevant disability provision.'

There is an exception by subsection (6) when: **8.120**

... a question that A asks in so far as asking the question is necessary for the purpose of—

(a) establishing whether B will be able to comply with a requirement to undergo an assessment or establishing whether a duty to make reasonable adjustments is or will be imposed on A in relation to B in connection with a requirement to undergo an assessment,
(b) establishing whether B will be able to carry out a function that is intrinsic to the work concerned,
(c) monitoring diversity in the range of persons applying to A for work,

(d) taking action to which section 158 would apply if references in that section to persons who share (or do not share) a protected characteristic were references to disabled persons (or persons who are not disabled) and the reference to the characteristic were a reference to disability, or

(e) if A applies in relation to the work a requirement to have a particular disability, establishing whether B has that disability.

Medical evidence on disability

8.121 A tribunal is under a duty to summarise and take into account medical evidence which is produced on behalf of the employee in its decision; and if it rejects that evidence, it must explain the reasons for that rejection (*Edwards v Mid Suffolk District Council* [2001] IRLR 190). General directions as to how medical evidence is to be treated in such claims were given in the EAT case of *De Keyser Ltd v Wilson* [2001] IRLR 324. These include that the joint instruction of a single expert is a preferred course; that any letter of instruction should specify in as much detail as can be given any particular questions which the expert is being invited to answer, or more general subjects which he is to be asked to address; and that such instructions should as far as possible avoid partisanship. It is wrong for the tribunal to refuse to make findings on expert medical evidence because it had not been before the employer at the time when it rejected the applicant for a position (*Surrey Police v Marshall* [2003] IRLR 843).

Reasonable adjustment discrimination

8.122 There are several statutory provisions to consider about the unusual form of reasonable adjustment discrimination. Unlike other aspects of discrimination the employer must take positive steps to accommodate disabled persons, in particular to ensure that they are not disadvantaged because workplaces and jobs are not adapted for them.

8.123 In s 20(2) the duty to make adjustments comprises the following three requirements:

(a) '... where a provision, criterion or practice of A's puts a disabled person at a substantial disadvantage in relation to a relevant matter in comparison with persons who are not disabled, to take such steps as it is reasonable to have to take to avoid the disadvantage'.

(b) '... where a physical feature puts a disabled person at a substantial disadvantage in relation to a relevant matter in comparison with persons who are not disabled, to take such steps as it is reasonable to have to take to avoid the disadvantage'.

(c) '... where a disabled person would, but for the provision of an auxiliary aid, be put at a substantial disadvantage in relation to a relevant matter in comparison with persons who are not disabled, to take such steps as it is reasonable to have to take to provide the auxiliary aid'.

8.124 By s 20(7), 'A person (A) who is subject to a duty to make reasonable adjustments is not (subject to express provision to the contrary) entitled to require a disabled person, in relation to whom A is required to comply with the duty, to pay to any extent A's costs of complying with the duty.'

8.125 Substantial disadvantage is defined by s 20(9) so that:

In relation to the second requirement [set out above], a reference in this section or an applicable Schedule to avoiding a substantial disadvantage includes a reference to—

(a) removing the physical feature in question,
(b) altering it, or
(c) providing a reasonable means of avoiding it.

(See also s 108(4).)

Schedule 8, para 20, says that the duty to make reasonable adjustments does not arise if **8.126** the person to whom it would apply 'does not know and could not reasonably be expected to know ... in the case of the applicant or potential applicant that an interested disabled person may be an applicant for the work in question'.

It is not possible to justify reasonable adjustment discrimination as it was before 2004. **8.127**

As a general summary, the Code of Practice provides that 'an employer must ... do all **8.128** they can reasonably be expected to do to find out whether a person is disabled' but that 'when making enquiries about disability, employers should consider issues of dignity and privacy and ensure that personal information is dealt with confidentially' (para 6.19).

These principles have been developed in the case law: **8.129**

(a) It is not necessary for a claimant to satisfy the tribunal that someone who does not have a disability but whose circumstances were otherwise the same as hers would have been treated differently (*Fareham College Corporation v Walters* [2009] IRLR 991).

(b) In order to find that there was a breach of a duty to make reasonable adjustments, the tribunal must find that there was a provision, criterion, or practice which placed a disabled person not simply at some disadvantage viewed generally but at a disadvantage which was substantial when viewed in comparison with persons who were not disabled. The focus was on the practical result of the measures that could be taken and not on the process or reasoning leading to the making or failure to make a reasonable adjustment (*RBS v Ashton* [2011] ICR 632; see also *Secretary of State for Work and Pensions v Alam* [2010] ICR 665; *Callaghan v Glasgow City Council* [2001] IRLR 724; *Johnson & Johnson Medical Ltd v Filmer* [2002] ICR 292; *Environment Agency v Rowan* [2008] IRLR 20; *Wright v Governing Body of Bilton High School* [2002] ICR 1463).

(c) It is, however, necessary to carry out a proper assessment of what needs to be done (*Mid Staffs General Hospitals NHS Trust v Cambridge* [2003] IRLR 566). The House of Lords saw this in terms of a duty positively to discriminate in *Archibald v Fife Council* [2004] IRLR 651. The claimant was a roadsweeper who was unable to walk because she suffered a complication after undergoing surgery. She applied for various office jobs but lost out because of her lack of relevant experience. It was held to be a reasonable adjustment for the employer to transfer her to an appropriate office job when it fell vacant without requiring her to compete with other candidates. The effect which the tribunal has to consider in assessing whether the reasonable adjustment 'would prevent the effect in question' is the placing of the claimant at a substantial disadvantage compared with an employee who is not disabled (*Johnson & Johnson Medical Ltd v Filmer* [2002] ICR 292). It was neither appropriate nor sufficient to ask (as did this tribunal) whether the adjustment 'would have prevented the effect on the applicant worsening' (on the burden of proof, see *Project Management Institute v Latif* [2007] IRLR 579).

A new post: The duty goes as far as the employer needing to consider creating a new post **8.130** for the disabled employee. *Southampton City College v Randall* [2006] IRLR 18 concerned a lecturer whose voice had broken down. The tribunal found that the employers had a duty to devise a job which would take account of the effects of the claimant's disability, and the EAT found that the Disability Discrimination Act 1995 (DDA 1995) did not as a matter of law preclude the creation of a new post in substitution for an existing post from being a reasonable adjustment. The employers should it was held have considered voice amplification as a reasonable adjustment. It may be a reasonable adjustment to swap jobs or even create a new post (*Chief Constable of South Yorkshire v Jelic* [2010] IRLR 744).

8.131 In an associated area, in order to determine whether frustration of contract applied, the tribunal must first consider whether the employer was in breach of the duty to make reasonable adjustments (*Warner v Armfield Retail & Leisure Ltd* [2014] ICR 239).

8.132 *Pay for sickness absence*: In *O'Hanlon v HM Revenue and Customs* [2007] IRLR 404, the claim was that the employee did not receive full pay for sickness absence, in particular after six months of absence. It was held not to be a reasonable adjustment to aggregate periods of illness or to make full payment. The employer need not disapply normal sick pay contractual rules for a disability-related absence.

8.133 The cost of an adjustment in itself may be sufficient to find an adjustment unreasonable (*Cordell v FCO* [2012] ICR 280). There is no objective measure of how much it is reasonable for the employer to be expected to spend; it is for the tribunal to make a judgement as to what it considers just and reasonable. The relevant considerations might include the size of any budget dedicated to reasonable adjustments, what the employer had spent in comparable situations, what other employers were prepared to spend, and any collective agreement or other indication of an appropriate level of expenditure by other representative organisations.

8.134 *Dismissal*: Employers must also observe the duty to make reasonable adjustments in the arrangements they make for dismissing (*Morse v Wiltshire County Council* [1998] IRLR 352). The test of reasonableness is directed at the steps to be taken to prevent the employment from having a detrimental effect upon the disabled employee (*Beart v HM Prison Service* [2003] IRLR 238).

8.135 *Monetary benefits*: The provision applies to monetary benefits as well as to other arrangements (*London Clubs Management Ltd v Hood* [2001] IRLR 723). 'Arrangement' could for example include a condition that the employee could carry a full service radiator cabinet (*Smith v Churchills Stairlifts plc* [2006] IRLR 41).

8.136 In *Kenny v Hampshire Constabulary* [1999] IRLR 76, the EAT decided that the duty did not, however, extend to providing a personal carer to help a worker to go to the lavatory. In its view, the duty related only to adjustments to the workplace or work practices, and not the provision of personal care to employees.

8.137 *Post Office v Jones* [2001] IRLR 34 was a landmark decision in that it raised the inter-relationship between the DDA 1995 and the employer's duties which might have criminal sanctions under the Health and Safety at Work etc Act (HSAWA) 1974. The HSAWA requires that a risk assessment be carried out, and the employer said that the terms of that risk assessment (in this case that a diabetic should be restricted from driving duties) should provide justification for its action in restricting driving for the purposes of the DDA 1995. The Court of Appeal said that Parliament did not intend to confer on employment tribunals the general powers which were used to decide whether the employer's assessment of risk is correct. The tribunal thus cannot go to the extent of disagreeing with a risk assessment which is properly conducted based on the properly formed opinion of suitably qualified doctors and which produces an answer which is not irrational. A reason may be material and substantial under the Act, and thus the defence of justification be made out, even if the tribunal would have come to a different decision as to the extent of the risk. A tribunal is also not permitted to make up its mind on justification on the basis of its own appraisal of the medical evidence and to conclude that the reason is not material or substantial, because the medical opinion on the basis of which the employer's decision was made is not to be treated as inferior to a different medical opinion expressed at the tribunal. The task is not very different from that which tribunals have to conduct in relation to unfair dismissal, coming within a range of reasonable responses approach (see also *Williams v J Walter Thompson Group Ltd* [2005] IRLR 376).

D THE SCOPE OF PROHIBITED DISCRIMINATION

The scope of unlawful discrimination is necessarily very widely drawn and naturally **8.138** encompasses every stage of employment.

The most general employment provisions are found in s 39. Section 39(1) states that: **8.139**

> (1) An employer (A) must not discriminate against a person (B)—
> (a) in the arrangements A makes for deciding to whom to offer employment;
> (b) as to the terms on which A offers B employment;
> (c) by not offering B employment.

Further, by s 39(2)

> (2) An employer (A) must not discriminate against an employee of A's (B)—
>
> (a) as to B's terms of employment;
> (b) in the way A affords B access, or by not affording B access, to opportunities for promotion, transfer or training or for receiving any other benefit, facility or service;
> (c) by dismissing B;
> (d) by subjecting B to any other detriment.

Arrangements for deciding to whom to offer employment

A claimant may claim if she or he is put off applying for a job by reason of, for example, **8.140** the way in which an interview is set up, the questions asked there, or being left off a shortlist (*Saunders v Richmond LBC* [1977] IRLR 362). This may include a volunteer training programme (*Murray v Newham CAB* [2001] ICR 708).

When a claimant became unable to walk after a rare complication of surgery, the employer **8.141** interviewed her for a sedentary post but chose to appoint a more qualified individual and dismissed her. This was held to be an 'arrangement' which qualified (*Archibald v Fife Council* [2004] IRLR 651 HL). It is no defence to such a claim that the employer has so made arrangements in order to keep an overall balance between the sexes. In *Brennan v J.H. Dewhurst Ltd* [1983] IRLR 357 a tribunal found that the conduct by the local manager of a butcher's shop at an interview suggested that he did not want a woman for the job on offer, but that there was no discrimination since no one had ultimately been appointed to the job. The EAT thought differently since the subsection covered the discriminatory operation of *arrangements* for selection as well as discriminatory *selection*. This is in line with EU case law. In *Centrum voor Gelijkheid van Kansen en voor Racismebestrijding v Firma Feryn NV* [2008] IRLR 732, the ECJ held that a statement by an employer that it would not recruit employees of a certain ethnic or racial origin constituted direct discrimination. Such a public declaration is clearly likely strongly to dissuade certain candidates from applying for jobs.

Not offering employment

This is one of the few areas where a *potential* employee can complain of discrimination. **8.142**

Opportunities for promotion, transfer, or training

Example Harry, a West Indian, proves to be an excellent delicatessen manager but Eric **8.143** refuses to promote him to be assistant manager of the store because he fears that some employees might object. This is prima facie direct discrimination in access to promotion.

Differentiation in this respect is generally unlawful, but there is a defence to an action **8.144** where the employer is taking steps to train minorities and the racial group favoured has been under-represented in the company during any time in the previous twelve months.

Contract workers

8.145 By s 41(1):

> (1) A principal must not discriminate against a contract worker—
>
>   (a) as to the terms on which the principal allows the worker to do the work;
>   (b) by not allowing the worker to do, or to continue to do, the work;
>   (c) in the way the principal affords the worker access, or by not affording the worker access, to opportunities for receiving a benefit, facility or service;
>   (d) by subjecting the worker to any other detriment.

8.146 This is necessary because normally it is the client company for whom the 'temp' works (although he is employed by the agency) that has the scope for discrimination. It is not, however, sufficient under this head that work is done by one person for the benefit of another unless there is an *undertaking* to support the work. It thus does not include a taxi owners' collective, which patrons phone to ask for a taxi (*Rice v Fon-a-Car* [1980] ICR 133) and probably not Uber. However, it might include individuals working in concessions inside a department store (*Harrods Ltd v Remick* [1998] ICR 156; see also *Jones v Friends Provident Life Office* [2004] IRLR 783).

Dismissal

8.147 If an employee is dismissed solely because of his colour, or if two employees have stolen from the employer and one culprit is white and one black, but only the black person is dismissed, the latter may have a claim. Normally it would be easier to claim unfair dismissal, but an employee might not be qualified to do so because he has not served for a sufficient period of continuous employment. Further, there is no upper limit on compensation in discrimination claims. Recommendations also may be made by the employment tribunal to prevent such acts in the future in discrimination cases (but not in unfair dismissal).

8.148 Constructive dismissal is included within the term 'dismissal' in the Equality Act (*Derby Specialist Fabrication Ltd v Burton* [2001] IRLR 69).

Any other detriment

8.149 Although 'detriment' is a word of deliberately wide import and this is a residual subsection, some action is clearly too insignificant to fall within its scope. There have been several cases on the meaning of detriment. In *Ministry of Defence v Jeremiah* [1979] IRLR 436, where the requirement that men undertake particularly dirty work was sufficient, Brandon LJ paraphrased the word to mean 'putting under a disadvantage'. It was irrelevant that the employer paid an extra 4p an hour to compensate for the dirty work, since it could not thus 'buy' a right to discriminate. In *Peake v Automotive Products Ltd*, as already mentioned, the Court of Appeal decided that the rule allowing women to leave five minutes early was not serious enough and this *ratio* survives the overruling of most of the decision in the later Court of Appeal decision in *Jeremiah*.

8.150 In *St Helens MBC v Derbyshire* [2007] ICR 841, it was held that 'distress and worry' that might be induced by an employer's honest and reasonable conduct in the course of his defence or in the conduct of any settlement negotiations would not normally constitute detriment. The question whether there was detriment was to be determined primarily from the perspective of the alleged victim. It was held that for the Council, which was engaged in equal pay litigation involving catering staff, to point out that a successful claim was likely to lead to the cost of school meals rising to such an extent that the Council would have to cease providing them, went further than was reasonable in protecting its interests in litigation. Lord Neuberger said that the main focus of the tribunal in such a case should be on the question whether those who were claiming victimisation had been subjected to detriment. This was to be decided by reference to the viewpoint of a 'reasonable worker'. While 'distress and worry which may be induced by the employer's honest and reasonable conduct in the course of his defence or in the conduct of any settlement negotiations cannot ... constitute "detriment"' save in exceptional circumstances.

In *Cordant Security Ltd v Singh* [2016] IRLR 4, the EAT held that it was inappropriate for a tribunal to find that there was discrimination when the employer had failed to investigate the employee's fabricated racial abuse allegation. The employee could not in truth demonstrate any detriment in this situation; a sense of grievance or injustice was insufficient. He had not suffered any substantive disadvantage by the allegation not being investigated as if it had been considered it would have been found to be untrue. **8.151**

In order to qualify as a detriment, it must be such that a reasonable worker by reason of the acts complained of takes the view that he was thereby disadvantaged in the way in which he would have to work (*De Souza v Automobile Association* [1986] IRLR 103). It does not, however, have to amount to a constructive dismissal so as to qualify. It is also not restricted to 'an occasion connected with the dismissal or during disciplinary proceedings' (*Kapur v Barclays Bank* [1991] ICR 208). **8.152**

The House of Lords in *Shamoon v Chief Constable of the RUC* [2003] ICR 337 formulated the proposition that if a reasonable worker would or might take the view that the treatment accorded to her had in all the circumstances been to her detriment it was not necessary to demonstrate some physical or economic consequences. Chief Inspector Shamoon was thus found to have suffered a detriment when after complaints about her behaviour in carrying out her role in the appraisal of staff, her counselling responsibilities for staff were taken from her. **8.153**

The following have also been found to amount to detriments: **8.154**

(a) transfer to a less interesting job (*Kirby v Manpower Services Commission* [1980] IRLR 229);
(b) failure to investigate an allegation of discrimination (*Eke v Commissioners of Customs and Excise* [1981] IRLR 334);
(c) a restriction on females standing at the bar of a Fleet Street wine bar (*Gill and Coote v El Vinos Co Ltd* [1983] IRLR 206);
(d) when, for reasons connected with her ethnic origins, an investigation by the employer into the employee's activities was continued longer than an ordinary investigation would have been, even though she was unaware that the investigation was continuing (*Garry v London Borough of Ealing* [2001] IRLR 681).

On the other hand, there was *no* detriment within the Act when: **8.155**

(a) a local authority refused to permit a woman librarian to job share, since job sharing was not available to any librarians (*Clymo v London Borough of Wandsworth* [1989] ICR 250);
(b) there were transitory hurt feelings but no more (*Jiad v Byford* [2003] IRLR 232);

(c) The outing that someone was gay when he had previously made known his homo-
sexuality in a different office of the same employer (*Land Registry v Grant* [2011]
ICR 1390).

(d) Adopting an aggressive stance on costs because there was no detriment beyond what
was properly involved in the honest and reasonable conduct of a case for the respondent (*Bird v Sylvester* [2008] IRLR 232; see also *HM Prison Service v Ibimidin* [2008]
IRLR 940).

Exceptions

8.156 There are exceptions under Sch 9 para 1(1) so that:

(1) A person (A) does not contravene a provision ... by applying in relation to work a requirement to have a particular protected characteristic, if A shows that, having regard to the
nature or context of the work—

(a) it is an occupational requirement,

(b) the application of the requirement is a proportionate means of achieving a legitimate
aim, and

(c) the person to whom A applies the requirement does not meet it (or A has reasonable
grounds for not being satisfied that the person meets it).

There are then special provisions for religious requirements relating to sex, marriage etc,
and sexual orientation, so that by para 2:

(1) A person (A) does not contravene a provision mentioned in sub-paragraph (2) by applying in relation to employment a requirement to which sub-paragraph (4) applies if
A shows that—

(a) the employment is for the purposes of an organised religion,

(b) the application of the requirement engages the compliance or non-conflict
principle, and

(c) the person to whom A applies the requirement does not meet it (or A has reasonable
grounds for not being satisfied that the person meets it).

Further, by subsection (3):

(3) A person does not contravene section 53(1) or (2)(a) or (b) by applying in relation to a
relevant qualification (within the meaning of that section) a requirement to which sub-
paragraph (4) applies if the person shows that—

(a) the qualification is for the purposes of employment mentioned in sub-paragraph (1)
(a), and

(b) the application of the requirement engages the compliance or non-conflict principle.

By para 2(4) the provision applies to these requirements:

- to be of a particular sex;
- not to be a transsexual person;
- not to be married or a civil partner;
- not to be married to, or the civil partner of, a person who has a living former spouse
or civil partner;
- relating to circumstances in which a marriage or civil partnership came to an end;
- related to sexual orientation.

8.157 The law is unclear where the discrimination is applied on the basis of the identity of the
individual's spouse or partner. A Jewish organisation, for example, may require its rab-
bis and religious teachers to be Jewish but it would be hard pressed to make the same
requirement of cleaners, social workers, or teachers in a Jewish school of subjects other
than religion because religious beliefs are not necessary to be congruent to the employer's.

By para 2(5), 'The application of a requirement engages the compliance principle if the **8.158** requirement is applied so as to comply with the doctrines of the religion.'

The principle of non-conflict with the religious doctrines is engaged 'if, because of the **8.159** nature or context of the employment, the requirement is applied so as to avoid conflict-ing with the strongly held religious convictions of a significant number of the religion's followers' (para 6).

Further, by para 3: **8.160**

> 3 A person (A) with an ethos based on religion or belief does not contravene a provision
> ... by applying in relation to work a requirement to be of a particular religion or belief
> if A shows that, having regard to that ethos and to the nature or context of the work—
> (a) it is an occupational requirement,
> (b) the application of the requirement is a proportionate means of achieving a legitimate
> aim, and
> (c) the person to whom A applies the requirement does not meet it (or A has reasonable
> grounds for not being satisfied that the person meets it).

There is a positive obligation under the Act to make reasonable adjustments, which **8.161** includes allowing disabled persons to trump applicants for other jobs even if they were not the best candidate provided that they were suitable to do that work.

E CLAIMANTS AND RESPONDENTS

Relationships which have ended

By s 108 of the Equality Act 2010: **8.162**

> (1) A person (A) must not discriminate against another (B) if—
> (a) the discrimination arises out of and is closely connected to a relationship which used
> to exist between them, and
> (b) conduct of a description constituting the discrimination would, if it occurred during
> the relationship, contravene this Act.

This is extended to harassment. It even applies to relationships which ended before the Equality Act came into force (subsection 3).

Respondents

Secondary liability

It is natural that the employer is made liable for acts of the employee (s 109) and similarly **8.163** a principal for an agent (s 109(2)) and this is decreed regardless of knowledge or approval (subsection 3). It is, however, a defence (subsection 4):

> ... for B to show that B took all reasonable steps to prevent A—
> (a) from doing that thing, or
> (b) from doing anything of that description.

A person also must not instruct or induce another to do an act contravening the Act **8.164** (s 111(1)). This extends to an attempt to cause or induce the person to do so (s 111(8)). The same applies to aiding a contravention (s 112).

The arc of potential liability is thus wide. 'Aiding' has no technical meaning and connotes **8.165** the help and assistance which is given to one person by another, whether or not that help was substantial and productive, provided it was not negligible (*Anyanwu v South Bank*

Student Union [2001] ICR 391; *Allaway v Reilly* [2007] IRLR 864). In order to 'aid' discrimination a person must, however, have done more than merely create an environment in which discrimination can occur, according to *Gilbank v Miles* [2006] IRLR 538. The employer could be responsible for aiding even if the employer itself were not liable (*Hurst v Kelly* [2013] ICR 1225).

8.166   An individual may also be personally liable for acts of discrimination committed by him in the course of employment against a fellow employee even though he was not that employee's employer and even though the employer was held not to be vicariously liable for his conduct. He might be found to have 'knowingly' aided the unlawful act by the employer (*Yeboah v Crofton* [2002] IRLR 634).

8.167   As to inducement, in *Commission for Racial Equality v Imperial Society of Teachers of Dancing* [1983] IRLR 315, the EAT decided that the words 'procure' and 'attempt to procure' should be construed widely and included the use of words that brought about a certain course of action. 'Inducement' means to persuade, or to prevail upon, or bring about. It declared to be unlawful a request by the respondent's secretary in charge of records to the head of careers of a local school not to send along for an assignment a 'coloured person' since that person 'would feel out of place as there were no black employees'.

8.168   The term 'in the course of his employment' is flexible and should be interpreted according to its natural everyday meaning and not by reference to the complex common law concept of vicarious liability (*Jones v Tower Boot Co Ltd* [1997] ICR 254). It will not cover discrimination perpetrated in a purely social context, but may include a work-related social environment, such as an office party (eg *Waters v Commissioner of Police of the Metropolis* [1997] ICR 1073; *Chief Constable of Lincolnshire Police v Stubbs* [1999] IRLR 81) or an assault during a works family day out at Thorpe Park (*Sidhu v Aerospace Composite Technology Ltd* [2001] ICR 167).

8.169   As to taking 'such steps as were reasonably practicable to prevent the employee from doing that act, or from doing in the ... course of his employment acts of that description', in *Canniffe v East Riding of Yorkshire Council* [2000] IRLR 555, the employment tribunal had decided that there was nothing that the employer could have done to have stopped its employee from sexually assaulting the claimant. This was not the proper approach according to the EAT, which was rather to identify, first, whether the employer took any steps at all to prevent the employee from doing the act or acts complained of in the course of his employment; and, secondly, having identified what steps, if any, it took, to consider whether there were any further steps that it could have taken which were reasonably practicable. Whether taking such steps would have been successful in preventing the acts of discrimination is not determinative, although it may be relevant (see also *Balgobin v London Borough of Tower Hamlets* [1987] IRLR 401; *Croft v Royal Mail Group Ltd* [2003] IRLR 592).

8.170   The prohibitions extend beyond *employers* to other providers of services:

  (a) By s 55:

      (1) A person (an employment service-provider) concerned with the provision of an employment service must not discriminate against a person—
        (a) in the arrangements the service-provider makes for selecting persons to whom to provide, or to whom to offer to provide, the service;
        (b) as to the terms on which the service-provider offers to provide the service to the person;
        (c) by not offering to provide the service to the person.

(b) By s 96(1) and (2), qualifications bodies must not discriminate:

   (1) A qualifications body (A) must not discriminate against a person (B)—
      (a) in the arrangements A makes for deciding upon whom to confer a relevant qualification;
      (b) as to the terms on which it is prepared to confer a relevant qualification on B;
      (c) by not conferring a relevant qualification on B.
   (2) A qualifications body (A) must not discriminate against a person (B) upon whom A has conferred a relevant qualification—
      (a) by withdrawing the qualification from B;
      (b) by varying the terms on which B holds the qualification;
      (c) by subjecting B to any other detriment.

Appeals by complainants must be made in this case to the normal appeal body for the body, for example, the High Court in the case of the General Medical Council, and not to tribunals or the ordinary civil courts. It does not extend to a political party since the party's activities were for its own political purposes (*Ali v McDonagh* [2002] ICR 1026). An application for admission to a set of chambers as a pupil was also not an application for membership of a trade organisation (*1 Pump Court Tax Chambers v Horton*, The Times, 30 August 2004).

(c) *The Crown* is dealt with by s 205 of the EA 2010, but this does not extend to the selection of justices of the peace (*Knight v Attorney-General* [1979] ICR 194; *Arthur v Attorney-General* [1999] ICR 631), or rent officers (*Department of the Environment v Fox* [1979] ICR 736). A special policeman is covered (*Sheikh v Chief Constable of Greater Manchester Police* [1989] 2 All ER 684). Special procedural provisions apply to discrimination claims brought by members of the armed forces.

(d) *Barristers* are included by s 47.

There is a controversial area of exclusion where a person sits in a quasi-judicial capacity. **8.171** In *Heath v Metropolitan Police Commissioner* [2005] ICR 329, there was an allegation by a civilian employee that a police inspector had sexually assaulted her. The Commissioner appointed an all-male board under the Police (Discipline) Regulations 1985 and a complaint was brought of sex discrimination. The tribunal held that it had no jurisdiction to hear the complaint since it involved judicial or quasi-judicial proceedings which were immune from suit. This was upheld by the Court of Appeal. The question to be asked was whether the body was recognised by law, considered an issue akin to that of the courts, whether its procedures were akin to the courts, and whether the result of its procedures led to a binding determination of the civil rights of the party. The same applied to a police misconduct panel in *P v Commissioner of Police for the Metropolis* [2016] IRLR 301; see also *Lake v BTP* [2007] ICR 301).

F 'REVERSE DISCRIMINATION'

Normally, as already stated, the motive of the respondent (good or bad) for the act of **8.172** discrimination does not matter, and differentiation on the prohibited grounds is unlawful whatever the underlying reason and however benign the purpose behind it. However, the discrimination legislation was introduced on both sides of the Atlantic in order to improve the position of ethnic minority groups and women. In recognition of this, the US statutes contain power to decree affirmative action to promote the hiring of a particular under-represented race or sex until a fixed quota is reached. Moreover, private schemes of a similar nature were upheld in the important case of *Regents of the University of California v Bakke* 438 US 265 (1978) as long as the quotas were not too rigid.

8.173 There is a form of positive discrimination in the disability provisions in that there is no equivalence of the non-disabled with disabled and there is the need for reasonable adjustments to be made. There are also more general provisions, however.

By s 158:

(1) This section applies if a person (P) reasonably thinks that—
   (a) persons who share a protected characteristic suffer a disadvantage connected to the characteristic,
   (b) persons who share a protected characteristic have needs that are different from the needs of persons who do not share it, or
   (c) participation in an activity by persons who share a protected characteristic is disproportionately low.
(2) This Act does not prohibit P from taking any action which is a proportionate means of achieving the aim of—
   (a) enabling or encouraging persons who share the protected characteristic to overcome or minimise that disadvantage,
   (b) meeting those needs, or
   (c) enabling or encouraging persons who share the protected characteristic to participate in that activity.

Subsection (6) states, however, that 'This section does not enable P to do anything that is prohibited by or under an enactment other than this Act.'

Section 159 deals with recruitment and promotion so that:

(1) This section applies if a person (P) reasonably thinks that—
   (a) persons who share a protected characteristic suffer a disadvantage connected to the characteristic, or
   (b) participation in an activity by persons who share a protected characteristic is disproportionately low.
(2) Part 5 (work) does not prohibit P from taking action within subsection (3) with the aim of enabling or encouraging persons who share the protected characteristic to—
   (a) overcome or minimise that disadvantage, or
   (b) participate in that activity.

Subsection 4(b) says that the provision applies only where the person relying on it 'does not have a policy of treating persons who share the protected characteristic more favourably in connection with recruitment or promotion than persons who do not share it.'

G ENFORCEMENT MECHANISMS

Individual complaint

8.174 An individual's claim for any type of discrimination must be presented to an employment tribunal within three months of the act complained of, unless the tribunal considers it just and equitable to extend the limit (EA 2010, ss 118, 123, 140). The power to extend time is rather wider than the analogous provision in respect of unfair dismissal (12.06–12.27). It is, however, the exception rather than the rule (*Robertson v Bexley Community Centre* [2003] IRLR 434; *DCA v Jones* [2008] IRLR 128). In *Hutchison v Westward TV Ltd* [1977] ICR 279, the EAT emphasised the width of the discretion so provided, and 'deprecated [the] very simple wide words becoming encrusted by barnacles of authority'. The EAT would interfere only if the decision of the employment tribunal was wrong in law or perverse. It was not a general principle that it was just and equitable to extend time for presenting a discrimination complaint because the employee was pursuing an appeal against dismissal (*Robinson v Post Office* [2000] IRLR 804). This was just one of the matters to be taken into account in making an overall assessment of the facts (also *Rathakrishnan v Pizza Express (Restaurants) Ltd* [2016] ICR 283).

The relevant time thus runs in the normal case from the date of the act of discrimination **8.175** which is complained of, but this is not always easy to identify. In a discriminatory dismissal case, the 'act complained of' arose when the claimant found himself out of a job rather than the date on which he was given notice (*Lupetti v Wrens Old House Ltd* [1984] ICR 348; *Gloucester Working Men's Club & Institute v James* [1986] ICR 603; see also *Adlam v Salisbury and Wells Theological College* [1985] ICR 786). The continuing failure of the employer to prevent racial abuse and discrimination was an act extending over a period (*Derby Specialist Fabricators Ltd v Burton* [2001] ICR 833). Extension of time was allowed when it was at a much later date found out there had been discrimination in connection with appointment nine years before (*Southwark LBC v Afolabi* [2003] ICR 800).

There are further provisions as to the scope of the act complained of. By s 140(3) of the **8.176** EA 2010:

(a) conduct extending over a period is to be treated as done at the end of the period;
(b) failure to do something is to be treated as occurring when the person in question decided on it.

The following principles have been established in the case law as to the act complained **8.177** of from which the time is measured (now slightly changed to 'the act in respect of which complaint is made' in the Equality Act 2010):

(a) there is an important distinction drawn between a one-off act of discrimination and a continuing discriminatory arrangement. In *Kapur v Barclays Bank* [1989] IRLR 57, East African Asians who were first employed by Barclays Bank in 1970 alleged that the bank discriminated against them by refusing to credit their African service for pension purposes, whereas the past service of those of European origin was so credited. The EAT, however, held that such discrimination was an act which was done in 1970; but this was overturned by the Court of Appeal ([1989] IRLR 387, whose conclusion was itself upheld by the House of Lords [1991] IRLR 137). A job applicant cannot complain of a policy of continuing discrimination extending over a period (*Tyagi v BBC World Service* [2001] IRLR 465). The refusal of his application is a one-off event. There may be an act extending over a period notwithstanding that the claimant had been off work sick for twelve months prior to her tribunal complaint. There was according to the Court of Appeal (*Hendricks v Commissioner of Police for the Metropolis* [2003] IRLR 96) no warrant for the tribunal to concentrate on whether the concepts of a policy, rule, scheme, regime, or practice as such, applied in accordance with which decisions affecting the treatment of workers are taken fitted the facts of the case. They were merely examples of when an act extends over a period and should not be treated as a complete and constricting statement of the indicia of such an act. Instead, the focus should be on the substance of the complaints that the respondent was responsible for an ongoing situation or continuing state of affairs in which female ethnic minority officers were treated less favourably. The question was whether there was such an act as distinct from a succession of unconnected or isolated specific acts for which time would begin to run from the date when each specific act was committed.
(b) Where an employee brings an *appeal* against dismissal, the date will be that act, which is not necessarily the same as the effective date of termination for unfair dismissal

purposes (*Adekeye v Post Office* [1993] IRLR 324). Time does not run in respect of a discriminatory dismissal claim until the notice of dismissal expires and the employment ceases (*British Gas Services Ltd v McCaull* [2001] IRLR 60).

(c) When the complaint is based upon *omitting to offer* to a person employment, the act complained of cannot arise until the alleged discriminator is in a position to offer such employment (*Swithland Motors plc v Clarke* [1994] ICR 231).

(d) Where a discrimination complaint is based on the *denial of a particular benefit*, the employee may be able in effect to reactivate the time limit by making another request for the benefit in question. The time limit will then begin to run again from the date on which the latest request is refused (*Rovenska v General Medical Council* [1997] IRLR 367).

(e) *Clarke v Hampshire Electro-Plating Co Ltd* [1992] ICR 312 illustrates a common scenario in which the employee is aware or suspicious of the act of which he complains within three months of it occurring but does not have *evidence* that it was actually a discriminatory act until a later date, when a person of another sex or race is appointed to the relevant position. In such a case, time starts to run from the date of that person's appointment, or whatever else may be the triggering event.

(f) In respect of an unsuccessful *application for promotion* the relevant act is the date when the decision was taken to reject the internal appeal rather than the following day when he was notified of it; an act is done when it is completed (*Virdi v Commissioner of Police of the Metropolis* [2007] IRLR 24).

Problems of proof

8.178 In many ways, the claimant in discrimination cases is like a fettered runner. Those who are most prone to suffer acts of racial discrimination, for example, are likely to have language difficulties, and may find the legal system to be a hostile maze. Legal aid is not available. Application and success rates compare most unfavourably with the analogous jurisdiction in unfair dismissal cases and American experience of not dissimilar provisions (see Lustgarten (1977) 6 ILJ 212).

Burden of proof and inferences

8.179 Those alleging discrimination are sometimes met by a smokescreen defence and all sorts of alternative and spurious reasons put forward for the less favourable treatment that has been meted out. In order to reflect this fact and to implement the European Directive on the burden of proof in cases of discrimination based on sex (79/80), the burden of proof in discrimination cases was amended by statutory instruments. The position is now found in s 136 of the EA 2010, which provides that where the complaint is that the respondent has committed unlawful discrimination or an act of harassment, and the complainant proves facts from which the tribunal or court *could conclude in the absence of an adequate explanation* that the respondent has committed such an act of discrimination or an act of harassment, the tribunal shall uphold the complaint unless the respondent proves that he did not commit the act.

8.180 Proof is often found in drawing inferences from the established facts. Important guidance on the changed burden of proof was promulgated in *Barton v Investec Ltd* [2003] IRLR 332 which drew support from *King* and included these principles:

(4) It is important to remember that the outcome will usually depend on what inferences it is proper to draw from the primary facts ...

(5) these inferences can include in appropriate cases any inferences that it is just and equitable to draw ... from an evasive or equivocal reply to a questionnaire

(12) Since the facts necessary to prove an explanation would normally be in the possession of the respondent, [a tribunal] would normally expect cogent evidence to discharge that burden of proof.

(See also *Dresdner Kleinwort Wasserstein Ltd v Adebayo* [2005] IRLR 514 cf *Network Rail Infrastructure Ltd v Griffiths-Henry* [2006] IRLR 865.)

One of the guidelines was slightly modified by the EAT in *Chamberlain Solicitors v* **8.181** *Emokpae* [2004] IRLR 592 so that it read that 'To discharge the burden on the employer the respondent must prove on the balance of probabilities that the treatment was not significantly influenced on the grounds of sex.'

It is also important to note that the tribunal must first arrive at a conclusion that there **8.182** is a prima facie case that the respondent has treated the applicant less favourably on the prohibited grounds before the burden is inverted (*University of Huddersfield v Wolff* [2004] IRLR 534). Thus, the burden of proof does not shift at such stage as the claimant establishes a difference in status and in treatment. Those bare facts only indicate a *possibility* of discrimination and are not sufficient that a tribunal 'could conclude' that on a balance of probabilities the respondent had committed an unlawful act of discrimination.

The leading case is now *Igen Ltd v Wong* [2005] ICR 931, where the Court of Appeal **8.183** decided that it is for the claimant to prove on the balance of probabilities facts from which the employment tribunal could conclude in the absence of an adequate explanation that the employer has committed an act of discrimination. Whether the claimant has proved such facts will usually depend on what inferences it is proper to draw from the primary facts found by the tribunal. The burden of proof then moves to the employer, and it is for the employer (or other respondent) to prove that he did not commit the act by proving on the balance of probabilities that the treatment was in no sense whatsoever on the ground of sex. A tribunal is thus required to assess not merely whether the employer has proved an explanation for the facts from which the inferences can be drawn, but whether it is adequate to discharge the burden of proof on the balance of probabilities that sex (or some other protected characteristic) was not a ground for the treatment in question. It was not enough to found discrimination that the employee had been treated badly or with incompetence and insensitivity (*HM Prison Service v Johnson* [2007] IRLR 951).

The words 'could conclude' in the statutory formulation meant 'a reasonable tribunal could **8.184** properly conclude' from all the evidence before it (*Madarassy v Nomura International plc* [2007] IRLR 246; see also *Brown v LB of Croydon* [2007] IRLR 259; *Appiah v Governing Body of Bishop Douglass RC High School* [2007] IRLR 264). Unfair treatment was, however, not enough to displace the burden of proof (*BMA v Chaudhary* [2007] IRLR 800). It should be noted that the inversion of the burden of proof does not apply to claims of race victimisation (*Oyarce v Cheshire CC* [2008] IRLR 653).

The scope of the inquiry

The nature of the evidence that may be relevant to a discrimination claim is potentially **8.185** very wide. In the important decision of *Anya v University of Oxford* [2001] IRLR 377, the Court of Appeal said that evidence that one or more members of a selection panel were not unbiased, or that equal opportunities procedures were not used when they should have been, may point to the possibility of conscious or unconscious racial bias having entered into the process. It is impossible to consider the drawing of relevant inferences without making some findings of primary fact. It is the task of the tribunal in the first instance not simply to set out relevant evidential issues but to follow them through to a reasoned conclusion, except to the extent that they become otiose; and if they do become otiose, the tribunal needs to say why they are so. It was not sufficient in *Anya* that the tribunal said that race did not play any significant role in the selection decision because it accepted as truthful the evidence of the claimant's supervisor and member of the interview panel that his reasons for not choosing the claimant were to do entirely with the genuine assessment of his strengths and weaknesses. The Court of Appeal stressed that the credibility of the relevant witnesses is not necessarily the end of the road since the witness may be credible, honest, and yet mistaken. It is precisely because a witness, who by himself comes across as essentially truthful, may be shown by documentary evidence or by inconsistency to be less reliable than he seems that the totality of the evidence has to be evaluated. In the present case there was no useful way of approaching the totality except through its constituent parts. The tribunal, for example, had (a) failed to record such inferences or conclusions as it should have reached from the fact that, in breach of the University's policy, no person specification was drawn up until minutes before the interview and no references were taken up on the candidates; (b) erred in directing itself that if an employer behaves unreasonably towards a black employee, it is not to be inferred without more evidence that the reason for this is attributable to the employee's colour in that the employer might very well behave in a similarly unreasonable fashion to a white employee. Instead, such hostility may justify an inference of racial bias if there is nothing else to explain it. Whether there was an explanation such as that posited by the tribunal will depend not upon the theoretical possibility that the employer behaves badly to employees of all races but on evidence that he does.

8.186 There was, however, soon an important corrective to the wide scope of *Anya*. In *Miriki v Bar Council* [2002] ICR 505, the Court of Appeal stated that the tribunal was *not* required to make express findings on *every* piece of circumstantial evidence, however peripheral to the case brought, merely because the claimant chose to make it the subject of complaint.

8.187 Importantly, a tribunal is not entitled to draw an inference of discrimination from the mere fact that the employer has treated the employee unreasonably. Elias J held in *The Law Society v Bahl* [2003] IRLR 640 that all unlawful discriminatory treatment is unreasonable but not all unreasonable treatment is discriminatory. The fact that the victim is black or a woman does no more than raise the possibility that the employer could have been influenced by unlawful discriminatory considerations. Absent some independent evidence supporting the conclusion that this was indeed the reason, no finding of discrimination may be made. A tribunal must ensure that it has taken into consideration all potentially relevant non-discriminatory factors which might realistically explain the conduct of the alleged discriminator.

8.188 In the case of sexual orientation, statements suggestive of the existence of a homophobic recruitment policy which were made by a person appearing to play a leading role in the management of a football club but who did not have the actual legal capacity to determine its recruitment policy were capable of constituting 'facts from which it may be presumed that there has been ... discrimination' within Art 10 of Directive 2000/78. An employer's failure clearly to distance itself from such discriminatory statements was a factor which could be taken into account in assessing the facts (*Asociaţia ACCEPT v Consiliul Naţional pentru Combaterea Discriminării* [2013] ICR 938).

Statistical evidence

8.189 In the USA, 'statistics speak loudly, and the courts listen' is an oft-repeated *dictum*. They are accepted as of great significance in both class and individual actions brought under the Civil Rights Act 1964. The demonstration of a large disparity between the number of females or members of minority groups in a work force and the local or national population establishes a prima facie case (*Kaplan v International Alliance of Theatrical Operatives*, 525 F(2d) 1354); while in some cases, statistics have been held 'dispositive' of the whole case.

Jalota v IMI [1979] IRLR 313 appeared to close the door on the effective use of statis-   **8.190**
tics in direct discrimination cases. The Indian applicant claimed that, although amongst payroll employees in the respondent's rolled mill division there were a number of black employees, only one or two minority workers had succeeded on the staff side for which he was applying. He thus sought, among other things, information on the race, colour, and ethnic origins of other applicants for the position in question, and the number of black persons employed at the date when he submitted his application. Talbot J thought that such revelation could not be directly relevant; the claim was 'wholly unreasonable, irrelevant and should not be answered'. Instead he commended the respondent for not categorising the colour of its employees. He inquired, 'What could be more undesirable and more divisive than keeping such records?'

Jalota was disapproved in *West Midlands Passenger Transport Executive v Singh* [1988]   **8.191**
ICR 614. The Court of Appeal held that statistical material might establish a discernible pattern of treatment by the employer towards a racial group from which an employment tribunal could infer that discrimination had been the effective cause of the applicant's failure to (in this case) obtain promotion. It might also assist the applicant to rebut the employer's contention that it *in fact* operated an equal opportunities policy (see also *Carrington v Helix Lighting Ltd* [1990] IRLR 6).

Relevant evidence

The circumstances from which inferences of discrimination may be drawn are wide and var-   **8.192**
ied. The EAT decided in *Chattopadhay v Holloway School* [1981] IRLR 487 that evidence of events which were *subsequent* to the discrimination complained of should be admitted where these are logically probative. Here it satisfied the test, since the claimant sought to bring evidence of his treatment after he was turned down for the post of Head of History at the respondent school, to prove that his previous treatment was racially motivated, but Browne-Wilkinson J counselled against his judgment being taken as a charter for the wholesale introduction of irrelevant evidence. The tribunal is entitled to consider evidence about the conduct of the alleged discriminator before and after the act of which complaint is made so that the total picture is looked at (*Rihal v LB of Ealing* [2004] IRLR 642).

Remedies

An employment tribunal which upholds a complaint under the Equality Act may grant   **8.193**
three types of remedies. First, it may make a *declaration of the rights* of the parties (EA, s 124(2)(a)). The other two remedies dealt with here are a recommendation and compensation.

Recommendation

By s 124(3):   **8.194**

> ... a recommendation [may be made] that within a specified period the respondent takes specified steps for the purpose of obviating or reducing the adverse effect of any matter to which the proceedings relate—
>
> (a) on the complainant;
> (b) on any other person.

Subsection 7 supplements this as follows:

If a respondent fails, without reasonable excuse, to comply with an appropriate recommendation in so far as it relates to the complainant, the tribunal may—

(a) if an order was made under subsection (2)(b), increase the amount of compensation to be paid;
(b) if no such order was made, make one.

By s 2 of the Deregulation Act 2015, the tribunal may make recommendations only that bear on the complainant and not the wider workforce.

8.195 The recommendation cannot be used to 'top up' compensation as the employment tribunal appeared to suggest it could in *Irvine v Prestcold Ltd* [1981] IRLR 281, when it recommended an increase in wages to the claimant who had been discriminated against by not being promoted. The tribunal also cannot recommend *positive* action. The following cases illustrate the use of this remedy:

(a) in *Ministry of Defence v Jeremiah* [1980] ICR 13, the suggestion that the employer provide showers for women was overturned;
(b) in *Bayoomi v British Railways Board* [1981] IRLR 431, the employment tribunal refused to make a general recommendation affecting the employer's recruitment policies on the ground that it could only obviate or reduce the adverse effect on the applicant; instead, it decreed the entry of a reference on the applicant's personal file explaining that his dismissal was due to discrimination;
(c) an employment tribunal should not make a recommendation that a health authority seek the authorisation of the Secretary of State for Health to dispense with its statutory obligations to advertise its next vacancy for a consultant in order to accommodate the applicant who was found to have been discriminated against on a previous occasion (*Noone v North West Thames Regional Health Authority* [1988] IRLR 530; see the analogous situation in *British Gas plc v Sharma* [1991] ICR 19);
(d) a recommendation that the Deputy Chief Constable should interview named police officers and discuss with them relevant parts of the decision was acceptable, but it was not appropriate that each of the officers should be invited to apologise in writing to the claimant. This was because the officers had not had the opportunity to make their position clear to the employment tribunal, before which they were not parties; neither was there any means of enforcing the recommendation (*Chief Constable of West Yorkshire Police v Vento (No 2)* [2002] IRLR 177).

Compensation

8.196 There is no limit on compensation for discrimination. The measure of compensation is, however, the same as that adopted by the ordinary courts in tort (EA s 124(6) except that it may expressly include injury to feelings (s 66(4)), provided that the tribunal considers that it is just and equitable to award compensation. The following principles of calculation are the most important:

8.197 **(1) The general approach** The proper question for the tribunal which has made a finding of unlawful discrimination is what would have happened were it not for the unlawful act, because discrimination is specifically rendered a statutory tort and compensation is in the nature of tortious damages (*Ministry of Defence v Sullivan* [1994] ICR 193). The most exhaustive consideration of the approach to compensation is to be found in the decision by the EAT in ten conjoined cases of dismissal from the armed services on the ground of pregnancy in *Ministry of Defence v Cannock* [1994] IRLR 509. These cases were brought directly under the then extant EC Equal Treatment Directive, but the same principles would apply under the UK statute. These women served under fixed-term contracts. Morison J held that the proper measure of damages was not contractual. The Ministry of Defence had argued that the servicewomen who became pregnant were entitled to loss only to the end of their fixed-term service engagements and not beyond. On the contrary, held the EAT, the claimants must be put in the position in which they would be in but for the unlawful conduct in dismissing them by reason of their pregnancy. The employment tribunal should crucially assess the chance of the employee returning to work after the birth of the child. It was necessary to consider the length of service which she hypothetically lost out on, including within this calculation the possible extension of the period of engagement, her chances of promotion, and other relevant contingencies. There should not be any separate award for loss of congenial employment since this overlapped with the award for injury to feelings.

The following principles also appear from the case law: **8.198**

(a) Contingencies must be taken into account as per the *Polkey* principle so that the tribunal must assess what would have happened if the discriminatory act had not occurred, in other words a counter factual (*Tower Hamlets LBC v Wooster* [2009] IRLR 980; *Abbey National Plc v Chagger* [2010] ICR 397).

There is no limitation of the amount which can be compensated for to losses which are reasonably foreseeable consequences of the wrong (*Essa v Laing Ltd* [2004] ICR 746).

(b) The full amount of a deduction for a failure to mitigate should be applied to a compensatory award for loss of earnings, so that a discount of 10 per cent reflecting the chance that the claimant might not have completed her service should 'have been applied to the award before making the deduction for failure to mitigate (*Ministry of Defence v Bristow* [1996] ICR 544).

(c) If a discriminatory dismissal not only shortened the claimant's period of employment but also altered his subsequent career path, the employee may be able to gain compensation for career-long loss from the tribunal (*Abbey National Plc v Chagger* [2010] ICR 397).

(d) It does not automatically follow that if somebody was liable to suffer depression or another psychiatric injury then the extent to which that might have been caused by non-tortious causes should necessarily have been eliminated if it had been possible to distinguish between the tortious and non-tortious cause (*BAE Systems (Operations) Ltd v Konczak* [2014] IRLR 676).

(e) Earnings which a claimant would have earned had it not been for a failure to mitigate loss should be deducted before rather than after the percentage chance figure of the prospect that the employee would return to work following pregnancy was applied to the resulting sum (see *Ministry of Defence v Hunt* [1996] ICR 554).

(f) The EAT must take account of the fact that the employee receives compensation for future loss and has the benefit of receiving immediately what he would otherwise have had to wait for in order to receive it in instalments; it was not appropriate for the EAT simply to make a single deduction of 5 per cent of the total compensation when that loss covered two and a half years' future earnings and ten years' pension payments (*Bentwood Bros (Manchester) Ltd v Shepherd* [2003] ICR 1000).

(g) Payments made by the underwriters of a health insurance policy for which premiums were paid by the tortfeasor without contribution from the claimant should be deducted from disability discrimination awards (*Atos Origin IT Services Ltd v Haddock* [2005] ICR 277). The same applied here as in personal injury cases.

(h) It was appropriate not to deduct anything from the award for failure to mitigate where an employee who was dismissed from his job as a security officer retrained in a different field in computers (in which he had no relevant experience), because the reason why he did not pursue work in security was that he needed a clean record and his dismissal meant that his record was not clean (*ICTS (UK) Ltd v Tchoula* [2000] IRLR 643).

8.199 **(2) Injury to feelings** At first, appeal bodies were reluctant to permit very large awards to be made for injury to feelings. In *Skyrail Oceanic Ltd v Coleman* [1981] IRLR 398, the Court of Appeal thought that no more should be awarded for injury to feelings than is given in comparable defamation cases, and rejected the employment tribunal's award of £1,000. Their Lordships thought that there could be no damage to the claimant's reputation on the facts and that £100 was thus suitable as recompense. In *Noone v North West Thames Regional Health Authority* (see 8.195) an award of £5,000 for injury to feelings was held to be too high even though the applicant, a medical consultant, suffered substantial injury to her feelings. The sum of £3,000 was substituted by the Court of Appeal. It is important that victims of discrimination are not given over-generous treatment by too great sums being awarded for injury to feelings (*Ministry of Defence v Kemeh* [2014] ICR 625).

8.200 In sexual harassment cases, an employment tribunal is entitled to take into consideration the fact that the claimant wore clothes which were 'scanty and provocative', as it found in *Wileman v Minilec Engineering Ltd* [1988] IRLR 144. Its award of only £50 under this head would thus not be overturned (see *Sharifi v Strathclyde Regional Council* [1992] IRLR 259; *Duffy v Eastern Health and Social Services Board* [1992] IRLR 251; *Ministry of Defence v Sullivan*, above; *Murray v Powertech (Scotland) Ltd* [1992] IRLR 257).

8.201 There is no need for the employee to have knowledge of the discriminatory motivation of the employer (*Taylor v XLN Telecom Ltd* [2010] IRLR 499); the distress and humiliation may, however, be as a general rule greater where the discrimination is overt.

8.202 In principle, awards for injury to feelings and psychiatric injury are distinct. In practice the two types of injury are not always easily separable to realise the risk of double recovery. In a given case it may be impossible to say with any certainty of decision when the distress or humiliation which may be inflicted on the victim of discrimination becomes a recognised psychiatric illness, such as depression; injury to feelings can cover a very wide range (*HM Prison Service v Salmon* [2001] IRLR 425).

8.203 The Court of Appeal laid down some guidance as to the appropriate level of such awards in *Vento v Chief Constable of West Yorkshire Police (No 2)* [2003] ICR 318 where an award of £50,000 for injury to feelings had been made in addition to £15,000 for aggravated damages and £9,000 for psychiatric injury. The court stressed that subjective feelings of upset, frustration, worry, anxiety, mental distress, fear, anguish and the degree of their intensity is incapable of objective proof or of measurement in monetary terms, but tribunals have to do the best they can. The award by the employment tribunal in the case was seriously out of line with guidelines compiled for the Judicial Studies Board and with cases reported in the personal injury field. The court laid down three broad bands for injury to feelings:

(a) the top band between £15,000 and £25,000 to be awarded in the most serious cases such as where there has been a lengthy campaign of harassment;

(b) the middle band between £5,000 and £15,000 for serious cases that do not merit an award in the highest band;

(c) between £500 and £5,000 for less serious cases where the act of discrimination is an isolated or one-off occurrence.

8.204 Where different forms of discrimination (eg race and disability) have contributed to the claimant's injury to feelings, the tribunal must consider what part of that injury to feelings is caused by each form of discrimination (*Al Jumard v Clywd Leisure Ltd* [2008] IRLR 345). Each is a separate wrong for which damages should be provided. The EAT pointed out that the level of award should not necessarily be the same for different forms of discrimination as the offence, humiliation, or upset may vary if, for example, the act is one of deliberate racial discrimination as contrasted with a 'thoughtless' failure to comply with the duty to make reasonable adjustments in respect of disability. At the end of the exercise the tribunal must stand back and have regard to the overall magnitude of the global sum to ensure that it is proportionate and that there is no double counting in the calculation.

Stigma damages

There is a further head of loss which may be awarded called stigma damages. An employer **8.205** who has dismissed an employee on discriminatory grounds may be liable for the consequences of the stigma which might attach to the employee if future employers decided not to employ him because of his proceedings against the employer. Where damage to a claimant's employment prospects from stigma would be the only potentially recoverable head of future loss, in the event that the evidence of stigma difficulties is sufficiently strong, it would be open to a tribunal to make an award of future loss for a specific period. If, however, the evidence showed that stigma was only one of the claimant's difficulties, it may be that a modest lump sum would be appropriate to be awarded (*Abbey National Plc v Chagger* [2010] ICR 39). It is in each case necessary to ask whether such stigma had had a real or substantial effect and, if so, how great was the effect. There needed to be more than a suggestion or suspicion that stigma had been the cause of failure to gain employment (*Ur-Rehman v Ahmad* [2013] ICR 28).

(3) Oppressive etc acts of government Aggravated damages may be awarded if the con- **8.206** duct falls within the categories recognised in *Rookes v Barnard* and *Cassell v Broome* [1972] AC 1027. These include oppressive, arbitrary, or unconstitutional acts of government, including organs of local government (*Deane v Ealing LBC* [1993] ICR 329; *City of Bradford MBC v Arora* [1991] IRLR 165). Where the defendant had behaved high-handedly, insultingly, or oppressively in committing the act of discrimination, as it was found that prison officers had in *Alexander v Home Office* [1988] ICR 685, an amount of aggravated damages should be awarded. The sum of £50 awarded by the trial judge was too low. Exemplary or aggravated damages are not appropriate to be awarded when there is no evidence that either party knew or believed that the discriminatory policy was unlawful when the events actually occurred (*Ministry of Defence v Mutton* [1996] ICR 590).

As a matter of EU law, there is no need for punitive damages as a remedy for sex dis- **8.207** crimination according to the CJEU in *Arjona Camacho v Securitas Seguridad España SA* [2016] ICR 389.

To avoid duplication, aggravated damages should be treated as part of the overall award **8.208** of injury to feelings and not as an extra sum to be awarded over and above that amount (*McConnell v Police Authority for Northern Ireland* [1997] IRLR 625).

The tribunal could make separate awards for aggravated damages and injury to feelings **8.209** if it chose. In *ICTS (UK) Ltd v Tchoula* [2000] IRLR 643, it was appropriate to do so given that senior managers were consciously motivated by the claimant's claims of racial discrimination when they purported to find him in dereliction of his duty and the disciplinary procedure was seriously flawed. The tribunal could regard this as amounting to high-handed, insulting, or oppressive behaviour. The overall award of £27,000 was reduced to £7,500 for injury to feelings and £2,500 as aggravated damages. Quantification in this field remains an even less precise exercise than in the personal injury field.

8.210 **(4) Contributory fault** There is no provision for reduction of compensation on the ground of contributory fault (see *Gubala v Crompton Parkinson Ltd* [1977] IRLR 10; *Roadburg v Lothian Regional Council* [1976] IRLR 283; *Thorndyke v Bell Fruit (North Central) Ltd* [1979] IRLR 1), although misconduct by the employee may have some impact on the amount awarded for injury to feelings.

8.211 **(5) Personal injuries** An award may include compensation for personal injuries suffered, in particular stress-related illness (*Sheriff v Klyne Tugs (Lowestoft) Ltd* [1999] IRLR 481).

8.212 **(6) Joint liability** A salon manager might be jointly and severally liable with the employer for acts of pregnancy discrimination against the claimant even though some of the acts of discrimination were carried out by other managers (*Gilbank v Miles* [2006] IRLR 538).

8.213 **(7) Perverse awards** An appellate court can correct a quantification of compensation by the employment tribunal only where an incorrect principle of assessment had been adopted, or the tribunal had arrived at a figure at which no tribunal properly direct-ing itself could arrive (*Gbaja-Biamila v DHL International (UK) Ltd* [2000] ICR 730; *Noone v North West Thames Regional Health Authority* (above); *Wileman v Minilec Engineering Ltd* (above)). An award of compensation may be so excessive as to amount to an error of law and to fall outside the permissible bracket for awards (*ICTS (UK) Ltd v Tchoula* [2000] IRLR 643).

8.214 **(8) Effect of illegality** An employee was entitled to compensation for sex discrimination even though she knew that her employers were not paying tax on part of her wages and therefore her contract of employment was tainted with illegality. The Court of Appeal so held in *Hall v Woolston Hall Leisure Ltd* [2000] IRLR 578. A complaint of sex discrimi-nation by dismissal is not based on the contract of employment. Sex discrimination is a statutory tort. The question for the tribunal would be whether the claim arises out of or is so inextricably bound up with illegal conduct that the court should not permit the claim-ant to recover compensation without the court appearing to condone that conduct. Here there would be no such condonation since the illegality consisted only of the employer's mode of paying wages. The claimant herself was not guilty of any illegal conduct, and she received no benefit from the employer's failure to deduct tax and national insurance and to account for the same to the Inland Revenue. Where the contract of employment is neither entered into for an illegal purpose nor prohibited by statute, the illegal perfor-mance of the contract will not render the contract as unenforceable unless, in addition to the knowledge of the facts which make the performance illegal, the employee actively participates in the illegal performance. It is a question of fact in each case whether there has been a sufficient degree of participation by the employee (see also *Governing Body of Addey & Stanhope School v Vakkante* [2003] ICR 290, where an asylum seeker obtained employment in breach of a condition of leave to remain).

8.215 Importantly, illegality in the performance of a contract does not affect claims which do not depend on the contract of employment itself, such as harassment (*Wijesundera v Heathrow 3PL Logistics Ltd* [2014] ICR 523). The question to be considered is whether the claim is so clearly connected or inextricably bound up with the claimant's illegal conduct that the tribunal would be appearing to condone that conduct if it permitted the claimant to recover compensation.

Commission enforcement

8.216 The CRE and EOC were abolished by the Equality Act 2006 and replaced by the new Commission on Equality and Human Rights. The powers of this body are more flexible than those of the previous commissions. The Commission must 'monitor the effectiveness of the equality and human rights enactments' (s 11 Equality Act 2006) and may advise central government about their effectiveness. The powers of the Commission include publishing and disseminating ideas or information, undertaking research, providing education, and giving advice and guidance (s 13 Equality Act 2006). It may conduct an inquiry into any matter within its jurisdiction (s 16 Equality Act 2006) and an investigation as to whether an unlawful act has been committed (s 20 Equality Act 2006), which may lead to the issue of an unlawful act notice (s 21 Equality Act 2006). Such a notice may require the person who is subject to it to 'prepare an action plan for the purpose of avoiding repetition or continuation of the unlawful act'. This is subject to an appeal to the court or tribunal on the grounds that the unlawful act was not committed or that the action plan requirement was unreasonable (s 21(5) Equality Act 2006). The Commission may enter into an agreement for an undertaking not to commit an unlawful act of a specific kind (s 23 Equality Act 2006). The amount of money available to provide legal support to claimants is much less than under the previous regime.

Other enforcement mechanisms

The Commission may put together an action plan under s 22. By s 23:　　　　　　**8.217**

(1) The Commission may enter into an agreement with a person under which—
　　(a) the person undertakes—
　　　　(i) not to commit an unlawful act of a specified kind, and
　　　　(ii) to take, or refrain from taking, other specified action (which may include the preparation of a plan for the purpose of avoiding an unlawful act).

If the Commission thinks that a person is likely to commit an unlawful act, it may apply **8.218** to the county court for an injunction restraining the person from committing the act.

By s 30(1), 'The Commission shall have capacity to institute or intervene in legal proceed- **8.219** ings, whether for judicial review or otherwise, if it appears to the Commission that the proceedings are relevant to a matter in connection with which the Commission has a function.'

Further, by s 142(1) of the Equality Act 2010, a 'term of a contract is unenforceable **8.220** against a person in so far as it constitutes, promotes or provides for treatment of that or another person that is of a description prohibited by this Act'. Also, a 'term of a contract is unenforceable by a person in whose favour it would operate in so far as it purports to exclude or limit a provision of or made under this Act' (s 144(1)). This also applies to a term of a collective agreement (s 144(1)).

9

PART-TIME AND FIXED-TERM WORKERS

A PART-TIME WORKERS REGULATIONS 9.01
  The right not to be treated less
  favourably 9.07

Claims 9.16
B FIXED-TERM WORKERS 9.17
C AGENCY WORKERS 9.21

It is a common place that one of the characteristics of the current labour market is flexibility. This has led to an increase in employment relationships based on part-time working, temporary employment, seasonal work and the like. (*Matthews v Kent Fire Authority* [2005] ICR 85.)

A PART-TIME WORKERS REGULATIONS

9.01 A significant development in discrimination law occurred with the House of Lords decision in *R v Secretary of State for Employment, ex p EOC* [1994] ICR 317, to the effect that the minimum hours provisions in the Employment Protection (Consolidation) Act 1978 were unlawful because they were indirectly discriminatory against women. The EU made provisions to deal with discrimination against part-time workers head on. One result of the incoming Labour Government's decision to waive their predecessors' 'opt-out' from the 'Social Chapter' of the 1992 Maastricht Treaty was that the UK became liable to implement the provisions of the European Directive on Part-time Work (No 97/81) into domestic law. This contains the framework agreement on part-time work which was signed by the 'social partners' in June 1997. Clause 4 of the agreement forbids discrimination against part-time workers in respect of employment conditions (so long as these are not justified on objective grounds) and requires that the pay and conditions of such workers should be calculated on a 'pro rata' basis.

9.02 Out of a workforce of twenty-nine million nearly eight million worked part-time in 2011. Part-time work often involves segregation in that the part-time workforce is overwhelmingly female.

9.03 The scope of the Directive is wide. A recorder is an office-holder and covered by the Part-time Workers Directive (*O'Brien v Ministry of Justice* [2010] IRLR 883; [2013] ICR 499).

9.04 This Directive was implemented in UK law by the Part-time Workers (Prevention of Less Favourable Treatment) Regulations 2000 (SI 2000/1551). This and the Fixed-term Workers Regulations derive from EU Directives which they faithfully copy out. The Regulations define a full-time worker as a person who is 'paid wholly or in part by reference to the time he works and, having regard to the custom and practice of the employer in relation to workers employed … under the same type of contract, is identifiable as a full-time worker' (reg 2(1)). Anyone else is a part-time worker, who is paid wholly or by reference to the time when he works. The part-timer can compare herself with a full-time worker only if both are employed by the same employer under the same type of contract, and are engaged in the same or broadly similar work, having regard, where relevant, to whether they have a similar level of qualification, skills, and experience; and the full-time worker works or is placed at the same establishment as the part-time worker, or is based at a different establishment satisfying the requirement set out above.

There is some limited assistance provided in considering the question of whether the workers are employed under the same type of contract by reg 2(3), which defines, as being employed under different types of contract, 'employees employed under a contract that is neither for a fixed term nor a contract of apprenticeship', for example. There is an unusual sweep-up provision at reg 2(3)(f) so that employees are under different types of contract if they are 'any other description of worker that it is reasonable for the employer to treat differently from other workers on the ground that workers of that description have a different type of contract'. **9.05**

In *Matthews v Kent & Medway Towns Fire Authority* [2004] IRLR 697, [2006] IRLR 367, the Court of Appeal held that the categories (a) to (f) of reg 2(3) were mutually exclusive so that since full-time and retained fire fighters were both employed under contracts which were 'neither for a fixed term nor a contract of apprenticeship' within (a) they could not fall within (f) as 'any other description of worker'. Retained and full-time fire fighters were employed under a 'contract that is neither for a fixed term nor a contract of apprenticeship' for the purposes of reg 2(3)(a) and were thus employed under the 'same type of contract' so that a comparison might be made between them. It was not the case that retained fire fighters fell under reg 2(3)(f) which covers 'any other description', which is a long stop or residual category. The House of Lords held that in the light of the underlying purpose of the Directive the aim of reg 3 was to distinguish between different kinds of relationship rather than different types of contract. **9.06**

The right not to be treated less favourably

The crucial enactment is reg 5(1), which accords to the part-time worker the right not to be treated by his employer less favourably than the employer treats a comparable full-time worker— **9.07**

(a) as regards the terms of his contract; or
(b) by being subjected to any other detriment by any act, or deliberate failure to act, of his employer.

The part-time status need not be the sole cause of the less favourable treatment for discrimination to be made out but rather the effective and predominant cause (*Carl v University of Sheffield* [2009] IRLR 617). **9.08**

In making the assessment whether the part-time worker has indeed been treated less favourably the 'pro rata principle' is to be applied, 'unless it is inappropriate' (reg 5(3)). The principle is defined as the right of the part-timer to 'receive or be entitled to receive not less than the proportion of that pay or benefit that the number of his weekly hours bears to the number of weekly hours of the comparable full-time worker' (reg 1(2)). The claim may succeed only if the 'treatment is on the ground that the worker is a part-time worker' (reg 5(2)(a)), so that if there are other reasons at work, the claim fails. **9.09**

In *McMenemy v Capita Business Services Ltd* [2006] IRLR 761 the claimant was a part-timer who worked only on Wednesday to Friday. She was not treated less favourably than a comparable full-time worker because she did not gain the benefit of public holidays **9.10** which fell on Mondays and was not given any additional days off in lieu. The tribunal was correct to find that the detriment suffered was not on the ground that she was a part-timer but was instead due to the fact that she did not work Mondays and the employer's policy that employees were entitled to public holidays only where these fell on an employee's normal working day.

9.11 The part-time nature of the worker's status need not be the sole reason for the discriminatory treatment for it to fall within the unlawful conduct under the Regulations (*Sharma v Manchester CC* [2008] IRLR 336).

9.12 In *Matthews v Kent & Medway Towns Fire Authority* [2006] IRLR 367, the House of Lords overturned the decision of the tribunal because it had concentrated on the differences between the work of retained and full-time fire fighters rather than the weight to be given to the similarities of their roles which was the key. The work will inevitably be different from each other to some extent. Where both full- and part-timers do the same work but the full-timers have extra activities with which to fill their time this should not prevent the work being regarded as the same or broadly similar overall. The importance of the same work which they do to the work of the enterprise as a whole is also of great importance in this assessment.

9.13 In an unusual demonstration of the scope of the provisions it was held that part-time property judges had been treated less favourably than full-time tax judge comparators in relation to fees paid for decision-making; the former received it as a matter of discretion whereas the latter were entitled to it (*Ministry of Justice v Burton* [2016] IRLR 100).

9.14 Further, the employer may justify the treatment 'on objective grounds' (reg 5(2)(b)). The employer, however, in *Ministry of Justice v O'Brien* [2013] ICR 499 failed to demonstrate that part-time judges needed pensions less than full-timers; the reasons given were not sufficiently precise and transparent.

9.15 A worker has the right to receive a written statement of the reasons for less favourable treatment (reg 6).

Claims

9.16 The Regulations give to the part-time worker a free-standing right to complain independently of any claim of sex discrimination which may also be available. The complaint may be made to the employment tribunal within three months beginning with the date of the less favourable treatment or detriment to which the complaint relates or, where an act or failure to act is part of a series of similar acts or failures comprising the less favourable treatment or detriment, the last of them (reg 8(2)). Time may be extended if it is just and equitable to do so.

B FIXED-TERM WORKERS

9.17 The Fixed-term Employees (Prevention of Less Favourable Treatment) Regulations 2002 (SI 2002/2034) follow largely the legislative method of the Part-time Workers Regulations. An employee is a comparable permanent employee if at the time of the less favourable treatment he is employed by the same employer and 'engaged in the same or broadly similar work having regard where relevant to whether they have a similar level of qualification and skills' (reg 2(1)(a)). Such a fixed-term employee must not be treated less favourably than a comparable permanent employee as regards contractual terms or by being subject to any detriment (reg 3(1)) but the right is conferred only if the treatment is on the ground that the employee is a fixed-term employee, and it is not justified on objective grounds (reg 3(3)). The termination of a fixed-term contract by effluxion of time could not itself constitute less favourable treatment by comparison with a permanent employee (*Webley v Department for Work and Pensions* [2005] ICR 577). If a person was treated as he was by reason of being a member of an employee group which consisted of fixed-term contractors, it did not matter that the employer excluded other employee groups (*Coutts & Co v Cure* [2005] ICR 1098).

The treatment of justification of fixed-term contracts may be seen clearly in *Sec of State for Schools v Fletcher* [2011] ICR 495. This involved teachers seconded from Britain to schools which were established to provide education for the children of EU officials. Under the relevant Convention the secondment could last no more than nine years. The Government provided a probationary period of two years and then a further three years. Baroness Hale said that the true mischief to which the Directive was addressed was manipulation of them to disguise what was in effect permanent employment. The use of fixed terms in this case was justified here. **9.18**

The objective need for temporary replacements was considered in *Kucuk v Land Nordrhein-Westfalen* [2012] ICR 682. In an administration with a large workforce so that temporary replacements would be frequently necessary due to the unavailability of employees on leave, there was a temporary replacement of employees (see also *Márquez Samohano v Universitat Pompeu Fabra* [2014] ICR 609). When there is conversion to a permanent contract there must not be material amendments to the contractual terms for it to pass muster (*Huet v Université de Bretagne occidentale* [2012] ICR 694). **9.19**

Where the employee has been engaged on a fixed-term contract or succession of such contracts for four years or more, the employer must treat him as permanent unless there is objective justification not to do so (reg 8). **9.20**

C AGENCY WORKERS

The Agency Workers Directive 2008/104 only requires that there be no discrimination in respect of hours and pay, not that agency workers should be treated as equivalent in access to posts with employed staff. The Directive recognised that it was a fundamental exercise for employers to protect the position of permanent employees in a restructuring exercise (*Coles v Ministry of Defence* [2016] ICR 55). **9.21**

The twelve-week period may be made up of assignments from different agencies. The test for unequal treatment is to decide how the agency worker would have been treated if he 'had been recruited directly by [the user] undertaking to occupy the same job'. **9.22**

10

MATERNITY, PARENTAL, AND DOMESTIC CARE RIGHTS, AND FLEXIBLE WORKING

A ORDINARY MATERNITY LEAVE 10.07
  Notifying the employer of pregnancy . . .10.08
  Length of ordinary and compulsory
  maternity leave 10.12
  Notifying the employer of the return to
  work 10.15
  Terms and conditions of employment
  on return 10.16

B ADDITIONAL MATERNITY LEAVE 10.21
  Notifying the employer of return to
  work 10.22
  Terms and conditions of employment . . . 10.23

C STATUTORY MATERNITY AND
  PATERNITY PAY 10.29

D PATERNITY LEAVE 10.35

E ADOPTION LEAVE AND PAY 10.38

F ANTENATAL CARE 10.39

G SUSPENSION ON MATERNITY GROUNDS . . .10.40

H SHARED PARENTAL LEAVE 10.46
  The right 10.47
  Qualifying conditions 10.48
  Administering parental leave 10.51

I CONTRACTUAL RIGHTS 10.54

J DEPENDANT CARE LEAVE 10.55
  The right 10.56
  Qualifying conditions 10.58
  Length of time off 10.63
  Notifying the employer 10.65

K DISMISSAL 10.66
  Unfair dismissal 10.66
  Exception 10.74

L DETRIMENT 10.77

M FLEXIBLE WORKING 10.78

10.01 The Employment Protection Act 1975 recognised for the first time the problems faced by the pregnant employee who wished to return to work after having her baby. It thus closely supplemented the protection afforded to women under the Equal Pay and Sex Discrimination Acts, and built on the widespread provisions in collective agreements. However, the complexity and rigidity of the Act's provisions (especially after amendments made by the TURERA 1993) weakened its effectiveness and threatened to bring the system of maternity rights into disrepute (see, eg, *Lavery v Plessey Telecommunications Ltd* [1982] ICR 373).

10.02 The Government's response to these criticisms was the maternity provisions of the Maternity and Parental Leave etc Regulations 1999 (SI 1999/3312), which have subsequently been much amended.

10.03 As well as generally reforming the law on maternity leave, the 1999 Regulations were designed to implement the European Parental Leave Directive (96/34/EC), now repealed and replaced by Directive 2010/18. The Regulations introduced, for the first time, a statutory right to parental leave (albeit unpaid) for both male and female employees. The effect of the Regulations, together with further amendments to the ERA 1996 which introduced a right to dependant care leave, and what remains of the old employment protection legislation, was to create a varied framework of 'family-friendly' rights in the workplace, including:

(a) 'ordinary' and 'additional' maternity leave;
(b) statutory maternity and paternity pay;
(c) time off for antenatal care;
(d) protection against suspension on maternity grounds;
(e) shared parental leave;
(f) dependant care leave;
(g) protection against dismissal or detriment for reasons connected with some of the above rights; and
(h) flexible working.

Amendments were made in the Employment Act 2002 and then by further amendment **10.04** regulations (2006/ SI No 2014). These removed the requirement for six months' service for an employee to claim additional maternity leave and introduced the new concept of 'keeping in touch days' so that the employee could agree with her employer to work for up to ten days during the statutory maternity leave period without that work bringing the period of maternity leave to an end. Although a woman has fifty-two weeks in which to return, most in fact come back after thirty-nine when the right to statutory maternity pay expires.

The Children and Families Act 2014 removed the need for caring responsibilities before a **10.05** person could seek flexible working and created shared parental leave which could be used by both parents. Many companies allow women to take longer career breaks notwithstanding the lack of legal necessity.

The resulting mix of measures is complex. Indeed, Ward LJ in *Halfpenny v IGC Medical* **10.06** *Systems Ltd* [1999] ICR 834 commented that 'it is surely not too much to ask of the legislature that those who have to grapple with this topic should not have to have a wet towel around their heads as the single most important aid to the understanding of their rights'.

A ORDINARY MATERNITY LEAVE

The Trade Union Reform and Employment Rights Act (TURERA) 1993 granted female **10.07** employees, for the first time, a right to fourteen weeks' maternity leave. The maternity provisions contained in the 1999 Regulations reproduce and improve upon this right. They provided that all employees are entitled to eighteen weeks' statutory maternity leave regardless of their length of service or hours of work. The now twenty-six-week period is referred to as 'ordinary maternity leave'. By contrast, the right to twenty-six weeks' 'additional maternity leave' (see 10.21–10.28 below) applies only to women with the appropriate qualifying service.

Notifying the employer of pregnancy

An employee must, not later than the end of the fifteenth week before the expected date of **10.08** childbirth (or, if that is not reasonably practicable, as soon as is reasonably practicable), notify her employer of:

(a) her pregnancy;
(b) the expected week of childbirth (EWC); and
(c) the date on which she intends her ordinary maternity leave period to start (reg 4(1)(a)).

This notice must be in writing if the employer requests it to be in writing (reg 4(2)). The **10.09** employee has also to comply with any request by her employer to produce for inspection a certificate from a registered medical practitioner, or a registered midwife, stating the EWC (reg 4(1)(b)).

10.10 The earliest date that an employee can notify to her employer as the date of intended absence is the beginning of the eleventh week before the EWC (reg 4(2)). The woman also must not work beyond the date of the birth of her child except where the maternity leave period is triggered automatically, namely:

(a) where childbirth occurs before the maternity leave period would otherwise commence; or

(b) where the employee is absent from work wholly or partly because of pregnancy or childbirth after the beginning of the sixth week before the EWC.

Both of the above situations will affect the notice requirements since an employee who has not already done so will be unable to give twenty-one days' notice. The Regulations recognise this and provide for a modification of the type of notice to be given. Regulation 4(4) specifies the notice that a woman must give where her maternity leave is triggered by premature childbirth. It provides that the woman in such a case is not required to notify her employer of the date on which she intends to take her leave. However, she is not entitled to ordinary maternity leave unless she notifies him as soon as is reasonably practicable after the birth that she has given birth. This notification must be given in writing, if the employer so requests. 'Childbirth' is defined in reg 2(1) as 'the birth of a living child or the birth of a child whether living or dead after twenty-four weeks of pregnancy'. A woman whose child is born early, or who suffers a stillbirth after twenty-four weeks of pregnancy, will therefore begin her 18-week maternity leave period automatically.

10.11 Regulation 4(3) modifies the notice provisions where an employee is absent from work after the beginning of the sixth week before the EWC wholly or partly because of pregnancy or childbirth. In these circumstances the employee must notify her employer as soon as is reasonably practicable that she is absent for that reason. This notification must be given in writing, if the employer so requests.

Length of ordinary and compulsory maternity leave

10.12 An employee's ordinary maternity leave lasts for a period of up to twenty-six weeks or until the end of the compulsory maternity leave period (reg 7(1), see below).

10.13 Compulsory maternity leave is a two-week period that is sometimes added to ordinary maternity leave when an employee's baby is very late. Compulsory maternity leave commences on the day on which childbirth occurs (reg 8). Its purpose is to ensure that a mother has at least two weeks' leave after the birth of her baby even if, owing to the late arrival of her baby, she has technically exhausted her entitlement to eighteen weeks' leave. Ordinary maternity leave may also be extended where there are health and safety provisions which prevent an employee who has recently given birth from working after the end of her ordinary maternity leave. Where this occurs, a woman is prevented from working until the period of prohibition is over (reg 7(2)). One example of such a provision is the Public Health Act 1936, s 205, which prohibits employment of a woman in a factory or workshop within four weeks of her giving birth. There are also restrictions in the aviation field.

10.14 A worker must be allowed to take the paid annual leave to which she is entitled under the Working Time Directive during a period other than the period of her maternity leave (*Merino Gomez v Continental Industrias del Caucho SA* [2004] IRLR 407).

Notifying the employer of the return to work

A woman returning to work after a period of ordinary maternity leave simply presents **10.15**
herself for work at the end of the eighteen-week period. Where she wishes to return *before*
the end of the eighteen-week period, however, reg 11(1) provides that she must give to her
employer not less than eight weeks' notice of the date on which she intends to return (this
was formerly twenty-eight days). If she attempts to return to work without giving the
required notice, her employer is entitled to postpone her return to a date that will ensure
that the employer has eight weeks' notice of her return (reg 11(2)). The employer is not
entitled, however, to postpone the employee's return to work to a date after the end of the
relevant maternity leave period (reg 11(3)). An employee whose return to work has been
postponed has no right to receive remuneration until the date to which her return was
postponed if she returns to work before that date (reg 11(4)).

Terms and conditions of employment on return

Employees who are absent on ordinary maternity leave are entitled to the benefit of all **10.16**
their contractual terms and conditions except for 'remuneration' (ERA 1996, s 71(4)
and (5)). Some, however, will qualify for maternity allowance or statutory maternity
pay for eighteen weeks, provided that they satisfy certain conditions (see 10.31 below).
In other cases, the contract of employment may provide more favourable maternity
pay arrangements. About two-fifths of women who return from maternity leave in
fact seek part-time employment and there are provisions about flexible working which
are considered below (although they apply beyond the field of the returning maternity
leavers).

Meaning of 'remuneration'

Regulation 9 clarifies the definition of 'remuneration' for the purposes of determining to **10.17**
what a woman is entitled during ordinary maternity leave to some extent, by providing
that only salary and wages are to be treated as remuneration. Accordingly, women taking
twenty-six weeks' ordinary maternity leave will be entitled to the benefit of all their contractual terms and conditions except salary and wages. The employer must also continue
to pay pension contributions at the normal rate for the first twenty-six weeks' leave and
for any further period during which the woman receives maternity pay. If a woman pays
contributions, they are calculated by reference to her actual maternity pay while she is
receiving it.

The position on returning to work

An employee who takes ordinary maternity leave is entitled to return to a job of a pre- **10.18**
scribed kind (ERA 1996, s 71(4)(c)) (as to meaning of job see *Blundell v Governing Body
of St Andrews RC Primary School* [2007] IRLR 652). The right to return does not give
a right to return on different terms on a part-time basis. (*Simpson v Endsleigh Insurance
Services Ltd* [2011] ICR 75). As a matter of EU law the employee should not be disadvantaged by the method of assessing workers in the context of the abolition of a post
(*Riežniece v Zemkopības Ministrija* [2013] ICR 1096; see also *Betriu Montull v Instituto
Nacional de la Seguridad Social* [2013] ICR 1323).

In addition, she is entitled to return with her 'seniority, pension rights, and similar **10.19**
rights' as they would have been had she not been absent, and on terms and conditions
not less favourable than those which would have applied if she had not been absent
(s 71(7)).

Unfavourable treatment by reason of pregnancy

10.20 By s 18(2):

> A person (A) discriminates against a woman if, in the protected period in relation to a pregnancy of hers, A treats her unfavourably—
>
> (a) because of the pregnancy, or
> (b) because of illness suffered by her as a result of it.

Further, by s 18(3): 'A person (A) discriminates against a woman if A treats her unfavourably because she is on compulsory maternity leave.'

By s 18(4): 'A person (A) discriminates against a woman if A treats her unfavourably because she is exercising or seeking to exercise, or has exercised or sought to exercise, the right to ordinary or additional maternity leave.'

Section 18(6) provides that:

> the protected period, in relation to a woman's pregnancy, begins when the pregnancy begins, and ends—
>
> (a) if she has the right to ordinary and additional maternity leave, at the end of the additional maternity leave period or (if earlier) when she returns to work after the pregnancy;
> (b) if she does not have that right, at the end of the period of 2 weeks beginning with the end of the pregnancy.

If treatment for a pregnancy-related reason had taken place after the end of a protected period of maternity leave the claimant could not rely on s 18 ERA (*Lyons v DWP Job Centre Plus* [2014] ICR 668).

B ADDITIONAL MATERNITY LEAVE

10.21 The most fundamental right of a pregnant employee is that she may return to work within twenty-nine weeks following her absence. The 1999 Regulations preserve this right in the provisions on 'additional maternity leave'. Additional maternity leave commences on the day after the last day of an employee's ordinary maternity leave period (reg 6(3)). Many of the same principles apply as to ordinary maternity leave.

Notifying the employer of return to work

10.22 An employee who intends to return to work *before* the end of her additional maternity leave must give to her employer not less than eight weeks' notice of the date on which she intends to return. If the employee attempts to return to work without giving this notice, her employer is entitled to postpone her return to a date that will ensure he has at least eight weeks' notice of her return (reg 11(1) and (2)). The employer is not entitled, however, to postpone the employee's return to work to a date after the end of the additional maternity leave period (reg 11(3)). An employee whose return to work has been postponed is not entitled to be paid remuneration until the date to which her return was postponed if she returns to work before that date (reg 11(4)).

Terms and conditions of employment

10.23 Any one who takes parental leave is entitled, during the period of leave, to the benefit of her employer's implied obligation of trust and confidence and any terms and conditions of her employment relating to:

(a) notice of the termination of the employment contract by the employer;
(b) compensation in the event of redundancy; and
(c) disciplinary or grievance procedures (reg 17).

At the same time, the employee will be bound by her implied obligation to the employer **10.24** of good faith and any terms and conditions of her employment relating to:

(a) notice of the termination of the employment contract by her;
(b) the disclosure of confidential information;
(c) the acceptance of gifts or other benefits; and
(d) the employee's participation in any other business (reg 17).

Once ordinary maternity leave has ended, a woman will not be entitled to the benefit of **10.25** any of her normal terms and conditions of employment, save for those specified above in reg 17. This means, for example, that an employee may be entitled to keep her company car during ordinary maternity leave, but could be asked to return it in the period of additional maternity leave. It should be noted, however, that women taking additional maternity leave will continue to accrue holiday leave under the Working Time Regulations 1998 even though they are not entitled to do so under their contracts. This is because the Working Time Regulations do not exempt employees on maternity leave from the statutory right to accrue four weeks' holiday. An employee on additional maternity leave is not, however, entitled to any remuneration unless her contract provides otherwise.

Returning to work

An employee who takes additional maternity leave is entitled to return from leave to the **10.26** job in which she was employed before her absence, or, if it is not reasonably practicable for the employer to permit her to return to that particular job, then to another job which is both suitable for her and appropriate for her to do in the circumstances (reg 18(2)). Her terms and conditions in respect of remuneration must not be less favourable than those which would have been applicable to her had she not been absent from work at any time since the commencement of ordinary maternity leave. The employee is also entitled to her seniority, pension rights and similar rights as she would have been if the period or periods of her employment prior to her additional maternity leave period were continuous with her employment following her return to work.

As already stated, women returning to work after maternity leave may want to return on **10.27** different terms and conditions, for example, on a part-time or job share basis. The Court of Appeal has confirmed, in *Cast v Croydon College* [1998] ICR 500, that an employer's refusal to accede to, or even consider, such a request may constitute indirect discrimination under what is now the Equality Act 2010.

Exclusion from consideration for a bonus because of absence on additional maternity **10.28** leave would also amount to sex discrimination (*GUS Home Shopping Ltd v Green* [2001] IRLR 75).

C STATUTORY MATERNITY AND PATERNITY PAY

The rate of payment for the first six weeks of statutory maternity pay (SMP) will be the higher **10.29** of 90 per cent of normal weekly earnings or £139.58 per week. The rate for the remaining twenty weeks is £139.58 per week or 90 per cent of normal weekly earnings, whichever is less.

Backdated pay increases must be taken into account in calculating 'normal weekly earn- **10.30** ings' by reason of the Statutory Maternity Pay (General) Amendment Regulations 1996

(SI 1996/1335) (which were introduced to put into effect the second *ratio* in *Gillespie v Northern Health and Social Services Board* [1996] ICR 498 that an employee absent on maternity leave was entitled to any increase in pay awarded to similar employees during her absence (see also 7.98)) (see also *Fletcher v Blackpool Fylde & Wyre Hospitals NHS Trust* [2005] IRLR 689; *Hoyland v ASDA Stores Ltd* [2005] IRLR 438). The ECJ held that payment of wages to a worker in the event of illness falls within pay for the purposes of Art 141. A rule of a sick leave scheme that provides for a reduction in pay where the absence exceeds a certain duration as regards both female workers absent prior to maternity leave by reason of an illness related to their pregnancy and male workers absent by reason of any illness does not constitute discrimination on grounds of sex so long as the amount of payment is not so low as to undermine the objective of protecting pregnant workers (*North Western Health Board v McKenna* [2005] IRLR 895).

10.31 Statutory maternity pay is payable to any woman who (by the Statutory Maternity Pay (General) Regulations 1986):

(a) is an employee;

(b) has been continuously employed by the same employer for at least twenty-six weeks, continuing into the fifteenth week before the week when her baby is due;

(c) has average weekly earnings of not less than the lower earnings limit for national insurance contributions during the eight weeks up to and including the qualifying week;

(d) is still pregnant at the eleventh week before the baby is due or has given birth by this time;

(e) has given twenty-one days' notice of the date on which she intends to stop work or as much notice as was reasonably practicable in writing if the employer requests it; and

(f) presents medical evidence of the date on which the baby is expected.

10.32 Any woman who satisfies these criteria is entitled to receive SMP even though she is not returning to work after her maternity leave has ended. The SMP cannot start earlier than eleven weeks before the expected date of childbirth, but it can be as late as the week immediately following the week in which the woman gives birth. An employer who refuses to pay SMP must give written reasons for not doing so.

10.33 As is the case with most issues of continuity of employment, the following absences from work and transfers of employment do not break continuity of service for the purposes of SMP (reg 11 Statutory Maternity Pay (General) Regulations 1986 (SI 1986/1960), as amended):

(a) periods of incapacity for work of less than twenty-six weeks;

(b) weeks which fall between the date of a woman's dismissal which is found to be unfair and her reinstatement;

(c) a transfer of business;

(d) transfer of employment to an associated employer.

10.34 The employee cannot validly sign away her right to SMP, nor can the employer validly require her to contribute towards the costs incurred by him. Any such agreement to the contrary is void (Social Security Contributions and Benefits Act 1992, s 164(6)).

D PATERNITY LEAVE

10.35 Pursuant to s 80A of the ERA 1996, regulations provide for two weeks' paternity leave for each child (Paternity and Adoption Leave Regulations 2002/2788). This must be taken before the end of a period of fifty-six days beginning with the child's birth. Following payment, the employer could formerly claim reimbursement from the state by way of retention of national insurance contributions which he would otherwise have to pay by the Paternity and Adoption Leave Regulations. New Additional Statutory Paternity Pay gives the father or partner the right to take over any unclaimed SMP from the mother if she returned to work early.

Many of the requirements and privileges of the other periods of leave and payment are **10.36** the same as for maternity leave. The main features of the right to paid paternity leave in cases of birth are:

(a) In order to qualify for the new right employees must:
    (i) have twenty-six weeks' continuous service at the beginning of the fourteenth week before the EWC;
    (ii) have or expect to have responsibility for the upbringing of the child; and
    (iii) be the biological father of the child or married to, or the partner of, the child's mother. Same-sex couples are included in these cases so a female employee can take paternity leave.
(b) The employee must notify the employer of his intention to take paternity leave in the fifteenth week before the EWC.
(c) Paternity leave will need to be taken within fifty-six days of the child's birth (or the EWC if it is a premature birth).
(d) The right to return from paternity leave will be the same as for ordinary maternity leave, that is, to the same job.

The Statutory Paternity and Adoption Pay Regulations 2002 (SI 2002/2820 and SI 2002/ **10.37** 2822) also provide:

(a) Where there is a joint adoption, the partner who has not taken adoption leave is entitled to paternity leave.
(b) Employees will only qualify for paternity leave (adoption) if they:
    (i) have twenty-six weeks' continuous service when the adopter is matched with the child;
    (ii) are not taking adoption leave;
    (iii) have or expect to have responsibility for the upbringing of the child; and
    (iv) are married to or the partner of the child's adopter, (same-sex couples are included so a female employee can take paternity leave).
(c) The employee must notify the employer of his intention to take paternity leave within seven days of the date the adopter is matched with the child.
(d) Paternity leave will need to be taken within fifty-six days of the day the child is placed for adoption.
(e) The right to return from paternity leave will be the same as for ordinary maternity leave, that is, to the same job.

E ADOPTION LEAVE AND PAY

Chapter 1A of the ERA 1996 contains enabling provisions for regulations on a new right to a **10.38** period of paid adoption leave. They apply to adoptive parents of children placed or matched for adoption. The detailed provisions substantially mirror maternity leave as follows:

(a) in cases of joint adoption, either partner (but not both) can take adoption leave;
(b) ordinary and additional adoption leave will each be for a twenty-six-week period, one after the other;

(c) to qualify for adoption leave an employee must have twenty-six weeks' continuous service when matched for adoption and give notice to take adoption leave within seven days of being matched for adoption;

(d) employers will be required to write to an employee stating her expected date of return within twenty-eight days of the notification to take adoption leave;

(e) adoption leave can start on the date the child is placed for adoption or up to fourteen days before that date;

(f) if the placement does not go ahead or is disrupted after adoption leave has started (for example, because the child dies or the placement is ended), adoption leave will end eight weeks later; and

(g) the amount of notice required to return early from adoption leave will be twenty-eight days.

Statutory Adoption Pay is £139.58 per week or 90 per cent of normal weekly earnings, whichever is less, for the whole twenty-six weeks.

F ANTENATAL CARE

10.39 The right to time off for antenatal care was introduced in 1980 (now in ERA 1996, s 55), following concern at the extent of perinatal mortality and handicap. The right is available to all women employees irrespective of length of service or hours of work. In order to claim it, the employee may, however, be required to produce a doctor's or midwife's certificate of pregnancy, and appointment card. If she does, she should be paid at the appropriate hourly rate for the time taken off, and if this is unreasonably refused, she may complain to an employment tribunal within three months. It may be reasonable to refuse such time off if an employee can reasonably make arrangements for an appointment outside normal working hours (*Gregory v Tudsbury Ltd* [1982] IRLR 267). A similar right is given to agency workers by s 57ZA ERA which was inserted by the Agency Workers Regulations 2010.

G SUSPENSION ON MATERNITY GROUNDS

10.40 The TURERA 1993 introduced new rights with regard to suspension of employees from work on maternity grounds where the employee is prohibited from continuing working (ERA 1996, ss 66–8). If an employee is suspended from work by her employer either because she is pregnant, has recently given birth, or is breastfeeding a child, she has a number of rights, but only where the suspension is in consequence of any requirement imposed by or under any relevant provision of any enactment, or of any instrument made under any enactment, or any recommendation in any relevant provision of a code of practice issued or approved under s 16 of the Health and Safety at Work, etc Act 1974 (ERA 1996, s 66(1)).

10.41 The first right which a woman has where she cannot continue working as a result of any requirement or recommendation is that she should be offered any suitable alternative work which is available before she is suspended (s 67(1)). The alternative work must be suitable by reference to the same principles as relate to the redundancy provisions in s 77(3). The work offered was held not to be suitable, for example, when crew members were given basic pay when they were employed on alternative ground-based work and did not receive flying allowances to which they were entitled when working normally (*BA (European Operations at Gatwick) Ltd v Moore & Botterill* [2000] IRLR 296; see also *New Southern Railway Ltd v Quinn* [2006] IRLR 266).

If the woman is not offered work, in contravention of s 67(1), then she may complain to an **10.42** employment tribunal, which may make an award of such compensation as it considers to be just and equitable having regard to the extent of the employer's infringement and any loss attributable to that breach (s 70(4)–(7)). Any complaint must be lodged within three months of the first day of the suspension, unless it is not reasonably practicable to present a complaint within those three months (s 70(5)).

If the employee is actually suspended pursuant to s 66, then she is entitled to be paid **10.43** remuneration by her employer while she is suspended (s 68). The suspension lasts as long as the employee continues to be employed but is not provided with work or—excepting alternative work under s 67—does not do the work which she did before suspension.

Complaint of breaches of s 68 is made to an employment tribunal. The application must **10.44** be brought within three months of any day on which the appropriate remuneration is not paid, unless the employment tribunal considers that it was not reasonably practicable to complain within this period (s 70(2)). If the tribunal finds that the complaint is well founded then it must order the employer to pay the amounts of remuneration which it finds due to the woman (s 70(3)).

Where a worker is suspended on maternity grounds, the provisions of ss 66–70 of the **10.45** ERA 1996 operate as a code so that no equal pay claim may be brought (*BA (European Operations at Gatwick) Ltd v Moore & Botterill*, above). There is also a cognate provision about the ending of the supply of an agency worker on maternity grounds introduced by the Agency Workers Regulations 2010 as s 68A ERA. This is followed by the right to an offer of alternative work (by inserted s 68B).

H SHARED PARENTAL LEAVE

While the maternity provisions of the 1999 Regulations built upon an already-existing system **10.46** of maternity rights, those implementing the European Parental Leave Directive (96/34/EC) created an entirely new legal entitlement of up to thirteen weeks' (unpaid) parental leave.

The right

By the Statutory Shared Parental Leave General Regulations 2014, the key aspects of the **10.47** statutory right to parental leave are as follows:

(a) the maximum leave that an employee can take per child is thirteen weeks;
(b) the right is an individual right, so both parents are entitled to parental leave;
(c) the employee's rights to take the leave will last until the child's fifth birthday or—in the case of adoption—until five years have elapsed following placement of the child with the parents;
(d) parents of disabled children will be able to use their leave over a longer period. The Regulations provide that in their case parental leave can be taken up to the child's 18th birthday. Whether a child is disabled or not is determined by whether the child is entitled to disability living allowance;
(e) the employee will remain employed while on parental leave; some terms, such as contractual notice and redundancy terms will still apply; and
(f) at the end of parental leave the employee is guaranteed the right to return to the same job as before, or, if that is not practicable, to a similar job which has the same or better status, terms and conditions as the old job; where the leave taken is for a period of four weeks or less, the employee will be entitled to go back to the same job.

Qualifying conditions

10.48 The qualifying conditions for parental leave are dealt with in reg 13 of the MPLS Regulations. An employee has the right to be absent from work on parental leave if he or she has at least one year's continuous service with the employer and:

(a) is the parent, and is named as such on the birth certificate, of a child who is under five years old; or

(b) has adopted, on or after 15 December 1999, a child under the age of 18 (this right lasts for five years from the date on which the child is placed for adoption or until the child's 18th birthday, whichever is the sooner); or

(c) has, under the Children Act 1989 or the Children (Scotland) Act 1995, acquired formal parental responsibility for a child under five years old.

Parents will be able to start taking parental leave either when a child is born or placed for adoption, or when they have completed one year's service with their employer, whichever of these two dates is the later.

10.49 During parental leave the employee is bound by terms of good faith, notice of termination by the employee, disclosure of confidential information, the acceptance of gifts or other benefits, or the employee's participation in any other business (reg 17 MPLS Regulations).

10.50 The leave must be taken between twenty weeks and twelve months from the date of the birth of the child. Shared parental leave was inserted by the Children and Families Act 2014 and Shared Parental Leave Regulations 2014/3050. Parents may take leave concurrently or switch places altogether so long as leave is taken in week blocks and does not amount to more leave or pay than the mother would have under her maternity leave pay provisions.

Administering parental leave

10.51 The intention of the 1999 Regulations is that employers and employees should be encouraged to agree a scheme on the specific implementation of the rules, in terms of the notice that should be given and the time off that can be taken at any time. Therefore, the Regulations give employers and employees the option of making their own agreements about how parental leave will operate in the workplace. This can be done through workforce or collective agreements or individual agreements. Such agreements can be used to improve upon the key elements set out above, but they cannot offer rights that are less favourable than those above.

The statutory 'fall-back' scheme

10.52 The Regulations are in effect the rules that will apply in the absence of any agreement. Where employers and employees have not entered into an agreement about these matters, or until they have done so, the fall-back scheme set out in the Regulations applies. This provides that employees can take parental leave only subject to the following rules:

(a) leave can be taken only in blocks or multiples of one week;

(b) employees must give a minimum of twenty-eight days' notice;

(c) employees can take only four weeks' leave in a year; and

(d) leave may be postponed by the employer for up to six months where the business would be unduly disrupted; however, leave cannot be postponed when the employee gives notice to take it immediately after the time the child is born or is placed with the family for adoption.

The fall-back scheme provides that parents of disabled children may take up to eighteen weeks' leave. Where there is a collective or workforce agreement, this may be less favourable to the employee than the fall-back scheme.

Keeping records

There is nothing in the Regulations that requires employers to keep statutory records of **10.53** parental leave taken, although many will want to do so for their own purposes. When an employee changes jobs, employers will be free to make enquiries of a previous employer or seek a declaration from the employee about how much parental leave he or she has taken. Similarly, the employer may request that the employee demonstrates proof of his or her entitlement to parental leave. Under the statutory fall-back scheme it is provided that the employee must, where requested, provide details of the fact that he or she has responsibility for the child; the child's date of birth; and, where appropriate, the details of the child's entitlement to disability living allowance.

I CONTRACTUAL RIGHTS

Some employers make contractual provision for maternity and parental leave. It is not **10.54** uncommon, for example, for an employee to have a basic statutory right to ordinary maternity leave as well as a contractual right to maternity leave. Where this happens, the employee may take advantage of whichever right is, in any particular respect, the more favourable (reg 21). She cannot, however, select parts from each, for example, attempting to combine the contractual offer of part-time employment with retaining under statute her previous terms and conditions (*Bovey v Hospital for Sick Children* [1978] IRLR 241; *Kolfor Plant Ltd v Wright* [1982] IRLR 311).

J DEPENDANT CARE LEAVE

The provisions of the European Parental Leave Directive (96/34/EC) also required the **10.55** UK to implement measures providing employees with a legal right to take time off work for certain family and domestic reasons. These measures are now contained in the ERA 1996, ss 57A and 57B. By s 57A ERA, which was introduced in 1999, an employee may take a reasonable amount of time off for emergencies, for example, 'to provide assistance on an occasion when a dependant falls ill, gives birth or is injured or assaulted' or 'in consequence of the death of a dependant'.

The right

Section 57A(1) states that an employee is entitled to take a reasonable amount of time off **10.56** during working hours in order to take action which is necessary:

(a) to provide assistance on an occasion when a dependant falls ill, gives birth or is injured or assaulted;
(b) to make arrangements for the provision of care for a dependant who is ill or injured;
(c) in consequence of the death of a dependant;
(d) because of the unexpected disruption or termination of arrangements for the care of a dependant; or
(e) to deal with an incident which involves a child of the employee and which occurs unexpectedly in a period during which an educational establishment which the child attends is responsible for him or her.

10.57 There is no right under the statute to *payment* during dependant care leave. Any rights that the employee does have will stem from his or her contract of employment, or from custom and practice.

Qualifying conditions

Employees

10.58 The right applies to employees. There is no qualifying period for the right, so it applies on the first day of employment.

Who is a dependant?

10.59 The statutory definition of a dependant includes an employee's wife, husband, civil partner, child, parent, or someone who lives in the same household as the employee but who is not his or her employee, tenant, lodger, or boarder (s 57A(3)). This clearly covers non-married partners, but also potentially extends to family members or friends who live together. The definition also covers children who are not the employee's children but who live in the same house.

10.60 There is a further category of dependants provided for by s 57A(4), which states that a dependant also includes any person who reasonably relies on the employee either for assistance on an occasion when the person falls ill or is injured or assaulted, or to make arrangements for the provision of care in the event of illness or injury. Furthermore, where the time off relates to unexpected disruption or termination of arrangements for the care of a dependant, then a dependant will also include any person who reasonably relies on the employee to make arrangements for the provision of care.

What situations are covered?

10.61 As noted above, an employee can claim time off in order to take action that is 'necessary':

    (a) if a dependant falls ill or has been injured or assaulted;
    (b) when a dependant is having a baby;
    (c) to make longer-term care arrangements for a dependant who is ill or injured;
    (d) to deal with the death of a dependant;
    (e) to deal with an unexpected disruption or breakdown of care arrangements for a dependant; or
    (f) to deal with an unexpected incident involving the employee's child during school hours.

10.62 What is 'necessary' will depend on all the circumstances of the case. There may, for example, be instances where a dependant has a physical or mental illness which does not necessitate full-time care but suffers from occasional relapses which require assistance from the employee. There may also be many cases where the employee's presence is not 'necessary' from a medical point of view, but may be needed with regard to both the employee's and the dependant's psychological needs in difficult circumstances, such as attendance at an important medical examination. The practical realities of the action that needs to be taken will be very relevant. So, for example, while it might perhaps be necessary for both parents of a child to take time off when the child is seriously ill, it would not be necessary for both of them to take time off if the childminder did not turn up—although it would be necessary for one of them to take time off.

Length of time off

10.63 Unlike maternity and parental leave, there is no express limitation on the amount of time off that an employee can take. The amount of time is merely limited by the fact that it should be 'reasonable' and will therefore vary by reference to the circumstances. The government guidance suggests that, for most cases, one or two days should be sufficient to deal with the problem and gives the example that 'if a child falls ill with chickenpox, the leave should be enough to help the employee cope with the crisis—to deal with the immediate care of the child, visiting the doctor if necessary, and to make longer-term care arrangements'.

In determining what action is necessary, the factors that are to be taken into account include **10.64** the nature of the incident, the closeness of the relationship between employee and dependant, and the extent to which anyone else was available to assist; the disruption and inconvenience to the employer were irrelevant (*Qua v John Ford Morrison* [2003] ICR 482).

Notifying the employer

There are no formalised notice requirements for exercising the right. All that an employee **10.65** must do is notify his or her employer as soon as is reasonably practicable of the circumstances giving rise to the leave. The notification does not need to be in writing.

K DISMISSAL

Unfair dismissal

By s 18 EA an employer discriminates against a woman if he treats her unfavourably **10.66** (a) because of the pregnancy or (b) because of illness suffered by her as a result of it or because she is on maternity leave or is attempting to exercise maternity rights or to return from maternity leave. Article 10 of the Pregnant Workers Directive 92/85 requires member states to take the necessary measures to prohibit the dismissal of workers during the period from the beginning of their pregnancy to the end of the maternity leave (save in exceptional circumstances which are not connected with their condition). An employee who is dismissed is treated as unfairly dismissed for the purposes of the ERA 1996, Pt X, if the reason or principal reason for his or her dismissal is:

(a) the pregnancy of the employee;
(b) the fact that the employee has given birth to a child;
(c) the application of a relevant requirement, or a relevant recommendation, as defined by s 66(2) of the ERA 1996;
(d) the fact that the employee took, sought to take, or availed herself of the benefits of, ordinary maternity leave;
(e) the fact that he or she took or sought to take additional maternity leave, parental leave, or dependant care leave;
(f) the fact that he or she declined to sign a workforce agreement for the purposes of the Regulations;
(g) the fact that, as a workforce representative for the purposes of a workforce agreement on parental leave, or as a candidate in an election for such a representative, the employee performed (or proposed to perform) any of the functions or activities of such a representative or candidate (Maternity and Parental Leave etc Regulations 1999, reg 20(1) and (3)).

For automatic unfairness of pregnancy the employer must know of the existence of the pregnancy and it was not sufficient that the symptoms of pregnancy simply existed (*Ramdoolar v Bycity Ltd* [2005] ICR 368).

There is a difference between protection under reg 10 (redundancy during maternity **10.67** leave) of the 1999 Regulations and s 18 EA 2010; the latter requires a finding of unfavourable treatment because of pregnancy or maternity leave whereas under reg 10 during the relevant maternity period the woman was entitled to special protection and would be treated as unfairly dismissed if that was denied.

10.68 IVF treatment should be treated as equivalent to pregnancy for the purposes of determining whether less favourable treatment of a woman constitutes sex discrimination only for the stage between the follicular puncture and the immediate transfer of the in vitro fertilised ova (*Sahota v Home Office* [2010] ICR 772).

10.69 Likewise, a woman who is made redundant during her ordinary or additional maternity leave periods will have a claim for automatic unfair dismissal against her employer if he failed to offer her a suitable alternative vacancy in accordance with reg 10. Lastly, an employee is treated as unfairly dismissed if he or she is dismissed for redundancy, but it is shown:

    (a) that the circumstances constituting the redundancy applied equally to one or more employees in the same undertaking who held positions similar to that held by the employee and who have not been dismissed by the employer; and

    (b) that the reason, or principal reason, for which the employee was selected was a reason of a kind specified in (a) to (g) above (reg 20(2)).

10.70 In relation to the offer of suitable alternative employment this must be made as soon as the decision to delete a position and the employee was potentially redundant (*Sefton BC v Wainwright* [2015] ICR 652).

10.71 None of the above alters the separate principle in *Webb v EMO Air Cargo* [1995] ICR 1021, that a dismissal on grounds of pregnancy is automatically sexually discriminatory but it is now usually unnecessary to use that cause of action (see 8.26). Sex discrimination cannot, however, be claimed after a protected period of maternity leave (*Lyons v DWP Jobcentre Plus* [2014] ICR 668) and would not apply to absence for postnatal depression. On the distinction between direct and indirect discrimination in pregnancy see *Metropolitan Police Commissioner v Keohane* [2014] ICR 1073.

10.72 The borderline between maternity rights and discrimination is maintained by s 76 of the Equality Act, which provides that 'The relevant pregnancy and maternity discrimination provision has no effect in relation to a term of the woman's work that is modified by a maternity equality clause or rule.' Further, by s 76(1A), the relevant pregnancy and maternity discrimination provision has no effect in relation to a term of the woman's work—

    (a) that relates to pay, but

    (b) in relation to which a maternity equality clause or rule has no effect.

10.73 While the protection of the special position of employees who are pregnant or on maternity leave might sometimes require them to be accorded treatment more favourable than that accorded to their colleagues, it does not extend to favouring such employees beyond what is reasonably necessary to compensate them for the disadvantages occasioned by their condition (*Eversheds Legal Services v De Belin* [2011] ICR 1137).

Exception

10.74 The exception, which appears at reg 20(7) of the Maternity and Parental Leave etc Regulations 1999 SI 1999/3312, covers all forms of statutory leave. The effect of this provision is that a dismissal which would otherwise fall within reg 20(1) shall nevertheless not be treated as automatically unfair if:

    (a) it was not reasonably practicable, for a reason other than redundancy, for the employer (who may be the same employer or a successor of his) to permit the employee to return to a job which is both suitable for the employee and appropriate for him or her to do in the circumstances;

(b) an associated employer offers the employee a job of that kind; and

(c) the employee accepts or unreasonably refuses that offer.

Clearly it would be anomalous to give women a right not to be dismissed on pregnancy- **10.75** related grounds regardless of service and not to give them a right to a written statement of the reasons for dismissal unless they have been employed for a year. This is recognised by the ERA 1996 s 92(4), which provides that:

> An employee is entitled to a written statement under this section without having to request it and irrespective of whether she has now been continuously employed for any period if she is dismissed—
>
> (a) at any time while she is pregnant, or
> (b) after childbirth in circumstances in which her ordinary or additional maternity leave period ends by reason of the dismissal.

The general nature of an employer's breach of the obligation to provide written reasons is **10.76** changed from an 'unreasonable refusal' to 'an unreasonable failure' (ERA 1996 s 93(1)).

L DETRIMENT

Employees are entitled, by virtue of s 47C of the ERA 1996, not to be subjected to any det- **10.77** riment by any act, or any deliberate failure to act, by an employer because the employee:

(a) is pregnant;

(b) has given birth to a child;

(c) has taken time off;

(d) is the subject of a maternity suspension within the meaning of s 66(2) of the Act;

(e) took, sought to take, or availed herself of the benefits of ordinary maternity leave;

(f) took or sought to take:
   (i) additional maternity leave,
   (ii) shared parental leave, or
   (iii) dependant care leave;
   (iv) ordinary or additional adoption leave;

(g) declined to sign a workforce agreement for the purposes of the Regulations; or

(h) was a workforce representative for the purposes of a workforce agreement on parental leave, or a candidate in an election for such a representative, and performed (or proposed to perform) any of the functions or activities of such a representative or candidate (reg 19) (see *Sarkatzis Herrero v Instituto Madrileno de la Salud* [2006] IRLR 296).

M FLEXIBLE WORKING

By s 80F of the ERA 1996, an employee may apply to the employer for a change of terms **10.78** and conditions if the change relates to the hours he is required to work, the times when he is required to work, where (as between his home and the employer's business) he is required to work, or such other aspects as may be specified by regulations, if the purpose of the change is to enable him to care for someone who at the time of application is a child in respect of whom he satisfies conditions as to relationship to be specified by regulations. This applies beyond mothers returning after pregnancy. Flexible working is not only about hours but also concerns working from home.

10.79 The employee may only make the request if she has at least twenty-six weeks' continuous service; is the mother, father, adopter, guardian, or foster parent of the child or married to or the partner of the child's mother, father, adopter, guardian, or foster parent; and expects to have responsibility for the child's upbringing (Flexible Working Regulations 2014 (SI 2014/1389) reg 4). An application must be made in writing, state whether the employee has previously made any such application to the employer, and be dated. A flexible working application is taken as made on the day when it is received. The employee may only make one application for flexible working a year (ERA 1996, s 80F(4)).

10.80 The employer may refuse the flexible working requested only if (s 80G) he considers that one or more of the following grounds applies:

(a) the burden of additional costs;
(b) detrimental effect on ability to meet customer demand;
(c) inability to reorganise work among existing staff;
(d) inability to recruit additional staff;
(e) detrimental impact on quality;
(f) detrimental impact on performance;
(g) insufficiency of work during the periods the employee proposes to work;
(h) planned structural changes; and
(i) such other grounds as may be set out in regulations (so far none have been specified).

10.81 If the request is granted, unless otherwise agreed, changes to the employee's contract are permanent in character and the employee has no right to revert to the previous terms. Pay and other benefits may be reduced pro rata to take account of any fall in hours.

10.82 The Flexible Working (Procedural Requirements) Regulations 2002 (SI 2002/3207) provide that:

(a) a meeting to consider an application for contract variation must be held within twenty-eight days of the application (reg 3);
(b) the employer must give notice of his decision within fourteen days of the meeting (reg 4);
(c) any appeal must be made within fourteen days of the notice being given (reg 6);
(d) the parties may agree to an extension (reg 12).

10.83 The right to complain to the employment tribunal is available only if the employer has failed to nominate the grounds of refusal; has failed to comply with the procedural requirements set out in the regulations handling the governing of the procedure; has rejected the application on a ground that is not a permitted business reason for refusal (s 80H(1) of the ERA 1996), or if the decision to reject was 'based on incorrect facts' (s 80H(1); see *Commotion Ltd v Rutty* [2006] ICR 290). An employer who falls foul of these provisions may only be required to reconsider the employee's application, following a declaration by the employment tribunal (ERA 1996, s 80I), but may have to pay compensation, as the tribunal considers just and equitable, of up to eight weeks' pay (2002 Regulations, reg 7). It may also order reconsideration of the request for flexible working (s 80I(1) of the ERA 1996). An application must be made in writing, be dated, and specify that it is made under the ERA. When the request has been received the employer must hold a meeting with the employee within twenty-eight days unless within that time the employer sends written notice specifying that the changes have been accepted and the date from which they will take effect (Flexible Working (Procedural Requirements) Regulations 2002 (SI 2002/3207)). If agreement cannot be reached, the employee must send the employer an appeal notice within fourteen days after the date on which notice of the decision is given (regs 6, 7 of the Flexible Working (Procedural Requirements) Regulations 2002 (SI 2002/3207)).

The employee has an additional right under the ERA 1996, s 47D, not to be subjected to **10.84** any detriment arising from exercising these rights, or certain acts preparatory to that, as specified (dismissal is excluded). Where the employee is dismissed in these circumstances, that will be considered to be an automatically unfair dismissal (ERA 1996, s 104C).

11

CONTINUITY OF EMPLOYMENT

A BACKGROUND 11.01
    Change of duties 11.04
    Presumption of continuity 11.05
B MONTHS AND YEARS OF SERVICE 11.06
C WEEKS IN WHICH THERE IS NO CONTRACT
    OF EMPLOYMENT 11.07
    Temporary cessation of work 11.13
    Arrangement or custom 11.22
    Strikes 11.27

Reinstatement .11.28
Miscellaneous .11.29
D CHANGE OF EMPLOYER 11.30
    Transfer of business 11.32
    Associated employer 11.41
    Change of partners 11.49
    Unincorporated associations 11.50
E ESTOPPEL 11.51

A BACKGROUND

11.01 Statutory continuity of employment is centrally important to most statutory employment protection rights including redundancy pay, maternity pay, and unfair dismissal. The concept is vital in determining: (a) whether the employee has served the appropriate qualifying period; and (b) if so, what is the appropriate amount of award or payment due.

11.02 Continuity is extensively defined in the ERA 1996, Pt XIV, ch I. The aim of the statute is broadly to overcome the common law rule that every change of terms was a new contract, which would artificially restrict employee rights.

11.03 The length of continuous service is so important that it must be stated in the written statement of terms provided under the 1996 Act. The period of service must, however, be lawful employment so that in *Hyland v J.H. Barker (North-West) Ltd* [1985] IRLR 403, the employee was not able to count a vital month in which he received an illegal lodging allowance. Time spent 'in work wholly or mainly outside Great Britain' counts towards continuity save for the purposes of building service for a redundancy payment (ERA 1996, s 215(1) and (2)).

Change of duties

11.04 Continuity is preserved even though, during an employee's service, the duties required by his contract and other incidental terms vary greatly (this is very different to the equal pay provisions where, in effect, continuity is defined by reference to the particular contract under which the employee is engaged at the particular time). He may rise in status from cleaner to managing director and fall all the way back again, but he still retains his continuity. In *Wood v York City Council* [1978] IRLR 228, for example, the employee worked for York City Council for three years in various capacities, finishing up in the Treasurer's Department. He resigned from this post in order to take up a position with the council's York Festival office and, on being made redundant a year later, he qualified to receive redundancy payment since his employment in both capacities was continuous, notwithstanding the change of his duties and intermediate resignation (see also *Jennings v Salford Community Service Agency* [1981] IRLR 76; *Tipper v Roofdec Ltd* [1989] IRLR 419; cf *Ryan v Shipboard Maintenance Ltd* [1980] IRLR 16).

Presumption of continuity

Where an employee works for one employer, there is thus a statutory presumption of continuity and the onus is then on the employer to disprove that the service was continuous (ERA 1996, s 210(5); *Nicholl v Nocorrode Ltd* [1981] IRLR 163). The presumption, however, applies only to employment with one employer; an exceptional case in which continuity bridges service with two or more different employers, such as a transfer of business or between associated employers, must thus be proved on the balance of probabilities by the employee (*Secretary of State for Employment v Cohen* [1987] IRLR 169; see further discussion at 11.32). The presumption of continuity was evident in *Cornwall CC v Prater* [2006] ICR 731. The claimant, a home tutor, worked for the Council for ten years under a series of assignments of different durations. She had a different contract for each pupil. The Court of Appeal held that she was engaged under contracts of employment because on acceptance of the work she had to teach the pupil and the council had to pay her. Although there were gaps in assignments they were covered by the notion of the 'temporary cessation of work' which did not break continuity.   **11.05**

B MONTHS AND YEARS OF SERVICE

The units adopted to measure continuity are calendar months and years. The period of continuity begins on the day when the employee 'starts work' (ERA 1996, s 211(1)(a)). This concept is itself not free from difficulty as shown in *General of the Salvation Army v Dewsbury* [1984] ICR 498. The EAT decided that it referred to the beginning of the contractual period of employment rather than necessarily the date when the full range of the employee's responsibilities began. Thus, a teacher whose post commenced on 1 May, a Saturday, but who did not begin her full teaching load until 4 May because of the intervening bank holiday, was held to have started work on 1 May. The end of continuous service depends on the employment protection right in question, being the effective date of termination in unfair dismissal and the relevant date for redundancy purposes (see 14.92).   **11.06**

C WEEKS IN WHICH THERE IS NO CONTRACT OF EMPLOYMENT

Section 212(1) of the ERA 1996 provides that, 'Any week during the whole or part of which an employee's relations with his employer are governed by a contract of employment counts in computing the employee's period of employment.' It is irrelevant that there is a voluntary termination of employment by the employee, a gap and then a resumption, provided that the requirements of this section are satisfied (see *Sweeney v J. & S. Henderson (Concessions) Ltd* [1999] IRLR 306 and *Carrington v Harwich Dock Co Ltd* [1998] ICR 1112). The section is not concerned with cases where there has been a change of employment (cf in the case of two consecutive employers on a transfer of business, *Gibson v Motortune Ltd* [1990] ICR 740). In *Roach v CSB (Moulds) Ltd* [1991] ICR 349, the EAT held that an employee's employment was not continuous owing to a ten-day break in his employment, even though there was no complete week in which he did not work. Where there is a contract of employment there is continuity even though   **11.07** there is nothing requiring actual performance of work (*Welton v Deluxe Retail Ltd* [2013] ICR 428).

11.08   Generally, if a week is not one of employment, continuity is broken, so that the employee would have to start again to secure continuity. There are, however, exceptions to this principle, especially where the employee is not working for reasons not of his own making, yet he would be considered to be still 'on the books'.

11.09   In the following cases the employee is treated as retaining continuous employment notwithstanding that the contract of employment has ceased to exist. By ERA 1996, s 212(3), the continuity of an employee who is not working is protected in so far as the absence is:

(a) in consequence of sickness or injury up to twenty-six weeks (see *Scarlett v Godfrey Abbot Group Ltd* [1978] IRLR 456);

(b) on account of a temporary cessation of work; and

(c) by arrangement or custom.

11.10   'Absent from work' in all these subparagraphs means 'not only that the employee is not doing any actual work for the employer but that there is no contract of employment subsisting between him and his employer that would entitle the latter to require him to do any work' (*Ford v Warwickshire County Council* [1983] IRLR 126). Although the heading to what was then Sch 13, para 9, read 'Periods in which there is *no* contract of employment', the court held that 'absent from work' meant 'not performing in substance the contract that previously existed between the parties' (*G.W. Stephens & Son v Fish* [1989] ICR 324).

11.11   The vital issue is the *reason* why there is no contract for a particular period not the reason for termination of a contract, whether it be dismissal, frustration, or agreement (*Tipper v Roofdec Ltd* [1989] IRLR 419).

11.12   In *Pearson v Kent County Council* [1992] ICR 20, the employee worked for the county council from 1955 until he decided to resign on the grounds of ill health on 31 May 1984. He accepted the offer of a less demanding position and commenced that work on 11 June. There had been an agreement that there should be a ten-day gap for the purpose of pension arrangements. When he was declared redundant in 1988, he argued for continuity going back to 1984 but the tribunal rejected the claim on the ground that during the ten-day gap he had not been incapable of work in consequence of sickness. The EAT upheld the decision on the ground that during the ten days, there was no medical reason for absence. Further, when the employee was to return in a new position, the employment tribunal had to be satisfied that he was incapable of carrying out that position as well.

Temporary cessation of work

11.13   A temporary cessation of work usually signifies a short-term closure of a workplace due to, say, lack of orders, a fire, an explosion (*Newsham v Dunlop Textiles Ltd (No 2)* (1969) 4 ITR 268), or a strike at suppliers (although a dispute at the employee's plant would not fall within this rubric: *Hanson v Fashion Industries (Hartlepool) Ltd* [1980] IRLR 393). The reason for the temporary cessation is irrelevant (*Welton v Deluxe Retail Ltd* [2013] ICR 428). Another sequence which used to be common occurred in *Hunter v Smith's Dock Co Ltd* [1968] 2 All ER 81. During the applicant's forty years of working for the respondent, he was accustomed to being laid off for a week or two at various times until trade picked up. These were treated as temporary cessations of work and his continuity was maintained.

Whose work must have ceased temporarily?

It is sufficient that the employer's need for work to be done by the particular employee **11.14** has ceased even if the other aspects of the business run as normal. The issue received the attention of the House of Lords in *Fitzgerald v Hall, Russell & Co Ltd* [1970] AC 984. There, although the applicant welder was laid off for an extended period, many of his colleague welders were not, and the employer thus argued that there had been no cessation of welding work from their viewpoint. The House of Lords, however, decided that the relevant consideration was that there 'was no longer work available for him [the employee] personally' and Lord Upjohn continued, 'The question whether at the same time the whole works would close down or a department was closed down or a large number of other employees were laid off at the same time would seem to be irrelevant in a computation essentially personal to the particular workman.'

Where work is in fact available for an employee to perform but it is merely not offered to **11.15** him, there is no cessation of work for statutory purposes (*Byrne v City of Birmingham DC* [1988] ICR 480). Three questions must be posed in each case:

(a) Was there a *cessation* of the employee's work?
(b) Was the employee's absence *on account* of that cessation?
(c) Was the cessation *temporary*?

What is temporary?

(1) **The nature of the breaks** The temporary issue has received most attention naturally in **11.16** respect of schoolteachers. In *Rashid v ILEA* [1977] ICR 157, the EAT held that the school holidays were not a temporary 'cessation of work' for the claimant, a supply teacher, who was not paid during them since 'at the end of each term that job finished; at the beginning of the next term he started another one'. This was, however, overruled in the House of Lords decision in *Ford v Warwickshire CC* [1983] IRLR 126 where the employee had been engaged on eight successive contracts lasting for one academic year each. Their Lordships did not consider that it made any difference that the absences for the holidays were foreseeable, predictable, and regular; nor were they attracted by the 'job by job' argument. Whilst it would not be so in every case, here it was conceded that having regard to the length of the total period of employment the holiday absences were temporary. Lord Diplock had in mind also seasonal absences in agriculture and the hotel and catering trade (see also *McLeod v Hellyer Brothers* [1987] IRLR 232, CA). Furthermore, absence because an employer is short of funds to pay the worker qualifies as absence on account of a temporary cessation of work since work in this context means *paid* work, according to the EAT in *University of Aston in Birmingham v Malik* [1984] ICR 492.

In *Letheby & Christopher Ltd v Bond* [1988] ICR 480, it was held that there cannot be **11.17** such an absence when the employee was engaged under a series of single separate contracts (see also *G. W. Stephens & Son v Fish* [1989] ICR 324). This is increasingly common in zero hours or on-call contracts.

(2) **Reviewing temporary breaks** 'Temporary' means in this context transient, that is, **11.18** lasting only for a relatively short time in relation to the total relationship of employment (*Ford*'s case). The temporary nature of the cessation of work is to be reviewed *ex post facto* and what the parties intended at its inception is only marginally relevant to this question. A projected temporary closure may prove permanent because, say, a drop in orders lasts longer than anyone expected. This is a question of fact in each case, and Phillips J stated in *Bentley Engineering Co Ltd v Crown* [1976] IRLR 146 that, 'The Tribunal is enjoined to look at the matter as the historian of a completed chapter of events

and not as a journalist describing events as they occur from day to day.' An employee may during the temporary cessation take a job elsewhere (*Thompson v Bristol Channel Ship Repairers* (1969) 4 ITR 262) and still qualify. In *Bentley Engineering Co Ltd v Crown*, a two-year gap was held to be temporary in the circumstances, and Phillips J indicated these as some factors to be taken into consideration in determining whether the intervening period was temporary: the nature of the employment; the length of prior and subsequent service; the duration of the break; what happened during the break; and what was said on re-engagement.

11.19 (3) **Aggregation** In *Lewis v Surrey County Council* [1987] IRLR 509, the House of Lords determined that the respondent, a part-time teacher, did not meet the necessary continuous service requirements when she was employed by the appellant on a term-by-term basis under three separate and independent concurrent contracts. An interval between separate contracts as opposed to intervals between successor and predecessor contracts also could not amount to a temporary cessation of work. Each series of contracts has to be considered in isolation from any other. On the other hand, Lord Ackner accepted the EAT's view that where an unscrupulous employer deliberately subjects the employment relationship to a mosaic of separate contracts for the purpose of specifically depriving an employee of the rights to which he would have been entitled had the whole of his engagement been incorporated in a single employment contract, the employment tribunal could penetrate the superficial disguise, look at the substance of the arrangements, and arrive at a conclusion that purported multiple contracts were in reality one single contract. It might suggest that there was also a unifying umbrella contract which was collateral to those separate contracts under which the minimum hours requirement was satisfied.

11.20 (4) **The mathematical approach** A strictly mathematical approach to the concept of temporary cessation, however, is not appropriate in all cases. In *Flack v Kodak Ltd* [1986] IRLR 255, the Court of Appeal said that in determining this issue in relation to persons who had worked intermittently over a period of years, the tribunal must have regard to all the circumstances and should not confine itself to taking the percentage that the gap of work bore to the periods of work immediately adjoining it. Moreover, the whole period of intermittent employment should be considered, and not only those in the two-year period which formed the qualifying time.

11.21 'Temporary' in relation to the cessation of work has to be construed in the sense of a relatively short time compared with the period in work. In *Sillars v Charrington Fuels Ltd* [1989] IRLR 152, the employee who drove fuel delivery lorries had, over a total period of fifteen years, spent about half of each year in the respondent's employment and the remainder out of it. Thus, the finding that there was not a temporary cessation would be upheld. Where seasonal workers had a pattern of work of twenty-three weeks in work and twenty-nine weeks out of work, there was no continuity; a cessation could not be temporary when it was greater than the period in work (*Berwick Salmon Fisheries Co Ltd v Rutherford* [1991] IRLR 203).

Arrangement or custom

11.22 In order to maintain continuity by reason of 'arrangement or custom' there must be an agreement or understanding at the time of departure from work of the employee that the employee will be so absent and return. The lack of such mutuality of expectation was fatal to this claim in *Murphy v A. Birrell & Sons Ltd* [1978] IRLR 458. The claimant had worked for the respondents for nineteen years before taking another job (although not officially resigning) because of an argument with the manager. When things were smoothed over, she returned and the newly appointed managing director told her that 'her old contract stood'. This could not *ex post facto* convert the absence into one which was by arrangement.

An 'arrangement' requires that *in advance of the break*, there must have been some dis- **11.23** cussion or agreement to the effect that the parties regard the employment relationship as continuing despite the termination of the contract of employment. This was so held in *Booth v USA* [1999] IRLR 16, irrespective of the fact that the employer may pur- posely have introduced breaks in employment to defeat the application of the legislation. Morison J stated that, 'if by so arranging their affairs, an employer is lawfully able to employ people in such a manner that the employees cannot complain of unfair dismissal or seek a redundancy payment, that is a matter for him' (para 16). As in the case of tem- porary cessation, an employee may be considered as continuing in the employment of one employer even though he takes a position with another. Rather unusually, in *Ingram v Foxon* [1984] ICR 685 a reinstatement agreement made some months after the employ- ment ceased and after tribunal proceedings had been issued, was held to constitute such an arrangement (although see *Morris v Walsh Western UK Ltd* [1997] IRLR 563, which refused to follow *Ingram*). This, however, does not include a resignation for a child break scheme with all the financial consequences of cessation of employment and the emphasis on re-employment as an option at the end of the period (*Curr v Marks & Spencer plc* [2003] IRLR 74; *Evans v Malley Organisation Ltd* [2003] ICR 443).

Secondment to another company is the best example of arrangements which fit under this **11.24** rubric. In *Wishart v National Coal Board* [1974] ICR 460, the claimant was employed by the NCB from 1946 to 1973 except for one year when he worked for Cementation Ltd, which carried out development work for the NCB. Since he remained a member of the Mineworkers' Pension Scheme and the two companies worked closely together, the EAT considered that he was working for Cementation by arrangement with the NCB.

A similar practice was found among shipyard workers whose contracts lasted only as **11.25** long as there was work to be done but who would expect to be re-engaged as soon as work picked up (*Puttick v John Wright & Sons (Blackwall) Ltd* [1972] ICR 457; see also *Brown v Southall and Knight* [1980] IRLR 130; *Duff v Evan Thomas Radcliffe & Co Ltd* [1979] ICR 720). Continuing to pay an employee during a break normally points towards there being such an arrangement.

The EAT somewhat widened the provision in the case of *Lloyds Bank Ltd v Secretary of* **11.26** *State for Employment* [1979] ICR 258, where the employee, who worked one week on, one week off, was held to be absent from work on her off weeks by arrangement or cus- tom. This decision was reached notwithstanding that the cross-heading to the statutory provision indicated that it only applies where there is *no contract*, and here the agree- ment clearly still subsisted. The case was indeed distinguished in *Corton House Ltd v Skipper* [1981] IRLR 78, and its authority must be considered very doubtful in the light of *Ford*'s case in which the House of Lords decided that 'absent from work' meant more than merely not at work; rather it was when there was no contract which could require the employee to work.

Strikes

Special rules apply to the treatment of strikes. Their effect on continuity is an unusual **11.27** hybrid in that, while a week during which for any part of that week the employee is engaged in a strike does not breach continuity, it is not counted as a week of employment (see *Hanson v Fashion Industries (Hartlepool) Ltd* [1980] IRLR 393). Nice questions may also arise in this regard as to when a strike actually begins and ends (eg *Winnett v Seamarks Brothers Ltd* [1978] IRLR 387). The weeks of a lock-out are deducted in a similar manner. It also does not matter that an employee took work elsewhere during the strike or lock-out.

Reinstatement

11.28 Where an employee successfully claims to have been unfairly dismissed and is reinstated or re-engaged by his employer, a successor employer, or associated employer, his continuity is preserved and he can include in his continuous service the time in between dismissal and reinstatement. This applies where re-employment is as a result of an employment tribunal order, an agreement made through the good offices of an ACAS conciliation officer, or by a valid settlement agreement (Employment Protection (Continuity of Employment) Regulations 1996 (SI 1996/3147)). A similar preservation of continuity applies to voluntary reinstatement outside the ACAS or tribunals systems (*Ingram v Foxon*, above). This does not, however, apply to a redundant employee when the weeks of the interval count only for the purpose of redundancy payment qualification.

Miscellaneous

11.29 (a) In the case of redundancy payments, a week does not count if the employee worked outside Great Britain during the whole or part thereof and no employer's Class 1 national insurance contributions were payable by the employer (ERA 1996, s 215(2)).

(b) Periods spent in the armed forces do not break continuity but also do not count as periods of employment if the employee is entitled to apply to his former employer under the Reserve Forces (Safeguard of Employment) Act 1985 and he rejoins that employer within six months of leaving (ERA 1996, s 217(1)).

D CHANGE OF EMPLOYER

11.30 The common law position was that every contract of employment was discrete, and for the good reason that if employees might be transferred at will from contract to contract, they would, in the words of Lord Atkin in *Nokes v Doncaster Amalgamated Collieries Ltd* [1940] AC 1014, be 'serfs and not servants'. However, this can act as a boomerang against employees in the different circumstances of a statutory floor of employment protection rights. Thus, there are five important rules for maintaining continuity when an employee works in sequence for *different* employers. The periods are considered continuous where:

(a) 'a trade or business, or an undertaking ... is transferred from one person to another' (s 218(2));

(b) 'an employee of an employer is taken into the employment of another employer who, at the time when the employee enters the second employer's employment, is an *associated employer* of the first employer ...' (s 218(6));

(c) one *body corporate* is substituted for another body corporate as the employer by or under an Act of Parliament (s 218(3));

(d) the employer *dies* and his personal representatives or trustees keep on the employee (s 218(4)), even where the employee is also the personal representative (*Rowley, Holmes and Co v Barber* [1977] ICR 387); and

(e) there is a *change in the partners*, personal representatives, or trustees who employ him (s 218(5)). This is necessary since the employees of a partnership are in law employed by the individual partners jointly, so that each time there is a change of partners continuity would be lost if it were not for this provision in the ERA 1996, s 218.

In applying these rules the *capacity* in which the worker is employed with the second **11.31** company is irrelevant. The House of Lords established this important principle in *Lord Advocate v De Rosa* [1974] 2 All ER 849. The majority thought that all that was required was employment continuously first by one employer, and then by another to whom the business had been transferred. It was irrelevant that the first employer had terminated the contract and the second had not continued the employment by a suitable alternative offer. The same rule applied both to initial entitlement to rights and assessment of the value of the rights where this depended on length of service.

Transfer of business

The Transfer of Undertakings (Protection of Employment) Regulations 2006 achieve an **11.32** automatic continuation of the contract of employment on a transfer which falls within their scope. Continuity provisions are probably rights arising 'under or in connection with the contract of employment', which is the bundle of rights transferred under the Regulations. The result will in any event inevitably be the same under the continuity statute and transfer regulations since the definition under the 2006 Regulations is virtually coincident with that under s 218(2) (see Chapter 18). That provision applies to the transfer of a 'trade or business, or an undertaking' and the only further definition is that business includes a trade or business or any activity carried on by a body of persons whether corporate or unincorporate. 'Undertaking' includes the functions of a minister or government department. Although there is no express reference to transfer of *part* of an undertaking, employment tribunals should read this concept into the statute (eg *Gibson v Motortune Ltd* [1990] ICR 740).

Transfer

In *Melon v Hector Powe Ltd* [1981] ICR 43 Lord Fraser declared that there was an 'essen- **11.33** tial distinction between the transfer of a business, or part of a business, and a transfer of physical assets ... in the former case the business is transferred as a going concern so that the business remains the same but it is in different hands ... whereas in the latter the assets are transferred to the new owner to be used in whatever business he chooses'.

The Court of Appeal decision in *Woodhouse v Peter Brotherhood Ltd* [1972] 2 QB 520 **11.34** went further. Crossleys Ltd had for many years manufactured diesel engines at their Sandiacre factory. It removed this part of its operation to Manchester and sold to Peter Brotherhood Ltd the factory and much of the plant and machinery therein. The latter company ultimately turned it to the production of spinning machines, compressors, and steam turbines. They first completed four large engines on which Crossleys was engaged at the time of the sale. The two employees who claimed redundancy payments had been engaged for the last six months of their service on the same engines as before. The National Industrial Relations Court's test for transfer was whether the 'working environment' had changed, and it decided it had not done so. Thus, continuity was preserved. It was particularly impressed by the fact that, since the entire workforce had been taken over, most employees were unlikely to realise that they should at this point claim redundancy payments if continuity was indeed broken.

11.35   The Court of Appeal, however, rejected this straightforward approach, and decided that 'the new owner did not take over the business as a going concern, but only the physical assets, using them in a different business'. Although 'the same men are employed using the same tools, the business is different'. The EAT was again overruled by the higher courts in *Melon v Hector Powe Ltd* (above). The respondents were multiple tailors who owned a factory at Blantyre where they had, for many years, manufactured men's suits made to measure. In 1977, due to a fall in demand, Executex Manufacturing Ltd took over the factory, including work in progress which they undertook to complete. One-hundred-and-twenty employees sought redundancy payments on the takeover. Hector Powe Ltd defended these claims on the ground that there was a transfer of business and pointed in particular to the continuation of work in progress. Lord Fraser dismissed this factor as 'merely a temporary expedient to help Executex through the initial stages'. The House of Lords decided that the issue was one of fact for the employment tribunal. They also rejected the contention that this was at least a transfer of *part* of a business since such a change 'will ... seldom occur except when that part is to some extent separable and severable from the rest of the business either geographically or by reference to products or in some other way'.

11.36   The distinctions drawn may seem somewhat narrow. In *Crompton v Truly Fair (International) Ltd* [1975] ICR 359, for example, the EAT decided that since the new employer was manufacturing children's clothing rather than men's trousers, the business was different and had not been transferred.

11.37   There may be a transfer between partners (*Jeetle v Elster* [1985] IRLR 227) but there must be an actual transfer of some sort, and it is insufficient that another company may have assumed *de facto* control whilst negotiations for purchase of a business took place (*SI (Systems and Instrumentation) Ltd v Grist and Riley* [1983] IRLR 391; cf *Dabell v Vale Industrial Services Ltd* [1988] IRLR 439).

Employment 'at the time of transfer'

11.38   There are two possible interpretations of the statutory phrase that it applies to those in employment 'at the time of transfer':

(a) that the *relationship of employer and employee* must subsist at that time; or
(b) that the *period of employment* accumulated counts.

Both interpretations, however, require that the concept of 'transfer' has a starting and end point. The most searching, but ultimately unsatisfactory, discussion of the concept is found in the Court of Appeal decision in *Teesside Times Ltd v Drury* [1980] IRLR 72. The applicant had been employed by Champion Publications Ltd for six years, when the company ran into financial difficulties and negotiations were opened with the appellants with a view to a takeover. These reached fruition in a general agreement at about 3pm on Friday, 17 November 1975. A few hours later Champion's receiver dismissed all its employees, but this was still some time before the formal contract was signed. Although the appellant's management assured the staff that they would be re-engaged, the applicant was dismissed three days after takeover. He had to establish that there was a transfer of business to claim unfair dismissal. The appellants argued that he was not employed at *the* 'time' of transfer', since he had been dismissed before the formalities of the sale had been completed. All three Lord Justices found for the respondent on the ground that he was, under the then provisions of Sch 13 to the EPCA 1978, to be taken to have been employed for the whole of the week, and therefore his continuity was preserved until the following Monday.

On the conceptual issue, Eveleigh LJ adopted the first view set out above so that there was **11.39** continuity 'so long as the dismissal was a step towards the re-engagement'. Stephenson LJ on the other hand considered that a contract must be in effect during the transfer. This was, however, 'a complex of operations which are part of a continuous process through different stages, including dismissal and re-engagement of staff'. The full extent of the transfer was a 'question of fact and degree in the light of common sense'. Goff LJ defined it more narrowly as 'the moment when the transaction of transferring the business is effected'.

An ample view is most in line with the policy of both the European Directive and the UK **11.40** legislation. This would include at least the stages within the transfer process of general agreement, the dismissal, and re-engagement of employees and the entry into possession, and transfer of full legal title. Should the employee be under a contract at any of these stages, continuity would be preserved (see *Litster v Forth Dry Dock Engineering Co Ltd* [1989] ICR 341 with respect to transfers of undertakings). This approach has been confirmed as correct by the Court of Appeal in *Clark & Tokeley Ltd v Oakes* [1998] IRLR 577; *Celtec v Astley* [2001] IRLR 788.

Associated employer

Section 231 of the ERA 1996 gives 'associated employer' a technical and rather limited **11.41** meaning:

... any two employers shall be treated as associated if—

(a) one is a company of which the other (directly or indirectly) has control, or
(b) both are companies of which a third person (directly or indirectly) has control.

Exhaustive definition

The vital question for determination of the status of 'associated employer' is whether **11.42** the subsection was exhaustive or had merely illustrative status. The Court of Appeal determined in *Gardiner v London Borough of Merton* [1980] IRLR 472 that the former was the correct view. In that case, the appellant's local government career began in 1965 and he had worked for four different authorities before his dismissal in 1977. He sought to count all twelve years. The Court of Appeal restricted the definition to limited companies and in any event doubted whether anyone had sufficient control of the various councils to fall within the subsection. Griffiths LJ pointed to the problems which might arise if the section were not construed as exhaustive. It would then be necessary to give some other meaning to 'associated'. There were a myriad of possibilities including 'associated in a common purpose, associated through a common element of control or associated through a common interest or associated through common negotiation with a trade union'. This would necessitate 'far-ranging and complex inquiries into the activities of a complainant's present and previous employers'. To predict the outcome of such litigation would prove hazardous. The change from 'company' to employer in the 1975 Act merely intended to include the case of the sole trader who became a limited company. Further, if the section was not intended to be exhaustive, it would not be appropriate for s 153(4) to conclude with the phrase 'and the expression "associated employer" shall be construed accordingly' (see to the same effect *Hasley v Fair Employment Agency* [1989] IRLR 106—where it was held that the Northern Ireland Fair Employment Agency and the Equal Opportunities Commission were not associated employers—but a partnership of companies may be associated: *Pinkney v Sandpiper Drilling Ltd* [1989] ICR 389).

11.43	In the normal case, for continuity to be preserved the second employer must be an associated employer *at the time when the employee enters the employment* of the second employer. The courts have rejected the proposition that there may be no gap at all between the first and second employment (*Bentley Engineering Co Ltd v Crown* [1976] IRLR 146; *Charnock v Barrie Muirhead Ltd* [1984] ICR 641).

11.44	Since it defeated the reasonable expectations of employees who had spent all of their working life in local government, the result in *Gardiner* was altered for the purpose of redundancy payments by the Redundancy Payments (Local Government) (Modification) Order 1983 (SI 1983/1160). This has been amended on several subsequent occasions (see especially SI 1999/2277), primarily in order to extend the number of bodies within the (already extensive) definition of local government employer. The bodies now include most education, planning and development, public transport, police fire and civil defence, and social service institutions. Likewise, the ERA 1996, s 218(8), preserves continuity for employees moving from one health service employer to another as part of their professional training. The employers include Strategic Health Authorities, Primary Care Trusts, NHS Foundation Trusts, NHS Trusts, and Local Health Boards.

11.45	Further, by the ERA 1996, s 218(7), continuity is preserved in the special case of an employee who moves from employment by a local education authority to the service of governors of a local education authority maintained school and vice versa and in certain other narrowly defined circumstances.

The meaning of control

11.46	The concept of control by one company of another was at first flexibly construed. It had regard to the direction of operations not merely the ownership of shares (*Zarb and Samuels v British & Brazilian Produce Co (Sales) Ltd* [1978] IRLR 78). This liberal approach was limited by the EAT in *Secretary of State for Employment v Newbold and David Armstrong (Catering Services) Ltd* [1981] IRLR 305, with unfortunate results for the applicant, and possible opportunities for avoidance for employers. David Armstrong Junior owned 46 per cent of the shares of the applicant's first employer, Armstrong Bakers Ltd, and 99 per cent of the second employer, David Armstrong (Catering Services) Ltd. They were not, however, associated according to Bristow J, because:

> In the law affecting companies, control is well recognised to mean control by the majority of votes attaching to shares exercised in General Meeting. It is not how or by whom the enterprise is actually run. Control rests in those who by the constitution of the company can say to the management 'Thou shalt do this; thou shalt not do that; thou art no longer the management'.

The applicant lost his valuable continuity rights notwithstanding that: the share ownership was beyond his ken; he had no written contract; and David Armstrong was 'the mainspring of the family business'.

11.47	In *Washington Arts Association Ltd v Forster* [1983] ICR 346, a transfer between the appellants, a guarantee company, and an arts centre which it in effect ran was held not to be a transfer between associated employers. Further, in *Hair Colour Consultants Ltd v Mena* [1984] ICR 671, a claim for continuity failed where the applicant had started work as a hair stylist at a salon run by Interhair Ltd which was owned jointly by two brothers, each of whom held 50 per cent of the shares. She then went to the respondent company in which one brother owned 85 per cent of the shares, but the other had none. Negative control of just 50 per cent of the shareholding was not enough to satisfy the stringent conditions of the statute (see also *South West Launderettes Ltd v Laidler* [1986] ICR 455).

Zarb's case is, however, still authority for the proposition that the persons who control two companies may be a group acting in concert. They must be the *same* group of individuals in each company (*Poparm Ltd v Weekes* [1984] IRLR 388). The approach in *Zarb* was preferred in *Harford v Swiftrim Ltd* [1987] ICR 439 and *Tice v Cartwright* [1999] ICR 769 (cf *Strudwick v IBL* [1988] ICR 796; *Payne v Secretary of State for Employment* [1989] IRLR 352).

A company qualifies as an associated employer even if it is incorporated overseas, provided that it is a body which can be likened in its essentials to a company limited under the Companies Act 2006 (*Hancill v Marcon Engineering Ltd* [1990] ICR 103). **11.48**

Change of partners

Where there is a change of the partners who employ the applicant, continuity is preserved. In *Harold Fielding Ltd v Mansi* [1974] 1 All ER 1035, it was held that this did not apply where employment by a partnership is followed by work for one of the former partners on his own account. It can hardly be supposed that such a technical limitation was intended by Parliament and the case was narrowly distinguished in *Allen & Son v Coventry* [1979] IRLR 399 as applying only when different businesses were involved. Moreover, in *Jeetle v Elster* [1985] IRLR 227, the transfer from four doctors to one was held to fall within the paragraph, and the *Mansi* case was disapproved. **11.49**

Unincorporated associations

A change in the composition of the management committee of an unincorporated association will not have the effect of breaking the continuity of service of the association's employees. Such employees are to be treated as employed by the management committee as constituted from time to time (*Affleck v Newcastle MIND* [1999] ICR 852). **11.50**

E ESTOPPEL

Continuity is a purely *statutory* concept. Thus, a second employer who told an employee that he would recognise fifty years' previous employment as continuous with the new job could not be held to his statement under statutory remedies, although possibly by contract enforceable in the county court. Certainly the Department of BIS would not have had to pay a rebate for such period, as it was not privy to the arrangement. **11.51**

In *Evenden v Guildford AFC* [1975] QB 917, the Court of Appeal had suggested that a statement by the respondent football club that the appellant could carry forward his previous service with the Guildford Supporters Club (which was not associated with the Football Club within the meaning of the Act) operated by way of proprietary estoppel, so that the club could not go back on it. Lord Denning MR further thought that the statutory presumption of continuity of employment applied to employment by successive employers. **11.52**

The doctrine of *Evenden* was overruled by the House of Lords in *Secretary of State for Employment v Globe Elastic Thread Co Ltd* [1979] 2 All ER 1077. The Department of Employment (which was then responsible for these payments; now BIS) refused to give a redundancy rebate to the respondent in respect of the dismissal of Mr Wyazko. This was calculated to include not only the five years' work for Globe but also twenty-two years for Heathcotes, which was not an associated company. Further, no business had **11.53** been transferred from one to the other. There had, however, been a statement, on which Mr Wyazko relied, that the service would be treated as continuous. The *ratio* of the decision was that the redundancy payment had not been 'made under the Act' so that the Department of Employment was not obliged by statute to pay a rebate, and could not be estopped from denying continuity. Their Lordships stated that any arrangement worked not by estoppel but by contract between Globe and Wyazko, and went on:

> Any employer is perfectly entitled to make his own arrangement with his employees, and no doubt many employers do so, departing in various ways from the terms of the Act. Such arrangements may have the force of a contract, and be enforceable as such, but they cannot commit the Minister to make a rebate. The Minister is only liable to do so in respect of payments made strictly under the Act.

Although this leaves open the possibility of a contractually binding statement by the second employer, this could only at the time have been established in the county court and it might be difficult to prove the employee had provided consideration (see also *Collison v British Broadcasting Corporation* [1998] ICR 669, in which *Globe Elastic* was applied).

11.54   The 'two-way' estoppel case of *Smith v Blandford Gee Cementation Ltd* [1970] 3 All ER 154 remains good law. The applicant thought he was employed by the respondent as an underground waller on repairs for the National Coal Board. By a Task Work Agreement between the respondent and the NCB, Blandford Gee was agent for the NCB for employment purposes. Since it was Blandford Gee who behaved as his employer and gave the applicant his written statement of terms it could not deny it was his employer for the purposes of redundancy payment.

12

THE SCOPE OF STATUTORY PROTECTION: UNFAIR DISMISSAL AND REDUNDANCY

A QUALIFYING PERIOD 12.04

B LIMITS IN TIME 12.07

The normal time limit 12.08

The power to extend time: General
principles 12.11

The power to extend: Particular
examples 12.17

C ILLEGALITY 12.25

Knowledge of illegality 12.28

Severance 12.33

D GEOGRAPHICAL LIMITATIONS 12.34

E THE NATURE OF THE EMPLOYER 12.42

F THE NATURE OF THE EMPLOYMENT 12.43

G EXCLUSION BY AGREEMENT 12.44

Agreement between management and
union 12.48

Individual agreement 12.50

H MISCELLANEOUS 12.58

Only employees are eligible for most employment protection rights; independent con-   **12.01**
tractors are not covered. Before examining the main statutory rights for employees of
redundancy and unfair dismissal, it must be noted that the employee should also have
completed the minimum qualifying period of service which is different for each right
(12.04–12.06), and make his claim in time (12.07–12.16). There are also several exclusions, most of which are common to unfair dismissal, redundancy, and most of the other
employment protection rights, although any necessary distinctions will be identified.

There have been several changes in the scope of these exclusions, including the repeal of   **12.02**
the exemption of employers of fewer than five workers which was found in the Industrial
Relations Act 1971, and varying the length of qualifying periods on several occasions as
governments have changed.

Once it is established that the claimant is an employee of the employer, the onus is on the   **12.03**
latter to show that the employee was excluded from the statutory entitlements (*Kapur v
Shields* [1976] ICR 26). Most exclusions, however, go to establish the very jurisdiction of
the tribunal to hear the claim itself so that even if neither party raises them, the tribunal
itself must enquire whether they are satisfied (*BMA Ltd v Lewis* [1978] ICR 782). It is
normally appropriate for an employment tribunal to consider the question as a separate
preliminary issue.

A QUALIFYING PERIOD

The qualifying period in redundancy payments has always been two years' continuous   **12.04**
service, but the time for unfair dismissal has varied with the differing policies of different
governments. It is now two years in most cases.

12.05   The *Seymour-Smith* cases ([1999] IRLR 253 and [1997] IRLR 315, for the ECJ and House of Lords judgments respectively) tested whether the two-year period was in breach of the EU Equal Treatment Directive. The ECJ merely said that the national court 'must verify whether the statistics available indicate that a considerably smaller percentage of women than men is able to fulfil the requirement imposed'; and as to justification 'it is for the Member State to show that the rule reflects a legitimate aim of its social policy, that that aim is unrelated to any discrimination based on sex and that it could reasonably consider that the means chosen were suitable for attaining that aim'. In *R v Secretary of State for Employment, ex p Seymour Smith (No 2)* [2000] ICR 244, the House of Lords finally decided by 3:2 that the evidence adduced as to the proportion of men and women who were able to satisfy the two-year qualifying period showed a persistent and constant disparity over a long period so as to amount to indirect discrimination for the purposes of Art 119 of the Treaty of Rome unless shown to be justified by objective factors. It held, however, that this was a reasonable response to a legitimate aim which was unrelated to discrimination based on sex, of encouraging recruitment by employers.

12.06   There are just two modifications to the two-year rule:

(a) Where the dismissal is on the grounds of one of the automatically unfair grounds, such as trade union membership or activities, health and safety activities or assertion of a statutory right, or unlawful discrimination, or the employee is dismissed by reason of pregnancy, or as a protected Sunday worker or as an employee representative, or as an occupational pension fund trustee, or because he made a protected disclosure under the Public Interest Disclosure Act 1998 (now ERA s 47B), there is no qualification period at all (ERA 1996, s 108); these are day 1 rights.

(b) Where the dismissal follows a refusal by the employer to pay an employee who is suspended from work on medical grounds, there is a one-month qualification period (ERA 1996, s 65(1)).

B   LIMITS IN TIME

12.07   'The intention of the Act is that claims for compensation should be presented promptly' (*Westward Circuits Ltd v Read* [1973] ICR 301 NIRC).

The normal time limit

12.08   The following principles apply:

(a) The employee has three months from the effective date of termination (defined at 14.92) inclusive of the first day in which to present a claim to an employment tribunal for unfair dismissal, and six months for redundancy and where strikers claim unfair dismissal under the TURL(C)A 1992, ss 237–9. Thus, if the effective date of termination is 31 August, the last date for presentation would be 30 November (*Pruden v Cunard Ellerman Ltd* [1993] IRLR 317; *University of Cambridge v Murray* [1993] IRLR 460; *Pacitti Jones v O'Brien* [2005] IRLR 888; for full discussion see Mansfield *et al, Blackstone Employment Practice*, OUP, 2015).

(b) It is important that the employment tribunal first identifies the precise cause of action relied on by the claimant and the appropriate limitation periods before determining the date from which time begins to run and, therefore, whether the applicant is out of time (*Taylorplan Services Ltd v Jackson* [1996] IRLR 184).

(c) A claim is 'presented' when it is delivered to the relevant Office of Employment Tribunals (*Hammond v Haigh Castle & Co Ltd* [1973] ICR 148; *Post Office v Moore* [1981] ICR 623).

(d) A solicitor should operate a system which enables him to find out contemporaneously whether the conduct of business is taking a normal course and to check at or near the time that replies from the employment tribunal which should have been received at a given date have in fact been received. Such a system was not operating where it involved no more than a check several weeks after the solicitor expected an acknowledgement from the employment tribunal (*Camden & Islington Community Services NHS Trust v Kennedy* [1996] IRLR 381). The 'ordinary course of email', without any contrary indication that an email message has not been sent, is to expect delivery within a reasonable time thereafter, perhaps half an hour up to an hour (see *Initial Electronic Security Systems Ltd v Avdic* [2005] IRLR 671).

(e) Whether the claim is presented in time goes to the jurisdiction of the tribunal to hear the claim. As Lord Denning MR said in *Dedman v British Building & Engineering Appliances Ltd* [1974] ICR 53, 'If [an application] arrives a minute after midnight on the last day the clerks must throw it out; the tribunal is not competent to hear it'.

(f) Section 111(3) of the ERA 1996, however, permits a premature application but only in the case of unfair dismissal, so that where a dismissal takes place with notice, the employee may make an application during that notice period.

(g) An appeal varied the date on which termination took effect: *Hawes & Curtis Ltd v Arfan* [2012] ICR 1244.

When an employee is dismissed by letter the three-month limitation period for bringing a claim runs from the date when the employee has actually read the letter or has had a reasonable opportunity of reading it rather than the date when the letter was posted or delivered, or the date when the employer decided to dismiss: *Gisda Cyf v Barratt* [2010] IRLR 1073. General common law principles do not necessarily apply in this arena. **12.09**

The effective date in notice cases is the date on which notice expires. In this context the law takes no account of any fractions of a day so that notice which is given during one day does not take effect until the following day, and in the absence of an express or implied agreement in the contract of employment or letter of dismissal that notice is to start immediately on receipt; that rule should be applied to notices of dismissal regardless of whether the notice was oral or in writing (*Wang v University of Keele* [2011] ICR 1251). **12.10**

The power to extend time: General principles

The time limit often proves inadequate and the employment tribunal may thus allow a reasonable further period 'in a case where it is satisfied that it was not reasonably practicable for the complaint to be presented before the end of that period of three months' (ERA 1996, s 111(2)). The Court of Appeal considered that this statutory phrase was 'not really apt in the particular context'. The best approach was to read the word 'practicable' as the equivalent of feasible '... and to ask colloquially and untrammelled by too much legal logic—was it reasonably feasible to present the complaint to the employment tribunal within the relevant three months' (*Palmer v Southend-on-Sea BC* [1984] IRLR 119). **12.11**

The early cases tended to view this as a general equitable principle, to be 'considered in the light of general standards of ordinary people in industry'. More guidance, however, was given by Lord Denning MR's so-called liberal approach in *Dedman v British Building & Engineering Appliances Ltd* [1974] IRLR 379, then construing the twenty-eight-day period for unfair dismissal: **12.12**

> If in the circumstances the man knew or was put on inquiry as to his rights, and as to the time limit then it was practicable for him to have presented his complaint within the four weeks, and he ought to have done so. But if he did not know and there was nothing to put him on inquiry, then it was not practicable and he should be excused.

12.13   The working out of this principle did not prove so liberal primarily because the Master of the Rolls went on to say:

> If a man engages skilled advisers to act for him and they mistake the time limit and present it too late—he is out. His remedy is against them.

This may weigh against less-well-advised employees. Moreover, the concept of the 'skilled adviser' was widely interpreted to include not only a solicitor (as in *Dedman*) but also such persons as a trade union official and a Citizens Advice Bureau adviser. In *Riley v Tesco Stores Ltd* [1980] IRLR 103, the Court of Appeal, however, disapproved of construction of the title 'skilled adviser' as if it were itself a part of a statute. Stephenson LJ regarded this as 'bewildering and deplorable'.

12.14   The fault of an adviser is to be treated as the fault of the claimant for these purposes (*Trevelyans (Birmingham) Ltd v Norton* [1991] ICR 488). It has subsequently been held that there is, however, no absolute rule about skilled advisers to the effect that in each case where such an adviser has been consulted, the claimant may never demonstrate that it has not been reasonably practicable to present his or her complaint in time (*London International College Ltd v Sen* [1993] IRLR 333, see also *Harber v North London Polytechnic* [1990] IRLR 198; *Capital Foods Retail Ltd v Corrigan* [1993] IRLR 430). The time limit may indeed be extended on the basis that the employee was given erroneous legal advice (*Hawkins v Bell* [1996] IRLR 258).

12.15   The issue is one of fact and degree and the appeal tribunal and Court of Appeal deprecate appeals. Thus, in *Walls Meat Co Ltd v Khan* [1979] ICR 52, Shaw LJ stated:

> The test is empirical and involves no legal concept. Practical common sense is the keynote and legalistic footnotes may have no better result than to introduce a lawyer's complication into what should be a layman's pristine province. These considerations prompt me to express the emphatic view that the forum to decide such questions is the Industrial Tribunal and that their decision should prevail unless it is plainly perverse or oppressive.

12.16   A fundamental attack on the present arrangements on discrimination grounds failed in *Biggs v Somerset CC* [1996] ICR 364. This was an attempt by a part-time teacher working fourteen hours per week who had been dismissed in August 1976, to apply to an employment tribunal in 1994 after the decision of the House of Lords that the then qualifying thresholds for part-time employees were incompatible with EC law. The Court of Appeal decided that the expression 'reasonably practicable' was directed to difficulties faced by an individual claimant, whereas the applicant's mistake as to what her rights were constituted a mistake of law. It was further contrary to the principle of legal certainty to allow past transactions to be reopened and limitation periods to be circumvented because the existing law had not then been explained or fully understood. Further, Art 119 (now 141) of the EC Treaty could not be read so as to spell out a right to compensation for unfair dismissal when there was no sex discrimination.

The power to extend: Particular examples

Internal proceedings

12.17   Some general principles have been established for the more common types of valid excuse for delay which are put forward. One frequently encountered example is that internal proceedings about the dismissal were pending at the same time, and that it was reasonable to delay the application to the tribunal in order not to prejudice them (*Bodha v Hampshire AHA* [1982] ICR 200; see also *Croydon Health Authority v Jaufurally* [1986] ICR 4). In *Walls Meat v Khan* (12.15 above), Shaw and Brandon LJJ gave as examples of valid excuses physical impediment, absence abroad, or a postal strike, while in *Dedman* Scarman LJ spoke of 'some untoward and unexpected turn of events'. In *Porter v Bandridge* [1978] IRLR 271, Stephenson LJ thought that the tribunal should consider whether the employee 'was discouraged or impeded or misled or deceived'.

In *Aniagwu v London Borough of Hackney* [1999] IRLR 303, the EAT held that the time **12.18** limit in respect of an employer's refusal to accept a grievance ran not from the date of the decision of the grievance panel involved, but rather from the date on which that decision was communicated to the employee. This was because a claimant must be able to identify the detriment to which he has been subjected before he can present a complaint. The EAT appeared to lay down a general principle that unless there is some particular feature about the case or some particular prejudice which the employers can show has occurred, every tribunal would inevitably conclude that it is a responsible and proper attitude for someone to seek to redress a grievance through the employer's internal grievance procedure before embarking on legal proceedings (see also *Apelgun-Gabriels v London Borough of Lambeth* [2002] IRLR 116).

Discovery of new facts outside the three-month period

There needs to be a different approach to the strictness of the time limit where new **12.19** facts are discovered beyond the three-month period and the period is then extended. In *Churchill v A. Yeates & Sons Ltd* [1983] IRLR 187, the employee excused his delay by reason of the discovery outside the three-month period that his old job which had been declared redundant had in fact been filled. Although this was only one of the five grounds on which he challenged the fairness of his dismissal, the EAT decided that it was not reasonably practicable to bring a complaint until the applicant knew of a fundamental fact which rendered the dismissal unfair (cf *Belling & Lee v Burford* [1982] ICR 454).

According to the Court of Appeal in *Machine Tool Industry Research Association v* **12.20** *Simpson* [1988] IRLR 212, it is thus not reasonably practicable to bring a claim if during the period of three months there were crucial or important facts unknown and reasonably unknown to the applicant which later became known to him and which were such facts as to give him a genuine belief that he had a claim before the employment tribunal. At this stage, it is not necessary for the employee to establish in evidence the veracity of the facts which led him belatedly to make the claim. In the instant case, it was appropriate to extend time where the employee only knew after her dismissal that another employee had been re-engaged. She claimed that this called into question whether the real reason for dismissal was redundancy as the employer claimed. The Court of Appeal held that it was proper to extend time, notwithstanding that she had not as yet proved that anyone else had *in fact* been re-engaged (see also *Post Office v Sanhotra* [2000] ICR 866).

It has subsequently been decided that even where an offer of re-employment in a lower **12.21** grade at a reduced salary had been made by the employer and accepted by the claimant within the three-month time limit but was withdrawn after its expiry, the existence of the new job offer was not a fact which is fundamental to the employee's right to present a claim in the sense of affecting the factual basis on which the application was brought (*London Underground Ltd v Noel* [1999] IRLR 621). Time for presentation was thus not to be extended on that basis.

Other examples

12.22   The following have, however, been found not to support an extension on the basis of reasonable practicability (although each case must be considered on its own merits):

(a) the holding of union negotiations (*Times Newspapers Ltd v O'Regan* [1977] IRLR 101);

(b) that criminal proceedings were on foot at the same time (*Norgett v Luton Industrial Co-operative Society Ltd* [1976] IRLR 306; *Union Cartage Co Ltd v Blunden* [1977] ICR 420; *Trevelyans (Birmingham) Ltd v Norton* [1991] ICR 488);

(c) misleading advice from, for example, the Free Representation Unit (*Croydon Health Authority v Jaufurally* [1986] ICR 4);

(d) In *Marks and Spencer v Williams-Ryan* [2005] IRLR 562 the Court of Appeal upheld a tribunal's decision that it had not been reasonably practicable for an employee to bring an unfair dismissal claim in accordance with the applicable three-month time limit where, having received advice from a Citizens Advice Bureau, the employee had believed it necessary to exhaust the employer's internal appeal procedure before bringing her claim; and

(e) the fact that an ex-employee has entered into a commission arrangement with his employer: this may make it a matter of commercial convenience and interest that he should not issue proceedings against his former employer, but it does not render it not reasonably practicable to do so (*Birmingham Optical plc v Johnson* [1996] ICR 459).

(See also *Cambridge & Peterborough NHS Foundation Trust v Crouchman* [2009] ICR 1306.)

12.23   On the other hand:

(a) there is no principle that mistaken advice by any third party will prevent an employee establishing that it was not reasonably practicable to make a claim in time. The mistake in *Rybak v Jean Sorelle Ltd* [1991] ICR 127 arose from a combination of tribunal staff and the CAB advisers;

(b) in *James W. Cook & Co (Wivenhoe) Ltd v Tipper* [1991] IRLR 386, the Court of Appeal held that it was not reasonably practicable to present applications for redundancy where the employees thought that work soon would pick up again. The time should run in such a case from the moment that the business closed down and the dismissals were recognised as irrevocable (see also *Machine Tool Research Association v Simpson* [1988] 1 Ch 558; *Marley (UK) Ltd v Anderson* [1996] IRLR 163); and

(c) the fact that the result of an internal appeal had been received only six hours before the expiry of the time limit rendered it not reasonably practicable to present the complaint (*Ashcroft v Haberdashers' Aske's Boys' School* [2008] IRLR 375).

A second complaint

12.24   The assessment of reasonable practicability of presenting a complaint depends on the awareness of the specific grounds of complaint, not of the right to complain in general terms. The fact that the employee is precluded from bringing a complaint by lapse of time does not prevent him from proceeding on a second complaint on different grounds brought within a reasonable period of the discovery of those fresh grounds. The case in which this principle was propounded, *Marley (UK) Ltd v Anderson* [1996] ICR 728, had unusual facts in that the claimant was given notice of redundancy on 15 November 1991. Some four months later he first learnt of matters which gave him reasonable grounds for believing either that there was no redundancy at all, or that he had been unfairly selected for redundancy. He thus issued a fresh application after the expiry of the three-month period.

C ILLEGALITY

The principle of public policy is this: *ex dolo malo non oritur actio.* (*Holman v Johnson*   **12.25**
per Lord Mansfield (1775) 1 Cowp 341, translated by A.P. Herbert as 'The dirty dog gets
no dinner here'.)

The general principle in English law is that an employee cannot claim employment protec-   **12.26**
tion rights when his contract is tinged by illegality, for as Bristow J has stated, 'The rights,
though creatures of statute ... depend on or arise from the contract just as do the common
law rights which arise from the contract itself' (*Tomlinson v Dick Evans 'U' Drive Ltd*
[1978] IRLR 77). Thus, an employee cannot claim for unfair dismissal or redundancy
payment if his contract is illegal, nor count a week spent on an illegal contract in determining the length of continuous employment. This denial of such rights may, however,
be out of all proportion to any wrong committed by the employee. All sorts of incidental
breaches of the law, whether of statutory provisions or at common law on the ground of
public policy, have been held to avoid a contract. In *Napier v National Business Agency
Ltd* [1951] 2 All ER 264 Lord Evershed MR said:

> There is a strong legal obligation placed on all citizens to make true and faithful returns for
> tax purposes and, if parties make an agreement which is designed to do the contrary, i.e. to
> mislead and delay, it seems to me impossible for this court to enforce that contract at the suit
> of one party to it.

(See also *Hyland v J.H. Barker (North-West) Ltd* [1985] IRLR 403.) The burden of proof
of illegality rests on the person trying to prove illegality (*Colen v Cebrian (UK) Ltd*
[2004] ICR 568).

The courts have also gone some way to mitigate its effect by adopting two doctrines: **12.27**

(a) that the employee must *know* of the illegality;
(b) that *incidental illegality* does not avoid the contract.

Knowledge of illegality

In *Davidson v Pillay* [1979] IRLR 275, the EAT stated that the employee must actually   **12.28**
participate in the illegality to be fixed with the consequence of it; while in *McConnell v
Bolik* [1979] IRLR 422, the employer's failure to disclose to the Inland Revenue income
derived from the sale of two calves did not automatically make the whole contract illegal,
since there was nothing to suggest the employee was privy to the arrangement.

In *Hall v Woolston Hall Ltd* [2000] IRLR 578, the EAT and Court of Appeal held that   **12.29**
it is irrelevant if a contract of employment is tainted with illegality for the purpose of the
SDA 1975 because the claim for sex discrimination is not founded upon or seeking to
enforce contractual obligations. When a husband and wife shared commission payments
on the basis of what was most tax efficient they were not participating in an illegality
(*Colen v Cebrian (UK) Ltd* (supra)).

When the party to an illegal contract knew what was being done, which was illegal, it did   **12.30**
not matter that he did not *know* that the same was illegal (*Salveson v Simons* [1994] ICR
409; cf *Wilkinson v Lugg* [1990] ICR 599). In *Lightfoot v D.J. Sporting* [1996] IRLR 64,
it was not necessarily illegal for an employee's wife to be paid part of his salary solely to
reduce his tax liabilities if this was entered into in good faith, was a proper method of
reducing tax, and was fully declared to the Revenue. Further, a contract was not avoided
because an employee in its course was engaged in a fraud on the company by way of an

agreement between the employee and his manager that he be given an unofficial pay rise after the managing director decided not to increase his pay (*Broaders v Kalkare Property Maintenance Ltd* [1990] IRLR 421). This was held to be quite different from an agreement between employer and employee for an illegal element in the contract such as a fraud on the Revenue.

Incidental illegality

12.31   In a case where the employee did not have proper identity documents *Hounga v Allen* [2014] ICR 847, the Supreme Court decided by 3:2 that the defence of illegality to a claim in tort was based on the public policy of preserving the integrity of the legal system by not allowing a claimant to profit from wrongful conduct. The proper test to be applied generally was whether the claimant's claim was so closely or inextricably linked to her illegal conduct that by permitting her to recover compensation the court might appear to condone the illegality. Here the illegality provided no more than the *context* for the discriminatory acts so that the connection was insufficient to bar the claim. In this situation the public policy in support of the application of the defence of illegality should give way to the public policy against trafficking.

12.32   Illegality may, however, be inextricably bound up with a complaint to the tribunal such that had it allowed the claim for compensation the tribunal would have appeared to condone a complainant's illegal conduct of breaching his limited leave to remain in the UK and falsely stating that he had a right to work in the UK (*Vakante v Governing Body of Addey and Stanhope School (No 2)* [2005] ICR 231; see also on a case of a work permit expiring *Kelly v University of Southampton* [2008] ICR 357; *Hounslow LBC v Klusova* [2008] ICR 396).

Severance

12.33   The courts have also sometimes allowed severance of illegal terms so as to leave the remainder of the contract valid and enforceable in respect of employment rights. They have also in some cases permitted the less blameworthy party to the contract to enforce it where he has been the victim of fraud, duress, or oppression by the other party. Beldam LJ said in *Hewcastle Catering Ltd v Ahmed and Elkanah* [1992] ICR 626, in which the employees made no personal gain from the illegality perpetrated by their employer:

> the fact that a party has in the course of performing a contract committed an unlawful or immoral act will not by itself prevent him from further enforcing that contract unless the contract was entered into with the purpose of doing that unlawful or immoral act or the contract itself (as opposed to the mode of its performance) is prohibited by law.

(See also *Blue Chip Trading Ltd v Helbawi* [2009] IRLR 128.)

D GEOGRAPHICAL LIMITATIONS

12.34   The Employment Relations Act 1999, s 32, abolished the previous rules on geographical limitations for statutory rights without replacing them so that the courts had to step in without much guidance from Parliament. The key employment protection rights apply only to 'employment in Great Britain'; although the residence of the parties might be relevant, the emphasis must be on the place of employment itself. The leading case in the House of Lords is *Lawson v Serco Ltd* [2006] IRLR 289, which held that the right not to be unfairly dismissed generally applies to an employee who is working in Great Britain at the time of his dismissal. What was contemplated at the time when the contract was made and the prior history of the contractual relationship may, however, be relevant to whether the employee is really working in Great Britain or whether he is merely on a casual visit, but ordinarily the question should simply be whether he is working in Great Britain at the time of his dismissal. In the case of peripatetic workers, such as airline pilots and international management consultants, the old base test (formulated when there was a statutory provision covering the area) for statutory purposes remains valid. This treated the base of the peripatetic workers as his place of employment.

In discrimination cases the person may be ordinarily residing in more than one country at **12.35** a time: *Neary v Service Children's Education* [2010] IRLR 1030. The place of residence must be voluntarily adopted; there must be a degree of settled purpose although that may be for a limited period.

Whether on given facts a case falls within the territorial scope of s 94(1) is a question of **12.36** law, but it is a question of degree on which the decision of the principal fact finder is entitled considerable respect. The House of Lords in *Lawson v Serco Ltd* rejected the argument that jurisdiction was governed by the terms of the Employment Tribunal Rules of Procedure, or the substantial connection test formulated by the EAT in *Jackson v Ghosh* [2003] IRLR 824. They thus held that the claimant who was employed in providing security on Ascension Island on a British base was employed in Great Britain because it was unrealistic to regard him as having taken up employment in a foreign community (see also *Crofts v Cathay Pacific Airways* [2005] IRLR 624). The examples given in *Serco* are just illustrations (*Ministry of Defence v Wallis* [2010] IRLR 1035; [2011] ICR 617). The emphasis is on location at the date of dismissal rather than at the outset of the relationship (*YKK Europe Ltd v Heneghan* [2010] ICR 611).

Compulsory training in the UK counted as work in Great Britain (*BA v Mak* [2011] **12.37** ICR 735).

Unfair dismissal only covered employees who worked or were based abroad where **12.38** the employment had much stronger connections with Great Britain and with British employment law than with any other system of law. In *Duncombe v Secretary of State for Children, Schools and Families (No 2)* [2011] ICR 1312 the claimant's employer was not just based in Britain but was the British Government itself and he was employed under a contract governed by English law in an international enclave that had no particular connection with the country in which it happened to be situated. The employment had such an overwhelmingly close connection with Britain and British law that it was held to be right to conclude that he should enjoy protection from unfair dismissal.

The central question to be asked was where was the place with which by comparison **12.39** with any other location the claimant's employment had the closest connection; while the proper law of the contract, reassurance as to the availability of UK employment law, and commuting from home in Great Britain could not be regarded as determinative, they were relevant to the issue. These tipped the balance in *Ravat v Halliburton Manufacturing and Services Ltd* [2012] ICR 389 in favour of accepting jurisdiction even though the claimant had been working in Libya for the benefit of an associated German company and the decision to dismiss was taken in Cairo.

There have been some important further cases on what is the strongest jurisdictional **12.40** connection (*Dhunna v CreditSights Ltd* [2013] ICR 909 [2015] ICR 105; *Powell v OMV Exploration & Production Ltd* [2014] ICR 63). The question of sufficiently close connection is generally one of fact for the tribunal of fact (*Olsen v Gear Bulk Services Ltd* [2015] IRLR 185).

12.41   The question of geographical jurisdiction in discrimination cases depends on the facts at the time of the complaint and cannot be conferred retrospectively by virtue of the fact that the acts might amount to an act extending over a period (*Tradition Securities and Futures SA v X* [2008] IRLR 934; *Bleuse v MBT Transport Ltd* [2008] ICR 488). The territorial reach of the Equality Act should be taken as the same as that under the Employment Rights Act 1996 (*R (ota Hottak) v Secretary of State for Foreign and Commonwealth Affairs* [2015] IRLR 827).

E THE NATURE OF THE EMPLOYER

12.42   Statutory protection of certain special groups of employees is modified as follows:

(a) *Crown servants* The definition and coverage of Crown servants has already been considered (2.40). Employees of central government are not covered by the redundancy payment scheme. Section 159 of the ERA 1996 also exempts those employed in certain government employment from statutory redundancy payments.

   On the other hand, civil servants are specifically *included* within the scope of the unfair dismissal provisions (ERA 1996, s 191). This is notwithstanding that they hold office at the pleasure of the Crown and thus cannot claim to have been wrongfully dismissed. The provisions also extend to House of Commons staff (s 195), although they and other employees may be excluded by reason of national security (s 193).

(b) *Overseas governments* Redundancy payments legislation does not apply 'to any person in respect of his employment in any capacity under the government of an overseas territory' (ERA 1996, s 160(1)). Further, the doctrine of sovereign immunity applied to a clerk at the Indian High Commission in London since the dismissal was an act done in pursuance of the Republic of India's public function (*Sengupta v Republic of India* [1983] ICR 221; see also the State Immunity Act 1978, s 4(1)).

F THE NATURE OF THE EMPLOYMENT

12.43   The following are excluded from some or all employment protection rights:

(a) *Share fishermen* who are 'remunerated only by a share in the profits or gross earnings of the vessel' (ERA 1996, s 199(2)), but this does not apply to a person who shares in the profits of a whole *fleet* of vessels (*Goodeve v Gilsons* [1985] ICR 401).

(b) *Domestic servants* in a private household where the employer is a close relative cannot claim redundancy payments (ERA 1996, s 161(1)).

(c) Members of the *armed forces* (ERA 1996, s 192(1)), that is, the naval, military, and air forces of the Crown.

G EXCLUSION BY AGREEMENT

12.44   It would render the unfair dismissal provisions virtually meaningless if employers and employees could agree between themselves to exclude their operation, particularly given the normally greater bargaining power of the employer in this respect. Thus, by s 203 of the ERA 1996, any provision in an agreement is void in so far as it purports to exclude or limit the operation of the unfair dismissal provisions or in so far as it precludes any person from pursuing a claim for unfair dismissal. This has a wide scope especially since it may exclude even accepting a contractual variation. Its aim has been described as to 'protect employees from entering perhaps into misguided bargains before their claim is heard by the employment tribunal' (*Times Newspapers Ltd v Fitt* [1981] ICR 637) or 'hasty and imprudent agreements' (*Council of Engineering Institutions v Maddison* [1977] ICR 30). It is public policy to encourage early settlements so that the Enterprise and Regulatory Reform Act 2013 requires ACAS conciliation to be completed before tribunal proceedings are commenced. It also prohibits any evidence being given of protected conversations, that is, discussions with a view to achieving settlements.

In *Tocher v General Motors (Scotland) Ltd* [1981] IRLR 55 EAT, the employers concluded an agreement with the union to deploy employees made redundant on new work removing other employees whose positions were not redundant (a so-called 'bumping' agreement). The claimant who was a lorry driver volunteered for redundancy, but since the employers wished to keep him they put him in the less skilled position of washer operator for which he received £6 per week less. He tried it but resigned after ten days. The employment tribunal said that his acceptance of the job amounted to an agreed variation of contract, so that on his resignation, since there had been no dismissal, he could not claim a redundancy payment. The EAT allowed an appeal on the ground that although the agreement was incorporated into the contract of employment, it was rendered void since it purported to exclude or limit the operation of the redundancy payments and deprived the employee of his right to a trial period in the alternative employment (see also on effect on continuity and s 203, *Hanson v Fashion Industries (Hartlepool) Ltd* [1981] ICR 35). **12.45**

Section 203 may also apply to an agreed reduction in an employee's hours. In *Secretary of State for Employment v Deary and Cambridgeshire CC* [1984] IRLR 180, the EAT held that if employees could not meet the service qualification of the necessary hours worked for redundancy payments when they were dismissed, whereas prior to the reduction in their hours they would have qualified, it was the reduction in their hours which deprived them of their rights, and an agreement to that effect was rendered void by reason of what is now s 203 (see *Igbo v Johnson Matthey Chemicals Ltd* [1986] IRLR 215). **12.46**

Notwithstanding the amplitude of s 203, there are certain strictly defined circumstances in which an agreement, whether collective (12.48–12.49) or individual (12.50–12.57), might exclude these vital forms of employment protection. Compromise agreements may be reached between the parties. **12.47**

Agreement between management and union

The Secretary of State may by statutory instrument exclude parties to a dismissal procedure agreement or redundancy payments agreement from the scope of the legislation (ERA 1996, s 110(3)), and similar provisions apply to handling redundancies and guarantee payments. They are all designed to encourage domestic procedures tailored to the particular needs of different industries. The statutory requirements have proved too stringent for their widespread development. **12.48**

In the case of unfair dismissal pacts (s 110(3)): **12.49**

(a) Every union party to it must be *independent*.
(b) Procedures must be available *without discrimination* to all employees of the description covered by it.
(c) The *remedies* must be on the whole as beneficial as in the statute.
(d) The final stage must involve recourse to an *independent body* or the employment tribunal.
(e) It must be possible to determine with *reasonable certainty* whether a particular employee is covered by the agreement.

The Secretary of State may revoke an order if that is the desire of all the parties to it, or it has ceased to fulfil all the statutory conditions.

Individual agreement

Agreement to settle through an ACAS conciliation officer

12.50   The unfair dismissal legislation seeks as a matter of policy to promote conciliation. Even though the statute does not normally countenance such agreements excluding the right to claim, there are some circumstances in which they may bind the parties. The compromise reached by the statute in this regard is that, to be enforceable, agreements must be made under the guidance of an ACAS conciliation officer. This is in effect a form of insurance against an employer using his extra bargaining power to prevail on an employee. The importance of the conciliation officer's role as a 'sieve', and the utility of conciliated settlements, are both shown by the fact that the majority of unfair dismissal applications which go through conciliation officers are settled or withdrawn without a hearing. The following general principles apply:

(a) By s 203(1)(b) of the ERA 1996, any agreement which purports to exclude any person from presenting a complaint to an employment tribunal is void unless a conciliation officer has *'taken action'* under s 18 of the Employment Tribunals Act 1996. The general statutory duty of the officer is to endeavour to promote a settlement or, where appropriate, to seek to promote agreement on a sum in compensation. The conciliator need not do much, however, so as to support the enforceability of a conciliated settlement to have taken such action according to the House of Lords. In *Moore v Duport Furniture Products Ltd* [1982] ICR 84, the claimant was suspended on suspicion of stealing from his employers. An ACAS conciliation officer was contacted for advice and eventually the employer and employee agreed on the payment of a lump sum for the latter's resignation in return for the employee withdrawing his claim to the employment tribunal. The officer took no part in these negotiations, but did record the details of the settlement in the standard ACAS form COT3. Later the employee sought to go back on the arrangement and claimed to have been unfairly dismissed. The Court of Appeal and House of Lords held that the minimal 'action' taken here by the conciliation officer was sufficient to make the agreement binding. Moreover, there was no duty resting on the officer to promote a *fair* settlement (as the claimant had argued). It seemed to Cumming Bruce LJ 'inconceivable or extremely unlikely that Parliament intended to make it impossible for parties who have arrived at a settlement between them before a conciliation officer arrives on the scene to render that settlement valid to exclude a complaint to an employment tribunal'.

(b) Section 203 does not, however, avoid a genuine agreement to terminate a contract of employment since this is not to exclude but rather to apply the provisions of the ERA 1996 so that there may be an agreed termination and not a dismissal (see 14.64–14.72; *Logan Salton v Durham CC* [1989] IRLR 99).

(c) An agreement through ACAS need not be in writing, and is enforceable even though the standard ACAS COT3 form is left unsigned (*Gilbert v Kembridge Fibres Ltd* [1984] IRLR 52).

(d) In *Slack v Greenham (Plant Hire) Ltd* [1983] IRLR 271, an agreement was not avoided because the conciliation officer did not advise the employee of the possibility that he could claim future loss of earnings. The officer's duty must depend on the circumstances of each case, and here the claimant was an intelligent man who was keen to have a settlement without delay.

(e) An agreement might, however, be set aside if (which would be very unusual) the officer were to act in bad faith or adopt unfair methods when promoting the settlement. In *Hennessey v Craigmyle & Co Ltd and ACAS* [1986] ICR 461, the Court of Appeal confirmed that the doctrine of duress could apply to settlements of employment tribunal proceedings, but this will be established only in the most exceptional circumstances. Here the settlement was not invalidated by the fact that at the date of its signing the claimant had not been dismissed or given notice of dismissal (see also *Courage Take Home Trade Ltd v Keys* [1986] IRLR 427).

(f) A Citizens Advice Bureau officer has ostensible authority to enter into an agreement to settle a claim, as has counsel, a solicitor, or law centre member named as a representative by a party to proceedings before employment tribunals (*Freeman v Sovereign Chicken Ltd* [1991] ICR 853; *Gloystarne & Co Ltd v Martin* [2001] IRLR 15).

(g) In *Livingstone v Hepworth Refractories Ltd* [1992] ICR 287, the EAT held that an agreement reached under the auspices of a conciliation officer does not prevent the employee bringing a claim under discrimination legislation. Section 203 applies only to matters within the 1996 Act which have been settled.

(h) An employee who enters into such a void agreement which involves a payment to him of a sum greater than the statutory maximum may still bring a claim under the Act, on the grounds that the employee has the right to have his compensation assessed by a tribunal, according to the EAT in *NRG Victory Reinsurance Ltd v Alexander* [1992] ICR 675.

(i) An agreement does not in any way affect an employee's continuity of employment should he choose to continue to work for the employer following the agreement (*Collison v British Broadcasting Corporation* [1998] ICR 669, EAT; *Fitzgerald v University of Kent at Canterbury* [2004] ICR 737 CA).

(j) The ACAS officer has no responsibility to see that the terms of the settlement are fair on the employee and the expression 'promote a settlement' must be given a liberal construction capable of covering whatever action by way of such promotion as is applicable in the circumstances of the particular case (*Clarke v Redcar & Cleveland BC* [2006] IRLR 324). The ACAS Officer must, however, never advise a party as to the merits of the case.

Compromise agreements

By the ERA 1996, s 203(3), certain agreements not to take proceedings before employment tribunals are exempted from the general rule that such agreements are void. Such agreements must now comply with the following stringent conditions: **12.51**

(a) the agreement must be written;
(b) the agreement must relate to the particular complaint;
(c) the employee must have received independent legal advice from any 'relevant independent adviser';
(d) there must be in force, when the adviser gives the advice, a 'contract of insurance or an indemnity provided for members of a profession or professional body' or a Fellow of the Institute of Legal Executives (Compromise Agreements (Description of Person) Order 2004 (SI 2004/754));
(e) the agreement must identify the adviser; and
(f) the agreement must state that the 'conditions regulating compromise agreements under this Act are satisfied'.

A single compromise agreement may cover claims under more than one statute (*Lunt v Merseyside TEC* [1999] IRLR 458), but it cannot seek to exclude potential claims that have not yet arisen on the off-chance that they might be raised. If a series of claims has **12.52** been raised by the employee, whether in correspondence or the claim itself, all may be covered by a compromise agreement. A compromise agreement which is expressed as being in full and final settlement of 'any claim' fails to comply with s 203. The agreement is made void, however, only in respect of statutory claims. It remains enforceable to the extent to which it contains a compromise of contractual claims.

12.53 Sometimes it is necessary to construe exactly what claims fall into a restriction in bringing proceedings and this may raise difficulties. A 'full and final settlement of all or any claims ... of whatsoever nature that exist or may exist' was held not to apply to claims for damages in respect of disadvantage on the labour market which at the time the agreement was entered into was not considered to be a possibility (*BCCI SA v Ali* [2003] IRLR 292). The clause could not be read literally, the House of Lords held. Lord Nicholls said that 'the employee signed an informal release when he lost his job, in return for an additional month's pay. The ambit of the release should be kept within reasonable bounds. Mr Naeem cannot reasonably be regarded as having taken upon himself the risk of a subsequent retrospective change in the law'.

12.54 The agreement should specify each claim which the employee agrees not to bring against the employer, so that in *Hinton v University of East London* [2005] ICR 1260, although there was an intention by the parties to settle all claims whether statutory or common law, there was no mention of a public interest disclosure claim so that the agreement was not proof against it being brought. The Court of Appeal stated that it is good practice for particulars of proceedings and of the particular allegations made in them to be inserted in the compromise agreement in the form of a brief factual and legal description.

12.55 The question to be posed is what, in constructing such a contract, looking at the compromise agreement objectively, was the intention of the parties (*Royal National Orthopaedic Hospital Trust v Howard* [2003] IRLR 849). If the parties seek to achieve such an extravagant result that they release claims of which they have (and can have) no knowledge, whether those claims have already come into existence or not, they must do so in language which is absolutely clear and leaves no room for doubt as to what it is they are contracting for.

12.56 According to the EAT in *Horizon Recruitment v Vincent* [2010] ICR 491, while s 203(2) ERA permitted parties to make a valid compromise agreement precluding a claimant from proceeding in the employment tribunal, the employment tribunal had to ensure that any purported agreement was valid, including the consideration as to whether it should be avoided at common law on grounds of duress and misrepresentation before deciding whether it satisfied the statute.

12.57 A settlement given by a public body must not be irrationally generous (*Gibb v Maidstone & Tunbridge Wells NHS Trust* [2010] IRLR 786) and at the time of writing the Government were anticipating the introduction of the Public Sector Exit Regulations to set a cap on the amounts which might be paid.

H MISCELLANEOUS

12.58 (a) By s 209(1) of the ERA 1996 the Secretary of State has *residuary power*:
  (i) to bring specifically excluded employees or holders of certain public offices within the scope of the Act; and
  (ii) to exclude employees otherwise included in its coverage.

(b) A person employed in the *police service* is excluded from all rights derived from the TULR(C)A 1992 and the ERA 1996, but not the right to a written statement of terms, minimum notice, or redundancy payments. 'Police service' here means service as a member of a statutory constabulary or in any other capacity by virtue of which the person has the powers and privileges of a constable. It includes prison officers (*Home Office v Robinson and Prison Officers' Association* [1981] IRLR 524). A prison officer has a right to complain to the Civil Service Appeal Board, which must give reasons for its decisions (*R v Civil Service Appeal Board, ex p Cunningham* [1990] IRLR 503). 'Police' includes the British Transport Police (*Spence v BRB* [2001] ICR 232).

(c) The Redundancy Payments Office Holders Regulations 1965 (SI 1965/2007) extended the scope of redundancy payments to offices such as Clerk of the Peace, airport police, rent officers, and registrars of births and deaths.

13

TERMINATION OF CONTRACT
AND WRONGFUL DISMISSAL

A AUTOMATIC TERMINATION BY
   SUPERVENING EVENT 13.02

B TERMINATION BY NOTICE 13.03
   Notice at common law 13.03
   Statutory minimum notice 13.04
   Probationary periods 13.09

C TERMINATION BY BREACH 13.10
   Must a breach be accepted by the
   innocent party? 13.13

D TERMINATION BY DISMISSAL 13.20
   Employees 13.20

Office holders 13.21
Summary dismissal 13.30

E REMEDIES FOR WRONGFUL DISMISSAL . . . 13.40
   Specific performance and
   injunctions 13.41
   Exceptions 13.43
   Declaration 13.49
   Judicial review 13.51
   Damages 13.53
   Modification of the principles in
   relation to damages 13.69

13.01 There are several ways in which the contract of employment may be terminated at common law—that is, by:

(a) supervening event;
(b) notice given by either party;
(c) breach;
(d) dismissal;
(e) agreement;
(f) performance; and
(g) frustration.

The first four will be considered here while the last three are more appropriately covered in Chapter 14 on Unfair Dismissal, to which the same principles apply.

A AUTOMATIC TERMINATION BY SUPERVENING EVENT

13.02 The contract of employment is terminated by automatic operation of law without action by employer or employee in the following circumstances:

(a) a fundamental change in *partners* in a firm where the contract of employment is personal to the partners (*Brace v Calder* [1895] 2 QB 253; *Phillips v Alhambra Palace Co* [1901] 1 KB 59; *Briggs v Oates* [1990] ICR 473);
(b) compulsory *winding up* of a company, although there is no termination where a company voluntarily resolves to wind itself up (*Fox Bros (Clothes) Ltd v Bryant* [1978] IRLR 485; *Golding and Howard v Fire Auto & Marine Insurance Co Ltd* (1968) 3 ITR 372);
(c) appointment of a *receiver* (*Hopley-Dodd v Highfield Motors (Derby) Ltd* (1969) 4 ITR 289, see *Nicoll v Cutts* [1985] BCLC 322 and, for further discussion, 16.70–16.74);

(d) permanent *closure* of the employee's place of employment (*Glenboig Union Fireclay Co Ltd v Stewart* (1971) 6 ITR 14); and

(e) *death* of an employer (*Farrow v Wilson* (1869) LR 4 CP 744),

but not by an intervention by the Law Society into a solicitors' firm (*Rose v Dodd* [2005] IRLR 977).

B TERMINATION BY NOTICE

Notice at common law

Save in the case of a fixed-term contract, an employee is employed for an indefinite period **13.03** but this is always subject to termination by a reasonable period of notice. The length of notice is usually expressly agreed between the parties and, if so, it must now be stated in the written particulars of employment. Otherwise, the common law will imply a period of reasonable notice depending on the circumstances of the particular employment. This has regard to the big differences of worker status which are found. Thus, a year was held to be reasonable notice for a newspaper editor (*Grundy v Sun Printing and Publishing Association* (1916) 33 TLR 77), and six months for a manager of 120 cinemas (*Adams v Union Cinemas Ltd* [1939] 3 All ER 136) and a journalist (*Bauman v Hulton Press Ltd* [1952] 2 All ER 1121). An airline pilot was entitled to three months (*Nicoll v Falcon Airways Ltd* [1962] 1 Lloyd's Rep 245). This proceeds by implied term and where there is an express term, which gives the employer an express and unrestricted power to terminate employment without cause at any time during the contract period, that must be given effect (*Reda v Flag Ltd* [2002] IRLR 747).

Statutory minimum notice

The common law picture was modified by minima which were first introduced in the **13.04** Contracts of Employment Act 1963, then amended, and are now to be found in the Employment Rights Act 1996 (ss 86, 87). The statutory rule is that the employer must give one week's notice to an employee who has been employed by him between one month and two years and thereafter one week for each year served up to a maximum of twelve weeks for twelve years. The employee in return must give at least one week's notice of resignation if employed for more than one month (s 86(2)). These provisions do not, however, apply to servants of the Crown and House of Commons' staff. Further, the statute does not:

(a) prevent either party from *waiving* the right to notice;

(b) affect the rights of either party to terminate the contract as a result of the *conduct* of the other (s 86(6)); or

(c) prevent a party from accepting a payment *in lieu of notice* (s 86(3)). Employers often take the realistic view that an employee under notice is unlikely to be a hard or willing worker. If (s)he has another job to go to the employer may fear that (s)he will abuse confidential information. He may give him/her money instead, essentially as settlement of damages for breach of contract (on the true nature of payment in lieu of notice, see *Delaney v Staples* [1992] ICR 331). It is not clear whether the employer has a right to make such payment in the unlikely event that the employee demands to work out his notice. The general lack of a right to be provided with work suggests a negative answer (*Marshall (Cambridge) Ltd v Hamblin* [1994] ICR 363); where there is an express term to that effect (see *The Scotts Co (UK) Ltd v Budd* [2004] ICR 299).

13.05 The Court of Appeal has held, in *Trotter v Forth Ports Authority* [1991] IRLR 419, that where the right to waive notice is exercised, the right to payment in lieu is lost. Despite the fact that there is nothing in s 86(3) ERA 1996 expressly to this effect, this would appear to be consistent with viewing payments in lieu as damages for breach of contract, for where notice is waived, there is no breach of contract, according to the Court of Appeal in *Rex Stewart Jefferies Parker Ginsberg Ltd v Parker* [1988] IRLR 483 (see also *Baldwin v British Coal Corporation* [1995] IRLR 139).

13.06 The Employment Rights Act 1996 also lays down the rate of pay which must be maintained during the period of statutory notice (ss 88–91). The employer must pay a normal week's pay even though his employee does not work, if (s 88(1)): (a) he is ready and willing to work but the employer has no work for him;

(b) he is incapable of work through sickness or injury (*The Scotts Company (UK) Ltd v Budd* [2003] IRLR 145);

(c) she is absent from work wholly or partly because of pregnancy or childbirth; or

(d) he is away on holiday.

13.07 Any sickness or industrial injury benefit which is paid during any such period may be deducted from the sum to which the employee is entitled under this provision. There is no right to payment where:

(a) the employee takes time off (s 91(1));

(b) the employee breaks his contract during the notice period (s 91(4)); or

(c) the employee has given notice and he then goes on strike during the notice period (s 91(2)).

In the case of an employee without normal working hours, the right to remuneration is conditional upon that employee being 'ready and willing to do work of a reasonable nature and amount to earn a week's pay' (s 89(2)).

13.08 Fringe benefits like holiday stamps are not included in the assessment of holiday pay (*Secretary of State for Employment v Haynes* [1980] ICR 371). A remedy for failure to make any payment during the notice period may be sought in the civil courts or in the employment tribunals up to £25,000 under the Employment Tribunals (Extension of Jurisdiction) Order 1994 (SI 1994/1623).

Probationary periods

13.09 Employees may be given probationary periods and difficulties frequently arise on the construction of the terms relating thereto. In *Dalgleish v Kew House Farm Ltd* [1982] IRLR 251, the letter of appointment provided that 'Your position will be probationary for a period of three months at the end of which time your performance will be reviewed and if satisfactory you will be made permanent.' The claimant was dismissed after three weeks and was given one week's pay in lieu of notice. The Court of Appeal determined that this was not a breach of contract.

C TERMINATION BY BREACH

13.10 As a general approach:

> ... it is really very desirable that in relations between employers and workmen and the workmen's union there should be so far as can possibly be achieved simplicity: academic discussions as to the operation in certain circumstances in the law of contract of repudiations and

acceptances, and acceptances of offers and novations and counter offers and so on should not be allowed to produce a waste of time and energy (Per Winn LJ in *Marriott v Oxford and District Co-operative Society (No 2)* [1970] 1 QB 186 at 193).

A party to a contract of employment is discharged from performance by a fundamental breach, that is a breach which: **13.11**

(a) the parties regard as vital (*The Mihalis Angelos* [1971] 1 QB 164);
(b) is so serious in its consequences as effectively to deprive the other party of what he had contracted for (*Hong Kong Fir Shipping v Kawasaki Kisen Kaisha* [1962] 2 QB 26); or
(c) shows that the other party no longer intends to be bound by one or more of the essential terms of the contract (*Western Excavating (ECC) Ltd v Sharp* [1978] QB 761).

MacCardie J put it thus in *Re Rubel Bronze & Metal Co* [1918] 1 KB 315 at 322: **13.12**

> In every case the question of repudiation must depend on the character of the contract, the number and weight of the wrongful acts or assertions, the intentions indicated by such acts and words, the deliberation or otherwise with which they are committed or uttered and on the general circumstances of the case.

The fundamental breach may be made up of a series of small breaches, the last providing the straw which breaks the camel's back (*Pepper v Webb* [1969] 2 All ER 216; *Garner v Grange Furnishing Ltd* [1977] IRLR 206).

Must a breach be accepted by the innocent party?

One of the fundamental questions of labour law is whether or not a repudiation of a contract of employment, including a dismissal itself, needs to be accepted. This apparently academic issue is practically important when deciding: **13.13**

(a) the date when termination took place;
(b) whether strikers by the very act of striking, that is, in fundamental breach of contract, put an end to their contract;
(c) whether a termination/repudiation comes within the definition of direct or constructive dismissal for unfair dismissal (14.10ff) and redundancy; and
(d) to what date the employee must be paid.

The normal contractual doctrine is that 'an unaccepted repudiation is a thing writ in water', and this was restated in *Photo Production Ltd v Securicor Transport Ltd* [1980] AC 827. Many cases have determined that this holds true for contracts of employment also. There are, however, special difficulties in this area since a contract of service cannot be specifically performed, so that even if a breach is not accepted the court has no mechanism to force the parties to continue in harmony, and employment depends more than most contracts on the existence of mutual trust and cooperation between the parties. **13.14**

This discussion is closely related to the converse concept of 'self-dismissal'. The courts at one time threatened to exclude a whole range of terminations from the statutory definition of dismissal, and thus from examination on their merits, by concluding that the employee himself brought the contract to an end when he committed acts of misconduct. **13.15**

In *Sanders v Neale Ltd* [1974] ICR 565, a group of employees went on strike, but after an ultimatum on 11 May presented themselves for work the next day. The question for the NIRC was whether, by their action, the employees could claim that they had refused to accept the employer's repudiation in the ultimatum. Donaldson P thought not, as 'the repudiation of a contract of employment is an exception to the general rule'. It terminates **13.16** the contract without necessity for acceptance by the injured party. Megarry V-C reviewed an extensive array of cases in *Thomas Marshall (Exports) Ltd v Guinlé* [1979] Ch 227, where the employer was suing the employees. The defendant had been employed as managing director of the plaintiff company under a ten-year service contract, but in 1977 he resigned and the company discovered that during his contract he had been soliciting business for himself away from the employer in breach of his implied duties of good faith. In response to the company's application for an interlocutory injunction to prevent the defendant from so acting, the defendant claimed that, with effect from the date of his resignation, the contract had automatically terminated, so that he was no longer bound by its conditions. Megarry V-C rejected this on three grounds:

(a) *Policy:* Why should a person who makes a contract of service have the right at any moment to put an end to his contractual obligations? No doubt the court will not decree specific performance of the contract, nor will it grant an injunction which will have the effect of an order for specific performance: but why should the limitation of the range of remedies for the breach invade the substance of the contract?

(b) *Authority,* since any other decision was difficult to reconcile with, *inter alia, Lumley v Wagner* (1852) 1 De GM & G 604, and *William Robinson & Co Ltd v Heuer* [1898] 2 Ch 451.

(c) *Justice:* 'the courts must be astute to prevent a wrongdoer from profiting too greatly from his wrong', and this is supported by the discussion of the House of Lords on the general law of contract in *Photo Production Ltd v Securicor Transport Ltd* [1980] AC 827.

13.17   The latest word on the subject from the Supreme Court is that the repudiatory breach does not terminate the contract unless the other party elected to accept it; if an employer wishes to exercise a contractual right to dismiss an employee by making a payment in lieu of notice it has to notify the employee in clear and unambiguous terms that such a payment has been made and that it was made in exercise of that right (*Geys v Société Générale, London Branch* [2013] ICR 117).

13.18   In *Cavanagh v William Evans Ltd* [2012] ICR 1231 a managing director was appointed under a contract by which the company could terminate summarily by paying salary in lieu of the required notice period. The company did so but before the claimant received the sums which were due to him the company discovered that the claimant, prior to the termination of his role as managing director, had wrongly procured payment of £10,000 to his pension provider. The company thus refused to make the payments which it had promised to make. The Court of Appeal held that the agreement was lawfully terminated and a debt by the company had accrued. The company could not then resile from the contractual consequences of its choice by later following the different route of accepting the repudiation.

13.19   The question of when a repudiatory breach has been accepted is one of fact for the employment tribunal (*F.C. Shepherd & Co Ltd v Jerrom* [1986] IRLR 358) and can be very significant for many purposes. In *Pendlebury v Christian Schools North West Ltd* [1985] ICR 174, it occurred, for example, when the employer sent the applicant his final wages and Form P45. The EAT also stressed in *Shook v London Borough of Ealing* [1986] IRLR 46, that an employee could not assert that by reason of a breach of the dismissal procedure by her employer, she had never been lawfully dismissed. The acceptance of such repudiation must have occurred at the latest by the end of her case before the employment tribunal. An appeal against dismissal by the employee is not, however, inconsistent with an acceptance of repudiation (*Batchelor v British Railways Board*

[1987] IRLR 136; see also *Octavius Atkinson & Sons Ltd v Morris* [1989] IRLR 158; *Marsh v National Autistic Society* [1993] ICR 453; *Rigby v Ferodo Ltd* [1988] ICR 29).

D TERMINATION BY DISMISSAL

Employees

The general view of the common law is that a dismissal with proper notice is lawful, **13.20** except in the rare event that procedural protections for termination are expressed in the contract (eg *Tomlinson v LM & S Railway* [1944] 1 All ER 537). In *Sarker v South Tees Acute Hospitals NHS Trust* [1997] IRLR 328, the EAT held that an employment tribunal would have jurisdiction to consider the claimant's claim for damages for breach of contract, in circumstances in which she had contracted to work for the respondent employers but the contract was terminated before she had commenced work under it. There is no general implication of the rules of natural justice (eg *McLory v Post Office* [1992] ICR 758), although the implied duty of trust and confidence often achieves a similar result.

Office holders

There are some cases in which the court will grant judicial review remedies to restrain or **13.21** control dismissal. Office holders and occupants of statutory positions have this greater security, first, because the law implies into the terms of their office a right to natural justice and, second, because a declaration might issue that the dismissal was invalid and unlawful. In *Ridge v Baldwin* [1964] AC 40, for example, the dismissal of the Chief Constable of Brighton was declared void because he had not been given an opportunity to give his explanation for alleged misconduct. *Malloch v Aberdeen Corporation* [1971] 1 WLR 1578 was an analogous case, the appellant being a Scottish teacher whose terms were set out mainly in statute, and here Lord Wilberforce sought to clarify the relevant distinctions:

> All requirements of the observance of rules of natural justice are excluded [in] ... what have been called 'pure master and servant' cases which I take to mean cases in which there is no element of public employment or service, no support by statute, nothing in the nature of an office or a status which is capable of protection. If any of these elements exist, then in my opinion, whatever the terminology used and even though in some *inter partes* aspects the relationship may be called that of master and servant, there may be essential procedural requirements to be observed, and failure to observe them may result in a dismissal being declared to be void.

(See also *Chief Constable of North Wales v Evans* [1983] 1 WLR 141; *R v Chief Constable of Thames Valley Police, ex p Cotton* [1990] IRLR 344.)

Hodgson J in *R v East Berkshire Health Authority, ex p Walsh* [1984] ICR 743 thought **13.22** that judicial review was appropriate to quash a breach of a health authority's procedure since 'the applicant is an officer of a profession recognised as a profession by Parliament'. Judicial review was only unavailable to review activities 'of a purely private or domestic kind'. This was, however, heretical in the view of the Court of Appeal [1984] IRLR 278. Employment by a public authority did not *per se* inject any element of public law into the process. The relationship, which incorporated the Whitley Council collectively agreed terms, fell into the category of 'pure master and servant', and the rules of natural justice could not be implied.

13.23   The decision was narrowly distinguished by Hodgson J in *R v Secretary of State for the Home Department, ex p Benwell* [1985] IRLR 6. The applicant, a prison officer, was charged with disobedience to orders. After an inquiry had recommended that he should receive a severe reprimand, the Home Office dismissed him after considering notes on his disciplinary file of which he was unaware, and which he had obviously had no opportunity to answer. Hodgson J decided that, if the case were considered on the proper material, no reasonable Home Secretary would have dismissed. Accordingly, the decision to dismiss was quashed (see also *R v Secretary of State for the Home Department, ex p Broom* [1986] QB 198; *McClaren v Home Office* [1990] IRLR 338).

13.24   In recent years, the common law, moving in step with the statutory unfair dismissal jurisdiction and modern ideas of personnel management, has indicated a somewhat wider scope to the need for an unbiased hearing. In *Stevenson v URTU* [1977] ICR 893, the claimant, a full-time employee of the defendant trade union, was dismissed by its executive after disciplinary proceedings, and the Court of Appeal upheld his claim that this was invalid because he was not given an adequate opportunity to defend himself.

13.25   In *R v BBC, ex p Lavelle* [1982] IRLR 404, Woolf J went further and indicated, albeit *obiter*, that when there is a procedure for dismissal in an employment not covered by statute at all, employers must comply with that procedure for the dismissal to be valid. If the contractual procedure was infringed, an injunction should issue to prevent the dismissal. This view was partly based on the notion that employment protection legislation had substantially changed the position at common law, so that 'the ordinary contract between master and servant now has many of the attributes of an office'. Judicial review was not the appropriate remedy here because there was no statutory element in the employment, but an injunction could issue in an appropriate case.

13.26   The rules of natural justice 'must depend on the circumstances of the case, the nature of the inquiry, the rules under which the tribunal is acting, the subject-matter that is being dealt with and so forth' (*Russell v Duke of Norfolk* [1949] 1 All ER 109; *R (on the application of McNally) v Secretary of State for Education* [2002] ICR 15). In employment cases, the essentials are, as in the concept of fair procedure in unfair dismissal, the rights to be heard by an unbiased tribunal, to have proper notice of charges of misconduct, to be heard in answer to the charges, and to appeal from the initial decision. These have been supplemented by the following principles:

(a) that the employee should see reports about his dismissal (*Stevenson v United Road Transport Union* [1977] 2 All ER 941);

(b) that the body determining the truth of allegations should adopt a higher standard of proof the more serious the charges are (*R v Hampshire CC, ex p Ellerton* [1985] ICR 317); and

(c) that an appeal should be heard by persons who had not been involved in the decision to dismiss (*Re John Snaith* [1982] IRLR 157).

13.27   A dismissal has also been held to be unlawful at common law in the following circumstances:

(a) the contract stated that the employee could be dismissed only on a limited number of grounds and that selected did not fall within them (*McClelland v Northern Ireland General Health Services Board* [1957] 2 All ER 129);

(b) a statutory body dismissed for a *mala fides* reason (*Short v Poole Corporation* [1926] Ch 66);

(c) a police authority failed to inform the appellant police officers for two and a half years that complaints had been made against them, since this seriously prejudiced their ability to defend themselves (*Calveley v Merseyside Police* [1989] 1 All ER 1025); and

(d) an allegation against a college lecturer could not fall within the terms of the disciplinary procedure (*Jones v Gwent CC* [1992] IRLR 521).

In *Barros D'Sa v University Hospital Coventry and Warwickshire NHS Trust* [2001] **13.28** IRLR 691, a consultant general surgeon was suspended following allegations of serious professional misconduct. An inquiry panel investigated and reported on the allegations. The panel decided that the dismissal was wholly unjustified for the one allegation which it found to have been partially proved. The next stage was to be a hearing before the chief executive. At this stage the management sought to rely on an alleged breakdown of the relationship of trust and confidence as a result of allegations which the claimant had made against management, but the Court of Appeal upheld an injunction granted against such allegations being used as disciplinary matters against the claimant. This was on the ground that it would be contrary to the principles of natural justice for the allegations of a subsequent breakdown in trust and confidence to be taken into account at the disciplinary hearing.

In *West London Mental Health NHS Trust v Chhabra* [2014] IRLR 227, the Supreme **13.29** Court said that:

(a) The court will be prepared to intervene in a disciplinary process if it is demonstrated that the proceedings are being conducted on a basis which makes their conduct a breach of contract such that the pursuit would also be a breach;
(b) Breaches must be sufficiently serious such that they make the continued pursuit of the disciplinary process unfair in a manner which cannot be remedied within the proceedings themselves;
(c) Nonetheless the court will not micromanage an employment disciplinary procedure.

The employer failed to follow its own disciplinary procedure and the Supreme Court granted an injunction to prevent it from accusing the employee of gross misconduct because her wrongdoing was insufficiently serious.

The court may make a pre-emptive strike in the case of disciplinary proceedings which are out of kilter. Where there was no genuinely serious misconduct which permitted a disciplinary hearing, the court could intervene by awarding an injunction in a doctor's disciplinary case to prevent the disciplinary process (*Mezey v SW London & St George's Mental Health NHS Trust* [2010] IRLR 512).

Summary dismissal

'The principles [of summary dismissal] are but rarely revealed.' (*Re Rubel Bronze &* **13.30** *Metal Co Ltd* [1918] 1 KB 315.)

There are some cases in which a dismissal without notice may be lawful at common law. The general test of whether summary dismissal is justifiable was stated in *Laws v London Chronicle (Indicator Newspapers) Ltd* [1959] 1 WLR 698 as:

> whether the conduct complained of is such as to show the servant to have disregarded the essential conditions of the contract of service ... One act of disobedience or misconduct can justify dismissal only if it is of a nature which goes to show (in effect) that the servant is repudiating the contract or one of its essential conditions; and for that reason therefore I think you find ... that the disobedience must at least have the quality that it is 'wilful'; it does (in other words) connote a deliberate flouting of the essential contractual conditions. (See also *Freeth v Burr* (1874) 9 CP 208 at 213.)

Such conduct may be found in just one action committed by the employee (*Blyth v The Scottish Liberal Club* [1983] IRLR 245).

13.31   It should be noted that the court is not performing a reviewing role in wrongful dismissal so it is not appropriate to apply a test of the range of reasonable responses such as applies in unfair dismissal (*Boardman v Nugent Care Society* [2013] ICR 927).

13.32   Conduct amounting to gross misconduct must so undermine the trust and confidence inherent in the particular contract of employment that the employer should no longer be required to retain the employee (*Dunn v AAH Ltd* [2010] IRLR 709).

13.33   Summary dismissal has thus been held to be lawful in cases of:

(a)   a strike (*Simmons v Hoover Ltd* [1977] ICR 61) and probably in most cases of work to rule (*Secretary of State for Employment v ASLEF (No 2)* [1972] 2 QB 455);

(b)   dishonesty, for example, where a betting shop manager took money from the till for his own purposes (*Sinclair v Neighbour* [1967] 2 QB 279);

(c)   a series of incidents of drunkenness (*Clouston & Co Ltd v Corry* [1906] AC 122);

(d)   the taking of a secret commission in breach of the employee's duty of fidelity (*Boston Deep Sea Fishing & Ice Co v Ansell* (1888) 39 ChD 339);

(e)   gross negligence, for example, where the manager of the life insurance department of an insurance company negligently recommended the insurance of a life which a few days earlier the managing director had refused to insure (*Jupiter General Insurance Co Ltd v Shroff* [1937] 3 All ER 67);

(f)   wilful disobedience to orders such as refusal to attend meetings (*Blyth v The Scottish Liberal Club* (above)). In *Laws v London Chronicle (Indicator Newspapers) Ltd* (above), however, the fact that a female employee defied the managing director's orders not to leave the room with her superior following a row between the two men was insufficiently serious since 'one act of disobedience or insubordination or misconduct can justify dismissal only if it is of a nature which goes to show in effect that the servant is repudiating the contract or one of its essential conditions'.

13.34   The court may be asked to determine in advance whether the allegations could amount to gross misconduct. Where there was no genuinely serious misconduct which permitted a disciplinary hearing, the court could intervene by awarding an injunction in a doctor's disciplinary case (*Mezey v SW London & St George's Mental Health NHS Trust* [2010] IRLR 512).

13.35   As to disclosure of confidential information as gross misconduct, see *Farnan v Sunderland AFC* [2016] IRLR 185.

13.36   The lawfulness of the dismissal may (according to the particular circumstances) depend *inter alia* on:

(a)   the position of the employee;

(b)   his past record;

(c)   the social conditions of the time; so that many old cases are thus to be treated as unreliable as precedents today, since as Edmund Davies LJ said in *Wilson v Racher* [1974] ICR 428 at 430B, they:

date from the last century and may be wholly out of accord with current social conditions. What would today be regarded as almost an attitude of Czar-serf, which is to be found in some of the older cases where a dismissed employee failed to recover damages, would, I venture to think, be decided differently today.

In *Wilson*'s case, the employee, a gardener, was dismissed by the defendant following a **13.37** heated argument about his early departure on the previous Friday. This culminated in his saying: 'Get stuffed'. There was no background of inefficiency or insolence as in *Pepper v Webb* [1969] 1 WLR 514, an earlier case with otherwise similar facts. The test which the Court of Appeal applied was 'whether the plaintiff's conduct was insulting and insubordinate to such a degree as to be incompatible with the continuance of the relation of master and servant'. Here it was not so serious and the dismissal was therefore wrongful (see also *Hamilton v Argyll and Clyde Health Board* [1993] IRLR 99).

The employer may rely on facts discovered *after* the dismissal to justify his action in **13.38** giving his employee the sack. This is the very opposite of the rule developed in unfair dismissal (*Boston Deep Sea Fishing & Ice Co v Ansell* (1888) 39 ChD 339; cf *W. Devis & Sons Ltd v Atkins* [1977] AC 931).

In the absence of gross misconduct, the employee dismissed without notice may claim **13.39** for wrongful dismissal and this exists today alongside statutory unfair dismissal but is used by higher earning employees. One of the greatest reforms wrought by the introduction of the latter was the new importance of procedure in dismissal, and consequent lessening of the power of summary dismissal (and the need to find that a role was an office to which the principles of natural justice applied). This does not, however, mean that summary dismissal is not still valid in some cases.

E REMEDIES FOR WRONGFUL DISMISSAL

The potential remedies for wrongful dismissal are: specific performance and injunction; **13.40** declaration; judicial review remedies; and damages.

Specific performance and injunctions

A central defect of the common law of wrongful dismissal from the point of view of **13.41** employees is that the courts will not enforce a broken contract by specific performance, so that if an employee has been unlawfully sacked, there is no way he can regain his job through the courts. The following reasons have been advanced for this conclusion:

(a) It would amount to *forced labour*. Thus, Fry LJ in *De Francesco v Barnum* (1890) 43 ChD 165 was:

> very unwilling to extend decisions the effect of which is to compel persons who are not desirous of maintaining continuous personal relations with one another to continue those personal relations ... I think the courts are bound to be jealous lest they should turn contracts of service into contracts of slavery.

(b) It would be inconsistent with the *trust and confidence* which must exist between employer and employee, although this is less valid in modern times when the employer is likely to be a large impersonal corporation.
(c) If the effect of dismissal is to terminate the employment, equity will not act on the basis that it is still alive.
(d) It offends against the doctrine of *mutuality* since to force an employer to reinstate cannot be balanced by forcing an employee to work.
(e) The court cannot *supervise* performance of the contract.
(f) *Damages* are usually an adequate remedy.

Some of these are unconvincing reasons. Section 236 of the TULR(C)A 1992 specifically enacts part of this principle, providing that 'no court shall issue an order compelling an employee to do any work or attend at any place for the doing of any work'.

13.42   The courts have long held that these rules do not prevent the court enforcing an agreement not to *compete* with the employer whether during or after employment, even where this may have the indirect effect of pressurising him to carry on working in that employment. Thus, in *Warner Bros Pictures Inc v Nelson* [1937] 1 KB 209, Bette Davis, the famous actress, broke her agreement to work solely for the company and Branson J granted it an injunction by adopting the negative provision that she should work for no other motion picture or stage producer. She could work in other fields and the judge was not impressed by the argument that: 'The difference between what [she] can earn as a film artiste and what she might expect to earn by any other form of activity is so great that she will in effect be driven to perform her contract.' The court will not, however, enforce a provision not to take any employment at all for a period after termination of the contract of service. For this would constitute a thinly disguised form of compelling service (see *Page One Records Ltd v Britton* [1967] 3 All ER 822; *Lumley v Wagner* (1852) 1 De GM & G 604; *Evening Standard Co v Henderson* [1987] IRLR 64, discussed at 6.14). In *Warren v Mendy* [1989] IRLR 210, Nourse LJ said that: 'Compulsion is a question to be decided on the facts of each case, with a realistic regard for the probable reaction of an injunction on the psychological and material, and sometimes the physical, need of the servant to maintain the skill or talent.'

Exceptions

13.43   Some exceptions have been developed to this general rule. The Court of Appeal in *Hill v CA Parsons and Co Ltd* [1972] 1 Ch 305 went considerably further than precedent, to grant an injunction which had the effect of specific performance although only in very particular circumstances. The claimant was dismissed after thirty-five years working for the defendant company as a chartered engineer, because he would not join the union DATA with which the employer had just signed a closed shop agreement. The Court of Appeal, with Stamp LJ dissenting, would have granted an interim injunction preventing the employer from implementing the dismissal. Lord Denning MR and Sachs LJ thought that in this case the normal arguments deployed against such enforcement did not apply, since:

(a) there was a continued relationship of confidence between employer and employee, as it was the union and not the company who sought to remove him; and

(b) damages would not here be an adequate remedy.

13.44   It may also have been significant that at the time of the decision the unfair dismissal provisions were due to take effect in two months' time when the remedy of reinstatement would become available. The case was distinguished in *GKN (Cwmbran) Ltd v Lloyd* [1972] ICR 214; *Sanders v Ernest A. Neale Ltd* [1974] ICR 565; and *Chappell v Times Newspapers Ltd* [1975] ICR 145. It was followed, however, in:

(a) *Jones v Lee* [1980] ICR 310, where the Court of Appeal issued an injunction to prevent managers of a Roman Catholic primary school from dismissing its headmaster without the consent of the local council and without affording him the opportunity to be heard, both of which were required in his contract; and

(b) *Irani v Southampton and South West Hampshire Health Authority* [1985] IRLR 203, where an ophthalmologist was dismissed by the authority without the procedural protection which was required to be afforded by the Whitley Council. Warner J considered it important that, just as in *Parsons*, damages would not be an adequate remedy since Mr Irani would become virtually unemployable throughout the National Health Service and would lose the right to use NHS facilities to treat his private patients (see also *Marsh v National Autistic Society* [1993] ICR 453).

In the absence of special provision in the contract of employment, there was no right for the employer to increase the disciplinary sanction on appeal (*McMillan v Airedale NHS Foundation Trust* [2015] ICR 747). **13.45**

An injunction may normally be granted only where there is the necessary trust and confidence remaining between employer and employee, as was the case in *Irani* and *Powell v London Borough of Brent* [1987] IRLR 466. The courts will, however, scrutinise carefully an employer's assertion that trust and confidence has broken down in order to ensure that there are facts on which that assertion is based. This must be judged by reference to all the circumstances of the case including the nature of the work, the people with whom the work must be done, and the likely effect on the employer and employer's operations if he is required by the injunction to suffer the employee to remain in his position (cf *Ali v Southwark LBC* [1988] ICR 567; see also *Alexander v STC plc* [1990] ICR 291; *Wishart v NACAB* [1990] ICR 794; and *Gryf Lowczowski v Hinchingbrooke Healthcare NHS Trust* [2006] IRLR 100). **13.46**

In *Wadcock v London Borough of Brent* [1990] IRLR 223, the High Court granted an injunction even though it was impossible to say that trust and confidence remained between the parties. Nevertheless, the judge felt that the employee was competent and would be well able to work in the post to which he had been assigned if he were minded to obey his superiors. There are also cases where the employee seeks an injunction, not to remain in his job, but to treat the original dismissal as *void* in order to recover pay until the proper procedures are gone through. In this event, as the High Court pointed out in *Robb v London Borough of Hammersmith and Fulham* [1991] ICR 514, the retention of trust and confidence is not material. **13.47**

A decision to suspend may be restrained by injunction. The duty of mutual trust and confidence meant that any implied power to suspend must be exercised in a way which was no less favourable to doctors than the provisions of a Department of Health circular which included suspension. This was even though the circular was not in itself binding (*Mezey v South West London and St George's Mental Health NHS Trust* [2007] IRLR 237). **13.48**

Declaration

The declaration has some importance as a remedy in the area of dismissals and it has been for some time used in cases involving statutory status and offices (*Vine v National Dock Labour Board* [1956] 1 QB 658; *Stevenson v United Road Transport Union* [1977] ICR 893). **13.49**

The Court of Appeal in *Gunton v Richmond-upon-Thames LBC* [1980] ICR 755 countenanced an extension in the use of this remedy to declare that the employee's contract remained in being. It indicated that it was not issued because of any special statutory status of the applicant; it may be particularly appropriate for declaring that a contract still exists and a repudiation has not been accepted by the other party. **13.50**

Judicial review

Where the employer is a statutory authority, quashing and staying orders may be sought in the Administrative Court, a Division of the High Court (*University Council of the* **13.51**

Vidyodaya University v Silva [1965] 1 WLR 77). In *R v East Berkshire Health Authority, ex p Walsh* [1984] ICR 743, the Court of Appeal stressed that judicial review was available only where an issue of public law was involved. A breach of the contract of employment even by a public authority was not, however, a matter of public law. Lord Donaldson MR explained that it was the existence of special statutory provisions bearing directly upon the right to dismiss which distinguished this case from the cases of *Ridge v Baldwin* [1964] AC 40 and *Malloch v Aberdeen Corporation* [1971] ICR 893 where judicial review was granted.

13.52 The following have not been held to raise issues of public law so that judicial review was not available as a remedy:

(a) the termination of the contract for services between a deputy police surgeon and a county council (*R v Derbyshire CC, ex p Noble* [1990] ICR 808); and

(b) a decision of a probation committee to phase out a mileage allowance on financial grounds (*Doyle v Northumbria Probation Committee* [1992] ICR 121).

Damages

13.53 Damages are the normal remedy for breach of the employment contract, and the usual contractual measure is the wages and benefits that the employee would have earned if due notice had indeed been given (*Radford v De Froberville* [1977] 1 WLR 1262; *Shove v Downs Surgical plc* [1984] IRLR 17). For that is the only period when he is entitled by contract to continue in employment. If, by way of example, his contract can be determined by three weeks' notice he cannot claim his loss over the next three years even though he is unemployed for that length of time; for at any time within that period he might have been dismissed with three weeks' notice. (This is a quite different basis to unfair dismissal compensation.)

13.54 If the basis of claim is not the failure to give notice, the result may be different. In the case of an employer's breach of contract in dismissing an employee without first having followed a contractual disciplinary procedure, the appropriate measure of loss is based on an assessment of the time for which, had the procedure been followed, the employee's employment would have continued, not on an analysis of the chances that if the procedure had been followed the employee might never have been dismissed (*Janciuk v Winerite Ltd* [1998] IRLR 63).

13.55 It is not the case that disciplinary procedures are nor are they intended to give a right to damages if they are breached (*Edwards v Chesterfield Royal Hospital NHS Foundation Trust* [2012] ICR 201). Damages are not recoverable in relation to the manner of dismissal even where the breach was of an express term of the contract relating to disciplinary procedures leading to dismissal. This is a complex case and the Supreme Court split four to three and the reasoning of the majority is split between different judgments.

Treatment of benefits

13.56 All contractual fringe benefits are taken into account and an important element for consideration in *Shove v Downs Surgical plc* (above) was the provision of a Daimler car. Sheen J rejected the employer's submissions that:

(a) the correct method of assessment was by reference to the tax charge imposed by the Finance Acts;

(b) the employee was entitled to compensation only in respect of such a vehicle as he could expect to be provided with in his position; and

(c) the absence of contractual entitlement to petrol meant that it could not be claimed
even though it had been provided to him free by the company for many years.

Damages may also include the loss of pension rights for the relevant period (*Silvey v
Pendragon plc* [2001] IRLR 686).

A common component of remuneration packages, especially for senior executives, is *share*   **13.57**
options in the company. Most schemes, however, expressly provide that they are not exer-
cisable after termination of employment, save typically in cases of sickness or redundancy
(ie factors which are not created by employer or employee), and that loss of the options
on termination shall give no rights to damages or compensation for wrongful or unfair
dismissal. It seems likely that such clauses would be upheld. For this argument to succeed,
it would be necessary to show that they were standard terms of a company's business,
which would be difficult (eg *Micklefield v SAC Technology Ltd* [1990] IRLR 218). In
Levett v Biotrace International plc [1999] ICR 818, the Court of Appeal held that an
employee who was summarily dismissed was entitled to exercise an option to purchase
shares notwithstanding that a contractual clause had been entered into which provided
that the option would lapse if the employee was dismissed following disciplinary action,
as the dismissal was unlawful so that the employer was not entitled to rely on it to deprive
the employee of his rights.

A provision in a service agreement that the 'executive's salary shall be reviewed annu-   **13.58**
ally and be increased by such amount if any as the board shall in its absolute discretion
decide' was held to be a contractual obligation upon the employers to provide an annual
upward adjustment in salary. It was only the amount of such increase which was in the
absolute discretion of the board, and in that respect the board must not act capriciously
or in bad faith. The Court of Appeal decided that in awarding wrongful dismissal damages, it was not to be assumed that the discretion would be exercised so as to give the
least possible benefit to the claimant if that was not realistic on the facts (*Clark v BET plc*
[1997] IRLR 348). The burden of proving that no rational bank in the City would have
paid the employee a bonus of less than his line manager recommended was a heavy one
to discharge: *Commerzbank AG v Keen* [2007] IRLR 132. This was because so much
must depend on the discretionary judgement of the bank in fluctuating market and labour
conditions.

Damages for distress etc

The leading case in this area of law for many years was *Addis v Gramophone Co Ltd*   **13.59**
[1909] AC 488. *Addis* held that no damages were recoverable for loss of reputation even if
the dismissal led to difficulty in getting a job in the future. The House of Lords in *Malik
v Bank of Credit and Commerce International* [1997] ICR 606, however, held that the
claimants were entitled to bring a claim for their loss of reputation, difficulty in finding
new employment, and subsequent financial losses following their dismissal in a very unusual fact situation. This was because their employer's fraudulent behaviour had caused
a stigma to be attached to them, even though they were themselves innocent of any such
behaviour. The House of Lords in *Johnson v Unisys Ltd* [2001] ICR 480 rejected the
attempt to depart from *Addis*. Courts cannot award damages merely for the manner of
dismissal, although they may be available in unfair dismissal.

The House of Lords in *Unisys* rejected the implication of the term of mutual trust and   **13.60**
confidence in the manner or grounds of dismissal.

In *Edwards v Chesterfield Royal Hospital NHS Foundation Trust* [2012] ICR 201, Lords   **13.61**
Dyson, Mance, and Walker applied the *Johnson* exclusion to the claims and held that

although a contractual disciplinary procedure might have some legal effects, a breach of that procedure could not provide the basis for a claim for compensation for damage to reputation resulting in economic loss because such a claim under the common law would circumvent the carefully circumscribed limits established by Parliament for claims for unfair dismissal.

13.62 Lady Hale and Lords Kerr and Wilson would not extend the *Johnson* exclusion to cover breaches of express terms (as opposed to the implied term of trust and confidence) that had been broken by the employer during the performance of the contract. Lord Philips, although he agreed with the result preferred by the first group, doubted whether it was possible to deprive a contractual disciplinary term of legal effect by reference to the presumed intent of Parliament. Instead he decided that *Addis* had concluded that a claim for damages to reputation which results from dismissal or the fact of dismissal was not recoverable and that the same rule should apply to breach of contractual disciplinary procedures leading up to dismissal.

13.63 The upshot is that any breach of contract, whether express or implied, which results in or leads directly to a dismissal cannot afford damages at common law other than the notice period and any extension on the basis of cases like *Gunton*.

13.64 It is clear that no damages are recoverable for the humiliating way in which the employee was dismissed (*Addis*), or for stress and anxiety (*French v Barclays Bank plc* [1998] IRLR 647). There will be also no award for:

(a) *bonuses* which are solely within the discretion of the employer (*Lavarack v Woods of Colchester Ltd* [1967] 1 QB 278); or

(b) share options which are purely in the discretion of the employers (*O'Laiore v Jackel International Ltd* [1991] ICR 718).

13.65 Extra damages may also be available where the parties envisage a greater return from the contract of employment than simply pay for hours worked. Thus, an American actress who was wishing to establish her name in London who contracted to play a part for the defendant was held to have done so in return not only for money but also for full publicity, and her damages were thus enhanced (*Marbe v George Edwardes (Daly's Theatres) Ltd* [1928] 1 KB 269). There is also an old exception in cases of apprenticeships (eg *Dunk v George Waller & Sons Ltd* [1970] 2 QB 163).

Loss of a chance

13.66 In *Robert Cort & Son Ltd v Charman* [1981] IRLR 437, Browne-Wilkinson J suggested *obiter* that damages might include a sum for the loss of the right to compensation for unfair dismissal which the employee would have successfully claimed had the correct notice of termination been given. In *Raspin v United News Shops Ltd* [1999] IRLR 9, a similar result was reached on the basis that the employer was in breach of the contractual obligation to follow the required disciplinary procedure and, therefore, in order to accord with the principle that an employee who sustains a loss by reason of the employer's breach of contract is to be placed in the same position as if the contract had been performed, the court should determine the value to the employee of the above breach, that is, the right to claim unfair dismissal, because had the proper disciplinary procedure been carried out, the employee would have been employed long enough to claim unfair dismissal (see also *FOCSA Services (UK) Ltd v Birkett* [1996] IRLR 325; *Morran v Glasgow Council of Tenants Association* [1998] IRLR 67).

Where a dismissal was wrongful on purely procedural grounds (and this finding would   **13.67**
itself depend on a finding that the disciplinary procedure was contractually binding), the
proper amount of damages is such sum as would have been earned from the date of the
unlawful dismissal to the date when the contract could lawfully be terminated, according
to Hodgson J in *Dietman v London Borough of Brent* [1987] IRLR 259. The claimant
would not, however, be entitled to a sum to reflect the fact that she had lost the statutory
minimum notice period which she had built up since she might have been lawfully dismissed in the near future had the proper procedure been followed.

Very large measures of damages are available only where the contract is for a fixed term   **13.68**
and cannot be terminated by notice. This is most usually the case in high status occupations such as company directors, football club managers, and accountants. The measure
of damages is then similarly the amount which would have been earned in the unexpired
part of the fixed term, but here there might be four or five years to run.

Modification of the principles in relation to damages

From the amount of damages so made up must be deducted sums to take account of: miti-   **13.69**
gation; taxation; and benefits received.

Mitigation

As in every breach of contract claim, the employee claimant must mitigate his loss as a   **13.70**
result of the breach. He cannot sit back at home and mount up his losses in the confident
expectation that he will be able to claim them from his former employer. In particular, he
must take reasonable steps to obtain another job, and if he succeeds any wages which are
earned in the new position will be deducted from wages due as damages over the period
of notice. If, on the other hand, he does not try to find another post, a sum is taken away
to represent his lack of effort (see also *Westwood v Secretary of State for Employment*
[1984] IRLR 209).

Each case depends on its own facts but the dismissed employee does not normally have to   **13.71**
take the first job which comes along in order to be found to have mitigated his loss. He
may also act reasonably in refusing to take another position in the company which has
just dismissed him. He is entitled to wait for a suitable skilled job, so that a painter is not
necessarily expected to take work as a general labourer (*Edwards v SOGAT* [1971] Ch
354) nor a managing director as an assistant manager (*Yetton v Eastwoods Froy* [1967] 1
WLR 104). A similar approach is taken to that of suitable alternative employment offers
after redundancy (16.33ff).

The employee must also give credit for any benefits and opportunities gained as a result of   **13.72**
his dismissal, but not where these arise only indirectly. In *Gregory v Wallace* [1998] IRLR
387, the facts were somewhat unusual. The employee's contract of employment specified a
two-year contractual notice period with a power by the employer to pay this in lieu. The
contract further provided that the employee would be entitled to accept other employment during such notice period. The employee was summarily dismissed, and the Court
of Appeal held that the employee was entitled to a full two years' salary notwithstanding
that he had obtained other employment within that period, because the employee would
have been entitled to this even if the contract had not been breached by the employer.
Further, in *Lavarack v Woods of Colchester Ltd* [1967] 1 QB 278, the claimant was, after
dismissal, able to take shares in a competing company, which was profitable, but this was
too indirect a benefit to be brought into account.

13.73 There is no duty to mitigate, however, in a case where the contract of employment provides for a specific period of payment on termination which may be thus recovered as a debt. This controversial decision in *Abrahams v Performing Right Society Ltd* [1995] ICR 1028 arose out of an unusual factual situation since the employee's terms included the provision that in the event of termination he 'would be entitled, other than in the case of dismissal for gross misconduct, to a period of two years or the equivalent payment in lieu' (at 1030H). The Court of Appeal found that this was not a case in which damages were being awarded for wrongful dismissal but the employee was instead exercising his entitlement to a debt pursuant to the contract. This was a liquidated damages claim so that the duty to mitigate did not arise. In *Cerberus Software Ltd v Rowley* [2001] IRLR 160, a clause providing that the employers 'may make a payment in lieu of notice to the employee' did not have this effect. This gave to the employer a choice, and was wholly inconsistent with the employee having a contractual right to insist on the payment being made. The employee thus was under a duty to mitigate (see also *Murray v Leisureplay plc* [2005] IRLR 946).

Taxation

13.74 Since the relevant damages are based on lost wages, the court deducts from them the amount of tax which the employee would have paid if he had received the money week by week or month by month rather than in a lump sum. This is the same rule as applies generally to damages in tort (*BTC v Gourley* [1956] AC 185) and is based on the assumption that damages are not taxable in the hands of the claimant, but this is not always the case in all damages claims for wrongful dismissal (s 403 Income Tax (Earnings and Pensions) Act 2003). The Inland Revenue has intervened in respect of termination of employment contracts to prevent 'golden handshakes' being used as tax avoidance devices so that payments of over £30,000 are subject to tax in the claimant's hands. The rule in *Gourley's* case therefore applies only to the first £30,000 of an award or settlement. Section 148(2) applies to 'any payment ... which is made, whether in pursuance of any legal obligation or not, either directly or indirectly in consideration or in consequence of, or otherwise in connection with, the termination of the holding of the office or employment or any change in its functions or emoluments ...'. (On the treatment of injury to feelings awards see *Orthet Ltd v Vince Cain* [2004] IRLR 857; *Timothy James Consulting Ltd v Wilton* [2015] IRLR 368; *Moorthy v HM Revenue & Customs* [2016] IRLR 259.) In *Shove v Downs Surgical plc* [1984] IRLR 17, Sheen J decided that the assessment of the claimant's loss should be increased by such amount as was necessary to leave him after deduction of tax with the net compensation due to him, so as properly to put him in the same position as if the contract had been properly performed.

Other benefits

13.75 There may be other sources of assistance during unemployment caused by the dismissal besides recourse to the courts for damages. These must be balanced against damages so that the dismissed employee does not recover twice. The following rules apply to such other benefits:

(a) the *jobseeker's allowance* received during the period of notice for which damages can be gained are deducted (*Parsons v BNM Laboratories Ltd* [1964] 1 QB 95; *Cheeseman v Bowater Paper Ltd* [1971] 3 All ER 513; *Nabi v British Leyland (UK) Ltd* [1980] 1 All ER 667; *Lincoln v Hayman* [1982] 1 WLR 488);

(b) *redundancy payment* is not deducted since it is not a substitute for wages but a lump sum recognition of the loss of past employment (*Yorkshire Engineering & Welding Ltd v Burnham* [1974] ICR 77; *Basnett v J. & A. Jackson Ltd* [1976] ICR 63; *Stocks v Magna Merchants Ltd* [1973] ICR 530; *Wilson v National Coal Board* (1980) 130 NLJ 1146);

(c) the sum of national insurance contributions which the employee has not had to pay while unemployed is deducted (*Cooper v Firth Brown Ltd* [1963] 1 WLR 418);

(d) unfair dismissal compensation is deducted, at least the amount awarded for loss of earnings (*Berry v Aynsley Trust Ltd* (1976) 127 NLJ 1052), but the court will not be able to do this if the unfair dismissal award is for the maximum figure then available and the tribunal has not apportioned that amount to any particular period when the employee was out of work (*O'Laiore v Jackel International Ltd* [1991] ICR 718); and

(e) occupational pension benefits are not deductible (*Hopkins v Norcross plc* [1994] IRLR 18).

Normally unfair dismissal is the more efficacious remedy for dismissal, but wrongful **13.76** dismissal maintains a residual utility where:

(a) the employee is a *higher earner* and may claim the full extent of his loss beyond the maximum on unfair dismissal claims;

(b) the employee *cannot claim* the statutory right because he is disqualified or, for example, he has not applied within three months of dismissal (Chapter 12);

(c) the dismissal is *fair* but in breach of contract; or

(d) a declaration or judicial review is required.

14

UNFAIR DISMISSAL

A THE BACKGROUND 14.01

B OUTLINE 14.06

C DISMISSAL 14.10

   Direct dismissal (s 95(1)(a)) 14.13

   Contracts terminating by a limiting
event (s 95(1)(b)) 14.22

   Constructive dismissal 14.23

   Statutory extensions of dismissal 14.54

   Terminations which are not
dismissals 14.64

   Frustration 14.80

D EFFECTIVE DATE OF
TERMINATION 14.92

E THE REASON FOR DISMISSAL 14.94

   Later discovered reason 14.95

   Written reasons for dismissal 14.100

   Statutory reasons for dismissal 14.103

F FAIRNESS OF DISMISSAL:
GENERAL .14.106

G INCAPABILITY 14.112

   Incompetence 14.113

   Health 14.123

   Qualifications 14.135

H MISCONDUCT 14.136

   Disobedience to reasonable
instructions .14.137

   Rules 14.146

   Offences 14.152

   Conduct checklist 14.171

I PROCEDURE 14.172

   Agreed procedures 14.173

   Warnings 14.174

   Hearings 14.181

   Appeals 14.185

J REDUNDANCY 14.191

   Reasonableness: The residuary
question 14.195

   Criteria of selection 14.200

   Consultation 14.206

   Alternative employment 14.210

K SOME OTHER SUBSTANTIAL
REASON .14.213

   Quasi or reorganisational
redundancy 14.223

   Contractual changes: A blow to the
sanctity of contract? 14.232

   Temporary workers: A recognition
of the dangers 14.235

   Subverting the other
gateways: Conduct 14.238

   Outside pressure 14.240

L ILLEGALITY 14.242

M SPENT OFFENCES 14.245

N DISMISSAL DURING STRIKE OR
LOCK-OUT 14.247

   The meaning of strike, other
industrial action, or lock-out 14.251

   Official action 14.262

   Dismissal during unofficial industrial
action 14.271

   Protected industrial action 14.273

O DISMISSAL BY REASON OF
RECOGNITION ACTION 14.276

P DISMISSAL FOR ASSERTION OF
A STATUTORY RIGHT 14.278

Q JURY SERVICE 14.284

R DISMISSAL: PRESSURE ON EMPLOYER
TO DISMISS 14.286

S REMEDIES 14.287

   Reinstatement 14.288

   Re-engagement 14.298

   Failure to comply with reinstatement
or re-engagement order 14.299

   Compensation: Basic award 14.302

   The compensatory award 14.310

   Deductions .14.334

   Contributory fault 14.337

   Mitigation .14.349

   Jobseeker's allowance 14.357

   Other issues 14.361

T UNFAIR DISMISSAL: OVERVIEW 14.362

The expression 'unfair dismissal' is in no sense a common sense expression capable of being understood by the man in the street. (Phillips J in *W. Devis & Sons Ltd v Atkins* [1976] ICR 196.)

A THE BACKGROUND

Unfair dismissal was a completely new concept when ushered in as a minor part of the controversial Industrial Relations Act 1971. It is different from common law wrongful dismissal since, as Phillips J said in *Redbridge LBC v Fishman* [1978] ICR 569, many dismissals are unfair although the employer is contractually entitled to dismiss the employee. In contrast, some dismissals are fair even though the employer was not contractually entitled to dismiss as he did dismiss. The new superstructure was, however, built on a common law base in that many of the underlying concepts arose directly from the law of contract. Dismissal, gross misconduct, and the failure to obey reasonable orders can hardly be understood apart from these roots.   **14.01**

The statutory jurisdiction seeks to meet the following shortcomings of the common law of wrongful dismissal: **14.02**

(a) the low level of damages, generally compensating only for the appropriate notice period;
(b) the inability of the dismissed employee in most cases to regain his job;
(c) the artificiality and archaism of the principles of summary dismissal; and
(d) the lack of express procedural protections for most employees.

The right can be seen embodied in various international treaties. The EU Charter of Fundamental Rights, Art 30, states: 'Every worker has the right to protection against unjustified dismissal in accordance with Community law and national laws and practices.'   **14.03**

ILO Convention 158, Art 4, states: 'The employment of a worker shall not be terminated unless there is a valid reason for such termination connected with the capacity or conduct of the worker or based on the operational requirements of the undertakings, establishment or service.' (See also European Social Charter, Art 24.)   **14.04**

What was intended as a central remedy of reinstatement, that is, putting an unfairly dismissed employee back in his old job, is granted in only about 1 per cent of cases.   **14.05**

B OUTLINE

The central provisions have remained remarkably little changed since 1971. The amendments contained in the Trade Union and Labour Relations Act 1974, the Employment Protection Act 1975, and the Employment Acts 1980, 1982, and 1988 concerned, in the main, the way this individual protection affects the trade unions and the closed shop, and the remedies it provides. Further changes were made by the TURERA 1993 in respect of dismissal for assertion of statutory rights and on the ground of maternity, and by the TULR(C)A 1992. The provisions are now consolidated in Part X of the Employment Rights Act 1996.   **14.06**

Section 94 of the ERA 1996 proclaims generally that, subject to exceptions, 'An employee has the right not to be unfairly dismissed by his employer.' The elaboration of what is in effect a slogan caused Phillips J, after rejecting the idea that it was a common-sense concept, to explain: 'It is narrowly and to some extent arbitrarily defined ... it is a form of   **14.07** words which could be translated as being equivalent to dismissal "contrary to statute" and to which the label unfair dismissal has been given' (*W. Devis & Sons Ltd v Atkins* [1976] ICR 196). Moreover, in some ways the statute does not adopt the most direct approach to the definition of an unfair dismissal.

14.08   Once (a) eligibility, and (b) dismissal have been established (themselves very complicated in concept), the necessary determination is twofold:

(a)   The employer must prove the reason or *principal reason* for the dismissal. Some reasons are automatically unfair (discrimination, union membership or activity, health and safety grounds, and pregnancy), but the five most important statutory reasons are only *potentially* fair and have to be tested against the standard of the reasonable employer. These reasons are: capability or qualifications, conduct, redundancy, statutory prohibition, and some other substantial reason for dismissal.

(b)   To be actually fair in any particular case it must be *reasonable* in all the circumstances for the employer to treat the reason he has given as a reason to dismiss (see 14.106 for full formula).

14.09   This process, according to Viscount Dilhorne in the leading case of *W. Devis & Sons Ltd v Atkins* (above), directs the tribunal to focus on the conduct of the employer and not on whether the employee in fact suffered any *injustice*. It involves consideration of substance and procedure, the latter being most clearly set out in the ACAS codes of practice which are non-binding but persuasive in employment tribunals in the same way as the Highway Code (while not having the force of law) receives marked respect from the criminal courts.

C DISMISSAL

14.10   At common law there were only two types of terminations of employment which might found an action for wrongful dismissal:

(a)   a sending away by the employer; and

(b)   a radical change of the employee's terms and conditions which amounted to a repudiatory breach of his contract (*Marriott v Oxford Co-op Society (No 2)* [1970] 1 QB 186).

An extended definition, however, became necessary as first the Redundancy Payments Act 1965 and later the Industrial Relations Act 1971 with its unfair dismissal provisions, attempted to meet the perceived deficiencies of the common law.

14.11   In order to claim either type of remedy, the employee first has to prove that he was dismissed, and both statutes adopted virtually the same codification of the concept, which has remained largely intact throughout several re-enactments. The three main headings of dismissal are now to be found in s 95(1) (and repeated in s 136(1) for redundancy) of the ERA 1996. An employee shall be treated as dismissed by his employer only in the following circumstances:

(a)   *Direct dismissal*—when the contract under which he is employed by the employer is terminated by the employer, whether it is so terminated by notice or without notice.

(b)   *Termination of limited term*—where under that contract he is employed for a limited term, that limited term terminates without being renewed under the same contract. Limited term here means '(a) the employment under the contract is not intended to be permanent and (b) provision is accordingly made in the contract for it to terminate by virtue of a limiting event', that is, expiry of a fixed term, performance of a specific task, or the occurrence or non-occurrence of an event where the contract provides for termination on such occurrence or non-occurrence.

(c) *Constructive dismissal*—when the employee terminates that contract, with or without notice, in circumstances such that he is entitled to terminate it without notice by reason of the employer's conduct.

All three species of dismissal focus on the termination of *the contract* of employment rather than necessarily of the *relationship* of the employer and employee. The last remaining doubt in this respect concerned constructive dismissal and it was removed by *Western Excavating (ECC) Ltd v Sharp* [1978] 1 All ER 713, as reiterated by the Court of Appeal in *Bournemouth University HEC v Buckland* [2011] QB 323. One consequence is that an employee can claim to have been dismissed even though taken back by the same employer under a different contract, although it is then unlikely that unfairness would be found (see *Hogg v Dover College* [1990] ICR 39; *Alcan Extrusions Ltd v Yates* [1996] IRLR 327).

The difficulties under each paragraph will now be examined, and then we turn to those terminations which remain outside their scope. The employee must prove dismissal, so that if there is any dispute on this point he goes first before an employment tribunal (*Horsell v Heath* (1966) 1 ITR 332). The question whether or not there has been a dismissal is one of fact for the tribunal (*Martin v MBS Fastenings (Glynwed) Distribution Ltd* [1983] ICR 511). **14.12**

Direct dismissal (s 95(1)(a))

Words of dismissal

The concept of direct dismissal appears obvious at first sight. Some cases, however, are not clear-cut, and courts and tribunals have required that words of dismissal should be unequivocal and set a date for the end of employment. It is essential to distinguish clearly words of dismissal from words which are equivocal or uttered in the heat of the moment. Where words are not obvious but the employee has interpreted them as amounting to a dismissal, tribunals have been counselled to concentrate on the employer's intention and the employee's reaction to it. The approach of the EAT is revealed in the following cases: **14.13**

(a) In *Tanner v D.T. Kean Ltd* [1978] IRLR 110, the respondent's manager lost his temper on finding that the employee had taken the company's van and he ended his somewhat vitriolic attack by saying, 'You're finished with me.' The EAT decided that these words were spoken in anger, and were not meant to be an effective dismissal.

(b) A worker on Hull docks was so anxious to finish his job for the day quickly that his foreman was moved to comment that if he did not like the job he could 'fuck off'. In interpreting the words in the light of the language normally heard on Hull docks, as it was necessary to do, the tribunal held that the words were not indicative of dismissal (*Futty v D & D Brekkes Ltd* [1974] IRLR 130).

(c) In *J. & J. Stern v Simpson* [1983] IRLR 52, the claimant was told to 'go, get out, get out' by Mrs Stern who was ill at the time and had just overheard a heated discussion between her son and the claimant. Tudor Evans J emphasised the need to consider all the surrounding circumstances. Here it should have been clear that the words were not intended to be a dismissal (see also *Martin v Yeomen Aggregates Ltd* [1983] IRLR 49).

(d) If the employee is told he faces a disciplinary process for misconduct but agrees to resign to avoid this, or if he is otherwise responding to a 'resign or be sacked' ultimatum, this will be regarded as a dismissal, not a resignation (*Sandhu v Jan de Rijk Transport Ltd* [2007] ICR 1137).

(e) A forced change for an employee to self-employed status was not a dismissal where the employer made clear soon after the words were uttered that this was a mistake (*Willoughby v CF Capital plc* [2012] ICR 1038). The overall test was whether the person to whom the words were addressed was entitled to assume that they represented a conscious and rational decision on the part of the employer and here he was not so entitled.

(f) The dispatch of a Form P45 to the employee may be evidence, although not conclusive, that an employee has been dismissed (*Makin v Greens Motor (Bridport) Ltd*, The Times, 18 April 1986).

14.14 The jurisdiction to make a complaint of unfair dismissal after an employee has been given notice but before that termination takes effect is unaffected by a subsequent summary dismissal (*Patel v Nagesan* [1995] IRLR 370).

14.15 Secondly, to be effective, a dismissal, although it may be with or without notice, must set a date for termination or at least make it possible to ascertain such a date. Thus, a dismissal would be valid which was to take effect on the Queen's birthday, since that is easily identifiable, whereas a sacking to become effective when Grimsby Town FC win the FA Cup would not be. A vital distinction is thus drawn between an actual dated dismissal and advance warning thereof (*Hicks v Humphrey* (1967) 2 ITR 214). As Lord Parker CJ stated in *Morton Sundour Fabrics Ltd v Shaw* (1967) 2 ITR 84: 'As a matter of law you cannot dismiss an employee by saying "I intend to dispense with your services in the coming months."' This is not to deny that a very long period of notice, even a year in length, may be given, but a final date must always be set and communicated to the individual concerned. While in *Shedden v Youth Hostel Association (Scotland)* (1966) 1 ITR 327, there *was* a dismissal where the employee was told, 'We are moving in six months' time but you are not coming with us', a mere announcement of factory closure, even fixing a general date, was not sufficient. In *Doble v Firestone Tyre Co Ltd* [1981] IRLR 300, the respondent declared towards the end of 1979 that its Brentford factory would shut on 15 February 1980, and its statement continued with the assurance that: 'Obviously we will be keeping these plans under constant review and any change will be notified to you.' Less comforting was the indication that 'notices of termination will be issued as they become due'. In the atmosphere of insecurity thus engendered, the appellant naturally saw his best course as securing alternative employment as quickly as possible. He took this up on 17 December 1979, and claimed both a redundancy payment and unfair dismissal. The EAT upheld the employer's contention that he had not been dismissed and Waterhouse J echoed Lord Widgery's statement in *Morton* that (at 87):

> The employee has the perfectly secure right if he thinks fit to wait until his contract is determined, to take his redundancy payment, and then see what he can do in regard to obtaining other employment. If he does, and one can appreciate that there may be compelling reasons, choose to leave his existing employment before the last minute in order to look for a new job before the rush of others competing with him comes, then it is up to him. The effect of the employer's warning is not in any way to derogate from his statutory rights but to give him an alternative which, if he is so minded, he can accept.

(See also *Tunnel Holdings Ltd v Woolf* [1976] ICR 387.)

14.16 A letter from the employer informing an employee that if he did not return to work by a particular date he would be treated as having terminated his contract on that date did not itself amount to a dismissal with notice; rather the termination took effect summarily on that date (*Rai v Somerfield Stores* [2004] IRLR 124).

14.17 The rule can, however, work with particular harshness when a cloud of uncertainty descends on a workplace, yet the employee who leaves has no remedy. An indication that his job is at risk, even that the place where he works 'will close within a year', is not an anticipatory breach of contract according to the EAT in *Haseltine Lake & Co v Dowler* [1981] IRLR 25 (see also *International Computers v Kennedy* [1981] IRLR 28). This is because for such a breach to occur it must be *inevitable* that an actual breach will happen in due course because the other party to the contract has renounced it, whether by showing that he intends not to be bound by it or that he has rendered performance impossible by putting it beyond his power to perform it. However, a termination with proper notice cannot constitute a repudiation (*Land and Wilson v West Yorkshire MCC* [1981] IRLR 87).

The same rules formulated in *Morton* as to dates of dismissal apply to resignations **14.18** (*Hughes v Gwynedd AHA* [1978] ICR 161), so that a statement that the applicant intended to leave her job to have her baby and would not return was not sufficient since it was merely a statement of present intention and nothing more than that. On the other hand, an announcement that 'I am resigning' contains no ambiguity according to the Court of Appeal in *Sothern v Franks Charlesly & Co* [1981] IRLR 278, and is to take effect at once. The context is, however, the key. The matter was to be examined there in the context of a senior secretary who had taken a considered decision. There may, however, be circumstances permitting the employment tribunal to find that words were uttered in the heat of the moment and thus did *not* amount to a true resignation. In so deciding in *Sovereign House Security Services Ltd v Savage* [1989] IRLR 115, the Court of Appeal came down in favour of the objective test. Further, if he seeks to assume that the employment has come to an end, it is necessary for that employer to set out in the clearest possible terms the manner in which that employment has been so terminated. Otherwise, if ambiguity exists, the tribunal will be entitled to look at what a reasonable employee would understand the position to be, with the terms of any notice of termination being construed strictly against the employer (*Widdicombe v Longcombe* [1998] ICR 710).

Repudiation as dismissal

There is a termination by the employer, and thus direct dismissal, when he repudiates **14.19** the contract of employment. This may be constituted, for example, by his insistence on a change in terms (*Marriott v Oxford and District Co-operative Society (No 2)* [1970] 1 QB 186), or by making it impossible for the employee to continue by closing the factory at which the employee worked (*Maher v Fram Gerrard Ltd* [1974] ICR 31). This is more normally treated as a constructive dismissal, but the fact that it is a termination by the employer within s 55(2)(a) does have some consequences in respect of the effective date of termination and the acceptance of breach (see discussion of *Geys v Société Générale, London Branch* [2013] ICR 117 at 13.17).

Termination of one series of tasks where a contract is severable does not amount to a **14.20** dismissal according to the Court of Appeal in *Land and Wilson v West Yorkshire MCC* [1981] IRLR 87. Thus, when the respondents terminated the retained part-time duties of the appellant firemen, they were not dismissed.

Once given, notice of termination may not be retracted without the agreement of the **14.21** other side (*Harris & Russell Ltd v Slingsby* [1973] ICR 454).

Contracts terminating by a limiting event (s 95(1)(b))

The Acts from the earliest days of unfair dismissal provided for a dismissal where a fixed **14.22** term expired but there was great controversy as to what was a fixed-term contract, which is fully discussed in earlier editions of this book. As from 1 October 2002 this formula was accordingly changed to 'employment under a limited term contract and that contract terminates by virtue of the limiting event without being renewed under the same contract'. This brings within the scope of dismissal contracts that are terminated by performance as well as fixed-term contracts as before.

Constructive dismissal

14.23 Section 95(1)(c) of the ERA 1996 reflects the common law position that an employee may be entitled to resign in reaction to his employer's behaviour and yet claim to have been dismissed. Otherwise the employer could make life so difficult for the employee that he had to leave, yet escape liability since he had not actually terminated his contract. The most difficult questions raised by the statutory codification of the concept are:

(a) what is the nature and degree of conduct which entitles the employee to leave (14.24–14.37); and
(b) whether the particular worker has in fact genuinely *reacted* to that conduct in leaving (14.43–14.51) and a delay after such conduct may be a barrier to such a finding.

This section should be read together with the section on implied terms (3.21) especially the implied duty of trust and confidence.

What conduct entitles the employee to terminate?

14.24 To claim constructive dismissal, the requirement is that the employee must be *entitled* to terminate his contract by reason of his employer's conduct, and two alternative criteria have struggled for recognition as the proper construction of 'entitled'. The broad view, propounded *inter alia* in *George Wimpey Ltd v Cooper* [1977] IRLR 205, was that the statute required only 'conduct of a kind which in accordance with good industrial relations practice no employee could reasonably be expected to accept'. This test, however, received its quietus in *Western Excavating (ECC) Ltd v Sharp* [1978] QB 761, where the Court of Appeal held that the employer must be in breach of contract. It was a case with particularly strong facts which left the higher courts with little sympathy for the employee. He was originally suspended from work for taking an afternoon off to play cards and in his consequent self-inflicted financial plight he asked the company for his accrued holiday pay or a loan. When the employer refused, he resigned. The tribunal decided in his favour on the preliminary issue of dismissal, but the Court of Appeal found this to be perverse. The determination of whether the employee was 'entitled to terminate' his contract was in its view, a purely contractual matter. Lord Denning MR said:

> If the employer is guilty of conduct which is a significant breach going to the root of the contract of employment or which shows that the employer no longer intends to be bound by one or more of the essential terms then the employee is entitled to treat himself as discharged from any further performance. If he does so, then he terminates the contract by reason of the employer's conduct. He is constructively dismissed. The employee is entitled in those circumstances to leave at the instant without giving any notice at all, or alternatively he may give notice and say he is leaving at the end of his notice. But the conduct in either case must be sufficiently serious to entitle him to leave at once.

The employee could not claim to have been dismissed since the appellant had committed no breach of contract. The Court of Appeal gave several reasons for preferring this more stringent contractual approach:

(a) the statute *distinguished* between dismissal and unfairness and it was anomalous to have the same test of reasonableness applying to both;

(b) the words in paragraph (c), 'terminate' and 'entitled', had a *legal*, and hence *contrac-tual*, connotation;

(c) the test of unreasonableness was *too indefinite* by far, and had, according to Lord Denning MR, led to decisions on 'the most whimsical grounds'; and

(d) any person of *common sense* could apply the contractual test.

The reasonableness test, however, appeared to be subtly reintroduced in *Woods v WM Car Services (Peterborough) Ltd* [1982] IRLR 413, when Watkins LJ commented, in determining whether the employee had been constructively dismissed, that: **14.25**

> Employers must not in my opinion be put in a position where, through the wrongful refusal of their employees to accept change, they are prevented from introducing business methods in furtherance of seeking success from their enterprise.

It appears that this *obiter* remark must be confined to the facts of the case since the EAT emphasised in *Wadham Stringer Commercials (London) Ltd v Brown* [1983] IRLR 46 that neither the circumstances inducing the fundamental breach by the employer nor the circumstances which led the employee to accept the repudiation were relevant to the ques-tion of constructive dismissal (see also *Millbrook Furnishing Industries Ltd v McIntosh* [1981] IRLR 309).

Two important general points emerged from the Court of Appeal decision in *Bournemouth University HEC v Buckland* [2010 ICR 908: **14.26**

(a) A repudiatory breach once complete is not capable of being remedied; and

(b) The range of reasonable responses test has no application in this respect.

Employer's duty of good faith

One consequence of the *Western Excavating* case has been to encourage the develop-ment at common law of manifold implied contractual terms specifically related to dis-missal. The courts have taken to heart the words of Bristow J that 'implied terms should reflect the changes in the relationship between employer and employee as social standards change'. Most room for manoeuvre has been found in the developing obligation of the employer to act towards his employee in good faith and with trust and confidence (see also 3.26–3.33). The fount of this stream of authority of 'reverse fidelity' is *BAC v Austin* [1978] IRLR 332. Mrs Austin was supposed to wear goggles at work, but did not find those provided to be suitable. She accordingly complained bitterly to management about them and when they failed to respond in any meaningful way, she resigned. The EAT found that the employer had indeed been in breach of a contractual obligation to act rea-sonably in dealing with safety and complaints, and more fundamentally, Phillips J uttered the widely quoted (albeit *obiter*) words: **14.27**

> If employers behave in a way which is not in accordance with good industrial practice to such an extent that the situation is intolerable or the situation is such that the employee cannot be expected to put up with it any longer that is a breach of an implied term of the contract.

The distinction between this and the old reasonableness test is wafer thin and it has stimulated a creative approach to implied terms in several cases.

In *Courtaulds Northern Textiles Ltd v Andrew* [1979] IRLR 84, Phillips J identified an implied term that the employer would not, 'without reasonable and proper cause conduct themselves in a manner calculated or likely to destroy or seriously damage the relation-ship of confidence and trust between the parties'. This has heralded a revolution in the very conceptual foundations of the contract of employment, moving it in stages from a relationship of subordination to one necessitating trust and cooperation on each side. It **14.28** imposes a 'proper purposes' doctrine on the use by management of its power. The actions of the employer must be either calculated or likely to destroy the relation of trust and confidence; *Baldwin v Brighton & Hove City Council* [2007] ICR 680, EAT.

14.29   An unusual situation arose in *RDF Media Group plc v Clements* [2008] IRLR 207. The employee had, unbeknown to the employer at the time, already breached the implied term of trust and confidence before the employer subsequently breached the term. The employee had probably disclosed confidential information to a prospective employer and had assisted the prospective employer in press briefings to put pressure on the existing employer. In deciding whether the employer has breached the implied obligation it is important to consider the state of the relationship at the time when the breach is alleged to have taken place. The court found that since Mr Clements was himself in repudiatory breach of a mutual obligation he was not entitled to accept any repudiation by RDF.

14.30   In the later case of *Tullett Prebon plc v BGC Brokers LP* [2010] IRLR 648, it was held that when an employee brings a claim for wrongful or unfair constructive dismissal the employee cannot rely on conduct unless he leaves by reason of it. *RDF Media* was said to be wrong in so far as it suggested otherwise.

14.31   The various obligations which have been imposed under this rubric include:

(a) not to treat employees *'arbitrarily,* capriciously or inequitably' with respect to increases in pay (*Gardner (F.C.) Ltd v Beresford* [1978] IRLR 63) whilst, on the other hand, an employee has no right to an annual pay rise (*Murco Petroleum Ltd v Forge* [1987] IRLR 50);

(b) not to *undermine the authority* of senior staff over subordinates;

(c) not to *falsely accuse* an employee of theft (*Robinson v Crompton Parkinson Ltd* [1978] IRLR 61); nor to threaten to call in the CID if she did not resign (*Allders International Ltd v Parkins* [1981] IRLR 68);

(d) not to expect employees to work in *intolerable conditions* (*Graham Oxley Tool Steels Ltd v Firth* [1980] IRLR 135);

(e) not persistently to attempt to vary the employee's conditions of service. In *Woods v WM Car Services (Peterborough)* [1981] IRLR 347, there was a potential repudiation when the new management of the company within a few months of a takeover tried to reduce the pay of the long-serving applicant, who had been its chief secretary, and also insisted that she work longer hours, gave her unjustified warnings as to conduct, issued new terms, and gave her a job specification which was more than one person could handle. In fact, the EAT did not interfere with the tribunal's finding of fact that here there was no fundamental breach. The Court of Appeal upheld this view and Lord Denning MR said that, 'Just as a servant must be good and faithful so an employer must be good and considerate' (see also *Wadham Stringer Commercials (London) Ltd v Brown* [1983] IRLR 46);

(f) to *encourage positively,* and maintain appraisal of, a probationer during his trial period in particular by giving guidance and advice (*White v London Transport Executive* [1981] IRLR 261);

(g) not to undermine the authority of the football club manager as would happen when a player whom he did not want was brought in by the club over his head (*Keegan v Newcastle United FC Ltd* [2010] IRLR 94). There was an implied term that Kevin Keegan as manager would have the final say as to transfers into Newcastle United Football Club;

(h) to treat staff with dignity, being guarded in the use of foul language, particularly where the employee is in a close personal relationship with the employer; thus, in *Isle of Wight Tourist Board v Coombes* [1976] IRLR 413, a director of the appellant said of his secretary, in front of another employee: 'She is an intolerable bitch on a Monday morning.' This clearly shattered the relationship of complete confidence which must exist in the circumstances so that she could resign and claim constructive dismissal;

(i) not to require without reasonable cause the claimant to undergo a psychiatric examination (*Bliss v South East Thames Regional Health Authority* [1985] IRLR 308);

(j) not to impose a disciplinary punishment (even though expressly provided for in the contract of employment) if it is out of proportion to the 'offence' committed (*BBC v Beckett* [1983] IRLR 43; *Cawley v South Wales Electricity Board* [1985] IRLR 89);

(k) not to seek to change an employee's job specification by underhand means (*Chapman, Lowry & Puttick Ltd v Cox*, EAT 270/85).

The EAT warned of the limits of this general doctrine in *Post Office v Roberts* [1980] IRLR 347, although it found a breach of contract on the facts. The employee was a clerical assistant who worked for the respondent in Brighton. She applied to be transferred to a similar position in Croydon but was turned down ostensibly on the ground that there were 'no suitable vacancies' in the area. She soon discovered, however, newspaper advertisements in the Croydon district announcing the availability of the very positions which she was seeking. It was only several weeks later, and after much probing, that she discovered the real reason for her initial 'brush-off'; that she had been given a bad report which she had not been shown. In the view of Talbot J, this constituted a breach of the employer's implied duty of trust and confidence. He rejected the respondent's contention that a repudiation must be deliberate and in bad faith, but considered that it was going too far to say that an employee had to be treated in a reasonable manner. The behaviour must be, and here was, 'such that its effect judged reasonably and sensibly is to disable the other party from properly carrying out its obligations' (see also *Lewis v Motorworld Garages Ltd* [1985] IRLR 465). A finding that there has been conduct which amounts to a breach of the implied term of trust and confidence will mean inevitably that there has been a fundamental or repudiatory breach going necessarily to the root of the contract and entitling the employee to resign and claim constructive dismissal (*Morrow v Safeway Stores plc* [2002] IRLR 10). **14.32**

It is always an objective test of whether trust and confidence has been destroyed; the subjective intention of the employer is irrelevant (*The Leeds Dental Team Ltd v Rose* [2014] ICR 94). **14.33**

Other breaches of contract justifying resignation

Other breaches of express and implied terms which have been held sufficient to justify resignation include: **14.34**

(a) A deliberate reduction in pay, since: 'The basic rate of pay is a fundamental element in any contract of employment and in our opinion it cannot be said that there is no material breach on the part of an employer who proposes to reduce the basic rate even for good reasons and to a relatively small extent.' This was even though in *Industrial Rubber Products v Gillon* [1977] IRLR 389 (at 390), from which this quotation derives, the reduction was dictated by government pay policy. It is, however, subject to the *de minimis* rule, so that the sharing out with fellow employees of 1½p per hour bonus for lifting crates of empty bottles, which would at most reduce the applicant's wages by £1.50 per week out of a total of £60, was held not to be fundamental. On the other hand, abolition of a 1 per cent commission was held repudiatory, even though the introduction of a new scheme might eventually at least restore that loss. The crucial point was that at the time of resignation this could only be a matter for speculation (*R.F. Hill Ltd v Mooney* [1981] IRLR 258). It may be sufficient that the employer fails to increase pay in line with the contractual entitlement (*Pepper & Hope v Daish* [1980] IRLR 13). The circumstances in which a failure to pay would not be repudiatory would be where it reflected no more than a temporary fault in the employer's technology, an accounting error or simple mistake, or was by way of unexpected events (*Cantor Fitzgerald International v Callaghan* [1999] IRLR 234).

(b) A change in *job content or status*: in one case an acting manager had his 'most interesting and enjoyable duties' of buying greengroceries removed from him, and this constituted constructive dismissal (*Coleman v S & W Baldwin* [1977] IRLR 342). The nature of the change is a question of degree and, in assessing the scope of job duties, it is pertinent to examine not only the employee's statement of terms, but also the advertisement by which he was attracted to the post and all surrounding circumstances in order to build up a full picture of what he was employed to do (*Pedersen v Camden London Borough* [1981] IRLR 173). Requiring an employee to cease doing what has been his principal job and to take up a new role will almost always be capable of being a repudiatory breach of contract. Whether in a particular case the breach is sufficiently material to be repudiatory has to be judged objectively by reference to its impact on the employee. The question whether the proposed change was justified is a different and distinct question (*Hilton v Shiner Ltd* [2001] IRLR 728).

Temporary changes are treated less severely than permanent imposed variations and the EAT has held that:

> If an employer under the stresses of the requirements of his business directs an employee to transfer to other suitable work on a purely temporary basis and at no diminution in wages that may in the ordinary case not constitute a breach of contract. However, it must be clear that 'temporary' means a period which is either defined as being a short fixed period ... or which is in its nature of limited duration.

In *Millbrook Furnishing Industries Ltd v McIntosh* [1981] IRLR 309, where Browne-Wilkinson P enunciated this principle, a transfer of highly skilled sewing machinists in the respondent company's upholstery department to unskilled work in its bedding section was a breach; for it was to last until work picked up in the former section and this could not be at all accurately estimated at the time of the application (see also *McNeill v Charles Crimin (Electrical Contractors) Ltd* [1984] IRLR 179).

(c) Substantial change in the *place of work* (see *Hawker Siddeley Power Engineering Ltd v Rump* [1979] IRLR 425; and *Little v Charterhouse Magna Assurance Co* [1980] IRLR 19). Whether a forced move is a fundamental enough breach of contract 'is a question of degree to be determined according to all the circumstances such as the nature of the work, the circumstances in which it is performed and the circumstances of the place to which the work is to be transferred'. Thus, neither the move of Times Newspapers from Printing House Square to Grays Inn Road (*Times Newspapers Ltd v Bartlett* (1976) 11 ITR 106), nor of a restaurant from Holborn to Regent Street, was a *fundamental* breach of contract (*Managers (Holborn) Ltd v Hohne* [1977] IRLR 230), but a requirement to move fifteen miles from Mosshill Industrial Estate, Ayr, to Irvine was a fundamental breach (*McAndrew v Prestwick Circuits Ltd* [1988] IRLR 514).

In *Courtaulds Northern Spinning Ltd v Sibson and TGWU* [1988] IRLR 305, the Court of Appeal decided that it was not a fundamental breach to instruct the respondent HGV driver to transfer to another depot one mile away in order to avoid conflict with the union. It was not correct to postulate that an implied term to transfer from depot to depot was subject to the qualification of reasonableness and that the move had to be for genuine operational reasons (see also *United Bank Ltd v Akhtar* [1989]

IRLR 507). There is an implied term that reasonable notice of a transfer should be given (*Prestwick Circuits Ltd v McAndrew* [1990] IRLR 191; cf *White v Reflecting Roadstuds Ltd* [1991] ICR 733).

(d) Change in *hours of work* (*Derby CC v Marshall* [1979] ICR 731).

(e) *Suspension* by the employer without contractual authority.

(f) Failure to *provide work* where this is an implied term, for example, refusal to allow the employee to perform his contractual duties while working out his notice.

(g) Failure to provide such assistance as was customary, for example, in a hairdressers' salon (*Seligman & Latz v McHugh* [1979] IRLR 130).

(h) Failure to provide a *safe system of work* (*Keys v Shoefayre Ltd* [1978] IRLR 476), including enhanced security after an armed robbery.

(i) Failure to follow a contractual disciplinary procedure (*Post Office v Strange* [1981] IRLR 515).

(j) Imposition of a disproportionate penalty of a final written warning for leaving the workplace for one hour (*Stanley Cole (Wainfleet) Ltd v Sheridan* [2003] ICR 297).

(k) Making public remarks about an employee which are highly damaging to his reputation (*RDF Media Group Ltd v Clements* [2008] IRLR 207).

(l) Appointing someone to an internal interview panel whom the employee perceives to be prejudiced against transsexuals when the employer did not know the employee was a transsexual (*Baldwin v Brighton & Hove City Council* [2007] ICR 680).

In *Transco plc v O'Brien* [2002] IRLR 441, the permanent workforce was given a new **14.35** contract on better terms. By mistake, the employer missed out the claimant as he thought the employee was not on a permanent contract. Although there was no bad faith, the exclusion was a breach of the implied term of trust and confidence.

There is, however, no contractual right for the employer to abide by statutory rights such **14.36** as the right to carry out trade union activities; thus the failure by the employer to accord such rights could not found a claim for constructive dismissal (*Doherty v British Midland Airways Ltd* [2006] IRLR 90).

The following principles also apply: **14.37**

(a) A constructive dismissal may arise by way of an *anticipatory* breach. In *Norwest Holst Group Administration Ltd v Harrison* [1985] IRLR 240, the Court of Appeal decided that an employer who threatened a breach was entitled to withdraw the threat at any time before the innocent party communicated his unequivocal acceptance of the repudiation. In that case the employee was engaged as director and chief engineer, but was told by letter on 14 June 1982 that he would lose his directorship as from 1 July 1982. The employee replied by letter headed 'Without prejudice' that he was not prepared to accept the loss of the directorship. Faced with this, the company withdrew the threat but later on that day the employee sought to accept the repudiation. The Court of Appeal did not think that this was a constructive dismissal.

(b) The employee may complain of conduct such as a reprimand by a member of management even though that person would have no authority actually to dismiss. The proper question is whether that person was acting within the scope of his employment in delivering the reprimand (*Hilton International Hotels (UK) Ltd v Protopapa* [1990] IRLR 316).

(c) There may be a fundamental breach of contract when an employer threatens that unless employees change their hours, the employer will dismiss them with due notice (*Greenaway Harrison Ltd v Wiles* [1994] IRLR 380).

(d) The employee can rely on a matter as giving rise to a constructive dismissal even though the body purporting to carry out the act which amounts to the fundamental breach of contract relied upon had no power to do so on behalf of the respondent (*Warnes v Cheriton Oddfellows Social Club* [1993] IRLR 58).

(e) A council may constructively dismiss an employee by the action of an individual councillor (*Moores v Bude-Stratton Town Council* [2000] IRLR 676).

14.38 There is special provision in the TUPE situation. An employee can claim constructive dismissal on the takeover or merger of his employer only if a substantial change is made in his working conditions to his material detriment under reg 4(9) of the Transfer of Undertakings (Protection of Employment) Regulations 2006 (SI 2006/246) but not simply by reason of the change of employer (see 18.59ff).

The breach must be fundamental

14.39 In all these cases the breach in question must be fundamental. The conduct of the employer must be of a serious nature and, in the normal case, take place over a period of time. However, what is not normally a fundamental breach in respect of a new employee may be sufficient to justify resignation where the employee has given long and good service. A small straw may break this doughty camel's back. The question is always one of degree, but the following are illustrations of cases where the breach was *not* fundamental:

(a) failure to interview candidates for redundancy in accordance with the appropriate collective bargain (*British Leyland Ltd v McQuilken* [1978] IRLR 245);

(b) failure to pay the employee on the due date because of cash flow problems, since he was assured of full settlement in the near future (*Adams v Charles Zub Associates Ltd* [1978] IRLR 551);

(c) failure by the employer to investigate a complaint against it by the employee (*GLC v Canning* [1980] IRLR 378);

(d) absence of consultation over the appointment of a subordinate and not telling an employee of pay increases received by subordinates when his own increment was withheld (*Walker v Josiah Wedgwood & Sons Ltd* [1978] IRLR 105; see also *Kenneth McRae & Co Ltd v Dawson* [1984] IRLR 5);

(e) failure to take further measures to limit the risk of criminal attacks at a building society agency (*Dutton & Clark Ltd v Daly* [1985] IRLR 363); and

(f) failure to treat an allegation of sexual harassment seriously (*Bracebridge Engineering Ltd v Darby* [1990] IRLR 3).

The last straw

14.40 Where the course of conduct or series of events led to a breach of implied term, the final event which brought about the employee's resignation need not itself be a breach of contract (*Meikle v Notts CC* [2005] ICR 1) so long as it is more than trivial and is capable of contributing to a breach of the implied term of mutual trust and confidence and has been preceded by blameworthy or unreasonable conduct in the past. The essential feature of the final straw is that it is an act in a series the cumulative effect of which amounted to the breach. This is an objective, not a subjective, test so that there will be no breach simply because the employee subjectively feels that such a breach has occurred no matter how genuinely that belief is held (*Omilaju v Waltham Forest LBC* [2005] IRLR 35). Examples of what might constitute the last straw could include a reduction in the number of hours worked, or a requirement to move workplace to some distance away, even if the contract allows such changes to be made, provided this has been preceded by previous unreasonable behaviour towards the employee. However, it will be an unusual case where the 'final straw' consists of conduct which viewed objectively as reasonable and justifiable satisfies the final straw test. In 'last straw' cases, one does not need to review whether the action was within the range of reasonable responses (*GAB Robbins (UK) Ltd v Triggs* [2008] IRLR 317).

There are some cases dealing with disputed contractual construction, in particular: *Frank Wright & Co (Holdings) v Punch* [1980] IRLR 217; *Financial Techniques v Hughes* [1981] IRLR 32; *Ready Case Ltd v Jackson* [1981] IRLR 312; cf *BBC v Beckett* [1983] IRLR 43; *Bliss v South East Thames Regional Health Authority* [1985] IRLR 308; *Brown v JBD Engineering Ltd* [1994] IRLR 568; *Transco plc v O'Brien* [2002] IRLR 441; and *Bridgen v Lancashire CC* [1987] IRLR 58. **14.41**

A question of fact

The Court of Appeal in *Woods v WM Car Services (Peterborough) Ltd* [1982] IRLR 413 decided that there was no rule of law for determining whether a particular set of facts constitutes a repudiatory breach. The EAT should interfere with the decision of the employment tribunal only if it is shown that the tribunal misdirected itself in law so that the decision was such that no reasonable tribunal could reach it (see also *Pedersen v Camden London Borough* [1981] IRLR 173; cf *McNeill v Charles Crimin (Electrical Contractors) Ltd* [1984] IRLR 179; *Scott v Coalite Fuels and Chemicals* [1988] IRLR 131). **14.42**

The resignation must be in reaction to the fundamental breach

There must be evidence that an employee's resignation was really in reaction to, and motivated by, a fundamental breach by the employer, and thus an acceptance, in orthodox theory, of his repudiation. While the worker need not use such technical language, he 'must indicate the reason why he is going and must make it plain that he is accepting a breach on the part of his employers' (*Genower v Ealing AHA* [1980] IRLR 297). **14.43**

A long period between breach and resignation will be difficult to explain without good reason, and may amount to waiver of any breach (*Bashir v Brillo Manufacturing Co* [1979] IRLR 295). **14.44**

Lord Denning MR said in *Western Excavating v Sharp* [1978] QB 761, that: **14.45**

> the employee must make up his mind soon after the conduct of which he complains; for if he continues for any length of time without leaving, he will lose his right to treat himself as discharged.

Thus, in *Jeffrey v Laurence Scott* [1977] IRLR 466, where the employer's conduct occurred some three and a half months before the resignation, the employee was held not to have been constructively dismissed. On the other hand, mere delay alone will not amount to affirmation or waiver of the breach (*Cook v MSHK Ltd* [2009] IRLR 838). **14.46**

The lapsing of a few weeks will probably not amount to waiver, particularly if the claimant is looking for other work in that time, or clearly objects to the breach of contract (see *W.E. Cox Toner International Ltd v Crook* [1981] IRLR 443; *G.W. Stephens & Son v Fish* [1989] ICR 324; *Reid v Camphill Engravers Ltd* [1990] IRLR 268). There may even be as long as eighteen months' delay between the last straw and the resignation (*Logan v Commissioners of Customs and Excise* [2004] IRLR 63) without affirmation being found. Affirmation is essentially the legal embodiment of the everyday concept of 'letting bygones be bygones' (*Cantor Fitzgerald International v Bird* [2003] IRLR 867). Giving notice does not amount necessarily to affirmation of the contract following a repudiatory breach (*Cockram v Air Products plc* [2014] ICR 1065). **14.47**

It is not necessary for an employee to give a reason for leaving at the actual time, especially in cases where the employer gives outrageous or embarrassing instructions, as the **14.48** employee may not wish to argue the point there and then. The tribunal should look at each case on its own facts (*Weathersfield Ltd v Sargent* [1999] ICR 425, CA). It was incorrect to ask whether a repudiatory breach of contract had played a part in the resignation of an employee rather than to look for the 'effective' cause of the resignation (*Wright v North Ayrshire Council* [2014] ICR 77).

14.49   Even if an employee has not treated a breach of an express contractual term as a wrongful repudiation in and of itself, he may add such a breach to other actions which taken together may cumulatively amount to a breach of the implied obligation of trust and confidence (*Lewis v Motorworld Garages Ltd* [1985] IRLR 465; cf *Reid v Camphill Engravers* (above) in which a failure to pay in accordance with relevant Wages Council orders was characterised as a continuing breach).

14.50   Before a contract of employment is terminated, there must have been some communication by words or by conduct such as to inform the other party to the contract that it is at an end. Thus, an employee alleging constructive dismissal must communicate in some way to the employer the fact that he is terminating his employment (*Edwards v Surrey Police* [1999] IRLR 456).

14.51   The latest time for the employee to accept the employer's repudiatory breach is at the close of his unfair dismissal claim before the employment tribunal (*Shook v London Borough of Ealing* [1986] IRLR 46). There is, however, no need for an employee to take the precaution of an express reservation of the right to accept repudiation when the employer had expressly allowed the employee time to make up his mind (*Bliss v South East Thames Regional Health Authority* [1985] IRLR 308).

Constructive dismissal and fairness

14.52   It is a commonly held misconception that a constructive dismissal is necessarily an *unfair* dismissal. The fact that there has been a breach of contract (however fundamental) by the employer means only that the employee has crossed the first hurdle of establishing dismissal. This is because the employer may still seek to justify the reason for his actions as being fair. The proper question to be asked was formulated in *Savoia v Chiltern Herb Farms Ltd* [1982] IRLR 166, as whether, though in fundamental breach of contract, the employer had in all the circumstances behaved fairly, and the facts of the instant case provide a good example of a positive answer to that question. The employer decided to reorganise its business operation after one of its foremen died. It moved the claimant to the dead man's position because it had certain complaints about his performance in his previous job. He refused what was described by the employer as a 'promotion', claiming that it would expose him to conjunctivitis. The Court of Appeal found that the reorganisation was necessary and that the employer had in the circumstances done all that it could to ease the changeover by offering him a higher salary. On the other hand, he had refused to undergo a medical so that it could judge whether his claims of potential sickness were genuine. Thus, the constructive dismissal was fair (see also *Stephenson & Co (Oxford) Ltd v Austin* [1990] ICR 609).

14.53   The EAT has naturally indicated that cases of this sort will be rare (*F.C. Shepherd & Co Ltd v Jerrom* [1985] IRLR 275, overturned on appeal on other matters). Moreover, it is perverse of an employment tribunal to decide that an employee has been constructively dismissed because he has received a disciplinary penalty out of all proportion to the offence he had committed and still decide that he has been treated fairly in all the circumstances. Waite J said that, 'Considerations of fairness on the one hand and the considerations affecting constructive dismissal on the other are two sides of the same coin' (*Cawley v South Wales Electricity Board* [1985] IRLR 89).

Statutory extensions of dismissal

There are several circumstances in which the notion of an employer termination has been **14.54** widened beyond the common law, because of potential injustice if these situations lie outside the concept of dismissal. There are four statutory enlargements which operate in favour of the employee, although the first two have some counterpart at common law.

Leaving early

If the employee is under notice of dismissal but wishes to leave early in order to take **14.55** another job, it would be unjust to hold that he has thus resigned and lost his rights to claim unfair dismissal and redundancy payments. Section 136(3) of the ERA 1996 enacts that there is still a dismissal for redundancy provided that the employee gives notice in writing that he wishes to leave prematurely.

If, on the other hand, the employer does protest at the premature termination, an employ- **14.56** ment tribunal must decide, on the justice and equity of the whole case, whether to grant a redundancy payment, and if so, to do this in part or in full. For redundancy this declaration of intention must be given within the 'obligatory period of notice', that is, within the period of notice required to be given either by statute or under the employee's contract. The EAT has wavered between applying this requirement strictly and flexibly. It does not apply to unfair dismissal as is (*Ready Case Ltd v Jackson* [1981] IRLR 312; *CPS Recruitment v Bowen and Secretary of State for Employment* [1982] IRLR 54), but there are similar provisions. By s 95(2) of the ERA 1996:

> (2) An employee shall be taken to be dismissed by his employer for the purposes of this Part if—
>   (a) the employer gives notice to the employee to terminate his contract of employment, and
>   (b) at a time within the period of that notice the employee gives notice to the employer to terminate the contract of employment on a date earlier than the date on which the employer's notice is due to expire;
>
> and the reason for the dismissal is to be taken to be the reason for which the employer's notice is given.

The passing on of a copy of a claim form by the employment tribunal to the employer did **14.57** not constitute notice by the employee to terminate the contract within the forerunner to s 95(2) (*Cardinal Vaughan Memorial School Governors v Alie* [1987] ICR 406).

Example Gibbon tells Harvey in week 1 that he will be dismissed in week 14. Harvey **14.58** has been employed for ten years, and gives notice that he wishes to leave in week 10. The employment tribunal then has to decide in its discretion whether he still deserves redundancy pay. There are as yet no reported cases on how the discretion will be exercised. If Harvey seeks to leave in week 2 he forfeits all rights to redundancy pay because this is not within the 'obligatory notice period', that is, ten weeks for ten years (= 14–10) which begins in week 4.

Taking a new job for a trial period

After a dismissal from one position with an employer, the employee may take on another **14.59** post with the same or an associated employer intending to try it out. This is particularly so where the termination is by way of the employer's repudiatory conduct. It would penalise the employee who attempted in this way to make a new start if he were not still entitled to claim the statutory remedies should things not work and he then resigned. At common law, the courts thus often characterise the employee's acceptance of such new post after a breach of contract by an employer as qualified and conditional. If he leaves after a reasonable period for assessing the new job, the termination relates back to the employer's original action of repudiation and he can claim his rights. This notion of a 'trial period' is found in the ERA 1996, s 138(3). An employee has four weeks to decide whether he accepts the new terms (16.35–16.37) and this relates to actual weeks and not weeks in which work was actually carried on (*Benton v Sanderson Kayser Ltd* [1989] IRLR 19). This may be extended, although rather restrictively, only for the purposes of retraining (s 138(6)).

14.60 **Example** Blake worked as a machinist for Coleridge Textiles Ltd for ten years. The managing director announces that henceforth he must do the work of presser. He is not sure whether to take it; the statute gives him four weeks to make up his mind. If in that time he decides he does not like it, he can still claim unfair dismissal and/or redundancy pay.

14.61 The EAT has, however, held that the legislation does not supplant the common law but rather runs concurrently with it. This gives the employee a reasonable time in which to make up his mind before the four weeks begin to run, and may make the statutory provision virtually redundant. Thus, in *Air Canada v Lee* [1978] IRLR 392, the airline moved staff including the claimant from one office to another in breach of her contract. She agreed to go on a trial basis, but after two months she decided it was not for her and left the employment. The EAT held that she had never finally and without qualification accepted the proffered new terms and conditions. The statutory trial period had never begun to run, since the termination of her original contract only occurred 'when, before the expiry of the reasonable period of the common law trial period, she made up her mind that she did not wish to continue to be employed'. In *Turvey v C.W. Cheyney & Sons Ltd* [1979] IRLR 105, the EAT said that the trial period 'provides an improvement on rather than a restriction of the employee's common law rights'.

Lay-off and short-time

14.62 An employee may be left in a state of limbo by his employer, being given little or no work but not actually dismissed. Again statute protects him, but in this respect only allows him to claim he has been dismissed for the purposes of redundancy payments. Sections 147–52 of the ERA 1996 provide a species of 'implied dismissal' where, for at least four consecutive weeks or at least six weeks spread over not more than thirteen weeks, the employee is 'laid-off' (no work provided at all for a week—s 147(1)), or on 'short-time' (ie where the employee receives less than half a week's pay, not including bonus—s 147(2)). The employee may then give notice in writing equivalent to the period of notice required by his contract to his employer, indicating his intention to claim a redundancy payment (see *Walmsley v C. & R. Ferguson Ltd* [1989] IRLR 112). The employer may react by issuing a counter-notice that he will contest the claim, in which case the matter will be referred to an employment tribunal to decide whether 'it was reasonably to be expected that the employee would ... not later than four weeks after that date enter on a period of not less than thirteen weeks during which he would not be laid off or kept on short-time for any week' (ERA 1996, s 152(1)(a)).

Implied termination

14.63 Section 136(5) of the ERA 1996, which provides for 'implied termination', is unique to redundancy, and reads:

> (5) Where in accordance with any enactment or rule of law—
>   (a) an act on the part of an employer, or
>   (b) an event affecting an employer (including, in the case of an individual, his death),
>   operates to terminate a contract under which an employee is employed by him, the act or event shall be taken for the purposes of this Part to be a termination of the contract by the employer.

Again, this is an example of the statute rather obscurely building on the quicksand of the common law. It comprises all the automatic dismissals already discussed in 13.02, including death of a personal employee, dissolution of partnership, appointment of a receiver, and liquidation of a company, and also a frustrating event affecting the employer, such as a fire at his sole place of business, or his imprisonment. This means that even though the employee is not entitled to claim unfair or wrongful dismissal, he may be eligible for redundancy payment, although only if the frustrating event affects the employer. Where a solicitors' practice was disposed of as a going concern following intervention by the Law Society, that intervention did terminate contracts of employment within the meaning of s 136(5) of the ERA 1996 (*Barnes v Leavesley* [2001] ICR 38); the position would be different if the firm simply ceased trading.

Terminations which are not dismissals

One of the main aims of the unfair dismissal provisions is to give employees a hearing of **14.64** their grievances on their merits, and to narrow the concept of dismissal nips that policy in the bud. However, although the statutory concept of dismissal is somewhat wider than at common law, many species of terminations of the contract of employment still do not qualify. We now consider the common law principles from time to time adopted by the employers to exclude dismissal.

Agreement to terminate

If there is a genuine agreement between employer and employee that a contract of **14.65** employment shall terminate, there is no dismissal, either at common law or by statute (*Strange Ltd v Mann* [1965] 1 All ER 1069). The same is true where there is a 'pure' resignation, rather than one which is given in response to a repudiatory breach of the employer, that is, constructive dismissal. The main problem lies in identifying and construing any purported agreement, and assessing whether it is reached under employer pressure, in which case it will be treated as a dismissal. It was reiterated in *Sandhu v Jan de Rijk Transport Ltd* [2007] ICR 1137 that 'Resignation implies some form of negotiation and discussion; it predicates a result which is a genuine choice on the part of the employee.'

A statement that it was in the mutual interest of both parties to part company after the **14.66** employer had given notice is not enough to amount to an agreed termination (*Harman v Flexible Lamps Ltd* [1980] IRLR 418). Moreover, tribunals have been astute not to recognise a consensus between the parties where the initiative to terminate has clearly been taken by the employer. In *McAlwane v Boughton Estates Ltd* [1973] 2 All ER 299, Donaldson J said that tribunals 'should not find an agreement to terminate employment unless it is proved that the employee really did agree with full knowledge of the implications it had for him' (see also *Hellyer Bros Ltd v Atkinson* [1992] IRLR 540).

An agreement to terminate does not itself fall foul of s 203 of the ERA 1996. In *Logan* **14.67** *Salton v Durham CC* [1989] IRLR 99 Wood J said:

> In our judgment ... in the resolution of industrial disputes, it is in the best interests of all concerned that a contract made without duress, for good consideration, preferably after proper and sufficient advice, and which has the effect of terminating a contract of employment by mutual agreement (whether at once or on some future date) should be effective between the contracting parties, in which cases there will probably not have been a dismissal within [ERA 1996, s 95].

Resignation under threat

14.68　The courts are understandably reluctant to hold that there has been no dismissal where an employee is prevailed upon to resign under threat that if he does not do so he will be dismissed (*Scott v Formica Ltd* [1975] IRLR 104; *East Sussex CC v Walker* (1972) 6 ITR 280). Further, the threat of dismissal need not be the sole factor inducing the employee to resign; there may be other facts operating (*Jones v Mid-Glamorgan County Council* [1997] IRLR 685, CA; *Jones v F. Sirl & Son (Furnishers) Ltd* [1997] IRLR 493). However, the fact that disciplinary proceedings are in train does not in itself amount to sufficient pressure (*Staffordshire CC v Donovan* [1981] IRLR 108) to avoid an agreed termination.

14.69　In *Sheffield v Oxford Controls Co* [1979] IRLR 133, the EAT sought to lay down a general principle to be applied in such cases by means of a rule of causation. The claimant had been a director and employee of the respondent company until a boardroom row, when he was threatened that, if he did not resign, he would be dismissed. After negotiations he signed an agreement to leave in return for certain financial benefits, including £10,000, but then claimed to have been unfairly dismissed. The EAT began from the premise that an employee who resigns as a result of a threat is dismissed, but there was in this case an intervening cause: 'He resigns because he is willing to resign as the result of being offered terms which are to him satisfactory terms on which to resign' (see *Catherall v Michelin Tyres plc* [2003] ICR 28; *Lassman v De Vere University Arms Hotel* [2003] ICR 44).

14.70　There was, however, held to be a dismissal in *Caledonian Mining Co Ltd v Bassett and Steel* [1987] IRLR 165, where the employment tribunal found that the employer had falsely inveigled the employees to resign with the express purpose of avoiding liability for redundancy payments.

Words of resignation

14.71　The courts look for unambiguous, unequivocal words uttered by the employee in order to find a resignation (*Hughes v Gwynedd AHA* [1978] ICR 161); and did not so find, for example, where the employer knew that the employee had learning difficulties and he uttered the words in the heat of the moment after an argument (*Barclay v City of Glasgow DC* [1983] IRLR 313). Ordinarily, the employer can treat unambiguous words of resignation as a termination of employment, but if there are special circumstances, such as the particular character of the employee, the employer should allow reasonable time for facts to come to light which may cast doubt on the proposition that these were intended to be words of resignation.

14.72　Should the employer not investigate the matter, he might not be able to rely on those words (*Kwik Fit (GB) Ltd v Lineham* [1992] IRLR 156). An employer may not rely on a letter of resignation which the employee is induced by the employer to sign on the basis of a misrepresentation (*Makin v Greens Motor (Bridport) Ltd,* The Times, 18 April 1986).

'Voluntary redundancy'

14.73　It is often difficult to characterise on which side of the dismissal/resignation line an application for voluntary redundancy falls. In *Birch v University of Liverpool* [1985] ICR 470, the claimants wrote to the University making a formal application to retire under a premature retirement compensation scheme and received a reply that, 'The University hereby confirms that it is in the managerial interests for you to retire ... and requests you to do so ...'. The EAT overturned the employment tribunal's decision that, since the offer of retirement was subject to the University's approval, it was the giving of that approval which terminated their employments. Instead, both in form and in substance, this was a termination by agreement (see also *Morley v C. T. Morley Ltd* [1985] ICR 499 in relation to a family business).

In *Scott v Coalite Fuels and Chemicals Ltd* [1988] IRLR 131, there was no dismissal **14.74** when employees who had received notice of redundancy accepted voluntary early retirement as an alternative thereto. It was not the case that once a notice of dismissal has been served to take effect on a future date, nothing which occurs in the interim can alter that position. Section 140 of the EPCA 1978 on agreed termination (now ERA 1996, s 203) was not relevant, since the agreement to resign was only necessary to a consideration of whether one of the applicable provisions of the Act had been satisfied, rather than an exclusion or limitation of rights under the Act itself.

There may be a dismissal where an employee agrees to continue working on a temporary **14.75** basis beyond the date on which his redundancy notice expired pending a permanent position becoming available (*Mowlem Northern Ltd v Watson* [1990] IRLR 500).

Late return after extended leave

Where an employee signs an undertaking that he will return to work on a stated date in **14.76** order to gain extended leave of absence from his employment, and he fails to come back at the agreed time, the trend of authority has ebbed and flowed between accepting the undertaking as an agreed termination and viewing it as a dismissal.

In *British Leyland Ltd v Ashraf* [1978] ICR 979, the claimant sought five weeks' unpaid **14.77** leave of absence to visit his native Pakistan, and this was granted subject to the condition that there be no further holiday. He signed a form stating: 'You have *agreed* to return to work on 21/2/77. If you fail to do this, your contract of employment *will terminate* on that date' (author's italics). The EAT took this at face value as a subsidiary contract and agreed termination, stressing the employee's full knowledge of its terms and open acceptance. It had in mind the fact that these were conditions attached to a *privilege*, since the claimant had no contractual right to leave of absence; they also pointed out that such failure to return was becoming a widespread problem in British industry. The danger of this approach is that it might be extended to an agreement that the contract would end if the employee was late even once. These draconian implications, which would mean that in such circumstances the employee could not test the fairness of the employer's action since there would be an agreed termination, were indeed spelt out by Phillips J who commented that the employer's argument would prevail even if the return flight 'had been hijacked or diverted because of fog'.

The case was, however, distinguished in *Midland Electric Manufacturing Co Ltd v Kanji* **14.78** [1980] IRLR 185, on somewhat narrow grounds. Mrs Kanji's leave of absence was conditional on the 'warning that if you fail to return ... for whatever reason the company will *consider* that you have terminated your employment'. She failed to return on the specified date because of illness, but the EAT found the letter to be a mere statement of intention by the employer as to what would happen in the event of failure to return, that is, she would be dismissed. Referring to the more ambiguous wording here than in *Ashraf*, Slynn J was generally mindful 'not to defeat the objects of the employment protection legislation or in particular to fly in the face of the intent of [what is now] ERA 1996, s 203'.

A similar line was taken in *Igbo v Johnson Matthey Chemicals Ltd* [1985] IRLR 189. **14.79** Mrs Igbo was given leave of absence after signing a 'contractual letter for the provision of extended holiday absence'. It stated *inter alia* that 'if you fail [to return on 28 September 1983], your contract of employment will automatically terminate on that date'. She did not report to work on that day but instead sent a medical certificate. The Court of Appeal thought that such an agreement fell foul of s 140 and was void ([1986] IRLR 215). The effect of the agreement was to 'limit' the operation of what is now ERA 1996, ss 94 and 95. It was not correct, as was argued by the respondent, that the effect of the arrangement was only to bring the contract to an end by consensual termination, that is, otherwise than by one of the ways which constitute dismissal for the purposes of what is now ERA 1996, s 94. If this were so, the Act could be circumvented by a term in the contract of employment that if the employee were late for work on any day, no matter for what reason, the contract would automatically terminate. Their Lordships took the opportunity to overrule the *Ashraf* case.

Frustration

14.80 There is no dismissal where the contract of employment is frustrated. The general contractual test for frustration is that:

> Frustration occurs whenever the law recognises that without default of either party a contractual obligation had become incapable of being performed because the circumstances in which the performance is called for would render it a thing radically different from that which was undertaken by the contract. (Lord Radcliffe in *Davis Contractors Ltd v Fareham UDC* [1956] AC 696.)

14.81 Donaldson J formulated the appropriate test in employment cases in *Marshall v Harland & Wolff* [1972] ICR 101, primarily with cases of long sickness or injury in mind, when he asked:

> Was the employee's incapacity to work of such a nature that further performance of his obligations in the future would be either impossible or be something radically different from that which he undertook under the contract?

(See also *Williams v Watsons Luxury Coaches Ltd* [1990] IRLR 164.)

Frustration and ill health

14.82 Donaldson J went on to counsel tribunals to take account of (author's italics):

(a) *The terms of contract* including the provisions as to sickness pay. The whole basis of weekly employment may be destroyed more quickly than that of monthly employment and that in turn more quickly than annual employment. When the contract provides for sickness pay, it is plain that the contract cannot be frustrated so long as the employee returns to work, or appears likely to return to work, within the period during which such sick pay is payable. But the converse is not necessarily true. The right to sick pay may expire before the incapacity has gone on for so long as to make a return to work impossible or radically different from the obligations undertaken under the contract of employment.

(b) How long the employment was *likely to last* in the absence of sickness. The relationship is less likely to survive if the employment was inherently temporary in its nature or for the duration of a particular job, than if it was expected to be long-term or even life long.

(c) The *nature of the employment*—where the employee is one of many in the same category, the relationship is more likely to survive the period of incapacity than if he occupies a key post which must be filled and filled on a permanent basis if his absence is prolonged.

(d) The *nature of the illness* or injury and how long it has already continued and the prospects of recovery. The greater the degree of incapability and the longer the period over which it has persisted and is likely to persist, the more likely it is that the relationship has been destroyed.

(e) The period of *past employment*—a relationship which is of long standing is not as easily destroyed as one which has but a short history.

In *Williams v Watsons Luxury Coaches Ltd* (above), Wood J added another considera- **14.83** tion, that is, the terms of the contract as to the provisions for sickness pay, if any, and also a consideration of the prospects of recovery. Donaldson J said that: 'These factors are interrelated and cumulative, but are not necessarily exhaustive of those which have to be taken into account.' In particular, they are hardly appropriate to short-term periodic contracts where the more likely event anyway is dismissal on short notice (*Harman v Flexible Lamps Ltd* [1980] IRLR 418; cf *Notcutt v Universal Equipment (London) Ltd* [1986] 1 WLR 641).

In *Egg Stores (Stamford Hill) Ltd v Leibovici* [1977] ICR 260, Phillips J added four extra **14.84** considerations in this context:

(a) the *need* of the employer for the work to be done, and the need for a replacement to do it;
(b) the risk to the employer of *acquiring obligations* in respect of redundancy payments or compensation for unfair dismissal to the replacement employee;
(c) whether *wages* have continued to be paid; and
(d) the *acts and the statements* of the employer in relation to the employment, including the dismissal of, or failure to dismiss, the employee.

He asked as a matter of common sense: 'Has the time arrived when the employer can no longer be expected to keep the absent employee's place open?' and this was a similar conclusion to that which had to be reached in determining whether a dismissal for sickness was fair.

In *Chakki v United Yeast Co Ltd* [1982] ICR 140, the EAT declared that in order to deter- **14.85** mine whether the imposition of an eleven-month prison sentence frustrated the contract, it was essential to determine precisely when it had become commercially necessary for the employer to decide to employ a replacement; to have regard to what, at that time, a reasonable employer would have considered to be the probable duration of the employee's absence and to decide whether the employer had acted reasonably in employing a permanent rather than a temporary replacement.

It is instructive to distinguish two cases on either side of the wafer-thin frustration/dis- **14.86** missal line. In *Hart v Marshall* [1977] ICR 539, the employee was a night service fitter, and described by his employer as a 'key worker'. In 1974 he contracted industrial dermatitis which continued for about twenty months, and during this time he regularly sent to his employers medical certificates of his unfitness to work, which were received without any comment. On his recovery, he was told that he had been permanently replaced. The EAT decided that, because he was such an important employee 'this is one of the comparatively rare cases where it can be said that a short-term period contract of employment has been frustrated'.

On the other side of the line stands *Hebden v Forsey and Son* [1973] ICR 607. The **14.87** respondent ran a small factory employing two sawyers—Mr Forsey's son, and the applicant, who had worked for the business for many years when he had to undergo an operation on one of his eyes. Since the necessary equipment was not available at the local hospital, it would be two years before he could work again. Mr Forsey, with whom the claimant maintained frequent contact, agreed with him that it would be better if he waited on the sick list, drawing state benefits, until his eye was fully recovered. There was insufficient work for him to do when he was completely fit, so that he could not return. On these facts it was held that the employer had not discharged the burden resting on him to prove frustration; he had in fact dismissed him. Frustration cannot occur because of the risk of *future* illness (*Converfoam (Darwen) v Bell* [1981] IRLR 195). Matters foreseen will not be a frustrating event (*Villella v MFI Furniture Centres Ltd* [1999] IRLR 468).

Other examples of frustration

14.88   Although illness is the most common frustrating event, contracts have also been held to be frustrated when the employee was:

(a) called up to the army (*Morgan v Manser* [1948] 1 KB 184); and
(b) suspended from medical practice for twelve months and his name temporarily removed from the register (*Tarnesby v Kensington, Chelsea and Westminster AHA* [1981] IRLR 369).

The contract was also frustrated when the employer's property was destroyed by fire (*Taylor v Caldwell* (1863) B & S 826).

14.89   There have been differing views of the effect of imprisonment. In *Hare v Murphy Brothers* [1974] ICR 603 and *Harrington v Kent CC* [1980] IRLR 353, the contract was held to be frustrated, even though the sentence was quashed on appeal (see also *Four Seasons Healthcare Ltd v Maughan* [2005] IRLR 324). In *F.C. Shepherd & Co Ltd v Jerrom* [1986] IRLR 358, a four-year apprenticeship was held to be frustrated by a borstal sentence of six months. The Court of Appeal decided that, contrary to the argument on behalf of the employee, what affected performance of the contract was the sentence of borstal training which was the act of the judge, and not that of the employee himself. Thus, the doctrine of self-induced frustration could not be applied to the case. Moreover, the apprentice should not be allowed to plead his own default in order to establish his right to claim compensation for unfair dismissal. *Hare*'s case was not binding authority since the legal basis on which the court decided the case was not clear. Since the borstal sentence was a substantial break during the period of training, the contract was radically different from what had been envisaged and had indeed been frustrated. The employee thus could not make an application for unfair dismissal.

14.90   Frustration must be due to an occurrence 'for which neither contracting party was in any way responsible' (Salmon LJ in *Denmark Productions Ltd v Boscobel Productions Ltd* [1969] 1 QB 699 at 725). In respect of the prison sentence in *Hare*'s case, the court addressed the employer's argument that the frustration was self-induced because the employee committed an assault by noting that the actual disabling event was the sentence of the court. In *Norris v Southampton City Council* [1982] IRLR 141, however, the EAT held that imprisonment was a self-induced event (for the unlikelihood of frustration where the employee is highly skilled, see *Gryf Lowczowski v Hinchingbrooke Healthcare NHS Trust* [2006] IRLR 100).

14.91   The difficulty found in the decisions on ill health shows the inappropriateness of the concept of frustration in this area. In the sphere of commercial contracts it provides a narrow exception, a defence, to parties who are strictly liable for contracts. It assumes that each side knows its rights and can take advice on major unforeseen circumstances. In unfair dismissal and redundancy, however, it breaks down the statutory definition of fault, and leaves complainants fettered at the starting line for statutory protections. It has thus in fact been rarely upheld as a defence in statutory claims.

D EFFECTIVE DATE OF TERMINATION

Where there has been a dismissal, it is necessary to pinpoint the actual date of termina- **14.92**
tion of employment for several statutory purposes:

(a) the *qualifying period* before a claim may be made, for example, one year for unfair
dismissal (12.04–12.06);
(b) the *date of calculation* of the employee's week's pay for working time payments, redundancy payment, and unfair dismissal basic award;
(c) when an employee may seek *written reasons* for his dismissal (14.100); and
(d) to decide whether the employee has brought his *claim in time*, since the claim must
be submitted generally within three months or six months of that date for unfair dismissal or redundancy respectively (12.07–12.16).

This important stage is called the 'effective date of termination' in the unfair dismissal **14.93**
provisions and the 'relevant date' for redundancy payments. In most respects the concepts
coincide and the term 'effective date' is used here to denote both concepts, except where
it is necessary to distinguish between them. The appropriate dates can both best be considered in the following series of propositions (ERA 1996, s 92(6)):

(a) Where the employee is dismissed *with notice* the effective date is the date on which
the notice expires. Where the employer orally gives the employee 'a week's notice
from now', this means seven clear days excluding the day on which the employee
started work and was actually given notice (*West v Kneels Ltd* [1987] ICR 146).
(b) Where the dismissal is *lawfully without notice*, that is, summary dismissal usually
for gross misconduct, the effective date of termination is the date on which the termination takes *effect*. It is not sufficient that the employer *characterised* a dismissal
as being one on the grounds of gross misconduct. According to the Scottish EAT in
Lanton Leisure Ltd v White and Gibson [1987] IRLR 119, it was necessary to inquire into the merits of whether there was *in fact* such misconduct as would enable
the employer to terminate without notice.
    The date of termination has generally been assumed to be the date when the employer
tells the worker he is fired, but there was scope for argument since this implicitly assumes
that the dismissal automatically terminates the contract. If, instead, it is brought to an
end only on the other party's acceptance of that breach, it may be thought that the
correct effective date is the date of acceptance of the repudiation. In *Robert Cort &
Son Ltd v Charman* [1981] IRLR 437, the EAT held that, on the authorities, the effective date of termination was that of the repudiation. The contract in fact terminated at
once for this purpose irrespective of whether, as a matter of contract law, the employer
ought to have given notice. In *Stapp v The Shaftesbury Society* [1982] IRLR 326, the
EAT held that the effective date of termination was the actual date of termination of the
employment whether the employment was lawfully or wrongfully terminated.

The situation where communication of termination is not instantaneous was considered
by the EAT in *Brown v Southall and Knight* [1980] IRLR 130, and it was held that the
effective date of termination when dismissal was by letter was generally the date when the
letter was received. Slynn J stated:

> In our judgment the employer who sends a letter terminating a man's employment summarily
> must show that the employee has actually read the letter or at any rate had a reasonable op-
> portunity of reading it. If the addressee of the letter to the employee does not deliberately
> open it or goes away to avoid reading it he might well be debarred from saying that notice of
> his dismissal had not been given to him.

The following further principles have been established:

(i)   Where the employer dismisses an employee immediately but with a payment to cover the period of notice which should have been given, this payment in effect is damages for instant dismissal, so the effective date is that of immediate dismissal itself (*Adams v GKN Sankey Ltd* [1980] IRLR 416).

(ii) An employee can waive the right to notice so that the contract is brought to an end immediately (*Secretary of State for Employment v Staffordshire CC* [1989] IRLR 117).

(iii) In construing an ambiguous letter of dismissal, the tribunal should adopt the construction which a reasonable employee receiving it would understand (see *Chapman v Letherby & Christopher Ltd* [1981] IRLR 440; *TBA Industrial Products v Morland* [1982] ICR 686; *Leech v Preston BC* [1985] ICR 192; *Stapp v The Shaftesbury Society* (above); *Widdicombe v Longcombe* [1998] ICR 710).

(iv) The date on which tax form P45 is sent to the employee has no special significance for these purposes (*London Borough of Newham v Ward* [1985] IRLR 509) unless the dismissal itself was effected by service of the P45.

(v)   A clear notice of immediate dismissal takes effect at once, notwithstanding that the employer did not operate the disciplinary procedure properly in relation to the dismissal. The employee may have an action at common law against the employer but that does not affect the effective date of termination (*Batchelor v British Railways Board* [1987] IRLR 136).

(vi) It does not matter that the meeting at which the decision was taken to dismiss was not properly constituted (*Newman v Polytechnic of South Wales Students Union* [1995] IRLR 72).

(vii) Dismissal is not effective on the date when the employee might reasonably be expected to receive notice as the employee must actually know that he is being dismissed; but the position might be otherwise if the employee deliberately avoids the communication of his dismissal (*McMaster v Manchester Airport plc* [1998] IRLR 112).

(c)   Where notice *should* have been given to the employee of a longer period than that which is in fact given or where no notice is given, the proper *statutory minimum notice* is added to the actual date of the dismissal in order to pinpoint the effective date for statutory purposes (ERA 1996, s 97(2); see also *Secretary of State for Employment v Staffordshire CC* (above)). The reasoning is that it is unfair that by the employer's own wrongful act in terminating the contract of employment in breach of the statutory notice requirement he might reduce the employee's entitlement, whether the amount of basic award or taking into account a later pay rise in calculating a week's pay.

Moreover, if the employee's contract provides that a period of longer than the statutory minimum notice must be given to the particular employee, still only the minimum number of weeks required by statute need be added if notice has not in fact been given to the employee.

This statutory concept does not apply, however, to the cases of summary and constructive dismissal (*Slater and Secretary for Employment v John Swain Ltd* [1981] IRLR 303) nor to:

(i)   the start of the period for bringing a complaint to a tribunal;

(ii) written reasons for dismissal;

(iii) whether the employee was striking at the application to the employment tribunal for interim relief;

(iv) the start of the seven-day period for an application to the employment tribunal for interim relief;

(v) redundancy consultation; or

(vi) the requirement that an offer of renewal or re-engagement be made before the ending of the employment.

Example Jack's contract provides for eight weeks' notice. He is dismissed after fifty weeks of employment without notice. He can claim a statutory extension to week 51 because he is entitled by the ERA 1996 to one week's minimum notice, but cannot add the eight weeks. If the employer in fact gives eight weeks' notice, the effective date of termination is week 58 and he would be entitled then to claim unfair dismissal.

(d) Where the contract is for a limited *term* and dismissal is by reason of the expiry of the limited term, the date is when the fixed term expires.

(e) Where the employee is dismissed by reason of a *strike* or other industrial action, even when terminated by notice the effective date is, by reason of a special statutory exception (see TULR(C)A 1992, s 238(5)), the date on which the notice is given; otherwise the above rules apply, as appropriate.

(f) The courts have generally rejected attempts to extend the effective date of termination to cover periods during which an *appeal* is being heard under an internal disciplinary procedure. In *J. Sainsbury Ltd v Savage* [1980] IRLR 109, this refusal was notwithstanding that the internal disciplinary procedure provided for 'suspension without pay' pending appeal. Brightman LJ stated that: 'If an employee is dismissed ... on terms that he then ceases to have the right to work under the contract of employment and that the employer ceases likewise to be under an obligation to pay the employee, the contract is at an end' (approved by the House of Lords in *West Midland Co-operative Society Ltd v Tipton* [1986] IRLR 112; see also *Crown Agents v Lawal* [1978] IRLR 542; cf *Drage v Governing Body of Greenford High School* [2000] ICR 899).

(g) The same result was reached in *Board of Governors, National Heart and Chest Hospital v Nambiar* [1981] IRLR 196, even though the employee was paid for a ten-month period while his appeal was pending. The principle does not depend on there being any express term providing for this result (*Howgate v Fane Acoustics Ltd* [1981] IRLR 161), but instead rests on the policy reason of the uncertainty of any other course, and the desirability that speed be of the essence in enforcing employment rights.

(h) The effective date of termination is a statutory construct and cannot be changed by agreement (*Fitzgerald v University of Kent at Canterbury* [2004] ICR 737).

(i) The effective date for a *constructive dismissal* is not necessarily the date when the relevant resignation takes effect; rather, it may be when the relationship of employer and employee has ceased. In the case in which this proposition was laid down, the facts were such that the effective date was properly when the employee ceased to be director, and thereby chairman, of the company (*BMK v Logue* [1993] ICR 601). Where an employee communicated by fax his immediate acceptance of his employers' repudiation of his contract of employment, the effective date of termination was the date when the employee's fax was received and not any later date when it was actually read or acted upon (*Potter v R KJ Temple plc*, The Times, 11 February 2004).

E THE REASON FOR DISMISSAL

Several cases have laid down these principles in defining the reason for dismissal: **14.94**

(a) The onus of proof rests on the employer to establish on the balance of probabilities the reason for dismissal. If the employer cannot prove any reason at all for dismissal, the dismissal is automatically unfair (*Adams v Derby City Council* [1986] IRLR 163). This includes public interest disclosures (*Kuzel v Roche Products Ltd* [2008] ICR 799; *Nunn v Royal Mail Group Ltd* [2011] ICR 162).

(b) The employer's reason for dismissal, on the basis of which the employment tribunal must go on to determine the fairness, is 'the set of facts known to the employer or beliefs held by him which cause him to dismiss the employee' (*Abernethy v Mott Hay and Anderson* [1974] ICR 323, as approved by the House of Lords in *W. Devis & Sons Ltd v Atkins* [1977] AC 931). This does not necessarily imply automatic acceptance by the tribunal of the reason which is put forward by the employer if there are grounds to think that it was not in fact the real cause. Thus, many employers claim that they are dismissing employees for reasons of redundancy although this is in reality a cloak for getting rid of particular employees. The 'reason for dismissal' which must be determined is that 'uppermost in the mind of the employer at the time of dismissal' (*Abernethy*).

(c) The reason may, however, incorporate a series of incidents and not merely one single event (eg *Turner v Wadham Stringer Commercials (Portsmouth) Ltd* [1974] ICR 277), and where there is more than one ground the tribunal must establish what was the *principal* factor motivating the dismissal (*Carlin v St Cuthberts Co-op Association Ltd* [1974] IRLR 188).

(d) When the employer mistakenly construes as a resignation an equivocal expression of an intention to resign by the employee, that may constitute a reason for dismissal (*Ely v YKK Fasteners (UK) Ltd* [1994] ICR 164). An employer can only rely on its own reason (*Hynd v Armstrong* [2007] IRLR 338).

(e) A reason cannot be treated as a sufficient reason for dismissal when it has not been established as true or there were no reasonable grounds on which the employer could have concluded that it was true (*Smith v City of Glasgow District Council* [1987] IRLR 326).

(f) To be believed the employer must tell a consistent story, and will probably not be believed if he puts forward a different reason:

  (i)   at the tribunal, from that which he stated in his response; or
  (ii) on appeal, from that relied upon before the employment tribunal (*Nelson v BBC* [1977] ICR 694); or
  (iii) on an internal appeal, from that initially tendered.

  For the employer to make alternative claims as to the reason for the dismissal is tempting but may be dangerous for the employer (*Murphy v Epsom College* [1983] IRLR 395).

  In *Monie v Coral Racing Ltd* [1981] ICR 109, for example, the claimant was dismissed for dishonesty and he exercised his contractual right of internal appeal. This was heard by the managing director, who confirmed the dismissal, but since he found no evidence of dishonesty against Mr Monie, he gave as the reason that his failure to exercise the authorised cash control procedures justified dismissal. The court thought that the reason must be that which operated on the minds of the employer at the time of the dismissal. The internal appeal made no difference. If the employer has no reason for dismissal such sacking is automatically unfair.

(g) A tribunal is not entitled to find a dismissal to be fair on a ground not pleaded or argued where the difference in grounds goes to facts and substance of the case and where there would, or might have been, some substantial or significant difference in the way the case was conducted, had another reason been put forward. On the other hand, where the different grounds are in effect different *labels* for the same set of facts (such as redundancy or some other substantial reason for dismissal), a tribunal is justified in finding that the true reason for dismissal was one which was not pleaded (*Hannan v TNT-IPEC (UK) Ltd* [1986] IRLR 165).

In *Hotson v Wisbech Conservative Club* [1984] IRLR 422, the employer's response gave the reason for dismissal as 'inefficiency', but their representative at the tribunal agreed with the chairman's remark that 'in effect what you are claiming is that the [applicant] was dishonest'. The tribunal decided that the employee had been fairly dismissed on the ground of reasonably suspected dishonesty. The EAT would not let the decision stand since the suspicion must be stated at the outset by the employer. Whilst the employer would not be necessarily tied to a 'label' which he put on the facts on which he relied, he could not substitute dishonesty for negligence at so late a stage because it did not give the employee sufficient opportunity to meet the challenge. The EAT, however, in *Clarke v Trimoco Motor Group Ltd* [1993] ICR 238, decided that where it is obvious to the employee what the real reason was for the dismissal, that change does not render the dismissal unfair.

(h) An employment tribunal cannot pick out and substitute a reason for dismissal which was neither given nor entertained by the employer merely because the tribunal considers that it was a better reason or one which would justify dismissal whereas the employer's stated reason would not. The tribunal can, however, find that the reason proffered by the employer is *not* the real or principal reason provided that the employee shows that there is a real issue whether that was the true reason. The onus then shifts back to the employer to show his real reason (*Maund v Penwith DC* [1984] IRLR 24 in the case of trade union dismissals; *Kuzel v Roche Products Ltd* [2008] ICR 279 in the case of whistleblowing).

(i) An error of characterisation of the reason for dismissal by the tribunal is an error of law which can be corrected on appeal (*Wilson v Post Office* [2000] IRLR 834). Here, a dismissal for failing to improve the employee's attendance record was not a reason relating to capability on the grounds of health. Although ill health was the cause of poor attendance, ill health was not the reason for dismissal.

Later discovered reason

The employer cannot dismiss for an insubstantial reason and then hunt round for misconduct to justify it. In this there is a vital distinction from the position on wrongful dismissal where this is indeed permissible (*Ridgway v Hungerford Market* (1835) 3 Ad & El 173; *Boston Deep Sea Fishing & Ice Co v Ansell* (1888) 39 ChD 339; *Item Software (UK) Ltd v Fassihi* [2003] IRLR 769). The rule in the statutory jurisdiction was clearly established by the House of Lords in the leading case of *W. Devis & Sons Ltd v Atkins* [1977] AC 931. The respondent, who managed the appellant's abattoir, was dismissed on the ground that he refused to implement his employer's purchasing policy. Later they found evidence of much dishonest conduct while he was employed, and sought to advance that as the reason for dismissal, even though they did not know of it at the time. Their Lordships thought that the statutory language that fairness must be determined 'having regard to the reason shown by the employers' could only mean the set of facts known to him *at the time of dismissal*. **14.95**

The overall effect of this decision is somewhat limited, however, because, although they can have no influence on the reason and fairness, subsequently discovered matters may diminish the amount of compensation awarded; in the *Devis* case itself no compensation at all was granted on the grounds that he suffered *no loss* (14.310ff). **14.96**

Moreover, what happens between the date of notice and expiry of notice, especially of a procedural nature, such as hearings and appeals, *is* relevant to the determination of fairness. In *Rank Xerox (UK) Ltd v Goodchild* [1979] IRLR 185, for example, the fact that appeals from employees were heard after the date of termination did not mean that **14.97** aspects affecting their fairness could not be taken into account in determining reasonable-ness. Otherwise the procedural provisions at the heart of the unfair dismissal jurisdiction would be rendered unenforceable. In *West Midlands Co-operative Society Ltd v Tipton* [1986] IRLR 112, the House of Lords re-emphasised the need to consider all things which came to the employer's knowledge on appeal from his initial decision to dismiss. The appeal is inextricably bound up with the employer's action of dismissal. Lord Bridge of Harwich could 'see nothing in the language of the statute to exclude from consideration [of] "equity and the substantial merits of the case" evidence relevant to show the strength or weakness of the real reason for dismissal which the employer had the opportunity to consider in the course of an appeal...'.

14.98	Although the facts of the instant case concerned a contractually binding appeal, this principle applies also to a non-contractual appeal (*Greenall Whitley plc v Carr* [1985] IRLR 289; *Whitbread & Co plc v Mills* [1988] IRLR 501; see also *White v South London Transport Ltd* [1998] ICR 293). The employment tribunal may also take into account medical information about the employee which comes to light in the course of his appeal against dismissal (*Board of Governors, National Heart and Chest Hospital v Nambiar* [1981] IRLR 196), or after notice of dismissal for medical grounds has been given (*White v South London Transport Ltd* above).

14.99	In *Parkinson v March Consulting Ltd* [1998] ICR 276, the Court of Appeal held that the employer's reason for dismissal had to be determined by reference to his reasons both at the time when the dismissal occurred *and* at the time when notice was given. This deci-sion was given a gloss, however, by *West Kent College v Richardson* [1999] ICR 511, in which the EAT held that an admissible reason for dismissal has to remain constant throughout the process of dismissal, beginning with the moment of notice and ending with termination and for all the period in between. In the instant case, the claimant was a full-time lecturer and chairman of the local branch of his union. He was given notice that he was to be made redundant although, during his notice period, sufficient teaching hours became available to justify his retention. The claimant was still dismissed, and the employment tribunal found that the true reason for his dismissal was his union activities. The EAT remitted the case for rehearing (see also *Stacey v Babcock Power Ltd* [1986] IRLR 3 and *Alboni v Ind Coope Retail Ltd* [1998] IRLR 131).

Written reasons for dismissal

14.100	Statute facilitates the employee's discovery of the reasons for dismissal by according to the employee a right to a written statement of them. The employee can under the ERA 1996 request such written reasons if he is given notice of dismissal, is dismissed without notice, or the employer does not renew his limited-term contract (but not if he is constructively dismissed). He must also have completed one year's continuous employment with the employer (ending with the last complete week before the effective date of termination).

14.101	The employer must, if it is reasonably possible, reply to an employee's request for rea-sons within fourteen days and give true and adequate particulars (ERA 1996, s 92(2)) (on the meaning of 'true' in this context, see *Harvard Securities plc v Younghusband* [1990] IRLR 17). This document is available as evidence before an employment tribunal (s 92(5)), and an employer may be effectively estopped from denying the accuracy of the particulars which have been given. If the statement as given by the employer is untrue or inadequate, the employment tribunal may decide what the employer's reasons really were, looking at all the evidence and drawing inferences, and make a declaration as to the true reason.

The following principles have also been established by the cases: **14.102**

(a) The written statement must 'at least contain a simple statement of the essential reasons for the dismissal' (*Horsley Smith and Sherry Ltd v Dutton* [1977] IRLR 172), otherwise 'no particular technicalities are involved and no particular form is required. It can be perfectly simple and straightforward'.

(b) A written statement can refer to letters previously written to an employee, according to the Court of Appeal in *Kent CC v Gilham* [1985] IRLR 16. The respondent dinner ladies refused to accept terms put forward by the County Council to economise on the school meals service. The council sent out an explanatory letter to the dinner ladies explaining the reasons for the changes and a week later gave them notice of termination referring back to the earlier letter, which was held legitimate. Furthermore, it was adequate compliance with the Act to send the reasons to their representative rather than to the employees personally.

(c) The employee may complain to an employment tribunal if there has been: (i) an *unreasonable refusal* by the employer to provide the necessary written statement; or (ii) the statement given is untrue or inadequate. Any claim must be made during notice of dismissal or within three months after the effective date of termination, although the employment tribunal has the usual discretion to extend the time limit if it was not reasonably practicable to comply (see 12.11).

(d) A claim may be brought before the tribunal only if a specific request for reasons had been made of the employer (*Catherine Haigh Harlequin Hair Design v Seed* [1990] IRLR 175).

(e) If the employer is found to be in default of his obligations, the tribunal must award two weeks' pay to the employee under this section. The provision is generally strictly construed since according to the EAT in *Charles Lang & Sons Ltd v Aubrey* [1977] IRLR 354, 'it is a penal section. Parliament was intending to impose a penalty on a contumacious employer who decides he is not going to give the employee the required statement'.

(f) A general request to the employer by the police not to communicate with the employee was not a reasonable ground for refusing to provide reasons (*Daynecourt Insurance Brokers Ltd v Iles* [1978] IRLR 335); but in *Brown v Stuart Scott & Co* [1981] ICR 166, it was held reasonable not to give reasons where the employer had a conscientiously formed belief that there was no dismissal.

Statutory reasons for dismissal

The statute proceeds to divide reasons for dismissal into three categories. **14.103**

(a) *Potentially fair reasons*: these are by far the most important category of reasons demanding an analysis of the overall fairness of the dismissal. They are thus necessary but not sufficient conditions for showing a dismissal was fair. Those specified in the ERA 1996, s 98 are:
    (i) a reason related to the *capability or qualification* of the employee for performing work which he was employed by the employer to do (14.112ff);
    (ii) a reason related to the *conduct* of the employee (14.136ff);
    (iii) *redundancy* (14.191ff);
    (iv) that the employee could not continue to work in his position without contravention by him or his employer of a *duty or restriction* imposed by or under an enactment (14.242); and
    (v) some *other substantial reason* of a kind such as to justify the dismissal of an employee holding the position which that employee held (14.213).

(b) *Automatically fair reasons:*

    (i) where the decision was taken 'for the purpose of safeguarding *national security*', and a certificate signed by or on behalf of a minister is conclusive evidence of this fact (see *Council of Civil Service Unions v Minister for the Civil Service* [1985] IRLR 28); and

    (ii) dismissal whilst taking part in unofficial industrial action.

(c) *Automatically unfair reasons since the employment tribunal has no jurisdiction to consider the issue of fairness:*

    (i) dismissal of a woman because she is *pregnant* or for a reason connected therewith (10.66) or for a reason related to parental leave/dependant care leave;

    (ii) dismissal for *trade union membership or activities,* or because of refusal to join a trade union, or because the employee was not a member of any trade union or of one of a number of particular trade unions, or had refused or proposed to refuse to become or remain a member, or by reason of health and safety activities (20.73ff);

    (iii) dismissal because of a *conviction* which is spent under the Rehabilitation of Offenders Act 1974 (14.245);

    (iv) where the reason for dismissal was connected with a transfer of undertaking (reg 7 of the Transfer of Undertakings (Protection of Employment) Regulations 2006), save where there are 'economic, technical or organisational reasons entailing changes in the workforce' (18.99ff);

    (v) dismissal of a protected shop worker or an opted-out shop worker in respect of Sunday working;

    (vi) dismissal for assertion of a statutory right (14.278ff);

    (vii) dismissal of an occupational pension fund trustee because he performed his functions;

    (viii) dismissal of an elected representative because he performed any functions or activities as such;

    (ix) dismissal of an employee who has made a protected disclosure (15.18);

    (x) dismissal in relation to claiming the national minimum wage;

    (xi) dismissal in connection with claims for trade union recognition;

    (xii) dismissal of strikers during a protected twelve-week period (subject to appropriate extension periods in certain cases);

    (xiii) dismissal of a part-time worker or fixed-term employee (Part-time Workers (Prevention of Less Favourable Treatment) Regulations 2000 (SI 2000 No 1551, reg 7);

    (xiv) dismissal for taking leave for family reasons;

    (xv) dismissal for seeking to benefit from tax credits;

    (xvi) dismissal for performing functions relating to transnational information and consultation (Transnational Information and Consultation of Employees Regulations 1999 (SI 1999/3323));

    (xvii) dismissal because of absence on jury service (14.285ff).

14.104 The Exclusivity Terms in Zero Hours Contracts (Redress) Regulations 2015/2021 provide that any dismissal of a zero hours contract employee is automatically unfair if the principal reason is that he breached a contractual clause prohibiting him from working for another employer (and this does not have any qualifying period).

14.105 Qualifying periods do not apply to an employee dismissed because of political opinions because of a change in legislation made in response to the decision of the ECtHR in *Redfearn v UK* [2012] ECHR 1878.

F FAIRNESS OF DISMISSAL: GENERAL

In all cases which are not rendered automatically unfair or automatically fair by statute, **14.106**
where the tribunal has determined the reason for the dismissal, s 98(4) of the ERA 1996
provides as follows:

> (4) Where the employer has fulfilled the requirements of subsection (1), the determination of
> the question whether the dismissal is fair or unfair (having regard to the reason shown
> by the employer)—
>
> (a) depends on whether in the circumstances (including the size and administrative
> resources of the employer's undertaking) the employer acted reasonably or unreason-
> ably in treating it as a sufficient reason for dismissing the employee, and
>
> (b) shall be determined in accordance with equity and the substantial merits of
> the case.

Section 34 of the Employment Act 2002 inserted a new s 98A into the ERA 1996 and **14.107**
reversed the rule enunciated by the House of Lords in *Polkey v Dayton Services Ltd* [1988]
ICR 142. Breach by the employer of a statutory procedure on dismissal, which sets down
the minimum procedural requirements, meant that the dismissal is automatically unfair
(s 98A(1)). The Employment Act 2008 repealed all the rigid provisions about statutory
discipline and grievance procedures and s 98A of the ERA but, by a new s 207A of the
TURL(C)A, if there is a breach of an ACAS code of practice by the employer and the failure
was unreasonable the tribunal may, if it considers it just and equitable to do so, increase
any award by no more than 25 per cent. By the same token if the employee is in breach
the amount may be reduced by no more than 25 per cent. By Sch A2 this applies to most
procedures.

In general, there is no burden of proof of fairness operating either way (see *Abbots* **14.108**
& Standley v Wesson-Glynwed Steels Ltd [1982] IRLR 51; *Murray MacKinnon*
v Forno [1983] IRLR 7; *Post Office Counters v Heavey* [1990] ICR 1). An appeal
is indeed likely to be upheld if the employment tribunal misdirected itself that the
employer must prove fairness (*Howarth Timber (Leeds) Ltd v Biscomb* [1986]
IRLR 52).

Secondly, tribunals must have regard to the size of the respondent employer's undertaking **14.109**
(see eg *Henderson v Granville Tours Ltd* [1982] IRLR 494), although the small size of
an employer cannot excuse it, for example, from making any effort at all to consult over
a redundancy (eg *De Grasse v Stockwell Tools Ltd* [1992] IRLR 269). It may, however,
affect the nature, extent, or formality of the consultation process.

The following principles have been developed: **14.110**

(a) The fairness of a dismissal is essentially a question of fact, and the employment
tribunal as an industrial jury is best equipped to deal with the decision, using its
employment experience and knowledge of local conditions. Tribunals are directed
by appeal bodies to approach the matter with common sense and common fairness,
eschewing technicalities. The cases which follow are offered merely as examples of
the approach of tribunals, and more particularly the Employment Appeal Tribunal
and Court of Appeal, in so far as they have offered guidance. They are not, however, to be taken as binding precedents (*Jowett v Earl of Bradford (No 2)* [1978]
ICR 431).

(b) Two tribunals may on similar facts reach opposite conclusions, yet this does not necessarily amount to an error of law to be corrected by the appeal bodies (*Kent CC*
v Gilham (No 2) [1985] ICR 233). The Court of Appeal set the tone for the current

orthodox position in *Bailey v BP Oil (Kent Refinery) Ltd* [1980] IRLR 287, where Lawton LJ said:

> The wording [of s 98(4) of the ERA 1996], which is clear and unambiguous, requires the tribunal, which is the one which hears the evidence, not the one which hears the legal argument, to look at every aspect of the case ... Each case must depend on its own facts. In our judgment, it is unwise for this court or the Employment Appeal Tribunal to set out guidelines and wrong to make rules and establish presumptions for employment tribunals to follow or take into account.

(See also *Retarded Children's Aid Society v Day* [1978] ICR 437.)

(c) In *The County Council of Hereford and Worcester v Neale* [1986] IRLR 168, the Court of Appeal re-emphasised the narrowness of the perversity jurisdiction. May LJ said (at para 45) 'Deciding these cases [of unfair dismissal] is the job of employment tribunals and when they have not erred in law, neither the EAT nor this Court should disturb their decision unless one can say in effect: "My goodness, that was certainly wrong"' (see also *British Telecommunications plc v Sheridan* [1990] IRLR 27; *Yeboah v Crofton* [2002] IRLR 634). The decision in *Piggott Brothers & Co Ltd v Jackson* [1991] IRLR 309 went even further and pronounced that the EAT should interfere with the decision of an employment tribunal only if that conclusion was not a permissible option, that is that it was not supported by *any* evidence (but cf the powerful *dicta* of the EAT in *East Berkshire HA v Matadeen* [1992] IRLR 336).

(d) It is, however, necessary to consider not only whether the dismissal fell within the bounds of reasonable responses, but also whether the procedure used in reaching the decision to dismiss was fair (*Whitbread plc v Hall* [2001] IRLR 275). The range of responses test applies as much to the investigation into suspected misconduct as to the decision to dismiss (*J Sainsbury plc v Hitt* [2003] ICR 111). The Court of Appeal decided that it was 'necessary to apply the objective standards of the reasonable employer to *all* aspects of the question whether the employee had been fairly and reasonably dismissed' (see also *Boardman v Nugent Care Society* [2013] ICR 927; *Capita Hartshead Ltd v Byard* [2012] ICR 1256). The judicial policy is thus to avoid the tribunal stepping directly into the shoes of the employer. In *Sarkar v West London Health NHS Trust* [2010] EWCA Civ 289, the Court of Appeal said that improper substitution is what happens when the members of a tribunal decide what they would have done if they were the employer; this is an error of law. The function of the tribunal is to judge the fairness of the actions of the employer objectively (see also *Secretary of State for Justice v Lown* [2016] IRLR 22 on the 'substitution mindset'). In *Bowater v Northwest London Hospitals Trust* [2011] IRLR 331, Longmore LJ stressed the corrective that 'the employer cannot be the final arbiter of its own conduct in dismissing an employee'.

(e) The appeal bodies have varied in their willingness to lay down guidelines for tribunals. The approach of the EAT has often reflected the approach of its President for the time being. Browne-Wilkinson J pioneered the use of 'guidelines', concerned as he was that there was little uniformity between different tribunals. Such guidelines were distillations of good industrial practice so that: 'properly instructed employment tribunals would know [them] to be the principles which, in current industrial practice, a reasonable employer would be expected to adopt'. In the *locus classicus* of this position, *Williams v Compair Maxam Ltd* [1982] IRLR 83, the EAT formulated five guidelines for a redundancy dismissal which it would 'expect ... to be departed from only where good reason is shown to justify such departure'. It counselled, however, that there should 'be no attempt to say that an employment tribunal which did not have regard to or give effect to one of these factors has misdirected itself in law. Only in cases where a genuine case for perversity on the grounds that the decision flies in the face of commonly accepted standards of fairness can be made out are these factors directly relevant' (see also *Grundy (Teddington) Ltd v Plummer and Salt* [1983] IRLR 98). In fact, guidelines of this nature have been laid down to cover the most important aspects of misconduct and procedure in *British Home Stores Ltd v Burchell* [1978] IRLR 379 and *British Labour Pump Co Ltd v Byrne* [1979] ICR 347, and had been expressly approved by the Court of Appeal in *W. Weddel & Co Ltd v Tepper* [1980] ICR 286 and *W. & J. Wass Ltd v Binns* [1982] ICR 486 respectively.

(f) The EAT is reluctant to interfere with the decision of a tribunal provided that the tribunal directed itself by statute, however much the EAT might disagree with the outcome. It is indeed astute not to allow issues of fact to be dressed up as issues of law. Together with the limited role of employment tribunals as reviewers of the decisions of employers, this has added great strength to managerial prerogative. Tribunals are regarded by appeal bodies not as being in the seat of management but rather as having to decide whether what management did was reasonable. It is for management to lay down the standards, and only if dismissal was not 'within the range of reasonable responses of the reasonable employer' should a tribunal decide that the dismissal is unfair (*British Leyland UK Ltd v Swift* [1981] IRLR 91; also *Vickers Ltd v Smith* [1977] IRLR 11, *N.C. Watling & Co Ltd v Richardson* [1978] ICR 1049, *Iceland Frozen Foods Ltd v Jones* [1982] IRLR 439, reiterated in *Securicor Ltd v Smith* [1989] IRLR 356; *Brent LBC v Fuller* [2011] ICR 806).

(g) It is clearly important that the employment tribunal considers fairness in the light of matters which are known, or which should have been known, to the employer at the time of dismissal and not on the basis of the evidence which comes out at the employment tribunal for the first time (*Linfood Cash & Carry Ltd v Thomson* [1989] IRLR 235).

(h) The appeal body will need to find it clear from the tribunal's decision that they have directed themselves by reference to s 98(4) of the ERA 1996 for a decision to be correct in law (*United Distillers v Conlin* [1992] IRLR 503).

(i) The fact that an employee has been dismissed without notice cannot in itself render a dismissal unfair (*BSC Sports & Social Club v Morgan* [1987] IRLR 391).

The general approach here followed is to discuss the case law on each of the reasons given for dismissal, and then attempt a general overview of the procedures needed in most cases for a fair dismissal. **14.111**

G INCAPABILITY

The only guidance to be found in the ERA 1996 in relation to capability as a reason for dismissal is its definition to include 'skill, aptitude, health or any other physical or mental quality' (s 98(3)(a)). 'Qualifications' means 'any degree, diploma or other academic, technical or professional qualification relevant to the position which [the employee] held' (s 98(3)(b)). The ground which is put forward by the employer need only *relate to* capability. It need not be a circumstance which is so incapacitating as to prevent the employee performing all work of the kind he was employed to do (*Shook v London Borough of Ealing* [1986] IRLR 46). The relevant case law will be considered under the headings of: incompetence; health; and qualifications. **14.112**

Incompetence

14.113 The general principle is that 'the employee's incapacity as it existed at the time of dismissal must be of such a nature and quality as to justify dismissal'. It need not, however, be reflected in any one particular incident but may arise from several indications (*Miller v Executors of John Graham* [1978] IRLR 309). Thus, in *Lewis Shops Group Ltd v Wiggins* [1973] ICR 335, a shop manageress was fairly dismissed when she left her shop dirty and untidy, cash registers failed to operate properly, and stock was not put away.

Evidence of incompetence

14.114 Employment tribunals may find it difficult to measure intangible examples of poor work performance. In *Taylor v Alidair Ltd* [1978] IRLR 82, Lord Denning MR said:

> Wherever a man is dismissed for incapacity or incompetence it is sufficient that the employer honestly believes on reasonable grounds that the man is incapable or incompetent. It is not necessary for the employer to prove that he is in fact incapable or incompetent.

The case had particularly strong facts since the claimant was an airline pilot, who was dismissed because he was thought to be at fault for a bad landing which had caused serious damage to the respondent's aircraft. According to the Court of Appeal, the employer had reasonably demanded a high degree of care and fairly dismissed him when he failed to measure up to it on one occasion. He was engaged in a special category of:

> activities in which the degree of professional skill which must be required is so high, that the potential consequence of small departures from that high standard is so serious that the failure to perform in accordance with those standards is sufficient to justify dismissal.

The Court of Appeal specifically approved Bristow J's examples of other such employees as, 'the scientist operating the nuclear reactors, the chemist in charge of research into the possible effects of, for example, thalidomide, the driver of the Manchester to London Express, the driver of an articulated lorry full of sulphuric acid'. Few procedural safeguards were necessary in relation to such employees, but in *ILEA v Lloyd* [1981] IRLR 394, the Court of Appeal restricted this principle to cases where safety was in question.

14.115 There should normally be some other evidence, besides the opinion of the employer, of the employee's incapacity. The EAT did, however, say in *Cook v Thomas Linnell & Sons Ltd* [1977] IRLR 132 that: 'When responsible employers genuinely come to the conclusion that over a reasonable period of time a manager is incompetent, we think that it is some evidence that he is incompetent.' This recognises that although ideally there should be more objective assessments, when one is dealing with such imponderables as quality of management, this may be almost impossible to provide. The tribunal must, however, ensure that the employer's standards are attainable.

14.116 In *Gray v Grimsby Town FC* [1979] ICR 364, the EAT accepted a football club manager's assessment of a player's capabilities (or lack thereof) in the first team. The industrial jury were hardly in a proper position to review his decision. Evidence of staff and consumer complaints (*Dunning and Sons (Shopfitters) Ltd v Jacomb* [1973] ICR 448), or a fall-off in trade, even though this was not directly attributable to the claimant's own failure (*Cook v Thomas Linnell & Sons Ltd* (above)), will, however, be important evidence.

Incompetence and procedure

14.117 One difficult procedural question is how far the stringent guidance found in the ACAS Code, mainly provided for dealing with conduct cases, should apply to dismissal on the grounds of incapacity. This goes to the heart of the policy behind such procedural requirements; if they are enacted because warnings and hearings might lead the employer to change his mind, they are unlikely to be of much value in relation to those employees who have shown themselves manifestly incapable of doing the job in any event. If, on the other hand, the intention is to give to the employee a chance to prove or improve himself there is no reason to distinguish between incompetence and misconduct. It is, in fact, often difficult in practice to draw the line. The result is that, according to the NIRC in *James v Waltham Holy Cross UDC* [1973] IRLR 202 (author's italics):

> An employer should be very slow to dismiss upon terms that an employee is incapable of performing the works which he is employed to do without first *telling the employee* of the respects in which he is failing to do his job adequately, *warning him* of the possibility or likelihood of dismissal on this ground, and giving him an *opportunity to improve* his performance.

Appraisal

The employer may not be able to prove that he has adequately taken a reasonable view **14.118** of the employee's incapacity without a proper system of appraisal. This is particularly important in cases at opposite ends of the spectrum of experience, that is:

(a) where a long-service employee has to adapt to new methods; and
(b) in the case of a probationer who will need to know what standard he is required to meet.

In *Post Office v Mughal* [1977] IRLR 178, Cumming Bruce J formulated these tests for **14.119** tribunals:

> Have the employers shown that they took reasonable steps to maintain appraisal of the probationer throughout the period of probation, giving guidance by advice or warning when such was likely to be useful or fair; and that an appropriate officer made an honest effort to determine whether the probationer came up to the required standard having informed himself of the appraisals made by supervising officers and any other facts recorded about probationers?

A dismissal of a probationer was subsequently held to be unfair where the employing authority did not realise his status for the first seventeen months (*ILEA v Lloyd* [1981] IRLR 394).

Warnings

A warning is less vital in the case of incapability than for misconduct. It is most important **14.120** where the required level of performance is uncertain, and independent judgement thereof difficult. Sir Hugh Griffiths graphically gave the reason in *Winterhalter Gastronom Ltd v Webb* [1973] IRLR 120, thus:

> There are many situations in which a man's apparent capabilities may be stretched when he knows what is being demanded of him; many do not know that they are capable of jumping a 5-barred gate until the bull is close behind them.

Where the prospects of an employee improving are next to nil, however, a warning and **14.121** opportunity of improvement can be of no benefit to the senior employee and may constitute an unfair burden on the business (*James v Waltham Holy Cross UDC* (above); cf *McPhail v Gibson* [1976] IRLR 254). This is also the case in situations with very serious consequences, such as a gaming inspector who failed to notice a serious fraud being conducted under his nose (*Turner v Pleasurama Casinos Ltd* [1976] IRLR 151). There is no requirement to offer such an employee an alternative position (*Bevan Harris Ltd v Gair* [1981] IRLR 520). However, in other circumstances length of service may have the opposite effect in that dismissal may be too serious a sanction for a single act of negligence by an old employee (*Springbank Sand & Gravel Ltd v Craig* [1973] IRLR 278).

14.122   An employer may rely on a final written warning when deciding whether to dismiss provided that the warning was issued in good faith, there was at least prima facie grounds for imposing it, and that it was not manifestly inappropriate to issue it (*Davies v Sandwell MBC* [2013] IRLR 374). It may also be appropriate to consider whether there had been an appeal made against that warning. It is not, however, for the tribunal to conduct a primary fact-finding exercise.

Health

14.123   Cases on dismissal because of ill health demonstrate clearly the role of the unfair dismissal provision in mediating between the economic interest of keeping production moving and maximising profits, on the one hand, and humanitarian requirements on the other. The EAT in *Spencer v Paragon Wallpapers Ltd* [1977] ICR 301 most generally reconciled this tension by stating:

> The basic question which has to be determined in every case is whether in all the circumstances the employer can be expected to wait any longer and if so how much longer ...

for an employee to return. This is not so widely different from the test for frustration on account of sickness discussed earlier (14.82ff) (see *Tan v Berry Brothers and Rudd Ltd* [1974] ICR 586). In neither case is there a fixed period that the employer has to wait, each situation depending on its own facts.

14.124   The Court of Appeal in *Hooper v British Railways Board* [1988] IRLR 517 decided that if an employee is declared by his doctor to be fit for that work which he can reasonably be expected to do, he is not 'incapable' within the statutory definition even though he is not capable of returning to his own particular job on which he was in fact engaged before his absence through sickness.

Medical opinion and consultation with the employee

14.125   The most important procedural requirement in health cases is that the employer should take an informed view on the basis of proper medical information. Best practice includes consultation with the employee, as stressed in the leading case of *East Lindsey DC v Daubney* [1977] ICR 566, approved by the Court of Session in *A. Links & Co v Rose* [1991] IRLR 353. There the employer council's own physician asked a doctor to examine the employee and as a result of his short advice recommended retirement. The procedure was inadequate since the employer had not seen the medical report and had not extended to Mr Daubney the opportunity to obtain and present his own version. The EAT thought that such requirements were far from futile since:

> Discussion and consultations will often bring to light facts and circumstances of which the employers were unaware and which will throw new light on the problem, or the employee may wish to seek medical advice which, brought to the notice of the employer's medical advisers, will cause them to change their opinion.

(See also *First West Yorkshire Ltd v Haigh* [2008] IRLR 182.)

14.126   The medical evidence must be more detailed than a mere statement of unfitness if the employer is to take the necessarily 'rational and informed decision'; but dismissal is a personnel and not a medical decision, and in this the employer may have to use his own discretion in choosing between conflicting medical opinions (*BP Tanker Co v Jeffries* [1974] IRLR 260). There is no countervailing duty on the employee to keep the employer informed as to his progress (*Mitchell v Arkwood Plastics (Engineering) Ltd* [1993] ICR 471).

It is irrelevant in considering the fairness of a sickness dismissal that the illness was caused **14.127** by action of the employer (*London Fire & Civil Defence Authority v Betty* [1994] IRLR 384). The question is whether the employee at the time of dismissal was incapable of performing his job duties. If an employer or someone for whom the employer is responsible has acted maliciously or wilfully, causing an employee incapacitating ill health which results in dismissal, there is no reason why that should not lead to a finding of unfair dismissal (*Edwards v Governors of Hanson School* [2001] IRLR 723). Fairness requires the reasonable employer to give proper consideration to an ill health retirement scheme before dismissing for long-term sickness (*First West Yorkshire Ltd v Haigh* [2008] IRLR 182).

Intermittent absences

The tribunals have also significantly lowered the procedural threshold where a series **14.128** of *intermittent absences* apparently for illness cause serious hardship to the employer. In *International Sports Co Ltd v Thomson* [1980] IRLR 340, the employee had been away for 25 per cent of her last eighteen months' employment. She had submitted various medical certificates to cover these absences, specifying dizzy spells, anxiety and nerves, bronchitis, and viral infection. Four warnings were given to no avail, and the company claimed that it was excused from having her examined by its doctor, because none of her illnesses could be subsequently and independently verified. The EAT agreed that this was a dismissal on the grounds of misconduct rather than ill health, and Waterhouse J said:

> What is required ... is, firstly, that there should be a fair review by the employer of the attendance record and the reasons for it; and, secondly, appropriate warnings after the employee has been given the opportunity to make representation.

The EAT in *Rolls Royce v Walpole* [1980] IRLR 343, took a similar line and found the **14.129** meagre requirements to have been satisfied. The claimant's attendance record was around 50 per cent for the last three years of employment. He received several warnings, and even counselling to discover the reason for his absences, some two years before his actual dismissal, but, on termination, no medical evidence was sought. In an important statement of principle, the EAT declared that:

> Frequently there is a range of responses to the conduct or capacity of the employee on the part of the employer, from and including summary dismissal downwards to a mere informal warning, which can be said to have been reasonable.

The employer's reaction could not be said to be outside this spectrum, and the dismissal was fair (see also *Lynock v Cereal Packaging Ltd* [1988] ICR 670).

A sick note from a doctor may not be conclusive of the genuineness of an employee's **14.130** illness. In *Hutchinson v Enfield Rolling Mills Ltd* [1981] IRLR 318, the employee was held fairly dismissed without any procedure being followed when he was seen at a union demonstration in Brighton on a day when certified as off work by reason of sciatica (see also *Patterson v Messrs Bracketts* [1977] IRLR 137).

Other factors

While a medical opinion is normally necessary for fair dismissal in pure sickness cases, it **14.131** is not quite sufficient. In determining whether the employer was reasonable, an employment tribunal can here be expected to have particular regard to 'the size and administrative resources of the employer's undertaking', as directed by s 98(4) of the ERA 1996.

An employer who has, however, culpably caused or contributed to the incapacity of an **14.132** employee is not precluded for ever from effecting a fair dismissal on the ground of the employee's incapacity to perform his work (*Royal Bank of Scotland v McAdie* [2008] ICR 1087).

14.133   Amongst the several additional factors which the employer must weigh in the balance are:

(a) the employee's past and likely future *service*;

(b) the *likely duration* of the illness (*Luckings v May and Baker* [1975] IRLR 151), and how far this can be accurately predicted;

(c) how readily a *temporary replacement* could be trained or recruited if necessary;

(d) the *status* of the employee, since the more important his position the more likely that his dismissal will be fair (*Spencer v Paragon Wallpapers Ltd* [1976] IRLR 373);

(e) whether it is possible for the employee to perform some of his *functions from home*;

(f) whether the prospect of the job remaining open might be a major *promoter of recovery*;

(g) whether the results of the illness and in particular any *lasting disability* will prevent the employee in fact or by law doing his old job;

(h) whether reasonable alternative employment is available; if so, it should usually be offered to him. Thus, an employer was held to have acted unreasonably in not giving consideration to finding the employee a job in circumstances where although he was not fit to do shift work he could do a day job. Slynn P said here: 'Employers cannot be expected to go to unreasonable lengths in seeking to accommodate someone who is not able to carry out his job to the full extent' (*Garricks Caterers Ltd v Nolan* [1980] IRLR 259; see *Shook v London Borough of Ealing* [1986] IRLR 46);

(i) a contractual clause providing for a certain number of days off (*Smiths Industries Aerospace and Defence Systems v Brookes* [1986] IRLR 434). There may be complex collective agreements covering sickness absence which are incorporated into the individual contract of employment, and if so, the employment tribunal is bound to adopt the ordinary canons of contractual construction of the agreements, including the principle that an agreement cannot normally be construed in the light of the subsequent actions of the parties (*Hooper v British Railways Board* [1988] IRLR 517). The fact that the employee is dismissed while in receipt of his contractual entitlement to sick pay does not, however, in itself make the termination unfair. The only relevance of this right to payment is that its duration may be evidence of the period during which the business could do without the employee; and

(j) while an alternative position should be offered even if it is likely that the employee will refuse, for example because it carries a lower rate of pay, the authorities fall short of suggesting that there is a duty on the employer to 'create a special job for an employee however long serving he may be' (*Merseyside & North Wales Electricity Board v Taylor* [1975] IRLR 60; see also *Spencer* (above)), nor where to propose it would breach an agreement with the unions.

Other situations in which the employee's health may be relevant

14.134   There are other situations in which health may be relevant:

(a) the EAT has held that an employer cannot fairly dismiss an employee on the ground that there is a *risk* of a heart attack unless that risk is of such importance as to make it unsafe for the employee to continue in the job (*Converfoam (Darwen) Ltd v Bell* [1981] IRLR 195), which might include a sole wireless operator on a sea-going ship; and

(b) failure to state illness in an *application* for a job may justify a dismissal if it is serious and job-related, for example, mental illness (*O'Brien v Prudential Assurance Co Ltd* [1979] IRLR 140).

Qualifications

Although the word 'qualifications' is widely defined in the ERA 1996, s 98(3)(b), it does **14.135** not extend to the personal characteristic of trustworthiness (*Singh v London Country Bus Services Ltd* [1976] IRLR 176) and must be related to 'performing work of the kind which he was employed by the employer to do'. Thus, in *Blue Star Ship Management Ltd v Williams* [1979] IRLR 16, authorisation as a registered seafarer was irrelevant to the employee's position so that lack of this could not be a reason for dismissal. The requirement of a clean driving licence need not be set out in a written contract of employment to be a qualification (*Tayside Regional Council v McIntosh* [1982] IRLR 272).

H MISCONDUCT

Dismissals relating to misconduct will be discussed under these general rubrics: breach of **14.136** employer's reasonable orders and rules; and commission of criminal offences. In general, conduct must be action of such a nature, whether committed in the course of employment or not, as to reflect in some way on the employer–employee relationship. The fact that an employee had caused damage to the employer's petrol pump did not in any way affect her capacity to perform her duties, and so did not amount to conduct under the Act (*Thomson v Alloa Motor Co Ltd* [1983] IRLR 403). In another case it was found to be difficult to see how the action of an employee acting in self-defence in pushing another person onto a sofa in a domestic situation could be such as to reflect upon the employer–employee relationship (*CJD v Royal Bank of Scotland* [2014] IRLR 25).

Disobedience to reasonable instructions

'There must be considered not only the nature of the order but the circumstances sur- **14.137** rounding the giving of the order ... and also the reason for not carrying out the order.' (Talbot J in *Union of Construction Allied Trades and Technicians v Brain* [1980] IRLR 357.)

The unfair dismissal jurisdiction maintains the fundamental principle of the contract **14.138** of employment that the employee must obey the lawful and reasonable instructions of the employer. There must, however, be a serious breach of the rules to justify dismissal just as at common law, and, moreover, the employee must not only be *warned* as to the consequence of a breach of the rule, but also have an *opportunity to state his side of the story*. More generally, the ACAS Code of Practice provides that, rules should be 'specific and clear' and 'employees and where appropriate their representatives should be involved in [their] development'.

Instructions and the contract

The scope of lawful instructions must be determined primarily by construing the contract **14.139** of employment. This may require analysis of the written statement of terms, custom and practice, works rules, and collective agreement, particularly with regard to job duties, hours of work and location. Thus, in *Deeley v BRE Ltd* [1980] IRLR 147, the original letter of engagement gave the right to the respondent company's managing director to transfer the employee to whatever duties he saw fit. Although the advertisement referred to the claimant's post as Sales Engineer Export and he had always, in fact, been engaged in export sales, a requirement to work on home sales was not in breach of contract. His dismissal for refusal to carry out these duties was thus fair.

14.140 If an employee is dismissed for refusing or failing to do something which was not within his contractual duties to do, the dismissal is likely to be unfair, although any compensation may be reduced because of the employee's contributory fault in failing to react reasonably in the circumstances. In *Redbridge LBC v Fishman* [1978] ICR 569, the claimant was appointed to be in charge of the resources centre at a large comprehensive school. At first she did little teaching, but the school's new headmistress informed her that henceforth she would have to take eighteen English lessons a week; she refused and was dismissed, unfairly in the tribunal's and EAT's view, since she had been recruited for special duties which would largely absolve her from general teaching duties. The instruction was not within her contractual duties and she could reasonably refuse it.

14.141 Phillips J, however, warned against the imposition of a contractual straitjacket in approaching this question. In particular, the employee's duties may be considerably wider than what he has actually been accustomed to doing on a day-to-day basis. Flexibility may be called for on the part of the employee, particularly in a small business (*Glitz v Watford Electric Co Ltd* [1979] IRLR 89; *Coward v John Menzies (Holdings) Ltd* [1977] IRLR 428; *Simmonds v Dowty Seals Ltd* [1978] IRLR 211). Where an employee agrees under protest to work under varied terms, a subsequent failure to observe those varied terms may amount to misconduct justifying dismissal (*Robinson v Tescom Corporation* [2008] IRLR 408).

Reasonableness of the instruction

14.142 One important way in which the modern law differs from wrongful dismissal is that it focuses on the *reasonableness* of the employer's order as well as its *legality* by contract. The most wide-ranging review of the principles is to be found in *Farrant v The Woodroffe School* [1998] ICR 184, where the EAT held that when an employer relied on the employee's conduct in refusing to obey an instruction, the lawfulness of the instruction, although relevant, is not decisive as it would be in a claim for wrongful dismissal. In *UCATT v Brain* [1981] IRLR 225, the claimant employee was publications officer of the respondent union when a libel action was brought against him and the union in respect of articles in the union journal. As a part of its settlement, the applicant was required by the union to sign a statement that neither he nor any officers, servants, or agents would repeat the defamatory statement, but he refused to do so on the grounds that he would be thereby making himself liable for the acts of others over whom he had no control. His persistence in this stance led to his dismissal and the Court of Appeal upheld a finding of unfairness on the ground that the instruction was manifestly unreasonable. This directly points the difference from wrongful dismissal where the only question is whether the employer's order was contractual.

14.143 Determining the scope of fair dismissal for disobeying instructions is indeed vital in delimiting the bounds of the managerial prerogative of the employer. For example, the EAT in *Boychuk v H.J. Symons Holdings Ltd* [1977] IRLR 395 suggested that an employer can still dictate his employee's appearance in the workplace. The claimant, an audit clerk, was held to have been fairly dismissed because of her insistence on wearing badges proclaiming her lesbianism. The EAT considered that: 'a reasonable employer ... can be allowed to decide what upon reflection and mature consideration, can be offensive to the customers and the fellow employees'. In another case, it was held to be fair to dismiss a woman school cleaner who insisted on bringing her young child to school even though he distracted her attention from her work and had caused accidents (*Lawrence v Newham LBC* [1978] ICR 10).

As in the common law of wrongful dismissal, it is not fair to dismiss an employee where **14.144** he refuses to obey an *unlawful* order. Thus, in *Morrish v Henlys (Folkestone) Ltd* [1973] ICR 482, the appellant was sacked for refusing to acquiesce in the alteration of accounts on drawing diesel oil from petrol pumps; and this was held unfair.

The dividing line is not easy to draw, so that the dismissal of a finance director of an NHS **14.145** Trust because his manner and management style had led to a breakdown in his relationship with other members of the senior executive team was held to be by reason of conduct rather than some other substantial reason. Personality of itself could not be a ground for dismissal but an employee's personality may manifest itself in such a way as to bring the actions of the employee within s 98 (*Perkin v St George's Healthcare NHS Trust* [2005] IRLR 934).

Rules

The need for clear rules

The employer will normally codify the instructions and requirements for his employees **14.146** into a series of disciplinary rules relating to everything from time sheets and attendance, to standards of appearance and rudeness. The employee's written statement of terms must include 'any disciplinary rules that apply' and the ACAS Code of Practice on Disciplinary Practice and Procedure 2009 lays down detailed guidance supplemented by the ACAS Guide 2014 'Discipline and Grievances at Work'. This is not to say that every 'i' need be dotted and every 't' crossed.

In *Pringle v Lucas Industrial Equipment Ltd* [1975] IRLR 266, the EAT said that 'if **14.147** employers wish to dismiss automatically for certain misconduct which is short of inherently gross misconduct they must be able to show that management has unequivocally brought to the attention of employees what that conduct is and what its consequences will be'. To cover a series of offences in company rules does not, however, mean that matters falling outside their terms cannot merit dismissal because of their absence from the 'code'.

It is indeed reasonable for an employer to expect that his workforce are aware of the most **14.148** obvious prohibitions. This was confirmed with respect to fighting in *C.A. Parsons & Co Ltd v McLoughlin* [1978] IRLR 65. Although it was not included in the respondent company's rules as gross misconduct, Kilner Brown J thought that 'it ought not to be necessary for anybody, let alone a shop steward, to have in black and white in the form of a rule that a fight is something that is going to be regarded very gravely by management'. The effects here of an assault near machinery on the factory floor were obviously serious, but the position may be different when the action is not so grave. Thus, in *Meyer Dunmore International Ltd v Rogers* [1978] IRLR 167, a summary dismissal for fighting was held to have been unfair and Phillips J declared:

> If employers wish to have a rule that employees engaged in what could properly and sensibly be called 'fighting' are going to be summarily dismissed, as far as we can see there is no reason why they should not have a rule provided—and this is important—that it is plainly adopted, that it is plainly and clearly set out, and that great publicity is given to it so that every employee knows beyond any reasonable doubt whatever that if he gets involved in fighting he will be dismissed.

Whether a set of facts falls on one side or other of the distinction between the *Parsons* **14.149** and *Meyer* cases must be a matter of fact and degree, but several cases have emphasised the need for clear rules in regard to, for example, overstaying leave and drinking alcohol during working hours (*Hoover Ltd v Forde* [1980] ICR 239; *Dairy Produce Packers*

Ltd v Beverstock [1981] IRLR 265; and *Distillers Co (Bottling Services) Ltd v Gardner* [1982] IRLR 47).

14.150   Disciplinary rules are indeed particularly important in emphasising to employees those less serious breaches which the employer proposes to visit with the severe sanction of dismissal. In this way, the rule acts as a form of preliminary warning of dismissal. Instant dismissal has thus been considered fair following breach of clearly stated rules relating, for example, to clocking on (*Dalton v Burton's Gold Medal Biscuits Ltd* [1974] IRLR 45) and working for a competitor (*Golden Cross Hire Co Ltd v Lovell* [1979] IRLR 267).

Where dismissal for breach of rules is unfair

14.151   Even where there is in place a disciplinary rule and it is broken, a tribunal is still likely to find a dismissal in consequence to be unfair in the following situations, although each case depends on its own facts:

(a) Where the rule breached is of *no relevance* to the employment (see *Greenslade v Hoveringham Gravels Ltd* [1975] IRLR 114).

(b) Where the rule is *ambiguous*: thus, Kilner Brown J in *Meridian Ltd v Gomersall* [1977] IRLR 425 found that a works notice that 'anyone found clocking cards on behalf of other personnel will render themselves *liable* to instant dismissal' was insufficiently precise. The authority of this decision has, however, been undermined by the opposite result by the EAT on similar facts in *Elliot Brothers (London) Ltd v Colverd* [1979] IRLR 92.

(c) Where the 'punishment' of dismissal is disproportionate in that it does *not fit the 'crime'*. Thus, in *Ladbroke Racing Ltd v Arnott* [1983] IRLR 154, where three betting shop employees were summarily dismissed for placing bets on behalf of relations in breach of a clearly stated rule in the respondent's disciplinary code, the tribunal's determination of unfairness was upheld by the EAT and the Court of Session on the grounds that instant dismissal was an unreasonable response in all the circumstances. The full extent of their misconduct was that one employee had placed just one bet for his brother on one occasion, the second occasionally for two old-age pensioners, and the third was the office manager who had apparently condoned the practice (see also *Richards v Bulpitt & Sons Ltd* [1975] IRLR 134). A similar principle was applied in *Unkles v Milanda Bread Co* [1973] IRLR 76; although rules existed to restrict smoking, dismissal for breach was too severe since the employee's conduct in breaking the rule was inadvertent rather than wilful.

    Employers should also normally take into account length of service when determining on the application of disciplinary rules. In *Johnson Matthey Metals Ltd v Harding* [1978] IRLR 248, an employee with fifteen years' unblemished service was dismissed when he was found in possession of a fellow worker's wrist watch six months after it had been lost. The EAT held that the amount of previous years' service was 'plainly a matter to be taken into consideration' and held that the dismissal was unfair. Past work did not, however, weigh against the serious and proved misconduct in *AEI Cables Ltd v McLay* [1980] IRLR 84, where the claimant had made false claims for reimbursement for diesel fuels and had been presenting such fraudulent vouchers for the last two years.

(d) Where there is no semblance of *consistency* in application of the rules. It may be that breaches of clear disciplinary rules are waived with such regularity that an employee is lulled into a false sense of security, but this will be comparatively rare. Employers often acquiesce, for example, in breaches of rules (say) prohibiting drinking in the lunch hour or leaving the night shift early when all allocated work has been completed. Several decisions have stressed that a clear warning is necessary if there is to be a 'purge' on a particular breach which has not before been visited with disciplinary sanction:

(i) An employer is entitled to treat two similar cases of misconduct differently, provided that the employer acted within the band of reasonable responses open to him and was not so irrational that no employer could reasonably have dismissed an employee in those particular circumstances (*Securicor Ltd v Smith* [1989] IRLR 356; see also *London Borough of Harrow v Cunningham* [1996] IRLR 256).

(ii) In *Post Office v Fennell* [1981] IRLR 221, the employee was summarily dismissed after assaulting a fellow employee in the works canteen. His case was that many other workers had been guilty of similar offences but were not punished in this way. The Court of Appeal upheld a decision that the dismissal was unfair for that reason on the basis that the statutory reference to 'equity and the substantial merits of the case' comprehended the concept that employees who behave in much the same way should receive similar punishments (see also *Parr v Whitbread & Co plc* [1990] ICR 427).

(iii) In *Hadjioannou v Coral Casinos Ltd* [1981] IRLR 352, the EAT limited the applicability of this case by stating that an appeal to consistency was only relevant when:

(1) there was evidence that employees had been led to believe that certain categories of conduct would either be overlooked or at least not dealt with by dismissal;

(2) evidence in relation to other cases supports the inference that the employer's purported reason for dismissal was not the real reason; and

(3) the circumstances in other cases were truly parallel.

Here these conditions were not fulfilled so that the EAT upheld a finding by a tribunal that the appellant's dismissal for socialising with customers was in breach of company rules and was fair. In *Paul v East Surrey District Health Authority* [1995] IRLR 305, the Court of Appeal went on to apply *Hadjioannou*. Beldam LJ stated that, ultimately, the question for the employer is whether in the particular case dismissal is a reasonable response to the misconduct proved.

(iv) It is no answer to a claim to consistency for the employer merely to assert that the decisions in the cases of other employees were taken by different employees or agents of the employer (*Cain v Leeds Western HA* [1990] ICR 585).

(v) The employer should consider truly comparable cases of which he has knowledge, or of which he ought reasonably to have known, but not every case of leniency should be considered a deviation from a declared policy (*Procter v British Gypsum Ltd* [1992] IRLR 7). (On the tension between the desirability of consistency and flexibility, see *United Distillers v Conlin* [1992] IRLR 503.)

(e) Where the employer did not consider the facts of the *individual case* but simply dismissed because it was his policy to do so in the class of cases concerned, for example, assault (*Taylor v Parsons Peebles NEI Bruce Peebles* [1981] IRLR 119).

(f) Where the employee is then suddenly faced with *a stale allegation of misconduct* (*Allders International Ltd v Parkins* [1981] IRLR 68, *Refund Rentals Ltd v McDermott* [1977] IRLR 59). In *Marley Homecare Ltd v Dutton* [1981] IRLR 380, for example, it was held to be unfair to inform an employee of the result of test purchases which pointed to the claimant cashier's dishonesty seven days after the event. She could not then be expected to remember the particular incident, and the EAT suggested that it would have been much fairer to suspend the suspect at the time, so that she could identify the transaction, albeit that a disciplinary hearing might not be effected until some time later. Moreover, a dismissal may be unfair because of delay in bringing disciplinary proceedings even though there was no evidence that delay had actually prejudiced the employee's position (*RSPCA v Cruden* [1986] ICR 205).

Offences

Does commission of the offence merit dismissal?

14.152   The tribunals and courts naturally draw a distinction between offences committed at work and those committed outside. Whether the commission of a criminal offence outside of his job merits an employee's dismissal depends above all on the degree of its relevance (if any at all) to the individual's duty as an employee. The tribunal in each case should take into account: the *status* of the employee; the *nature* of the offence; the employee's *past record*; his access to *cash*; and proximity to members of the *public*. Thus, in *Rentokil v Mackin* [1989] IRLR 286, for example, dismissal for theft of a milkshake from a customer was held to be unfair.

14.153   The 2009 ACAS Code of Practice provides in para 30 that:

> If an employee is charged with, or convicted of, a criminal offence, this is not normally in itself reason for disciplinary action. Consideration needs to be given to what effect the charge or conviction has on the employee's suitability to do the job and their relationship with their employer, work colleagues and customers.

The EAT has, however, emphasised that in these cases reasonable employers may reach different decisions, and 'it does not necessarily mean if they decide to dismiss they have acted unfairly because there are plenty of situations in which more than one view is possible' (*Trusthouse Forte Leisure Ltd v Aquilar* [1976] IRLR 251). It is also not a valid argument for the claimant that he has suffered already in the criminal courts by way of fine (*British Leyland (UK) Ltd v Swift* [1981] IRLR 91; see also *British Gas plc v McCarrick* [1991] IRLR 305). The EAT has, however, concluded that a second offence of deliberate fraud by an employee on his employers so obviously strikes at the fundamental relationship of trust and confidence between the employer and employee that there would have to be some clear reason to justify a finding that the decision fell outside the range of reasonable responses open to an employer (*United Distillers v Conlin* [1992] IRLR 503).

14.154   The employer is also entitled to take into account aggravating factors such as a previous poor disciplinary record (*London Borough of Harrow v Cunningham* [1996] IRLR 256).

14.155   Tribunals have, for example, upheld as fair these dismissals:

(a) A film cameraman after a conviction of indecent assault on a young girl, since his employer would henceforth have to be selective in the assignments which it might give him (*Creffield v BBC* [1975] IRLR 23).

(b) Lecturers who taught students between the ages of sixteen and eighteen when they were found guilty of gross indecency (*Gardiner v Newport County Borough Council* [1974] IRLR 262; and *Nottinghamshire CC v Bowly* [1978] IRLR 252).

(c) A drama teacher for possessing and cultivating cannabis (*Norfolk CC v Bernard* [1979] IRLR 220; see also *Mathewson v R. B. Wilson Dental Laboratory Ltd* [1988] IRLR 512).

(d) A shop assistant who had stolen from a nearby store (*Moore v C & A Modes* [1981] IRLR 71).

On the other hand, dismissal following a conviction for incest has been held to be unfair since it was 'an isolated incident, it had nothing to do with the applicant's work, his work did not bring him into contact with female staff' (*Bradshaw v Rugby Portland Cement Co Ltd* [1972] IRLR 46).

14.156   An employee may be fairly dismissed where he conceals from his employer a criminal conviction which was imposed before his employment began (*Torr v British Railways Board*

[1977] IRLR 185) or where the employee has been sentenced to three months' imprisonment for a serious offence (*Kingston v British Railways Board* [1984] IRLR 146).

Degree of proof

Tribunals have steered a middle course in relation to dismissal for offences, both at work **14.157** and outside, between demanding such proof of guilt as would be necessary in a criminal court and allowing dismissal on mere suspicion of crime. The crucial question (which applies to all misconduct cases) was formulated by Arnold J in *BHS Ltd v Burchell* [1978] IRLR 379, as whether the employer:

> entertained a reasonable suspicion amounting to a belief in the guilt of the employee of that misconduct at that time ... First of all, there must be established by the employer the fact of that belief; that the employer did believe it. Secondly, that the employer had in his mind reasonable grounds upon which to sustain that belief. And thirdly, we think that the employer at the stage at which he formed that belief on those grounds, at any rate at the final stage at which he formed that belief, had carried out as much investigation into the matter as was reasonable in all the circumstances of the case.

(See also *Scottish Special Housing Association v Cooke* [1979] IRLR 264; *ILEA v Gravett* [1988] IRLR 497; *Salford Royal NHS Foundation Trust v Roldan* [2010] IRLR 721.)

In approving this test in *Weddel and Co Ltd v Tepper* [1980] IRLR 96, Stephenson LJ did, **14.158** however, emphasise the requirement that belief on reasonable grounds entailed that employers must not 'form their belief hastily without making the appropriate enquiries' (see also *Trusthouse Forte Leisure Ltd v Aquilar* [1976] IRLR 251; *Trusthouse Forte Hotels Ltd v Murphy* [1977] IRLR 186; *Scottish Midland Cooperative Society Ltd v Cullion* [1991] IRLR 261). Similar principles were applied in the case of suspected serious negligence in *McPhie & McDermott v Wimpey Waste Management Ltd* [1981] IRLR 316, and generalised in *Distillers Co (Bottling Services) Ltd v Gardner* [1982] IRLR 47. *Burchell* should, however, be understood as a 'guideline not a tram-line' (*Boys' and Girls' Welfare Society v McDonald* [1996] IRLR 129; *Scottish Daily Record Ltd v Laird* [1996] IRLR 665).

The need for a reasonable belief in the responsibility of the employee for misconduct is **14.159** illustrated by *Ferodo Ltd v Barnes* [1976] IRLR 302. The claimant was dismissed when it was thought that he had committed an act of vandalism in the company's toilets. The fact that the employer could not prove that the employee had committed the offence was not relevant save as evidence that the employer acted reasonably or otherwise in concluding that the employee had so behaved. The vital question was the state of evidence and information known to the employer at the time of dismissal. Thus, a dismissal may be fair even though a criminal court decides that the offence was not in fact committed by the applicant (*Harris (Ipswich) Ltd v Harrison* [1978] IRLR 382). One reason for this is that while the criminal court must be convinced of guilt beyond reasonable doubt, the employment tribunal works on the less exacting standard of balance of probabilities (*Lees v The Orchard* [1978] IRLR 20). Conversely:

> If an employer thinks that his accountant may be taking the firm's money but he has no real grounds for so thinking, and dismisses him for that reason, he acts wholly unreasonably notwithstanding that it was later proved that the accountant had been guilty.

(*Earl v Slater and Wheeler (Airlyne) Ltd* [1972] ICR 508; see also *Lovie Ltd v Anderson* [1999] IRLR 164.)

While the law generally rejects blanket dismissals of several employees (*Scottish Special* **14.160** *Housing Association v Cooke* [1979] IRLR 264; *Gibson v British Transport Docks Board* [1982] IRLR 278), there is a difference where the net of reasonable suspicion rests on the heads of *two* employees, and both may be dismissed if the true culprit cannot be identified. This was established in the difficult case of *Monie v Coral Racing Ltd* [1980] IRLR 464. The appellant worked as an area manager with control and supervision over nineteen betting shops, and only he and his assistant knew the combination for the safe in the area headquarters. While Mr Monie was on holiday, his assistant discovered that £1,750 was missing from this safe. There were no indications that either the premises or the safe had been forcibly entered, and the respondent's security officer thus concluded that one or other, or both, must have been involved in the theft. The two were dismissed, and this decision was confirmed by a director. The ordinary application of the test demanding reasonable belief in the applicant's guilt would result in a finding that both dismissals were unfair and the EAT so held.

14.161   On appeal, however, all three Lord Justices confined the *Burchell* principle to those cases in which only one employee is under suspicion. Here, 'looking at the matter as an ordinary businessman', Sir David Cairns thought that the tribunal had correctly inquired 'whether there were solid and sensible grounds on which the employer could reasonably *infer or suspect* dishonesty' (author's italics), and had rightly answered in the affirmative. The fact that the two employees would have the right to be acquitted on a criminal charge of theft on this evidence was immaterial. An employer will need to show that the most careful investigation has been undertaken in such a case. Moreover, it should not be forgotten in applying its principle that in *Monie* both suspects were in senior positions and handled money in a business in which security and honesty were obviously vital.

14.162   This principle was taken further in *Whitbread & Co plc v Thomas* [1988] ICR 135, where three employees were dismissed who *might* have been responsible for stock losses at an off-licence. The EAT held that where an employer could not identify the individual(s) who were responsible for an act or acts of commission or omission, an employer was entitled to dismiss a group of employees on grounds which would justify dismissing an identified individual, provided that the employer had carried out a proper investigation and could show that the acts had been committed by one or more of the group and each member of that group had been individually capable of having committed the acts complained of (see also *Parr v Whitbread & Co plc* [1990] IRLR 39).

14.163   The converse application of the principle is that where any one or more of a group of employees *could* have committed a particular offence or deed of misconduct, the fact that one was not dismissed does not make the dismissals thereby unfair, provided that the employer can demonstrate sensible grounds to differentiate between those dismissed and those not dismissed (although these factors do not have to be related to the relevant offence) (*Frames Snooker Centre v Boyce* [1992] IRLR 472).

Investigation

14.164   There are no hard and fast rules governing an employer's investigations of criminal offences. The main principle was enunciated by Viscount Dilhorne in *W. Devis & Sons Ltd v Atkins* [1976] IRLR 314: 'It cannot be said that the employer acted reasonably ... if he only did so in consequence of ignoring matters which he reasonably ought to have known'. The ACAS Code states (at para 5):

> It is important to carry out necessary investigations of potential disciplinary matters without unreasonable delay to establish the facts of the case.

Often there will be agreed procedures for such fact-finding processes and if these are followed the dismissal is likely to be fair (see *Bentley Engineering Co Ltd v Mistry* [1978] IRLR 436; *ILEA v Gravett* [1988] IRLR 497).

The employer, not the tribunal, is the proper person to conduct the investigation into **14.165** alleged misconduct. The function of the tribunal is to decide whether that investigation is reasonable in the circumstances, and whether the decision to dismiss in the light of that investigation is a reasonable response to the results of the investigation. In *Wilson v Post Office* [2000] IRLR 834, the Court of Appeal interfered with the decision of the employment tribunal that the employer's determination that the applicant should be dismissed because his attendance record had not met requirements of the agreed attendance procedure was not a substantial reason. Although the claimant's ill health was the cause of this poor attendance, ill health was not the reason for his dismissal.

There is no need for a detailed inquiry where, for example: **14.166**

(a) a thief admits guilt or is caught red-handed (*Scottish Special Housing Association v Linnen* [1979] IRLR 265; *Royal Society for the Protection of Birds v Croucher* [1984] IRLR 425);
(b) the employee makes a tacit acknowledgement of guilt (eg, *Parker Bakeries Ltd v Palmer* [1977] IRLR 215); and
(c) the employee has pleaded guilty to the criminal offence (in *P v Nottinghamshire CC* [1992] IRLR 362, to an offence of indecency).

The following principles apply to an employer's investigation, whether of an offence or **14.167** breach of the employer's own internal rules:

(a) where there has been a confession and then a retraction of it by the employee, the tribunal should decide whether the employer behaved reasonably in relying on the admission (*University College at Buckingham v Phillips* [1982] ICR 318);
(b) where there are large numbers of alleged offenders, each case must still be dealt with individually (*Gibson v British Transport Docks Board* [1982] IRLR 228);
(c) the requirements of criminal procedure generally do not apply (*Morley's of Brixton Ltd v Minott* [1982] IRLR 270);
(d) where a complaint is received about an employee, the employer should inquire whether there has indeed been any misconduct and the extent of its gravity and not rely solely on the integrity of the complainant (*Henderson v Granville Tours Ltd* [1982] IRLR 494);
(e) it is improper for police to be present at an internal inquiry without the foreknowledge and consent of the employee (*Read v Phoenix Preservation Ltd* [1985] IRLR 93);
(f) police statements may be taken into account even though they would be inadmissible in criminal proceedings; the weight to be attached to them is a matter for the employment tribunal (*Dhaliwal v British Airways Board* [1985] ICR 513);
(g) the use of informers in investigations is problematic; in *Linfood Cash & Carry Ltd v Thomson* [1989] IRLR 235, the EAT gave this general guidance:
    (i) the information given by the informant should be reduced into writing in one or more statements. Initially these statements should be taken without regard to the fact that in those cases where anonymity is to be preserved, it may subsequently prove to be necessary to omit or erase certain parts of the statements before submission to others—in order to prevent identification;
    (ii) tactful inquiries may well be thought advisable to be conducted into the character and background of the informant or any other information which may tend to add to or detract from the value of the information;
    (iii) if the informant is prepared to attend a disciplinary hearing, no problem will arise, but if the employer is satisfied that the fear is genuine a decision will need to be made whether or not to continue with the disciplinary process; and

      (iv) the written statement of the informant—if necessary with omissions to avoid identification—should be made available to the employee and his representatives.

    (h) in investigating serious allegations of criminal misbehaviour the employer should focus inquiries no less on any potential evidence that may exculpate or at least point towards the innocence of the employee as on the evidence directed towards proving the charges (*A v B* [2003] IRLR 405); and

    (i) a delay in the conduct of an investigation may itself render an otherwise fair dismissal to be unfair (*A v B* [2003] IRLR 405).

14.168 Where the employer was a large organisation the investigation of an allegation of misconduct would normally be delegated to a person within the organisation who had sufficient knowledge, skill, and experience to carry it out effectively, and that would be the person whose knowledge or state of mind counted as that of the employer (*Orr v Milton Keynes Council* [2011] ICR 704).

14.169 Where an employee was dismissed following an unsolicited disclosure to his employer by the police or a responsible public authority that he posed a risk to children but the suspicion was based not on an established criminal conviction but on untested information, the focus of the tribunal's inquiry should be on whether the employer reacted reasonably to the disclosure not on whether it was true (*A v B* [2010] ICR 849; *Leach v Office of Communications* [2012] ICR 1270 CA). In principle and subject to certain safeguards, the employer must be entitled to treat the information as reliable and is not expected to carry out an independent investigation to test the reliability of the information, nor was it necessary for the employer to believe in the truth of what he had been told.

Hearing

14.170 The following principles may be drawn together from EAT decisions about hearings:

    (a) At the stage of investigation there is no need to involve the employee, but once the facts are fully garnered, they must be put before him at a hearing. The two processes often merge into one, especially when only the employee can give information about the incident; in that case a distinct second stage of hearing is unnecessary.

    (b) When police inquiries and internal procedures are being held simultaneously, employees have naturally sought to prevent the latter prejudicing them in any criminal charges, but *dicta* (eg Lord Macdonald in *Carr v Alexander Russell Ltd* [1976] IRLR 220) that employment procedures should be suspended while a prosecution was pending have been later disapproved.

    (c) There is also no general requirement that employees should be suspended on full pay whilst awaiting the outcome of criminal proceedings, although this commonly happens (*Conway v Matthew Wright & Nephew Ltd* [1977] IRLR 89).

    (d) The employee should not be left in a state of uncertainty. Thus, in *Portsea Island Mutual Cooperative Society v Rees* [1980] ICR 260, the employer was held to have acted unreasonably when at the date of dismissal the incident relied on was six weeks old and the employee had already been reprimanded for it.

    (e) It is not necessarily unfair to fail to disclose to the employee or to his representative the witness statements which formed the basis of the decision to dismiss, when the employee knew exactly what was being alleged against him. (*Fuller v Lloyds Bank plc* [1991] IRLR 336).

    (f) The tribunal should not 'second guess' the employer's appreciation of a witness at an internal hearing (*Linfood Cash & Carry Ltd v Thomson* [1989] IRLR 235; *Morgan v Electrolux* [1991] IRLR 89).

Conduct checklist

It is impossible to catalogue all types of misconduct dismissals but the following are fur- **14.171**
ther examples, and in most the courts have demanded the same degree of investigation
into the facts and fairness in applying the sanction as above:

(a) failure to cooperate with the employer (eg *Retarded Children's Aid Society v Day*
[1978] ICR 437);
(b) insubordination (eg *Chantrill v W. F. Shortland Ltd* [1974] IRLR 333);
(c) assault (eg *Parsons (C.A.) & Co v McLoughlin* [1978] IRLR 65; *Stevenson v Golden
Wonder Ltd* [1977] IRLR 474);
(d) breach of hygiene and safety standards (eg *Unkles v Milanda Bread Co Ltd* [1973]
IRLR 76);
(e) absenteeism and bad timekeeping (eg *City of Edinburgh DC v Stephen* [1977]
IRLR 135);
(f) disclosing confidential information (*Archer v Cheshire & Northwich Building
Society* [1976] IRLR 424);
(g) disloyalty by entering into competition with the employer (*Golden Cross Hire Co Ltd
v Lovell* [1979] IRLR 267), especially where this is accompanied by lies about such
action (cf *Laughton and Hawley v Bapp Industrial Supplies Ltd* [1986] IRLR 245; cf
Marshall v Industrial Systems & Control Ltd [1992] IRLR 294);
(h) covert deals by a managing director with members of his own family so that his
personal interests and the interests of the company might conflict (*Maintenance Co
Ltd v Dormer* [1982] IRLR 491);
(i) taking a holiday without permission (*Brandon and Goold v Murphy Bros* [1983]
IRLR 54);
(j) deliberate use of an unauthorised password in order to enter a computer known to
contain information to which the employee was not entitled (*Denco Ltd v Joinson*
[1991] IRLR 63, and this was dismissal for a single offence);
(k) making nuisance telephone calls to other members of staff whilst on duty as a mental
health night charge nurse (*East Berkshire Health Authority v Matadeen* [1992] IRLR
336); and
(l) using the telephone for personal purposes (*John Lewis v Coyne* [2001] IRLR 139).

I PROCEDURE

'Good industrial relations depend upon management not only acting fairly but being **14.172**
manifestly seen to act fairly.' (Sir John Donaldson, *Earl v Slater & Wheeler Ltd (Airlyne)*
[1972] ICR 508.) Lord Bridge said in *Polkey v Dayton Services Ltd* [1988] ICR 142:

> In the case of misconduct, the employer will normally not act reasonably unless he investi-
> gates the complaint of misconduct fully and fairly and hears whatever the employee wishes
> to say in his defence or in explanation or mitigation.

There are two axes to the reasonableness of a dismissal—the substantive merits and procedural fairness—and it is to the latter that we now turn. It focuses on the 'equity' part
of the s 98(4) test and is most conveniently dealt with here because most of the cases in
which it is relevant concern capacity or misconduct.

Agreed procedures

Tribunals have strained to uphold union agreed procedures in accordance with the leg- **14.173**
islative policy. *East Hertfordshire DC v Boyten* [1977] IRLR 347 is the highpoint of

that trend, even referring to the agreed code as the 'Bible'. The applicant refuse collector had been dismissed for fighting which was witnessed by two fellow employees who made statements about it. On appeal, the employer did nothing to ensure the presence of the witnesses, as appeared to be necessary to give the appellant a fair hearing. Yet Forbes J overturned the tribunal's determination of unfairness since the employer had followed the agreed code of procedure to the letter, and tribunals should not rush in where management and unions fear to tread. His Lordship said:

> The point is that there is a code, carefully agreed between the parties, and ... it is not for the Industrial Tribunal, or indeed, this Appeal Tribunal to rewrite an agreed code of that kind which has been hammered out by both sides of industry. No employer, it seems to us, should be accused of acting unreasonably in those circumstances if that employer follows a code which has been arrived at in that way.

Warnings

14.174 It is good sense and reasonable that in the ordinary way for a first offence you should not dismiss a man on the instant without any warning or giving him a further chance (*Retarded Children's Aid Society v Day* [1978] ICR 437).

14.175 An employee should generally be given a warning about his misconduct or incompetence before being dismissed if that dismissal is to be considered to be fair. Warning in this context is shorthand for 'efforts to try to make the employee change and (an indication) to him of the consequence if these efforts are unsuccessful' (*Plasticisers Ltd v Amos*, EAT 13/76). A warning is intended to deter and reform the employee, and should be administered to the worker individually. Exceptionally, however, a general warning to all staff might be acceptable (*Connely v Liverpool Corporation* (1974) 9 ITR 51).

14.176 Although the latter stage of the process should be in writing, 'there is no special magic' about it (*McCall v Castleton Crafts Ltd* [1979] IRLR 218). Its value is that it invests the process with a more official character, and its seriousness is also shown by the supplementary provision that the employee may be represented by a union official or friend before the final warning is administered.

14.177 To have its proper effect, the warning must be *sufficiently specific*. An employer's insistence, for example, that 'you undertake these responsibilities and duties forthwith if you are to continue as Deputy Head of the Documentary Credit Department', did not suffice in *UBAF Bank Ltd v Davis* [1978] IRLR 442 (see also *Littlewoods Organisation Ltd v Egenti* [1976] ICR 516).

14.178 In most cases a warning on ground 'A' should not be used as a step in procedure to dismiss on a completely different ground 'B'. Previous warnings may be considered even if the conduct for which the employee is dismissed is different in character (*Auguste Noël Ltd v Curtis* [1990] ICR 604). Although confidential records should be kept at all stages, if the employee improves, the warning should be removed; usually a six-month period is reasonable and a specific time will often be inserted in disciplinary rules (*Charles v SRC* (1977) 12 ITR 208). This brings to the forefront of practice the aim to deter and reform. An employer is entitled to take into account an employee's misconduct even if a warning for it has expired under the employer's procedure. In *Airbus UK Ltd v Webb* [2008] IRLR 309, Mr Webb, in August 2004, received a final warning for gross misconduct for fraudulent use of company time. The letter confirmed that the warning would be placed on his personal file for twelve months and would be subsequently removed, provided that his conduct reached certain standards. The letter concluded that the likely consequence of further misconduct was dismissal. About three weeks after the expiry of that warning, he and four others working on the night shift were found to be watching television outside of the normal break time. He was dismissed for gross misconduct but the other four were not. The Court of Appeal decided that the lapsed warning might be taken into account. Mummery LJ said (at para 74) 'The relevance of the previous misconduct and the expired warning was to the reasonableness of the response of Airbus to the later misconduct, that is, whether dismissal of Mr Webb was within the range of reasonable responses' (cf *Diosynth Ltd v Thomson* [2006] IRLR 284).

The general requirement of a warning represents one of the most important improve- **14.179** ments in the employee's protection from the law of wrongful dismissal, so that instead of summary dismissal, the employee is to be given a reasonable opportunity to improve. Disciplinary procedures should ensure that, except for gross misconduct, no employees should be dismissed for a first breach of discipline. This is particularly important where a rule has lain dormant for a considerable time (*Wilcox v Humphreys & Glasgow* [1975] ICR 333. See also *Ayub v Vauxhall Motors Ltd* [1978] IRLR 428).

Many disciplinary procedures have provisions for appeals to be heard against a warning. **14.180** There is, however, no general rule that an employee may not be dismissed while his final warning is under appeal (*Stein v Associated Dairies Ltd* [1982] IRLR 447). The tribunal is not to sit in judgement on whether the employee should or should not have received such warning. Rather, it is sufficient that the final warning has been issued in good faith and that there was at least prima facie ground for following the procedure. If, however, there was anything to suggest that the warning had been issued for an oblique motive or that it was manifestly inappropriate, the tribunal could take that into account in reaching its general decision on fairness (*Tower Hamlets Health Authority v Anthony* [1989] IRLR 394). It was not open to the tribunal to reopen a final warning when it came to consider dismissal unless it was given in bad faith (*General Dynamics Information Technology Ltd v Carranza* [2015] ICR 169).

Hearings

The principle that there should be a meeting to discuss misconduct was given statutory **14.181** support in Sch 2 to the Employment Act 2002 but after 6 April 2009 this was replaced by a requirement to abide by the new ACAS Code of Practice in default of which the tribunal might award up to a maximum of 25 per cent uplift (see 14.356). In the normal case the following aspects are required for hearings to be fair:

> To explain the purpose of the meeting; identify those present; if appropriate, arrange rep-
> resentation; inform the employee of the allegation or allegations being made; indicate the
> evidence, whether in statement form or by the calling of witnesses; allow the employee and
> representatives to ask questions; ask whether the employee wishes any witnesses to be called;
> allow the employee or the representative to explain and argue the case; listen to the argument
> from both sides upon the allegations and any possible consequences, including any mitiga-
> tion; ask the employee whether there is any further evidence or enquiry which he considers
> could help his case. (*Clark v Civil Aviation Authority* [1991] IRLR 412 at para 20.)

The right for the employee to be heard before dismissal is one of the most important ele- **14.182** ments in the natural justice which is an inherent part of unfair dismissal law. Its remit is to consider whether the allegations of misconduct or incapability are proved, and, if so, what should be the proper penalty. The following principles have been established in the cases although each case depends ultimately on its own facts:

(a) The hearing should be conducted as fairly as possible in the circumstances, but the EAT has been anxious to guard against the rigid imposition of judicial-style proceedings in inappropriate domestic situations. The operation of the hearing requirements can be seen in two contrasting cases. In *Bentley Engineering Co v Mistry* [1979] ICR 47, the dismissal was unfair because the employee did not know what evidence the employers had against her when she approached the 'hearing'. On the other hand, in *Khanum v Mid-Glamorgan AHA* [1978] IRLR 215, the lack of opportunity to cross-examine and to see statements of witnesses to alleged misconduct did not render the hearing unfair (see *Ulsterbus Ltd v Henderson* [1989] IRLR 251; *Santamera v Express Cargo Forwarding* [2003] IRLR 273). The EAT in *Khanum* summarised the three guiding principles:

   (i)   that the employee should know of the accusations he has to meet (see also *Bell v Devon & Cornwall Police Authority* [1978] IRLR 283);

   (ii) that he should be given an opportunity to state his case; and

   (iii) that the internal tribunal act in good faith.

(b) A dismissal may be unfair because the hearing of a complaint against the applicant was conducted in breach of the rules of natural justice. In *Moyes v Hylton Castle Working Men's Social Club & Institute Ltd* [1986] IRLR 482, two officials of the employer, a working men's club, acted as witnesses of the incidents of sexual harassment and later as judges of the truth of the allegations by sitting on the committees which took the decision to dismiss. The EAT decided that such a procedure rendered the procedure unfair.

(c) A hearing is completely useless if it is not held *before* the final decision to dismiss is taken (*Earl v Slater & Wheeler Airlyne) Ltd* [1972] IRLR 115; *Clarke v Trimoco Motor Group Ltd* [1993] ICR 238); and (probably) it is to be heard by those who will actually take that decision (*Budgen & Co v Thomas* [1976] IRLR 174).

(d) A hearing should take place as soon as possible after the alleged misdemeanour; thus a delay of nine months was severely criticised in *Distillers Co (Bottling Services) Ltd v Gardner* [1982] IRLR 47.

(e) The employee should have the opportunity to present mitigation of penalty as well as arguments on 'liability' for the misconduct (*Siggs & Chapman (Contractors) Ltd v Knight* [1984] IRLR 83).

(f) A hearing may proceed in the absence of the employee provided that he or she has been given fair and proper opportunity to attend, especially if represented (*Pirelli General Cable Works Ltd v Murray* [1979] IRLR 190). It should, however, be adjourned if the employee is not in a fit state to go through with it (*Tesco Group of Companies (Holdings) Ltd v Hill* [1977] IRLR 63) although there is no obligation in every case to postpone it until criminal proceedings have ended which may be years later.

(g) If an employee chooses to say nothing because it might prejudice a pending criminal case, the dismissal may still be fair provided that he has been given the opportunity to present his case (see *Murray v British Rail* [1976] IRLR 382).

(h) The presence of the police at an internal inquiry without the claimant's foreknowledge and consent would be wholly improper (*Read v Phoenix Preservation Ltd* [1985] IRLR 93).

(i) An employee should always be informed of allegations against him. In *Pritchett & Dyjasek v J. McIntyre Ltd* [1987] IRLR 18, the Court of Appeal held that the tribunal's conclusion that the employers had evidence which was so clear and overwhelming that a reasonable employer could assume that there was no sensible possibility of an explanation or mitigating circumstances being advanced, was perverse (see *Spink v Express Food Group Ltd* [1990] IRLR 320). In *Coxon v Rank Xerox (UK) Ltd* [2003] ICR 628 a dismissal was unfair because it was based on unparticularised allegations of gross misconduct and breach of trust. The charge against the individual should be precisely framed and the evidence should be confined to the particulars given in that charge (*Strouthos v London Underground Ltd* [2004] IRLR 636).

(j) The employee should also see any written statements where an employer intends to rely on the same in disciplinary proceedings, and any other procedure would be prima facie unfair (*Louies v Coventry Hood and Seating Co* [1990] IRLR 324). Where there had been an investigation which had led to a belief that there had been misconduct on the part of the employee, the subsequent dismissal procedure had to be conducted in such a way that the fairness of the procedure balanced the initial belief of misconduct.

(k) A failure to keep notes at a hearing and to provide them to the employee during the hearing may be a procedural error (*Vauxhall Motors Ltd v Ghafoor* [1993] ICR 376).

(l) In *Whitbread plc v Hall* [2001] ICR 699, the tribunal found that the dismissing officer had acted as complainant, judge, and jury and failed to consider any penalty other than dismissal. The band of reasonable responses applied to both procedural and substantive complaints, and there was open to the tribunal the possibility of a finding of unfair dismissal even though the employee had admitted the complaints against him.

The right to be represented

The employee has a concomitant right, which is the right to be accompanied at a hear- **14.183** ing by a trade union representative or fellow employee; and because of the sensitivity of the shop steward's position no disciplinary dismissal should be implemented without the involvement, usually at the hearing stage, of a senior trade union representative or full-time official. Again, however, the lack of this representation by itself is unlikely to make the dismissal unfair (*Bailey v BP Oil Ltd* [1980] IRLR 287). This right is now enshrined in statute (s 10 of the Employment Relations Act 1999).

The recognised exceptions to the right to a hearing include cases where: **14.184**

(a) 'The employee, as part of the conduct complained of, states in terms why he adopted that attitude [and] it is clear that this is the employee's considered view and not merely the result of a passing emotion', or the conduct is of such a nature that whatever his explanation, his continued employment is not in the interests of the employer's business (*James v Waltham Holy Cross UDC* [1973] ICR 398).

(b) A serious theft has been admitted by the employee (*Carr v Alexander Russell Ltd* [1976] IRLR 220), or conversely where the employee so strongly denies the matter to the police that an internal opportunity to state his case would not advance matters further (*Conway v Matthew Wright & Nephew Ltd* [1977] IRLR 89).

(c) The circumstances were so grievous (ie in the instant case five serious and costly errors) that although an explanation might conceivably have been produced, it was wildly unlikely that it would be (*Lowndes v Specialist Heavy Engineering* [1976] IRLR 246; see also *Cardiff City Council v Condé* [1978] IRLR 218).

(d) The employee was reasonably required to work overtime and was dismissed on refusal (*Martin v Solus Schall* [1979] IRLR 7).

Appeals

There should be an appeal from an initial decision to dismiss. This was given statutory **14.185** support in Sch 2 to the Employment Act 2002 but after 6 April 2009 this was replaced by a general requirement to follow the ACAS Code of Practice. The general terms of an appeal procedure should be stated in the written statement of terms (ERA 1996, s 3(1)(a)).

14.186 The importance of a properly conducted appeals procedure was emphasised in *Whitbread & Co plc v Mills* [1988] IRLR 501. The EAT held that in certain circumstances, defects in disciplinary and dismissal procedures may be remedied on appeal but whether they are so corrected depends on the degree of unfairness at the original hearing. If it is to remedy procedural defects at that hearing, the appeal must be of a comprehensive nature, that is in essence a rehearing and not merely a review. Wood J said that while a minor departure from a contractual appeal process may be ignored, a total failure to comply with it may entitle an employment tribunal to find the dismissal unfair (see also *Qualcast (Wolverhampton) Ltd v Ross* [1979] IRLR 98).

14.187 In *Sartor v P&O European Ferries Ltd* [1992] IRLR 273, a defect could not be cured since the manager hearing the appeal had already been involved in earlier stages of the disciplinary process. Where the first stage of the disciplinary process is seriously flawed it is essential, if the appellate process is to be treated as establishing fairness, that it should be able to stand on its own merits as conferring on the employee all the rights which should have been accorded at the initial stage, especially proper notice of the complaint and a proper opportunity to state the employee's case. A review would be insufficient (*Clark v Civil Aviation Authority* [1992] IRLR 503; *Byrne v BOC Ltd* [1994] IRLR 505).

14.188 Normally the person taking an appeal should be more senior than the employee who decided on dismissal, but the dismissal can be fair notwithstanding that this did not happen (*Adeshina v St George's University Hospitals NHS Foundation Trust* [2015] IRLR 704). Here the appeal process was sufficient to cure earlier irregularities.

14.189 The following propositions appear from the cases:

(a) An employee should be *informed* of his right to appeal (*Tesco Group of Companies (Holdings) Ltd v Hill* [1977] IRLR 63) and have the right to be *represented* (*Rank Xerox (UK) Ltd v Goodchild* [1979] IRLR 185).

(b) The appeal body should be composed of *different persons* from those who took the original decision to dismiss (*Johnson Matthey Metals Ltd v Harding* [1978] IRLR 248).

(c) An employer need not grant the employee's request to be accompanied by his solicitor.

(d) In small companies, to provide an appeal at all where there is only one level of management may prove an 'Elysian standard' (eg *Tiptools Ltd v Curtis* [1973] IRLR 276).

(e) A full judicial-style hearing is unnecessary. The procedure adopted in *Rowe v Radio Rentals Ltd* [1982] IRLR 177 thus did not conflict with the rules of natural justice, even though the person hearing the appeal had been informed of the decision to dismiss before it took place, and the person who took that decision was also present throughout the appeal hearing. Such a procedure should not be cramped by legal requirements imposing impossible burdens on companies in the conduct of their affairs. Nevertheless, any previous dealings with the claimants by those hearing the appeal should be made known to the employee.

(f) The cutting short of an appellate process by way of a dismissal effected before a decision is given by the person hearing the appeal is a procedural defect in itself (*Rao v Civil Aviation Authority* [1992] IRLR 203).

(g) Failure by the employee to appeal does not constitute acquiescence in the decision to dismiss (*Chrystie v Rolls Royce Ltd* [1976] IRLR 336) although in one case it indicated a failure to mitigate loss (*Hoover Ltd v Forde* [1980] ICR 239).

(h) The employer is expected to comply with the full requirements of an appeal procedure in its own disciplinary code (*Stoker v Lancashire County Council* [1992] IRLR 75); but the fact that the appeal procedure provided by the employer's disciplinary code has not been followed to the letter does not mean that the decision to dismiss is necessarily unfair (*Westminster City Council v Cabaj* [1996] IRLR 399; *Blundell v Christie Hospital NHS Trust* [1996] ICR 347).

The fact that the appeal takes place *after* the effective date of termination does not mean **14.190** that it should be ignored in relation to the fairness of the dismissal (*Rank Xerox (UK) Ltd v Goodchild* [1979] IRLR 185); and there are specific provisions on compensation in the case of an employee who fails to use an appeal procedure which is available to him (see 14.356).

J REDUNDANCY

The definition of redundancy is in s 139 of the ERA 1996. The presumption that a dis- **14.191** missal is for redundancy unless it is proved otherwise does not, however, apply in unfair dismissal cases as it does where a statutory redundancy payment is claimed. There are three primary ways in which a redundancy dismissal may be unfair:

(a) Selection for redundancy by reason of membership of, or activities at an appropriate time in, an independent trade union, or because he was not a member of any trade union or of one of a number of particular trade unions, or had refused or proposed to refuse to become or remain a member, is a protected or opted-out shop worker, was a trustee of an occupational pension scheme or an employee representative, has asserted a relevant statutory right or has acted in connection with recognition of a trade union, or is a part-time worker (ERA 1996, s 105). The burden of proof here is heavy on the claimant (*Taylor v Butler Machine Tool Ltd* [1976] IRLR 133), and it is more appropriately discussed in connection with the general question of dismissal for trade union activities.

(b) The *general reasonableness* test posited by s 98(4) of the ERA 1996, for all cases of unfair dismissal; for the employment tribunal must still consider, even in the absence of any agreed procedure, whether the employer 'acted reasonably ... in treating [re-dundancy] as a sufficient reason for dismissing the employee' (14.191ff).

(c) Selection of a woman for redundancy because she is pregnant and will require mater-nity leave is dismissal for a 'reason connected with her pregnancy' within s 99 of the ERA 1996 and is automatically unfair (*Brown v Stockton on Tees BC* [1988] IRLR 263).

The employer does not have to justify his declaration of redundancy itself unless it **14.192** is an obvious sham (*Goodwin Ltd v Fitzmaurice* [1977] IRLR 393). Thus, in *Moon v Homeworthy Furniture (Northern) Ltd* [1977] ICR 117, the employees claimed that there was no true redundancy because the factory from which they were dismissed was still economically viable. Kilner Brown J thought that if the courts were to decide such questions they would be in danger of being utilised as a forum for the decisions as to industrial disputes. Therefore 'there could not ... be any investigation into the rights and wrongs of the declared redundancy' (see also *Campbell v Dunoon & Cowal Housing Association Ltd* [1993] IRLR 496). These are the outer limits of non-intervention.

In *Ladbroke Courage Holidays Ltd v Asten* [1981] IRLR 59, the EAT required that if the **14.193** employer sought to give as a reason for dismissal that he needed to reduce his wage costs he should produce evidence of the need for economy; while Slynn J in *Orr v Vaughan* [1981] IRLR 63 thought that the employer must act on reasonable information which was properly acquired when choosing a method of reorganisation.

14.194   An employer used to be deemed to be acting unfairly if employees were selected for redundancy in breach of a customary arrangement or agreed procedure, where 'the circumstances constituting the redundancy applied equally to one or more employees in the same undertaking who held positions similar to that held by [the applicant]'. This was repealed, however, by the Deregulation and Contracting Out Act 1994. Tribunals may, however, treat a failure to follow agreed or customary procedure as a factor in establishing unfairness of dismissal pursuant to the ERA 1996, s 98(4).

Reasonableness: The residuary question

14.195   'In the case of redundancy, the employer will normally not act reasonably unless he warns and consults any employees affected or their representative, adopts a fair basis on which to select for redundancy, and takes such steps as may be reasonable to avoid or minimise redundancy by redeployment within his own organisation' (Lord Bridge in *Polkey v Dayton Services Ltd* [1988] ICR 142).

14.196   The manner in which tribunals should approach the residuary question of reasonableness under s 98(4) in the case of redundancy is highly controversial. In *Atkinson v George Lindsay & Co* [1980] IRLR 196, the Court of Session thought that it would 'in most cases be extremely difficult for any tribunal to hold' that a dismissal was unfair under this general test if it survived the agreed selection hurdle. These cases have tended to treat the employer as though he were an administrative agency whose decisions in this respect should be challenged only *in extremis*. The same test of perversity has been applied here as to judicial review of administrative action. This is notwithstanding the unambiguously objective terms of the general test of reasonableness in unfair dismissal. It does, however, reflect the limited options open to an employer at a time of crisis. Thus, in *Vickers Ltd v Smith* [1977] IRLR 11, the EAT thought that the tribunal should have asked 'whether the decision of management was so wrong that no sensible or reasonable management could have arrived at the decision which the employers [reached]'. In *Jackson v General Accident, Fire and Life Assurance Co Ltd* [1977] IRLR 338, Lord Macdonald commented, 'whilst where the ground of dismissal is capability or conduct and there has been some procedural failure ... it can readily be seen how the employer could be held to have acted unreasonably ... it is not so easy to envisage this where the ground is redundancy' (see *Valor Newhome Ltd v Hampson* [1982] ICR 407).

14.197   This trend appeared to be halted in *Williams v Compair Maxam Ltd* [1982] IRLR 83, where the EAT laid down guidelines of good industrial practice in redundancies. The tribunal was directed to consider in each case whether objective selection criteria were chosen and fairly applied, whether the possibility of transfer to other work was investigated, whether employees were warned and consulted, and whether the union (if there was one) was consulted over the most equitable manner of implementing the redundancies. The background in the *Compair Maxam* case was a major redundancy in an employer with a recognised union.

14.198   Notwithstanding that the case was approved by the Northern Ireland Court of Appeal in *Robinson v Carrickfergus BC* [1983] IRLR 122, Lord Macdonald thought that the guidelines were 'becoming overworked and increasingly misapplied' in cases of small non-unionised employers such as in *Simpson v Reid & Findlater* [1983] IRLR 401. The facts of the case concerned the dismissal of two out of three employees. In such a context the EAT felt that the guidelines should not be used by tribunals 'like a shopping list'. Further, in *Buchanan v Tilcon Ltd* [1983] IRLR 417, the Court of Session reverted to the restrictive approach of the *Jackson* case (see also *Eaton Ltd v King* [1995] IRLR 75).

These latter cases also questioned the appropriateness of the appeal tribunal's role in offering guidelines at all in the light of certain Court of Appeal *dicta*. Browne-Wilkinson J, however, defended this role for the EAT in *Grundy (Teddington) Ltd v Plummer and Salt* [1983] ICR 367 on the ground that it was a useful and proper part of the appeal tribunal's function in a limited number of cases to give guidance on the general approach as to what constitutes reasonable conduct (see also *Gray v Shetland Norse Preserving Co Ltd* [1985] IRLR 53; *Rolls Royce Motors Ltd v Dewhurst* [1985] IRLR 184). More recently, however, in *Langston v Cranfield University* [1998] IRLR 172, the EAT held that the *Compair Maxam* guidelines are so fundamental that they should be treated as being in issue in every unfair dismissal case by reason of redundancy, and the tribunal should consider them even if they are not specifically raised by the employee. The Court of Appeal has since emphasised that it was inappropriate for an employment tribunal to place the bar so high that it asked whether the employer acted in bad faith (*Northgate HR Ltd v Mercy* [2008] IRLR 222). In *Morgan v Welsh Rugby Union* [2011] IRLR 376, the *Williams* guidelines were understood to be not principles of law but rather the standards of behaviour to be applied in most cases. Only in those situations where there is genuine perversity would the factors be directly relevant. Interview processes involving an employer's assessment of which candidate will best perform the new role are likely to involve a substantial element of judgement with which the tribunal is unlikely to interfere. **14.199**

Criteria of selection

In an important statement of principle, in *British Aerospace Ltd v Green* [1995] IRLR 433, the Court of Appeal said that: **14.200**

> ... in general the employer who sets up a system of selection which can reasonably be described as fair and applies it without any overt sign of conduct which mars its fairness will have done all that the law requires of him ... The tribunal is not entitled to embark upon a re-assessment exercise ... it is sufficient for the employer to show that he set up a good system of selection and that it was fairly administered, and that ordinarily there is no need for the employer to justify all the assessments on which the selection for redundancy was based.

This demonstrates the generally laissez-faire approach which has been taken by appeal courts over many years to employers' decisions on redundancy selection.

The employer should, however, have some settled criteria for the selection of employees to be dismissed. In *Compair Maxam*, the criterion used for selection was of those employees 'who in the opinion of the managers concerned would be able to keep the company viable'. This, above all, rendered unfair the dismissals, because the criteria should be capable of being objectively checked against such matters as attendance record, job efficiency, experience, and/or length of service. In *Cox v Wildt Mellor Bromley Ltd* [1978] IRLR 157, the EAT held that the employer must 'show how the employee came to be dismissed for redundancy, upon what basis the selection was made and how it was applied in practice' (see also *Greig v Sir Alfred McAlpine & Son (Northern) Ltd* [1979] IRLR 372; *Graham v ABF Ltd* [1986] IRLR 90). On the other hand, the question for the tribunal should be whether 'the selection [was] one which a reasonable employer could have made, not would we have made that selection' (*BL Cars v Lewis* [1983] IRLR 58). The tribunal should not simply substitute its decision for that of the employer. **14.201**

The pool of selection must be reasonably defined, so that in *GEC Machines Ltd v Gilford* [1982] ICR 725, selection from a section rather than the whole department was held to be unfair since the work was interchangeable between employees within the department. **14.202**

The idea that the employer has to produce direct evidence to support his selection received some support in *John Brown Engineering Ltd v Brown* [1997] IRLR 90. Lord Johnston in the EAT stated that a policy decision to withhold all markings in a particular selection process may result in individual unfairness and, in choosing not to publish 'league tables', the employer must run the risk that he is not acting fairly in respect of individual employees.

14.203   The following matters have also been considered in the cases:

(a) **Attendance figures** Employers often use comparative attendance figures as a criterion for selection for redundancy but where they do so, they must go further and ascertain the *reason* for the absence. It is unfair to dismiss without such investigation (*Paine and Moore v Grundy (Teddington) Ltd* [1981] IRLR 267). Unlike in a case of dismissal for misconduct or incapability, the employer need not, however, warn an employee that his poor attendance may lead to his being selected for redundancy (*Gray v Shetland Norse Preserving Co Ltd* [1985] IRLR 53).

(b) **'Bumping'** An employer may decide to declare the redundancy not in the section in which the work requirements have themselves diminished but instead to move employees from other sections to cover that work and make the redundancies elsewhere in the establishment. Thus, in *Thomas & Betts Manufacturing Co Ltd v Harding* [1980] IRLR 255, the Court of Appeal approved a tribunal decision that a woman who was employed making fittings and had two years' employment was unfairly dismissed where a packer who had served for a few weeks was retained (see also *Forman Construction Ltd v Kelly* [1977] IRLR 469). The Scottish EAT, however, has held that this was not necessarily a general 'hard and fast' principle which must be followed in every case (*Green v A & I Fraser (Wholesale Fish Merchants) Ltd* [1985] IRLR 55).

(c) **Participating in a strike** In *Cruikshank v Hobbs* [1977] ICR 725, a redundancy arose after a dispute at the employer's Newmarket racing stables. The employer chose five out of the six stable lads who had gone on strike, and the EAT thought that this was a fair reaction, having regard to the loyalty of the other twenty-four lads shown during the dispute. The result would have been different, however, if the redundancy had been merely a pretext to remove the strikers.

(d) **Last in first out** This is the criterion which is most often advocated by trade unions, but employers are often reluctant to accede to it on the ground that after a redundancy, it will leave them with the oldest and least fit workers. The Court of Appeal commented in *Bessenden Properties Ltd v Corness* [1977] ICR 821 that, 'it is generally regarded as fair to retain the services of that employee who has been longest in service'. Employers often temper this by the need to maintain a balanced workforce or by taking into account attendance and conduct records, and in recent times tribunals have been reluctant to criticise an employer's selection unless it is manifestly unfair.

(e) **Discriminatory selection** Selection which is unlawful because it is on one of the protected grounds will probably render the dismissal unfair as well as entitling the dismissed employee to claim under the Equality Act. This applies to indirect as well as direct discrimination, as seen in *Clarke v Eley (IMI) Kynoch Ltd* [1982] IRLR 482. The EAT decided that the commonly applied criterion of dismissing part-time workers first was indirectly discriminatory against women since a considerably smaller proportion of women than men could comply. In *Kidd v DRG (UK) Ltd* [1985] IRLR 90, however, the EAT decided that dismissal of a part-time employee before full-timers was not discriminatory, and even if it had been, it would have been justifiable because of the marginal advantages in cost and efficiency involved in operating one shift.

In *Pinewood Repro Ltd v Page* [2011] ICR 508, the EAT stated that it might be too broad **14.204** a principle to require in every case an employer to provide an explanation of why an individual had received the redundancy scores which he had been awarded. Fair consultation included the provision of adequate information on which an employee could respond and argue his case.

There is no absolute requirement for a right of appeal in a selection case (*Robinson v* **14.205** *Ulster Carpet Mills Ltd* [1991] IRLR 348), although giving an appeal may remedy defects in procedure which arise at an earlier stage (*Lloyd v Taylor Woodrow Construction Ltd* [1999] IRLR 782).

Consultation

According to the *Compair Maxam* case, the employer must consult the union as to the **14.206** best means by which the desired management result of redundancies can be achieved with as little hardship to the employees as possible. This principle receives specific statutory embodiment in the TULR(C)A 1992. An employee who is affected by such failure is entitled to compensation by way of a protective award (Chapter 17).

The EAT, in *Mugford v Midland Bank plc* [1997] IRLR 209, considered the existing **14.207** authorities relating to consultation and laid down the following principles:

(a) where no consultation of any kind has taken place, the dismissal will normally be unfair, unless the tribunal finds that a reasonable employer would have concluded that consultation would be an utterly futile exercise in that particular case;
(b) consultation with the trade union over selection criteria does not of itself release the employer from considering with the employee individually, who is identified for redundancy; and
(c) it will be a question of fact and degree for the tribunal to consider whether consultation with the individual and/or his union was so inadequate as to render his dismissal unfair, viewing the overall picture up to the date of termination.

Consultation is 'one of the fundamentals of fairness' (*Holden v Bradville Ltd* [1985] **14.208** IRLR 483; cf *F. Lafferty Construction Ltd v Duthie* [1985] IRLR 487). To fail to consult is not a matter of mere discourtesy to the employee, but rather it deprives the employer of the opportunity to consider whether there may be another slot for the worker to fit into (*Abbots & Standley v Wesson-Glynwed Steels Ltd* [1982] IRLR 51) and how he might ameliorate the blow for the employee (*Graham v ABF Ltd* [1986] IRLR 90; *Freud v Bentalls Ltd* [1982] IRLR 443). Even the small size of an employer cannot excuse it from making any effort at all to consult over a redundancy (eg *De Grasse v Stockwell Tools Ltd* [1992] IRLR 269), although a long drawn-out process will not then be required. A procedural defect in failing to consult might be cured at an appeal stage if the appeal is a rehearing (*Lloyd v Taylor Woodrow Construction Ltd* [1999] IRLR 782).

The Court of Session, in *King v Eaton Ltd* [1996] IRLR 199, ruled that the union should **14.209** be consulted at a time when it could influence the criteria for selection and not after the criteria have been set in stone. Consultation may, however, be held to be utterly futile (*Polkey v Dayton Services Ltd* [1988] ICR 142; see also *Huddersfield Parcels Ltd v Sykes* [1981] IRLR 115).

Alternative employment

The principle that the employer should take reasonable steps to seek alternative employ- **14.210** ment for his employees was first enunciated in *Vokes Ltd v Bear* [1974] ICR 1. This was a strong case for the employee since the respondent company was part of a large group of companies in which there existed several vacancies in the type of senior management positions which the claimant had occupied before his redundancy. The failure to offer such a position rendered the dismissal unfair. A contrasting case is *MDH Ltd v Sussex* [1986] IRLR 123, where the claimant was employed by Dent & Hellyer Ltd, which was also part of the same group as in *Vokes*. Dent & Hellyer was merged with another company to form MDH Ltd. When the applicant was made redundant the tribunal thought that there was an obligation to look for alternative opportunities *throughout* the Tilling Group. The EAT thought that this was an error of law.

14.211   In *British United Shoe Machinery Co Ltd v Clarke* [1977] IRLR 297, the EAT counselled against unreal or 'Elysian standards' being expected of an employer, and in *Barratt Construction Ltd v Dalrymple* [1984] IRLR 385, the Scottish EAT decided that the appellant employer did not have to look for alternatives in other parts of the Barratt group for more junior jobs than that which the employee had occupied. Lord Macdonald thought that the change in the onus of proof in s 57(3) of EPCA 1978 (now ERA 1996, s 98(4)) had altered the scope of the *Vokes* principle, and:

> Without laying down any hard and fast rule we are inclined to think that where an employee at senior management level who is being made redundant is prepared to accept a subordinate position he ought, in fairness, to make it clear at an early stage so as to give his employer an opportunity to see if this is a feasible solution.

(Cf *Avonmouth Construction Co Ltd v Shipway* [1979] IRLR 14, *Modern Injection Moulds Ltd v Price* [1976] ICR 370.) An employer who can offer alternative employment must make any such offer sufficiently clear so that an employee may make an informed decision. In some cases, this obligation to consider offering alternative work has meant that another employee has to be dismissed (*Thomas & Betts Manufacturing Co Ltd v Harding* [1980] IRLR 255).

14.212   The Court of Appeal has indicated that an employer only has a duty to provide such alternative employment as is available whilst the employee remains in the employment of the employer. In *Octavius Atkinson & Sons Ltd v Morris* [1989] IRLR 158, new employment became available in between the employee leaving work, having been summarily dismissed, and arriving at his home on the same day. Although the EAT had found that the employee remained in employment until he reached home, the Court of Appeal held that the employers had acted reasonably in not offering the employee the alternative employment.

K SOME OTHER SUBSTANTIAL REASON

14.213   This provision has been variously described as a 'dustbin category' or 'employer's charter', although it was intended as a safety net to catch substantial reasons for dismissal which did not fall within other potentially fair gateways to dismissal. It has a 'rubber band' quality which arguably has been stretched too far (see J Bowers and A Clarke, 10 ILJ 34). Its language is indeed rather wider than the provisions of ILO Recommendation No 119 on which most of the unfair dismissal legislation was based.

14.214   The test was explained by the Court of Appeal in *Kent CC v Gilham* [1985] IRLR 16 as follows:

> The hurdle over which an employer has to jump at this stage of an enquiry into an unfair dismissal complaint is designed to deter employers from dismissing employees for some trivial

or unworthy reason. If he does so, the dismissal is deemed unfair without the need to look further into its merits. But if on the face of it the reason *could* justify the dismissal, then it passes as a substantial reason, and the enquiry moves on to [s 98(4)] and the question of reasonableness.

According to Sir John Donaldson MR, 'different types of reason could justify the dismissal of the office boy from those which could justify the dismissal of the managing director' (see also *Harper v National Coal Board* [1980] IRLR 260). Very few reasons have failed this preliminary test because they are not substantial and there is a tendency in this area to conflate the issue of 'other substantial reason' with the question of whether the employer acted reasonably. **14.215**

These, and other, developments have important implications for the whole policy of unfair dismissal. For the delicate balance at its heart between employer and employee may thus be subtly tilted in favour of the employer. Central to this imbalance is the fact that rejection of management-instituted reorganisation is often portrayed as an undesirable curb on employer prerogative. **14.216**

In three respects, subsequent judgments have not lived up to what general statements there have been in the NIRC and EAT about 'some other substantial reason'. Most importantly, Brightman J in *RS Components Ltd v Irwin* [1973] ICR 535, while deciding that the subsection was not to be construed *ejusdem generis* with the other headings, did go on to say that: 'It ought not as a matter of good industrial relations and common fairness to be construed too widely against the employee.' Subsequently, however, a conglomeration of reasons, usually flowing from management-pronounced notions of 'business efficiency', have come through the wide-open door. **14.217**

Secondly, the NIRC was at pains to keep distinct the separate issue of the employer's reasons for dismissal and the reasonableness thereof. In *Mercia Rubber Mouldings v Lingwood* [1974] IRLR 82, Donaldson J commented: 'The reason must be one which can justify dismissal, not one which *does* justify the dismissal.' This has proved rather easier to formulate than apply, as demonstrated by the relative paucity of cases in which 'another substantial reason' has been found, and yet the dismissal has been subsequently held unfair. **14.218**

Thirdly, although the EAT roundly declared in *Trusthouse Forte Leisure Ltd v Aquilar* [1976] IRLR 251, that 'the employer's description of the reason for dismissal is by no means conclusive', this principle has recently been honoured more in the breach than in its observance. The most extreme expression of non-intervention is to be found in the acceptance by tribunals of the employer's policy on reorganisation. As Arnold J formulated it in *Banerjee v City and East London AHA* [1979] IRLR 147 (at para 19): **14.219**

> If an employer comes and says 'we have evolved such and such a policy' ... it seems to us that it must inevitably follow that this enunciation by the employer of the policy as a matter of importance ... can be seen to be the subject of a substantial other reason.

The reasons laid down by statute as being substantial reasons are dismissals of employees: **14.220**

(a) taken on temporarily to replace permanent employees who are medically suspended or pregnant (in both cases the replacement must be warned of the temporary nature of the job on engagement (ERA 1996, s 106)); and

(b) where there are 'economic, technical or organisational reason[s] entailing [a change] in the workforce of either the transferor or transferee before or after a relevant transfer' on a transfer of undertaking (reg 7(2) of the Transfer of Undertakings (Protection of Employment) Regulations 2006).

14.221 If an employer wishes to rely on this reason for dismissal, he must expressly raise it before the tribunal, or at the very least relate the full facts establishing it before the tribunal (*Murphy v Epsom College* [1983] IRLR 395).

14.222 The five most important categories of cases under this rubric are as follows.

Quasi or reorganisational redundancy

14.223 It is in the area of 'quasi redundancies', that is, reorganisations which fail to satisfy the detailed requirements of ss 135 and 139 of the ERA 1996 for redundancy, that the EAT has found most scope for a dynamic interpretation of s 98(1)(b). It has allowed the undertaking which reorganises or regroups, and finds that it has 'surplus staff', to escape both redundancy payments and unfair dismissal. That there should be some flexibility for employers to reorganise cannot be gainsaid, but it may be argued that the threshold for use of this heading has been lowered.

14.224 When this notion crystallised is difficult to pinpoint. Phillips J in *Gorman v London Computer Training Centre* [1978] IRLR 22, however, dwelt on the 'clear distinction' recognised between redundancy (s 98(2)(c)) and quasi 'redundancy' (s 98(1)(b)). The learned judge said:

> An employer may say 'I was overmanned, so we had to get rid of someone so A and B had to go, they were redundant.' The wording of [now ERA 1996, s 139] may show he was wrong, but these grounds may well form a substantial reason.

14.225 It is difficult to define the criteria attached to reorganisation beyond the need for a 'policy', and 'this is not an onus which it is at all difficult to discharge'. Only where there is no evidence at all is the claim open to challenge. In *Banerjee v City and East London AHA* [1979] IRLR 147, a consultancy had been held jointly by two part-time employees. One left and the Authority decided to create a single full-time appointment so that the claimant Dr Banerjee, the other part-timer, was consequently dismissed. The defendant stated that this was determined in accordance with its 'policy of rationalisation, and the custom and practice of amalgamating part-time posts', but the EAT thought that was not enough and called on the Authority to produce relevant minutes of meetings to prove that due consideration had been given to all relevant matters in formulating the policy. There was no evidence of this at all.

14.226 Once there is evidence of a policy, however, the next stage which would appear crucial to the substantiality of the reason has become much less strict over time. In *Ellis v Brighton Co-operative Society* [1976] IRLR 419, there was a properly consulted-upon and trade union-agreed reorganisation which, if not done, would 'bring the whole business to a standstill'. In *Robinson v British Island Airways Ltd* [1978] ICR 304, the EAT required a 'pressing business reason', and in *Hollister v NFU* [1979] ICR 542, the Court of Appeal pointed to the necessity for a 'sound good business reason'. After *Banerjee*, however, all that need be shown is that the changes were considered to be 'matters of importance' or to have 'discernible advantages to the organisation'. The EAT in *Bowater Containers Ltd v McCormack* [1980] IRLR 50 required that the reorganisation be 'beneficial' (see also *Genower v Ealing, Hammersmith & Hounslow AHA* [1980] IRLR 297).

14.227 It was in *Hollister v NFU* (above) that the Court of Appeal formalised the close relation between reorganisation and managerial prerogative. The appellant was one of the respondent union's group secretaries, and received a modest wage and commission on insurance policies sold. The union reorganised its business in a drastic way, so that insurance was no longer dealt with locally, and the appellant's income was substantially cut as a result. On his refusal to sign a new contract, he was dismissed. Not only was this found to be 'some other substantial reason', but the Court of Appeal decided that there was no requirement for consultation with the employee.

In this area more than elsewhere, the tribunal has to weigh the economic interests of employer and employee. In *Evans v Elemeta Holdings Ltd* [1982] IRLR 143, the EAT suggested that if it was reasonable for an employee to decline new terms offered by the employer, it would be unreasonable to dismiss him for it. In *Chubb Fire Security Ltd v Harper* [1983] IRLR 311, the EAT dissented from this view, however, and stressed that the only proper question is the reasonableness of the employer's conduct in dismissing: was the employer reasonable in determining that the advantages to it of implementing the proposed reorganisation of terms outweighed any disadvantage it should have foreseen that the employee might suffer? (see also *Richmond Precision Engineering Ltd v Pearce* [1985] IRLR 179).   **14.228**

The crucial question is not the reasonableness of the offer of the new terms but the overall decision to dismiss which follows the refusal to agree to them: to concentrate on the offer may blind the employment tribunal to the important issue of what happened between the time when the offer was made and the dismissal. The proper enquiry, therefore, is whether the *dismissal* was reasonable in all the circumstances, and that would be affected by the question of whether only 1 per cent or as many as 99 per cent of the other employees had accepted the offer. The situation may be one in which the employer's legitimate interests and the employee's equally legitimate interests are irreconcilable, but if there is a sound business reason for the particular reorganisation, the reasonableness of the employer's conduct must be considered in the context of that reorganisation (*St John of God (Care Services) Ltd v Brooks* [1992] IRLR 546). The tribunal should examine the employer's motive for the changes and satisfy itself that they are not to be imposed for arbitrary reasons (*Catamaran Cruisers Ltd v Williams* [1994] IRLR 386). It is also important to bear in mind whether the trade union accepted the changes (*Catamaran Cruisers Ltd*). The EAT did 'not accept as a valid proposition of law that an employer may only offer terms which are less or much less favourable than those which pre-existed if the very survival of his business depends upon acceptance of the terms' (para 19).   **14.229**

Tribunals should scrutinise the basis on which the employer acts to dismiss. In *Orr v Vaughan* [1981] IRLR 63, the EAT stressed that the employer must act on reasonable information which is reasonably acquired as to its business needs. Here, the employer could not be satisfied on the information available that it was at the particular salon where the respondent was employed that the business was losing money. The employer must indeed provide evidence that there was a need for economy there and it is material for the employment tribunal to know whether the company was at the time making profits or losses (*Ladbroke Courage Holidays Ltd v Asten* [1981] IRLR 59).   **14.230**

Where the employer decides to dismiss an employee and uses a reorganisation as a pretext to achieve this covert aim, the dismissal is unfair (*Oakley v The Labour Party* [1988] IRLR 34).   **14.231**

Contractual changes: A blow to the sanctity of contract?

Another frequent use of 'other substantial reason' is where an employer insists on a change in the employee's contractual terms and conditions without a general reorganisation of   **14.232** duties. Thus, in *RS Components Ltd v Irwin* [1973] ICR 535, the company was losing profits because of the activities of some ex-employees who had set up in competition to them. They thus required their ninety-two current salesmen to sign a restrictive covenant. Four refused and the NIRC held their consequent dismissal fair. Brightman J posited:

> a case where it would be essential for employers embarking, for example, on a new technical process to invite existing employees to agree to some reasonable restriction on their use of the knowledge they acquire of the new technique.

14.233 Unfair dismissal provisions have provided no protection against unilateral changes in:

(a) job content (eg *Robinson v Flitwick Frames Ltd* [1975] IRLR 261);
(b) location (eg *Farr v Hoveringham Gravels Ltd* [1972] IRLR 104);
(c) pay (*Industrial Rubber Products Ltd v Gillon* [1977] IRLR 389); and
(d) night shift working (*Martin v Automobile Proprietary Ltd* [1979] IRLR 64).

These cases emphasise that what would be a constructive dismissal is not necessarily unfair (14.11ff). Yet it is ironic that the unfair dismissal provisions, which were intended to give employees broader rights than at common law, should recognise as a reason for dismissal a compulsory change in contractual terms which would be unlawful at common law.

14.234 It is not for the tribunal to decide on the reasonableness of a restrictive covenant which it is proposed to introduce under this rubric (*Willow Oak Developments Ltd v Silverwood* [2006] IRLR 28). If the proposed covenant appears to the tribunal to be plainly unreasonable and was being put forward as all or nothing or not severable, it may be easier for the tribunal to conclude that there was unfairness (see also *Forshaw v Archcraft Ltd* [2005] IRLR 600).

Temporary workers: A recognition of the dangers

14.235 One of the clearest perceptions of British individual employment law is that it provides a form of 'job security' only to employees who have been with the undertaking for more than a minimal amount of time. This principle might be infringed if employees were too readily held to be 'temporary', and thus not deserving of protection. The 'other substantial reason' heading has been at times adopted to cover dismissals of temporary workers, but the dangers of an over-extended definition have been recognised.

14.236 In the leading case, *Terry v East Sussex CC* [1976] ICR 536, the EAT stressed that in every instance the tribunal must ensure that the description was 'a genuine one, where an employee has to his knowledge been employed for a particular job on a temporary basis'. In *Cohen v London Borough of Barking* [1976] IRLR 416 EAT, Slynn J emphasised that, while the fact that the contract was not assured of continuance beyond a fixed term was a material factor to be considered, it was not at all conclusive. The temporary employee ought to be given the opportunity of being considered if a full-time position becomes available (*Beard v St Joseph's School* [1978] ICR 1234), and tribunals must not omit a 'full consideration of the circumstances surrounding a decision to dismiss at the end of a temporary fixed-term contract'. In the case of *North Yorkshire CC v Fay* [1985] IRLR 247 the Court of Appeal dealing with a teacher's contract decided that there was a fair 'other substantial reason' if it is shown that the fixed-term contract was adopted for a genuine purpose and that fact was known to the employee, and that the specific purpose for which the contract was adopted had indeed ceased.

These cases show a welcome recognition of the underlying intentions of the Act, refusing **14.237** to allow 'some other substantial reason' too easily to deny protection for the temporary employee. They need to be considered now in the light of the Fixed Term Employees Regulations which will provide a more direct route for the claimant to succeed (9.17).

Subverting the other gateways: Conduct

The ERA 1996 defines with some particularity conduct, redundancy, and contravention **14.238** of an enactment which may give rise to a fair dismissal, but tribunals have used 'other substantial reason' to extend these concepts. While conduct connotes active behaviour by the employee, 'another substantial reason' includes omissions. In *O'Brien v Prudential Assurance Co Ltd* [1979] IRLR 140, an employee failed to disclose a long period of mental illness when applying for the job and this was some other substantial reason justifying dismissal. The argument that the reason had to be directly referable to the employee's work for the employer failed, as it did in a series of cases in which activities outside and before the job have been included under s 98(1). Some raise philosophical issues about how far the managerial prerogative strays into the employee's private life. The cases include dismissals on the grounds of:

(a) The wish of the employer to appoint his son to the employee's job (*Priddle v Dibble* [1978] ICR 149).
(b) The employee's epileptic attacks which frightened fellow employees (*Harper v National Coal Board* [1980] IRLR 260).
(c) The employee's plan to join another firm (*Davidson and Maillou v Comparisons Ltd* [1980] IRLR 360).
(d) A woman employee's plans to marry a man who worked for a rival travel company (*Skyrail Oceanic v Coleman* [1980] ICR 596), and this fell within the section notwithstanding that the two clerks had no financial interest in their respective companies. It was found to be unfair in all the circumstances, however, because the employer had given no warning of dismissal so that there was no opportunity to find alternative employment.
(e) A breakdown in relationships between employees has often been characterised as some other substantial reason, but the EAT in *Turner v Vestric Ltd* [1980] ICR 528 counselled that the employer must take reasonable steps to try to improve the relationship and examine all options short of dismissal to obviate the situation (see also *Treganowan v Robert Knee* [1975] ICR 405).
(f) A three-month prison sentence for a serious offence (*Kingston v British Railways Board* [1984] IRLR 146).
(g) The employee's husband having been dismissed as bar manager where the employer required a husband and wife team (*Kelman v G. J. Oram* [1983] IRLR 432).
(h) A refusal by the employee to work at weekends (*Yusuf v Aberplace Ltd* [1984] ICR 850).
(i) The removal of an employee who was a chief executive because he ceased to be a director of the company and who under his contract of employment would cease to be chief executive if he ceased to be a director of the company (*Cobley v Forward Technology* [2003] ICR 1051).

(See also *Henderson v Connect (South Tyneside) Ltd* [2010] IRLR 466.)

On the other hand, the following reasons have been held to be insubstantial and thus not **14.239** to qualify as some other *substantial* reason:

(a) a rumour that the employee would leave to set up a rival business;

(b) a rescinded decision to depart (*Ready Case Ltd v Jackson* [1981] IRLR 312); and

(c) the fact that the applicant's wife had been convicted of many offences of dishonesty (*Wadley v Eager Electrical Ltd* [1986] IRLR 93).

Outside pressure

14.240 There are several decisions in which an outside source of pressure on the employer has been seen as constituting some other substantial reason. In *Scott Packing and Warehousing Co Ltd v Paterson* [1978] IRLR 166, the EAT held that it might be justifiable to dismiss an employee in response to an ultimatum from the company's major customer. The US naval authorities refused the claimant's services because of a suspected theft, of which no evidence was presented. This could hardly be a fair dismissal for misconduct, since the employing company had been fully aware of the facts for a full six weeks before dismissal, but it was some other substantial reason.

14.241 *Moody v Telefusion Ltd* [1978] IRLR 311 takes this further, since the EAT held fair a dismissal because the employee was unable to secure a fidelity bond. In deciding whether the reason was substantial the EAT failed to enquire into the reasonableness of requiring a fidelity bond (see also *Dobie v Burns International Security Services (UK) Ltd* [1984] IRLR 329). In *Grootcon (UK) Ltd v Keld* [1984] IRLR 302, the EAT stressed that the employer must provide convincing evidence of the outside pressure he was under.

L ILLEGALITY

14.242 The employer may prove as a reason for dismissal 'that the employee could not continue to work in the position which he held without contravention (either on his part or on that of his employer) of a duty or restriction imposed by or under an enactment' (ERA 1996, s 98(2)(d)). To qualify, the statute must in any case be related to the work which the claimant was actually employed to do, so that a clear example is the determination by the Secretary of State for Education under his statutory powers that a teacher is unsuitable (*Sandhu v Department of Education and Science* [1978] IRLR 208). Dismissal often, for example, follows the disqualification from driving of an employee who must use his car for work.

14.243 Even in these cases the resulting dismissal is not automatically fair. In *Sutcliffe & Eaton Ltd v Pinney* [1977] IRLR 349, the claimant, a hearing aid dispenser, was sacked when he failed to pass the Hearing Aid Council's examination and was thus removed from the appropriate register of dispensers. It was an offence for him to continue to so act under the Hearing Aid Council Act 1968. Since, however, it was possible for him to obtain an extension of time in which to take the exam and prosecution was unlikely, his dismissal was held unfair by the EAT because the employer had not inquired of the likely position. Reasonableness may also require the employer to offer suitable alternative employment if appropriate. Thus, the disqualified driver may be transferred to a stationary task (eg *Appleyard v Smith (Hull) Ltd* [1972] IRLR 19).

14.244 Dismissal of an employee because he has not obtained a proper work permit often falls under this head, but if the employer is mistaken as to the requirement for the permission the appropriate subsection is 'some other substantial reason' (*Bouchaala v Trusthouse Forte Hotels Ltd* [1980] ICR 721).

M SPENT OFFENCES

The aim of the Rehabilitation of Offenders Act 1974 is that a convicted criminal may put **14.245**
his past behind him and make a fresh start. When the rehabilitation period appropriate
to his sentence has elapsed, the conviction is 'spent' and should not be taken into account
for any purpose including employment. Thus, s 4(3)(b) provides that a spent conviction
or the failure to disclose a spent conviction shall be an automatically unfair ground for
dismissing someone from any office, profession, occupation, or employment, or for preju-
dicing him in any way. The length of the rehabilitation period depends on the nature of
the sentence imposed; the most important are as follows:

Sentence	Rehabilitation period
Imprisonment between 6 and 30 months	10 years
Imprisonment under 6 months	7 years
Fine	5 years
Borstal	7 years
Detention centre	3 years

The effect is limited by subsequent regulations (Rehabilitation of Offenders Act 1974 **14.246**
(Exceptions) Order 1975 (SI 1975/1023), as subsequently amended in 2001 and 2013),
which make exemptions from these provisions in the case of certain sensitive professions, including medical practitioners, lawyers, accountants, dentists, nurses, police,
and social services workers (see *Hendry v Scottish Liberal Club* [1977] IRLR 5). By the
Rehabilitation of Offenders Act 1974 (Exceptions) (Amendment) Order 1986 (SI 1986/
1249), a general exception exists for any office or employment which is concerned in
the provision of accommodation, leisure and recreational facilities, schooling, social services, supervision, or training to persons under 18 years, where the holder of the office
or employment would have access to such minors in the normal course of his duties, or
if the duties are carried out wholly or partly on the premises where such provision takes
place. There is no exception in respect of security guards (*Property Guards Ltd v Taylor
and Kershaw* [1982] IRLR 175; see also *Wood v Coverage Care Ltd* [1996] IRLR 264).

N DISMISSAL DURING STRIKE OR LOCK-OUT

The provisions of the TULR(C)A 1992, ss 237–9, concerning dismissal during lock-out, **14.247**
strike, or other industrial action are a borderline where collective and individual labour
law meet. The interconnection is not altogether happy, and the tensions are apparent in
the case law. One can see in particular the natural desire of the employment tribunals to
avoid determining the merits of industrial disputes. The predecessor of s 237 was used,
for example, by News International plc management in January 1986 to dismiss 5,500
print workers in the 'Wapping dispute' and by P & O in the Dover ferry dispute in 1988.
(For fuller consideration, see J Bowers, M Duggan, and D Reade, *The Law of Industrial
Action and Trade Union Recognition*, OUP, 2011.)

By s 238 of the 1992 Act a tribunal has no jurisdiction to determine whether a dismissal **14.248**
is unfair if at the time of the dismissal, the employer was conducting a lock-out or the
employee was taking part in a strike or other industrial action and if all so participating
are dismissed, and none re-engaged within three months of the dismissal. There are more

stringent provisions against unofficial action, whereby any single participant may be dismissed without the employment tribunal having jurisdiction (see below 14.271). The employer does not have to prove that the industrial dispute was the *reason* for the dismissal, merely that such termination coincided with the industrial action. The employer may even deliberately provoke the stoppage to remove his workforce with financial impunity. The position was, however, amended by the Employment Relations Act 1999 in an important way, so that in certain limited cases of protected action employees may claim unfair dismissal when dismissed while on strike. This is considered at 14.273–14.275.

14.249   In *Hindle Gears Ltd v McGinty* [1984] IRLR 477, Waite J said that the general immunity

> is subject ... to stringent sanctions, designed to deter employers from abusing the immunity by treating a strike as a pretext for dismissing the unwanted elements in their workforce and retaining the remainder ... Motive is irrelevant. Inadvertance makes no difference. The rule is wholly rigid and inflexible. The result (as the authorities show) has been to turn the process of dismissal of a striking workforce into something like a game of hazard in which the winner takes all, in which defeat or victory turns upon the fall of a single card and in which the stakes increase dramatically according to the number involved.

14.250   As Browne-Wilkinson J stated in *Coates v Modern Methods and Materials Ltd* [1982] ICR 763, in these cases 'it is of great importance to employers that they should so far as possible know the consequences of their acts before they decide to dismiss and who to retain or reengage'. The costs of 'getting it wrong' from the employer's point of view may indeed be colossal, especially if the tribunal were to decide that the employees were not dismissed in the course of a strike and that the reason for dismissal was the trade union activities of the workforce. (On issue estoppel in such cases, see *Munir v Jang Publications Ltd* [1989] IRLR 224.)

The meaning of strike, other industrial action, or lock-out

What is a strike?

14.251   'Strike' is undefined for the purposes of the TULR(C)A 1992, ss 237 to 239. In one case, the EAT incorporated by reference its definition for continuity purposes in Sch 13 to the EPCA 1978 (now ERA 1996, ss 210–19 and 235(5)). Lord Denning's definition of a strike in the contractual case of *Tramp Shipping Corporation v Greenwich Marine Inc* [1975] ICR 261 has also been applied in this context and this is rather more appropriate. The then Master of the Rolls considered that a strike was 'a concerted stoppage of work by men done with a view to improving their wages or conditions or giving vent to a grievance or making a protest about something or other or sympathising with other workmen in such endeavours'. An individual protest would not usually qualify (*Bowater Containers Ltd v Blake*, EAT 522/81; cf *Lewis and Britton v E. Mason & Sons* [1994] IRLR 4; see below).

What is other industrial action?

14.252   Tribunals and appeal bodies have been reluctant to place a rigid limit on the activities which might constitute other industrial action for the purposes of the TULR(C)A 1992, ss 237 to 239. They again see it as a question of fact in each case; the categories are certainly not closed. The phrase includes a go-slow, work-to-rule, concerted non-cooperation, and probably a picket of the employer's premises. Most such activity will break the implied contractual duty that an employee shall not disrupt the employer's enterprise (*Secretary of State for Employment v ASLEF (No 2)* [1972] 2 QB 455; see also *Miles v Wakefield Metropolitan District Council* [1987] ICR 368).

The phrase is not, however, restricted to such a breach of contract; thus a concerted **14.253** withdrawal of cooperation over admittedly voluntary overtime constituted 'other industrial action' according to the Court of Appeal in *Faust v Power Packing Casemakers Ltd* [1983] IRLR 117. It was sufficient that the action applied pressure against management, and was designed to extract some benefit from management for the workforce. In *Lewis and Britton v E. Mason & Sons* [1994] IRLR 4, this was somewhat surprisingly held to apply to a protest by a lorry driver about driving a particular vehicle from Wales to Edinburgh because it did not have an overnight heater, unless he was given an extra £5 for overnight subsistence. The EAT was concerned to uphold the decision of the tribunal on the ground that it was a matter of fact for it to determine.

Controversy has arisen over participation in unauthorised mass meetings. In some busi- **14.254** nesses, the disruptive union meeting at the peak point of production is a well-worn union tactic (see also *Rasool v Hepworth Pipe Co Ltd (No 1)* [1980] ICR 494).

It may indeed be difficult in some cases to distinguish between a strike and other indus- **14.255** trial action. In *Thompson v Eaton Ltd* [1976] ICR 336, for example, employees stood round a new machine for a short time to prevent their employers from testing its operation. The EAT held that this could qualify under either heading.

Withdrawal by an employee of his labour, even if there is a breach of contract, will not, **14.256** however, necessarily and in every conceivable circumstance justify dismissal, but where large numbers of employees deliberately absent themselves from work in an unofficial strike action in a manner which is plainly liable to do serious damage to the employer's business, dismissal of those taking part in the action will be within the range of responses even if the absence is not very prolonged (*Sehmi v Gate Gourmet London Ltd* [2009] IRLR 807).

Unauthorised and unexplained absence from work at a time when industrial action is in **14.257** progress will constitute participation in industrial action (*Sehmi* (supra)).

What is a lock-out?

The ERA 1996, s 235(4), defines lock-out (which has rarely been used by employers in **14.258** recent years) for the purposes of continuity of service as 'the closing of a place of employment, suspension of work, refusal by an employer to continue to employ any number of persons employed by him in consequence of a dispute done with a view to compelling those persons to accept terms and conditions of or affecting employment'. These words were applied to what was the predecessor subsection in *Fisher v York Trailer Co Ltd* [1979] ICR 834, but the Court of Appeal sought to take a broader view in *Express & Star Ltd v Bunday* [1988] ICR 379. In the course of a dispute over the introduction of new technology into a local newspaper, the employer refused the employees access to the premises where they worked, with the exception of one door which was manned by members of management. When employees arrived through this door, they were taken at once to a meeting at which those who refused to work with new machinery were suspended without pay.

The Court of Appeal decided that the definition of 'lock-out' could not be applied word **14.259** for word to these facts, but May LJ said that 'they may give an indication of the sort of ingredients that one should look for'. May and Croom-Johnson LJJ regarded the question of whether the employers were in breach of contract as a 'material consideration' in determining whether there was a lock-out. Glidewell LJ, dissenting, thought that as a matter of law an employer who refuses to let all employees work unless they undertake to perform the terms of their contract cannot be regarded as conducting a lock-out. In the result, the Court of Appeal decided that the tribunal was correct as a matter of fact in determining that the employees were taking part in industrial action at the date of their dismissals rather than that the employer was conducting a lock-out.

Can an employer provoke industrial action and then dismiss those who participate in it?

14.260   It appears that an employer may deliberately engineer a dispute and then dismiss without compensation those who participate in it. The test is merely whether the employee was dismissed *in the course of the industrial action*. Whether the action was the real *reason* for the sacking is irrelevant to this issue (see *Faust*'s case at 14.253). This principle has the advantage of keeping the employment tribunals away from the merits of the dispute. Moreover, as Phillips J said in *Thompson v Eaton* (above): 'It is rare for a strike or other industrial action to be wholly the fault of one side or the other. Almost always there is some blame on each side' (see also *Marsden v Fairey Stainless Ltd* [1979] IRLR 103).

14.261   Employers who follow this strategy must be careful, however, not to repudiate the contracts of employment of their employees since the workforce might accept such a breach as a constructive dismissal, and then claims would be made on grounds not of the employer's choosing. The question for the employment tribunal would then be whether in breaching the contract, the employer acted reasonably in all the circumstances of the case (the normal s 98(4) test). The fact of going on strike in itself will probably not, however, be treated as the acceptance by the employee of the employer's repudiation (*Wilkins v Cantrell & Cochrane (GB) Ltd* [1978] IRLR 483).

Official action

Was the dismissed employee participating in the action?

14.262   Importantly, the section has effect in giving immunity to the employer only if the dismissed employee was participating in the strike or other industrial action on the *date of dismissal*. Stephenson LJ in *Coates*'s case considered that this vital issue on which the jurisdiction of the tribunal depended was 'just the sort of question which an industrial jury is best fitted to decide' (see to the same effect *Hindle Gears Ltd v McGinty* [1984] IRLR 477). This position was criticised with great force by the EAT in *Naylor v Orton & Smith Ltd* [1983] IRLR 233. There, thirty-three employees were dismissed for participating in an overtime ban. Two others had voted in favour of such action at a meeting but later signed a form sent out by the employers to say that they would work normally. The tribunal decided that these two were not to be taken as participating in industrial action, and the EAT President considered that the appeal body could not intervene in the light of the Court of Appeal's pronouncements in *Coates*'s case. It is, however, clear that participation must be personal and direct, and not vicariously through the agency of a shop steward (*Dixon v Wilson Walton Engineering Ltd* [1979] ICR 438).

14.263   In *McKenzie v Crosville Motor Services Ltd* [1989] IRLR 516, the EAT decided that the employer had immunity if he dismissed all those whom he reasonably *believed* to be participating in the industrial action; but in *Manifold Industries Ltd v Sims* [1991] IRLR 242, another division of the EAT preferred the approach taken in *Bolton Roadways Ltd v Edwards* [1987] IRLR 392, so that the matter was one of objective fact, not the knowledge of the employer (see also *Jenkins v P&O European Ferries (Dover) Ltd* [1991] ICR 652). A genuine belief by the employer that the employee took part in a strike is not enough to justify the employer's action in dismissing (*Thompson v Woodland Designs Ltd* [1980] IRLR 423). Moreover, the onus is on the employer to prove that the employee took part in the strike, but participation in a strike need not be *known* to the employers before it can qualify as conduct taking part in a strike (*McGinty*'s case (above)).

Two categories of employee have engaged particular attention: **14.264**

(a) *The frightened employee*: In *Coates*'s case (above) a Mrs Leith went on strike, not because of her support for the cause in dispute, but because she was frightened that she would be abused by her fellow workers if she did not. The tribunal decided that she was nevertheless participating in the strike, so that it had jurisdiction to hear the claims of other workers who had been dismissed while she had been re-engaged after the end of hostilities. Kerr LJ did not think that the employee's reasons or motives for participating in the strike were of any moment. Such an enquiry would not be 'correct or practicable'. It would not be relevant 'to consider whether [the employee's] utterances or actions, or silence or inaction showed support, opposition or indifference in relation to the strike'. Stephenson LJ took the direct view that: 'In the field of industrial action, those who are not openly against it are presumably for it.' Eveleigh LJ, however, dissented on the ground that an employee must act in concert with the strikers to be participating in the strike, and this Mrs Leith did not do.

(b) *The sick employee*: An employee genuinely on sick leave or holiday during a strike could not normally be said to be participating in it, even though he might have spoken to pickets when attending work to present his sickness certificate (*McGinty*'s case (above)). The position is, however, different if the employee has already taken part in the action before he goes off sick. In *Williams v Western Mail and Echo Ltd* [1980] ICR 366, members of the NUJ were given an ultimatum to discontinue industrial sanctions by a certain day or face dismissal. The claimant was away sick at the time but made clear that he would not have submitted to the ultimatum had he been well. Slynn J was not impressed by the argument that he was not to be considered as taking part in industrial action (see also *McKenzie v Crosville Motor Services Ltd* [1989] IRLR 516).

In a case where there was no clear finding by the employment tribunal that had the employee not been ill she would have taken part in industrial action, there was insufficient factual foundation for the inference that she took part in strike action (*Rogers v Chloride Systems Ltd* [1992] IRLR 198). **14.265**

The importance of the date of dismissal

The employee must be taking part in the appropriate action on the *date of dismissal* for the employer to remain immune from an unfair dismissal claim. The 'date of dismissal' has been construed as the actual time of dismissal, and this has potentially important consequences. In *Heath v J. F. Longman (Meat Salesmen) Ltd* [1973] ICR 407, a dispute about overtime payments for Saturday working provoked the employer to declare that if the employees did not work on the following Saturday, they would be dismissed. The claimant and two colleagues went out on strike in response to this ultimatum, but after seeing their union representatives, one of them told the employer that the strike of all of them was at an end. Even so, the employer dismissed all three. The National Industrial Relations Court was of the view that, 'once the men had telephoned and told the employer that they no longer wished to withdraw their labour and wanted to come back to work, they had in our view clearly ceased to be on strike'. The rule that a part equalled the whole day was not appropriate in this context. The essence of the decision was that the return to work had been communicated to the employer. **14.266**

14.267   The employer may not dismiss with impunity those employees who have merely announced their intention of going on strike but have not yet begun their action (*Midland Plastics v Till* [1983] IRLR 9). If, on the other hand, a strike has already begun, and an employee who is off duty states a clear intention to become involved in it as soon as his shift starts, he is treated as participating from the time at which he makes his intention clear even if his shift has not started at the time of dismissal (*Winnett v Seamarks Brothers Ltd* [1978] ICR 1240). There are three important questions to be asked:

(a) By what time does the tribunal decide whether all relevant employees have been dismissed? In *P&O European Ferries (Dover) Ltd v Byrne* [1989] IRLR 254, the Court of Appeal determined that the question had to be asked at the *conclusion* of the tribunal hearing. If only some have been dismissed by this time, the tribunal must examine whether the employer was fair or unfair in deciding who was to remain and who was to go. This introduces a certain arbitrary element since the length of time between dismissal and hearing can vary greatly. Moreover, the reason for dismissal of the comparative employees need not be by reason of the strike but may be, for example, because of redundancy.

(b) What is the position if participants in industrial action have returned to work by the time of the claimant's dismissal? Any participant in strike action who has returned to work at the time of the claimant's dismissal does not amount to a 'relevant employee'. Thus, the employer need not dismiss all those who are on strike at any time, but merely all those participating in the disruptive action at the time of the claimant's dismissal. He may thus issue an ultimatum to his employees on strike to return or else face the consequences of dismissal. Moreover, only those participating in the action at the establishment 'at or from which' the complainant worked are to be considered.

(c) Must all the employees be involved in the *same* strike? This issue was considered in *McCormick v Horsepower Ltd* [1981] IRLR 217, where the appellant was one of a number of boilermakers who struck for increased pay. A fitter's mate in a different department (this was before the restriction to the particular establishment was introduced) refused to cross the picket lines of the boilermakers. The appellant claimed that the other employee was a relevant employee for the purposes of what was EPCA 1978, s 62, who had not been dismissed. The Court of Appeal disagreed on the ground that there was no agreement between the parties to take industrial action.

Relevant employees in a lock-out

14.268   A different regime applies to dismissals in a lock-out. A relevant employee there is one 'directly interested in the dispute in contemplation or furtherance of which the lock-out occurred'. In *Fisher v York Trailer Co Ltd* [1979] ICR 834, the EAT decided that locked-out employees who subsequently returned to work were 'relevant employees' if their colleagues were subsequently dismissed. In *H. Campey & Son Ltd v Bellwood* [1987] ICR 311, a haulage contractor decided unilaterally to vary the terms and conditions of its employees. The employer gave notice that because of threatened industrial action the operation of the company was to be suspended forthwith. The employer dismissed only those who had failed to return to work, and argued before the EAT that *Fisher* was wrongly decided. The EAT did not accede to this submission and thought that the test was a retrospective one and had to be looked at when the lock-out occurred.

Re-engagement

14.269   As already mentioned, a tribunal must consider whether all those participating in a strike or other industrial action have been dismissed and whether some have been re-engaged. The re-engagement need not be at the same site as that from which the employee was dismissed, nor need the employer realise that it was re-engaging an employee previously dismissed from one of its sites (*Bigham v GKN Kwikform Ltd* [1992] ICR 113). There was, however, no offer of re-engagement within the meaning of the statute when the employers placed notices at their bus depot, made press and local radio announcements that they were recruiting, and so advised local job centres (*Crosville Wales Ltd v Tracey* [1993] IRLR 60). What was made available to employees in this case was merely the *opportunity* of having an offer made to them, not an offer of re-engagement itself. If not all have been dismissed *or* some but not others have been re-engaged, the tribunal has jurisdiction to consider the reason for the non-dismissal or re-engagement of some but not others on its merits in each case.

(a) *The time of re-engagement.* The tribunal has to consider whether any employee has been re-engaged within the three months following dismissal of the relevant employee. Thereafter, the employer can re-engage employees without any effect on unfair dismissal claims at all. The Scottish EAT decided in *Highlands Fabricators Ltd v McLaughlin* [1985] ICR 183 that the employment tribunal had no jurisdiction where all the striking employees, including the claimant, had been offered re-engagement before the end of three months even though in an original offer of re-engagement, the claimant was one of 400 employees who did not receive the offer and had gained work elsewhere. Lord McDonald considered that 'it would wreck all chances of negotiations on what is frequently a delicate and tense situation if a limited offer of re-engagement were to confer immediately on employees to whom the offer was not directed a vested right to complain of unfair dismissal'. The three months was in effect a 'cooling off' period.

(b) *What are suitable terms of re-engagement?* An offer of re-engagement is defined as an offer to work in the same job as that which was held before dismissal or in a different job which would be reasonably suitable in the case of the employee. This focuses the scope of the tribunal's inquiry on the nature of the work and the place where it is to be carried on. An offer may so qualify even though it requires that the employee be treated as on the second warning stage of the disciplinary procedure (*Williams v National Theatre Board Ltd* [1982] ICR 715). The question of suitability is, however, one of fact and degree for the employment tribunal to determine.

Discriminatory selection

Where there is a selective dismissal or re-engagement, the employer must reveal the criteria on which he made his choice of who should go and who should stay. He must show that his selection criteria are fair in all the circumstances of the case so that if the reason for picking and choosing between employees would be invalid if there were no strike, it is likely to be invalid in this situation. The fact that the employee was on strike may itself be taken into account. The EAT in *Laffin and Callaghan v Fashion Industries (Hartlepool) Ltd* [1978] IRLR 448 said that 'a valid matter to be considered is the loyalty of those who serve during the strike but ... by the same token to give *carte blanche* to the loyalty of those who did work is likely to cause indignation among those who ... did not stay loyal to the management'. **14.270**

Dismissal during unofficial industrial action

By s 237 of the TULR(C)A 1992, no employee can complain of unfair dismissal if at the time of his dismissal he was taking part in unofficial industrial action. Action will be taken to be unofficial unless the employee is a member of a trade union and the action is authorised or endorsed by that union, or 'he is not a member of a trade union but there **14.271** are among those taking part in the industrial action members of a trade union by which the action has been authorised or endorsed'.

14.272 In similar circumstances, there will be no immunity under s 223 of the TULR(C)A 1992 if the act is done because an employee has been dismissed in circumstances such as by virtue of s 237 he cannot complain of unfair dismissal.

Protected industrial action

14.273 Section 238A of the TULR(C)A 1992 provides that a dismissal is to be treated as unfair if the reason or principal reason for it is that the employee participated in 'protected' industrial action. This covers by far the majority of strikes. The action is 'protected' if it has been *lawfully* organised under s 219 of the 1992 Act, which includes the requirement that there is a primary trade dispute and a properly conducted ballot. The dismissal will thus be automatically unfair if:

(a) it takes place within twelve weeks of the day on which the employee started to take protected industrial action (s 238A(3)); or

(b) it takes place after the end of this twelve-week period, but the employee has stopped taking part in the industrial action before twelve weeks has expired (s 238A(4)); or

(c) twelve weeks have passed and the employee is still taking part in the industrial action but the employer has not taken 'such procedural steps as would have been reasonable for the purposes of resolving the dispute' (s 238A(5)). Whether such procedural steps have been taken is to be determined without reference to the merits of the dispute but by reference to (s 238A(6)):

   (i) whether the employer or a union had complied with procedures established by any applicable collective or other agreement;

   (ii) whether the employer or union offered or agreed to resume negotiations after the start of the protected industrial action;

   (iii) whether the employer or union unreasonably refused, after the start of the protected industrial action, a request that conciliation or mediation services be used.

14.274 Section 238A(7D) adds to the normal twelve-week period an extension period when the employee was subject to a lock-out. As to (i), s 238B specifies matters to be taken into account in this respect as:

(a) whether at meetings arranged by the service provider, the employer or union was represented by an appropriate person;

(b) whether the employer or union cooperated in the making of arrangements for meetings to be held with the service provider;

(c) whether the employer or union fulfilled any commitment which was given by it during the provision of the service to take particular action and regard may be had to any timetable that has been agreed for the taking of the action in question or, if no timetable was agreed, to how long it was before the action was taken;

(d) whether at meetings arranged by the service provider between the parties making use of the service, the representatives of the employer or union answered any reasonable question put to them concerning the matter subject to conciliation or mediation.

14.275 If the union repudiates the industrial action, so that it becomes unofficial, employees will lose their protection from unfair dismissal if they continue taking action after the end of the working day following the union's repudiation (s 238A(8)). Provision is made so that applications for reinstatement or re-engagement cannot be heard until the end of the dispute.

O DISMISSAL BY REASON OF RECOGNITION ACTION

There is a necessity for protection of employees caught up in recognition disputes beyond   **14.276**
those available for trade union activities. By Sch A1 to the TULR(C)A 1992, a worker has
the right not to be subjected to any detriment, including dismissal, by the employer by
reason of any act, or any deliberate failure to act, on the grounds that the worker:

(a) acted with a view to obtaining or preventing recognition of a union by the employer
     or the ending of bargaining arrangements under the Schedule;
(b) indicated that he supported or did not support recognition or the ending of bargain-
     ing arrangements under the Schedule;
(c) influenced or sought to influence the way in which votes were to be cast by other work-
     ers, or to influence other workers to vote or abstain, in a ballot under the Schedule;
(d) voted in a ballot under the Schedule; or
(e) proposed to do, failed to do, or proposed to decline to do any of the above.

By way of exception, however, a worker may be subjected to a detriment for doing any of
the above things if his so doing would be a breach of the worker's contract with the employer or an 'unreasonable act or omission' by the worker (Sch A1, para 161(2)).

A complaint under Sch A1, para 161, can be made to an employment tribunal. The ordi-   **14.277**
nary unfair dismissal time limit applies. The three months runs from the date of the act
or failure to which the complaint relates or, if it is part of a series of acts or failures, the
last of them (Sch A1, para 157(1)). Where a complaint is made under Sch A1, para 161, the
burden is on the employer to show the reason for the act or omission of which complaint
is made (Sch A1, para 158). If the complaint is upheld, the tribunal must make a declaration to that effect and may award compensation (Sch A1, para 159). If the victimisation
takes the form of dismissal of an employee or selection for redundancy, the dismissal will
be automatically unfair (Sch A1, para 162).

P DISMISSAL FOR ASSERTION OF A STATUTORY RIGHT

Section 104 of the ERA 1996 renders the dismissal of employees automatically unfair   **14.278**
where they assert that their employer has breached a statutory right. The dismissal is
unfair if the reason, or the principal reason, was that the employee brought proceedings
against his employer to enforce a relevant statutory right (s 104(1)). No qualifying period
of employment is needed in order to claim the right.

In order to exercise the right, the employee need not specify the right that he claims has   **14.279**
been infringed (s 104(3)).

The relevant rights which may be asserted to give rise to the claim are all those under   **14.280**
the ERA 1996 and the TULR(C)A 1992 for which the remedy is a complaint to an
employment tribunal. These are, in particular, the rights to written particulars of
employment, guarantee payments, suspension from work for medical grounds, protection against dismissal and other detriments in health and safety cases, time off for
public duties and to look for work or to make arrangements for training, time off for
antenatal care, to return to work after pregnancy, to be given a written statement of
reasons for dismissal, to claim redress for unfair dismissal, redundancy payments, to
reclaim unauthorised deduction from wages, require employer to end check-off, object
to political fund contribution, protection against action short of dismissal related to

union membership or activities, payment for time off for union duties, and time off for trade union activities.

14.281   In addition, the right found in the ERA 1996, s 86, to receive a minimum period of notice is expressly included (s 104(4)(b)) even though it is not enforceable solely in an employment tribunal.

14.282   It is immaterial whether the employee actually has the right or whether it has in fact been infringed or not (s 104(2)). So long as the employee claims in good faith that the right has been infringed, the protection of s 104 applies. The relevant time within which a complaint must be presented is three months (ERA 1996, s 111).

14.283   In the first important case on the provisions, *Mennell v Newell & Wright (Transport Contractors) Ltd* [1997] ICR 1039, a clause in a new draft contract provided that the employer would recover certain training costs by a deduction from payment of final salary on termination of employment. The claimant refused to sign the contract and alleged that he was told that if he did not sign he could expect dismissal. He was indeed eventually dismissed. He claimed that the dismissal was automatically unfair because he had been asserting a right then conferred by the then current Wages Act 1986. The employer contended in response that there was no infringement of a right under that statute of which complaint could be made, but the EAT decided on the contrary that there need be no actual infringement or any claim brought (see also *McLean v Rainbow Homeloans Ltd* [2007] IRLR 14).

Q JURY SERVICE

14.284   An employee must not suffer detriment because he has been summoned for jury service (new s 43M of the ERA).

14.285   A dismissal because of needing to do jury service is automatically unfair (new s 98B of the ERA) unless the employer shows that:

(a) the circumstances were such that the employee's absence in pursuance of the summons was likely to cause substantial injury to the employer's undertaking;
(b) the employer brought those circumstances to the attention of the employee;
(c) the employee refused or failed to apply to the appropriate officer for excusal from or deferral of the summons; and
(d) the refusal or failure was not reasonable.

R DISMISSAL: PRESSURE ON EMPLOYER TO DISMISS

14.286   The employer cannot argue either as a defence or in mitigation of compensation that he was forced to dismiss an employee because of the threat of a strike, whether the pressure was implicit or explicit (ERA 1996, ss 107 and 123(5)). The former was illustrated in *Colwyn Borough Council v Dutton* [1980] IRLR 420 EAT, where the applicant's trade union branch refused to act as crew of the applicant's dustcart because they considered his driving dangerous, and he was dismissed in consequence. The test propounded in *Ford Motor Co Ltd v Hudson* [1978] ICR 482, was whether:

> the pressure exerted on the employers [was] such that it could be foreseen that it would be likely to result in the dismissal of those employees in respect of where the pressure was being brought?

S REMEDIES

The remedies for unfair dismissal are: reinstatement; re-engagement; and compensation. **14.287**
After a finding of unfairness the claimant elects whether or not he wishes to be reinstated,
re-engaged, or gain only a monetary award, and the employment tribunal must explain to
him the consequences of each course (*Pirelli General Cable Works Ltd v Murray* [1979]
IRLR 190), although a failure to do so does not render the decision a nullity (*Cowley v
Manson Timber Ltd* [1994] ICR 252). Interim relief may be gained in the case of pen-
sion trustees, employee representatives, whistleblowers, and under the Working Time
Regulations.

Reinstatement

Reinstatement is an order that 'the employer shall treat the complainant in all respects as if **14.288**
he had not been dismissed' and must include benefits payable in respect of the period since
dismissal and rights and privileges, including seniority and pensions (ERA 1996, s 114(2)). It
was originally designed to be the primary remedy for unfair dismissal, and is an order akin
to the specific performance which the common law generally refused to grant in the case
of contracts of employment. In general, only 1 per cent of cases which went to an employment tribunal hearing resulted in a reinstatement or re-engagement order. The explanation
is partly that claimants do not wish to return to employers who in their view have treated
them disgracefully, and partly because tribunals and judges, imprisoned by common law
training, have not been adventurous in its application (see Hart *et al*, 10 ILJ 160).

The principles in awarding reinstatement

Reinstatement should not be ordered if it is 'not practicable' for the employer to comply **14.289**
with it or it would be unjust to do so because the employee contributed to the dismissal.

There are two separate occasions when the issue of practicability may arise. The first is a **14.290**
preliminary view by the ET at this stage of deciding whether the order should be made,
since if an order is made and the employer does not comply with it, the employer may
show (and then the onus is on him) that it was not practicable for the employer to comply. This somewhat strange provision caused Knox J to comment in *Mabrizi v National
Hospital for Nervous Diseases* [1990] IRLR 133, 'although it might be that a cherry
that is rejected at the first date will be likely to be indigestible at the second, there is in
our view no doubt at all that two bites are allowed'. This concept of practicability is to
be applied in the same way as reduction of compensation (see 14.337). In *Boots Co plc v
Lees-Collier* [1986] IRLR 485, the EAT held that it is unnecessary to decide contributory
fault under separate headings for the two different purposes.

At the first stage of determining whether an order should be made, the decision as to **14.291**
practicability is necessarily provisional; it is not final in the sense that it creates an estoppel or limits the employer at the second stage to relying on facts which occurred after the
order for re-engagement was made (*Port of London Authority v Payne and Others* [1994]
IRLR 9).

'Practicability' is only one of the considerations to be taken into account at the initial **14.292**
stage in exercising the discretion and the tribunal need not make a definite finding on this
aspect (*Timex Corporation v Thomson* [1981] IRLR 522; see also *Nairne v Highlands
and Islands Fire Brigade* [1989] IRLR 366 and *Motherwell Railway Club v McQueen*
[1989] ICR 418). The general meaning of practicability was considered by the Court
of Appeal in *Coleman v Magnet Joinery Ltd* [1974] IRLR 343, where, in rejecting the

employee's contention that it depended solely on whether a job was available, Stephenson LJ said:

> The tribunal ought to consider the consequences of re-engagement in the industrial relations scene in which it will take place. If it is obvious as in the present case that re-engagement would only promote further serious industrial relations strife, it will not be practicable to make the recommendation.

(See also *Meridian Ltd v Gomersall* [1977] ICR 597.)

14.293 The matter is one which is pre-eminently for the tribunal's exercise of its independent discretion, and appeals are only rarely entertained. The EAT would not order reinstatement where:

(a) it would *poison the atmosphere* in a factory either generally or among particular workers (*Coleman v Toleman's Delivery Service Ltd* [1973] IRLR 67);

(b) the employee has shown that she distrusts the employer, and has made allegations of a serious nature against them (*Nothman v London Borough of Barnet (No 2)* [1980] IRLR 65);

(c) a *genuine redundancy* or reorganisation has arisen in the position since dismissal (*Trusler v Lummus Co Ltd* [1972] IRLR 35);

(d) it would lead to *strike* action (*Langston v AUEW (No 2)* [1974] ICR 510);

(e) the employee is not fit to return (*McAulay v Cementation Chemicals Ltd* [1972] IRLR 71); and

(f) a local education authority had grave doubts as to the abilities of a teacher (*ILEA v Gravett* [1988] IRLR 497).

In *Boots v Lees-Collier* (above), the EAT held that the tribunal had not erred in deciding that it was practicable for the appellants to reinstate the respondent even though his ultimate manager was convinced that he was guilty of theft from the company.

14.294 The employer does not have to go so far as to require voluntary severances in his workforce before it can demonstrate that it was not practicable to reinstate or re-engage the claimants (*Port of London Authority v Payne and Others* [1994] IRLR 9). It was stressed in *Payne* that the proper test under the statute is the *practicability* of reinstatement or re-engagement, not the *possibility* of reinstatement or re-engagement. Although the employment tribunal should carefully scrutinise the reasons which are advanced by the employer for not reinstating or re-engaging, due weight should be given to the commercial judgement of management, but in doing so the standard must not be set too high as to the practicability of reinstatement or re-engagement. The employer cannot, in particular, be expected to explore *every* possible avenue which ingenuity may suggest as to jobs which might be provided for the claimant.

14.295 The most important general restriction upon the remedy was introduced in *Enessy Co SA v Minoprio* [1978] IRLR 489, where Lord McDonald said, *obiter*: 'In our view it was not realistic to make an order of this nature in a case where the parties involved were in close personal relationships with each other such as they were in the present situation. It is one thing to make an order for reinstatement where the employee concerned works in a factory or other substantial organisation. It is another to do so in the case of a small employer with a few staff' (see also *Wood Group Heavy Industrial Turbines v Crossan* [1998] IRLR 680).

14.296 Appeals as to practicability on grounds of perversity are virtually impossible (*Clancy v Cannock Chase Technical College* [2001] IRLR 331).

Dismissal of replacement for reinstated employee

The fact that the employer has engaged a replacement for the dismissed employee before **14.297**
the tribunal hears the case is irrelevant and does not make it impracticable to reinstate
unless the employer shows that:

(a) it was not practicable for him to arrange for the dismissed employee's work to be done
without engaging a permanent replacement for him; and

(b) he engaged the replacement after the lapse of a reasonable period without having
heard from the dismissed employee that he wished to be reinstated or re-engaged
and that when the employer engaged the replacement, it was no longer reasonable for
him to arrange for the dismissed employee's work to be done except by a permanent
replacement (ERA 1996, s 116(5)).

Re-engagement

Re-engagement resembles reinstatement in its effect except that the employee does not **14.298**
return to the *same* post on the same terms. The job must still be comparable with the
previous post and suitable for the employee, however, and so far as is reasonably practicable as favourable as the previous position (ERA 1996, s 115(1)). The re-engagement
may, however, be with an associated or successor employer and the tribunal decides what
terms should apply and the date by which compliance must be made (*British Airways plc
v Valencia* [2014] IRLR 683).

Failure to comply with reinstatement or re-engagement order

Should the employer not comply with an order for reinstatement or re-engagement, the **14.299**
only remedy is extra compensation (*O'Laiore v Jackel International Ltd* [1990] ICR
197). The tribunal has no power to commit to prison for contempt of court, or fine the
employer if he ignores an order to reinstate or to re-engage, but the sacked worker can
apply for an '*additional award*'—a special form of exemplary or punitive damages—
which amounts to between twenty-six and fifty-two weeks' pay in all cases (s 117(3)
(b)). The week's pay is subject, as usual, to a maximum of £479 (14.304). The employment tribunal must properly exercise its discretion in determining where in the range
the additional award should be fixed (*Morganite Electrical Carbon Ltd v Donne* [1987]
IRLR 363). The factors to be taken into account in this respect include the conduct of
the employer in refusing to comply with the order, the extent to which the compensatory award has met the actual loss suffered by the applicant, and mitigation (*Mabrizi
v National Hospital for Nervous Diseases* [1990] IRLR 133). It is not based on loss to
the employee (see *Electronic Data Processing Ltd v Wright* [1986] IRLR 8). Further, in
respect of the amount ordered to be paid by way of salary and benefits between dismissal
and reinstatement, there is no statutory maximum on the amount which the employer
may be ordered to pay.

The employer may avoid an additional award only if he 'satisfies the tribunal that it **14.300**
was not practicable to comply with the order' (s 117(4)). The criteria are different from
the determination in respect of the order for reinstatement itself. There practicability is
merely one consideration amongst others; here the onus is on the employer specifically to
prove impracticability and if he cannot, the additional award will be made (*Freemans plc
v Flynn* [1984] IRLR 486).

14.301 Various issues of jurisdiction have arisen under this rubric:

(a) An employment tribunal may not order that an employee be re-engaged on terms significantly *more* favourable than those he would enjoy if reinstated (*Rank Xerox (UK) Ltd v Stryczek* [1995] IRLR 568).

(b) There is no jurisdiction to reduce the amount of arrears of pay between the date of termination and the date of re-engagement to reflect a finding that had the appellant pursued her complaint more expeditiously before the employment tribunal she would have been re-engaged at an earlier date (*City and Hackney Health Authority v Crisp* [1990] ICR 95; *Conoco (UK) Ltd v Neal* [1989] IRLR 51; *O'Laiore v Jackel International Ltd* [1991] IRLR 170).

(c) An employment tribunal must not give both a compensatory award, if an order of reinstatement is not complied with, *and* a sum by way of back-pay as if such an order had been complied with. The latter will be included within the general compensatory award (*Selfridges Ltd v Malik* [1998] ICR 268; *Parry v National Westminster Bank plc* [2005] IRLR 193).

Compensation: Basic award

14.302 Unfair dismissal compensation in most cases consists of two components, the basic and compensatory awards (ERA 1996, s 118) and both may be reduced owing to contributory fault. Failure to mitigate the loss can limit, however, only the compensatory element. The unfairly dismissed employee claims as basic award so many weeks' pay for each year of continuous employment with his own or any associated or predecessor employer before the effective date of termination, irrespective of whether the unfair dismissal has caused any loss to him. This head is intended at the same time not only to convey disapproval of the employer's action but also to compensate for the loss of job security. It performs a similar function to a redundancy payment and it is appropriate that they should be calculated in almost the same way (ERA 1996, s 119).

14.303 The amount of basic award depends on the age of the employee in this way:

(a) for each year which consists wholly of weeks in which the employee was over forty-one, one and a half week's pay;

(b) for each year which consists wholly of weeks not within (a) but in which the employee was not below twenty-two, one week's pay; and

(c) for any year wholly consisting of weeks in which the employee was under twenty-two, half a week's pay (s 119(2)).

14.304 No account is to be taken of any time employed beyond twenty years (s 119(3)) or of any week's pay over £479. The sum is index-linked to the retail prices index (Employment Relations Act 1999, s 34) and must be updated every September.

14.305 There is now no minimum basic award, except £5,853 in cases of dismissal by reason of carrying out health and safety functions, or acting as an occupational pension fund trustee or employee representative (ERA 1996, s 120); and there is a two weeks' maximum of basic award where the reason for dismissal was redundancy and the employee unreasonably refuses to accept a renewal of the contract or suitable alternative employment or where the employee during a trial period unreasonably terminates the contract (ERA 1996, s 121).

14.306 The amount of the basic award may be reduced:

(a) if the employee had unreasonably refused an offer of reinstatement (ERA 1996, s 122(1)); and

(b) because of any conduct before the dismissal with the exception of a dismissal for redundancy (ERA 1996, s 122(2)).

The latter is designed to mitigate the effect of the sort of case exemplified by *Devis v Atkins* [1977] AC 93 where the dismissal is unfair because the employer did not know at the time of the facts for which he could reasonably dismiss. Unlike contributory fault in assessing the compensatory award, it does not matter under this subsection whether there was a causal link between the claimant's conduct and the dismissal.

Since the basic award performs the same function and is assessed in a similar way, any redundancy pay is fully deducted from it. However, the EAT in *Chelsea Football Club & Athletic Co Ltd v Heath* [1981] IRLR 73, held that the basic award was not automatically to be reduced by any money paid by the employer *ex gratia* although it was presumed to be referable expressly or impliedly to the basic and compensatory award. It is a matter of construction of the basis of the *ex gratia* payment in each case. **14.307**

Any amount paid by way of a settlement which has been made should normally be deducted from the compensatory award for the same dismissal (*Optimum Group Services plc v Muir* [2013] IRLR 339). The tribunal should thus not award a sum which exceeds the loss which has been suffered. If a claimant seeks compensation from more than one respondent (say in a TUPE case), sums which already have been received from one should be deducted. **14.308**

Where the employer makes a larger redundancy payment than is required by statute, any excess goes to reduce the compensatory award where the dismissal is found to be by reason of redundancy (s 122(4)). In *Boorman v Allmakes Ltd* [1995] IRLR 553, however, an employee was paid an *ex gratia* sum which was expressed to include statutory redundancy payment, but it was held that it did not fall to be deducted from the basic award when he was ultimately found to have been unfairly dismissed on a ground other than redundancy (see also *Darr v LRC Products Ltd* [1993] IRLR 257). **14.309**

The compensatory award

The compensatory award provides what is just and equitable as compensation having regard to the loss suffered as a result of the dismissal so far as that loss is attributable to action taken by the employer (ERA 1996, s 123(1)). This was subject to a maximum of £12,000 until 26 October 1999 but was then markedly increased to £50,000 (Employment Relations Act 1999, s 34(4)) with further annual increases. By s 124(1ZA) ERA, introduced by the Enterprise and Regulatory Reform Act 2013, the amount is now, since 2013, the lower of £78,962 and fifty-two multiplied by the week's pay of the claimant. There is no limit, however, in respect of dismissals which are rendered unfair under the Public Interest Disclosure Act 1998, and in respect of dismissal for health and safety matters (Employment Relations Act 1999, s 37(1)). **14.310**

The test for assessing the award within the maximum sum has remained generally consistent since the introduction of unfair dismissal in 1971. In *W. Devis & Sons Ltd v Atkins* [1977] ICR 662, Viscount Dilhorne thought that it in truth had two elements: **14.311**

> [Section 123(1)] does not ... provide that regard should be had only to the *loss* resulting from the dismissal being unfair. Regard must be had to that but the award must be just and equitable in all the circumstances, and it cannot be just and equitable that a sum should be awarded in compensation when in fact the employee has suffered no injustice in being dismissed. (Emphasis added.)

14.312 These principles have been established by case law:

(a) If the employee has suffered *no loss* because, for example, he has immediately gained a better-paid job, he can claim nothing under this head, although he may still be entitled to the basic award. Thus, in *BUSM Co Ltd v Clarke* [1978] ICR 70, where a redundancy dismissal was held unfair because there was no consultation, the EAT would not give the employee compensation because he would have been made redundant at a later stage anyway. Phillips J commented:

> In some cases it will happen that the employment tribunal reaches the conclusion that had everything been done which ought to have been done it would not have made the slightest difference ... where the employment tribunal finds that the dismissal was unfair it will be necessary for them to proceed to assess compensation and for that purpose to make some estimate of what would have been the likely outcome had that been done which ought to have been done. This is often a difficult question, but one which the employment tribunal in their capacity as industrial jury are well suited to answer, and in respect of which they will not go wrong if they remember that what they are trying to do is to assess the loss suffered by the claimant and not punish the employer for his failure in industrial relations.

(See also *Winterhalter Gastronom Ltd v Webb* [1973] IRLR 120; *Mansfield Hosiery Mills Ltd v Bromley* [1977] IRLR 301; *Barley v Amey Roadstone Corporation Ltd* [1977] IRLR 299.)

(b) On the other hand, the *degree of unfairness* of the dismissal is probably not a relevant consideration in the assessment of what award is just and equitable. The tribunal is not entitled at this stage to take into consideration, for example, that the employer had no wish to treat the employee in anything other than a fair manner (*Morris v Acco Co Ltd* [1985] ICR 306; cf *Townson v Northgate Group Ltd* [1981] IRLR 382).

(c) There is no remoteness or foreseeability test, so that when an unfairly dismissed employee had to sell back 60,000 shares in the company on leaving at the then price of £1.70 but they later rose to £5.85 some months later because of a takeover of the employer, it was just and equitable to award the difference; it was not too remote (*Leonard v Strathclyde Buses Ltd* [1998] IRLR 693). Compensation may be reduced under both the just and equitable rubric and contributory fault head at the same time (*Rao v Civil Aviation Authority* [1994] IRLR 240). The reductions should indeed be applied in that order (see also *Campbell v Dunoon & Cowal Housing Association Ltd* [1993] IRLR 496). A nil award may be justified in exceptional cases (*Chaplin v Rawlinson* [1991] ICR 553).

(d) An employment tribunal may take into account in measuring compensation that the employee resigned in a peremptory manner without any warning being given (*TGWU v Howard* [1992] IRLR 170).

(e) Conduct after dismissal, such as the claimant selling a story about his case to a national newspaper, is not relevant and cannot be taken into account in reducing an award (*Soros v Davison* [1994] IRLR 264).

There may be contributory conduct even in the case of constructive dismissal (*Frith Accountants Ltd v Law* [2014] ICR 805).

14.313 The EAT has frequently called upon tribunals to take a broad brush approach to compensation questions, and will interfere with a decision on this matter only if there is some manifest misdirection in assessing it or it is perverse (*Manpower Ltd v Hearne* [1983] IRLR 281). Moreover, in *Courtaulds Northern Spinning Ltd v Moosa* [1984] IRLR 43, Browne-Wilkinson J accepted that 'the assessment of compensation in employment tribunals cannot be as scrupulously accurate as, say, in an action for personal injuries in the High Court'.

Tribunals have also been counselled not to act 'in a general benevolent manner according to the conception of what they think will be fair in the circumstances' (*Lifeguard Assurance Ltd v Zadrozny* [1977] IRLR 56). The burden of proving loss is firmly on the complainant, although: 'It is not therefore to be expected that the precise and detailed proof of every item of loss will be presented.' (*Norton Tool Co Ltd v Tewson* [1972] ICR 501 per Donaldson J.) The *Norton* case also required tribunals to set out their findings in appropriate subheadings, and this is now expressly formulated in the Employment Tribunal Rules of Procedure 2004 as 'either by a table showing how the amount or sum [of compensation] has been calculated or by a description of the manner in which it has been calculated'. **14.314**

Many of the criteria adopted for compensation derive from the principles adopted in awarding damages for personal injuries. The usual headings include the following: **14.315**

(a) immediate loss of wages;
(b) future loss of wages;
(c) loss of benefits;
(d) expenses in seeking work;
(e) loss of pension;
(f) loss of future employment protection; and
(g) manner of dismissal.

Immediate loss of earnings

This heading seeks to replace loss of net earnings from the date of dismissal to the hearing, and receipt of jobseeker's allowance is ignored for this calculation because the Department of Work and Pensions can recoup such benefits from the employer of a successful claimant. It was at one time thought that no deduction was to be made for anything which was or could have been earned during the notice period (*Everwear Candlewick Ltd v Isaac* (1974) 8 ITR 334; *Norton Tool Co Ltd v Tewson* [1972] ICR 501), so that where proper notice was not given, payment in lieu thereof was the irreducible minimum to be awarded as compensation. This was, however, doubted in *Tradewinds Airways Ltd v Fletcher* [1981] IRLR 272, where the EAT confirmed that compensation is to be awarded for actual financial loss, and if, as in the instant case, the employee proceeds to take another position within the notice period, earnings therefrom must be fully deducted. In *Babcock FATA Ltd v Addison* [1987] IRLR 173, however, the Court of Appeal indicated that this was not a rule of law (see below). The current position is that an employee is not entitled to unfair dismissal compensation based on full pay in respect of the notice period because such was in accordance with good industrial practice: *Burlo v Langley* [2007] IRLR 145. Statutory sick pay was held to be the correct measure of loss during the notice period. **14.316**

In *Finnie v Top Hat Frozen Foods Ltd* [1985] ICR 433, the EAT stressed that the general rule was that *ex gratia* payments on account of wages and other benefits should be deducted from any award (see also *Roadchef Ltd v Hastings* [1988] IRLR 142; *Horizon Holidays Ltd v Grassi* [1987] ICR 851). **14.317**

Norton Tool is no longer an appropriate juridical basis for awarding full compensation for the notice period given that it was inconsistent with the analysis of the House of Lords in *Dunnachie v Kingston upon Hull CC* [2004] IRLR 727 (cf *Voith Turbo Ltd v Stowe* [2005] IRLR 228). **14.318**

Before it is able to award compensation, the employment tribunal must first determine what salary the employee should have been receiving if there is disagreement on the contractual terms between the employer and employee (*Kinzley v Minories Finance Ltd* [1988] ICR 113). **14.319**

14.320 If the claimant was unable to work because of an accident, the tribunal should not award full loss (*Burlo v Langley* [2007] IRLR 145; *Hilton International Hotels (UK) Ltd v Faraji* [1994] IRLR 267; *Puglia v C. James & Sons* [1996] IRLR 70; and *Rubenstein v McGloughlin* [1996] IRLR 557).

Future loss of earnings

14.321 The amount to be awarded under this element depends on how long the dismissed worker is likely to be unemployed, and whether he has already taken (or soon will have to take) a job at a lower rate than his previous employment. The proper comparison to be drawn is between net (and not gross) pay in the two positions. Tribunals must:

> compare his salary prospects for the future in each job and see as best they could how long it would have been before he reached with [the second employer] the equivalent salary to that which he would have reached if he had remained with his old employers. Then the amount of shortfall during the period before he reached parity would be the amount of his future loss.

(*Tradewinds v Fletcher* (14.316 above).)

14.322 The following principles have been established in the cases:

(a) There is a considerable body of conflicting case law on the vital question whether a summarily dismissed employee should lose anything from his compensatory award because he has earned money in the period during which he should have received his period of notice. A strictly compensatory principle suggests the full duty to mitigate loss during that period, so that any earnings in the alternative position *should* indeed be deducted. The counter-argument runs to the effect that if the employer had given *proper* notice, the employee would have received full payment of wages. The early authorities took the latter approach (eg *Norton Tool Co Ltd v Tewson* [1972] IRLR 86) but the EAT departed from this practice in *Tradewinds Airways Ltd v Fletcher* (above) (see also *Finnie v Top Hat Frozen Foods Ltd* [1985] IRLR 365).

In the Court of Appeal in *Babcock FATA Ltd v Addison* [1987] IRLR 173, Ralph Gibson LJ said that:

> In the absence of an agreement, express or implied, to the contrary effect it seems to me to be clear that the respondent employer is to be given credit for all payments he has made to the employee on account of any claim for wages and other benefits ... circumstances may arise in which, having regard to the length of notice required and the known likelihood of the employee getting new employment within a short period of time, or for other sufficient reason, an employer may show that a payment less than the wages due over the full period of notice did not offend good industrial practice ... The number of cases in which an employer will be able, in the view of the employment tribunal, to justify a departure from the general practice will probably be small.

There was no rule of law to either effect (see also *Horizon Holidays Ltd v Grassi* [1987] ICR 851; and cf *Rushton v Harcros Timber and Building Supplies Ltd* [1993] ICR 230, where the EAT appeared not to apply the decision of the Court of Appeal in *Babcock* but said that an *ex gratia* redundancy payment made on the dismissal ought *always* to be taken into account).

In *Hardy v Polk (Leeds) Ltd* [2004] IRLR 420 the EAT decided that a compensatory award was based on compensation and subject to mitigation in all circumstances; it was not to be awarded in full for the period of notice which should have been given.

(b) Where an employee set up in business immediately after his dismissal and received gross earnings some £10,000 in excess of his previous earnings, the EAT in *Isleworth Studios Ltd v Rickard* [1988] IRLR 137 decided that he was to receive no compensatory award (see also *Trico Folbeith Ltd v Devonshire* [1989] IRLR 396).

(c) Normally the tribunal then adopts a sum as multiplier and multiplicand, as in tort cases, so that the proper sum is the difference between earnings in the new job and the old multiplied by a reasonable estimate of how long any shortfall will last. In *Cartiers Superfoods Ltd v Laws* [1978] IRLR 315, since the shortest period when the claimant would be expected to work was two to three years and the longest ten, the tribunal were held correct in applying a multiplier of three (see also *Adda International Ltd v Curcio* [1976] ICR 407). There may be a discount for accelerated receipt of earnings which may as a lump sum be invested and bear interest, and to take account of a whole range of possible future contingencies, although the EAT has criticised over-complicated analysis of this factor. If the employee has not found other employment before the tribunal hearing, the tribunal must consider the local job market and the following circumstances may be relevant:

(i) If the employee is in poor health or has defective eyesight (*Fougère v Phoenix Motor Ltd* [1976] ICR 495; also *Penprase v Mander Bros Ltd* [1973] IRLR 167) or was injured in a fight which led to his dismissal (*Brittains Arborfield Ltd v Van Uden* [1977] ICR 211), it may prove more difficult for him to find other work, so that a higher award is appropriate, and again this resembles the principle in tort—of taking the victim as one finds him. It is wrong in principle not to make a compensatory award because the employee was unfit for work ever since dismissal since the tribunal should consider loss of sickness benefits which attach to the former employment (*Slaughter v C. Brewer & Sons Ltd* [1990] ICR 730).

(ii) The tribunal may award compensation for a time beyond the compulsory *retiring age* if it finds that in its assessment the employee would probably have stayed in a job beyond that time (*Barrel Plating Co Ltd v Danks* [1976] 3 All ER 652).

(iii) An employee who was engaged in, say, a sophisticated *high technology area* where there are few other jobs may recover a longer period of loss of earnings.

(iv) If the employee might have been fairly *dismissed in the near future*, the period of future loss will be thereby reduced to last only until the date of fair dismissal. In *Evans v George Galloway & Co Ltd* [1974] IRLR 167, for instance, the claimant was dismissed because of poor productivity. The tribunal thought that the five weeks he had been given to improve his performance was insufficient, but that he was hardly likely to turn the corner even if given a longer period in which to do so. They thought six months was a reasonable period in which to test his capabilities and that he could have been fairly dismissed at the end of it, and they thus limited future loss of earnings to this period (see also *Winterhalter Gastronom Ltd v Webb* [1973] IRLR 120). In some cases this may mean that no compensation at all is awarded although the practice has proved very controversial, not least because it renders a finding of unfairness virtually useless to the claimant. Even so, in *Devis & Sons v Atkins* (above), the House of Lords rejected the claimant's argument that the statutory provision to the effect that the tribunal 'shall' award compensation altogether precluded a nil award. They did this on the ground that in the circumstances of the subsequently discovered fraud it was neither just nor equitable to award compensation. In *O'Donoghue v Redcar and Cleveland Borough Council* [2001] IRLR 615, the employment tribunal found that although the claimant had been unfairly dismissed and victimised on the grounds of sex because she embarrassed council members by raising in her previous tribunal proceedings remarks which those members had made which prima facie were sexist, her divisive and antagonistic approach to her colleagues was such that it would inevitably have led to her dismissal anyway within a period of six months from the date of the actual unfair dismissal which took place. The tribunal was entitled, therefore, to regard the date of six months after the termination as a cut-off point for the purposes of calculating compensation. Where the tribunal was satisfied that the claimant was on an inevitable course towards dismissal, it was legitimate to avoid the complicated problem of some sliding scale percentage estimate of her chances of dismissal as time progressed, by setting a safe date by which the tribunal was certain that dismissal would have taken place in making an award of full compensation in respect of the prior period. Imponderables can be taken into account by assessing the period of weeks when, if the procedural unfairness had not taken place, the employee would still be employed or a percentage reduction to take account of the chance that the employee would not have been dismissed at all if the proper steps had been taken (*Contract Bottling Ltd v Cave* [2015] ICR 146). In assessing future loss where a tribunal had found an employer wanting in the procedure adopted to effect a dismissal, the tribunal had to determine how likely it was that, acting fairly, the employer would have dismissed the employee. In doing so, the tribunal was not deciding what it would have done if it was the employer but instead was assessing the chances of what the actual employer would have done. The spectrum may range between the extremes of certainty that the employer would have dismissed to the certainty he would not. It should not apply a band of reasonable responses test to this different point (*Hill v Governing Body of Great Tey Primary School* [2013] ICR 691). Even if the outcome would inevitably have been the same had the dismissal been procedurally correct, that did not necessarily mean that there would be no compensatory award to be made since the employment might have continued for a longer period (*Greenwood v NWF Retail Ltd* [2011] ICR 896).

In most cases it can be assessed that the employment would not have continued forever even without the unfair dismissal being effected (*Scope v Thornett* [2007] IRLR 155). Any such question is bound to operate by way of prediction and inevitably involves a speculative element (see also *Software 2000 Ltd v Andrews* [2007] IRLR 568). The tribunal might, however, decide that there was a 100 per cent chance of dismissal at the relevant time or in due course (*Perkin v St George's Healthcare NHS Trust* [2005] IRLR 934. See also *Constantine v McGregor Cory Ltd* [2000] ICR 938).

(d) The English and the Scottish courts have diverged over whether a distinction should be made between a dismissal which is unfair on 'merely' procedural grounds and a dismissal which is substantively unfair. The Scottish Court of Session in *King v Eaton Ltd (No 2)* [1998] IRLR 686 held that the distinction will often be of some practical use. The Court of Session further held that the *Polkey* principle of awarding a percentage of what would otherwise have been the compensatory award to reflect the degree of procedural default does not entitle an employer to ask for a finding as to the likelihood of the employee having been dismissed had the proper procedures been followed, if the tribunal considers that the employer's failure to consult 'goes to the heart of the matter'. However, the Scottish EAT has also held, in *Fisher v California Cake & Cookie Ltd* [1997] IRLR 212, that where the tribunal determines that the evidence supports the position that dismissal would have occurred in any event, it is necessary that it addresses the question of whether dismissal would have occurred in percentage terms at least in respect of the grounds on which it happened in fact (*Devonshire v Trico-Folberth Ltd* [1989] IRLR 396); and if it fails to do this, its approach will be flawed. The English decisions do not, however, consider the distinction made in *King* to be helpful (see *Boulton & Paul Ltd v Arnold* [1994] IRLR 532 and *O'Dea v ISC Chemicals Ltd* [1995] IRLR 599). There is, according to these cases, no straitjacket on the awarding of compensation for failure to consult: in some cases it may cover the time during which further consultation should have taken place; whilst in others it may include disadvantage in the job market by not being informed earlier of the impending dismissal (*Elkouil v Coney Island Ltd* [2002] IRLR 174).

(e) When calculating the compensatory award, a deduction on the grounds of what is just and equitable is to be deducted *after* reducing the award to reflect payments, such as an enhanced severance payment, which are made to the employee on termination of employment (*Digital Equipment Co Ltd v Clements (No 2)* [1997] IRLR 141). A redundancy payment offsetting the basic award should not be subject to a *Polkey* percentage reduction, with such reduction only being applied to the compensatory award (*Taylor v John Webster Buildings Civil Engineering* [1999] ICR 561). This case further held that the six weeks' net pay should also not be subject to the deduction because it constituted pay in lieu of lack of notice, and the claimants would have been entitled to this amount in any event.

(f) The fact that the employee has been *accused of* gross misconduct may increase compensation (*Vaughan v Weighpack* [1974] ICR 261), while the possibility of *redundancy* in the old and new job may lead to its reduction (*Marcus v George Wimpey Co Ltd* [1974] IRLR 356; *Youngs of Gosport v Kendall* [1977] ICR 907).

(g) It is important to ask when the compensation 'clock' should stop ticking in a case where the employee gets another job and promptly loses it. In *Courtaulds Northern Spinning Ltd v Moosa* [1984] ICR 218, the EAT decided that compensation should be granted only up to the time when the employee secures alternative employment. The position may be different, however, where the employee takes a temporary job to mitigate his loss (*Ging v Ellward Lancashire Ltd* (1978) 13 ITR 265). In *Dench v Flynn & Partners* [1998] IRLR 653, the Court of Appeal held that a loss which is consequent upon unfair dismissal does not necessarily cease when a claimant gains employment of a permanent nature at an equivalent or a higher salary than the employee previously enjoyed. The question which the employment tribunal must determine is whether the particular loss was *caused* by the unfair dismissal or by some other cause. Thus, when an employee loses alternative employment after having been unfairly dismissed, the chain of causation may not have been broken depending on all of the circumstances. The earlier case of *Simrad Ltd v Scott* [1997] IRLR 147 held that the claimant was not entitled to claim for loss of earnings due to a career change after having been unfairly dismissed, as the EAT in Scotland did not consider a career change to be an immediate cause of the dismissal. It is, however, an error of law to make a compensatory award for a period beyond the time at which the employers' premises close, even though the employees allege that if the employers had acted reasonably, the premises would have continued for a longer period (*James W. Cook & Co (Wivenhoe) Ltd v Tipper* [1991] IRLR 386).

(h) Where the claimant is paid less than the national minimum wage that is a matter which must be investigated by the tribunal when assessing the proper level of both the basic and compensatory award (*Paggetti v Cobb* [2003] IRLR 861).

(i) The use of the Ogden Tables (which are normally adopted in personal injury claims to calculate the period for loss of earnings) will be rare and should only be relied on where it is established that there is a prima facie career-long loss (*Kingston upon Hull CC v Dunnachie No 3* [2003] IRLR 843). In such a case and where the tribunal has arrived at an annual figure for estimated loss and an estimated period up to a likely retirement at a particular age, the tables can be a useful tool for accurate calculation of a discount for accelerated payment and the general risks. It was not, however, appropriate to assess a career-long loss when the tribunal had found on the evidence it had heard that the claimant had a 70 per cent chance of returning to banking in an equivalent job in a few years; the Court of Appeal decided that the tribunal had wrongly approached the claimant's case on the assumption that an award had to be made up to the point that it was sure that the claimant would find an equivalent job (*Wardle v Credit Agricole Corporate & Investment Bank* [2011] ICR 1290).

(j)   In *Gover v Propertycare Ltd* [2006] ICR 1073 the Court of Appeal held that the tribunal had to decide whether the unfair departure from what should have happened was of a kind that made it possible to say that the failure had made no difference and an appellate court must tread very warily when asked to substitute its own impression for that of the tribunal.

(k)   The tribunal may decide that the employment would continue indefinitely, in which case compensation will be assessed on normal principles. This decision should only be reached where the evidence is so scant or unreliable that it should be ignored because, even with a certain amount of legitimate speculation, it is impossible to reconstruct what might have happened if the dismissal had not occurred (*Software 2000 Ltd v Andrews and Others* [2007] IRLR 568, EAT).

Loss of fringe benefits

14.323   By s 123(2) of the ERA 1996, recoverable loss includes 'any expenses reasonably incurred by the complainant in consequence of the dismissal, and ... loss of any benefit which he might reasonably be expected to have had but for the dismissal'. This has covered, in various cases, a company car (*Mohar v Granitstone Galloway Ltd* [1974] ICR 273), commission, free housing, food, special travel allowance, and benefits under a share participation scheme (*Bradshaw v Rugby Portland Cement Ltd* [1972] IRLR 46). Non-contractual bonuses, such as Christmas gifts, cannot be claimed; while tronc tips are subject to differing decisions (*Palmanor Ltd v Cedron* [1978] ICR 1008; *Nerva v R. L. & G. Ltd* [1997] ICR 11).

14.324   It is not appropriate to take into account loss of such allowances as are paid free of tax in the former employment since they go towards reimbursing the employee for expenses which are necessarily incurred in the course of his job and there should be no profit element thereon (*Tradewinds Airways Ltd v Fletcher* [1981] IRLR 272). Similarly, nothing can be awarded where a company car was only to be used for business purposes (so that there was no private benefit). On the other hand, where the employee has lost tied free accommodation, the loss will be the rent which he has to pay on new accommodation (*Scottish Cooperative Wholesale Society Ltd v Lloyd* [1973] ICR 137).

Expenses in looking for work

14.325   The sacked employee may have to move house to gain appropriate work and will inevitably have other expenses such as travel, and buying trade journals to search the appointments columns (*Cooperative Wholesale Society v Squirrell* (1974) 9 ITR 191), although now this will largely be done through internet sites. This is part of his necessary mitigation of loss and the dismissed employee can claim compensation for the costs incurred in seeking it. Legal expenses in fighting a claim are not, however, recoverable under this head, although they may, in certain restricted circumstances, be included in a costs order. The tribunal may also in a proper case award expenses incurred in a reasonable attempt to set up a new business (*Gardiner-Hill v Roland Berger Technics Ltd* [1982] IRLR 498; *AON Training Ltd v Dore* [2005] IRLR 891) or in having to move away for the purposes of a new job.

Loss of pension right

14.326   Loss of pension entitlement can in some cases amount to a very large sum, and its calculation often proves difficult. Guidance is provided in *Employment Tribunals Compensation for Loss of Pension Rights*, which is a guide drawn up by three tribunal chairmen with the assistance of the Government Actuary Department. The third edition was published in November 2003. It is not, however, binding authority (*Bingham v Hobourn Engineering Ltd* [1992] IRLR 298) and it is open to the parties to call their own expert actuarial evidence if they wish to (*Port of Tilbury (London) Ltd v Birch and Others* [2005] IRLR 92; *Griffin v Plymouth Hospital NHS Trust* [2014] IRLR 963).

There are basically two forms of pension loss which may be suffered, the loss of pension position earned thus far, and loss of future pension opportunity (*Copson v Eversure Accessories Ltd* [1974] ICR 636). Usually it is most appropriate to base the sum which has been lost on the amount of employee's and employer's contributions which are made to a future pension (*Willment Brothers Ltd v Oliver* [1979] IRLR 393), and this is reached by applying the conventional multiplier and multiplicand method. Where, however, the employee is approaching retirement, tribunals may instead determine how much it would cost to purchase an annuity to produce the pension which he has lost and award this amount subject to a discount for accelerated payment (*Smith, Kline & French Laboratories v Coates* [1977] IRLR 220). In the leading case, *Powrmatic v Bull* [1977] IRLR 144, it was also necessary to take into consideration that the thirty-two-year-old employee was unlikely to remain in the same job for the next thirty-three years and that he might go on to another job with much better pension prospects, the scheme might be altered, or he might die prematurely. There were a number of imponderables. A multiplier of fifteen was adopted instead of the actual number of years to take account of these contingencies. A withdrawal factor as high as 70 per cent may be justified in recognition of the high probability that an employee's poor performance would sooner or later result in his dismissal (*TBA Industrial Products Ltd v Locke* [1984] IRLR 48). **14.327**

A system of computation which is based on the value of the employer's contributions is not appropriate in assessing loss of pension rights under a scheme which yields not only an income benefit but also a lump sum arising as a right by commutation of pension (*Clancy v Cannock Chase Technical College* [2001] IRLR 331). Conversely, payments under the employer's occupational pension scheme which the claimants decided to take early following their dismissals should not be offset against their compensatory awards (*Knapton v ECC Card Clothing Ltd* [2006] IRLR 756). **14.328**

Loss of employment protection

It will take a sacked employee two years in a new job to build up such continuous employment as is sufficient to found a claim for unfair dismissal, and for a redundancy payment, and the entitlement to continuous service in both will also be correspondingly lower. A nominal sum is thus awarded on account of loss in respect of unfair dismissal, while the basic award is intended to serve this purpose for loss of redundancy payment (*Norton Tool Co Ltd v Tewson* [1972] ICR 501; see generally *Mono Pumps Ltd v Froggatt and Radford* [1987] IRLR 368). The tribunal may also take into account the fact that an employee's dismissal may deprive him of his entitlement under the employer's redundancy scheme through lack of service (*Lee v IPC Business Press Ltd* [1984] ICR 306). The EAT has declared that an amount to reflect loss of notice entitlement in a new job is *especially* necessary in a time of high unemployment (*Daley v A.E. Dorsett* [1981] IRLR 385). The sum most usually awarded is £150. **14.329**

Manner of dismissal

A sum may be awarded if the way in which the employee's sacking was handled makes him less acceptable to another employer (*John Mill and Sons v Quinn* [1974] IRLR 107; *Brittains Arborfield Ltd v Van Uden* [1977] ICR 211). In *Johnson v Unisys Ltd* [2001] ICR 480, Lord Hoffmann appeared to suggest that loss was not restricted to financial loss **14.330** but included compensation for 'distress, humiliation, damage to reputation in the community or to family life', and this threatened to extend greatly the range of awards but this was not part of the *ratio decidendi* of the case. He had commented: 'The emphasis is upon the tribunal awarding such compensation as it thinks just and equitable. So I see no reason why in an appropriate case it should not include compensation for distress, humiliation, damage to reputation in the community or to family life.'

14.331 In *Dunnachie v Hull City Council* [2004] IRLR 727, the House of Lords (including Lord Hoffmann) decisively concluded that tribunals had no jurisdiction to make awards for non-economic loss, and held that the comment of Lord Hoffmann in *Johnson* was *obiter*. Their Lordships concluded unanimously that on the proper construction of the statute, non-economic loss was thus not recoverable. They considered that read in context the word 'loss' had a plain meaning which excludes non-economic loss. It did not cover *injury* to feelings and its terms were to be contrasted with the discrimination acts, which all expressly provide for compensation for injury to feelings, albeit 'for the avoidance of doubt'. Further, it could not be said that the meaning was different when re-enacted in the 1996 Act from that which it bore in 1971 when unfair dismissal was introduced.

14.332 Lord Steyn took as a further support for his conclusion as to non-economic loss being irrecoverable, that any wider meaning of 'loss' would permit an award of aggravated or exemplary compensation by way of penalisation of the conduct of the employer and that this could not be 'seriously suggest[ed]' as the meaning intended by Parliament.

14.333 In his concurring speech, Lord Rodger of Earlsferry accepted that it would be wholly anomalous if non-pecuniary awards could be made as compensation whilst the direct remedies of reinstatement or re-engagement referred only to 'sums payable', which was clearly financial only.

Deductions

14.334 These sums must be considered:

(a) *Ex gratia* sums: employers should give close attention to how they structure *ex gratia* payments if they envisage the possibility of an unfair dismissal claim. The EAT in *Chelsea Football Club v Heath* [1981] IRLR 73 held that if an employer admits that he has unfairly dismissed an employee and pays him an amount specifically referable to the basic award the employer may properly contend that he has made a basic award and need not pay again. Whether a general payment covers the basic award is 'a question of construction in each case'. Here the letter was really to be read as an offer without prejudice to legal rights.

In *McCarthy v British Insulated Callenders Cables plc* [1985] IRLR 94, the EAT decided whether an *ex gratia* payment should be deducted from the amount which would otherwise have been awarded and then the maximum compensatory award applied, or alternatively should merely be deducted from the maximum compensatory award. This may make a major practical difference. Here, the employee had been given an *ex gratia* sum of £1,274. Compensation was assessed by the tribunal at £15,820. The tribunal reduced the sum to £7,000, then the maximum award, and deducted £1,274 from that. The EAT thought that this was the wrong approach. The £1,274 should be deducted from the amount which would be awarded irrespective of the maximum. The claimant thus received the then £7,000 maximum. The same process applies to deduction for contributory fault (*Walter Braund (London) Ltd v Murray* [1991] IRLR 100).

Where the employment tribunal has not stated the period for which it is awarding compensation, such sum is not to be deducted from an award for wrongful dismissal on the basis that the claimant was unable to point to any double recovery (*O'Laiore v Jackel International Ltd* [1991] IRLR 170, CA).

(b) Discrimination compensation: s 126 of the ERA 1996 states that where compensation falls to be awarded for unfair dismissal and discrimination, an employment tribunal must wholly offset the compensation under one head against the others.

(c) Tax rebate: a tax rebate need not be deducted (*MBS Ltd v Calo* [1983] IRLR 189; cf *Lucas v Lawrence Scott and Electromotors Ltd* [1983] IRLR 61).

(d) Sickness benefits: where an employee had received after his dismissal statutory sick pay for six months and invalidity benefit for more than three years, it has been held that it is appropriate to deduct all sums thus received (*Puglia v C. James & Sons* [1996] ICR 301; *Sun and Sand Ltd v Fitzjohn* [1979] ICR 268; *Morgans v Alpha Plus Security Ltd* [2005] IRLR 234; see also *Homan v A1 Bacon Co Ltd* [1996] ICR 721) but this is not a unanimous view (eg *Hilton International Hotels (UK) Ltd v Faraji* [1994] IRLR 267). A middle course of deducting half of the amount was taken in *Rubenstein v McGloughlin* [1996] IRLR 557.

(e) Death in service benefit (*Fox v British Airways plc* [2013] ICR 1257).

(f) Redundancy payments: s 123(7) of the ERA 1996 states that where a redundancy payment is made to the employee, an amount equivalent to the basic award will be set off against the basic award and the surplus then is set off against the compensatory award.

(g) An employee cannot as part of a constructive dismissal claim secure compensation for future loss of earnings caused by the employer's breach of the implied term of trust and confidence (*GAB Robins (UK) Ltd v Triggs* [2008] IRLR 318).

(h) Where an employee is prevented after dismissal from working owing to ill health, the tribunal must decide whether the ill health was caused to any material extent by the dismissal itself (*Dignity Funerals Ltd v Bruce* [2005] IRLR 189).

(i) A question which may make a big difference to the amount of the compensatory award actually awarded is whether this is set off as part of the overall assessment of loss or only after reductions under the principle in *Polkey v Dayton* or if contributory fault had been made from the award. In *Digital Equipment Ltd v Clements (No 2)* [1998] ICR 258, the Court of Appeal held that as a matter of statutory construction, it was to be taken off the compensatory award as finally determined, that is the compensatory award *after* deductions.

In asking would a person have been dismissed in any event, this is inevitably a matter of impression and judgement for a fact-finding tribunal (*Lyons v DWP Jobcentre plus* [2014] ICR 668). **14.335**

As to contribution to compensation, see *Thaine v LSE* [2010] ICR 1422; *Hackney LBC v Sivanandan* [2011] ICR 1374, [2013] ICR 672. **14.336**

Contributory fault

Blameworthy and causative

The power to make a deduction from an award for contributory fault allows a tribunal a wide discretion to reduce compensation in a case where they find the claimant employee to be to some degree at fault. By s 123(6) of the ERA 1996, 'where the tribunal finds that the dismissal was to any extent caused or contributed to by any action of the complainant' compensation may be reduced by 'such amount as it considers just and equitable'. The tribunals possess a slightly differently worded power to deduct for contributory fault from **14.337** the basic award (s 122(2)). Viscount Dilhorne called contributory fault an 'industrial form of contributory negligence' in *W. Devis & Sons Ltd v Atkins* [1977] AC 931.

14.338   Sir Hugh Griffiths said in *Maris v Rotherham Corporation* [1974] 2 All ER 776 that the concept 'brings into consideration all the circumstances surrounding the dismissal, requiring the tribunal to take a broad common sense view of the situation, and to decide what, if any, part the applicant's own conduct played in contributing to his dismissal and then in the light of that finding, decide what, if any, reduction should be made in the assessment of this loss'. The onus lies on the employer to prove that the employee contributed to his dismissal by conduct which is 'culpable or blameworthy' and unreasonable in the circumstances. His action need not, however, amount to a breach of contract or tort in order to qualify (*Nelson v BBC (No 2)* [1979] IRLR 346; *Gibson v British Transport Docks Board* [1982] IRLR 228). In *Nelson's* case, Brandon LJ thought that it 'includes conduct which is ... perverse or foolish or, if I may use the colloquialism, bloody-minded. It may also include action which, though not meriting any of those more pejorative epithets, is nevertheless unreasonable in the circumstances'. These principles apply:

(a)   it is only the complainant's conduct which may be taken into account, and not all the circumstances of the case (*Parker Foundry Ltd v Slack* [1992] ICR 302); and

(b)   tribunals must concentrate on the conduct of the employee and not probe his state of mind (*Ladbroke Racing Ltd v Mason* [1978] ICR 49).

14.339   The employee's misdeeds also need not relate to the reason which is given by the employer for the dismissal (*Robert Whiting Designs Ltd v Lamb* [1978] ICR 89), but according to the EAT in *Hutchinson v Enfield Rolling Mills Ltd* [1981] IRLR 318 there must be 'a causal link between the actions of the employee and the dismissal'. In that case, the employee was dismissed for attending a union demonstration in Brighton, notwithstanding that he had presented a sick note for the day to his employer in which he gave sciatica as the reason for absence. The EAT considered that the tribunal was wrong to take any of the following as amounting to contributory fault: that he had been a 'troublemaker' throughout his employment; that he intended to picket his union leaders in Brighton; and that his political views were affecting his work. None of these was, however, causative of the dismissal, but his attendance in Brighton *was* and in itself justified a reduction for contributory fault. The need for causation was re-emphasised in *Tele-Trading Ltd v Jenkins* [1990] IRLR 430.

14.340   The following situations raise conceptual difficulties for the issue of contributory fault and have thus received attention from the EAT:

(a)   Incapability cases: in the normal case, fault consists of some misconduct by the employee and there has been much discussion as to whether it is appropriate to deduct when the complaint is about the employee's incapability. There are, however, many borderline cases between conduct and capability. Kilner Brown J in *Kraft Foods Ltd v Fox* [1978] ICR 311 drew this distinction:

In the case of a man who falls short, he may not try. He may not be doing his best. That is something over which he has control. However, if he is doing his best and his best is not good enough, it does not seem to us to be proper to say that in those circumstances he has contributed.

(See also *Moncur v International Paint Co Ltd* [1978] IRLR 223; *Sutton & Gates (Luton) Ltd v Boxall* [1978] IRLR 486; *Slaughter v C. Brewer & Sons Ltd* [1990] IRLR 426). One example would be where the employee blatantly and persistently refuses to obtain appropriate medical reports or attend for medical examination.

(b) Constructive dismissal: a reduction is only exceptionally appropriate in a case of constructive dismissal since the finding itself involves a conclusion that there has been a fundamental breach by the employer (*Holroyd v Gravure Cylinders Ltd* [1984] IRLR 259). One such rare case was *Garner v Grange Furnishing Ltd* [1977] IRLR 206, where the EAT criticised the employee's 'oversensitivity and his most unfortunate choice of time for taking the step of walking out' (see now *Morrison v ATGWU* [1989] IRLR 361). Further, in *Polentarutti v Autokraft Ltd* [1991] ICR 757, the EAT held that there need not be found a reason for dismissal to which the employee specifically contributed for contributory fault to be awarded.

(c) Post-dismissal conviction: in *Ladup Ltd v Barnes* [1982] IRLR 7, the EAT sanctioned a deduction for contributory fault in the light of a subsequent conviction of the employee for the possession of cannabis, which was promulgated after compensation had been assessed. Bristow J considered the employer's application for a review 'unanswerable' since the conviction made the original award a 'blatant unfairness'.

(d) Selective re-engagement: it had been argued that the general principle should be modified in a case under ss 237–9 of the TULR(C)A 1992, in that the tribunal should concentrate not on the conduct leading to the dismissal but instead conduct contributing to the employer's resolve not to take the striker back after the dispute. This contention was, however, firmly rejected in *Courtaulds Northern Spinning Ltd v Moosa* [1984] ICR 218.

Examples of contributory fault

The case law offers the following examples of contributory fault: **14.341**

(a) refusal to take alternative work offered by the employer (*Nelson v BBC (No 2)* [1979] IRLR 346);

(b) threats by the claimant of violence when allegations of financial misdeeds were made (*Munif v Cole & Kirby Ltd* [1973] ICR 486);

(c) participation in violence towards work colleagues who ignored an overtime ban even though it could not be proved precisely what part the claimant played (*Gibson*'s case (above));

(d) setting up a rival business (*Connor v Comet Radiovision Services Ltd*, EAT 650/ 81);

(e) placing the wrong body in a coffin (*Coalter v Walter Craven* [1980] IRLR 262); and

(f) not returning a cheque to the employer which the employer had mistakenly sent to the claimant (*Allen v Hammett* [1982] IRLR 89).

On the other hand, the following matters have been held not to constitute contributory fault: **14.342**

(a) failure to exercise a right of appeal under the employer's internal procedure (*Hoover Ltd v Forde* [1980] ICR 239) (see below 14.356);

(b) failure by an employee to disclose a criminal conviction which he had no need to reveal by reason of the Rehabilitation of Offenders Act 1974 (*Property Guards Ltd v Taylor and Kershaw* [1982] IRLR 175); and

(c) ill health (*Slaughter v C. Brewer & Sons Ltd* [1990] ICR 730).

Participation in industrial action was for many years held to fall outside this rubric (*Courtaulds Northern Spinning Ltd v Moosa* (above)) since this would require tribunals to attach blame to the respective parties in industrial disputes, but the EAT departed from this principle in *TNT Express Ltd v Downes* [1994] ICR 1, on the basis that it was not warranted by the statutory language.

This controversial issue was finally resolved by the House of Lords. The broad position   **14.343**
in *Moosa* was restored in *Tracey v Crosville Wales Ltd* [1997] ICR 862, on the basis that

this was the presumed intention of Parliament, especially given that many who had been involved in the same industrial action would have been offered re-engagement. There is, however, an important caveat that where complainants have been shown to be responsible for some additional conduct of their own over and above mere participation in the industrial action, the fact that such conduct occurred during and as part of the industrial action does not preclude the tribunal from examining it separately and considering whether it contributed to the dismissal (see especially at 880G).

Amount of reduction

14.344   Once a causal link has been established, the *amount* of deduction is an issue which is at large for the tribunal. It takes a percentage from such compensation as the employee would otherwise be entitled to. In extreme cases the award may be reduced to nil, but this should only occur where the unfairness is highly technical, perhaps a minor breach of procedure, and the employee's own conduct was highly provocative. If the tribunal decides that there has been blameworthy conduct on the part of the employee which caused his dismissal, it must reduce the compensatory award (*Optikinetics Ltd v Whooley* [1999] ICR 984).

14.345   There has been a major difference of opinion as to the acceptability of large deductions. Although the English EAT reduced compensation by 100 per cent in *Maris v Rotherham Corporation* [1974] IRLR 147, it commented in *Trend v Chiltern Hunt Ltd* [1977] ICR 612 that reductions should rarely exceed 80 per cent. Lord McDonald, on the other hand, in the Scottish EAT in *Courtney v Babcock & Wilcox (Operations) Ltd* [1977] IRLR 30 could see nothing wrong in principle or practice with a 100 per cent reduction, adding that the English EAT's approach savoured of a tariff which was unacceptable. This line was indeed approved in *Devis & Sons v Atkins* (above). The question of what is just and equitable is directed to the proportion of the reduction and not whether there should be any reduction at all, which is simply a question of causation (*Warrilow v Robert Walker Ltd* [1984] IRLR 304; see also *Friend v Civil Aviation Authority* [2002] IRLR 819). A full 100 per cent reduction was described as a permissible but unusual finding in *Steen v ASP Packaging Ltd* [2014] ICR 56.

14.346   The deduction for contributory fault is made from the losses of the employee, as assessed without regard to the statutory maximum award of compensation. Thus, if the tribunal computes the potential award as £70,000 but considers a 50 per cent reduction appropriate, £35,000 is deducted from £70,000 notwithstanding that the statutory maximum is presently £52,600. That only operates as a ceiling on the *final* figure awarded (see *Parker & Farr Ltd v Shelvey* [1979] IRLR 435; *UBAF Bank Ltd v Davis* [1978] IRLR 442). The termination payment made should be deducted before making the *Polkey* reduction (*Digital Equipment Co Ltd v Clements (No 2)* [1997] IRLR 141).

14.347   There has also been some conflict of authority as to whether a tribunal errs in law in making a reduction for contributory fault from only the compensatory award whilst leaving intact the basic element. The Northern Ireland Court of Appeal in *McFall & Co v Curran* [1981] IRLR 455 thought that this showed unacceptable inconsistency, but the EAT in *Les Ambassadeurs Club v Bainda* [1982] IRLR 5 saw no objection. In most cases, however, the same percentage should be deducted from both awards (*RSPCA v Cruden* [1986] IRLR 83). An example of different percentage deductions is, however, to be found in the case of *Charles Robertson Ltd v White* [1995] ICR 349.

14.348   The EAT will generally not intervene in a tribunal's finding of contributory fault, still less in the *amount* of deduction. In *Hollier v Plysu Ltd* [1983] IRLR 260, the Court of Appeal advised tribunals to take a broad common-sense view. It was a matter of 'impression, opinion and discretion' (see also *Warrilow v Robert Walker Ltd* (above); *Yate Foundry Ltd v Walters* [1984] ICR 445; *F. C. Shepherd & Co Ltd v Jerrom* [1986] IRLR 358).

Mitigation

Reduction in compensation will be made if the employee failed to take reasonable steps to gain another job or otherwise keep down his loss, as at common law (ERA 1996, s 123(4)). The onus of proof of failure of mitigation rests on the employer (*Sturdy Finance Ltd v Bardsley* [1979] IRLR 65; *Fyfe v Scientific Furnishings Ltd* [1989] IRLR 331). **14.349**

In *Wilding v BT* [2002] IRLR 524, the Court of Appeal held that it is the duty of the employee to act as a reasonable person who is unaffected by the prospect of compensation from the former employer. The test of reasonableness is objective and based on the totality of the evidence heard; the circumstances in which the offer was made and refused, the attitude of the former employer, the way in which the employee had been treated whilst employed, and all the surrounding circumstances, including the employee's state of mind should be taken into account. Further, the tribunal should not be too stringent in its expectations of the injured party. The duty only arises *after* dismissal, so a refusal to accept other employment before that date does not affect the judgment (*Savoia v Chiltern Herb Farms Ltd* [1981] IRLR 65). Indeed, in general, conduct prior to dismissal cannot feature in an allegation of failure to mitigate loss (*Prestwick Circuits Ltd v McAndrew* [1990] IRLR 191). **14.350**

The employee cannot, however, sit back and mount up an unreasonable extent of losses after termination in the confident expectation that they will be met by the respondent. The proper test for tribunals to apply was set out by the Court of Appeal in *Bessenden Properties v Corness* [1974] IRLR 338, as whether, 'if the complainant had had no hope of recovering compensation from anybody else and if he had consulted merely his own interests and had acted reasonably in all the circumstances, would he have accepted the job in mitigation of the loss which he had suffered' (see also *Archbold Freightage v Wilson* [1974] IRLR 10; *Scottish and Newcastle Breweries Ltd v Halliday* [1986] IRLR 291; *Morganite Electrical Carbon Ltd v Donne* [1987] IRLR 363; cf *Fyfe v Scientific Furnishings Ltd* [1989] IRLR 331). **14.351**

This is a question of fact in each case, and reference may be made to the authorities on the similar question for wrongful dismissal (Chapter 13). The claimant need not show that he took steps in mitigation *before* he was actually dismissed (*McAndrew v Prestwick Circuits Ltd* [1988] IRLR 514). **14.352**

Broadly speaking, although the employee need not take the first job that comes along (*Gallear v Watson* [1979] IRLR 306), it will be reasonable after a period of unemployment to accept a post at a lower rate of pay than he enjoyed before (*Daley v A. E. Dorsett* [1981] IRLR 385; *Hardwick v Leeds AHA* [1975] IRLR 319). To make one job application in eight weeks has been held to be unreasonable (*O'Reilly v Welwyn and Hatfield District Council* [1975] IRLR 334; *Sweetlove v Redbridge & Waltham Forest AHA* [1979] IRLR 195). The proper approach to calculation involves assessing how long the employee would be out of work if he had properly mitigated his loss, rather than reducing the global sum by a percentage as in contributory fault (*Smith, Kline & French Laboratories Ltd v Coates* [1977] IRLR 220). A similar process is to be applied to loss of pension rights. **14.353**

Tribunals realistically recognise that a former employee who starts a new business after dismissal will probably earn little in the initial period, but this does not mean that he is **14.354** not reasonably mitigating his loss. In *Gardiner-Hill v Roland Berger Technics Ltd* [1982] IRLR 498, the claimant was dismissed from his position as managing director of the respondent consultancy service when he was 55 years old and decided then to set up on his own account. In the six and a half months between the time of the dismissal and the tribunal hearing he had earned only £1,500. The employer argued that this did not reflect a reasonable attempt to mitigate his loss and the tribunal decided that since he was spending some 90 per cent of his time on the new business and not looking for alternative employment, his compensation should be reduced by 80 per cent. The EAT thought that the claimant's strategy was a reasonable one and that in any event it was wrong to make a percentage reduction in relation to mitigation. Rather, the tribunal should have decided on a date when, if the ex-employee had used reasonable efforts, he would have gained other employment at a similar level (see also *Lee v IPC Business Press Ltd* [1984] ICR 306; *Savage v Saxena* [1998] IRLR 182).

14.355   An employee is well advised to keep a list of all jobs for which he has applied and the answers he has received in order to demonstrate to a tribunal that he has tried as hard as he can to find alternative work.

Effect of failing to comply with procedures

14.356   As from 1 October 2004, if the statutory procedures set out in Sch 2 to the Employment Act 2002 were not completed before proceedings were begun in the employment tribunal (s 31(2)), and the non-completion was wholly or mainly attributable to failure by the employee to comply with a requirement of the procedure or to exercise a right of appeal under it, the tribunal had to reduce any award by 10 per cent and might, if it considered it just and equitable to do so, reduce it by a further amount up to 50 per cent of the award. If, on the other hand, the failure was that of the employer to provide these procedures, the tribunal had, save in exceptional circumstances, to increase any award by 10 per cent and could, if it considered it just and equitable to do so, increase it by a further amount up to 50 per cent. This was, however, abolished by the Employment Act 2008, but by a new s 207A of the TURL(C)A, if there is a breach of an ACAS code of practice by the employer and the failure was unreasonable the tribunal may if it considers it just and equitable to do so increase any award by no more than 25 per cent. By the same token if the employee is in breach the amount may be reduced by no more than 25 per cent. By Sch A2 this applies to most procedures.

Jobseeker's allowance

14.357   Jobseeker's allowance and unfair dismissal cover similar types of loss through a period of unemployment. After initial doubts whether they should be set off one against the other, the relationship between them is now governed by regulations.

14.358   By the Employment Protection (Recoupment of Jobseeker's Allowance and Income Support) Regulations 1996 (SI 1996/2349), the Department of Work and Pensions has the first claim on the amount of compensation for the days on which the allowance or social security has already been paid out. The employee should not recover twice over. An employment tribunal thus has to set out an amount of the 'prescribed element' of compensation, that is, immediate loss of earnings up to the tribunal hearing, if any, and this must not be paid over by the employer until the Department has determined whether to recoup the allowance paid. If so, the Secretary of State must serve a recoupment notice within twenty-one days after the hearing, or nine days after the decision has been sent to the parties, whichever is later. There is no appeal against the amount of money stated in the notice.

Where the payment represents remuneration which the employment tribunal considered **14.359** the employee might have earned for a particular day, he cannot receive an allowance. This applies even if the former employer is insolvent so that the sum due is *not* in fact paid (*Morton v Chief Adjudication Officer* [1988] IRLR 444).

Where the case is settled without a tribunal hearing there is no provision for recoupment, **14.360** and this has undoubtedly been an additional spur to settlement of claims.

Other issues

(a) There is no limit on compensation in discrimination cases and interest may be **14.361** awarded for a discriminatory dismissal under the Equality Act, but there remains a limit to the unfair dismissal jurisdiction.
(b) The employment tribunal must make an award of interest if an award is unpaid forty-two days after the decision is promulgated (Employment Tribunals (Interest) Order 1990 (SI 1990/479) and there are special provisions for sex discrimination and equal pay claims (Sex Discrimination and Equal Pay (Remedies) Regulations 1993 (SI 1993/2798)).

T UNFAIR DISMISSAL: OVERVIEW

> The Industrial Relations Act 1971 was a remarkable piece of social legislation. Parliament recognised that even if the employer had the right in strict law to dismiss the employee there were circumstances in which it would be unfair for the employer to exercise that right (per Lord Salmon, *Nothman v Barnet LBC* [1979] IRLR 35, para 4).

Of the whole panoply of employment protection rights which began to be enacted in **14.362** the mid-1960s, the unfair dismissal provisions have had by far the most effect in changing personnel practices and collective bargaining arrangements. They were intended to accord to employees a form of property in their jobs. Such was the employee's compensation for his relative lack of property in the capital that employs him. If taken away unjustly, he should be reinstated in his job, or at the least gain compensation for loss suffered. No longer could an employer autocratically terminate an employee's contract at whim.

On its procedural side it has important implications for the development of rules for **14.363** industrial justice which go far beyond dismissal alone. Some 42 per cent of employment tribunal applications concern unfair dismissal and its effect is in inverse proportion to the degree of unionisation in a particular factory or plant, so that in poorly organised industries, such as construction and distribution, claims are disproportionately high. BIS figures show that a quarter of all claims are made against firms employing fewer than twenty. However, there are disturbing indications that those most at risk from the 'hire and fire' mentality of management are least aware of the legislation, and are often persuaded to become independent contractors and to accept unfavourable settlements. Moreover, in times of high unemployment, many workers feel that to bring an unfair dismissal application will mark them as a 'troublemaker' and, whether they win or lose, render it more difficult to gain another job.

It is also necessary to keep its practical impact in perspective. Far less than 1 per cent of **14.364** employees leaving their jobs make such claims, and each year only one out of 100 firms with fewer than 200 employees is likely to be faced with such application.

15

PUBLIC INTEREST DISCLOSURES: DISMISSAL AND DETRIMENT CLAIMS

A	DISCLOSURE	15.03	**C** DETRIMENT	15.17
	The scope of protected disclosures	15.06	**D** THE REASON TEST	15.18
	Persons to whom disclosure may be made	15.08	**E** BURDEN OF PROOF	15.19
	Reasonable belief in the truth	15.09	**F** SCOPE	15.20
	Good faith	15.12	**G** JOINT LIABILITY	15.21
B	WIDER DISCLOSURE	15.13	**H** TIME LIMIT	15.24

15.01 The Public Interest Disclosure Act 1998 (which inserted a new Pt IVA into the ERA 1996) was implemented to protect individuals who make disclosures of information in the public interest. All statutory references in this chapter are to the ERA 1996. It was passed with support from all parties and followed the lobbying activities of Public Concern at Work amongst others. (For full coverage see Bowers, Lewis, Fodder, and Mitchell, *Whistleblowing: Law and Practice* OUP, 2017, 3rd edn.)

15.02 An employee who makes a protected disclosure may claim in respect of a detriment or dismissal which is caused thereby. In analysing this provision, it is necessary to consider what is a qualifying disclosure and then whether that disclosure is protected, and this issue depends crucially on the question to whom the disclosure is made and how it is made.

A DISCLOSURE

15.03 Disclosure is an ordinary word and has no special meaning (*Bolton School v Evans* [2007] IRLR 140) in this context. A disclosure may be constituted from a series of separate emails (*Norbrook Laboratories (GB) Ltd v Shaw* [2014] ICR 540).

15.04 There is a distinction between conveying information and making an allegation; the ordinary meaning of information is to convey facts and disclosure has to be more than a communication. A solicitor's letter in *Cavendish Munro Professional Risks Management Ltd v Gould* [2010] ICR 325 was held to be merely a statement of the claimant's position which was communicated in the course of negotiations between the parties alleging that the claimant was an oppressed minority shareholder, but it did not convey let alone disclose information (see also *Kilraine v LB of Wandsworth* [2016] IRLR 422).

15.05 Facts may relate to an omission (eg the wards have not been cleaned for the last two weeks) as well as to a positive action (eg the sharps were left lying around) (*Millbank Financial Services Ltd v Crawford* [2014] IRLR 18).

The scope of protected disclosures

Protected disclosures are defined as disclosures concerning crime, breach of a legal   **15.06**
obligation, miscarriage of justice, danger to health or safety or to the environment,
and attempts to conceal any of these. In *Parkins v Sodexho Ltd* [2002] IRLR 109,
the applicant claimed that he was dismissed after complaining about lack of adequate
on-site supervision which, he maintained, gave rise to a breach of contract. This was
a protected disclosure as it revealed a breach of a legal obligation. There was no need
to distinguish between an obligation arising from the contract of employment and any
other obligation. Such information cannot be protected by a duty of confidentiality in
a contract because this is rendered void (s 43J of the ERA). The term 'worker' is very
widely defined for these purposes and includes third-party contractors and trainees
(s 43K).

A protected disclosure may occur after termination of employment (*Onyango v Berkeley*   **15.07**
[2013] IRLR 338). The sections define a qualifying disclosure as one which is made by the
worker with no express requirement that the worker was in any particular employment
let alone the employment in which he claimed to have been subjected to a detriment; the
act could be inspired by a disclosure made at an earlier time when he had worker status,
whoever the employer then was (*BP plc v Elstone* [2010] ICR 879).

Persons to whom disclosure may be made

There are different hurdles to be satisfied depending on who is the person to whom the   **15.08**
disclosure is made:

(a) The worker is entitled to disclose a relevant failure to his employer if he has a reason-
     able belief that malpractice has occurred (s 43C); and
(b) to his legal adviser if the disclosure is made in the course of obtaining legal advice
     (s 43D).
(c) He is further entitled to disclose relevant information to a person prescribed by an
     order made by the Secretary of State specifically for this purpose, provided that he
     reasonably believes 'that the information disclosed, and any allegation contained in
     it, are substantially true'. He must also reasonably believe that the relevant failure
     falls within any description of matters in respect of which that person is so pre-
     scribed (s 43F). Prescribed persons include regulators such as the Financial Conduct
     Authority, the General Medical Council, and OFCOM (Public Interest (Prescribed
     Persons) Order 2014 (SI 2014/2418)).

Reasonable belief in the truth

The standard of belief in the truth of what was disclosed is not such as to require the worker   **15.09**
to hold the belief that both the factual basis of the disclosure and what it tends to show were
substantially true (*Darnton v University of Surrey* [2003] ICR 615). That phrase 'tends to
show' is important as the crucial regulator of the scope of the provision. The reasonable
belief has to be based on the facts as they are understood by the worker to be at the time of
the disclosure, not as actually found to be the case after a tribunal hearing.

It is sufficient if the employee reasonably believes that the matters on which he relies   **15.10**
amount to a criminal act or found a legal obligation; they do not have to do so in fact
(*Babula v Waltham Forest College* [2007] IRLR 346). This is because the purpose of the
statute is to encourage responsible whistleblowing, and to expect employees to have a

detailed knowledge of, for example, the criminal law sufficient to enable them to determine whether or not particular facts which they reasonably believe are true are capable as a matter of law of constituting a particular criminal offence is unrealistic, and to require this would work against the grain of the statute.

15.11   In *Babula v Waltham Forest College* (supra), the Court of Appeal decided that the reasonable belief test applies to whether there is a criminal offence or legal obligation. Mr Babula, an American citizen, was employed by the respondent college as a business studies lecturer. He was told by his students that his predecessor had used lesson time to teach religious studies, dividing the class into Islamic and non-Islamic groups, and had told the Muslim students that he wished that an incident such as 11 September 2001 would occur in London. Mr Babula raised the matter with a supervisor, who took the view that no action was required to be taken against him. Concerned that there might be a threat to national security and believing that at the least an offence of incitement to racial hatred had been committed, and that the College had failed to comply with a legal obligation to report it, Mr Babula himself contacted the CIA and FBI and informed the College that he had done so. The disclosure led to a series of actions by the College which Mr Babula felt had left him with no choice but to resign. The employment tribunal struck out his claim as having no reasonable prospect of success, on the ground that, on the basis of the facts asserted by Mr Babula, any incitement was to religious, not racial, hatred, which was not an offence at the time, and, therefore, the disclosure was not a qualifying disclosure complying with s 43B(1) ERA. In rejecting this view, the Court of Appeal emphasised that if a worker reasonably believed that a criminal offence had been committed, was being committed, or was likely to be committed, and provided his belief was found by the tribunal to be objectively reasonable, neither the fact that the belief turned out to be wrong nor the fact that the information which he believed to be true did not in law amount to a criminal offence was sufficient, of itself, to render the belief unreasonable. The Court noted that this approach was also supported by policy considerations. As Wall LJ said (at para 80):

> It is also, I think, significant that section 43B(1) uses the phrase 'tends to show' not 'shows'. There is, in short, nothing in section 43B(1) which requires the whistleblower to be right. At its highest in relation to section 43B(1)(a) he must have a reasonable belief that the information in his possession 'tends to show' that a criminal offence has been committed: at its lowest he must have a reasonable belief that the information in his possession tends to show that a criminal offence is likely to be committed. The purpose of the statute, as I read it, is to encourage responsible whistleblowing. To expect employees on the factory floor or in shops and offices to have a detailed knowledge of the criminal law sufficient to enable them to determine whether or not particular facts which they reasonably believe to be true are capable, as a matter of law, of constituting a particular criminal offence seems to me both unrealistic and to work against the policy of the statute.

Good faith

15.12   Good faith is a separate issue and used to be required for liability to be established. It is now an issue only in relation to remedy so that the older cases are still relevant but only to that extent. These include a decision that the fact that the employee believed that the material disclosed was true does not conclude the issue of good faith in his favour since the motive for which the employee had made the disclosure could change its character from good to bad. This calls for a difficult fact-sensitive judgment by the tribunal. The employee might, for example, be promoting the disclosure merely for reasons of personal antagonism. In judging this sensitive issue of motive, the tribunal is entitled to consider facts arising both before and after the time of disclosure (*Street v Derbyshire Unemployed Workers Centre* [2004] IRLR 687).

B WIDER DISCLOSURE

There are other circumstances in which workers may validly make a wider disclosure. **15.13** Section 43G provides that where the worker makes the disclosure to any other person, believes that the information is substantially true, is not making the disclosure for purposes of personal gain, and meets one of the following conditions, the disclosure will be protected provided that it is reasonable for the worker to make the disclosure in all the circumstances of the case. The conditions are as follows:

(a) that, at the time when he makes the disclosure, the worker reasonably believes that he will be subjected to detriment by his employer if he discloses the relevant failure either to his employer or to a prescribed person; or
(b) that, in a case where there is no prescribed person, the worker reasonably believes that it is likely that evidence relating to the relevant failure will be destroyed if he discloses information to his employer; or
(c) that the worker has already made the disclosure to his employer or to a prescribed person.

The criteria to be used to determine the reasonableness of the disclosure include the identity of the person to whom the disclosure is made, the seriousness of the disclosure, and whether the failure detailed in the disclosure is likely to occur in the future (s 43G(3)).

There is a further category where the employee discloses information concerning an **15.14** *exceptionally* serious failure. The requirements that the worker needs to satisfy in order to disclose such information (such as suspected child abuse) are less stringent, and do not require him to believe that he would be victimised or to have already raised his concerns with his employer or a prescribed person (s 43H).

If the action of the employer takes effect by reason of the making of a public interest **15.15** disclosure, an employee may claim unfair dismissal and a worker as well as an employee may claim in respect of detriment.

A dismissal on this ground is automatically unfair and there is no cap on compensation **15.16** for it (s 103A of the ERA). There is also a right to claim interim relief.

C DETRIMENT

By s 47B of the ERA a worker has 'the right not to be subjected to any detriment by **15.17** any act, or any deliberate failure to act, done on the ground that the worker has made a protected disclosure'. This does not apply to a dismissal. If a course of events harmful to a worker was ongoing, to fail to stop it could amount to a deliberate failure to act (*Abertawe Bro Morgannwg University Health Board v Ferguson* [2013] ICR 1108).

D THE REASON TEST

It is necessary to show that the fact that the protected disclosure had been made caused **15.18** or influenced the employer to act or not to act in the way complained of. Merely to demonstrate that 'but for' the disclosure, the act or omission would not have occurred is not enough to succeed (*London Borough of Harrow v Knight* [2003] IRLR 140). Thus where an employee hacked into the employer's computer system, he was found to have been disciplined for that and not because he had made a protected disclosure. Whilst a tribunal should look with care at arguments that the dismissal was because of acts related to the disclosure rather than the disclosure itself, here there was no reason to attribute ulterior motives to the employer (*Bolton School v Evans* [2007] IRLR 140). The proper question is whether the protected disclosure materially influences (in the sense of being more than a trivial influence on) the employer's treatment of the whistleblower (*Fecitt v NHS Manchester* [2012] ICR 372).

E BURDEN OF PROOF

15.19 The appropriate burden of proof in protected disclosure dismissal cases was considered in *Kuzel v Roche Products Ltd* [2007] IRLR 309, [2008] EWCA Civ 380. In relation to ordinary unfair dismissal (under s 98(4) of the ERA) the burden is on the employer to establish the reason for dismissal. If the employer fails to establish a potentially fair reason, the dismissal is unfair, but it does not follow that it is automatically unfair under s 103A of the ERA. The proper approach to the burden of proof was summarised as follows (at para 47 of the EAT judgment):

(1) Has the Claimant shown that there is a real issue as to whether the reason put forward by the Respondent, some other substantial reason, was not the true reason? Has she raised some doubt as to that reason by advancing the s 103A reason?
(2) If so, has the employer proved his reason for dismissal?
(3) If not, has the employer disproved the s 103A reason advanced by the Claimant?
(4) If not, dismissal is for the s 103A reason.

In answering those questions it follows:

(a) that failure by the employer to prove the potentially fair reason relied on does not automatically result in a finding of unfair dismissal under s 103A;
(b) however, rejection of the employer's reason, coupled with the Claimant having raised a prima facie case that the reason is a s 103A reason entitles the Tribunal to infer that the s 103A reason is the true reason for dismissal, but
(c) it remains open to the employer to satisfy the Tribunal that the making of the protected disclosures was not the reason or principal reason for dismissal, even if the real reason as found by the Tribunal is not that advanced by the employer;
(d) it is not at any stage for the employee (with qualifying service) to prove the s 103A reason.

This formulation was approved by the Court of Appeal ([2008] EWCA Civ 380).

F SCOPE

15.20 Agency workers are brought expressly within the scope of the Act by s 43K(1)(a) of the ERA but in respect of detriment only. In *Croke v Hydro Aluminium Worcester Ltd* [2007] ICR 1303 the EAT held that in construing the extended definition, it is, by analogy with other statutory provisions relating to discrimination or victimisation, appropriate to apply a purposive construction. The legislation is therefore to be construed, where this can properly be done, so as to provide protection rather than to deny it. Where, as in *Croke*, an individual supplied his services to an employment agency through his own company, and the employment agency in turn provided the services of that company to an end user, if the individual did work for the end user the tribunal could conclude that he was a worker of the end user for the purposes of s 43K(1)(a) of the ERA. This is subject to satisfying the statutory requirement that the terms upon which he worked were substantially determined not by the worker but by the person for whom he worked (the end user), or by a third person (which might be the employment agency) or both. Police officers are included within this scope (*Lake v British Transport Police* [2007] ICR 47). Further, the supply of an individual could include a person introduced by an agency even where that person was operating through their own service company (*Keppel Seghers UK Ltd v Hinds* [2014] ICR 1105).

G JOINT LIABILITY

In *Cumbria County Council v Carlisle-Morgan* [2007] IRLR 314 the issue arose as to the   **15.21**
application of principles of vicarious liability in the context of detriment on the grounds of a protected disclosure. The claimant, Mrs Carlisle-Morgan, worked at a supported residential home as a support worker for two men with severe learning difficulties. She made protected disclosures to her supervisor, and to her supervisor's line manager, relating to concerns as to how a colleague, Mrs Horsman, who was another support worker, had been treating residents at the home. The tribunal found that the claimant was then subjected to detrimental treatment by Mrs Horsman on the grounds of the protected disclosures. This included being shouted at and called a 'bitch', being ignored by her, and being the subject of a threatening remark.

The employment tribunal found that the County Council was vicariously liable for   **15.22**
actions of Mrs Horsman, and therefore had subjected the claimant to a detriment on the grounds of a protected disclosure. On appeal, it was argued that the principle of vicarious liability had no application to the ERA 1996. In support of this it was said that claims under s 47B ERA do not create statutory torts and, unlike in relation to other discrimination legislation, there is no express provision for such vicarious liability. The arguments that the employer could only be liable for the acts of an employee where the employee had express or implied authority to do that which was complained of were rejected by the EAT, and the decision of the employment tribunal was upheld. The EAT emphasised that an employer may be liable for the acts of its employees done in the course of employment whether or not what the employee did would be actionable against another employee. The EAT also said it was wrong to draw a line between acts of someone in authority over the claimant and the acts of other employees. The proper approach was (at para 42):

> to see whether as a matter of fairness and justice, turning, in the circumstances of each case, on the sufficiency of the connection between the breach of duty and the employment and/or whether the risk of such breach was one reasonably incidental to it.

In *Fecitt v NHS Manchester* [2012] ICR 372, the Court of Appeal said that the employer   **15.23**
would not be liable for victimisation carried out by workers who were not employees (see also *Blackbay Ventures Ltd v Gahir* [2014] ICR 747).

H TIME LIMIT

By s 48(3) of the ERA 1996, a tribunal may not hear a case on detriment unless it is pre-   **15.24**
sented 'before the end of three months beginning with the date of the act or failure to act to which the complaint relates or where that act or failure is part of a series of similar acts

or failures the last of them'. The last part of this phrase is designed to cover a case which cannot be characterised as an act extending over a period by reference to a connecting rule, practice, scheme, or policy but where there is some link between the acts which makes it just and reasonable for them to be treated as in time and for the claimant to be able to rely on them (*Arthur v London Eastern Railway Ltd* [2008] IRLR 58).

16

REDUNDANCY PAYMENTS

A INTRODUCTION 16.01
  Justifying the scheme 16.04
B DEFINITION OF REDUNDANCY 16.08
  Dismissal and proof 16.11
  Total cessation of the employer's
  business 16.13
  Cessation of business at place of
  employment 16.15
  Diminution in the requirements
  of the business 16.19
C OFFER OF NEW EMPLOYMENT 16.33
  The statutory provisions 16.33
  Trial period 16.35
  Acceptance of job offer 16.40
  Refusal of job offer 16.41
D DISQUALIFICATION FROM REDUNDANCY
  PAYMENT 16.50

  Misconduct 16.51
  Industrial action 16.54
  Early leaving 16.55
E CALCULATION OF REDUNDANCY
  PAYMENT 16.56
  Normal working hours 16.57
  Remuneration 16.60
  Calculation date 16.61
  The week's pay of particular
  workers 16.63
  The method of calculation 16.64
F CLAIMING A REDUNDANCY
  PAYMENT 16.68
G INSOLVENCY 16.69
  Preferential creditor status 16.69
  Direct Government payment 16.75

A worker of long standing is now recognised as having an accrued right in his job, and his right gains in value with the years. So much so, that if the job is shut down, he is entitled to compensation for loss of a job—just as a director gets compensation for loss of office. The director gets a golden handshake. The worker gets a redundancy payment. It is not unemployment pay. I repeat 'not'. Even if he gets another job straightaway, he nevertheless is entitled to full redundancy payment. It is, in a real sense, compensation for long service. (Lord Denning MR in *Lloyd v Brassey* (1969) 4 ITR 100.)

Ironically, a major function of redundancy law has changed; from protecting a particular kind of job right for the innocent worker, it has become in part a package for legitimation of his dismissal. (KW Wedderburn, *The Worker and the Law*, Penguin, 1988, 3rd edn.)

A INTRODUCTION

The redundancy payments scheme was introduced by the Redundancy Payments Act **16.01** 1965 as the first of the substantial statutory individual employment rights. In retrospect its chief significance was that, 'for the first time it turned dismissal into a prima facie compensable event rather than a generally non-compensable event' (Davies and Freedland, *Labour Law: Text and Materials*, Weidenfeld & Nicholson, 1984, at 395).

The current law has been substantially consolidated in the Employment Rights Act 1996. **16.02** The original structure, however, remains intact and requires that the employer make a lump sum payment designed to tide an employee over the period of uncertainty and hardship after dismissal or redundancy. If the employer is insolvent the employee can gain his full entitlement directly from the National Insurance Fund.

16.03 The amount of redundancy payment increases, like basic award for unfair dismissal, with the number of years' continuous service of the employee. His entitlement is in the bank, as it were, only maturing at dismissal, but payment is denied if the employee unreasonably refuses a suitable alternative offer of employment from his employer, his employer's successor, or an associated employer. A measure of the importance of the scheme is that about a quarter of a million people receive such payments each year and the numbers are likely to increase with the effects of the credit crunch.

Justifying the scheme

16.04 Various justifications of the scheme have been proffered, but few explain all its features. Some have described it as establishing a 'proprietary interest in the job'.

16.05 It seeks to assist training and resettlement and thus to stimulate mobility of labour, the lack of which has been diagnosed as one of the major problems of Britain's economy. Other commentators see the payment less idealistically as a bribe to employees to go quietly.

16.06 Professor C Grunfeld described the scheme more pragmatically as:

> just one lubricant of this particular unavoidable component [loss of employment] in the process of adaptation to the larger changes rolling relentlessly forward in the modern world as countless businesses close down to lighten existing or make way for new enterprises and as heavily-manned, long-established industries drive to sharpen their efficiency and reduce or remove their dead weight in relation to the total economy.

(*Law of Redundancy*, Sweet & Maxwell, 1989, 3rd edn.)

16.07 At the outset of the legislation, it was in the interests of employers to disprove redundancy since that was the only reason for dismissal which would cost them money, but with the Industrial Relations Act 1971 and its introduction of unfair dismissal, management began to put it forward as a potentially fair reason for dismissal. The battle lines were redrawn; the decisions drew different distinctions; the patchwork became more complicated.

B DEFINITION OF REDUNDANCY

16.08 Redundancy is quite strictly defined in the ERA 1996. It is not uncommon to hear that a man has been 'made redundant' in day-to-day speech when in fact he has really been dismissed for misconduct or incapability. The statute uses the same definition for three different purposes:

(a) determining entitlement to redundancy payments;
(b) establishing a potentially fair reason for dismissal; and
(c) requiring consultation with unions although for this purpose the definition is now somewhat wider (Chapter 17).

16.09 Under s 139(1) of the ERA 1996, an employee is dismissed for redundancy where the dismissal is attributable wholly or mainly to:

(a) the fact that his employer has ceased, or intends to cease, to carry on the business for the purposes of which the employee was employed by him, or has ceased, or

intends to cease, to carry on that business in the place where the employee was so
employed; or
(b) the fact that the requirements of that business for employees to carry out work of a particular kind, or for employees to carry out work of a particular kind in the place where
he was so employed, have ceased or diminished or are expected to cease or diminish.

After some doubt, it has been held that an employee who is dismissed on a transfer of **16.10**
undertaking may be able to claim a redundancy payment (*Gorictree Ltd v Jenkinson*
[1984] IRLR 391; *Anderson & McAlonie v Dalkeith Engineering Ltd* [1984] IRLR 429).

Dismissal and proof

A dismissal is a condition precedent to a redundancy payment just as it is the basis for **16.11**
a claim of unfair dismissal (14.10–14.63). Its definition has already been considered and
the slight differences in respect of redundancy payments noted. The frequently used term
'voluntary redundancies' is also apt to be misleading, since for a claim for redundancy
payment to succeed the initiative must come from the employer; an employee who resigns
except in reaction to a fundamental breach of contract is not entitled to a redundancy
payment (*Walley v Morgan* (1969) 4 ITR 122). An employee engaged on a succession of
fixed-term contracts is treated as dismissed for redundancy on the expiration of each one
(*Pfaffinger v City of Liverpool Community College* [1996] IRLR 508).

After dismissal has been proved, for the purposes of redundancy payment alone and not **16.12**
unfair dismissal, redundancy is presumed to be the reason 'unless the contrary is proved'
(ERA 1996, s 163(2)).

Total cessation of the employer's business

There are three discrete parts to the definition of redundancy. The first limb applies when **16.13**
a worker's employer completely closes the business in which the applicant was employed.
The term business, by statute, includes any trade or profession or activity carried on by
a body of persons, and it is not necessary to prove that the employer owns the business
in question in order to succeed in claiming a payment on its closure. Thus, in *Thomas
v Jones* [1978] ICR 274, the claimant was hired and dismissed by a sub-postmistress,
although the Post Office actually owned the business in which she worked. The EAT held
that the former was correctly named as respondent.

Early decisions refused to countenance a redundancy payment where an employee was **16.14**
in effect himself responsible for the redundancy caused (*Marsland v Francis Dunn Ltd*
(1967) 2 ITR 353). However, this was rejected as authority for any general principle of
self-induced redundancy in *Sanders v Ernest A. Neale* [1974] ICR 565, where dismissal
followed a strike.

Cessation of business at place of employment

If the employee works at a particular factory, office, or shop of the employer company **16.15**
which closes, his dismissal then will be on grounds of redundancy notwithstanding that
the employer continues to carry on business elsewhere. This will also be the case when
the employee ceases the work of a particular kind in the place where the employee was
employed. This puts into focus the *place of employment* of the employee and, according
to the NIRC: 'These words do not mean "where he in fact worked". They mean "where
under his contract of employment he could be required to work".'

16.16   In the case where this principle was established, *UK Atomic Energy Authority v Claydon* [1974] IRLR 6, the employee's conditions reserved to the employing Authority 'the right to require any member of their staff to work at any of their establishments in Great Britain or in posts overseas'. The claimant, a draughtsman, was originally employed at Orford Ness, and was dismissed when the work on which he was engaged moved to Aldermaston and he refused to go with it. The court upheld the employer's contention that requirements for workers had not ceased 'in the place where he was employed', since he was obliged to work at any place in Great Britain where the employer so chose. In *Bass Leisure Ltd v Thomas* [1994] IRLR 104, the EAT held that the 'place' where an employee was employed did not extend to any place where he could *contractually* be required to work. The location and extent of that place must be ascertainable whether or not the employee is in fact to be required to move, that is therefore, before any such requirement is made, if it is made, and without knowledge of the terms of any such requirement or of the employee's response, or of whether any conditions upon the making of it have been complied with. This principle has now been affirmed by the Court of Appeal in *High Table Ltd v Horst* [1997] IRLR 513.

16.17   A general term of mobility will only rarely be implied into the contract of employment (see *United Bank Ltd v Akhtar* [1989] IRLR 507). In *O'Brien v Associated Fire Alarms Ltd* (1968) 3 ITR 182, the employing company installed fire and burglar alarms throughout the United Kingdom, but the claimant electrician worked for its north western area, which covered a very large area (at least 200 miles long) and was controlled from the Liverpool office. He lived in Liverpool and generally worked within commutable distance of his home. When the employer's requirements for employees in that area diminished, the management sought to compel him to work 120 miles away in Barrow-in-Furness claiming that it was implied in his contract that he would work anywhere in the north west. It thus claimed that there was *no* diminution in the place where he was required to work. The Court of Appeal would only imply a term that the employee should work within daily travelling distance of his home and no further. His dismissal by way of the employer's repudiation *was* thus due to a diminution of work in the relevant *place* where he was employed (see *F. Little v Charterhouse Magna Assurance Co Ltd* [1980] IRLR 19; cf *Jones v Associated Tunnelling Co* [1981] IRLR 477; see for full discussion of mobility issues).

16.18   Where there is a clear term of mobility and an employee's refusal to move results in his dismissal, the statutory reason for it will be disobedience to orders, that is misconduct, and not because his employer has ceased to carry on business at a place where he is employed, so that he cannot claim redundancy (*Rowbotham v Arthur Lee & Sons Ltd* [1974] IRLR 377; see also *Sutcliffe v Hawker Siddeley Aviation Ltd* (1974) 9 ITR 58 DC, express term; *Parry v Holst and Co Ltd* (1968) 3 ITR 317, collective agreement; *Bective Electrical Co Ltd v Warren* (1968) 3 ITR 119, custom).

Diminution in the requirements of the business

16.19   The third limb of the statutory definition of redundancy comprises a reduction in requirements for *employees* because of, say, a fall-off in demand or rationalisation of the business altogether or in the particular place where the employee was employed, or because fewer men and women (as opposed to machines or new techniques) are necessary, and it is the most difficult to construe. The vital question is not whether less work was required but whether there was less need for *employees* to carry on that work (*McCrea v Cullen & Davison Ltd* [1988] IRLR 30). Thus, although the work in question remains to be done, an employee is redundant if the company has so organised its affairs that the work required is done by fewer employees, whether this is achieved by improved mechanisation, automation, other technical advance, or the reallocation of functions.

Further, the proper question is not the reason *why* the employer's requirement has ceased **16.20** but the *fact* that it *has* ceased. The EAT decision in *Association of University Teachers v University of Newcastle upon Tyne* [1988] IRLR 10 concerned the dismissal of a temporary lecturer in the training of teachers of the deaf. The teacher had been engaged on a three-year fixed-term contract, which was not renewed because funding for the course had run out. The tribunal held that there was no redundancy but the EAT criticised it for considering the cause of the cessation of the employer's requirements rather than merely the fact that there *was* a cessation of need for an employee (see also *Lamont v Fry's Metals Ltd* [1985] ICR 566 and *Macfisheries v Findlay* [1985] ICR 160).

Work of a particular kind

Only if the requirements for employees to carry out the *particular work* which the employee **16.21** was contracted to perform have ceased or diminished is the employee redundant under this heading. But that focuses attention on the precise meaning of 'work of a particular kind'. The NIRC declared it to mean 'work which is distinguished from other work of the same general kind by requiring special aptitudes, special skills or knowledge' (*Amos v Max-Arc Ltd* [1973] IRLR 285 and *O'Neill v Merseyside Plumbing Ltd* [1973] ICR 96). Fine lines sometimes have to be drawn to characterise jobs, and the EAT and Court of Appeal have frequently stated that it is a matter of fact and degree for the employment tribunal (*Murphy v Epsom College* [1984] IRLR 271), as the following cases demonstrate:

(a) In *Vaux and Associated Breweries Ltd v Ward* (1968) 3 ITR 385, the employer decided to relaunch one of its hotels by employing young 'bunny girls' in place of older barmaids, and the vital question in deciding whether one of the dismissed middle-aged barmaids was entitled to redundancy payment concerned whether 'the work that the barmaid in the altered premises was going to do was work of a different kind to what the barmaid in the unaltered premises had been doing'. The Divisional Court found that the *work* was not different, even though the type of *person* required to fill the position was, and, therefore, the applicant was not entitled to redundancy payment.

(b) On the other hand, in *Archibald v Rossleigh Commercials Ltd* [1975] IRLR 231, the tribunal held that the work of an emergency unsupervised night mechanic could be distinguished from that of an ordinary mechanic. The test clearly focuses on the characteristics of the job and whether these have gone, rather than the aptitudes of the employee filling it (*Pillinger v Manchester AHA* [1979] IRLR 430 EAT).

(c) To dismiss two plumbers to make way for a heating engineer was a redundancy even though the work done was broadly the same and the total number of employees did not change. The employees, however, had different qualifications and skills (*Murphy v Epsom College* (above)).

(d) Although a reorganisation of two departments within an NHS Hospital Trust changed the work that its employees in one department were required to carry out, it did not necessarily follow that the Trust's requirements for the employees to carry out a particular form of work had diminished (*Shawkat v Nottingham City Hospital NHS Trust (No 2)* [2001] ICR 7). The employer proposed to reorganise the work of thoracic surgeons by cutting down their thoracic work and requiring them also to carry out cardiac work. The Court of Appeal upheld the finding of the tribunal that there was no reduction in the amount of thoracic surgery that was required to be performed, or in the number of employees required to do that work. It was not conclusive that where an employee of one skill is replaced by an employee of a different skill, requirements for work of a particular kind have ceased or diminished. It is merely a consideration which the tribunal may take into account. The mere fact of reorganisation is also not conclusive of there being a redundancy. These were essentially matters of fact for the tribunal to decide.

16.22   The scope and extent of the business in which a redundant employee is employed is also a question of fact for the tribunal to determine. The relevant factors include the similarity of the work done at each establishment, the skilled nature of the work, and the degree of interchangeability between members of staff (*Babar Indian Restaurant v Rawat* [1985] IRLR 57).

Function or contract?

16.23   A related issue is whether the tribunals should consider what the employee actually *did* when he was made redundant or what he *could*, pursuant to his contract, be asked to do which may be much wider. These have been called the function and contract tests respectively. The resolution of this issue also has an effect on the relationship between ordinary redundancy and 'bumping' redundancy, that is, when an employee who is himself redundant is moved to another position and the person occupying that other job is dismissed. The authorities were in some chaos before order was restored by the speech of Lord Irvine LC in *Murray v Foyle Meats Ltd* [1999] IRLR 562.

16.24   The EAT in *Haden v Cowen* [1982] IRLR 314 had derived from *Nelson v BBC* [1977] ICR 649 the principle that the tribunal should focus not on the work that the employee actually did before dismissal, but rather on the work which he could be expected to do under his contract of employment (approved in *Pink v White and White & Co (Earls Barton) Ltd* [1985] IRLR 489).

16.25   The case of *Safeway Stores plc v Burrell* [1997] IRLR 200 further developed the law by stating that both the contract test and the function test were flawed. In this case, the claimant was employed as a petrol station manager but, following reorganisation of the business, his job disappeared and he was instead asked to apply for the job of petrol filling station controller at a lower salary. The applicant refused this offer and presented a complaint of unfair dismissal, claiming that the new position was exactly the same in substance to his old job so that he was not redundant (see *Church v West Lancashire NHS Trust* [1998] IRLR 5; *BBC v Farnworth* [1998] ICR 1116).

16.26   However, there is now approval at the highest level of *Safeway Stores* in the House of Lords decision of *Murray*. The claimants were employees of a slaughterhouse company. They were 'meat plant operatives', normally working in the slaughter hall, but they could be ordered under their contracts to work elsewhere, and occasionally did so in the boning hall. Faced with retrenchment, the company decided to close down one of the two killing lines in the hall, thus requiring fewer employees. It formulated selection criteria for redundancy with the union, and these resulted in the claimants being selected. On their complaint of unfair dismissal, the employers argued that they were redundant (ie dismissal was wholly attributable to the fact that the requirements of the business for employees to carry out work of a particular kind, on the slaughter line, had diminished). The claimants responded that they were *not* redundant. Lord Irvine LC stated that the two simple questions to be asked were:

(a) Were the requirements of the employer's business for employees to carry out work of a particular kind diminished irrespective of the employee's own functions or the terms of his contract?

(b) Was the dismissal wholly or mainly attributable to that state of affairs?

It may be that an employee who is dismissed could have been redeployed or was carry-ing out work which was unaffected by the diminution of the employer's need for work of a particular kind, but the establishment of a causal link under the second part of Lord Irvine's test is an issue of fact and not one of law (see also *Shawkat v Nottingham City Hospital NHS Trust* [1999] IRLR 340, [2001] IRLR 555; *Delanair Ltd v Mead* [1976] ICR 522; *North Riding Garages Ltd v Butterwick* (1967) 2 ITR 229).

Reorganisation of terms or reduction in requirements?

A mere reorganisation of the work programme of the employer leading to a dismissal is **16.27** not a redundancy dismissal. Thus, where duties are different or hours have been changed, but the overall needs of the persons doing the collection of those duties, that is the job, is not less, the courts have not awarded a redundancy payment. The essential question is whether the process 'results in the employee's work being encompassed in other posts and whether the employer's business is such that it no longer has a requirement for a separate and additional employee to carry out the work' (*Sutton v Revlon Overseas Corporation Ltd* [1973] IRLR 173). Only in this case is there a redundancy. The employee's skill and qualifications and hours of work are irrelevant. Night shift as opposed to day shift work may, however, qualify as work of a particular kind (*Macfisheries Ltd v Findlay* [1985] ICR 160).

The distinction between the job description and the job itself is sometimes little short **16.28** of metaphysical. The most that perhaps can be done is to accept Phillips J's statement that: 'In truth all these cases of redundancy claims ultimately raise questions of fact and the decided cases are only of value in enunciating the principles.'

A good illustration of the difficulty is *Chapman v Goonvean and Rostowrack China* **16.29** *Clay Ltd* [1973] ICR 310, where seven workers used to travel to work each day on a bus which was provided by the employers. As this became uneconomical it was decided to cut off the service. The employees claimed to be thus constructively dismissed by reason of redundancy and argued that if they had not been dismissed, the employers would be running the business at a loss which would eventually have led to redundancy. Lord Denning MR, however, held that, 'the requirements of the business—for the work of these seven men—continued just the same as before. After they stopped work the firm had to take on another seven men to replace them ... it would be necessary to import the words on the existing terms and conditions to justify the employees' arguments'. Redundancy did not cover a change of terms. (See also *Lesney Products & Co Ltd v Nolan* [1977] ICR 235.)

The distinction between different terms and different jobs is further illustrated by the **16.30** important Court of Appeal decision in *Johnson v Nottinghamshire Combined Police Authority* [1974] ICR 170. The two employees had worked as clerks in one of the respondent's police stations for some years, coming in between 9.30am and 5.30pm or 6pm from Monday to Friday. In 1974, the Authority sought to introduce a shift system of 8am to 3pm and 1am to 8am, which both women refused, and they were dismissed. The Court of Appeal decided that the sacking was not by reason of redundancy, since the clerical work for which they were employed had neither ceased nor diminished, even though there was no need for women doing those hours. The NIRC declared: 'Work of a particular kind refers to the task to be performed not to the other elements which go to make up the kind of job which it is.' Moreover, 'an employer is entitled to reorganise his business so as to improve its efficiency'. Since it was 'the same job done to a differ-ent time schedule', the dismissal was not attributable to redundancy (see also, to the same effect, *Blakely v Chemetron Ltd* (1972) 7 ITR 224; *North Riding Garages Ltd v*

Butterwick (1967) 2 ITR 229; cf *Kykot v Smith Hartley Ltd* [1975] IRLR 372; *Macfisheries Ltd v Findlay* (above)).

Replacement

16.31 If an employee is replaced in the same job there can be no redundancy. Thus, in *Wren v Wiltshire CC* (1969) 4 ITR 251, no redundancy payment could be claimed where an unqualified teacher was replaced by one with qualifications; the employers still required employees to do the same kind of work. It is, however, only the requirement of the business for *employees* that need cease or diminish; if they are replaced by self-employed workers, there would probably be a redundancy (*Bromby and Hoare Ltd v Evans* [1972] ITR 76; *Amos v Max-Arc Ltd* [1973] IRLR 285; *Ladbroke Courage Holidays Ltd v Asten* [1981] IRLR 59).

16.32 *Variations on the theme*

(a) It does not matter that the employee knows from the beginning of his job that his work is going to diminish, as shown by *Nottinghamshire CC v Lee* [1979] IRLR 294, where the employee was offered a post as a temporary lecturer for one year, at the end of which period the post was extended for another twelve months. He knew that there would be no further extension of the term since the College's requirements had already ceased. Slynn J found that this was not included in the statutory definition since the employer's requirements had not diminished *during* his second period of employment and that it would be unfair in the circumstances if a redundancy payment be required. The Court of Appeal overruled this interpretation, applying the very precise words of the statute. The claimant's contract was not renewed because the employer's requirements for employees had diminished. The statute did not mean that the requirement must cease or diminish *during the period of employment*. The case also serves to re-emphasise that the fairness of the dismissal has nothing to do with redundancy payment.

(b) The diminution in requirements must arise in the job being done, so that, as in *North East Coast Ship Repairers Ltd v Secretary of State for Employment* [1978] IRLR 149, there is no redundancy where an apprentice is not taken on at the end of his apprenticeship as a journeyman because there is not enough work for him to do.

(c) There is a redundancy where the employer takes on additional workers in the hope of increased production which never in fact materialises (*O'Hare and Rutherford v Rotaprint Ltd* [1980] IRLR 47).

(d) By s 139(1) and (2) of the ERA 1996, if the employee is dismissed because of an overall reduction in requirements within a group of associated employers (defined in 11.41–11.48), he can claim a redundancy payment even if there is no redundancy on his particular employer's part. Further, it is enough that redundancy is the main reason where there is more than one cause for dismissal, or that requirements are expected to cease or diminish in the future, so that a claim may be brought *before* the closure actually takes place.

(e) It has been questioned whether a dismissal is attributable wholly or mainly to redundancy if the reason for dismissal actually uppermost in the employer's mind is something other than redundancy, notwithstanding that a redundancy situation may exist. In *Hindle v Percival Boats Ltd* (1969) 4 ITR 86, the Court of Appeal decided that, provided that the employer honestly believes that dismissal is justified by another reason, here, because the applicant boatbuilder was 'too good and too slow' to adapt to new techniques with fibreglass boats, it did not matter that he was also redundant. At the time, this decision meant that he could claim nothing: now he would be entitled to claim unfair dismissal. Lord Denning MR dissented on the ground that if redundancy was a prominent cause of the dismissal it was not necessary that the employer should have it in mind as his reason, and this, it is submitted, is the better view.

C OFFER OF NEW EMPLOYMENT

The statutory provisions

If the employee accepts the renewal of his contract on the same terms as before, he is not **16.33** entitled to a redundancy payment, and the same applies if he is re-engaged in a *suitable alternative* position (ERA 1996, s 138(1), *Camelo v Sheerlyn Productions Ltd* [1976] ICR 531). In either case the offer is also valid if it comes from an associated employer, on trans-fer of the business, or involves a move to Crown service. The Act does not apply where an offer is made by a third party (*Farquharson v Ross* (1966) 1 ITR 335). It is not intended to prevent the award of a redundancy payment simply because the redundant worker gains another job. Where the old job ends on a Friday, Saturday, or Sunday, it suffices if the new employment begins on the following Monday or within four weeks of that Monday (s 146(2)). A job offer by a company associated with the employee's employer counts as an offer by an associated employer even though at the time of the offer the company making the offer was dormant and had no employees of its own. The EAT so held in construing s 84 of the EPCA 1978 (now ERA 1996, s 138) in *Lucas v Henry Johnson (Packers & Shippers) Ltd* [1986] ICR 384.

Section 138 applies only for the purposes of redundancy pay. It does not extend to unfair **16.34** dismissal (*Hempell v W.H. Smith & Sons Ltd* [1986] IRLR 95). The section is merely designed to provide a defence for an employer which is faced with a claim for a redun-dancy payment in circumstances where the employee, even before his dismissal, has obtained another job with the same or an associated employer (see *EBAC Ltd v Wymer* [1995] ICR 466).

Trial period

Application

If the proffered new contract differs as to capacity or place of employment, the offer must **16.35** be made before the redundancy takes effect, and the employee is entitled to a trial period of up to four weeks to test the new terms (ERA 1996, s 138(4)–(6)). This does not apply where the differences are *de minimis*, for example, where his pay is 5p less (*Rose v Henry Trickett & Sons Ltd (No 2)* (1971) 6 ITR 211), but it does not matter that the new condi-tions are better than the old (*Baker v Gill* (1971) 6 ITR 61).

The aim is that during the relevant four-week period, the employee can decide whether **16.36** to take the new position or to leave. If he finds it disagreeable and resigns, he can claim a redundancy payment, being treated as dismissed, and the statutory reason for dismissal is the reason for the original dismissal, that is, before the trial period began. Further, the four-week trial period may be extended for such longer period as is agreed between the employer and employee or his representative in writing, provided that the following restrictive conditions are fulfilled:

(a) the agreement is reached before the employee starts the work;
(b) the extra time is for training purposes only; and
(c) the parties specify the date of the end of the longer period and the terms and condi-tions to apply after it.

After such a period the employee could not assert constructive dismissal (*Optical Express Ltd v Williams* [2007] IRLR 936).

16.37   The trial period is four *calendar* weeks even though not all days during that period were working days (*Benton v Sanderson Kayser Ltd* [1989] ICR 136). Moreover, the employer can end the trial period if he can show a reason connected with or arising out of the change in terms, such as reorganisation or redundancy or the employee's incompetence in the position (s 138(4)). If the employer takes this step the original dismissal stands and the employee may claim a redundancy payment unless the employer makes a more successful offer of suitable alternative employment at that stage.

Resigning after the trial period

16.38   If the employee leaves *after* the four-week period of grace he is treated as having resigned in the normal way and cannot claim a redundancy payment or unfair dismissal. The strictness of the rule is shown by *Meek v Allen Rubber Co Ltd and Secretary of State for Employment* [1980] IRLR 21. The employee used to drive a lorry for the first respondent on a shuttle between Lydney and Whitecroft, and when the latter depot was closed down he was offered the alternative of a London to Lydney route. Part of the deal was that he might try it out for at least *six months* and at the end of this period he decided that it was not for him. Notwithstanding the six months offer, it was held that he could not claim a redundancy payment when he then resigned, since he was taken to have accepted the offer of alternative employment, and the four statutory weeks had elapsed. The EAT also rejected a submission that his acceptance of the new route was conditional on his satisfaction.

Trial period at common law

16.39   If, but only if, the dismissal is a repudiation of contract by the employer's unilateral change in his worker's contractual terms, the employee can claim time to make up his mind in what is effectively a trial period at common law (16.34–16.38). He may say that he never properly accepted the new terms but worked under duress or in order to test them (*Shields Furniture Ltd v Goff* [1973] ICR 187), and this doctrine, which was enunciated by the courts before the statutory trial period was introduced (*Marriott v Oxford and District Co-operative Society Ltd (No 2)* [1970] 1 QB 186), was set out by Bristow J in *Turvey v C. W. Cheyney & Sons Ltd* [1979] IRLR 105 EAT, thus:

> At common law, where the employer has repudiated the contract, the employee has an option. He can either treat the contract as at an end or he can take a new job with the employer on trial. If he takes the job on trial he has a reasonable period in which to make up his mind whether he will accept the new job before he will be taken to have made a new contract or renewed the old one with variations ...

(*Air Canada v Lee* [1978] ICR 1202).

Such a trial period may last even as long as twelve months (*McKindley v William Hill (Scotland) Ltd* [1985] IRLR 492) and possibly may even cover circumstances where the employee accepts a new position at another organisation but subsequently withdraws the acceptance and decides that he wants to accept his previous employer's offer of redundancy (*East Suffolk Local Health Services NHS Trust v Palmer* [1997] ICR 425).

Acceptance of job offer

16.40   If the employee accepts the job which has been offered there is no problem as there is no redundancy. The fact that it may be wildly unsuitable and he is forever unhappy about the decision is irrelevant. He retains his continuous service, provided that, if there are changes in conditions, the offer was made before the former redundant employment terminated.

Refusal of job offer

If, on the other hand, the employee refuses the new offer there are two more complicated **16.41** situations:

(a) where the new terms do not differ from the old, the tribunal must decide whether his refusal was *reasonable* and it is for the employer to prove that it was not (s 141(2)); and

(b) if the proffered terms do *differ*, the employer must prove that the offer was of *suitable* alternative employment and that the employee was *unreasonable* in refusing it, if he is to avoid liability to make a redundancy payment (s 141(3)(b)).

We now look at the requirements for an offer to be valid (16.43–16.49), when the alterna- **16.42** tive is likely to be found suitable (16.45–16.46), and when the employee will be regarded as reasonable in refusing it (16.48–16.49).

The offer

The offer of new terms must be sufficiently certain, unconditional, and duly commu- **16.43** nicated (*Havenhand v Thomas Black Ltd* (1968) 3 ITR 271; *Rosseyer Motors Ltd v Bradshaw* (1972) 7 ITR 3), although it may be addressed to a group of workers (*McCreadie v Thomson & MacIntyre (Patternmakers) Ltd* [1971] 2 All ER 1135) rather than solely to the individual. The offer need not be in writing but it must contain specific information about 'the capacity and place and other terms and conditions of employment' (*Roberts v Essoldo Circuit (Control) Ltd* (1967) 2 ITR 351).

Moreover, the employer must have a reasonable expectation of fulfilling the offer made **16.44** (*Kane v Raine & Co* [1974] ICR 300); it is not good enough to pluck a post out of the air in a desperate effort to avoid a redundancy payment.

Suitability

This question is one of fact in every case, and Bridge J suggested in *Collier v Smith's Dock* **16.45** *Ltd* (1969) 4 ITR 338 that appeal bodies should not interfere with the decisions made by tribunals apart from cases where a job is so obviously unsuitable that the tribunal must have misdirected itself in finding to the contrary or where the tribunal has failed to take account of relevant circumstances. In *Carron Company v Robertson* (1967) 2 ITR 484 at 489, the court gave this general survey:

> Now suitability is an imprecise term, but I accept that in deciding as to the suitability of employment in relation to an employee, one must consider not only the nature of the work, hours and pay, the employee's strength, training, experience and ability but such matters as status in the premises of the employer.

Neill LJ in *Spencer v Gloucestershire CC* [1985] IRLR 393 considered that it was con- fusing to 'draw too rigid a distinction between' suitability and reasonableness because 'some factors may be common to both aspects of the case'.

This point was brought out neatly in the EAT's decision in *Cambridge and District* **16.46** *Cooperative Society Ltd v Ruse* [1993] IRLR 156, when it held that, even though the tribunal felt that the alternative job offered was suitable, where the employee thought that it was not (owing to his perceived drop in status), that did not mean that his refusal to accept the offer was unreasonable. Reasonableness did not relate merely to the personal factors of the employee which were extraneous to the job.

16.47 The effect of the most important factors has been considered in several cases:

(1) **Pay** The most important criterion of pay concerns what is actually earned in the new position, including bonuses, and not basic wage alone (*F. Kennedy v Werneth Ring Mills Ltd* [1977] ICR 206; *Tocher v General Motors (Scotland) Ltd* [1981] IRLR 55).

(2) **Hours of work** A change from day to night work will often render a job offer unsuitable (*Morrison & Poole v Ceramic Engineering Co Ltd* (1966) 1 ITR 404).

(3) **Status** The leading case is *Taylor v Kent CC* (1969) 4 ITR 294, where the headmaster of a boys' secondary school was, on its closure, offered a post in a pool of mobile staff, meaning that he would have to teach in any school where he was required. Although he would still be remunerated on his old scale as a headmaster, the Divisional Court (which then heard appeals from tribunals) held that this was not suitable because of the large drop in status.

(4) **Skill** In *Dutton v Hawker Siddeley Aviation Ltd* [1978] IRLR 390, Phillips J said:

> Great care has to be exercised before it can be said that an employee who is skilled and with a particular trade can be required to move to some other in a case where his contract does not provide for it.

> A patternmaker has been held reasonable in rejecting work as a progress clerk (*Souter v Balfour Ltd* (1966) 1 ITR 383), and a gantry cranedriver as an articulated lorry driver (*Watson v Bowaters UK Pulp & Paper Mills Ltd* (1967) 2 ITR 278).

(5) **Place of work** That the new offer involves greater distance to travel from home may render a job offer to be unsuitable, unless this disadvantage is counterbalanced by higher pay or travel expenses (*Gotch & Partners v Guest* (1966) 1 ITR 65; cf *McIntosh v British Rail* (1967) 2 ITR 26).

Reasonable refusal

16.48 It is for the employer still to go on to show, even if he has established that the alternative offer was suitable, that the employee's rejection of it was unreasonable (*Jones v Aston Cabinet Co Ltd* [1973] ICR 292). Objections on the following grounds have figured in the case law and have been held to be reasonable:

(a) travel difficulties: although an offer which would maintain the same rate of pay together with nine months' travelling expenses and altered working hours to fit in with travelling times was held unreasonably refused (cf *Hitchcock v St Ann's Hosiery* (1971) 6 ITR 98);

(b) the unsociability of shiftwork (*Silver v Jel Group of Companies* (1966) 1 ITR 238);

(c) bad health and safety conditions (*Denton v Neepsend Ltd* [1976] IRLR 164);

(d) the necessity for the individual to change his skills;

(e) family problems which make it difficult to travel (*Wilson-Undy v Instrument Co Ltd* [1976] ICR 508);

(f) the lateness of the offer, especially when the employee has by that time made alternative arrangements (*Barratt v Thomas Glover & Co Ltd* (1970) 5 ITR 95);

(g) lack of housing in the vicinity of the job (*Bainbridge v Westinghouse Brake & Signal Co Ltd* (1966) 1 ITR 55);

(h) ill health: in *Daniels Elliott & Hare v Thomas Glover Ltd* (1966) 1 ITR 283, an offer to the female applicant was reasonably refused because it entailed heavy physical labour and she had come out of hospital only ten days before; and

(i) loss of status (*Cambridge and District Co-operative Society Ltd v Ruse*, at 16.46 above).

Tribunals take into account the existence or otherwise of other local employment (*Laing* **16.49** *(John) & Son Ltd v Best* (1968) 3 ITR 3) (or in the area of business more generally) in assessing the reasonableness of the refusal of the job, but have held that an offer is not in itself unreasonable because it is in an industry, for example, coal, which is contracting so that the new job in it is unlikely to be permanent (*James and Jones v National Coal Board* (1969) 4 ITR 70). This was held notwithstanding that the tribunal thought that the claimants had made a wise decision to leave the declining industry and appeared sympathetic to the worker who, having just undergone one trauma, did not wish to uproot himself again. It may be inevitable, however, at a time of recession when industries are in sharp decline. For similar reasons, the refusal of an offer which 'on any view was to last 12 to 18 months' though not necessarily for ever (*Morganite Crucible v Street* [1972] ICR 110), was held to be unreasonable. It is all a matter of degree, so that in *Thomas Wragg & Sons Ltd v Wood* [1976] ICR 313, on the other hand, uncertainty of future prospects, combined with the fact that the employee was fifty-six, had accepted a job elsewhere, and that the offer came very late, provided valid grounds for refusal (see also *Paton Calvert & Co Ltd v Westerside* [1979] IRLR 108). In *Spencer v Gloucestershire CC* (16.45 above), the Court of Appeal disagreed with the proposition of the EAT that it was not legitimate for school cleaners to refuse reduced hours of work on the ground that they did not consider that they could do a satisfactory job in the time and with the numbers available. The EAT thought that this was a matter for the employer alone to decide. The Court of Appeal considered, however, that there was no rule of law that questions of standards are irrelevant to the decision; it was a question of fact and the EAT should not have interfered with the decision of the employment tribunal that the employees were *not* unreasonable in refusing the offered positions.

D DISQUALIFICATION FROM REDUNDANCY PAYMENT

An employee may lose his entitlement to redundancy payment or part thereof even though **16.50** he satisfies other requirements so far considered, by reason of:

(a) misconduct;
(b) strike action;
(c) leaving during notice; or
(d) grant of pension.

Misconduct

An employee may not gain a redundancy payment if the employer was entitled to termi- **16.51** nate the employment by reason of his misconduct (ERA 1996, s 140(1)). For this exception to apply, the contract must be terminated either without notice, or with shorter notice than was contractually necessary. Where the misconduct occurred before notice of redundancy the employer must either sack instantly or give a written statement that he is entitled to dismiss at once.

This is a strange provision, since if the employer dismisses the employee for cause, **16.52** whether incapability or misconduct, that is not a dismissal for redundancy because it would not fall in the terms of the ERA 1996, s 139. The reason that the provision was inserted is because the Redundancy Payments Act 1965, in which it is first found in exactly the same form, predated the wider unfair dismissal jurisdiction. Its continuance now is more problematic. *Sanders v Ernest A. Neale Ltd* [1974] ICR 565 suggests that the subsection is intended to apply where the employee is dismissed in fact for redundancy when he *could have been* sacked for cause (see *Bonner v Gilbert Ltd* [1989] IRLR 475).

16.53   If the dismissal for gross misconduct takes place *during the statutory period of notice*, the employee may apply to a tribunal, which can pay all or some of the redundancy payment and will make this decision on the basis of the justice and equity of the case. In *Simmons v Hoover Ltd* [1977] ICR 61, the majority of the EAT decided that a strike could be considered to be misconduct, but went on to say that action in response to deliberate provocation or unreasonable demands by an employer would not prejudice the employee's rights.

Industrial action

16.54   There are three further specific provisions about strikes:

(a) if the employee takes part in a strike within the period of notice of termination which the employer must give, and the employer then terminates the contract for that reason, s 140(1) does not apply and he remains entitled to a redundancy payment (s 140(2));

(b) if the employer dismisses for any other reason during this time, an employment tribunal may award the whole or part of the redundancy payment to which the employee would have been otherwise entitled if this appears just and equitable (s 140(3)); and

(c) where a redundant employee goes on strike the employer may require him by 'notice of extension' to make up the time lost in the strike if he is still to be entitled to redundancy payment (s 143(2)). It must warn the employee that the employer will dispute the employee's right to redundancy payment if he does not comply (s 143(2)(c)).

Early leaving

16.55   If the employee is under notice of redundancy and wishes to leave before the notice runs out, for example, to start another job, he may himself give notice. If the employer objects to him leaving early, he can request the employee to withdraw the notice and warn him that he will contest his redundancy payment. The tribunal must then decide whether to award all or part of the redundancy payment, reviewing all the circumstances (s 142). The provision has been little used.

E CALCULATION OF REDUNDANCY PAYMENT

16.56   Redundancy pay, like the basic award in unfair dismissal, is calculated by reference to the week's pay in accordance with the ERA 1996, ss 221–9. The Employment Act 2008 adds a new s 163(5) of the ERA so that the tribunal may award 'such amount as the tribunal considers appropriate in all the circumstances to compensate the worker for any financial loss sustained by him which is attributable to the non-payment of the redundancy payment'. The basis of calculation depends first on whether or not the employee has normal working hours and secondly whether he is paid by time, piece, or is on shift or rota work. First the vocabulary will be explained, then the mode of calculation.

Normal working hours

16.57   Section 234 of the ERA 1996 defines normal working hours as where the contract fixes the number, or the minimum number, of hours in a week, whether or not those hours can be reduced in certain circumstances. The number of hours must be included in the written statement of terms. The working of overtime involves manifold complications because it is unusual to find hours of overtime expressly fixed by a contract of employment. The more common situation was examined by the Court of Appeal in *Tarmac Roadstone Holdings Ltd v Peacock* (1973) 8 ITR 300. The employee's standard hours were forty but his contract also stated 'workers shall work overtime in accordance with the demands of the industry', and in fact they regularly laboured fifty-seven hours. The court considered that the decisive issue was whether the contract not only obliged the employee to work overtime, which it did, but also required the employer to provide it, which was not so here. A unilateral obligation on the employee is, in fact, much more frequent. The 'normal working hours' were held to be forty and the claimant's redundancy pay consequently amounted to less than the amount which he normally took home in his pay packet each week (see also *Fox v C. Wright (Farmers) Ltd* [1978] ICR 98; *Lotus Cars Ltd v Sutcliffe and Stratton* [1982] IRLR 381; *Bamsey v Albion Engineering Ltd* [2004] IRLR 457).

Moreover, the EAT is reluctant to infer a variation of contract by reason of practice (*Friend v PMA Holdings Ltd* [1976] ICR 330; cf *ITT Components (Europe) Ltd v Kolah* [1977] ICR 740) although this is not unknown. In *Dean v Eastbourne Fishermen's and Boatmen's Protection Society Ltd* [1977] ICR 556, for example, the claimant worked fixed bar sessions and at other times as and when his employer needed him. The regular periods which were demanded amounted to less than the twenty-one hours which was then necessary to gain employment protection. The EAT held that in the absence of any express term as to the number of hours worked, the tribunal should have inferred a term of obligation from what actually happened in practice; and that since during the two years necessary to qualify for the redundancy payment he was claiming he had worked for more than the statutory minimum on eighty-six occasions, he was entitled to claim. **16.58**

Several cases concern a conflict between the hours of work laid down in national and in local collective agreements. In *Loman and Henderson v Merseyside Transport Services Ltd* (1969) 4 ITR 108 the Divisional Court adopted the former. **16.59**

Remuneration

Having worked out the normal hours of work it is then necessary to determine the pay for them. For these purposes the week is deemed to end on Saturday, unless pay is calculated on a weekly basis, in which case the week ends on the day on which the employee is regularly paid (s 235(1)). These rules are relevant: **16.60**

(a) The remuneration is by statute '*money paid under the contract of employment by the employer*' (*Lyford v Turquand* (1966) 1 ITR 554). A useful definition which gives some flavour of the width of remuneration was found in the Prices and Charges (Notification of Increases and Information) Order 1977 (SI 1977/1281), para 16(2), as including 'any benefit, facility or advantage, whether in money or otherwise, provided by the employer or by some other person under arrangements with the employer whether for the employee or otherwise, by reason of the fact that the employer employs him'.

(b) The concept refers to the *gross* amount of weekly pay (*Secretary of State for Employment v John Woodrow & Sons (Builders) Ltd* [1983] IRLR 11).

(c) The wage which is taken for these purposes is that to which the employee is *contractually* entitled, even if the employer does not (eg, because it is in breach of the minimum wage) pay that sum (*Cooner v P. S. Doal & Sons* [1988] IRLR 338). The week's pay certainly does not include the value of, for example, a company car or free accommodation but it does cover bonuses, allowances, and commission, if they are provided for by an express or implied term in the contract of employment (eg *Lawrence v Cooklin Kitchen Fitments Ltd* (1966) 1 ITR 398).

(d) The remuneration is only that which is paid in respect of hours 'when the employee was actually working', thus excluding that which is apportioned to rest days (*British Coal Corporation v Cheesbrough* [1990] ICR 317).

(e) Section 221(3) of the ERA 1996 provides that if bonuses are annual payments, or in any other way do not coincide with the periods of normal pay, a proportionate amount is to be included (*J.S. Buckley Ltd v Maslin* [1977] ICR 425). The average hourly rate is to be calculated by reference to all of the hours which are worked and all remuneration including overtime payments is calculated at the rate attributable to normal working hours.

(f) A Christmas bonus payable *ex gratia* is clearly excluded (*Skillen v Eastwoods Froy Ltd* (1967) 2 ITR 112), while the treatment of *tips* depends on their precise nature. Where a restaurant levied a compulsory service charge, and shared this each week between its waiters, for example, their right was contractually enforceable and included in the relevant remuneration (*Tsoukka v Potomac Restaurants Ltd* (1968) 3 ITR 259), but tips paid direct to the employee, on the other hand, are not so reckoned (*S & U Stores Ltd v Lee* (1969) 4 ITR 227), since they are not money paid by the employer (see also *Cofone v Spaghetti House* [1980] ICR 155).

(g) The week's pay includes a site bonus where there was by custom a term that when the main contractor paid such an extra sum to the sub-contractor the respondent sub-contractor would divide it amongst his employees (*Donelan v Kerrby Constructions Ltd* [1983] ICR 237).

(h) For similar reasons *state benefits*, like industrial injuries benefits, are not included (*Wibberley v Staveley Iron & Chemical Co Ltd* (1966) 1 ITR 558), while *holiday pay* is outside the definition since it is referable to weeks of *absence*, not normal working time (*Secretary of State for Employment v Haynes* [1980] IRLR 270).

(i) Items described as *expenses* are taken into account only where they represent a profit over actual outlay (*S & U Stores Ltd v Wilkes* [1974] ICR 645), but nothing is awarded where the relevant arrangement is illegal as a fraud on HM Revenue & Customs.

Calculation date

16.61 The relevant pay and hours for redundancy payment purposes are those governing at the 'calculation date' as specified in the ERA 1996, s 226. This is generally the last date of working under the employee's contract of employment, but some modification is made to prevent employers escaping liability to pay higher amounts (because of a pay rise) by giving shorter notice than that to which the employee is entitled by virtue of his contract. The calculation date is then treated as the date on which notice would have expired had the employer given the minimum notice as required by s 86 of the ERA 1996. The proper method to calculate this is to find the statutory period and work backwards from the relevant date of termination. Thus, if the employee has worked for ten years and is dismissed in week twenty, the calculation is in week ten whether or not the necessary ten weeks' notice has in fact been given. If he has worked for two years, the calculation date is week eighteen.

16.62 Doubts surround the treatment of a pay agreement which has been backdated to the calculation date; where, for example, the agreement is announced in week twenty-five but starts in week fifteen and the employee is dismissed in week twenty. Since the vital words are 'is payable' it is thought that it should be included in the remuneration to be so calculated. This view has been upheld (*obiter*) in *Leyland Vehicles Ltd v Reston* [1980] IRLR 376, where there was evidence that wages were annually increased on a particular date, and it may be confined to these special facts. In fact the particular claimant was not entitled since he was not employed on the starting date. If the backdated agreement is announced after the calculation for redundancy payment falls to be made, a new claim may be submitted (*Cowan v Pullman Spring Filled Co Ltd* (1967) 2 ITR 650).

The week's pay of particular workers

Having set out the relevant vocabulary, it is now possible to apply these general provisions in the concrete situation of particular workers, that is, time workers, piece-workers and shift workers. **16.63**

(a) A *time worker* has normal working hours and his 'remuneration for employment in normal working hours (whether by the hour or week or other period) does not vary with the amount of work done in the period' (ERA 1996, s 221(2)). His week's pay is that 'payable' under the contract of employment in force on the calculation date.

In the case of a sales representative in *Evans v Malley Organisation Ltd* [2003] ICR 432, pay did not vary with the amount of work done in so far as it meant the amount of work done to achieve a particular contract; payment of commission was based on the outcome of the work whether fortuitous or due to good performance. It was intended to cover piece-work. Pill LJ said (para 23) 'Work is done and the amount of work does not depend on the number of contracts obtained. Time spent attempting unsuccessfully to persuade a client to sign a contract is as much work as a successful encounter with the client.'

(b) A *piece-worker* has normal working hours, but his pay varies with the amount of work done; this may take the form of payment for every piece of work he does, an incentive bonus, or a commission related to output. One arrives at his 'week's pay' by multiplying the normal hours worked by the average hourly rate of remuneration in the twelve weeks before the last complete week before the calculation date (ERA 1996, s 221(3)). It does not matter whether these previous weeks were full working weeks or not (*Sylvester v Standard Upholstery Co Ltd* (1967) 2 ITR 507), although any week in which no pay at all was received in the relevant twelve-week period is ignored and an earlier week used. Overtime premium rates are to be excluded even when the hours are counted.

(c) *Shift and rota workers* are defined by statute as those whose hours 'differ from week to week or over a longer period so that the remuneration payable for ... any week varies according to the incidence of those days or times' (ERA 1996, s 222(1)). Here one multiplies the *average* weekly hours by the average hourly rate of remuneration. Both calculations are again made by taking an average of the twelve weeks preceding the calculation date if that date is the last day of a week, or otherwise ending with the last complete week before the calculation date. The average hourly rate of remuneration is the average pay for the hours actually worked in the twelve weeks preceding the calculation date, if that should be the last day of the week, or in other circumstances the last complete week before the calculation date. Again, the remuneration to be considered is only that which is paid in respect of hours 'when the employee was actually working', so excluding rest days.

Example Edward has been employed for fifteen years as a shift worker. He is given five weeks' notice in week thirty. The calculation date is week twenty-three because the relevant date of termination is week thirty-five from which the minimum period of notice, that is twelve weeks' maximum, must be taken. The tribunal then looks at the previous twelve-week period, thus:

Week	Basic	Overtime
1	45	5
2	40	5
3	35	5
4	45	5
5	40	5
6	35	5
7	45	5
8	40	5
9	35	5
10	45	5
11	40	5
12	35	5

The average weekly hours are forty, notwithstanding that there is regular overtime of five hours, unless there is an obligation on the company to provide it as well as on the employee to work when it is provided.

(d) *No normal working hours*: some employees, such as university teachers, salespersons on commission, and those employed in a managerial, administrative, or professional capacity have no normal working hours at all. None of these is employed on a strict 9am to 5pm basis or any basis linked to time. Here again, an average of a twelve-week period is taken (ERA 1996, s 224(2)). There are, however, some cases in which the employee has not been employed in the same job for twelve weeks, yet is still able to claim employment protection rights, because continuity is preserved from a previous employment. If this is so, the weeks of that previous job are taken into account; but if this would not be appropriate or is impossible, the employment tribunal is directed to reach a computation which it considers to be just in all the circumstances.

The method of calculation

16.64 The appropriate redundancy payment is reached by multiplying the week's pay by a multiplier depending on age:

(a) 1½ for every year during the whole of which the employee was forty-one or over;
(b) 1 for every year during the whole of which the employee was between twenty-two and forty; and
(c) 1½ for every year in which the employee was below twenty-one.

(ERA 1996, s 102(2).)

16.65 The maximum payable is thus thirty weeks and this would be appropriate where an employee has been working for twenty years' continuous employment over forty-one. The amount of remuneration to be awarded for redundancy payment, as for unfair dismissal basic award, is subject to a *maximum limit*, and the Secretary of State has a statutory duty to review this sum annually and may do so more often. The present maximum stands at £479 per week, and this clearly reduces the compensation which would otherwise have been awarded to a large section of the workforce. The sum is index linked to the retail prices index (Employment Relations Act 1999, s 34) and must be updated every year.

The rules of continuity already discussed (see Chapter 11) apply in determining the proper **16.66** multiplier. The following points should also be noted:

(a) *overseas employment* may be counted only if the employee remained employed for the purposes of social security legislation (s 215(2)); weeks which do not count for this reason do not, however, break the continuity of employment;
(b) payment of an *earlier redundancy payment* breaks the continuity of service (s 214(2));
(c) where there is a *gap* of up to four weeks on the renewal of employment following a redundancy, and the offer of an alternative job or renewal of the old one, this counts towards continuity.

Just as with ordinary weekly pay (4.03–4.20), the employer must give the redundant **16.67** worker a written statement setting out how his amount of redundancy payment has been calculated (ERA 1996, s 165). An employer in default is liable to a small fine, and if no statement is given the employee may in writing demand it by a specified date giving at least one week to reply (s 165(3) and (4)).

F CLAIMING A REDUNDANCY PAYMENT

The employer usually offers the correct redundancy payment to his employee without **16.68** any formal claim being necessary. In the event of dispute the employee should submit a written claim, making it clear to the employer what he is seeking. In this respect, a call for a meeting to 'discuss the position' of the employee who was made redundant while off sick was insufficiently precise (*Hetherington v Dependable Products Ltd* (1971) 6 ITR 1). If this does not succeed, the next step is to refer the matter to an employment tribunal within six months of the relevant date of dismissal by submitting an application to the tribunal (ERA 1996, s 164). This may be combined with a complaint of unfair dismissal, but the claim cannot be made until the dismissal actually takes effect (*Watts v Rubery Owen Conveyancer Ltd* [1977] 2 All ER 1; *Pritchard-Rhodes Ltd v Boon* [1979] IRLR 19). If the employee fails to take any of these steps within six months he may have an extension of up to six months, but only if the tribunal thinks it to be 'just and equitable that the employee should receive a redundancy payment' (s 164(2)). A complaint of unfair dismissal presented within six months may entitle the claimant to a redundancy payment if the tribunal decides that the reason for dismissal was redundancy even where there is no claim as such for a redundancy payment (*Duffin v Secretary of State for Employment* [1983] ICR 766; see also *Secretary of State for Employment v Banks* [1983] ICR 48). If the employee has died in the meantime the right to redundancy payment devolves with his estate, and the ERA 1996 allows a special representative to be appointed solely for the purposes of tribunal proceedings.

G INSOLVENCY

Preferential creditor status

A worker whose employer becomes insolvent risks losing all his employment protection **16.69** rights in the financial wreck of the company, partnership, or individual who was the employer. He does, however, have preferential creditor status in the assets of the insolvent employer, so that he ranks to be paid out of company funds, along with PAYE tax and VAT, before anything goes into the pool for ordinary creditors. This may mean that the employees are paid in full or pro rata. Employees' preferential debts under the Insolvency Act 1986, s 175, Sch 6 are:

(a) four months' wages;
(b) guarantee payment;
(c) payment for time off for trade union duties or for antenatal care; and
(d) protective award for failure to consult over redundancies.

Similar provisions are contained in s 328 of and para 9 of Sch 6 to the Insolvency Act 1986. Any other sums due and owing may be claimed as an unsecured debt and proof of debt forms may be gained from the trustee or liquidator, but the process may take a very long time.

16.70 In *Nicoll v Cutts* [1985] BCLC 322, the plaintiff argued that a receiver appointed under a debenture was himself liable for his wages under s 492(3) of the Companies Act 1985 which provided that: 'A receiver ... shall to the same extent as if he had been appointed by an order of a court, be personally liable on any contract entered into by him in the performance of his functions, except in so far as the contract otherwise provides ...'. The Court of Appeal decided that if the receiver had entered into a new contract with the employee he would be personally liable but this had not occurred by the receivership itself. This has been largely reversed by s 40 of the Insolvency Act 1986.

16.71 In the combined appeals of *Powdrill v Watson* and *Talbot v Cadge*, the House of Lords ([1995] IRLR 267) construed s 19 of the Insolvency Act 1986 which provided that:

> Any sums payable [by the administrator] in respect of ... contracts entered into or contracts of employment adopted by him ... shall be charged on and paid out ... in priority ... For this purpose, the administrator is not to be taken to have adopted a contract of employment by reason of anything done or omitted to be done within 14 days after his appointment.

16.72 There is a similar but not identical provision for administrative receivers by s 44 of the 1986 Act with the main difference being that administrative receivers become liable for all liabilities 'on' contracts which extend to all liabilities whether incurred before, during, or after the receivership. The receivers had in all the conjoined cases sent to employees letters stating that they were not to be taken to have adopted their contracts of employment. Lord Browne-Wilkinson decided that a contract of employment is adopted if the employee is continued in employment for more than fourteen days after the appointment of the administrator or receiver and it is not possible to avoid this result or alter its consequences unilaterally by informing employees that he is not adopting the contract or only doing so on terms, but the consequence of adoption is to give priority only to liabilities incurred by the administrator or receiver during his tenure of office.

16.73 Immediately after the decision in *Powdrill* was reached in the Court of Appeal, Parliament rushed through the Insolvency Act 1994 by which the liability of receivers and administrative receivers on contracts of employment adopted by them on or after 15 March 1994 is restricted to payment of wages, salary, and contributions to a pension scheme in respect of services rendered after the adoption of the contract of employment.

16.74 Arrears of pay does not mean sums payable under the contract so that employees' contractual payments in respect of a period of lay-off is not recoverable (*Benson v Secretary of State for Trade and Industry* [2003] ICR 1082).

Direct Government payment

16.75 The Employment Rights Act 1996 builds on earlier legislation to offer three further ways of ensuring that the employee's position is somewhat protected where:

(a) an individual has been declared bankrupt or has made a composition or arrangement with his creditors;

(b) an individual's estate is being administered in accordance with an order under s 421 of the Insolvency Act 1986; or

(c) a company is wound up by a shareholders' resolution.

The provisions do not go so far as to cover an individual firm or company which is only unable to meet its debts as they fall due (*Pollard v Teako (Swiss) Ltd* (1967) 2 ITR 357).

National Insurance Fund

Speedy and safe recourse may be made to the Government's National Insurance Fund in the case of the following debts (ERA 1996, s 182): **16.76**

(a) up to eight weeks' *wages* including guarantee pay, medical suspension pay, union duties pay, antenatal care pay, statutory sick pay, and protective award (s 184(1)(a)), up to a maximum of £479 per week (this is higher than the preferential creditor maximum);

(b) minimum pay during *notice* under s 86 of the ERA 1996 or damages for failure to give such notice (s 184(1)(b)), but not including the appropriate holiday pay during notice according to the EAT in *Secretary of State for Employment v Haynes* [1980] IRLR 270 (see also *Secretary of State for Employment v Jobling* [1980] ICR 380);

(c) up to six weeks' accumulated holiday pay during the last twelve months preceding the relevant date (s 184(1)(c));

(d) basic award made by an employment tribunal for unfair dismissal (s 184(1)(d)); and

(e) reimbursement of premiums or fees paid for *apprenticeship* or articles of clerkship (s 184(1)(e)).

Item (d) may be reclaimed in full, but the other payments are subject to a weekly maximum, for, it would appear, each type (s 186(1)). In the unusual case where the employer has a cross-claim against the employee, for example, in respect of a loan, this may be set off (*Secretary of State for Employment v Wilson and BCCI* [1996] IRLR 330). This maximum is subject to reduction if the employee earns from another source or receives state benefits during the period of his notice. In *Westwood v Secretary of State for Employment* [1984] IRLR 209 the House of Lords also decided that the employee need only account for *net* benefits received during the period of unemployment. This had an important effect in the case of Mr Westwood who had been unemployed for more than a year and was entitled to a refund which was based on the loss arising from exhaustion of unemployment benefit after a year. This was, however, cleared up by the Social Security (General Benefit) Amendment Regulations 1984 (SI 1984/1259), which provide that days covered by payments made under the insolvency provisions do not count in establishing eligibility to what was known as unemployment benefit (now jobseeker's allowance; see also *Secretary of State for Employment v Cooper* [1987] ICR 766).

It was decided by the EAT in *Titchener v Secretary of State for Trade and Industry* [2002] ICR 225 that it was compatible with European law for s 186(1) of the ERA 1996 to set a limit on the amount which had to be paid out in the case of insolvency. The relevant department, BIS, may apply the limit before making deductions in respect of income tax and national insurance contributions (*Morris v Secretary of State for Employment* [1985] IRLR 297, approved in *Titchener*). **16.77**

The claims arise on the 'relevant date', which is defined as the latest of the following dates: when the employer becomes insolvent; when the employment came to an end; and where the debt is a basic award for unfair dismissal or a protective award for failure to consult the union over redundancies, the date when the award was made. **16.78**

16.79 Gaining these payments involves much form filling. A written application must be first made to the Department for Business, Energy & Industrial Strategy (BEIS) certifying that one of the appropriate debts was owing on the 'relevant date'. The payments are not actually made until a trustee or liquidator is appointed, since he must then submit to BEIS a statement of what is due to each employee as soon as reasonably practicable. If there is no such statement within six months of the submission of the written request, the Department has a discretion to pay without it, but if the Department refuses to pay what the employee claims he is entitled to, he can refer the matter to an employment tribunal within three months of the alleged default. If the Secretary of State is satisfied that he does not require a statement in order to determine the amount of the debt owed to the employee, he may make a payment without having received such a statement.

Pensions

16.80 The right to unpaid employer's pension contributions from BEIS extends to:

(a) arrears accrued within twelve months prior to insolvency;
(b) arrears certified by an actuary to be necessary to pay employees' benefits on dissolution of the scheme; and
(c) 10 per cent of the last twelve months' payroll for the employees covered by the scheme.

The maximum is the lowest of these figures. Again, the Department defers until a trustee or liquidator is appointed before paying, and recourse is to an employment tribunal in the event of dispute.

Redundancy payments

16.81 An employee can claim a redundancy payment direct from the National Insurance Fund where he is entitled to such a payment in the usual way, and he has taken all reasonable steps to obtain payment besides resorting to legal proceedings, or the employer is insolvent as defined in s 166(5) of the ERA 1996. The worker then receives his normal redundancy payment less any payment in fact already made towards it by the employer. The employee's rights and remedies are taken over by (subrogated to) the Secretary of State (s 167), who may take proceedings against the employer, while disputes over these payments may be referred to an employment tribunal (s 170).

Maternity payments

16.82 There are similar provisions for a claim from the Maternity Fund save that the employer need not be insolvent (Statutory Maternity Pay (General) Regulations 1986 (SI 1986/1960), regs 7 and 30), and the employee is entitled to her maternity pay even though the employer is put into liquidation in the course of her absence (*Secretary of State for Employment v Cox* [1984] IRLR 437). Where the Secretary of State makes any such payments the rights and remedies of the employee in the bankruptcy are vested in the Secretary of State (s 189 ERA 1996).

17

CONSULTATION ABOUT REDUNDANCY

A DEFINITION OF REDUNDANCY 17.07

B TRADE UNION RECOGNITION 17.09

C ELECTED EMPLOYEE REPRESENTATIVES . . .17.16

D CONSULTATION IN GOOD TIME BEFORE
DISMISSALS TAKE
PLACE 17.23

E MEANING OF ESTABLISHMENT 17.33

F INFORMED CONSULTATION 17.38

G THE DEFENCE OF 'SPECIAL
CIRCUMSTANCES' 17.41

H SANCTION: THE PROTECTIVE
AWARD 17.44
Application 17.44
The amount of the protective award . . . 17.47

I WHO ARE THE UNION'S AUTHORISED
REPRESENTATIVES? 17.55

The consultation may result in new ideas being ventilated which avoid the redundancy situation altogether. Equally it may lead to a lesser number of persons being made redundant than was originally thought necessary. Or it may be that alternative work can be found during a period of consultation. (Slynn J in *Spillers-French Holdings Ltd v USDAW* [1980] ICR 31 at 37D.)

17.01 Part IV of the Employment Protection Act 1975 for the first time extended collective bargaining to cover consultation over redundancies. Sections 99 to 107 imposed the duty on employers who recognise a trade union to consult with its 'authorised representatives' when even only one employee of the class for which the union is recognised is to be made redundant, and whether or not the worker(s) in question is a member of the union. The provisions were consolidated into the Trade Union and Labour Relations (Consolidation) Act (TULR(C)A) 1992. The sanction on the employer for default is a protective award unless the tribunal decides that there are special circumstances explaining his omission.

17.02 The legislation in effect has an English mother and European father. The EEC Council Directive 75/129 was the chief European impetus, while the British genesis is found in the Donovan Commission Report. Consultation was embodied in the Code of Industrial Relations Practice but only in an advisory capacity. Council Directive 75/129 has been replaced by Directive 98/59. Civilian staff of a military base are excluded from Directive 98/59 as workers employed by a public administrative body but there is no exclusion from domestic legislation (*USA v Nolan* [2015] ICR 1347, SC). It is one of the areas where the UK may cut down the scope of coverage given the Brexit vote.

17.03 From the same European source derives a parallel obligation to inform representatives of recognised unions about takeovers and mergers, enacted in the Transfer of Undertakings (Protection of Employment) Regulations 2006, which are discussed in Chapter 18.

17.04 The provisions were introduced domestically after the ECJ in *Commission of the European Communities v UK* [1994] ICR 664 held that UK law was not then in accordance with EC Directive 75/129 on Collective Redundancies (now replaced by Directive 98/59) because it contained no provision for information and consultation in a case where the employer refused to accord recognition to a trade union. This omission was rectified, albeit inadequately, by measures contained in the Collective Redundancies and Transfer of Undertakings (Protection of Employment) (Amendment) Regulations 1995 (SI 1995/ 2587). These allowed for the election of employee representatives with whom the employer would be expected to consult during a collective redundancy situation. The UK was held further to be in breach of the Directive in these respects:

(a) its narrow definition of redundancy for these purposes. The ECJ paid particular attention to the failure to cover 'cases where workers have been dismissed as a result of new working arrangements within an undertaking unconnected with its volume of business';

(b) the failure to require consultation 'with a view to reach agreement' and to 'cover ways and means of avoiding collective redundancies or avoiding the number of workers affected or reducing the number of workers affected'; and

(c) the low 'penalty' which could be awarded by way of protective award.

17.05 By the time that the ECJ had delivered judgment in the case, these points had, however, already been addressed by a wider definition of redundancy for these consultation purposes, a new scope of consultation, and the higher ceiling on protective awards introduced by the TURERA 1993. In *Griffin and Others v South West Water Services Ltd* [1994] IRLR 15, Blackburne J held that the Collective Redundancies Directive was not capable of being directly enforced against a state authority by a union which did not enjoy recognition because it was not 'unconditional and sufficiently precise'.

17.06 The UK Government in 1999 moved a step closer towards fulfilling its obligations under the 1975 Directive (as amended by Council Directive 92/156), by the Collective Redundancies and Transfer of Undertakings (Protection of Employment) (Amendment) Regulations 1999 (SI 1999/1925), which strengthened the position of union-authorised representatives vis-à-vis elected representatives and include new arrangements designed to underpin the independence of representatives who are elected by the employees. The threshold for consultation includes those with apprenticeships and assisted contracts (*Association de médiation sociale v Union des sydicats* [2014] ICR 411).

A DEFINITION OF REDUNDANCY

17.07 The definition of redundancy for these purposes only includes 'dismissal for a reason not related to the individual concerned or a number of reasons all of which are not so related' (TULR(C)A 1992, s 195). In *University of Stirling v UCU* [2015] ICR 567, the Supreme Court held that a reason 'related to the individual concerned' if it was something to do with him such as something he was doing, or something he had done, as distinct from a reason relating to the employer, such as the need to effect business change. These cases illustrate the meaning of this important phrase:

(a) The ending of a research project or a particular course was not related to such a reason (see also *Capital Energy Solutions v Arnold* [2015] ICR 611).

(b) Where an employer unilaterally and to the detriment of the employee makes significant changes to the essential elements of the employment contract for reasons not related to the individual employee concerned, that is a redundancy for the purposes of the Collective Redundancies Directive according to the CJEU (*Pujante Rivera v Gestora Clubs Dir SL* [2016] IRLR 51).

The other important concept to consider is the 'proposal to dismiss'. In *GMB v Man* **17.08**
Truck and Bus UK Ltd [2000] IRLR 636, after the merger of two independent businesses the respondent wanted to harmonise the terms and conditions of the two groups
of employees. The alterations were imposed by serving notice to terminate the contracts
of the employees with an order of re-engagement under new terms. The tribunal found
that the respondent did not intend the employees to lose their jobs so that there was no
'proposal to dismiss' under s 188. The EAT corrected this, since there was a dismissal for
statutory purposes and the extended definition of redundancy for consultation purposes
was satisfied here. These were not 'technical dismissals' since there was no such concept.
There may be such a *proposal* even though the employers anticipate redeploying employees (*Hardy v Tourism South East* [2005] IRLR 242; *Leicestershire CC v UNISON*
[2006] IRLR 810).

B TRADE UNION RECOGNITION

A vital question in establishing liability is whether the union(s) is(are) recognised by **17.09**
the employer. This is a mixed question of fact and law. The only definition of this
concept, important though it is throughout modern labour law, is to be found in the
statutory recognition provisions of the TULR(C)A 1992, s 178(3). It is self-reflexive,
citing 'recognition of the union by an employer to any extent for the purpose of collective bargaining'. Collective bargaining is then extensively construed in the TULR(C)A
1992 (19.52ff).

The matter is straightforward in the paradigm case of a written agreement to recognise, **17.10**
or an order for recognition which has been made by the Central Arbitration Committee
(CAC). At the other end of the scale a right to be consulted about terms and conditions is
not enough. Much more problematic is the factual situation arising in the leading case,
the Court of Appeal decision in *National Union of Gold, Silver and Allied Trades v
Albury Brothers Ltd* [1978] IRLR 504, where the union sought to prove recognition on
the ground that the company was a member of a trade association, the British Jewellers'
Association, which had negotiated a series of agreements on terms and conditions with
it. The Court of Appeal emphasised the heavy burden of proof resting on the union
since 'recognition was such an important matter involving serious consequences on both
sides'. In the absence of an actual agreement, only clear and distinct conduct signifying
implied accord would suffice and Eveleigh LJ thought 'a point must be reached where
one can use the expression "it goes without saying"'. That position was not reached on
the facts.

What more is required is illustrated in *National Union of Tailors and Garment Workers v* **17.11**
Charles Ingram & Co Ltd [1977] IRLR 147, where not only was the employer a member
of a bargaining trade association, but the manager of the factory in question had 'over
a substantial period of time' discussed terms and conditions of employment, and grievances raised by the shop steward, with the local union official. It was powerful evidence
also that the employer had stated on a government form that the union was recognised.
In *Joshua Wilson & Bros Ltd v USDAW* [1978] IRLR 120, the union qualified as recognised because management followed Joint Industrial Council wage agreements, allowed
the shop steward to put up a notice announcing a particular increase, and consulted with
the shop steward over changes in employees' duties. The company had also talked with
an area organiser of the union.

17.12   There is no place for automatic recognition to be thrust on an employer by a third party over whom he had no control. In *Cleveland CC v Springett* [1985] IRLR 131, the Association of Polytechnic Teachers claimed that it was recognised at what was then Teesside Polytechnic because although it had been refused recognition despite requests over many years, enquiries by union representatives concerning conditions at work were answered and the union was encouraged to send representatives to meetings of the Polytechnic Health and Safety Committee. Further, in 1981 the Secretary of State for Education decided that it should be represented on the Burnham Pay Committee. The EAT thought that the action of the Secretary of State was in no way decisive as the tribunal had thought that it was, and that the other matters did not add up to recognition for the purposes of the statute.

17.13   The cases make clear that discussion about matters of mutual interest on a 'one-off' basis is not enough to constitute recognition. In *NUGSAT v Albury* there were a few letters and one meeting, whilst in *TGWU v Dyer* there was very limited and unwilling contact over the reinstatement of a union member; in neither case did the events found an inference of recognition. As Lord McDonald put it, there must be *consensus ad idem* on recognition, and this must be without any misapprehension, the employer realising the significance of the step he is taking (*TGWU v Courtenham Products Ltd* [1977] IRLR 9). It is not enough that the employer has been wont to negotiate with two employees who happen to be Amalgamated Union of Engineering Workers members but are not accredited stewards of the union (*AUEW v Sefton Engineering Co Ltd* [1976] IRLR 318).

17.14   Regulation 6 of the Transfer of Undertakings (Protection of Employment) Regulations 2006 provides that a transferee must maintain the same recognition as the transferor had operated, but only 'where after a relevant transfer the undertaking or part of the undertaking transferred maintains an identity distinct from the remainder of the transferee's undertaking'.

17.15   Policy considerations appear to lie behind the difficult decision of the EAT in *Union of Shop, Distributive and Allied Workers v Sketchley* [1981] IRLR 291. The applicant union had reached a formal 'recognition for representation agreement' with the respondents in May 1978; clause VIII clearly provided that 'this agreement does not confer recognition by the company for negotiation of terms and conditions'. Even so, in January 1980 the company agreed to a meeting to discuss wages, and when it began to select candidates for redundancy, on 28 February, it fully discussed the crisis with the union. This meeting resulted in a memorandum of agreement providing that, *inter alia*, union officials would be given two hours' notice before any redundancy proposal was discussed, one of them would be available for discussion with staff, and that volunteers for redundancy would be encouraged. The EAT upheld the employment tribunal's decision that the 1978 agreement did not amount to recognition. They saw a clear distinction between, on the one hand, the role of a trade unionist who, under existing grievance procedures, is entitled to make representations on behalf of a worker and, on the other, the brief of another who has the right to negotiate over what the procedures themselves should be. Browne-Wilkinson P was particularly concerned about the cost to orderly industrial relations in the multi-union situation, if every union which obtained the right to represent its own members was thereby considered recognised. The EAT commented that an employer who enters into an agreement with a union relating to terms and conditions of employment of union members runs a severe risk that the inference will be drawn that the employer has recognised the union as having negotiating rights in that field.

C ELECTED EMPLOYEE REPRESENTATIVES

The 1995 Amendment Regulations extended the definition of those who are to be con- **17.16** sulted to 'employee representatives elected by the relevant employees'. Such employee representatives must be so employed at the time when they were elected, so it is not possible to draft in someone from outside the employing company. Section 188A of the TULR(C)A 1992 provides in detail for the conduct of elections of employee representatives and imposes a duty on the employer to make such arrangements as are reasonably practicable to ensure that the election is fair. Any employee who may be affected by the proposed dismissals or by measures taken in connection with them is entitled to vote in the election and, if he wants to do so, to stand as a candidate. The election should be conducted, so far as is reasonably practicable, in secret and votes must be accurately counted. Representatives' terms of office should be long enough for them to be fully informed and consulted in accordance with s 188.

The employer is required to consult union representatives where it recognises an independ- **17.17** ent trade union in respect of a group of affected employees (s 188(1B) of the TULR(C)A 1992). It is only where such a recognition arrangement does not exist that the employer is required to consult with non-union representatives and if the employees have not elected representatives then with the employees themselves.

By s 188(7B) of the TULR(C)A 1992, in the absence of an election, if the employer has **17.18** invited employees to elect employee representatives and they have failed to do so within a reasonable time, the employer must give information instead to all the affected employees individually. Redundancy consultation rights were conferred on trade union and elected representatives only. Where there was no such representative, the employer's duty was to consult with each individual employee but there was nothing to suggest that an individual could be considered to represent other employees in similar circumstances where he had not been elected to do so (*Independent Insurance Co Ltd v Aspinall* [2011] ICR 1234).

The representatives need not be elected only for the specific purposes of consultation **17.19** about redundancies for them to qualify under the statute, but where they have been elected for other purposes it must be appropriate for the employer to consult them over redundancies in order for the duty to arise. Thus, it would be appropriate for the employer to consult members of a works council, but probably not those who were elected as, for example, canteen representatives.

Where the employers put forward two names for employee representatives and no objec- **17.20** tion was taken, it was held that there was no need to conduct a ballot to elect where the number of candidates fell short of or equalled the number of representatives to be elected (*Phillips v Xtera Communications Ltd* [2012] ICR 171).

The elected representative and candidates for such posts also have a right not to be sub- **17.21** jected to detrimental treatment or to dismissal on the grounds of the carrying out of their functions or activities and they must also be accorded reasonable time off with pay, for the purposes of their activities (*Howard v Millrise Ltd* [2005] ICR 435).

In addition, s 189(1) of the TULR(C)A 1992 gives dismissed or affected employees, **17.22** employee representatives, and the union rights (as appropriate) to complain to an employment tribunal in circumstances where the employer has failed to perform any of the duties set out in s 188 and s 188A (see above).

D CONSULTATION IN GOOD TIME BEFORE DISMISSALS TAKE PLACE

17.23 By the TULR(C)A 1992, s 188 as originally enacted, the overriding duty resting on an employer when he *proposed* to dismiss employees as redundant was to begin consultation with the recognised union 'at the earliest opportunity'. The 1995 Regulations amended this so that consultation shall 'begin in good time', which is a somewhat less exacting test. The word 'proposal' is important in this formulation. It means more than a remote possibility of dismissal (*National Union of Public Employees v General Cleaning Contractors* [1976] IRLR 362), and requires, as the EAT put it in *Association of Patternmakers and Allied Craftsmen v Kirvin Ltd* [1978] IRLR 318, 'a state of mind directed to a planned or proposed course of events'. The employer must thus have formed some view of how many are to be dismissed, when this is to take place and how it is to be arranged. The duty arises only when matters have reached a stage when a specific proposal has been formulated (*Hough v Leyland DAF Ltd* [1991] ICR 696). That was a later stage than the diagnosis of the problem leading to the dismissals and the realisation that one answer to that problem would be redundancies.

17.24 There was, however, a strong argument for saying that this approach does not satisfy European obligations. This is because EC Council Directive 75/129 requires that where an employer is *contemplating* large-scale redundancies (replaced by Directive 98/59), he should consult with the union to consider at least ways to avoid the redundancies. It may be claimed that a firm proposal is too late a stage in the process of decision-making for realistic consultation to take place. This argument was, however, rejected by the EAT in *Hough* on a matter of the linguistic construction of the words used in UK legislation. Indeed, the EAT considered the French language version of the Directive before concluding that 'contemplating' did not require a wider construction than they placed on it. In *Re Hartlebury Printers Ltd* [1992] ICR 560, Morritt J held that 'contemplating' in Art 2(1) of Council Directive 75/129/EEC was to be construed in the same sense as 'proposing' in s 99 of the EPA 1975.

17.25 The EAT, in *UK Coal Mining Ltd v National Union of Mineworkers (Northumberland Area)* [2008] IRLR 4, however, made clear that the consultation obligations under s188 extend to consulting on the principle of the decision whether to declare the redundancies, even if that embraces the decision to close a specific business. Thus, in *UK Coal* they ought to have consulted with the recognised trade union about the decision to close a coal mine, with a potential for 400 job losses, before taking the final decision to close the mine. That consultation should have been for a period of at least ninety days before termination notices were given.

17.26 In *R v British Coal Corporation and Secretary of State for Trade and Industry, ex p Price and Others* [1994] IRLR 72, the meaning of consultation was considered for the purposes of s 46(1) of the Coal Industry Nationalisation Act 1946, a parallel provision involving:

(a) consultation when the proposals are still at a formative stage;
(b) adequate information on which to respond;
(c) adequate time in which to respond; and
(d) conscientious consideration by the employer of the response to consultation.

17.27 In *Green & Son (Castings) Ltd v ASTMS & AUEW* [1984] IRLR 135 the employer claimed that it had consulted the unions on the very day that redundancy notices were issued, and that this constituted the start of statutory consultations. The EAT reiterated its decision in *National Union of Teachers v Avon County Council* [1978] IRLR 55 that this could not constitute consultation in any meaningful sense of the word. It was also insufficient to inform the unions that the criteria for selection would 'be determined in consultation with union representatives' as this was too vague. The employer had rather to inform the unions of its proposed method before consultation began, and this must be done before notices of dismissal were dispatched, as union representatives must be able properly to consider the proposals put to them. In *Transport and General Workers' Union v Ledbury Preserves (1928) Ltd* [1986] IRLR 492, where dismissal notices were sent out half an hour after a meeting with union representatives took place at which redundancy proposals were put to them for the first time, the EAT had little difficulty in deciding that this was a sham exercise which would not qualify.

On the other hand, in *NALGO v National Travel (Midlands) Ltd* [1978] ICR 598, the **17.28** EAT stated that, 'This legislation never envisaged a requirement for a trade union to be involved in preliminary policy considerations which are a managerial responsibility.' Consultation thus does not need to extend to the economic background or context in which the proposal for redundancy arises (*Securicor Omega Express Ltd v GMB* [2004] IRLR 9; *MSF v Refuge Assurance plc* [2002] IRLR 324).

There is no automatic cut-off date after which information is seen to be 'spent'. An **17.29** employer could thus rely on information provided to the union in compliance with s 188(4) in relation to dismissals some twenty-two months later where the consultation deals with the same employees and the same prospective redundancies (*Vauxhall Motors Ltd v TGWU* [2006] IRLR).

Minimum periods of time are laid down by s 188(1A): where 100 or more men are to be **17.30** made redundant at one establishment within a period of ninety days or less, at least forty-five days must be left for consultations (reduced from ninety in 2013) before the first of the dismissals takes effect. Thirty days must be allowed for this process where between twenty and ninety-nine are to be dismissed within thirty days.

The Secretary of State for Business (now BEIS) has power to vary further this provision **17.31** (s 197(1)) as long as he does not reduce it to less than thirty days. These workers do not have to be entitled to redundancy pay so that it includes those with less than two years' service. It does not, however, apply to employees on fixed-term contracts for twelve weeks or less or those taken on to perform a specific task which is not expected to last more than twelve weeks. The duty arises even if the employees are not actually members of the recognised trade union which is being consulted (*Governing Body of the Northern Ireland Hotel and Catering College v NATFHE* [1995] IRLR 83).

Where people volunteered for redundancy because they were invited to do so in circum- **17.32** stances where the employer sought volunteers to mitigate the impact of those redundancies, it was held to be wrong to examine each employee's psychological process or motives for volunteering (*Optare Group Ltd v TGWU* [2007] IRLR 932). Instead they could be treated as having been dismissed.

E MEANING OF ESTABLISHMENT

The minimum amount of time for consultation depends on the number of persons to be **17.33** made redundant at the 'establishment' in question. This concept derives from the EC Directive itself and is not a term of art in English labour law.

The courts have sought guidance in the definition of this same word (for the different **17.34** purposes of selective employment tax) which focused on:

(a) the exclusive occupation of premises;
(b) the degree of permanence;

(c) organisation of workers; and

(d) how administration is organised.

(*Barratt Developments Ltd v UCATT* [1978] ICR 319; see also *Barley v Amey Roadstone Corp Ltd* [1977] ICR 546, referring to *Secretary of State for Employment and Productivity v Vic Hallam Ltd* (1970) 5 ITR 108.)

17.35 In *Green & Son (Castings) Ltd v ASTMS and AUEW* [1984] IRLR 135, the three appellant companies were all subsidiaries of the same holding company, operated from the same site, and shared the same accounting and personnel services. The tribunal sought to decide the number of employees to be made redundant at one establishment by aggregating the numbers employed by the three companies on the one site. Nolan J considered that this approach was misconceived. The first question is the identity of the employer, and only within the one company can numbers at a particular establishment be aggregated.

17.36 Establishment must be understood as a matter of European law as designating the unit to which the worker made redundant was assigned to carry out his duties (*Rockfon A/S v Specialarbejderforbundet i Danmark* [1996] IRLR 168; *Athinaïki Chartopoïïa AE v Panagiotidis* [2007] IRLR 284, see also *MSF v Refuge Assurance plc* [2002] IRLR 324).

17.37 *USDAW v Ethel Austin Ltd* [2015] ICR 675 is now the leading case and holds that establishment designates the unit to which the redundant workers were assigned to carry out their duties; it was not essential that such a unit was endowed with management that could independently effect collective redundancies and it did not have any legal, economic, financial, administrative, or technological autonomy (see also *Moyer-Lee v Cofely Workplace Ltd* [2015] IRLR 879).

F INFORMED CONSULTATION

17.38 By the TULR(C)A 1992, s 188(6), there is no exhaustive definition, but consultation must include consultation about 'ways of (a) avoiding the dismissals; (b) reducing the numbers of employees to be dismissed and (c) mitigating the consequences of the dismissals'. Further, the employer must undertake the consultation 'with a view to reaching agreement with trade union representatives' so that there is a need for good faith to be applied in the consultation. A breach of this provision is likely to be difficult to substantiate, for it is not clear how far actual negotiation must take place. However, talks must proceed on an informed basis, so that the employer is required at the beginning (s 188(4)) to disclose in writing to union representatives: the reason for the loss of jobs; the number, although not the names, of those to be dismissed; the total number of workers employed; and the proposed method of selection. The details should also include how much notice the employer intends to give, and whether he will be making any enhanced severance payments.

17.39 The employer's attempt to comply with the Act in *Electrical and Engineering Association v Ashwell-Scott* [1976] IRLR 319 was not good enough, since its letter only gave general notification of impending redundancies, and went on 'if there is any further information you should require please communicate ...'.

17.40 Tribunals have sought guidance on the meaning of consultation in the administrative law case of *Rollo v Minister of Town and Country Planning* [1947] 2 All ER 488, which decided that it means the communication of a genuine invitation, extended with a receptive mind, to give advice. It was not enough to commence consultation for the union to be sent merely a copy of the notification by the employer of redundancies to the then

Department of Employment (now BEIS) since this did not say anything about which divisions of the company might be affected or in what proportion (*MSF v GEC Ferranti (Defence Systems) Ltd (No 2)* [1994] IRLR 113).

G THE DEFENCE OF 'SPECIAL CIRCUMSTANCES'

An employer may plead 'special circumstances' as a partial exemption from the require- **17.41**
ment to consult with recognised union or employee representatives, although he must
still 'take all such steps towards compliance ... as are reasonably practicable' (TULR(C)A
1992, s 189(6)). The employer may not, however, rely upon 'a failure on the part of a
person controlling the employer (directly or indirectly) ... to provide information to the
employer' (TULR(C)A 1992, s 188(7), inserted by the TURERA 1993, s 34(2)). The
defence reflects the problems which affect particular trades and industries, especially
construction. In *Amalgamated Society of Boilermakers v George Wimpey Ltd* [1977]
IRLR 95, the employers contended that it was not reasonably practicable for them to comply since the building site at Grangemouth, where the redundancies were declared, was
subject to resignations, unexpected delays, uncertain weather, and design changes. These
were precisely the arguments which were unsuccessfully used in Parliament to justify an
amendment excluding the building trade altogether from the scope of the provisions, and
the EAT decided that such matters *could* provide an acceptable excuse, but did not do so
in this case, since the employers had not done their best to comply in the circumstances.
No protective award was granted to the employees, however. On the other hand, in what
may seem a harsh decision, where a builder was wrongly informed by the Department
of Employment that he could make a man redundant without first consulting the union,
this misleading advice was held not to be a 'special circumstance' (*Union of Construction
Allied Trades and Technicians v H. Rooke and Son (Cambridge) Ltd* [1978] IRLR 204).
Section 188(7) looks at the actual events which occurred and decides whether or not those
events rendered it not reasonable to consult (*E Ivor Hughes Educational Foundation v
Morris* [2015] IRLR 696).

The most common set of special circumstances to come before tribunals in respect of **17.42**
the defence concerns the last breaths of a dying business. The employers in *Clarks of
Hove Ltd v Bakers Union* [1978] ICR 1076 had carried on business for many years as
manufacturers and retailers of confectionery. By the early autumn of 1976 they were
in grave financial difficulties, but in October it was apparent that their last hopes of
survival had failed. Yet it was only two hours before the night shift came to work on
the final day at 7pm that a notice was posted on their numerous factory and bakery
premises announcing that the workforce were then dismissed. The Court of Appeal
confirmed the decision of the employment tribunal that 'special' circumstances must,
to qualify, be 'out of the ordinary run of events, and, in this context, commercial and
financial events, such as a destruction of the plant, a general trading boycott or a sudden withdrawal of supplies from the main supplier'. Insolvency *alone* was not a 'special'
circumstance, but it might be so if it were proved that the employer had continued trading in the face of adverse economic pointers in the genuine but nonetheless reasonable
expectation that redundancies would be avoided. Here, on the other hand, the company's management knew of the closure plans long before the date of dismissal and it
ought to have seen that there was little chance that it could ward it off, and thus should
have consulted the unions earlier.

In *Association of Patternmakers and Allied Craftsmen v Kirvin Ltd* [1978] IRLR 318, **17.43**
Lord Macdonald drew a valuable distinction between a foreseeable insolvency as in

Clarks' case, which could not be a special circumstance, and carrying on business in the reasonable hope that the company would be sold as a going concern, which would obviate the need for redundancies and which might be within the scope of the excuse. The Employment Appeal Tribunal thought that *Kirvin*'s case was in the latter category. Here, there were potential purchasers in the field, and potential government subsidies, and it was accepted that consultation would be fatal to delicate negotiations surrounding a 'rescue operation'. It might be thought that this was exactly the sort of circumstances for which these procedural sections were envisaged, but Lord Macdonald did warn that an employer will not prove special circumstances 'if he shut his eyes to the obvious'. In *Union of Shop, Distributive and Allied Workers v Leancut Bacon Ltd* [1981] IRLR 295, the respondent company's directors had for some time been negotiating for the purchase of its shares by a third party; on the breakdown of these talks, the receiver declared redundancies without the necessary consultations taking place. This was held to be a special circumstance, even though, unlike in *Hamish Armour,* where the future depended on the discretion of a government department, all factors were within the employer's knowledge. It is not, however, sufficient to amount to 'special circumstances' that the business could not be sold and that there were no orders anticipated by the employers (*GMB v Rankin and Harrison* [1992] IRLR 514), or to an expected decision of the US parent company to withdraw financial support and work from the employer (*GMB & AMICUS v Beloit Walmsley Ltd* [2004] IRLR 18). This is to be ignored since they were potentially decisions which did have the effect of requiring dismissal by reason of redundancy by the employers and the persons who made them must have contemplated that they would have that consequence.

H SANCTION: THE PROTECTIVE AWARD

Application

17.44 The remedy for failure to comply with the duty to consult on any of the procedural requirements of the section lies in the 'protective award' (TULR(C)A 1992, s 189(3)). This is an unusual hybrid in that it may be sought in an employment tribunal by a recognised union, employee representative, or individual (if there is no union nor elected representative), but is made in favour of, and can ultimately be enforced by, the individual employee dismissed as redundant. It is an entitlement 'to be paid remuneration by the employer for the protected period' (s 190(1)), conditional upon, in the main, the employee being available for work should management wish to use his services. Besides a maximum in all cases of ninety days' pay, the only guidance provided for employment tribunals is that the award must be 'just and equitable in all the circumstances having regard to the employer's default' (s 189(4)). The award may only be made in favour of those in respect of whom a complaint of breach has been proved so that where a claim is made by a trade union the award inures only for the benefit of those whom the union represents. Other employees must make their own claim (*TGWU v Brauer Coley Ltd (in administration)* [2007] IRLR 207).

17.45 An application must be presented to the tribunal 'before the proposed dismissal takes effect or before the end of the period of three months beginning with a date on which the dismissal takes effect' or within a further period which the tribunal finds it just and equitable to grant, by way of extension. The question of whether an individual employee who may not be a trade union member can force the recognised union to make a claim on his behalf remains unanswered (see *Northgate HR Ltd v Mercy* [2008] IRLR 222).

The time limit imposed by s 192(2)(a) of the 1992 Act required that an application to a **17.46** tribunal against an employer which failed to pay any remuneration at all in respect of a protected claimant must be made within a period of three months beginning with the last day of the protected period, even where a protected award was made well after the expiry of the protected period (*Howlett Marine Services Ltd v Bowlan* [2001] IRLR 201).

The amount of the protective award

The primary judicial guidance on the size of the award is to be found in *Talke Fashions* **17.47** *Ltd v Amalgamated Society of Textile Workers and Kindred Trades* [1977] ICR 833, where the EAT emphasised that it was discretionary and in no way a penal provision. Tribunals should weigh the loss suffered by the employees and the seriousness of the employer's conduct in relation to them.

In *Barratt Developments Ltd v UCATT* [1978] ICR 319, the EAT thought the appropri- **17.48** ate award was the 'amount of money, either by way of wages or in lieu of notice, that the employee would have got if the proper consultation procedures required by the Act had been applied'. This was adopted by Slynn J in *Spillers-French Holdings Ltd v USDAW* [1980] ICR 31, where the employer argued that it was not liable to make an award to redundant employees at thirteen of the bakeries which it had closed, because they had immediately secured jobs with the transferee company. The EAT remitted the case to the employment tribunal to examine the number of days' consultation lost and the serious- ness of the default. On the latter, it pointed to a difference of substance between disclos- ing certain matters orally which should have been in writing and failure to give reasons for the redundancy at all, and went on:

> If the employer has done everything that he can possibly do to ensure that his employees are found other employment ... a tribunal may well take the view that either there should be no award or if there is an award it should be minimal.

Remuneration paid by another employer during the protected period was to be disre- garded (see *GKN Sankey Ltd v National Society of Motor Mechanics* [1980] IRLR 8).

Section 189(4) of the TULR(C)A 1992 provides that the protected period for award 'shall **17.49** be a period beginning with the date on which the first of the dismissals to which the complaint relates takes effect'. In *Transport and General Workers' Union v Ledbury Preserves (1928) Ltd* [1986] IRLR 492, the EAT decided that the relevant time runs from the *proposed* date of the first dismissal rather than the actual date. There, twenty-five employees were given notice of redundancy without any consultation with the union. In fact one of the employees left (and was by statute treated as having been dismissed) two months before the proposed date of termination. The maximum protective award at the time was thirty days and if that time began to run with the first actual dismissal, his own, the other employees would receive no award. The words 'takes effect' mean take effect in accordance with the proposal in s 188(3).

An employment tribunal may make a nil award even where liability is established. Thus, **17.50** in *Association of Scientific, Technical and Managerial Staffs v Hawker Siddeley Aviation Ltd* [1977] IRLR 418, the parties had already agreed on payment by the employer of wages in lieu of notice so that, even though the first employee left only nine days after the beginning of consultation, the tribunal awarded no compensation. Also, where the breach was only lack of written information this was treated as a technical default, since the workers were kept fully informed, and the EAT made no protective award (*Amalgamated Society of Boilermakers v George Wimpey* [1977] IRLR 95). In *Sovereign Distribution* *v TGWU* [1989] IRLR 334, however, the EAT decided that a protective award should be made even though consultation would have been unlikely to have made any difference to the final outcome.

17.51 The futility of any consultation given the circumstances of the business is not relevant to the making of a protective award (*Susie Radin Ltd v GMB* [2004] IRLR 400; *Smith v Cherry Lewis Ltd* [2005] IRLR 86; *AMICUS v GBS Tooling Ltd* [2005] IRLR 683). The required focus is not on compensating the relevant employees but instead on the seriousness of the employer's default in complying with the statutory obligation. The default in compliance may indeed vary greatly in seriousness from the technical default to a complete failure to provide any of the required information and to consult. The deliberateness of the failure may be relevant as may the availability to the employer of legal advice. A proper approach by the tribunal in a case where there has been no consultation at all is to start with the maximum period and reduce it only if there are mitigating circumstances justifying a reduction to an extent that the tribunal considers appropriate.

17.52 Moreover, the employee loses entitlement to a protective award if during the period covered he:

(a) is not ready and willing to work;
(b) goes on strike;
(c) is fairly dismissed for a reason other than redundancy;
(d) unreasonably terminates his contract;
(e) is offered suitable new employment; or
(f) has his old contract renewed to take effect before or during the protected period.

Protective awards are treated as earnings for social security purposes, and national insurance contributions are taken off.

17.53 The employee may not claim jobseeker's allowance throughout the period of the protective award. The normal situation is that benefit is paid in the first instance because of uncertainty whether an award will be made, but when made it is subject to recoupment as ordered by the employment tribunal. The award must not be paid to the relevant employees until social security received has been returned to the Department of Work and Pensions. They are treated as golden handshakes for tax purposes and are thus usually exempt.

17.54 An insolvent employer may not set off, in relation to failure to consult over redundancies, sums which are not paid for failure to give statutory minimum notice (*Secretary of State for Employment v Mann* [1996] IRLR 4) and the award is enforceable as a contingent liability in an insolvency (*Haine v Day* [2008] IRLR 642) but not in priority to the expenses of the administration (*Krasner v McMath* [2005] IRLR 995).

I WHO ARE THE UNION'S AUTHORISED REPRESENTATIVES?

17.55 It is difficult in some cases to decide who are the appropriate representatives of the union who should be consulted in the absence of a legally created plant-level body such as exists in most European countries. Section 196 of the TULR(C)A 1992 identifies 'an official or other person authorised to carry on collective bargaining with the employer in question by that trade union'. In *General and Municipal Workers' Union v Wailes Dove Bitumastic Ltd* [1977] IRLR 45, an employment tribunal rejected the union's complaint that the employer had not discharged his statutory duty because he had consulted the shop steward with whom he bargained over plant matters, rather than the full-time organiser of the union, since the latter had never carried on collective bargaining with the company.

18

TRANSFERS OF UNDERTAKINGS

A A RELEVANT TRANSFER 18.04
  Introduction 18.04
  The essential question 18.10
  European authority 18.11
  The UK cases .18.22
  The present position: Summary 18.33
  Service provision change 18.34
  Transfer by way of two or more
  transactions 18.40
  Exclusions and waiver 18.41

**B WHOSE CONTRACTS ARE
TRANSFERRED?** 18.43
  Employment by the transferor in the
  part transferred 18.43
  Employed by the transferor? 18.51
  Employment immediately before the
  transfer 18.55

**C EFFECT OF TRANSFER ON THE CONTRACT
OF EMPLOYMENT** 18.59
  Rights and duties transferred 18.63
  Rights which are not transferred 18.69
  Contractual rights separate from the
  contract of employment 18.76
  Variation of terms on transfer 18.77

**D THE POSITION OF THE
EMPLOYEE** 18.85
  Relief 18.98

**E DISMISSAL ON TRANSFER OF
UNDERTAKING** 18.99
  Is the dismissal a nullity? 18.100
  Is there a need for a specific
  transfer? 18.101
  What qualifies as an economic
  reason? 18.102
  Entailing changes in the workforce . . .18.107
  The test of fairness 18.110
  Dismissal by the vendor at the behest
  of the purchaser 18.111

**F CONSULTATION WITH THE
RECOGNISED UNIONS OR ELECTED
REPRESENTATIVES** 18.116
  The information to be given 18.116
  The expanding scope of
  consultation .18.119
  The defence .18.121
  The rights of elected representatives . . . 18.124

G TRADE UNION RIGHTS 18.126
  Notification of employee liability
  information .18.129

> The objective of the Directive [77/187 on Acquired Rights] is to ensure as far as possible the continuation without change of the contract of employment or the employment relationship with the transferee in order to avoid the workers concerned being placed in a less favourable position by reason of the transfer alone. (*Landsorganisationen i Danmark v Ny Mølle Kro* [1989] IRLR 37 at para 28.)

It was fundamental to the common law that each contract of employment was a discrete **18.01** unit, and for the best of reasons, since if an employee could be forcibly transferred from one employer to another, they would be 'serfs and transferred as though they were property' (*Nokes v Doncaster Amalgamated Collieries Ltd* [1940] AC 1014; *Bolwell v Redcliffe Homes Ltd* [1999] IRLR 485). This may, however, act against an employee's interest in the context of modern employment rights where preserving continuity of service is important. As required by the European Directive 77/187 on Acquired Rights, the Transfer of Undertakings (Protection of Employment) Regulations 1981 (SI 1981/1794) considerably altered the position and this was amended by the 2006 Regulations (for detailed commentary, see J Lewis, J. Bowers, *et al, Transfer of Undertakings: Encyclopaedia*, Sweet & Maxwell). The Government may restrict some of the rights accorded to employees under TUPE following the Brexit referendum result.

18.02 The original Regulations were found to be flawed as a matter of the proper implementation of the Directive. Following enforcement proceedings against the UK Government brought by the European Commission in 1992, amendments were made by the Collective Redundancies and Transfer of Undertakings (Protection of Employment) (Amendment) Regulations 1995 (SI 1995/2587). In 2001, the EU amended the Acquired Rights Directive itself and this led to the 2006 amended TUPE Regulations (SI 2006/246) which wholly replaced the original version.

18.03 TUPE may apply to a transfer of a business where, following the transfer, it is based outside both the UK and the European Union (*Hollis Metal Industries Ltd v GMB* [2008] IRLR 187). It is indeed unlikely that employees will want to transfer abroad but they will be entitled to their information and consultation rights on the transfer, with the possible penalty of up to thirteen weeks' pay, as well as the possibility of bringing claims for unfair dismissal for a transfer-related reason.

A A RELEVANT TRANSFER

Introduction

18.04 The Regulations apply only where there is a transfer of an undertaking situated in the UK at the time of transfer. There is no definition of 'an undertaking' as such, but economic entity means 'An organised grouping of resources which has the objective of pursuing an economic activity whether or not the activity is central or ancillary' (reg 3(2)). In general, therefore, the transfer of an undertaking will involve the transfer of a trade or business.

18.05 There are now two different situations which constitute a transfer. The first is where there is a transfer of an economic entity, which is the original model of a transfer derived from the EU Directive. The second is where there is an organised group of employees which is dedicated to performing a specific service and there is a change in service provider, which has been introduced into the 2006 Regulations as a purely domestic extension of the law.

18.06 The purchaser may simply purchase the undertaking in order to lease or sell and yet it remains a transfer (see *Premier Motors (Medway) Ltd v Total Oil (GB) Ltd* [1984] ICR 58). Although normally the transfer will be achieved by sale, reg 3(2) expressly provides that it may be involuntary, being by operation of law, for example on succession, and also that it may be a voluntary transfer activated otherwise than by sale, for example, by gift or exchange. The Regulations will also apply where there is a change in the identity of the person operating an 'economic entity' which is transferred. It is not necessary for the transferee actually to acquire the ownership of that entity.

18.07 The transfer of shares is, however, outside the scope of the Regulations even though it is adopted with the purpose of avoiding their consequences (*Brookes v Borough Care Services* [1998] IRLR 636). The onus of proof that there has been a transfer rests on the party (usually the claimant employee) who so asserts.

18.08 This was reaffirmed in *Millam v Print Factory (London) 1991 Ltd* [2007] IRLR 526, but it was held that this did not apply on the facts of the case where Mr Millam was employed by a company which was sold by its parent company by way of a share sale agreement to M Ltd. He was told that the identity of his employer was not changing, but, despite the fact that it was a share sale, he was also informed that his employment had continued under TUPE 1981 and that it was the purchaser's intention fully to incorporate the business of the employer into its own business. In 2005 M Ltd went into administration and he was dismissed. On the following day, the business was acquired by PF(L) Ltd. M brought proceedings against PF(L) Ltd. An employment tribunal found that on the sale by the parent company there was a relevant transfer under the Regulations to M Ltd. The Court of Appeal held that a change in the legal control of the original corporate employer, such as occurred on a share sale of the kind that took place in the present case, did not of itself constitute a relevant transfer of the business for the purposes of the Regulations. The proper question to be asked, however, was whether as a matter of fact the business in which Mr Millam was employed had been transferred from one company to another. The employment tribunal, properly directed, had concluded that there was such a transfer, and the EAT had accordingly misdirected itself in referring to the issue in terms of piercing the corporate veil. The question was not truly whether the two companies existed as separate legal entities, which they clearly did, but whether the business of the subsidiary had, in fact, been transferred up to the parent company. Although a lack of independence was typical of a subsidiary and did not of itself demonstrate that the parent company owned the subsidiary's business, the tribunal had made specific findings that their business activities had been integrated to such a degree that the business carried on by the subsidiary, and not simply the shares, had transferred to the purchasing company.

18.09 A transfer 'may take place whether or not any property is transferred to the transferee by the transferor'. It may also 'be effected by a series of two or more transactions'. This reflects the considerable European case law to this effect (eg *Bork International v Foreningen af Arbejdsledere i Danmark* [1989] IRLR 41; *Foreningen af Arbejdsledere i Danmark v Daddy's Dance Hall A/S* [1988] IRLR 315). It may also occur between two companies which are in the same group (*Allen v Amalgamated Construction Co Ltd* [2000] IRLR 119, ECJ).

The essential question

18.10 In so far as there is one general formulation which may be derived from the complex and extensive case law, both UK and European, it is as follows: Has there been a change in the legal or natural person responsible for carrying on the business and is there an economic entity which has retained its identity and is transferred from one to another? There is thus a difference between a change in ownership (which is not required for a transfer of undertaking) and a change in employer (which is a prerequisite for it but is not itself sufficient). The question must be answered by reference to the substance of the transaction, not necessarily its form (see *Council of the Isles of Scilly v Brintel Helicopters Ltd* [1995] IRLR 6; and *Kelman v Care Contract Services Ltd* [1995] ICR 260).

European authority

The pre-Süzen cases

18.11 The European authority on the meaning of 'transfer' has become ever more important and has greatly influenced the whole approach to the question. The proper starting point is *Spijkers v Gebroeders Benedik Abattoir CV* [1986] 2 CMLR 296, which concerned a transferor company which had entirely ceased activity and dissipated its goodwill by the time it had sold its assets (a slaughterhouse and appurtenant premises and goods). The ECJ in this case said that the proper question was whether the entity retained its identity; all the circumstances had to be considered, but the mere sale of the assets of an enterprise did not constitute a transfer. Advocate General Sir Gordon Slynn said (at para 29): 'That at the time of transfer the business is still active, that machinery is being used, customers supplied, workers employed and that all the physical assets and goodwill are sold are strong indications that a transfer ... has taken place.' It was not, however, conclusive against a transfer taking place that 'goodwill or existing contracts are not transferred', or that there was a gap before trading was resumed after transfer. This was all a matter of fact to be determined by the national court. The court stated (at para 303) that:

> To decide whether these conditions [for transfer] are fulfilled it is necessary to take account of all the factual circumstances of the transaction in question, including the type of undertaking or business in question, the transfer or otherwise of tangible assets such as buildings and stocks, the value of intangible assets as at the date of transfer, whether the majority of staff are taken over by the new employer, the transfer or otherwise of the circle of customers, the degree of similarity between activities before and after the transfer and the duration of any interruption in those activities. It should be made clear, however, that each of these factors is only a part of the overall assessment which is required and therefore they cannot be examined independently of each other.

18.12 In the cases of *Bork International v Foreningen af Arbejdsledere i Danmark* [1989] IRLR 41; *Landsorganisationen i Danmark v Ny Molle Kro* [1989] IRLR 37, *Berg and Busschers v Besselsen* [1989] IRLR 447; and *Foreningen af Arbejdsledere i Danmark v Daddy's Dance Hall A/S* [1988] IRLR 315, discussed further below, the ECJ emphasised that the key question is whether there has been a transfer of an economic entity.

18.13 These cases reflected a very broad approach to the question of when there is a transfer, and suggested that in the case of contracting out, mere continuation of the same activity (at least at the same location) would often suffice.

The Süzen case and its aftermath

18.14 The ECJ somewhat ironically reversed itself at the same time that the UK courts were extending the boundaries of a transfer, and has narrowed down the scope of a transfer. The process started with the decision in *Ledernes Hovedorganisation acting on behalf of Ole Rygaard v Dansk Arbejdsgiverforening, acting on behalf of Strø Mølle Akustik A/S* [1996] IRLR 51, where the ECJ appeared for the first time to have pulled back from the ample extent of the concept of transfer in other cases, and stressed that the economic entity which is alleged to have been transferred must be a stable one. The firm had been entrusted by SAS Service Partner with the construction of a canteen, but was informed by the main contractor that part of the work on ceilings and joinery work should be completed by the respondent. The second contractor refunded the first for the cost of materials supplied. The alleged transferor was declared bankrupt and the employee sued the respondent for wrongful dismissal. The Advocate General found that the identity of the operation was retained since there were the same or similar economic activities being conducted before and afterwards. The ECJ reiterated that the central test was whether the business in question retained its identity, but it interpreted it and applied it to the facts in a way which was somewhat out of line with previous ECJ decisions. The ECJ rejected the claim because the transfer must 'relate to a *stable* economic entity whose activity is not limited to performing one specific works contract'. It could fall within the terms of the Directive only if it included the 'transfer of a body of assets enabling the activities or certain activities of the transferor undertaking to be carried on in a stable way'. That was not the case here. There is also to be detected the more liberal interpretation of the Directive in *Merckx v Ford Motor Co Belgium SA* [1996] IRLR 467, which concerned the application of the Directive to the transfer of a motor vehicle dealership covering a particular geographical area from one undertaking to another. The employers argued in essence that one undertaking had terminated and another had commenced, so that there was no transfer between them. The ECJ, however, concluded that the second company had carried on the activity, which was performed by the first without interruption, in the same sector and subject to similar conditions. It had taken on part of the staff of the first company and was positively recommended to the customers of the first in order to ensure continuity in the operation of the dealership. The ECJ held that neither the transfer of tangible or intangible assets nor the partial preservation of the transferor's undertaking was crucial to the application of the Directive.

The ECJ's next important decision was *Süzen v Zehnacker Gebäudereinigung GmbH* **18.15** *Krankenhausservice* [1997] IRLR 255, a decision so disruptive of previously held assumptions about the meaning of 'transfer' that it may be said that the courts have still to recover their bearings. The circumstances of the case were familiar, in that it concerned a contracting out situation. Mrs Süzen was dismissed when the company which employed her lost its contract to clean a school to another contractor. Although approving the previous decisions in the *Spijkers, Redmond, Merckx,* and *Schmidt* cases, the ECJ appeared to deviate from them by stating that:

> the mere fact that the service provided by the old and new awardees of the contract is similar does not therefore support the conclusion that an economic entity has been transferred. An entity cannot be reduced to the activity entrusted to it. Its identity also emerged from other factors, such as its workforce, its management staff, the way in which its work is organised, its operating methods or indeed, where appropriate, the operational resources available to it.

Applying these principles, the ECJ held that in a labour-intensive business, such as the **18.16** instant case, the fact that the transferor does not transfer significant tangible or intangible assets, or the transferee has not taken on a majority of those working on the contract, would count against a relevant transfer having taken place (see also *Balfour Beatty Power Networks Ltd v Wilcox* [2006] IRLR 258). This is a very strange conclusion to reach in that it appears to give the parties in a contracting out situation a measure of control over whether the Directive is to apply. It also directly contradicts the ECJ's own approach in the *Merckx* case (above). As we see below, the UK courts have started to move away from an initial grudging acceptance of the ECJ's decision in *Süzen* towards an attempt to minimise the significance of the case.

The ECJ cases of *Francisco Hernández Vidal SA v Gómez Pérez* [1999] IRLR 132 and **18.17** *Sánchez Hidalgo v Asociación de Servicios Aser and Sociedad Cooperativa Minerva* [1999] IRLR 136 concerned second generation contracting out (where the initial contract to Company A expires, is re-tendered, and goes to Company B). The ECJ reiterated that the Acquired Rights Directive applies to such situations.

The ECJ in *Temco Service Industries v Imzilyen* [2002] IRLR 214 considered a change of **18.18** cleaning contractors at Volkswagen plants in Belgium. The central question was whether there can be a transfer even in the absence of a contractual link between the two contractors, and the ECJ decided that there could be. It is sufficient if the transaction is 'part of the web of contractual relations'. The decisive criterion it decided was whether the business retains its identity. In *Liskojärvi v Oy Liikenne Ab* [2002] ICR 155, the ECJ decided that the award of bus routes by tender was not a transfer of an undertaking where no transfer of significant tangible assets occurred. Bus transport could not be characterised as an activity based essentially on manpower. There need be no significant tangible or intangible assets as a matter of European law (*Jouini v Princess Personal Service GmbH* [2007] IRLR 1005).

18.19 More recently it has been held that the retention of identity required the retention not of the specific organisation of the elements of production but of such a functional link of interdependence and contemplementarity between those elements as enabled the transferee to use them to pursue an identical or analogous economic activity even if after the transfer they were integrated into a new and different organisational structure (*Klarenberg v Ferrotron Technologies GmbH* [2009] ICR 1263). Further, the mere fact that the activity carried out by the defendant company and that carried out by the municipal authority were identical did not mean that an economic entity had retained its identity, since an entity could not be reduced to the activity entrusted to it but rather emerged from several indissociable factors such as its workforce, its management staff, and the way in which it was operated (*CLECE SA v Martin Valor* [2011] ICR 1319).

18.20 Where an economic entity was transferred to multiple transferees which included the original transferor, there was no relevant transfer and any liability on the claimant's employment remained with the original company but on a joint and several basis (*Hyde Housing Association Ltd v Layton* [2016] ICR 261).

Public sector transfers

18.21 Surprisingly, the ECJ in *Henke v Gemeinde Schierke* [1996] IRLR 701 decided that there was no transfer of undertaking when a municipal administration was dissolved and its tasks were transferred to a regional authority. In *Collino v Telecom Italia SPA* [2002] ICR 38, however, the ECJ held that under Art 1(1) the transfer for value following decisions of the public authorities, and in the form of administrative concession of an entity managed by a public body within the state administration to a private law company whose capital was held by another public body, came within the scope of the Directive provided that the persons employed by the transferor did not have public law status but were subject to private employment law (see also *Mayeur v Association Promotion de L'Information Messine* [2000] IRLR 788). Regulation 4(4)(a) of TUPE now provides that the Regulations apply to 'public and private undertakings engaged in economic activities whether or not they are operating for gain'.

The UK cases

Before Süzen

18.22 Several early UK cases modified greatly the approach taken to the concept of transfer and gave it a much more European flavour. In *Wren v Eastbourne DC* [1993] IRLR 425, the Council terminated its existing arrangements for refuse collection and made fresh arrangements by way of contract with the Onyx Company. A major degree of control was retained by the Council, of which refuse collection was one of its statutory functions, and the tribunal thus held that there was no transfer of undertaking within the Regulations (see especially at para 32). The EAT overturned the decision and remitted the case for rehearing in accordance with the correct legal principles, in particular to consider:

> whether there is a recognisable entity, a going concern (this can include the provision of services), which is run or operated or carried on by the alleged transferor ... and which is being continued by the alleged transferee ... One must look at the substance of what has occurred and not the form ... There is no necessity for the transfer of assets ... All these questions are questions of fact and degree.

Cases after Süzen

18.23 Soon after the ECJ's decision in *Süzen* (see 18.15), the Court of Appeal was called upon to reconsider its previously liberal approach in contracting out cases. *Betts v Brintel*

Helicopters Ltd [1997] IRLR 361 concerned a contract for helicopter services which was transferred from a supplier in one part of the country to another elsewhere. The latter, KLM Helicopters, had no need for either the assets or the staff who had previously worked on the contract, and so they took on neither. Adopting the same approach as the ECJ's in *Süzen*, the Court of Appeal differentiated between labour-intensive undertakings and others. Whereas in the latter case, the court was entitled to embark on a wide-ranging enquiry as to whether the identity of the economic entity has been preserved, in the former this question could be answered relatively simply by asking whether the activity in question is resumed with substantially the same staff. If not, then no transfer of an undertaking will have occurred. This argument suffers from a rather circular quality.

As time has passed, the UK courts appear to have become less willing to ascribe the same **18.24** significance to the *Süzen* case. In *ECM (Vehicle Delivery Service) Ltd v Cox* [1999] IRLR 559, the Court of Appeal decided that the importance of this case had been 'overstated'. The ECJ in *Süzen* had, Mummery LJ said, not overturned but expressly approved the approach taken in its earlier decisions in *Spijkers* and *Schmidt*. These cases had made clear that national courts *should* take into account 'all the facts characterising the transaction in question', in order to determine whether the undertaking has continued and retained its identity albeit in different hands. *Süzen* simply set limits on the application of the Directive by indicating that the mere fact that the service provided continues to be similar will not be enough to show that an economic entity has been transferred. Other factors need to be taken into account. The question of whether the majority of the employees are taken on by the transferee is just one of these factors, as are the similarity of the pre-and post-transfer activities and the type of undertaking concerned (eg in labour-intensive sectors). In these circumstances, the Court of Appeal was prepared to uphold the employment tribunal's decision that a transfer of an undertaking had indeed occurred when a vehicle delivery contract was switched from one contractor to another without any significant transfer of assets or employees. As Mummery LJ said, 'the customers were the same and the work going on was essentially the same, ie cars were unloaded at Grimsby, were put onto transporters and were driven to VAG dealers. The result was the same'. The court also held that the tribunal was entitled to take into account the reason why, in the present case, the transferee had refused to take on the transferor's employees, which was that it wished to avoid possible unfair dismissal claims (see also *Kerry Foods Ltd v Creber* [2000] IRLR 10).

Sometimes there may be in truth no economic entity at all. In *Wynnwith Engineering Co* **18.25** *Ltd v Bennett and Others* [2002] IRLR 170, the claimants worked for British Aerospace (BAe) at its aircraft manufacturing plant, in skilled positions for varying, lengthy periods, until they volunteered for redundancy in 1995 when BAe needed to shed labour. The claimants were aged over fifty and were entitled to take early retirement and receive a pension. BAe operated a Special Early Release Programme (SERP) for the employees. In 1996 business improved again and BAe needed to recruit. To bring back the skills required at short notice, BAe re-engaged on short-term contracts about thirty of those who had taken early retirement under the SERP scheme, including the applicants. Following negotiations with the unions, Wynnwith became the exclusive agency for the ongoing provision of temporary labour. The thirty or so 'SERP' workers, after differing and disparate periods of employment under short-term contracts with BAe, registered with Wynnwith and worked in all parts of BAe's Broughton plant. The SERP workers covered a wide range of skilled trades and occupations: they did not work as one group within the plant, but rather alongside other 'core' workers, new recruits, and other temporary workers recruited by Wynnwith and placed with BAe.

18.26 It is not unusual for one employment agency to take over the supply of 'temps' to an end user from another agency. *Wynnwith* shows that in such a case it is unlikely that the employees who cease to work for one agency and begin working for another the next day—albeit for the same end user—will be regarded as transferred as part of an economic entity.

18.27 There will be no transfer where there has been an irretrievable insolvent liquidation and cessation of business (*Perth & Kinross Council v Donaldson* [2004] IRLR 121), but a stable economic entity may comprise just a single employee (*Dudley Bower Building Services Ltd v Lowe* [2003] IRLR 260).

The significance of the transfer of staff

18.28 One important question to be asked (and already touched upon) in the case particularly of labour-intensive organisations is the extent to which the transferee takes over 'a major part in terms of numbers and skills of the employees specially assigned by the predecessor to the task', but the absence of the movement of significant assets or a major part of the workforce does not necessarily deny the existence of a relevant transfer (*Kerry Foods Ltd v Creber* [2000] IRLR 10; *RCO Support Services & Aintree Hospital Trust v UNISON* [2000] IRLR 624). The emphasis on the latter point rendered putative transferees naturally reluctant to take on any of the workforce of the putative transferor. Further, there is some authority that if the reason for the refusal by the putative transferee is specifically to seek to avoid the application of the Regulations, that fact will be ignored. This was the basis of the decision in *ECM (Vehicle Delivery Service) Ltd v Cox* [1999] IRLR 559 (see also *ADI (UK) Ltd v Willer* [2001] IRLR 542).

18.29 Thus, it is not merely open to a tribunal to investigate this issue of why the employees were not taken on and resolve it. It *must*, in an appropriate case, consider the question. This is an aspect of giving a purposive construction to the Regulations.

18.30 *RCO Support Services Ltd v UNISON* [2002] IRLR 401 involved not only a change of contractor but also a change of location (from Walton to Fazakerley) where the operation was to be carried on. RCO had submitted that *Süzen* should be interpreted as stating that, as a matter of Community law, there could never be a transfer of an undertaking in a contracting out case if neither assets nor workforce are transferred. Since none of the workforce had been taken on by RCO, no transfer could have taken place. Mummery LJ rejected this contention because it was contrary to the 'multifactorial approach' to the retention of identity test laid down by the ECJ in *Spijkers* (and *Süzen* does not overrule *Spijkers*). Whether or not the majority of employees are taken on by the new employer is, he said, only one of the many factors to be considered in making an overall assessment as to whether there is a transfer. Single factors must not be considered in isolation.

18.31 During the run-up to the 'transfer', RCO had positively said, in the context of a disagreement as to whether the TUPE Regulations applied, that it would take the cleaners employed by the 'transferor' (Initial) into the operation in Fazakerley Hospital, but only if they resigned from Initial first. The employment tribunal had taken this statement into account. Mummery LJ considered that RCO's willingness to take on the workforce by way of re-employment on its terms and conditions, in preference to automatic employment on the terms and conditions applicable as a result of a transfer under the Regulations, was relevant to the crucial issue of retention of identity. That RCO:

(a) needed a workforce to operate the contract at Fazakerley; and
(b) was willing to re-employ at Fazakerley the workforce employed at Walton,

and the workforce would have been taken on by RCO, if they had accepted RCO's offer to re-employ them on RCO's terms and conditions, was 'relevant evidence pointing to, rather than away from, RCO's own recognition of the reality of the continuity of the entities and the retention of identity'. Mummery LJ continued that: 'A subjective motive of the putative transferee to avoid the application of the Directive and TUPE is not the real point.'

Thus, the state of mind of the putative transferee as regards whether the Regulations will apply is irrelevant. The putative transferee's acts (and omissions) may be taken into account as one of the factors going to the overall question of whether there is an entity whose identity is preserved, but they are not to be considered for the purpose of drawing an inference as to the state of the corporate mind on the question of TUPE avoidance. This is a matter of fact and degree. It was held that the failure of a new contractor to take over an essential part of the staff of its predecessor who were employed to perform the same activity is not sufficient to preclude the transfer of an entity in a sector such as catering where the activity is based essentially on the equipment used (*Abler v Sodexho MM Catering Gesellschaft mbH* [2004] IRLR 168). **18.32**

The present position: Summary

The law on transfers of undertakings remains somewhat unsettled but this is less impor- **18.33** tant because of the extension of the concept to incorporate service provision changes. Nevertheless, the following principles are compatible with the domestic case law:

(a) The employment tribunal should take a robust and realistic view of the facts (*Spijkers* [1986] 2 CMLR 296 at 299; *Kenny v South Manchester College* [1994] IRLR 336).

(b) The tribunal should take a snapshot before and after the alleged transfer and see how an ordinary person would consider the circumstances; it is not sufficient that the same activity is going on before and after the putative transfer (*Kenny v South Manchester College* (above), *Süzen* (above)).

(c) One viable approach is to ask whether there is an economic entity which retains its identity and is transferred from one to another (*Rastill v Automatic Refreshment Services* [1978] ICR 289 at 295; *Spijkers* (above); *ADI* (above)).

(d) The employment tribunal should take into consideration all the circumstances characterising the operation concerned (*Dines v Initial Services Ltd* [1994] IRLR 336).

(e) The tribunal should look at the substance and not the form of the transaction (*Spijkers* (above); *Wren v Eastbourne DC* [1993] IRLR 425; *Dines* (above)).

(f) The fact that the activity transferred is only an ancillary activity of the transferor's business (not necessarily related to its objects) may count against there being a transfer of undertaking.

(g) The fact that goodwill is not transferred is not a factor telling conclusively against there being a transfer, but if no goodwill is transferred this counts as a factor against a transfer being established (*Spijkers* (above)).

(h) Although there is no requirement of a transfer of assets or property (eg *Kelman v Care Contract Services Ltd* [1995] ICR 260), such a transfer (or lack of it) will still be one of the factual circumstances to be taken into account (*ECM (Vehicle Delivery Service) Ltd v Cox*, above).

(i) There may only be one employee involved in the transfer (*Schmidt v Spar* [1995] ICR 237).

(j) The assets transferred do not have to be for independent commercial use by the transferee (*Gurney-Gorres v Securicor Aviation* [2006] IRLR 305).

(k) There may be a transfer when a company has been dissolved but the business which it conducted is then carried on by the main shareholders in the company (*Charlton v Charlton Thermosystems (Romsey) Ltd* [1995] ICR 56).

(l) An activity of itself is not an entity: the identity of an entity emerges from other factors such as its workforce, management staff, the way in which its work is organised, its operating methods, and, where appropriate, the operational resources available to it (*Cheesman v R. Brewer Contracts Ltd* [2001] IRLR 144). There would be no stable economic entity when an operation depends for its existence on a day-to-day handout of work to which it is not contractually entitled and could be terminated at any time (*Perth & Kinross Council v Donaldson* [2004] IRLR 121).

A stable economic entity is to be contrasted with one which was carrying out a single contract or operation which was likely to have a limited duration. In *NUMAST v P&O Scottish Ferries* [2005] ICR 1270, the ferry service in issue had been provided by the respondent for many years and was in fact a stable economic entity. Even though the ships were not transferred the new provider took over numerous premises and piers which were integral to the operation of that service and the government subsidy; further, a high percentage of seafarers were taken on by the new provider, the service continued to be used by the same passengers, and there was a high degree of similarity in the activities taken on (see also *Balfour Beatty Power Networks Ltd v Wilcox* [2006] IRLR 258).

(m) A tribunal may have regard to the fact that both transferor and transferee considered at the time of the putative transfer that the Regulations indeed applied to it; it is 'appropriate to consider not only the events directly constituting the transaction but also the surrounding circumstances. Those ... may include the attitudes adopted by a party in anticipation of the transaction' (*Lightways (Contractors) Ltd v Associated Holdings Ltd* [2000] IRLR 247, at para 23).

(n) There may be a transfer of business even though an envisaged merger which caused an employee to work for another company was subsequently called off. In *Dabell v Vale Industrial Services (Nottingham) Ltd* [1988] IRLR 439, the employee had been working for Vale Industrial Services for eight years when discussions started with Nofotec Co with a view to Vale joining that group. An agreement was reached in principle and Vale's orders, machines, and other items and materials were transferred. Twenty-two days after he started being paid by Nofotec, Mr Dabell resigned. Thereafter, the merger was called off. The Court of Appeal decided that whether there had been a transfer of business had to be determined as at the date when the act of which the employee complains occurs, and at this stage there was indeed a transfer of undertaking. The EAT had also erred in determining that there could be no transfer of ownership of a business without a written agreement (*SI (Systems and Instrumentation) Ltd v Grist and Riley* [1983] IRLR 391).

Service provision change

18.34 This provides a second definition of a transfer of undertaking and is a purely domestic UK creation. For this purpose it is first of all necessary to identify relevant activities, which is a question of fact and degree for the tribunal of fact (*SNR Denton UK LLP v Kirwan* [2013] ICR 101). Regulation 3(1)(b) defines the service provision change as a situation in which:

(i) activities cease to be carried out by a person ('a client') on his own behalf and are carried out instead by another person on the client's behalf ('a contractor'),

(ii) activities cease to be carried out by a contractor on a client's behalf (whether or not those activities had previously been carried out by the client on his own behalf) and are carried out instead by another person ('a subsequent contractor') on the client's behalf, or

(iii) activities cease to be carried out by a contractor or a subsequent contractor on a client's behalf (whether or not those activities had previously been carried out by the client on his own behalf) and are carried out instead by the client on his own behalf and in which the conditions set out in paragraph (3) are satisfied.

The key case law has decided as follows: **18.35**

(a) The Court of Appeal in *Hunter v McCarrick* [2013] ICR 235 decided that reg 3(1)(b)(ii) was consistent only with the situation where there was the same client throughout.

(b) The singular included the plural in relation to clients in reg 3(1)(b) of TUPE provided that the identity of such clients remained the same before and after the service provision change and that they were sufficiently linked so that a common intention could be identified for satisfying the condition in reg 3(3)(a)(ii) (*Ottimo Property Services Ltd v Duncan* [2015] ICR 859).

(c) it includes the transfer of part of a service or activity (*Arch Initiatives v Greater Manchester West Mental Health NHS Foundation Trust* [2016] IRLR 406).

This concept covers an activity which is outsourced to a contractor, taken by one con- **18.36** tractor from another or taken back in-house. It is not derived from European law but is a domestic invention. The conditions referred to are that:

(a) there must be an organised group of employees before the change which have as their principal purpose the carrying on of activities on behalf of the client. The provision excludes cases where there is no organised group of identifiable employees as it will be unclear who is to transfer; and

(b) the client intends that the activities will be carried out by the transferee other than in connection with a single specific event or task of short-term duration. A single specific event connoted short duration (*Liddell's Coaches v Cook* [2013] ICR 547). Whether or not a client intended certain activities to be carried out in connection with a task of short-term duration was an issue of fact (see also *SNR Denton UK LLP v Kirwan* [2013] ICR 101). This involved the tribunal drawing an inference from all the relevant surrounding circumstances, including both contemporaneous expressions of intent and actions, and subsequent events or non-events which are capable of casting light on the intention of the relevant party at the relevant date (*ICTS UK Ltd v Mahdi* [2016] ICR 274). A single person may constitute an organised group (*Rynda (UK) Ltd v Rhijnsburger* [2015] ICR 1300).

Kimberley Group Housing Ltd v Hambley [2008] IRLR 682 stands as authority that **18.37** a service might be transferred to more than one transferee but that it was not correct to divide liabilities for employees between them on a percentage basis as the tribunal had done.

In a services provision change case, there is no need for a formal list of factors which the **18.38** tribunal must consider before it can make a decision whether there was or was not a relevant transfer (*Metropolitan Resources Ltd v Churchill Dulwich Ltd* [2009] IRLR 700).

Further, it is not the intention that the concept of services provision change should not **18.39** apply because of some minor differences between the natures of the tasks carried on or in the way they are performed. A common sense and pragmatic approach is required. A difference in location is highly significant but is unlikely on its own to be determinative. The addition of some new duty or function to the duties of the replacement contractor who is performing all of the services carried out by his predecessor is unlikely to negate the existence of a transfer unless the addition is of such substance that the activity then being carried on is no longer essentially the same (*Metropolitan Resources Ltd v Churchill Dulwich Ltd* [2009] IRLR 700).

Transfer by way of two or more transactions

18.40   Regulation 3(6)(a) provides that, where a transfer is effected by a series of two or more transactions, reg 4 will bite on the contract of a person employed *immediately before* any of those transactions. A transaction will only form part of a series for the purposes of reg 3(6)(a), however, if it is instrumental in effecting the transfer; it is not sufficient that it forms part of a chain of events leading up to the transfer (*Longden v Ferrari Ltd and Another* [1994] IRLR 157).

Exclusions and waiver

18.41   Any agreement to contract out of the Regulations is void (reg 18; see *Foreningen af Arbejdsledere i Danmark v Daddy's Dance Hall A/S* (above)).

18.42   A party may take advantage of variations on a transfer which he considers to be in its interest. In *Regent Security Services Ltd v Power* [2008] IRLR 66, the Court of Appeal held that changes which were made to the benefit of the transferring employee could be enforced by the employee whilst those to the employee's detriment would be void. This is on the basis that there should be nothing in TUPE to prevent employees gaining additional rights. Thus, negotiating a new package which includes additional benefits in return for a reduction in transferred obligations can, if the reason for the changes is shown to be the transfer or a reason connected with it, leave the employer with the liability to pay the additional benefits and the employees still able to assert their original rights.

B WHOSE CONTRACTS ARE TRANSFERRED?

Employment by the transferor in the part transferred

18.43   The question of whose employment is actually transferred when only a part of an undertaking is transferred is a crucial issue.

18.44   By reg 4(1) TUPE 2006, 'except where objection is made under paragraph (7), a relevant transfer shall not operate so as to terminate the contract of employment of any person employed by the transferor and assigned to the organised grouping of resources or employees that is subject to the relevant transfer, but any such contract shall have effect after the transfer as if originally made between the person so employed and the transferee'. The only limited further guidance given on the face of the regulations is by reg 2(1), which provides that: 'assigned' means assigned other than on a temporary basis.

18.45   The scope of assignment was considered most authoritatively by the ECJ in the case of *Botzen v Rotterdamsche Droogdok Maatschappij BV* [1986] 2 CMLR 50. Certain specific departments of a company were sold following a liquidation of the company, and the question arose whether employees employed in general departments which provide services for them (eg personnel, porters' services, general maintenance) were also transferred. It was accepted that they carried out certain duties for the benefit of the transferred part of the undertaking, as well as for other departments of the business.

However, the ECJ held that the staff were not transferred merely because they used assets **18.46** which were located in the part transferred or carried out work which benefited that part. There had to be more, since they had to be *assigned* to the part transferred. In reaching this conclusion, the ECJ adopted the view of the European Commission, who had described in argument before the court that the 'decisive criterion' was 'whether or not a transfer takes place of the departments to which they were assigned and which formed the organisational framework within which their employment relationship took effect'.

Sometimes, the contract of employment will expressly define the section or department **18.47** in which the employee is required to work; in other cases the answer to that question will have to be implied or inferred from all the surrounding facts and circumstances (see *Northern General Hospital NHS Trust v Gale* [1994] IRLR 292). In order to be assigned to the part which has been transferred, it is clearly unnecessary for the employee to work exclusively in that part; the question is one of fact to be determined by considering all the relevant circumstances. In *Buchanan-Smith v Schleicher & Co International Ltd* [1996] ICR 613, Morison J said:

> There will often be difficult questions of fact for industrial tribunals to consider when deciding who was 'assigned' and who was not. We were invited to give guidance to industrial tribunals about such a decision, but declined to do so because the facts will vary so markedly from case to case. In the course of argument a number were suggested, such as the amount of time spent on one part of the business or the other; the amount of value given to each part by the employee; the terms of the contract of employment showing what the employee could be required to do; how the cost to the employer of the employee's services had been allocated between different parts of the business. This is, plainly, not an exhaustive list; we are quite prepared to accept that these or some of these matters may well fall for consideration by an industrial tribunal which is seeking to determine to which part of his employer's business the employee had been assigned.

(See also *CPL Distribution Ltd v Todd* [2003] IRLR 28.)

Time spent by the employee on the relevant duties can, however, be a blunt tool to analyse **18.48** the true underlying situation as to assignment, particularly where senior management is concerned. Senior management are likely to have duties which extend to the whole of a business and not merely to a specific part of it. That part may, however, have experienced particular difficulties which required more management time than others. This would not appear to lead to the conclusion that the member of senior management who was concerned was assigned to that part, as they were no more assigned to that part than to any other part of the business given their duty to manage the whole. One can see this principle at work in *Jones and Kingston v Darlows Estate Agency* (unreported, 6 July 1998, CA). Mr Kingston and Ms Jones were employed by the transferor estate agency in positions (as Regional Operations Director and PA respectively) where they had regional responsibility for Wales (twenty branches) and the West of England (eleven branches). They were both based in Cardiff. There was then a TUPE transfer involving a transfer of the Welsh branches. They were subsequently dismissed by the transferor and complained that this was in fact an automatically unfair dismissal by the transferee. The Court of Appeal upheld the employment tribunal's finding that, since they had been responsible for the entire region, and not just for the Welsh part, they had not been assigned to the part of the undertaking which has been transferred but were in fact assigned to the whole business of the transferor.

One consequence of assessing the relevant assignment at the point which was immediately **18.49** before the transfer is that it opens up the possibility of transferors being able to 'cherry-pick' key employees who will remain with the transferor and also being able to move unwanted employees into the undertaking to be transferred. As set out below, it will not be permissible to avoid employees transferring by temporarily assigning them artificially to a different part of the undertaking. However, a permanent reassignment away from the transferred undertaking is permissible and will be given effect.

18.50   These cases illustrate how tribunals should approach the issue of assignment:

(a) Where an order had been made by a council to remove a person from work on a particular contract as they were entitled to do, there was no change in the assignment. Regulation 4 contemplates assignment by or with the authority of the putative transferor, not by the unilateral act of a third party without the employer's intervention or authority (*Jakowlew v Nestor Primecare Services Ltd* [2015] IRLR 813).

(b) Suspending an employee on full pay pending disciplinary proceedings did not have the effect of removing her from the organised grouping of employees to which she belonged (*Jakowlew*).

(c) An employee on long-term sickness absence could not be considered to be assigned (*BT Managed Services Ltd v Edwards* [2016] ICR 733).

Employed by the transferor?

18.51   A related question concerns whether the employee is actually employed by the transferor of the undertaking, in which case he transfers, or by some other party, when he would not do so. In *Webb (Duncan) Offset (Maidstone) Ltd v Cooper* [1995] IRLR 633, the EAT considered the case where a person is employed by X to work on Y's business and Y transfers that business to Z. It decided that prima facie the Regulations would not apply but that '[Employment] tribunals will be astute to ensure that the provisions of the Regulations are not evaded by devices such as service companies or by complicated group structures which conceal the true position'. Such tribunals were advised to 'keep in mind the purpose of the Directive and the need to avoid complicated corporate structures from getting in the way of a result which gives effect to that purpose'. This focuses on restricting the possibilities for evasion and requires the adjudicating body to be astute to the possibility of stripping away the veil of incorporation in appropriate circumstances.

18.52   An apparently altogether more radical approach was taken by the EAT sitting in Scotland in *Sunley Turriff Holdings Ltd v Thomson* [1995] IRLR 184. Mr Thomson was employed as company secretary and chief accountant for Lilley Construction Ltd and Lilley Construction (Scotland) Ltd. His contract was with Lilley Construction Ltd. On 18 January 1993 the business of Lilley Construction (Scotland) Ltd was transferred to Sunley Turriff Holdings Ltd and Mr Thomson was not on the list of employees who were transferred; in effect he claimed that he should have been. He was dismissed on the grounds of redundancy on 1 March 1993 by the Receivers of Lilley Construction Ltd and he claimed against Sunley Turriff Holdings Ltd as transferee. The Regulations applied since the part transferred included Lilley Construction (Scotland) Ltd for whom Mr Thomson provided services and accordingly Mr Thomson was held to be assigned to the part transferred. The crucial question, however, was whether the claimant was an employee in that undertaking (para 13). The EAT said that 'The tribunal did not focus on that question; an employee may well work in a particular undertaking but not be employed by the transferor or anyone connected with the transferor. We have in mind, in particular, secondees and contractors working within an undertaking but not employed by the transferor.'

18.53   It was argued by the putative transferees that, in any event, Mr Thomson had entered into a new contract and was thus retained by the transferor, but this contention was rejected by the tribunal and the EAT because Mr Thomson had been constantly seeking to establish what his employment position was. The EAT thus had to focus on whether he was transferred, notwithstanding that on a purely contractual analysis he was not employed by the transferor. The *Peters* case (below) (which had at that stage been decided but not reported) was not cited to the EAT in *Sunley Turriff*. Further, in *Sunley Turriff*, there was much confusion about the shape of the organisation (see eg para 3). Nevertheless, the purported application of the *Botzen* test to reach the result that Mr Thomson could be said to be assigned to these subsidiary companies is still somewhat surprising since *Botzen* is not a case in which the employee might have been employed by either of two companies, so that the issue now under discussion did not arise in *Botzen*.

The decision in *Peters (Michael) Ltd v Farnfield and Peters (Michael) Group plc* [1995] **18.54** IRLR 190 is more orthodox. Mr Farnfield was chief executive of the Michael Peters Group plc and was responsible for the financial management of all twenty-five subsidiary companies in the group. The group went into receivership on 27 August and Mr Farnfield on that date was made redundant. Three days later four subsidiary companies were sold to CLK and the subsidiary companies were named as the seller. CLK also acquired part of the assets of the parent company which belonged to the subsidiary companies. Mr Farnfield failed in his claim against the transferee on the ground that he worked for the group as a whole and not exclusively for the subsidiaries sold. He was thus not employed by the transferor. The decision might have been otherwise, however, if Mr Farnfield had been employed by the group company but had worked almost exclusively for the subsidiary.

Employment immediately before the transfer

Only persons who are employed 'immediately before the transfer' are considered to be in **18.55** the group of employees who are transferred (reg 4(1)). The appeal bodies have, however, been reluctant to give 'immediately' its literal meaning because it would allow the transferor employer to dismiss and deprive the employee of his rights, but they have been just as cautious in defining what leeway is permissible. In *Apex Leisure Hire Ltd v Barratt* [1984] ICR 452, the EAT withdrew from this conundrum by suggesting that it was a question of fact in each case. An employee dismissed by the transferor after contracts of sale were exchanged but before completion was employed 'immediately before the transfer' (*Kestongate Ltd v Miller* [1986] ICR 672). Reading the Regulations as a whole, Wood J thought that there was no difficulty in construing transfer as a period of time rather than a specific point in time.

In *Secretary of State for Employment v Spence* [1986] IRLR 248 the employer went **18.56** into receivership in November 1983. At 11am on 28 November 1983 all employees were dismissed, and the business was sold three hours later to a company which re-engaged the entire workforce. The transferor then went into liquidation and the litigation arose when the Secretary of State for Employment refused to make a redundancy payment from the Redundancy Fund on the sole ground that such employees were not employed by the transferor immediately before the transfer. The Court of Appeal took a very narrow view of 'immediately before' and overturned the decision. There was an express finding of fact by the employment tribunal that there was no 'collusion' between transferor and transferee to ensure dismissal by the former before the transfer took place and this was important in reaching the result.

The reason why the receivers in *Spence* had decided to dismiss the workforce was that **18.57** until a contract could be renegotiated with the company's principal customer, there was no prospect of any work for the business. The case was narrowly distinguished by the House of Lords in *Litster v Forth Dry Dock & Engineering Co Ltd* [1989] IRLR 161.

The House implied words into TUPE (in the words of Lord Keith) 'in order that the manifest purpose of the Regulations might be achieved and effect given to the clear but inadequately expressed intention of Parliament certain words must be read in by necessary implication'. This principle justified not taking a narrow approach to the phrase 'a person employed immediately before the transfer' in the Transfer Regulations. To do so would indeed render the Regulations 'capable of ready evasion through the transferee arranging with the transferor for the latter to dismiss its employees a short time before the transfer becomes operative', said Lord Keith. Lord Oliver (at para 50) thought it necessary to remember in this regard that the purpose of the Directive and Regulations was to 'safeguard' the rights of employees on transfer and that there was a mandatory obligation to 'provide remedies which are effective and not merely symbolic to which the Regulations are intended to give effect. The remedies ... in the case of an insolvent transferor are largely illusory unless they can be exerted against the transferee as the Directive contemplates'. Thus, the then reg 5(3) (now 4(3)) had to be construed on the 'footing that it applies to a person employed immediately before the transfer or who would have been so employed if he had not been unfairly dismissed before transfer for a reason connected with the transfer' (Lord Templeman at para 19; see also *Macer v Aberfast Ltd* [1990] ICR 234; and *Thompson v SCS Consulting Ltd* [2001] IRLR 801, EAT).

When does the transfer take place?

18.58 The implications of the transfer mean that it will frequently be necessary to identify the precise point at which the transfer occurred. It is the better view that it takes place at the moment of completion rather than on exchange of contracts (*Wheeler v Patel and J. Golding Group of Companies* [1987] IRLR 211). This is compounded by the fact that neither the transferor nor transferee is able to alter the date on which transfer takes place. There was at first some debate as to whether a transfer could take place over a period of time or whether a point in time has to be identified. This has now been resolved by the ECJ requiring the identification of a single point in time at which the transfer occurs. That relevant point is the time at which responsibility as employer for carrying on the business of the unit transfers passes from transferor to transferee (*Celtec Ltd v Astley* [2005] IRLR 647, ECJ). The crucial date is not when contracts were entered into but the date of operation of the Regulations (*Housing Maintenance Solutions Ltd v McAteer* [2015] ICR 87).

C EFFECT OF TRANSFER ON THE CONTRACT OF EMPLOYMENT

18.59 These provisions lie at the heart of TUPE. Regulation 4(1) states:

> Except where objection is made under paragraph (7), a relevant transfer shall not operate so as to terminate the contract of employment of any person employed by the transferor and assigned to the organised grouping of resources or employees that is subject to the relevant transfer, which would otherwise be terminated by the transfer, but any such contract shall have effect after the transfer as if originally made between the person so employed and the transferee.

18.60 The centre point of the enacting provision of TUPE is Reg 4(2), which goes on:

> Without prejudice to paragraph (1), but subject to paragraph (6), and regulations 8 and 15(9), on the completion of a relevant transfer—
>
> (a) all the transferor's rights, powers, duties and liabilities under or in connection with any such contract shall be transferred by virtue of this regulation to the transferee; and

(b) any act or omission before the transfer is completed, of or in relation to the transferor in respect of that contract or a person assigned to that organised grouping of resources or employees, shall be deemed to have been an act or omission of or in relation to the transferee.

The case of an appeal is interesting. An internal appeal panel can reverse or vary the **18.61** original decision to dismiss and any success on appeal means that the dismissal did not take effect. Thus, if the appeal succeeds the employment contract is revived and is thus transferred in accordance with the terms of reg 4 (*Salmon v Castlebeck Care (Teesdale) Ltd* [2015] ICR 735).

A temporary absence or cessation of work immediately before activities were carried **18.62** out by a new contractor did not preclude the existence of a grouping of employees. Whether a group maintained its identity was an issue of fact (*Inex Home Improvements Ltd v Hodgkins* [2016] ICR 71; *Mustafa v Trek Highways Services Ltd* [2016] IRLR 326—a temporary cessation by a transferor because of a contractual dispute with other contractors).

Rights and duties transferred

The effect of the transfer is in the nature of a statutory novation of the contract of employ- **18.63** ment so that the purchaser simply stands in the shoes of the vendor as far as the vendor's employment responsibilities are concerned. Anything done by the transferor before the transfer in respect of the employee's contract is deemed to have been done by the transferee (reg 4(2)). In addition to transferring rights and liabilities, reg 4(2)(b) of TUPE 2006 provides that any act or omission of or in relation to the transferor before the transfer is treated after the transfer as being an act or omission of or in relation to the transferee after the transfer. The general principle is that the terms of employment offered by the transferee to an employee must be overall no less favourable than those which he enjoyed with the transferor (*Scattolon v Ministero dell'Istruzione* [2012] ICR 740).

This does not apply in the case of those on fixed-term contracts if the contracts would not **18.64** have continued in the absence of the Regulations (*Ralton v Havering College of Further & Higher Education* [2001] IRLR 738).

There is an important right, however, which was introduced for the first time in 1993, **18.65** for an employee to object to being transferred (see below, 18.86). More specifically, the transferee of the undertaking takes over all 'rights, powers, duties and liabilities under or in connection with any such contract' (reg 4).

The phrase 'in connection with' is probably ample enough to include statutory continuity **18.66** rights. Regulation 15(9) of TUPE 2006 provides for the first time that: 'The transferee shall be jointly and severally liable with the transferor in respect of compensation payable under sub-paragraph (8)(a) or paragraph (11)'.

A claim by an employee who has been injured at work that his employer owed him a **18.67** duty of care and had been negligent arose 'in connection with' the contract of employment (*Martin v Lancashire CC* [2001] ICR 197). An employee was able to bring a disability discrimination claim against the transferee even though she objected to transfer where the transferee had made her a job offer (*NHS Direct NHS Trust v Gunn* [2015] IRLR 799).

The effect of TUPE is not to confer additional rights on the employee or improve the **18.68** situation of the employee. The effect of the deeming provision is not to give a transferred employee access to employment benefits other than those to which he was entitled before the transfer (*Jackson v Computershare Investor Services plc* [2008] IRLR 70).

Rights which are not transferred

18.69   There is a specific exclusion from the Regulations in respect of the transfer of occupational pensions and criminal liabilities.

Regulation 10(1) TUPE 2006

18.70   Robert Walker J in *Adams & Others v Lancashire CC and BET Catering Services Ltd* [1996] ICR 935 considered a case where Lancashire County Council put its school catering service out to tender. BET acquired the contract and offered to take the transferred employees into its own pension scheme, but this excluded many of the transferred staff, including the claimants. They sought declarations to the effect that the local authority pension rights were protected on a transfer. Essentially their argument was as follows:

(a)   Notwithstanding the different language used in limbs (a) and (b) of Art 3(3) (ie all severance rights in limb (a), and rights to immediate or prospective entitlement in limb (b)), the two limbs were intended to cover the same rights.

(b)   The primary analysis was that Art 3(3) applies only to accrued rights in both limbs, so that the transferee remained liable for securing future pension provision.

(c)   The secondary and alternative submission was that both limbs covered all pension rights, so that although there was no liability on the transferee, the State was responsible for securing both accrued pension rights and future pension rights. It was further contended that if this was indeed the correct analysis, the second limb was directly effective and could be enforced as against the Council in respect of future pension rights.

The judge rejected both arguments. He did not accept that the two limbs were symmetrical, in the sense of covering the same ground. He held that it was an *acte clair* as a matter of European law (so as not to require consideration by the ECJ) that limb (a) excluded all pension rights, and that limb (b) merely protected accrued rights. Furthermore, he held that in any event, even if his construction was wrong, it would not be possible so to construe reg 7 as to give effect to the claimants' construction of Art 3(3). It would, thought the judge, involve an impermissible distortion of the Regulation, going beyond the legitimate scope recognised in such cases as *Litster*. Robert Walker J's decision was subsequently upheld when the case reached the Court of Appeal (reported in [1997] IRLR 436) (see also *Frankling v BPS Public Sector Ltd* [1999] IRLR 347).

18.71   In *Beckmann v Dynamco Whicheloe Macfarlane Ltd* [2002] IRLR 578 the important question arose in the ECJ about the treatment of pension benefits paid as part of a package on redundancy under s 45 of the General Whitley Council terms and conditions. This provided for premature retirement with immediate payment of superannuation and compensation in the cases of dismissal for redundancy, retirement in the interests of the service, or premature retirement on organisational change. The transferee employers contended that these were excluded from the scope of the TUPE Regulations by reason of the pensions exception. The ECJ disagreed on the grounds that only benefits which were paid from the time when an employee reaches the end of his normal working life, as laid down by the general structure of the pension scheme in question, can be classified as 'old age benefits' falling within Art 3(3) of the Directive. That exception must be construed in a narrow sense. It did not matter that the benefits were calculated by reference to the rules for calculating normal pension benefits. They still went across on transfer.

Rights contingent on dismissal or the grant of early retirement by agreement fall within **18.72** the scope of the rights which are transferred. Early retirement benefits arising by agreement between the employer and the employee to employees who have reached a certain age are not old age, invalidity, or survivors benefits under supplementary company or inter-company pension schemes within the exception provided by Art 3(3) ARD (*Martin v South Bank University* [2004] IRLR 75 ECJ).

Pensions Act 2004

The UK has taken up the right under the EU Acquired Rights Directive for member **18.73** states to require pension provision on transfer in a limited way. These are not under the TUPE regulations themselves but in the Transfer of Employment (Pension Protection) Regulations 2005 (SI 2005/649) which were made under the Pensions Act 2004 and took effect from 6 April 2005. A transferee must provide a minimum level of pension provision going forward if the transferred employees enjoyed access to an occupational pension scheme prior to the transfer.

Restrictive Covenants

In *Morris Angel Ltd v Hollande* [1993] ICR 71, the court held that if the literal transposi- **18.74** tion of a term would impose wider obligations than those originally contemplated by the parties, the term in question must be construed purposively, so that it has the same effect post-transfer as it did pre-transfer.

Equal pay

An important issue is the interconnection between equal pay liability and TUPE. Where **18.75** there has been a TUPE transfer, time begins to run under the Equal Pay Act 1970 for the purpose of a claim against the transferor on the operation of an equality clause for an occupational pension scheme from the date of the TUPE transfer rather than from the end of the employee's employment with the transferee; *Powerhouse Retail Ltd v Burroughs* [2006] IRLR 381; *UNISON v Allen* [2007] IRLR 975; *Gutridge v Sodexo Ltd* [2009] IRLR 721.

Contractual rights separate from the contract of employment

It has been argued that where a right is contained in a contract which is separate from **18.76** the contract of employment the right will not necessarily be transferred, even though it exists as an agreement between employer and employee. Thus, in *Chapman and another v CPS Computer Group plc* [1987] IRLR 462, CA, entitlements under a share option scheme, governed by a contract separate from the contract of employment, did not transfer. Where, however, a share option entitlement is part of the contract of employment, there is no reason why the employee's entitlements should not go across to the transferee. This decision may be open to question in the light of the definition of 'contract of employment' under the Regulations. Sometimes the difficulty will arise not with the term itself which passes across, but with the consequences which this has for other arrangements. For example, suppose that a transferring employee had the benefit of private medical cover in his employment with the transferor. The obligation to provide private medical cover clearly passes to the transferee, but if the employee was receiving treatment for a particular condition at the time of transfer, the insurer providing the new cover in the transferee's employment may not be prepared to take on the incoming employee into the existing scheme. In that case the transferee employer will have to carry the cost of the private medical insurance himself.

Variation of terms on transfer

18.77 The decision of the EAT in *Wilson v St Helens Borough Council* [1996] IRLR 320 suggested that employers and employees could not vary the contract of employment by agreement at the time of transfer. The orthodox concept of the Regulations is that they hold a mirror at the time of transfer, and anything which could be achieved with the transferor employer by his employees, such as a consensual variation, could be done in the same manner by the transferee. The appellants were teachers or carers at a school which was formerly owned by trustees and controlled by Lancashire County Council. The County Council decided to withdraw and St Helens Borough Council agreed to take over the School. The appellants received an Extraneous Duties Allowance from the County Council, but St Helens Borough Council made it clear that it would not continue to pay this. The tribunal rejected the employees' claim under the then Wages Act 1986 on the basis that new contracts of employment were agreed with the Borough Council which operated to vary the appellants' terms and conditions as previously enjoyed with the County Council.

18.78 The EAT, however, allowed the appeal. The crucial question was 'what is the total amount of wages properly payable to the employee'. The central point was 'the identity of the reason for the alteration or variation in the terms of the contracts of employment which the [appellants] had with the transferor County Council'. Mummery J relied on the ECJ decision in *Daddy's Dance Hall* for the proposition that the policy of the Directive, and thus of the 1981 Regulations, precluded even a consensual variation in the terms of that contract if the transfer of the undertaking was the reason for the variation. The parties would, however, be free to vary an agreement if the reason was something else. This is a question of fact in each case. There was no possibility here of relying upon the exception in reg 8(2) (now reg 7(2)) for 'an economic, technical, or organisational reason for dismissal' since the employees had not been dismissed. In summary 'there was no break in the causal link in the variation between the terms and conditions and the transfer of the undertaking. The cause of the variation was the transfer itself. For that reason the variation was ineffective. The terms of the original contracts of employment with the County Council remained in force'.

18.79 In the Court of Appeal, *Wilson* was joined with another case covering the same issue, *British Fuels Ltd v Baxendale*. This involved two workers who were made redundant by their employer, the transferor, and then re-employed on less favourable terms by the transferee. Both claimed in subsequent applications to a tribunal that the purported variation of their terms and conditions should be treated as invalid. This claim was rejected both by the tribunal and the EAT. In its decision (reported in [1998] ICR 387), the Court of Appeal overturned the EAT's decision in both cases. Its essential reasoning was that where an employee was dismissed by the transferor for a reason connected with the transfer and was then taken on by the transferee (*Baxendale*), the dismissal would be ineffective and the employee would be employed by the transferee on the terms of the original contract. However, where the dismissal was for an 'economic, technical, or organisation reason entailing changes to the workforce' (*Wilson*), this would not be the case and the terms of the new contract of employment would therefore apply.

18.80 The House of Lords ([1998] IRLR 706) overturned the Court of Appeal's decision in *Baxendale* but upheld its decision in *Wilson*. Their Lordships rejected the proposition that a variation of contract is invalid only if it is agreed on as part of the transfer itself. The variation may still be due to the transfer and for no other reason even if it comes later in the sequence. However, the time would come when the link between the transfer is broken or should be treated as no longer effective. When this would be was not a live issue in the *Baxendale* case since the House of Lords had already decided that the dismissal in that case had been effective (for further comment on this part of the decision). In the *Wilson* case, the House of Lords held that the tribunal had been entitled to find that the transfer of the undertaking did not constitute the reason for the variation. It could be said to be a variation of contract 'to the same extent as it could have been with regard to the transferor', such as was identified as being compatible with the Directive in the *Daddy's Dance Hall* case (above).

The House of Lords added that although on or after a transfer the employees' previously **18.81** existing rights against the transferor are enforceable against the transferee and cannot be amended by the transfer itself, this did not mean that there cannot be a contractual variation for reasons which are not themselves due to the transfer, either at the time of the transfer of the undertaking or later. Admittedly, it may be difficult to decide whether the variation is due to the transfer or attributable to some separate cause; however, if the variation is not due to the transfer, it can be validly made. Where the reason for a change in terms was expiry of the employees' fixed-term contracts, it was not because of the transfer within the meaning of Art 4(2) of the Directive. The correct test was whether the variation was *solely* by reason of the transfer rather than whether it was for a reason connected with the transfer (*Ralton v Havering College of Further Education & Higher Education* [2001] IRLR 738). A compromise agreement may be valid on transfer of undertaking where it merely compromised a financial claim that the employee had on the termination of the employment contract. The employer was not purporting to vary the contract but merely to compromise a dispute as to its value (*Solectron Scotland Ltd v Roper* [2004] IRLR 4).

The 2006 Regulations provide clear wording generally prohibiting variations, but subject **18.82** to a particular type of variation. Regulation 4(4) provides that:

> Subject to regulation 9, in respect of a contract of employment that is, or will be, transferred by paragraph (1), any purported variation of the contract shall be void if the sole or principal reason for the variation is—
>
> (a) the transfer itself; or
> (b) a reason connected with the transfer that is not an economic, technical or organisational reason entailing changes in the workforce.

Although the restriction on variations is imposed in the interests of employee protection, it is not possible for an employer to argue that the variation is on balance favourable to the employee. An argument to this effect was addressed by the Court of Appeal in *Credit Suisse First Boston (Europe) Ltd v Lister* [1998] IRLR 700.

Variation and insolvency

In the context of insolvency there is a limitation on the operation of the transfer of liabili- **18.83** ties. Where there are 'relevant insolvency proceedings' affecting the transferor, reg 8(5) provides that reg 4 will not operate to transfer liability for the sums payable to the relevant employee under the relevant statutory schemes (which relate to certain payments to be made by the Secretary of State, who may then seek to bring the claims against the transferor, these being such elements as notice pay and statutory redundancy payments) (see *Secretary of State for Trade and Industry v Slater* [2007] IRLR 928).

Further, it is provided that reg 4 will not apply where the transferor is the subject of **18.84** bankruptcy proceedings or any analogous insolvency proceedings which have been instituted with a view to the liquidation of the assets of the transferor and which are under the supervision of an insolvency practitioner (reg 8(6)). The issue whether insolvency proceedings were instituted with a view to the liquidation of the transferor is an issue of fact and not of domestic insolvency law (*Oakland v Wellswood (Yorkshire) Ltd* [2009] IRLR 250).

D THE POSITION OF THE EMPLOYEE

18.85 By reg 4(7), the employee loses the right he would have at common law to resign on a change of identity of his employer. He can claim constructive dismissal only if there is actually a: 'substantial change in his working conditions to [his] material detriment' (reg 4(9)). It is likely that this will be construed in a way which is on all fours with the test in *Western Excavating Ltd v Sharp* [1978] QB 761.

18.86 In *Katsikas v Konstantinidis* [1993] IRLR 179, the ECJ decided that the Acquired Rights Directive did not prevent an employee from refusing the transfer to a transferee of his contract of employment or employment relationship. The Directive does not require member states to provide that the contract of employment should be maintained with the transferor in the event that the employee freely decides not to continue the contract of employment with the transferor. The ECJ said that: 'Such an obligation would undermine the fundamental rights of the employee who must be free to choose his employer and cannot be obliged to work for an employer.' Further, it leaves to member states the right to determine the fate of the contract in the event of a transfer. On the basis of this doctrine, the TURERA 1993 introduced a new reg 5(4A) (now 4(7)) into the Regulations. This disapplies the automatic transfer principle 'if the employee informs the transferor or transferee that he objects to becoming employed by the transferee' in which case, by reg 5(4B), the transfer operates 'to terminate his contract of employment with the transferor' but he 'shall not be treated, for any purpose, as having been dismissed by the transferor' (*Hay v George Hanson (Building Contractors) Ltd* [1996] IRLR 427; and *Senior Heat Treatment Ltd v Bell* [1997] IRLR 614).

18.87 The EAT case of *Tapere v S London & Maudsley NHS Trust* [2009] IRLR 972 concerned a mobility clause to the effect that 'there may be occasions when you are required to work either temporarily or permanently at other locations within the trust'. When the employers insisted on a move it was held that there was a constructive dismissal. The contract had to be construed at the point when the contract was entered into. In considering whether there was any material detriment, what had to be considered was the impact of the proposed change from the employee's point of view. It was not an issue to be objectively determined. Here the change of location meant potential disruption to child care arrangements and a longer journey.

18.88 The ECJ has subsequently held that where the contract is terminated by the employee on account of a substantial detrimental change in his or her working conditions, the member state must provide that the employer is to be regarded as responsible for the termination (*Merckx v Ford Motor Co Belgium SA* [1996] IRLR 467).

18.89 In *Photostatic Copiers (Southern) Ltd v Okuda and Japan Office Equipment Ltd* [1995] IRLR 11, the EAT held that reg 5(1) does not take effect in relation to an employee's contract of employment unless and until the employee is given notice of both the fact of the transfer and the identity of the transferee. However, this conclusion was subsequently rejected by the EAT in *Secretary of State for Trade and Industry v Cook* [1997] IRLR 288.

The transferee would not be liable for constructive dismissal if the employee was never in **18.90** its employment (*SITA (GB) Ltd v Burton* [1997] IRLR 501). The conduct of a potential transferee cannot be regarded as sufficiently affecting the employer's obligation of mutual trust and goodwill where the employee's complaints or fears relate solely to the terms and conditions of the contract and the substance of those complaints is protected under the Regulations.

Thus, in a case where the employee objects to the employment being transferred because **18.91** he or she does not wish to work for the transferee, the employment is terminated by the transfer itself and the employee is not able to claim that there has been a dismissal by the transferor. This is not the position where there will be a substantial and detrimental change in an employee's terms and conditions and the employee resigns in consequence (reg 4(9)). Then the liability is that of the transferor (*University of Oxford v Humphreys* [2000] IRLR 183).

Rossiter v Pendragon plc [2001] IRLR 256 considered the scope of constructive dismissal **18.92** under the Regulations. After a takeover the claimant complained that the new employer altered the rate of commission payable, had decided no longer to pay holiday pay on the basis of average commission earnings during the preceding twelve months, and that his responsibilities had been reduced. The employment tribunal found that there had been no fundamental breach of contract and dismissed the claim under reg 5(5). This was overturned on appeal to the EAT on the basis that the same test did not apply as governed constructive dismissal. The reasoning was that reg 5(5) did not give rise to any new, free-standing right to claim unfair dismissal on the grounds of constructive dismissal but simply preserved common law and statutory rights to terminate a contract of employment where a substantial change was made in the employee's working conditions to his detriment. It was not necessary to find a breach of contract in order to give rise to entitlement to claim. This was in turn reversed in the Court of Appeal ([2002] IRLR 488) on the basis that reg 5(5) was not intended to create a new right to claim constructive dismissal. Rather, its language was designed to be consistent with the general right to claim constructive dismissal in s 95(1) of the ERA 1996, and only conduct by the employer amounting to a repudiation of the contract would entitle the employee to terminate the contract without notice.

There is, however, the core requirement of objection. There must thus be a genuine objec- **18.93** tion to a transfer, amounting to a refusal to transfer and not merely a protest falling short of this. Tribunals must also consider whether there is an objection in reality and not merely as a matter of form. In *Senior Heat Treatment Ltd v Bell* [1997] IRLR 614, the EAT held that although the employees had expressly purported to exercise their right to 'opt out', they had not in fact done so with the rather surprising result (on the particular facts of the case) that the employees in question were able to obtain double recovery of redundancy payments, once from the transferor and also the transferee. The employees working in the undertaking had been given three options:

(a) alternative employment within the transferor;
(b) transfer to the transferee under the terms of TUPE; or
(c) exercise of the right under TUPE to 'opt out' of the transfer in which case they would be offered a severance package by the transferor.

The employees in question took the third option and, on the date when the transfer took place, their employment with the transferor ceased and they received redundancy payments in accordance with the severance package. However, by that date, they had already entered into contracts with the transferee and they did take up employment with the transferee in the undertaking immediately after the transfer. When ten months later they were dismissed on the grounds of redundancy, they argued that they had two years' continuous employment, entitling them to bring claims for unfair dismissal and redundancy payments. The question was whether their case fell within the 'employee objection' exception. The EAT held that although the employees had volunteered to opt out of the transfer, this did not constitute a genuine objection to the transfer as they had in fact agreed to go and work for the transferee. Accordingly, their contracts of employment had not for TUPE purposes terminated at the time of transfer and they had the relevant continuity of employment.

18.94   The consequences of this were that the applications for unfair dismissal and redundancy payments could be made. Furthermore, the payments by the transferor at the time of transfer in the severance package could not be taken into account and set off against any statutory entitlement to those redundancy payments which were now due from the transferee. These payments would have to be calculated on the basis of the whole of the employees' continuous service with both transferor and transferee.

The position of an employee who objects is thus as follows: if the employee is unable to:

(a)   assert that there has been a constructive dismissal; or
(b)   rely on reg 4(9)

the employee's option is to object to the transfer, but this has the effect of terminating the employment upon the transfer without there being a dismissal. The employee would then be unable to make any claim in respect of redundancy, wrongful dismissal, or unfair dismissal, all of which require the establishment of a dismissal as a first stage of any claim (see also *Capita Health Solutions Ltd v McLean* [2008] IRLR 595).

18.95   The effect of TUPE on secondment arrangements and provision for employees to remain with the transferor are important. There must be a specific agreement if the employee is to remain with the transferor, but this must be shown to be the result of a freely made decision by the employee. This emerges from the difficult decision of the ECJ in *Celtec Ltd v Astley and Others* [2005] IRLR 647. The principal issue was as to whether a transfer must be regarded as having been completed at a particular point of time or whether this could be seen to have occurred instead over a period of time. The ECJ held that a particular time must be identified. The case concerned a transfer from the Department of Employment to Training and Enterprise Councils (TECs). In order to assist the fledgling TECs in their early years, civil servants were seconded rather than have the TECs incurring liabilities to their own employees. The civil servants therefore took up direct employment with the TECs over a long period of time. This also benefited the civil servants in that they could see how the TECs progressed before choosing to take up employment with them, and they would also maintain favourable civil servant terms, such as in relation to pensions, in the meantime. However, the ECJ decision gave rise to the possibility that the transfer had been completed several years before the secondment from the Department of Employment came to an end.

18.96   The ECJ decided that notwithstanding that all parties had operated on the basis that the civil servants had worked as secondees, the consequences of the transfer were automatic. The ECJ stated (at para 37) that:

> As the Court has already held, implementation of the rights conferred on employees by Article 3(1) of Directive 77/187 may not be made subject to the consent of either the transferor or the transferee nor to the consent of the employees' representatives or the employees themselves, with the sole reservation, as regards the workers themselves, that, following

a decision freely taken by them, they are at liberty, after the transfer, not to continue the employment relationship with the new employer (see case 105/84 *Danmols Inventar* [1985] ECR 2639, para 16, and *D'Urso*, cited below, para 11).

The principles set out in *Celtec* are thus merely an application of the employee's entitlement to object to a transfer. An employee who agrees to stay on with the transferor may be said to have thereby informed the transferor that he objects to being transferred, so that the exclusion from TUPE found in reg 4(7) comes into play.

Normally, any objection must be taken by the employee before the transfer but there are **18.97** exceptions. In *New ISG Ltd v Vernon* [2008] IRLR 115, the employees learned of the identity of the transferee only after the transfer had happened, and they objected to the transfer. The matter came before the High Court where the transferees of the goodwill of the business were attempting to enforce post-termination restraints. They failed because it was held that the objecting employees did not transfer, even though they did not voice their objections until after the transfer had happened. Thus, they never actually became employees of the new employer. They also immediately ceased to be employees, as a consequence of the objection, and thus it was not even possible to enforce notice periods to prevent them competing.

Relief

It is not possible to gain an injunction to prevent a transfer of undertaking taking place. **18.98** In *Newns v British Airways plc* [1992] IRLR 575, British Airways decided to hive off part of its business to a subsidiary, but employees were told only on 11 June that this would occur on 26 June. Notwithstanding this, the appellant did not have an arguable case on an application for an injunction that the transfer of a contract of employment or a proposal to so transfer was a repudiatory breach by the employer which the employee was entitled to restrain. The only remedy is compensation which will of course be awarded long after the transfer takes place (see, to the same effect, *Betts v Brintel Helicopters* [1996] IRLR 45).

E DISMISSAL ON TRANSFER OF UNDERTAKING

The Regulations render a dismissal automatically unfair if the transfer or a reason con- **18.99** nected with it is the sole or principal reason for dismissal (the words were amended by the Collective Redundancies and Transfer of Undertakings (Amendment) Regs 2014 SI No 16). The only escape for the employer is where the reason or principal reason was 'an economic, technical, or organisational reason *entailing changes in the workforce of either the transferor or transferee* before or after a relevant transfer' (reg 7(1) with emphasis added). In such a case, the reason is automatically treated as 'some other substantial reason for dismissal' and then the normal fairness principles apply. The following important questions arise.

Is the dismissal a nullity?

The House of Lords indicated in *Wilson v St Helens Borough Council* [1998] IRLR **18.100** 706 that a dismissal effected by the transferor for reasons connected with the transfer is not to be treated as a nullity. Accordingly, the dismissal takes place then, and not when the transferee subsequently refuses to employ the person who is so dismissed. However, doubts have been expressed about whether the House of Lords' judgment in

Wilson can be squared with the ECJ's view in *P Bork International A/S v Foreningen af Arbejdsledere i Danmark* [1989] IRLR 41, that transfer-related dismissals should be treated as ineffective.

Is there a need for a specific transfer?

18.101 A pivotal question in applying this provision generally is whether the dismissal must be by reason of a specific transfer, or whether a dismissal designed to enhance the prospects of any transfer being effected will suffice. In *Harrison Bowden Ltd v Bowden* [1994] ICR 186, the EAT held that a dismissal was unfair if it was designed so as to facilitate a transfer, even though the identity of the employer was not known at the time. A later EAT decision (*Ibex Trading Ltd v Walton* [1994] ICR 907) did not follow the *Bowden* case and held that the dismissal must be by reason of a specific transfer to qualify. Morison J said:

> ... A transfer is not just a single event: it extends over a period of time culminating in a completion. However, here the employees were dismissed before any offer had been made for the business. Whilst it could properly be said that they were dismissed for a reason connected with a possible transfer of the business, on the facts here we are not satisfied that they were dismissed by reason of *the* transfer or for a reason connected with *the* transfer. A transfer was, at the stage of the dismissal, a mere twinkle in the eye and might well never have occurred.

In a third decision, however (*Morris v John Grose Group Ltd* [1998] IRLR 499), the EAT preferred *Bowden* to *Ibex*.

What qualifies as an economic reason?

18.102 In *Meikle v McPhail* [1983] IRLR 351, the purchaser established an economic reason for dismissal when it made some employees redundant shortly after the transfer when it realised that the pub transferred could not be run economically with so many staff. In the important case of *Wheeler v Patel and J. Golding Group of Companies* [1987] IRLR 211, however, the EAT indicated that an economic reason must be connected with the conduct or running of the business and not merely be a dismissal made in order to achieve a better price for the entity transferred (see to the same effect *Wendelboe v LJ Music ApS* [1985] ECR 457; *Gateway Hotels Ltd v Stewart* [1988] IRLR 287).

18.103 In *Trafford v Sharpe & Fisher (Building Supplies) Ltd* [1994] IRLR 325, the EAT held that the rights of workers not to be dismissed on the transfer of an undertaking may be outweighed by economic reasons.

18.104 The narrowness of the distinctions drawn are illustrated by *Kavanagh v Crystal Palace FC Ltd* [2014] ICR 251. An administrator sought to sell a football club as a going concern and received expressions of interest from a consortium. He decided to protect the core operations of the club in the closed season but asked that non-essential staff be identified for redundancy. Eventually an agreement was reached for the sale of the club to a consortium. The tribunal decided that the reason for dismissal was connected with the transfer and was an ETO. The Court of Appeal held that the tribunal had to make a subjective fact-intensive analysis of the reason for dismissal, taking care not to enable an artificially contrived reason to avoid the regime under the Regulations. There were unique features pertaining to the financial affairs of a failing football club whose business was seasonal and whose most valuable and realisable assets were its contracted players, which meant that liquidation left few or no assets to be realised for the benefit of creditors. It was a justifiable distinction drawn by the tribunal between the administrator's reason for dismissing the employees, namely to reduce the wages bill to continue running the business to avoid liquidation, and his ultimate objective, the early sale of the club in time for the new football season.

An organisational reason may be established if the transferee can show that a change **18.105** in the way the business is run creates a need for new skills which the employee does not possess (*Porter and Nanayakkara v Queen's Medical Centre (Nottingham University Hospital)* [1993] IRLR 486; see also *Kerry Foods Ltd v Creber* [2000] IRLR 10).

One interpretation of the Regulations has now been laid to rest. There was initially doubt **18.106** whether an employee could claim a redundancy payment on a transfer dismissal (*Canning v Niaz* [1983] IRLR 431; *Meikle v McPhail* (above)), but the EAT has now decided that he can, if s 135 of the ERA 1996 is in the normal way satisfied (*Gorictree Ltd v Jenkinson* [1984] IRLR 391; *Anderson & McAlonie v Dalkeith Engineering Ltd* [1984] IRLR 429; see also *Dynamex Friction Ltd v AMICUS* [2008] IRLR 515).

Entailing changes in the workforce

A significant limitation on the scope of this exception to automatic unfairness is that **18.107** the reason, whether economic or technical or organisational, must itself entail changes in the workforce. In *Berriman v Delabole Slate Ltd* [1984] ICR 636, the employee was constructively dismissed. He resigned because he would not accept new disadvantageous terms required by the transferee employer who sought to standardise his contract with that of other existing employees. This neither had the objective of effecting, nor did it bring about, a change in the workforce as required by the Regulations for the case to fall within the relevant exception. Changes in the identity of individuals who make up the workforce do not constitute changes in the workforce itself if the overall numbers and functions of the employees as a whole remain unchanged. Their Lordships thought, however, that a change in the *function* of the workforce would suffice and the consequences of this *dictum* have still to be worked out. Entailing changes in workforce meant changes in the actual numbers who are employed or in the jobs which the employees did (*Manchester College v Hazel* [2014] ICR 989). This did not include the introduction of adverse changes in the terms of transferred staff in order to achieve harmonisation with the terms of existing staff nor a move in workplace, although the Regulations were soon changed so that change in location counted (*RR Donnelley Global Document Solutions Group Ltd v Besagni* [2014] ICR 1008).

'Workforce' means the workforce as an entity separate from the individuals who make **18.108** up that workforce. It does not include limited companies such as corporate franchisees which have a separate identity from their directors or controlling shareholders (*Meter U Ltd v Ackroyd* [2012] ICR 834).

The issue under the Regulations is whether the reason for dismissal involved a change in **18.109** that workforce. There could be such a change even if the same people were retained but were given different jobs by the transferee (*Crawford v Swinton Insurance Brokers Ltd* [1990] ICR 85; see also *D'Urso v Ercole Marelli Elettromeccanica General SpA* [1992] IRLR 136; *Trafford v Sharpe & Fisher Ltd* [1994] IRLR 325; cf *Wilson v St Helens Borough Council* [1997] IRLR 505).

The test of fairness

Where there is a relevant reason entailing changes in the workforce, the tribunal must **18.110** then decide in the normal way whether the dismissal is fair within the rubric of s 98 of the ERA 1996 (see *McGrath v Rank Leisure Ltd* [1985] ICR 527). The EAT has seen little difference between this and the conclusions reached on 'some other substantial reason' on business reorganisation (*Richmond Precision Engineering Ltd v Pearce* [1985] IRLR 179).

Dismissal by the vendor at the behest of the purchaser

18.111   One vital issue, however, concerns dismissal by the vendor at the behest of the purchaser. In *Anderson & McAlonie v Dalkeith Engineering Ltd* [1984] IRLR 429, the Scottish EAT decided that this was an 'economic, technical, or organisational reason' and that the motives of the purchaser in requiring the dismissals were irrelevant. The mere fact that it was under pressure by the transferee rendered the dismissal by the vendor fair (cf *Gateway Hotels Ltd v Stewart* [1988] IRLR 287).

18.112   *BSG Property Services and Mid Beds DC v Tuck* [1996] IRLR 134 raised many issues of everyday concern on dismissals on contracting out, in that case as part of compulsory competitive tendering. The employees were all employed by the Mid Bedfordshire District Council in the Housing Maintenance Direct Services Organisation ('DSO') in bricklaying, carpentry, and plumbing work. The Council contracted with its own DSO for a five-year period. The DSO board, however, decided to terminate the contract and not put in a bid for a further contract since it had failed to make the required 5 per cent return on capital and thus was in breach of the appropriate regulations. They were given notice by the Council on 12 February 1993 to expire on 15 May 1993. One day before the expiry of the notice, the Council concluded a contract with BSG for the provision of day-to-day jobbing maintenance work by self-employed tradesmen. The Council and BSG argued that there was no transfer of undertaking, but the EAT upheld the decision of the employment tribunal that the relevant economic entity was 'the provision of maintenance services to council tenants in the Area concerned' and that there was a transfer.

18.113   The tribunal had also decided that the reason for dismissal was an economic or organisational reason and the dismissals were fair in all the circumstances. Several issues arose for consideration on appeal:

(a) What was the appropriate date for determining the reason for dismissal in the circumstances, whether the date when notice was given, when the claimants were engaged by the council, or the date of expiry of the notice when they had transferred (briefly) to the service of BSG. The EAT held that the crucial question was the Council's reason for dismissal as at the date when notice was given.

(b) As a result, the Council could not have any economic or organisational reasons since they did not believe that the TUPE Regulations applied. BSG, the transferee, inherited the liabilities of the Council and was deemed to have given the notice of termination which had already been sent by the Council, but did nothing in relation to the dismissals 'because they did not believe that they had to do anything about the dismissal of the Applicants'.

(c) If BSG was liable for dismissing them, it was for a reason fixed by the deeming effect of the Regulations, not because they (BSG) dismissed for *its own reason*. BSG was therefore stuck with the reason of the Council. Thus, there was no economic or organisational reason for dismissal on the part of the Council, and there was in fact no valid reason for dismissal at all and the dismissals were automatically unfair.

18.114   By way of contrast, in *Whitehouse v Blatchford & Sons Ltd* [1999] IRLR 492, the EAT did not take such a rigorous approach as in the *BSG* case. The case involved the outsourcing of a contract for the supply of prosthetic services to a Sheffield hospital which B Ltd successfully obtained in a competitive tender. The NHS Hospital Trust made it clear in the course of the tender process that it required the new service provider to provide the service with only twelve employees, rather than the then current complement of thirteen employees, and as a result, shortly after the TUPE transfer, B Ltd made one of the transferring employees redundant. The EAT held that this was a valid 'economic, technical, or organisational' reason as B Ltd would not have won the contract unless it had agreed to operate the contract with only twelve employees. In this context, the EAT's decision in *Wheeler v Patel* (see 18.102 above) was distinguished, since the hospital's economic requirements could constitute the basis of an economic, technical, or organisational reason.

In *Thompson v SCS Consulting Ltd* [2001] IRLR 801, the EAT upheld the conclusion **18.115** of an employment tribunal that the dismissal of an employee prior to the sale of his employer's insolvent business by receivers was not automatically unfair because there was no prospect of the business continuing as a going concern unless the workforce was reduced. The reason for dismissal was thus an economic, technical, or organisational one. In reaching this decision, the tribunal is 'entitled to take into account as relevant factual material whether there was any collusion between transferor and transferee and whether the transferor or those acting on its behalf had any funds to carry on the business or any business at the time of the decision to dismiss'. This was essentially a factual matter for the tribunal, and since the tribunal had concluded that 'the business was overstaffed, inefficient in terms of sales and insolvent and that the only way in which it could be made viable for the future and continued as a going concern was for the workforce to be reduced in size', and 'this was not a case of collusion', this qualified as an economic, technical, or organisational reason.

F CONSULTATION WITH THE RECOGNISED UNIONS OR ELECTED REPRESENTATIVES

The information to be given

Recognised trade unions, elected representatives, and (in some situations) individuals **18.116** have similar rights to consultation over transfers of undertakings as on redundancies being made. There is also a duty on the employer to inform them of an upcoming transfer. The transferor has a duty to inform a union or unions, where its members may be affected by the transfer or by 'measures' to be taken (and the union is recognised for that grade) in connection with it, of:

(a) the fact that the relevant transfer is to take place;
(b) when the transfer is to take place;
(c) the reasons for the transfer;
(d) the legal, economic, and social implications for affected employees; and
(e) the measures which he envisages the transferor or the transferee will take or if there will be no such measures, that fact (reg 13(2)).

TUPE does not require consultation post-transfer concerning measures to be taken in connection with the transfer (*AMICUS v City Building (Glasgow) LLP* [2009] IRLR 253).

The word 'measures' is a curious one, which is not found in any other area of employ- **18.117** ment law. In *Institution of Professional Civil Servants v Secretary of State for Defence* [1987] IRLR 373, Millett J construed the similar language of s 1 of the Dockyard Services Act 1986, which re-enacted reg 10 of the Transfer of Undertakings Regulations 1981 for the special purpose of the 'privatisation' of the naval dockyards. He considered that 'measures' was a word of wide import, including 'any action, step or arrangement'. 'Envisages' in this sense meant 'visualises' or 'foresees'. Whilst manpower projections were not measures, reductions in the level of manpower would be. Where information to be divulged under the equivalent of reg 10(2) (now reg 13(2)) is not factual but is based on appraisal or judgment, such as manpower forecasts, the employer need only divulge the result of his deliberations; the union may not demand information on the calculations or assumptions on which the appraisal or judgment is based.

18.118 The relevant information must be given to a 'relevant person ... long enough before a relevant transfer to enable the employer of any affected employees to consult all the persons who are the appropriate representatives of any of those affected employees'. The employers need only actually consult if any 'measures' are to be taken, in which case management must consider any representations which the union may make. The definition of 'affected employees' were those employees who would or might be transferred or whose jobs were in jeopardy by reason of the transfer or who had job applications within the organisation which were pending at the time of transfer but did not extend to the whole workforce (*UNISON v Somerset CC* [2010] ICR 498).

The expanding scope of consultation

18.119 The original requirement for consultation to take place only with recognised unions was not compatible with EU law following the decision by the ECJ in *Commission of European Communities v UK* [1994] ICR 664 (see full discussion in Chapter 17). As a result, the Collective Redundancies and Transfer of Undertakings (Protection of Employment) (Amendment) Regulations 1995 (SI 1995/2587) widened the scope of those to be informed and consulted from merely those representatives of a recognised independent trade union to 'employee representatives elected by' the employees. Until 1 November 1999 whether the employer consulted elected representatives or representatives of a recognised union was entirely a matter for the employer to determine. The Collective Redundancies and Transfer of Undertakings (Protection of Employment) (Amendment) Regulations 1999 (SI 1999/1925) removed this freedom of choice by requiring the employer to consult union representatives where it recognises an independent trade union in respect of a group of affected employees (reg 10(2)). It is only where such recognition does not exist that the employer will be entitled to consult with non-union representatives.

18.120 Regulation 14 governs the conduct of elections of employee representatives. It imposes a duty on the employer to make such arrangements 'as are reasonably practicable' to ensure that the election is fair. It is still open to doubt whether the employer must ensure that an election is actually held. Any employee who may be affected by the proposed dismissals or by measures taken in connection with them is entitled to vote in the election and, if he wants, to stand as a candidate. The election should be conducted, 'so far as is reasonably practicable', in secret and votes must be accurately counted. The terms of office of such representatives should be long enough for them to be fully informed and consulted in accordance with the 2006 Regulations. Regulation 15(1) gives to affected employees, employee representatives, and the union rights to complain to an employment tribunal in circumstances where the employer has failed to perform any of its duties in relation to consultation or elections.

The defence

18.121 The only defence for the employer is where it is faced by 'special circumstances rendering it not reasonably practicable' for it to conform (reg 15(2)). This exception is construed in much the same restrictive manner as under the redundancy consultation provisions. In *Angus Jowett & Co Ltd v NUTGW* [1985] IRLR 326, the financial circumstances which gave rise to the appointment of a receiver were neither sudden in onset nor unforeseeable and the employment tribunal had correctly decided that there was no special circumstance. Regulation 15(3) provides that 'the transferee shall give the transferor such information at such time as will enable the transferor to perform the duty imposed on him ...'.

Any complaint of default must be made to the employment tribunal within three months **18.122** of the default or such longer period as the tribunal considers reasonable. Subject to the maximum limit of thirteen weeks' pay, the tribunal should award such compensation for breach of the consultation provisions as 'the tribunal considers just and equitable having regard to the seriousness of the failure of the employer to comply with his duty'. The amount is a question of fact with which the EAT is unlikely to interfere (*Angus Jowett* case). The principle in *Susie Radin* (see 17.51) applies in a TUPE case (*Sweetin v Coral Racing* [2006] IRLR 252) so that the normal expectation is that the maximum protective award will be made unless there are mitigating circumstances.

These important principles are established by the recent case law: **18.123**

(a) Article 7 of the Acquired Rights Directive did not require the imposition of any obligation on a transferee to inform employees of the transferor of measures which it envisaged taking in connection with a transfer, nor did it require the conferring of any right on those employees to pursue a claim against the transferor (*Allen v Morrisons Facilities Services Ltd* [2014] ICR 792).

(b) Regulation 13(2) TUPE 2006 did not contemplate warranty of the legal accuracy of the information provided as opposed to a genuine view expressed by the employer (*Royal Mail Group Ltd v CWU* [2010] ICR 83).

(c) The obligation to consult with employees always lay with the subsidiary company which employed the workers and never with the parent company, irrespective of whether the decision in connection with collective redundancies was made by the parent or the subsidiary, and it was the subsidiary which bore the consequences of any failure to carry out consultation even if it had not been immediately and properly informed of a decision by the parent making decisions on redundancies necessary. The time when the consultation procedures had to be started was when a strategic or commercial decision taken within the group compelled collective redundancies to be contemplated or planned for (*Akavan Erityisalojen Keskusliitto v Fujitsu Siemens Computers Oy* [2010] ICR 444).

The rights of elected representatives

There are certain rights which go with the post of elected representative. The elected **18.124** representative and union representative are accorded the right not to suffer detriment as a consequence of carrying out the functions or activities of an employee representative or a candidate for such elections, and time off for such purposes (ERA 1996, ss 47(1), 61(1)). A dismissal will be automatically unfair if the reason or principal reason is that the employee performed or proposed to perform any functions as an employee representative. The 1999 Amendment Regulations extended these rights to cover any employee dismissed or subjected to a detriment by reason of his participation in an employee representatives' election (ERA 1996, ss 47(1A) and 103(2)).

Further, the employer must provide elected representatives or trade union representatives **18.125** with access to the affected employees (reg 10(6A)), such as by use of the telephone, and they should be allowed time off to undergo training in their functions (ERA 1996, s 61).

G TRADE UNION RIGHTS

18.126 Regulation 5 requires that rights and duties arising under a collective bargain should be transferred to the transferee, but this is expressly enacted as being without prejudice to the non-binding nature of such agreements (TULR(C)A 1992, s 179; *Werhof v Freeway Traffic Systems GmbH & Co KG* [2006] IRLR 400).

18.127 After much debate in the case law it was held that Art 3(1) of the Acquired Rights Directive did not bear a dynamic interpretation of the burden of transferees of employment contract terms fixed by reference to collective agreements negotiated from time to time so that a transferee was only committed to the terms of any collective agreement until such agreement terminated, expired, or was replaced (*Alemo-Herron v Parkwood Leisure Ltd* [2010] ICR 793; [2013] ICR 1116). The CJEU took into account the fact that as the transferee was unable to participate in the collective bargaining process it could neither assert its interests effectively in a contractual process nor negotiate aspects determining changes in working conditions with a view to its future activity (also *Österreichischer Gewerkschaftsbund v Wirtschaftskammer Österreich* [2014] ICR 1152).

18.128 Further, a transferee is obliged to succeed to and honour the transferor's union recognition arrangements but only 'where after a relevant transfer the undertaking or part of the undertaking maintains an identity distinct from the remainder of the transferee undertaking' (reg 6).

Notification of employee liability information

18.129 There is a duty which is new to the 2006 Regulations (reg 11(1)) on the part of the transferor to notify the transferee in relation to employee liability information of any person employed by him who is assigned to the organised grouping of resources or employees that is the subject of a relevant transfer. This may be done in writing or by making it available to him in a readily accessible form.

18.130 There are thus five categories of information:

(a) the employees;
(b) the details under their statements of terms and conditions;
(c) details of any disciplinary or grievance procedures in the previous two years;
(d) details of any court or tribunal case, claim, or action brought within the previous two years or that the transferor has reasonable grounds to believe that an employee may bring against the transferee arising out of the employee's employment with the transferor; and
(e) information of any collective agreement which will have effect after the transfer.

The information has to be supplied in relation to any assigned employee transferring and any person who might have transferred if he or she had not been automatically unfairly dismissed under reg 7. On or after a relevant transfer, the transferee may present a complaint to an employment tribunal that the transferor has failed to comply with any provision of reg 11.

18.131 Where an employment tribunal finds that such a complaint is well-founded, the tribunal shall make a declaration to that effect and may make an award of compensation to be paid by the transferor to the transferee.

The amount of the compensation shall be such as the tribunal considers to be just and **18.132** equitable in all the circumstances having particular regard to:

(a) any loss sustained by the transferee which is attributable to the matters complained of; and

(b) the terms of any contract between the transferor and the transferee relating to the transfer under which the transferor may be liable to pay any sum to the transferee in respect of a failure to notify the transferee of employee liability information.

The amount of compensation awarded is not less than £500 per employee in respect of **18.133** whom the transferor has failed to comply with a provision of reg 11, unless the tribunal considers it just and equitable, in all the circumstances, to award a lesser sum. The normal rules of mitigation apply.

The only direct change under the new regulations, originally reg 7, is that the relevant **18.134** definition of occupational pension scheme is changed, which is now the same as under the Pension Schemes Act 1993.

19

TRADE UNIONS AND COLLECTIVE BARGAINING

A THE BRITISH SYSTEM OF COLLECTIVE BARGAINING 19.01

B THE LEGAL STATUS OF TRADE UNIONS AND EMPLOYERS' ASSOCIATIONS 19.03

C LISTING 19.07

D INDEPENDENCE OF TRADE UNIONS 19.11

Purpose 19.12

Definition of independence 19.14

Criteria of independence 19.15

E THE RIGHT TO JOIN A TRADE UNION 19.18

The common law and the 'right to work' 19.19

Statute 19.21

Unjustifiable discipline of members by a union .19.31

Review of internal disciplinary hearings 19.41

F UNION LIABILITY IN TORT 19.43

G ENFORCEMENT OF COLLECTIVE BARGAINS 19.49

General principles 19.49

Enforcement of a statutory method of collective bargaining 19.52

H THE AUXILIARY ROLE OF THE LAW 19.55

I RECOGNITION 19.57

Statutory recognition 19.58

Other statutory provisions 19.100

J RIGHT OF TRADE UNIONS TO INFORMATION IN SUPPORT OF COLLECTIVE BARGAINING 19.103

Trade Union and Labour Relations (Consolidation) Act 1992 . . . . .19.104

Health and safety 19.113

Pensions 19.114

K INFORMATION AND CONSULTATION ON TRAINING 19.116

Qualifying conditions 19.117

Employer's duty to disclose information before meeting 19.118

Enforcement and remedies 19.120

L THE ADVISORY, CONCILIATION AND ARBITRATION SERVICE (ACAS) 19.121

Conciliation 19.124

Mediation .19.127

Advice 19.128

Inquiry 19.129

Arbitration .19.130

M CENTRAL ARBITRATION COMMITTEE (CAC) 19.131

N CODES OF PRACTICE 19.134

O HEALTH AND SAFETY AND COLLECTIVE BARGAINING 19.138

P EUROPEAN WORKS COUNCILS 19.141

Scope 19.142

Establishing the EWC 19.143

Employee representatives 19.145

Disputes and enforcement 19.147

The Information and Consultation of Employees Regulations 19.148

Societas Europaea 19.150

It is of the essence of the right to join a trade union for the protection of their interests that employees should be free to instruct or permit the union to make representations to their employer or to take action in support of their interests on their behalf. If workers are prevented from doing so, their freedom to belong to a trade union for the protection of their interest becomes illusory. (*Wilson v UK* (2002) 35 EHRR 20, para 46.)

A THE BRITISH SYSTEM OF COLLECTIVE BARGAINING

Collective bargaining grew in the nineteenth century to replace customary rates of pay set **19.01** by the masters in each particular district and industry as had formerly pertained. With the impulse of the 'new model unions', and then the unskilled general unions, national bodies emerged as the forum for negotiations (usually annual) between a union or several unions and the appropriate employers' association.

There has, in recent years, been a steep decline in the scope of collective bargaining as tra- **19.02** ditional highly unionised industries have declined, many employers have derecognised trade unions, or have set up greenfield sites without any degree of union recognition. More recently the growth of the 'gig' economy and zero hours contract has made the field even less favoura- ble to unionisation. Indeed, it was public policy during the period in office of the Conservative Government of 1979–97 to *discourage* collective bargaining. The most celebrated exam- ple of derecognition was by the Government itself at the Government Communications Headquarters at Cheltenham (which went further, in that employees were not permitted to be members of trade unions at all and could only join a staff association which was subsequently held by the EAT not to qualify as an independent trade union). The GCHQ ban was reversed by the incoming Blair Labour Government, which improved unions' chances of establish- ing collective bargaining rights more generally by means of the recognition provisions of the Employment Relations Act 1999 but this has been little used. The New Labour Governments of Messrs Blair and Brown have been at best lukewarm to collective bargaining and the Coalition Government of 2010 and Conservative Government from 2015 have returned to the positive hostility seen in the Thatcher Period. One of the constitutional obligations of the ILO is, however, still to 'further among the nations of the world programs which will achieve ... the effective recognition of the right of collective bargaining'.

There is a marked gap now between public and private sector in terms of union density with the 2013 figures showing only 14.4 per cent of private sector workers yet 55.4 per cent in the public sector.

B THE LEGAL STATUS OF TRADE UNIONS
AND EMPLOYERS' ASSOCIATIONS

The advent of the Industrial Revolution was also the dawn of organised labour. The **19.03** realisation of this, coupled with the hysteria amongst Britain's aristocracy caused by the French Revolution, made for a very twitchy ruling class in the nineteenth century. Coercive measures were used to stamp out Britain's fledgling trade unions. The Tolpuddle Martyrs, for example, were exiled abroad simply for organising workers in Dorset vil- lages. Trade unions were held by the courts to be unlawful associations because they restricted the terms on which each member would sell his labour (*Hornby v Close* (1867) 2 LRQB 153), and it was therefore necessary to make special provision even just to render them lawful organisations.

A trade union is an unincorporated association at common law, which means prima facie **19.04** that it is not a separate entity from its members, and its property must rest in the hands of trustees. It is in this respect, as a matter of law, more like a members' club than a company, although several cases have suggested that it has a quasi-corporate status and it may be sued as such by reason of s 10(1) of the TULR(C)A 1992. The most notorious and historic in its significance was the decision in *Taff Vale Railway Company v Amalgamated Society of Railway Servants* [1901] AC 426, which concluded from the fact that they were registered under the Trade Union Acts 1871 and 1876 that unions could be sued in tort in their registered name.

19.05   The issue next arose in the rather different context of deciding whether an employee could sue a trade union for breach of rules by its officers. In *Bonsor v Musicians' Union* [1956] AC 104, Lord Morton said that a union was 'a body distinct from the individuals who from time to time compose it'; Lord Parker thought it 'an entity, a body, a "near corporation"'. As part of its aim to make unions pay for the consequences of their industrial action, the Industrial Relations Act 1971 went further and imposed corporate status on all unions. This was, however, reversed by the Trade Union and Labour Relations Act 1974 and has not been re-enacted.

19.06   Although the legal form of a trade union is thus different from corporate entities, the reality underneath is not, since s 10(1) of the TULR(C)A 1992 confers on unions many of the characteristics of legal corporate status. Thus, it provides that:

(a)   a union is capable of making contracts in its own name;
(b)   all union property must be vested in trustees who hold it in trust for the trade union; if they were ordinary unincorporated associations it would be in trust for the members or otherwise void as a purpose trust and perpetual;
(c)   a union is capable of suing or being sued in its own name;
(d)   proceedings may be brought against a union for a criminal offence; and
(e)   a union is liable for enforcement of judgments as though it were a body corporate.

Section 11 of the TULR(C)A 1992 now provides that no trade union *purposes or rules* should be unlawful or unenforceable on the ground of restraint of trade.

C LISTING

19.07   By the TULR(C)A 1992, s 2, the Certification Officer is charged with the duty of keeping a voluntary list of trade unions and employers' associations. The following unions are automatically listed:

(a)   any union registered under the Trade Union Act 1871 on the day of the coming into force of the Industrial Relations Act;
(b)   unions registered under the Industrial Relations Act; and
(c)   TUC-affiliated unions.

19.08   Outside of this rubric the Certification Officer grants a listing to a union if he is satisfied that the organisation comes within the appropriate definition. He retains a copy of the rules, a list of officers, and its address; and the union must pay the prescribed fee. Further, to be registered a union's name must not be too similar to an existing union's appellation nor likely to deceive the public (TULR(C)A 1992, s 3(4)).

19.09   The Certification Officer may remove a union from the list, which is open to public view, if it ceases to fall within the definition or to exist altogether (TULR(C)A 1992, s 4). An appeal against either refusal to register or against removal from the register lies to the EAT on a point of fact or law (TULR(C)A 1992, s 9).

There are only minor differences between listed and non-listed unions, in that listing **19.10** provides:

(a) a precondition for a certificate of *independence* which itself confers many additional benefits (19.11–19.17);
(b) entitlement to *tax relief* on income and chargeable gains applied for provident benefits (Income and Corporation Taxes Act 1988, s 467);
(c) prima facie *evidence* that the organisation is a trade union, should the matter arise in any legal proceedings (TULR(C)A 1992, s 2(4)); and
(d) express identification as a 'permissible donor' for the purpose of making donations to a registered political party (Political Parties, Elections and Referendums Act 2000, s 54(2)(d))—although an unlisted trade union, as an 'unincorporated association', may also make such donations (s 54(2)(h)).

D INDEPENDENCE OF TRADE UNIONS

'What Parliament will not tolerate is the recognised and certificated existence of a band **19.11** of people claiming to be an independent trade union when in reality they are unable to offer a vigorous challenge to the employers on behalf of their members whether collectively or individually.' (Kilner Brown J in *Association of HSD (Hatfield) Employees v Certification Officer* [1978] ICR 21, at 23H.)

Purpose

An employer who fears that a union is about to gain strength among his employees has **19.12** several cards up his sleeve to resist it. He may pay more than the union rates in order to convince his workers that there is no need for outside intervention, or he can stimulate and nurture a staff association (a quasi-union active solely within his firm). Such a 'house union' may represent its members only feebly. However, the consequence of their dependence is that they cannot now claim the advantages of important statutory rights, including the possibility of statutory recognition.

This idea that such groups of workers do not merit the privileges accorded to unions, **19.13** derives originally from the ILO Convention No 98 of 1951; and now under ss 5 to 9 of the TULR(C)A 1992, the characterisation rests with the Certification Officer, with a right of appeal by the union to the Employment Appeal Tribunal on both law *and fact*. It is a vital criterion for conferring the following rights:

(a) to take part in trade union activities;
(b) to gain information for collective bargaining purposes (TULR(C)A 1992, s 181);
(c) to secure consultation over redundancies and transfers of undertakings;
(d) to take time off for trade union duties and activities;
(e) to appoint health and safety representatives;
(f) to apply to the Central Arbitration Committee for an award of statutory recognition (TULR(C)A 1992, Sch A1; see further 19.57–19.102);
(g) to appoint learning representatives;
(h) to negotiate collective agreements modifying statutory entitlements under various provisions (eg Working Time Regulations 1998); and
(i) to advise workers on entering into a compromise agreement.

Definition of independence

19.14 By s 5 of the TULR(C)A 1992 a union is independent if it is:

(a) not under the domination or control of an employer; and
(b) not liable to interference by an employer (arising out of provision of financial or material support or by any other means tending towards such control).

The second limitation is the more difficult to apply since it demands a subjective approach and a good deal of speculation about the union's likely future performance. In *Squibb UK Staff Association v Certification Officer* [1979] ICR 235, the Court of Appeal determined that the proper question was whether the union was 'exposed to, vulnerable to, or at the risk of, interference'.

There is, however, no statutory requirement that a union be *effective* in its activities to be independent.

Criteria of independence

19.15 Although each case must ultimately depend on its own facts, this 'critique calls for a subtle assessment', and the main criteria are most helpfully set out in the Certification Officer's Report for 1976. The substance is now contained in a booklet Guidance for trade unions wishing to apply for a certificate of independence (Certification Officer, 2000). Its predecessor booklet was approved by the EAT in *Blue Circle Staff Association v Certification Officer* [1977] ICR 224, and will provide the basis for treatment of the subject here.

(a) *History*: where the union was set up at the behest of management, the more recent the connection with the employer's coat tails, the less likely it is that the union is genuinely independent therefrom. Thus, in the *Blue Circle SA* case (above) it was important to the EAT's decision refusing independence that the Association had been formed only six months earlier with complete employer control; the change of rules since then was treated as a mere facade. The Certification Officer did, however, state that 'it was not unusual for a staff association to start as a creature of management and grow into something independent' (at 231).

(b) *Membership base*: a single-company union is more vulnerable to employer interference than one which draws its membership from many sources. This cannot be taken too far, however, since the members of the National Union of Mineworkers (at the time) derived from a single employer, yet no one would doubt its sturdy independence and effectiveness.

(c) *Finance*: a low bank balance may make a union dependent, while a direct employer subsidy would probably be decisive against independence.

(d) *Employer-provided facilities*: a major influence in the refusal of a certificate in the *Squibb* case (a decision ultimately approved by the Court of Appeal), was the fact that the employer accorded, *inter alia*, time off with pay for its officials; free use of office accommodation; free stationery; and internal mailing facilities. This suggested dependence on the employer, yet the irony is that when a union *has* established its independence, the employer is actively encouraged to make provision of this sort. Generally, the Certification Officer should enquire what would be the effects of the removal of employer-provided facilities from a small organisation.

(e) *Collective bargaining record*: although the Certification Officer has stated that 'a robust attitude in negotiation is regarded as an item on the credit side', in *Blue Circle*, the EAT 'deplored any suggestion that a record of bad relations is an index of freedom from domination or control'.

(f) *Organisation and structure*: one of the major elements arguing against independence in *Blue Circle* was the limited role which ordinary members might play in the union. Only employees of three or more years' service were eligible for election as area committee representatives; the employer could insist on the withdrawal of credentials of a union representative on the Joint Central Council, the chairman of which was always nominated by the employer. The EAT said:

> The main requirement is that the union should be organised in a way which enables the members to play a full part in the decision-making process and excludes any form of employer involvement or influence in the union's internal affairs.

The Government Communications Staff Federation which was formed at GCHQ after the ban on union membership instituted by the Thatcher Government, was held not to be independent by a five-member EAT in *Government Communications Staff Federation v Certification Officer* [1993] IRLR 260. The Federation was determined to be vulnerable to or exposed to the risk of interference by the employer because its continued existence was dependent on the approval of the Director of GCHQ. Further, it was a condition of service that staff were not allowed to be members of other unions and any attempt to affiliate with another union would probably lead to derecognition. **19.16**

In order to preserve the single channel of adjudication in the Certification Officer the Act provides that, if the question of independence arises in any legal proceedings (whether at an employment tribunal, the Employment Appeal Tribunal, the Central Arbitration Committee, or the Advisory, Conciliation and Arbitration Service), those proceedings must be stayed until the Certification Officer has decided whether or not to issue a certificate of independence (TULR(C)A 1992, s 8(4)). The certificate is then conclusive evidence that the union is independent (s 8(1)). **19.17**

E THE RIGHT TO JOIN A TRADE UNION

Unions are in essence voluntary associations like the Boy Scouts or a youth club and in few such organisations is there an automatic right to join. However, in the case of unions, different considerations obtain, particularly in the case of the formerly widespread practice of a pre-entry closed shop, since failure to be admitted into the appropriate union may mean the inability to gain a particular job at all. We will consider common law and then statutory attempts to subject this power to legal control. **19.18**

The common law and the 'right to work'

In controlling admission to unions, the basic difficulty for the ordinary common law is that the prospective union member cannot claim that any contract has been broken by reason of refusal of his application. His grudge is rather that there *is no* contract of membership and he wants one. He complains of deprivation of an expectation for which, in the absence of a previous relationship or tort, there is normally no legal remedy. **19.19**

The Court of Appeal, however, in several cases suggested that the so-called '*right to work*' provides a basis for judicial control of the admission process and that natural justice applies to such dashing of legitimate expectations, for example, *Nagle v Feilden* [1966] 2 QB 633 (see also *Boulting v ACTT* [1963] 2 QB 606; and *Faramus v Film Artistes' Association* [1964] AC 925). **19.20**

Statute

19.21 The Trade Union and Labour Relations (Consolidation) Act 1992 accords the employee a right not to be *unreasonably* refused, or excluded from, membership of a trade union. This right remains alongside the more general provisions on unjustifiable discipline by trade unions. *Unreasonable delay* by the union in determining an application to a union is deemed to be tantamount to refusal of an application, but it is a nice point as to what delay is unreasonable.

19.22 The doctrine of 'constructive expulsion' cannot be fitted into the statutory language. In *McGhee v TGWU* [1985] IRLR 198, the claimant argued that this was similar in concept to constructive *dismissal*. The trade unionist had resigned his membership as a consequence of being treated as in arrears with subscriptions when he had not paid a fine imposed for criticising the union's leadership, but he was not entitled to claim under what was then s 4 of the Employment Act 1980. The claimant can, however, claim if he is offered membership only of a particular, unfavourable, class of membership, according to *Kirkham v NATSOPA* [1981] IRLR 244, but the refusal of a union to allow a member additional shifts in the printing industry did not mean that he had thereby been refused membership of a branch or section of the union (*Goodfellow v NATSOPA* [1985] IRLR 3). Exclusion does not include suspension from the benefits of union membership (*NACODS v Gluchowski* [1996] IRLR 252).

19.23 A claim may fall within the TULR(C)A 1992, s 174, even if the applicant to the union has no specific job in view but is merely seeking employment in a closed shop industry (*Clark v NATSOPA* [1985] IRLR 494). Article 11 of the European Convention on Human Rights cannot be interpreted as imposing an obligation on organisations to admit whoever wishes to join; *ASLEF v UK* [2007] IRLR 361. This was decided in the case of a train driver who was a member of the British National Party.

19.24 The exclusion or expulsion of an individual from a trade union is permitted if and only if he does not satisfy an 'enforceable membership requirement'; he does not qualify because the union operates only in a particular part of Great Britain; where the union regulates relations between its members and one particular employer or a number of particular employers and he is not employed by that employer or employers; or neither the exclusion nor expulsion is entirely attributable to conduct (other than excluded conduct) which is not protected conduct (s 174(2)). It is thus necessary to consider the definition of 'excluded conduct' which by s 174(4) means conduct consisting of his ceasing to be a member of another trade union; his having ceased to be employed by a particular employer or at a particular place; or conduct under s 65 for which he may not be disciplined. By s 174(4A) protected conduct consists of the individual's being or ceasing to be a member of a political party but does not include conduct as such a member.

19.25 It is not necessary to exhaust all the union's internal procedures before using the tribunal.

19.26 The remedial mechanism is of some complexity and has more stages than in an unfair dismissal claim. It begins with a declaration of unreasonableness. The award made by the employment tribunal at this stage serves to compensate for the loss sustained by the union's earlier refusal subject to the usual duty of the worker to mitigate his damage, and also to a reduction if the complainant caused or contributed to the union's action (TULR(C)A 1992, s 176(5)). The maximum award is thirty weeks' pay plus the maximum compensatory award for the time being in respect of unfair dismissal (TULR(C)A 1992, s 176(6)).

19.27 If the union refuses to abide by the tribunal's initial declaration of unreasonableness, having been given four weeks to put matters right, the sanction becomes more severe. The complainant may now go to the employment tribunal within six months of the original refusal, giving what is usually an appeal body its only original jurisdiction (TULR(C)A 1992, s 176(2)).

The maximum is now thirty times the maximum week's pay plus the maximum compensatory award available in an employment tribunal (TULR(C)A 1992, s 176(6)) and shall not be less than £8,868. **19.28**

There are four potential heads of compensation: loss of earnings during the period of unemployment; net loss of earnings resulting from the dismissal; loss of earning opportunity generally as a result of being denied union membership; and non-pecuniary loss. In *Howard v NGA* [1985] ICR 101, the EAT reduced the award by 15 per cent because the claimant had contributed to the refusal of membership by the union when he took a job with a company which he knew subscribed to the closed shop agreement whilst his application for union membership was under consideration (see also *Saunders v Bakers, Food and Allied Workers' Union* [1986] IRLR 16; *Day v SOGAT (1982)* [1986] ICR 640). **19.29**

The Trade Union and Labour Relations (Consolidation) Act 1992 provides in this respect that the rights which it confers are in addition to and not in substitution for any other right whether by statute or at common law. The Equality Act 2010 incidentally impinges on the right of admission in that it makes it illegal to discriminate against an applicant for a trade union or employers' association on the ground of race, sex, disability, age, or sexual orientation. In addition, the 1992 Act states that if a union has a political fund, it must not make contribution thereto a condition of admission nor discriminate against a non-contributor. Sections 64 to 67 of the 1992 Act provide a general prohibition of unjustifiable discipline of trade union members. **19.30**

Unjustifiable discipline of members by a union

A union is prohibited from disciplining a member for not taking part in industrial action notwithstanding that a majority of that member's colleagues voted in favour of the action in a properly held ballot. **19.31**

The grounds

The most important grounds (TULR(C)A 1992, s 65(2)) on which discipline of a trade union member is to be taken as unjustifiable are: **19.32**

(a) failure to support a strike or industrial action by members of his own trade union or any other;
(b) failure to participate in a strike or industrial action by members of his own trade union or any other (on the definition of 'industrial action', see *Fire Brigades Union v Knowles* [1996] IRLR 617);
(c) indication of opposition to a strike or industrial action by members of his own trade union or any other;
(d) indication of lack of support for a strike or industrial action by members of his own trade union or any other;
(e) failure to contravene a contract of employment or any other agreement between the member and 'a person for whom he normally works' (this is a concept wider than 'employee' or 'worker', see 2.06–2.20);
(f) the making of an assertion that the union, or any official, representative, or trustee thereof, has contravened or is proposing to contravene a requirement imposed by the union rules;
(g) consulting the Certification Officer or asking him to provide advice or assistance;

(h) failure to agree to the making of a deduction of subscriptions arrangement;

(i) resigning from one union to join another;

(j) working with individuals who are not members of that union or another union;

(k) working for an employer who employs or has employed individuals who are not members of that union or another union; or

(l) requiring the union to do an act which the union is, pursuant to the TULR(C)A 1992, required to do on the requisition of a member.

19.33 'Discipline' is widely defined in the Act and includes advice that another trade union or branch or section of another trade union should be encouraged or advised not to accept that individual as a member and subjecting the individual to any detriment (*Medhurst v Dental Estimates Board Branch of NALGO and NALGO* [1990] IRLR 459). Detriment may take the form of the publication of her name in a circular or newsletter circulated to all branch members (*NALGO v Killorn and Simm* [1990] IRLR 464).

Exclusion

19.34 The section does not apply to discipline for criticism of the union's leadership if the relevant assertion was false and the person making it or attempting to vindicate it acted:

(a) in the belief that it was false; or

(b) otherwise in bad faith,

and there was no other reason for disciplining him which was within the grounds of unjustifiable discipline (TURL(C)A 1992, s 65(6)).

Procedure for claiming unjustifiable discipline

19.35 In order for a member to claim, there must be a 'determination' by the union, that is, its decision has to dispose of the issue of discipline once and for all and not, as in *TGWU v Webber* [1990] IRLR 462, merely to be a recommendation of a Regional Council to the General Executive Council of the union, when the latter body was the only one which could decide on the implementation of it.

19.36 A union member may complain of unjustifiable discipline to an employment tribunal within three months of the unjustifiable discipline being imposed (s 66). The tribunal has a power to extend this period if it considers it reasonable to do so, if it was not reasonably practicable to present the application within that period, and the delay is wholly or partly attributable to any reasonable attempt to appeal against such determination (s 66(2)).

19.37 A member whose complaint is upheld by the employment tribunal may claim compensation; such an application is to be made to the employment tribunal. The application for compensation must be presented between four weeks and six months after the declaration has been made by the employment tribunal (s 67(3)). The employment tribunal may make such an award of compensation as it considers 'just and equitable in all the circumstances' (s 67(5)).

19.38 The following principles, however, apply, which are similar to those relevant to the unfair dismissal compensatory award:

(a) the common law rules of mitigation of loss (s 67(6)); and

(b) contributory fault by the claimant, in which case the relevant body should 'reduce the amount of the compensation by such proportion as it considers just and equitable' having regard to such conduct (s 67(7)).

Compensation may be awarded for injury to feelings (*Bradley v NALGO* [1991] ICR 359), but within a reasonable bracket and not where the injury arose not from the discipline itself but from the calculated behaviour of certain members after the claimants had been expelled in that they wrote articles criticising the claimants. What is important is the duration and intensity of the injury to feelings, that is, the result of the wrongful act(s) (*Massey v UNIFI* [2007] IRLR 902) (see on remedy, *NALGO v Courteney-Dunn* [1992] IRLR 114).

The maximum special award was thirty times a week's pay, together with the maximum **19.39** compensatory award currently available. Where the application is because the union has not complied with the declaration made by the employment tribunal, the amount is at least £8,868 (s 67(8)).

Moreover, if an individual is unjustifiably disciplined under these provisions, no one may **19.40** enforce:

(a) the payment of any sums; or
(b) the performance of any other obligation.

Review of internal disciplinary hearings

The courts insist that meetings to dispense discipline must be properly called, so that an **19.41** expulsion has been held void because two members of the branch committee who decided to expel the plaintiff did not receive the papers relating to his case (*Leary v NUVB* [1971] Ch 34), and a similar result was reached where a meeting was called with only a few minutes' notice (*MacLelland v NUJ* [1975] ICR 116). By s 174(4H) of the TULR(C)A 1992, the union must act in a way that is procedurally fair so it must give notice of and the reasons for exclusion or expulsion and an opportunity to make representations.

The courts will not normally, however, review the facts as found by the internal union **19.42** tribunal (*Weinberger v Inglis* [1919] AC 606), as long as it acts honestly, in good faith, and in accordance with its rules (*Maclean v Workers Union* [1929] 1 Ch 602) and the internal tribunal reaches a decision at which a reasonable tribunal could arrive (*Radford v NATSOPA* [1972] ICR 484).

F UNION LIABILITY IN TORT

A union is fully liable in tort except where it acts in contemplation or furtherance of **19.43** a trade dispute, but this immunity was further reduced by the Employment Acts 1980 and 1982. There is, however, a maximum level of damages to be awarded under what is now s 22 of the TULR(C)A 1992 depending on the membership of the union as follows: £10,000 when the union has fewer than 5,000 members; £50,000 where it has between 5,000 and 25,000; £125,000 between 25,000 and 100,000 members; and £250,000 where more than 100,000 belong. The only way that this may be circumvented is if there is a claim to breach of free movement of capital or labour under EU law (see 21.158). Curiously, this maximum has remained unchanged since 1982. Interest may be awarded in addition to the appropriate sum (*Boxfoldia v National Graphical Association (1982)* [1988] ICR 752).

For the union to be liable, the action must have been authorised or endorsed by a respon- **19.44** sible person, and this is defined as: the principal executive committee; any person empowered by the rules to give endorsement; the president or general secretary; any employed official or a union committee to whom an employed official regularly reports; any committee of the union (whether employed by it or not); or a group of persons, the purposes of which include organising or coordinating industrial action (TULR(C)A 1992, s 20; see *Gate Gourmet London Ltd v TGWU* [2005] IRLR 881).

19.45 Unions, however, have power by the statute to repudiate actions which are purported to be taken on their behalf by their lay officials, but only if they do so 'as soon as reasonably practicable after it has come to [their] knowledge' and if the person who takes the action 'has been notified in writing and without delay'. In order to preserve this status the principal executive committee or president or general secretary must not thereafter 'behave in a manner which is inconsistent with the purported repudiation' (TULR(C) A 1992, s 21(5); see *Express & Star Ltd v NGA* [1986] IRLR 222; *Thomas v National Union of Mineworkers (South Wales Area)* [1985] IRLR 136; *News Group Newspapers v SOGAT 82* [1986] ICR 716).

19.46 For the union to repudiate action, written notice must be given to the official or committee who has or which has authorised or endorsed the relevant action without delay. Further, the union must 'do its best to give individual written notice of the fact and date of repudiation without delay (i) to every member of the union who the union has reason to believe is taking part, or might otherwise take part, in industrial action as a result of the act and (ii) to the employer of every such member'. Such a notice must include a 'health warning' in the following terms:

> Your union has repudiated the call (or calls) for industrial action to which this notice relates and will give no support to unofficial industrial action taken in response to it/them. If you are dismissed while taking unofficial action, you will have no right to complain of unfair dismissal. (TULR(C)A 1992, s 21(3)).

19.47 The union must also confirm such repudiation on any request which is made to the union's principal executive committee, president, or general secretary within six months of the repudiation by 'a party to a commercial contract whose performance has been or may be interfered with as a result of the act in question'.

19.48 Where damages are awarded no execution may be levied against:

(a) property belonging to union trustees or members otherwise than on behalf of the union; and
(b) the union's political fund or provident benefit funds (TULR(C)A 1992, s 23).

G ENFORCEMENT OF COLLECTIVE BARGAINS

General principles

19.49 The central legal question raised by collective bargaining used to be whether agreements so produced can be enforced in the courts. Most controversy has surrounded whether the employer can sue the union for taking strike action before the procedure for settling disputes laid down in the collective bargain has been pursued. There is no problem with privity here; the vital question is instead whether they are intended to have legal effect.

19.50 Collective agreements are usually not drafted with the precision to which a lawyer is accustomed, rarely covering all eventualities and this is particularly so at local level. It was primarily for these reasons that, in the leading case at common law, *Ford Motor Co v AEU* [1969] 2 QB 302, Geoffrey Lane J found that the Ford Motor Company's collective agreement was not intended to create legal relations, and therefore not open to construction and enforcement by the courts. He also referred to 'the general climate of opinion on both sides of industry' and 'the vague aspirational wording' of the agreement before him, and went on: 'Agreements such as these, composed largely of optimistic aspirations, presenting grave practical problems of enforcement and reached against a background of opinion adverse to enforceability are, in my judgment, not contracts in the legal sense.' He said, on the general issue of intention:

> If one applies the subjective test and asks what the intentions of the various parties were, the answer is that so far as they had any express intentions they were certainly not to make the agreement enforceable at law. If one applies an objective test and asks what intention must be imputed from all the circumstances of the case the result is the same.

(See also *Edwards v Skyways Ltd* [1964] 1 WLR 349; *Adams v British Airways plc* [1996] IRLR 574; *Whent v T. Cartledge Ltd* [1997] IRLR 153; *Edinburgh Council v Brown* [1999] IRLR 208.) In *Monterosso Shipping Ltd v International Transport Workers' Federation* [1982] ICR 675, the Court of Appeal decided that the collective bargain was not a contract at all for the purposes of private international law.

The nature of the collective bargain was further explored in *National Coal Board v* **19.51** *National Union of Mineworkers* [1986] IRLR 439. The NCB agreed in 1946 with the NUM for reference of disputes to a national reference tribunal. In 1985, following the miners' strike, the NCB gave six months' notice of its intention to terminate the agreement. The NUM did not accept that this was valid, arguing that the agreement was legally binding since it actually stated that the parties were 'bound'. Scott J thought that this was insufficient to replace the presumption in what is now the TULR(C)A 1992, s 179, that collective bargains are *not* intended to be legally binding. The union also sought to argue that the agreement was incorporated into the contracts of employment of individuals. This was rejected on the basis that such incorporation refers to substantive terms such as wages and conditions and not to collective procedural matters such as arose in this case.

Enforcement of a statutory method of collective bargaining

A limited exception to the general rule that collective bargaining arrangements are not **19.52** enforceable at law is found in the statutory recognition provisions introduced in 1999. Where the Central Arbitration Committee (CAC) has made a declaration of recognition, there is a further procedure under which either side may apply to it to impose a 'method of collective bargaining' (in effect a bargaining procedure), where the parties have failed to arrive at such a method voluntarily. The method which is imposed by the CAC will have the force of a binding contract between the union and the employer, and will be enforceable by an application to the civil courts for specific performance (see *BALPA v Jet2.com* [2015] IRLR 543).

Similar provisions apply where the CAC imposes a method of collective bargaining on **19.53** parties who have entered into a semi-voluntary form of recognition known in the Act as an 'agreement for recognition'; where the parties agree to vary a method of collective bargaining imposed by the CAC; and where, following a change in the bargaining unit, the parties' established method of collective bargaining transfers across to the new bargaining unit (see further 17.12).

Further, notwithstanding this lack of direct legal enforcement, reg 5 of the Transfer of **19.54** Undertakings (Protection of Employment) Regulations 2006 (SI 2006/246) provides that on a transfer of undertaking, 'any collective bargain agreed by the transferor shall have effect as if made by the transferee' (see 18.126).

H THE AUXILIARY ROLE OF THE LAW

19.55 The general duty laid on ACAS by the TULR(C)A 1992 (s 209) is 'the improvement of industrial relations ...'. The legislation which was originally introduced by Labour Governments also recognised that successful bargaining can be carried out only when employees achieve a sufficient degree of organisation. Thus, the TULRA 1974 and the EPCA 1978 sought to enhance union strength and cohesion by such provisions as time off for union activities, and banning discrimination against members (Chapter 20).

19.56 We look in turn at the following statutory provisions and common law developments as supports for collective bargaining:

(a) recognition of trade unions (19.57);
(b) rights to information (19.103);
(c) information and consultation on training (19.116);
(d) ACAS (19.121);
(e) the Central Arbitration Committee (19.131);
(f) codes of practice (19.134);
(g) health and safety (19.138); and
(h) European Works Councils (19.141).

I RECOGNITION

19.57 'Recognition entails accepting a trade union to some extent as the representative of the employees for the purpose of carrying on negotiations in relation to or connected with one of the matters set out in [s 178(2) of the TULR(C)A 1992]. Thus, it entails not merely a willingness to discuss but also to negotiate in relation to one or more such matters. That is to say, to negotiate with a view to striking a bargain upon an issue and this involves a positive mental decision.' (Eveleigh LJ in *National Union of Gold, Silver and Allied Trades v Albury* [1978] IRLR 504.)

Statutory recognition

19.58 After a largely unsatisfactory and controversial experiment with statutory recognition during the 1970s, recognition reverted from 1980 onwards to being a matter for voluntary agreement between unions and employers. However, this changed to a new and more successful regime with the coming into force of the recognition provisions of the Employment Relations Act 1999, now contained in the TULR(C)A 1992 as Sch A1 (and somewhat amended). It provides enormous detail in the schedule, running to 172 paragraphs.

19.59 Part I of the Schedule sets out a procedure under which an independent trade union has the right to apply to the Central Arbitration Committee (CAC) for a declaration awarding it recognition for collective bargaining purposes in respect of a particular 'bargaining unit' (ie group of workers) (for definition of independence see 19.12–19.22). If the CAC does issue such a declaration, the award of statutory recognition should, if all goes well, last for a minimum of three years, and can normally be terminated only through one of the derecognition procedures described in 19.86–19.92, below.

'Collective bargaining' in Sch A1 has, however, a much narrower meaning than else- **19.60** where in the TULR(C)A 1992. For the purposes of this statutory recognition, it refers to negotiations only about 'pay, hours, and holidays', and nothing else, although the union and the employer are free to add to, or subtract from, this list by mutual agreement (para 3) (see *BALPA v Jet 2* [2015] IRLR 543). Negotiations relating to pay were held by the CAC to include pensions (*UNIFI v Union Bank of Nigeria plc* [2001] IRLR 713) but this was reversed by statute so that pay does not include membership of or rights under contributions to an occupational or personal pension scheme (para 171A introduced by the ERA 2004).

With the exception of derecognition of non-independent unions (discussed briefly at **19.61** 19.89), the Schedule is not intended to affect voluntary recognition arrangements, either those entered into before its coming into force, or after. Part II of the Schedule is, as we shall see, involved with a hybrid form of recognition which is, perhaps, better described as 'semi-voluntary' (see further 19.85).

Application for statutory recognition

The statutory recognition procedure, under Pt I of the Schedule, begins when a union **19.62** sends a request to an employer to recognise it as entitled to conduct collective bargaining on behalf of a particular 'bargaining unit' (para 4). This request will be valid only if the union possesses a certificate from the Certification Officer that it is independent and the employer and any associated employers must employ at least twenty-one workers (paras 6 and 7). The procedure allows the parties to agree to recognition voluntarily at this stage, but, failing this, the union will normally then be entitled to apply to the CAC (paras 10 to 12) but the CAC will accept the union's application for further consideration only if it complies with the various admissibility criteria set out in paras 33 to 42. One of the most important of these is the requirement that 10 per cent of the workers in the proposed bargaining unit must already belong to the union (or unions) making the application and that a majority of workers in the bargaining unit 'would be likely' to vote in favour of recognition of the union in a ballot (para 36).

An application is not admissible if an agreement is already in force in respect of any of **19.63** the workers who fall within the relevant bargaining unit. This may be so even though the agreement had not been used to determine terms and conditions and the recognised union had at most one member amongst the workers (*R (on application of the NUJ) v CAC* [2006] IRLR 53). An agreement is in force when it can be shown to be binding on the parties to it. When challenged, this was held not to be incompatible with Art 11 of the European Convention on Human Rights because of the mechanism of derecognition being available (*R (ota Boots Management Services Ltd) v CAC* [2014] IRLR 887).

In order to discourage competing applications by rival unions, the CAC must reject appli- **19.64** cations covering any part of the same bargaining unit where there is already a collective agreement in place (paras 38(2) and 51(1)). However, it will accept a single, joint application made by two or more unions where they can show they will cooperate with each other and will accept 'single-table bargaining' if this is what the employer wants to occur (para 37).

The CAC may require information from the union or employer in order for it to make a **19.65** decision (para 170A). If a party fails to comply the CAC 'may draw an inference against the party concerned' (para 170A(7)).

19.66 By para 18A(1), within five working days starting with the day after that on which the CAC gives the employer notice of acceptance of the application, the employer must supply the following information to the union:

(a) a list of the categories of worker in the proposed bargaining unit;
(b) a list of the workplaces of the workers in the proposed bargaining unit; and
(c) the number of workers the employer reasonably believes to be in each category at each workplace.

The lists and numbers which are supplied under this paragraph must be as accurate as it is reasonably practicable to be in the light of the information in the possession of the employer at the time when he complies with the duty.

Bargaining unit for statutory recognition purposes

19.67 Once the CAC has accepted an application as admissible, the next stage will depend on whether or not the parties have already agreed the appropriate bargaining unit for collective bargaining purposes. The CAC may extend time for the parties to agree a bargaining unit if it sees fit. Where they have agreed the scope of the bargaining unit, the CAC will go on to consider the issue of recognition straight away (see below). Otherwise, it must first help the parties to try once more to agree the bargaining unit. If a voluntary solution still proves elusive, the CAC will have to select the bargaining unit itself and impose this on the parties. In doing so, it will have to take various factors into account, but the overriding consideration must be the compatibility of the unit with effective management (paras 18 and 19). The factors to be taken into account in this connection (and subject to the overriding criterion) are:

(a) the views of the employer and of the union (or unions);
(b) existing national and local bargaining arrangements;
(c) the desirability of avoiding small, fragmented bargaining units within an undertaking;
(d) the characteristics of workers falling within the proposed bargaining unit and of any other employees of the employer whom the CAC considers relevant; and
(e) the location of workers.

19.68 *R v CAC, ex p Kwik Fit (GB) Ltd* [2002] IRLR 395 remains the crucial judgment on the definition of the bargaining unit, and in effect decided that a light touch should be taken to this issue by the CAC. The only matter in issue between the parties as to the scope of the bargaining unit was its geographical scope rather than the nature of the workers to be comprised within it (which is often a further source of controversy at this stage). Kwik Fit presented evidence before the CAC (which was uncontested) to the effect that it was an integrated, nationally run operation with standard basic terms and conditions of employment. Notwithstanding this, the CAC decided that Greater London on its own was an appropriate bargaining unit in the circumstances. The Court of Appeal concluded that the CAC's task is to start with the only proposal that it has before it, which is that contained in the union's request for recognition, and to determine whether that proposal is 'appropriate', and that the statutory test is set at the comparatively modest level of 'appropriateness' rather than the optimum or best possible outcome (para 7). The CAC thus has a broad discretion on the appropriateness of the bargaining unit with which the Administrative Court will be reluctant to interfere (*R (on application of Cable & Wireless Services UK Ltd) v CAC* [2008] IRLR 425). Irrationality includes a failure to have regard to a material matter or the taking into account of an irrelevant matter and an error of law will usually comprise a failure to construe and so to apply a statutory provision correctly.

Paragraph 19 was clarified by the ERA 2004 so that by subsection (3) if the CAC decides **19.69** that the proposed bargaining unit is not appropriate, it must also decide within the relevant decision period a bargaining unit which is appropriate. Further, the role of the employer is such that: 'In taking an employer's views into account for the purpose of deciding whether the proposed bargaining unit is appropriate, the CAC must take into account any view the employer has about any other bargaining unit that he considers would be appropriate.' This seeks to clarify the position further in favour of the employer following the decision in *Kwik Fit*.

A union's entitlement to recognition will depend on the amount of support which it has **19.70** within the bargaining unit in question, which is usually measured by means of a secret ballot of all the workers in the unit. However, a ballot may be unnecessary where a majority of those employed in the bargaining unit are already union members. If this is the case, the CAC will merely make a declaration ordering the employer to recognise the union without further ado. The only exception is where the CAC decides that a ballot should be held anyway, either because a significant number of union members have indicated that they do not support recognition, or because there is evidence to suggest that the membership figures may have given a misleading impression of the degree of genuine support for recognition in the bargaining unit, or 'in the interests of good industrial relations' (para 22).

When ACAS seeks to bring about a settlement of a recognition dispute it may, on the **19.71** request of the parties, itself hold a ballot of workers involved in the dispute or ascertain the union membership of such workers (s 210A of the TULR(C)A). There is a right of unions to communicate with workers by para 19C so that long before the ballot period, the union may apply for the appointment of a 'suitable independent person' to handle communication following the acceptance of the application and ending with any of these stages: withdrawal of the application; a declaration of invalidity; a declaration of recognition; or the decision to appoint a person to conduct a ballot. The employer must give to the independent person the names and home addresses of the relevant workers or those who later become such a relevant worker. The costs are to be borne by the union(s) who sought the appointment (para 19E(2)). If the employer fails to fulfil a duty which it is under, the CAC may order the employer to remedy the defect by a 'remedial order' and the CAC may declare a union to be recognised if the employer fails to comply with such a remedial order.

Statutory recognition: Ballots

Where the union membership is short of a majority of members in the bargaining unit, the **19.72** CAC will hold a secret ballot to determine the level of support for recognition within the bargaining unit (para 23). The CAC does not conduct the ballot itself, but delegates the supervision of this task to a 'qualified independent person', whom it must appoint. The ballot may take place either by post, or in the workplace or workplaces concerned, and, in certain circumstances, the CAC will be able to specify a mixture of methods to be adopted (para 25). If an employee is absent during a workplace ballot he may be given an opportunity to vote by post (para 25(6A)).

In order to ensure the fairness of the balloting process, the Schedule imposes a number **19.73** of duties on the employer, including a general duty to cooperate with the union and the independent person and an obligation to allow the union 'reasonable' access to the workforce during the run-up to the ballot itself (para 26). Where an employer fails to fulfil any of its duties under para 26, the CAC has the power initially to issue an order requiring it to do so, and, where the employer persists in its default, may issue a declaration granting the union recognition without the need for a ballot (para 27), although this has not yet occurred to date.

19.74 During the ballot, the employer must not make any offer to any worker within the bargaining unit, which 'has or is likely to have the effect of inducing any or all of them not to attend any relevant meeting between the union(s) and the bargaining unit workers and is not reasonable in the circumstances' (para 26(4A)). Further, the employer must not take or threaten any action against a worker on that ground (new para 26(4B)). The employer must also not refuse a request for a meeting between the union and the relevant workers in the bargaining unit in the absence of the employer or any representative of his. He must not seek to record or otherwise be informed of the proceedings at any such meeting or refuse to give an undertaking that he will not seek to record or otherwise be informed of such proceedings. This is designed to curb what were seen to be heavy-handed tactics by some employers in the period leading up to a ballot aimed at reducing support for recognition. The CAC has general jurisdiction to intervene in respect of the propriety of ballots (*R (on the application of Ultraframe (UK) Ltd) v CAC* [2005] IRLR 641).

19.75 By para 27A, a party uses an unfair practice if, with a view to influencing the result of the ballot, that party:

(a) offers anything to a worker entitled to vote in the ballot in return for the worker's agreement to vote in a particular way or to abstain from voting;
(b) coerces or attempts to coerce a worker entitled to vote in the ballot to disclose—
    (i)   whether he intends to vote or to abstain from voting in the ballot, or
    (ii) how he intends to vote, or how he has voted, in the ballot;
(c) dismisses or threatens to dismiss a worker;
(d) takes or threatens to take disciplinary action against a worker;
(e) subjects or threatens to subject a worker to any other detriment; or
(f) uses or attempts to use undue influence on a worker entitled to vote in the ballot.

19.76 A party may complain to the CAC that another party has failed to comply with these requirements (para 27B(1)) but a complaint must be made on or before the first working day after the date of the ballot or the last date of the ballot if spread over several days (para 27B(2)). A complaint will only succeed if the CAC is satisfied that the use of the unfair practice 'changed or was likely to change in the case of a worker entitled to vote in the ballot his intention to vote or abstain from voting; his intention to vote in a particular way; or how he voted' (para 27B(4)). If the CAC decides that the complaint is well founded it may order the party concerned to take any action specified or give notice that it intends to hold a secret ballot on recognition (para 27C(3)).

19.77 The action to be taken must be such as 'the CAC consider reasonable in order to mitigate the effect of the failure of the party to comply with its duty' (para 27C(5)). Similar provisions are made for derecognition ballots (para 119) as a mirror image. There are special provisions if the unfair practice consists in or includes the use of violence or dismissal of a union official (para 27D(1)). If the party concerned is the employer, the CAC may award recognition without more (para 27D(3)) and if it is the union which is in default, it may make a declaration conversely that the union is not entitled to be recognised.

19.78 The costs of the ballot are to be shared equally between the employer and the union, and where two or more unions are involved the 'union half' will be apportioned equally between them unless they indicate a contrary intention to the person conducting the ballot (para 28). An appeal against a demand for costs may be made to the employment tribunal (para 165A).

Once all of the votes have been counted, the qualified independent person will notify the **19.79**
CAC of the result of the ballot. The CAC will issue a declaration awarding the union
recognition only if a majority vote is in favour of this, and the number so voting must constitute at least 40 per cent of the total number of workers in the bargaining unit (para 29).

Method of bargaining following a declaration of recognition

A declaration of recognition by the CAC does not put an end to the process. The union **19.80**
and employer have to move on to negotiations about the contents of what the Schedule
calls the 'method of collective bargaining' (para 30). This is the bargaining procedure
that the parties will undertake to observe during the lifetime of the statutory recognition arrangement (ie covering such matters as when collective bargaining negotiations
are to take place, who is to attend, what provisions are to be made in the event of a
failure to agree, etc). The CAC will be asked to impose a method of collective bargaining where the parties are unable to agree (para 31), although it is unusual that they
cannot agree. If they have to adjudicate, the CAC must take into account the model
contained in the Trade Union Recognition (Method of Collective Bargaining) Order
2000 (SI 2000/1300). Even when the parties have had a method of collective bargaining imposed on them in this way, the Schedule allows them to vary this by mutual
agreement in writing (para 31(5)), thus emphasising voluntariness as throughout the
schedule.

The method imposed by the CAC will have the force of a binding contract between the **19.81**
union and the employer, unless the parties agree otherwise in writing (para 31(5)). The
only means of enforcing a legally binding method of collective bargaining is, however, by
an application to the civil courts for specific performance (para 31(6)), although the parties may apply to the CAC for 'assistance' in certain circumstances (para 32).

Change in bargaining unit

Part III of the Schedule contains important provisions where a change occurs that may **19.82**
affect the continued viability of statutory recognition. The change can be any of the
following:

(a) a change in the organisation or structure of the business carried on by the employer;
(b) a change in the activities pursued by the employer in the course of business carried on
     by him; or
(c) a substantial change in the number of workers employed in the original bargaining unit.

Where either side believes that, because of any such change, the original bargaining **19.83**
unit is no longer appropriate, it may apply to the CAC, which will (if the parties are
unable to reach their own agreement) determine if this is in fact the case and, if so,
select a new bargaining unit (or units) as appropriate to the changed circumstances
(paras 66–73). Under a similar procedure, the union has the right to make an application to the CAC where the employer informs it that the employer believes the original bargaining unit to have ceased to exist on account of one of the changes listed
above and wishes to bring statutory recognition to an end (paras 74–81). Where the
CAC imposes one or more new bargaining units under either of these procedures, it
must be satisfied that this does not disrupt any other collective bargaining arrangements (either statutory or voluntary) and that the difference between the original and
new bargaining units is not such as to require a fresh test of support for recognition
(paras 82–6).

Where the CAC is not satisfied of the latter, it will hold a ballot of workers in the new **19.84**
unit, organised along much the same lines as before (paras 88–9). A ballot will not be

necessary, however, where a majority of workers in a new unit already belong to the union, unless (on the same grounds as in para 22 above) the CAC decides to hold a ballot anyway in the interests of good industrial relations (para 87). The CAC will issue a new declaration awarding the union statutory recognition in respect of the new bargaining unit if the new unit has a majority of union members, or the union wins majority support for recognition in a ballot.

Voluntary recognition

19.85 Part II of the Schedule gives to the union the option, once it has invoked the statutory recognition procedure under Pt I, to bring it to an early halt on the ground that the employer has agreed to recognise it voluntarily. From the union's perspective the main advantages of recognition under Pt II over entirely voluntary recognition are: (1) that the employer may not bring the former to an end before three years have elapsed unless the parties agree otherwise (para 56(4)) (whereas the union may terminate the agreement for recognition at any time); and (2) recognition under an agreement for recognition allows either side to apply to the CAC to impose a method of collective bargaining in the same way as for statutory recognition (see above).

Derecognition

19.86 Parts IV, V, and VII contain various procedures allowing either the employer or workers in the bargaining unit to apply to the CAC to bring statutory recognition to an end after a period of three years (these provisions do not apply to 'voluntary' recognition under Pt II).

19.87 Generally speaking, these procedures take a very similar form which is in a mirror image to that for statutory recognition under Pt I, including the ultimate test of a secret ballot of all the workers in the bargaining unit concerned. Under Pt IV, the employer may apply for de recognition on the ground that it now employs fewer than the threshold figure of twenty-one workers (paras 99–103), or that there is no longer majority support for recognition within the bargaining unit (paras 104–11). One or more workers in the bargaining unit can also apply to end the statutory bargaining arrangements on the ground that there is no longer majority support for recognition within the bargaining unit (paras 112–16).

19.88 Part V provides the employer with a slightly different procedure in cases where the CAC originally awarded the union 'automatic' statutory recognition (ie on the basis that a majority of workers already belonged to the union, without the need for a ballot). Under this procedure, the CAC will first examine whether the union has in fact lost a majority of membership within the bargaining unit and, if so, hold a ballot to test whether it nevertheless enjoys majority support (paras 122–33).

19.89 Part VI of the Schedule is almost unique, in that it allows the CAC to interfere with purely voluntary recognition arrangements, which, as we already have seen, are normally out of bounds to it. Paragraph 137 allows one or more workers to apply to the CAC to end an employer's voluntary recognition of a *non-independent* trade union in respect of the bargaining unit to which they themselves belong. The procedure after this largely follows that for derecognition under Pt IV, including the test of a secret ballot of all the workers in the bargaining unit (paras 134–48).

19.90 Part VII covers the situation where a previously independent trade union loses its certificate of independence (a virtually unheard-of occurrence). The effect of such a loss will be to convert any statutory recognition arrangement that the union has into a voluntary recognition arrangement. In principle, this would leave the union open to attack by a disgruntled workforce by means of an application for derecognition under Pt VI.

The balloting provisions for Pts IV–VI of the Schedule are mainly contained in paras **19.91** 117–21. They are, for the most part, a mirror image of those for statutory recognition, described above.

The mechanism which was available of derecognition meant that the process in para **19.92** 35 did not infringe ECHR law (*R (ota Boots Management Services Ltd) v CAC* [2014] IRLR 887).

Detriment/dismissal in relation to recognition or derecognition

Part VII contains provisions to protect 'workers' from suffering a detriment on grounds **19.93** related to recognition or derecognition under the Schedule. Paragraph 156(1) states that a worker must not be subjected to a detriment by any act or any deliberate failure to act by his or her employer which takes place on any of the following grounds:

(a) the worker acted with a view to obtaining or preventing the employer recognising a union under the Schedule;
(b) the worker indicated that he or she supported or did not support the employer recognising a union under the Schedule;
(c) the worker acted with a view to securing or preventing the ending of bargaining arrangements under the Schedule;
(d) the worker indicated that he or she supported or did not support the ending of bargaining arrangements under the Schedule;
(e) the worker influenced or sought to influence the way in which votes were to be cast by other workers in a ballot arranged under the Schedule;
(f) the worker influenced or sought to influence other workers to vote or to abstain from voting in such a ballot;
(g) the worker voted in such a ballot; or
(h) the worker proposed to do, failed to do, or proposed to decline to do, any of the above.

The employer will not be liable for inflicting a detriment in cases where the worker's act or omission (as described above) is deemed to have been unreasonable (para 156(3)).

Where a worker alleges that he has suffered a detriment in breach of para 156, the rem- **19.94** edy may be gained from a complaint to an employment tribunal. This should be brought within three months of the act or failure complained of, unless the tribunal is satisfied that it was not reasonably practicable for the worker to do so, in which case it will accept the complaint so long as the worker manages to present it within whatever further period the tribunal regards as reasonable (para 157). The burden of proof lies on the employer to show the ground on which it has acted or failed to act (para 158).

If the tribunal finds the worker's complaint to be well founded it must make a declaration **19.95** to this effect and may order the employer to pay compensation. The amount awarded should be whatever 'the tribunal considers to be just and equitable in all the circumstances having regard to the infringement complained of and to any loss sustained by the complainant which is attributable to the act or failure which infringed his [or her] right', including but not limited to:

(a) any expenses reasonably incurred by the complainant in consequence of the act or failure to act complained of; and
(b) loss of any benefit which the complainant might reasonably be expected to have had but for that act or failure (para 159).

The tribunal may reduce an award of compensation where the complainant has failed **19.96** to mitigate his loss, or where action by the complainant caused or contributed to the employer's detrimental act or failure to act. There is a limit on compensation in cases where the detriment complained of is the termination of a contract other than a contract of employment. In this situation, a successful complainant will be entitled to a sum which is no greater than the total of the basic and compensatory awards which he would have received if the claim had been one for unfair dismissal (para 160).

19.97 Paragraph 161 prohibits dismissal of an employee on grounds relating to recognition or derecognition under the Schedule. Such a dismissal is treated as automatically unfair if the reason, or main reason, for it is one of those already set out above in relation to detriment (although para 161 naturally refers to 'employee' rather than 'worker'). The employer's defence that the employee's action or omission was 'unreasonable' also applies (see above). As in other categories of automatically unfair dismissal, there is no qualifying period for such claims. Claims are governed by the normal rules for unfair dismissal cases (on time limits, compensation etc).

19.98 In common with some other types of claimant, an employee who claims to have been unfairly dismissed on one of the grounds listed above will be entitled to apply to the tribunal for interim relief, so long as he or she does so within the seven days immediately following the effective date of termination. Interim relief, in this context, will consist of an order for reinstatement, re-engagement or the continuation of the employee's contract (ss 128 and 129 of the ERA 1996).

19.99 Paragraph 162 states that the dismissal of an employee will be treated as 'automatically' unfair if:

(a) the reason or main reason for the dismissal was that the employee was redundant; but
(b) the circumstances constituting the redundancy situation applied equally to other employees in the same undertaking who held positions similar to that held by the employee in question and who have not been dismissed by the employer; and
(c) the reason or main reason why the employee in question was selected was one of those already listed above in relation to detriment.

Other statutory provisions

19.100 A further statutory provision for recognition is contained in the Transfer of Undertakings (Protection of Employment) Regulations 2006. Where there is a transfer of undertaking 'whether by sale or by some other disposition or by operation of law', the transferee must continue to recognise any trade union recognised by the transferor, provided that 'the undertaking or part of the undertaking transferred maintains an identity distinct from the remainder of the transferee's undertaking' (reg 6). There is, however, no specific enforcement provision and it may thus remain rather a pious exhortation (see Chapter 18).

19.101 It is also unlawful on the ground of a requirement of union membership to:

(a) fail to include any person or company on a list of approved suppliers of goods or services;
(b) terminate a contract for the supply of goods or services;
(c) exclude anyone from the list on which tenders are invited;
(d) fail to permit a person to submit a tender; or
(e) otherwise determine not to enter into a contract with a person for the supply of goods or services.

(TULR(C)A 1992, s 145.)

The Act also outlaws a requirement that another party to a contract recognise a trade **19.102** union or negotiate or consult with it. Sections 186 and 187 of the TULR(C)A 1992 provide an action for breach of statutory duty to a person who is subject to such a condition. That may be any other party to the contract or 'any other person who may be adversely affected by its contravention'. There is no trade dispute immunity under s 219 of the TULR(C)A 1992 for a union which seeks to enforce the union membership requirement (see 21.154).

J RIGHT OF TRADE UNIONS TO INFORMATION IN SUPPORT OF COLLECTIVE BARGAINING

A vital factor in facilitating collective bargaining is the provision of information by the **19.103** employer to the unions so that discussion may proceed on an informed basis. It was only with the EPA 1975 (now the TURL(C)A 1992, ss 181 to 185) that the disclosure of information so long advocated in trade union circles became a reality, and then arguably in a most attenuated form. One major defect is that, based as it is on a threshold of recognition, an employer can resist the disclosure of information on a particular subject by refusing to bargain at all on that issue (*General and Municipal Workers' Union et al & BL Cars Ltd*, CAC Award No 80/65). The right may take on a new lease of life as unions come to achieve recognition through the statutory mechanism against hostile employers.

Trade Union and Labour Relations (Consolidation) Act 1992

What must be disclosed

The employer must 'disclose to any recognised union, information: **19.104**

(a) without which the trade union representative would be to a material extent impeded in carrying on with him ... collective bargaining; and
(b) which it would be in accordance with good industrial relations practice that he should disclose to them for the purposes of collective bargaining' (TULR(C)A 1992, s 181(2)).

Collective bargaining is defined by s 178 of the TULR(C)A 1992 as concerned with: **19.105**

(a) terms and conditions of employment, or the physical conditions in which any workers are required to work;
(b) engagement or non-engagement, or termination or suspension of employment or the duties of employment of one or more workers;
(c) allocation of work or the duties of employment between workers or groups of workers;
(d) matters of discipline;
(e) a worker's membership or non-membership of a trade union;
(f) facilities for officials of trade unions; and
(g) machinery for negotiation or consultation, and other procedures, relating to any of the above matters, including the recognition by employers or employers' associations of the right of a trade union to represent workers in such negotiation or consultation or in the carrying out of such procedures.

These are largely the same as for trade disputes.

It may be difficult for a union to say it is impeded in collective bargaining through lack **19.106** of information when it has *ex hypothesi* managed without it for many years past. The general test was stated in CAC Award No 78/353 para 20 as being: 'Is the information sought in this case relevant and important in general terms?'

19.107 The relevant ACAS code of practice (last revised 1998) directs negotiators to:

> take account of the subject-matter of the negotiations and the issues raised during them; the level at which negotiations take place (department, plant, division, or company level); the size of the company; and the type of business the company is engaged in.

19.108 Joint understandings are especially encouraged. The Code sets out the following list of subjects in which information should be provided but they are not the only evidence of good practice; they serve neither as a checklist nor are they intended to be exhaustive:

(a) *pay and benefits*: principles and structure of payment systems;
(b) *conditions of service*: policies on recruitment, redeployment, redundancy, training, equal opportunity and promotion; appraisal systems; health, welfare, and safety matters;
(c) *manpower*: numbers employed analysed according to grade, department, location, age and sex; labour turnover; absenteeism; overtime and short-time; manning standards; planned changes in work methods, materials, equipment, or organisation; available manpower plans; investment plans;
(d) *performance*: productivity and efficiency data;
(e) *financial*: cost structures; gross and net profits; sources of earnings; assets; liabilities; allocation of profits; details of government financial assistance; transfer prices; loans to parent and subsidiary companies and interest charged.

This does not extend to commercial information about the market share of products, cash flow, and government assistance.

19.109 The details which are sought must be relevant for the description of workers in which the union is recognised, and the application must be made in writing by a representative of the union, defined as: 'an official or other person authorised by the trade union to carry on such collective bargaining' (TULR(C)A 1992, s 181(1)). It is not, however, sufficient to disclose material to representatives only on condition of its not being available to full-time officers of the union or denying access to individual members (*IPC Ltd and the National Union of Journalists*, CAC Award Nos 80/4, 78/711, 80/73). The union may require the information to be given in writing but not that any particular documents be produced. It is possible that the employer could be sued for misstatement in the event of false information being provided.

Restrictions on disclosure

19.110 There is a list of exceptions from the right to information which must normally be proved by the employer (TULR(C)A 1992, s 182). They relate to cases where:

(a) Disclosure would contravene a prohibition imposed by *statute*. This served, for example, to exclude a survey of earnings in an industry since the copyright was in the surveying company (*Joint Credit Card Co & NUBE*, CAC Award No 78/2/2).
(b) Information has been communicated to the employer *in confidence* or where he has obtained it in consequence of the confidence reposed in him by another person.
(c) Information which relates to an *individual*, unless that person has consented to its disclosure. This arises particularly where grading schemes are in issue. While the CAC in *Rolls Royce Ltd & ASTMS*, CAC Award No 80/30 said that such information should be given even where it might enable an individual to be identified, in Award No 79/121 an application for information about a directors' pension scheme was refused since it related only to individuals.

(d) Disclosure would cause *substantial injury* to the employers' undertaking. The Code of Practice suggests as examples where the employer might lose customers to competitors, where suppliers will refuse to supply necessary materials, and where the ability to raise funds to finance the company would be seriously impeded. It does not, however, allow the argument that the use of the information in negotiations would harm the company.

(e) The information has been obtained for the purpose of bringing or defending any *legal proceedings* (TULR(C)A 1992, s 182(1)(f)).

(f) The compilation or assembly of the information would involve an amount of work or expenditure out of all reasonable proportion to the value of the information in the conduct of collective bargaining (TULR(C)A 1992, s 182(2)(b)).

(g) Disclosure would involve a breach of *national security* and a certificate to this effect signed by the Minister is conclusive evidence that the information must be withheld (TULR(C)A 1992, s 182(1)(a)).

Remedies for failure to disclose collective bargaining information

To gain a remedy for failure to provide information is a lengthy process. Like the right **19.111** itself, it is a hybrid between the collective and individual enforcement (TULR(C)A 1992, s 183) and consists of these stages:

(a) The union applicant makes a *complaint* to the Central Arbitration Committee.

(b) The CAC may refer the matter to ACAS for settlement by *conciliation*, failing which—

(c) The CAC conducts a *hearing* at which anyone whom it considers to have a proper interest in the matter may be heard and the CAC must give reasons for its findings.

(d) If the CAC upholds the complaint it may make a *declaration* of the information which ought to be disclosed and a final date by which this must be done.

(e) If the employer still fails to comply, the union may make *a further complaint*, and also seek changes in those parts of the individual contract in respect of which the union is recognised (s 184).

The Act merely states that the CAC may award the terms claimed or others as it considers appropriate. There is no appeal from this finding.

There are also two other duties of disclosure, to which we now turn. **19.112**

Health and safety

Provided that a safety representative gives the employer reasonable notice, he may inspect **19.113** (and take copies of) any document which the employer is required to keep by virtue of the statutory health and safety provisions. There is also the more general duty on the employer to make available to him information which is within his knowledge and which is necessary for the safety representative to fulfil his functions. The Health and Safety Commission Code of Practice: Safety Representatives and Safety Committees (1978), reg 6 exemplifies:

(a) plans and performance of the undertaking, and any changes affecting the health and safety at work of the employees;

(b) technical data about hazards and necessary precautions; and

(c) accident records.

Pensions

Schedule 2 to the Social Security Act 1985 introduced twelve new sections into the Social **19.114** Security Pensions Act 1975 giving the Secretary of State for Social Services the power to make provisions for disclosure by trustees to members of a pension scheme and to a register of pensions schemes. They also prescribe the contents of a scheme's annual report and require schemes to obtain reports from qualified auditors and actuaries.

19.115 The Occupational Pension Schemes (Disclosure of Information) Regulations 1996 (SI 1996/1655) provide, *inter alia*, that documents containing the constitution of an occupational pension scheme must be made available by the trustees for inspection by members and prospective members, spouses, beneficiaries, and independent trade unions recognised in respect of members or prospective members. Copies of the actuarial valuation of the scheme (which must be carried out at least once every three and a half years) must also be open to inspection by the same persons and bodies.

K INFORMATION AND CONSULTATION ON TRAINING

19.116 Section 70B of the TULR(C)A 1992 entitles any trade union satisfying the qualifying conditions described below to be invited by the employer 'from time to time' to send representatives to a meeting to be:

(a) consulted about the employer's policy on training for workers within the bargaining unit;

(b) consulted about the employer's plans for training for those workers during the period of six months starting the day of the meeting (or, if the employer indicates that a shorter period is to elapse before the next meeting, that period); and

(c) informed about training provided for those workers since the previous meeting.

The employer must hold the first of these meetings no longer than six months after the union meets the qualifying conditions described below, and subsequent meetings no more than six months after the previous meeting.

Qualifying conditions

19.117 The right will apply only where:

(a) the trade union has obtained recognition for collective bargaining purposes as a result of a declaration by the CAC under Pt I of Sch A1 to the TULR(C)A 1992;

(b) the CAC has imposed a method of collective bargaining on the parties; and

(c) the parties have not subsequently agreed that the imposed method should not be legally binding, or have varied or replaced the method by agreement (s 70B(1)).

Where two or more trade unions satisfy these requirements, the right to consultation and information will apply to each of them (s 70B(7)).

Employer's duty to disclose information before meeting

19.118 At least two weeks before each meeting, the employer must provide the trade union with whatever information is required in order to ensure that the union's representatives can participate properly in the meeting and to comply with good industrial relations practice. This obligation is subject to the same limitations as the already established duty of disclosure during collective bargaining under s 181 of the TULR(C)A 1992 (see 19.102ff).

19.119 In fact, the union's power to do anything to influence training policy is extremely limited. The employer merely needs to 'take account of' the union's reservations, and even then only if they are presented in writing within four weeks of the meeting (s 70B(6)).

Enforcement and remedies

Where the employer fails to comply with its obligations under s 70B, the union has the **19.120** right to complain to an employment tribunal under s 70C of the TULR(C)A 1992. Where the tribunal finds the union's complaint well founded, it will make a declaration to this effect and may order the employer to pay compensation to each individual in the bargaining unit concerned (s 70C(3)). This compensation cannot exceed two weeks' pay, calculated in accordance with ch II of Pt XIV of the ERA 1996 and subject to the limit on 'a week's pay' specified in s 227(1) of that Act (s 70C(4) and (5)).

L THE ADVISORY, CONCILIATION AND ARBITRATION SERVICE (ACAS)

The policy of the statutes is to exclude 'trade disputes' ... from judicial review of the courts ... There is substituted for judicial review of trade disputes an advisory conciliation and arbitration process with ACAS as the statutory body to operate it. (Court of Inquiry into a dispute between Grunwick Processing Laboratories Ltd and members of APEX, Cmnd 6922, 1977.)

It is in the interests of everyone, above all the general public, that industrial disputes are **19.121** resolved peacefully and quickly. From early times, government services have therefore been made available independently to assist warring industrial parties. The role used to be filled mainly by the Ministry of Labour but its functions were transferred in 1969 to the quasi-autonomous Commission for Industrial Relations, the brainchild of the Donovan Commission. The Advisory Conciliation and Arbitration Service (ACAS) took over all the CIR's functions in 1974, originally on a non-statutory basis, although its constitution was soon laid down by EPA 1975 and it was given the duty:

of promoting the improvement of industrial relations, and in particular of encouraging the extension of collective bargaining and the development, and where necessary, the reform of collective bargaining machinery.

Its main strength in this respect lies in its complete independence from both of the two sides of industry and from the Government. The TULR(C)A 1992 clearly provides that it is not to be 'subject to directions of any kind from any Minister of the Crown as to the manner in which it is to exercise any of its functions under any enactment' (s 247(3)). The Service is instead controlled by a Council which is responsible for policy matters and consists of nine members serving part-time, and the chairman who holds office for five years. All are appointed by the Secretary of State of BEIS—three after consultation with employers and three on the recommendation of the unions, while the rest sit as independents. The Council was thus intended, like ACAS itself, to reflect whatever consensus existed in British industrial relations, and to be the constructive side of dispute management.

The chief functions of ACAS under the TULR(C)A 1992 include: **19.122**

(a) assistance in the settlement of complaints to *employment tribunals* for which purpose it employs about 200 conciliation officers;
(b) *arbitration* before independent arbitrators;
(c) *general advice* on industrial relations;
(d) *holding inquiries* into questions relating to industrial relations generally or in a particular industry;
(e) responsibility for various pieces of collective bargaining, usually in the public sector; and
(f) issuing some *codes of practice* (19.134–19.137).

19.123 The most important role of ACAS is its peacekeeping and firefighting functions, trying to prevent industrial action at the very first stages. It must, however, strike a fine balance between intervening too readily in disputes and yet being available if the parties desire its assistance. It thus has power where a *trade dispute* (as defined) exists 'by way of conciliation or by other means to offer assistance to the parties to the dispute with a view to bringing about a settlement'. The following methods, which are selected according to the circumstances of each particular dispute, will be considered in turn:

(a) conciliation (19.124);
(b) mediation (19.127);
(c) advice (19.128);
(d) inquiry (19.129); and
(e) arbitration (19.130).

Conciliation

19.124 Conciliation involves not so much making suggestions to the two parties, but rather providing a forum for discussion and procedural guidance to bring them together. Thus, the Service does not involve itself unless both sides agree, and not until internal procedures under the collective bargain have been exhausted (TULR(C)A 1992 s 210(1)). The hope is that it can then flexibly react to particular problems involved.

19.125 This process of conciliation requires considerable reserves of psychological analysis, and Professor Phelps Brown has described the conciliator's role thus (*The Growth of British Industrial Relations*, 1960, at 127):

> When the parties lose their tempers with one another too easily to be able to talk face to face he can go backwards and forwards between them. He may be able to devise proposals new in form or substance, which go some way to reconcile conflicting claims, or provide a rough compromise, or make it easier to give ground without losing face ... Especially when both sides have stuck fast, thinking it a sign of weakness to be the first to climb down, he can get them to make concessions because he can tell them what the other will do in return.

19.126 ACAS conciliation officers are also involved in conciliation on an individual level, since every complaint to an employment tribunal is examined by them to see whether a settlement is feasible.

Mediation

19.127 Mediation is a more intrusive and active process than conciliation, for the mediator, who may or may not come from the ACAS staff, usually makes recommendations of his own for a way out of an industrial dispute, and the parties then consider his suggestions.

Advice

19.128 ACAS not only offers advice on particular matters as exemplified in the TULR(C)A 1992, s 213, but also on aspects of industrial relations in general. Included are a telephone advice service and a comprehensive industrial relations handbook.

Inquiry

19.129 The offer of a far-ranging independent inquiry can sometimes defuse an apparently intractable industrial dispute by providing a calmer atmosphere in which to review all the underlying issues involved (TULR(C)A 1992, s 214). The generally held convention is that the parties call off their strike or lock-out pending the results of the inquiry. The TULR(C)A 1992 accords power to the Secretary of State to refer any matter connected with a trade dispute to a court of inquiry conducted either by one person or a board. Such 'courts' have been set up to consider some of the most damaging industrial disputes. The hearing before the court is invariably formal in procedure and it has power to compel witnesses, whose evidence may be heard on oath. It may otherwise generally regulate its own procedure, but it must lay a report before Parliament (s 215(3)). This method has been little used in recent years.

Arbitration

Arbitration is a much stronger step for the parties in dispute since it in effect delegates the industrial relations autonomy of both sides to a third party over whom they can have no control. A trade dispute may be referred to arbitration by ACAS with the consent of all parties and provided that internal bargaining procedures have already been adopted, unless there is a 'special reason' for by-passing such procedures. Further, before so referring it ACAS must have considered the likelihood of the dispute being settled by conciliation (TULR(C)A 1992, s 212(2)). The Service may itself appoint an arbitrator or a board of arbitrators, but none of them should be on the ACAS staff (s 212(1)(a)). Alternatively, the case may be referred to the CAC. **19.130**

M CENTRAL ARBITRATION COMMITTEE (CAC)

The Central Arbitration Committee replaced the Industrial Arbitration Board in 1975 but it traces its descent to the Industrial Court set up in 1919 and continues to act as an independent focus for arbitration, along with the following statutory jurisdictions (TULR(C)A 1992, s 259(1), Sch 3, para 7): **19.131**

(a) adjudication on complaints of failure to disclose information to a recognised trade union for the purposes of collective bargaining (TULR(C)A 1992, ss 183 to 185) (19.103);

(b) determination of applications relating to statutory recognition of trade unions for collective bargaining purposes under Sch A1 of the TULR(C)A 1992 (19.57) and in respect of European Works Councils.

Like employment tribunals, the CAC consists of a chairman sitting with 'wingmen' who are representatives of employers and employees; they seek to reach unanimous decisions, and where this is impossible the chairman acts as an umpire, his decision counting even if outvoted by the wingmen. Its procedure is flexible, and the Arbitration Acts do not apply (TULR(C)A 1992, s 263(6); *Imperial Metal Industries (Kynoch) Ltd v AUEW* [1978] IRLR 407). It has no power to summon witnesses nor to punish anyone for contempt and usually first considers written representations which are then amplified at a formal hearing, normally held in public.

While there is no appeal, its decisions are subject to judicial review by the Administrative Court of the High Court Queen's Bench Division but only where there is an error of law or a procedural irregularity. The judges have overly refrained from intervening in the CAC. Lord Widgery CJ inferred, from the lack of any appeal, that 'Parliament intended these matters to be dealt with without too much assistance from the lawyers' (*R v CAC, ex p TI Tube Divisional Services Ltd* [1978] IRLR 183; reiterated in *R v CAC, ex p Kwik Fit (GB) Ltd* [2002] IRLR 395). **19.132**

19.133 Like most administrative bodies, the CAC is not obliged to give reasons for its decisions (except when upholding a complaint of failure to disclose information for collective bargaining purposes) (TULR(C)A 1992, ss 183(3) and 184(2)), but it has broken from the practice of the old Industrial Court and sets out the 'general considerations' behind its awards. They are, however, to 'be read by the parties as a guide—not as a precise legal judgment'.

N CODES OF PRACTICE

19.134 Codes of practice are a fertile source of quasi-law and sometimes of confusion in the industrial relations area. A distinction must be now drawn in procedure and effect between codes promulgated by ACAS and BEIS. Section 199 of the TULR(C)A 1992 requires that ACAS provide guidance by codes of practice on disclosure of information and time off for trade union duties and activities, both of which were only generally defined in the statute. In the exercise of its discretion it has also published a code on disciplinary practice and procedures. All of these are intended as authoritative statements of proper practice.

19.135 Section 203 of the TULR(C)A 1992 now gives concurrent power to the BEIS Department also to issue codes of practice. The procedure here requires the Secretary of State to consult ACAS, issue a draft, consider representations, if necessary amend the draft, and then lay it before Parliament for approval. The codes of practice so far promulgated in this manner are on picketing, industrial action ballots, and access to the workforce prior to a recognition/derecognition ballot under Sch A1 of the TULR(C)A 1992. Significantly, the statutory aim of the codes is stated by the TULR(C)A 1992, s 203(1)(a), to be the promotion of improvement of industrial relations.

19.136 Section 207(1)) of the TULR(C)A 1992 clearly states that:

> a failure on the part of any person to observe any provision of a Code of Practice shall not of itself render him liable to any proceedings

but any such code is admissible in evidence, with the same persuasive but not decisive authority as the Highway Code has in road traffic cases. An important difference between ACAS and Secretary of State codes is that the latter may be referred to in the courts as well as employment tribunals and the CAC. This may be particularly important with regard to picketing, which often strays into the criminal area (see use of the code in *Thomas v NUM (South Wales Area)* [1985] IRLR 136).

19.137 Section 203(1)(b) of the TULR(C)A 1992 gives the Secretary of State for BEIS the power to issue codes of practice for the purpose of 'promoting what appear to him to be desirable practices in relation to the conduct by trade unions of ballots and elections and trade union learning representatives'. The ECtHR and Health and Safety Executive also have similar powers under their respective enabling Acts.

O HEALTH AND SAFETY AND COLLECTIVE BARGAINING

19.138 Health and safety matters were not considered to be issues for joint industry–management regulation before 1975. The Health and Safety at Work etc Act 1974 provided for the election of safety representatives by all employees at the appropriate workplace but this was soon repealed by EPA 1975, which channelled their appointment through recognised unions. The detail is contained in the Safety Representatives and Committees

Regulations 1977 (SI 1977/1500 as amended by SI 1992/2051), which provide for their appointment where one or more workers are employed by the employer which recognises the union. They are empowered to inspect the workplace, to investigate potential hazards and complaints, and to make representations to management. To enable them to do these tasks effectively, they must be provided with relevant documents and information by management, and, like union officials, they can take time off with pay to perform their statutory duties (Health and Safety at Work etc Act 1974, s 2(7) (20.55)).

Safety committees are plant level institutions and must be formed when at least two safety **19.139** representatives make such a written request to the employer. Guidance on all these issues is provided by a Health and Safety Commission Code of Practice, breach of which has the same effect as that of other such codes. Otherwise, there is no sanction on the employer for failure to carry out these responsibilities.

Consistent with the changes made to consultation over transfers of undertakings and **19.140** redundancy, the Health and Safety (Consultation with Employees) Regulations 1996 (SI 1996/1513) provide that where there are no union safety representatives, consultation must take place with employees directly or 'one or more persons in the group who were elected ... to represent that group for the purposes of such consultation' (reg 4(1)). They have the same rights to time off and protection against victimisation as other employee representatives. What is particularly noticeable about this structure is that the employer may consult employees individually should it so choose.

P EUROPEAN WORKS COUNCILS

The European Works Council Directive (94/45) requires organisations employing at **19.141** least 1,000 staff across the European Economic Area (the twenty-seven EU States, plus Norway, Iceland, and Liechtenstein), and at least 150 in two or more states, to establish a mechanism at European level for informing and consulting staff about transnational issues.

Scope

The Transnational Information and Consultation of Employees Regulations 1999 (SI **19.142** 1999/3323) apply to all multinationals of the requisite size, by virtue of inclusion of UK staff, whose central management is located in the UK. They do not apply to organisations which establish a European consultative body voluntarily, in accordance with Art 13 of the Directive; nor to multinationals which have already come under an obligation to establish a European Works Council (EWC) by virtue of their staff in other EEA states where the Directive has been implemented for some time.

Establishing the EWC

If no voluntary EWC agreement existed by 15 December 1999, either 100 employ- **19.143** ees, their representatives, or management might trigger a process leading to negotiations to set up an EWC or equivalent body. These should take place between central management and employee representatives in a Special Negotiating Body (SNB). The Regulations state that the SNB should consist of one representative from each EEA state where the company operates plus, where appropriate: one extra seat for a state where 20 to 39 per cent of the workforce within the EEA is employed; two extra for 40 to 60 per cent; and three extra for over 60 per cent. UK members of the SNB are to be elected by a general ballot of the UK workforce, although where more than one SNB seat is allocated to the UK, management has the option of dividing the workforce into equal constituencies.

19.144 If management refuses to enter into talks about setting up an EWC within six months of a request by the employees or their representatives, or fails to negotiate an EWC within three years thereof, a statutory EWC will be set up in accordance with the Annex to the Directive, which is attached to the Regulations.

Employee representatives

19.145 Employee representatives (including representatives of an independent trade union recognised for collective bargaining purposes) who are in place prior to the formation of an SNB or EWC have the right to request information concerning staff numbers to ascertain whether a company is covered by EWC legislation; to submit a written request to management for the creation of an EWC, or equivalent procedure; and to elect or appoint from their own ranks members of the EWC who represent the whole workforce.

19.146 Members of the SNB and EWC have rights to paid time off to perform their duties, and protections against detriment and unfair dismissal under ERA 1996. Management may withhold information from the SNB or the EWC only if disclosure could be harmful to the company. SNB and EWC members are also forbidden to disclose information provided to them in confidence.

Disputes and enforcement

19.147 Disputes arising in the UK about matters prior to the establishment of an EWC are referred to the Central Arbitration Committee. Disputes about the operation of an EWC, or failure to set one up within the three-year period, are handled by the EAT, except for challenges to the withholding of information, which are referred to the CAC.

The Information and Consultation of Employees Regulations

19.148 The Information and Consultation of Employees Regulations 2004 (SI 2004/3426) implement the further Information and Consultation Directive 02/04 for UK undertakings. The information and consultation procedure may be initiated by employees or the employer. If this process is initiated by employees, at least 10 per cent must seek it subject to a minimum of fifteen employees. The request must be written and must contain the names of the employees. The employer must initiate negotiations for an information and consultation procedure. Where there are pre-existing agreements the employer must show that they have been approved (*Stewart v Moray Council* [2006] IRLR 592).

19.149 If the CAC declares that the employer was in default the complainant may within three months apply to the EAT which must impose a financial penalty on the employer unless it can satisfy the EAT that his default resulted from a reason beyond his control or that he has 'some other reasonable excuse' (reg 20(7)). The maximum penalty is £75,000 (reg 23(2)).

Societas Europaea

19.150 A Societas Europaea may be incorporated under EU Regulation 2157/01 as implemented by the European Public Limited Liability Company Regulations 2004 (SI 2004/2326).

Such a company must give specified information to the employees or their representatives (reg 18).

The Occupational and Personal Pension Schemes (Disclosure of Information) Regulations **19.151** 2013/2734 provides for disclosure of information generally about the conduct of occupational pension schemes initially to the members themselves but also to recognised unions to any extent for collective bargaining in relation to members and prospective members of the scheme in question.

20

PROTECTION OF TRADE UNION AND COGNATE ACTIVITIES

A THE RIGHTS 20.01

B ACTIVITIES 20.08

   Scope 20.08

   Limitations 20.13

C WHAT TIME IS APPROPRIATE FOR TRADE
   UNION ACTIVITIES? 20.26

D DETRIMENT 20.28

E PROOF 20.32

F TIME OFF FOR TRADE UNION
   DUTIES 20.35

   Meaning of industrial relations
   duties 20.39

   Reasonableness of the time off
   sought 20.49

   Union learning representative 20.51

G TIME OFF FOR TRADE UNION ACTIVITIES . . 20.52

H TIME OFF FOR INDUSTRIAL RELATIONS
   TRAINING 20.54

I TIME OFF FOR HEALTH AND SAFETY
   REPRESENTATIVES 20.55

J PROTECTION OF HEALTH AND
   SAFETY ACTIVITIES 20.57

K RIGHTS OF PENSION FUND TRUSTEES . . . 20.67

L REMEDIES 20.69

   Detriment short of dismissal 20.70

   Failure to permit time off 20.72

   Dismissal: Compensation 20.73

   Interim relief .20.76

Workers shall enjoy adequate protection against acts of anti-union discrimination in respect of their employment. (Art 1(1), ILO Convention Concerning Application of the Principles of the Right to Organise and Bargain Collectively, No 88.)

Workers without distinction whatever shall have the right to establish and subject only to the rules of the organisation to join organisations of their own choosing without previous authorisation. (Art 2, ILO Convention Concerning Freedom of Association and Protection of Right to Organise, No 87.)

A THE RIGHTS

20.01 The rights of an employee to join an independent trade union and take part in its activities are safeguarded in many countries by their constitutions (eg France, Germany). In Britain the rights were enacted only in 1971 and are protected in these important ways by the Trade Union and Labour Relations (Consolidation) Act (TULR(C)A) 1992:

(a) By s 146, he has 'the right not to be subjected to any detriment', so that there must be no discrimination against him on this ground any more than by reason of race or sex (20.26). Section 14 of the EA 1980 and s 10 of the EA 1982 also outlawed acts short of dismissal designed to compel an employee to join a union.

(b) Under s 152, dismissal is regarded as automatically unfair (and it is as a reason in selecting an employee for redundancy) (TULR(C)A 1992, s 153) if the reason was that the employee:

(i) was, or proposed to become, a member of an independent trade union;

(ii) had taken, or proposed to take, part at any appropriate time in the activities of an independent trade union; or

(iii) had refused, or proposed to refuse, to become or remain a member of a trade union which was not an independent trade union.

The rights have been extended to cover employees with particular functions which are cognate to trade union duties, that is, those involved in health and safety activities, whether on behalf of a trade union or not, employee representatives (for consultation purposes), union learning representatives, and occupational pension fund trustees.

An employee so dismissed may claim statutory remedies even though he does not have the length of service normally necessary to apply, or even though he is over normal retiring age. Moreover, interim relief (under s 161), in the form of reinstatement or suspension on full pay until final determination of the complaint, is available to him (20.76).

(c) Officials and members of recognised unions are given the right to time off without pay (20.35), while union officials may take time off *with* pay to carry out their *duties* in connection with collective bargaining.

Important new provisions were introduced in 2004 outlawing various inducements relating to union membership and activities in order to accommodate the terms of the ECtHR judgment in *Wilson & Palmer v UK* [2002] IRLR 568. First, by a new s 145A of the TULR(C)A, a worker has the right not to have an offer made to him by his employer for the sole or main purpose of inducing the worker not to be (or seek to become) a member of an independent trade union, not to take part at an appropriate time in its activities, not to make use at an appropriate time of trade union services, or to be or become a member of any trade union. The notion of 'trade union services' is defined by statute as services which are made available to the worker by the union by virtue of his membership. **20.02**

Secondly, s 145B of the TULR(C)A provides that a worker who is a member of a recognised trade union has the right not to have an offer made to him by the employer if acceptance of the offer would have the result that the worker's terms of employment or any of them are no longer determined by collective agreement negotiated by or on behalf of the union. This is subject to the employer's sole or main purpose being to achieve that result. An award of £3,830 must be made if the employer is in breach of these provisions (s 145E(3)). **20.03**

Further, if an offer in breach of either section is accepted by the worker, and the acceptance results in the worker agreeing to vary his terms of agreement, the employer cannot enforce the agreement to vary. **20.04**

Thirdly, s 146 restricts any detriment where the employer seeks to prevent or deter the worker from using trade union services. **20.05**

Under powers introduced in the Employment Relations Act 1999, the Government passed the Employment Relations Act 1999 (Blacklists) Regulations 2010 (SI 2010/493). Regulation 3 prohibits the compilation, use, sale, or supply of a 'prohibited list', that is, a list which 'contains details of persons who are or have been members of trade unions or persons who are taking part or have taken part in the activities of trade unions' and which is drawn up 'with a view to being used by employers or employment agencies for the purposes of discrimination in relation to recruitment or in relation to the treatment of workers'. The remedy is an award of compensation with a minimum of £5,000 and **20.06** a maximum of £65,300. The tribunal may also recommend 'that the respondent take within a specified period action appearing to the tribunal to be practicable for the purpose of obviating or reducing the adverse effect of any conduct to which the complaint relates' (reg 8(1)(b)).

20.07 We first examine the scope of trade union activity (22.08–22.12) and the appropriate time when it may be carried out (22.26–22.27), which are central to all three rights. Whether the trade union is independent must be considered. It should, however, be emphasised that while the employee need not usually belong to a union *recognised* for the purposes of collective bargaining where there is a closed shop in operation, only members of the specified trade union(s) have these rights. Moreover, the general provisions do not apply to the police and armed forces (Police Act 1996, s 64, and ERA 1996, ss 192, 200).

B ACTIVITIES

Scope

20.08 The interpretation of the phrase 'activities of an independent trade union at any appropriate time' is key to s 146 and s 152 rights. It is also necessary to construe the words 'had refused or proposed to refuse to become or remain a member' of a trade union. The underlying tension in the case law was well expressed by Phillips J in *Lyon v St James Press Ltd* [1976] ICR 413 (a dismissal case):

> The special protection afforded to trade union activities must not be allowed to operate as a cloak or an excuse for conduct which may ordinarily justify dismissal; equally the right to take part in the affairs of a trade union must not be obstructed by too easily finding acts done for that purpose to be a justification for dismissal.

In *Dixon and Shaw v West Ella Developments Ltd* [1978] IRLR 151, the same judge said:

> [Section 58 of the EPCA 1978, now TULR(C)A 1992, s 152] was intended, and must have been intended, to discourage employers from penalising participation in activities of a fairly varied kind ... and should be reasonably, and not too restrictively, interpreted.

He gave little guidance to expand this statement but some examples are contained in the ACAS Code of Practice on Time Off for Trade Union Duties and Activities 2010: in para 37, where it details attendance at workplace meetings to discuss and vote on the outcome of negotiations with the employer, meeting full-time officers to discuss issues relevant to the workplace, and voting in union elections.

20.09 The cases have established that the following activities are among those protected: collecting union subscriptions; discussing union affairs (*Zucker v Astrid Jewels Ltd* [1978] IRLR 385); seeking advice from union representatives on industrial issues (*Stokes and Roberts v Wheeler-Green Ltd* [1979] IRLR 211); posting union notices (*Post Office v Crouch* [1974] 1 WLR 89); speaking at a recruitment forum (*Bass Taverns Ltd v Burgess* [1995] IRLR 596); and seeking recognition for a union (*Taylor v Butler Machine Tool Ltd* [1976] IRLR 133). The protection extends to criticism of the union itself (*British Airways Engine Overhaul Ltd v Francis* [1981] IRLR 9), and union recruiting activities even where, as in *Lyon v St James Press Ltd* (above), the employees cloaked their attempt to start a union chapel with utmost secrecy, and thus caused considerable ill feeling in the small respondent company. The EAT did say, however, that:

> unreasonable and malicious acts done in support of trade union activities might be a valid ground for dismissal.

The scope of trade union activities does not extend to strike action. It may, however, pro- **20.10** tect the enlisting by a member of the help of a union official to elucidate and negotiate the terms and conditions of her employment since this was 'to use a prayer book expression the outward and visible manifestation of trade union membership' (*Discount Tobacco Ltd v Armitage* [1990] IRLR 14). In *Speciality Care plc v Pachella* [1996] IRLR 248, the EAT supported the principle laid down in *Armitage* and held that the tribunal may consider whether the introduction of a union representative into the employment relationship had led to the employer dismissing the employee.

The trade union activities must have been at least part of what operated on the operations **20.11** manager's mind to make him do what he did (*Miller v Interserve Industrial Services Ltd* [2013] ICR 445). There was a genuine distinction between the operations manager being motivated by resentment at what he regarded as unacceptable pressure from the trade union official, as was the finding here, and being motivated by the characteristics of the shop stewards being put forward.

A controversial issue concerns the holding of union meetings in company time, with con- **20.12** sequent loss of production. On one view, this is tantamount to a strike, yet an employer should give reasonable time to his employees to attend union meetings which are necessary for the proper functioning of collective bargaining. In *Marley Tile Co Ltd v Shaw* [1980] ICR 72, Goff LJ was 'inclined to doubt' whether this was a protected activity, where the caller of the assembly in question was an unaccredited shop steward. Eveleigh LJ, however, thought that nothing should be done to 'fetter the judgment of members of employment tribunals'. All the Lord Justices agreed that the question should 'not be dressed up as a point of law'. However, it is difficult for employment tribunals to decide this issue, since the Court of Appeal gave no guidance as to criteria, even though in the instant case the Lord Justices criticised the 'industrial jury' for their 'broad brush approach'. The ACAS Code advises that meetings are protected where to hold the meeting is 'reasonable because of the urgency of the matter or where to do so would not adversely affect production or services'.

Limitations

Activities of trade union or trade unionist

An assault has been made on the generality of 'activities of a trade union' from at least **20.13** five directions. The first, a distinction between the activities of a *union* and a trade *unionist*, owes its provenance to *Gardner v Peaks Retail Ltd* [1975] IRLR 244, but this was criticised in *Palmer* and *Wilson* (see above 20.02). The claimant in *Gardner* was dismissed for having made various complaints to management about the unsatisfactory state of the staff room. She was not protected since 'individual complaints may be of a trouble-making kind ... if supported by a union this provides some guarantee that they have substance'. Kilner Brown J made the point forcefully in *Chant v Aquaboats Ltd* [1978] 3 All ER 102:

> The mere fact that one or two employees making representations happen to be trade unionists and the mere fact that the spokesman happens to be a trade unionist does not make such representations a trade union activity.

In this case a round-robin petition protesting against unsafe machinery was held not to be a trade union activity.

What authorisation must proceed from the union for the activities, and in what form, **20.14** is left unclear. It is not enough, however, that the claimants are trade union officers and considered a course of conduct to be in the interests of their members (*Stokes and Roberts v Wheeler-Green Ltd* (22.09 above)). A difficult case arises where there may be a union policy, contained in a conference resolution, to resist a particular management decision on the ground that such is inimical to employers' obligations regarding health and safety. If the union member wrongly takes that as a sanction for resisting management, is his action included? In *Drew v St Edmundsbury BC* [1980] ICR 513, a parks gardener was dismissed because of his refusal to clear snow during an official go-slow and his long-standing one-man campaign against the council's health and safety record. The EAT rejected his contention that he had been sacked for an inadmissible reason, first because the employment tribunal had no jurisdiction where he was dismissed during industrial action even though this constituted a continuation of his own campaign. The second ground for rejecting it was that he had no official standing in the union. It is submitted that a more suitable interpretation is that the protection should cover activities of the sort carried out by a trade union, even if in the particular circumstances, the precise *modus operandi* has not been referred to, nor received express approval from, the official union hierarchy. This would at once recognise the independent power of shop stewards, and deal more satisfactorily with the facts in *Chant*, for example.

Activities before employment

20.15 Secondly, in early cases the sections were held not to extend to activities *before* the applicant's employment began. In *City of Birmingham v Beyer* [1977] IRLR 211, a blacklisted trade unionist had to resort to a false name to get a job with the appellant and was sacked when recognised. Kilner Brown J said that union activity protected by the section 'could not conceivably refer to activities outside and before the employment began'.

20.16 Although the same conclusion was reached by the EAT in *Fitzpatrick v British Railways Board*, this was overturned by the Court of Appeal [1992] ICR 221. The Court of Appeal distinguished *Beyer* as dealing with a case where the reason for dismissal was obtaining employment by deceit. It was, however, perfectly possible in a general sense for what happened in a previous employment to form the reason for the dismissal in subsequent employment (per Woolf LJ at para 18). It is also unnecessary to identify precise activities (para 22). The political activities of the applicant were subsidiary to her trade union activities so that the dismissal was on trade union grounds.

Activities contrary to union rules

20.17 The third potential restriction relates to the position where the union activity is contrary to a particular union rule. This was accepted as a principle in *Marley Tile Co Ltd v Shaw* (20.12 above), although, on the facts, the court held that the action did not infringe rule 13 of the rules of the Amalgamated Union of Engineering Workers. In *McQuade v Scotbeef Ltd* [1975] IRLR 332, the employment tribunal went so far as to say that activities were not protected under this rubric if they were in breach of a union–management procedure agreement, while a shop steward who advised his members to strike was held not to have engaged in trade union activity since this was contrary to union policy as laid down in the Shop Stewards Handbook (*Fortune v Thames Water Authority*, IDS Brief 161, at 7).

Claim to recognition

20.18 The Court of Appeal in *Therm-A-Stor Ltd v Atkins* [1983] IRLR 78 narrowly construed the provision so that it did not apply to employees who were dismissed because the employer objected to the *recognition* of their union. Rather the section was concerned only with the *individual* employee's activities in the trade union. The situation in the *Atkins* case should be contrasted with that in *Farnsworth v McCoid* [1999] IRLR 626, where the employer objected not to the union but to the conduct of a particular individual while he was acting as shop steward. In these circumstances, the Court of Appeal concluded that a tribunal had been entitled to find that the employer's decision to remove his accreditation as a shop steward constituted action taken against the employee for his trade union activities even though the employer's reasons related to him uniquely and personally.

Strikes

Trade union activities cannot comprise strike action. Even so, this phrase may prove difficult to construe. One possibility is that it includes anything in breach of contract, but does a refusal to work voluntary overtime, which may not involve breach of contract, come within it? Is it confined to collective union action, or does it comprise individual protests? Would a demonstration to protest at government policy be included? An argument was raised in *Winnett v Seamarks Bros* [1978] ICR 1240 that the strike is a well-recognised activity of an independent trade union, but this was summarily rejected. Two rationales have been put forward for this result: **20.19**

(a) in *Brennan v W. Ellward (Lancs) Ltd* [1976] IRLR 378, that the activity was not at 'an appropriate time: The Employment Protection Act cannot extend to ... suddenly downing tools and leaving the premises, in order to consult their union officials elsewhere'; and

(b) in *Drew v St Edmundsbury BC* [1980] ICR 513, the EAT based its *obiter* conclusion on the fact that there was a different provision in the legislation for strike dismissals.

The fact that an employee carries out acts which are preparatory to a strike may, however, constitute trade union activities according to the EAT in *Britool Ltd v Roberts* [1993] IRLR 481.

In *Rath v Cruden Construction Ltd* [1982] IRLR 9, the EAT held that the protection against dismissal on grounds of trade union membership did not extend to inter-union disputes. **20.20**

Proposal to refuse to remain a member of a trade union

The Employment Act 1988 removed the limited remaining protection for the closed shop, and placed dismissal on the ground that an employee is not a member of any trade union or of one of a number of particular trade unions or has refused or proposes to refuse to become or remain a member, on exactly the same footing as dismissal on the grounds of trade union membership or activities whether or not there is a union membership agreement. **20.21**

In *Crosville Motor Services Ltd v Ashfield* [1986] IRLR 475, the claimant made it clear that unless there were changes in union policy and organisation, he would leave the union. The EAT held that the words in what is now the TULR(C)A 1992, s 152, rendering unfair a dismissal where an employee 'proposed to refuse to ... remain a member [of a trade union]', covered such a contingent event. Garland J said that the subsection 'is saying that if somebody refuses to remain a member of a union he can do it now; he can do it with effect from next week, or next month, or in six months' time ... That is something which can be conditional or contingent on something occurring or not occurring as the case may be'. **20.22**

Refusal of employment on trade union grounds

20.23 The Employment Act 1990 outlawed the last remnants of the closed shop by rendering unlawful the *pre-entry* closed shop. It has since been unlawful to refuse to a person employment on the ground that:

(a) he is a member of a trade union;
(b) he is not a member of a trade union;
(c) he will not agree to become a member of a trade union; or
(d) he will not cease to be a member of a trade union (now TULR(C)A 1992, s 137).

This includes refusal of employment on the grounds that an employee had at some time been engaged in trade union activities (*Harrison v Kent County Council* [1995] ICR 434). Where an advertisement indicates that employment is open only to a member of a trade union or a person who is not a member, a person who applied for but was refused employment is conclusively presumed to have been refused unlawfully. 'Advertisement' is also widely defined.

20.24 The provisions specifically tackle informal practices which were still common in some industries. Thus, it is unlawful where there is an arrangement or practice under which employment is offered only to persons who are put forward or approved by a trade union, and where the trade union puts forward or approves only persons who are members of the union, a person who is not a member of the union and who is refused employment in pursuance of the arrangement or practice is treated unlawfully. The term 'Refusal of employment' extends to a person who is made a 'spurious offer of employment which he does not accept', that is, when 'the terms are such as no reasonable employer who wished to fill the post would offer'. These prohibitions extend to an employment agency, and anyone who is refused the services of that agency may complain in a similar way.

20.25 A person thus refused employment may only complain to an employment tribunal. A complaint must be presented 'before the end of the period of three months beginning with the date of the conduct to which the complaint relates' subject to an extension if such complaint is not reasonably practicable (TULR(C)A 1992, s 139). Compensation is to be 'assessed on the same basis as damages for breach of statutory duty and may include compensation for injury to feelings' (TULR(C)A 1992, s 140(2)), but the total is subject to the limit for the compensatory award now £78,962 (s 140(4)). The sum is index linked to the retail prices index (Employment Relations Act 1999, s 34) and must be updated every September. The tribunal may also make a recommendation of action which 'appears practicable for the purpose of obviating or reducing the adverse effect on the complainant'; and if the respondent fails to comply with this, further compensation may be granted (s 140(1)(b)). Relief may also be directed against a trade union which puts pressure on an employer to act in breach of the above sections (s 142(1)). The appeal provisions and restrictions on contracting out found in the unfair dismissal area apply to this jurisdiction, and there are similar exclusions for Crown employees, those in police service, mariners, and offshore employees.

C WHAT TIME IS APPROPRIATE FOR TRADE UNION ACTIVITIES?

20.26 The appropriate time for trade union activities is defined as not only occasions 'outside the employee's working hours' but also time 'within working hours at which, in accordance with arrangements agreed with, or consent given by his employer, it is permissible for him to take part in those activities' (TULR(C)A 1992, ss 146(2), 152(2), 170(2)). In

Post Office v UPW [1974] ICR 378, Lord Reid declared that, 'it does not include periods when in accordance with his contract the worker is on his employer's premises, but not actually working'. He went on to cut down the scope of his judgment by saying that 'the incursion of these rights on the employer's rights ... must be reasonable' and the employer must not be caused substantial inconvenience. He continued: 'It is a very different matter to use facilities which are normally available to the employer's workers or to ask him to submit to some trifling inconvenience.' He went on:

> Discrimination against a man's trade union generally affects him personally. The prejudice to the man himself may be so small as to be negligible. But where it is substantial and a necessary consequence of the discrimination against the trade union and this must have been known to the employer the employer has in fact so acted as to worsen the man's position in comparison with that of a man in another union against which there has been no discrimination.

Interpreting 'arrangement' and 'consent' in the definition was central to the decision in **20.27** *Marley Tile Co Ltd v Shaw* [1980] ICR 72. The EAT had held that a meeting of maintenance men to protest about the shop steward's lack of credentials during working hours was 'at an appropriate time', because the legislation had to be construed in the light of 'actual industrial practice'. The Court of Appeal, however, disapproving of this 'broad brush approach', viewed the issue more narrowly. While consent might be implied, it could not arise by way of extension from the position at other workplaces, custom, and practice at the plant in question, nor the employer's silence. The EAT and employment tribunal were overruled because they 'considered too much the reasonableness of the behaviour and the reactions of the employees'.

D DETRIMENT

The Employment Relations Act 1999 replaced the term 'action short of dismissal' with the **20.28** broader term 'detriment', bringing this part of the TULR(C)A 1992 into line with other measures to protect union and employee representatives. 'Detriment' can be suffered as a result of 'any act, or any deliberate failure to act, by his employer' (s 146 of the TULR(C) A 1992). Consequential amendments are made to ss 147 and 148, to take account of the inclusion of deliberate omissions in the concept of 'detriment'.

There is exemption from liability where the employer's purpose includes the furthering of **20.29** 'a change in his relationship with all or any class of his employees'.

The employment tribunal, in deciding whether the dismissal was carried out on the **20.30** grounds of trade union activities, must consider why the employee was not considered by the employer for alternative work (*Driver v Cleveland Structural Engineering Co Ltd* [1994] ICR 372) as well as the reason for the dismissal itself. A discriminatory motive is not required, however (*Dundon v GPT Ltd* [1995] IRLR 403).

In *O'Dea v ISC Chemicals Ltd* [1995] IRLR 599, Mr O'Dea spent half of his time on **20.31** union activities and the remainder working as a packaging operator. He claimed under s 153 of the TULR(C)A 1992 that 'the circumstances constituting the redundancy applied equally to one or more employees ... who held similar positions [to those] held by him and who have not been dismissed by the employer' and that the reason for differentiation was on the grounds of his trade union activities. The question for the Court of Appeal was whether Mr O'Dea should be treated as in a 'special position' because of his union activities, or whether he should be compared with others in similar circumstances. The tribunal should have left out of account the fact that he spent half his time as a trade union official and limited their consideration to his status as a skilled manual worker, the nature of his work as a packaging operator, and his terms and conditions as a technical services operator (see also *Smiths Industries Aerospace and Defence Systems v Rawlings* [1996] IRLR 656).

E PROOF

20.32 Discrimination, whether on the grounds of race, sex, or trade union activities, is, as we have already seen, most difficult to prove. Unless the employer blatantly says, 'no trade unionists here', the evidence is likely to take the form of inferences, nods, and winks.

20.33 Lord Denning MR, dissenting in *Smith v Hayle Town Council* [1978] IRLR 413, said that the weight of the burden at least must depend 'on the opportunities and knowledge with respect to the facts to be proved which may be possessed by the parties respectively'. The other two Lord Justices took the orthodox approach, confirming *Goodwin Ltd v Fitzmaurice* [1977] IRLR 393, that the burden fell squarely on the claimant. The latter case also stands as authority for the rule that a tribunal must first decide whether the dismissal was for trade union activities before examining whether it was redundancy or some other ground (see also *Maund v Penwith DC* [1984] IRLR 24; and *Kuzel v Roche Products Ltd* [2007] IRLR 309 in respect of public interest disclosures).

20.34 Another problem in this area concerns the nature of collective decisions. In *Smith v Hayle Town Council* (above), the employee was dismissed by a one vote majority of the respondent council. Although he proved that at least one councillor was motivated by his dislike of trade unionists, this did not prove that it was the principal reason for the decision to dismiss. The task is slightly easier for an employee claiming to have suffered a detriment on trade union grounds. Section 148(1) of the TULR(C)A 1992 in that case places the burden on the employer to prove the purpose for which he acted or failed to act. Where he fails to do so, an employment tribunal may draw an adverse inference (*Southwark LBC v Whillier* [2001] ICR 1016, CA).

F TIME OFF FOR TRADE UNION DUTIES

20.35 Where his union is recognised, an official is entitled to time off with pay 'to carry out those duties … which are concerned with industrial relations between his employer and any associated employer and their employees' (s 168(1) of the TULR(C)A 1992), and this is in accordance with ILO Convention No 135. This is restricted to those duties concerned with negotiations about matters within s 244 of the TULR(C)A 1992 'in relation to which the trade union is recognised by the employer' or 'any functions related to or connected with any [such] matters … and the employer has agreed may be so performed by the trade union'. If the employer refuses, the official can complain to the employment tribunal and seek a declaration and compensation; however, he should not ignore the employer's refusal and take the time off regardless, since the statutory provisions do not allow that (*Ryford Ltd v Drinkwater* [1996] IRLR 16). 'Official' is defined as any officer of the union or branch and any other person elected under the union rules to represent the members or some of them (TULR(C)A 1992, s 119), thus clearly including a shop steward.

20.36 A part-timer serving as a trade union safety representative was held to be entitled to receive the same payment for the time which she spent attending a union training course as a full-time colleague (*Davies v Neath Port Talbot County BC* [1999] IRLR 769). The right to paid time off does not include time off between the hours of 7pm and 11pm when these are not normal hours of work (*Hairsine v Kingston upon Hull CC* [1992] ICR 212).

The ACAS Code of Practice on Time Off 2010 gives some indication of the duties for **20.37** which time off should be granted:

(a) collective bargaining with the appropriate level of management;
(b) informing constituents about negotiations or consultations with management;
(c) meetings with other lay officials or with full-time officials;
(d) interviews with and on behalf of constituents on grievance and disciplinary matters;
(e) appearing on behalf of constituents before an outside body; and
(f) explanations to new employees whom he or she will represent of the role of the union.

We will consider first the meaning of 'duties' and then the reasonableness of the time **20.38** taken off.

Meaning of industrial relations duties

The central problem with the section is that the essential terms 'industrial relations' and **20.39** 'duties' are nowhere defined, nor does the Code of Practice grasp this nettle. Moreover, there is an inevitable tension in that what is phrased as a right is, in reality, a privilege, since employers retain a significant degree of control over what time off is reasonable and when it should be taken.

In three EAT decisions these ambiguities surfaced and difficulties, especially in rela- **20.40** tion to unions organising in a group of companies, became apparent. In *Sood v GEC Elliott Process Automation Ltd* [1979] IRLR 416, an official of the union ASTMS claimed that he should be granted time off with pay to attend a meeting of his union's Telecommunications, Electronics and Automation Product Advisory Committee (PAC). This was a collection of representatives from GEC plants where the appropriate products were manufactured. It had no powers to represent anyone or negotiate with any GEC companies. Its brief was, instead, threefold:

(a) to exchange information and experience;
(b) to supply information to the ASTMS National Executive Committee; and
(c) to coordinate activities in relation to the affairs of members working with the relevant products.

The employment tribunal and Employment Appeal Tribunal considered that this was **20.41** 'a useful body,' so that by attending its meetings the members became 'better representatives'. The EAT's judgment, given by Slynn J, first made it clear that the section did not only cover those areas of collective bargaining for which the union was recognised. Further, the right was not only concerned with meetings with representatives of management; it also comprised planning, strategy, and discussion with other workers who were negotiating with their employers. Yet the EAT went on to refuse the instant application. Slynn J drew two distinctions in the crucial section of the judgment (author's italics):

> Although it was no doubt *beneficial* to the union members that their representatives should attend such meetings, attendance was *not required* in order to enable the official to carry out his duties ... We do not consider that the mere exchange of information between trade union officials themselves necessarily qualifies.

20.42 It may be argued, however, that 'duties' in s 168 of the TULR(C)A 1992 is used in the layman's sense of 'business, office or function' (*Shorter Oxford Dictionary*), rather than in the sense of distinguishing between what an official was and was not obliged to do. Thus, the adoption of the employee's contention that any meetings reasonably likely to be relevant to industrial relations are covered by the section, would be closer to the intention of Parliament.

20.43 In *Sood*, Slynn J also took a narrow definition of 'industrial relations'. Having said that 'industrial relations is capable of covering many matters', he then applied it to collective bargaining and nothing else (see also *RHP Bearings Ltd v Brookes* [1979] IRLR 452).

20.44 A wider approach to industrial relations duties was evident in the case of *Young v Carr Fasteners Ltd* [1979] IRLR 420. It concerned the analogous training subsection of s 168, which for these purposes uses the same concepts. Mrs Young, a GMWU shop steward, attended a course at the union's college called 'Pensions and Participation'. The EAT, reversing the view of the employment tribunal, held that she was, indeed, entitled to paid time off for this purpose. It was irrelevant that there were no negotiations in progress about pensions at the company. The judge thought that: 'Employees may well wish to consider making representations to the company ...'. It was, further, not a conclusive objection that the pension scheme was administered in such a way that no employee could at that time be a trustee, or that the scheme was substantially administered in accordance with the advice of an insurance company. On the narrow view in *Sood* it might be thought that for these reasons pensions were hardly within the duties of Mrs Young as a shop steward; a broader approach was clearly taken.

20.45 The problems with Slynn J's twofold distinction were also clearly demonstrated in *RHP Bearings Ltd v Brookes* (above). The RHP joint shop stewards' committee decided in 1978 to change its former practice and henceforth meet in working time. As a test case, Mr Brookes, a committee member, claimed paid time off in connection with the first such meeting. The employment tribunal allowed the application, but was criticised by the EAT, since it had not looked in detail at what took place at the meeting. In remitting the case, Bristow J said that:

> The approach of the new tribunal should be to examine each item discussed in the minutes and to consider, in its capacity as 'an industrial jury', whether it is a matter in which Mr Brookes was doing his duty as a union official concerned with industrial relations between the company and other employers in the group and the group work force.

The judgment goes on to give guidance that if 'only a proportion of time was spent on s 168 matters the Industrial Tribunal will probably think that only a proportion of the time should reasonably be paid for'.

20.46 A wider view was taken by the EAT in *Beal v Beecham Group Ltd* [1982] ICR 460. The ASTMS National Advisory Committee for the Beecham Group organised two subgroups on Products and Pharmaceuticals, and members sought time off to attend such meetings claiming they were trade union duties. The EAT thought that the subsection was not restricted to the actual transaction of industrial relations business; it was more generally concerned with industrial relations, but not, as such, a mere exchange of information. The test was not whether the meeting was essential. Here, 'a coordinated approach in industrial relations is a legitimate objective even though the negotiating groups comprise disparate groups of employees who might in the end achieve varied settlements'. The Court of Appeal agreed with this analysis. Moreover, the time off could not be made subject to a condition that it should be unpaid (*Beecham Ltd v Beal (No 2)* [1983] IRLR 317).

Unless the recognised union expressly or impliedly requires the attendance of an official **20.47** at a meeting, his attendance at the meeting cannot be a duty 'as such an official' within the statutory language. The right does not extend to functions which the shop steward as opposed to the union considers desirable (*Ashley v Ministry of Defence* [1984] IRLR 57). In *Adlington v British Bakeries (Northern) Ltd* [1989] IRLR 218, attendance at a union workshop on the implications of the proposed repeal of the Baking Industry (Hours of Work) Act 1954 was held to be within 'industrial relations duties'. The question was whether the meeting was 'sufficiently proximate' to actual negotiations with the employers to constitute 'industrial relations'. In this case there was a very close connection between repeal of the legislation and employees' working conditions.

This may also include meetings prior to negotiations, provided that there is sufficient **20.48** nexus between the collective bargaining and the duty involving the preparation for that particular issue (*London Ambulance Service v Charlton* [1992] ICR 773).

Reasonableness of the time off sought

The time taken off must be reasonable as to amount and the circumstances when it is **20.49** taken. The ACAS Code of Practice 2010 directs attention to, *inter alia*, the exigencies of production, services, and shifts in process industries, the size of the enterprise and the size of the workforce. An employer may also properly consider the occasions on which an applicant for time off had previously enjoyed time off in assessing the reasonableness of a further request. In *Wignall v British Gas Corporation* [1984] IRLR 493, the claimant had already been granted twelve weeks' leave for union business when he sought a further ten days for the preparation of a union district monthly magazine. The EAT upheld the tribunal's decision that it was reasonable for the employers to refuse the further time.

In *Thomas Scott & Sons (Bakers) Ltd v Allen* [1983] IRLR 329, the Court of Appeal **20.50** emphasised that the question of the reasonableness of the time off sought was a matter of fact for the employment tribunal, and the Court of Appeal would accordingly not interfere with the tribunal's view that it was unreasonable to seek leave for all eleven shop stewards at the same time. Moreover, May LJ appeared to suggest that the tribunal had to decide not only whether it was reasonable for them to attend the meeting, but also whether it was reasonable that they should be paid for so doing. This analysis is difficult to square with the wording of the section.

Union learning representative

By s 168A of the TULR(C)A 1992, introduced in 2002, an employer must permit an **20.51** employee who is a union learning representative time off for the purposes of carrying on these activities in relation to qualifying members of the trade union: analysing learning or training needs; providing information and advice about learning or training matters; arranging learning or training and promoting the value of learning or training; consulting the employer about carrying on such activities; or preparing for these matters. The representative must have undergone sufficient training to enable him to carry on these activities and the union must give to the employer notice of this fact. The amount of time off and the purposes for which it is taken are those that are reasonable in all the circumstances.

G TIME OFF FOR TRADE UNION ACTIVITIES

20.52 By s 170 of the TULR(C)A 1992, a trade union member is to be allowed reasonable time off during working hours *without pay* to take part in the *activities* of an independent trade union recognised by the employer for the purposes of collective bargaining. These activities need have nothing to do with industrial relations, provided they are reasonable. As the ACAS Code of Practice on Time Off for Trade Union Duties and Activities 2010 (para 35) states: 'To operate effectively and democratically, trade unions need the active participation of members in certain union activities.'

20.53 The issue is one of fact for the employment tribunal. The EAT held in *Luce v London Borough of Bexley* [1990] ICR 159 that whilst the words 'any activity of an independent trade union' should not be construed restrictively, it was not the intention of Parliament to include *any* activity at all. Rather, it had to be within the ambit of the relationship between employer and employee and that trade union. It must be linked with the employment relationship. The EAT thus upheld an employment tribunal decision that the applicant, the Honorary Treasurer of the Bexley Branch of the National Union of Teachers, was not allowed time off as a matter of right to attend a Trades Union Congress lobby of Parliament in connection with the Education Reform Bill which was then under consideration by Parliament. A lobby intended to convey only political or ideological objections to proposed legislation could not qualify under the relevant section. The Bexley Schools Subcommittee recommended that the local authority should refuse requests for trade union members to attend any parliamentary lobbies arranged by their trade unions. The EAT held that the resolution of the Bexley Schools Subcommittee was far too sweeping because it failed to consider the details of each case; some activities directed at Parliament might fall within the scope of s 170(1), such as those of a trade union which had developed specialist technical knowledge relevant to a measure before Parliament concerned with health and safety. In such a case representations arising out of such expertise might well satisfy s 170(1).

H TIME OFF FOR INDUSTRIAL RELATIONS TRAINING

20.54 Reasonable time off must also be given by the employer to a trade union *official* for training which is relevant to industrial relations duties and which is approved by the TUC or the claimant's own union (on relevance see *Ministry of Defence v Crook and Irving* [1982] IRLR 488). However, approval by the union alone is not sufficient and this was the message demonstrated by *Menzies v Smith & McLaurin Ltd* [1980] IRLR 180. The EAT decided that an employee had been properly refused time off to attend a union course on redundancy because its syllabus was not relevant to industrial relations duties, being far too general in scope. It covered issues like North Sea oil, import controls, and responses to the EEC, and the employee had failed to establish that anything he learned on the course would be of direct value to him in negotiations with the company. He was allowed time off as a union activity but he had no right to be paid for it.

I TIME OFF FOR HEALTH AND SAFETY REPRESENTATIVES

20.55 A duly appointed health and safety representative has a right to reasonable time off with pay to perform his function and to train therefor (Safety Representatives and Safety Committee Regulations 1977 (SI 1977/1500), reg 4, para 2). Where the employer provides an adequate internal course it is not necessarily reasonable to seek time off also to attend a TUC sponsored school (*White v Pressed Steel Fisher Ltd* [1980] IRLR 176).

The code of practice issued by the Health and Safety Commission states that safety rep- **20.56** resentatives should be given basic training as soon as possible after appointment and such further training thereafter as may be appropriate.

J PROTECTION OF HEALTH AND SAFETY ACTIVITIES

Section 44 of the ERA 1996 gives an employee 'the right not to be subjected to any det- **20.57** riment by any act, or any deliberate failure to act, by his employer' on the ground that:

(a) having been designated by the employer to carry out activities in connection with preventing or reducing risks to the health and safety of employees at work, he carried out or proposed to carry out any such activities;

(b) if a representative of employees on matters of health and safety at work, he performed or proposed to perform any functions as such;

(c) if a member of a safety committee formed in accordance with any enactment or acknowledged as such by the employer, he performed or proposed to perform any functions as such;

(d) he left or proposed to leave his place of work or any dangerous part of his place of work in circumstances of danger which was serious and imminent and which he could not reasonably have been expected to avert; or

(e) he took or proposed to take appropriate steps to protect himself or other employees from danger in circumstances of serious and imminent danger.

In a case where there is no safety representative or safety committee appointed, or it was **20.58** not reasonably practicable for the employee to raise a health and safety issue with those persons, the employee is protected if he brings to the employer's attention, by reasonable means, circumstances connected with his work which he reasonably believes were harmful or potentially harmful to health and safety. Taking industrial action is a reasonable means of bringing health and safety concerns to the employer's attention (*Balfour Kilpatrick Ltd v Acheson* [2003] IRLR 683).

The appropriateness of such steps must be judged by reference to all the relevant circum- **20.59** stances including his knowledge and the facilities available to him at the time (s 44(2)). There is no protection for an employee 'if the employer shows that it was (or would have been) so negligent for the employee to take the steps which he took (or proposed to take) that a reasonable employer might have treated him as the employer did' (s 44(3)). The term 'in circumstances of danger' is without any express limitation and applies to dangers caused by the behaviour of fellow employees (*Harvest Press Ltd v McCaffrey* [1999] IRLR 778).

This right derives from an EU directive on measures to encourage improvements in the **20.60** health and safety of workers at work (89/391) to the effect that the employer 'should take action and give instructions to enable workers in the event of serious, imminent and unavoidable danger to stop work and/or immediately to leave the workplace and proceed to a place of safety'.

The right is given to a worker to complain about infringement of his rights to an employ- **20.61** ment tribunal, and the onus is on the employer to show the ground on which any act or failure to act was done (s 48(2) of the ERA 1996). Any such complaint must be presented before the end of three months beginning with the date of the act or failure to act to which the complaint relates, or where the act or failure is part of a series of similar acts or failures, the last of them (s 48(3)(a)). There is the normal extension power found in applications, for example, for unfair dismissal, where it was not reasonably practicable for the complaint to be presented within the three-month period, in which case it must be presented within such further period as the employment tribunal considers reasonable (s 48(3)(b)). A deliberate failure to act is treated as done when it was decided upon (s 48(4)(b)), that is, when he does an act inconsistent with doing the failed act or if he does no such inconsistent act when the period expires within which it might reasonably have been expected to do the failed act if it was to be done.

20.62 An employment tribunal has power to award compensation and this award of compensation is on a similar basis to compensation for unfair dismissal, that is, what the tribunal considers just and equitable in all the circumstances having regard to the infringement complained of and to any loss which is attributable to the act or failure which infringed the applicant's right (s 49(2)). That loss includes any expenses which have been incurred and the loss of any benefit which the applicant 'might reasonably be expected to have had but for that failure' (s 49(3)). The principles of mitigation and contributory fault apply just as they do in analogous unfair dismissal proceedings (s 49(4) and (5)).

20.63 There is a new species of automatically unfair dismissal to go alongside the remedies for dismissal on trade union grounds if dismissal is by reason of any of the circumstances that give rise to the right not to suffer detriment in health and safety cases. A selection for redundancy on these grounds is also automatically unfair (s 105 of the ERA 1996). This is achieved in respect of dismissal by s 100 of the ERA 1996, but there is an exception in that the dismissal is not to be regarded as unfair if the employer shows that it was or would have been so negligent for the employee to take the steps which he took or proposed to take that a reasonable employer might have dismissed him for taking or proposing to take them (s 100(3)).

20.64 There is no qualifying period to make a claim (s 108) and no maximum on a compensatory award for dismissals falling within s 100. The law is, however, neutral in the sense that such representatives have no right to positive discrimination in their favour, so that in *Smiths Industries Aerospace and Defence Systems v Rawlings* [1996] IRLR 656, the EAT overturned a decision of the employment tribunal that in deciding on selection for redundancy the employer should have taken into account the skills and qualities shown by the employee in performing his representative duties.

20.65 The similarity with trade union dismissal cases is taken further by the ability of a person dismissed on these health and safety grounds to apply for interim relief (s 128(1)) (see also the Health and Safety (Consultation with Employees) Regulations 1996 (SI 1996/1513), as amended).

20.66 A degree of publicity is required as a result of the Trade Union Act 2016 so that by a new s 172A of the TULR(C)A 1992, regulations may be made to require public sector employers to publish information about 'how many of an employer's employees are relevant union officials ... the total spent by an employer ... on paying relevant union officials for facility time ... the percentage of the total pay bill spent on facility time'. There are attached reserve powers by which the relevant Minister can set out his concerns about the amount of facility time in the particular employer's case and inform the employer that the Minister may exercise his reserve powers (s 14 Trade Union Act 2016). These may seek to ensure that the amount of facility time does not exceed a percentage that is set down.

K RIGHTS OF PENSION FUND TRUSTEES

A pension fund trustee has protection from any detriment by any act or any deliberate **20.67** failure to act by the employer done on the grounds that he was a trustee of a relevant occupational pension scheme (s 46(1) of the ERA 1996). A dismissal on those grounds is automatically unfair (s 102).

Pension fund trustees have similar rights to time off to perform their duties and to undergo **20.68** training as trade union officials. In determining the reasonableness of the time off sought, the employment tribunal must again consider 'the circumstances of the employer's business and the effect of the employee's absence on the running of that business' (ss 58–60).

L REMEDIES

If the claimant has mounted the foregoing hurdles, the remedies available to him are **20.69** several, depending on the way in which his rights to participate in union activities have been infringed.

Detriment short of dismissal

A declaration may be granted and compensation which is 'just and equitable in all the cir- **20.70** cumstances having regard to the infringement of the complainant's rights' (TULR(C)A 1992, s 149(2)). The EAT in *Brassington v Cauldon Wholesale Ltd* [1978] IRLR 479 determined that 'compensation for the employee, not a fine on the employer, however tactfully wrapped up, is the basis of the award'. The claimants could thus recover their expenses in going to the employment tribunal, and also non-pecuniary losses such as 'the stress engendered by such a situation' and compensation if a 'deep and sincere wish to join a union ... had been frustrated' with all the benefits of help and advice which that might entail (see also *Cleveland Ambulance NHS Trust v Blane* [1997] ICR 851). In *Cheall v Vauxhall Motors* [1979] IRLR 253, the claimant could show no financial loss but the tribunal awarded him £50 on account of his frustration and stress for not being allowed to have his case presented by his own representative while he was still a member of one trade union. The normal reasonable mitigation of loss provision applies, and the remedy can be sought by complaint within three months to an employment tribunal (see *Adlam v Salisbury and Wells Theological College* [1985] ICR 786). The employer or employee may unusually reclaim such compensation by joining in proceedings any union or person pressurising him to take such action (TULR(C)A 1992, s 150(1)).

Trade union discrimination is not to be treated as a lower level than other forms of dis- **20.71** crimination when assessing injury to feelings (*Saunders v APCOA Parking UK Ltd* EAT, 18 March 2003; *London Borough of Hackney v Adams* [2003] IRLR 402).

Failure to permit time off

Breach of this provision similarly entitles the complainant to a declaration and just and **20.72** equitable compensation (TULR(C)A 1992, s 172). A trade union official cannot, however, be held to have been refused time off if the employer did not know of the request for that time off to be taken (*Ryford Ltd v Drinkwater* [1996] IRLR 16).

Dismissal: Compensation

20.73   In the case of a Trade Union or Health and Safety dismissal, there is a two-stage test; the issue is the employee's state of mind when engaged in the activity in question and not whether the employer agrees with that assessment (*Oudahar v Esporta Group Ltd* [2011] ICR 1406).

20.74   The usual remedies of compensation up to £78,962 (plus the basic award), reinstatement, and re-engagement are available on a dismissal for trade union membership or activities. There are the same provisions for enhanced payments as apply to dismissals for refusal to join a trade union, that is, a basic award minimum of £4,700. The sum is index-linked to the retail prices index (Employment Relations Act 1999, s 34) and must be updated every September.

20.75   In assessing compensation, by the TULR(C)A 1992, s 155(2), the tribunal must ignore any breach of or refusal to comply with or objection to a requirement to be a member of any trade union or a particular trade union, or to cease membership or not to take part in such activities. In *TGWU v Howard* [1992] ICR 106, the claimant was employed by and was a member of the TGWU. She resigned and joined another union and was dismissed by the union. The tribunal found that the dismissal was automatically unfair within the TULR(C)A 1992, s 152, and that the claimant had contributed to her dismissal in that her conduct in resigning was unreasonable but that s 155(2) of the TULR(C)A 1992 required the tribunal to disregard that conduct. The EAT upheld appeals by the TGWU on the ground that there was a distinction between what was done by the applicant and the way in which it was done, and that if the conduct of the applicant prior to dismissal deserved to be criticised, the tribunal could make an appropriate deduction.

Interim relief

20.76   The applicant may also claim interim relief, a special emergency interim procedure which reflects the serious industrial relations consequences that often ensue in a tense industrial relations stand-off, especially from the dismissal of a shop steward (ERA 1996, s 128). It does not, however, apply to selection for redundancy for an inadmissible reason; it does extend to an employee dismissed for refusing to join a union and to those dismissed for whistleblowing, health and safety activities, as trustees of occupational pension schemes, and as employee representatives.

20.77   An application must be made to the employment tribunal within seven days of the effective date of termination, supported by a written certificate signed by an official of the employee's union who is specifically so authorised. This should contain the reasons why it is said that the particulars fall within the scope of interim relief (*Stone v Charrington & Co* [1977] ICR 248), although tribunals have eschewed technicalities in the interpretation of this provision. Thus, it was accepted that a union regional organiser was an authorised official notwithstanding that he had no such express appointment (cf *Farmeary v Veterinary Drug Co Ltd* [1976] IRLR 322). Moreover, the tribunal may read together an application lodged within the time limit which does not comply with s 161(2) of the TULR(C)A 1992 and a letter presented after the period has expired which does so comply (*Barley v Amey Roadstone Ltd* [1977] ICR 546). Where, however, the authority of the official to give such a certificate is challenged by the employers before the tribunal, the onus lies on him to prove that he has actual or implied authority to sign the certificate, and if he had not, the certificate is defective and the claim must fail (*Sulemany v Habib Bank Ltd* [1983] ICR 60). If an employee has ostensibly been dismissed for redundancy, the tribunal may still order interim relief if it believes the employee may well succeed in an argument that the redundancy was fabricated to obscure the fact that dismissal was really for one of the specified activities, such as his trade union activities (*Bombardier Aerospace v McConnell* [2008] IRLR 51). There is no set pattern for the scope of interim relief hearings so that it is for the discretion of the employment judge as to how much evidence to hear.

The tribunal must hear an interim relief application as quickly as possible (TULR(C)A **20.78** 1992, s 162(1)), and to expedite matters, its chairman may sit alone. The crucial issue is whether it is 'likely' that the tribunal will, at the end of the day, make a finding of unfair dismissal on account of an inadmissible reason. If so, it should at this stage order reinstatement or re-engagement pending final determination (TULR(C)A 1992, s 164). 'Likely' has been interpreted as demanding more than a reasonable chance of success; the prospects must be 'pretty good' (*Taplin v C. Shippam Ltd* [1978] IRLR 450). On the other hand, Slynn J did not 'think it right in a case of this kind to ask whether the applicant has proved his case on a balance of probabilities'.

An employer or employee may apply for the revocation or variation of an order once **20.79** made (TULR(C)A 1992, s 165). Such an application may be determined by a different employment tribunal from that which made the original order (*British Coal Corporation v McGinty* [1988] IRLR 7).

21

STRIKES AND OTHER INDUSTRIAL ACTION

A A RIGHT TO STRIKE? 21.01
History 21.01
Justification of freedom to strike 21.02
Legal liabilities 21.03

**B INDUSTRIAL ACTION AND THE INDIVIDUAL
CONTRACT** 21.06
Notice to terminate 21.07
Suspension of contract 21.09
Repudiatory breach 21.10
Damages 21.13
Other forms of industrial action 21.14
Industrial action by the employer 21.15

**C THE LEGALITY OF INDUSTRIAL ACTION: THE
QUESTIONS FOR THE COURT** 21.16

D INDUCING BREACH OF CONTRACT 21.18
Importance of the tort 21.18
Different modes of committing
the tort 21.20
Direct inducement 21.21
Indirect inducement 21.22
Procuring breach of contract 21.23
Knowledge of contract 21.26
Inducement 21.28
Breach of contract 21.31
Causation 21.33
Unlawful means 21.35
Justification 21.38
Immunity 21.40

E INTERFERENCE WITH CONTRACT 21.44
The tort 21.44
Unlawful means 21.52
Immunity 21.56

F INTIMIDATION 21.57
The tort 21.57
Immunity 21.61

G CONSPIRACY 21.62
The tort 21.62
Justification 21.66
Immunity 21.68
Criminal conspiracy 21.69

H TRADE DISPUTE IMMUNITY 21.71
The section 21.71
Trade dispute .21.77
Parties 21.79
The dispute 21.83
Subject matter 21.85
'Relate wholly or mainly' 21.96
Contemplation or furtherance of a
trade dispute 21.100

**I STATUTORY CONTROL OF SECONDARY
ACTION** 21.103

J STRIKE BALLOTS 21.106
When a ballot is required 21.107
The scope of the constituency 21.114
Trade Union Act 2016 . . . . .21.122
Industrial action at different
workplaces 21.124
The ballot paper 21.128
Protection of the voter 21.129
Call before the ballot 21.132
Notice of the ballot 21.133
Notice of industrial action 21.142
Member's right to remove
authorisation for strikes and industrial
action 21.145
Persons authorised to call industrial
action 21.149

K UNION RECRUITMENT STRIKES 21.154

**L STATUTORY RESTRICTIONS ON INDUSTRIAL
ACTION** 21.155
Restrictions on classes of workers 21.155
Emergencies .21.156

M CONSUMER ACTIONS 21.157

**N EU LAW ON FREEDOM OF
ESTABLISHMENT** 21.158

O INJUNCTIONS 21.159
Use of injunctions in strikes 21.159
Principles determining whether
injunctions are to be granted 21.161
Injunctions to restrain criminal
offences 21.168

[The period since 1906 has seen] a shifting pattern of Parliamentary assertions and judicial responses, a legal point and counterpoint which has been more productive of excitement than of harmony. (Lord Scarman in *NWL Ltd v Woods* [1979] 3 All ER 614 at 630.)

A A RIGHT TO STRIKE?

History

There is no general right to strike in Britain, unlike in several other countries where indus-   **21.01**
trial action is protected by the relevant constitution. Strikes are indeed discouraged by criminal, civil, and administrative means, and benefits are withheld from strikers. Such liberty as exists to take industrial action has been established by way of statutory immunity from the law of tort and its extent has been a constant political football, not only between the political parties, but also between the legislature and the courts (see generally John Bowers, Michael Duggan, and D Reade, *The Law of Industrial Action and Trade Union Recognition*, OUP, 2011, 2nd edn). In 2013 there were 443,600 working days lost from 114 work stoppages. Tony Blair said in the Fairness at Work White Paper in 1998 'the days of strikes without ballots, mass picketing, closed shops and secondary action are over', and there was largely agreement between recent Conservative and New Labour Governments about the way forward.

Justification of freedom to strike

Professors Kahn-Freund and Hepple isolated four rationales for a right or freedom to   **21.02**
strike (*Laws Against Strikes, Fabian Society 1972*, pp 5–8):

(a) the *equilibrium argument*: that labour needs a sanction to resist the otherwise total prerogative of management;
(b) the need for *autonomous sanctions* to enforce collective bargains, self-help being stronger than legal enforcement could be;
(c) the *voluntary labour argument*, that compulsion to work is tantamount to serfdom; and
(d) the *psychological argument*, which sees strikes as a necessary release of tension.

The authors conclude that 'the imperative need for a social power countervailing that of property overshadows everything else'. More recently, the right to strike has been viewed as one of the fundamental human rights. This was expressed with most force in *Demir v Turkey* [2009] IRLR 766 by the CJEU. The right to bargain collectively with the employer has become one of the essential elements of the right to form and join trade unions for the protection of one's interests.

Legal liabilities

'You cannot make a strike effective without doing more than is lawful.' (Lindley LJ in   **21.03**
Allen v Flood [1898] AC 1.)

There are eight different ways in which common law and statute now regulate and control   **21.04**
strikes and other industrial action:

(a) breach of the worker's contract of employment;
(b) liability of unions for economic torts of inducing breach of contract, interference with contract, or trade or business intimidation and conspiracy;

(c) government emergency powers;

(d) residual criminal liability, which is mainly concerned with conspiracy and control of picketing;

(e) a union member's right to remove authorisation by the union for strikes and industrial action held without a proper ballot;

(f) the right of a member to complain against his union about unjustifiable discipline (TULR(C)A 1992, ss 64 to 67);

(g) the right of a member to complain of indemnification by his union of individuals who take part in industrial action (TULR(C)A 1992, s 15); and

(h) the right of a member to complain of unlawful application of union assets by trustees of unions (TULR(C)A 1992, s 16).

Moreover, separate and extensive codes of practice now cover strike ballots and the conduct of picketing.

21.05   The potential legal liabilities will be considered in turn and then the 'golden formula' which gives an individual or union immunity from torts when acting 'in contemplation or furtherance of a trade dispute'.

B   INDUSTRIAL ACTION AND THE INDIVIDUAL CONTRACT

21.06   The effect of strikes and other industrial action on the individual contract of employment is rarely of direct importance. Employers normally do not wish to disturb post-strike calm by resorting to the courts to sue individual workers for breach of contract, although this has sometimes occurred (eg *Boxfoldia Ltd v National Graphical Association (1982)* [1988] ICR 752). The effect of industrial action on the contract of employment is still vital indirectly, for it provides the illegality which is central to the economic torts of intimidation, inducing breach of contract, and conspiracy. In this way management may seek redress from strike leaders and unions unless they are acting in contemplation or furtherance of a trade dispute as defined. The most valuable remedy is an injunction to prevent a strike taking place at all. Basically the law is still as stated in *Allen v Flood* [1898] AC 1:

> A strike may be legal if due notice is given, that is, if the employee gives the minimum he must give to terminate his employment.

Notice to terminate

21.07   There is a statutory minimum of one week for an employee's notice to terminate the contract of employment, but longer periods are often demanded by the terms of the individual contract. If such notice is given in a strike by each employee, the effect is that the employee has resigned, although this rarely happens in practice, since the object of industrial action is not to sever relations with the employer but to impose different terms on which that continuing relationship is to be carried on. As Donovan LJ said in *Rookes v Barnard* [1963] 1 QB 623:

> It would, however, be affectation not to recognise that in the majority of strikes no such notice to terminate the contract is either given or expected. The strikers do not want to give up their jobs; they simply want to be paid more for it or to secure some other advantage in connection with it. The employer does not want to lose his labour force; he simply wants to resist the claim. Not till the strike has lasted some time, and no settlement is in sight, does one usually read that the employers have given notice that unless the men return to work their contracts will be terminated and they will be dismissed.

Lord Denning MR recognised that:

> The strike notice is nothing more nor less than a notice that the men will not come to work. In short, they will break their contract ... (*J.T. Stratford and Son Ltd v Lindley* [1965] AC 269.)

Moreover, there might be difficulties in a union giving notice to terminate on behalf of its members, not only because it is not their agent but also because employee A may have to give eight weeks under his contract, B three weeks, and C one week. Davies LJ, dissatisfied with the ramifications of the notice idea, saw strike notices as notices to terminate the present contractual conditions coupled with an offer to work on new terms (*Morgan v Fry* [1968] 2 QB 710). Thus, the striker does not intend to put an end to the employment altogether. Only if the employee is subject to a non-strike agreement between his employer and union, would he then be acting in breach of contract. There is also no rule that notice of a strike is to be construed as giving notice of a breach of contract rather than terminating the contract, but in the particular case the union had no authority from its members to act as their agents to terminate their contracts of employment (*Boxfoldia Ltd v National Graphical Association (1982)* [1988] ICR 752; see also *Solihull Metropolitan Borough v National Union of Teachers* [1985] IRLR 211).   **21.08**

Suspension of contract

Another contention which has at times attracted the courts is that a strike suspends the contract of employment. This focuses on the reality that there is clearly no right to pay during a strike and everyone anticipates that after the strike is over normal service will be resumed. Thus, in *Morgan v Fry* (21.08 above), Lord Denning MR held that there was an implied term that each side to a contract agreed to its suspension by strike action after the giving of notice which could determine the contract. He said (at 728): 'If a strike takes place the contract of employment is not terminated. It is suspended during the strike and revives again when the strike is over.' The Donovan Commission, however, rejected the general adoption of this idea on the ground of 'considerable technical difficulty', including problems over its application to unofficial, unconstitutional strikes and other forms of industrial action like a go-slow and work-to-rule. It is also unclear what would happen if a strike were never settled, or if the employer sought to dismiss all the strikers.   **21.09**

Repudiatory breach

The courts thus generally see a strike without proper contractual notice as amounting to a repudiation of their contracts by the strikers. The EAT in *Simmons v Hoover Ltd* [1977] ICR 61 at 76, said, 'It seems to us to be plain that it was a [repudiation] for here there was a settled, confirmed and continued intention on the part of the employee not to do any of the work which under his contract he had been engaged to do; which was the whole purpose of his contract.' Phillips J thought that *Morgan v Fry* was not 'intended to revolutionise the law on this subject' and held to the view that a strike is a repudiatory breach, citing *Bowes & Partners v Press* [1894] 1 QB 202, for it is a failure by the employee to perform the most fundamental duty under his contract—to work.   **21.10**

The employer has a choice whether or not to accept the repudiation by the strikers; if he does (which is the less usual course), he reacts by dismissing them and this counts as a termination of contract by the employer. Those cases which suggested that a strike, and indeed any other repudiatory breach, automatically brings the contract to an end   **21.11** as a form of 'constructive resignation' are now regarded as unsound (*London Transport Executive v Clarke* [1981] IRLR 166. Striking employees can thus claim unfair dismissal since they have been dismissed, but will succeed only in the circumstances set out in the TULR(C)A 1992, ss 237 to 239. The situations in which a dismissal will be unfair were expanded by the Employment Relations Act 1999 (see further 14.248ff).

21.12 The other major consequence of the breach principle is that the employer is clearly not obliged to pay employees during a strike; the employee must prove that he is ready and willing to work for payment to be due (*Henthorn and Taylor v CEGB* [1980] IRLR 361) (see 4.18–4.20). The situation was not affected by the regulation of deductions in ss 13–20 of the ERA 1996. The general principle is that deductions from pay are regulated by agreement between the parties. There is, however, an exception by ERA 1996, s 14(5): 'where the worker has taken part in a strike or other industrial action and the deduction is made by the employer on account of the worker's having taken part in that strike or other action'. Further, strikers may not gain an injunction to prevent their employers dismissing them since they do not come to equity with clean hands (*Chappell v Times Newspapers Ltd* [1975] ICR 145; on the attempted use of the clean hands doctrine against the employer, see *Ministry of Justice v POA* [2008] IRLR 380).

Damages

21.13 When the employer sues strikers for damages (which is a very unusual course), a major difficulty arises in their calculation. The courts have rejected a proportionate share of overhead expenses during lost days as the appropriate measure (*Ebbw Vale Steel, Iron and Coal Co v Tew* (1935) 79 SJ 593). In *National Coal Board v Galley* [1958] 1 WLR 16, the Court of Appeal ignored the breaches of contract by other employees, and awarded the employers of the defendant, a colliery deputy engaged on safety work, only the cost of hiring a substitute—the princely sum of £3 18s 2d—and not a proportional amount of the whole loss as they had claimed. If the factory were running at a loss only nominal damages could be secured, and sometimes strikes may even enhance a company's chance of profitability by reducing wage costs. In reality, very few employers take the risk of further exacerbating industrial relations by suing for damages after the end of a dispute. As the CBI said in evidence to the Donovan Commission (para 413 of the Report): 'The main interest of the employer is in the resumption of work and the preservation of good will.'

Other forms of industrial action

21.14 The strike is not the only method of bringing industrial pressure to bear on the employer. The following forms of action do not lead necessarily to full loss of wages for the individuals involved:

(a) The *work-to-rule* and *go-slow* are particularly common on the railways. Employees may purport to follow work rules meticulously. Forms may be completed in great detail, and usually ignored provisions activated. All this slows down the rate of work progress and the Court of Appeal has held that this withdrawal of cooperation can amount to a breach of contract (*Secretary of State for Employment v ASLEF (No 2)* [1972] 2 All ER 949; *British Telecommunications plc v Ticehurst* [1992] ICR 383; on go-slow see *General Engineering Services Ltd v Kingston and St Andrew Corporation* [1988] 3 All ER 867).

(b) Overtime bans have traditionally occurred most frequently in the newspaper industry and on the railways, and are a breach of contract only if overtime is compulsory, which is rarely the case. This tactic is often combined with a ban on shift working.

(c) Employees may work normally but refuse to perform the particular duty about which they are protesting. Thus, bus drivers on one-man buses may refuse to collect fares, and teachers may refrain from dinner duties (*Gorse v Durham CC* [1971] 2 All ER 666), or refuse to cover for absent colleagues (*Sim v Rotherham Metropolitan Borough Council* [1986] IRLR 391).

(d) Sit-ins, which normally take place after the termination of the contract of employment in order to preserve open a factory, would normally constitute the tort of trespass and can be restrained by injunction. In general, an employee is not entitled to remain on the employer's property without the employer's consent (*City and Hackney Health Authority v NUPE* [1985] IRLR 252).

In *Miles v Wakefield Metropolitan District Council* [1987] ICR 368, Lord Templeman stated that any form of industrial action by a worker is repudiatory, since it is a breach of contract intentionally to harm the employer's business.

Industrial action by the employer

The employer does not often have to resort to overt industrial action, since he retains **21.15** the prerogative to make changes in his business. Thus, the employer's main offensive tactic against his workforce, the lock-out, has been little used in Britain, unlike in the US.

C THE LEGALITY OF INDUSTRIAL ACTION: THE QUESTIONS FOR THE COURT

The court must essentially ask itself three questions to test the legality of most indus- **21.16** trial action. The stages were first adumbrated as such by Brightman LJ in *Merkur Island Shipping Corporation v Laughton* [1983] IRLR 218, and approved by Lord Diplock in *Dimbleby & Sons Ltd v NUJ* [1984] 1 WLR 427 at 434F. The questions are:

(a) Whether the claimant employers have a cause of action at common law.
(b) Whether the defendants are acting in contemplation or furtherance of a trade dispute against the claimant. If so, s 219 of the TULR(C)A 1992 gives immunity from action which:
  (i) induces a person to break a contract of employment;
  (ii) threatens that a contract of employment will be broken;
  (iii) interferes with the trade, business or employment of a person; or
  (iv) constitutes an agreement by two or more persons to procure the doing of any such act.
(c) Whether the immunity is removed on some ground.

In order to retain the immunity from certain torts, there must be an affirmative ballot **21.17** amongst those likely to be called out in the action; and if the industrial action is to take place at different workplaces, the complex requirements of s 228 of the TULR(C)A 1992 must also be satisfied. Action to enforce union membership is also unlawful. The liability of trade unions in tort has already been discussed (19.43). We will first consider here the main economic torts used in strike claims, and then turn to the immunities. It is also necessary to take into account the Code of Practice on Industrial Action Ballots and Notice to Employers 2005.

D INDUCING BREACH OF CONTRACT

Importance of the tort

21.18   This tort is centrally important and is committed where a person directly or indirectly induces a party to a contract to break it without legal justification. It will be almost always in play in a strike which breaches not only the contracts of employment of the strikers, but also commercial contracts entered into by the employer who has been struck against. The tort has thus always been at the forefront of regulation of strikes and it formed the basis for the short-lived concept of unfair industrial practice introduced by the Industrial Relations Act 1971.

21.19   In the first authority on inducement, *Lumley v Gye* (1853) 2 E & B 216, the defendant theatre owner persuaded an opera singer to sing for him at Her Majesty's Theatre, thus inducing breach of her exclusive engagement for three months to the plaintiff at the rival Queen's Theatre. The court held that there was a cause of action and thus generalised the existing action for enticement of a servant. Since then it has been applied to all manner of agreements. Lord Watson later stated the principle in *Allen v Flood* [1898] AC 1 at 107, that:

> He who wilfully induces another to do an unlawful act which, but for his persuasion, would or might never have been committed, is rightly held to be responsible for the wrong which he procured.

Different modes of committing the tort

21.20   There are several different ways of committing this tort in a strike, and although nomenclature varies and the categories are by no means watertight, they will be dealt with under the headings:

(a)   direct inducement (21.21);
(b)   indirect inducement by unlawful means (21.22); and
(c)   procuring breach of contract by unlawful means (21.23).

In the following diagrams the *dramatis personae* are:

Union organiser—Bill
Employer in dispute—Slim Trousers
Employee of Slim—Joan
Suppliers to Slim Trousers—Bright Buttons
Employee of Bright Buttons—Kevin

(a)   Direct inducement

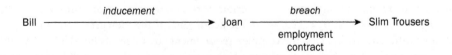

Bill pressures Joan to break her contract of employment with Slim Trousers.

(b) Indirect inducement

Bill ——————*inducement*——————▶ Bright ———————*breach*———————▶ Slim Trousers
Buttons   commercial
contract

Bill induces Bright Buttons to breach its commercial contracts to supply Slim Trousers.

(c) Procuring breach

Bill ——*procuring*——▶ Kevin ——*breach*——▶ Bright ——*breach*——▶ Slim Trousers
Buttons

employment   commercial
contract   contract

Bill tells Kevin not to switch on the machine which makes buttons which will be supplied to Slim Trousers. This prevents Bright Buttons from performing its contract to
supply buttons to Slim Trousers. Slim will lose profits and is likely to seek an early
settlement of the dispute. Here two contracts are broken: the employment contract
between Bright and Kevin and the commercial contract between Bright and Slim. Bill
has *induced* breach of the former by persuasion of Kevin, but only indirectly *procured*
breach of the latter.

Direct inducement

Most commonly in strikes, the tort is committed when a shop steward directly operates   **21.21**
on an employee and persuades him to breach his contract of employment.

Indirect inducement

Another common factual situation used to be a boycott or 'blacking' where union   **21.22**
organisers take action against suppliers or distributors of the employer with whom it
is in dispute and so induce breach of the employer's commercial contracts. This is an
essential feature of solidarity action and *Torquay Hotel Co Ltd v Cousins* [1969] 2
Ch 106 is a good example. The owner of the plaintiff hotel company had criticised the
defendant union's action in an inter-union dispute already affecting other hotels in the
area. The defendant thus contacted the drivers for Esso Ltd, which supplied the plaintiff hotel with fuel, and stated that it would prevent all oil supplies. The non-delivery
of oil was a result of the employees' inducement and a majority of the Court of Appeal
held there was a breach of contract. The inducement was, however, indirect and for it
to be illegal required unlawful means to be used. There were unlawful means, however, in the information conveyed to Esso Ltd that if they did not cut off oil supplies,
the union would be calling on its members in that company to break their contracts of
employment.

Union official ——————*threat*——————▶ Esso Ltd ———————*breach*———————▶ Torquay Hotel
commercial
contract

Procuring breach of contract

21.23   The tort is also committed if the strikers unlawfully interfere with any contract by actually preventing performance by, for example, removing essential tools, or kidnapping an employee (examples given in *Thomson (D.C.) & Co v Deakin* [1952] Ch 646; *GWK v Dunlop* (1926) 42 TLR 376), or switching off the lights at a theatre to prevent the production of a play. This, again, requires unlawful means. Blacking the goods of a particular employer is the example *par excellence* of procurement, and often two contracts will thereby be broken: that of the employee who procures it, and the employer's agreement with the outside party. *J.T. Stratford and Son Ltd v Lindley* [1965] AC 269 provides a good illustration of this *modus operandi*. The plaintiff was the chairman of companies A and B. A owned Thames motor barges while B hired them out to firms which employed their own crews. Forty-five of A's employees were members of the Transport and General Workers Union, while three belonged to the much smaller competitor, the Watermen's Union. Both organisations sought negotiating rights with Stratford for Company A. When the TGWU made a breakthrough by negotiations, the WU sought to use whatever industrial muscle it had to compel the same end. It had no power to attack Company A directly since it had very few members there, and instead it put pressure on B by calling on its members in companies to which B's barges were hired not to return them to the moorings when the contracts ended. The breaches of these agreements were thus achieved indirectly but were no less successful in securing their end. The High Court granted an injunction, since the union had induced the hirers' employees to act in breach of their contracts of employment in order to procure a breach of contract between their employers and Company B on whom the union was seeking to exert pressure. Procuring breach of contract most commonly constitutes secondary action, the restriction on which is considered later (21.103–21.105).

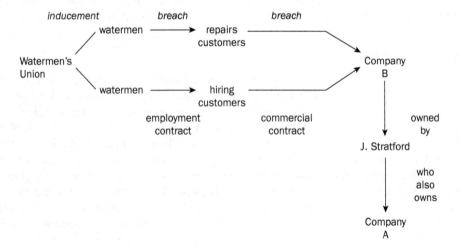

21.24   In *Thomson v Deakin* [1952] Ch 646 at 697, Jenkins LJ stated the general principle that for this variant of the tort to be committed it must be shown (author's italics):

> first, that the person charged with actionable interference *knew* of the existence of the contract and intended to procure its breach; secondly that the person so charged did *definitely and unequivocally* persuade, induce or procure the employees to breach their contracts of employment with the intent mentioned; thirdly, that the employees so persuaded, induced or procured did *in fact break* their contracts of employment, and fourthly, that the breach of the contract forming the alleged subject of interference

ensued as a *necessary consequence* of the breach of the employees concerned of their contracts of employment.

This *dictum* has been approved by the House of Lords in *Merkur Island Shipping Corporation v Laughton* [1983] 2 AC 570.

The four elements will now be considered in order and then we will look at unlawful means, justification, and the statutory immunity.   **21.25**

Knowledge of contract

Economic torts require intention by the defendant, which means that he must foresee the   **21.26** possibility of a breach of contract and desire that result. The older cases demanded that the defendant have *actual knowledge* of the contract breached and some cognisance of its terms (*Thomson v Deakin* [1952] Ch 646; also *Long v Smithson* (1918) 88 LJ KB 223 at 225; and *Smithies v National Association of Operative Plasterers* [1909] 1 KB 310), but the threshold has been reduced over time. Ignorance may be bliss but it will not always excuse liability for inducement. Thus, in *Cunard SS Co Ltd v Stacey* [1955] 2 Lloyd's Rep 247, strike organisers were taken to know that, on their calling a strike, union members would thereby break their articles as seamen. Similarly, the Master of the Rolls took the more objective view in his wide statement of principle:

> Even if [the Defendants] did not know of the actual terms of the contract, but had the means of knowledge which they deliberately disregarded—that would be enough.

Diplock LJ thought that the defendant is liable if he intends to have the contract ended by breach if it cannot be ended lawfully; again, motive enters the field. He could not 'turn a blind eye to it', and Russell LJ agreed. Here they found that the defendants did intend a breach, for even though the defendants said they assumed that the contracts could be terminated lawfully, they were in the end indifferent whether they did so or not (see also *British Industrial Plastics Ltd v Ferguson* [1938] 4 All ER 504; *Emerald Construction Co Ltd v Lowthian* [1966] 1 WLR 691; *Merkur*'s case (above)). In *Greig v Insole* [1978] 3 All ER 449 at 488, Slade J said:

> It will suffice for the plaintiff to prove that the defendant knew of the *existence* of the contract, provided that he can prove also that the defendant intended to procure the breach of it ... ignorance of the precise terms may in particular circumstances enable him to satisfy the court that he did not have such intent; ignorance of this nature, however, does not alone suffice to show absence of intent to procure a breach.

One case where the union was held to have insufficient knowledge for liability to attach   **21.27** was *Timeplan Education Group Ltd v National Union of Teachers* [1997] IRLR 457. The NUT was in dispute with Timeplan, a teachers' supply agency. After the union persuaded a New Zealand teachers' magazine to stop carrying Timeplan's advertisements, the company sued the NUT for unlawful interference with its continuing advertising contract with the magazine. The Court of Appeal rejected the claim. Although the union was aware of the contract and the law did not require knowledge of precise terms, there was no evidence that the NUT knew there was a *continuing* contract. The union reasonably assumed that Timeplan would have paid for advertisements placed in the past; but there was no suggestion that it ever occurred to the union that there was a subsisting contract extending to future advertising. The court rejected Timeplan's submission that the union was under a duty to make enquiries about whether there was such a contract (see also *Solihull Metropolitan Borough v NUT* [1985] IRLR 211). In *OBG Ltd v Allan* [2007] IRLR 21 the House of Lords reiterated that actual knowledge and a deliberate intention to induce a breach of contract are necessary ingredients of the tort of inducing breach of contract. There are two relevant torts, inducing breach of contract and causing loss by unlawful means. They could arise on the same set of facts but they are not properly viewed as subdivisions of one larger tort. Lord Hoffmann said that the extension of economic torts into areas such as mere interference with contract was inappropriate. Further, the tort of intimidation is not to be considered as a separate form of liability but rather only as a factual example of the tort of causing economic loss by unlawful means. Lord Hoffmann summarised the position that 'unlawful means therefore consists of acts intended to cause loss to the claimant by interfering with the freedom of a third party in a way which is unlawful as against that third party and which is intended to cause loss to the claimant. It does not in my opinion include acts which may be unlawful against a third party, but which do not affect his freedom to deal with the claimant'.

Inducement

21.28   Inducement must be carefully distinguished from the giving of friendly advice, but the line of distinction is very difficult to draw and apply in particular cases. It is not enough that a union official tells employees that the boss is going to cut overtime payments from next week, and they immediately strike in protest against it. The Court of Appeal thus held that there was no inducement in *Thomson v Deakin* (21.24 above) because the defendants simply stated the facts as they knew them. In *Torquay Hotel Co Ltd v Cousins* [1969] 2 Ch 106, Winn LJ, however, thought that mere advice could be an inducement, going on to say:

> A man who writes to his mother-in-law telling her that the central heating in his house has broken down may thereby induce her to cancel an intended visit.

In *J.T. Stratford and Son Ltd v Lindley* [1965] AC 269 at 333, Lord Pearce abstracted from the case law the proposition that:

> The fact that an inducement to break a contract is couched as an irresistible embargo rather than in terms of seduction does not make it any the less an inducement.

It would be enough if the union members were threatened with loss of their union membership if they did not take part in particular action.

21.29   It does not matter that the recipient of information is willing to break the contract. In *Camellia Tanker SA v ITF* [1976] ICR 274, it was held that the defendant in informing its members of negotiations with the plaintiff, did not induce them to break their contract in support, since there was no 'pressure, persuasion or procuration'. The breach of the commercial contract was not the *necessary* result of the union's action, only being reasonably likely, and this was not sufficient.

21.30   Section 127 of the Criminal Justice and Public Order Act 1994 created a new statutory tort of inducing a prison officer to withhold his services or to commit a breach of discipline. This was introduced because of judicial doubt whether prison officers had contracts of employment. There is a ban on prison officers striking under ss 138 to 139 of the Criminal Justice and Immigration Act 2008.

Breach of contract

21.31   A *breach* of contract is a fundamental requirement for the commission of this tort, although there is a little used wider tort of interference which does not require breach (see further 21.44–21.56). Thus, in *Allen v Flood* [1898] AC 1, the defendant boilermakers' action in informing management that they would 'knock off work if the plaintiff shipwrights were not dismissed' was not unlawful since they were free to leave at any time without breaking their contracts. The fact that the motive for their leaving was to injure the plaintiffs was irrelevant. A malicious or bad motive did not render the act unlawful. The tort has no application where the term of the contract breached is itself void for illegality, nor is there 'a tort of wrongfully inducing a person not to enter into a contract' (see Megarry J in *Midland Cold Storage v Steer* [1972] Ch 630; *Solihull Metropolitan Borough v NUT* (21.27 above); *Hadmor Productions Ltd v Hamilton* [1983] 1 AC 191).

Breach of an equitable duty suffices, so that in *Prudential Assurance Co v Lorenz* (1971) **21.32** 11 KIR 78, trade union members who refused to submit insurance premiums they had collected to their head office were enjoined from this course of action, since it was inducing breach of their equitable duty to account, which they owed as agents to their principal, the plaintiff.

Causation

Thomson v Deakin [1952] Ch 646 shows the need for a chain of causation between **21.33** inducement and breach of contract. The plaintiff printers had a policy of refusing to employ trade unionists and they required workers to sign a written undertaking that they would not join one. This was challenged by the union NATSOPA, who called out on strike their seventy-five secret members at the company and asked other unions to disrupt the company's activities as a sign of solidarity. TGWU members at Bowaters, a non-associated company, responded by stating that they would not deliver paper to Thomson and another union refused to load it. In fact, the threats never materialised into a breach of contract by the employees, although there was a breach of the contract to supply between Bowaters and Thomson. This was held not to be due to any inducement of the employees but to Bowater's decision not to supply, for it could not be proved conclusively that this had been caused by messages from the union. Lord Evershed said (at 686): 'The links in the chain which connect the defendants with the plaintiffs are ... very insubstantial'. In any event, the employees were not in breach of their contracts so that the necessary unlawful means were not present. Jenkins LJ said (at 697): 'A person who advocates the objects without advocating the means is [not] to be taken to have advocated recourse to unlawful means.'

The fact that the contracted party may be perfectly willing to break the contract does not **21.34** mean that the inducement is not effective.

Unlawful means

As to the tort of interference by unlawful means, Lord Hoffmann said in *OBG Ltd v Allan* **21.35** [2008] AC 1 'The essence of the tort therefore appears to be (a) a wrongful interference with the actions of a third party in which the claimant has an economic interest and (b) an intention thereby to cause loss to the claimant'.

21.36 Unlawful means are necessary in the tort variants of indirect inducement and procuring breach of contract. To return to the diagrammatic example in 21.20, if Bill had simply stood peacefully outside Bright Buttons factory with a placard stating 'Employers are rogues', there would be no tort, since there Bill would not be adopting any unlawful means to put his point across. His protest would have been well within his lawful rights. In the example, the unlawful means for procuring the breach of the commercial contract is provided by the inducing of the breach of the employment contract by Kevin. Unlawful means may be constituted by way of tort, breach of contract, or any other form of civil liability. This is a vital restriction because of the enormous potential width of this tort if it were not observed. Otherwise, for example, a wholesaler's action in persuading a retailer to cancel his supply contract with a competitor because of its lower prices might be illegal, yet this is generally considered fair in a free market economy.

21.37 Lord Denning suggested that there was a tort even if lawful means were adopted, in *Daily Mirror Newspapers v Gardner* [1968] 2 QB 762, but he retracted this view a year later in *Torquay Hotel Co Ltd v Cousins* [1969] 2 Ch 106 at 138, with the salient comment that the 'distinction [between lawful and unlawful means] must be maintained, else we should take away the right to strike altogether'. He went on to explain:

> Nearly every trade union official who calls a strike ... knows that it may prevent the employers from performing their contracts. He may be taken even to intend it. Yet no one has supposed hitherto that it was unlawful; and we should not render it unlawful today. A trade union official is only in the wrong when he procures a contracting party directly to break his contract or when he does it indirectly by unlawful means.

Unlawful means in the indirect inducement of breach of commercial contracts may be found in the direct inducement of breach of employment contracts, as *Emerald Construction Co Ltd v Lowthian* [1966] 1 WLR 691 shows. The main contractor for a CEGB power station had entered into a lump labour contract with the plaintiff, but this was not to the liking of the union's officers, who were opposed to such arrangements in principle. The union called its bricklayer members out on strike, and as a result the work fell behind, which put the plaintiff in breach of its contract with the main contractor. The Court of Appeal held that there was a prima facie case that the union's action was intended to procure a breach of contract; the unlawful means used were the inducement of the employees' breaches. Moreover, there was no statutory protection at the time, since the breach induced was not of a contract of employment.

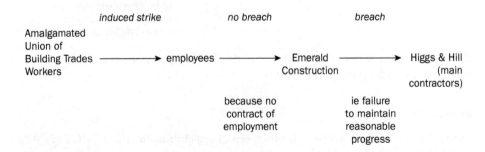

Justification

Justification is more narrowly circumscribed as a defence to inducement than to the other economic torts. Indeed, it has succeeded only in *Brimelow v Casson* [1924] 1 Ch 302, and there in very special circumstances. Chorus girls employed by the defendant, a notorious impresario at the time, were paid so little that they had to resort to immorality to make ends meet. A strike in protest at these conditions was held to be justified in the circumstances, even though it induced breach of the employer's contract to perform his 'King Wu Tut' review for the good burghers of Dudley. **21.38**

The wider argument that the defence is available where there is no ill will towards the employer (thus attempting to generalise from *Brimelow*'s case), was scotched in *South Wales Miners' Federation v Glamorgan Coal Co Ltd* [1905] AC 239 (see *British Motor Trades Association v Salvadori* [1949] Ch 556; *Camden Nominees Ltd v Forcey* [1940] Ch 352). Moreover, in *Greig v Insole* [1978] 3 All ER 449, where the International Cricket Council was found to have induced breach of cricketers' contracts with the Kerry Packer World Cricket Series, Slade J held that the Council's contention that it had acted from 'disinterested and impersonal motives' did not amount to justification. **21.39**

Immunity

There have been successive amendments to the immunity for the tort. The original immunity was enacted in the Trade Disputes Act 1906 for inducement to breach a contract in contemplation or furtherance of a trade dispute, but applied only in the case of *employment* contracts. It endured until 1971 when the Industrial Relations Act converted certain methods of inducing breach of contract briefly into unfair industrial practices, for example, where a person was acting outside the scope of authority and calling a strike without notice, and only gave immunity to registered unions (s 96). The position which existed in 1906 was restored by the Trade Union and Labour Relations (Amendment) Act 1976 which inserted s 13(1)(a) into the TULRA 1974 (now TULR(C)A 1992, s 219). **21.40**

This provided that an act done by a person in contemplation or furtherance of a trade dispute shall not be actionable in tort on the ground only: **21.41**

(a) that it induces another person to break a contract or interferes or induces any other person to interfere with its performance; or
(b) that it consists of his threatening that a contract (whether one to which he is a party or not) will be broken or its performance interfered with, or that he will induce another person to break a contract or to interfere with its performance.

The Employment Act 1980 reduced its scope by excluding from protection certain secondary action, that is, to bring pressure to bear on a party not in dispute, and also declared that any act of picketing leading to inducement of breach of contract was not lawful unless conforming to the now stricter immunity for picketing (TULR(C)A 1992, s 220). The Labour Government further amended the provision (see Chapter 22 on picketing). **21.42**

Example Slim Trousers' workers strike and in order to exert pressure on Slim Trousers his workers picket Bright Buttons Ltd and persuade its workers not to make buttons required by Slim. They have induced breach of the workers' contracts of employment, and since the picketing does not meet the conditions of s 220 of the 1992 Act, as amended by the 1980 Act, because the picketing is not of Slim's premises, they are not protected from the tort of inducing breach of contract. **21.43**

E INTERFERENCE WITH CONTRACT

The tort

21.44   Lord Denning MR, on several occasions, stated that a wide tort exists of interference with contract by unlawful means, of which inducement of breach and intimidation are but two examples. This opens the prospect of a much wider arc of liability—there need be no breach of contract and the claimant need not be a party to the contract broken, but need only have an interest capable of protection. It may also extend to the prevention of an *expectation* that a contract would be made (*Brekkes Ltd v Cattel* [1972] Ch 105). In *Barretts & Baird (Wholesale) Ltd v IPCS* [1987] IRLR 3, Henry J stated the basic elements of the tort as follows:

> first that there should be interference with the plaintiffs' trade or business....; secondly, that there should be the unlawful means ...; thirdly, that that should be with the intention to injure the plaintiffs ...; and, fourthly, that the action should in fact injure [the plaintiffs].

21.45   The central significance of such a development for labour law is that it lies altogether *outside* the trade dispute immunity. In *Merkur Island Shipping Corporation v Laughton* [1983] 2 AC 570 at 609, Lord Diplock regarded the tort of 'interfering with the trade or business of another person by doing unlawful acts' as a 'genus of torts' of which procuring breach of contract is a 'species'.

21.46   The history of the tort is a complex one and its definition is still imprecise. The House of Lords in *Allen v Flood* [1898] AC 1 said that an individual was not liable per se for intentionally inflicting economic loss on another, if the means which were used were otherwise lawful. The presence of malice or bad motive did not constitute the border post between lawfulness and unlawfulness. Thus, the defendant union official could with impunity threaten to call on the boilermakers who worked for the plaintiff to strike unless shipwrights also so employed were dismissed. Neither action was in breach of contract and so was quite legal even though the reason it was taken was to punish the shipwrights. This was always difficult to reconcile with *Quinn v Leathem* [1901] AC 495, also a decision of the House of Lords, and there were some straws in the wind before Lord Denning's series of pronouncements. For example, in *J.T. Stratford and Son Ltd v Lindley* [1965] AC 269, Lord Reid doubted whether breach of contract was essential to constitute a tort, although Lord Donovan thought this argument 'as novel and surprising as I think the members of this House who decided *Crofter Handwoven Harris Tweed Co Ltd v Veitch* would have done'.

21.47   The issue arose directly in *Torquay Hotel Co Ltd v Cousins* [1969] 2 Ch 106, the facts of which have already been given (21.22). There was a clause in the agreement between the fuel suppliers and the hotel that the former, Esso, would not be liable in contract for failure to supply should that be due to industrial dispute. Russell LJ narrowly interpreted this as 'an exception from liability for non-performance' (so that there was a breach of contract) and considered it as an ordinary inducement of breach of contract. Winn LJ suggested that if the contract allowed performance in mode A or mode B it would be tortious to prevent performance in mode A even if it could still be performed in mode B (see also *Greig v Insole* [1978] 3 All ER 449). However, Lord Denning MR, disagreeing, made an ample formulation that ([1969] 2 Ch at 130):

> ... if one person deliberately interferes with the trade or business of another, and does so by unlawful means, that is, by an act which he is not at liberty to commit, then he is acting unlawfully.

He thought this was the basis as properly understood of *Stratford v Lindley* (above) and *Rookes v Barnard* [1963] 1 QB 623, and defined the requirements of the tort of interference in some detail (at 139):

> First, there must be interference in the execution of a contract. The interference is not confined to the procurement of a *breach* of contract. It extends to a case where a third person prevents or *hinders* one party from performing his contract, even though it be not a breach. Second, the interference must be deliberate. The person must know of the contract, or, at any rate, turn a blind eye to it and intend to interfere with it: see *Emerald Construction Co Ltd v Lowthian* [1966] 1 WLR 691. Third, the interference must be *direct*. Indirect interference will not do.

21.48 The existence of the tort was affirmed by the House of Lords in *Hadmor Productions Ltd v Hamilton* [1983] 1 AC 191, where the plaintiff alleged that ACTT (Association of Cinematograph Television and Allied Technicians) officials threatened to persuade union members to refuse to transmit television programmes produced by the plaintiff. The plaintiff claimed that this was interference with the plaintiff's business by unlawful means. Thames TV had acquired a licence to transmit the programmes but was not contractually *bound* to do so. The House of Lords accepted the plaintiff's proposition that it could complain since the company's commercial *expectation* that the programmes would be broadcast was 'shattered' by the 'blacking'.

21.49 The tort was further rationalised in *Merkur Island Shipping Corporation v Laughton* [1983] 2 AC 570. The facts followed the familiar pattern in international shipping cases. The International Transport Workers Federation organised blacking of the plaintiff's Liberian registered ship after a crew member complained of low wages. When the ship sought to leave the Port of Liverpool, tugmen and lock-keepers refused to assist its free passage. The House of Lords agreed with Parker J's formulation that the tort of 'interfering by unlawful means' consisted of 'procuring the tugmen and the lockmen to break their contracts of employment by refusing to carry out operations on the part of the tugmen and the port authorities that were necessary to enable the ship to leave the dock'. The contractual duty under the charter was to 'prosecute voyages with the utmost dispatch'. The plaintiff could not rely on procurement of breach of contract since there was a *force majeure* clause. This provided an exclusion from liability, *inter alia*, 'in the event of loss of time due to boycott of the vessel in any port or place by shore labour or others'. Lord Diplock distinguished for these purposes between the primary obligations of the parties to perform under the contract, and their secondary obligations, to pay damages for breach, and said (at 608B):

> All prevention of due performance of a primary obligation under a contract was intended to be included [in the definition of interference] even though no secondary obligation to make monetary compensation thereupon came into existence, because the second obligation was excluded by some *force majeure* clause.

21.50 As to knowledge of the contract breached, Lord Diplock thought that there 'can hardly be anyone better informed than the International Transport Workers Federation as to the terms of the sort of contracts under which ships are employed' (see also *Dimbleby & Sons Ltd v NUJ* [1984] 1 WLR 427; *Thomas v NUM (South Wales Area)* [1985] IRLR 136; *Messenger Newspaper Group v NGA* [1984] IRLR 397).

21.51 The tort of interference may also cover such interference with future contracts not yet in existence (*J.T. Stratford and Son Ltd v Lindley* [1965] AC 269 at 339; *Union Traffic Ltd v TGWU* [1989] ICR 98 at 105). This was not made out by the distribution of leaflets outside supermarkets urging members of the public to boycott the employer's mushrooms (*Middlebrook Mushrooms Ltd v TGWU* [1993] ICR 612). The plaintiff was not able to prove a causal connection between the defendant's action and a contract breaker. Since the leaflet was directed at the public and not the management of the supermarkets, any pressure or inducement to act in breach of contract would come from the public and only indirectly from the defendants, so that the action was not tortious at all. To be tortious, the persuasion had to be directed at one of the parties to the commercial contract in issue.

Unlawful means

21.52 Indirect interference can be restrained only if unlawful means are adopted. Interference appears to include any hindrance upon the freedom of either party to perform the contract (see also *Acrow (Automation) Ltd v Rex Chain Belts Inc* [1971] WLR 1676 at 1682). In *Torquay Hotel Co v Cousins* (21.22 above), the majority held that there were breaches of contract, but Lord Denning MR returned to a similar theme in *BBC v Hearn* [1978] 1 All ER 111 and *Beaverbrook Newspapers Ltd v Keys* [1978] IRLR 34, where he said that coercive interference with another's freedom of action was in itself unlawful. In *Associated Newspapers v Wade* [1979] ICR 664, he widened the principle still further by suggesting that some matters (here interference with freedom of the press) could be so contrary to public policy that they could themselves amount to unlawful means. Thus, the National Graphical Association's blacking of advertisements in a local newspaper with which it was in dispute was held to be unlawful means, partly because it prevented some public authorities and local councils from complying with their statutory duties to publish formal notice of proposed actions. It did not matter that neither party could enforce the unlawfulness by an independent cause of action. An act contrary to the Restrictive Practices Act 1956 has also been held, albeit *obiter*, to suffice (*Daily Mirror Ltd v Gardner* [1968] 2 QB 762).

21.53 The Court of Appeal has indicated that inducing breach of statutory duty may constitute unlawful means (*Meade v Haringey LBC* [1979] 2 All ER 1016), notwithstanding that some such breaches are only technical and almost incidental to the strike action itself. In *Associated Newspapers Ltd v Wade* (above), the defendant and the executive of the National Graphical Association ordered the blacking of all advertisements of advertisers who continued to use the Nottingham Evening Post with which the union was engaged in a bitter industrial dispute. This incidentally made it difficult for many public bodies to fulfil their statutory duties to make public announcements, and provided the unlawful means for indirect inducement. Further, Lord Denning MR thought the action would anyway have been unlawful as an infringement of Art 10 of the European Convention on Human Rights. Inducing such a breach of statutory duty lies outside the trade dispute immunity which refers only to inducing breach of *contract*. The presence of unlawful means depends on the true construction of the appropriate statute (*Lonrho v Shell Petroleum Co Ltd (No 2)* [1982] AC 173).

21.54 Inducing a breach of statutory duty may thus constitute unlawful means, but that was not the case in:

(a) *Barretts & Baird (Wholesale) Ltd v IPCS* [1987] IRLR 3, since there was nothing in the relevant statutes which imposed a statutory duty that the Meat and Livestock Commission should produce a strike-free system.

(b) *Associated British Ports v TGWU* [1989] IRLR 399, since there was, properly construed, no statutory obligation by clause 8(1)(b) of the National Dock Labour Scheme 1967 requiring registered dock workers to work. It provided that: 'A permanent worker ... shall ... (b) work for such periods as are reasonable in his particular case.' The House of Lords upheld the judgment of Millett J (which had been overturned by the Court of Appeal) and decided that this was not a statutory obligation but rather a condition of applicability of the scheme to registered dock workers.

This finding by the House of Lords that clause 8(1)(b) did not impose a statutory duty meant that they did not have to consider the judgments of the Court of Appeal as to the scope of the tort.

In *Barretts & Baird Wholesale Ltd v IPCS* (above), Henry J found an arguable case that a **21.55** striker's own breach of his contract of employment constituted unlawful means. In order to render an individual striker liable in tort to any third party damaged by that strike, it is necessary that his predominant purpose be injury to the claimant rather than his own self-interest.

Immunity

There was an immunity from a species of this tort which dated back to the Trade Disputes **21.56** Act 1906. Section 13(2) of the TULRA 1974 provided:

> For the avoidance of doubt it is hereby declared that an act done in contemplation or further-ance of a trade dispute is not actionable in tort on the ground only that it is an interference with the trade, business or employment of another person or with the right of another person to dispose of his capital or his labour as he will.

This was, however, repealed by s 19(1) of the EA 1982.

F INTIMIDATION

The tort

In 1793 the master of a slave trading ship (A) in the Cameroons fired at a canoe which was **21.57** about to do business with another vessel (B), and the natives in panic ceased to trade with B as a result of the volley. On an action by vessel B, the Court of Common Pleas held that the defendant, the master of ship (A), was liable in damages for intimidation since the plain-tiff had lost financially as the result of a threat of violence (*Tarleton v McGawley* (1793) 1 Peake 270). This may seem far removed from the modern industrial dispute, but in *Rookes v Barnard* [1964] AC 1129, the House of Lords developed this tort to include threat of a breach of contract or other unlawful act as well as threats of violence. This was one of the most con-troversial cases of the century and the result was reached notwithstanding that Pearson LJ in the Court of Appeal had described the tort as 'obscure, unfamiliar and peculiar' ([1963] 1 QB 623 at 695). The Association of Engineering and Shipbuilding Draughtsmen threat-ened to withdraw its labour if a non-unionist was not removed by British Overseas Airlines Corporation (a predecessor of BA) within three days, in order to preserve its informal closed shop. Inducement of breach of contract was not here available as a cause of action, since the employee was lawfully dismissed with notice, but the House of Lords held that this anyway constituted the tort of intimidation and awarded exemplary damages to the employee con-cerned. The unlawful threat was contained in threatening to act in breach of contract, since it had been conceded by counsel for the union that a no-strike clause of a collective agree-ment had been incorporated into the contracts of individual workers.

The objection that allowing breach of contract to be a threat enabled a person not a party **21.58** to a contract to sue on it was summarily rejected by the House of Lords. The principle seems to be that the claimant can sue the defendant for intimidation if he could succeed in an action for breach of contract had the defendant carried out the threat. Liability in *Rookes* was for an unlawful threat against BOAC, a third party which indirectly but unintentionally caused the plaintiff loss. The decision gave rise to much controversy, both academic (eg 1964 CLJ 159, 81 LQR 116) and political.

21.59   **There must be proof of loss** to constitute the tort. Thus, referring back to our earlier example, if Bill says to Slim that unless it shuts its factory he will break all of its windows, and Slim keeps the factory open and Bill does not carry out his threat, Slim has no cause of action. There must be a threat and damage resulting therefrom—if a union organiser says to the employer that if he does not concede higher wages he will paralyse the company's operations, and the employer does not give an increase and the union leader finds his fierce words not backed up by his members' actions, the employer has no cause of action in intimidation. *Hodges v Webb* [1920] Ch 70 defined a threat as 'an intimation by one to another that unless the latter does or does not do something, the former will do something which the latter will not like'. The difficulty is to distinguish in particular cases between a threat and a warning or mere advice.

21.60   It has also been suggested that the party who submits to a threat may claim the loss flowing therefrom (*DC Builders v Rees* [1966] 2 QB 617 at 625). This is known as two party intimidation. It is probably necessary that the defendant must then have the claimant directly in mind when making the threat. However, the threat must be 'of sufficient consequence to induce the other to submit' (Lord Denning in *Morgan v Fry* [1968] 2 QB 710 at 724).

Immunity

21.61   The development of the tort of intimidation caused an outcry in the trade union movement as it would potentially render every strike illegal. Thus, the Trade Disputes Act 1965 soon afterwards extended trade dispute immunity to the newly coined tort where the person acted 'in contemplation or furtherance of a trade dispute'. Section 13(1)(b) of the TULRA 1974 (now s 219(1)(b) of the TULR(C)A 1992) continued with that policy by granting immunity to action 'where it consists in threatening that a contract (whether one to which he is a party or not) will be broken or its performance interfered with, or that he will induce another person to break a contract or interfere with its performance'. The provision was further widened in 1976 to cover breaches of commercial as well as employment contracts, but there is no protection against intimidation for secondary action (21.103–21.105).

G CONSPIRACY

The tort

21.62   It was only a few years after the abolition of the criminality of trade unions for conspiracies (Conspiracy and Protection of Property Act 1875, s 3) that the courts developed a *tort* of conspiracy with precisely the same components. Since injunctions were granted freely its effects were also similar. It was described by Willes J in *Mulcahy v R* (1868) LR 3 HL 306 at 317, as consisting 'in the agreement of two or more to do an unlawful act, or to do a lawful act by unlawful means'. A conspiracy to commit a crime or a tort is clearly included in this class whereas whether it includes agreement to commit a breach of contract is less certain (see *Rookes v Barnard* [1964] AC 1129, Lord Devlin at 1210).

It is, however, the second part of the definition—'unlawful means' conspiracy—which **21.63** is the most difficult and invidious, because it makes unlawful when done by two or more what would have been quite lawful when performed by an individual, for example, *Kamara v DPP* [1974] AC 104. A conspiracy to injure consists of an agreement to cause deliberate loss to another without cause or excuse with the intention of injuring the claimant (eg *Huntley v Thornton* [1957] 1 All ER 234). The unlawful means of pursuing the strike must, however, be integral to the aims of the conspirators and not peripheral to them. Similarly, it would not render it unlawful that the strike organiser broke the speed limit as he raced to a mass meeting. The scope of the tort appeared to have been cut down by the House of Lords in *Lonrho Ltd v Shell Petroleum Ltd (No 2)* [1982] AC 173 (see also *Metall und Rohstoff AG v Donaldson Lufkin & Jenrette Inc* [1989] 3 All ER 14) in so far as Lord Diplock was taken to have suggested that even in an unlawful means conspiracy, the court had to determine that the predominant purpose of the defendants was to injure the claimants. In the case of *Lonrho plc v Fayed* [1992] AC 448, however, the House of Lords clarified that this was requisite only in a lawful means conspiracy.

In *Quinn v Leathem* [1901] AC 495, officials of the union asked the respondent butcher to **21.64** dismiss a non-unionist, and, on his refusal to do so, told him that an important customer would be warned to cease dealing with him under threat of strike if he persisted in denying their request. The matter went before a jury which found that the union's motive was to *injure* the respondent and not to promote the interests of the union. On appeal, five members of the House of Lords decided that this was actionable as a tortious conspiracy notwithstanding that the defendants had not committed any otherwise unlawful act in inducing the butcher no longer to trade with the plaintiff; there had been no crime, tort, or breach of contract. This decision was also reached notwithstanding that *Allen v Flood* [1898] AC 1 showed that action done with the desire to injure was not in itself necessarily tortious. In *Mogul Steamship Co v McGregor, Gow and Co* [1892] AC 25, the House of Lords delineated the threefold requirements of the tort as:

(a) *combination* by at least two persons;
(b) intentionally causing *loss*; with
(c) the *predominant purpose* not to further a legitimate interest.

(See an attempted reconciliation in *Thomas v NUM (South Wales Area)* [1985] 2 WLR 1081.)

The claimant must thus always prove an agreement between the parties, not merely coin- **21.65** cidental action on their part.

Justification

Traders often combine in an attempt to create a monopoly and this has received the bless- **21.66** ing of the common law in, for example, the *Mogul Steamship* case, where it was said that 'otherwise most commercial men would be at risk of legal liability in their legitimate trading practices and competition would be dead'. The most important justification case involving trade unions is *Crofter Handwoven Harris Tweed Co v Veitch* [1942] AC 435, where the TGWU combined with Stornaway dockers to prevent yarn imports from the mainland in order to achieve a closed shop. The House of Lords found this conspiracy to injure justified since the predominant purpose was the promotion of the combiners' legitimate interest, for they wished to secure the elimination of price competition which was holding down wages at the largest spinning mill where their members were employed (see also *Reynolds v Shipping Federation* [1924] 1 Ch 28). Lord Wright said that: 'The true contrast is between the case where the object is the legitimate benefit of the combiners and the case where the object is deliberate damage without any such just cause'.

21.67   Courts have also held legitimate: attempts to force an employer to abandon a policy of refusing to employ trade unionists (*D. C. Thomson & Co Ltd v Deakin* [1952] Ch 646); a campaign against a colour bar in a club (*Scala Ballroom (Wolverhampton) Ltd v Ratcliffe* [1958] 3 All ER 220); and the enforcement of a closed shop (*Reynolds v Shipping Federation* [1924] 1 Ch 28). *Huntley v Thornton* [1957] 1 All ER 234 was an exception, since most members of a union district committee who expelled their fellow member acted merely out of personal grudge and a desire for vengeance, although two were acquitted of such motivations and thus were not liable for the tort. The bitterness arose because he had not complied with union instructions to stop work some twenty-four hours before.

Immunity

21.68   In most cases in the trade union area, an immunity against liability for conspiracy is superfluous since the motivation with which it is carried on would amount to justification in itself at common law. Out of an abundance of caution, immunity is provided generally by what is now the TULR(C)A 1992, s 219(2), so that:

> An agreement or combination by two or more persons to do or procure the doing of any act in contemplation or furtherance of a trade dispute shall not be actionable in tort if the act is one which, if done without any such agreement or combination, would not be actionable in tort.

Criminal conspiracy

21.69   The law of criminal conspiracy was the most potent weapon against the early trade unions, both as in restraint of trade and for restricting strike action. Section 3 of the Conspiracy and Protection of Property Act 1875 provided a first small step towards the modern immunities when it excluded criminal liability for acts in contemplation or furtherance of a trade dispute which would not be punishable as a crime if done by an individual. It also removed liability for conspiracy to injure committed without use of unlawful means. This was repeated by the Criminal Law Act 1977, a general statute reforming criminal conspiracy which provides a specific statutory form of conspiracy (s 1(3)), normally biting on actions which would be crimes by individuals.

21.70   It is, however, specifically provided for trade unionists that where the acts agreed upon are to be done in contemplation or furtherance of a trade dispute any offence that would be committed shall be disregarded so long as it is a summary offence which is not punishable with imprisonment.

H TRADE DISPUTE IMMUNITY

The section

21.71   When Parliament originally granted immunities to the leaders of trade unions, it did not give them any rights. It did not give them a right to break the law or to do wrong by inducing people to break their contracts. It only gave them immunity if they did and 'such statutes are to be construed with due limitations so as to keep the immunity within reasonable bounds' (*Express Newspapers Ltd v McShane* [1980] ICR 42).

We have already considered under the heading of each tort how immunity safeguards trade **21.72** unionists against liability for each individual tort, but must return to the overall structure of s 19 of the TULR(C)A 1992. It begins: 'An act done by a person in contemplation or furtherance of a trade dispute shall *not be actionable in tort on the ground only*'—and then sets out the specific torts in respect of which immunity is conferred against. Every word counts. The section protects a defendant against a claim for an injunction as well as a claim for damages (*Torquay Hotel Co Ltd v Cousins* [1969] 2 Ch 106 at 141, 144–6).

The meaning of 'not actionable'

The words used only render the strike *'not actionable'* and do not make it lawful for all **21.73** purposes. Thus, for example, in *J.T. Stratford and Son Ltd v Lindley* [1965] AC 269, the plaintiff could not sue for the direct inducement by the union of the employee's breach of contract of employment since that clearly fell within the immunity. However, that illegality provided the *unlawful means* for procuring breach of commercial contract and the strike could be restrained on that ground. To remedy this anomaly, s 13(3)(b) of the TULRA 1974 declared that a tort involving breach of contract within the 'golden formula' (see 21.100–21.102), 'shall not be regarded as the doing of an unlawful act or as the use of unlawful means for the purpose of establishing liability in tort'.

The subsection was, however, repealed by the Employment Act 1980, and the true effect **21.74** of the repeal arose in *Hadmor Productions Ltd v Hamilton* [1983] 1 AC 191. The plaintiff company produced a series of programmes ironically called 'Unforgettable' featuring pop musicians. Their *modus operandi* involved hiring freelance members of the Association of Cinematograph Television and Allied Technicians (ACTT), rather than direct employment, and was viewed with suspicion by the union. This hostility had led in the past to a complete blacking of programmes made by facility companies (as they were called), but by the time of Hadmor's foundation in August 1979 this stance had softened somewhat, as was confirmed in a letter from the union. As a result, Thames TV informally undertook to purchase the relevant series, but the ACTT shop stewards at Thames were unhappy, threatened to black the series, and consequently the company withdrew its transmission. As we have seen, the House of Lords held that the defendant shop stewards had interfered with the plaintiff's business by unlawful means. They disagreed with Lord Denning MR, who thought that owing to the repeal of s 13(3) of the TULRA, the blacking in breach of the technicians' contracts constituted unlawful means.

Other torts

There are certain other torts which may be committed in strike situations, such as tres- **21.75** pass and inducement of breach of statutory duty against which no statutory protection is given by the 'golden formula'. Another possible flanking movement is a claim in restitution for duress. This was canvassed without success in *Universe Tankships Inc of Monrovia v ITWF* [1983] AC 366. The plaintiff claimed to recover money paid to the defendant Federation's Welfare Fund on the ground that it had been paid under duress. The action was framed in restitution rather than tort, but the House of Lords paid regard to the intention of the TULRA 1974 to exempt all forms of industrial action from liability. Thus, where there were alternative remedies of restitution and damages available, the plaintiff should not be allowed to circumnavigate the Act by recovering by a restitutionary remedy what he could not gain as damages. There is a difficult line to be drawn between hard bargaining by a union and illegitimate coercion.

Dimskal Shipping Co SA v International Transport Workers Federation [1992] ICR 37, **21.76** [1992] IRLR 78, concerned the blacking of the vessel 'Evia Luck' at Uddevalla, Sweden, in pursuance of the ITF's campaign against the registration of vessels under flags of convenience. Under pressure, the plaintiffs paid over US$110,000 to the ITF, and thereafter sought restitution thereof, and damages for the torts of intimidation and interference with contractual rights. The judge found that the industrial action was lawful under Swedish law. The House of Lords, with Lord Templeman dissenting, held that the material or essential validity of the contract was governed by its proper law, which in this case was English law, and that illegitimate economic pressure, including blacking of a ship, was duress, which avoided the contract made between the ITF and the shipowners.

Trade dispute

21.77 To be protected, the individual must be acting in contemplation or furtherance of *a trade dispute*, and by s 244(1) of the TULR(C)A 1992, this means importantly: 'A dispute between workers and their employer, that is to say, which relates wholly or mainly to one of the following:

(a) terms and conditions of employment, or the physical conditions in which any workers are required to work;

(b) engagement or non-engagement, or termination or suspension of employment or the duties of employment, of one or more workers;

(c) allocation of work or the duties of employment as between workers or groups of workers;

(d) matters of discipline;

(e) the membership or non-membership of a trade union on the part of a worker;

(f) facilities for officials of trade unions; and

(g) machinery for negotiation or consultation, and other procedures, relating to any of the foregoing matters, including the recognition by employers or employers' associations of the right of a trade union to represent workers in any such negotiation or consultation or in the carrying out of such procedures'.

This is commonly termed the 'golden formula' and dates back to the Conspiracy and Protection of Property Act 1875, although in that statute it dealt with picketing alone. It was, however, extended in the Trade Disputes Act 1906, passed by the Liberal Government to give protection to trade unionists specifically against the decision sanctioning tortious conspiracy, *Quinn v Leathem* [1901] AC 495, since this case threatened to make most strike action unlawful.

21.78 The Industrial Relations Act 1971 altered the nomenclature to 'industrial dispute' and restricted the scope of the immunity to exclude disputes between groups of workers. After this short-lived experiment the substance of the 1906 provisions was re-enacted with some extensions in the TULRA 1974, amended by the Trade Union and Labour Relations (Amendment) Act 1976, and then again restricted by the Employment Acts 1980 and 1982 and Trade Union Act 1984. Since then, legislative activity has been confined to the ballot requirements. All this material is now consolidated by the TULR(C)A 1992. It does not add up to a general right to strike. The economic torts, as we have seen, reign supreme where the variant of tort committed is not precisely within those which are granted immunity, and where the act is not carried out in contemplation or furtherance of a trade dispute, as defined. This has left the judges much room for manoeuvre, and AWR Carothers has described the area as exhibiting 'a seesaw vendetta between the courts and the legislature' (*Collective Bargaining Law in Canada*, at 57). The discussion of trade disputes here is divided into the definition of:

(a) parties (21.79–21.82);

(b) dispute (21.83–21.84);

(c) subject-matter (21.85–21.95);
(d) 'relates wholly or mainly to' (21.96–21.99; and
(e) in contemplation or furtherance of (21.100–21.102).

We then turn to:

(f) secondary action (21.103–21.105);
(g) strike ballots (21.106ff);
(h) union recruitment strikes (21.154); and
(i) particular statutory restrictions on industrial action (21.155ff).

'Secondary action' means action directed against an employer's suppliers or customers, that is, those in a business relationship with him, rather than at the employer himself, which is primary action (TULR(C)A 1992, s 224).

Parties

The freedom to strike afforded by the 'golden formula' used to extend to a dispute between   **21.79**
employers and workers, or between workers and workers, and thus protected demarcation disputes or arguments over union recognition which used to be quite frequently encountered. This was restricted, however, by s 18(2) of the EA 1982 to disputes between 'workers and their employer'.

The operative word is 'workers' and this used to include those who seek to work, and   **21.80**
those reinstated after dismissal. Section 244(5) of the TULR(C)A 1992, however, now excludes a person who has ceased to be employed unless:

(a) his employment was terminated in connection with the dispute; or
(b) was one of the circumstances giving rise to that particular dispute.

It is irrelevant that the employer may change his business identity during the course of the conflict. Thus, Lord Denning said 'the words "employers" and "workers" in [s 244(5)] apply to employers whatever the particular hat those particular employers may wear from time to time' (*Examite Ltd v Whittaker* [1977] IRLR 312; *The Marabu Porr* [1979] 2 Lloyd's Rep 331). The veil will not, however, normally be lifted as between separate companies in respect of secondary action (*Dimbleby & Sons Ltd v NUJ* [1984] 1 WLR 427; see 21.103–21.105).

The immunity may be claimed by any person who is sued when acting in contemplation   **21.81**
or furtherance of a trade dispute, whether or not he is an officer of the union, and there is thus no distinction at all between official and unofficial action save in respect to the ballot provisions which apply only to official action. Disputes between employer and employer are not granted immunity (*Larkin v Long* [1915] AC 814), so that union activity to support one side or another is not protected.

A dispute will relate to employees' terms and conditions only where it concerns their   **21.82**
relationship with their *current* employer. This was the Court of Appeal's conclusion in *University College Hospital NHS Trust v UNISON* [1999] IRLR 31, in which a hospital trust obtained an injunction preventing UNISON calling its members out on strike. The dispute had arisen after the Trust refused the union's demand that it enter into an agreement with a consortium taking over the hospital which bound the consortium, 'its associates, subcontractors and successors', for a period of up to thirty years, to provide terms and conditions equivalent to those applying under the Trust. The court was persuaded that the strike would be unlawful since it related to employers other than the Trust and, in view of the length of the guarantee sought, to employees who would never have worked

for the Trust. (The case was taken by the union to the ECtHR but failed ([2002] IRLR 497).) According to the Court of Appeal in *Westminster City Council v UNISON* [2001] ICR 1046, however, a dispute about a proposal to transfer an undertaking, including its employees, from the local authority to a private company was a trade dispute, provided that the dispute was predominantly about the change in the identity of the employer and not about public policy issues. Pill LJ remarked that 'The court is concerned with the nature of dispute between individual employees and their employer and not with any stance taken by UNISON itself save in so far as it reflects the views of employees in dispute'.

The dispute

21.83   Lord Denning said that a dispute 'exists whenever a difference exists, and a difference can exist long before the parties become locked in combat ... It is sufficient that they should be sparring for an opening' (*Beetham v Trinidad Cement Ltd* [1960] AC 132). A dispute need not be in existence to provide immunity. According to *Conway v Wade* [1909] AC 506, it may be 'an objective event or situation ... likely to occur' (Lord Atkinson at 517) or 'a real thing imminent' (Lord Shaw at 512) (see *Associated British Ports plc v TGWU* [1989] IRLR 399).

21.84   There may be a dispute even if the employers concede to the demands of the union. Section 244(4) of the TULR(C)A 1992 provides that 'an act, threat or demand done or made by one person or organisation against another which, if resisted, would have led to a trade dispute with that other, shall, notwithstanding that because that other submits ... [and] no dispute arises, be treated as being done ... in contemplation of a trade dispute with that other'. This provision reverses the decision in *Cory Lighterage Ltd v TGWU* [1973] ICR 339, where the employer was at one with the union in seeking to preserve a closed shop, but could not gain permission from the National Dock Labour Board to dismiss the employee whose sacking the union sought. Buckley LJ decided (at 362):

> If someone threatens me with physical injury unless I hand over my wallet and I hand it over without demur, no one could, in my opinion, sensibly say that there had been any dispute about my handing over my wallet.

Thus, there was no immunity for the union's action since there was no dispute; but s 244(4) is a statutory reversal of this interpretation and a clear illustration of the effect of the statute was provided in *Hadmor Productions Ltd v Hamilton* [1983] 1 AC 191, where Thames TV submitted without a fight to the union's demand not to show a series made by a TV facility company. There is, however, no immunity for any action which is taken *after* a dispute has been settled (*Stewart v AUEW* [1973] ICR 128).

Subject matter

21.85   A trade dispute must relate wholly or mainly to one or more of the matters set out in s 244 of the TULR(C)A 1992, a list of matters which is intended to separate the sheep of industrial grievances, which it is legitimate for trade unions to pursue, from the goats of political or personal grievances with which, according to the policy of statute, they should not concern themselves. The 1906 immunity was restricted to disputes 'connected with the employment or non-employment, terms of employment or conditions of labour of any person'. This was then greatly extended in several directions, but the EA 1982 restricted it again, especially by requiring that the dispute relate *wholly or mainly* to the listed matters rather than merely being connected therewith, the lesser requirement under s 29(1) of the TULRA 1974 as originally enacted. The 1982 Act also removed immunity from pressure to impose an unlawful union membership only requirement, and this itself was modified by the Employment Act 1988.

The fact of the strike itself cannot be a trade dispute; it must rather be the manifestation **21.86** of a grievance over something comprised within the definition of trade dispute. This was clearly demonstrated in the important case of *BBC v Hearn* [1977] IRLR 273. The BBC sought to enjoin television technicians who were threatening to prevent transmission of the FA Cup Final to South Africa because of the policy of the Association of Broadcasting Staffs (of which the defendant was General Secretary) to oppose racial discrimination in that country. The Court of Appeal rejected the union's claim that this in itself amounted to a dispute about whether there should be a condition that employees should not be compelled to transmit to South Africa while its government practised apartheid. There had been no such demand for a term to be incorporated before the strike was called and accordingly no trade dispute existed. Lord Denning MR described the union's actions as 'coercive interference', and not falling within s 29(1), even though he thought the definition included:

> not only the contractual terms and conditions but those terms which are understood and applied by the parties in practice, or habitually or by common consent, without ever being incorporated into the contract. If the union had only asked: 'We would like you to consider putting a clause in the contract by which our members are not bound to take part in any broadcast which may be viewed in South Africa,' and the BBC had refused, they *would* then have been cloaked with the immunity.

Lord Diplock confirmed in *NWL Ltd v Woods* [1979] 3 All ER 614 (at 633–4) that the ratio of *Hearn*'s case would be strictly construed (cf also *Hadmor Productions Ltd v Hamilton* [1983] 1 AC 191 at 227).

There are *dicta* that the dispute must be about the current contract and that the claims of **21.87** a union may be so preposterous as not to be genuine but these arguments rarely succeed. One of the defendant union's arguments in *Dimbleby & Sons Ltd v NUJ* [1984] 1 WLR 427 (at 433) was that there was a dispute over terms and conditions in that there was an implied term in the journalists' contracts entitling them to refuse to comply with instructions given to them by the employers to provide copy of the kind they were employed to obtain if the NUJ gave them an instruction to the contrary. Lord Diplock stated that 'it passes beyond the bounds of credibility that any responsible newspaper proprietor would agree to such a term in contracts of employment with his journalists' (see also 21.27 and *Universe Tankships Inc of Monrovia v ITF* [1983] AC 366 at 388; *London Borough of Wandsworth v National Association of Schoolmasters/Union of Women Teachers* [1993] IRLR 344).

In *P v The National Association of School Masters/Union of Women Teachers* [2001] **21.88** ICR 1241, the Court of Appeal held that there was a trade dispute when employees refused to teach a particular pupil who, it was claimed, was disruptive in class. The reality was that the teachers' working conditions were in dispute, as to instructions given to them by the headteacher. Thus, a dispute about the reasonableness of an instruction may be about terms and conditions. The court explained *BBC v Hearn*, where an injunction was granted, as being a case where no dispute had arisen between employers and employees about anything.

We will now consider the following strikes which fall *outside* the definition of trade **21.89** dispute:

(a) disputes motivated by personal malice (21.90–21.91);
(b) political strikes (21.92–21.94); and

(c) foreign disputes (21.95).

Personal disputes

21.90   It may be a matter of some difficulty to identify properly what a strike is connected with, especially when it is called for a variety of different reasons. However, in some cases the reasons for action clearly have nothing to do with pursuing a trade dispute, for example, in *Conway v Wade* [1909] AC 506, at 512, Lord Loreburn said:

> If, however, some meddler sought to use the trade dispute as a cloak beneath which to inter-fere with impunity in other people's work or business, a jury would be entirely justified in saying that what he did was done in contemplation or in furtherance, not of a trade dispute, but of his own designs, sectarian, political or purely mischievous as the case might be.

21.91   *Huntley v Thornton* [1957] 1 All ER 234 was a strong case which fell outside of pro-tection. As a result of the plaintiff's refusal to take part in a one-day strike, his work-mates declined to work with him and the Hartlepool District Committee of his union attempted to ensure that he did not get another job in the area. They threatened to organise strikes to secure the success of this policy. The atmosphere was poisonous and Harman J decided that even if there had been a trade dispute in the first place, the union was now acting merely out of ruffled dignity in a personal vendetta. Similarly, in *Torquay Hotel Co Ltd v Cousins* [1969] 2 Ch 106, the court found that the black-ing of the plaintiff's hotel by the defendant union was motivated by a desire to suppress criticism by its manager of their existing dispute; there was no trade dispute between the defendant and plaintiff so that there was no immunity. In *J.T. Stratford and Son Ltd v Lindley* [1965] AC 269, the House of Lords held that there was no trade dispute because the union's contentions were really not about terms and conditions, but because the Watermen's Union was annoyed with the employer in the course of rivalry with the TGWU (see 21.22–21.24).

Political strikes

21.92   Political strikes are not trade disputes, and there has never been any immunity for them. The distinguishing features of a political strike are, however, by no means easy to deline-ate. As Roskill LJ commented in *Sherard v AUEW* [1973] IRLR 188 (at para 20):

> It is all too easy for someone to talk of a strike as being a political strike when what that person really means is that the object of the strike is something of which, as an individual, he objectively disapproves.

The most famous determination that there was a political rather than a trade dispute was in respect of the General Strike of 1926 which was thus deprived of immunity by Astbury J (*National Sailors and Firemen's Union of GB and Ireland v Reed* [1926] 1 Ch 536).

21.93   Strikes held to protest against government policies have received the same treatment, whether called, as in *Associated Newspapers Group Ltd v Flynn* (1970) 10 KIR 17, to protest against the Industrial Relations Bill, or, as in *Beaverbrook Newspapers Ltd v Keys* [1978] IRLR 34, as part of the unions' collective 'day of action' against the Government's economic policies. One outstanding characteristic of these disputes is that the employer is in no position to concede the demands of those who are taking the industrial action. Thus, in *Gouriet v UPW* [1978] AC 435, the Post Office, whose employees threatened to stop mail to South Africa, could have no direct effect on the racialist government there. Similarly, there is no immunity where employees strike with the aim of bringing about a change in their employer's political policy, for example, objecting to the contribution of the employer to the Conservative Party, local government workers protesting about their employer council's policy of investing in South Africa, or hospital workers rejecting the principle of pay beds. On the other hand, in *Sherard*'s case the Court of Appeal would not enjoin a one-day strike against the Government's wage freeze, for the union had some members who were employed by the Government and objected to their pay being restrained in this way, and this was a typical industrial grievance. Further, union members are protected if they are directly affected by the government policies protested against in other ways, for example, concerning denationalisation as in *General Aviation Services UK Ltd v TGWU* [1974] ICR 35, since this might lead to redundancies (see also *Hadmor Productions Ltd v Hamilton* [1983] 1 AC 191; *Associated British Ports plc v TGWU* [1989] IRLR 399; *University College Hospital NHS Trust v UNISON* [1999] IRLR 31).

It is necessary in this area to distinguish the role of the Government as national guardian and also as employer. The 'golden formula' does not cover the former, but in the latter capacity it is no different from any other management. Moreover, a dispute between a minister and workers may be a trade dispute, even where he is not the employer, if he must approve a settlement of the dispute (TULR(C)A 1992, s 244(2)). Examples closer to the dividing line include road workers striking against a decision not to build a motorway, or prison officers against any increase in prison numbers which they fear may lead to violent confrontation. Action designed by union members above all to change the policies of the union's own executive is, however, outside the scope of the immunity (*PBDS National Carriers v Filkins* [1979] IRLR 356). **21.94**

Foreign disputes

By s 244 of the TULR(C)A 1992, a trade dispute exists 'even though it relates to matters occurring outside the United Kingdom' provided that 'the person or persons whose actions in the United Kingdom are said to be in contemplation or furtherance of a trade dispute relating to matters outside the United Kingdom are likely to be affected in respect of one or more of the matters specified in s 244 [of TULR(C)A] ... by the outcome of that dispute' (s 244(3)). This sanctions the taking of action in solidarity with colleagues working for the same multinational abroad, but only if their pay or conditions are likely to have an effect on those in the UK. **21.95**

'Relate wholly or mainly'

Until 1982 a dispute needed only to be 'connected with' the acceptable subjects of the 'golden formula' to gain immunity. The provision of the 1982 Act that it must 'relate wholly or mainly' to one or more such subjects was among the most important reforms ushered in by that legislation. The industrial issue need not be predominant in the minds of the strikers. **21.96**

The significance of the reform arose first in *Mercury Communications Ltd v Scott-Garner* [1984] Ch 37. The union objected to the Government's liberalisation of telecommunications from which the company, as one of the first licensed operators besides British Telecom, stood to gain. The claimant planned to establish a digital communications network partly using the BT network. The National Executive Committee of the Post Office Engineers Union, however, instructed its members, the vast majority of whom were employed by BT, not to connect Project Mercury to the BT system. The Court of Appeal decided that the dispute was wholly or mainly about government policy. Although the union honestly and fervently believed that their campaign was in the best interests of the jobs and conditions of service of employees in the industry, it did not follow that industrial action in the course of that campaign constituted a dispute 'wholly or mainly' about the threat of redundancy if the monopoly were not maintained. **21.97**

21.98   Sir John Donaldson MR thought that (at 79):

> In context the phrase 'wholly or mainly relates to' directs attention to what the dispute is
> about and, if it is about more than one matter, what it is mainly about. What it does *not*
> direct attention to is the reason why the parties are in dispute ... A contributory cause of the
> dispute and possibly the main cause is the belief that redundancy ('termination ... of employ-
> ment' in the words of the section) is just around the corner, but the dispute is not about that
> or, if it be preferred, relates wholly or mainly to pay ...

He considered that Parliament 'intended a relatively restricted meaning to be given to the
phrase "relates wholly or mainly to"' and that the most obvious way to find out what
a particular dispute is wholly or mainly about 'is to inquire what the men concerned ...
said to management at the time'. Here it was fatal that the union at no stage referred to
the job security agreement, which it would have done had the dispute been truly about
redundancies.

21.99   May LJ commended an 'ordinary common-sense approach' analogous to that which is
adopted when a court has before it a question of causation. He saw the present action as
springing from 'a political and ideological campaign seeking to maintain the concept of
public monopoly against private competition'. This may be contrasted with the case of
University College Hospital NHS Trust v UNISON [1999] IRLR 31, where the Court of
Appeal held that the fact that the union was opposed in principle to hospital privatisation
did not mean that industrial action aimed at protecting employees' terms and conditions
on the transfer of their employment to a private consortium was unlawful because it
was political, although it was declared unlawful for other reasons. A particular cause of
industrial action, they said, may have broader, political objectives as well as more limited
aims, namely to alleviate the anticipated consequences of the general policy. The more
limited aim can be the reason for taking action and, if so, will satisfy the requirements
of s 244 (see also *Associated British Ports plc v TGWU* [1989] IRLR 291). The case was
taken by the union to the European Court of Human Rights as *UNISON v UK* [2002]
IRLR 497 but was dismissed.

Contemplation or furtherance of a trade dispute

Contemplating a dispute

21.100   As we have seen, there needs to be a starting point to the coverage of the immunity; simply anticipating a fight as a future possibility is not enough. The words in 'contemplation'
meant, according to Lord Loreburn in *Conway v Wade* [1909] AC 506, 'that either a
dispute is imminent and the act is done in expectation of and with a view to it, or that the
dispute is already existing and the act is done in support of one side to it' (see also *Bent's
Brewery Co Ltd v Hogan* [1945] 2 All ER 570). On the other hand, in *Health Computing
Ltd v Meek* [1980] IRLR 437, NALGO sought, as a matter of policy, to ensure that its
members in the National Health Service had nothing to do with the plaintiff, a private
company which sought to supply computer systems to the NHS. Goulding J upheld the
union leaders' contention that a dispute was contemplated as likely to arise between its
members and any Health Service employers who engaged the plaintiff's services, notwithstanding that there was apparently no original demand made to management (cf *J.T.
Stratford and Son Ltd v Lindley* [1965] AC 269 and *BBC v Hearn* [1977] IRLR 273).

A remoteness test for secondary action

21.101   In several highly controversial cases the words 'in contemplation or furtherance' were
fashioned by the Court of Appeal into a 'remoteness' test to enjoin secondary action

but this was struck down several times by the House of Lords. The Court of Appeal, mainly under the influence of Lord Denning MR, had held that a union could not properly claim immunity for such secondary action because it found, objectively reviewing the evidence before it, that it was not furthering its trade dispute but was too remote from it (*Star Sea Transport Corp of Monrovia v Slater* [1978] IRLR 507 CA; *Express Newspapers Ltd v McShane* [1979] 2 All ER 760; *Associated Newspapers Ltd v Wade* [1979] 1 WLR 697; *PBDS v Filkins* [1979] IRLR 356; *Beaverbrook Newspapers Ltd v Keys* [1978] ICR 582). The House of Lords, however, decided that the only proper consideration was whether the defendant *honestly and genuinely believed* the action that he was taking would contribute in the disputes (*NWL Ltd v Woods* [1979] 3 All ER 614; *Express Newspapers v McShane* [1980] AC 672; and *Duport Steels Ltd v Sirs* [1980] 1 All ER 529).

In *NWL Ltd v Woods* (above) the International Transport Workers Federation threatened to black the *Nawala*, a ship owned by the plaintiff company, in pursuance of their longstanding protest against flags of convenience. They wanted to force the owners to pay higher wages in line with the ITF norm, but the Court of Appeal decided that this was not connected with matters listed in what is now s 244 of the TULR(C)A 1992 because the employers *could not* accede to the union's demands. The House of Lords overruled this and Lord Diplock stated (at 624A): **21.102**

> If a demand on an employer by the union is about terms and conditions of employment the fact that it appears to the court to be unreasonable because compliance with it is so difficult as to be commercially impracticable or will bankrupt the employer or drive him out of business, does not prevent its being a dispute connected with terms and conditions of employment. Immunity under s 13 [of TULRA 1974] is not forfeited by being stubborn or pig-headed.

(See also *Norbrook Laboratories Ltd v King* [1984] IRLR 200.)

I STATUTORY CONTROL OF SECONDARY ACTION

One of the central themes of the Thatcher Government's union policy was to cut down what these cases had shown to be the wide scope of the trade dispute immunity, by the popularly called 'secondary action' provisions of the Employment Act 1980. The sections operated by making an exception to the immunity which strikers would normally enjoy; they thus made strikers liable for action which causes breach of commercial contracts against other employers besides their own. This was subject to restricted exceptions which were still cloaked with the immunity and constituted permitted secondary action. **21.103**

Section 17(2) of the EA 1980 first defined 'secondary action' as: **21.104**

When, and only when, a person—

(a) induces another to break a contract of employment or interferes or induces another to interfere with its performance, or
(b) threatens that a contract of employment under which he or another is employed will be broken or its performance interfered with, or that he will induce another to break a contract of employment or to interfere with its performance,

if the employer under the contract of employment is not a party to the trade dispute.

A contract of employment for these purposes includes work done by independent contractors who undertake to perform the work personally. Section 4 of the Employment Act **21.105**

1990 finally removed all immunity for secondary action other than secondary picketing which is peaceful.

J STRIKE BALLOTS

21.106   The other main plank of the general Thatcherite restriction of strikes was the introduction of ballots before strikes could take place. Part II of the Trade Union Act 1984 (now ss 226–34 of the TULR(C)A 1992) removed the immunity of unions and individual strike organisers from certain actions in tort unless a majority of union members likely to be called out in industrial action have approved that action in a properly held ballot. The section applies, however, only to the torts of: inducing an employee to break his contract of employment; inducing an employee to interfere with the performance of his own contract of employment; and indirectly procuring a breach of or interference in a commercial contract by the unlawful means of inducing a breach of a contract of employment. It does not apply to intimidation or conspiracy to injure. Ballots were introduced in 1984 and the duty to give notice was enacted in 1993 and then amended in 1999 and 2004. Significant amendments were made by the Trade Union Act 2016.

When a ballot is required

21.107   A ballot is required only in respect of 'an act done by a trade union'; that is, if it is authorised or endorsed by the principal executive committee, the president or general secretary, or some other person in accordance with the rules of the union. This is the same codification as governs the vicarious liability of a union in tort actions under the TULR(C)A 1992 (see 19.43–19.47).

21.108   The general rule is that the first authorisation or endorsement of the strike or other industrial action must be given within four weeks from the date the ballot is taken. Since 1999, the union and the employer may extend this period by agreement for up to another four weeks. This gives the union the flexibility to hold a ballot at the start of negotiations and then, with the employer's agreement, wait until the result is known up to eight weeks later before putting it into effect. This may give more valuable time for negotiations. In the event that unofficial action is later given official backing (ie endorsed, in the language of the statute), the ballot must be held before, but not more than four weeks before, the union declares it official.

21.109   The time limits focus on a 'relevant act' being within four weeks (or between four and eight weeks if there is an agreement to extend time). 'Relevant act' is defined in the TULR(C)A 1992, s 226, as an act of inducing a person to breach his contract of employment or interfere with its performance. There is, however, no need for the inducement of members to be successful for it to be such a relevant act. The Court of Session in *Secretary of State for Scotland v Scottish Prison Officers' Association* [1991] IRLR 371 had to consider whether the instruction by the Association's executive to hold meetings of members during working hours without permission was a relevant act. It was held to be such even though, in the event, no breach of contract occurred in fact because the meetings called by the POA were authorised by the employers.

21.110   Authorising or endorsing by the union does not, however, extend to communicating the decision to authorise a ballot with a view to more extensive industrial action, and it was entitled to be partisan in this respect (*Newham London Borough Council v NALGO* [1993] ICR 189). The union was demonstrating that it wanted industrial action to be extended to members in addition to those already on strike but it was not calling on them to strike.

In the national docks dispute in 1989 the TGWU was prevented from calling industrial **21.111** action during this period of four weeks after the result of the ballot was announced because of an injunction. In similar circumstances the union may now apply for an extension of time of up to twelve weeks, but no application may be made more than eight weeks after the ballot (TULR(C)A 1992, s 234). If on the basis of evidence presented to the court the ballot no longer appears to represent the views of the members, the court may not grant the extension. This means that the courts are to some extent thus drawn into the merits of the dispute. The Trade Union Act 2016 introduced a further curb on the period after which the ballot ceases to be effective of six months or 'of such longer duration not exceeding nine months as is agreed between the union and the members' employer' (new s 234(1) of the TULR(C)A 1992).

Some strikes commence and are then suspended for talks to take place, or for the parties **21.112** to reconsider their respective positions. In *Monsanto plc v TGWU* [1987] ICR 269, the union held a lawful ballot and received a mandate for a strike, which then took place. After some weeks, however, the union suspended the action while it negotiated with the employers, but then reimposed the action when the negotiations failed. The Court of Appeal held that the union did not have to hold a further ballot since the resumption of action was in connection with the original trade dispute (cf *Boxfoldia Ltd v NGA (1982)* [1988] ICR 752).

There may be a long campaign of action provided that it was sufficiently continuous and **21.113** self-contained. Whether it is or is not is a question of fact in each case (*Post Office v Union of Communications Workers* [1990] IRLR 143). As Lord Donaldson MR put it: 'The question the court has to ask itself is whether the average reasonable trade union member, looking at the matter shortly after any interruption in the industrial action would say to himself, "the industrial action has now come to an end", even if he might also say, "the union may want us to come out again if the dispute continues"'.

The scope of the constituency

The union must ballot those whom it reasonably expects to call on to participate in indus- **21.114** trial action and no others (s 227(1)). The industrial action loses the support of the ballot if the union calls out a member or ex-member who ought to have been given the right to vote but was not so given it (s 232A). Each person must have one and only one vote. No one else may be permitted to vote, not even those who will be subject to lay-off as a result. The ballot is required even if there are no individual members of the union and the rules do not make any provision for a ballot (*Shipping Company Uniform Inc. v ITWF* [1985] ICR 245). In *P v NASUWT* [2001] IRLR 532, the union did not lose immunity when it inadvertently failed to send ballot papers to two members.

On the other hand, in *National Union of Rail, Maritime and Transport Workers v* **21.115** *Midland Mainline Ltd* [2001] IRLR 813, twenty-five people who were employed by the company as operational train crew and were members of the union had not been balloted. It was held that this meant that the union had not accorded entitlement to vote in the ballot equally to members who it was reasonable, at the time of the ballot, for the union to believe would be induced to take part in the industrial action. The proper approach was to ask two separate questions: first, who did the union, at the time of the ballot, believe would be induced to take part in the industrial action; and secondly, was such a belief a reasonable one on the part of the union?

21.116 The union may call out members who had joined it since the date of a ballot, and to do so does not lose the union any immunity which it would otherwise have. The Court of Appeal so decided in *London Underground Ltd v RMT* [1996] ICR 170 on the basis that it was the industrial action which required to be supported by a ballot, not that industrial action in which a particular person has been induced to take part. The Court of Appeal rejected the proposition put forward by the employers that the industrial action which had been called was thus different from that on which the ballot had been held. They disapproved some comments of Lord Donaldson MR to this effect in *Post Office v UCW* (see above).

21.117 In *British Railways Board v National Union of Railwaymen* [1989] IRLR 349, Lord Donaldson MR indicated that there is a profound difference between *denial* of a right to vote and inadvertently failing to give a member an opportunity to vote. The latter is governed by s 230(2) of the TULR(C)A 1992, which provides that the opportunity must be given 'as far as reasonably practicable'. Where, as in the instant case, the trade union does its best in good faith to comply with the balloting provisions, the mere fact that some members are missed out does not in itself mean that s 230 is not satisfied. This approach is given statutory force by a new s 232B (inserted by the Employment Relations Act 1999), which provides that overlooking some members during the balloting process will not invalidate the final result if the omission of these individuals was 'inadvertent and on a scale unlikely to affect that result' (see *P v NASUWT* [2001] IRLR 532, at 21.114ff above).

21.118 In *RMT v London & Birmingham Railway Ltd*, the union had mistakenly informed the employer that fifty-four rather than fifty-two workers would be taking part in the strike. The accidental inclusion of the two members not entitled to vote was decided by the Court of Appeal to be trivial and excusable. It was stated that it was not the role of the court 'to set traps and hurdles for the union which have no legitimate purpose or function'.

21.119 In *Balfour Beatty Engineering Services Ltd. v UNITE* [2010] ICR 822, the issue arose because the union claimed that there were particular difficulties in identifying members employed by the claimant because in construction, workers frequently move from site to site. The Court of Appeal stressed that there was a balance to be struck between democratic legitimacy and imposing unrealistic burdens on unions. Thus, union officers were entitled to base themselves on information in their possession without having to ensure that it was definitive.

21.120 The term 'reasonably necessary' in s 231 TULR(C)A diminished the strict ordinary meaning of the word 'necessary' and allowed for a measure of focus on practical realities, the words carrying with them the notion of what a reasonable and prudent person would do in the particular circumstances. In *British Airways plc v UNITE* [2010] ICR 1316, this meant that in publishing the results the union was not required to prove that every eligible member had been sent his or her own individual report of the full results and in the context of union members who were highly computer literate the required information could be posted on union websites.

21.121 There is a right to strike under Art 11 ECHR. The legislation should, however, be construed in the normal way without presumptions one way or the other. The 1992 Act should be given a likely and workable construction (*NURMT v Serco Ltd* [2011] IRLR 399). In the defence open to the union of demonstrating 'accidental failures which were unlikely to affect the result of the ballot', a failure is 'accidental' even where the union has failed to take reasonable steps that could have prevented it. The High Court Judge had been wrong to decide that the failure must be both unintentional and unavoidable. This put the matter too high. The union was required to disclose the information it possessed and not to seek out further material (see also *Metroline Travel Ltd v Unite the Union* [2012] IRLR 749).

Trade Union Act 2016

The Trade Union Act 2016 increased the vote which is needed for normal ballots from 50 per cent of those voting to 'at least 50% of those who were entitled to vote in the ballot did so' and then at least 50 per cent of those actually voting must vote yes (amended s 226(2)). In relation to 'important public services' there is an additional requirement that 'at least 40% of those who were entitled to vote answered yes' (new s 226(2C)). These are to be defined in regulations but may only be within these categories: health, education of those under seventeen, fire services, transport services, decommissioning of nuclear installations, and border security. Further, there is to be an independent review 'on the delivery of secure methods of electronic balloting' and for pilot schemes (s 4 Trade Union Act 2016). **21.122**

Until 1990 the ballot requirements applied only to persons engaged in industrial action who were employees. Section 5 of the 1990 Act, however, extended the provisions of s 10 of the Trade Union Act 1984 (no immunity in tort for industrial action without a ballot) and s 1 of the Employment Act 1988 to those who work pursuant to contracts for services. **21.123**

Industrial action at different workplaces

A union intending to organise industrial action must conduct separate ballots for each place of work, subject to certain important exceptions. Industrial action may not be taken at a particular workplace unless the union has obtained a majority vote for the action at that workplace. **21.124**

By the TULR(C)A 1992, s 228, in so far as the union believes, and it is a reasonable belief, that the persons to be induced to take part in a strike or other industrial action are engaged at different places of work, it must hold a ballot at each such place of work. This provision does not apply, however, where there are common features between workplaces, that is, some factor: **21.125**

(a) which relates to the terms, conditions, or occupational description of each member entitled to vote; and
(b) which that member has in common with some or all members of the union who have the same employer.

The High Court held in *University of Central England v NALGO* [1993] IRLR 81 that it is not necessary for entitlement to vote in a ballot to be restricted to employees of only one employer. This is because while it would have been easy for reference to be made to a restriction to one employer in the TULR(C)A 1992, s 288, none was made.

'Place of work' means the premises at or from which the employee works, or that with which he has the closest connection if he works from more than one. **21.126**

If the union fails to comply with these provisions, it will:

(a) lose its immunity from action in pursuance of a trade dispute; and
(b) be open to a claim by a member of the union under s 235A(1) of the TULR(C)A 1992.

21.127 The Employment Relations Act 1999 established important exceptions. Section 228A of the TULR(C)A 1992 provides that the union need not ballot different workplaces separately because of s 228 in any of the following situations:

(a) at least one union member in a workplace is directly affected by the dispute in question;

(b) entitlement to vote is restricted to union members who have an occupation (or occupations) of a particular kind and are employed by a particular employer (or any of a number of employers) with whom the union is in dispute; or

(c) entitlement to vote is restricted to union members who, according to the union's *reasonable belief*, have an occupation (or occupations) of a particular kind and are employed by a particular employer (or any of a number of employers) with whom the union is in dispute.

The ballot paper

21.128 The Employment Relations Act 1999 made further changes to the required contents of the ballot paper. The ballot paper must also:

(a) ask the relevant members (using whatever words) whether they are willing to take part in a strike (if a strike is proposed by the union) or other industrial action (if that is recommended) or, separately, both questions (if action of both kinds is proposed); and

(b) make no comment or qualification upon the required statement as set out above (TULR(C)A 1992, s 229(2), (4)).

The ballot form must state 'If you take part in a strike or other industrial action, you may be in breach of your contract of employment', and then:

> However, if you are dismissed for taking part in strike or other industrial action which is called officially and is otherwise lawful, the dismissal will be unfair if it takes place fewer than eight weeks after you started taking part in the action, and depending on the circumstances may be unfair if it takes place later.

For the purposes of the ballot wording (but for no other purpose) an overtime or call-out ban will be treated as industrial action short of a strike (new s 229(2A) of the TULR(C)A 1992, reversing the effect of the Court of Appeal's decision in *Connex South Eastern Ltd v National Union of Rail Maritime and Transport Workers* [1999] IRLR 249).

Protection of the voter

21.129 There is nothing to prevent the union from including tendentious campaigning material with the ballot papers which it sends out. It may not, however, merely ask in the ballot whether the members agree with the union's negotiating position. Rather it must put the member being balloted on the spot as to whether *he or she* is prepared to *participate* in the action proposed.

21.130 There are also provisions protecting the voter which are similar to those found in Pt I of the TULR(C)A 1992, relating to the election for the principal executive committee. There must be no interference with or constraint in exercising his or her rights to vote, nor should he or she have to bear any costs in so doing (TULR(C)A 1992, s 230(1)). The ballot paper should be available so far as reasonably practicable to the potential striker before, immediately after, or during his or her working hours. Again, subject to the reasonable practicability defence, the voting must take place in secret.

A majority of the votes must be cast in favour of the action in question for the union to **21.131** have immunity. Thus, spoiled votes in effect count *against* support for the action. The union must also take reasonably practicable steps to inform those who are entitled to vote of the complete result of the ballot, although here again it can exempt overseas members. Any inaccuracy in counting the votes is to be disregarded if it is accidental and on a scale which could not affect the result of the ballot (TULR(C)A 1992, s 230(4)).

Call before the ballot

The industrial action will not be treated as supported by the ballot if there has been a 'call' **21.132** for such action before the date of the ballot (TULR(C)A 1992, s 233(3)). 'Call' means that the actual action is positively announced. However, the Court of Appeal held in *Newham London Borough Council v National and Local Government Officers Association* [1993] ICR 189 that s 233(3) does not require the union to take a neutral stance in relation to the ballot. A union can thus indicate its desire for industrial action to be held without that amounting to a call for, or authorisation or endorsement of, such action.

Notice of the ballot

A further important requirement for the validity of a ballot is found in s 226A of the **21.133** TULR(C)A 1992. The trade union must 'take such steps as are reasonably necessary to ensure that not less than the seventh day before the opening day of the ballot' there is received, by every person whom it is reasonable for the union to believe will be the employer of those persons who will be entitled to vote in the ballot, a written notice to the effect that the union intends to hold a ballot, specifying the opening date of the ballot and describing the category of employees who will be entitled to vote therein.

The burden of notifying the employer was reduced somewhat by provisions contained **21.134** in the Employment Relations Act 1999. Under these, the duty is merely to include 'such information in the union's possession as would help the employer to make plans and bring information to the attention of those of his employees'. Where the union possesses information as to the number, *category*, or workplace of the employees, the notice to the employer should communicate this, but there will be no requirement to name individuals (new s 226A(3A)). Notices served on the employers by the appellant union relating to the pay strike action by 'all members of the union employed in all categories at all workplaces' did not comply with the requirements of ss 226A and 234A of the 1992 Act (*National Union of Rail, Maritime and Transport Workers v London Underground Ltd* [2001] IRLR 229).

It was, however, sufficient for a union to tell the employer of its intention to ballot 'all **21.135** Assessment and Advice Unit workers at Harrow Road who pay their union dues via the deduction of contributions at source scheme' (only about forty-five workers). This was a category of employees (*Westminster CC v UNISON* [2001] IRLR 524). The court held that 'category' is a very broad word: 'It means no more than a reference to the general type of workers.' In *Metrobus* [2010] IRLR 173, the fax sent by the independent scrutineer containing the ballot result went astray and the local union official waited for authorisation from the general secretary before giving notice to the employer. This led to a delay of forty-eight hours in notifying the employer of the ballot result. This was not as soon as was reasonably possible.

Information is in a union's possession if it is possessed by any official of the union who, **21.136** in accordance with the union's rules and normal operating procedures, is concerned with maintaining records kept for the union's purposes. This includes senior officials at union headquarters and branch secretaries (*NURMT v London Underground*, above).

21.137 In *BT plc v CWU* [2003] EWHC 937, the CWU informed the employer that it was calling on 'all Engineering members currently in BT Customer Services Field Operations and BT Northern Ireland (MJE1 4 5)'. It was known that some 90 per cent of those affected by the voluntary introduction of the Self Managed Teams (the reason for the industrial dispute) were members of the union. Although many paid their dues by deduction from their salaries, others paid in other ways. There were various respects in which the employer might wish to make plans, for example, to notify customers of the unavailability of services during the period of a strike or to organise teams of non-striking employees to carry out work having priority. The union did give to the employer the total number of those to be called out on strike. The judge found that BT had raised a triable issue because although there was 90 per cent union membership, this could not be assumed to be uniform across the UK. It would be of practical assistance to BT to have those numbers broken down. There was a triable issue that the union indeed possessed information as to the number and category of employees beyond that which it had communicated.

21.138 The employer must be sent not later than the third day before the opening date of the ballot a sample voting paper. The employer must be informed of the ballot result (TULR(C)A 1992, s 231A).

21.139 Section 226A(2)(c) provides that unions must provide lists and figures or where some or all employees pay by deductions from wages those lists and figures. The lists are to define the categories of employee and the workplaces concerned. The figures must be 'as accurate as is reasonably practicable in the light of the information in the possession of the union at the time when it complies'. The information counts if it is in a document whether in electronic or other form and in the possession or under the control of an officer or an employee of the union.

21.140 The duty to provide lists and figures of those union members who were being balloted was limited by reference to the information possessed by the union, and while a union was obliged to obtain and collate information to enable it to supply the relevant lists and figures as accurately as it reasonably could and it would be a breach of duty to provide information the union knew to be wrong, the duty was no more than simply one to replicate the information in the union's possession (*London & Birmingham Railway Ltd v ASLEF* [2011] ICR 848). The general doctrine of ignoring matters which were *de minimis* would be available to the union where it had wrongly identified two out of more than 600 members whom it understood fell to be balloted. If the union had conferred the opportunity to vote on those whom it must have known would not subsequently be induced to take part in the strike it could not rely on the exception.

21.141 The union must, following the passing of the Trade Union Act 2016, provide the number entitled to vote; the number of votes cast; the number saying yes and no; the number of spoiled voting papers; whether the number of votes cast is at least 50 per cent of those who were entitled to vote in the ballot; and whether of those at least 40 per cent voted yes. This was passed in order to prevent calls for strikes by the narrowest of margins.

Notice of industrial action

21.142 By s 234A of the TULR(C)A 1992, the union must give advance notice of industrial action to the affected employer(s). Indeed, the trade union must 'take such steps as are reasonably necessary to ensure that the employer receives' a specified notice of industrial action, that is, fourteen days before the starting date of the action or seven days if the employer and union so agree (s 234A(4)(b), inserted by the Trade Union Act 2016).

As with notice of the ballot, the burden of notifying the employer was reduced by the **21.143** Employment Relations Act 1999. The duty is to include 'such information in the union's possession as would help the employer to make plans and bring information to the attention of his employees'. Where the union possesses information as to the number, category, or workplace of the employees, the notice to the employer should communicate this, but there is no requirement on the union to name individuals (s 234A(5A)).

The balance of convenience must be carefully weighed in deciding whether to grant an **21.144** injunction when there has been no ballot as may be seen in *Solihull Metropolitan Borough v National Union of Teachers* [1985] IRLR 211. The NUT issued guidelines to its members to refuse to cover for such absences of colleagues as known in advance and various other tasks. No ballot had been held and Warner J granted an injunction that the union must rescind its instructions. Whilst he saw detriment to the claimant in the harm done to the children in their schools, which could not be remedied in damages, there would be little inconvenience to the union. It was merely a matter for the union of choosing between holding a ballot and accepting arbitration.

Member's right to remove authorisation for strikes and industrial action

When the obligations to hold a ballot before strike action were introduced in 1984, the **21.145** only enforcement mechanism was in the hands of the employer, in that, as we have seen, the union's immunity from action was taken away. Section 62 of the TULR(C)A 1992 now accords the right to the ordinary member not to have his union make official a strike or other industrial action which is not supported by a ballot. Alternatively, it covers the situation where a ballot has been held but its terms infringe the requirements of the TULR(C)A 1992, ss 226 to 232 (see 21.146–21.153). These provisions have been little used.

Application

Section 62 of the TULR(C)A 1992 applies where a trade union authorises or endorses **21.146** strike or industrial action. This is defined in the same way as for other acts of authorisation, and bites on an inducement by the union even though such a 'call to arms' has not succeeded in its object of calling employees out on strike or to participate in other industrial action: it may be one which would be ineffective because the member was 'unwilling to be influenced by it or for any other reason'. 'Strike' is specifically defined as 'any concerted stoppage of work'.

A member of the relevant union may apply to court for an order that the union withdraw **21.147** any authorisation or endorsement for the strike or other industrial action in the event that a proper ballot has not been held. To apply, the member must be a person who is likely to be or has been induced by the union to take part in the action. The action called for need not have actually yet commenced for an order to be made.

The court order

On such an application, the court may make such order as it considers appropriate to **21.148** require the union to take steps to ensure that there is no, or no further, inducement of members to take part in such action. The statute specifically mentions in this respect an order for 'the withdrawal of any relevant authorisation or endorsement'. The order may not, however, require the union expressly and positively to hold a ballot. It might nevertheless restrain the union from paying strike pay to those taking part in a strike not supported by a ballot. It is likely that most cases will come before the courts by an application for an interim injunction.

Persons authorised to call industrial action

21.149   By TULR(C)A 1992, s 229(3), an industrial action ballot paper must specify who is authorised for the purposes of calling members to take part or continue to take part in industrial action. There will be no immunity for the trade union if action supported by a ballot is not in fact called by the person who is named in the ballot paper. Further, there must be no call by the trade union to take part or to continue to take part in industrial action *before* the date of the ballot (see *Govia Thameslink Railway Ltd v ASLEF* [2016] IRLR 686).

21.150   Section 233(3) does not require an unequivocal call by the specified person which is free of all conditions. Some matters may be left for the judgement of those on the ground who must decide how and when as a matter of common sense the call for action should be put into operation. On the other hand, it is not consistent with the purpose of the Act for a specified person to give blanket authority for a local union official to go ahead with negotiations on the basis that a strike could then be treated as authorised if things did not go well (*Tanks & Drums Ltd v TGWU* [1992] ICR 1).

21.151   The Secretary of State's Code of Practice on Trade Union Ballots on Industrial Action was issued by the then Department of Employment pursuant to the Employment Act 1988 and draws together the threads of the TULR(C)A 1992 on industrial action together with various non-statutory guidance. The purpose of this Code (as last revised in 2005) is proclaimed in para 1 to be 'to provide practical guidance to promote the improvement of industrial relations and desirable practices in relation to the conduct by trade unions of ballots about industrial action'. The most noteworthy provisions of this Code, which go beyond existing statutory provisions, are that:

(a)   an industrial action ballot should not take place before agreed procedures which might lead to the resolution of a dispute without the need for industrial action have been completed (para 6);

(b)   a ballot should be held only if the union is contemplating industrial action and it would be lawful to organise it (para 6); and

(c)   voters should not be misled or confused by the framing of the question and should not, for example, be led to believe that they are being asked to agree to an opinion about the union's view of the merits of a dispute (para 31).

The immunity is not lost by minor failures regarding the provision of information about the results to union members (*BA plc v Unite the Union* [2010] IRLR 809). This includes websites and email.

21.152   In *BA plc* [2010] IRLR 423, the employer had set up a voluntary redundancy scheme such that about 1,000 employees would have left by the time the strike took place. These employees should have been excluded from the ballot. Even though their voting did not affect the ballot result the union could not rely on s 232B because it did not have a reasonable belief within s 227 that it was balloting the correct people.

21.153   As a further method of putting pressure on the unions, the union has to make a return to the Certification Officer of the nature of any trade dispute in which it took part in the annual return of the union (TULR(C)A, s 32(ZA) inserted by the Trade Union Act 2016).

K UNION RECRUITMENT STRIKES

Section 225(1) of the TULR(C)A 1992 limits immunity from claims in tort in relation **21.154** to disputes over the closed shop or to promote trade union membership. Neither a union nor its officials have trade dispute immunity where the reason or one of the reasons for the act of the union is the fact or belief that an employer is employing, has employed, or might employ a person:

(a) who is not a member of any trade union;
(b) who is not a member of a particular trade union; or
(c) who is not a member of one of a number of trade unions.

Alternatively, the pressure may be brought because the employer is failing, has failed, or might fail to discriminate against any such person in that he treats: (a) employees; (b) applicants for employment, differently according to whether or not those persons are such members and is more favourable to such people who *are* members of trade unions in general or of a particular trade union. Membership of a trade union in this context may mean membership of a particular branch or section of a trade union.

L STATUTORY RESTRICTIONS ON INDUSTRIAL ACTION

Restrictions on classes of workers

There is nothing in Britain like the wide restrictions on strikes by *Beamte*, established **21.155** public servants, in Germany. There are, however, several statutory limitations on the right to withdraw labour for various classes of workers, and these generally concern the public sector:

(a) *Armed forces* Any member of the armed forces who engages in disruptive activity in order to redress a grievance can be disciplined under the Army Act 1955, Airforce Act 1955, or Naval Discipline Act 1953; and s 1 of the Incitement to Disaffection Act 1934 also makes it an offence 'if any person maliciously and advisedly endeavours to seduce any member of her Majesty's forces from his duty or allegiance to her Majesty'.
(b) *Police* Section 91 of the Police Act 1996 enacts the offence of causing disaffection or inducing a policeman to withhold his services or commit breaches of discipline.
(c) *Merchant seamen* Section 58 of the Merchant Shipping Act 1995 makes it a crime to endanger a ship, life, or limb in breach of duty.
(d) *Postal workers* The Post Office Act 1953, ss 58 and 68 and the Telegraph Act 1863, s 45, render it an offence wilfully to delay or procure the delay of any post packet or message (*Gouriet v UPW* [1978] AC 435; see also Telecommunications Act 1984, ss 44 and 45).
(e) *Aliens* The Aliens Restriction (Amendment) Act 1919, s 3(2), makes it a crime punishable by three months' imprisonment for an alien to promote industrial unrest unless engaged *bona fide* in the same industry for at least two years. This measure was passed to seek to insulate Britain from the shockwaves of the Russian revolution.
(f) *Endangering life* Section 240(1) of the TULR(C)A 1992 states, 'where any person wilfully and maliciously breaks a contract of service or of hiring, knowing or having reasonable cause to believe that the probable consequences of his so doing, either alone or in combination with others, will be to endanger human life or cause serious bodily injury, or to expose valuable property whether real or personal to destruction or serious injury', he is guilty of an offence punishable by fine or imprisonment for three months (Criminal Justice Act 1991, s 17(2)). This includes doctors, firemen,

nurses, and also lorry drivers, within its scope. There is no record of prosecution under this section, but it may be a ground for an injunction.

(g) *Prison officers* The Criminal Justice and Public Order Act 1994 rendered it unlawful to induce a prison officer to withhold services or to commit a breach of discipline. This could be enforced by the Home Secretary. The terms were disapplied by the Labour Government but then reinstated in the Criminal Justice and Immigration Act 2008, ss 138 and 139.

Emergencies

21.156   The current emergency powers are in the Civil Contingencies Act 2004. Emergency regulations may not 'prohibit or enable the prohibition of participation in, or any activity in connection with, a strike or other industrial action' (s 23(3)(b); see G Morris, *Strikes in Essential Services*, Mansell Publishing, 1986).

M CONSUMER ACTIONS

21.157   Consumers have statutory rights to pursue trade unions in respect of unlawful industrial action by s 235A of the TULR(C)A 1992. An individual may apply to the High Court where he claims that any trade union or other person has done, or is likely to do, an unlawful act to induce any person to take part, or to continue to take part, in industrial action, and an effect, or a likely effect, of that industrial action is or will be to prevent or delay the supply of goods or services, or reduce the quality of goods or services supplied to that individual. That individual need not actually have an entitlement, contractual or otherwise, to be supplied with the particular goods or services in question (s 235A(3)). The normal remedy will be an interim injunction to restrain such action, and it appears that such an application may be considered by the court even if an application is also made by an employer. The union may thus have to fight at very short notice on two separate fronts. The only reported instance of this right being exercised concerned a disruptive pupil who pursued an unsuccessful claim against teachers who had refused to continue teaching him (*P v NASUWT* [2001] IRLR 532).

N EU LAW ON FREEDOM OF ESTABLISHMENT

21.158   Domestic strike law must be considered alongside EU principles of freedom of movement and establishment. *International Transport Workers' Federation v Viking Line ABP* [2008] IRLR 143 concerned industrial action by FSU, the Finnish affiliate of the London-based ITF, aimed at stopping the employers from reflagging a ferry from Finland to Estonia, and staffing it with a cheaper Estonian crew. The ECJ characterised the right of establishment as 'a fundamental freedom', which is horizontally binding on persons within the EU. It is capable of conferring rights on a private employer which may be relied on against a trade union. The ECJ ruled that the right to strike does not fall outside the scope of regulation by EU competition rules. In effect, this means that trade union activity is potentially reviewable by the courts under EU law and, if it infringes the rights of employers, the courts may examine the reasons for the industrial action to see whether they conform to the principles of proportionality. This is likely to have major implications, in particular because employers may say that the limit on the amount of awards against trade unions may be circumvented (see also *Laval un Partneri Ltd v Svenska Byggnadsarbetareförbundet* [2008] IRLR 160).

O INJUNCTIONS

Use of injunctions in strikes

Most employers are not, as already stated, concerned to claim damages from striking **21.159** employees. The employer wants them back to work to prevent any further losses of production, rather than to claim monetary judgments which would be difficult to enforce. He thus turns to the equitable remedies. As we have seen, it is only in very exceptional circumstances that the courts have countenanced specific performance of a contract of employment; it savours too much of forced labour. Section 236 of the TULR(C)A 1992 provides that no court may by an order for specific performance of a contract of employment or by an injunction to restrain breach thereof compel an employee to work (see also *Barretts & Baird (Wholesale) Ltd v IPCS* [1987] IRLR 3).

The courts feel no such restraint in granting injunctions to prevent torts, and these have **21.160** very much the same effect. Application may be speedily made to the Chancery Division or the Queen's Bench Division. Although the claimant must in most circumstances give two days' notice, this may be dispensed with and an application may even predate the issue of a claim form. If an interim injunction without notice is granted, the absent defendants will be given leave to apply to discharge it on short notice (see further, Civil Procedure Rules 1998, Pt 25). Actions in trade disputes differ from most (though not all) other areas of law in which injunctions are sought, since they rarely go to trial.

Principles determining whether injunctions are to be granted

The balance of convenience

Before 1975, the claimant had to establish a prima facie case before he was entitled to **21.161** injunctive relief (*J.T. Stratford and Son Ltd v Lindley* [1965] AC 269), so that the merits of the case were at least partially aired in court at this early stage. What is now the leading case arose in the completely different jurisdiction of patent law. In *American Cyanamid Ltd v Ethicon* [1975] AC 396, the House of Lords postulated that it was only necessary that the claimant have an arguable case, and that there was a serious issue to be tried. The only other consideration was the balance of convenience of giving or refusing the injunction. The court was thus not justified in embarking on anything resembling a trial of the action on conflicting affidavits in order to evaluate the strength of each party's case. The court should not indeed at this stage express a concluded opinion as to the law unless it is reasonably clear (*Associated British Ports plc v TGWU* [1989] IRLR 305). This makes it considerably easier for a claimant employer to gain an interim injunction against a strike not covered by immunity. It is balanced only to some degree by the claimant having to give an undertaking in damages, promising to compensate the defendant if he has suffered loss as a result of its issue and the trial court determines, on reviewing all the evidence, that the injunction should not in fact have been granted. This is, however, of little use in dispute cases to a union enjoined because, first, full trials rarely take place and, second, the financial loss which the union could prove that it has suffered by not being able to strike is likely to be nominal in money terms, save that it may be able to recover the costs incurred in holding a ballot (cf *Cayne v Global Natural Resources plc* [1984] 1 All ER 225).

For the same reason, the balance of convenience frequently sways in favour of preserving **21.162** the status quo, which, in the case of a trade dispute, means maintaining production. The particular union concern here is that it is easy to portray the employer losing immediately and irretrievably by a strike, and the union as suffering little tangible hardship. The general principle is that if there is only a risk of unquantifiable damage to the defendant yet a certainty of unquantifiable damage to the claimant, an injunction should be issued. The industrial reality is, however, that the impetus of the workers' case is inevitably lost when it is restrained even for a short period of time; once postponed it is difficult to revive. Further, the employer can organise to defeat a subsequent strike, including making alternative arrangements for supplies or sub-contracting his work to other firms. Lord Diplock realised this when he said in *NWL Ltd v Woods* [1979] 3 All ER 614:

> It is in the nature of industrial action that it can be promoted effectively only so long as it is possible to strike while the iron is hot; once postponed it is unlikely to be revived.

21.163   In *Associated British Ports plc v TGWU* [1989] IRLR 305, the Court of Appeal stated that the status quo was to be understood in the sense that work was still proceeding at the time the claim was issued, so that was the position as the status quo. In the High Court, Millet J had decided that the court had to balance the status quo of the union's position in negotiations (especially given that its declared aim was to preserve the existing contractual position after the abolition of the National Dock Labour Scheme).

21.164   The Labour Government reacted to the judicial developments in *American Cyanamid* by enacting the TULRA 1974, s 17(1) (now TULR(C)A 1992, s 221), which provided that if there *might* be a 'trade dispute' defence to an injunction, the court must not grant without notice relief unless all reasonable steps have been taken: (a) to notify the other side of the application; and (b) to give them an opportunity of putting their side of the story. Further, subsection (2) stated that on an application for an interim injunction the court must 'have regard' to the fact that the defendant would succeed at trial with a trade dispute defence. Employers have since raised the argument that the court may consider it, yet find that it was outweighed by the damaging consequences of the dispute in question. The House of Lords in *NWL v Woods* (above), however, indicated that if the defendant had shown that it was *more likely than not* that he could prove he was within the trade dispute definition the injunction should be refused. This was subject to an exception, where the seriousness of the consequences for the employer, a third party, or the general public demanded a higher degree of probability of the case. Lord Diplock thought the subsection was a reminder to judges that:

> they should in exercising their discretion whether or not to grant an interlocutory injunction put into the balance of convenience in favour of the defendant those countervailing practical realities, and in particular that the grant of an injunction is tantamount to giving final judgment against the defendant.

In cases which fall outside the trade dispute defence, however, the ordinary principles of *Cyanamid* apply (*Dimbleby & Sons Ltd v NUJ* [1984] 1 WLR 427 at 431–2; see also *Associated British Ports plc v TGWU* [1989] IRLR 288 HL, [1989] IRLR 305 CA).

Public interest

21.165   The court may treat as weighing heavily in favour of granting an injunction immediate threats to health and safety if a strike went ahead (*Beaverbrook Newspapers Ltd v Keys* [1980] IRLR 34). Lord Scarman applied this to a dispute by journalists in *Express Newspapers Ltd v MacShane* [1980] IRLR 35, thus:

> In a case where action alleged to be in contemplation or furtherance of a trade dispute endangers the nation or puts at risk such fundamental rights as the right of the public to be informed and the freedom of the press, it could well be a proper exercise of the court's discretion to restrain the industrial action pending trial of the action.

In *Duport Steels Ltd v Sirs* [1980] IRLR 116, Lord Scarman took the opposite view on the facts in relation to the 1980 national steel strike, commenting:

> The economic damage threatened by the extension of the strike to the private sector, though very serious, is not so immediate as to justify intervention by the court granting relief to which it is probable that the plaintiff was not entitled.

(See also *Associated British Ports plc v TGWU* [1989] IRLR 305.)

The balance of convenience where no strike ballot has been held was considered in **21.166** *Solihull Metropolitan Borough v NUT* [1985] IRLR 211 (see also in a picketing case *Union Traffic Ltd v TGWU* [1989] ICR 98).

A failure to provide by enactment or agreement compensatory measures which are said **21.167** to accord with the provisions of international treaties which are not incorporated into English law cannot amount to inequitable conduct for the purposes of the doctrine of 'clean hands'. Further, Art 11 of the European Convention on Human Rights confers no right to strike (*Ministry of Justice v POA* [2008] IRLR 380).

Injunctions to restrain criminal offences

Where a strike constitutes a crime it may also be restrained by injunction, but the private **21.168** citizen does not usually have *locus standi* to maintain such an action. Instead he must ask the Attorney-General to proceed for a relator action. The House of Lords declared this still to be the law in the case of *Gouriet v UPW* [1978] AC 435. The Post Office unions were there alleged to be about to commit offences under the Post Office Act 1953 if they implemented plans to boycott mail to South Africa. The Attorney-General's refusal to bring a relator action was upheld by the House of Lords.

22

PICKETING AND PUBLIC ORDER

A INDUSTRIAL BACKGROUND 22.01

B OFFENCES AND PICKETING 22.05

   Obstruction of the highway 22.06

   Obstructing a police constable 22.07

   Assaults 22.11

   Public Order Act 1986 . . . . .22.12

   Unlawful assembly 22.15

   Affray and riot 22.16

   Public nuisance 22.18

   Trade Union and Labour Relations
(Consolidation) Act 1992, s 241 . . . . . 22.21

   Public processions and assemblies 22.26

   Offences under the Protection from
Harassment Act 1997 . . . . 22.27

C CIVIL LIABILITY 22.29

   Private nuisance 22.30

   Trespass to the highway 22.32

   Interference with contracts 22.33

   Statutory tort of harassment 22.35

D IMMUNITY 22.36

   History 22.37

   Secondary picketing 22.38

   Place of work 22.39

   Limitations of the immunity 22.41

   Number of pickets 22.43

   Right to stop vehicles? 22.45

   Union supervision 22.46

E THE CODE OF PRACTICE 22.47

There is no legal right to picket as such, but peaceful picketing has long been recognised as being lawful. (Code of Practice on Picketing, 1992 para 2.)

A INDUSTRIAL BACKGROUND

22.01 Picketing is an ill-defined term which covers various methods of strengthening strike action by employees standing at the gates of work premises. It has over time subtly changed its function and is much less to the fore in industrial disputes than in times past. At the beginning of the last century, the picket was mainly concerned to prevent blackleg labour being taken in to replace strikers. Later it became a medium of protest, while the 1970s witnessed a growth in 'secondary picketing', broadly aimed at parties which were extraneous to the actual trade dispute to bring pressure on the employer in dispute. By this means, union members seek to prevent goods leaving their employer's factory and to stop him moving his production elsewhere. The target may be fellow workers who have not joined the strike or substitute labour who have been brought in to break it. The modern phenomenon is also a recognition that employers are increasingly organised on a multi-plant, if not multi-national, basis and that such solidarity action by strong unions is of particular value to weakly organised sectors. Some of the cases below may need re-examination in the light of developments under Art 11 ECHR. The Trade Union Act 2016 introduced further restrictions on picket organisers.

22.02 Picketing was used to particular effect during the two miners' strikes of the 1970s, when picketing by various groups of workers prevented the delivery of replacement oil to power stations, and made the strike much more effective in bringing almost the whole of industry to a halt. There was indeed unprecedented picket-line violence during the year-long miners' strike in 1984/5; no fewer than 10,372 criminal charges were brought (*The Times*, 20 March 1985). Its impact has declined in recent years.

The central justification of peaceful picketing lies in the right to freedom of speech and peaceful protest, and in many countries it is protected by the constitution. Typically, in Britain what freedom exists has traditionally been found in the interstices of a narrow immunity from several general and particular prohibitions of common law and statute by way of crimes and torts, although it may raise issues under the European Convention on Human Rights, especially Art 11 of the Convention, which establishes the right to freedom of association and peaceful assembly (see below and Chapter 23). **22.03**

Unlike other areas of trade disputes, this is phrased as a 'right' to picket. Much in reality depends on the practice of police on the spot in controlling pickets. The Employment Act 1980, however, restricted the right to picket to the workers' own place of work. There is a Code of Practice on picketing which supplements this body of law and which was found to be of persuasive influence in *Thomas v NUM (South Wales Area)* [1985] IRLR 136. **22.04**

B OFFENCES AND PICKETING

Pickets may commit the following crimes: **22.05**

(a) obstruction of the highway (**22.06**);
(b) obstructing a police constable in the execution of his duty (22.07–22.10);
(c) assault (22.11);
(d) Public Order Act offences (22.12–22.14);
(e) unlawful assembly (22.15);
(f) affray and riot (22.16–22.17);
(g) public nuisance (22.18–22.20);
(h) offences under the TULR(C)A 1992, s 241 (22.21–22.25);
(i) refusing to obey conditions imposed on public assembly (22.26); and
(j) harassment, or putting a person in fear of violence, under the Protection from Harassment Act 1997 (22.27–22.28).

Obstruction of the highway

By s 137 of the Highways Act 1980, 'if a person without lawful authority or excuse in any way wilfully obstructs the free passage along the highway, he shall be guilty of an offence ...'. This is a charge which is frequently brought against pickets. The illegality of an obstruction is in all cases a question of fact, and depends on, *inter alia*, 'the length of time the obstruction continues, the place where it occurs, the purpose for which it is done, and of course whether it does in fact cause an actual obstruction as opposed to a potential obstruction' (*Nagy v Weston* [1965] 1 WLR 280 at 284 per Lord Parker CJ). In *Lowdens v Keaveney* [1903] 2 IR 82, the judge said: 'No body of men has a right to appropriate the highway and exclude citizens from using it. The question whether use is reasonable or not is a question of fact to be determined by common sense with regard to ordinary experience.' *Mens rea* is not, however, a requirement of the offence (*Arrowsmith v Jenkins* [1963] 2 QB 561), which is committed by anyone freely causing an obstruction; it is irrelevant that he *bona fide* believes he has a right to picket or demonstrate (see also *Broome v DPP* [1974] AC 587). There is statutory control of processions and assemblies under ss 11 to 16 of the Public Order Act 1986 (see 22.26). **22.06**

Obstructing a police constable

22.07   Section 51(3) of the Police Act 1964 makes it criminal to obstruct a police constable in the execution of his duty and that duty is to prevent trouble where he reasonably apprehends a breach of the peace as a 'real possibility' (*R (on application of Laporte) v Chief Constable of Gloucestershire Constabulary* [2007] 2 AC 105). Very few magistrates' courts will *ex post facto* doubt the policeman's opinion at the time, and this provides wide discretion for the police to control picketing. It allows a constable to tell demonstrators all to go home or reduce their number and visit any resistance to these instructions with prosecution for the Police Act offence. Thus, in *Kavanagh v Hiscock* [1974] QB 600, a policeman claimed that he had reason to believe there would be a breach of the peace if an exit from a hospital was not completely clear of pickets, and he thus proceeded to remove those who were waiting to harangue 'blacklegs' being transported to work by bus. The court held that the offence of breach of the peace had been committed and the pickets had no legal right to stop a vehicle without the consent of the driver.

22.08   In *Piddington v Bates* [1960] 3 All ER 660, the defendant was prevented from reaching a factory entrance by a constable who told him that two pickets were enough. The report quaintly states that he 'pushed gently past the policeman and was gently arrested'. Although this occurred without obstruction or threats of violence, Lord Parker CJ held that a policeman was entitled to 'take such steps as he thinks proper', including limiting the number of pickets. He continued (at 663B):

> ... it is not enough that his contemplation is that there is a remote possibility but there must be a real possibility of a breach of the peace. Accordingly in every case it becomes a question whether on the particular facts there were reasonable grounds on which a constable charged with this duty reasonably anticipated that a breach of the peace might occur.

It is immaterial whether the breach of the peace is likely to be caused by the pickets themselves, the picketed, or bystanders (*Kavanagh v Hiscock* (above); see also *Austin v Metropolitan Police Commissioner* [2007] EWCA Civ 989).

22.09   In *Moss v McLachlan* [1985] IRLR 76 the Divisional Court determined that the offence might be committed when pickets ignore orders given by the police some distance from the site to be picketed if the policeman in question honestly and reasonably fears an imminent breach of the peace if the accused continues with his journey.

22.10   A constable can arrest without warrant in the case of obstruction if that obstruction was such that it actually caused or was likely to cause a breach of the peace (*Wershof v Metropolitan Police Commissioner* [1978] 3 All ER 540).

Assaults

22.11   There is no such specific crime or tort of assault, unless the capacity to carry into effect the intention to commit a battery is present at the time of the overt act indicating an immediate intention to commit a battery. There was thus no liability in *Thomas v NUM (South Wales Area)* [1985] IRLR 136 where threats uttered by the picketing miners were made from the side of the road to working miners who were in vehicles which the pickets could not reach.

Public Order Act 1986

22.12   By s 4 of the Public Order Act 1986, a person is guilty of an offence if he:

(a) uses towards another person threatening, abusive, or insulting words or behaviour; or

(b) distributes or displays to another person any writing, sign, or other visible representation which is threatening, abusive, or insulting with intent to cause that person
to believe that immediate unlawful violence will be used against him or another by
any person, or to provoke the immediate use of unlawful violence by that person or
another or whereby that person is likely to believe that such violence will be used or
it is likely that such violence will be provoked.

By s 5 of the Act, a person commits an offence if he: **22.13**

(a) uses threatening, abusive, or insulting words or behaviour, or disorderly behaviour; or
(b) displays any writing, sign, or other visible representation which is threatening, abusive, or insulting, within the hearing or sight of a person likely to be caused harassment, alarm or distress thereby.

The requirement that another person must be present is intended as a safeguard, although
it is not necessary for the prosecution to show that that person was actually alarmed,
harassed, or distressed.

Further, by s 4A of the Public Order Act 1986, a person is guilty of an offence if he,   **22.14**
with intent, causes another person harassment, alarm, or distress by using threatening,
abusive, or insulting words or behaviour or disorderly conduct or by displaying any writing, sign, or other visible representation which is threatening, abusive, or insulting. It is
a defence for an accused person to prove that his conduct was reasonable in the circumstances of the case. The offence carries a maximum penalty of six months' imprisonment,
or a fine not exceeding level 5 on the standard scale or both. It is an arrestable offence.

Unlawful assembly

An unlawful assembly at common law consists of the assembly of three or more persons   **22.15**
with the intention of fulfilling a common purpose in such a manner as to endanger the
public peace. By s 2 of the Public Order Act 1986:

> Where three or more persons who are present together use or threaten violence and the con-
> duct of them (taken together) is such as would cause a person of reasonable fitness present at
> the scene to fear for his personal safety, each of the persons using or threatening violence is
> guilty of violent disorder.

Affray and riot

Affray and riot are other possible charges which may be brought in relation to picketing.   **22.16**
The former offence at common law meant unlawful fighting by one or more persons in a
public place in such manner that reasonable people might be frightened or intimidated.
Section 3 of the Public Order Act 1986 clarifies this offence.

The common law definition of a riot was the collection of at least three people with a   **22.17**
common purpose, and an intent to help one another by force, if necessary, in the execution of that object, against anyone who may oppose them. Further, force or violence had
to be displayed in such a manner as to alarm at least one person of reasonable firmness
(see eg *Field v Receiver of Metropolitan Police* [1907] 2 KB 853). By s 1(1) of the Public
Order Act 1986:

> Where 12 or more persons who are present together use or threaten violence for a common
> purpose and the conduct of them (taken together) is such as would cause a person of reason-
> able firmness present at the scene to fear for his personal safety, each of the persons using
> unlawful violence for the common purpose is guilty of riot.

Public nuisance

22.18 It is an offence at common law to obstruct the public in the exercise or enjoyment of rights common to all, including free passage along the highway. Picketing often falls foul of this prohibition, but picketing in itself without more probably does not constitute nuisance. In *J. Lyons & Sons v Wilkins* [1899] 1 Ch 255 Lindley LJ thought it did, since it constituted an attempt to persuade, regardless of any obstruction. Lord Denning MR in *Hubbard v Pitt* [1975] ICR 308, however, considered that this view 'has not stood the test of time ...'. He was concerned not to restrict free speech and assembly by restricting picketing. He decided, dissenting, that a group of non-industrial protesters standing on the pavement outside an estate agents premises, in reasonable numbers and orderly manner, to protest against the 'gentrification' of Islington was quite lawful and not a nuisance. He commented (at 318H):

> There was no obstruction, no violence, no intimidation, no molestation, no noise, no smells, nothing except a group of six or seven people standing about with placards and leaflets outside the plaintiff's premises, all quite orderly and well-behaved. That cannot be said to be a nuisance at common law.

He considered that, in any case, the real grievance of the plaintiff concerned the defendant's placards and leaflets and that to enjoin these would be an interference with free speech: 'These are rights which it is in the public interest that individuals should possess: and indeed that they should exercise without impediment so long as no wrongful act is done ... As long as all is done peaceably and in good order, without threats or incitement to violence or obstruction to traffic, it is not prohibited.' He saw no reason to distinguish between picketing connected with a strike and for other purposes. The majority of the Court of Appeal, on the other hand, merely affirmed the use by Forbes J of his discretion in deciding to grant an interlocutory injunction to the plaintiffs, and said little on the general principle (see also *Mersey Dock and Harbour Co v Verrinder* [1982] IRLR 152; *News Group Newspapers Ltd v SOGAT 82 (No 2)* [1987] ICR 181; *DPP v Jones* [1999] 2 All ER 257).

22.19 In *Tynan v Balmer* [1967] 1 QB 91, forty people walking in a circle outside premises was held unreasonable and a nuisance: that a passer-by might avoid the obstruction by a detour, did not make it lawful. Further, the pickets were held not to be protected by the precursor of the TULRA 1974 immunity because they were doing more than was absolutely necessary for conveying information about their own cause. In *Thomas v NUM (South Wales Area)* [1985] IRLR 136, Scott J decided that regular picketing of a person's home would in itself be a common law nuisance.

22.20 Public nuisance is a tort as well as a crime but civil proceedings may be brought only with the consent of the Attorney-General. He has, however, complete discretion whether or not to allow it, and a private individual can only act if he can show that he has suffered damage greater than that borne by the general public (*Gouriet v UPW* [1978] AC 435).

Trade Union and Labour Relations (Consolidation) Act 1992, s 241

22.21 It was originally an offence under the Combination Act 1825 'by threat or intimidation or by molesting or in any way obstructing another, to endeavour to force any workman or other person not being employed from accepting employment'. This very general prohibition was abolished by the Conspiracy and Protection of Property Act 1875, but re-enacted therein as specific offences, which still exist in s 241 of the TULR(C)A 1992. This makes it a criminal offence if a person 'wilfully and without legal authority':

(a) uses violence or intimidates another;

(b) persistently follows another from place to place (see *Smith v Thomasson* (1890) 62 LT 68);

(c) hides any tools, clothes, or other property owned or used by such other person, or deprives him of, or hinders him in the use thereof;

(d) watches or besets the house or other place where such other person resides, or works, or carries on business or happens to be, or the approach to such house or place; or

(e) follows such other person with two or more other persons in a disorderly manner in or through any street or road.

In each case the action must be done without any legal authority for it to constitute a crime.

The case of *J. Lyons and Sons v Wilkins* [1896] 1 Ch 811 decided that the wrongful action **22.22** might consist solely of the trespassing of the provisions of the section in itself, whereas *Ward Lock & Co v Operative Printers' Assistants Society* (1906) 22 TLR 327, suggested that it must be independently unlawful. Fletcher Moulton LJ summed up the provision thus: 'It legalises nothing and it renders nothing wrongful that was not so before. Its object is solely to visit certain selected classes of acts which were previously wrongful, i.e. which were at least civil torts, with penal consequences.' Scott J decided in *Thomas v NUM (South Wales Area)* (above) that conduct must first be tortious in order to constitute an offence under what is now s 241. The purpose of the Act was merely to render certain acts unlawful in the *criminal* sense.

Most of the subsections add little to the tort of common law nuisance but subsection (a) **22.23** is of importance, especially since James LJ in *R v Jones* [1974] ICR 310 construed 'intimidate' so as to include 'putting persons in fear by the exhibition of force or violence or the threat of violence, and there is no limitation restricting the meaning to cases of violence or threats of violence to the person'. Hence violence against buildings was sufficient and even 'harsh words' might qualify (see also *Gibson v Lawson* [1891] 2 QB 545; *Elsey v Smith* [1983] IRLR 292). Occupying property as a 'sit-in' may amount to 'watching and besetting'.

The fact that the defendant's actions are protected from civil liability within the meaning **22.24** of s 219 of the TULR(C)A 1992 does not mean that they could not be done 'wrongfully and without legal authority' for the purposes of criminal proceedings. There is nothing in the language of what is now s 219 which can convert what was a wrongful act into one which is legally innocent (*Galt v Philp* [1984] IRLR 156).

The Public Order Act 1986, Sch 2, para 1, makes the maximum sentence six months' **22.25** imprisonment or a fine not exceeding level 5 on the standard scale or both. Further, a police constable may arrest without warrant anyone whom he reasonably suspects is committing an offence under the section.

Public processions and assemblies

The Public Order Act 1986 gave the police powers to impose conditions on public proces- **22.26** sions and assemblies with the threat of criminal sanctions for failure to obey these conditions. Since pickets are usually stationary, only the latter powers are considered here. Section 14 applies if the senior police officer present at an assembly

having regard to the time or place at which and the circumstances in which any public assembly is being held or is intended to be held, reasonably believes that:

(a) it may result in serious public disorder, serious damage to property or serious disruption to the life of the community, or

(b) the purpose of the persons organising it is the intimidation of others with a view to compelling them not to do an act they have a right to do, or to do an act they have a right not to do.

He may then give directions imposing on the person organising or taking part in the assembly such conditions as to the place at which the assembly may be (or continue to be) held, its maximum duration, or the maximum number of persons who may constitute it as appears to him necessary to prevent such disorder, damage, disruption, or intimidation. Failure to obey such conditions is a criminal offence. The intimidation limb of the section was clearly drafted with picketing in mind. The effect has been watered down, however, by the addition of a definition of public assembly, in s 16, as being an assembly of more than twenty persons in a public place.

Offences under the Protection from Harassment Act 1997

22.27   Although the Protection from Harassment Act 1997 was passed to tackle the problem of stalkers, it also has repercussions for picketing. Section 1 establishes that it will be an offence for someone to pursue a course of conduct that amounts to harassment of another and which he knows, or ought to know, amounts to harassment. 'Harassment' is not defined in the Act, but can include 'alarming the person or causing the person distress' (s 7). It is also an offence (under s 4) to embark on a course of conduct that causes another person to fear, on at least two occasions, that violence will be used against him.

22.28   A person who is found guilty of an offence under either s 1 or s 4 is liable to a term of imprisonment or a fine. He may also be made subject to a restraining order under s 5 of the Act. However, an individual will have a defence to a charge under ss 1 or 4 if he can establish one of the following:

(a) that the course of conduct was pursued for the purpose of preventing or detecting crime;
(b) that the course of conduct was pursued under any enactment or rule of law; or
(c) that the pursuit of the course of conduct was reasonable for the protection of himself or herself or another, or for the protection of his or her property or the property of another (ss 1(3) and 4(3)).

C CIVIL LIABILITY

22.29   Picketing is not actionable per se but only if a tort is committed by the pickets (*News Group Newspapers Ltd v SOGAT 82* [1986] IRLR 337) as it often will be. Civil liability is indeed important in relation to picketing, just as in strike cases, not because damages are often sought, but owing to the availability of injunctive relief, particularly of an interim nature.

Private nuisance

22.30   Private nuisance is an unlawful interference with an individual's enjoyment or use of his land. To sue for the tort, the claimant must have some proprietary interest in the land and this action is most likely to be relevant where pickets block an access route to premises. Picketing accompanied by violence, or even merely noise, may be a private nuisance. Scott J in *Thomas v NUM (South Wales Area)* [1985] IRLR 136 thus held that mass picketing at the gates of five collieries in South Wales during the miners' strike of 1984/5 was tortious and could be restrained at the suit of the plaintiffs who were working miners. The picketing was of such a nature and was carried out in such a manner that it represented an unreasonable harassment of the claimants in the exercise of the right to use the highway in order to go to work. While picketing of itself was not a nuisance, this was different since by sheer weight of numbers it blocked the entrance to premises or prevented the entry thereto of vehicles or people to the mines. Where feelings ran high, the court held that the presence of substantial numbers of pickets was almost bound to have an intimidatory effect on those going to work, especially as here some fifty to seventy striking miners attended at the gates each day. Even if nothing at all was said by the pickets, the action could not fail to be highly intimidatory. Scott J held that the public right to use the highway was a sufficient proprietary interest to support an action in nuisance. This was, however, doubted by Stuart Smith J in *News Group Newspapers Ltd v SOGAT 82* (above). In *Hunter v Canary Wharf Ltd* [1997] AC 655, the facts of which did not concern picketing, the House of Lords re-established the orthodox position that only those with a proprietorial interest in the land in question may sue in private nuisance and that no common law tort of intentional harassment exists (but see the statutory tort created by the Protection from Harassment Act 1997, at 22.27–22.28).

Mersey Dock and Harbour Co v Verrinder [1982] IRLR 152 was a case where the picket-ing was entirely peaceful. Judge McHugh nevertheless decided that there was a nuisance since the pickets had mounted 'an attempt ... to regulate and control the container traffic to and from the company's terminals' and so their intention was not merely to obtain or communicate information. This rather puts the cart of determining the scope of the immunity before the horse of establishing the tort committed (see also *Messenger Newspaper Group Ltd v NGA* [1984] IRLR 397; *British Airports Authority v Ashton* [1983] 1 WLR 1079; *News Group Newspapers Ltd v SOGAT 82 (No 2)* [1987] ICR 181). **22.31**

Trespass to the highway

A person commits a tort if he uses the highway 'otherwise than reasonably for passage and repassage and for any other purpose reasonably incidental thereto' (*Hickman v Maisey* [1900] 1 QB 752; see also *Hubbard v Pitt* [1975] ICR 308), and pickets may trespass even though moving around in a circle (*Tynan v Balmer* [1967] 1 QB 91). The proper claimant is the owner of the soil beneath the relevant highway—usually abutting landowners have such rights up to the midpoint in the road, or the local authority. The liability is more theoretical than real since few such landowners would be able to show special damage from the picketing. There was no right to sue in tort for obstruction to the highway for working miners since no special damage was caused to them (*Thomas v NUM (South Wales Area)* (above)). **22.32**

Interference with contracts

The existence of a picket-line may be sufficient in itself to induce another person to break his contract of employment and not attend for work (*Union Traffic Ltd v TGWU* [1989] ICR 98). Alternatively, it may be an interference with a commercial contract, but it is then necessary that a primary obligation under the contract is interfered with (see *Thomas v NUM (South Wales Area)* (above)). **22.33**

Where there is such evidence, in order for the defendant to be immune from claim, the action must fall within the limited immunity for 'secondary action' (see 22.38–22.39) even if it takes place at the pickets' own place of work. This is achieved by s 224 of the TULR(C)A 1992, which provides that secondary action 'done in the course of attendance declared lawful by s 220 of the 1992 Act' retains the protection of s 219 of the TULR(C) A 1992 if done by a worker employed by a party to the trade dispute or by a trade union official whose attendance is lawful. **22.34**

Statutory tort of harassment

22.35 As well as creating the criminal offences described in 22.27–22.28 above, the Protection from Harassment Act 1997 establishes a statutory tort of harassment. Section 3 of the Act provides that a victim of an offence under s 1 may bring civil proceedings against the alleged harasser, and the same applies where someone has merely been threatened with harassment under s 1. The remedies available consist of damages and/or an injunction. Damages may include compensation for any anxiety caused by the harassment as well as financial loss.

D IMMUNITY

22.36 The immunity for picketing is found in s 220 of the TULR(C)A 1992, which reads:

> It shall be lawful for a person in contemplation or furtherance of a trade dispute to attend
>
> (a) at or near his own place of work, or
> (b) if he is an official of a trade union, at or near the place of work of a member of that union whom he is accompanying and whom he represents,
>
> for the purpose only of peacefully obtaining or communicating information, or peacefully persuading any person to work or abstain from working.

History

22.37 The provision derives in part from the protection against the watching and besetting offence in the Conspiracy and Protection of Property Act 1875. It offered immunity for attendance 'merely to obtain or communicate information' (see *J. Lyons & Sons v Wilkins* [1896] 1 Ch 811). The Trade Disputes Act 1906 added the proviso that picketing be carried on 'peacefully' and restricted it to action 'in contemplation or furtherance of a trade dispute' (for the definition of which, see 21.77ff). It thus does not extend to picketing for non-industrial purposes, for example, to protest against the practices of a shopkeeper or estate agents (as in *Hubbard v Pitt* [1975] ICR 308), and this fact has led to claims that trade unionists have privileges beyond those open to other members of the community. The Industrial Relations Act 1971 was similar in its terms except that it removed protection for picketing outside an individual's home, and this was undisturbed by the TULRA 1974.

Secondary picketing

22.38 A secondary picket is not liable for economic torts, such as inducing breach of contract, where he pickets his own place of work and his employer is:

(a) an immediate supplier or customer of the employer in dispute, *and* the aim is to disrupt services between them; or
(b) an associated employer of the employer in dispute, and the aim is to cut off substitute goods or services which would normally have been provided to or by the employer in dispute (TULR(C)A 1992, s 224).

Place of work

22.39 Even if he fulfils all the other requirements of secondary action, the picket must also be picketing at or near his *place of work* in order to attract immunity (see *Mersey Dock and Harbour Co v Verrinder* [1982] IRLR 152). According to the Code of Practice on

Picketing, 'place of work' means 'an entrance to or an exit from the factory, site or office at which the picket works'. There are some statutory elaborations:

(a) If an employee works at *more than one place* or it is impossible to attend that place (eg, if it is a North Sea oil rig or a pit), he can picket the administrative headquarters of his employer (TULR(C)A 1992, s 220(2)).

(b) A person *dismissed* during an industrial dispute in question may picket his former place of work (s 220(3)).

(c) A *union official* appointed or elected for a section of union members may lawfully protest at property other than his own place of work but he must in that case be representing members for whom he is responsible in order to qualify (s 220(1)(b), (4)); thus national officials have 'licence' to picket any place where their members are working, but a regional union officer may only accompany members of a branch within his region. There is thus no recognition of support by one union of another, an aspect of secondary picketing.

(d) There is a location restriction against picketing at an employer's home.

Where the place from or at which employees used to work has been closed down, pickets **22.40** may have nowhere where they can lawfully picket. The place of work to qualify must be the person's principal place of work or base (see *News Group Newspapers Ltd v SOGAT 82* [1986] IRLR 337; *Union Traffic Ltd v TGWU* [1989] ICR 98). In *Rayware Ltd v TGWU* [1989] IRLR 134, the claimant carried on business on a private trading estate along with twenty other companies. As part of the dispute between the company and its employees, pickets stood at the gate going from the road into the trading estate, about seven-tenths of a mile away. The Court of Appeal held that this was 'at or near' their place of work within what is now s 220(1)(a) of the TULR(C)A 1992. The phrase was to be understood in a geographical sense in accordance with the intent and purpose of the legislation, although it was a question of fact and degree in each case.

Limitations of the immunity

The immunity has also been severely limited by case law. It legalises only the *attendance* **22.41** of the pickets for peaceful communication and not their activities while so attending. As Lord Salmon said in *Broome v DPP* [1974] ICR 84: 'The section gives no protection in relation to anything the pickets may say or do whilst they are attending if what they say or do is itself unlawful ... The section therefore gives a narrow but nevertheless real immunity to pickets. It clearly does no more'. Lord Reid said, at 89F:

> I see no ground for implying any right to require the person whom it is sought to persuade to submit to any kind of constraint or restriction of his personal freedom ... But if a picket has a purpose beyond those set out in the section, then his presence becomes unlawful and in many cases such as I have supposed it would not be difficult to infer as a matter of fact that pickets who assemble in unreasonably large numbers do have the purpose of preventing free passage. If that were the proper inference then their presence on the highway would become unlawful.

The section offers no immunity from criminal or tortious activities of pickets as opposed to their mere attendance. For example, the immunity does not prevent a picket being liable in trespass whether at common law or under British Airports by-laws at Heathrow (*Larkin v Belfast Harbour Commissioners* [1908] 2 IR 214; *British Airports Authority v Ashton* [1983] IRLR 287; see also *Elsey v Smith* [1983] IRLR 292). Moreover, it covers only those purposes which are stated and not, for instance, where the pickets go further and also seek to prevent access to the gates by vehicles (*Tynan v Balmer* [1967] 1 QB 91). 'Peacefully' in this context means without a breach of the peace (*Charnock v Court* [1899] 2 Ch 35).

22.42 It is important to identify who is and who is not a picket for the purposes of the immunity. There is no statutory definition, and references in the case law were rare until the case of *News Group Newspapers Ltd v SOGAT 82* [1986] IRLR 337. There, the word 'picket' was held to comprehend both the six official union pickets who stood each day by the entrance to News International's Wapping printing plant and also the fifty to 200 'demonstrators' who stood each day some eighty yards away from the entrance behind barriers. It did not, however, not include the 700 to 7,000 who marched twice a week to hold a protest meeting addressed by speakers. In so far as some of these broke ranks and attempted to rush the main gates, it was arguable that they too were pickets.

Number of pickets

22.43 The statute contains no specific restriction on the number of pickets, but clearly large numbers may intimidate more easily than the actions of the few. Lord Reid's opinion has already been reviewed. The Code of Practice issued in 2009 describes mass picketing as 'obstruction if not intimidation' and para 31 recommends ensuring that 'in general the number of pickets does not exceed six at any entrance to a workplace: frequently a smaller number will be appropriate'.

22.44 In *Thomas v NUM (South Wales Area)* [1985] IRLR 136 Scott J decided that the attendance of between fifty and seventy striking miners at colliery gates could not fall within the immunity. He could not understand the need for so many people to attend if the aim was merely peaceful persuasion: threats of violence and intimidatory language were inconsistent in any event with such peaceful persuasion. Normal insults were not in themselves against the peace, but here the language was carried to extremes and persisted in over a long period. The judge thought that the Code of Practice provided a sensible guide as to the maximum number of pickets, beyond which, simply by weight of numbers, pickets will commit intimidation (*News Group Newspapers Ltd v SOGAT 82 (No 2)* [1987] ICR 181).

Right to stop vehicles?

22.45 Much controversy has surrounded the claim of pickets to stop vehicles in order to convey their message, often somewhat forcefully, to drivers who may be bringing in supplies in order to keep the plant open, and which it is the aim of the pickets to prevent. Picketing may otherwise be wholly ineffective. In *Broome v DPP* [1974] ICR 84, the House of Lords put a decisive brake on any flexibility in the current law. The defendant stood with a poster in front of a lorry trying to enter a factory and was convicted for his temerity even though there was no violence, and the whole incident lasted only nine minutes. Lord Reid could see:

> no ground for implying any right to require the person whom it is sought to persuade to submit to any kind of constraint or restriction of his personal freedom. One is familiar with persons at the side of the road signalling to a driver requesting him to stop. It is then for the driver to decide whether he will stop or not. That, in my view, a picket is entitled to do. If the driver stops, the picket can talk to him but only for as long as the driver is willing to listen.

Union supervision

22.46 The Trade Union Act 2016 introduced further restrictions on pickets so that by a new s 220A(2) a union must appoint a picket supervisor who is 'an official or other member of the union who is familiar with the Code of Practice'. The union must tell the police his name, where picketing will be taking place, and how to contact the picket supervisor. While the picketing takes place, the picket supervisor must 'be present where it is taking place or be readily contactable by the union and the police and able to attend at short notice'. The picket supervisor must wear something readily identifying him as such.

E THE CODE OF PRACTICE

Trade unions have accepted that some actions of pickets have not been in the interests of the wider trade union movement. The TUC thus advised that official pickets wear distinctive armbands and consider restriction of numbers. The BIS code of practice issued in 1992 includes this advice but goes considerably further, including the following 'guidance': **22.47**

(a) 'mass picketing ... is not picketing in its lawful sense of an attempt at peaceful persuasion and may well result in a breach of the peace or other criminal offence. Moreover, anyone seeking to demonstrate support for those in dispute should keep well away from any picket-line so as not to create the risk of a breach of the peace ...' (para 30);

(b) 'large numbers ... exacerbate disputes and sour relations not only between management and employees but between pickets and their fellow employees';

(c) an experienced person should be in charge of the picket-line with a letter of authority from the union (para 32);

(d) pickets should maintain close contact with the police by advance consultation and accepting directions as to reasonable numbers (para 33);

(e) there should be cooperation where several unions are picketing;

(f) pickets on an entrance also used by workers of other companies should not call on them to join the dispute;

(g) where possible, picketing should take place as near as feasible to the workplace;

(h) pickets should not assert that they are official unless organised and endorsed by the union; and

(i) pickets should not jeopardise activities essential to maintenance of important plant and machinery.

The code is also concerned to maintain essential services and supplies: this is a direct response to picketing associated with widespread strikes in the public sector and especially among health service manual workers. It includes under this rubric medical and pharmaceutical products, supplies essential to health and welfare institutions, heating for schools, etc, 'other supplies for which there is a crucial need during a crisis in the interests of public health and safety (eg chlorine, lime, and other agents for water purification), ... and the operation of essential services, such as police, fire, ambulance, medical, and nursing services ...'. **22.48**

The Code seeks to influence union discipline by providing that: 'Disciplinary action should not be taken against a member on the ground that he crossed a picket-line which it had not authorised or which was not at the member's place of work.' An exclusion or expulsion, therefore, is likely to be unlawful. **22.49**

The Code is 'admissible in evidence' by a court and must be 'taken into account'. These phrases do not, however, indicate the weight to be attached to its provisions nor to what is relevant. Unlike the ACAS codes, many of its provisions go considerably further than previous legislation and judicial determinations. Scott J in *Thomas v NUM (South Wales Area)* (above) relied on the code for the proposition that no more than six pickets should be allowed at each entrance to the workplace. He said that: 'This paragraph simply provides a guide as to a sensible number for a picket-line in order that the weight of numbers should not intimidate those who wish to get to work.' **22.50**

23

EMPLOYMENT LAW AND HUMAN RIGHTS

A THE IMPACT IN EMPLOYMENT
LAW 23.01
Article 3: Degrading treatment 23.02
Article 4: Prohibition of slavery
and forced labour 23.03
Article 6: Right to a fair trial 23.08

Article 8: Right to respect for private
and family life 23.24
Article 9: Freedom of thought,
conscience, and religion 23.37
Article 10: Freedom of expression 23.46
Article 11: Freedom of assembly and
association 23.53
Article 14: Discrimination 23.70

A THE IMPACT IN EMPLOYMENT LAW

23.01 The articles of the European Convention on Human Rights of most importance in relation to labour law are:

(a) the right not to be subjected to inhuman or degrading treatment (Art 3);
(b) the right not to be required to perform forced or compulsory labour (Art 4);
(c) the right to a fair trial (Art 6);
(d) the right to respect for private life (Art 8);
(e) the right to freedom of thought (Art 9);
(f) the right to freedom of expression (Art 10);
(g) the right to freedom of peaceful assembly and to freedom of association with others,
     including the right to form and to join trade unions (Art 11); and
(h) the right to enjoy the substantive rights and freedoms set forth in the Convention
     without discrimination (Art 14).

Article 3: Degrading treatment

23.02 Article 3 of the Convention states that 'No one shall be subjected to torture or to inhuman or degrading treatment or punishment.' This is (not surprisingly) an absolute right
and may be relevant to issues of serious racial or other types of harassment.

Article 4: Prohibition of slavery and forced labour

23.03 Article 4 of the Convention provides:

1. No one shall be held in slavery or servitude.
2. No one shall be required to perform forced or compulsory labour.
3. For the purpose of this Article the term 'forced or compulsory labour' shall not include:
    (a) any work required to be done in the ordinary course of detention ... or during condi-
         tional release from such detention;
    (b) any service of a military character;

(c) any service exacted in case of an emergency or calamity threatening the life or well-being of the community;

(d) any work or service which forms part of normal civic obligations.

This Article was itself based on the ILO Convention No 29 on forced and compulsory labour. The Convention defines such labour as 'all work or service which is exacted from any person under the menace of any penalty and for which the said person has not offered himself voluntarily'. **23.04**

The word 'forced' in Art 4 connotes physical or mental constraint. In *van der Mussele v Belgium* [1984] 6 EHRR 163, from which this test derives, it was held that an obligation on pupil barristers to provide services free to those without legal aid did not amount to forced or compulsory labour. Economic duress will thus not suffice. Further, the services to be rendered by such pupil barristers did not fall outside the ambit of the normal activities of an advocate and they contributed to the applicants' general training. The burden on the applicants was not in any sense disproportionate, accounting as it did for a small proportion of their time. If, however, 'the service imposed a burden which was so disproportionate to the advantages attached to the future exercise of that profession that the service could not be treated as having been voluntarily accepted beforehand' then it would breach the Article. **23.05**

In *van Droogenbroeck v Belgium* [1982] 4 EHRR 433, the Commission said that 'in addition to the obligation to provide another with certain services, the concept of servitude includes the obligation on the part of the "serf" to live on another's property and the impossibility of changing his condition'. **23.06**

The topics which may be the subject of challenge include the long hours worked by particular groups of workers who are presently excluded from the Working Time Regulations 1998. **23.07**

Article 6: Right to a fair trial

Article 6(1) of the Convention provides (in material part): **23.08**

1. In the determination of his civil rights and obligations ... everyone is entitled to a fair and public hearing within a reasonable time by an independent and impartial tribunal established by law ...

The basic requirements

The basic requirements of Art 6(1) in civil proceedings are: **23.09**

(a) a fair and public hearing;

(b) an independent and impartial tribunal;

(c) a trial within a reasonable period;

(d) a public judgment (although there are some exceptions to this); and

(e) a reasoned decision to be given.

It may also require in some cases the opportunity to cross-examine witnesses and to give and receive adequate disclosure of documentation. Certain features have been held to be implied in the Article, such as the right to be present, or at least represented, at any determination of the case (*X v Sweden* (1959) 2 YB 354).

This Article is central to the Convention as a whole, since it sets out the fundamentals of the rule of law itself. The scope of the Article in employment issues often turns on the **23.10** autonomous Convention concept of 'determination of a civil right or obligation', which alone gives rise to claims under Art 6.

23.11   There have been several important cases on the extent to which Article 6 rights are engaged:

(a) A teaching assistant at a primary school did not have any right to be represented at an internal disciplinary hearing by a lawyer even though he ran the risk of being placed on the children's barred list as a result of such discipline being exacted (*R (G) v X School* [2012] 1 AC 167). It was only in the second set of proceedings to decide whether he be placed on the barred list (so that he could no longer operate his profession) that Art 6 rights were engaged (see also *Leach v Office of Communications* [2012] ICR 1269).

(b) Unfair dismissal did not determine civil rights under Art 6 but the right to carry on one's profession did (*Mattu v University Hospitals Coventry & Warwicks NHS Trust* [2013] ICR 271; see also *MOJ v Parry* [2013] ICR 311).

(c) It could not be said that the decision of the charity Action for Children would influence any decision of the General Social Care Council so that it was not subject to Art 6 (*R (on the application of Kirk) v Middlesbrough BC* [2010] IRLR 699).

Public tribunals

23.12   **(1) Lengthy delays** The European Court of Human Rights has underlined more than once in employment cases 'the importance of rendering justice without delays which might jeopardise its effectiveness and credibility' (*H v France* (1990) 12 EHRR 74). In *Obermeier v Germany* (1991) 13 EHRR 290, the Court said more specifically that 'an employee who considers that he has been wrongly suspended by his employer has an important personal interest in securing the judicial decision of the lawfulness of that measure promptly'. Lengthy delays of the sort which were commonplace in tribunals a decade ago are now happily long forgotten, but a very long time can still elapse where a case goes on appeal to the Court of Appeal, is then remitted, and after reconsideration by the employment tribunal again goes up the judicial hierarchy.

23.13   There are also some cases where there are long, drawn-out internal procedures before the matter reaches the tribunal system at all. The most obvious case is in the medical arena, where there are many stages of the process in the case of hospital consultants, and it was from there that the leading case of *Darnell v UK* (1994) 18 EHRR 205 arose. There was a nine-year delay between dismissal and final disposal of the case. The European Court of Human Rights found the UK to be in default for allowing such a delay to occur (see also *Somjee v UK* [2003] IRLR 886).

23.14   **(2) Equality of arms** Another feature inherent in the concept of a fair trial is the equality of arms between the parties. This may render the inability to gain legal help in employment tribunals open to challenge. It is no part of Strasbourg jurisprudence that the lack of legal help in *every case* is a breach of the principle of a fair trial, but there have been some circumstances in which the unavailability of legal assistance in respect of complicated issues has been held to be a breach of the principles of a fair trial. The leading case is *Airey v Ireland* (1979–89) 2 EHRR 305. The applicant complained that she could not enforce her civil right to separate from her alcoholic and violent husband because she could not afford legal representation in the separation proceedings. The Irish Government countered with the proposition that she could represent herself, but this received short shrift in Strasbourg. The Court stated that:

The Convention is intended to guarantee not rights that are theoretical or illusory but rights that are practical and effective. This is particularly so of the right of access to the courts in view of the prominent place held in democratic society by the right to a fair trial. It must therefore be ascertained whether [the applicant's] appearance ... without the assistance of a lawyer would be effective in the sense of whether she would be able to present her case properly and satisfactorily.

It was held that this was not so for Mrs Airey because of the legal and factual complexity of the case in which she was involved, and the emotional involvement of the applicant in it.

23.15 Later cases have resisted the notion that *Airey* can be used to provide a general right to legal help. For example, an application to the effect that the refusal of legal aid in defamation cases was in breach of the Convention failed in *Munro v UK* (1987) 52 DR 158.

23.16 **(3) Restriction on publicity of hearings** This issue raises the use in employment tribunals of restricted reporting orders and private hearings. There are exceptions in the Convention itself to the general rule that hearings should be held in public. Those which are most relevant to the tribunals are where 'the protection of the private life of the parties so require, or to the extent strictly necessary in the opinion of the court in special circumstances where publicity would prejudice the interests of justice' (Art 6(1)). This requires the court to weigh in each case whether the restriction on publication is necessary and proportionate to the risk involved. In *BBC v Roden* [2015] IRLR, the EAT said that when an anonymity order was made the court was reconciling three Convention rights, Arts 6, 8, and 10. There must be a fact-specific assessment of the public or other interest in full publication.

23.17 **(4) Access to the court** Whether a fair trial is still possible is a crucial factor in an employment tribunal deciding whether to strike out an application or notice of appearance. In *De Keyser Ltd v Wilson* [2001] IRLR 324, where the claimant sought to strike out a notice of appearance, it was held to be disproportionate to strike out a notice of appearance because a tendentious letter of instruction had been written to a medical expert, since a fair trial was still possible.

23.18 Other relevant issues found in the caselaw are:

(a) that it was an incurable breach of the right to a fair hearing for there to be individuals who had made recommendations for the judge's dismissal to sit on the panel which decided whether or not to remove him from office (*Volkov v Ukraine* [2013] IRLR 480).

(b) Office holders have a right to be given a proper opportunity to explain their conduct before a decision is taken to terminate (*R (Shoesmith) v Ofsted* [2011] ICR 1195).

Private hearings

23.19 **(1) Professional disciplinary bodies** Article 6 may also have scope in disciplinary hearings before professional disciplinary bodies. These have been held to fall within the concept of determining 'civil rights and obligations' within Art 6(1) in several Strasbourg cases (eg *Le Compte v Belgium* (1982) 5 EHRR 183; *König v Germany* (1979–80) 2 EHRR 170). The term 'civil rights and obligations' is treated as an autonomous Convention concept, so that it is not appropriate to apply UK notions of what is a civil right to its construction. The lines of distinction between the cases on what are and what are not 'civil rights' are not, however, easy to draw. Thus, the term has covered a disciplinary hearing in relation to disqualification of a doctor by the French Medical Association, a private body regulated to some extent by statute (*Diennet v France* (1995) 21 EHRR 554), or the UK

General Medical Council (*Wickramasinghe v UK* (1998) 22 EHRR 318), or a decision to re-admit a barrister to the Ordre des Avocats (*H v Belgium* (1988) 10 EHRR 339).

23.20   **(2) Recruitment, employment, and dismissal of public officials** Generally, disputes relating to the recruitment, employment, and retirement of public servants have been held to fall outside the scope of Art 6(1). There is also some jurisprudence excluding disputes about the recruitment, employment, and dismissal of public officials, although as with much Strasbourg jurisprudence the rationale and precise scope of the doctrine has not been clearly spelt out (eg *Neigel v France* (1997) 21 EHRR 424).

23.21   There is a civil right within Art 6(1) where the 'claims in issue relate to a "purely economic right" such as payment of a salary or pension' (*Huber v France* (1998) 26 EHRR 457). Violation by a public authority of the Article has been found where there has been a dismissal or threat of dismissal (*Vogt v Germany* (1996) 21 EHRR 205), or a suspension or reprimand (*Morissens v Belgium* (1988) D&R 127). In *Balfour v Foreign and Commonwealth Office* [1994] ICR 277, however, a former diplomat was unable to rely on Art 6 to challenge the use of public interest immunity certificates in an employment tribunal case which he brought on the termination of his service.

23.22   If a matter is within the scope of civil rights the issues which may there arise include the employee being on an equal footing with the employer; the right to representation at the hearing; access to documents and witnesses; the need for a reasoned decision; and the public nature of the hearing. It may, however, be particularly difficult to fit impartiality and independence into the conduct of disciplinary matters in a small organisation.

23.23   The fact that the determination of illegality effectively stops further litigation of an action is not a breach of Art 6 but rather is part and parcel of the substantive law of contract (*Soteriou v Ultrachem Ltd* [2004] IRLR 870; see also *Heath v Metropolitan Police Commissioner* [2005] ICR 329).

Article 8: Right to respect for private and family life

23.24   Article 8 of the Convention provides:

> 1. Everyone has the right to respect for his private and family life, his home and his correspondence.
> 2. There shall be no interference by a public authority with the exercise of this right except such as is in accordance with the law and is necessary in a democratic society in the interests of national security, public safety or the economic well-being of the country, for the prevention of disorder or crime, for the protection of health and morals, or for the protection of the rights and freedoms of others.

This right includes respect for personal identity, including sexual identity, moral or physical identity, sexual activities and personal relations, gender identification, name, sexual orientation and sexual life, right to identity and personal development, and the right to establish relationships with other human beings and the outside world (*Pay v UK* [2009] IRLR 139). It is to be noted that the word used is 'respect' for privacy, so that there is no absolute right to privacy.

23.25   The right to respect for private life, however, clearly does not stop at the doors of the workplace. This has a number of implications for employers in relation to security measures, dress codes, disclosure, medical checks, and email intrusion.

23.26   The sexuality of the employee is a matter of private life. An employee had, however, been fairly dismissed from a job working with youth offenders after he had been cautioned for gross indecency with another man in a public toilet (*X v Y* [2004] IRLR 625). The claimant's conduct was held not to take place in his private life since it happened in a place to which the public had access. Further, it was a criminal offence that is normally a matter of legitimate concern to the public and it led to a caution for the offence that was relevant to the applicant's employment and should have been disclosed by him to his employer.

The Court also decided that if a dismissal was for the claimant's private conduct and was   **23.27**
in breach of Art 8, that would be relevant to the determination for an unfair dismissal claim whether or not the employer was a public authority. Under s 3 of the HRA 1998 the employment tribunal had, if possible to do so, to read the ERA in a way compatible with Convention rights. The employment tribunal is itself a public authority for these purposes (see also *Brumfitt v MOD* [2005] IRLR 4).

In another case, the employer found that the claimant who was a senior train conductor   **23.28**
had printed a substantially higher number of faulty tickets than any of her colleagues. This led to her dismissal. The CA held that a finding of dishonesty here damaged the employee's reputation so that Art 8 might be engaged but that it would not be applicable where the employee had brought such consequences on herself by her own wrongdoing established by a properly conducted, procedurally fair process. The range of reasonable responses test was compatible with Art 8 (*Turner v East Midlands Trains Ltd* [2013] ICR 525).

In *Schüth v Germany*, 23 September 2010, the ECtHR found a breach of Art 8 when   **23.29**
the German labour court did not decide a dismissal to be unfair where the organist and choirmaster of a Catholic Church was dismissed for an extramarital affair (see also on reasonable expectation of privacy, *Garamukana v Solent NHS Trust* [2016] IRLR 476).

Security measures

Security measures at work may also fall within the scope of the Article; thus a search of   **23.30**
a lawyer's office was held to be in breach of Art 8 (*Niemitz v Germany* (1993) 16 EHRR 97). The Court said that 'to interpret the words "private life" and "home" as excluding certain professional or business activities or premises would not be consonant with the essential object and purpose of Art 8'. In *Halford v UK* [1997] IRLR 471, the absence of domestic legislation dealing with an employer's right (or lack of right) to 'tap' telephone calls at work was found to be a breach of Art 8. The claimant (who was a senior police officer) had alleged that her office telephone was being tapped by her employers in order to obtain evidence to use in a sex discrimination claim which she had brought. The European Court of Human Rights held that to tap an office telephone was prima facie a breach of Art 8, unless the employer warned the employee that it was being done. At that time there was no statutory basis for the telephone tapping (see now 'Interception' in Regulation of Investigatory Powers Act 2000, s 1(3)).

In *Leander v Sweden* (1987) 9 EHRR 433 the ECtHR decided that storing information   **23.31**
about a job applicant in a secret police register and releasing it to a prospective employer breached the applicant's right to respect for private life. This interference could be justified, however, as 'necessary in a democratic society' (the defence in Art 8(2)). Whether it was so justified in a particular case would depend on whether the action taken was proportionate to the risk which was posed. The use of such information for vetting candidates for posts which are *not* of importance for national security may be harder to justify.

Adopting CCTV to monitor employees at work is increasingly common. It may be justi-   **23.32**
fied on the grounds that it is necessary for the protection of health (eg, on an assembly line), or to protect the rights of others (the employer); but it must be a proportionate

response in each case, so that its indiscriminate use throughout the workplace may not be proportionate.

23.33　Likewise, employers interfering with emails at work may prima facie breach the right to respect for correspondence under Art 8. In some cases, such interference may be justified on the basis that it is necessary to protect the rights of others (either the employer—to prevent employees wasting time at work, or to check that employees are not acting against the employer's interests by working for a competitor—or fellow employees, by monitoring to ensure that employees are not sending offensive emails which might amount to harassment). Proportionality is the key to resolving the point. The Employment Practices Data Protection Code 2011 deals with data such as emails relating to salary, notes about specific workers, and application forms, and gives guidance on when it is appropriate to store sensitive personal data. In *Bărbulescu v Romania* [2016] IRLR 235, the employee created at the employer's request an internet instant messaging service to respond to clients' enquiries. The employer told him that the communications had been monitored and the records showed that he had been using the internet for personal purposes which was contrary to internal regulations. He claimed that he was only using it for personal matters, including on subjects such as his health and sex life. The ECtHR decided that his Art 8 rights had not been violated because the state had struck a fair balance between his right to respect for private life and his employer's interests. He had been able to raise his right to privacy before the domestic courts.

Dress codes

23.34　Dress codes may be subject to challenge under both Art 8 and Art 10 (freedom of expression; see also 23.46). An employee may seek to 'express her personality' by wearing, for example, a nose-ring which the employer finds offensive and off-putting to customers or clients. She may be able to argue that she has a right to express herself by wearing a nose-ring, and that the employer is failing to respect her right to express herself or her right to a private life. Again, the real issue is the proportionality of the response to the harm caused to others.

Medical checks

23.35　The collection of medical data and the maintenance of medical records fall within the sphere of private life (*Chare née Julien v France* (App No 14461/88) DR 141), and there may be interference when the employer collects highly sensitive health-related information about its employees. There was thus a potential breach in *MS v Sweden* (1997) 3 BHRC 248, where the applicant injured her back at work and claimed compensation under the Industrial Injury Insurance Act. The clinic which treated her disclosed her medical records in full to the Social Insurance Office without her permission. While this was a potential breach, it was held to be proportionate in the pursuit of the legitimate aim of protecting the economic well-being of the country by ensuring that public funds were allocated only to deserving claimants. The Court said that 'the domestic law must afford appropriate safeguards to prevent any such communication or disclosure of personal health data as may be inconsistent with the guarantees in Art 8'. It was wrong to find references to the applicant's private life in a letter of instruction by the respondent's solicitor to a medical expert who was to prepare a medical report for a disability discrimination case. This breached Art 8 (*De Keyser Ltd v Wilson* [2001] IRLR 324) given that the recipient doctor would have been bound by conventional medical confidence. An employee may by his conduct in submitting false timesheets force the employer to investigate the matter. Surveillance which operated to quantify the number of times that the claimant left his house to go to the employer's plant was also not in breach of Art 8 (*McGowan v Scottish Water* [2005] IRLR 167).

Article 8 has also been interpreted to apply to respect for the right to work as required by **23.36** the European Social Charter (*Sidabras v Lithuania* [2004] ECHR 395).

Article 9: Freedom of thought, conscience, and religion

Article 9 of the Convention provides: **23.37**

1. Everyone has the right to freedom of thought, conscience and religion; this right includes freedom to change his religion or belief and freedom, either alone or in community with others and in public or private, to manifest his religion or belief, in worship, teaching, practice and observance.
2. Freedom to manifest one's religion or beliefs shall be subject only to such limitations as are prescribed by law and are necessary in a democratic society in the interests of public safety, for the protection of public order, health or morals, or for the protection of the rights and freedoms of others.

The scope of the religion and conscience which is protected by this Article is wide, so that **23.38** in *Arrowsmith v UK* (1980) 3 EHRR 218, the Commission accepted that 'the attitude of pacifism may be seen as a belief protected by Article 9(1)'. A balance is to be struck between the needs of the religion and wider societal requirements, including the concerns of employers, which was most clearly articulated in *X v UK* (1984) 6 EHRR 583, where the Commission stated that:

> Article 9 primarily protects the sphere of personal beliefs and religious creeds ... In addition, it protects acts which are intimately linked to these attitudes, such as acts of worship or devotion which are aspects of the practice of a religion or a belief in a generally recognised form. However, in protecting this personal sphere, Art 9 of the Convention does not always guarantee the rights to behave in the public sphere in a way which is dictated by such a belief, for instance by refusing to pay certain taxes because part of the revenue so raised may be applied for military expenditure.

The Article clearly protects not only ideas which are favourably received, but also the expression of ideas which would be regarded as offensive to all or a sector of the population. This is another important right, which has the potential to cover a variety of situations.

First, and most obviously, it presents employees of public authorities with a general enti- **23.39** tlement to practise their religion and, more importantly, not to be disciplined or dismissed for doing so.

The early guidance from Strasbourg did not, however, suggest that Art 9 is a licence **23.40** for employees to insist on time off to practise their religion during working time. For example, in *Ahmed v UK* (1982) 4 EHRR 126, a Muslim schoolteacher wanted to pray at his mosque for forty-five minutes every Friday. The Inner London Education Authority (ILEA) refused permission and relied on the contract of employment, which required the teacher to work on Fridays. The European Court of Human Rights held that the ILEA's refusal did not infringe Art 9, since the employee had voluntarily accepted a teaching post which prevented his attendance at prayers (and had not complained, or requested time off, during his first six years at work). The Court identified the crucial issue as being whether, in relying on the contract of employment, the ILEA was arbitrarily disregarding the right to freedom of religion (see also *Copsey v WWB Devon Clays Ltd* [2005] IRLR

810 on Sunday working; *Knudsen v Norway* (1985) 142 DR 247). This is not the line taken in the more recent jurisprudence.

23.41   Secondly, Art 9 has implications for working on religious holidays and Sundays. However, in *Stedman v UK* (1997) 23 EHRR 168, the applicant was dismissed for refusing to work on Sundays in accordance with her religious belief. The Commission rejected her claim on (it seems) the grounds that she was not dismissed because of her religious beliefs but because she refused to work her contractual hours. It did not consider at any length the point that her refusal to work contractual hours was *because* of her religious beliefs (cf *Prais v EC Commission* [1976] ECR 1589).

23.42   The Court has also emphasised that a balance must be struck between the applicant's religious views and the essential needs of the particular job, including the ethos of the organisation in which the applicant works. In *Kalac v Turkey* (1999) 27 EHRR 152, for example, the application was brought by a judge advocate in the air force with the rank of group captain who was the high command's director of legal affairs. He was compulsorily retired from that post because his 'conduct and attitude revealed that he had adopted unlawful fundamentalist opinion'. The principle of secularism was at the time inherent in the Turkish armed forces and the Court did not think that his rights were infringed.

23.43   The key case now is *Eweida v BA* [2013] IRLR 231, which was the consideration of four contrasting cases with quite different results. Overall the ECtHR decided that the manifestation of religious belief may take the form of worship, teaching, practice, and observance. Not every act which is in some way inspired, motivated, or influenced by religious belief constitutes a 'manifestation' of belief. In order to fall within Art 9 the act must be intimately linked to the particular religion or belief. The existence of a sufficiently close and direct nexus between the act and the underlying belief must be determined on the facts of each case. There is no requirement on the applicant to establish that he acted in fulfilment of a duty *mandated* by the particular religion. In the lead case of Ms Eweida, her wearing a cross visibly at work was a manifestation of her religious belief and the refusal by BA to allow her to remain in her post whilst wearing one was an interference with her right to manifest her religion. The vital question for the ECtHR was whether her right freely to manifest her religion was sufficiently secured within the domestic order. It was not; the religious manifestation was a fundamental right which was to be set against the employer's wish to project a certain corporate image. In deciding that this was proportionate the domestic courts had not made a proper balance. There was no evidence that the wearing of other previously authorised items of religious clothing, such as turbans and hijabs, by other employees had any negative impact on the employer's brand or image. This was to be contrasted with the combined case of Ms Chaplin who wanted to wear a cross but in the context of working in a hospital, where there were genuine health and safety concerns on a ward. Health and safety was an area where domestic authorities had a wide margin of appreciation. The hospital managers were better placed than a court to make decisions about clinical safety. The measures taken by the employer were not disproportionate.

23.44   In another combined case, Ms Ladele was a registrar of births, deaths, and marriages who believed that same-sex civil partnerships were contrary to God's law. A disciplinary process was applied. The ECtHR recalled that differences in treatment based on sexual orientation required particularly serious reasons by way of justification. The aim pursued of providing a registration service for same-sex couples was legitimate, while the consequences for the applicant were serious but the local authority's policy aimed to secure the rights of others which were also protected under the Convention. National authorities had a wide margin of appreciation when it came to striking a balance between competing

Convention rights. Mr McFarlane worked as a counsellor for Relate Avon Ltd, which provided a confidential sex therapy and relationship counselling service. He refused to work with same-sex couples for religious reasons. The ECtHR decided that he had enrolled voluntarily on Relate's postgraduate training programme knowing that it operated an equal opportunities policy and that the filtering of clients on the ground of sexual orientation was not possible. The most important factor was that the employer's action was intended to secure the implementation of its policy of providing a service without discrimination. The state authorities benefited from a wide margin of appreciation in deciding where to strike the balance between Mr McFarlane's right to manifest his religious belief and the employer's interest in securing the rights of others. This margin was not exceeded on the facts.

Section 13 of the HRA 1998 makes specific provision for a court or tribunal, in deter- **23.45** mining any question which 'might affect the exercise by a religious organisation ... of the Convention right to freedom of thought, conscience and religion', to have regard to the 'importance of that right'. This arose from the concerns felt by some such organisations that their ethos might be challenged by the Act—for example, that they would have to allow gay priests or marriages, or engage persons who were hostile to their beliefs.

Article 10: Freedom of expression

Article 10 of the Convention provides: **23.46**

1. Everyone has the right to freedom of expression. This right shall include freedom to hold opinions and to receive and impart information and ideas without interference by public authority and regardless of frontiers ...
2. The exercise of these freedoms, since it carries with it duties and responsibilities, may be subject to such formalities, conditions, restrictions or penalties as are prescribed by law and are necessary in a democratic society, in the interests of national security, territorial integrity or public safety, for the prevention of disorder or crime, for the protection of health or morals, for the protection of the reputation or rights of others, for preventing the disclosure of information received in confidence, or for maintaining the authority and impartiality of the judiciary.

In this respect, 'expression' covers not only words, but also pictures, images, and actions **23.47** intended to express an idea or to present information (*Stevens v UK* [1986] D&R 245). The exceptions to the right should be 'narrowly interpreted' and 'convincingly established'. The right applies not only to ideas which are favourably received or regarded as inoffensive, but also to those which 'offend, shock or disturb the state or any sector of the population. Such are the demands of pluralism, tolerance and broadmindedness'. In the employment sphere, the cases may be analysed under various heads.

The right to political views and to manifest them

The crucial case is *Vogt v Germany* (1996) 21 EHRR 205. A teacher was dismissed because **23.48** of active membership of the German Communist Party. She had already been appointed to a tenured position and this dismissal was held to infringe her Art 10 rights. On the other hand, previous applications by office holders have been held not to be protected (*Glasenapp v Germany* (1986) 9 EHRR 25; *Kosiek v Germany* (1987) 9 EHRR 328).

Ahmed v UK [1999] IRLR 188 was an important challenge in Strasbourg to the restric- **23.49** tion on senior local government officers engaging in political activity, set out in the Local Government (Political Restrictions) Regulations 1990. The first issue was that the restriction was prescribed by law (although there was some uncertainty, it was inevitable that such measures were couched in broad terms given that they were laying down rules of general application). It was in pursuance of one or more legitimate aims (to protect the rights of the council members and the electorate to effective political democracy at the highest level); local government has long relied on a bond of trust between elected members and permanent corps of local government officers who both advise them on policy and assume responsibility for implementation of policies adopted, and this was necessary in a democratic society. The appropriate test was whether there was a pressing social need, and states have a wide margin of appreciation in assessing whether such need exists. Thus, the Regulations satisfied the test in Art 10.

23.50 Some types of employment may require a degree of restriction of freedom of speech. Thus, in *Morissens v Belgium* [1988] D&R 127, the Commission said that 'by entering the civil service [as a teacher] the applicant accepted certain restrictions on the exercise of her freedom of expression, as being inherent in her duties'. In *B v UK* (1985) 45 D&R 41 the disciplining of an Aldermaston atomic weapons worker, who criticised atomic weapons on a TV programme, was found to be justified.

23.51 In *Rekvényi v Hungary* (2000) 30 EHRR 519, the Court considered a provision in the Hungarian constitution whereby members of the armed forces and police could not join any political party or engage in political activity. The Court recognised (especially in the light of Hungary's recent history) the legitimacy of the public being able to expect that 'in their dealings with the police they are entitled to be confronted with politically-neutral officers who are detached from the political fray'.

23.52 Freedom of expression is relevant to the fairness of what occurred in a claim for breach of confidentiality (*Hill v Governing Body of Great Tey Primary School* [2013] ICR 691).

Article 11: Freedom of assembly and association

23.53 Article 11 of the Convention provides:

1. Everyone has the right to freedom of peaceful assembly and to freedom of association with others, including the right to form and to join trade unions for the protection of his interests.
2. No restrictions shall be placed on the exercise of these rights other than such as are prescribed by law and are necessary in a democratic society in the interests of national security or public safety, for the prevention of disorder or crime, for the protection of health or morals or for the protection of the rights and freedoms of others. This article shall not prevent the imposition of lawful restrictions on the exercise of these rights by members of the armed forces, of the police or of the administration of the State.

There are various respects in which this Article may give rights to workers.

Closed shop

23.54 The Strasbourg Court first examined the closed shop in 1980 in *Young, James, and Webster v UK* [1981] IRLR 408. This case concerned three British Rail employees dismissed pursuant to a closed shop agreement, and the closed shop provisions of the TULRA 1974 and the TULR(A)A 1976. All three had principled—but not religious— objections to belonging to a trade union. It was a strong case because the claimants had joined British Rail before the closed shop agreement was entered into.

23.55 Eighteen of the twenty-one judges found for the sacked employees; three against. The necessary foundation of the majority's decision was its finding that the very notion of *freedom* of association implied 'some measure of freedom of choice as to its exercise'. In other words, the freedom to associate included, to some extent, the freedom not to associate.

On the facts of the case, the majority held the threat of dismissal, involving loss of liveli- **23.56**
hood, 'a most serious form of compulsion ... [which] strikes at the very substance of the
freedom guaranteed by Art 11 ... [rendering that freedom] non-existent or so reduced
to be of no practical value'. Because of the three workers' principled objections to trade
union membership, the majority also held their treatment to have been in violation of
their rights of freedom of thought and expression.

Lastly, the Court rejected the UK's submission that the closed shop legislation was never- **23.57**
theless necessary in a democratic society and proportionate, and hence lawful under the
provisions of Art 11(2). Its judgment did not mean that closed shop arrangements would
always be in contravention of the right to freedom of association: indeed, '[a]ssuming
that Article 11 does not guarantee the negative aspect of that freedom on the same footing as the positive aspect, compulsion to join a particular trade union may not always be
contrary to the Convention'.

Since *Young, James, and Webster* the Court has held compulsion to join a particular **23.58**
trade union to be lawful under the Convention. in *Sibson v UK* (1994) 17 EHRR 193, Mr
Sibson was a lorry driver who objected when he was given the choice of joining the trade
union at his existing depot (because it was a closed shop) or moving to another depot.
This followed his being expelled from his union when he made allegations of dishonesty
against a branch official. The Court did not uphold the application and distinguished the
facts of this case from those pertaining in *Young, James, and Webster* in two respects.
First, in this case there was not the same threat of dismissal leading to loss of livelihood.
Mr Sibson had the alternative of moving depots, and the employer was contractually
entitled to move staff between depots. Secondly, Mr Sibson had no principled objections
to trade union membership, unlike Messrs Young, James, and Webster.

Article 11 cannot be interpreted as imposing an obligation on organisations to admit **23.59**
whoever wishes to join them (*ASLEF v UK* [2007] IRLR 361). This was decided in the
case of a train driver who was a member of the British National Party.

(On Victimisation of trade unionists, see *Palomo Sanchez v Spain* [2011] ECHR 1319.)

Right of union to be heard but not to be recognised

Establishing and joining a trade union may be of little practical value if the employer **23.60**
does not recognise the union as its employees' representative in negotiations over pay
and conditions. The Court considered the extent to which Art 11(1) protected more than
just the right to *join* a trade union in *Swedish Engine Drivers' Union v Sweden* (1979–
80) 1 EHRR 617. This case concerned the refusal of the Swedish National Collective
Bargaining Office to enter into a collective agreement with the Engine Drivers' Union.
The union asserted that this represented a violation of Art 11(1). The union lost because
the Court held that Art 11(1) did not oblige a member state to treat trade unions in any
particular way. The right to negotiate through collective bargaining was not inherent in
the right to form and join a trade union.

In the *Engine Drivers* case, the Court considered the extent to which a state should assist **23.61**
trade unions and their members to conform with its duties under Art 11. It observed that
Art 11(1) obliges public authorities to protect an individual's 'right to form and to join
trade unions *for the protection of his interests*' (emphasis added). It refused to 'accept the
view expressed by the minority in the Commission who describe the phrase "for the protection of his interests" as redundant'. 'These words', the Court continued, 'clearly denot-
ing purpose, show that the Convention safeguards freedom to protect the occupational
interests of trade union members by trade union action, the conduct and development of

which the Contracting States must both permit and make possible. In the opinion of the Court, it follows that the members of a trade union have a right, in order to protect their interests, that *the trade union should be heard*' (emphasis added). It was a matter for the state to determine how this right would be provided.

23.62   This may be argued to mean that under Art 11(1) there is some form of compulsory consultation by employers, although states have a discretion as to how this should be done. The Court said that 'the Article does not secure any particular treatment of trade unions, or their members, by the state, such as the right that the state should conclude any given collective agreement with them'. In the European Court of Human Rights in *Wilson & Others v UK* [2002] IRLR 568, the employees' and unions' complaint, primarily based on Art 11 of the European Convention, succeeded on the basis that a trade union must thus be free to strive for the protection of its members' interests, and the individual members have a right, in order to protect their interests, that the trade union should be heard. Since there was at the time that the case arose no legal obligation on employers to recognise trade unions for the purposes of collective bargaining, there was no remedy in law by which the applicants could prevent the employers from derecognising the unions and refusing to renew the collective bargaining agreements. The Court decided that the union and its members must, however, be free, in one way or another, to seek to persuade the employer to listen to what the union has to say on behalf of its members. It is of the essence of the right to join a trade union for the protection of their interests that employees should be free to instruct or permit the union to make representations to their employer, or to take action in support of their interests on their behalf. If workers are prevented from so doing, their freedom to belong to a trade union, for the protection of their interests, becomes illusory. UK law permitted employers to treat less favourably employees who were not prepared to renounce a freedom that was an essential feature of union membership. Such conduct constituted a disincentive or restraint on the use by employees of union membership to protect their interests. The statutory recognition procedure does not transgress Art 11 because the right to be recognised for collective bargaining is not a right guaranteed by Art 11 (*R (on the application of NUJ) v CAC* [2006] IRLR 53).

Rules about which unions are appropriate for the worker

23.63   The Convention may protect those employees who are required to join particular unions by reference to rules drawn up between the unions themselves. *Cheall v UK* (1986) 8 EHRR 74 was an action brought by a worker expelled from his new union (APEX) because, in breach of the TUC's Bridlington Principles which applied to limit inter-union disputes, it had not checked that his old union was content with the change of his membership. The TUC Disputes Committee intervened pursuant to rules set up by agreement. The Commission found against Mr Cheall, explaining that in 'the exercise of their rights under Art 11(1), unions must remain free to decide, in accordance with union rules, questions concerning admission to and expulsion from the union'. The role of the state was limited, in such circumstances, to protecting 'the individual against any abuse of a dominant position by trade unions … [such as] might occur … where exclusion or expulsion was not in accordance with union rules or where the rules were wholly unreasonable or arbitrary or where the consequences of exclusion or expulsion resulted in exceptional hardship such as job loss because of a closed shop'. The Court said that 'the State must protect the individual against any abuse of dominant position by trade unions'.

Restrictions on rights of the union to organise

23.64   The best known challenge to the restrictions on the rights of unions failed. The Thatcher Government banned unions recruiting at the Government Communications Headquarters.

The complaint against this on human rights grounds was rejected by the Commission because of the wide discretion in matters of national security accorded to nation states (*CCSU v UK* (1988) 50 DR 228).

The following points can be drawn from the Commission's decision and Art 11(2) itself: **23.65**

(a) Whether a worker is a member of the 'administration of the state' is important when determining if his or her rights under Art 11(1) have been violated.

(b) The first sentence of Art 11(2) is directed towards workers, other than those engaged in the army, the police or the administration of the state, who might endanger others' rights, morals, property, or persons by embarking on mass industrial action. Health professionals, members of the emergency services, and prison officers are probably to be included in this category. Restrictions on the freedom of these groups to form and join trade unions are thus subject to the requirements that they are (i) lawful; (ii) necessary in a democratic society to serve one of the important social goods set out in Art 11(2); and (iii) proportionate to the seriousness of the mischief that they are designated to prevent.

Right to take industrial action

There is also no general right to strike guaranteed by the Convention. This was the   **23.66**
clear conclusion reached by the Court in *Schmidt and Dahlström v Sweden* (1979–80) 1 EHRR 632. This case concerned collective bargaining practices in Sweden. In the event that national pay negotiations continued beyond the date on which the annual pay increase was due to take effect, the normal practice was to give retroactive effect to the pay increase when it was finally agreed. However, it was a principle of the system that the members of any union which chose to strike during this period would automatically forfeit the right to benefit from this retroactive effect. The applicants in *Schmidt and Dahlström* claimed that this practice violated their rights under Art 11. However, the Court found against them. It reasoned that the right to strike was not inherent in the right to freedom of association, and accordingly the state was free to restrict the right to strike as it saw fit.

UNISON v UK [2002] IRLR 497 concerned an injunction to prevent strike action   **23.67**
by UNISON members at University College Hospital (known as *UCLH v UNISON* [1999] ICR 204 in the domestic courts). The Strasbourg Court considered that the prohibition of the strike must be regarded as a restriction on the union's power to protect those interests and therefore disclosed a restriction on the freedom of association. However, the Court went on to decide that the restriction was justified under Art 11(2). The Court was satisfied that UCLH could claim that its ability to carry out its functions effectively including the securing of contracts with outside bodies might be adversely affected by the actions of the union so that measures taken to prevent the strike may be regarded as concerning the 'rights of others', that is, UCLH (para 39). The state had not exceeded that margin of appreciation accorded to it in regulating trade union action (para 42).

The Court reached a similar result in *Federation of Offshore Workers' Trade Unions v*   **23.68**
Norway (App No 38190/97). The Norwegian Government had issued an ordinance preventing a strike of workers on offshore gas platforms, and compelling the disputing parties to participate in a compulsory arbitration process. The Court held that restrictions imposed by a contracting state on the exercise of the right to strike do not in themselves give rise to an issue under Art 11. The question is whether the law of the contracting state, looked at as a whole, adequately protects the freedom of trade unions to pursue their members' interests.

23.69 *International Transport Workers' Federation v Viking Line ABP* [2008] IRLR 143 involves EU law rather than human rights but there is an important consideration in the case of whether there is a right to strike. It concerned industrial action by FSU, the Finnish affiliate of the London-based ITF, aimed at stopping the employers from reflagging a ferry from Finland to Estonia, and staffing it with a cheaper Estonian crew. The ECJ characterises the right of establishment as 'a fundamental freedom'. It is capable of conferring rights on a private employer which may be relied on against a trade union. The ECJ holds that the right to strike does not fall outside the scope of regulation by EU competition rules. In effect, this means that trade union activity is potentially reviewable by the courts under EU law and, if it infringes the rights of employers, the courts may examine the reasons for the industrial action to see whether they conform to the principles of proportionality.

Article 14: Discrimination

23.70 Under Art 14 of the Convention:

> The enjoyment of the rights and freedoms set forth in this Convention shall be secured without discrimination on any ground such as sex, race, colour, language, religion, political or other opinion, national or social origin, association with a national minority, property, birth or other status.

23.71 This Article is narrower in some important respects than might be anticipated, but wider than the national law in the variety of statuses which are prohibited as grounds for discrimination. It does *not* prohibit discrimination by public bodies; rather, it prohibits public bodies from discriminating on the above grounds (which include the vague ground 'status') when complying with other Convention requirements. In that sense it is *dependent* on the other rights; there need be no breach of the particular article but the allegation must come within the ambit of one of them (see eg *Jones v 3M Healthcare Ltd* [2002] ICR 341). A key example of the operation of this aspect was *Abdulaziz Cabales & Balkandali v UK* (1985) 7 EHRR 471. The applicants were lawfully and permanently settled in the UK. They complained that their husbands were refused permission to join them. There was no breach of Art 8 alone but there was a breach of Art 14 in conjunction with Art 8. Although it was legitimate to restrict admission of non-national spouses to the UK, it was not legitimate to distinguish between non-national spouses of males (who were permitted entry) and non-national spouses of females (who were not).

23.72 The use of the words 'such as' and 'other status' indicates that the categories of prohibited discrimination are not closed; they include sexual orientation, marital status, military status, status as a trade union, and imprisonment. Article 14 extends to any ground for adverse treatment of a group or class that lacks objective and reasonable justification (*Belgian Linguistics case* (1968) 1 EHRR 252).

23.73 Further, Art 14 covers a much wider range of subject areas than does domestic law, which is restricted to discrimination in employment, education, and the provision of goods and services.

23.74 Discrimination under this Article can be justified by an 'objective and reasonable justification' for the differential treatment. This depends on the aim and effect of the measure; whether there is a reasonable relationship of proportionality between the means employed and the aims sought to be realised.

INDEX

Accounting *see* **Duty to Account and disclose**
Additional awards 14.299–14.301
Adoption
  detriment 10.77
  time off work 10.38
Advisory, Conciliation and Arbitration
    Service (ACAS)
  determination of fair terms 3.44
  disciplinary and grievance procedures 4.52
  functions 19.122–19.123
  methods of dispute settlement
    advice 19.128
    arbitration 19.130
    conciliation 19.124–19.126
    independent inquiry 19.129
    mediation 19.127
  misconduct hearings 14.181
  overview 19.120–19.121
  settlement agreements 12.50
Affray 22.16–22.17
Age discrimination
  justifications 8.104–8.105
  protected characteristic 8.14
Agency workers
  employee status 2.48–2.53
  national minimum wage 5.21
  non-discrimination 9.21–9.22
  protected disclosures 15.20
  working time regulation 5.51
Agreements to terminate 14.65–14.67
Annual leave
  pay 5.62–5.63
  relationship with sick pay 5.64–5.66
  relevant pay 5.67
  statutory rights 5.61
Antenatal care 10.39
Appeals
  Commission enforcement 8.216
  flexible working 10.82
  procedural fairness 14.185–14.190
  selection for redundancy 14.205
Apprentices
  capacity to enter contract 3.45
  national minimum wage 5.23
  special contract requirements 3.50
  special work status 2.43
  working time regulation 5.51
Arbitration
  ACAS dispute settlement 19.130

Central Arbitration Committee (CAC)
  determination of fair terms 3.44
  enforcement of collective
    agreements 19.52–19.53
  EWC disputes 19.147–19.149
  judicial review 19.132
  reasoned decisions 19.133
  recognition of trade unions 19.62–19.71
  statutory jurisdiction 19.131
Armed forces
  continuity of employment 11.29
  exclusion from all protection rights 12.43
  exclusion from working time
    regulation 5.55
  freedom of assembly (Art 11) 25.53
  national minimum wage 5.24
  restrictions on industrial action 21.55
Assaults 22.11
Assemblies
  freedom of assembly (Art 11)
    closed shop 23.54–23.59
    ECHR text 23.53–23.69
    industrial action 23.66–23.69
    national security 23.64–23.65
    recognition of trade unions 23.60–23.62
    union rules 23.63
  public order offences 22.26
  unlawful assembly 22.15
Assertion of statutory rights
  automatically unfair grounds
    for dismissal 14.278–14.283
  qualifying period of employment 12.06
  Sunday trading 5.80
Associative discrimination 8.116
Automatically fair grounds for
    dismissal 14.103
Automatically unfair grounds for dismissal
  assertion of statutory rights 14.278–14.283
  dismissal during strike or lock-out
    action provoked by
      employers 14.260–14.261
    date of dismissal
      important 14.266–14.267
    discriminatory selection 14.270
    official action 14.262–14.265
    'other industrial action' 14.252–14.257
    overview 14.248–14.250
    protected industrial
      action 14.273–14.275

Automatically unfair grounds for dismissal (*Cont.*)
  re-engagement 14.269
  statutory provisions 14.247
  'strike' defined 14.251
  unofficial industrial action 14.271–14.272
  jury service 14.284–14.285
  recognition disputes 14.276–14.277
  spent convictions 14.245–14.246
  statutory provisions 14.103
  Sunday trading 5.80
  transfer of undertakings 18.99

Ballots
  background to modern era
    Cameron governments 1.29
    Employment Act 1980 1.12
    Industrial Relations Act 1971 1.06
  'calls' for action before ballot 21.132
  contents of ballot paper 21.128
  different ballots for each
    workplace 21.124–21.127
  enforcement by members 21.145–21.148
  notice of ballot 21.133–21.141
  notice of industrial action 21.142–21.144
  number of votes required 21.122–21.123
  person authorised to call for
    action 21.149–21.153
  person to be balloted 21.114–21.121
  statutory provisions 21.106
  voter protection 21.129–21.131
  when required 21.107–21.113
Basic awards 14.302–14.309
Beliefs *see* **Religion and belief**
Benefits
  calculation of redundancy payments 16.60
  damages for wrongful
    dismissal 13.59–13.65
  during notice period 13.08
  part of compensatory
    award 14.323–14.324
  reasonable adjustment
    discrimination 8.135–8.137
'Blacklisting' 20.15, 20.06
Breaches of contract
  consequences 4.46
  constructive dismissal
    general principles 14.37–14.38
    good faith 14.27–14.33
    need for fundamental breach 14.39
    question of fact 14.42
    reaction to fundamental
      breach 14.43–14.51
    'the last straw' 14.40
    variation of contracts 14.34–14.36

  effect of industrial action 21.06
  inducing breaches of contract
    causation 21.33–21.34
    different ways of committing
      tort 21.20
    direct inducement 21.21
    immunity 21.40–21.43
    importance 21.18–21.19
    indirect inducement 21.22
    inducement 21.28–21.30
    justification 21.38–21.39
    knowledge of contract 21.26–21.27
    picketing 22.33–22.34
    procuring breaches 21.23–21.24
    requirement for breach 21.31
    unlawful means 21.35–21.37
  interference with contracts or businesses
    immunity 21.56
    importance 21.44–21.51
    unlawful means 21.52–21.55
  intimidation
    immunity 21.61
    key requirements 21.57–21.60
  repudiatory breaches
    industrial action 21.10–21.12
    variation of contracts 14.19–14.20
  termination of employment
    general principles 13.10–13.12
    need for acceptance 13.13–13.19
Business reorganisations
  diminution in requirements of business
    distinguished 16.27–16.30
  qualifications 12.26
  quasi redundancy 14.223–14.231

Cadets 2.43
Capacity to enter contract 3.45
Care and safety *see* **Health and safety at work**
Carers *see* **Dependant care leave**
Casual workers
  employee status 2.11, 2.47
  lay-offs and short-time working 4.53
  sham contracts 2.14
Central Arbitration Committee (CAC)
  determination of fair terms 3.44
  enforcement of collective
    agreements 19.52–19.53
  EWC disputes 19.147–19.149
  judicial review 19.132
  reasoned decisions 19.133
  recognition of trade unions
    application procedure 19.62–19.66
    ballots to determine support for
      recognition 19.67–19.71
  statutory jurisdiction 19.131

Cessation of business
insolvency 18.27
at place of employment 16.15–16.18
total 16.13–16.14
Closed shop
background to modern era
Employment Act 1980 1.12–1.13
Industrial Relations Act 1971 1.06
freedom of assembly (Art 11) 23.54–23.59
refusal of employment on union
grounds 20.23–20.25
refusal to remain a union
member 20.21–20.22
union recruitment strikes 21.154
Codes of practice
BEIS powers 19.135, 19.137
disciplinary and grievance procedures 4.52
enforcement 19.136
function of ACAS 19.122
harassment 8.106
misconduct hearings 14.181
picketing 22.47–22.50
reasonable adjustment discrimination 8.128
status 19.134
Collective agreements
background to modern era
Industrial Relations Act 1971 1.06
Labour legislation 1997–2009 1.24
basis of incorporation 3.10–3.13
criteria for independent union 19.15
details required in written statement of
terms 3.63
effect of transfer of
undertakings 18.126–18.128
effect on individual contracts 3.06–3.09
enforcement
general principles 19.49–19.51
statutory provisions 19.52–19.54
equal pay 7.94–7.95
history and development of collective
bargaining 19.01–19.02
information rights
exceptions 19.110
importance 19.103
remedies 19.111–19.112
what must be disclosed 19.104–19.109
overview 3.04–3.05
priority for national agreements 3.20
recognition of trade unions
agreement on bargaining
unit 19.67–19.71
agreement on method of
bargaining 19.80–19.81
changes in bargaining unit 19.82–19.84
termination 3.14–3.15

terms inappropriate for
incorporation 3.16–3.18
working time 5.70
Commencement of employment
see also **Continuity of employment**
details required in written statement of
terms 3.63
entitlement to annual leave 5.61
Commission on Equality and Human Rights
creation 8.02
enforcement of discrimination
claims 8.216–8.220
Common law
different policy considerations 2.04
following instructions 4.42
importance of employee status 2.02
lay-offs
general principles 4.54–4.58
income maintenance 4.59
ownership of patents 6.41
right to work 19.19–19.20
termination of employment
by dismissal 13.20
by notice 13.03
terminations excluded from unfair dismissal
agreements to terminate 14.65–14.67
frustration 14.80–14.91
late return after time off 14.76–14.79
resignations 14.68–14.75
trial periods to avoid redundancy 16.39
unlawful terms 4.51
Compensation and damages
claims against strikers 21.13
claims of unjustified union
discipline 19.35–19.40
detriment arising from union
recognition 19.95–19.96
discrimination claims
aggravated damages 8.206–8.209
contributory fault 8.210
effect of illegality 8.214–8.215
general principles 8.196–8.198
injury to feelings 8.199–8.204
joint liability 8.212
personal injuries 8.211
perverse awards 8.213
stigma damages 8.205
exclusion from trade union
membership 19.28–19.29
failure to comply with reinstatement or
re-engagement 14.299–14.301
infringement of rights of safety
representatives 20.61–20.65
infringement of trade union rights
detriment short of dismissal 20.70

Compensation and damages (*Cont.*)
  failure to permit time off 20.72
  unfair dismissal 20.73–20.75
  redundancy consultation 17.44–17.54
  unfair dismissal
    basic awards 14.302–14.309
    compensatory awards 14.310–14.360
  wrongful dismissal
    benefits 13.56–13.58
    general principles 13.53–13.55
    loss of chance 13.66–13.68
    mitigation of losses 13.70–13.73
    non-economic losses 13.59–13.65
    taxation 13.74
Compensatory awards
  contributory fault
    amount of deduction 14.344–14.348
    examples 14.341–14.343
    relevant circumstances 14.337–14.340
  deduction of jobseeker's
    allowance 14.357–14.360
  deductions 14.334–14.336
  expenses for looking for work 14.325
  interest on awards 14.361
  jurisdiction 14.361
  loss of benefits 14.323–14.324
  loss of earnings
    future losses 14.321–14.322
    immediate 14.316–14.320
  loss of pension rights 14.328–14.328
  lost employment protection 14.329
  manner of dismissal 14.330–14.333
  method for assessing 14.311–14.315
  mitigation of losses
    general principles 14.349–14.355
    procedure 14.356
  statutory provisions 14.310
Competition *see* **Restraint of trade**
Compromise agreements 12.51–12.57
Conciliation 19.124–19.126
Confidence *see* **Duty of trust and confidence**
Confidentiality
  enforcement and remedies 6.23
  express contract terms 6.35–6.36
  freedom of expression (Art 10) 23.52
  permitted disclosures 6.39–6.40
  relevant information 6.24–6.34
  springboard injunctions 6.37–6.38
  summary dismissal for breach 13.35
Conservative Party
  Cameron governments 1.29
  Industrial Relations Act 1971 1.06–1.07
  legislation 1980–95 1.11–1.23
Conspiracy
  criminal conduct 21.69–21.70

  immunity 21.68
  justification 21.66–21.67
  key requirements 21.62–21.65
Constructive dismissal
  conduct entitling employee to
    terminate 14.24–14.26
  discrimination 8.148
  fairness of dismissal 14.52–14.53
  general principles 14.37–14.38
  implied terms 14.27–14.33
  need for fundamental breach 14.39
  question of fact 14.42
  reaction to fundamental
    breach 14.43–14.51
  statutory provisions 14.23
  statutory rights 14.36
  'the last straw' 14.40
  on transfer of undertakings 18.85, 18.92
  variation of contracts 14.34–14.36
Consultation
  see also **Information rights**
  European Works Councils 19.148–19.149
  health and safety at work 19.140
  redundancy 14.206–14.209
    authorised union representatives 17.55
    employee representatives 17.16–17.22
    failure to comply 17.44–17.54
    informed consultation 17.38–17.40
    overview 17.01–17.06
    'redundancy' defined 17.07–17.08
    'special circumstances'
      defence 17.41–17.43
    timing 17.23–17.37
    union recognition 17.09–17.15
  training 19.116–19.120
  transfer of undertakings
    employee representatives 18.119–18.120
    information rights 18.116–18.118
    'special circumstances'
      defence 18.121–18.123
Consumer actions 21.157
Continuity of employment
  armed forces 11.29
  'arrangements or customs' 11.22–11.26
  change of employer
    overview 11.30–11.31
    partnerships 11.49
    transfer of undertakings 11.32–11.48
    unincorporated associations 11.50
  compensatory award for lost employment
    protection 14.329
  entitlement to statutory rights 12.01–12.03
  estoppel 11.51–11.54
  flexible working 10.79
  importance 11.01–11.1103

measurement
  months and years 11.06
  period governed by contract of
    employment 11.07–11.12
  preservation during change of duties 11.04
  presumption of continuity 11.05
  redundancy payments 11.29, 12.04–12.06
  reinstatement 11.28
  strikes 11.27
  temporary cessations of work
    meaning of 'temporary' 11.16–11.21
    need for work ceased 11.14–11.15
    short interruptions 11.13
Contract workers
  sex discrimination 8.29
  statutory provisions against
    discrimination 8.145–8.146
Contracting out
  employee shareholders 2.80
  liability for employer's negligence 4.29
  statutory rights
    ACAS settlement agreements 12.50
    agreements between management and
      unions 12.48–12.49
    compromise agreements 12.51–12.57
    statutory provisions 12.44–12.47
  Sunday trading 5.80
  transfer of undertakings 18.41
  working time 5.70
Contractors
  control test 2.18
  importance of identification 2.01–2.02
  labour only sub-contractors 2.46
  sham contracts 2.14
  status 2.46
  statutory control of secondary
    action 21.105
  wages and sick pay 2.25
Contracts of employment
  capacity to enter contract 3.45
  collective agreements
    basis of incorporation 3.10–3.13
    details required in written statement of
      terms 3.63
    effect on individual contracts 3.06–3.09
    no-strike clauses 3.19
    overview 3.04–3.05
    priority for national agreements 3.20
    termination 3.14–3.15
    terms inappropriate for
      incorporation 3.16–3.18
  effect of industrial action
    breaches of contract 21.06
    damages 21.13
    notice to terminate 21.06–21.08

    repudiatory breaches 21.10–21.12
    suspension 21.09
  effect of transfer of undertaking
    employee's right to decline
      transfer 18.85–18.97
    overview 18.59–18.62
    rights and duties transferred 18.63–18.68
    rights not transferred 18.69–18.75
    rights separate to contract 18.76
    variation of contracts 18.77–18.84
  external factors
    custom and practice 3.40–3.42
    incorporation of rules and
      handbooks 3.36–3.39
    statutory provisions 3.43
    third party awards 3.44
  formalities of agreement
    ambiguities 3.48–3.49
    conditions and warranties 3.47
    general principles of
      construction 3.52–3.53
    intention to create legal relations 3.51
    offer and acceptance 3.46
    written requirements 3.50
  implied terms
    duty of trust and confidence 3.28–3.32
    general principles 3.21–3.25
    grounds for rejection 3.27
    relationship with express
      terms 3.34–3.35
    unfair dismissal 3.32–3.33
    wide scope 3.26
  overview 3.01–3.03
  variation
    general principles 3.54
    mere variations and wholly new contracts
      distinguished 3.55–3.56
    transfer of undertakings 3.61
    unilateral variation by
      employer 3.57–3.60
  written statement of terms
    remedy for failure to supply 3.75–3.76
    required details 3.63–3.64
    status of document 3.69–3.74
    statutory provisions 3.62
    supplementary provisions 3.65–3.67
Contributory fault
  compensatory awards
    amount of deduction 14.344–14.348
    examples 14.341–14.343
    relevant circumstances 14.337–14.340
  discrimination claims 8.210
Control test
  agency workers 2.50
  economic reality test 2.25

Control test (*Cont.*)
test of employee status 2.16–2.18
transfer of undertakings 11.46–11.48
Cooperation
general principles 4.25–4.28
implied term 4.23
meaning and scope 4.24
Cooperatives 2.55
Criminal conduct
conspiracy 21.69–21.70
intentional harassment 8.110
picketing
affray and riot 22.16–22.17
assaults 22.11
harassment 22.27–22.28
highway obstruction 22.06
intimidation 22.21–22.25
overview 22.05
police obstruction 22.07–22.11
processions and assemblies 22.26
public nuisance 22.18–22.20
threatening behaviour 22.12–22.14
unlawful assembly 22.15
potentially fair dismissals
checklist 14.171
hearings 14.170
investigation by employer 14.164–14.169
offences committed at work and outside
distinguished 14.152–14.156
proof 14.157–14.163
spent convictions 14.245–14.246
strike injunctions 21.168
summary dismissal 13.33
Crown servants
modification of statutory rights 12.42
national minimum wage 5.24
special work status 2.40–2.42
Custom and practice
continuity of employment 11.22–11.26
incorporation into employment
contract 3.40–3.42

Damages *see* **Compensation and damages**
Death
implied termination 14.63
redundancy payment claims 16.68
termination at common law 13.02
Declaration of rights
detriment arising from union
recognition 19.94
discrimination claims 8.193
infringement of trade union rights 20.70
wrongful dismissal 13.49–13.50
Deductions from wages
agreements to deduct 5.07–5.10

exceptions 5.12–5.14
failure or refusal to pay 5.06
policy 5.01–5.02
relevant 'wages' 5.03–5.05
special rules for retail employment 5.11
Degrading treatment (Art 3) 23.02
Delegation
EU approach 2.70
supervision of strike ballots 19.72
test of employee status 2.25, 2.12–2.13
Dependant care leave
detriment 10.77
EU law 10.55
length of time off 10.63–10.64
notice requirements 10.65
qualifying conditions 10.58–10.62
statutory rights 10.56–10.57
unfair dismissal
exceptions 10.74–10.76
scope of protection 10.67–10.73
statutory provisions 10.66
Detriment
employee representatives 18.124
exercise of family rights 10.77
flexible working 10.84
less favourable treatment
because of protected
characteristic 8.84–8.92
defined 8.76–8.77
dress codes 8.82–8.83
hypothetical comparators 8.78–8.81
part-time workers 9.07–9.15
pregnancy 10.20
reasons based on generalised
assumptions 8.93–8.95
pension fund trustees 20.67
protected disclosures 15.17
recognition of trade unions 19.93–19.99
safety representatives 20.57
scope of prohibited activities 8.149–8.155
trade union activities 20.28–20.31
enforcement and remedies 20.70–20.71
trade union services 20.05
working time protection 5.75
Direct discrimination
example 8.72
institutional racism 8.75
key questions for tribunal 8.73–8.74
less favourable treatment
because of protected
characteristic 8.84–8.92
defined 8.76–8.77
dress codes 8.82–8.83
hypothetical comparators 8.78–8.81
statutory provisions 8.70–8.71

Directors
employee status 2.56–2.63
workers under EU law 2.75
Disability
discrimination arising from disability
enquires about disability 8.119–8.120
need for medical evidence 8.121
reasonable adjustment
discrimination 8.122–8.137
statutory provisions 8.118
equal pay claims 7.89
impairments affecting day-to-day
activities 8.59–8.61
meaning and scope 8.31–8.47
mental impairment 8.54–8.56
severe disfigurements 8.48–8.53
treatable conditions 8.57–8.58
Disciplinary and grievance procedures
for breaches of contract 4.46
deductions from wages 5.12
details required in written statement of
terms 3.63
hearings
investigation of criminal conduct 14.170
Labour legislation 1997–2009 1.24
need for fairness and
transparency 4.48–4.50
right to be accompanied
enforcement and remedies 4.87
fair process 4.86
relevant hearings 4.83–4.84
relevant workers 4.85
statutory rights 4.81–4.82
statutory rights 4.52
Disclosure *see* **Duty to Account and disclose**
Discrimination
see also **Equal pay**
agency workers 9.21–9.22
background to modern era
Industrial Relations Act 1971 1.06
part of 'social contract' 1.10
deduction from compensatory
award 14.334
dismissal during strike or lock-out 14.270
ECHR Art 14 23.70–23.74
effect of transfer of undertaking 18.67
enforcement and remedies
Commission on Equality and Human
Rights 8.216–8.220
compensation 8.196–8.215
declaration of rights 8.193
individual complainants 8.174–8.177
proof 8.178–8.184
recommendations 8.194–8.195
relevant evidence 8.192

scope of inquiry 8.185–8.188
statistical evidence 8.189–8.191
fixed-term workers
justification 9.18–9.20
less favourable treatment 9.17
forms of discrimination
associative discrimination 8.116
direct discrimination 8.70–8.95
discrimination arising from
disability 8.118–8.137
harassment 8.106–8.110
indirect discrimination 8.96–8.105
transferred discrimination 8.116
victimisation 8.111–8.115
history and development of law 8.01–8.12
part-time workers
enforcement and remedies 9.16
EU law 9.01–9.06
less favourable treatment 9.07–9.15
pensions
enforcement and remedies 7.107
relevant differences 7.106
statutory provisions 7.105
protected characteristics
age 8.14
disability 8.31–8.61
gender reassignment 8.15–8.16
marital status 8.24
pregnancy 8.25–8.30
race 8.17–8.23
religion and belief 8.62–8.68
relationships which have ended 8.162
'reverse discrimination' 8.172–8.173
scope of prohibited activities
any other detriment 8.149–8.155
contract workers 8.145–8.146
dismissal 8.147–8.148
offers of employment 8.140–8.142
promotion, transfer or
training 8.143–8.144
statutory provisions 8.138–8.139
secondary liability 8.163–8.171
selection criteria for redundancy 14.203
trade union activities
detriment short of dismissal 20.70–20.71
trade union membership
overview 20.01
proof 20.32–20.34
refusal of employment on union
grounds 20.23–20.25
refusal to remain a member 20.21–20.22
Dismissal
see also **Unfair dismissal; Wrongful
dismissal**
at common law 13.20

Dismissal (*Cont.*)
  office holders 13.21–13.29
  for redundancy
    defined 16.09–16.10
    proof 16.11–16.12
  summary dismissal
    for breaches of contract 4.46
    effect on unfair dismissal claim 14.14
    general principles 13.30–13.39
Dispute settlement *see* **Settlements**
Domestic servants
  employee status 2.16
  exclusion from all protection rights 12.43
  exclusion from working time
    regulation 5.55
Donations 19.10
Donovan Report 1968 1.03–1.05
Dress codes
  direct discrimination 8.82–8.83
  right to respect for privacy (Art 8) 23.34
Duty of trust and confidence
  implied terms 3.28–3.32
  summary dismissal for breach 13.33
Duty to account and disclose 6.03–6.07

Economic reality test
  ministers of religion 2.32–2.34
  relevant factors 2.25
  self-description 2.26–2.31
  test of employee status 2.20–2.24
Economic reasons
  age discrimination 8.105
  dismissal on transfer of undertaking
    dismissals at behest of
      purchaser 18.111–18.115
    fairness 18.110
    meaning and scope 18.102–18.106
    need for change to
      workforce 18.107–18.109
Effective date for dismissal
  general propositions 14.93
  importance 14.92
Employee representatives
  consultation on transfers 18.119–18.120
  European Works Councils 19.145–19.146
  health and safety role 19.138–19.140
  redundancy consultation
    authorised union representatives 17.55
    employee representatives 17.16–17.22
  safety representatives
    protection of activities 20.57–20.66
    time off work 20.55–20.56
  statutory rights 18.124–18.125
Employee status
  purpose and importance 201–2005

  question of law or fact 2.77–2.78
  tests of status
    control 2.16–2.18
    economic reality test 2.20–2.34
    integration 2.19
    mutuality of obligation 2.06–2.15
Employees
  access to medical reports 4.79–4.80
  confidentiality
    enforcement and remedies 6.23
    express contract terms 6.35–6.36
    permitted disclosures 6.39–6.40
    relevant information 6.24–6.34
    springboard injunctions 6.37–6.38
  defined 2.02
  details required in written statement
    of terms 3.63
  duty to account and disclose 6.03–6.07
  implied terms
    care and safety 4.33
    cooperation 4.23–4.28
    following instructions 4.42–4.45
    holidays 4.41
    pay 4.03–4.22
    place of work 4.73–4.75
  new classes of worker
    employee shareholders 2.80
    zero hours contracts 2.81–2.83
  other work relationships
    agency workers 2.48–2.53
    apprentices 2.43
    cadets 2.43
    casual workers 2.47
    Crown servants 2.40–2.42
    directors 2.56–2.63
    merchant seamen 2.65
    office holders 2.35–2.39
    partnerships 2.64
    students 2.44
    sub-contractors 2.46
    unincorporated associations 2.54
    workers cooperatives 2.55
    youth schemes 2.45
  ownership of patents 6.41–6.47
  restraint of trade
    competition with employer while
      employed 6.08–6.12
    construction and
      interpretation 6.56–6.58
    ex-employees 6.21–6.22
    general principles 6.48–6.51
    geographical area 6.52
    injunctions 6.70–6.72
    non-solicitation covenants 6.53–6.55
    in public interest 6.62–6.63

repayment clauses 6.73–6.75
severance 6.59–6.61
solicitation of other employees 6.68–6.69
where employer is in breach 6.64–6.67
right to be accompanied
enforcement and remedies 4.87
fair process 4.86
relevant hearings 4.83–4.84
relevant workers 4.85
statutory rights 4.81–4.82
workers
EU law 2.70–2.76
key requirements 2.68–2.69
statutory rights 2.66–2.67
Employers
details required in written statement of terms 3.63
effect of death
implied termination 14.63
termination at common law 13.02
implied terms
cooperation 4.26–4.28
health and safety at work 4.29–4.34
references 4.76–4.78
industrial action
unfair dismissal pacts 12.48–12.49
unilateral variation of contracts 3.57–3.60
vicarious liability
apprentices 2.43
control test 2.17
importance of employee status 2.02
policy considerations 2.04
protected disclosures 15.21–15.23
Employment Appeal Tribunal
see **Enforcement and remedies**
Employment law
background to modern era
Cameron governments 1.29
Conservative legislation
1980–95 1.11–1.23
Donovan Report 1968 1.03–1.05
General Strike 1926 1.02
Industrial Relations Act 1971 1.06–1.07
Labour legislation 1997–2009 1.24–1.28
'social contract' 1.08–1.10
effect of Brexit 1.30
history and development
collective agreements 19.01–19.02
picketing 22.01–22.04, 22.37
right to strike 21.01
transfer of undertakings 18.01–18.02
impact of human rights 23.01
Employment tribunals *see* **Enforcement and remedies; Time limits**
Enforcement and remedies
see also **Time limits**

breaches of confidentiality
general principles 6.23
springboard injunctions 6.37–6.38
breaches of contract 4.46
collective agreements 3.06
general principles 19.49–19.51
statutory provisions 19.52–19.54
deductions from wages 5.14
discrimination
Commission on Equality and Human
Rights 8.216–8.220
compensation 8.196–8.215
declaration of rights 8.193
individual complainants 8.174–8.177
proof 8.178–8.184
recommendations 8.194–8.195
relevant evidence 8.192
scope of inquiry 8.185–8.188
statistical evidence 8.189–8.191
equal pay
collective agreements 7.94–7.95
time limits for claims 7.82–7.92
equal value claims
jurisdiction 7.78
statutory provisions 7.79
work of equal value defined 7.80–7.81
European Works Councils 19.147–19.149
exclusion from trade union
membership 19.24–19.30
failure to supply written
statement 3.75–3.76
flexible working 10.83
information rights
collective bargaining 19.111–19.112
training 19.120
infringement of rights of safety
representatives 20.61–20.65
injunctions
breaches of confidentiality 6.23
for breaches of contract 4.46
during garden leave 6.13–6.20
restraint of trade 6.70–6.72
transfer of undertakings 18.98
itemised pay statements 5.18
national minimum wage 5.45–5.46
part-time workers 9.16
pension equality 7.107
redundancy consultation 17.44–17.54
restraint of trade
injunctions 6.70–6.72
repayment clauses 6.73–6.75
right to be accompanied 4.87
strike ballots 21.145–21.148
trade union activities
detriment short of dismissal 20.70–20.71

Enforcement and remedies (*Cont.*)
　　failure to permit time off 20.72
　　unfair dismissal 20.73–20.79
　unfair dismissal
　　compensation 14.302–14.360
　　overview 14.287
　　re-engagement 14.298–14.301
　　reinstatement 14.288–14.297
　working time 5.71–5.74
　written statement of terms
　　remedy for failure to supply 3.75–3.76
　　status of document 3.72
　wrongful dismissal
　　damages 13.53–13.74
　　declaration of rights 13.49–13.50
　　judicial review 13.51–13.52
　　specific performance and
　　　injunctions 13.41–13.48
Equal pay
　choice of comparator
　　EU law 7.19–7.24
　　UK law 7.17–7.18
　collective agreements 7.94–7.95
　consideration on term-by-term
　　basis 7.101–7.104
　effect of transfer of undertaking 18.75
　enforcement and remedies 7.82–7.92
　equal value claims
　　jurisdiction 7.78
　　statutory provisions 7.79
　　work of equal value defined 7.80–7.81
　EU law
　　importance 7.97
　　'pay' defined 7.98–7.100
　　Treaty provisions 7.96
　genuine material factors
　　general principles 7.30–7.41
　　grading systems 7.50–7.51
　　justification 7.60–7.66
　　not by reason of sex 7.52–7.59
　　part-time workers 7.42–7.43
　　'red-circled' jobs 7.45–7.49
　　sham bonus schemes 7.44
　job evaluation
　　alternative route to equal pay 7.67–7.69
　　challenges to job evaluation
　　　studies 7.76–7.77
　　chief types of scheme 7.70
　　defined 7.72–7.75
　like work 7.25–7.29
　maternity leave 7.93
　overview 7.01–7.10
　part of 'social contract' 1.10
　'same establishment' defined 7.13–7.16
　statutory provisions 7.11–7.12
Equal treatment *see* **Discrimination**

Estoppel
　continuity of employment 11.51–11.54
　overpayment by mistake 4.17
EU law
　associative discrimination 8.116
　dependant care leave 10.55
　early influence on employment law 1.15
　effect of Brexit 1.30
　equal pay
　　choice of comparator 7.19–7.24
　　genuine material factors 7.53
　　importance 7.97
　　'pay' defined 7.98–7.100
　　time limits for claims 7.85
　　Treaty provisions 7.96
　European Works Councils 19.141
　harassment 8.106
　industrial action 21.158
　part-time workers
　　implementation 9.04–9.06
　　incorporation into domestic law 9.01
　　scope 9.03
　prohibition of discrimination 8.03
　protection of safety representatives 20.60
　redundancy consultation 17.02–17.06
　Societas Europaea 19.150–19.151
　test of employee status 2.15
　transfer of undertakings
　　employee's right to decline transfer 18.86
　　history and development of
　　　law 18.01–18.02
　　relevant transfers 18.09, 18.11–18.21
　　variation of contracts 3.61
　workers
　　client exception 2.70–2.73
　　defined 2.74–2.76
　working time 5.47
European Works Councils
　applicable organizations 19.142
　consultation 19.148–19.149
　employee representatives 19.145–19.146
　enforcement and remedies 19.147–19.149
　establishment 19.143–19.144
　EU law 19.141
　information rights 19.148–19.149
Ex dolo malo non oritur actio 12.25
Ex gratia sums
　deduction from compensatory
　　award 14.334
　intention to create legal relations 3.51
　redundancy payments 16.60
Exclusion by agreement *see* **Contracting out**
Expenses
　calculation of redundancy
　　payments 16.60
　compensatory awards 14.325

Fair trial (Art 6)
  basic requirements 23.09–23.11
  ECHR text 23.08
  private hearings 23.19–23.23
  public tribunals 23.12–23.18
Fairness of dismissal
  automatically fair grounds 14.103
  automatically unfair grounds for dismissal
    assertion of statutory rights 14.278–14.283
    dismissal during strike or
      lock-out 14.247–14.275
    jury service 14.284–14.285
    pressure on employers to dismiss 14.286
    recognition disputes 14.276–14.277
    spent convictions 14.245–14.246
    statutory provisions 14.103
    transfer of undertakings 18.99
  constructive dismissal 14.52–14.53
  general considerations when assessing
    fairness 14.106–14.111
  potentially fair dismissals
    illegality 14.242–14.244
    incapability 14.112–14.135
    misconduct 14.136–14.171
    procedure 14.172–14.190
    redundancy 14.191–14.212
    some other substantial
      reason 14.213–14.241
    statutory provisions 14.103
Family rights
  adoption leave and pay 10.38
  antenatal care 10.39
  contractual provisions 10.54
  Labour legislation 1997-2009 1.26, 1.24
  maternity
    additional leave 10.21–10.28
    equal pay 7.93
    ordinary leave 10.07–10.20
    statutory payments 10.29–10.35
    suspension on maternity
      grounds 10.40–10.45
  overview 10.01–10.06
  paternity
    leave 10.35–10.37
    statutory payments 10.29–10.35
  shared parental leave
    administration 10.51–10.53
    qualifying conditions 10.48–10.50
    statutory rights 10.47
  unfair dismissal
    exceptions 10.74–10.76
    scope of protection 10.67–10.73
    statutory provisions 10.66
Fidelity
  breaches amounting to constructive
    dismissal 14.27–14.33

  confidentiality
    enforcement and remedies 6.23
    express contract terms 6.35–6.36
    permitted disclosures 6.39–6.40
    relevant information 6.24–6.34
    springboard injunctions 6.37–6.38
  duty to account and disclose 6.03–6.07
  overview 6.01
  patents 6.41–6.47
  restraint of trade
    competition with employer while
      employed 6.08–6.12
    construction and
      interpretation 6.56–6.58
    ex-employees 6.21–6.22
    garden leave injunctions 6.13–6.20
    general principles 6.48–6.51
    geographical area 6.52
    injunctions 6.70–6.72
    non-solicitation covenants 6.53–6.55
    in public interest 6.62–6.63
    repayment clauses 6.73–6.75
    severance 6.59–6.61
    solicitation of other employees 6.68–6.69
    where employer is in breach 6.68–6.69
  summary dismissal for breach 13.33
Fixed-term workers
  details required in written statement of terms 3.63
  economic reality test 2.25
  effect of transfer of undertaking 18.64
  less favourable treatment
    justification 9.18–9.20
    regulatory provisions 9.17
Flexibility clauses 4.73–4.75
Flexible working
  detriment 10.84
  enforcement and remedies 10.83
  procedure 10.82
  qualifying periods of employment 10.79
  refusal by employer 10.80
  statutory provisions 10.78
  terms and conditions 10.81
Following instructions
  common law obligation 4.42
  disobedience to reasonable instructions
    potentially fair dismissals 14.137–14.138
    'reasonableness' 14.142–14.145
    scope of lawful
      instructions 14.139–14.141
  disobedience to rules
    need for clear rules 14.146–14.150
    unfair dismissal 14.151
  illegal orders 4.44
  periods of illness 4.45
  reasonableness 4.43
  summary dismissal for breach 13.33

Forced labour (Art 4) 23.03–23.07
Formalities of agreement
  ambiguities 3.48–3.49
  conditions and warranties 3.47
  general principles of
      construction 3.52–3.53
  intention to create legal relations 3.51
  offer and acceptance 3.46
  written requirements 3.50
Freedom of assembly (Art 11)
  closed shop 23.54–23.59
  ECHR text 23.53–23.69
  industrial action 23.66–23.69
  national security 23.64–23.65
  recognition of trade unions 23.60–23.62
  union rules 23.63
Freedom of establishment 21.158
Freedom of expression (Art 10)
  ECHR text 23.46
  political views 23.48–23.52
  scope 23.47
Freedom of thought, conscience and belief
    (Art 9)
  ECHR text 23.37
  key cases 23.43–23.44
  need for balance 23.42
  scope 23.38–23.41
  statutory provisions 23.45
Frustration of contracts
  ill health 14.82–14.87
  no dismissal 14.80–14.81
  other examples 14.88–14.91

Garden leave injunctions 6.13–6.20
Gender reassignment
  harassment 8.106
  protected characteristic 8.15–8.16
General Strike 1926 1.02
Genuine material factors
  general principles 7.30–7.41
  grading systems 7.50–7.51
  justification 7.60–7.66
  not by reason of sex 7.52–7.59
  part-time workers 7.42–7.43
  'red-circled' jobs 7.45–7.49
  sham bonus schemes 7.44
Geographical limits
  restraint of trade clauses 6.52
  statutory rights 12.34–12.41
'Gig' economy 19.02
Government
  BEIS powers 19.135, 19.137
  Conservative Party policy
    Cameron governments 1.29
    Industrial Relations Act 1971 1.06–1.07
  legislation 1980–95 1.11–1.23
  Crown servants 2.40–2.42
  Labour Party policy
    legislation 1997–2009 1.11–1.23
    'social contract' 1.08–1.10
  payments for insolvent employers
    maternity pay 16.82
    National Insurance Fund 16.76–16.79
    pensions 16.80
    redundancy payments 16.81
    statutory provisions 16.75
  residuary powers to deal with statutory
      rights 12.58
Grading systems 7.50–7.51
Grievance procedures *see* **Disciplinary and
    grievance procedures**
Gross misconduct
  compensation on dismissal 13.73
  redundancy payments 16.53
  summary dismissal 13.30–13.39
  unfair dismissal
    background to modern era 14.01
    effective date for dismissal 14.93
    hearings 14.182
    need for clear rules 14.147
    warnings 14.178

Harassment
  defined 8.106
  hostile environments 8.109
  intentional harassment 8.110
  oppressive and unacceptable
      behaviour 8.108
  picketing
    civil liability 22.35
    criminal offence 22.27–22.28
  underlying rationale 8.107
Health and safety at work
  implied terms 4.29–4.34
  information rights 19.113
  reasonable adjustment discrimination 8.137
  safety representatives
    protection of activities 20.57–20.66
    time off work 20.55–20.56
  trade union role 19.138–19.140
  working time regulation 5.48
Hearings
  fair trial (Art 6)
    private hearings 23.19–23.23
    public tribunals 23.12–23.18
  investigation of criminal conduct 14.170
  procedural fairness
    meetings to discuss
        misconduct 14.181–14.182
    right to be accompanied 14.183–14.184

Highways
 obstruction 22.06
 trespass 22.32
History of employment law
 Cameron governments 1.29
 collective agreements 19.01–19.02
 Conservative legislation 1980–95 1.11–1.23
 Donovan Report 1968 1.03–1.05
 General Strike 1926 1.02
 Industrial Relations Act 1971 1.06–1.07
 Labour legislation 1997–2009 1.24–1.28
 picketing 22.01–22.04, 22.37
 right to strike 21.01
 'social contract' 1.08–1.10
 transfer of undertakings 18.01–18.02
Holidays
 annual leave
  pay 5.62–5.63
  relationship with sick pay 5.64–5.66
  relevant pay 5.67
  statutory rights 5.61
 details required in written statement
   of terms 3.63
 implied terms 4.41
Home workers
 national minimum wage 5.22
 test of employee status 2.25
Hours of work *see* **Working time**
Human rights
 Convention Articles
  degrading treatment (Art 3) 23.02
  discrimination (Art 14) 23.70–23.74
  fair trial (Art 6) 23.08–23.23
  freedom of assembly
   (Art 11) 23.53–23.69
  freedom of expression
   (Art 10) 23.46–23.52
  freedom of thought, conscience and belief
   (Art 9) 23.37–23.45
  prohibition of slavery and forced labour
   (Art 4) 23.03–23.07
  right to respect for privacy
   (Art 8) 23.24–23.36
 embodiment of unfair dismissal 14.03
 impact of HRA 1998 1.25
 impact on employment law 23.01
 prohibition of discrimination 8.01
 right to work 4.53
 trade union membership 19.23, 20.02

Ill health
 compensatory award for lost employment
   protection 14.334
 failure to follow instructions 4.45
 frustration of contracts 14.82–14.87

 potentially fair dismissals
  intermittent absences 14.128–14.130
  medical opinion and consultation with
    employee 14.125–14.126
  other factors 14.131–14.134
  other relevant situations 14.134
  overview 14.123–14.124
 sick pay
  deduction from compensatory
    award 14.334
  details required in written statement
    of terms 3.63
  economic reality test 2.25
  implied terms 4.06–4.12
  during notice period 13.07
  reasonable adjustment
    discrimination 8.132–8.133
  relationship with pay for annual
    leave 5.64–5.66
Illegality
 effect on discrimination
   claims 8.214–8.215
 effect on statutory rights
  general principles 12.25–12.27
  incidental illegality 12.31–12.32
  knowledge of illegality 12.28–12.30
  severance of terms 12.33
 employer's instructions 4.44
 industrial action
  conspiracy 21.62–21.70
  inducing breaches of
    contract 21.18–21.43
  interference with contracts or
    businesses 21.44–21.56
  intimidation 21.57–21.61
  key tests 21.16–21.17
 potentially fair dismissals 14.242–14.244
 terms unlawful at common law 4.51
Immunities
 see also **Ballots**
 conspiracy 21.68
 Employment Act 1980 1.13
 inducing breaches of contract 21.56
 interference with contracts or
   businesses 21.56
 picketing
  history and development of law 22.37
  limitations 22.41–22.42
  number of pickets 22.43–22.44
  at or near place of work 22.39–22.40
  secondary picketing 22.38
  statutory provisions 22.36
  stopping of vehicles 22.45
  union supervision 22.46
 trade disputes

Immunities (*Cont.*)
  acceptable subject matter 21.85–21.89
  connection with acceptable subject
    matter 21.96–21.99
  contemplating a dispute 21.100
  'disputes' 21.83–21.84
  disputes between 'workers and
    employers' 21.79–21.82
  exceptions for other torts 21.75–21.76
  foreign disputes 21.95
  'not actionable' 21.73–21.74
  personal disputes 21.90–21.91
  political strikes 21.92–21.94
  requirement for trade
    dispute 21.77–21.78
  secondary action 21.101–21.102
  statutory provisions 21.71–21.72
  union recruitment strikes 21.154
Implied termination 14.63
Implied terms
  constructive dismissal 14.27–14.33
  cooperation 4.23–4.28
  duty of trust and confidence 3.28–3.32
  following instructions 4.42–4.45
  general principles 3.21–3.25
  grounds for rejection 3.27
  health and safety at work 4.29–4.34
  holidays 4.41
  pay
    deductions for industrial
      action 4.18–4.22
    medical suspension pay 4.13–4.16
    overpayment by mistake 4.17
    overview 4.03
    payment for part contract 4.04–4.05
    sick pay 4.06–4.12
  place of work 4.73–4.75
  pre-employment medical
    examinations 4.77
  references 4.76–4.78
  relationship with express terms 3.34–3.35
  unfair dismissal 3.32–3.33
  wide scope 3.26
Incapability
  ill health
    intermittent absences 14.128–14.130
    medical opinion and consultation with
      employee 14.125–14.126
    other factors 14.131–14.134
    other relevant situations 14.134
    overview 14.123–14.124
  incompetence
    evidence 14.114–14.116
    general principle 14.113
    need for proper appraisal 14.118–14.119

    procedure 14.117
    warnings 14.120–14.122
  potentially fair dismissals 14.112
  qualifications 14.135
Incompetence
  evidence 14.114–14.116
  general principle 14.113
  need for proper appraisal 14.118–14.119
  procedure 14.117
  warnings 14.120–14.122
Incorporation of collective agreements
  basis of incorporation 3.10–3.13
  effect on individual contracts 3.06–3.09
  no-strike clauses 3.19
  priority for national agreements 3.20
  terms inappropriate for
    incorporation 3.16–3.18
Indirect discrimination
  importance 8.100
  justification 8.103–8.105
  new formulation 8.98–8.99
  'provision, criteria, practice'
    defined 8.101–8.102
  statutory provisions 8.96–8.97
Inducing breaches of contract
  causation 21.33–21.34
  different ways of committing tort 21.20
  direct inducement 21.21
  importance 21.18–21.19
  indirect inducement 21.22
  inducement 21.28–21.30
  justification 21.38–21.39
  knowledge of contract 21.26–21.27
  picketing 22.33–22.34
  procuring breaches 21.23–21.24
  requirement for breach 21.31
  unlawful means 21.35–21.37
Industrial action
  ACAS methods of dispute settlement
    advice 19.128
    arbitration 19.130
    conciliation 19.124–19.126
    independent inquiry 19.129
    mediation 19.127
  background to modern era
    Conservative legislation
      1980–95 1.11–1.23
    Donovan Report 1968 1.03–1.05
    General Strike 1926 1.02
    Industrial Relations Act 1971 1.06–1.07
    Labour legislation 1997–2009 1.24,
      1.24–1.28
    'social contract' 1.08–1.10
  consumer claims for unlawful
    action 21.157

deduction of pay 4.18–4.22
deductions from wages 5.12
disciplining of union members 19.31–19.32
entitlement to redundancy payments 16.54
EU law 21.158
illegality 21.56
 conspiracy 21.62–21.70
 inducing breaches of
  contract 21.18–21.43
 interference with contracts or
  businesses 21.44–21.56
 intimidation 21.57–21.61
 key tests 21.16–21.17
immunity for trade disputes
 acceptable subject matter 21.85–21.89
 connection with acceptable subject
  matter 21.96–21.99
 contemplating a dispute 21.100
 'disputes' 21.83–21.84
 disputes between 'workers and
  employers' 21.79–21.82
 exceptions for other torts 21.75–21.76
 foreign disputes 21.95
 'not actionable' 21.73–21.74
 personal disputes 21.90–21.91
 political strikes 21.92–21.94
 requirement for trade
  dispute 21.77–21.78
 secondary industrial
  action 21.101–21.102
 statutory provisions 21.71–21.72
official action 14.273–14.275
picketing
 civil liability 22.29–22.35
 code of practice 22.47–22.50
 criminal offences 22.05–22.28
 history and development of
  law 22.01–22.04
 immunity 22.36–22.46
protected industrial action 14.273–14.275
relationship with contract
  of employment
 breaches of contract 21.06
 damages 21.13
 by employers 21.15
 non-strike action 21.14
 notice to terminate 21.06–21.08
 repudiatory breaches 21.10–21.12
 suspension 21.09
secondary action
 remoteness test 21.101–21.102
 statutory control 21.103–21.105
statutory restrictions
 emergency powers 21.156
 specified workers 21.155

strikes
 ballots 21.106–21.153
 continuity of employment 11.27
 Crown servants 2.42
 dismissal during strike or
  lock-out 14.247–14.275
 freedom of assembly (Art 11) 23.66–23.69
 injunctions 21.159–21.168
 no-strike clauses 3.19
 right to strike 21.01–21.05
 selection criteria for redundancy 14.203
 summary dismissal 13.33
 union 'activities' 20.19–20.20
 union recruitment strikes 21.154
 unofficial industrial action 14.271–14.272
Information rights
 see also **Consultation**
 collective bargaining
  exceptions 19.110
  importance 19.103
  remedies 19.111–19.112
  what must be disclosed 19.104–19.109
 consultation on transfers 18.116–18.118
 European Works Councils 19.148–19.149
 redundancy consultation 17.38–17.40
 Societas Europaea 19.150–19.151
 trade unions
  collective agreements 19.103–19.111
  health and safety at work 19.113
  pensions 19.114–19.115
  training 19.114–19.115
 transfer of undertakings 18.89
Injunctions
 breaches of confidentiality
  general principles 6.23
  springboard injunctions 6.37–6.38
 for breaches of contract 4.46
 during garden leave 6.13–6.20
 strikes
  criminal conduct 21.168
  general principles 21.161–21.167
  overview 21.159–21.160
 transfer of undertakings 18.98
 wrongful dismissal
  exceptions 13.43–13.48
  general principles 13.41–13.42
Injury to feelings 8.199–8.204
Insolvency
 automatic termination of contract 13.02
 cessation of business 18.27
 redundancy consultation 17.42–17.43
 redundancy payments
  direct government payments 16.81
  preferential creditor status 16.69–16.74
 transfer of undertakings 18.83–18.84

Institutional racism 8.75
Instructions *see* Following instructions
Integration test 2.19
Interference with contracts or businesses
    immunity 21.56
    importance 21.44–21.51
    unlawful means 21.52–21.55
Intimidation
    immunity 21.61
    key requirements 21.57–21.60
    picketing 22.21–22.25
Itemised pay statements
    enforcement and remedies 5.18
    fixed deductions 5.16
    no request required 5.17
    statutory rights 5.15

Job evaluation
    alternative route to equal pay 7.67–7.69
    challenges to job evaluation
        studies 7.76–7.77
    chief types of scheme 7.70
    defined 7.72–7.75
Jobseeker's allowance
    deduction from compensatory
        award 14.357–14.360
    entitlement after three days 4.68
    statutory rights 4.67
Joint liability
    contributions 4.32
    discrimination claims 8.212
Judicial review
    CAC decisions 19.132
    CEHR powers 8.219
    control of dismissal 13.21–13.29
    exclusion of trade disputes 19.120
    wrongful dismissal 13.51–13.52
Jury service 14.284–14.285

Labour Party
    legislation 1997–2009 1.11–1.23
    'social contract' 1.08–1.10
'Last in first out' 14.203
Law *see* Employment law
Lay-offs
    common law
        general principles 4.54–4.58
        income maintenance 4.59
    continuity of employment 11.13
    overview 4.53
    statutory rights
        amount of payment 4.64–4.66
        conditions of entitlement 4.61–4.62
        exclusions 4.63
        guaranteed payments 4.60

    unfair dismissal 14.62
Leaving early 14.55–14.58
Less favourable treatment
    because of protected
        characteristic 8.84–8.92
    defined 8.76–8.77
    dress codes 8.82–8.83
    fixed-term workers
        justification 9.18–9.20
        regulatory provisions 9.17
    hypothetical comparators 8.78–8.81
    part-time workers 9.07–9.15
    pregnancy 10.20
    reasons based on generalised
        assumptions 8.93–8.95
Like work 7.25–7.29
Lock-outs
    continuity of employment 11.27
    dismissal during
        discriminatory selection 14.270
        'lock-out' defined 14.258–14.259
        overview 14.248–14.250
        re-engagement 14.269
        relevant employees 14.268
        statutory provisions 14.247
    redundancy payments 4.71
    right to payment 4.63
Loss of earnings
    future losses 14.321–14.322
    immediate loss 14.316–14.320
    part of compensatory award 14.315
Low Pay Commission 5.46

Marital status
    prohibited discrimination (Art 14) 23.70
    protected characteristic 8.24
Maternity rights
    additional leave
        commencement 10.21
        notification of return 10.22
        terms and conditions on
            return 10.23–10.28
    detriment 10.77
    equal pay 7.93
    ordinary leave
        length 10.12–10.14
        notification of pregnancy 10.08–10.11
        notification of return 10.15
        statutory provisions 10.07
        terms and conditions on
            return 10.16–10.20
    payments for insolvent employers 16.82
    statutory payments 10.29–10.35
    suspension on maternity
        grounds 10.40–10.45

unfair dismissal
    exceptions 10.74–10.76
    scope of protection 10.67–10.73
    statutory provisions 10.66
Mediation 19.127
Medical examinations and reports
    access to medical reports 4.79–4.80
    discrimination arising from disability 8.121
    pre-employment medical
        examinations 4.77
    right to respect for privacy (Art 8) 23.35–23.36
Medical suspension pay 4.13–4.16
Mental impairment 8.54–8.56
Merchant seamen
    employee status 2.65
    exclusion from working time
        regulation 5.55
    restrictions on industrial action 21.55
    special contract requirements 3.50
Ministers of religion
    classification as office holders 2.37
    employee status 2.32–2.34
    exclusion from working time
        regulation 5.55
    not 'workers' 2.68
Misconduct
    entitlement to redundancy
        payments 16.51–16.53
    gross misconduct
        compensation on dismissal 13.73
        redundancy payments 16.53
        summary dismissal 13.30–13.39
    potentially fair dismissals
        criminal offences 14.152–14.170
        disobedience to reasonable
            instructions 14.136–14.145
        disobedience to rules 14.146–14.151
        overview 14.136
        some other substantial
            reason 14.238–14.239
Mistake
    deductions from wages 5.12
    overpayments by mistake 4.17
Mitigation of losses
    compensatory awards
        general principles 14.349–14.355
        procedure 14.356
    damages for wrongful
        dismissal 13.70–13.73
Mobility clauses
    effect of transfer of undertaking 18.87
    implied terms 4.73–4.75
    redundancy 16.17–16.18
Mutuality of obligation
    ability to delegate 2.12–2.13

agency workers 2.52
sham contracts 2.14
test of employee status 2.06–2.11
volunteers 2.15
workers 2.68

National Insurance Fund 16.76–16.79
National minimum wage
    amount payable 5.25
    calculation 5.36–5.43
    enforcement and remedies 5.45–5.46
    exclusions 5.20–5.21
    record-keeping 5.44
    relevant hours 5.26–5.35
    relevant workers 5.22–5.24
    statutory rights 5.19
National security
    automatically fair grounds for
        dismissal 14.103
    exclusion of statutory rights 12.42
    restriction on human rights
        freedom of association
            (Art 11) 23.64–23.65
        freedom of expression (Art 10) 23.46
        right to respect for privacy
            (Art 8) 23.24, 23.32
    restriction on information rights 19.110
Natural justice
    dismissal at common law 13.21–13.26
    dismissal hearings 14.181
    'right to work' 19.20
    suspension 3.23
    union membership 1.06
Night workers 5.68–5.69
Non-discrimination *see* **Discrimination**
Non-economic losses
    compensatory award for manner of
        dismissal 14.330–14.333
    discrimination claims 8.199–8.204
    equal pay claims 7.104
    psychiatric damage 4.30–4.32
    wrongful dismissal
        distress 13.59–13.65
        loss of chance 13.66–13.68
Non-solicitation covenants 6.53–6.55
Notice of termination
    common law 13.03
    details required in written statement of
        terms 3.63
    directors 2.61–2.62
    probationary periods 13.09
    retraction 14.21
    statutory minimum periods 13.04–13.08
    unilateral variation of contracts by
        employer 3.57–3.60

Nuisance
civil liability 22.30–22.31
criminal offence 22.18–22.20

Obstruction
highways 22.06
police officers 22.07–22.11
Offers of employment
to avoid redundancy
acceptance of offer 16.40
refusal of offer 16.41–16.49
statutory provisions 16.33–16.34
trial periods 16.35–16.39
unfair dismissal 14.210–14.221
discrimination
interview procedures 8.140–8.141
refusal to offer job 8.142
mutuality of obligation 2.49
refusal of employment on union
grounds 20.23–20.25
variation of contracts 3.59
Office holders
dismissal at common law 13.21–13.29
special work status 2.35–2.39
Onus of proof *see* **Proof**

Parental leave
detriment 10.77
qualifying conditions 10.48–10.50
statutory rights 10.47
unfair dismissal
exceptions 10.74–10.76
scope of protection 10.67–10.73
statutory provisions 10.66
Part-time workers
enforcement and remedies 9.16
equal pay 7.42–7.43
EU law
implementation 9.04–9.06
incorporation into domestic law 9.01
scope 9.03
gender composition 9.02
less favourable treatment 9.07–9.15
statutory rights 2.67
Partnerships
automatic termination of contract 13.02
continuity of employment 11.49
employee status 2.64
Patents 6.41–6.47
Paternity rights
leave 10.35–10.37
statutory payments 10.29–10.35
Pay
see also **Equal pay**
adoption leave 10.38

annual leave
pay 5.62–5.63
relationship with sick pay 5.64–5.66
relevant pay 5.67
statutory rights 5.61
calculation of redundancy payments
relevant date 16.60
relevant remuneration 16.60
relevant workers 16.63–16.64
deductions from wages
agreements to deduct 5.07–5.10
exceptions 5.12–5.14
failure or refusal to pay 5.06
policy 5.01–5.02
relevant 'wages' 5.03–5.05
special rules for retail employment 5.11
details required in written statement of
terms 3.63
holidays 4.41
implied terms
deductions for industrial
action 4.18–4.22
medical suspension pay 4.13–4.16
overpayment by mistake 4.17
overview 4.03
payment for part contract 4.04–4.05
sick pay 4.06–4.12
itemised pay statements
enforcement and remedies 5.18
fixed deductions 5.16
no request required 5.17
statutory rights 5.15
jobseeker's allowance
entitlement after three days 4.68
statutory rights 4.67
lay-offs
common law 4.54–4.59
statutory rights 4.60–4.66
maternity leave
returners 10.17
statutory payments 10.29–10.35
national minimum wage
amount payable 5.25
calculation 5.36–5.43
enforcement and remedies 5.45–5.46
exclusions 5.20–5.21
record-keeping 5.44
relevant hours 5.26–5.35
relevant workers 5.22–5.24
statutory rights 5.19
during notice period 13.04–13.08
paternity leave 10.29–10.35
quantum meruit 4.02
redundancy payments
overview 4.69–4.72

Pensions
  contributions when employer
     insolvent 16.80
  details required in written statement of
     terms 3.63
  effect of transfer of
     undertaking 18.69–18.75
  equal treatment
     enforcement and remedies 7.107
     relevant differences 7.106
     statutory provisions 7.105
  information rights 19.114–19.115
  part of compensatory
     award 14.328–14.328
  protection of pension fund
     trustees 20.67–20.68
  Societas Europaea 19.151
Personal injuries
  discrimination claims 8.198, 8.211
Picketing
  civil liability
     harassment 22.35
     highway trespass 22.32
     importance 22.29
     inducing breaches of
        contract 22.33–22.34
     private nuisance 22.30–22.31
  code of practice 22.47–22.50
  criminal offences
     affray and riot 22.16–22.17
     assaults 22.11
     harassment 22.27–22.28
     highway obstruction 22.06
     intimidation 22.21–22.25
     overview 22.05
     police obstruction 22.07–22.11
     processions and assemblies 22.26
     public nuisance 22.18–22.20
     threatening behaviour 22.12–22.14
     unlawful assembly 22.15
  history and development of
     law 22.01–22.04
  immunity
     history and development of law 22.37
     limitations 22.41–22.42
     number of pickets 22.43–22.44
     at or near place of work 22.39–22.40
     secondary picketing 22.38
     statutory provisions 22.36
     stopping of vehicles 22.45
     union supervision 22.46
Place of work
  details required in written statement of
     terms 3.63
  effect of closure 13.02

implied terms 4.73–4.75
mobility clauses
   effect of transfer of undertaking 18.87
   implied terms 4.73–4.75
   redundancy 16.17–16.18
picketing 22.39–22.40
redundancy 16.15–16.18
Police officers
  classification as office holders 2.39
  exclusion from working time
     regulation 5.55
  obstruction 22.07–22.11
  restrictions on industrial action 21.55
Political strikes 21.92–21.94
Potentially fair dismissals
  illegality 14.242–14.244
  incapability 14.112–14.135
  misconduct 14.136–14.171
  procedure 14.172–14.190
  redundancy 14.191–14.212
  some other substantial
     reason 14.213–14.241
  statutory provisions 14.103
Practice *see* **Custom and practice**
Pregnancy
  antenatal care 10.39
  detriment 10.77
  less favourable treatment 10.20
  notification to employer 10.08–10.11
  protected characteristic 8.25–8.30
  unfair dismissal
     exceptions 10.74–10.76
     scope of protection 10.67–10.73
     statutory provisions 10.66
Pressure on employers to
     dismiss 14.240–14.241, 14.286
Prison officers
  dismissal at common law 13.23
  exclusion from all protection rights 12.58
  freedom of assembly (Art 11) 23.64
  inducement to withhold
     service 21.155, 21.30
  office holders 2.36
  restrictions on industrial action 21.55
Privacy *see* **Right to respect for privacy (Art 8)**
Private nuisance 22.30–22.31
Probationary periods *see* **Trial periods**
Procedure
  claims of unjustified union
     discipline 19.35–19.40
  compensatory awards 14.356
  disciplining of union members 19.41
  dismissal at common law 13.25–13.26
  flexible working 10.82
  implications for industrial justice 14.363

Procedure (*Cont.*)
  potentially fair dismissals
    agreed procedures 14.173
    appeals 14.185–14.190
    criminal conduct 14.164–14.169
    hearings 14.181–14.184
    incompetence 14.117
    procedural fairness 14.172
    warnings 14.174–14.180
  recognition of trade unions
    agreement on bargaining
      unit 19.67–19.71
    agreement on method of
      bargaining 19.80–19.81
    application to employer or
      CAC 19.62–19.66
    ballots to determine support for
      recognition 19.67–19.71
    changes in bargaining unit 19.82–19.84
    effect of voluntary recognition 19.85
    statutory provisions 19.58–19.61
  requirements for giving of written
      particulars of employment 3.65–3.67
  some other substantial reason (unfair
      dismissal) 14.221
Processions 22.26
Prohibition of slavery and forced labour
      (Art 4) 23.03–23.07
Proof
  break in continuity 11.05
  criminal conduct justifying
      dismissal 14.157–14.163
  detriment arising from union
      recognition 19.94
  discrimination claims
    inferences 8.179–8.184
    underlying problems 8.178
  genuine material factors 7.31
  infringement of rights of safety
      representatives 20.61
  justification for age
      discrimination 8.103–8.105
  protected disclosures 15.19
  redundancy dismissals 16.11–16.12
  trade union discrimination 20.32–20.34
  unfair dismissal 14.94
  victimisation 8.115
Protected characteristics
  age 8.14
  disability
    impairments affecting day-to-day
      activities 8.59–8.61
    meaning and scope 8.31–8.47
    mental impairment 8.54–8.56
    severe disfigurements 8.48–8.53
    treatable conditions 8.57–8.58

  gender reassignment 8.15–8.16
  less favourable treatment 8.84–8.92
  marital status 8.24
  pregnancy 8.25–8.30
  race 8.17–8.23
  religion and belief 8.62–8.68
Protected disclosures
  agency workers 15.20
  causation 15.18
  detriment 15.17
  disclosures
    good faith 15.12
    meaning 15.03–15.05
    persons to whom made 15.08
    reasonable belief in truth 15.09–15.11
    scope 15.06–15.07
  overview 15.01–15.02
  proof 15.19
  time limits for claim to tribunal 15.24
  validly made wider disclosures
      15.13–15.16
  vicarious liability 15.21–15.23
Protected industrial action 14.273–14.275
Protective awards 17.44–17.54
Psychiatric damage 4.30–4.32
Public interest
  restraint of trade 6.62–6.63
  strike injunctions 21.165–21.167
Public interest disclosures *see* **Protected**
      disclosures
Public nuisance 22.18–22.20
Public policy
  ex dolo malo non oritur actio 12.25
  vicarious liability 2.17

Qualifications
  business reorganisations 12.26
  genuine material factors 7.41, 7.31
  potentially fair dismissals 14.135
Qualifying periods of employment
      see **Continuity of employment**
Quantum meruit 4.02
Quasi redundancy 14.223–14.231

Race discrimination
  early legislation 8.02
  institutional racism 8.75
  less favourable treatment 8.87, 8.92
  protected characteristic 8.17–8.23
Re-engagement
  after dismissal during strike or
      lock-out 14.269
  after unfair dismissal
    failure to comply 14.299–14.301
    general principles 14.298
    discriminatory selection 14.270

Reasonable adjustment discrimination
  codes of practice 8.128
  creation of new posts 8.130–8.131
  dismissal procedures 8.134
  general principles 8.129
  monetary benefits 8.135–8.137
  sick pay 8.132–8.133
  statutory provisions 8.122–8.124
  'substantial disadvantage' defined 8.125
Reasons for dismissal
  general considerations when assessing
    fairness 14.106–14.111
  general principles 14.94
  later discovered reasons 14.95–14.99
  potentially fair dismissals
    incapability 14.112–14.135
    misconduct 14.136–14.171
    procedure 14.172–14.190
    redundancy 14.191–14.212
    some other substantial
      reason 14.213–14.241
  statutory provisions 14.103–14.105
  written reasons for
    dismissal 14.100–14.102
Recognition of trade unions
  derecognition 19.86–19.92
  dismissal during disputes 14.276–14.277
  freedom of assembly (Art 11) 23.60–23.62
  meaning and scope 19.57
  redundancy consultation 17.09–17.15
  statutory recognition
    agreement on bargaining
      unit 19.67–19.71
    agreement on method of
      bargaining 19.80–19.81
    application to employer or
      CAC 19.62–19.66
    ballots to determine support for
      recognition 19.72–19.79
    changes in bargaining unit 19.82–19.84
    effect of voluntary recognition 19.85
    statutory provisions 19.58–19.61
  transfer of undertakings 19.100
  unfair dismissal 19.93–19.99
  union 'activities' 20.18
Recommendations
  ACAS mediation 9.128
  discrimination claims 8.147, 8.194–8.195
  refusal of employment on union
    grounds 20.25
Record-keeping
  national minimum wage 5.44
  parental leave 10.53
'Red-circled' jobs 7.45–7.49
Redundancy
  cessation of business

  at place of employment 16.15–16.18
  total 16.13–16.14
consultation
  authorised union representatives 17.55
  employee representatives 17.16–17.22
  informed consultation 17.38–17.40
  overview 17.01–17.06
  'redundancy' defined 17.07–17.08
  'special circumstances'
    defence 17.41–17.43
  timing 17.23–17.37
  union recognition 17.09–17.15
defined 16.08
diminution in requirements of business
  examples 16.32
  reduced requirement for employees 16.19
  reorganisations
    distinguished 16.27–16.30
  replacement of employees 16.31
  what employee did or could be asked to
    do 16.23–16.26
  work of a particular kind 16.21–16.22
dismissal
  defined 16.09–16.10
  proof 16.11–16.12
implied termination 14.63
offers of new employment
  acceptance of offer 16.40
  refusal of offer 16.41–16.49
  statutory provisions 16.33–16.34
  trial periods 16.35–16.39
unfair dismissal
  alternative employment 14.210–14.221
  consultation 14.206–14.209
  overview 14.191–14.194
  reasonableness 14.195–14.199
  selection criteria 14.200–14.205
'voluntary redundancy' 14.73–14.75
Redundancy payments
  calculation
    method of calculation 16.64–16.67
    normal working hours 16.57–16.59
    overview 16.56
    relevant date 16.61–16.62
    relevant remuneration 16.60
    relevant workers 16.63–16.64
  claims 16.68
  continuity of employment 11.29,
    12.04–12.06
  deduction from compensatory
    award 14.334
  history and development of
    law 16.01–16.02
  insolvency
    direct government payments 16.81
    preferential creditor status 16.69–16.74

Redundancy payments (*Cont.*)
  justification for scheme 16.04–16.07
  loss of entitlement
    early leavers 16.55
    industrial action 16.54
    misconduct 16.51–16.53
    overview 16.50
  overview 4.69–4.72
  time limits for claim to tribunal
    examples of extensions 12.17–12.24
    extensions of time 12.11–12.16
    normal time limit 12.08–12.10
    requirement for promptness 12.07
References
  general principles 4.76
  investigation of employee's conduct 4.78
Reinstatement
  after unfair dismissal
    dismissal of replacement 14.297
    failure to comply 14.299–14.301
    general principles 14.289–14.296
    overview 14.288
  continuity of employment 11.28
Religion and belief
  freedom of thought, conscience and belief
      (Art 9)
    ECHR text 23.37
    key cases 23.43–23.44
    need for balance 23.42
    scope 23.38–23.41
    statutory provisions 23.45
  protected characteristic 8.62–8.68
Remedies *see* **Enforcement and remedies**
Reorganisations *see* **Business reorganisations**
Representation *see* **Employee representatives**
Repudiatory breaches
  industrial action 21.10–21.12
  variation of contracts 14.19–14.20
Resignations
  after trial period to avoid
      redundancy 16.38
  need for clear words 14.71–14.72
  under threat 14.68–14.70
  on transfer of undertakings 18.85
  'voluntary redundancy' 14.73–14.75
Restraint of trade
  see also **Confidentiality**
  competition with employer while
      employed 6.08–6.12
  construction and interpretation
      6.56–6.58
  effect of transfer of undertaking 18.74
  ex-employees 6.21–6.22
  garden leave injunctions 6.13–6.20
  general principles 6.48–6.51
  geographical area 6.52

  injunctions 6.70–6.72
  non-solicitation covenants 6.53–6.55
  in public interest 6.62–6.63
  repayment clauses 6.73–6.75
  severance 6.59–6.61
  solicitation of other employees 6.68–6.69
  where employer is in breach 6.64–6.67
'Reverse discrimination' 8.172–8.173
Right to be accompanied
  enforcement and remedies 4.87
  fair process 4.86
  misconduct hearings 14.183–14.184
  relevant hearings 4.83–4.84
  relevant workers 4.85
  statutory rights 4.81–4.82
Right to respect for privacy (Art 8)
  dress codes 23.34
  ECHR text 23.24
  medical checks 23.35–23.36
  scope 23.25–23.29
  security measures at work 23.30–23.33
Right to work
  basis for control of union
      membership 19.19–19.20
  garden leave injunctions 6.15
  human rights 4.53
  implied terms 3.27, 4.58
Riot 22.16–22.17
Rules
  incorporation into employment
      contract 3.36–3.39
  trade unions
    activities contrary to rules 20.17
    freedom of assembly (Art 11) 23.63
    legal status 19.05

Secondary industrial action
  background to modern era 1.12
  defined 21.104
  remoteness test 21.101–21.102
  statutory control 21.103–21.105
Secondary picketing 22.38
Service provision changes 18.34–18.39
Settlements
  ACAS agreements 12.50
  ACAS methods of dispute settlement
    advice 19.128
    arbitration 19.130
    conciliation 19.124–19.126
    independent inquiry 19.129
    mediation 19.127
  deduction from basic award 14.308
Severance of terms
  illegality 12.33
  restraint of trade clauses 6.59–6.61
Severe disfigurements 8.48–8.53

Sex discrimination
  see also **Equal pay**
  early legislation 8.02
  effect of illegal contract on claim 12.29
  less favourable treatment 8.91
Sexual orientation
  excepted situations 8.156
  harassment 8.106
  prohibited discrimination (Art 14) 23.70
  protected characteristic 8.05
  recruitment policy 8.188
  right to respect for privacy (Art 8) 23.24
Sham contracts
  directors 2.59
  mutuality of obligation 2.14
Shared parental leave
  qualifying conditions 10.48–10.50
  statutory rights 10.47
Shareholders
  employee shareholders 2.80
  status of directors 2.57
  transfer of undertakings 18.07
Short-time working
  overview 4.53
  unfair dismissal 14.62
Sick pay
  deduction from compensatory award 14.334
  details required in written statement of
    terms 3.63
  economic reality test 2.25
  implied terms 4.06–4.12
  during notice period 13.07
  reasonable adjustment
    discrimination 8.132–8.133
  relationship with pay for annual
    leave 5.64–5.66
Sickness *see* **Ill health**
Slavery and forced labour
    (Art 4) 23.03–23.07
'Social contract' 1.08–1.10
Societas Europaea 19.150–19.151
Some other substantial reason
  importance 14.216–14.219
  important categories of cases
    conduct 14.238–14.239
    quasi redundancy 14.223–14.231
    temporary workers 14.235–14.237
    variation of contracts 14.232–14.234
  key test 14.214
  pressure on employers 14.240–14.241
  procedure 14.221
  'rubber band' quality 14.213
  scope 14.215
  statutory reasons 14.220
Specific performance
  reinstatement 14.288

wrongful dismissal
    exceptions 13.43–13.48
    general principles 13.41–13.42
Spent convictions 14.245–14.246
Springboard injunctions 6.37–6.38
Statutory rights
  annual leave 5.61
  assertion of statutory rights
    automatically unfair grounds for
      dismissal 14.278–14.283
    qualifying period of employment 12.06
    Sunday trading 5.80
  compensatory award for lost employment
      protection 14.329
  constructive dismissal 14.36
  continuity of employment 12.01–12.03
  contracting out
    ACAS settlement agreements 12.50
    agreements between management and
      unions 12.48–12.49
    compromise agreements 12.51–12.57
    statutory provisions 12.44–12.47
  dependant care leave 10.56–10.57
  disciplinary and grievance
      procedures 4.52
  effect of illegality
    general principles 12.25–12.27
    incidental illegality 12.31–12.32
    knowledge of illegality 12.28–12.30
    severance of terms 12.33
  effect on contractual terms 3.43
  employee representatives 18.124–18.125
  employee shareholders 2.80
  excluded employees 12.43
  geographical limits 12.34–12.41
  importance of employee status 2.02
  itemised pay statements 5.15
  jobseeker's allowance 4.67
  lay-offs
    amount of payment 4.64–4.66
    conditions of entitlement 4.61–4.62
    exclusions 4.63
    guaranteed payments 4.60
  maternity and parenting 10.01–10.06
  modification or certain employees 12.42
  national minimum wage 5.19
  police officers 2.39
  residuary powers 12.58
  right to be accompanied 4.81–4.82
  safety representatives 20.57
  Sunday trading 5.76–5.80
  time off work 4.37–4.40
  workers 2.66–2.67
  working time 5.49–5.50
  wrongful dismissal 13.76
Stigma damages 8.205

Strikes
see also **Picketing**
ballots
'calls' for action before ballot 21.132
contents of ballot paper 21.128
different ballots for each
workplace 21.124–21.127
enforcement by members 21.145–21.148
notice of ballot 21.133–21.141
notice of industrial action 21.142–21.144
number of votes required 21.122–21.123
person authorised to call for
action 21.149–21.153
person to be balloted 21.114–21.121
statutory provisions 21.106
voter protection 21.129–21.131
when required 21.107–21.113
continuity of employment 11.27
Crown servants 2.42
deduction of pay 4.18–4.22
deductions from wages 5.12
dismissal during
action provoked by
employers 14.260–14.261
date of dismissal
important 14.266–14.267
discriminatory selection 14.270
official action
overview 14.248–14.250
protected industrial
action 14.273–14.275
re-engagement 14.269
statutory provisions 14.247
'strike' defined 14.251
unofficial industrial
action 14.271–14.272
entitlement to redundancy payments 16.54
freedom of assembly (Art 11) 23.66–23.69
General Strike 1926 1.02
illegality
conspiracy 21.62–21.70
inducing breaches of
contract 21.18–21.43
interference with contracts or
businesses 21.44–21.56
intimidation 21.57–21.61
key tests 21.16–21.17
immunity for trade disputes
acceptable subject matter 21.85–21.89
connection with acceptable subject
matter 21.96–21.99
contemplating a dispute 21.100
'disputes' 21.83–21.84
disputes between 'workers and
employers' 21.79–21.82

exceptions for other torts 21.75–21.76
foreign disputes 21.95
'not actionable' 21.73–21.74
personal disputes 21.90–21.91
political strikes 21.92–21.94
requirement for trade
dispute 21.77–21.78
secondary industrial
action 21.101–21.102
statutory provisions 21.71–21.72
injunctions
criminal conduct 21.168
general principles 21.161–21.167
overview 21.159–21.160
no-strike clauses 3.19
relationship with contract
of employment
breaches of contract 21.06
damages 21.13
notice to terminate 21.06–21.08
repudiatory breaches 21.10–21.12
suspension 21.09
right to strike
history and development of law 21.01
justifications 21.02
legal liabilities arising 21.03–21.05
selection criteria for redundancy 14.203
summary dismissal 13.33
union 'activities' 20.19–20.20
union recruitment strikes 21.154
Students 2.44
Sub-contractors
labour only sub-contractors 2.46
sham contracts 2.14
status 2.46
Summary dismissal
see also **Unfair dismissal**
for breaches of contract 4.46
effect on unfair dismissal claim 14.14
general principles 13.30–13.39
Sunday trading
freedom of thought, conscience and belief
(Art 9) 23.41
working time protection 5.76–5.80
Suspension
effect of industrial action 21.09
maternity 10.40–10.45
medical suspension pay 4.13–4.16
natural justice 3.23

Taxation
damages for wrongful dismissal 13.74
economic reality test 2.25
importance of employee status 2.03
non-listed unions 19.10

Temporary workers
agency workers 2.49
employee status 2.50
some other substantial reason (unfair
dismissal) 14.235–14.237
transfer of undertakings 18.25
Termination of employment
see also **Unfair dismissal; Wrongful
dismissal**
automatic termination by supervening
event 13.02
breaches of contract
general principles 13.10–13.12
need for acceptance 13.13–13.19
discrimination
reasonable adjustment
discrimination 8.134
scope of prohibited activities 8.147–8.148
by dismissal
common law 13.20
office holders 13.21–13.29
effect of industrial action 21.06–21.08
by notice
common law 13.03
statutory minimum periods 13.04–13.08
overview 13.01
summary dismissal
for breaches of contract 4.46
effect on unfair dismissal claim 14.14
general principles 13.30–13.39
Terms and conditions
employee confidentiality 6.35–6.36
external factors
custom and practice 3.40–3.42
incorporation of rules and
handbooks 3.36–3.39
statutory provisions 3.43
third party awards 3.44
family rights 10.54
flexible working 10.81
implied terms
cooperation 4.23–4.28
duty of trust and confidence 3.28–3.32
following instructions 4.42–4.45
general principles 3.21–3.25
grounds for rejection 3.27
health and safety at work 4.29–4.34
holidays 4.41
pay 4.03–4.22
place of work 4.73–4.75
pre-employment medical
examinations 4.77
references 4.76–4.78
relationship with express
terms 3.34–3.35

unfair dismissal 3.32–3.33
wide scope 3.26
incorporation of collective agreements
basis of incorporation 3.10–3.13
effect on individual contracts 3.06–3.09
no-strike clauses 3.19
priority for national agreements 3.20
terms inappropriate for
incorporation 3.16–3.18
lay-offs
common law 4.54–4.59
overview 4.53
pay
implied terms 4.03–4.22
quantum meruit 4.02
restraint of trade clauses
construction and
interpretation 6.56–6.58
general principles 6.48–6.51
geographical area 6.52
injunctions 6.70–6.72
non-solicitation covenants 6.53–6.55
in public interest 6.62–6.63
repayment clauses 6.73–6.75
severance 6.59–6.61
solicitation of other employees 6.68–6.69
where employer is in breach 6.64–6.67
returning from maternity
additional leave 10.23–10.28
ordinary leave 10.16–10.20
short-time working 4.53
superseding collective
agreements 20.03–20.04
terms unlawful at common law 4.51
time off work 4.37–4.40
unfair contracts 4.47
written statement of terms
remedy for failure to supply 3.75–3.76
required details 3.63–3.64
status of document 3.69–3.74
statutory provisions 3.62
supplementary provisions 3.65–3.67
Threatening behaviour 22.12–22.14
Time limits
claims of unjustified union discipline 19.36
detriment arising from union
recognition 19.94
discrimination claims 8.174–8.177
equal pay claims 7.83–7.92
exclusion from trade union
membership 19.27
failure to give time off 4.40
infringement of rights of safety
representatives 20.61
protected disclosures 15.24

Time limits (*Cont.*)
  redundancy consultation
    dependant on numbers in
      'establishment' 17.33–17.37
    before dismissals 17.23–17.32
  redundancy payment claims
    examples of extensions 12.17–12.24
    extensions of time 12.11–12.16
    normal time limit 12.08–12.10
    overview 16.68
    requirement for promptness 12.07
  service of written statement of terms 3.63
  trial periods to avoid
    redundancy 16.35–16.37
Time off work
  see also **Working time**
  adoption leave 10.38
  antenatal care 10.39
  dependant care leave
    EU law 10.55
    length of time off 10.63–10.64
    notice requirements 10.65
    qualifying conditions 10.58–10.62
    statutory rights 10.56–10.57
  holidays 4.41
  maternity leave
    additional leave 10.21–10.28
    equal pay 7.93
    ordinary leave 10.07–10.20
  paternity leave 10.35–10.37
  pension fund trustees 20.68
  selection criteria for redundancy 14.203
  shared parental leave 10.47
  statutory rights 4.37–4.40
  trade unions
    enforcement and remedies 20.72
    health and safety at work 20.55–20.56
    industrial relations training 20.54
    trade union activities 20.26–20.27,
      20.52–20.53
    trade union duties 20.35–20.51
  unfair dismissal for late
    return 14.76–14.79
Trade unions
  activities
    claims to recognition 20.18
    contrary to rules 20.17
    detriment 20.28–20.31
    before employment 20.15–20.16
    meaning and scope 20.08–20.12
    refusal of employment on union
      grounds 20.23–20.25
    refusal to remain a member 20.21–20.22
    strikes 20.19–20.20
    time off work 20.26–20.27

    union and unionist activities
      distinguished 20.13–20.14
  auxiliary role of law 19.55–19.56
  background to modern era
    Cameron governments 1.29
    Conservative legislation
      1980–95 1.11–1.23
    Donovan Report 1968 1.03–1.05
    General Strike 1926 1.02
    Industrial Relations Act 1971 1.06–1.07
    Labour legislation 1997–2009 1.24–1.28
    'social contract' 1.08–1.10
  collective agreements
    basis of incorporation 3.10–3.13
    criteria for independent union 19.15
    details required in written statement of
      terms 3.63
    effect of transfer of
      undertakings 18.126–18.128
    effect on individual contracts 3.06–3.09
    enforcement 19.49–19.54
    history and development of collective
      bargaining 19.01–19.02
    information rights 19.103–19.111
    no-strike clauses 3.19
    overview 3.04–3.05
    priority for national agreements 3.20
    termination 3.14–3.15
    terms inappropriate for
      incorporation 3.16–3.18
    working time 5.70
  consultation on training 19.116–19.120
  consultation on transfers
    employee representatives 18.119–18.120
    information rights 18.116–18.118
    'special circumstances'
      defence 18.121–18.123
  disciplining of members
    'discipline' defined 19.33
    fairness 19.41
    false assertions against leadership 19.34
    industrial action 19.31–19.32
    procedure 19.35–19.40
    statutory prohibitions 19.32
  effect of Brexit 1.30
  employee representatives
    consultation on transfers 18.119–18.120
    European Works Councils 19.145–19.146
    health and safety role 19.138–19.140
    redundancy
      consultation 17.16–17.22, 17.55
    statutory rights 18.124–18.125
    time off work for safety
      representatives 20.55–20.56
  freedom of assembly (Art 11)

recognition 23.60–23.62
rules 23.63
health and safety role 19.138–19.140
independence
  criteria 19.15–19.17
  defined 19.14
  key judicial pronouncement 19.11
  purpose 19.12–19.13
information rights
  collective agreements 19.103–19.111
  health and safety at work 19.113
  pensions 19.114–19.115
  training 19.114–19.115
legal status 19.03–19.06
liability in tort 19.43–19.48
listing
  non-listed unions distinguished 19.10
  role of Certification Officer 19.07–19.09
membership
  'blacklisting' 20.06
  common law difficulties 19.19–19.20
  detriment from use of services 20.05
  human rights 20.02
  non-discrimination 20.01
  refusal of employment on union
    grounds 20.23–20.25
  refusal to remain a member 20.21–20.22
  statutory provisions 19.21–19.30
  terms and conditions of
    employment 20.03–20.04
  union recruitment strikes 21.154
  unlawful requirements 19.101
  voluntary organisations 19.18
pension fund trustees 20.67–20.68
recognition
  derecognition 19.86–19.92
  dismissal during disputes 14.276–14.277
  meaning and scope 19.57
  redundancy consultation 17.09–17.15
  statutory provisions 19.58–19.102
  transfer of undertakings 19.100
  unfair dismissal 19.93–19.99
  union 'activities' 20.18
redundancy consultation
  authorised union representatives 17.55
  employee representatives 17.16–17.22
  informed consultation 17.38–17.40
  'special circumstances'
    defence 17.42–17.43
  timing 17.23–17.37
  union recognition 17.09–17.15
remedies for infringement of rights
  detriment short of dismissal 20.70–20.71
  failure to permit time off 20.72
  unfair dismissal 20.73–20.79

time off work
  enforcement and remedies 20.72
  health and safety at work 20.55–20.56
  industrial relations training 20.54
  trade union activities 20.26–20.27,
    20.52–20.53
  trade union duties 20.35–20.51
  unfair dismissal pacts 12.48–12.49
Training
  discrimination 8.139
  early statutory provisions 1.03
  national minimum wage 5.25
  pension fund trustees 20.68
  redundancy payments scheme 16.05
  response to new technology 3.56
  time off work 4.38, 20.54
  union consultation and information
    rights 19.116–19.120
Transfer of undertakings
  collective agreements 18.126–18.128, 19.54
  consultation
    employee representatives 18.119–18.120
    information rights 18.116–18.118
    'special circumstances'
      defence 18.121–18.123
  continuity of employment
    'associated employers' 11.41–11.48
    employed 'at time of
      transfer' 11.38–11.40
    regulatory provisions 11.32
    'transfer' defined 11.33–11.37
  contracting out 18.41
  effect on contracts of employment
    employee's right to decline
      transfer 18.85–18.97
    overview 18.59–18.62
    rights and duties transferred 18.63–18.68
    rights not transferred 18.69–18.75
    rights separate to contract 18.76
    variation of contracts 18.77–18.84
  history and development of
    law 18.01–18.03
  injunctions 18.98
  notification of employee
    liabilities 18.129–18.134
  part transfers 18.43–18.50
  protection of collective agreements 3.15
  recognition of trade unions 19.100
  relevant employment
    'immediately before
      transfer' 18.55–18.58
    third party employers 18.51–18.54
  relevant transfers
    EU law 18.11–18.21
    general formulation 18.10

Transfer of undertakings (*Cont.*)
  general principles 18.33
  multiple transactions 18.40
  overview 18.04–18.09
  service provision changes 18.34–18.39
  UK cases 18.22–18.32
  unfair dismissal
    automatically unfair grounds for
      dismissal 18.99
    economic reason defence 18.102–18.115
    effectiveness 18.100
    need for specific transfer 18.101
  union recognition 17.14
  variation of contracts 3.61
    EU law 3.61
    general principles 18.77–18.82
    insolvency 18.83–18.84
    waiver 18.42
Transferred discrimination 8.116
Trespass 22.32
Trial periods
  to avoid redundancy
    common law 16.39
    resignation after 16.38
    time limits 16.35–16.37
  termination of employment 13.09
  trial job with same employer
    to avoid redundancy 16.35–16.39
    unfair dismissal 14.59–14.61
Trust *see* **Duty of trust and confidence**

Unfair dismissal
  see also **Protected disclosures; Termination
    of employment; Wrongful dismissal**
  agreements between management and
    unions 12.48–12.49
  background and development of
    law 14.06–14.09
  background to modern era
    Employment Act 1980 1.12–1.13
    Industrial Relations Act 1971 1.06
  common law principles excluding
    dismissal
    agreements to terminate 14.65–14.67
    frustration 14.80–14.91
    late return after time off 14.76–14.79
    resignations 14.68–14.75
  effective date for dismissal
    general propositions 14.93
    importance 14.92
  family rights
    exceptions 10.74–10.76
    scope of protection 10.67–10.73
    statutory provisions 10.66
  implied terms 3.32–3.33
  importance of employee status 2.05

  infringement of rights of safety
    representatives 20.63
  infringement of trade union rights
    compensation 20.73–20.75
    interim relief 20.76–20.79
  overview 14.01–14.05
  procedural implications 14.363
  reasons for dismissal
    general considerations when assessing
      fairness 14.106–14.111
    general principles 14.94
    later discovered reasons 14.95–14.99
    potentially fair dismissals 14.112–14.241
    statutory provisions 14.103–14.105
    written reasons for
      dismissal 14.100–14.102
  recognition of trade unions 19.93–19.99
  redundancy
    alternative employment 14.210–14.221
    consultation 14.206–14.209
    overview 14.191–14.194
    reasonableness 14.195–14.199
    selection criteria 14.200–14.205
  remarkable and far-reaching effects 14.363
  remedies
    compensation 14.302–14.360
    overview 14.287
    re-engagement 14.298–14.301
    reinstatement 14.288–14.297
  statistics 14.364
  statutory enlargements in favour of
      employee
    implied termination 14.63
    lay-offs 14.62
    leaving early 14.55–14.58
    short-time working 14.62
    trial job with same employer 14.59–14.61
  statutory powers to extend
      protection 2.73
  termination of employment
    constructive dismissal 14.23–14.53
    contracts terminated by limiting
      event 14.22
    direct dismissal 14.13–14.21
    overview 14.10–14.12
  transfer of undertakings
    automatically unfair grounds for
      dismissal 18.99
    economic reason defence 18.102–18.115
    effectiveness 18.100
    need for specific transfer 18.101
  working time protection 5.75
Unincorporated associations
  continuity of employment 11.50
  employee status 2.54
  trade unions 19.04

Unlawful assembly 22.15
Variation of contracts
    changes to written statement of terms 3.67
    constructive dismissal 14.34–14.36
    general principles 3.54
    mere variations and wholly new contracts
        distinguished 3.55–3.56
    repudiation amounting to unfair
        dismissal 14.19–14.20
    some other substantial reason (unfair
        dismissal) 14.232–14.234
    transfer of undertakings
      EU law 3.61
      general principles 18.77–18.82
      insolvency 18.83–18.84
      waiver 18.42
    unilateral variation by employer 3.57–3.60
Vicarious liability
    apprentices 2.43
    control test 2.17
    importance of employee status 2.02
    policy considerations 2.04
    protected disclosures 15.21–15.23
    trade unions 21.107
Victimisation
    less favourable treatment 8.90
    motivation 8.112–8.113
    post-employment action 8.114
    proof 8.114
    statutory provisions 8.111
'Voluntary redundancy' 14.73–14.75
Volunteers
    prohibition of discrimination 8.12
    test of employee status 2.15

Wages
    deductions from
      agreements to deduct 5.07–5.10
      exceptions 5.12–5.14
      failure or refusal to pay 5.06
      policy 5.01–5.02
      relevant 'wages' 5.03–5.05
      special rules for retail employment 5.11
    economic reality test 2.25
    national minimum wage
      amount payable 5.25
      calculation 5.36–5.43
      enforcement and remedies 5.45–5.46
      exclusions 5.20–5.21
      record-keeping 5.44
      relevant hours 5.26–5.35
      relevant workers 5.22–5.24
      statutory rights 5.19
Warnings
    incompetence 14.120–14.122
    procedural fairness 14.174–14.180

Whistleblowers *see* Protected disclosures
Words of dismissal 14.13–14.18
Work
    details required in written statement of
        terms 3.63
    diminution in requirements of
        business 16.21–16.22
    equal pay
      equal value claims 7.80–7.81
      job evaluation schemes 7.67–7.77
      like work 7.25–7.29
    flexibility clauses 4.73–4.75
    during garden leave 6.15–6.16
    right to work
      basis for control of union
        membership 19.19–19.20
      garden leave injunctions 6.15
      human rights 4.53
      implied terms 3.27, 4.58
      natural justice 19.20
    unilateral variation by employer 3.55
Workers
    cooperatives 2.55
    EU law
      client exception 2.70–2.73
      defined 2.74–2.76
    key requirements 2.68–2.69
    statutory rights 2.66–2.67
Working time
    see also Time off work
    annual leave
      pay 5.62–5.63
      relationship with sick pay 5.64–5.66
      relevant pay 5.67
      statutory rights 5.61
    calculation of redundancy
        payments 16.57–16.59
      relevant workers 16.63–16.64
    contracting out 5.70
    defined 5.52–5.54
    details required in written statement of
        terms 3.63
    detriment 5.75
    enforcement and remedies 5.71–5.74
    exclusions 5.55–5.60
    key provisions 5.49–5.50
    night workers 5.68–5.69
    regulatory aims 5.48
    relevant workers 5.51
    statutory provisions 5.47
    Sunday trading 5.76–5.80
    unfair dismissal 5.75
Written reasons for dismissal 14.100–14.102
Written statement of terms
    remedy for failure to supply 3.75–3.76
    required details 3.63–3.64

Written statement of terms (*Cont.*)
 statutory provisions 3.62
 supplementary provisions 3.65–3.67
Wrongful dismissal
 see also **Termination of employment;**
  Unfair dismissal
 damages
  benefits 13.56–13.58
  general principles 13.53–13.55
  loss of chance 13.66–13.68
  mitigation of losses 13.70–13.73
  non-economic losses 13.59–13.65
  taxation 13.74
 declaration of rights 13.49–13.50
 judicial review 13.51–13.52

 other benefits available 13.75
 residual utility 13.76
 specific performance and injunctions
  exceptions 13.43–13.48
  general principles 13.41–13.42

Youth schemes 2.45

Zero hours' contracts
 effect on collective bargaining 19.02
 employee status 2.81–2.83
 national minimum wage 5.27
 temporary breaks 11.18
 time workers 5.27
 unfair dismissal 14.103–14.104